2 vols
70.⁰⁰

Duane P. Earley

Hiking the

Appalachian Trail

Hiking the Appalachian Trail

In Two Volumes   Volume Two

Edited by

James R. Hare

RODALE PRESS, INC.   EMMAUS, PA. 18049

Copyright 1975 by Rodale Press, Inc.
All rights reserved

SBN 87596-067-7
Library of Congress Catalog Number: 73-13180
Manufactured in the United States of America

FIRST EDITION

Contents of Volume Two

Illustrations in Volume Two

The First Step

By Eric Ryback

Started at MT. KATAHDIN on June 14, 1969
Finished at SPRINGER MOUNTAIN on September 3, 1969

This adventure really began when our family was visiting Harpers Ferry, West Virginia, during a summer vacation. My brother Tim was a great fan of the War Between the States and this trip had been planned around his interest.

When we arrived in the area the mountains seemed much more interesting to me. I wanted to climb one of them, but everyone else in the family was against it. In anger I accused them of "doing everything for Tim . . . this trip, everything . . . great old Tim." Tim was only 13, and it made me angry that he had an interest which absorbed him so completely.

My father can't stand fighting between members of the family. I have had family unity preached so hard for so many years that I shocked everyone, including myself, with my outburst. My father pulled the car to the side of the road, parked it, and said we were all going to climb. A little sign said APPALACHIAN TRAIL. I ran ahead. My parents called for me to come back, saying that we should all walk together.

My mother began to complain about the heat and the steep climb; she was exhausted and suffocating. My father has never been one to let my mother suffer too long. He suggested that we return to the car and find an air-conditioned restaurant and have dinner. He also reminded us that the motel had a pool. Tim and Kris agreed to go back. I was the only one who wanted to go on to the top of the mountain. As we descended I was angry and frustrated, vowing to all of them that someday I was going to "walk the whole darn thing."

We went to Gatlinburg, Tennessee, the following spring vacation.

APPALACHIAN TRAIL
MAINE TO GEORGIA

·LEGEND·

•••   APPALACHIAN TRAIL
1-2   NEW ENGLAND DISTRICT
2-3   NEW YORK·NEW JERSEY DISTRICT
3-4   PENNSYLVANIA DISTRICT
4-5   MARYLAND-VIRGINIA DISTRICT.
5-6   UNAKA DISTRICT
6-7   SOUTHERN DISTRICT

Appalachian
Trail
(MAINE to GEORGIA)

Scale in Miles

This trip was planned for my interests, so I could be near mountains. We visited the Sugarlands Visitors Center. I spotted a small booklet published by the Appalachian Trail Conference, and learned that the trail spanned over 2,000 miles. My goal never changed from that time on. It eventually led to my 2,023-mile walk of the entire trail during the summer of 1969, in 80 days.

For the next two summers I worked for neighbors and friends. I weeded, mowed grass, dug out embankments for seawalls. I asked for money instead of gifts for birthdays and Christmas. I accumulated $500. I read everything I could find about the Appalachian Trail and about hiking. I wrote for equipment catalogs and studied them.

My father supplied me with a camera and "all the film I could use." The shutter on my camera clicked almost 400 times before I ended my trek. I purchased my food supply with the money I had earned. I accepted only my plane fare to Bangor, Maine, and $30 in cash from my parents.

The Long Hike

The Appalachians greeted me with a clear path and a blue sky as I mounted the Abol Trail, leading to the summit of Mt. Katahdin, the northern terminus of the Appalachian Trail. It was June 14, 1969. I thought water would be abundant, so my canteen was empty as I set out to climb the mighty Katahdin, its massive head enshrouded in clouds.

The first miles were fun; then the sun emerged and the trail grew rockier and steeper. Soon I was resting at 30-foot intervals. My mouth grew parched; I felt a growing need for water. I stumbled and a loose rock sent me tumbling backward. I thrust out my hand. My fall was checked, but a jagged rock was embedded in the palm of my hand. A small river of blood started from the nasty gash. Getting out my first-aid kit, I wrapped some gauze around the cut before I continued.

Farther along the weight of my pack threw me against a boulder. I fell and was too exhausted to rise; I went to sleep right where I lay. The thought of never waking occurred to me and it was almost pleasant.

Upon awakening I saw that the beautiful day had been transformed by a monstrous grey sky that swirled overhead. I asked myself why I was walking *toward* such a storm, instead of seeking protection in the opposite direction.

After drinking water from crevices in the rocks, I continued toward the top of the mountain. By now the excitement was building in me as

I scrambled up small inclines, stepping from boulder to boulder, carefully watching each step. Stopping to rest and catch my breath, I looked upward as I had done many times before; this time I caught a glimpse of the summit of Mt. Katahdin through the fog. I felt tears roll down my face.

With a final burst of energy I bounded up the rocks straight to the sign which read NORTHERN TERMINUS OF THE APPALACHIAN TRAIL; I snapped a picture of the plaque dedicating this peak to Governor Baxter, and then took another picture of the cairn, remembering the tale the forest ranger at Abol Campground had told me: years ago the United States Geological Survey found that Mt. Katahdin was Maine's highest peak. In order to honor Governor Baxter, who had donated the land for the park, the state of Maine changed the name of Mt. Katahdin to Baxter Peak.

Years later another survey team discovered that Baxter Peak was *not* the highest point, but was actually ten feet lower than South Peak, which was close-by. This fact was kept as quiet as possible, and for most people Baxter Peak remained the highest mountain in the state.

One day a ranger told this story to a Boy Scout group. They decided to do something about it. They climbed to Katahdin's summit and made a 13-foot pile of rocks, thus raising Baxter Peak three feet above its neighbor. Now Mt. Katahdin really is the highest mountain in the state, although it had to be crowned with a cairn of rocks to maintain its royal position.

I made my descent to Katahdin Stream Campground by the Appalachian Trail and camped at the base of the mountain. I was feeling great because finally I was started on the trail.

During the night it was extremely cold. I was glad I had purchased a three-pound down sleeping bag. I burrowed myself into its cozy warmth. Later on, when I met other hikers and discussed hiking techniques and ideas, I found that all hikers agree on one thing: they loved their sleeping bags, and considered them their homes.

I didn't rest too well that night because I was so anxious to start hiking. I had camped near a stream, and could hear the water splashing most of the night. I awoke before the sun. It was great to hear birds chirping and the stream rushing down. It was a beautiful day for hiking, cold and crisp. I got out of my sleeping bag and walked to the stream to wash. The water was just melted snow coming down from the mountains. I practically froze as I bathed.

For breakfast I prepared oatmeal and scrambled eggs with bacon bits, using a Primus-type stove. Although I didn't enjoy the dehydrated foods I used on this trip, they satisfied my hunger without leaving me with a disagreeable taste all day. I would stuff the foods down, averaging 10 to 12 thousand calories a day. Even so, I had lost almost 14 pounds by the time I completed my trek.

After eating, cleaning my cooking utensils, and arranging my pack, I put on my boots and socks in the following manner: first I took off my jeans and slipped one pair of wool socks on. These came right below my knees. Then I slipped my jeans back on and put another pair of wool socks over the first pair and over the jeans, then folded them back halfway. Next I slipped my boots on and laced them up. I wore a T-shirt, sweat shirt, and a grey cotton shirt.

Dressed and ready, I shouldered my pack and started following the white blaze marks which were to guide me for over 2,000 miles. After a mile of fair trail, the ground became spongy, then swampy marshland. The farther I progressed, the deeper the water got and the fewer logs I could find to walk on.

Suddenly I realized I was not on the Appalachian Trail. Using my compass, I tried to work my way through the bog. The water entered my boots when I slipped off logs. The waterproofing grease was fine, but it couldn't keep my feet dry when I was standing in water up to my knees.

After eight miles I came to a nice long piece of forest trail covered with pine needles. By this time the sun was high and had melted the mist. It began to drizzle. At first I didn't mind this. It felt good. But the rain didn't stop, and I was getting soaked.

Oblivious to everything except forward movement, I kept going. Perhaps I was thinking too much about the rain, for suddenly I realized that I was completely lost. The lean-to was not where I expected it to be. Walking on, but at a slower and more cautious pace, I went deeper and deeper into the forest. Finally I stopped. I felt that I was going in the wrong direction.

Carefully I worked my way back, still looking for the lean-to. Panic began to unnerve me. I felt that if I didn't find the lean-to, which was my first landmark, I wouldn't be able to trust my judgment, and would have to return home.

Traveling back and forth for about 500 yards, I looked for the lean-to. Finally I had to face the fact that *I was lost*. Making my way back one more time I caught a glimpse of a shining object. Flash—then it was gone. I backed up 100 feet and started again. I saw the glint again. I made my way through the dense underbrush, pushing branches away, climbing over and under logs, slipping constantly on the moss.

I saw the log lean-to. I had a sense of wild elation. I told myself,

"The guy that put on that metal roof was really thinking, a great idea." It was the shiny metal roof I had seen.

When I reached the lean-to I was startled to see two hikers sleeping in it. Packs and equipment were scattered about.

Not wanting to disturb the sleepers, I removed my pack and wet sweatshirt as quietly as I could. Suddenly a soft voice said, "Hello." I introduced myself. The hiker's name was Chris; he was a biology teacher. His companion's name was Mary Joe.

We decided to push on in the rain and attempt to reach Rainbow Lake Lean-to, approximately seven more miles. In this way I could complete my mileage for the day and have companionship, too. They packed their gear and we started walking through the rainy cold forest. I didn't realize at the time how crazy it was to continue. We proceeded up the north slope of a mountain, slipping and sliding all the way. Mary Joe began to fall behind. Chris and I slackened our pace and then stopped to wait for her.

We finally made it to the top of the mountain, which was just a huge granite boulder, completely bald. I was beginning to feel the weight of my pack, a little over 65 pounds. Chris said his pack weighed about 45 pounds and Mary Joe probably had 30 pounds. We sat in the rain, looking for water. Believe it or not, we couldn't find any, so we made our way down the mountain heading toward Rainbow Lake.

It was late afternoon when we came to a stream. Chris led the way. He made it safely, hopping from rock to rock. He warned us that the rocks were slippery. I started to cross but my foot slipped. The weight of my pack made me lose my balance and I fell backward into the stream.

The water was rushing over me. I tried to stand up but with the pack I found it impossible. I tried to get into a sitting position but soon realized this wouldn't work. I rolled over sideways and got to my knees, finally managing to stand up in the river. Water was shooting out of my pack. Chris began to laugh, but quickly said that he had swallowed a blackfly and was just coughing. I had never seen a person try so hard not to laugh. Then I started laughing; it probably kept me from crying.

There I stood, soaking wet from the rain and the river. I told Chris and Mary Joe that I would go ahead to the lean-to. Perhaps I could build a fire and dry myself out before night.

I increased my pace to a trot. In 20 minutes or so I reached the lean-to. Fortunately, someone had been considerate enough to leave a few pieces of dry wood. I kindled a small fire and then roamed the dripping forest to pick up small branches which had been sheltered from the rain. With these I made the fire bigger, but it still seemed insufficient to dry my clothing. There were larger logs about, but I had only a machete. I needed Chris and his axe.

Within a few minutes Chris and Mary Joe arrived. Chris looked down and said, "Oh, come on, Eric, we can do better than that." With these words, he disappeared into the dense brush. I listened for sounds of the axe but heard only the river and the shuffling of Mary Joe in the lean-to.

Suddenly Chris emerged from the forest with a tree the size of a telephone pole slung over each shoulder. I thought my eyes had deceived me, but no, there was Chris, like a miniature Goliath, holding two giant trees.

"Here Eric, catch!" I sprang to my feet to avoid the giant log he hurled at me. Instinctively I fell backwards, but I found the log as light as if it had been balsa wood.

"Call me Goliath," Chris bellowed. Setting the other log down he disappeared again into the dripping woods. I followed and found myself in a forest of dead trees.

Most of these dead trees were still standing and I watched in amazement as Chris walked up to a large tree, put his arms around it, and ripped it out with a tremendous roar of victory. I tackled a smaller one and found myself tearing it from the ground. The woods boomed with waves of laughter as two giants uprooted tree after tree. We walked about the forest, intoxicated with our new power. We soon had a great stack of trees. We fell to the ground, exhausted and drunk with laughter.

Mary Joe must have been bewildered as we approached camp, booming and bellowing, each of us with a tree on each shoulder. It took us another 45 minutes to transport the timber, but we soon had a fire to end all fires, the heat driving us to the depths of the lean-to. We had a giant fire for the remainder of the night, and I spent my first comfortable night since the rain had started.

Mary Joe began to prepare their dinner and Chris put his axe to work. By darkness we had almost three cords of wood. No one would suffer from a lack of wood that summer at Rainbow Lake Lean-to.

The next morning I knew I should travel on quickly and make my mileage, but somehow it didn't seem as important as before. I knew I was going to be the first hiker through Maine that year. I probably would meet no other hikers, so I wanted to take advantage of the opportunity to be with Chris and Mary Joe. Being with Chris was fun.

I found he could teach me much about nature. He showed me various plants as we hiked. If you cleaned and boiled the roots of this one, he said, it would taste similar to potatoes. He taught me how to catch trout with my bare hands, and how to use pine sap for a fire starter.

Our companionship ended 14 miles beyond Rainbow Lake Lean-to. We sat fighting the black flies while eating lunch. I was eating dehydrated tuna fish salad. Chris was eating beef jerky and cheese, and Mary Joe had a water and malted milk mix. We sat fighting flies, lifting our face nets so we could take a quick bite before putting the face nets back down again. I told them I would like to go on hiking with them but if I wanted to hike the entire trail I would have to go faster.

I missed the companionship of Chris and Mary Joe, particularly the comments Chris made, which had us laughing most of the time. However, my pace picked up, and I was able to walk the miles I had originally planned for that day. The terrain was generally flat, and by evening I was at Wadleigh Pond Lean-to, where I spent the night. The stream ran under the lean-to, and I had to build a fire both outside and inside in order to combat the black flies, which were becoming worse.

The bites became so painful during the night that I burrowed my head, with net and fly dope on, deep into my sleeping bag. I remembered the day before when Chris had said, "My God, if they would just give me a moment's peace." To add to my misery, I heard a long high-pitched howl and figured wolves were near. I shuddered in the depths of my sleeping bag and wondered when the glorious part of my adventure would start.

The next day, as quoted directly from my journal: "Today was a long hard day; the walking started out level on the valley floor. The only problem is the black flies. If I stop for just a second they land on me and bite until blood comes, then more swarms come. It's all right when I am walking, then they can't get hold of me. The fly dope works until I start sweating, then it comes off. By 1:00 P.M. I ran out of dope and the bugs were eating me alive. My hands and neck were swollen twice as large as normal, and the stings hurt. The tops of the mountains saved me, as the black flies don't go that high. This is the first time I have wanted to go home."

Around lunchtime I came to Potaywadjo Spring. I sat down to rest; I wasn't feeling well after battling the flies all morning. As I bent to get a drink from the spring, a pine bough struck my eye. I removed my contacts, but as I leaned down one contact fell to the ground. I began a futile search. I carefully removed brush and leaves to expose the ground, but I had no success. Finally I gave up. I was glad that my mother had bullied me into slipping my glasses into my pack.

Farther along the trail I prepared my dinner. After eating, I found myself too exhausted from my 22-mile hike to even bother filling my canteen. Laying my sleeping bag on the platform of the lean-to, I left my pots and pans unwashed. Without removing my clothing, I crawled into my bag and immediately went to sleep. Even the sounds of the wild animals were unheard by me.

During the night I felt like I was having a nightmare. My body ached. My mouth felt like it was stuffed with cotton. Half awake, I reached for my canteen, aware that I must be completely dehydrated. There was barely a mouthful of water in the canteen. In desperation I groped my way toward the sounds of running water, my head spinning and aching. My flashlight was still in my pack. Stumbling forward I slipped and slid toward the stream in the complete blackness. My foot suddenly touched water. I threw myself down and drank and drank and drank. I stopped to catch my breath, and then drank some more.

After satisfying my thirst I filled my canteen and started to climb the steep embankment. I came to the place where I thought the lean-to should be, but couldn't find it. Finally, from exhaustion, I just lay down in the brush and went to sleep.

When I awoke I heard the stream running and the birds singing. I was shocked to find I was not in my sleeping bag. I got up and stretched, and then discovered that the shelter was about ten feet away.

Looking around and seeing everything misty, with the sun not quite breaking through, and everything cold and wet, I felt that my glorious adventure was beginning at last. I laughed at myself because I had been so close to the lean-to all the time and hadn't realized it. I was soon on my way, hoping to make the 20 miles to Antlers Camps before nightfall.

The forest became quite dense. Obscure trail marks caused me to lose my way. I was near a lake, traveling parallel to the shoreline but remaining in the forest. I knew I had to get to the other side of the lake, but couldn't find the trail. Sitting on a log, I tried to figure out my location by using the map. I finally located myself, or so I thought. I started to head back, but I couldn't find my way, so I turned around again. I got deeper and deeper into the woods. Fear crept through me, imperceptibly at first and then stronger, until I was crying without realizing it. I remembered what people had told me about Maine. If you get lost up there, you die. I pulled my compass out and tried to get my bearings. I was positive I was heading in a southwesterly direction, but the compass read northwest. Now I was really worried. The way I read the map, I was supposed to keep the lake always on my left, yet my compass indicated that I was traveling in the wrong direction. I became very upset and confused, and then I really cried. I thought I was going to die. I reached a point where I just wanted to be home with my family—not even talking to them, just sitting in a corner of the living room, listening to them talk and laugh.

I tried to pull myself together. I counted my resources. I had my food, my equipment, and most of all, I had my own personal strength and determination. Suddenly I knew I was going to be all right. I pulled my compass out again and the needle pointed southwest. I looked to see if the lake was on my left, and it was. I checked again. As I turned to shoulder my pack, the sun glinted off the frame, and I knew why my compass had failed. I had set the compass on the pack to take the reading. The steel D-rings of the pack had caused a distorted reading.

Exuberant, I worked some more with the map and compass but still couldn't find the trail, so I followed the lakeshore for about two miles and then headed toward a mountain peak. I didn't notice the terrain or the weather during this time. My goal was to get over that mountain and down to a smaller lake. I had to reach the other end of the small lake in order to accomplish my mileage for the day. When I reached the top of the mountain it was almost dark. I stepped up my pace—but how fast can you go in underbrush?

Finally I was traveling along the right lakeshore, through a pine forest. The wind picked up. There was rain in the air. The pine needles made the ground like a soft carpet. The wind started to blow through the pines, and the trees started to wave. I reached the top of a small rise and could see three buildings 800 yards away. I had found the place I was looking for.

Antlers Camps had been a fishing camp at one time. I made my way to the first building. I could see through the walls and the roof had fallen in. The second building was almost down, too. It looked desolate, perched there on the side of the hill. There were four buildings, all in ruins except for the fourth one. I went over to it and saw a rusty lock on the door. I looked through the window, and could see it was fairly well kept. I found another door and it opened when I pushed. I wondered if anyone lived in this old building. The wallpaper was hanging down and peeling off.

I entered the main part of the cabin—the entire structure was only about 12 by 15 feet. The first thing I saw was some bedsprings in one corner. Then I saw an old Franklin stove and an old table and two chairs. I was worried; perhaps I was in someone's house and they would think I was trespassing. Taking my canteen I went searching for water. I kept feeling that someone would appear and accuse me. I never did find the pump. I was so thirsty that I went to the lake. The water was crystal clear, so I bent over and drank. I filled the canteen and didn't even bother to use my halogen tablets, although later I had second thoughts and boiled the water. I never did use my halogen tablets, and later on this carelessness almost ruined my trek.

Entering the building again and looking farther I found dust about an inch thick on the table and floor. I decided no one lived here, and relaxed. Finding an old broom I cleaned the cabin. Then I built a fire in the stove and cooked my dinner. I kept the fire going all night. Because of my frightening experience during the day, it was wonderfully pleasant to wake during the night and find myself safe.

One of the most rewarding experiences of my trek through Maine was seeing the moose in velvet. The ranger at Abol Campground had told me that I was going through Maine too early in the year because of the black flies. He also said there was still a lot of snow in the mountains, that the rivers were running high, and that the valleys were wet and boggy. However, he told me I would be seeing a very beautiful sight: the moose in velvet. At this time of year a fuzzy growth formed on the antlers. Because the antlers were very soft at this stage and easily cut or damaged, the moose tended to walk on the deer paths or old logging roads, staying away from tree branches and brush as much as possible. For that reason more moose were seen at this time of year than at any other time. Moose were majestic as they moved through the woods; they made me think of soldiers who had battled triumphantly.

Another form of Maine wildlife was the beaver. They were the prime reasons many of the valleys had become swamps. They dam up the small streams and rivers, flood the valleys, and create marshland. When I would find beavers building their dams, I would stand for a bit and watch them work, enjoying their industriousness, yet angry because they were the ones who had created many of my problems. When I hear the phrase "busy as beavers," I know what it means.

In the valleys I was usually in marsh and bog. This was uncomfortable walking and I came to think of the lowlands as hellholes; I looked forward to the mountains. I would climb to the mountaintops and see the beautiful scenery and have a feeling of elation. Then, as if in punishment for feeling good, I would descend into the valleys and they were like a living hell to me.

When I left the abandoned Antlers Camps I started to ascend toward the headwaters of Cooper Brook, which were high in the mountains. The water kept getting louder and louder. The closer I got to the top the swifter and louder the noise became. The day was beautiful with the light filtering through the trees. I realized that I had made this trek for moments of perfect peace and joy like these. The pines formed an arch over the river as it cut through the mountain. I was still not sure I had found the trail, although I thought I saw traces of it now and then. Many of the blazes were gone because of the hard winter. Trees had been knocked down, and with the rivers and streams running high, many of the markers were under water.

There was an abundance of rabbits in Maine that year. One night it was extremely cold, and I had made a huge fire and spread my plastic ground cover and sleeping bag next to it. I had eaten my dinner and was writing in my diary. Suddenly I noticed a small rabbit hopping toward the fire. It came closer and must have seen me because it froze in its tracks, then darted to the other side of the fire and into the night. I continued writing and noticed three or four more rabbits coming from all directions. I didn't pay too much attention to them until the first rabbit had circled the fire and was right at my head. (I was lying down to write.) The rabbit moved cautiously, but did not seem to be afraid. I stopped writing and just looked at him. Then all of the rabbits came and sat by the fire, like little balls of fur. There must have been ten or more of them. The one by my head kept looking at me. I didn't have the nerve to touch him. I wanted to see if something was the matter with him, so I took a small pebble and tossed it near him. All he did was jerk; he didn't run away. I began to get a little disturbed because I felt they should be afraid of me, and they weren't. In fact, they were like little people. They wriggled their noses at me and seemed fearless. They didn't fit my ideas of how wild rabbits should act. Finally I got up and took a stick. I yelled and tossed the stick in the air. They darted in all directions, but didn't go far. They went perhaps ten feet from the fire and then sat and looked at me. I felt sorry for frightening them and began talking to them as if they were people. I said, "OK, you guys, come on back." Pretty soon they all came back. In fact they came close to me. I got into my bag and went to sleep. During the night when I woke up to put more wood on the fire, the rabbits were all lined up around my fire, some leaning on my sleeping bag. In the morning they were all gone.

The weather was getting warmer, and the next day was one of the nicest days I had in Maine. I ran into a small herd of deer. Unfortunately, my camera was in my pack. I didn't bother to get it out. Pictures didn't seem important at the time, so I have nothing to show of the beauty of these creatures as they made their way through the forest.

I was a little bit afraid of the moose. Some of them would come charging through the woods right in front of me. They would go about 20 feet beyond me and turn around and look, as if to say, "Oh, it's only you again." I would say to them, "Yes, it's just me plugging along." Sometimes I wished they could talk to me and keep me company.

White Cap Mountain was about 3,600 feet high. It was a long climb. I rested two or three times going up. I felt that there had to be a better way to climb these mountains. I had been walking fast, then resting for quite a while. I decided to change my procedure and hike continuously but at a slower pace. I was beginning to realize that there was more to hiking and climbing mountains than just walking. I needed a different pace and technique for different elevations and terrains.

After descending to the valley I came to a point where two rivers joined. I had to wade across. I removed my boots and socks. Holding my pack above my head, I crossed the river. It was about waist-deep. The cold shock, as the water gradually rose to my waist, almost caused me to turn back and seek an easier way. The distance was about 100 feet. When I finally got across, I sat down, dried my feet with my shirt, and put my wool socks back on. This warmed me a little, and I pulled on my boots.

I looked at my map and decided I could save five miles by taking a direct route to Chairback Mountain. I thought I was making good time but after I went about eight miles and still wasn't at the top, I began to worry. I got out my compass and found I was heading toward the wrong mountain. I became very angry with myself as I thought of all the miles I could have walked if I had gone the right way. I went back to the point where I had started, and that was the first and last of my shortcuts. I slept about halfway up Chairback Mountain.

The next morning I started at a pretty fast pace. I was going to attempt to reach Monson, where there would be a telephone and I could call my parents. I was beginning to worry about my feet. I had blisters that were broken and bleeding. My boots were not getting a chance to dry out. The pain I felt from the blisters could be overcome by mental effort. I have a strong capacity for overcoming fatigue, pain, and fear. Consequently I wasn't worried about the pain, but I knew that I could get a really serious foot infection from the blisters, and that would end my trek. I was very lonely and wanted to hear my family's voices. Suddenly I felt I would not be able to stand it if I didn't reach Monson, a distance of some 34 miles, that night.

I made my way to the crest of the mountain. Reaching the top, I ate some Bolton biscuits and started traveling the ridge crest. I told myself I would walk to a pond halfway down the crest, a total of 12 miles or so, before I ate breakfast. I didn't have any water to mix with my dehydrated food, anyway.

The sun climbed high. I was working so hard and getting so hot it seemed I would never reach the pond. Finally, during the afternoon, I reached a fire tower. I looked at the map to see where I was and found I had traveled the entire length of the crest, missing the pond where I was to get water. I was completely exhausted and dehydrated, having gone 17 miles without water. Looking for something which could be eaten dry, I came across the hot chocolate mix. I opened the package. Pouring some in my hand, I put it in my mouth and sat there gagging and fighting for breath. I finally swallowed the powder and then repeated the process until the entire bag was eaten. This satisfied my hunger to some extent. Resting, I rebuilt my strength enough to climb to the top of the fire tower, a practice I was to repeat many times during the next 2,000 miles. The fire towers became my box seats for Nature's performances.

As I approached the tower, I noticed a sign on the rail:

VISITORS WELCOME
COME UP FOR A FINE VIEW
PROPERTY OF STATE OF MAINE

I took my camera and slung the strap around my shoulder. I was soaking wet from sweat and felt the climb would be worthwhile just to feel the breeze. About halfway up I doubted the wisdom of my climb up the tower. My legs felt extremely weak. I reached the top, only to find the door bolted shut. There was a sign:

ANY PERSON FOUND ON THE TOWER
WILL BE PROSECUTED AND WILL PAY
A FINE OF $50.00 AND FIVE DAYS IN JAIL
PROPERTY OF STATE OF MAINE

I laughed my head off. I couldn't believe it. I stayed up there anyway, and the breeze dried my clothing and cooled me.

The trail became easier. I was descending the Barren Ledges. My legs were feeling very weak because now I was going beyond my accustomed mileage. I still intended to reach Monson. Suddenly my right foot plunged downward. There was nothing beneath it. I grabbed a branch to keep from falling and saw the valley and river far below. I was shaking. Pulling myself back on the trail I continued, but I made my way much more cautiously.

I was exhausted and felt the day would never end, but I was still determined to get to Monson. Loneliness welled up in me. I could feel tears trying to form but there wasn't enough water in my body to cry. I had never been away from home before and suddenly all the pain formed into one huge lump of loneliness. Never have I wanted anything as much as I wanted to hear the voices from home.

I reached Long Pond Stream and couldn't see any way to get across. The stream was extremely swift so I could not safely wade. I looked for boulders to cross on, but I couldn't find any. Again I felt like crying from frustration. The stream was about 15 feet across. Seeing a huge log near the bank, I took off my pack and pushed and pulled the log to the edge of the stream. Finally, after several failures, I was able to get the log between two boulders on the opposite shore. I was exhausted, but slung my pack on my back and started across the log. After two steps I almost lost my balance and had to go back. I tried two or three more times, and finally decided that I was walking too slow. I speeded up my pace. When I got to the middle of the stream, with the water really rushing below me, I started running and thus reached the other shore.

Coming to the remains of a lean-to, I sat down and had a late lunch. I had traveled that entire day without water. After eating my breakfast-lunch-dinner, I headed for Bodfish Farm.

I reached Monson at 8:30 P.M. on Saturday, June 21. There were only four or five buildings in the "business" area. I saw a telephone booth and called home. My parents were very anxious to hear from me. My mother told me that perhaps I should come home. My father was very practical, saying I should not be concerned about the daily mileage or finishing the trail by the time school started, but to take my time and really enjoy Maine. Relax and take it easy, he said. I laughed to myself. I told them about losing my contact lens and they promised to have another one at Glencliff, New Hampshire, which was to be my first food pickup.

As I talked with my parents I kept watching the light in the grocery store. It was blinking on and off and I was worried that it would go off completely before the conversation ended and I wouldn't be able to buy any fresh milk or food. My parents have told me that my entire conversation consisted of short "yeses" and "noes." They wanted to visit, and I wanted to get to the store. After hanging up, I ran to the grocery store. I just stood and stared at the rows and rows of food—not dehydrated food, but *real food*. There was no one in the store so I walked around and around looking at the food. I began to laugh. I couldn't believe I had finally made it to Monson. I just kept laughing and laughing. I saw some Oreo cookies and pulled a package off the shelf. Still laughing, I opened the package and started eating the cookies. Next I spotted some fresh fruit on the counter. That looked even better, so I tucked the cookie package under my arm and started stuffing fresh peaches down my throat. Then I started on bananas, meanwhile leaving a trail of chocolate cookies along the floor. I was laughing and eating when the store owner came out. I was so happy, sitting on the floor with all this food around me! I called, "Hi." He folded his arms and watched me eating his food. Finally he smiled and then started to chuckle and then he was laughing as hard as I was. He asked me where I had come from and I told him. He said, "You have been out a long time, haven't you?"

Paying him for the food I had eaten, and more to take with me, I walked out of the store into the black night. I was walking down the street when a man approached me and said, "Well, I see you got your groceries."

"Yes, sir, I have."

He asked me where I was heading, and I told him Georgia. He fell back against the wall and said, "Where?"

"Georgia."

"That's a long way from here."

"Yes, sir, it is."

"Well, where did you come from?"

"Mt. Katahdin."

Introducing himself as Donald MacPherson he said, "You come with me and have a nice soft bed tonight, or at least come and eat your food at my house."

His home was a nice two-story frame structure. He told me to sit down and eat my food while he asked me a few questions. He introduced me to his wife and explained why I was there. She sat down and listened, too. Mr. MacPherson asked me if I would like to stay in their home for the night. I said I sure would. It was 11:30 when I finally got to bed. I hadn't had a bath in almost ten days. I stunk like an animal, but I was so exhausted that I didn't even take a bath. I felt guilty about getting into that immaculate bed. The bedding and the entire room reflected the cleanliness and charm of a New England home. I really meant to sleep on the floor, but after I sat on the bed, I couldn't resist the luxury of it.

The next morning Mr. MacPherson asked me if I wanted a bath. I ended up taking two baths in order to wash off the many days of dirt and two bottles of fly dope on me. Mrs. MacPherson suggested I stay for breakfast, and my clothing could be washed during that time. That seemed like a fine idea.

I was putting on my dry socks, and she noticed the blisters on my feet. She was shocked at how bad they looked. I explained to her that I didn't feel the pain when my boots were laced tightly. She worried about infection and brought out some of her first-aid supplies. I put moleskin and ointment on the blisters and then bound my feet with bandages and tape. She gave me some additional supplies for my first-aid kit. She thought I should spend another day with them but as much as I wanted to, I couldn't. There was some driving force inside me that made me go on.

Mrs. MacPherson made me promise to do only 4 miles that day, but I did 12 when I was back in the wilderness. The next morning I was walking with my head down, watching the ground, when I heard a noise. I looked up and saw a mother bear and her cubs feeding in the middle of the trail about ten feet ahead of me. Glad for a chance to rest, I found a log and sat down to watch. I said, "It's a nice day. You have nice children," and went on making conversation as if with a human being.

Every once in a while the mother would raise her head and look at me, as if acknowledging my conversation. I started to worry about making my mileage and slung my pack on my shoulder, saying I would appreciate it if they would get out of the way because I really had to be going. When I said this the two cubs ran off, but the mother began eating again. Once again I asked if she would move, and started to walk cautiously toward her. She looked at me and started to move *in my direction.* I slowed down and Momma Bear veered to the left. I continued down the trail.

As I was moving along the trail instinct warned me I had made a mistake in coming between the mother and her cubs. I could feel the presence of the mother behind me and felt she would attack and probably kill me.

I began to run. The trail was extremely rocky. I could feel the bear lumbering along behind me. Just as she almost caught up with me, the cubs came out of the woods! Momma Bear turned to them! I began to make the best mileage of the trek—about ten miles in ten minutes—getting away from those bears. I saw quite a few deer that day, but after my adventure with the mother bear, nothing could add to the excitement.

My feet were still giving me trouble in the mornings when the dampness would penetrate the boots, but that trouble seemed minor after the black flies started to attack me. They would swarm around my head, their angry buzzing never ceasing. At night, when I would try to take my shirt off, it would be stuck to me with dried blood. I was becoming a mess but I never considered giving up and going home, even though loneliness troubled me as much or more than the flies. My rewards for the punishment I was taking were in the beautiful scenery and the good feeling of using my body to its limit every day. Eventually I would hike as much as 48 miles in one day, but at this point I wouldn't have believed such mileage possible.

I had one more mountain to cross before reaching Caratunk, which would be my second food stop since leaving Mt. Katahdin. Caratunk was some 150 miles from Mt. Katahdin. It was where I would cross the Kennebec River and I looked forward to it as a milestone.

It was raining when I reached Caratunk. Deciding to dry my boots and clean myself up before entering town, I built a fire and took most of my clothing off to dry. I put my boots near the fire. I felt that if my boots were dry it would solve part of my foot problem. I cooked some soup over the fire, and then checked my boots. They weren't drying as fast as I hoped so I set them nearer the fire. I ate my soup while studying maps for the next day. Suddenly I smelled leather and, sure enough, my boots were smoking. I grabbed them and looked inside. The toe leather was curled and split at the seam on one of the boots. The other boot also had a large split where the leather had shrunk. I took my canteen and poured water on the outside of the boots. The water sizzled and steamed but it didn't cool the boot much. Then I squeezed boot grease onto the burned area of the boot. I tore a corner off my sweatshirt and worked the grease into the boot, hoping to save the leather. The boots reminded me of the dwarf or fairy boots in nursery rhyme illustrations—the toes curled up. Putting a new pair of socks on, I rammed my foot down inside the boot until I came to the curled-up place. I couldn't get the boots on any farther. I found some sticks and rammed them inside the boots, then wedged the boots between rocks. After about five minutes I pulled the sticks out. As soon as I did that the boots curled up again. My only alternative was to make my foot conform to the shape of the boot.

I rammed my foot into the left boot because that foot was not quite as raw and sore as the other one, and the boot was not curled as much. After ramming my foot in as far as I could, I pounded the boot on the ground. Finally, I got the left boot on and stood up. My entire foot was compressed, and I couldn't walk very well. When I forced the other boot on in the same manner the bandages on my heel gave way. If my feet became infected, I couldn't walk, but if I couldn't wear my boots, I still couldn't continue. I decided not to take the boots off until morning, and slept with them on.

Caratunk had a few houses and a general store. The store was the post office, and seemed to be the town meeting hall, the library, and the center of the town's activities. I asked the store owner how I could get across the river. He said there was a boy with a canoe who took people across.

"At eleven o'clock, if you go out front and stand there, you can flag him down, and chances are if he isn't doing anything else, he will take you over."

I sat down and listened to the men of Caratunk as they visited together. They ignored me at first, but gradually they began to include me in the conversation. I spent the remainder of the morning listening to and enjoying these fine people. Time passed quickly. Shortly after eleven the jeep and the boy came by. I flagged him. He said that for three dollars he would be pleased to take me across.

The river was about 50 yards wide. He said we had to hurry because soon the logs would start down the river to the paper mill. We carried the canoe down to the river's edge. He gave me a paddle and we made our way across. I couldn't see the marker for the trail but I told him not to worry, I would find it as soon as I started walking.

The canoeist returned to the other side of the river. The drizzle was increasing so I put on my poncho before looking for the trail marker. After going up and down the bank for a mile or so and not finding a marker I decided to head toward a chain of mountains I could see not too far away. I started a circular pattern, increasing its size every time I headed out looking for the trail. I searched for five hours, in the rain, and couldn't find a trace of the trail. I was soaked to the bone. I decided to return to Caratunk. My only worry was getting back across the river. The road on the other side ran parallel to the river for a distance. I decided to sit on the logs that had been washed up on the banks and watch for a car.

I waited a long time before the first car came by. I waved and yelled, but the car didn't stop. I remembered the flare I had in my pack. I got it out and lit it. Another car soon came by and this time

I waved the flare and yelled. This car also drove on by. The only thing I accomplished was to burn holes in my poncho with the sulphur drippings from the flare. The flare would burn only two or three minutes more, so I decided to put it out and wait until another vehicle came along. In another fifteen minutes or so I saw a blue truck. Quickly lighting my flare—I was lucky because they usually don't light that easily—I stood up on the logs and screamed and yelled madly. The truck slowed down. The man looked through the window at me, but he, too, passed by. I increased my waving. He stopped. Then he went on, but he kept looking back. Finally he stopped and got out of his truck. He came to the edge of the river and asked me what I wanted. I told him I wanted to get back across the river. He asked me how I got over. I stood in the rain and asked myself, "My God, does it matter how I got over?" But I told the driver about the boy and the canoe. He kept saying, "What?" He finally said there was a county boat at a ranger station about a mile upstream and he would go and see if they would lend it to him. Anticipating my eventual return to the other side of the river, I relaxed. Shortly afterward the man returned and said the agent would not let the boat go any farther than the middle of the river, as that was the county line.

He said he would go back to the road and stop anyone who came by with a boat or canoe. I couldn't believe that a man would stand in the rain and flag down a car for someone he had never seen before. I never did get this man's name but if he ever reads this, I sure want him to know how much I appreciated his help.

Eventually a truck came by with a canoe on top, but the driver said he wouldn't take his canoe off to get me. My benefactor said he would keep trying. He returned to the bank in about five minutes, and said the same man returned and said he had changed his mind. The two men took the canoe about a quarter mile up the river in an attempt to paddle with the current and reduce the chance of logs hitting the canoe and capsizing them.

Finally they made it across to where I was standing on a pile of logs that extended a few feet out into the water. The owner told me to walk on the logs out to the canoe.

I said, "They're slippery. I would rather wade out to the canoe."

He said, "No, you will just get your boots wet."

I told him that I was already soaked all over, including my boots, and would rather wade out.

He said, "No, just do what I say."

It was impossible for me to argue with an adult, and right or wrong, he was an adult and it was his canoe. Taking off my pack, I held it

Photo courtesy Eric Ryback

Eric Ryback in Pennsylvania, near the midpoint of his hike.

Photo by Eric Ryback

Tim Ryback crossing Mill River Bridge in Vermont.

Breakfast from around 6:30 to 7:30.

Photos by Garnett W. Martin

Rattlesnake hunter with timber rattlesnake (15 rattles) on Salt Pond Road, Virginia.

Rhododendron blossoms on Potato Top, near Laurel Fork Gorge, Tennessee.

Photo by James R. Wolf

Graves of William and David Shelton, North Carolina
   infantrymen killed in the Civil War. The graves are
   south of Flint Gap, Tennessee.

item I needed, which had perhaps started at the top of the pack and worked its way down. One day I needed matches and knew there was a small pack somewhere in my belongings. I took everything from the main compartment, and then searched the pockets. Soon my entire pack had been emptied except for the back clothing compartment. In a final search of that compartment I found an untouched pack of matches, wrapped in a sweatshirt. When I finally had the matches in my hand, all of my food and equipment was scattered on the ground. I told myself that I had to organize my pack better.

I asked myself if I really needed every piece of equipment. I worked out a perfect location for every necessary item I was carrying, article by article and piece by piece. This proved to be an antidote for loneliness as I tried to make this jigsaw puzzle fit together in my mind. All the items would be laid out mentally, and I would work and rework the puzzle until each piece was in the most desirable position.

For my next trek I decided I would make a small bag for each pocket of the pack to serve as a liner. Then I could lift out the liner and find the item I needed; at present I had to dig around and remove almost everything from the pocket to find what I wanted.

Reading the Bible that had been presented to me back in New Hampshire became a nightly ritual. I would read passages and dispute their validity with myself. It was a new kind of reading for me. Although I had been reared in the Christian faith, I was not familiar with most of the Bible passages. Through hours of thinking about the purpose of God in creating man, I came to the conclusion that God didn't mean to create any religions or faiths; he just meant there should be God. This is the philosophy I have embraced, and it is a good one, for me.

I thought about my accomplishments. I'd overcome fatigue. I'd learned to live with Nature and sense her moods. My hiking techniques were more polished. I had come to feel that I knew something about God and His mysteries. Only they weren't mysteries. It was just that people got so caught up with things that they forgot how simple everything really was. I felt that I carried the key to the universe in my mind.

Continuing on through the valleys and over the crests, I made my way south. Each day was a new challenge, with new views and thoughts. This was a period of complete isolation. My only companion was my loneliness and my attempts to overcome it.

In living in isolation I learned to control but not to overcome my loneliness. When it would get too oppressive I would reflect on what I had accomplished; that gave me a measure of satisfaction and respect for myself.

Perhaps the most significant result of my loneliness was that I found *myself*. You sit and say, "My God, I am lonely." Then you contemplate this loneliness for about two weeks. Then you begin thinking about yourself. What have I done? What have I accomplished? And then you tell yourself loneliness doesn't exist any longer, and all of a sudden it doesn't! Now you are beginning to *know yourself*.

Actually this didn't happen all at once; it was gradual. I spent hours agonizing about myself. Just as I had taken my pack apart and rebuilt it mentally, so I took myself apart in those days of loneliness.

The first few days I was overwhelmed with all sorts of discoveries about myself. I tried to take my unflattering features and make excuses for them. I took features like my temper, impatience, and stubbornness, and tried to justify each of them. I said, "This is the result of being poorly treated in such a manner . . . this is because I had brothers . . . this is because I was oldest . . ." and so on. I felt pretty good at that point, because I had justified myself to myself. However, just like an ill-fitting pack, these ideas began to chafe me, and I was not at all happy with my conclusions. The loneliness was replaced with a feeling of inadequacy, a vague feeling of dishonesty.

Really angry at myself for attempting to hide myself from myself I said, "OK, God, here it is." Now I spent my long evenings with another type of jigsaw puzzle. I took my mind, my assets, my defects, each part of me, and laid them on a mental table. I sorted out the good qualities and the poor qualities, and then stood back to see how I looked. Then I had to fit all the pieces back together again.

I took each part of my personality and studied it, categorizing and putting it back where it belonged inside of me. This took hours of soul searching, and I tried to be honest with myself. I made no excuses, nor did I decide to change any part of me. I just took what was there and evaluated it.

In all honesty I can say that I really began to *know myself*. What I don't know is the reason, the *why* I am like I am, or what I should do to improve myself, or even if I should improve. My evaluation made me see that I needed to gain knowledge from real teachers, not merely "warm bodies in classrooms."

Now I felt anxious to return home, to finish my last year in high school and pray that the college I entered would give me what I was looking for, which was to learn how I could use my mind and body to get the most out of life.

The next morning, after I had made my final analysis of myself, I decided that I could now leave the mountains and search out human beings again. I felt like the young Indian boys must have felt when their puberty rites were completed. Just as I had isolated myself in the woods, they would be left alone with their Manitou, their God, in order to find what their special mission in life would be.

As I began studying my map to find the best way to reenter civilization from my self-imposed exile, I located a small campground about 32 miles away. I decided this would be a good place to see if I responded differently to people now that I felt I had the secret of knowing myself.

I traveled in a constant rain; it was not a storm, just a steady downpour. I was glad because I knew the snakes would not be out that day. The one fear I had left was a fear of snakes. Whenever I saw one I would become extremely agitated, and be unable to overcome my fear. When I saw a snake, which was fairly often, I had Emily Dickinson's "zero at the bone." If I killed a snake I would feel better, as if I had rid the world of one more evil.

I came down the side of the mountain, making my own path as I went. It was four miles of slipping and sliding. I didn't know if I could make it to the base of the mountain by nightfall, but I hated the thought of camping on the slopes after my bad experience in Pennsylvania.

Finally I came to the road. I couldn't see any sign of the campground, so I continued hiking along the road for a mile or so. A truck rumbled by and its headlight caught me and then moved on. After another mile another truck passed me. Then the driver changed his mind and stopped. The insignia of the U. S. Park Service was painted on the door.

The ranger asked me what I was doing. I replied with a question, asking how far it was to the campground. He said, "It's about a mile."

I thanked him, and he said, "I'm going that way. Would you like a lift?" I said sure, and put my pack into the back of the truck and hopped into the front seat.

He introduced himself as Bill Martin. He said he had to make one more round of checking the park, and after that he would take me to a camping spot. This was the only time on my entire trek that I had to sleep in a designated area. It surprised me. There was hard gravel on the spot I was given, but I was so tired I decided to camp there anyway.

Bill had inquired where I was from, and when I answered "Maine," he wanted me to tell him some of my adventures. However, I convinced him that after hiking 30 miles that day, I needed sleep. I told him I would be glad to talk in the morning. Although my stomach protested loudly against the mistreatment, I didn't eat even dehydrated food. I went to sleep almost immediately.

Early the next morning, as I prepared my breakfast over a small campfire, Bill appeared and began to examine some of my equipment. He said he had a Kelty, too, only a different model. We talked about equipment for awhile, and I related some of my experiences to him. He was amazed at the weight I had been carrying, but I assured him that the weight was not a big factor with me.

I was enjoying his company so much that I was disappointed when he said he had to leave. He said it was his day off and he was going snake hunting. He invited me to join him, saying I could be telling him about my trek while he was hunting. Usually people were amazed to hear about my trek, but now it was my turn to be startled. When he said "snake hunting" I was "zero at the bone" and just stared. I asked him if he really caught snakes.

"Yes, copperheads and rattlers."

"It would be worth taking a day off to see this, especially when I have been avoiding snakes at all costs, and killing them at times."

Bill was disturbed when I said I had killed snakes, and said he wasn't surprised to find that I was afraid of them. He asked me why I killed snakes. I told him I really didn't know, but that every time I saw one, I was afraid. Bill said he understood. My actions were like those of many people who just didn't know enough about snakes to understand them.

We went to his trailer and left my pack inside. Bill took some of his maps, a canvas bag, and a three-foot pole with a metal half-moon type hook on the end. He had constructed this snake catching pole himself.

As we drove away he told me to look at the map. It was a 7½-minute topographical map of the nearby mountain. It was quite similar to my maps. I asked him what the little circles on the map represented. He explained they indicated areas where snakes could be found. He knew all the major snake dens for 200 miles around.

He explained that snakes on the Eastern coast are generally on the mountainside facing south, in rocky areas where the sun's rays strike most of the day.

Arriving at the area he had selected I found we were in a gorge where a stream had slashed a wedge in the mountain range. There were steep slopes on both sides, with the river to our right. The grade was about 50°. The sun was showing through the cloud cover occasionally.

Bill explained that he had hunted here before, and that there should be quite a few snakes. He motioned me to follow him as he started zigzagging up the mountain. Bill's confidence reassured me; I was not worried about the snakes. I noticed that he was wearing old Army boots, with holes in the sides. The leather appeared to be extremely thin.

I couldn't resist asking him if he wasn't afraid the snakes would bite through his boot. He said no, he had worn those boots many times, and snakes probably couldn't bite through the leather, anyway. I told him I had always thought snakes had powerful jaws. He agreed, but said that when the leather was wrapped around your foot, like a boot is, the snake couldn't get the necessary leverage to puncture it.

I wasn't too worried about my own feet because my boots were insulated. I mentioned that I was glad I had purchased a high boot to protect my leg. He said it was unnecessary because snakes strike at the lowest level they can reach; they are not accurate when they strike high.

We had climbed about 400 feet. It became quite strenuous, zig-zagging and pushing our way through the brush. He motioned for me to come closer to him. He stopped, and began poking around as he had been doing before, using the odd-looking pole he had brought. He would thrust the pole under the rocks, and pull out leaves, twigs, and debris. He had mentioned earlier that because the sun wasn't shining we would have to dig into the dens to find the snakes, and that was what he was doing now. He explained all this as we kept moving up the mountain. I learned that if you want to catch snakes in a rocky area, always go up, never down. If you are going up you can always see ahead of you, whereas if you work your way down you can't see over the ledges and you may step onto a snake and be bitten.

By this time I was getting nervous. I wondered what I was sup-posed to do when he caught a snake. Would I just stand out of the way, or what? He poked again and said, "I've got one." I started to sweat as I heard the snake's rattle.

Bill quickly removed the canvas bag from his belt. He held the bag and the pole in the same hand and poked some more in the den. Then he pulled the pole out, bringing the snake with it. The snake began lashing about on the ground, trying to return to the den. Bill kept dragging it out. Then he got the hook part under the snake, near the middle, and lifted it off the ground and brought it forward in one smooth motion. With his free left hand he followed the snake's movements. When he found the right moment Bill reached out quickly and grabbed the snake, thrust it into the canvas bag, and closed the bag quickly. The snake was 30 to 36 inches long.

All of this activity was performed with quick, precise movements. Bill was as accustomed to snake catching as I was to walking. After closing the bag, he lifted it up and said, smiling, "Well, that's how it's done."

That made 286 snakes he had caught during the year, he said. My mouth dropped open. I asked what he did with them. He said, "I do research with them." He studied their habitats, what they ate, how large the snake areas were, how far they traveled; in fact, he knew a great deal about these snakes.

Bill wanted to catch a few more before it rained and said he would explain everything later. Opening the bag he dumped the snake out and it darted back into the underbrush.

As we traveled on I asked him how he happened to get started catching snakes. He said that when he was about ten years old he started going out with his father, who taught him to catch snakes like other fathers taught their sons to fish or hunt deer or bear. Bill said he had never been afraid of snakes. After catching them for a time he began to study their habits, and thus his unusual hobby had evolved. He caught two more snakes before the rain terminated the hunt and we headed down the mountain and back to the truck.

It was quite late in the day. He invited me to his trailer to visit a bit more and to get my pack. Entering the trailer, I noticed many topographic maps hung on the walls. I commented, "I see you like maps, too."

"Yes," he said. "There are a lot more maps over in the drawers."

I walked over, and there was the greatest collection of maps and charts imaginable. He showed me how to fold topographic maps properly, so I could read just a small portion at a time. This technique was to be of great use to me during the remainder of my trek.

Glancing at another wall, I saw books with handwritten numbers on the outside. These were filled with his data on snakes. One of the experiments included marking the snakes with a dye in order to study how far they would travel. He had caught some snakes three or four times, and found they usually didn't travel more than two or three miles from their dens. During mating season they never traveled in pairs. This contradicted what experienced hikers had told me. He said he had caught his largest snake out west—a six-foot specimen. Bill had also taken a trip to the Himalayas. I envied him that adventure, if not his snake-catching hobby.

Bill was the first truly knowledgeable man, in a specific field, that I had met on my trek. I wanted to stay with him and learn more, but, conscious of the miles ahead of me, I went on. After talking with Bill I regretted that I had killed snakes because of my fear. I decided I would never kill one again unless I was in danger. Thus I conquered one more of my own inner conflicts—my great fear of snakes. I had crossed another barrier to relaxed wilderness living.

The heat became almost unbearable. My clothing was saturated with sweat almost immediately after I began hiking. In a valley I spotted a small stream. Its source was the stagnant water of an abandoned millpond. I knew I shouldn't drink the water, at least not without purifying it. However, I was so thirsty I didn't bother with my halogen tablets, but just gulped the water down.

I found shelter for the night on top of the next mountain. My camp was nestled in a clump of trees. After locating a small spring, I built a fire. During my dinner I had an uneasy feeling in my stomach. Some hot chocolate seemed to soothe it. Then the pain came, forcing me to lie down. I rolled up in a ball on the shelter floor. Moving made the pain worse. I could scarcely breathe. Suddenly a thunderstorm added to my anxiety. Lightning slashed into the dark shelter, probing and reaching for me. It seemed to hit everywhere, and the thunder kept building up louder and louder, crashing around me. I kept telling myself that if I made it through the night alive I would be lucky. Finally sleep came and gave me release from both fear of the storm and the constant pain.

My first reaction the following morning was one of relief. The storm was over; looking out I noticed branches from trees lying on the ground. Evidently the storm was only starting when I fell asleep. Realizing that the pain of the night before was gone, I breathed a sigh of relief. I started to get up, only to feel sharp pains throughout my body. I screamed and the tears started to flow. I quickly curled my legs against my chest.

Reaching for my pack, I got out the map and found that I was some 40 miles from Pearisburg by trail. I looked for the nearest road. It was 10 miles away. From this dirt road it was another 5 miles to a paved road. I hoped people lived on the first road. Otherwise, it was going to be a long and painful 15 miles.

I forced on my jeans and my boots. The pain was getting worse. Walking in a hunched-over position, holding my stomach, feeling as if I were going to throw up at every step, I made my slow way. The heat was suffocating, but I felt that if I didn't keep moving I might never get out. My mouth was dry and sticky. Drinking the water I had obtained at the spring the night before made it worse. I vomited again.

It was late in the afternoon when I reached the paved road. Lying next to my pack, which I had placed near the road, I waited for someone to come along. The sun was beginning to sink when finally I heard a car coming! I eased myself into an upright position and waved my arms. The pain had increased. The car did not stop. Leaning against my pack, I waited. Soon I heard another car approaching from the opposite direction. Looking closely, I saw that it was the same car.

When the man stopped I asked him if he could take me to a hospital. He said yes, and that there was a hospital in Pearisburg. Between cramps I told him of my adventure. He introduced himself as W. Shaw, Jr. of Blacksburg, Virginia.

Upon reaching the hospital, Mr. Shaw took me to the emergency clinic. While we waited for a doctor, I telephoned my parents. They talked with Mr. Shaw, who told them that I seemed to be all right, but that I needed a bath.

The doctor decided that I had drunk bad water, or had eaten something that upset my system. He said I should rest for a few days and take the medicine he gave me. Mr. Shaw invited me to stay in his home until I recuperated. The medicine relieved the pain and stopped the nausea. I was able to walk, but I was afraid that I might have lost some of my strength. I had a lot of walking to do in order to complete the trail before school opened in September.

At the Shaws I had my first taste of traditional southern hospitality. When I was feeling better Mr. Shaw called the local newspaper and I was interviewed, the first of many talks with local people. Most of them wanted to know how my parents felt about my trek, particularly my mother. Then they would ask me about the animals and weather conditions. What really intrigued most people, however, was how I sustained myself for long periods of time in the woods, and how I coped with loneliness.

Monday morning Mr. and Mrs. Shaw and their son Dean drove me to the trail and dropped me off. I felt as if I were leaving my family. Thinking about my condition, I was glad Damascus was only a short distance ahead of me. That would be my fourth and last food drop.

After hiking for about 5 miles I had to stop and rest. I drank some of the medicine I had been given, and decided to move at a slower pace. I walked late that night in order to travel a full 25 miles.

I was glad it didn't rain. However, I had another problem—food. Since my stomach had been upset, I found it functioned better if I ate soft food, such as baby food. I had eaten baby food at the Shaws but now I was 25 miles away. Taking out the remaining dehydrated food, I found that every item contained some sort of harsh food, such as chunks of meat or vegetables. I tried to find something that would substitute for the baby food. My breakfasts were powdered pancakes in mixes. That was out of the question. Turning to the lunches, I noticed the Bolton biscuits. I placed a biscuit in my pot and then took my spoon and mashed it into a fine powder. I took two more and did the same thing. Then I added boiling water. The mixture looked exactly like baby cereal. I eagerly tasted it, and found that the taste was far from that of the baby cereal I had eaten the day before. To add flavor I sifted the sugar from my fruit cocktail mixture and sprinkled it over my homemade baby food. This satisfied my hunger without any bad effects on my aching stomach. The next morning I repeated the process and found the mixture rather tasty. My stomach was still shaky, although the pain was gone most of the time.

By the third night my stomach had settled enough to tolerate the dehydrated food. My strength had returned. The joy of being healthy again gave me renewed vigor. Just as I was starting to feel great, the rain began to fall. Finding a pine tree on the side of a gorge I made a shelter under its branches. Laying my sleeping bag near the tree's trunk, I put my poncho between the branches over the bag. This made an excellent improvised tent. Covering my pack with its rain cover, I propped it up against my side to prevent me from rolling down the mountain, as I had in Pennsylvania.

The next morning I awoke to find my pack, my sleeping bag, and myself completely dry. After eating breakfast, which was the last complete meal in my pack, I looked at my maps. Damascus was about 20 miles away.

Traveling in the early morning, in the humid heat that was found in the valleys and lowlands, I was confronted with wet leaves and brush for many miles of trail. If there was one thing I didn't like about early morning hiking, it was the wet underbrush, especially in the South. After about a mile, the wetness of the brush would saturate my jeans. My socks would get wet, too. This caused my feet to swell. My jeans, sticking to my legs, restricted my movement. I decided that on future trips I would not carry a poncho; it protected only the upper half of my body.

The idea of trying to save weight by using a poncho as a semi-tent as well as protection from the rain did not work for me. I vowed that next time I would take rain pants, a nylon tarp, and a rain parka. The extra ounces would not matter if I could be sure my legs wouldn't get wet.

Reaching the White Top Mountain and Mount Rogers area, I stopped to locate the new route. I saw that I would have to take the old route along the valley and then make a sharp left turn, traveling up the ridge to the top of 5,729-foot Mount Rogers. Coming to the junction, I looked down the overgrown path I would have taken if the trail had not been relocated. I asked myself why anyone would want to change the trail from nice level valley hiking to a steep mountain trail.

I began the ascent. After all, it was just one more mountain. After almost an hour of sweating what I felt must be gallons of water, I was standing on top of the mountain. I shed my pack, stretching and then relaxing my body, feeling the cool breeze drying my sweat-stained clothing.

Minutes later I reshouldered my pack and started along the crest, only to be greeted by a sign:

TRAIL NOT COMPLETED BEYOND THIS POINT

I sat down for a second time atop this mountain, this time not to admire the view but to laugh. I wondered whether to continue, or to go back to the old trail. Thinking back to the episode in Maine, I headed back down the mountain by the trail.

Later in the afternoon I was gazing down upon the small town of Damascus. It was nestled between the towering peaks of tree-covered mountains. I remembered I had no more food. I guessed it was about four o'clock, which left me very little time to get down the mountain to the the post office.

Practically running down the mountain, I wanted to shout that I was on my way, and not to close the post office yet. Suddenly I realized I could not stop running. I watched the trees whizz by in a blur. As I neared the base of the mountain I zeroed in on someone's back-yard and found a path between two houses. It was so narrow I was afraid I would bang into one of the houses. The momentum of the run down the mountain carried me along.

I saw a three-foot fence directly in front of me. I knew I would never be able to stop. My only alternative was to leap high in the air and hope I cleared it. Leap I did, and when I landed on the other side I was in the center of a giant mud puddle! I didn't have to worry about how to stop now; my feet were sinking into a foot of water plus a few inches of mud. I heard laughter behind me. Turning, I saw rows of elderly people sitting on porches. I walked out of the puddle and went down the sidewalk, trying to make it look as if I had planned it that way. I looked back and saw the smiling faces. I began to laugh with them.

Seeing the American flag, I ran down the street to the post office. I breathed a sigh of relief when I found it open. I asked if there was a package for me. The man behind the counter introduced himself as Mr. Grindstaff, the postmaster. He told me to follow him, and in the back office he handed me a box and told me to have a seat, courtesy of the Damascus Post Office. Then he asked me if I knew of any other post office that gave service like this. I told him no and he closed the door and left me with the box.

Looking at that food was one of my greatest pleasures on the whole trip. It was the last package I would pick up before I finished my trek. I wondered how I would make all of the food fit into the pack. It was for 20 days, the largest supply I had picked up. With the experience of 1,600 miles behind me, the heavier the pack, the more secure I felt. I knew I could go into the woods and stay for as long as the food lasted before coming back to civilization again.

Mr. Grindstaff came back and asked me if I was going to stay in town, and if I did, there was a small boarding house up the street which was run by three widows. The sun was sinking behind the mountains so I decided to stay.

The evening spent in the boarding house was one I will not forget. I stayed up late that night answering questions and relating some of my experiences to the three women. Finally I retired to a soft bed; too soft, for it finally drove me to the floor, which felt more like the ground I had slept on all summer.

The next morning I was greeted by Mr. Grindstaff, who wanted me to relate some of my experiences. When I was ready to leave, he asked me to look for his uncle's gravestone up in the mountains. His uncle had been a hermit. The postmaster had never seen the grave, but knew it was in the area I would be traveling.

I left Damascus in the hottest part of the day. An hour later I found myself on the Virginia–Tennessee border. Wanting to make as many miles as possible before night, I continued walking at a fairly rapid pace. Although at an approximate elevation of 4,000 feet, the mountains were rolling.

After I had walked 11 miles it started to get dark. I wanted to reach a nearby shelter, if possible. I began to go down the steep mountainside. I was soon almost falling down the trail, gripping small saplings to slow my descent. Suddenly the terrain leveled off, and a flat meadow lay before me.

I was winding through scattered clumps of trees in heavy underbrush. There was a gentle feeling about it, and although the sun had disappeared behind the mountain, I welcomed the peacefulness. Moonbeams came through the thick trees, illuminating sections of my path. I continued on, watching the ground very closely in the dim light, searching for any turns in the trail. The foliage became very thick and my feet would catch on roots and I would lose my balance.

I was beginning to worry, and tried to move more rapidly. The feeling of serenity left me. Suddenly the place seemed threatening, and I realized I was afraid. It was a new experience for me, because I was not lost. I had plenty of food and water. Nevertheless, I had a feeling of being pursued. The trees began to lose their individual shape and melt into each other. The long arms which had reached out over the trail now clasped each other, while all around the forest creatures whispered and sang. I was bewildered, surprised, and afraid.

Suddenly I felt myself falling forward, my legs gripped by some merciless force. I seemed to float to the ground, almost in slow motion, as if some force was gently lowering me. I felt a sudden jolt as I hit the earth. I had tripped over a log, upon which my ankles were now resting. For an instant I lay there, arms and legs all stretched out, like a sky diver who'd forgotten to open the chute. Then the pack hit my head, and I had a close-up view of what I had been walking on for 1,600 miles.

I struggled to get up. On the third try I was able to rise to my knees, remove the pack, and stand up. During my ordeal on the ground the forest had become an entirely different world. I realized I had lost my glasses in the fall. A few minutes of groping around and the glasses were again in my possession. The forest returned to normal.

After checking the pack I slung it back onto my shoulders but felt something awkward in its position. I found that the back band was beginning to tear.

I was concerned about the pack, but this only increased my determination to keep going. I came to an open field, and for the first time that night I saw the moon. How many thousands of men from the beginning of time had gazed upon that huge sphere? I felt good looking at it. I remembered my father telling my brothers and me that we were living in the greatest age of man, when more was known about the universe and about man than in any other age. I wanted to stand there and raise my voice and shout out, "I know all about you. We just landed there. Now the mystery is disappearing."

A half-demolished sign directed me toward a shelter. I had no idea how far away it might be. Sometimes the shelter would be a few feet from a sign like that, sometimes it would be a half or three-quarters of a mile away. I decided to walk a little way, and if the shelter didn't appear soon, I would come back and camp in the field. About 25 yards down the trail nestled the shelter, only its metal roof revealing its presence. I thought about Hillary when he talked about the high altitude camps, where men would set up tents for later use, and the feeling Hillary got when he saw the high-altitude camps after a day's climb. I felt the same way, even though my camp was not at 10,000 feet, or in snow.

Completely exhausted, I looked for a light to examine my damaged pack. Someone had left a huge candle. I found that the lower back band was torn in half. I decided to wait until morning to fix it, and turned my attention to food. Some juice and a few Bolton biscuits served as my meal.

I had used the last of my water for the juice, so taking the candle for light, I started down the trail to find water. The candle transformed the forest into a beautiful place, where the trees and branches became almost human forms, shifting and changing and sliding and creeping as the candle flickered.

After 40 feet or so I came to the spring. There was a tiny trickle of clear water coming from a pipe. Kneeling down, I drank, filled my canteen, and returned to the shelter, where I immediately got into my sleeping bag and fell asleep. During the night I heard heavy rain coming down and was glad for the safety of the shelter.

The next morning I tried to repair my pack, but after a few futile attempts I realized it needed machine sewing to withstand the pressure I was putting on it.

I took my nylon rope and wrapped it around the tubular frame to replace the broken back band. This kept my hips away from the metal frame. After eating, I left the shelter. The rope had a tendency to ride up the bars; I had to stop and pull it down fairly often.

Another problem was that my jeans were clinging to my legs. If I cut off the jeans and made them into shorts I would have problems with the briars. However, that seemed the lesser of two evils, so I removed my jeans and made them into shorts with my pocket knife.

I started walking again, and found I had much more freedom. I was moving so rapidly I began to laugh. It was unbelievable to be traveling at this pace! Then the briars began to cut into me. Even now, almost a year later, I am carrying scars from those briars. They ripped and tore me with a thousand tiny cuts. I finally reached Dennis Cove, and managed to hitch a ride into Elizabethton. Immediately I looked for the police station, to ask where I could have my pack repaired. The police station was usually my first stop when I was unfamiliar with a town.

The police reminded me that it was Sunday, and that all the stores were closed. I would have to wait until tomorrow. They offered me a cell for the night, and after we chatted about my adventures, the officer in charge called the local newspaper and radio station to inform them that a "minor celebrity" was in the area. The result was that I spent the night in the home of a local radio announcer, Mr. Beavers. He gave me my only souvenir for the entire trek: a bayonet which had been picked up after a Civil War battle. Mr. Beavers gave it to me for my brother Tim.

I saw the grave of Mr. Whitehead, "the man who killed 99 bear." As the story was told to me, Mr. Whitehead lived in the mountains with his wife and children. They all died many years before he did. He became a solitary figure, living alone in the mountains and killing bears. Even during his lifetime he was a legendary figure because of the great number of bears he had killed. When he was dying his record for bear killing stood at "99 bear." One of his neighbors went into the woods and found a small cub and brought it to him. Handing him the cub and a knife they asked him if he would like to kill it in order to have a score of 100. He was ready to kill the cub, but at the last minute changed his mind. He couldn't bring himself to kill any more, so the cub was released in the woods.

The graves of Mr. Whitehead and his family were high up in the mountains. It was a peaceful scene, with sunlight streaking through the trees onto the row of graves, each one carefully tended, with wild flowers on them. It is not known who puts the flowers there, but it is said that whenever anyone goes to the graves they are covered with flowers.

Another grave I saw was of great interest to me. It had two headstones which faced each other at a distance of about six feet. Beneath the stones were the remains of two brothers, one on top of the other, and facing each other. They had died over 100 years before, during the War Between the States. They'd fallen in combat and now they were together as brothers should be.

A wreath was placed in front of each stone and alongside, an American flag faded with age. I thought it ironical that two boys who had surrendered their lives for the Southern cause were now honored by the banner of their enemy. This disturbed me. I wanted to take the flag from the grave, but I left it stand.[1]

Another grave, not as elaborate or well-known as the one of the two brothers, was the resting place of 20 Union soldiers. They lay beneath an old oak tree on top of a mound in the field of a farmer. They were the victims of a Confederate who had constantly plagued the Union forces, Colonel John S. Mosby. These 20 soldiers had been captured and hung on the tree which still towers over them.

The long gnarled limbs which over a century ago had held the 20 men still reached out. A plaque on the tree commemorated the men.

As I traveled the crest I saw a man ahead of me. He was sitting on a large rock, his shoulders bent as if looking at the ground. I approached as noisily as I could, partly to warn him of my presence so he would not be startled, and partly to bolster my own courage at meeting a human being in "my sanctuary." Passing him, I nodded and said, "Good afternoon, sir." I hadn't gone five paces when his voice cut through the forest, "Boy, whare ya goin' in sech a rush?"

Immediately I turned around and stood facing an old man with a thick beard that hung well below his waist. His hair poked out from under an old hat and his eyes were a cold demanding blue.

I enjoyed telling him "up the trail a bit." That didn't satisfy him, and he demanded to know exactly "how fur up the trail."

When I told him he said, "Boy, you set raight here and tell me some of yore adventures." I told him one or two I thought he might enjoy, and suddenly he said, "What ya doin wearin' sech a shirt?" The cuffs of my shirt were gone, and what damage pack wear and the briars hadn't done, my elbows had. I told him it was the only one I had. He reached under his beard and began unbuttoning his brown one, which was so new the creases were still in it. He handed it to me and said, "Here, take it."

I didn't want to take the shirt right off his back, but he insisted, so I finally opened my pack to put the shirt in. Immediately he stopped me and said, "No, put it on right now." He reached over and began to unbutton my shirt, so I took it off and put his shirt on. Then

---

[1] Eric may be pardoned for his interpretation, for today only a Civil War buff equipped with a list of the fighting units of both sides would be likely to identify the side that the Sheltons served. Most southern mountaineers who took up arms in the conflict soldiered in the Northern cause. David Shelton, about 60, and his young nephew William joined North Carolina units of the Union army. On a visit home they were ambushed and killed by Confederates. Their tombstones were provided by the federal government. See "The Civil War Comes to the Mountains" in *Appalachian Trailway News* for September 1971.—ED.

I began to tell him some more adventures, but he stopped me and said, "No, no, I've heard enough. You can go now. I'll have a good night's sleep knowing that at least you have a decent shirt on your back."

As I left I asked him where he lived, and he pointed to a small cabin tucked away in the valley. I couldn't remember when anything had meant quite so much to me. The good feelings remained with me until later in the day, when a thunderstorm caught me.

The thunderstorms which were so prevalent in the South had forced me to change my camping habits. In the North it hadn't mattered if I slept on top of the mountain or in the valley, but in the South it made a great difference. If I camped in the valley and it rained, which it usually did, everything would be soaking wet when I woke up in the morning. I would have to waste time drying my equipment. Also, the mountains blocked the sunlight from the valleys, which meant I would have to start hiking later in the morning because of a lack of light. This "low camping," as I called it, was a psychological hindrance to my hiking, too, for upon awakening I would be faced with the prospect of a two or three thousand-foot climb.

The advantages of "high camping" were that I could see what I had accomplished that day, and also where I would be walking the next day. Coupled with this was the fact that the stiff breeze would quickly dry everything out, and in the morning I would find the hiking relatively easy because I would be walking downhill or moving along the ridge. The entire trail was a learning experience, presenting problems which I was forced to solve. My mind was a hiking manual, and I was the author, editor, teacher, and student of it.

The terrain grew quite rough soon after I left Elizabethton, and I really had to work to make my mileage. The Smokies were near, and I knew the trail would get worse. The peaks became higher and their slopes steeper, and with the burning southern sun, conditions were almost unbearable. As I pressed through the woods, a silence settled over everything as if the heat had made the forest creatures mute. The trail crept beneath my feet.

I'd gone about five miles when I decided to stop for a drink of water and a short rest, hoping the sweat would stop pouring from me. I set my pack against a tree, removed my canteen, and drank heavily. Suddenly a sound came from the underbrush. I paused, the canteen still pressed to my lips. A bear? Lowering the canteen, I turned toward the noise. There was only a fortress of briars. I listened intently, and thought it not likely to be a bear. A bear in a hurry crashes through everything in its path, raising quite a disturbance.

"No, it's not a bear," I told myself. "It could be a deer, grazing through the woods." I remembered in the Shenandoah forest watching a doe and three fawns amble contentedly through the woods, chewing on large pieces of tree fungus and the delicate ends of young saplings. They had moved along slowly, completely ignoring my presence.

Now I moved forward through the brush, which cracked beneath my feet. A path suddenly appeared. It was well used. I saw fresh footprints. I stood in bewilderment, unable to understand how such a path could appear in the middle of the forest. I'd followed footsteps in Maine for days on end, until I finally discovered they were made the preceding fall, then froze and were preserved through the winter. But this was midsummer, and the tracks were fresh. Almost every indentation was clear and precise.

The snap of a twig brought me from my study. Glancing up, I saw a man sitting on a stump. An ancient shotgun was across his knees. Startled, I didn't say a word. Something told me to keep quiet. "He must be a hunter," I thought, as all the mysterious pieces now fell into place, the noises, the lack of animal sounds, and the hidden trail. It was obvious he hadn't seen me, and I decided to approach him carefully. I knew some hunters were a little trigger-happy. He might mistake me for a bear. I'd sure hate to finish my trip that way, I thought. I gazed at the man, trying to figure out what his reactions would be if he got a glimpse of me. He was a short man, almost boyish in appearance except that a massive black beard enshrouded his head. His clothing was dirty and ragged. The shirt showed evidence of travel in briar country. The sleeves had a thick grime on the cuffs and collar. His hands were equally filthy. I watched as he removed chewing tobacco from a small leather bag and popped it into his mouth. Then he touched his tongue to his fingers, licking up the tiny pieces of tobacco.

"Good afternoon, sir," I said.

The response was a startled, "What the hell ya doin' here? Git out!" The gun barrel moved toward me as a further sign that my presence was not appreciated. I stood speechless, hoping he'd realize that I offered no harm.

"Did ya hear me?" he commanded, rising to his feet and spitting out the tobacco in an ugly brown wad. I watched it strike the sand and then said, "I'm not doing any harm. I'm just passing through."

"I don't give a damn watcha doin'. I told you to git, and I mean git. Don't tell me yer so innocent." he answered, glancing back over his shoulder at something in the woods. "I'd hate ta hurt ya."

My eyes followed his, and I saw two or three other men standing beside a large black object perched over a small fire. Immediately one word came to my mind. I plainly recognized the object. It was a *still*. I had heard about such oddities being hidden in the mountains. I also remembered hearing that the men who run them take no chances with outsiders. I could almost feel the bullets enter my flesh. Without even realizing it, I found myself replying to his first warning to "git out."

"Yes, sir, I'm leaving. I'm going right now. Ah, good afternoon."

And then I hightailed it out of there without even looking back. The briars, which I usually feared, were trampled without hesitation.

When I was back on the Appalachian Trail I didn't stop to see if I was being pursued, but whipped the pack up on my shoulders and kept running down the trail for the next few miles. I finally collapsed from exhaustion.

I continued at a rapid pace for the remainder of the day, frequently glancing about the forest. Every now and then I would see what appeared to be the flashing of clothing through the trees. This kept me moving at a rapid pace. I feared I was being followed to see if I was going to report the location of the still.

That night I stayed awake with Mr. Beavers's gift at my side, hoping the bayonet's 104 years of idleness would be extended to 105 years. I awoke with sunlight in my eyes. I realized I'd fallen asleep. Exhaustion had overcome fear. I was refreshed, and the fears of yesterday vanished beneath the prospects of the new day.

The terrain grew rougher with each mile. It was obvious that the Smokies were not too far away. That afternoon I met some hikers who were going north. They told me that two Explorer Scouts were a mile or so ahead of me, moving south. I continued hiking, almost at a trot, in an attempt to catch them. Sweat poured down my face and body in rivers, soaking my clothing.

The ground seemed to hold my feet as I stumbled along. Each step became a strain, a fight to overcome the mountains. Suddenly I felt a severe pain in my back. I jerked myself to a halt in time to avoid falling down a steep incline. I dropped to my knees, my back arched in pain. I discovered that the other back band on my pack had given way under the bouncing and juggling it was receiving on the rough terrain. I wrapped cord around the two metal bars, as I had done once before. This emergency repair would have to do until I reached Newfound Gap in the Smokies.

The delay gave me a few minutes to rest and catch my breath, but it had no effect on my sweating. After partially emptying the canteen of water over my head, I was on the trail again, pressing to make up for lost time. The repair rope on my pack hindered my hiking because it constantly slipped out of position and was very uncomfortable. An hour later, despite the difficulties of terrain, weather, and equipment, I overtook the two Explorer Scouts.

"Hey," I said, in not much more than a whisper. A second attempt produced a little more volume, and a third call brought a full-fledged mountain man bellow from somewhere inside me.

The two Scouts stopped, turned around, and looked up at me. "Hi there," one of them answered. I identified myself as Eric Ryback, from Michigan. They told me they planned to hike through the Smokies.

The trail, although rugged, was what I considered an expressway as trails go. It was wide, well-marked, and obviously well-traveled. We hiked a few more hours that day and then set up camp. This was one of the few occasions when I had the enjoyment of spending an evening around a campfire with other hikers, swapping tales, and just talking. The evening ended with a final story about bears by Mike, who concluded, "And those damn bears tore the hell outa' my pack. It makes me sick to think about it, a whole summer's work wiped out, sleeping bag, pack, even my camera!"

The next morning we got up pretty early and started hiking, pressing for those early miles before the southern sun reached its zenith. It was good to hike with someone else.

About two o'clock in the afternoon we were approaching False Gap Shelter when we heard noises in the distance. Curious, we quickened our pace. As we emerged from the woods the noises sounded like small explosions. The cause of all this noise was Mike's natural enemy— Bear. A bear was upside down in one of the trash containers. He had his back feet hooked onto the edge of the can and was pawing through the contents, happily unaware of our presence. His butt was high in the air.

Mike became a study in vengeance. He cautioned us to keep silent. He quickly patrolled the area, looking for a stick. When he emerged from the shelter with a five-foot two-by-four, both Jim and I grabbed our packs and scrambled on top of the shelter.

Mike's face was like that of a gladiator, ready for combat. As we stretched out on the tin roof, our noble Explorer approached the center of the arena. He advanced to within a few feet of the large hairy rump. He wavered for a moment, then took a step back and wound up like a baseball player in the world series. The two-by-four was his bat and there was no margin for error here. He swung, and as his board made contact with that bear's butt, his account with the bears was settled. There was a roar, then a squeal, then a boom that reverberated across the mountains. It grew in volume until we plugged our ears to shut out the deafening noise. The sound was one of fear, surprise, and pain, all mixed into one earsplitting bellow. We watched dumbfounded as the bear rose high into the air, giving out with bear lingo.

A fraction of a second later he bounced to the ground, landing square on his stricken area. The bear sat facing Mike, who was standing with the two-by-four, stunned by his own audacity. They were face-to-face for a moment. Mike gave a yowl, loud but not equal to the bear's. He dropped the two-by-four and began running around the lean-to, the bear in hot pursuit. Mike tried vainly to find a quick way to get onto the roof.

Realizing he couldn't make it, Mike began to run even harder. Whether from hope of shaking off the bear or from centrifugal force, Mike went flying off through the woods, crashing down brush and briars with the bear close behind.

We lashed Mike's pack to ours, and went on to the next shelter some five miles away. About ten o'clock that night a panting Mike entered the light of our campfire. Worn and haggard, his clothing torn, a blank expression on his face, Mike just stood and looked at the fire.

"Hey, Mike, what took ya?" I asked.

"Shut up Ryback, go to hell! Those damn bears!"

The next day we learned that just when Mike felt that he couldn't take another step, he came to a ravine. A limb from a tree was hanging over the edge. Mike grabbed for it, and the bear lunged and slid down the embankment. The bear sat at the foot of the embankment for a moment, turned to look at Mike, and then ambled off into the woods.

The night gave Mike time to cool off and rest up, and the next morning we were on our way again. My companions continued along the trail, while I descended to the Sugarlands Visitors Center to get my pack repaired.

Sugarlands was a one building complex, relatively modern and very inviting. Inside, posted on the walls, was information about interesting sights in the area. In a separate room there was a museum with stuffed animals illustrating the various species of wildlife found in the Smokies. Also, there were warnings about bears. Their lack of sociability was shown by a display of tin cans, lunch boxes, and other containers which bears had destroyed. There was nothing which was a part of the bears' natural habitat, except for some clawed tree limbs. This proved to me again that man not only ruins his own environment, but that of the bears and other animals, too.

I read all the bear warnings and laughed to myself. "The bears are my friends and I have no fear of them. They'd never harm me." Later I came to regret my feeling of security with regard to bears.

As a protective measure the lean-tos had been equipped with cyclone wire fencing across the open front. In other words, in the Smokies they cage the people, not the animals. The bears had gotten in the habit of coming into the lean-tos while the hikers slept. The unhappy hikers sometimes found their packs being mauled by a curious or hungry bear. The Great Smoky Mountains National Park was created for the enjoyment of the people and it would seem strange to tell them they couldn't stay in their own park because of the bears, so this unique device—the human cage—has been developed. Now the bear could peer in, inspect the unsuspecting camper, and leave whenever he wanted to. The humans could sleep easier, knowing they were subject to inspection only, and that the curious bears couldn't thrust their snouts into the sleeping bags or packs. Through that stretch of mountains almost every lean-to bunk is decorated with bear carvings. The language is not literally translatable, but the meaning is clear. Bear claw marks have a message most people can understand.

I inquired about pack repairs, and the assistance I received was most welcome. When the repairs were completed, I was given a shower, a hot meal, and a bed for the night—luxuries for which I was grateful.

During a discussion of my adventures someone mentioned a terrifying scream they had heard the day before. It had sent everyone outdoors to look up into the mountains. They thought that a bear had gone berserk, or had fallen off a cliff. I decided not to change their beliefs, and just listened.

By late afternoon I was on my way again. While in Sugarlands I had heard about three hikers who were moving south, and remembering the great time I'd had with the two Explorer Scouts, I decided to overtake them.

At a shelter that night I encountered a lone traveler, who was up in the mountains to watch birds. This struck me as being a little odd but I accepted the explanation without hesitation. Just having company was enough, although I couldn't figure out why he'd come into so primitive a place simply to watch a few feathery creatures.

He was lean and sinewy in appearance and with the binoculars around his neck he looked more like a frontline commander than a person in search of birds. After talking with him, though, I will never joke about "bird watchers." It's really more than a science, it's an art.

The moment a bird would chirp I would hear all about the creature's appearance, origin, mating, nesting, migratory habits, what he ate, and countless other facts. If I were a bird, I'd be proud to think that someone had such knowledge of my life. Our meal was interrupted many times; we both leaped to our feet as soon as a single chirp was heard. Actually, I had no real desire to break off my meal for a bird, but it seemed the polite thing to do, so I jumped up every time he did, without question. This was done in silence. He would begin to scan the trees with the long black binoculars which seemed almost a part of him. The binoculars would remain glued to his face as he walked forward; somehow he avoided the branches and other obstacles in his path.

That evening, as we sat around the campfire, I told him about my adventures, and he discussed his past. Fortunately, the birds had stopped chirping. Either they were tired of being talked about, or they sympathized with me and decided to give me a break.

A few years before, I was informed, he had been interested in judo and karate, taking lessons in both and becoming quite an expert, earning his brown belt. However, he encountered some unexpected difficulties, and two broken legs and two broken arms over a period of a few years made him lose interest in these sports.

I was hoping to get an early start the next morning and make up for the miles I had lost at Sugarlands. School would be opening on the fourth of September, and my senior year must be played out. It was a chore I had no real desire for, but I realized it was a necessity for the life I knew I had to conform to.

Quickly I drifted off into sleep, shutting out all sounds except the familiar ones of the forest. Suddenly I heard a chirp. My dozing was shattered by a hand clutching my shoulder. I moved a bit to shake the hand off, but the grip tightened. I opened my eyes, and standing over me was the bird watcher, his powerful hand clutching my shoulder and shaking me.

"What the ———," I muttered.

"Eric, Eric, there's a yellow-bellied, triwinged, dovetailed something or other I can't recall its real name out there. Come on, it's right outside," he whispered.

Wild-eyed, he dashed from the lean-to, lifting the binoculars to his face. I was too bewildered to move, realizing that some crazy bird had interrupted my sleep, not by his own chirp but by that of his admirer. Shortly afterward the bird watcher reentered the lean-to, explaining that he'd forgotten it was dark outside, and how he'd missed the chance of a lifetime.

"Boy, what would the guys back at the Audubon Society have said!" he exclaimed, grieving that such a rare bird had evaded him. I sat for another half hour as he described the bird and told of the few instances when men had "actually" seen the bird. Upon concluding his elegy he paused and then said, "You know, Eric, now I'm gonna have to buy a pair of infrared binoculars. This is too much. Do you realize that with infrared binoculars I could have studied that bird closer than any man ever has?" Then he went on to explain all the advantages and uses of an infrared setup, and the approximate costs.

As I listened to him, the words began to blend and mix together, losing clarity and meaning. He may have talked all night, for all I know, but ten minutes later I was dead to the world, not from boredom, but from exhaustion. For I have to admit that most of his explanations were interesting, and even helped me to distinguish some birds farther down the trail.

I left at an early hour the next morning, but the bird watcher was already up and about looking for "early birds." We had breakfast together and after the meal we both set out, each on his own business, he with his binoculars, me with my pack.

The heat of the morning became oppressive; it promised to be an unusually hot day. I was glad I had an early start. Afternoon came and the heat became relentless and unbearable. The trail was baked as solid as concrete. I was pondering over the condition of the trail when I heard a muffled puffing and the sound of footsteps. The sounds grew louder. I couldn't imagine who would be running down the trail under such bad conditions. The flash of a shirt caught my eye, and a man came around the turn. He didn't see me and kept moving toward me, each footstep falling exactly like the one before it. His head was completely bald and glistening with sweat in the sunlight. A bright band held the sweat from his eyes. He had on a plaid shirt. He was quite heavy, actually pudgy, and his stomach bulged out. His shorts were sweat-streaked and hung just to the knees; he had on knee socks of bright red and low hiking boots. As he approached me the snuffles and grunts grew louder. My first impulse was to take a picture of him. It would have made an interesting picture, but I didn't want to offend him.

When he caught sight of me he reached out for a tree for support. He removed the band from his head, wiped his face and neck vigorously, and introduced himself as a "fellow hiker." He asked me how far I had hiked and I told him from "up the trail a bit," and then enjoyed the shock when I told him the actual starting point of my hike. This was something I had perfected by this time. My listener's face and eyes reacted first in disbelief, then astonishment. Finally he grabbed me and insisted he would take me to Martha, "Oh, my gosh, oh, my gosh, Martha, Martha," he started shouting, meanwhile pushing me ahead of him, "let's go find Martha and the kids."

I detached myself from him and explained that I had a schedule to maintain. He said, "Wait right here, don't move, I'll go and get Martha and the kids, oh, my gosh." With that he was off and running while I called after him that I would be unable to wait.

I was now beginning to realize that the woods were not just for the animals and hikers. There was plenty of room for those who liked to trot through the forests, or sit for days on end watching birds. And this was the way it should be.

One night I hiked later than usual and had my own adventure with bears, less dramatic than Mike's, but exciting nevertheless. Darkness had come over the Smokies as I finished my meal. Retreating to the lean-to I closed the gate behind me and settled into one of the top bunks to watch the world that exists in the glowing coals of a fire. My mind was in that tranquil dreamlike state a tired hiker welcomes. I drifted into a half-sleep. An owl reported on its night watch, a tree frog gave a small chirp; then I heard something lazily lumbering through the woods.

Suddenly a large trash can came hurtling against the lean-to. I bolted upright in my sleeping bag and saw a bear clamoring about outside. The can boomed each time he struck it; the force of the blows actually made the can fly into the air.

Presently the bear was joined by two companions, and the trio really began having fun. First, the three of them completely demolished the trash can. Next they turned their attention to the latrine and knocked it over, splintered the wood, and knocked the pot to pieces. Then one of the bears fell into the privy hole and had a difficult time getting out. Finally they came to the register box which was on a pole. I had just signed it, "Eric Ryback, Maine to Georgia." The bears knocked the register box off and tore it to shreds.

I suddenly realized that the shelter was the only thing left. I checked the gate to the cyclone fence across the front of the shelter. I chained it and bolted it. Sure enough, in a short time all three of the bears came to the front of the lean-to. I had read about using live coals to scare animals. I tried brandishing some coals about, but these bears weren't afraid. I knew they were after my food, but I wasn't going to give it to them if I could help it.

A huge paw came crashing against the cyclone fencing. It gave me a good scare. I remembered hearing or reading that if you hit a bear hard enough on the nose he would go away (later I remembered that was the rule for sharks instead of bears). I grabbed a fair-sized stick and hit each snuffling nose a good whack. There was a quick response. The screams echoed against the walls of the lean-to and came roaring back to my ears.

The bears' assault began in earnest now. Those bears were smart, though. They soon realized that they were not going to get through the fence. One of the bears began to dig beneath the fencing. The huge paws easily cut through the moist earth, dragging out more and more dirt with each stroke.

Some thick logs had been used for seats. In desperation I rolled these logs into the holes the bear was making under the fence. The bear that was digging grew even more vicious when I did this. He pounded the earth and logs in a futile attempt to regain his lost advantage.

Meanwhile, one of the other bears began to pound on the tin roof, turning my fortress into a booming drum. The entire hut shook and reverberated at each stroke. I felt my position was growing more desperate as each second passed.

The third bear, who had been intent on trying to pound the walls down, now turned his attention to an eight-inch gap between the wooden side of the shelter wall and metal fencing over the open front.

The rest of the night was made up of moves by the bears to get at my food, and countermoves on my part to keep them from broaching my defenses. I was almost overwhelmed with fatigue when the first pale grey of dawn appeared. The bears, as if summoned by some unseen force, retreated into the woods. I was left alone on an abandoned battlefield. Still uneasy, I quickly shouldered my pack and left for Fontana Village. Surveying the damage as I left, I saw a scene of almost total destruction. The trash barrels were torn and chewed.

The latrine was now only scraps of lumber. Animal graffiti, written with claw and tooth on the outside walls of the lean-to, told a story that was obvious even to an inexperienced eye.

The night's experience made me feel a little closer to the human race than I had the day before. Reflecting back to the warnings about bears at Sugarlands, I regretted my egotism in thinking that I was completely in tune with the creatures of the forest.

By late morning I overtook the three hikers I had been hearing about. After my experiences of the night before, I was glad to have their companionship. They were from Tennessee and were also headed for Fontana Village.

Upon entering Fontana Village that afternoon we decided to have a good meal. A small restaurant that served fish was appealing, since the fish were freshly caught from a pond in front of the restaurant, cleaned, and cooked immediately.

We approached the restaurant, trail-worn in appearance, but too hungry to worry about it. We were about to enter when we decided to check our finances. Someone said, "Hey, I don't have enough money, someone will have to help me out a little." I stopped dead in my tracks, remembering that I was down to about 70 cents. Glancing about I saw both Jack and Jim standing there with empty palms. Gary was the only one who had money, but not enough to finance all of us, "Well, guys," he said, "looks like we're going to have to go back to dehydrated food." There was distress in his voice.

"Hey, wait a minute, I think I've got it," Jack said, triumphantly. He was notorious for his wild schemes. The other guys just kept walking. Apparently they knew that Jack's plans could lead to problems.

"Hey, come on, Gary, this one's foolproof. It won't fail and we'll have ourselves a good meal," Jack coaxed. Gary slowed down, but Jim said, "Just remember last time."

"Jim, think about me and Ryback with a good fish dinner when you're sitting over your dehydrated junk." The two paused, looked at each other, started to walk away, then turned and came back.

"All right, but this had better be good. If we get into any trouble ———"

"Don't worry. This idea can't fail. I've got everything down pat," Jack reassured us.

The three of us, like sheep to the slaughter, followed the shepherd without question. We found ourselves in front of the pond, gazing down at the long sleek fish gliding back and forth.

Jack took a thin metal wire from his pocket and quickly formed a small loop at one end. After threading the other end through the loop, forming a small noose, he put it around one of his fingers and pulled. The wire slid through the loop and tightened around his finger. Jack looked up and smiled, displaying the snare with pride.

The small wire loop was lowered into the water. Gary said, "Oh, no, Jim, you can't do that." I stayed, too intrigued to worry. The wire was practically invisible and the fish swam about freely, taking no heed of it. Jack kept trying to get it in the path of a fish, but they managed to evade the wire. From his pocket Jack took a small piece of Bolton biscuit and dropped it into the water. Immediately a fish spotted it and set a course straight for the floating morsel. Jack maneuvered the wire loop so that it was directly in the fish's path.

"Come on, just a little more, that's it, a little closer," Jack coached the fish in a gentle tone.

Warily, the fish approached the small piece of food, seeming to follow Jack's quiet commands. About a foot from the wire the fish slowed and then stopped, hovering in the water as if contemplating his next move.

"Come on, don't sit there, get that bread, just a little farther, come on, boy," Jack pleaded quietly, watching the silver body quiver and then inch forward. The fish suddenly darted forward, then stopped, his mouth a mere fraction of an inch from the loop.

"That's nice, take it easy, real slow," Jack begged.

I heard Gary say hello to someone. A shadow fell over me, and I glanced up. There were blue pant legs resting on shiny black shoes. My eyes followed upward and a pistol holster and black belt came into my line of vision. Then I saw the silver badge and blue shirt. I stumbled to my feet, smiling, a little apprehensive because I hadn't been to a barbershop since leaving home. Longhairs are not appreciated in the South.

"Uh, hello, officer," I managed, keeping relatively calm.

Jim, too, stood up to greet the policeman. Only Jack wasn't aware of the policeman's presence. He was still whispering quiet words to his friend of the deep.

Jack's talk bewildered the officer almost as much as his sudden appearance had startled us. He took a few steps forward to look into the pond to see what Jack was talking to. He leaned over the fence, gazing down beneath the rippled surface at the fish which hovered below Jack.

Jack's voice suddenly gained in volume and excitement, "I've got it, I've got it, just a l-i-t-t-l-e more," he said, stretching the word "little." "THERE!" he cried out, throwing a triumphant glance at the figure to his left. I had been standing there a few minutes before, but the policeman was there now. The policeman smiled at him, almost as excited as Jack. Jack threw a desperate glance at us, and then screamed at the top of his lungs, "My gosh, look at that fish jump!" The policeman almost fell over as the fish seemed to fly from the water, do a somersault in the air, and then plunge back into the water. The officer stared in sheer amazement, looking at the pond, then at Jack, and back at the pond again.

"How did he manage to do that?" he muttered.

Jack, realizing he had taken the officer by surprise, explained, "Oh, it's just an old trick my father taught me, kind of like fish psychology." The officer nodded appreciatively, not noticing the snare which Jack had dropped.

That evening we ate our dehydrated food and had a great time as we made camp on the steps to the visitors' center at Fontana Dam. I had already found one piece of equipment these guys carried that was superior to mine: their stove. It was a Svea. Mine, a Swiss import, had not been suitable to my needs. I had mailed it home from Glencliff, New Hampshire, and had used only wood fires since then. I was really studying equipment now, for I had decided to be the first person to hike the two longest mountain crest trails in the United States.[1] To do this I knew that I must improve my equipment, food, and techniques.

Jack disappeared while the rest of us talked. Later we learned that he had been prowling the countryside in search of a frog. When he had one that satisfied him, he climbed to the balcony above us and held the frog over Gary's sleeping bag and let go.

The smooth leggy creature did a few somersaults in the air and plopped down on Gary's face. Suddenly the night was filled with screams. Gary's bag seemed to explode. White down scattered in all directions. A giant mushroom of feathers floated lazily to the concrete. A laugh bellowed out, familiar to Gary and Jim, unknown to me: Jack in triumph. The frog had entered Gary's sleeping bag, hence the explosion. When things had quieted down, we recovered the frog and released him in the grass nearby.

The next morning we awoke to find tourists stepping around us.

[1] Eric completed the 2,500-mile Pacific Crest Trail on October 16, 1970; he was the first to hike the entire Pacific Crest Trail, and the first to hike *both* the Pacifc Crest and Appalachian trails. He told about his Pacific Crest hike in *The High Adventure of Eric Ryback*. In 1972 Eric and his brother Tim scouted a possible Continental Divide Trail from Canada to Mexico through five states. This adventure is recounted in Eric's and Tim's book, *The Ultimate Journey*.—ED.

The ranger came over and said that if we were going to sit around on the steps he would put us to work, so we had the pleasure of raising "Old Glory." Later that morning we said our good-byes after agreeing to do some hiking together in the snow.

The mountains were just as rough as before, but the struggle was made worthwhile by the sunrises, which were the most spectacular I had ever seen. These magnificent sunrises were often seen in southern Virginia, Tennessee, and North Carolina. From my maps I realized that the next morning might be the last time I would see such a sunrise on this trek. It was something most people would *never* see, so I decided to catch this "ceremony" of the sun's rising on film.

I came to an abandoned fire tower and decided to sleep in the cabin on top of the tower. I would try to get my perfect picture just as the sun rose. I could see that getting into the tower would not be an easy task. Taking only what I would need for the night, I hung my pack high in a tree so no animal could get into it.

The first 90 feet up the ladder was like a walk across the street. Within moments I was at the bottom of the cabin itself. It was locked. There was a small catwalk around the outside of the observation cabin, and I realized this catwalk would have to be my "key to the lock." An acrobatic act was necessary.

With my left hand on the top rung and my left foot down a little farther, I swung my body out toward the outer edge of the platform above me. My weight gave me great momentum, almost pulling my hand from the rung. I reached my right arm out for the edge of the platform, but was about two inches short. I was dangling 90 feet in the air, supported only by an arm and a foot. Did I want to risk my life for a photograph, or should I retreat to the ground? Remembering what I had been through for 2,000 miles—mountains, snow, heat, loneliness, battles with Nature and her moods—I felt that this was something I should be able to work out.

Knowing that a single error might be fatal, I pushed my left foot away from the ladder far enough to give me those extra inches. As my right hand clasped the edge of the platform, I released my left hand. I was hanging by five fingers some 90 feet in the air. For a second I regretted my decision as I hung there between life and death. Then I brought my free hand up. Ten fingers were the margin now. I stopped to catch my breath and to determine my next move. That wasn't too hard. There were only two alternatives, either climb up or fall down. For some reason, the first alternative appealed to me most. Now the punishment my body had taken over the past 2,000 miles paid off. I didn't have to wish for strength. It was there just waiting to be used. Swinging my body to and fro, I built up momentum, and my feet swung out away from the tower. For a second only the air was between me and the ground. Then I had my elbows on the catwalk. Slowly I pulled myself up. My chest was on the wooden floor. Then one leg, followed by the other, and I was completely on the catwalk.

I removed the equipment draped over me. The window to the cabin was unlocked. I lifted the frame and tossed my equipment in. Carefully I placed one foot into the cabin to make certain the floor would support my weight.

It was dark before I fell asleep. Several times during the night I got up to see if the sun was coming up yet. After about the fifth time I collapsed from fatigue and fell into a deep sleep.

I was awakened by a beam of light striking my eyes. I almost began to cry because I thought I'd missed the sunrise. I leaped to my feet, grabbed the camera, and glanced out the window. The sun was just lifting a fiery edge over the horizon. Tears of joy came to my eyes. *This was the happiest moment of my entire hike.* All the joys and sorrows had been transformed into this one second as I emerged from complete defeat to complete victory. I wiped the tears from my face and brought the camera up to get my picture.

Afterward I went from window to window photographing the panorama around me—the mountains, the forests, the clouds. I heard a bird sing out. It was answered by another. Everything was perfect. I loved it all. The world was my friend and companion.

Getting down from the fire tower proved to be more difficult than getting up, but I finally arrived safely on the ground. I removed my pack from the tree and ate a few gulps of baby food. An hour later I was at the Georgia border. It was my last state.

Coming to a road I discovered I was in Rabun County, Georgia. A sign pointed to a store some miles down the road and I started for it. I had gone back to eating baby food as I seemed unable to keep the dehydrated food in my stomach any more.

Some men inside the small store questioned me sharply. They were quite unimpressed with me and what I had accomplished. Their harsh accusations that I couldn't possibly have hiked all that way brought tears of anger to my eyes. I left the store and went to retrieve my pack.

As I reached for the pack a man who had been in the store, but was not one of my accusers, approached me and invited me to have lunch with his family at their summer home. I was not too eager, after the hostile reception by the men in the store, yet when I saw this man's gentle manner I felt secure. His wife and children were waiting for him in his car, and we drove to their summer home. I spent the evening with them, for their hospitality extended from lunch through dinner to a comfortable bed for the night.

The Charles L. Weltners, as I learned, were a family much like our own. Each member was his own individual self, respecting each other for what they were, respecting themselves enough to respect everyone. This family meant a lot to me, as did all the families who were good to me along the way.

Reflecting back on my journey I thought of the many people who had helped me. It seemed that whenever I needed help, there was always someone there to help. When I was sick the Shaws were there to take me in. When loneliness struck, I found myself. In finding myself, I found God. As I thought of all this, I was almost sorry to see the end of the trail.

I was really nearing the end. When I entered Vogel State Park the park superintendent called a reporter from the *Atlanta Journal and Constitution*. We sat for a long time talking about my trek, finally getting to bed when it was almost dawn.

In the morning I was escorted to the top of Blood Mountain and pictures were taken. The park superintendent's wife said it was a good thing I was leaving, because she would have sent me to the barber along with her summer crew of college boys. I assured her that I would be to a barber within hours after my parents saw me. However, I had really begun to enjoy long hair; it seemed to fit what I was doing.

I spent my last night sleeping in a field, a short 17 miles from Springer Mountain, the end of the trail.

I reflected back to the boy I had been when I started and the man I now felt I was. I knew one thing. I belonged to Nature and I would return; but first I had to finish my last year of high school. Suddenly I felt eager to be back in school. I wanted to see if everything else had changed as much as I felt I had. I wanted to have good teachers and to learn from them.

My thoughts turned to my parents. Everyone had asked me how my mother could let me go, and I had taken a certain pride in saying she worried. I know she worried and covered it up with smart sayings like "he's safer there than on the highway" or "you should see him drive to Ann Arbor." I wanted to talk to her and tell her I was grown up now and she needn't worry when she learned I would be leaving again.

My father was a different matter; I was certain that though he was worried, he just figured that I would be living up to his good opinion of me. Suddenly I remembered that my father and a friend of mine, Hans Jensen, were flying south at that very minute to meet me. I quickened my pace. Reaching the top of the mountain, I saw the sign which read:

SPRINGER MOUNTAIN

SOUTHERN TERMINUS OF THE APPALACHIAN TRAIL

A MOUNTAIN FOOTPATH EXTENDING 2,000 MILES TO

MT. KATAHDIN, MAINE

I signed my name and the date, September 3, 1969.

A Long Walk Home
By Jeffrey M. Hancock

Started at SPRINGER MOUNTAIN on June 2, 1969
Finished at MT. KATAHDIN on September 5, 1969

One evening in October, 1968, my parents and I began to talk about things we wanted to do. At 16 I wanted to go out and see the world, and do something exciting and different on my own. I thought motorcycling around the country would be a great adventure, but my mother didn't like the idea, and I didn't either after I'd thought more about it. After all, I had never even been on a motorcycle. Then I came up with the idea of hiking the Appalachian Trail, and my parents liked this idea better. They encouraged me to find out more about it.

I had joined the Boy Scouts when I was 12, and when I was 14 I went to Philmont Scout Ranch in New Mexico with a group of local Scouts. This rugged 138,000-acre preserve lies on the slopes of the Sange de Cristo Range of the Rocky Mountains. We hiked 75 miles in a trip that took 13 days, starting from a base camp located at over 6,000 feet. The higher peaks went over 13,000 feet! When I came home I began hiking regularly in the White Mountains. I set as my goal the summits of all the 46 peaks in New Hampshire that are over 4,000 feet.

In August of 1968, while hiking in the White Mountains, I saw an entry in the Guyot Shelter registry: *Howard Bassett, Wolcott, Conn. Hiking Appalachian Trail from Georgia to Maine.* I wrote down Mr. Bassett's address and after the talk with my parents, I wrote to Mr. Bassett. He invited me to visit. I prepared six pages of questions to ask him, and we spent a full day talking and looking at his large-scale maps of the Appalachian Trail. Howard had spent his spare time for a whole year in studying the Appalachian Trail guidebooks and making enlarged maps with a scale of four inches to the mile. He had transferred a lot of information from the guidebooks to these maps. He had updated his maps after returning from his own hike, so they contained much valuable information.

I decided that a cache system was the best method of food supply

1107

for me. Howard had used this system. I asked him for a copy of all of his cache descriptions, with the small maps he had made showing where each cache had been buried. I also asked him for a list of the stores, restaurants, and post offices along the trail.

I tried, without success, to find a hiking partner in my school. Realizing that I would need more than the normal 10-week school vacation, I asked for and received permission from the school committee to leave early in the spring and return late in the fall. I would be missing 4½ weeks of school. The principal, Mr. Peter N. Coffin, was of great help to me in obtaining this permission.

Using the guidebooks and maps, I prepared a trip plan. Then, using Mr. Bassett's 28 cache sites plus two more of my own, I figured out how much food to leave at each cache. I then prepared a food list showing the items that would be put into each cache. From January to mid-May many hours were spent in making the hiking itinerary and the food plans. I had hoped to spend several weekends learning more about my equipment by using it on camping trips, but I never found time to do this. Colin Fletcher's book *The Complete Walker* helped with the selection of gear. We picked up my custom-made summer hiking boots from Peter Limmer and Sons of Intervale, New Hampshire, in early April.

I purchased the food and the rest of the equipment in early May. All the food was spread out over our playroom. We broke all the Richmoor four-man packs in half. Enough powdered milk to make a quart a day, and enough Tang to make a pint a day, were put into individual plastic bags. In addition, a pound of peanuts and 13 ounces of raisins were allotted for each week. This made for quite a few hundred plastic bags! Also, a jar of Wesson oil, a jar of liquid soap, a plastic bag of salt, a plastic bag of sugar, a box of matches, and a plastic bag of napkins and paper towels were added to each cache. Of these items, I found I needed only the matches, napkins, and paper towels. The Wesson oil, soap, salt, and sugar were left in the caches.

The items for each cache were packed loosely into several one-gallon plastic jars. Later, the jars were repacked very tightly by my father, and my mother sealed them by dipping them, cover and all, into hot paraffin. We also planned to leave a quart soda bottle of white gas for my stove at each cache and my mother sealed these bottles with paraffin, too.

My brother Jon, Dad, and I buried caches 15 through 21 from Virginia to Massachusetts on the weekend of May 17–19. Right up until the night before we left for Georgia we were putting caches together.

The cache system takes a great deal of planning and a lot of travel by automobile, but the food is right on the trail waiting for the hiker when he arrives. This is also probably the most expensive type of food supply system, and cuts down on the fresh food a hiker would probably obtain if he were buying his food in stores along the way. Another disadvantage of the cache system is that all of those jars were still in the ground after my hike. The store system is probably cheaper, and it allows the hiker to adjust his diet as well as to meet more people, but stores are often closed at the wrong times.

As a greenhorn when I started, I relied on the opinions of others about food, but the only reliable guidelines are one's own taste buds. I included many packages of mixes to bake, as well as dehydrated egg breakfasts, pancakes, and French toast. I threw away most of these items, finding them too much bother to prepare and the pans too difficult to clean afterward. My stove had a very concentrated flame, so I found that my pancakes were burned in the center, while the outside was still doughy.

I used three kinds of food: supermarket, In-Flight, and dehydrated. The supermarket foods were items like Tang, tuna, instant pudding, hot chocolate, raisins, peanuts, and instant oatmeal. Through a friend I got the In-Flight food from an army PX. Each In-Flight meal consisted of four cans and an accessory pack: a can of crackers; a can of fruit such as peaches, pears, apricots, or fruit cocktail; a can of dessert such as chocolate nut roll, pound cake, or fruitcake; and a can of meat such as boned chicken, spiced beef with sauce, or chopped ham and eggs. The can of meat was heated in boiling water for several minutes before eating. Because of its weight, I generally scheduled the In-Flight food for the first two meals following the pickup from each cache. The canned fruits were excellent, as were the desserts. The meat was OK. I used the crackers with a meat spread for lunch. As they were in a can, these crackers kept better than other kinds.

The dehydrated foods that I used were of two varieties: energy foods and main meals. The energy items were Hershey's Tropical chocolate bars, cereal bars, beef jerky, fruit pemmican, trail cookies, and Kendall mint cake.

Here is the food list for cache 6 at Devil Fork Gap on the North Carolina–Tennessee border:

BREAKFAST	LUNCH	SUPPER	SNACKS
Day 18			
———	In-Flight meal ½ pkg. Kool-Aid	In-Flight ground meat and spa- ghetti meal ½ pkg. Kool-Aid	———

BREAKFAST	LUNCH	SUPPER	SNACKS
Day 19			
2 pkg. Ralston	4½-oz. can deviled	Lipton turkey meal	2 pkg. Enerzades
1 can Swift's bacon	ham	brownie mix	
Tang	⅓ pkg. Sea Pilot	½ pkg. green beans	
	crackers	Perma-Pak vege-	
	½ pkg. apple chips	table salad blend	
	2 trail cookies	½ pkg. Kool-Aid	
	2 sucrose tablets		
	½ pkg. Kool-Aid		
Day 20			
½ pkg. peach slices	1 can Spam spread	½ vegetable rice	1 fruit pemmican
1 box raisin bran	fruitcake	dinner	bar
pecan cake roll	⅓ pkg. Sea Pilot	1¼ oz. beef jerky	2 trail cookies
Tang	crackers	1 can crackers	2 sucrose tablets
2 pkg. hot chocolate	½ pkg. Kool-Aid	½ French apple	
		compote	
		½ pkg. Kool-Aid	
Day 21			
pancake mix			2 chocolate bars
maple syrup	———	———	
⅓ pkg. Familia			
Tang			

The supplies for this cache were in four jars, weighed 12 pounds, 3 ounces, and also included the following:

peanuts	sugar	matches
raisins	Wesson oil	towels
dried milk	liquid soap	film in can and mailer (every
3 chocolate bars	soap pad (every	second cache)
salt	third cache)	pen (every third cache)

Because I walked late into the evening I soon settled into a four-meal-per-day routine:

First lunch from 10:30 to 1:00.

Second lunch from 3:30 to 5:30.

Supper from 8:30 to 10:00.

BREAKFAST. As I have mentioned, I found that I disliked the eggs, pancakes, and French toast. My standard breakfast became a cup of hot chocolate, two packages of hot or cold cereal, a pint of Tang, two Pop-Tarts, and an instant breakfast preparation. Familia, bacon bars, and prefried bacon were treats. I varied the standard breakfast with the special items and an occasional supper dish. (I now use granola or some other type of natural cereal with powdered milk as the main component of my breakfasts. Hot Jello is fantastic for energy, especially in cold weather.)

FIRST LUNCH. I ate whatever I had left over from breakfast, such as a Pop-Tart or part of a bacon bar, with peanuts, raisins, and energy items.

SECOND LUNCH. This was the regular lunch that I had planned. A can of tuna was good, as were deviled ham, chicken spread, or corned beef—until I got tired of them. I didn't care for Spam spread at all. It is a good idea to vary these meats as much as possible.

I cached peanut butter and jelly in plastic bags and then found it was next to impossible to transfer these spreads from the plastic bags into Gerry squeeze tubes. I should have used Gerry squeeze tubes in each cache, or bought the peanut butter and jelly along the way and filled the tubes from the jar. I found dehydrated fruits delicious. To me, all crackers taste almost exactly alike. The In-Flight crackers and the Bolton biscuits (made by Chuck Wagon Foods) were practically indestructible, but all of the others crumbled badly. (I have recently learned that peanut butter and jelly on English muffins taste good, and the muffins last for some time.) The In-Flight desserts were *very* good. You can buy the canned fruitcake in most stores that serve hikers and climbers.

SUPPER. For dessert I found instant pudding, apple compote, and applesauce to be very good. Since my trip I have discovered the instant cheesecake mix that can be obtained in supermarkets, and the instant brownie mix from Richmoor. Freeze-dried ice cream from Mountain House is another recent find. I found the Lipton one-pot meals to be quite good, as well as most Richmoor supper dishes. Clam chowder, chili mac, and quick chicken dinners were all good. I like Chuck Wagon's vegetable rice dinner. The two-man package is just right for one hungry hiker. I also doubled the portions of the Richmoor and Lipton dinners. Mountain House and Tea Kettle put out rather expensive but delicious supper dishes. The two-portions-for-one hiker ratio still applies, though. These meals are convenient because all you do is add boiling water to the containers and stir. No messy pots! Perma-Pak makes a pretty good trail salad called vegetable salad blend, but I know of nothing that tastes like a good fresh salad! Freeze-dried vegetables by Richmoor and Mountain House are good. Pick the vegetables you like at home, and try the freeze-dried versions before starting on your hike.

My cache locations were as follows:

Cache number	Location
AA	In Neels Gap, Georgia (U.S. Routes 19/129)
1	In Dicks Creek Gap, Georgia (U.S. Route 76)
2	Across the Nantahala River at Wesser, North Carolina (U.S. Route 19)
3	Two miles south of Fontana Dam Village, North Carolina (North Carolina Highway 28)
4	In Newfound Gap, North Carolina–Tennessee (U.S. Route 441)
5	In Davenport Gap, North Carolina–Tennessee (North Carolina Highway 284/Tennessee Highway 32)
6	In Devil Fork Gap, North Carolina–Tennessee (North Carolina Highway 212/Tennessee Highway 81A)
7	In Iron Mountain Gap, North Carolina–Tennessee (North Carolina Highway 26/Tennessee Highway 107)
8	By Wilbur Lake, Tennessee, on Watauga Dam Road
9	Near Sugar Grove, Virginia (Virginia Highway 16)
10	Across the New River, Virginia (U.S. Route 460)
11	On Catawba Mountain, Virginia (Virginia Highway 311)
12	Near the military radar facility on Apple Orchard Mountain, Virginia (Lower Blue Ridge Parkway Crossing)
13	In Tye River Gap, Virginia (Virginia Highway 56)
14	On the Pocosin Fire Road in Shenandoah National Park, Virginia (Skyline Drive)
15	In Compton Gap in Shenandoah National Park, Virginia (Skyline Drive)
16	In Turners Gap, Maryland (U.S. Route 40A)
17	At Grier Point, Pennsylvania (Pennsylvania Highway 850)
18	Port Clinton, Pennsylvania (Pennsylvania Highway 61)
19	Near Delaware Water Gap, Pennsylvania, on a gravel road
20	Near Arden, New York, on Arden Valley Road
20 A	At Falls Village Bridge, Connecticut (Connecticut Highway 126)
21	Near Lee, Massachusetts, on Tyne Road
22	South of Vermont Highway 9
23	Gulf Lean-to, Vermont (dirt road)
24	In Kinsman Notch, New Hampshire (New Hampshire Highway 112)

Cache number	Location
25	In Pinkham Notch, New Hampshire (New Hampshire Highway 16)
26	By Long Pond, Maine (Maine Highway 4)
27	Bigelow Village, Maine (Maine Highway 27)
28	Two miles from Monson, Maine, on Elliotsville Road

PACK. I used a Kelty BB5 pack with an extra large frame. In the large back pocket I carried a water bottle, cup, dish, spoon, and the food I would eat between breakfast and supper. In the top pocket on the right I carried my raingear: rain pants, rain shirt, and pack cover. In the bottom pocket on the right was my camera with several extra cans of film. In the top pocket on the left side I carried a transistor radio, a thermometer, a Mallory flashlight with extra bulb and batteries, a Silva compass, and first-aid gear. In the bottom pocket on the left were glacier cream, mosquito repellent, rip-stop repair tape, and extra nylon cord. In the packbag I carried a large double plastic bag with my food. This was placed at the bottom of the packbag. On top of the food was a large stuff sack with my clothes, a second plastic bag with the cooking utensils and a gas bottle and funnel, and still another plastic bag with my space blanket.

From Fontana Village, North Carolina, northward I carried a pair of moccasins in a nylon stuff bag. I carried a tube tent as far as Crandon, Virginia, but sent it home because I had used it only once. My sleeping bag was in a stuff sack, and a Himalayan Industries shorty foam pad was rolled around it. This roll, containing my sleeping bag and the pad, was in turn fitted into an extra large Camp Trails stuff bag, which had been mailed to me at Hot Springs, North Carolina. Before that I had jammed my sleeping bag and foam pad into a plastic laundry bag, and then pulled another laundry bag over it from the opposite direction. These plastic bags ripped constantly, and I was lucky to reach Hot Springs without having to carry the sleeping bag and foam pad in my hands.

My pack usually weighed about 50 pounds. I definitely did not enjoy carrying that much, and I never did manage to carry that heavy pack with ease, yet there was nothing I wished to discard. However, I urge other hikers to do as I say and not as I did: *carry as little as possible.* You will feel better and hike faster.

COOKING GEAR. I used a Svea 123 stove with a Sigg Tourist Cook Set. If you use this stove, I suggest that you take an extra nozzle. I found this set to be light in weight, and inexpensive. You will want to carry a funnel and a gas bottle. I used up about a tankful of gas (one-third of a pint) per day in cooking supper and breakfast. Using a stove on the trail will become the rule in the future as wood supplies dwindle. Stoves are necessary, even now, in many locations in the White Mountains, the Great Smokies, and the Shenandoah National Park.

EATING GEAR. I carried a mediumweight Swiss army knife, a spoon, and a Sierra Club cup. I found this cup to be very handy for dipping water out of streams, and the long wire handle kept me from being burned by hot liquids. A large plastic dish completed my eating outfit.

SLEEPING GEAR. I used a space blanket for a ground cloth. It worked fine except for one evening north of Hot Springs, North Carolina. I set a hot pot on the space blanket and burned a hole in it. I carried the heavy space blanket so I could keep warm in case I took a bad fall and was unable to move. I carried an Icelandic Standard Sleeping Bag made by Black and Sons of Ogdensburg, New York. I picked this bag primarily because of the low price ($50). It was lined with cotton, and was not very light (four pounds). I would recommend a much lighter bag, around 2½ pounds, for most of the year on the Appalachian Trail. I carried a shorty foam pad because I was unable to sleep without it on the rough logs, concrete, wooden boards, or wire bunks found in the shelters.

CLOTHING. I wore the bare minimum: shorts and a T-shirt. I enjoyed the coolness and freedom of movement that come from wearing shorts, though briers and nettles made me uncomfortable at times. I carried a pair of army fatigue pants and a cotton shirt but usually wore them only when I was washing my other clothes. In addition to what I was wearing, I carried five T-shirts, three pairs of underwear, four pairs of cotton socks, and two pairs of wool socks. I carried the extra underwear so I could do almost all of my washing at laundromats. I wore my down vest almost every morning and evening, as there was usually a chill in the air. I could have used a sweater or a wool shirt at times, but on the whole I found my clothing adequate. In my left hand I normally carried a plastic bag with guidebook, map, pen, and notebook inside.

RAINGEAR. A hiker gets wet when it rains, either from the inside or the outside. In a warm rain I often walked without the rain suit, but sometimes it was necessary to wear it to hold in crucial body heat.

Photo by Eric Ryback

Firetower along the trail.

Photo courtesy Jeffrey M. Hancock

Jeffrey Hancock.

In high winds the Kelty pack rain cover tended to creep up the pack, exposing my sleeping gear to the rain. I spent several nights in a wet sleeping bag before figuring out how to correct this problem. I put two grommets at the bottom of the rain cover, and ran lines through the grommets and under the sleeping-bag roll to the packframe, where I tied the lines off.

CAMERA EQUIPMENT. I used three different Kodaks on my trip. They had built-in light meters, and cost about $35. each, bought used. The first camera malfunctioned in Saint Anthonys Wilderness in Pennsylvania, and the second one stopped working near Imp Shelter in New Hampshire after being dropped into a stream. I was without a camera for a sizable portion of my trip. I had buried a roll of 36-exposure Kodachrome II Daylight film and a Kodak mailer at every second or third cache. I took about 500 color slides in all, and noted the date, time, place, and subject of each picture in a little notebook. Without this record it would have been impossible for me to identify all the pictures.

FIRST-AID KIT AND BOOTS. These two items were closely linked on my hike. I started in Limmer boots and soon ran into trouble. My feet had grown since the previous fall when I had been measured for these boots.[1] I developed bad blisters on both heels, and secondary blisters on several toes on each foot. At first I used Band-Aids and first-aid cream. Then I tried moleskin with the ointment. I used Merthiolate on many of the blisters as they opened up. At Hot Springs, North Carolina, I mailed the heavy Limmers on to Damascus, Virginia, and purchased a pair of work boots. I soon regretted that I had not put something more than two coats of silicone on these work boots. Except for the first two days, they remained soaked all the way to Damascus.

My foot problems kept getting worse instead of better. I put Neosporin ointment, gauze pads, adhesive tape, and moleskin on the blisters every morning. In Damascus I received a pair of high-cut Browning kangaroo leather boots in the mail from home. I also went to Abingdon to see a doctor. He sent me on my way with a cheery prognosis and no bill. I sent the Limmer boots and the work boots home, and walked for two weeks in the Browning boots. They soon soaked

---

[1] In fairness to the Limmer boot, which is considered by many of its users to be the best hiking boot made, it should be pointed out that Jeffrey's problems with his Limmer boots are probably explained by this sentence—that is, he had grown since being measured, his feet were larger, and hence the boots no longer fit. No boot is satisfactory for hiking if it is too small.—ED.

through and after four days the toe on the right boot began to come apart.

Now, in the mornings, I began to pour tincture of benzoin over my feet after putting on Neosporin ointment, gauze pads, moleskin, and adhesive tape. This was to make my socks stick tightly to my feet, and, hopefully, reduce the blisters. At the Pinefield Shelter in the Shenandoah National Park I changed back to the Limmers. In five more days I had had enough. The Limmers were just too tight. Later I bought a pair of Italian Voyageurs, a lightweight, low-cut boot. They were very comfortable and my feet began to get better. Each morning and evening I spent from a half-hour to an hour fixing my feet very carefully. East of the Hudson River I alternated between the Voyageurs and a pair of Dunham Tyroleans for the rest of the trip. A noticeable improvement did not occur until southern New England, when calluses formed where the blisters had been. My advice to hikers is to be sure to get the right boots and break them in carefully.

I started my hike with a 5½-by-8½-inch diary, in which I intended to write my experiences at the end of each day. It soon became obvious that to keep to my schedule I would be walking late in the evening rather than stopping early to write in my diary. I spent the better part of June 17 in Hot Springs trying to catch up on my diary. From that point on I used small spiral notebooks, four in all, to write down my experiences along the trail. Whenever I reached a road crossing, or a shelter, or some scenic point on the trail, I would stop and write. This, I think, is the best way to keep a record of your hike. However, I lagged behind on this system too, and discontinued using the notebooks in southern Pennsylvania, at about the same time my first camera ceased to function. From then on, as I had done all along, I wrote notes in the margins of the guidebook pages.

THURSDAY, MAY 29. I went to school at 7:30 A.M. and worked until 5:20 P.M. putting together a 70-minute tape on population control for a history class project. Back at home, I packed some clothes and hiking gear for the trip to Georgia. We finished loading the Volkswagen bus after supper. At 8:15 P.M. my mother snapped several pictures of Jonathan, Joyce, Dad, and me, and off we went. Dad and I took turns driving all night.

FRIDAY, MAY 30. Morning found us still several hours from the Shenandoah National Park. We stopped at a roadside rest area and cooked breakfast on my little gasoline stove. Later we toured Manassas

National Battlefield Park and crossed the Appalachian Trail at Manassas Gap. We dug up cache 15 at Compton Gap in Shenandoah National Park and added the gas bottle which we had forgotten on our earlier trip. We stopped for lunch at the Jewel Hollow Parking Overlook off the Skyline Drive. After the meal I walked about a hundred feet to the Appalachian Trail and almost immediately met a man and his two sons from Marblehead, Massachusetts. As we were talking, Ed Garvey from Falls Church, Virginia, arrived. I had heard a lot about Mr. Garvey's hiking career, and was pleased when he agreed to meet me on my hike when I got near his home. We buried caches 14, 13, and 12 during the day, and enjoyed the beautiful views from the Blue Ridge Parkway and the Skyline Drive. That night we slept in a motel near Roanoke.

SATURDAY, MAY 31. Walking in on a fire road to bury cache 11 on Catawba Mountain, we heard a buzzing sound, just like the sound of the alien's spaceship on the television show "The Invaders." The sound came from the 17-year locusts that were stripping the leaves from the trees all along the trail. *From my diary:* "Whenever we see a high point and start toward it, we know the Appalachian Trail is on top. There is a brutally steep climb for the Volkswagen every time we make a cache. Usually the Appalachian Trail is right on top of the ridge, and we go steeply down the other side. Some of the roads we travel are just incredible. For instance, yesterday we left the Blue Ridge Parkway to drive down Virginia Highway 56 to bury cache 13. The curves on the road were so sharp that several times we almost ran over the back end of the Volkswagen before we completed the turn."

We buried caches 11 through 7, the last one at sunset in Iron Mountain Gap. We spent the night at a motel near Erwin, Tennessee, where I talked with a middle-aged couple who made me promise to mail them a postcard if I was successful in my adventure. I was able to keep this promise some months later.

SUNDAY, JUNE 1. We cooked an early breakfast and reached Devil Fork Gap at sunrise and buried cache 6. We buried three caches in the Smokies, where the mountains towered much higher above the surrounding country than anything we had seen previously. Stopped at the visitor center in Great Smoky Mountains National Park and watched a slide show, as we had done in Shenandoah National Park. Buried three more caches south of the park, and reached Dahlonega, Georgia, at 6:00 P.M. I wrote in my diary: "It has rained every day, and seems to be constantly hazy." Little did I know how much more I was to see of this blue haze, as well as of the rain! I packed the Kelty with my equipment for the first time, finishing around 1:00 A.M. Then I showered and went to bed.

Georgia, Chattahoochee National Forest

MONDAY, JUNE 2. We rose about 7:00 and went to a café of questionable cleanliness for breakfast. A man smoking a smelly cigar took our orders as the rain came down in sheets outside. I was ready to stay in the café all day, but we soon finished and left.

We drove from Dahlonega to Amicalola Falls State Park through rain and fog and occasional thunder. I got under a pavilion to put on raingear. We drove to the approach trail above the falls. After a few photographs and some rather sad good-byes I was off, going down an awfully lonely dirt road under cloudy skies.

I reached Frosty Mountain Fire Tower at 11:40. Sweat was dripping from me so I took off my rain clothes. Halfway up Springer Mountain I was forced to put on full raingear again as a storm let loose. I reached the summit at 2:15, signed the register, and took pictures of the SOUTHERN TERMINUS sign. It took me half an hour, standing in the rain reading the camera directions, to figure out how the flash attachment worked. I came to Big Stamp Gap Lean-to at 3:05 and found Jim Buchanan of Atlanta, Georgia, who was also spending the night there. It took me an hour to figure out how to make my stove work well enough to boil water for supper. My experiences with the camera and the stove indicated how unfamiliar I was with most of my equipment. A greenhorn out to walk 2,000 miles?

TUESDAY, JUNE 3. On trail at 8:10. Hung a wet sock on each side of the pack, attaching them with rubber bands to the wires that hold Kelty packbags to their frames. There were quite a few army trucks and jeeps at the forest service road at Three Forks when I arrived. At 11:20 I met five army men who were the "good guys" in the war games. They questioned me about what I had seen. Five minutes later I met about 10 men with blackened faces cutting through the woods. The leader ordered me to halt, and I was asked to show identification, answer questions, and explain what some of my equipment was used for.

I reached Hawk Mountain fire tower at noon and stopped for a snack while admiring the view. Later, crossing a fire road below the summit, I saw trucks several hundred yards away. I bent over and slunk across the road. Beyond, several trucks with soldiers passed me as I walked along. In Horse Gap I sat down and had food and water while reading the guidebook. As I was leaving I heard a noise and looked up. "Rat-a-tat-tat," echoed a machine gun about a hundred feet away. I jumped a couple of feet off the ground and took off fast. In less than five minutes I was stopped and questioned by a group of soldiers who were in opposition to the group who had just "killed" me. I continued up Sassafras Mountain, seeing many booby traps, much barbed wire, and several bunkers. This area is used by the U.S. Army Rangers for war games. Hikers beware! Reached Gooch Gap Lean-to at 6:15. Beef Stroganoff was the highlight of the menu that night. I fell asleep listening to cows lowing in a nearby field.

WEDNESDAY, JUNE 4. On trail at 7:50 today, meeting a road crew at work in nearby Woody Gap. Had my first good views of the trip on this very clear day. After picking up my first food cache, I hitched a ride from Neels Gap and called home for the first time from Vogel State Park. Dad, Joyce, and Jon had arrived home tired but safe. It was good to hear their voices!

Got a ride back to the trail from Steve Botti, a student from Georgia who had just finished his exams that day and intended to spend the night alone in Blood Mountain Shelter. Left Neels Gap and pushed the 5.7 miles to Tesnatee Gap Lean-to in the cool evening, arriving at 7:30. This old, run-down shelter was situated right next to the Richard B. Russell Memorial Highway. I spoke with a man who drove up just after I arrived. His was the only car to pass that night as far as I knew. I used Halazone tablets to purify the water and had an In-Flight meal plus potatoes and pudding for supper.

Shined the flashlight around just after getting into my sleeping bag and sawdust was sprinkling down. Carpenter ants and other insects were living in the shelter. I put my space blanket and sleeping bag down on a fairly level spot outside, but had to move under the overhang of the shelter in the early morning when it began to sprinkle.

THURSDAY, JUNE 5. On trail at 8:05 after burning some pancakes on my stove. The center got charred while the outside stayed raw. I met a Boy Scout troop strung out over two miles of trail north of Low Gap. The 28 boys and 4 leaders had come from Deep Gap, North Carolina, and were headed for Vogel State Park.

When I stopped for lunch I found a bad blister on my right foot, and soaked my feet for a while. This was the beginning of a foot problem that was to plague me all the way to New England. Walking on,

I reached Montray Lean-to at 7:00 on a beautiful spring night. As I washed my clothes and cooked some clam chowder for supper, something began to crash around in the nearby woods. Nothing appeared, but I kept my flashlight and a few rocks handy all night.

FRIDAY, JUNE 6. I started hiking at 8:15, meeting a Catholic church group of 10 people south of Addis Gap. Stopped at the gap for an orange nut roll and some Familia, which was delicious when mixed with a little water and powdered milk. I had lunch at Dicks Creek. It seemed like a lot of time had passed since my father, brother, and sister helped me bury this cache, but it had only been last Sunday! I had to refer to the sketch to find it.

Proceeded very slowly up what the guidebook described as "a gentle slope" but which I would call "a steep slope." A snake rattled at me from several yards off the trail. I didn't see him, just heard him, but that was enough! Plodded slowly onward, since I was too tired to worry about it. Reached Plumorchard Gap at 5:30 and decided to go on. Filled my water bottles to their combined five-quart capacity and walked on with a very heavy pack. Signed an Appalachian Trail register in an old rusty iron pipe, and found a campsite just beyond in a small field beside a tiny stream. I went to bed with clear skies, and prayed for the weather to hold.

North Carolina, Nantahala National Forest

SATURDAY, JUNE 7. It didn't rain, and I was on trail at 7:25. When I reached Bly Gap on the North Carolina–Georgia border I took a picture that has fooled almost everyone. I propped my pack against my hiking stick and put my hat on top of the stick. Everyone thinks that it's me in the photo, when actually it's just my pack and hat.

I climbed the side trail to Standing Indian twice. The second time was to recover my walking stick, which I had forgotten there. Had good views of the Nantahalas to the north. The rhododendrons on the summit were just starting to bloom. I was hiking the Appalachian Trail from south to north, yet for a while along here I was headed due south until the trail swung around to the north again in the late afternoon.

Passed by Pickens Nose, knowing that I also would see the Skookumchuck Trail and the Six Husbands Trail in the White Mountains as well as many other places with colorful names. South of Mooney Gap millions of beetles were mating; it sounded as if it were raining.

Several minutes passed before I figured out what was making the sound.

I met 30 soldiers from Ft. Bragg at Mooney Gap. They were on a 26-mile hike to Nantahala Lake. We talked for a few minutes, then they walked on up a jeep road and I turned onto the trail. One of the army men called and asked where I was going. I told him that I was following the Appalachian Trail. "See the white blazes?" He hailed his superior and said that the civilian knew where he was going, so the soldiers straggled back to the turnoff and followed me up Albert Mountain. It was a very steep and rocky climb for the last quarter of a mile, and the army men were not too pleased. They said the Appalachian Trail went over too many mountains! At times that was my feeling, too.

I met a troop of Boy Scouts camped at Big Spring Gap Lean-to. Their leaders were sleeping in a pop-up trailer. They moved the boys' packs ahead each day in this trailer.

That night I camped under the stars with three boys from North Carolina. The army platoon also moved in, so there was a line at the spring for water and also below it to wash dishes. I learned quite a bit about the army and their field communications systems from some of these men.

SUNDAY, JUNE 8. I was sorry to leave the busy campsite next morning but got my earliest start yet at 7:05, after a cold breakfast. Went through a poorly marked section of the trail beyond the shelter. I was like Daniel Boone, who, when asked if he had ever been lost, replied that he had been "a mite confused at times."

Met a second army platoon at Rock Gap Lean-to. The young officer was from Lowell, Massachusetts, which is near my home. We talked a little about my hike and then I walked on, making very good time on this rare cool day. Saw a doe as I reached Wallace Gap at 9:15. She was drinking at a stream, but flew up a steep slope when she caught sight of me.

Stopped for my early lunch break at 10:40 and enjoyed what was left of a can of Swift's prefried bacon that I had opened for breakfast. This cold bacon has a delicious flavor, better even than Wilson's bacon bars. The afternoon storm hit just as I arrived at the fine Siler Bald Lean-to. Later I reached a forest service picnic area with full rain-gear on. I was soaked! A wise little 10-year old rolled down a car window and asked me if I thought it was raining!

Off I went up the Wayah Bald Tower Road. Many cars passed, including a truckload of old acquaintances—a laughing waving army platoon. I reached the summit at 3:30, spoke with two elderly couples from North Carolina, then hiked on to the Cold Springs Trail Shelter, which was placed in a beautiful glen. I had seen many people in the last two days, but now I was alone again.

MONDAY, JUNE 9. Started my second week on the trail at 7:35. There was a complete circle of clouds at the 3,000-foot level as I looked down from the mile-high Wesser Bald Firetower. I passed the first house on Wesser Creek at 11:20, and as I walked down the road I fought off several packs of dogs with rocks and my hiking stick.

It had rained earlier in the morning and my feet were soaked. Squishing along U.S. Route 19 I decided to climb down the 20-foot bank and soak my feet in the river, then put on fresh Band-Aids and dry socks. A nice, warm feeling! I reached Wesser at 1:00 P.M. and stopped in the café for my first restaurant meal of the trip. Since the restaurant didn't have a telephone I thumbed a ride to Nantahala Station 3.5 miles away, to call home for the second time. I cried a bit while talking to my mother. I liked to call home, but when I hung up I felt very lonely for a while. Got a ride back to Wesser with the Clay County sheriff. He drove very fast around the corners and I was glad to get my feet on the ground again.

North Carolina, Cheoah Region

Left Wesser at 2:30 and quickly picked up a cache by the railroad tracks. Ascended very slowly into the Cheoah region, sweating profusely. At times like these the heat really hurt, especially when I remembered that I could have been swimming in a cool pool back home. I had been praying for rain to cool the ascent, but by 4:30, when I could see the thunderclouds building, I began praying for the storm to hold off. Reached an unmarked side trail to Sassafras Gap Trail Shelter at 6:30, and filled my water bottles from a small spring on the ridge, getting soaked by the rain and eaten by the mosquitoes in the process. The guidebook said that there probably would not be any water at the lean-to, but when I arrived I saw a stream some 50 feet away.

I met Dave Harper and his dog Appal there. Dave had left Springer Mountain two weeks earlier. He was headed for Maine, but said he might cut 500 or 1,000 miles out of the middle of the trail and do that part later on. He had just gotten his master's degree and wanted to enjoy a summer's vacation. The dog had started following him about five days before, and he had fed it. Finally the dog moved right into his sleeping bag one night, so now Dave had a dog. Dave and I both had Limmer boots, Svea stoves, Sigg cook sets, and Blacks sleeping bags. I cooked an In-Flight meal while we talked about our equipment and experiences. He had killed a snake at Woody Gap and had heard the beetles south of Mooney Gap. I took a couple of flash pictures before we crawled into our sleeping bags. It rained and rained and rained, coming down unbelievably hard. The shelter leaked and we shifted around, finally falling asleep around midnight.

TUESDAY, JUNE 10. On trail at 8:15 in a heavy rain. I was slow in starting because I did not want to leave Dave. He had played with his dog, looked out at the rain, and said, "I think I'll stay over today and catch up on my diary." With that he rolled over and went back to sleep, and I started hiking. If I wanted to get to Maine I would have to stay on schedule.

There was no view from Cheoah Bald because of the weather. I went down a slippery 30-degree slope for the last half-mile to Stekoah Gap. Two cars stopped and offered me a ride as I ate a snack in the rain, but I finished eating and trudged on up another steep section of the trail. In several places climbing ropes and pitons would have been helpful.

Stopped at Cable Gap Shelter at 4:30 to fix my glasses. One sidepiece had fallen off at Tesnatee Gap on June 5, so every once in a while I had to stick the piece back on with Scotch tape. I fell four or five times on the mud-slick descent to Fontana Dam, then I picked up cache 3, fought off another pack of dogs, and thumbed a ride into Fontana Village. In Fontana I called home, restocked my first-aid supplies, and got the cheapest room available. It was $12. I cooked a spaghetti dinner in my room. Three boys just down from a hike in the Smokies came in and we shared the room, so the night cost me only $3. after all. They drew lots and one of them slept on the floor, since the room had only three beds.

Great Smoky Mountains National Park

WEDNESDAY, JUNE 11. Got up at 8:10 and worked on my diary for an hour so the other boys could sleep. Left all my clothes at a laundry to be washed, and then enjoyed a restaurant breakfast of sausage, eggs, pancakes, syrup, and a honey bun. Mailed home my binoculars, and bought a pair of moccasins. I hoped that by wearing the moccasins in camp each evening I would help my feet.

I left at 1:00 P.M. and quickly got a ride to the trail. Hiking the section to Fontana Dam I met Terry Hubert, Paul Givan, and Doug Paradis, the boys from Columbia, South Carolina, with whom I had shared a room the previous night. One of them took my picture at the sign where the trail enters the park, and I was off toward Shuckstack Mountain where I had a good view from the fire tower. The graded trails in the park made for some very fast walking. With the steady grades a hiker can set a fast pace and keep it up for a long time. Reached Doe Knob and the main ridge of the Smokies at 7:05. A thunderstorm hit at 7:30 and the trail soon became a stream. Met Scoutmaster Jack Adams and Troop 523 of Hartsville, South Carolina, at Mollies Ridge Trail Lean-to. Ate an In-Flight meal while answering many questions from the Scouts, then put down my space blanket and sleeping bag on the floor of the crowded shelter.

The Scouts had set up a rope with cowbells on it in a half-circle around the front of the shelter to serve as a warning system against bears. After we had been in bed awhile the bells began to ring. I hurried out and took a picture of a bear that was some 20 feet away. The flash scared him off, but he soon returned and I took two more pictures, one from 12 feet, then one from 8 feet. I tried for a closer picture, but he ran away. All this time I had been standing in the 40-degree temperature in my underwear and moccasins, with the Scouts cheering me on from their warm sleeping bags. The bear returned and I moved in for a 3 to 5 foot close-up. The bear began to growl, then he began to stand up, and I began to move back—fast. He left for good this time, and we finally got to sleep.

THURSDAY, JUNE 12. Up at 6:00. Dropped the key from my stove and we looked for nearly two hours before a Scout found it. Left at 8:35. Met groups of hikers at the shelters all during the morning. Near Spence Field I saw a doe some 50 feet ahead. We looked at each other for nearly a minute, then I moved to get my camera and the doe was off, her white tail flashing. At Spence Field a cool 10-mph breeze was blowing across the large open fields and drying the tall damp grass. Mt. Le Conte rose majestically through the clouds on this fine morning.

From my diary: "Met Mr. Harold Huffaker and his troop from Knoxville, Tennessee, at Derrick Knob Lean-to; then a group of college students and a group of Boy Scouts and Girl Scouts later in the afternoon. Met Troop 333 from Avon, Ohio, at Silers Bald Lean-to. Now I know what hikers mean when they say that the Great Smoky Mountains National Park is crowded."

At 7:30 I reached Double Springs Gap Lean-to and found good *cold* water. Put my feet in the water below the spring pipe, and it was so cold I could stand it for only two minutes. Four young men walked in while I was cooking supper. Mark Franklin, John Lahr, and Roy Wasterburg were from Pittsburgh, and tall, mustached Gerry Bashein was from Albuquerque, New Mexico. Gerry said that he could not keep from getting heel blisters, such as I had on my right foot, when wearing his Limmer boots. Perhaps there was no escape for me! Went to bed at 11:00 after securing the door to the "bear cage." Practically all the shelters in the Great Smoky Mountains have these thick wire screens to prevent bears from paying destructive visits.

FRIDAY, JUNE 13. On trail at 7:30 after eggs with BacOs for breakfast. Ascended to Clingmans Dome, the highest point of the Appalachian Trail, through a spruce-fir forest which reminded me of the White Mountains. The group I met the night before had told me that a through hiker was coming south on the trail. With every group that I met, I knew that we were getting closer. I met Elmer L. Onstott of Ferguson, Missouri, at 10:30. He had hiked the entire Appalachian Trail in 1968, and was visiting the Smokies again.

I ate lunch at Newfound Gap and answered many questions from tourists. There were about 20 people at the Ice Water Spring Trail Shelters when I arrived, so I pushed on 3.5 miles to False Gap Trail Lean-to arriving at 6:05. I cooked an In-Flight supper, then boiled water for some Boy Scouts whose fire was not too successful. Many loud noises came from the woods as I worked on my diary, so I locked up the bear cage before going to bed.

SATURDAY, JUNE 14. On trail at 7:35. The Boy Scouts left at 7:10. Each Scout had two Pop-Tarts for breakfast. I don't think I could go very far on that! Met Troop 528 from Atlanta, Georgia, near Pecks Corner, then other groups from Washington, California, Florida, Mississippi, and Virginia. I think I have met someone from nearly every state while hiking through the park.

I dropped my pack and started to walk up the side trail to Mt. Cammerer fire tower, but when I remembered stories I had heard about bears carrying off packs I hurried back. What a relief when I saw that my pack was still lying where I had left it! Met Troop 1032 from Detroit, Michigan, just above the Davenport Gap Lean-to. I advised them not to walk in the dark, but they said the shelter was overflowing and went on. I found one empty bunk in the shelter—just room enough for me! Had a chili–beef dinner with corn, and pudding and hot chocolate for dessert. I got eaten by mosquitoes while washing my pans, cleaning my face, and soaking my feet below the spring.

It started to rain just after I crawled into bed and I had to move as the shelter leaked profusely.

Tennessee, North Carolina

SUNDAY, JUNE 15. On trail at 7:15. I had slept in the shelter with Troop 193 from Kettering, Ohio. Troop 52 from Mebane, North Carolina, had not fared too badly sleeping outside in the rain in their tube tents. A boy from Troop 1032 (the troop I had met near Davenport Lean-to) had been carried out by an emergency stretcher crew during the night. Hiking at night by inexperienced people is bad business. Just north of Davenport Gap I dug cache 5 out of the red mud with my bare hands. Tried to call home from a house near the Big Pigeon River, but the phone was not working. When I took off my left boot and socks there was a huge blister on my heel. After cleaning it out, I poured Merthiolate on it—and then I screamed! I should have paid more attention to my feet the night before. After putting on the dressings I hobbled along at a much slower pace. Made four miles in three hours on Snowbird Mountain; at one point a blacksnake slithered across the trail.

A thunderstorm hit as I stopped for lunch at a spring. Seven men on trail bikes appeared. After our curt conversation, they turned around and flew away at 20 mph. The Appalachian Trail is closed to all motor vehicles by federal law. The trail bikes had torn up the trail for the next five miles, making the walking more treacherous than it otherwise would have been.

Beautiful views from Max Patch Road. There were bare grassy ridges on either side, with cows grazing in many places and mountaineers' cabins along the road. I hoped someone would invite me in for the night. Perhaps I should have asked at one of the houses, but I passed on to Walnut Mountain Lean-to, arriving at 8:40. Walked 200 yards down an unmarked trail and luckily found the spring, then cooked an In-Flight meal.

MONDAY, JUNE 16. On trail at 9:45 after sleeping late and taking my time starting. Talked to a farmer at 1:15 in John Taylor Hollow Gap. He said that Everett and Nell Skinner had stopped here the year before. Descending to Hot Springs, I smelled a weird charcoal odor. Someone told me later that this probably was a still! Signed the register at the ranger station and arrived at the post office just before it closed. I sat on the sidewalk for half an hour reading part of my mail. After getting a good room at Henderson's Motel for $5, I bought a pint of ice cream and ate it while reading the remainder of my mail.

Worked on my diary while washing and drying my clothes at the laundromat. Called home, and it was great to talk to my family again. We agreed that I should mail my Limmer boots to Damascus and buy a lighter pair in Hot Springs.

TUESDAY, JUNE 17. Up at 8:00. Stocked up on medical supplies and some extra food, then purchased a pair of work boots at a dry goods store. I worked on my diary all day, calling home at 2:00. My mother and I decided that I should jot notes in a small notebook during the day rather than trying to write my thoughts in the larger diary at the end of the day. If I was tired the diary was the first thing to be forgotten. Bought some hamburger and several tomatoes for supper and left at 5:30. Fought off several packs of dogs before I reached the woods. I had found that merely leaning over, as if to pick up stones, was enough to drive most dogs away. I made the five miles from Hot Springs to Rich Mountain, with a 2,300-foot climb, in two hours and twenty minutes. The new shoes weighed about half as much as the old ones, and this really made a difference. I felt like I was flying. I camped by a spring and successfully kept the bugs away with Cutter's insect repellent. Had the hamburger and tomatoes for supper. It was a nice change in my diet, but cleaning the pan afterward was not so pleasant.

WEDNESDAY, JUNE 18. On trail at 7:50. Met a U.S. Forest Service maintenance crew north of Hurricane Gap. A new Little Laurel Lean-to had been built of stone to replace the shelter that had burned down. Never reached the top of Camp Creek Bald as the trail had been relocated around the summit because of a private development. I heard chain saws and bulldozers at work on this once wild mountain. The new Jerry Cabin Lean-to was full of trash as a jeep road runs right by it. As daylight waned and the temperature dropped, I pressed on for 5.5 miles after 6:00. Reached Locust Ridge Lean-to at 8:30 with 23.2 miles for the day! Retired at 10:00 and it started to rain at 10:30. The shelter leaked so badly that I had to put the space blanket over my sleeping bag.

THURSDAY, JUNE 19. Dug four cache jars out of the red mud north of Devil Fork Gap and transferred the food to my pack in the downpour. The rain stopped, but my boots still squished as I walked along. Talked with Mrs. Latta Shelton about the trail in the area and she told me that Andrew Giger had passed through about a week ago, headed for Maine. Near the crest of Frozen Knob my camera fell from the corner of the packframe where I carried it and began to bounce down the mountainside. I dropped my pack and gave chase and caught up with it after several hundred feet.

Along here the trail crossed barbed-wire fences, most of which did not have stiles. A mile south of Sams Gap I fell on one of the barbed-wire fences, ripping open the crotch of my walking shorts. Fortunately, only my clothing came in contact with the wire. Ten minutes later I walked through a pasture with a herd of cows in it. Several of the cows came toward me and one of them had to be dissuaded with my walking stick.

I called home from a house at Sams Gap, and then gulped down a quart of water. Later I watched a frisky brown horse in a pasture with Big Bald in the background to the north. After a hot day the cool twilight was most refreshing so I walked on, meeting three boys from Houston, Texas, who were hiking south on the trail. I bypassed the side trail to the springs at Big Stamp to try for another spring that was two miles down a side trail. This turned out to be one of the many times when trails to water sources were not marked. I missed the side trail and finally stopped in the trail at 9:10. I had only eight ounces of water. I warmed a can of spaghetti using some of the precious water, and then ate a can of pears, saving the remainder of the water for morning.

FRIDAY, JUNE 20. Last day of school for the kids at home. Ate a good snack and drank plenty of water when I reached the spring at Whistling Gap. It was like a furnace on Cliff Ridge above Unaka Springs. The scrub pine and laurel gave little relief from the heat of the midday sun, which reflected off the rocks. Called my father collect at his office from a house beside the trail. I told him my feet were killing me! The new cheap boots had not dried out from the rain around Devil Fork Gap. I had made a stupid mistake when I didn't waterproof them enough in Hot Springs. My father said he would buy a pair of Browning kangaroo leather boots and mail them to me.

I reached Curley Maple Gap Lean-to at 6:00 but pushed on for 5.5 more miles; the 4.5 miles on the dirt Unaka Mountain Road were much too hard for my sore feet. Erected my tube tent for the first time near Beauty Spot Gap. It took me more than half an hour in the dark. Had a delicious vegetable rice dinner and retired after 10:00, well satisfied with my long 24.2-mile day. Several drunks passed by in a car. I was afraid they might see my bright yellow tube tent and investigate, but they went away and I drifted into a peaceful sleep.

SATURDAY, JUNE 21. Dense fog this morning. Twice I practically bumped into parked cars that I couldn't see in the fog. People were sleeping in the cars. Hiked five miles on the Unaka Mountain Road before going off onto a graded trail. This long 9.5-mile section of road-walking should be relocated, and I understand the forest service will move the trail soon. *From my diary:* "Reached Cherry Gap Lean-to at 11:30; 6.45 miles in 3.5 hours. I'm just not moving today! All this push, push, push is starting to bother me."

Another hot day! Reached a cache 200 feet south of Iron Mountain Gap at 1:25. As I was digging up the food, the Mr. Buchanan mentioned in the guidebook drove up in his old truck. We talked about my method of food supply, and he took a picture of me with my fully loaded pack. I then staggered up the gravel road, very conscious of the 10 additional pounds.

A bright spot was meeting my first hikers in two days, a Mr. Andrew Neff and his son Brian. They were on a hike from U.S. Route 19E, near Elk Park, North Carolina, to Clingmans Dome in the Smokies. After a short but fierce lightning storm, I reached Hughes Gap at 7:30 with 17.5 miles for the day. Watched the lightning to the southwest as I contemplated the 2.6-mile 2,100-foot climb up Roan Mountain. I was 11 miles ahead of schedule, so why push on? It sure would be nice to stay with someone for the night. A truck came up the Tennessee side, and I flagged it. Mr. Donald Hughes stopped and his children piled out. They were out to see the rhododendron gardens on Roan Mountain but he sacrificed this trip so he could drive me to his uncle's grocery store, where he waited patiently while I gulped down two soft drinks and a candy bar. Then he went to his mother's house and I prepared to spend the night on the concrete floor of the workshed.

I called home, then talked with the Hugheses and had some fresh strawberries. I worked until 11:30 on my diary, and fixed my feet. They would just have to get better or I would never make it home by walking.

SUNDAY, JUNE 22. Enjoyed a good breakfast with food I had purchased at the store, and was waiting for Mr. Hughes when he arrived at 7:00 A.M. I enjoyed the ride up to the gap; it was easier than walking.

Very slippery trail up Roan Mountain. The spruce-fir forest near the summit again reminded me of my home country. At the rhododendron gardens I wandered about in the world's largest display of wild rhododendrons. I was one of the first through hikers to see this display, as the blooms last only a short time.

Beautiful views from the mile-high open balds beyond Roan Mountain. Rhododendrons and flame azaleas all about! Talked with several groups of hikers on day trips. I hiked in short spurts, spending a lot of time with the other hikers and with the beautiful flowers and mountains.

A feeling of loneliness returned when I went back into the woods. I saw thunderclouds in the distance and was hustling along when I fell on a barbed-wire fence at Yellow Mountain Gap. Fortunately, I was not badly hurt. I passed perhaps a hundred cows, and remembering my experience of the previous Thursday, hurried on by.

On the summit of Hump Mountain fog closed in. I lost the trail, but finally found it and reached U.S. Route 19E at 8:10 P.M. I asked the owners of the first house I came to if I could sleep in their shed or on the porch. Mr. Justice Winters said that I could sleep in his barn, but warned me not to light my stove because the barn was full of hay. I then went to the restaurant near the trail and called home after first ordering two complete meals. I asked the waitress to place one meal on each side of the table. First I ate my breaded veal cutlet dinner from beginning to end. Then I moved to the other side of the table and ate my haddock dinner. I bought several candy bars for a bedtime snack and returned to the Winterses' barn. Mr. Winters took my boots to the house to dry them, and invited me in to take a hot bath. I think this was partly a hint as well as an offer. He gave me one of his own T-shirts and a pair of underwear, and his wife washed my socks. Afterwards I had a cup of coffee with them and told them some of my adventures. I greatly enjoyed our conversation and didn't retire until 11:45, which was late for me on this hike. I fixed my feet before crawling into bed, since I found it easier to do this at night. In the morning I was always excited about the new day, and raring to go.

MONDAY, JUNE 23. Mr. Winters woke me at 7:00. I immediately lit my stove in the dewy grass outside the barn, ate a quick breakfast, passed up a proffered cup of coffee, and left at 7:50 A.M. I proceeded to get lost several times in the next mile, as the trail was poorly marked. I found the way only after getting directions from local residents. I enjoyed hiking over the small rolling hills and past the farms. I talked with two farmers and we all agreed that a storm was brewing. It did rain, from 12:30 to 3:00, and Laurel Fork Gorge was hidden in shadow as I passed.

I reached Tennessee Highway 67 about 7:30 P.M. With 18.8 miles covered I was ready to look for a place to stay. No one seemed too accommodating. Finally someone suggested that I see the Church of God minister. I did, and as a result I slept on Reverend Calhoun's garage floor that night. I also took my second hot shower in two nights. Stepping out of the shower in the dimly lit cellar of his house, I scraped my back on a saw hanging on the wall. This was certainly one of the more unusual hazards of hiking the Appalachian Trail! The minister gave me some lettuce and cake to supplement my chicken and rice dinner. Once again I spent half an hour fixing my feet before bed.

TUESDAY, JUNE 24. I had to do two 22-mile days to reach Damascus. I left at 8:00, soon meeting two leaders and nine Scouts from Troop 3 of Burlington, North Carolina, on a 60-mile hike to Iron Mountain. I picked up cache 8 near Wilbur Lake and staggered onward. After a snack I ascended very steeply, with some good views along the way. Then I descended very steeply on this 1.1-mile stretch in the woods. I hope all relocations on the Appalachian Trail aren't this brutal! A cool 20-mph breeze preceded the afternoon rainstorm, which lasted three hours. I reached Vanderventer Lean-to at 3:50 and took 40 minutes for lunch. I had 10 more miles to go for the day.

Reached Doe Valley Road at 9:15 and stopped at the nearest home, that of a Mr. Brinkley. I slept in his tobacco shed with the drying leaves hanging down from the rafters. I had developed burns on the inside of my legs near the knees from the constant rubbing of the rain pants on my bare skin. There had been many blowdowns and much overgrown brush on the trail; it seemed like a jungle. I got lost several times. I couldn't call home because the storm had knocked out the telephone lines, so I fixed my feet and went to bed in a damp sleeping bag. Mr. Brinkley didn't have any heat in his house so my boots would stay saturated. Oh, for those waterproof kangaroo leather boots I would get tomorrow!

WEDNESDAY, JUNE 25. Left Mr. Brinkley's at 7:45. I put on my rain pants before reaching U.S. Route 421. Stinging nettles made this necessary. When I brushed against these plants, which overgrew the trail in many places, the nettles became embedded in my exposed skin. Long pants would have been better for these sections, but I liked the freedom and coolness of shorts. Nevertheless, sweaty bare knees being rubbed by the rain pants really hurt.

I stopped at a roadside park and enjoyed a snack as I rested and studied the 15-mile stretch ahead on the map. Then I hurried along on Holston Mountain with no major elevation change for most of the hot and hazy afternoon. There was a good view from the hill overlooking Damascus, with the Blue Ridge to the north as a background.

I had no water, and asked several people sitting on their porches if I could get some at their houses. Several said that they didn't have any, but finally Mr. William K. Little invited me in. He asked me where I had come from and where I was going. I told him.

"Why don't you stay here for the night?"

"Well, I had planned on staying at Mrs. Keebler's, the lady who provides lodging for hikers."

"You're staying here tonight," said Mr. Little.

"I'd like to get downtown to the stores, the laundromat, and so on."

"We'll get you there. You're staying here tonight."

So I did. Later I learned that Mr. Little had been a sergeant in the army, and I believed it. He drove me to the laundromat after I put my things in their small guesthouse. I called home from a phone booth downtown. My parents urged me to see a doctor the next day about my feet. Had I been on my own, I probably would have walked until I could not go on any more.

Southwestern Virginia, Jefferson National Forest

THURSDAY, JUNE 26. Up at 7:50. I had awakened earlier and tried to go back to sleep, but it was impossible to turn off my mental alarm clock. After breakfast I went down to the post office and got my mail and packages, one of which contained the new boots. I took a half-hour bus ride to Abingdon, where I went to a medical clinic. I worked on my diary in the waiting room and then went out for several hamburgers and a milk shake at a nearby lunch counter. I finally saw one of the doctors around 2:00 P.M. He examined my feet and recommended a treatment he said would keep me walking and eventually clear up my foot problems. He was a hiker, too, so we talked for a while about the Appalachian Trail in Virginia. He refused any payment for his services. I took the bus back to Damascus, had a delicious supper at the Littles, and phoned my parents again. They would meet me on Monday, south of Pearisburg. Before I went to bed Mr. Little took a look at my feet and told me I'd "never get 15 miles on those feet."

FRIDAY, JUNE 27. I reached Feathercamp fire tower (3,700 feet) at 11:30 A.M. Visibility was less than two miles because of the haze. Reached Skulls Gap Road at 3:30, had a snack, then walked the 4.5 miles to Cherry Tree Lean-to in two hours, and the 5.5 miles to Virginia Highway 16 in 2.5 hours. The day's rest in Damascus seemed to have given me added speed, even though it was an uncomfortably hot day. The last 2.7 miles across overgrown fields and down past mountain houses on a small dirt road were most enjoyable in the cool evening. I reached Virginia Highway 16 at 8:40 P.M. At a lunch counter I had a bacon-lettuce-tomato sandwich, a hamburger, and two orange crush sodas. I walked 100 yards back up the dirt road and at the first house Mrs. Sam Di Maggio of Troutdale, Virginia, said I could spend the night in their garage. Obeying the doctor's instructions, I got a pail from Mrs. Di Maggio and soaked my feet in hot water. I put on some glacier cream to cool down the sunburn I'd acquired during the day, then covered myself with mosquito repellent as these pests were out in full force. I slept on top of my sleeping bag with the garage door open to enjoy the coolness of the night.

SATURDAY, JUNE 28. Arose at 6:00 and worked on my diary for a few minutes, then fixed my feet and cooked breakfast at the same time. Left at 8:10 and walked for 20 minutes on Virginia 16. Three ridges later I reached the top of High Point. Excellent views all along this section. While talking to two men in a truck on one of the secondary roads that the trail utilizes to cross the Rye Valley, I learned that the store in Teas was closed for good.

The abandoned manganese mines south of Virginia 16 definitely resembled the Badlands of South Dakota, as the guidebook suggested. They even had the searing heat that is associated with the Badlands. Picked up a cache north of the road. The flies in the damp woods caused me to walk even faster than usual. It was dark when I stopped at 9:15 at the intersection of U.S. Route 11 and Virginia Secondary Road 679. I had made 19.9 miles. The store had just closed, but I asked the owner, Mr. Manuel Catron, if he would open it for me, and he did. I bought three bananas, two cans of root beer, a pint of strawberry ice cream, a jelly roll, and several chocolate bars.

Two boys who were at the store said their parents would be glad to let me sleep on the porch, so I set my things on the porch of Mr. Frank Cox of Groseclose, Virginia. I was soaking my feet and talking with the two boys about my trip when Mr. Cox came and told me that the storekeeper had an old cottage, with a good mattress and an electric light in it, that I could use. I tried to tell Mr. Cox that I liked the cool porch better, but he insisted, so I moved to the cottage.

SUNDAY, JUNE 29. Awoke just before 6:00 and soaked my feet in cold water. I was doing this both in the morning and in the evening, and it gave me a good chance to catch up on my diary. I left at 8:15. After crossing Brushy Mountain I stopped beneath a big old pine tree by Reed Creek in Crawfish Valley for my first lunch. This isolated valley seemed to belong in the Old West, in New Mexico or Arizona, rather than in Virginia.

Some 1,400 feet up and 2.3 miles later, I reached the fire tower on Big Walker Mountain. Now it would be only 24 hours until I met my parents. I was counting the hours. Supper at the Lookout Restaurant compensated for the long eight-mile walk in the afternoon heat across flat Big Walker Mountain. Tourists were paying 50 cents to climb the lookout tower outside. I hurried on, preferring my own way of seeing the country. Several miles up the road toward Turkey Gap I stopped and poured a pint of water over my head to cool off. I planned to fill my water bottles at the Big Bend Recreation Area, but when I reached the recreation area and turned on the water spigot, nothing happened. The cistern was dry! How I wished I had back the water I had poured over my head! I walked for another three miles or so before I got out my sleeping gear and went to bed.

MONDAY, JUNE 30. *Today is the day!* Up at 6:00 and had two cups of water and two Pop-Tarts. Reached Turkey Gap at 7:50 and found a spring down the road from the gap. Ten minutes later I reached Turkey Gap Shelter and found a good supply of water from a spigot! I stopped for half an hour and had breakfast. From High Rock fire tower I looked down toward Crandon. I had only 3.5 miles to go! I forced myself to calm down and eat a chocolate nut roll and drink some water. I came to Virginia Secondary Road 608 at 1:47 and met my parents 12 minutes later! After a joyful reunion my father and I walked on to Crandon. After our short drive to Pearisburg I gave my parents the tube tent, a mosquito helmet, and some small items to take home. This decreased the weight of my pack by five pounds.

Supper was great, though I felt somewhat confined by the restaurant's four walls. I had a large T-bone steak, salad, rolls, milk, and pecan pie. Later I soaked my feet twice. The heel of my left foot was in bad shape. My left knee was also very sore, so we purchased an Ace bandage to give it added support.

TUESDAY, JULY 1. Woke at 6:00 A.M. and had a big breakfast of sausage, eggs, and pancakes. Ah, the rough life! We left Crandon at 9:00 A.M. My mother took my pack in the car and drove along the dirt roads that the trail followed here. My father walked along with me, discussing my trip. It was nice without the pack. We walked the 4.85 miles in an hour and forty-five minutes.

All too soon the time came to say good-bye. My feet were hurting, my knees were sore, and my 50-pound pack was pulling on my tired shoulders. Only 1,500 more miles to Katahdin! I limped away with tears running down my face, and waved a final good-bye as I rounded a turn in the road. If all went well I would see them again in five weeks in New York State.

A snake! I stepped gingerly around the copperhead in the middle of Dismal Creek Road and hurried on. It rained for half an hour and there was thunder and lightning almost all afternoon. *From my diary:* "Stopped at 4:19 for a second lunch in the shade of a rock. My parents haven't been gone quite six hours yet. I've adjusted to being by myself again, I suppose, but I sure miss them!"

So far I had experienced no difficulty in obtaining a place to sleep, or food, or a telephone to call home, or other necessities, but in Pearisburg it was different. Night had fallen by the time I knocked on someone's door to ask if I could sleep in their shed or garage. The answer was "no." To make a long story short, I was refused at all 14 houses where I asked. The people seemed either hostile or afraid. It was the only experience of this kind that I had. I finally went to a motel at 10:05 and paid $8.25 for a room. After eating in the restaurant adjacent to the motel I took a quick shower, soaked my feet, and collapsed into most welcome slumber.

WEDNESDAY, JULY 2. I picked up food at a cache and struggled along the relocated trail with my heavy pack. If it hadn't been for the relocation data I had read in the *Appalachian Trailway News,* I would have blundered ahead on the old trail, as the old paint blazes had not been obliterated. Sweating heavily, I chugged up Hemlock Ridge and met a forest service trail crew clearing brush off the trail. The grade up Peters Mountain was extremely steep, and the sun was hot.

As I left the ridge and started down the rocky stairway beside Pine Swamp Branch, I slipped on a rock and hurtled headfirst down the hill. Trying to protect my head and stomach, I landed on the rocks on my arms and legs. Slipping off my pack, I got out my first-aid gear while still lying down. I then crawled over to a stream some 50 feet away and bathed my wounds. After several aspirin, some food, and a short rest, I started off again, but I went slower than usual! I reached Bailey Gap Lean-to at 8:50. I was in a very lonely mood, and had almost passed up making the last 1.6 miles from Interior so I could stay at a farmer's house there. However, to get back to school when I had promised to be back, I had to keep to my schedule. At the shelter it took me 10 minutes to find the spring in the dark. The rough trail to the spring had been marked by pieces of cloth only recently. I was grateful to whoever tied up those bits of cloth.

THURSDAY, JULY 3. Only seven hours of sleep again. Up at 5:45 to soak my feet in cold water, then put on the ointment, gauze, tape, and moleskin. Another big breakfast: scrambled eggs with BacOs for the variety. The farther north I got the more dehydrated eggs, pancakes, biscuits, brownies, and cakes I left in the caches. It was easier to wait until I got to a store to buy food than to cook up these mixes, and this was an argument against the cache system. Reached War Branch Lean-to, situated in a beautiful hardwood forest beside a rushing stream, at 11:40. I tarried only a few minutes before pressing on.

On the ridge of Sinking Creek Mountain it took me half an hour to find the spring mentioned in the guidebook. Then I walked four more miles before bedding down in a grassy field under the stars.

FRIDAY, JULY 4. Woke at 5:00 but dozed off until 6:30. On the trail at 9:00. Just one of those days when I seem to start in slow motion. I passed a large family gathering on Virginia Secondary Road 651, and their holiday celebration reminded me of the parties on our porch and lawn at home. I longed for these people to invite me to share their festivities, but such was not to be. I settled for a snack at Trout Creek Lean-to on an uncomfortably hot hazy day. There was an interesting climb up Dragons Tooth and the cool breezes on top of this unique viewpoint were most welcome. The lunchroom at Catawba Mountain was closed, so I decided to hitch a ride down the highway toward Mason Cove to get water, as I had none left. The first car stopped and picked me up, but in 100 yards a house came into view, so I asked the driver to let me out, assuring him that I usually took longer rides.

The occupants of the house gave me two large soft drinks and a gallon of water, which was as precious to them as it was to me, because they had to haul it up from the valley. I picked up a cache on a fire road north of the highway in the dark, then stopped beside the road and had an In-Flight meal. After fixing my feet and going to bed at 11:15, I heard a car approaching. I got up quickly and shined my flashlight. The man was driving without lights and might have run over me.

SATURDAY, JULY 5. On trail at 7:50. The relocated trail in the woods was cooler than the old trail on the fire road would have been. Met five members of the Roanoke Appalachian Trail Club who were working on the trail, and continued on their yellow-ribboned relocation.

Stopped on Big Tinker Cliffs at 1:00 to take a picture and nearly stepped on a large timber rattler sunning himself on a warm rock. I respected his talents and steered around him. Two more steps and ————! It is interesting to note our exaggerated fear of snakes. More people die from being hit by lightning each year than are killed by snakes.

Met the MacCauleys from Alaska at 3:10. They had left Springer Mountain in May and were headed for the Delaware Water Gap on the Pennsylvania–New Jersey line. They had come over 600 miles, and were the first long-distance hikers I had met, though I had seen the names of Bill O'Brien and Andrew Giger, both headed for Katahdin, in the trail registers. The MacCauleys had hiked all the way without guidebooks. In fact, they didn't even know such things existed until they met hikers using them. They didn't seem to mind the inconvenience of not knowing what lay ahead, although they said that they had carried too much water at times, and had gone without it at other times. I stopped at a house on Virginia Secondary Road 605 for the night. Talked for more than an hour as I soaked my feet, then went to sleep on the porch at 11:20.

SUNDAY, JULY 6. Called the Sullivans in Lynchburg, Virginia, and arranged to meet them Tuesday morning at the James River. The Sullivans were friends of my family. Steep climb to the top of Full-hardt Knob, then steeply down again. Sometimes I wonder. . . . After 10 miles of graded trail I reached the Blue Ridge Parkway. No more private land or hot valley crossings for a while. At the Montvale Parking Overlook a group of picnickers gave me some water, a soda, and a most appreciated ham sandwich. Since 2:00 a thunderstorm had been booming away in the west. I put on my raingear, and the storm hit shortly thereafter. It lasted for only 20 minutes, but I was genuinely terrified. Since hitting the main Blue Ridge, I had seen a great many blowdowns along the trail. Early in 1969 an ice storm had devastated this area all the way to Jarmans Gap in Shenandoah National Park. I estimated that 20 percent of the trees had been blown down. No cleaning up had been done on the trail in the Jefferson National Forest when I passed through, and the blowdowns made for slow hazardous travel. Reached Cove Creek Lean-to at 9:00 after walking for half an hour by flashlight. A family of car campers from Roanoke was staying in the shelter. The mother was very nervous about my presence, so her husband got the warden to offer me a cabin several miles away. I declined, as it was a cold damp evening and I was ready to go to bed. The woman and her daughters finally left to sleep in a cabin with the warden's wife. Her husband was somewhat amused by all this. I had soft drinks and cake with him and we talked late into the night around a most welcome campfire.

MONDAY, JULY 7. Up at 6:35. Had awakened much earlier but was just too tired to get up. On trail at 8:55, another morning in slow motion. I had difficulty in finding the trail as it was in an open hardwood forest with fallen trees every few yards. Nearly all of the trees with the blazes had been knocked down. One time I found the trail after losing it for 20 minutes. The next time I got lost I was not so lucky! After searching for half an hour I was still unable to find the trail. I headed in a northeasterly direction through the woods and after 20 minutes of walking I came to a telephone line. I followed the telephone line and soon came out into the backyard of an old mountaineer. The kindly woman of the house gave me sandwiches, milk, and cake, and let me call home. She also told me how to get back on the trail. The traveling was better now, and I made the 6.5 miles to Cornelius Creek Lean-to in 3.5 hours. I was unable to find the food cache buried near a crossing of the Blue Ridge Parkway, and decided to come back with the Sullivans to find it the next day. I walked the last half-hour to Marble Spring Lean-to in the dark as my flashlight had quit working. I made up for getting lost that morning by walking late in the evening and finished with 20.2 miles for the day.

TUESDAY, JULY 8. Up at 6:30 and on trail at 8:50. I met Mrs. Dorothy Sullivan around 1:00 at the James River. A flood on this river was to take a number of lives several weeks later. We drove to the post office in Snowden, and then ate a picnic lunch Mrs. Sullivan had brought. I put almost everything from my pack into the car before starting the 2,600-foot climb back up the mountain. It would be wonderful to walk all the time with a pack this light.

There was cool wet fog blowing all afternoon, the kind I knew from the White Mountains. Reached the parkway at 7:30 P.M. No Sullivans! Mr. Sullivan arrived an hour later. He had been cruising back and forth on the highway, and had just missed me on his last trip. I had a good supper and shower at their home, and went to sleep on a fine soft mattress.

Southwestern Virginia, George Washington National Forest

WEDNESDAY, JULY 9. I bought a new and larger elastic support bandage for my left knee, having worn the first one constantly for the eight days since Crandon. Replenished my first-aid supplies and bought new batteries for my flashlight. I found the lost cache in five minutes, although it was raining heavily. I had been looking at the wrong parkway crossing!

Mrs. Sullivan let me out in the rain at Punchbowl Mountain Crossing, once again with a full pack. At 6.3 miles and 2:20 P.M. I reached Pedlar Lake Road. Going up the steep bank on the north side of the road my feet suddenly came out from under me and I fell face forward into the red mud. I was glad I was wearing my rain suit!

The section of trail on Long Mountain, north of U.S. Route 60, had not been cleared for some time. The undergrowth averaged eight feet in height, making trail-finding a difficult task. In the rain I stumbled many times over rocks covered by weeds. Reached the road at Hog Camp Gap in the dark and wandered down to Wiggins Spring Lean-to. Knocked on several trailer doors before finding the lean-to, which seemed to be in the middle of a trailer campground.

THURSDAY, JULY 10. Bacon bar for breakfast—one of my treats! Got a ride to the Appalachian Trail and started hiking, but 2½ hours later I found myself back at Hog Camp Gap! I had lost the trail in the high weeds and fog near the top of Tar Jacket Ridge, and when I finally found the trail I set off in what I thought was a northeasterly direction. In half an hour I found myself in a place that looked familiar! It turned out to be Hog Camp Gap. I should have used my compass when I became confused.

I had better luck the next time, and pressed on all afternoon over several 4,000-foot peaks including The Priest. I called home from Virginia Highway 56 and had a mild argument with Dad about the placement of the cache in this area. He insisted that I had passed it, so I hiked back 0.4 mile. He was right as usual, and I soon found the cache. I had missed the last two caches partly because I was hiking in the opposite direction to our direction of travel when we buried the caches. Because of this, it was often difficult for me to get oriented. A tip to hikers: if you're hiking north, bury the food on the *north* side of the road; if you're walking south, make your caches on the *south* side of the road. In that way it will be a lot easier to get oriented when you are trying to find them.

FRIDAY, JULY 11. This is the first day the sun has been out for any length of time since last Sunday! The 3,000-foot climb up Three Ridges went quickly in the cool morning. From a rocky viewpoint near the summit I had a good view of the 20-mile walk ahead to Rockfish Gap.

Watched six hawks for nearly half an hour as they glided about effortlessly. They would catch a wind current and ride it high into the sky,
then quickly plummet downward.

After my rest stop I really began to move, walking 4.8 miles in 70
minutes. North of Devils Knob Parking Overlook I met Robert Stephen-
son of Madison Heights, Virginia. We walked 3.5 miles together, reaching Laurel Spring Gap at 4:00. We rested and I had my lunch of tuna
fish, crackers, and Kool-Aid; then he took my pack in his car and said
he would meet me at Humpback Gap Picnic Area between 6:30 and
7:00. I made the five miles in two hours and paid him for the lemonade and pastries he had brought me. He left at 7:00 and I hiked the
six miles to Rockfish Gap in two hours; the last 2.1 miles were on very
pleasant roads. I stopped at the Skyline Motor Court and called Ed
Garvey. We made arrangements to meet on Sunday at the Pinefield
Shelter. Then I called home. I had made 740 miles in 40 days.

Shenandoah National Park

SATURDAY, JULY 12. Really living it up! Steak, french fries, onion
rings, tossed salad, bread, several sodas, and ice cream at Howard
Johnson's last night. Then a few candy bars and a good hot bath before going to bed at 11:30. This morning I had pancakes, eggs, sausages,
toast, rolls, and orange juice for breakfast. On trail at 8:00. Panoramic
views galore from Rockfish Gap to Jarmans Gap from the open slopes
of the balds. Passed several herds of cows that were friendlier than
those south of Sams Gap. The stiles over the barbed-wire fences here
were also much easier and safer than those in the Cherokee National
Forest. I stopped for the night on the stone porch of the Doyle River
Cabin, having made 24.8 miles. I broke the cleaning needle for my
Svea stove and tried to use a pin, but it broke off in the nozzle. I didn't
have a spare nozzle. It is a tiny 15-cent item and a spare should be
carried.

I built a fire to make supper, and went to sleep at 9:30. I was soon
awakened by a bold raccoon. He was dragging one of my pots with
tomorrow's breakfast in it. I quickly unzipped my sleeping bag and
tore after him in my underwear. He dropped almost everything and
disappeared over a ledge some 50 feet in front of the cabin. He came
back several times with no success. I took inventory of my supplies at
2:00 A.M. while eating a canned fruitcake and found that I'd lost
only an omelet and a package of milk.

SUNDAY, JULY 13. On trail at 8:15 after having breakfast and soaking my feet in the cold water that came gushing out of a two-inch

pipe. Had a second breakfast at the Loft Mountain Development store and later, on the trail, I met Ed Garvey and George Huber, outdoor editor of the *Washington Star*. We walked half a mile to the Pinefield Shelter. While Ed prepared a steak dinner, Mr. Huber interviewed me for his newspaper. I left my Browning boots with Ed, who had brought the Limmer boots. I asked George Huber how old he thought the Browning boots were, and he said, "Twenty years." They had actually been used for only three weeks and some 340 miles.

I left at 1:00 after a photographic session with Mr. Huber, whose article appeared a week later. He sent two spare Svea 123 stove nozzles to me at Thornton Gap, but they were not forwarded up the mountain from the park office until I had passed that point. I had supper at Swift Run Gap and then hitched a ride to Elkton, Virginia, to call home. At the South River Shelter I soaked my feet in the cold water below the spring; it numbed them so they didn't ache. My father and I had agreed that I needed new boots.

MONDAY, JULY 14. Up at 6:45. Soaked my feet once again. The boot was rubbing my right heel badly. On trail at 8:20 after a cold breakfast and walked 3.9 miles to a cache on the Pocosin Fire-road in 90 minutes. Lunch in the lodge at Big Meadows included the ever-welcome pint of ice cream. Watched a slide show in the visitor center, then walked a mile to the laundromat to wash and dry my clothes.

Took the side trail to Hawksbill and enjoyed the view from the last 4,000-foot peak I would climb for 800 miles, until I reached Killington Peak in Vermont. The walk to Skyland was most pleasant in the cool evening. The dining hall was closed, but I managed to get two sandwiches from the kitchen. I decided that a room was not worth the expense, so I walked 200 feet up the trail and put down my sleeping bag in a spot shielded from the resort's floodlights. There had been no answer at home when I telephoned. Not being able to talk to them made me realize how much I depended on my family's moral support to keep me going.

TUESDAY, JULY 15. Up at 6:00. Called home and talked to Mom. Arranged to meet the McLeishes on Wednesday. On trail at 8:15. Good views from Stony Man, The Pinnacle, and Marys Rock. Bought lunch again in Thornton Gap—what a life! The stove nozzle had not arrived yet so I called my father and he agreed that I should ask Mrs. McLeish for help. Passed several groups of Boy Scouts on the trail and met Troop 146 of Yorktown, Maryland, at Gravelly Springs Shelter. There was room for just one more in the shelter—me! I had a cold supper, soaked and fixed my feet, and listened to news of Apollo 11 on my radio. I had made 23.75 miles.

WEDNESDAY, JULY 16. On trail at 8:50. I listened to the lift-off of Apollo 11 on my radio from the outlook on North Marshall, and tuned in throughout the day until I heard that they had safely left earth orbit for the moon. Picked up a food cache at Compton Gap and left the beautiful Shenandoah National Park. Met Eric McLeish south of Manassas Gap and walked with him into Linden, where we met his sister, Cynthia, and his mother. We went to a shoe store in Front Royal to look for a pair of comfortable hiking boots. We had no success, so Mrs. McLeish agreed to meet us tomorrow with several pairs of boots for me to try on. She would also get the stove parts I needed. Looking through my mail from home, I discovered that the maps and guidebooks for the next section were missing, so Mrs. McLeish agreed to get these as well.

Northern Virginia

THURSDAY, JULY 17. On trail at 8:15. Reached Trico Firetower at 9:30 and Ashby Gap at 12:30. Walked on paved Virginia Highway 601 for many hot miles; Eric and I soon drank all of our water and began to wonder if we would ever reach Mt. Weather. We finally got there, and the guard gave us some water. We could feel the steam rising from the heavy undergrowth on this hot afternoon.

Reached Snickers Gap and met Mrs. McLeish and Cynthia once again. I tried on three pairs of boots, and a pair of Italian Voyageurs fit great! Mrs. McLeish also brought a new Svea 123 stove (the store didn't have any extra nozzles) and a precious guidebook and maps for the trail to the Susquehanna River. I greatly appreciated this kindness. Eric and I then walked on to Sand Spring where we met two local boys who were camping for the night in their tent.

FRIDAY, JULY 18. Woke about 5:40. Eric said that he hadn't slept well because of the boys' talking. They had left about midnight. Shortly after they left, Eric said, he had seen a skunk sniffing around my sleeping bag, near my head. I let Eric sleep another hour as I soaked my feet and cooked breakfast.

All the springs were dry, so we walked for more than eight miles without water. We took a side trail down into Harpers Ferry

National Historical Park, where Eric decided to return to Washington as his knee had been bothering him.

I followed the old towpath between the Chesapeake and Ohio Canal and the Potomac River to the north end of the Sandy Hook Bridge. Hiked up U.S. Route 340 to the Cindy-Dee Restaurant, which had been recommended to me by several local people. The food was good: roast beef, corn, mashed potatoes, salad, rolls, and lots of cold water. Blueberry pie and ice cream topped off the meal. I stepped back outside into what seemed to be an oven. Got five quarts of water at a gas station and reached Weverton Shelter at 9:00. Soaked my feet in the lukewarm and polluted Potomac River. Put my foam pad and sleeping bag on a picnic table under a pavilion, and slept on top of the sleeping bag as it was very warm. I heard Eric's train go by at 9:22, and wished I had slowed down a bit to give him a better chance of breaking into my tough routine. I didn't realize how much I valued a companion until I had lost him.

Maryland

SATURDAY, JULY 19. On trail at 8:15. Was disappointed that the fire tower on top of Lambs Knoll was fenced in; the view would have been fantastic. Reached Dodson's South Mountain House at 2:00 and bought a big lunch. Walked in the dark with a very weak flashlight to reach Wolfe Shelter, having made 26.53 miles for the day. I searched for the spring in the rain and found it dry, so I went to a house several hundred yards north on the trail. A man answered my plea for water by saying, "About 50,000 people have asked me for water. No, you can't have any." However, he did tell me how to find a springhouse nearby. I was cooking supper when four boys and girls from the University of Maryland came in. They were working six days a week and rock-climbing on Sundays.

SUNDAY, JULY 20. On trail at 9:00 after saying good-bye to the four boys and girls, who were members of the Terrapin Trail Club from College Park. Fifteen minutes later I almost stepped on a snake on the trail. Stopped in Pen Mar for a couple of sodas. Everyone was inside on this hot day.

Southern Pennsylvania

Reached the Log Cabin Inn in Caledonia State Park at 8:40. A college student who was working as a surveyor at a building project nearby drove me to Fayetteville, where I washed and dried my clothes while we talked. Back at the inn we watched Armstrong and Aldrin step out onto the moon!

MONDAY, JULY 21. *Today marks my 50th day on the trail!* Pleasant walking, primarily on woods roads, through Caledonia State Park. I seemed to pass a side trail or cross a road every few minutes all day long. Reached the Tagg Run Shelters at 8:15, with 26.1 miles covered. Tomorrow I leave the Blue Ridge, having walked 980 miles on it since I began hiking!

TUESDAY, JULY 22. Up at 6:20. On trail at 8:45. Reached the combined post office and store in Allen at 3:15. I had sent my mail to Churchtown, Pennsylvania, by mistake. Hikers should remember that the name of the post office is Allen, although the community itself is generally known as Churchtown. I sent the postmaster at Churchtown a card asking him to forward my mail to Delaware Water Gap, then called home.

The next 12 miles were almost entirely on roads. I was glad to be crossing the Cumberland Valley in the cool of evening. It began raining at 5:30 just before I crossed the Pennsylvania Turnpike. At first I didn't mind the rain as it cooled the air, but as the downpour continued, I was drenched. At 8:30 I reached Darlington Shelter. The area was a mess, with trash everywhere! I had mushroom soup, hot applesauce, pudding, and hot chocolate in an effort to drive out the chill.

WEDNESDAY, JULY 23. Up at 6:35. Soaked and fixed my feet as I cooked a leisurely breakfast and waited for the torrent to abate. The rain kept coming down, so I hit the trail at 9:15. Reached Grier Point at 10:00 and soon found cache 17. The cache was partly uncovered and one jar was partly open. Apparently a raccoon had managed to get the jar open far enough to allow ants to get in. A few items were ruined, but I didn't lose much. This was my only loss from the caches.

Northern Pennsylvania

Crossed the Susquehanna River at 2:30, then ascended Peters Mountain. Passed Susquehanna Shelter a few minutes later as the rain began to let up. In Duncannon I was told that six inches of rain had fallen in 21 hours. The mountainsides had been like huge streams all morning. The rain finally stopped around 3:30 and I reached the Earl

Shaffer Shelter at 5:15. After a quick snack I decided to hike to the highway, then go to Camp Shikellamy for the night. I just didn't want to go down a steep half-mile to Clarks Valley Shelter, and besides, I was lonely. I made good time all afternoon. The footway was rocky, but the ridge was quite level. I reached Pennsylvania Highway 325 at 8:00, and hitched a ride to the YMCA camp and slept in one of their empty buildings. Had made 25.9 miles.

THURSDAY, JULY 24. Met Eric Ryback of Belleville, Michigan, at 11:00. Eric had left Mt. Katahdin in Maine on June 14 and was to reach Springer Mountain in Georgia on September 3. He had made 10 miles that morning from Swatara Gap. He was really moving, averaging 25 miles a day!

Had a very late lunch at 3:15 at a restaurant near Swatara Gap and called Dad from a pay phone. He and Jon will hike with me next weekend in New York State. Had a bacon-lettuce-tomato sandwich, a fish sandwich, french fries, large tossed salad, a soda, and a strawberry milk shake. My restaurant meals were not too original, but I sure looked forward to them, especially to the big salads.

Reached Pennsylvania 501 at 9:20. It took me 40 minutes to find the shelter, and several more minutes to find the spring by flashlight. I had hiked 27.2 miles, the last mile or so by flashlight. This was the sixth day in a row that I walked more than 25 miles.

FRIDAY, JULY 25. Was awakened by a loud noise at 6:30. It sounded like glass and metal breaking! I thought I was having a dream, so I went back to sleep. Woke up again at 7:30, and as my curiosity had got the better of me, I went back to Pennsylvania Highway 501. A police officer walked out of the fog and explained that there had been an accident. Someone had tried to pass a truck on the hill in the fog and had collided head-on with an oncoming car.

It was hot walking on the road to Neys Shelter, which I reached at 1:30. Made Port Clinton at 4:00 and went to a camera shop in Hamburg. I was told my camera should be sent home, as water had probably got into the light meter as I walked in the rain south of the Susquehanna River.

I returned to Port Clinton and sent the camera home, after talking with Dad. I decided to hike a very long distance the next day, just to try the marathon hiking that others seemed to like.

SATURDAY, JULY 26. On trail at 7:20. Passed through Eckville at 11:00 on a hot, humid, overcast day. I bypassed the side trip to Hawk

Mountain Sanctuary, and later regretted it. I reached the George Outerbridge Shelter at 9:10, stumbling in as the last light was rapidly fading. Cooked a meal and collapsed into bed after briefly soaking my feet. It had been a 34.5-mile day, with little climbing but a very rough footway. I had proved that I could walk a long distance, but so what? I definitely preferred hiking fewer miles at a slower pace.

SUNDAY, JULY 27. Still tired from the previous day's exertion, I slept until 7:00, all alone in the large shelter. I started walking at 8:30 and reached Wind Gap at 7:30 in the evening. I was looking for a place to stay when two boys came up and asked many questions about my hike. In turn I asked them if they knew of a place where I could sleep. "Our clubhouse," they replied, and took me into the woods to their clubhouse.

MONDAY, JULY 28. Had some Familia for breakfast, got my mail at the post office, and headed out. Hiked in fog for the rest of the morning. It looked like there might be good rock-climbing on Wolf Rocks but the fog made it treacherous going for me. There was no view from Mt. Minsi at 3:30, and I was sorry to miss the view of one of America's more beautiful water gaps. I picked up cache 19 and walked down into the village of Delaware Water Gap, reaching the post office in the rain at 4:50, just before it closed. Today, for the first time in 18 days, I had walked less than 20 miles. I had walked the 400 miles from Rockfish Gap in 17 days and was glad to be done with the long flat ridges of eastern Pennsylvania. This stretch might have been more pleasant if I had been able to see anything, but the rain and fog barred any views. Seven states down and seven to go.

New Jersey and New York

TUESDAY, JULY 29. Reached Sunfish Pond at 10:30. The battle between the utility companies and the conservationists had been raging here for many years, and the area around the beautiful glacial pond had been badly overused and littered. The publicity that is needed to save an area prompts large numbers of people to visit it, and litter is the usual result.

Another hot, humid day. Reached the Blairstown Road at 2:45 and hitched a ride south to a store for ice cream, soda, and chocolate bars. Back on the trail at 3:20. Beautiful views of the lakes below, dotted with numerous camps. I stopped for a late lunch of tuna and crackers. I was invited in for a meal in the Blue Mountain Lakes development.

Photo by Jeffrey M. Hancock

Some of Jeffrey Hancock's supplies, ready for packing in plastic jars for caches.

Photo by Jeffrey M. Hancoe

Bear prowling near a shelter.

I only wanted to stop briefly for a drink of water, but the man insisted that I eat. I had several ears of corn, a slice of meat loaf, and a glass of milk before going on at 5:30. Life for the Appalachian Trail in this area was becoming increasingly tenuous because of real estate development.

Reached Stokes Lean-to at 8:30. My stomach had been a little upset, but I had not given it much thought. Cooked and ate a meal and went to bed outside the shelter, as it was full. A few minutes after going to bed I got sick. Never had I been so sick! I threw up three times in an hour. I finally got to sleep about midnight. I had eaten four meals in six hours, which might have accounted for my problem.

WEDNESDAY, JULY 30. On trail at 8:30. I ate a very small breakfast as my stomach had not yet recovered. It was a cool clear morning and Lake Owassa and Culvers Lake sparkled in the pleasant sunlight. I recovered my appetite at Worthington's Bakery on U.S. Route 206.

Huge holes had been shot through the roof at High Point No. 3 Lean-to. "More litter on the trail today than on any other day of my trip," I wrote in my diary. I walked into Unionville, New York, at 8:15 P.M. after five miles on roads. I had called the post office from High Point State Park, and Postmaster Julia H. Roche had brought my mail to her house. She also let me spend the night on her back porch.

THURSDAY, JULY 31. Either the blazes petered out on Pochuck Mountain or I lost the trail in an absentminded moment of reading the guidebook while walking. After several minutes of looking for the trail I came to a cornfield and walked all the way around it, though I am not sure why. I headed southeast by compass and reached County Route 565. Another 15 minutes of walking brought me back to the trail. I crossed the New York State line for the final time at 3:30. I was less than 800 miles from Katahdin!

It was a beautiful warm clear afternoon with great views along the trail above Greenwood Lake. On top of Mt. Peter I walked a quarter of a mile westward along New York Route 17A and saw what the guidebook had promised: the Shawangunk Mountains, famous as one of the best rock-climbing areas in the East, with Warwick Valley farms spread out below!

At the campground on Dutch Hollow Road I learned that Fitzgerald Falls would be a good place to camp. Reached the falls at 8:30. A brook dropped 25 feet down a moss-covered cliff into a shallow pool. I camped in the beautiful pine grove adjoining the falls. It was an extraordinary spot! The sound of the falling water drowned out all other sounds. I lay in bed for some time, thinking how lucky I was to be able to enjoy these sights and sounds.

FRIDAY, AUGUST 1. On trail at 7:30. Three very steep ascents, topped off by a descent of 660 feet in less than half a mile on Agony Grind. Picked up cache 20 near the Arden Valley Road and started walking on the historic first section of the Appalachian Trail, completed on October 1, 1923.

From my diary: "I continue to be surprised by the difficulty of the trail along here. The steep climbs through hardwood forests seem out of place. It looks like Vermont, not New York. Despite the fact that the trail in this area is but a half-hour's drive from New York City, I have met very few hikers. However, the scenic highways are crowded with cars."

I arrived at Bear Mountain Inn at 7:50. I walked into the lobby in my worn shorts and T-shirt and was told that the cheapest room was $15! The hot shower was good, anyhow. Called home and confirmed a meeting tomorrow with Dad and Jon. They will bury my caches in Vermont, then meet me around noon.

What a meal! Breaded veal with spaghetti, green beans, carrots, a loaf of hot bread, fruit cup with sherbet, a large salad, and deep-dish apple pie for dessert! The elegant dining room and fine food were costly but worth the price. Bought a *New York Times* and took it to my room, where I attempted to catch up on the news of the last two months while munching on the delicious bread I had saved from my supper in a doggie bag.

SATURDAY, AUGUST 2. The desk called me at 5:00 A.M. but I dozed off until 6:00. The museums and the entrance to the nature trail were locked, so I walked along U.S. Route 9W to the Bear Mountain Bridge. I paid the five-cent toll; it was the only toll I had to pay on the 2,000 miles of the Appalachian Trail. The elevation at the Bear Mountain Bridge tollgate is 176 feet. (The lowest point anywhere on the Appalachian Trail is at the museum's bear den, 115.4 feet.)

The Appalachian Trail had been relocated from an old woods road to a new trail up a mountain on the east side of the Hudson River. The sweat was dripping from me by the time I reached the top, despite the early hour. I reached U.S. Route 9 at Graymoor at 10:30 and Canopus Valley Crossroads at 2:00. I left napkins with a message on them at each road crossing so Dad and Jon could track me down. I became increasingly apprehensive as the day lengthened. Where were they? When I reached New York Route 301 at Canopus Lake at 5:15 and they were not there, I hiked back to headquarters in Fahnestock

State Park and called home. I learned that Jon had been sick, so it was late when they left home. I arranged with the superintendent to stay in a garage, and when he gave me a ride back to the trail at Canopus Lake that evening at 6:15—there they were! *From my diary:* "Now that I am practically in New England I will meet my family more often. It seems as if I am nearly home, though 750 miles of trail remain." We drove to Peekskill, but all the motels were full, so we eventually wound up back near Canopus Lake at the Monte Rosa Inn.

SUNDAY, AUGUST 3. After a big breakfast at the inn, Jon and I started hiking at 8:15. Dad drove the Volkswagen bus around to the Taconic State Parkway and walked back to meet us. Pesky deerflies were plentiful. They would light on our crusher hats where we could easily kill them, but they appeared in droves and it seemed that 10 would replace each one we killed.

I left Dad and Jon at the parkway at 11:10 and started on what is essentially 29 miles of road walking. It was a pleasant change from walking on a footpath. I enjoyed the hardwood forests and rolling countryside, as well as the innumerable stone walls, old farms, and abandoned fields.

I reached Pecksville North about 1:30, with 13.5 miles done. It was my best mileage for so early in the day. There were very few cars on the road; perhaps 20 passed me all day long. I stopped at 8:45 at a camp for young scientists administered by the National Science Foundation. I talked to the teen-age campers and the staff awhile, and was allowed to stay in one of their activity buildings. A quart of milk and two chicken sandwiches from the kitchen made a delicious supper. I had hiked 30.5 miles!

MONDAY, AUGUST 4. Three boxes of cereal and a quart of milk, again from the kitchen, plus an In-Flight meal from my own food supply, made up my breakfast. On trail at 8:15. Heavy rains hit at 9:10 as I approached Dog Tail Corners. I left the dirt roads that I had been following since the Appalachian Trail crossing of the Taconic State Parkway. At 10:20 I was on top of Schaghticoke Mountain in thick cloud cover and heavy rain. *New England at last!*

Connecticut

I reached Kent, Connecticut, at 12:30 after a very steep rock descent of Mt. Algo. Bought lunch in a restaurant, read my mail, and was back on the trail at 1:10. The rain subsided, but the day remained dark and damp. I soon passed Kent Rock and made a steep slippery descent over St. Johns Ledges, where Elmer Onstott had a close call in 1968.

It was fast traveling up the old River Road on the west bank of the Housatonic River. Just before I picked up a cache the rain really let loose. I dug the food out of the jars in a stone wall and had everything in my pack in three minutes. I jogged the next mile into Cornwall Bridge in 12 minutes, just beating the oncoming darkness. I stayed at a motel on U.S. Route 7, and cooked an In-Flight meal after a long hot shower.

TUESDAY, AUGUST 5. *I spent over an hour looking for my money!* I was helped by the owner of the motel, and we turned the room upside down but were unable to find the roll of traveler's checks in a plastic bag. Finally the owner lent me $15 and I left at 9:15. I was to stay that night at a cabin on the Mt. Riga Road, which is reached by a side trail from the Appalachian Trail south of Sages Ravine. That was 31 miles, with only 11 hours until dusk, so I had to do some *walking.* The hike up Dark Entry Ravine reminded me of St. Anthonys Wilderness in Pennsylvania, where I met Eric Ryback. I wished I had more time to look over this section of trail as it seemed very interesting, but I hurried on.

On the hard-surfaced River Road north of Falls Village I passed the Great Falls of the Housatonic. The guidebook says that the falls roar only at times of floodwater. They were so loud now that they drowned out the sounds of the cars on River Road. An old-timer from Falls Village told me that the water had never been so high. The same had been true south of Damascus, Virginia, in the Pisgah and the Cherokee National Forests, and in Pennsylvania. At the James River in Virginia I had preceded the floods by only a few weeks. It seemed that everywhere I had hiked there had been heavy rains.

From a green field north of Mt. Prospect I had a fine view of the Taconic Range, and for the first time in more than two months I saw my home state. Watched the sunset from the North Outlook on Lions Head at 8:20, then somehow missed the trail to the Mt. Riga Road. Even if I had found it, I doubt if I would have chanced the steep descent in the dark. Soon it began to sprinkle, and I looked for a cave or overhang. I crossed Ball Brook at 9:00 by flashlight and found an overhang to sleep under, with one rock squeezing my shoulder and another one nearly scraping my nose!

WEDNESDAY, AUGUST 6. On trail at 9:00 after a night of very ragged sleep. Reached the summit of Bear Mountain at 10:00. I spent a long time admiring the fine views, especially those to the east of the Housatonic River valley. A copperhead squirmed off the rocks on the trail as I descended into Sages Ravine.

Massachusetts

Spent some time looking for a place to cross the ravine. Here, as everywhere, the water was high. On Mt. Everett several groups were picking blueberries near the summit. I was delighted with the spectacular views all along the sparsely wooded ridge of the Taconic Range. After a short nearly vertical descent, I reached the valley floor. I stopped at a picnic area and was looking through the pockets of my pack when *I found the money I thought I had lost!* After that discovery I enjoyed my late lunch even more than usual.

The valley crossing here was one of my most pleasant experiences. I crossed the Housatonic River for the final time and stopped at 8:00 at a house on the far side of the valley to call home and make final plans for a meeting with my mother tomorrow afternoon near Tyringham. I took advantage of an offer of a bath from the man of the house, and when I got out of the tub I found two meat-loaf sandwiches and a glass of milk waiting for me!

THURSDAY, AUGUST 7. On trail at 7:45 on a downright cold morning. After 41 days of fixing my feet every morning, they were finally getting better. The Dunham Tyroleans that my father brought me on Sunday had definitely helped. I was lucky to get such a good fit, as I had not been able to try them on.

Hiking was more comfortable with the temperatures in the seventies. I was glad to be rid of the 80- to 90-degree temperatures of the previous six weeks or so. Met Mom, Jonathan, and my two youngest sisters, Jane and Jennifer, about half a mile north of Tyringham. They brought along a picnic lunch as well as fresh clothes for me. I exchanged the Tyroleans for the Italian Voyageur boots and arranged to meet Mom, Dad, and Jon on Saturday. Dad and Jon wanted to hike northward into Vermont with me.

I lost the trail on the east side of Upper Goose Pond but soon heard the traffic on the Massachusetts Turnpike. I quickly came to the fence that encloses the highway and crossed over it onto turnpike right-of-way. I had started walking eastward toward the trail when a state trooper stopped and gave me a ride to the concrete bridge over which the Appalachian Trail crosses the turnpike. He was not too happy that

I was hiking along the turnpike, and watched me until I had climbed the slippery bank up to the Appalachian Trail bridge.

I found cache 21 by the Tyne Road only by great good luck. It had been buried in a very rocky area, and the map description was too general to fit any particular spot. After a half-hour's search I happened to glance down and see the Appalachian Trail symbol we had scratched on a rock above the food supply. I slept by the trail, and took my water from a stream running right down the footpath.

FRIDAY, AUGUST 8. On trail at 8:00. Met a group of 25 girls camping next to the NO CAMPING sign at Finerty Pond. Reached Pittsfield Road at 10:48 and Mrs. Fred Hutchinson called to me. She had seen the articles about my hike in the *Boston Herald Traveler* and the *Washington Star* and was expecting me. She gave me a huge lunch, topped off by homemade pie. I added my name and comments to a book in which hikers had been writing for 40 years. Mrs. Hutchinson is truly a friend of all Appalachian Trail hikers! I reached the center of Dalton some 10 miles and 3½ hours later. Two-thirds of my trip was now completed!

I made good time all day, since the trail here is quite flat, with few steep spots. It is used for cross-country skiing in winter. Reached Cheshire at 8:10 and stayed at a boardinghouse a half-mile further north on the trail.

SATURDAY, AUGUST 9. On trail at 8:00. More and more this area seems like New Hampshire. The spruce and balsam bog beyond Saddle Ball Mountain is much like that between Mt. Jackson and the Mizpah Spring Hut in the White Mountains.

I reached the summit at 11:10 and met Mom, Dad, and Jon 10 minutes later. Fine views in all directions on this cool clear day. Dad, Jon, and I left at noon after a picnic lunch, while Mom returned home. Reached the Massachusetts–Vermont line at 5:23. I was genuinely surprised at the beauty and variety of the trail in my home state, although much of the trail was on roads and there were few shelters.

Vermont

Reached Seth Warner Shelter at 7:00. It was already occupied by Ed Jones and his son and his dog from Winchester, Massachusetts, and Frank Werner of North Tonawanda, New York. Little did I know at that time how much winter climbing I was to do with Ed in the coming years!

SUNDAY, AUGUST 10. Left at 7:30 in the rain. Reached Congdon Camp at 10:30 after a delightful walk through a pine forest near Stamford Stream. The rain let up but the fog continued, so all views were obscured. We reached the Molly Stark Highway (Vermont 9) and piled into the Volkswagen bus, which had been left there Saturday morning, to put on dry clothes and have a late lunch. At 2:00 I headed off alone, with a heavy pack and tears in my eyes. I had just become accustomed to having hiking companions, and now they were gone. Hiked rapidly all afternoon in the rain, trying to drive out my loneliness. Reached Stratton Road at 8:10, just before dark. Stopped at 8:30 on the porch of an old cabin and had my first real food since lunch, some 16.5 miles back. I had walked 28.2 miles in all.

MONDAY, AUGUST 11. Heavy fog and mist with cold breezes this morning. Reached Stratton Pond at 9:30. Fog down to the 3,000-foot level on Stratton Mountain. All four shelters around the pond were vacant, a rare situation in this busy area.

Reached Vermont Highway 11 at 1:00, called home from a nearby motel, then walked two-thirds of a mile to Bromley Camp. Ten campers and a counselor from a Vermont summer camp were already there, so I pushed on. I reached Mad Tom Shelter at 8:00 after a hard climb over Bromley Mountain. Visibility from the summit was 50 miles on this cool day.

TUESDAY, AUGUST 12. On trail at 7:45. The outhouse at Peru Peak Shelter had been badly chewed by porcupines. These pests do a lot of damage to forest service property each year. They will chew almost anything, including a hiker's shoes if they can get to them.

Another beautiful day! Reached Big Branch Shelter at 12:30 and stopped for lunch with a woman and two boys from Hong Kong. Reached Danby–Landgrove Road at 1:35. Some 40 years ago the trail for the next two miles had been built up into a smooth, well-graded path. It receives extremely heavy use as Little Rock Pond is only two miles from the road.

I met numerous groups at Little Rock Pond, swimming and picnicking for the day, but I pressed on to Greenwall Shelter. This five-mile stretch is maintained by the Green Mountain National Forest as a model section to demonstrate good maintenance techniques. It was in excellent condition. I reached Sunnsyide Camp at 7:30 and stayed with Troop 25 of Manchester, Connecticut. It was snug inside; there was just enough room for everyone. The Scouts battled off several porcupines during the night.

WEDNESDAY, AUGUST 13. Hiking by 8:00. Good views of Rutland and the surrounding countryside. Passed Governor Clement Shelter at 1:30 and started the 2,400-foot climb to Killington Peak. Haze prevented me from seeing the White Mountains from Killington. Reached Maine Junction at 7:20. Here the Long Trail continues north to Canada while the Appalachian Trail turns east across the Vermont hills. The 95 miles of the Long Trail were among the most enjoyable of my whole trip. I passed 29 shelters on this stretch, almost all of which were in excellent condition. The trail was generally well-marked. I told myself that I would return to the Long Trail, and I did, completing the 167 miles to Canada in 1970.

THURSDAY, AUGUST 14. Walked up and down the steep Vermont hills all day long. Picked up a cache at Gulf Lean-to at 4:30 and met my family at Barnard Brook Road at 5:30. This meeting was a typical "pit stop." The family would supply me with fresh clothes, first-aid supplies, and some additional food each time we met. After eating the picnic lunch they brought, I would be off in a different pair of boots, as I alternated between the Dunham Tyroleans and the Italian Voyageurs. These "pit stops" buoyed my spirits. From the meeting with Dad and Jon near the Hudson River my family met me at least once a week all the way to Katahdin. My hike became a family project for the summer.

After leaving my family I walked to the South Pomfret–Pomfret Road, then just beyond to a large farmhouse where I spent the night. My family had stopped there while looking for me and had arranged for me to stay there, so I had a hot supper and clean sheets for the night!

FRIDAY, AUGUST 15. Caring for my feet takes only a few minutes each morning now. It is amazing what good dry boots that fit properly will do. Reached West Hartford at 10:30, then "hustled" the eight miles to Norwich in three hours. Crossed the Connecticut River into Hanover, New Hampshire, at 2:00.

New Hampshire

Walked through the grounds of Dartmouth College and on to the

Etna–Hanover Center Road. I ran out of water and left the trail to find some. I came to the shop-home of Bill Robes, who runs Moose Mountain Pine, where he makes furniture. Mr. Robes gave me two glasses of Ma Robes's homemade root beer "for some power on the hills," he said.

The Moose Mountain Shelter appeared damp, dark, and uninviting, so I walked an additional mile to the summer home of Mr. B. C. Marcy of Broad Brook, Connecticut, where I stayed in their garage. Mr. Marcy and his wife had been in their yard when a plane hit Moose Mountain several years before. Apparently they were the only people who saw the crash.

SATURDAY, AUGUST 16. On trail at 7:30 and reached Clark Pond Cabin at 9:45. The pond was perfectly still in the early morning fog. The water was high in the many brooks south of Cummins Pond, and I had considerable difficulty in crossing some of them. I was crossing one of the streams on a narrow log, using my hiking stick for balance, when I slipped and fell on the stick, breaking it in half. I did not mind getting wet as much as I did breaking the trusty staff I had carried for 1,600 miles. I carried the pieces for the next two days, until I met my parents again. I wanted to repair this staff and preserve it as a memento of my trip.

Quite a difficult afternoon. Two long climbs over Smarts Mountain and Mt. Cube. At last the White Mountains were in sight! Reached Mt. Cube House on Highway 25A at 8:15. One of Mr. Meldrim Thomson, Jr.'s sons said that it would be OK for me to stay in one of their storage rooms. However, a few minutes later he came back and told me that I should move to an old house they owned. After I filled my water bottles he drove me about a mile down the highway to an old abandoned white house. Cooked up hash, corn, and applesauce before going to sleep on an old dusty bed.

SUNDAY, AUGUST 17. Thumbed a ride back to the trail and started hiking at 7:15. Reached New Hampshire Highway 25C at 9:45 and Glencliff at noon. Even on a Sunday morning I was able to get my mail at the post office. One of the advantages of small towns is that the post office people are willing to help the hiker as much as possible. Several times my mail was forwarded to a post office on the trail ahead, even without my asking.

The elevation at Glencliff is 1,540 feet and the summit of Mt. Moosilauke is 4,810 feet. I made the long hard climb entirely in fog, but I did not mind, as I was back on familiar territory at last.

About two miles beyond the summit the trail became very steep. I walked slowly down the badly eroded trail. Water running down the trail made it extremely slippery. At one of the steepest points I slipped on a root, slid 20 feet on my back down a ledge, then fell about 4 feet more until my feet hit a root. If it hadn't been for that root, I would have fallen another 20 feet into what the guidebook describes as "a beautiful cascade." When I fell I dropped my camera and hat, plus the plastic bag I carried in one hand, which had my guidebook, pen, and notebook in it. The waist strap on my pack had not been fastened so my pack flipped over onto my chest when I hit the root. I carefully turned so I was facing the cliff and grabbed a root with one hand and with the other moved the pack over my head to its correct position on my back.

I rested for a minute, then carefully made my way to a spot below where I had landed after falling. Apparently the fall of my camera had been broken when it hit a pine tree, for it still worked. Looking up the near vertical slope, I thanked God for putting that root in the right place.

I met my family in Kinsman Notch at 6:30 and we drove to our camp in the White Mountain National Forest. Dad cut me a new walking stick from a maple sapling.

MONDAY, AUGUST 18. Dad and I started hiking at 7:50. I left my Kelty pack in the car and carried a cruiser pack and frame with food and equipment for the day's hike. We reached the summit of South Kinsman at 1:45 after a tough 2,000-foot climb from Eliza Brook. Passed the first of the AMC huts at Lonesome Lake at 4:15. Many people were floating around the lake in boats or on air mattresses, but only a few hardy souls were swimming. We hurried through the 2.8 miles to the Whitehouse Bridge in an hour because of a supper date with the rest of the family. I left at 6:20, after arranging to meet the family around noon on Wednesday. My trip was to occupy their vacation, much as it had occupied the earlier part of their summer. They didn't mind; instead they urged me on and brought me whatever I needed.

I surprised myself by reaching the Liberty Spring Shelter in little more than an hour. The stretch was 2.4 miles long and 2,400 feet up. Met Mr. and Mrs. Atkinson from Medford, Massachusetts, at this old stone shelter. They were on their first camping trip and seemed glad to get some of the advice I offered, though most of our conversation was about my trip.

TUESDAY, AUGUST 19. On trail at 7:20. There was fog and a 30-mph wind on Franconia Ridge. Fortunately I had hiked this section in 1967 and again in 1968, so I had already seen the vistas that were hidden in the fog. Reached the summit of Mt. Lafayette at 9:30. Now there was a wet mist and a higher wind. I had thought that no one else was crazy enough to be on Franconia Ridge on a day like this, but I met three boys headed up the ridge near the Skookumchuck Trail.

What a relief to drop below tree line! Passed the Garfield Pond Cut-off in intermittent showers at 11:30. At 11:45 the rain stopped and it began to clear. By 12:00, when I reached Mt. Garfield, the sun was out with clear blue skies above. This is typical of the rapid weather changes in the White Mountains above timberline. Unfortunately, it works both ways. The temperature can drop from 75 degrees to 35 degrees and from clear skies, to rain, to snow, in just a few minutes.

Stopped at the AMC Galehead Hut for lunch, then climbed South Twin Mountain to find an incredible 360-degree view. I was able to pick out all the peaks I had climbed the previous summer!

WEDNESDAY, AUGUST 20. Slept in the men's dormitory at Zealand Falls Hut. Beautiful view down Carrigain Notch at sunrise as I cooked breakfast on the front porch. Hiked the easy 7.6 miles to U.S. Route 302 in Crawford Notch under clear skies. This is the only long, relatively flat stretch of the Appalachian Trail in the White Mountains. Met my family at 11:00 and left at 11:50 after getting clean clothes and more food. We arranged for another meeting at Pinkham Notch Camp.

Climbed very steeply on the Appalachian Trail up Webster Cliffs. One of the best days for hiking ever, with temperature in the sixties, clear blue skies, and cool breezes. Reached Mt. Jackson at 2:30 and met a teen-age group from Camp Walt Whitman. They had left the camp a week ago and had hiked 54 miles on the Appalachian Trail. They were heading for Pinkham Notch Camp. Beyond, I sped down the trail to make the Lakes-of-the-Clouds Hut in time for supper. To my surprise I soon arrived at Nauman Shelters. The Appalachian Trail had turned left while the side trail had continued straight ahead, and I had barreled on through. I returned to the trail and reached Lakes-of-the-Clouds Hut just in time for dinner. Went outside after eating and watched the most beautiful sunset I have ever seen. Slept for a while in one of the bunk rooms, then moved onto one of the dining room tables after all the people playing chess, checkers and cards, and just talking, went to bed. There were 105 people in the hut that night! I always like the friendly atmosphere in the huts after supper. The hut boys, and a few hut girls as well, are playing guitars in the kitchen while the "goofers" swap lies and play games in the main dining room. The food in the huts is not equaled in either quantity or quality by very many restaurants.

THURSDAY, AUGUST 21. Up at 6:00. Through the big windows by my head I saw dense fog all about. Left at 7:20 after cooking my own breakfast. The hutmen tore up my bill and wished me luck! Made the 1.5 miles up Mt. Washington in 50 minutes, shivering all the way! Had no more than 100-foot visibility, with half an inch of rime ice on the rocks near the summit. The observatory was recording a temperature of 27° F. with wind gusts of well over 40 mph. The chill factor was below zero. I was advised not to try to cross the northern Presidentials, as the conditions were supposed to remain bad all day. I had worn all the clothes I had coming up Mt. Washington, and was still cold, so I decided to follow the weather observer's advice and walk down the automobile road. I have since done the section I missed—all of it in summer hikes, and large parts of it in winter as well.

I turned off onto the Old Jackson Road at 10:40 and reached Pinkham Notch Camp at 11:20. I called the state police and one of the officers stopped at Bear Notch Camp to tell my father of my arrival. I hitched a ride 15 miles to Glen, New Hampshire, and met my Dad at 1:30. After lunch he took me to the Wildcat Ridge Trail. I reached the gondola lift summit building after a very steep climb over the Wild Kittens to Wildcat Peak E. It was clear everywhere but in the Presidentials, which were still shrouded in thick clouds. I crossed over Wildcat Peaks D, C, B, and A, then made the precipitous descent to Carter Notch Hut. I arrived at 5:59, just at suppertime! During the delicious supper I discovered that there was another long-distance hiker in the group, Professor John T. Cowles of the psychology department of the University of Pittsburgh. He had just hiked the 300 miles from Mt. Katahdin, and planned to walk through the White Mountains in the next few days. We stayed together in one of the rooms that night, talking for quite awhile about our hiking experiences. He had completed the Long Trail three times and had hiked extensively in the Adirondacks of New York as well as in Maine and New Hampshire.

FRIDAY, AUGUST 22. I made the summit of Carter Dome at 8:00. It was a cold clear day that was perfect for hiking, and I had a photographic field day as I walked over the Carters. About half a mile before the cutoff trail to the Imp Shelter I slipped while slabbing a rock ledge adjacent to a small brook. My camera flew off the top corner of the Kelty frame where it was attached and fell into the water. The camera bubbled several times before I fished it out. I tried to dry it, but soon realized that water had entered the light meter. I was to be without a camera for the next 200 miles.

At 4:00 I reached U.S. Route 2 and met my family. We drove into Gorham and ate supper at a hamburger stand, then I went to a store to buy additional food. Just as I was leaving a man turned partway toward me. He looked a lot like David Harper, the fellow I had left sleeping in a North Carolina trail shelter. Usually when this happens and you tap your "long lost buddy" on the shoulder, a stranger turns around and you realize that you have made a mistake. This time, however, I was right. From the morning of June 10, when I left in the rain with Dave still sleeping at Sassafras Gap Trail Shelter in North Carolina, he had hiked some 530 miles northward to the James River, then found the southern temperatures too hot and decided to knock off. Now he was staying with his family at a nearby campground for the week, on a family vacation.

We drove back to the Appalachian Trail and Dad and I walked a mile or so on a road to where the trail went into the woods. From there I headed into the rugged Mahoosuc Range. Since I had been meeting my family my pack had been lighter by at least 10 pounds, as I carried food and clothing for only a few days. Now, as I headed for Maine, I was carrying supplies to last me for 65 miles of hiking, which made for a heavy pack.

SATURDAY, AUGUST 23. Started hiking at 8:15 and reached the Mahoosuc Trail at 9:00. I walked up and down mountains of various sizes for the rest of the day. I crossed into Maine at 1:15. Now I had only one state and 283 miles to go!

Maine

The up-and-down trail continued. Reached Full Goose Shelter and stopped for a late lunch at 5:15. Climbed steeply over Fulling Mill Mountain, then descended even more steeply toward Mahoosuc Notch. I found a spring 100 yards down the trail and cooked supper. Slept in the trail for the second night in a row. I was beat after 14 brutal miles.

SUNDAY, AUGUST 24. Was awakened at 4:00 A.M. by a loud crash— lightning. Fortunately, there was no rain. I started through the notch at 8:30 and emerged from the treacherous 0.93 miles after two hours and 15 minutes. The notch looked like a giant had heaved boulders all around. The trail went over and under the boulders.

I had not seen anyone since 7:00 P.M. Friday. I was walking along on the north side of the notch with my head down, watching where I was going, when I heard a sudden "hello." I must have jumped two feet. It was a group of 24 Sierra Club members, hiking the Mahoosuc Range from Grafton Notch to Gorham, New Hampshire.

I reached Speck Pond Shelter at 12:30 after another steep climb and descent over Mahoosuc Arm. Then I made another steep climb to the observation tower on Old Speck. I could see the Presidential Range quite clearly, including the smoke rising from the cog train on Mt. Washington. From the summit of Old Speck down to Grafton Notch there is a descent of over 2,600 feet in 1.65 miles. This nearly ruined my knees, which were already sore from the rock hopping and constant pounding they had received from the ascents and descents of the previous 110 miles. I spent over two hours on the slow descent.

I reached Maine Highway 26 at 4:00 and decided to walk out my cramps over the Baldpates. Pushed up to West Peak, East Peak, and Little Baldpate. After walking past some spectacular falls on Frye Brook, I crossed the Andover-B Hill Road at 7:20. Hiked up the tote road to Surplus Pond just as fast, and arrived at 8:15. I slept on the porch of the only cabin on the lake. The mosquitoes were ferocious. I covered myself with repellent, but when this didn't work, I put on my rain suit, pulled the hood tight over my head, and tried to sleep face down. What a night!

MONDAY, AUGUST 25. Awoke at sunrise and began hiking at 6:10 A.M. after a quick breakfast. Reached Maine Highway 5 at 9:15. Ten miles already! I had been invited to spend a night at the nearby Sunset Camp on Lower Richardson Lake, but decided to keep hiking. There were good views from the many bumps of Bemis Mountain. I passed Sabbath Day Pond Lean-to at 5:30 and pulled in to Earl Townsend's camp on Long Pond at 7:30, too tired to do anything for the first few minutes but rest. I had hiked 31 miles over Maine mountains.

TUESDAY, AUGUST 26. Awoke early despite the previous day's exertion. Hit the trail at 8:00 and stopped at 10:30 at Piazza Rock Lean-to for an early lunch. It was a beautiful clear cool day. From Saddleback Mountain there was a picturesque view of the high peaks just north on the trail, with Maine lakes below as far as I could see. Stopped for an early second lunch, then hiked over the remaining three peaks of

Saddleback to Orbeton Stream, which I crossed on an old abandoned bridge. I reached Spaulding Mountain Lean-to at 7:00.

WEDNESDAY, AUGUST 27. On trail at 8:00. Reached the summit of Mt. Sugarloaf at 10:15. The Bigelows looked beautiful! Reached Maine Highway 27 at 12:30 and Avery Memorial Lean-to at 6:30. There was not much water in the spring, so I walked the 100 yards to the warden's cabin, where I met Darrell Atkinson and his wife from Wytheville, Virginia. Wytheville is near the Appalachian Trail on Big Walker Mountain. The Atkinsons had arrived on Bigelow in May and were to stay until October. They invited me in for supper, and after supper we talked for several hours before I said good-night around 9:00. I fell asleep listening to the wind rushing through the trees in the col.

THURSDAY, AUGUST 28. I was up early as I had been invited to breakfast. The temperature was in the thirties. Darrell and I left the cabin at 7:30 and walked up to the fire tower on top of Myron H. Avery Peak. He walked this stretch to work each morning then back again at night. He pointed out many of the nearby peaks from the tower, but we were unable to see Mt. Katahdin because of the overcast sky.

I left at 8:00 and hiked the 10 miles across Little Bigelow Mountain at a very fast pace as I wanted to reach Caratunk before dark. Reached the Long Falls Dam Road at 11:30, walking at breakneck speed all the way. I reached East Carry Pond Camps at 2:30 and left my pack there, having arranged to meet Mrs. Henry Spencer three miles south of the point where the Appalachian Trail crosses the Kennebec River. I reached the Kennebec at 5:00 and met Mrs. Spencer at 5:40, having jogged 13.5 miles in three hours. We reached Bingham by car at 6:30. I thanked her, then hitched a ride to Caratunk. I picked up my mail and called home, arranging to meet Dad, Jon, and Howard Bassett north of Monson on Saturday. I reached Pleasant Pond Mountain Lean-to at 9:00 that night, having hiked 35.68 miles on the trail, plus 3 additional miles back from the Kennebec River.

FRIDAY, AUGUST 29. The trail was badly overgrown along here. It was slow rough going to Moxie Bald Lean-to, but I sped past Bald Mountain Pond and Breakneck Ridge to Blanchard. Reached Monson at 7:30, with 1,900 miles now behind me. I called home and made final plans for a meeting with Dad the next day. Stayed at one of the boardinghouses in town after a fine meal at the coffee shop on Main Street.

SATURDAY, AUGUST 30. No rush today, as I have only 11.1 miles to hike. After breakfast at the restaurant, I picked up my last mail of the trip at the post office. Left Monson at 8:30 and hiked the two miles to cache 28. The 18 pounds of food would barely fit into my pack.

I passed the Old Stage Road Lean-to at 10:30, then walked past beautiful ponds and streams before reaching Jim Whyte's Lookout at 2:00. I was able to use this cabin through the kindness of the owner, Brent Schoffield. Dad, Jon, and Howard Bassett arrived about 4:30. Howard had spent a month in the West, hiking in Glacier National Park. He had faithfully sent me postcards as I hiked along the trail.

SUNDAY, AUGUST 31. We left the cabin at 7:15 and quickly reached Little Wilson Campsite. Jon, Mr. Bassett, and I walked without packs and Dad drove the Volkswagen bus ahead. We reached Bodfish Farm at 9:00, then walked the three miles to Long Pond Stream Lean-to where we said good-bye. With luck I would see them again in a few days at Katahdin Stream Campground.

I reached the Barren Mountain fire tower at 12:30. The views were limited on this hot hazy day. I walked all afternoon through a spruce-fir forest across rugged terrain. Became lost briefly on an overgrown stretch of trail near Cloud Pond, but as soon as I found the trail again I made a rapid descent to Long Pond, reaching Chairback Mountain Camps at 6:30. I hiked an additional three miles to Hay Brook and saw numerous groups of car campers, out for the Labor Day weekend. I was invited to a supper of soda, potato chips, tuna sandwiches, and cake. One man offered to let me use a pup tent which had already been set up. I was glad to meet these people, as I had been very lonely since leaving Dad, Jon, and Howard. Some mosquitoes were still around, so I appreciated the netting on the tent, too.

MONDAY, SEPTEMBER 1. The trail here was confusing because of many new logging roads. I passed White Brook Lean-to at 8:40, then stopped at 10:20 beside a spring at the ruins of the watchman's cabin. The water was bubbling down into a clear pool that was surrounded by spruce forest. I reached the summit of White Cap Mountain at 11:15 after a steep climb on a footpath that was overgrown by bushes and blocked by trees that had been blown down by winter storms.

The visibility from the White Cap Mountain fire tower was restricted by haze. When would I ever see Katahdin? I decided to move quickly again and reached West Branch Ponds Road at 12:45. I hiked the 10 miles to the Kokadjo-B Pond Road in four hours, then 6 more miles to

Cooper Brook Falls Lean-to, arriving there at 7:15. I can't keep hiking until 9:00 now, as the sun goes down before 8:00! I had been grinding out very good mileage on most days in Maine. I liked the going, and since I met virtually no one, I walked faster. I loved the beauty and solitude I found in the Maine woods.

TUESDAY, SEPTEMBER 2. *From my diary:* "Heard the sound of chain saws in the early morning air, the only sign of civilization in this beautiful wilderness." At 10:30 I reached the ruins of the former Antlers Camps on the shore of Lower Joe Mary Lake. On the old Wadleigh Valley Road I again heard chain saws. The road became a sea of mud that was from 3 to 10 inches deep. Soon I met one of the reasons why the road was muddy. A "squirmer" passed me with several chains dragging behind. Trees are cut near one of the logging roads, in this case the road over which the Appalachian Trail passed. Then a "squirmer," which is a heavy vehicle with huge tires six to eight feet in diameter, pulls the logs out of the woods by means of chains. When it rains the roadway becomes incredibly muddy.

I reached Wadleigh Pond Lean-to at 6:30. The pond was perfectly still. Cooked spaghetti and French apple compote, then spent some time stargazing. I heard wolves howling in the distance, and chills ran down my back.

WEDNESDAY, SEPTEMBER 3. Left the shelter reluctantly at 8:15. Reached Pollywog Stream and kept my boots on while fording it. Better to get my boots wet than to try it in my bare feet and perhaps slip on the rocks and soak everything. Crossed the outlet dam of Rainbow Lake at 12:00 and finally saw Mt. Katahdin, although it was covered by dense clouds. Reached Rainbow Lake Camps at 1:30 and just beyond the camp I spied a card on a tree. It was addressed to me and was from Ed Garvey! He was hiking the Appalachian Trail from Yoke Ponds to Katahdin. The card was dated September 3—*today!* I decided to abandon my plans for a leisurely hike to Hurd Brook and catch up with Ed.

From Rainbow Ledges there were some great views of Mt. Katahdin to the north, and of the many lakes and ponds to the south. I stopped at Hurd Brook Lean-to only long enough to "gas up" on Kendall Mint Cake and water.

Ed, Norm Greist, and George Ernst were just sitting down to supper at Abol Bridge Campsite when I arrived, and guess who joined them! Mashed potatoes, carrots, cold meat loaf, pumpernickel bread, coffee, custard pudding, and peaches for supper! Wow! Ed and the others left by car for Katahdin Stream Campground, and after watching a beautiful sunset I went to sleep under a picnic table.

THURSDAY, SEPTEMBER 4. Only 14.52 miles left! I was on trail at 8:50 and enjoyed a leisurely walk beside Nesowadnehunk Stream. Met Sidney N. Tappan of Beverly, Massachusetts, near Windey Pitch. He was cutting blowdowns from the trail. The day before he had repainted the blazes along the trail for some four miles. Sid maintained the stretch of trail from Abol Bridge to Baxter Peak, with some assistance from the state park people. Sid was typical of the people who selflessly devote their vacations and spare time to maintaining a stretch of trail. It is only because of people like Sid that hikes like mine are possible. I snapped a picture of Sid and hiked on. Later when I gave a lecture on my hike at a church in Danvers, Massachusetts, this picture was included among the slides. I said many of the things that I have written here about Mr. Tappan and his work on the trail. After the lecture I was shocked to learn that Sid Tappan had passed away the previous day. The Appalachian Trail had lost a good and faithful friend.

I saw my first and only moose wading in Grassy Pond north of Twin Pine Camps. Reached Katahdin Stream Campground at 3:00, checked in with the ranger, and set up camp for the night in one of the shelters. Ed Garvey, Norm Greist, and George Ernst came in from their hike up Mt. Katahdin before dusk, and Jon, Dad, and Howard Bassett arrived by car at about 8:00.

FRIDAY, SEPTEMBER 5. Left at 7:50 with Jon, Dad, and Howard to climb Mt. Katahdin. We followed the old route of the Appalachian Trail, on the advice of Ed's group and others. We stopped at the beautiful Katahdin Falls, then at the site of the former Hunt Spur Lean-to. We emerged above timberline at 10:00, then scrambled up Hunt Spur, making use of the iron bars set in the rock at the steeper spots. It was a perfect last day for me—cool and clear, with visibility of over 50 miles! With a mile to go, we stopped at Thoreau Spring for some good cold water. I began to hurry along and several times Dad asked me to slow down so the others could catch up. With a hundred yards to go I could see the summit! I hurried along and reached the summit at 12:15. Several hikers asked why we were so excited, and Dad told them. We photographed the views in all directions, as well as the NORTHERN TERMINUS sign on the summit and the plaque dedicated to

Percival Baxter. I was pleased with my accomplishment, but sad that the hike was over.

SATURDAY, SEPTEMBER 6. We arrived home in Wenham, Massachusetts, at about 2:00. Many cars were parked along the street in front of our house. What a crowd! I found a group of about 40 friends and relatives—my family, school friends, teachers, and friends from Wenham. I was especially pleased to meet Bill O'Brien for the first time. He was another through hiker, and I had seen his name in the registers all the way from Georgia to Maine. He had reached Mt. Katahdin on August 5. I talked with newspaper reporters from the *Boston Sunday Herald-Traveler*, the *Hamilton-Wenham Chronicle*, and the *Beverly Times*. Their articles appeared during the next week, and a television appearance on the Dave Garroway show in Boston soon followed.

I would like to thank the many people who helped me on my way. Most of all, thanks to my family, and most especially to my parents, who have encouraged all of my hiking. A yearning for the outdoors was born in me on this hike along the Appalachian Trail, and I like to think of it as one journey of my lifetime, but not the only one.

Hiking the Trail in 73 Days
By Branley Owen

Started at SPRINGER MOUNTAIN on April 2, 1970
Finished at MT. KATAHDIN on June 12, 1970

I was born and grew up in Brevard, North Carolina, which is a little mountain town about 30 miles southwest of Asheville. Some of my uncles were well-known bear and coon hunters, and I hunted with them. We also hunted deer and other game. I think my love of the outdoors comes from this background.

I got the idea of hiking the Appalachian Trail from end to end when I read a newspaper clipping telling about Grandma Gatewood and one of her hikes. I planned for about eight years to hike the whole trail, but never seemed to find the time or the money to do it. Finally I told my wife I just couldn't wait any longer, that I had to go. I quit my job, and she went to work.

I felt that I was pretty well prepared for the trip, physically. I had been in high school and college athletics for several years. In the Green Berets I had gone through ranger and jungle training. As additional training for my hike I ran up to five miles at a time, and lifted weights. Incidentally, after I started my hike I decided that I had trained in the wrong way. To be a good hiker you should be long and lean, rather than strong.

I wanted to go as light as possible, and I don't think my pack ever weighed more than 27 or 28 pounds. I used a Camp Trails pack and had one pair of walking shorts, one pair of long pants, two shirts, a change of underwear, one pair of hiking boots, a pair of tennis shoes, and three pairs of Wigwam socks. I wore only one pair of socks at a time. By the time I got to the end of the trail my clothes were pretty well-worn, but they lasted all the way. I had holes in the seat of my pants, so I took the pockets off and sewed them on the inside, over the holes.

For protection from the rain, and for use as a tent when I needed it, I carried a poncho. Fortunately, I had only about eight days of bad weather on the whole trip. Five of those days were all in a row, through the New York–Connecticut–Massachusetts area. I stayed wet the whole time, and was pretty miserable. I had the poncho, but if you walk in the rain long enough you are going to get wet, no matter what you wear. My worst day on the trail was going north from Bear Mountain Bridge in New York in a driving rainstorm. I became very cold, but there was no dry place to fix hot food or sleep so I just kept walking.

I started the hike with a pair of Raichle boots I got in Switzerland. They were about half worn out when I started. They lasted about halfway to Maine. Then I got a pair of $12.95 work shoes. In New Hampshire, when I had walked the soles off these shoes and had them tied on with a shoestring, I met some Green Berets who were training in the area. By this time I had a long beard and my hair was long and pretty dirty. I was talking to five or six of these soldiers when the captain rolled up in a jeep. He was pretty nasty to me, and said he didn't want his men associating with a dirty hippie. However, when he found out I had been a Green Beret, he became more friendly. They loaded me down with food and the captain wanted to know what else they could do to help me on my hike. I told him I needed a pair of boots more than anything else. He asked me what size I wore and I told him 11 or 12 or 13, that I didn't care just as long as I could get them on. I tried on a couple of pairs of tens. They were too short. The captain groaned, "Just my luck!" He was the only one who wore boots large enough to fit me. He sat down and took off his boots and gave them to me.

How to keep clean on the trail seems to be a fascinating subject to just about everyone, so here's what I did: I tried to wash my socks and underwear every day, but sometimes I missed a day or so. I went all the way to Hot Springs, North Carolina, before I took my first bath because I didn't care to bathe in a creek with ice on it. I averaged taking a bath about every third day. Sometimes it was a sponge bath and sometimes I could find a pool and take a dip. I carried a small bar of soap.

For sleeping I used a 56-by-84-inch space blanket and an Ensolite pad under a 3-pound down sleeping bag. The space blanket weighed 12 ounces and was practical when used as a ground cloth. It also protected my sleeping bag from the wire bunks in some of the shelters. However, a space blanket doesn't work very well if you try to wrap it around you. Although it had quite a few holes in it when I finished, my space blanket lasted the whole trip.

When I left Springer Mountain, Georgia, I carried food which I hoped would last me for two weeks, and I had a cache of food buried

near Damascus, Virginia. I bought food along the way for the remainder of the trip. When food got scarce, as it did several times
during my trip, I ate such things as cattail roots, wild greens, and
mushrooms, which I found along the way. I didn't depend on this as
a regular source of food, however. Connecticut, Maryland, and New
York were poke salad country. In the spring poke salad is all over
the place up there and when cooked it tastes pretty good. Incidentally, I was amazed at the number of hikers in the state of New York.
I went through on a weekend and saw groups of 45 and 50 people.
You had to go half a mile from the shelters to get firewood.

I didn't get nearly enough fruit, and missed it. One week, in the
New England area, I ate five pounds of flour and water. I just took
the flour and mixed it with water and fried it. I was so hungry that
it tasted pretty good. I met quite a few hikers along the trail who
had more food than they needed, and they often gave me their surplus. I also found quite a bit of food in the shelters. One time in
Vermont I found about a dozen cans of different types of food, including a big can of beef stew. I was so hungry I ate the whole can
of stew at one sitting, and didn't even bother to warm it up.

Because I was in such a hurry, I did very little cooking at the
shelters. However, I think more people should replenish the supply
of wood at the shelters. I always tried to do this because I knew what
it was like to come to a shelter late at night, perhaps in a rain with
most of my equipment wet, and not have enough wood to boil a
little water and fix something warm to eat before going to sleep.

After the first two weeks I cut down on the amount of food I
carried. For one thing, I was having a hard time digesting so much
of the concentrated, dehydrated foods. Also, I realized that I would
have to carry less weight if I wanted to maintain an average of 27
or 28 miles a day. Every day or two, or every third day at the most,
there was a place close enough to the trail so that I could get food
without losing too much time. In my opinion the long-distance hiker
on the Appalachian Trail should carry food for no more than four or
five days. You can have additional food shipped to you, or buy it
along the way.

My choice of food was determined pretty much by the thinness of
my wallet. By the time I reached Virginia I had learned that a loaf
of bread and a jar of peanut butter would make 20 sandwiches.
These 20 sandwiches would last me three days. I felt that this was
about the best source of protein I could afford, so I ate a lot of peanut butter sandwiches. One time I came to a country store having
a sale on pork and beans, 10 cans for a dollar. I bought 10 cans, and

found pork and beans made a pretty good trail food. I used a lot of rice because it was cheap and tasted good. Before I left home I made some beef jerky and carried it for the first part of the trip. I definitely liked my morning coffee, and carried it most of the time. I didn't have any food sent to me through the mail.

I tried to keep my equipment as simple as possible. I carried one old spoon, a Swiss army knife, and a one-quart cooking pot. I started with a small Mallory flashlight, but bought a standard two-cell flashlight when I began hiking at night. I planned to do the whole trail for a total of $60, in addition to what I had spent for equipment. However, when I was ready to start, I had only $40, so I completed the trip on that amount. I was offered money quite a few times, but never accepted any. I felt that accepting money would spoil the trip for me.

The only Appalachian Trail guidebook I owned was the one for Georgia and the Smokies, and as I had hiked that section a half-dozen times already, I didn't need that particular guidebook. I depended on Esso road maps to show me where I could buy food and where the highways were, in case of emergency. I depended on the blazes to keep me on the trail. I can't remember any place where the blazes were really bad except in some parts of Virginia, and I think this was because the trail was being rerouted.

Soon after I started my hike I heard a story about a fellow who had hiked about 1,000 miles on the trail and then got bitten by a dog and had to stay in the hospital for several weeks. I never did find out whether the story was true or not, but after hearing it I cut and carried a big stick in areas where I thought I might be bothered by dogs. When a dog came after me, I would go after him with the stick.

One of the first decisions I had to make was which direction to travel. I decided to start on the southern end of the trail, which I already knew, and go north with the spring. This gave me what was probably the longest spring I'll ever experience. I was about two weeks behind the peak of the spring season for most of my trip. For a long-distance hike on the Appalachian Trail starting in the spring, I think it is best to go from south to north. If the hike starts in late summer, the north-to-south direction is best. You can hike a lot better when it is a bit cooler. If you start in the middle of the summer from the southern end, it is so hot you don't feel like walking every day.

I started on April 2 from Springer Mountain, and a few nights later ran into four inches of snow. I kept going in the snow because I didn't want to get too far behind my schedule. The coldest temperature I had was around 15 degrees during those first few nights, and the hottest was a steaming 92 degrees in Maine. I was surprised to find that it could get so hot in Maine, especially that early in the year. I hit Maine at the peak of the blackfly season. There was a night near the Kennebec River when I don't think I slept a wink.

I slept in shelters about one-third of the time. Quite often I would come to a shelter and still need more miles to keep up my average, so after eating supper and resting a bit, I would walk another three or four miles. When the moon was shining it was pleasant to walk at night. If there was no moon I would walk with a flashlight. When it came time to go to sleep I would pick a spot that looked safe and put my space blanket down first, then my Ensolite pad, and my sleeping bag on top. If necessary, I used my poncho for a shelter. In making camp, the most important thing was to be near water. If I didn't know where the next spring was, or how good it was, I carried at least a pint of water. In the New Jersey–New York area I didn't trust the water. I carried Halazone tablets, and used them when I was in doubt. Shelters close to the road have quite a bit of garbage, and also quite a few mice, but you can learn to live with both if you are tired enough. If it was a pretty night I preferred to sleep in the open. I love to look at the stars, and if the sky was clear and I could find an open field with a good view of the stars, that was where I slept.

I started with the intention of hiking the trail in 70 days, which would be a record. This record meant everything to me when I started, but by the end of the hike it meant very little. I have been criticized, both in the press and in conversation, for trying to make this record. One lady, writing in a New York newspaper, said that I walked the trail so fast that I didn't see anything. What this lady didn't understand was that I wasn't particularly looking for scenery. I was looking for something inside myself, and I think I found it. However, I wasn't *always* rushing. If I saw something beautiful I sat down and admired it. I don't believe that just because a person takes 200 days to walk the trail he necessarily enjoys it more than I did. I think it depends on the hiker as to what he gets from his hike. Other critics have said that the trip took too much out of me, physically. That is an idea that is difficult for me to understand. I was in organized athletics all through high school and college, and hiking the trail didn't take any more out of me than some of those sports. To me, hiking to the limit of my endurance, really sweating, was part of the enjoyment. I will say that the people who understand my reasons for trying to set a record outnumber the critics by about ten to one.

As for my health, I can't remember spending 73 days when I had more perfect health. I can't remember coughing or sneezing a single time. I have always been lucky in that I don't get blisters, and I have no allergies. I am not affected by poison oak, poison ivy, or poison sumac. I did lose some weight. I weighed 217 pounds when I started hiking, and 178 pounds when I finished.

I tried to hike around 30 miles every day. My final average was between 27 and 28 miles a day for the 73 days. I tried to make around 12 miles before noon, and I walked an average of 14 or 15 hours a day. I am not an exceptionally fast walker, but I do have one advantage: I often feel as strong at the end of the day as I did when I started in the morning, and I can keep going as long as necessary. I can also move out of camp in the morning faster than most people. On this trip I tried to start at daylight and walk perhaps two hours before having breakfast. At first I tried a rest schedule something like the army has, that is, walking about an hour and then resting about 10 minutes. However, after I got in shape I found that I could walk three or four hours without taking my pack off. Incidentally, I think the most difficult section of the Appalachian Trail is around Wesser, North Carolina. The section near Standing Indian, North Carolina, is probably one of the most remote and unused sections of the trail. It is also beautiful, and would be a good place to vacation if you wanted to get away from crowds.

My family and I had a guessing game going. I called home once a week, give or take a day. I would call my dad, and after we had exchanged greetings, he would guess where I was. On the whole trip he never missed by more than 25 or 30 miles. I was pretty much on schedule until the last week of my hike, when I just seemed to run out of gas—perhaps because I wasn't eating very regularly or very well. When I reached Katahdin I was exhausted. If the trail had been a hundred miles longer I think I would have had to stop and rest a few days before going on. In spite of my experience during these last few days, however, I feel that long-distance hiking (for me, at least) is about 90 percent mental and 10 percent physical. It took a lot of determination to get up every day and do the same thing over and over; it took a lot of motivation to walk all day in the rain when I was tired.

The hike changed many of my attitudes about living things. When I was living in a house and saw an ant walk across the floor, my first impulse was to squash it. When I was out in the mountains and saw an ant, I somehow felt that he had a place in the universe the same as I did, and that perhaps man doesn't own the world, after all. I was in a shelter in Virginia one night and heard something beneath the bunk. I got my flashlight and looked, and a skunk looked right back at me. I decided the best course was just to leave it alone, so I went back to sleep. I saw approximately 20 wild turkeys one rainy drizzly day in Virginia. That was more wild turkeys than I had seen in my entire life before. I probably saw more game in the state of Virginia than in all the other states combined. However, I did see more deer in Pennsylvania. I'd seen moose before, but I had never been close to one until one day when I was on a ridge in Maine at about 4,000 feet. I was walking along a rocky ledge when I heard a snort. I turned and saw a female moose about 10 feet from me. She had big sad eyes and looked like that love-sick moose in the cartoons. I was afraid she might charge if I moved too fast, so I talked nice and slow to her, and eased away. I didn't want to be pushed off the ledge by a love-sick moose.

You meet many interesting people and have many interesting experiences on the trail. People who live near the trail seem to look forward to seeing hikers when spring comes. They are wonderful people, especially to through hikers. I didn't meet anyone on the entire trip who was really nasty. The only complaint I heard about hikers was in Virginia. A farmer told me his gate had been left open, and that it took him all day to get his cows back. Another time his gate had been torn off its hinges. He said that if the vandalism continued, he was going to ask that the trail be taken off his land. At a place called Max Patch I met a farmer working on a fence. I asked him how far it was to Hot Springs, North Carolina. "Oh, I don't know how many miles it is, but I've walked it many times in about four hours." I had about six hours of daylight left, so I thought I could reach Hot Springs that night. However, darkness caught me and I found an abandoned house and spent the night in it. The next morning I walked three hours before I finally reached Hot Springs. I have always wondered if that man really did walk that distance in four hours when he was in his prime. It took me about eight hours.

When I got to Hot Springs I called home, picked up some food, and asked the ranger about a place to spend the night. He directed me to a house where a lady rented me a room. During the night the house started to shake, and I thought I was in an earthquake. I opened the window and was about ready to jump when I heard a train whistle practically on top of me. The lady had forgotten to tell me that the train ran very close to her house. When she ran a board-inghouse the railroad crews stayed with her. Now, every time the trains passed by, they blew the whistle to say "hello" to her.

I was walking along a dirt road in Virginia late one afternoon when I came to some old buildings. It looked like a storm was coming, so I decided to ask if I could spend the night in the barn. An old fellow came to the door. When I explained what I wanted, he said, "Well, son, I don't have a barn, but you can sleep in the mission." I looked around and wondered where "the mission" was. The old gentleman asked me to have supper, and afterward invited me to attend the service. I figured a little bit of religion wouldn't hurt me, so I said I would attend. It turned out that the mission was the shabby old building we were in, and that the old gentleman was the preacher. About 20 people showed up for the service. For church music the preacher played a harpsichord and a harmonica at the same time. He could play all of the songs in the little songbook they used. After an old-time revival sermon, the preacher introduced me to the con-gregation and said he was happy that God had sent me by. The women of the congregation shook my hand, and gave me little prayer books to take with me. Soon after the service ended we had one of the worst thunderstorms I have ever experienced in my life, and I was very thankful to be warm and dry on the church floor, listening to the rain beat on the tin roof. About five o'clock the next morning the old preacher came out with a plate of biscuits, some honey, and a big pot of coffee, and we had breakfast together. Before I left he said a prayer for me, and wished me a safe journey. This experience was one of the highlights of my trip.

I had a breakfast of country ham and biscuits about five o'clock one morning in a little restaurant in Virginia. Late that afternoon I pulled into a little country store. The owner said I was the first through hiker he had seen that year, and asked me how far I'd hiked that day. I told him where I had started that morning. "You're a big fibber," he said, "nobody can walk that fast." We made a bet of $5 and he called back to the restaurant and asked if I had eaten break-fast there at about five o'clock that morning. "Yes, he certainly did," the lady said. She mentioned my hometown and what I had eaten for breakfast to prove it, and the man came across with the $5 and said I must really be moving, because he'd never seen it done before.

It was getting dark when I reached Pearisburg, Virginia, and I had no place to sleep. I decided to ask if I could spend the night in jail. At the sheriff's office I explained my hike and told the sheriff that I had enough money for a motel room but I needed it for food.

The sheriff called the jailer. I thought he was going to put me in jail right there, but he sent across the street to get me some food. He told me to put my pack down, and we sat and watched TV. After supper I made calls with him in the police car, beard and all. At about 10 o'clock, when I decided to get some rest, they locked me in the cell. This was quite an experience for me after spending so many nights in the woods watching the stars at night. The next morning the sheriff showed up bright and early and took me back to the trail. Just before we got to the trail he turned the siren on loud and then sat back and laughed. "I want to give you a royal send-off," he told me.

I picked up trash along the trail when I could. One day near the Delaware Water Gap in Pennsylvania I was picking up beer cans and singing to myself. A family was having a picnic at a roadside table. Curiosity was just killing the man. He came over and asked me where I was from and what I was doing. I told him. "What's a fellow from Tennessee doing picking up trash in Pennsylvania? That doesn't sound like much fun to me, walking halfway across the country picking up trash." He watched me for a moment, and then just walked off shaking his head.

I found northern Pennsylvania and New York so ugly that I traveled as fast as I could. Being born in the mountains of North Carolina, I am a lover of the high country. However, one nice thing did happen to me in Pawling, New York. I ran into a fellow who had been born in Knoxville, Tennessee. He asked me to spend the night in his home. I had a good bed and good food, and his wife even washed my clothes.

On the Long Trail in Vermont I ran into a fellow from Boston who had read a book on backpacking and decided to take it up as a hobby. He went to L. L. Bean's and bought a lot of equipment and had his wife drive him to the trail. He had started to do the 110-mile section to Rutland, Vermont, when I met him. I hiked with him for two days, and helped him as much as I could. When we got to the Long Trail Lodge he treated me to a nice big steak. He was overweight and didn't have the proper shoes but he completed his hike and probably got more out of it than I did out of hiking the whole Appalachian Trail.

When I crossed the White Mountains the weather was perfect, six of the prettiest days they had had in years, I was told. I was lucky about weather on the trip; I probably had fewer days of rain and bad weather than anybody who has ever made a through hike. The trail was often pretty crowded in New Hampshire. One Sunday after-noon in the Presidential Range I think I could have counted 45 or 50 hikers from where I was standing on Mt. Adams. At Mt. Washington I was looking out over the beauty of the Presidential Range when a tall slender girl came along. She was about six feet tall and looked like she weighed about 90 pounds. It turned out that we were head-ing for the same shelter, and I was delighted to have company. She set such a fast pace that after about two hours of hiking I asked her to stop and take a break. It was the first and only time a girl ever outwalked me. I had hiked some 1,700 miles of the trail, and she said this was her very first hike!

I saw hardly anyone at all in Maine. A few miles south of the Kennebec River I came to a fishing camp. A fellow at the camp was kind enough to phone Caratunk for someone to take me across the river when I got there. I waited two or three hours but the canoe didn't show up. Pulp logs were floating down the river. Using the 50 feet of nylon cord I had with me, I tied two of these pulp logs to-gether, took off my clothes, put my pack and clothes on top of the logs, and in I went. In spite of the many swiftly moving pulp logs, I managed to swim across.

In the Shenandoah Valley I had met a couple from Maine who told me that one of the peaks of Mt. Katahdin was the first place the sun strikes in the United States each day. The closer I got to Katahdin, the more I thought of this fact. When I got to Thoreau Spring, on my way up Mt. Katahdin, I could see the top. I was hoping some-body would be there so I could say, "Man, you know what I just did?" I wanted to share my joy, but there wasn't a darn soul up there. I touched the sign on top of Mt. Katahdin to signify that I had finally made it, and that it was all over. Then I decided that a more fitting way to end my trip would be to spend the night on top of Katahdin.

At about four o'clock the next morning I went out on the Knife-Edge and sat down where the sun was supposed to strike first. When the sun came up I jumped up and shouted and thought how wonder-ful it was to be the first person to feel the sun's rays in the United States that day.

When I hiked down from the summit the rangers were pretty mad at me for spending the night on the top, but I hadn't known about the rule against it so they let me go. The most satisfying moment of the whole trip was when I took one last look back at Mt. Katahdin and realized that it was all over. I hoped, and believed, that I was a better man than I was when I started my hike.

The Trail — By Accident

By Richard A. Hudson

Started near CHESTER GAP, VIRGINIA, on June 3, 1966
Finished at GRAFTON NOTCH, MAINE, on August 26, 1970

Like other day-dreaming hikers, I had wanted to walk the entire trail in one trip ever since I first learned of the Appalachian Trail. However, I cannot recall ever having decided to walk it piecemeal—at least not until I had finished most of it. For many years I had walked sections of the trail in the New York–New Jersey area. As a youth my parents often vacationed in the Great Smokies. Later I made trips there, walking many trails leading up from the Tennessee side as well as short sections of the Appalachian Trail from the cross-mountain road at Newfound Gap.

These trips left me with a desire to walk the Appalachian Trail all the way through the Great Smoky Mountains National Park. In 1966 I spent the spring months preparing for the trip. Guidebooks and other literature published by the Appalachian Trail Conference were ordered and studied. On the way down a stop was made in the Shenandoah National Park for conditioning purposes. I started at the northern end and walked through the northern and central sections. This was followed by a very successful trip through the Smokies.

That fall I returned to Shenandoah National Park and made day trips along the southern section. I decided to rewalk the New York–New Jersey section of the trail nearer home, and a week after the Virginia trip I began a series of day trips starting from Kent, Connecticut, and heading south. My father helped with the transportation by waiting for me at the end of the day or helping spot my car at the end of the section.

In the spring of 1967 I decided to walk the Long Trail in Vermont. That winter there had been a very heavy late snowfall. I started north from the Massachusetts border on June 1. The weather was warm but there was far too much snow on the ground for comfort. The trip ended after 145 miles when time and my food supply ran out. Later that year I returned to complete the Long Trail.

Every six weeks I was free for a three-day weekend. In the fall of 1967 I began to spend these weekends somewhere on the Appalachian Trail. During my vacation in 1968 I walked the trail from Damascus, Virginia, to the Smokies. This was the longest and most enjoyable trip I had made up until that time, even though much of it was in the rain. That August I started from the Maine–New Hampshire border, going through the White Mountains. Each night except the first two were spent in the Appalachian Mountain Club's huts. A subproject here was to climb as many of the 4,000-foot peaks as possible. Twenty-eight of the forty-six are on or near the Appalachian Trail.

Sometime during 1968 I was glancing through the guidebooks and by chance I added up the miles I had covered. I was surprised to learn how much of the trail I had walked. I realized that if I concentrated all of my hiking on the Appalachian Trail I would soon complete it. From then on all my vacations, days off, and long weekends were spent somewhere along the trail. My longest trip was made in 1969, when I covered over 300 miles from Waynesboro, Virginia, to Damascus, Virginia. My best mileage on this trip was 27 miles in one day going into Pearisburg and the same distance again on the day I left Pearisburg. It was much too many miles.

I had walked all of the trail sections in a north-south direction except for the Long Trail, so in the fall of 1969 I rewalked the Long Trail from Sherburne Pass to Massachusetts. My most active year was in 1970 when over 650 miles of trail were hiked, starting in the spring when I walked from Fontana Village to Springer Mountain, and ending with a final hike from Mt. Katahdin to the New Hampshire border. Sandwiched in between were various short sections not walked before. One of these was a ridiculous 36-mile trip in one day, in Pennsylvania. Another was the completion of the trail in Maryland. Here I had a real problem with transportation. Using a bicycle as my second vehicle, I covered the state in two days. After a long day on the trail the bike ride back to the car was a bit too much. The bike was also used a few times in Pennsylvania. The Maryland trip was followed by a quick drive to Virginia to walk 1.7 miles from Chester Gap to the Shenandoah National Park boundary. This was a section I had covered by taxi, not knowing I soon would be trying to walk the entire trail.

Walking the trail over several years had its advantages. Changes in diet and equipment were made as needed. The result was that each trip was an improvement over the last. My original source of information was the Potomac Appalachian Trail Club's equipment guide. The early editions gave specific suggestions on equipment, and some of these suggestions proved to be excellent ones. Peter Limmer boots were worn. Had I not done so much non-Appalachian Trail hiking, one pair with one resoling would have lasted the entire trail, but just before the final trip in Maine I was forced to buy another pair. A Kelty pack was used from the start, as well as a Holubar down sleeping bag. All cooking was done on a gasoline stove. Originally I used a Primus with the cookset that comes with it. This stove was later replaced with a Svea, but I continued to use the large pot and lid from the Primus cookset. A large spoon and a Sierra cup completed the cooking and eating equipment.

The first parka was by Holubar. It was lightweight and had excellent wind protection but I could not clean the dirt off. It was replaced by another brand which proved too heavy so I purchased another Holubar of a darker color. A foam pad was used on early spring or late fall trips for warmth. In other seasons the hardwood floor of a shelter can be very comfortable without a pad after a long day on the trail. A cheap plastic poncho served as both rain protection and ground cloth. I carried a tube tent but the only times it was used was on one occasion when a shelter was full, and twice in Virginia when the shelters had just been painted. The only extra clothes I carried were a down sweater, extra undergarments, and socks.

Even though I had plenty to eat I would still lose 10 to 15 pounds on each long trip. Breakfast consisted of Tang, Familia (a Swiss cereal prepacked at home with milk powder), and Swiss Miss Cocoa with marshmallow. Marshmallows were my luxury item and I always had plenty to munch on. Water was heated each morning for the cocoa and to pour over the cereal. It would usually take 45 minutes to an hour to get up, eat, and be on my way. The trips from the shelter each morning would hopefully begin as soon as it would be light enough to see the blazes.

Lunch consisted of a series of short stops when I munched from a bag of goodies consisting of nuts, raisins, Chunky Chocolate, and a two-ounce cheese stick. On a hot day stops would be made for Tang at springs or stream crossings. I liked to be at a shelter by midafternoon, to relax and investigate the surrounding area. The evening meal would be a long and enjoyable affair. With only one pot and one stove it took quite a bit of time. Originally I made up my own dinners from noodles, rice, or instant potatoes, along with dried meat and vegetables. One of my favorites was to make a white sauce from a package mix and add dried chipped beef. This was served over mashed potatoes that had been cooked with dried peas. On the last trips I discovered that the two-portion dinners of Stow-A-Way were

Photo by Robert Winslow

Dead chestnut tree at Big Meadows in the Shenandoah.

Photo by Elmer L. Onsto

View from the trail going up Mt. Katahdin.

ideal. Dinner began with hot Jell-O or bouillon, then the main dish, and for dessert a very large pot of tea and leftover lunch goodies. If a cold stream was near the shelter, Jell-O would set quicker in the stream than in the refrigerator at home.

The frequent road crossings gave access to motels and restaurants which I often used. For longer trips I would send a package to myself at a nearby post office. The logistics for even a short vacation were sometimes considerable. In fact, much of the pleasure was in the planning. Catalogs were ordered and read with great interest. Unfortunately, the Eastern Mountain Sports catalog did not become available until after I completed the trail. It is the best source of information on equipment that I know of. A copy can be obtained from 1041 Commonwealth Avenue, Boston, Massachusetts 02215. The guidebooks were read and reread. The sections to be covered were taken out and placed in a map case which hung around my neck. Maps were consulted and letters sent to bus and rail companies in order to arrange transportation to and from the trail. Frequently it was necessary to hitchhike or take a taxi, and I learned much local lore from these rides. Compared to my own New York area the taxi trips, though sometimes long, were usually cheap. However, in Maine it cost $17 to take a cab from Millinocket to Katahdin Stream Campground. The driver was a former logger and the stories of logging in the area almost made the expense worthwhile.

The trips in the South were in May before the schools were out. The result was that I had the trail to myself. The only hikers I met were through hikers going the full length of the trail. In August or September I would walk the New England sections, and on several occasions I again met the same through hikers I had met that spring in the South.

A hiker tends to go a little faster than he should when trying to cover a long section of trail in a short vacation or on a weekend trip. I've never been successful in slowing down. However, much that is fascinating is seen each day, even though less time is spent at some outstanding location than might be desirable. The hikers met along the way are always a joy to talk with because you share the same interests. Even though you have never met them before you can discuss the trail with them as if they were long lost friends.

That dream of walking the entire trail in one trip is still with me. If and when it is possible I would prefer to have another person or two along and also to take five or six months. Many sections would still be walked quickly but there are areas that it would be a crime to rush through.

Going a Journey

By Charles Konopa

One of the pleasantest things in the world is going a journey; but I like to go by myself.—Hazlitt, *On Going a Journey*

Started at SPRINGER MOUNTAIN on June 6, 1964
Finished the trail on September 19, 1970

In a flurry of reddish dust, the old sedan stopped on the dirt road which runs through Nimblewill Gap. I got out and shouldered my backpack. It bulged with sleeping bag, wool socks, rain poncho, alpine gas stove, food, and a clutter of gear I thought one couldn't walk a trail without.

Ernest Greer, who raises chickens on Route One, Gainesville, Georgia, shook my hand before driving away.

"Now don't you go straying from the trail," he said. "Lots of people have been lost in these hills. The country post offices used to list their names, and some names never did get off the list."

Mr. Greer grinned under his black hat, but it was plain that he was a little dubious. Looking back, I can see that my city complexion would hardly inspire confidence. I vowed (and I was really making a vow to myself) to stick to the narrow track as if my success as a backpacker depended on it—and in truth it did, for I was setting out to walk on the Appalachian Trail, the 2,000-mile footpath which crosses mountains in 14 Atlantic states to link northern Georgia with north central Maine.

Now the southern end of the Appalachian Trail is at the top of 3,782-foot Springer Mountain in the Chattahoochee National Forest. Where Mr. Greer dropped me off is the closest one can approach it by car; from Nimblewill Gap a connecting trail switchbacks among the hardwood trees to crest Black Mountain, dips into a ravine and climbs again. Two point three miles and 900 feet of vertical rise are required to deposit the traveler on Springer's summit.

It is a good introduction to the Appalachian Trail which, I soon discovered, never—well, almost never—is level; it's too busy running up mountains and down their backsides. Neither is it straight: no crowflight path this. It zigzags, serpentines, undulates, and meanders. At times the track even vanishes unexpectedly, leaving the hiker orphaned—seldom, fortunately, for very long.

But narrow, yes. As a rule the trail is from 20 to 30 inches wide, though on some hillsides it barely fits one's boot sole and is cambered the wrong way at that. And a few stretches, mercifully short, exist where the trail so steepens that hands become as necessary as feet. At other spots, trees and shrubbery provide the only safe handholds when precipitous footing is slippery from rain, mud, or ice.

In a number of places, there is no recognizable path, only a succession of blazes. This is what trail engineers mean by an "unworked footway."

The Appalachian Trail is blazed with two-inch by six-inch white rectangles painted on anything handy: tree trunks in the forest, boulders and wooden stakes in meadows, fences and telephone poles along the roads. But now and then—just where they are most needed, it seems at the time—there is a dearth of blazes. Frequently one sees nailed to trees small galvanized metal diamonds bearing the trail emblem: a black arrowhead formed by interlocking the letters A and T, and the words "Appalachian Trail—Maine to Georgia."

One thing the Appalachian Trail is, and all hikers heartily agree, it's the best no-pill guaranteed weight reducer in the Peach State, and the 13 other sovereign states, for that matter. If poundage is a problem and there is time to spare, take them both on the trail and find—as I did—why mountaineers are lean. If this is not reason enough, one might consider Trevelyan's observation. "I have two doctors," he said, "my left leg and my right."

There were to be moments ahead when this trail novice would mightily wish for, if not an extra pair of legs, then at least a second set of feet.

Foot blisters were my main problem; not even Army service had demanded so much continuous walking. The propagation, treatment, and care of the blister need not be explored here; but it was not until I was deep into Virginia, two months and 700 miles later, that feet had hardened to the task. Meantime, I had become—most reluctantly—an expert on blisters.

Fastened to the rock of Springer Mountain is a bronze plaque that is turning green with the passing years. It shows a man in the hiking garb of an older generation. (The Appalachian Trail wasn't completed until 1937.) In addition to a fine air of determination, he sports a felt hat (one clearly no longer suitable for town wear), long-sleeved shirt (only polo players and Britishers stationed in the tropics wore short sleeves in those more formal times), and breeches tucked into knee-length boots. The boots are of the type once known as high tops, and sometimes came equipped with a snap pocket to accommodate a jackknife (included with the purchase). They customarily took two minutes to draw on and another five to lace up, and gave the wearer a good deal of leg support and sense of security. Along with a generous lashing of bourbon, high tops were once regarded as the only sensible defense against ambush by poisonous reptiles.

Inscribed on the plaque, which faces ranges veiled in mysterious blue haze, are these words:

APPALACHIAN TRAIL—GEORGIA TO MAINE
A FOOTPATH FOR THOSE
WHO SEEK FELLOWSHIP
WITH THE WILDERNESS
THE GEORGIA APPALACHIAN TRAIL CLUB, 1934.

There was a soughing of wind through the trees, and I turned to gaze at the promontory called Pulpit Rock. It has been perhaps half a century since Pulpit Rock last was exercised for the purpose to which it owes its name. Then churches and roads were fewer, and hill people would gather once a year for protracted meeting. Here on the cool mountaintop they would camp for a week or more while being refreshed by the Word.

Revival is about to begin. The women are already seated on felled poplars serving as pews; expectant, uptilted faces are framed in silk or sateen Sunday poke bonnets, a few store-bought but most homemade. Squirmy kids have been pinned down by hushes and sharp eyeings. Their fathers and grandfathers, clad in spanking new blue denim overalls despite the hard times, rest powerful, work-reddened hands on their knees.

Silence falls as the evangelist—imported from distant Memphis or Atlanta—strides forward to mount Pulpit Rock. His shirt is as white as a dove's wing and his broadcloth suit is as dark as the black-bound Bible. A scattering of younger men, wiping backs of hands on mouths, break from the cover of the trees and advance to occupy safe seats at the rear, far from the mourners' bench. Those who neglected to remove hats snatch at them when reproving glances flash their way.

For a long moment the preacher stands on Pulpit Rock in stern contemplation of the assembly. Large, weighty, incased in jet morocco, the Good Book is slowly raised on high. A bony finger stabs at the Book, then at the people. Words heavy with portent rend the wilderness.

Y'all hear!

I Become a Saunterer

This was the jump-off point and I felt a little nervous. My first long hike was beginning. It had taken an hour and a half to climb from Nimblewill Gap to the top of Springer Mountain and already the pack was chafing my ribs and hanging heavily from my shoulders. These were new sensations and would take some getting used to.

Clouds milled overhead, thickened, and blotted out the blue of the sky. Chattahoochee Forest brooded. On a post squatted a box with the words, HIKING REGISTER—ALL HIKERS PLEASE REGISTER. I raised the lid and gazed at a page of penciled names and comments. Hikers starting or ending walks of a day, a week, or longer, had signed in. I wrote the date—June 6—then added my name to the roll. There was space for "Comments," but I left it blank; nothing had happened yet and I didn't have anything to say. A few drops of rain made dark spots on the page.

I set off slowly on the trail, which wound among the trees. The rain came down, hissing as its flight from the sun ended. There was a sudden commotion ahead. A grouse hen fluttered across my path, one wing dragging on the ground. I had approached her family of chicks too closely and she, having first hushed them under a bush, darted out to lure Two-Legs away with her wounded bird act. Though I looked about carefully, not a mite of reddish brown fluff could be detected. The game bird circled a few feet off, directing anxious glances in my direction. As I walked down the trail she flew onto a branch and I thought I heard fledglings cheeping.

When at noon the rain let up, I sat on a great fallen log and drank at the spring of pure mineral water that seethed from the rocky hillside. I had had no breakfast and now peeled a hard-cooked egg. Afraid lest my stomach get lonesome on the way, I had packed rations enough for two famished lumberjacks. Yet for three days I consumed very little—in all but two eggs, several sardines in a small tin, and a slice or two of that soft, white plastic-like mattress stuffing which is the only bread one can buy in many parts of the United States. After settling into the measured rhythm of walking and the calm flow of time my appetite returned. Later I was to find that I never ate so much on the trail as I did at home, where little exertion was required.

The days melded into a pattern of daybreak and dusk, sightings of black bear and deer, cold murmurous streams and the snapping of tiny brief campfires, sultry afternoons when nimbuses snarled overhead, leaden downpours, and sometimes brutally steep trails. I felt an expansion of my inner being. Simply, I was throwing aside the insulation by which our style of living separates man from nature: concrete everywhere to smooth the ground, a distaste for physical effort, electronic gadgetry to broadcast the clever but shallow thoughts of other confused men, writing scornful of the Decalogue, billboards serving only to ring what has increasingly become a cash register civilization.

In the Middle Ages, one who walked on a pilgrimage was known as a Saint Terrer, for he trod the sacred earth. From the phrase has derived the word saunterer. In this age a saunterer is not held in much regard. I am afraid that I was becoming a saunterer.

At any rate, the trail was returning me to contentment with elementary things.

Twelve days and 105 trail miles later I was eating fried chicken in a restaurant in Franklin, North Carolina, and making a list of supplies for the next leg north, the traverse of the Smokies.

I reflected that I would never again view with casual detachment these mountains which the Appalachian Trail crosses. The miles of hard up and down, walked so painfully at first, were the fee that had to be paid for my passport to an Appalachian world of vibrant life—a world to which I had been blind.

I took up walking because it would benefit my health, which was languishing from that common twentieth century ailment, a lack of regular exercise. At the beginning it took all my energy to surmount the ancient hills from one forest shelter to another. There were evenings when I didn't make shelter and threw myself on the mercy of the earth, drawing poncho over me when rain fell. Before folding hands in sleep I would listen to the frogs chanting "jug o' rum," "jug o' rum," while the owls, sitting in nightly parliament, boomed "I cook for myself, who cooks for you-all?"

My journey was begun without a trail guidebook. I had only

road maps from a filling station and found them all but useless to the walker. In consequence, at least once a day, at the onset, the route was lost. Every winding of the 2,000-mile footpath is meaningful, but visual directions are often sparse and not always where one might expect them to be, while vandals are busy in every season at filching the signboards or riddling them with gunshot. After a guidebook caught up with me at a mail stop, I became less anxious about my course and wasted fewer steps in straying.

When I eased into sleeping bag at day's end, my legs would tingle with what doubtless were "growing pains"; the aching intensity would bring me to the verge of screaming, though I think I never did. The soles of my feet, long accustomed to nothing harsher than the floor rug of a car, were so tender that I wore three pairs of socks at a time. Still, sharp pebbles made me wince. A veteran trail hiker I met casting for trout in a swift Tennessee run advised massaging the feet for five minutes every day. This helped, and in time my feet toughened. All the while heart and lungs had been strengthening, for Nature thrives when prodded.

My back carried everything requisite in a rig of metal and cloth called a backpack. Into it went clothing, camping gear, and food. A medical kit provided for emergencies from snakebite to toothache, but the trail never afflicted me with anything more dire than blisters. There were enough of those to gladden Dr. Scholls.

As an embryo backpacker, my equipment ran between 45 and 50 pounds, a weight to whip a wildcat. Experience taught me to use lighter items and before undertaking a hike to make two piles of them: those absolutely needed and those which might be needed, and then to throw away the second pile. Soon my pack was down to 30 pounds or less and rode easily. Only in Maine north of the Kennebec River was it necessary to carry provisions for more than four or five days at a stretch; along the rest of the trail food could be got at shorter intervals.

A good backpack is contoured to fit a normal person's anatomy. The first backpack I owned galled my ribs, its narrow straps dug into my shoulders, tubing broke, and stitching ripped on the packbag. It did not shed water, but maliciously soaked up rain, sweat, dew, and plain humidity. I bought the contraption from a nationwide mail-order house whose buyers had never carried anything heavier than a pint of rye in a briefcase. After 200 miles I took it back and found a model elsewhere that could do the job.

One night early in the trip, I was pulled awake by a powerful smell and a feeling of danger. Nearby a bear stood in the moonlight looking at me. The thought occurred then that I had been more observed than observing. From that time I began to look not merely ahead, but to each side of the slender track.

My ignorance was vast and indiscriminate. A tree was simply a tree, not an oak whose sire might have planked the immortal frigate *Constitution*, or a maple that blushed crimson as it shed summer dress. It seemed to me that I was on the rim of a new world; in truth, I was walking in the aisles of the most immense and diverse hardwood forest known to the temperate zones, one that had its origin in the Himalayas of Asia. But I knew none of these things, for I was a stranger in my native land.

I learned how the sight of a timber rattlesnake as thick as a man's arm, coiled and rattling furiously, chills the marrow. From this graceful creature emanates an almost palpable menace. The arrowlike head points directly at you, and its expressionless slit orbs are opaque windows to the mystery that is a serpent and the greater mystery of its creation.

The black bear has become timid, the passenger pigeon no longer clouds the upper air, the mountain lion is as seldom seen as a gold coin, the soaring trees are cut and humbled, the rivers are bridged, tunneled under, stripped of bed gravel and charged with foulness, and the internal combustion engine exults in its noisome chemistry. A meeting with a rattlesnake is one of the few original experiences left in the American outdoors.

The tattoo of its rattles, like the quickening beat of an Indian war drum, raises the hair and hones every sense to a sickle's edge. A tension is brought on which primitive man, in his vulnerable naked feet, knew well. It is primordial. I would no more forego the occasional session of castanets with a rattler than I would think of swapping five minutes with Cleopatra for the United States Army's Good Conduct Medal.

On the trail I learned, too, that the Appalachians mount guard over another manner of life, a tempo slower and more deeply breathing than most Americans now know. That life and these hills, their botany and zoology, the Indian knew in an intimate, even religious, way. When this basic man was betrayed and crushed a part of the wilderness ceased to exist. Along with him went an almost unremembered part of honest civilization: the ancestral knowledge that every living thing has its place under the sun.

Most of the trail was walked alone. I did so partly because the adventure of solitude was desired. And I knew that to wait on any long-distance hiker going in the same direction who wanted my company might mean a lengthy wait, indeed.

Not all the way is highland grandeur, untamed country, or the sweet smell of flowering herbs. The Appalachian Trail marches through a few towns: Hot Springs, North Carolina; Damascus, Virginia; Unionville, New York; Hanover, New Hampshire, and Monson, Maine, to name several. They are pleasant communities. A dozen or two hamlets and country stores are passed. The footpath also brings the Appalachian traveler by the outskirts of the most populous quarter of the hemisphere. From the pastoral banks of the Hudson he may look downriver over an increasingly building-choked landscape that culminates in a savage dark cloud of fumes. Beneath the foreboding pall is everything Western culture and ingenuity can devise. It seems unnatural that earthly Paradise should give off so much heat and smoke.

Gazing on this scene I knew that it is America's wild places which are her cathedrals.

A Lengthy Matter

Until a few years ago, the Appalachian Trail was counted as 2,028 miles long. Mount Oglethorpe in Georgia was the southern extremity, and rightly so, for it is southernmost mountain of the august Appalachian Range. But within two decades, logging demolished much of its proud mantle of forest, while motor traffic and a radar training school busied its tranquil summit. And the poultry-raising industry—of trenchant importance in the homeland of fried chicken —burgeoned: the vicinity of the peak named for the aristocratic founder of Georgia had come to be the breeding, hatching, and execution place of countless fryers.

The famished hiker might indeed welcome a plump pullet to his smoke-blackened pot, but the sight, smell, and cackle of hundreds of thousands of mindless birds make a fugitive of appetite. To one emerging from pine-scented woods, a new dimension is forever added to the word "chicken."

With a sigh, the Appalachian Trail Conference and the Georgia Appalachian Trail Club lopped Mount Oglethorpe and 21 miles from the route in 1958. This action placed the terminus atop Springer Mountain—still a fitting end, for Springer (3,782 feet) marks the southern limit of the enchanting Blue Ridge.

The super-trail begins and ends on mountaintops. Baxter Peak

(5,267 feet) on Mount Katahdin, a huge granitic monolith dominating central Maine, is its northern terminus.

Between the Peach and the Pine Tree States, the footway roves the skyline, a journey through 14 states on the rocky backbone of the Atlantic Seaboard. Someday it may be blazed into Canada; the Appalachians march craggily northward for an additional 100 miles in Maine, then cross the international border and proceed three hundred and some miles in Canada before sinking into the ocean on the tip of Newfoundland.

In the past several years relocations have added a few miles to the trail. It stood at 2,034.44 miles in mid-1973. Distances are determined by a meter that counts the revolutions of a measuring wheel which is pushed along the trail; the instrument looks like a unicycle with a handle instead of a seat. Mileages by states, starting with Georgia and heading north, are:

Georgia	79.04
North Carolina and Tennessee (the trail follows their common boundary for about 177 miles)	343.20
Virginia and West Virginia (the trail is shared between them for about 20 miles and runs in West Virginia for over 5 miles)	489.96
Maryland	37.41
Pennsylvania	222.40
New Jersey	61.55
New York	97.24
Connecticut	56.05
Massachusetts	83.80
Vermont	133.46
New Hampshire	153.54
Maine	276.79

Travelers on the full length of the Appalachian Trail, however, will walk more than its official 2,034.44 miles—at least seven and a half miles more, for that is the minimum required to approach or leave the summits where the trail begins and ends.

More of the Appalachian Trail is in Virginia—24 percent—than any other state. Ten of the states were among the original thirteen colonies: Georgia, North Carolina, Virginia, Maryland, New York, New Jersey, Pennsylvania, Connecticut, Massachusetts, and New Hampshire. Only three of the eastern states ridged by the Appalachians—Alabama, Kentucky, and South Carolina—are not serviced by the trail.

The Appalachian Trail winds through two national parks, Great Smoky Mountains and Shenandoah, and in central Virginia somewhat parallels the course of the Blue Ridge Parkway, which it frequently crosses. For a mile and a half in southern Maryland it uses the towpath of the C & O Canal National Historical Park. Two National Recreation areas—Mount Rogers in Virginia and Delaware Water Gap on the river boundary of New Jersey and Pennsylvania—are also traversed, as are eight national forests: the Chattahoochee in Georgia, Nantahala and Pisgah in North Carolina, Cherokee in Tennessee, Jefferson and George Washington in Virginia, Green Mountain in Vermont, and White Mountain in New Hampshire. It is a recreation trail, following the crest of the mountains, and not an Indian track as is sometimes reported. The southern half does parallel the age-old Great Indian Warpath which ran in the longitudinal valleys from Creek territory in Alabama north into Pennsylvania. But the trails blazed by red men followed the lowlands whenever possible, avoiding difficult mountain passages—quite the opposite of the intent of the Appalachian Trail.

White blazes, mostly on tree trunks, mark the main route except for a 38-mile stretch south of Davenport Gap in the Smokies and three spans in Vermont and New Hampshire. On both sides of the Vermont–New Hampshire line where it is used as a ski trail by the Dartmouth Outing Club, it is blazed with alternate orange and black stripes readily visible against a snowy background. And for much of its track through the White Mountains—actually from Kinsman Notch to Grafton Notch, about 112 miles—there are no paint marks of any sort, only signboards to guide the walker.

Blue paint blazes are used to mark side trails that lead off to shelters, waterholes, and viewpoints or are approach trails and alternate routes.

No year passes that modifications, usually minor, do not take place on the trail. Flood, landslide, and timbering obliterate short portions, requiring detours or relocations. An older route may be replaced by one more scenic when the opportunity is presented. Conversion of yet another New England landmark to ski resort might demand re-routing; crossing slopes scarred by removal of trees to make way for chair lifts and ski runs is aesthetically unappealing. The Appalachian Trail is concerned not only with linking North and South but with maintaining the primitive surroundings of its route.

Close to half of it is on private property. Thousands of generous, civic-minded persons allow it to cut through their lands. But odious statistics exist, too. Elmer Onstott, an end-to-ender, noted that while the trail "stands as a tribute to the effort of so many dedicated people of good will who are constructive instead of destructive, there is evidence that a vicious animal, better known as the vandal, is roaming the Big Woods."[1]

All too often trail users—nearly always nonhikers, it must be said —have damaged fences and buildings, left gates open, frightened livestock, dug up plants and wild flowers for resale, set fires, rutted the paths with motor bikes, and adorned innocent walls with graffiti and witless verbs remarkable for misspelling. Littering is a concern —as everywhere. Morons armed with weapons approximating the firepower of a medieval company of arquebusiers make targets of trail signs. On occasion, as farmers can testify, they even manage to mistake cows for deer, sheep for rabbits, and collies for foxes. Day and night have been made uncomfortable, frequently hideous, with portable blaring radios, pot parties gone out of hand, sonic shrieks, and manic laughter in areas devoted to quiet summer homes.

Then forebearance ends: the harried landowner may withdraw permission for passage. Local trail club volunteers apologize, clean up the mess, and clear a new footpath elsewhere. Sometimes, and this is a grievous matter injuring its essentially wilderness character, the trail must take to motor roads.

Continuing vandalism at the rustic log Hemlock Spring Shelter near Fort Montgomery, New York, has caused its abandonment; other shelters have been gutted, fired, and leveled to their foundation stones by the baleful. These miscreants are aware of their malice, as shown by the fact that government land has less of it. But federal and state property are guarded by fairly severe laws against human mischief. Owners of private property can seldom afford or demand the same amount of legal protection.

Add a gruesome statistic: benighted souls have even committed suicide in the shelters.

The remarkable foot trail—longest continuous path in the world —was the brain child of Benton MacKaye of Shirley Center, Massachusetts.

MacKaye was a forester who, in October, 1921, had published in an architectural journal an article entitled "An Appalachian Trail, A Project in Regional Planning."[2] His concept of a master trail through eastern states stirred quick response, for it was to be not

[1] *Appalachian Trailway News,* January 1969.

[2] In a letter to Stanley A. Murray, chairman of the Appalachian Trail Conference, that was printed in the *Appalachian Trailway News* for September, 1970, MacKaye recalled that except for the encouragement of two men, Charles Harris Whitaker, then editor of the *Journal of the American Institute of Architects,* and Clarence S. Stein, chairman of an American Institute of Architects committee, he might never have written this article which planted "the seed of our Trail."

merely a footway but a wilderness greenbelt to be preserved as a refuge from megalopolis. The following spring the first part of the Appalachian Trail was constructed in the Bear Mountain section of Palisades Interstate Park by New York and New Jersey trail groups; to it would be added existing trail systems in New York and New England. Within several years about 350 miles were open to cool the hiking hotfoot; still, the project had begun to falter—enthusiasm was waning.

Arthur Perkins, a retired citizen of Hartford, Connecticut, stepped in like a second wind to rescue the vision from its likely fate of subsiding into a campfire topic. He also enlisted the abiding interest of a younger man, Myron H. Avery, of Lubec, Maine.

As chairman of the Appalachian Trail Conference from 1931 to 1952, Avery rallied support up and down the East Coast. Local hiking clubs were formed and hundreds of members gave freely of time and work to further the dream.

The trail was officially opened in 1937.

These three men—MacKaye, who now in his mid-nineties lives in sprightly semiretirement, and Perkins and Avery, both now departed to stride loftier trails—were the principal founding fathers.

Anyone may walk the trail. Its use doesn't cost a nickel—except for the five-cent bridge toll exacted from pedestrians crossing the Hudson River 40 miles north of New York City. Another exception might be the crossing of Kennebec River in Maine. Coming to its banks, the hiker finds himself staring at a purposefully moving current five or six feet deep—sometimes less and sometimes more, depending upon the upstream release of water to float down logs—and one-fifth of a mile wide. No bridge or cable spans the river here.

Hikers have forded the Kennebec. Paul Macaulay, a reporter on the Worcester, Mass., *Telegram & Gazette,* did so with his 35-pound pack at "a low spot" when he couldn't find anyone to ferry him across. The experience was vivid. There were solemn moments when Mr. Macaulay was not too sure that he wasn't crossing the River Styx. "I was very lucky to succeed," he commented later, adding that he would not advise others to try the swift waters "under any circumstances." Mr. Macaulay went on to tramp the full length of the trail.

The Appalachian Trail guidebook recommends that advance arrangements be made for ferrying the Kennebec at Caratunk, Maine, a village of 90 citizens on its eastern bank. A Mr. Everett Thornton, care of the post office at Caratunk, used to take people across in his boat for a fee. The catch was that Mr. Thornton was not always home, nor could he divine without advance notice when a hiker would arrive under the large oak tree that marks the crossing point on the uninhabited western shore. At any rate, Mr. Thornton no longer lives there!

The southbound hiker can usually hire a boatman on his arrival in Caratunk. Paris Walters and I with our packs were canoed across by William York, owner of a sawmill south of town. His fee was a modest five dollars. Genial as are so many Mainers, Mr. York had several times that summer shut down his mill for an hour in order to row persons over the river.

A northbound hiker might just be lucky enough to find a fisherman on the river as he arrives (it does happen now and then), but the chances are greater that he will have to retrace his footsteps 11 miles to East Carry Pond Camps (a small resort) and then try to arrange transportation to the bridge at Bingham (population 1,308), where he may catch a bus to Caratunk, 15 miles north. Some back-packers step off the trail at Bigelow Village (no permanent popula-tion), get a ride around to Bingham and Caratunk (it is 70 miles via Maine Highways 27/16 and U.S. 201), ferry the river, walk the 41 trail miles back to Bigelow, and then return to Caratunk to resume the journey.

At a guess, a million walkers set foot on the Appalachian Trail every year. In this multitude are a few who hope to do the footway end-to-end. But bogs, steep hills, sore feet, stiff knees, and wet weather are notable dampeners. Despite the obstacles—and the trail in many places has the character of a training course for commandos —some of these hopefuls actually walk the full distance. Around five million steps are necessary.

Watchdog of the lengthy matter is the Appalachian Trail Con-ference, born in 1925 at the nation's Capital. It comprises about 10,000 individual members who pay annual dues, plus organizations and private persons (all volunteers) maintaining specific portions of the trail or otherwise contributing, and public officials and others whose duties may involve them with the trail. Associated with the conference are scores of regional hiking clubs, including the large Appalachian Mountain Club of Boston (over 14,000 members) and the influential Potomac Appalachian Trail Club of Washington, D.C. (2,000 members). Among the members is a certain "Mr. Apel Aitchen Walker, an outdoorsman of strong convictions."

The conference in its own words is a "volunteer, amateur recre-ational group—an experiment in amateurism on a very extensive scale." It is not affiliated with the federal government. Save for the executive director, Col. Lester L. Holmes, and a special projects coordinator, Peter H. Dunning, and occasional clerical help, salaries are unheard of, and expenses, as well as the labor of trail upkeep, are "contributions to the cause." Dues, bequests, and profits from the sale of guidebooks are the financial props.

From its headquarters in old Harpers Ferry, West Virginia 25425, the conference puts out maps, guides, and pamphlets dealing with trail subjects such as history, legislation, maintenance, and advice for hikers. A free information packet is sent to interested persons.[3] Since 1940, it has published the *Appalachian Trailway News*. This is a small magazine which in four issues a year details the triumphs and trials of the footpath. One of the conference's most popular publications, and a best seller in hiking circles, is the knowledgeable booklet entitled *Lightweight Equipment for Hiking, Camping and Mountaineering*.

As a footnote of sorts: the ATC long ago became resigned to receiving mail addressed to the "Appelation Trail Conference."

The trail has become more than a path of amazing extent and grandeur. In 1938, the National Park and United States Forest Services signed the Appalachian Trailway Agreement to preserve the route in a degree of isolation. Incompatible developments, as new paralleling roads, would not be built nearer than one mile to each side. (Timber felling—the loggers have a powerful lobby—and the Blue Ridge Parkway were exempted.) Similar accord was elicited from 13 of the 14 states for a zone one-fourth-mile wide on each side of the track where it crosses state parks and forests. In publicly owned areas Mr. MacKaye's greenbelt principle has been generally accepted and observed.

Since 682 miles of the Appalachian Trail cross federal lands and another 452 miles traverse state lands, the total of 1,134 miles represents about 56 percent of the length of the trail covered by zoning agreements. In practice, this has resulted in the genesis of a distinctive recreational area set aside "for the benefit of those who walk and camp." Breathing room has been found for the through trail and for those who "find their recreation by virtue of their own unaided efforts."

But what of the remaining 44 percent—the 900 miles crossing

---

[3] Since operating costs have been rising drastically, including postage and printing, the Conference suggests a contribution of a quarter or so to help with expenses.

private lands? This mileage is relatively defenseless except for gentlemen's agreements between hiking clubs and landowners, tenuous understandings which may be broken at any time. On these stretches there is no greenbelt. I was made painfully aware of this in northern Virginia.

Slabbing the hillside, the trail dipped into a ravine and came to Rock Spring. Trees arched overhead and their limbs shimmered on the water. I let the cool wetness run into my canteen and over my arms. On an overheated day a spring fills the eye like an oak log fire in the winter.

For a while I rested. A crow zigzagged past with a pair of finches in angry pursuit. From the shadows above, a rust colored spider with glowing red pinheads for eyes dropped on a monofilament. An inch from my nose it braked, became aware of my breath, and panicked back up the trembling line.

I tightened my shoelaces, got to my feet, stretched, yawned contentedly, and put on my pack. Ashby Gap was the next checkpoint north. The trail began to climb out of the ravine, but not halfway up it abruptly ended. Barbed wire was strung across the path. Nailed to trees were signs with light-reflecting red letters that screamed KEEP OUT and NO TRESPASSING. The most prominent sign was handwritten and said, redundantly I thought, NO TRESPASSING NOT ALLOWED.[4]

I dug out the guidebook and studied its usually informative pages. It prattled on with no mention of this blockade; there was not a hint of a detour. I backtracked to study the tree trunks for new blazes indicating a possible change in direction, but found only that the blazes ended where the barrier began.

The barbed wire and the signs were fresh, obviously put up within the previous few days. A yellow cottage peeped through the woods covering the ridge. There must be a road on top which I could follow. How else to proceed? Reasoning that I at least had the right of exit, I ducked under the wire and walked on. A dozen placards thundered trespass.

Now I could see that the white trail blazes had been obliterated with black paint.

Most householders below the Mason-Dixon Line are equipped with a shotgun, rifle, or pistol and a secret hankering to cut a notch in the stock. The homicide rate in Dixie is several times the national average. I looked about uneasily. My feelings were comparable to

---

[4] North of Sinking Creek Mountain the trail forsakes the trees to follow Virginia Secondary Highway 651. The reason is to be found on a sign along the road: POSTED! *Violators Will Be Shot At—Survivors Prosecuted By The Owner.*

those of a Yankee horse thief who discovers, while still deep in Confederate territory, that the mount he has stolen is Robert E. Lee's Traveller.

But there was no alarming glint of sunlight on gun barrel—nothing, in fact, more threatening than a scolding red squirrel. Soon I met with a dirt road and trudged it five miles to Ashby Gap. And then, instead of plunging back into the shaded woods, I had to pound the hard, hot pavement of Virginia Highway 601 for seven miles. The trail for a second time had been posted with lurid signs meant to intimidate.

The weak link in the Appalachian Trail system is not where it uses public forests and parks—for there its blithe presence is welcomed and gladly acknowledged as serving a public need—but where it must travel on private land. Here is the Achilles' heel.

Real estate development and logging are continuing hazards. Urbanization is reaching further into the mountains; the situation has become critical. There may be no end to people, but there is an end to land. Those who share Thoreau's belief that "in wildness is the preservation of the world" now share a feeling of desperation.

The only satisfactory solution is to acquire land for the trail where it leaves the public domain. Many property owners are willing to sell, or donate, some land for the purpose, especially since the pathway prefers locations where a tithe of wildness still exists. And often the terrain is so remote, jumbled, stone-bound, and precipitous that even frantic tax collectors have judged it to be of little monetary value.

For the few parcels whose owners refuse to sell or trade for other land, and where the Appalachian Trail cannot be re-routed and compromise is impossible, condemnation can be instituted to obtain easement. This is exactly what occurs when motor roads are constructed. Yet the hiker, who knows as well as any American the meaning of laissez-faire, would choose reasonable means.

Were the philosophy of private property the same in the United States as it is generally in Europe, much of Canada, and Mexico, the matter would be less serious. There, the property owner seldom objects to considerate use of it by pedestrians, whether knapsacking or on their way to work or market. Indeed, the public would think him a base and stingy fellow if he did.

Back in the period 1945–1948, legislation was drafted by the late Pennsylvania Congressman Daniel K. (Uncle Danny) Hoch to authorize the building and maintenance of a national system of foot trails, including the Appalachian Trail. It called for expenditure of

$50,000 for each of the first three years of the project, and sums as might be necessary thereafter. Part of this money would have gone to acquire easements on private land.

The Hoch Bill got exactly nowhere. Modesty was its undoing, in my opinion. The bill was not based on that soundest of national principles, "What's in it for me, Jack?" Fifty thousand units of exchange per annum is, after all, merely the income of a run-of-the-mill disciple of Hippocrates, and doesn't represent any house calls at that. Its lack of extravagance was held against it.

No, it wasn't much of a pork barrel for professional pols to roll and didn't have that lusty green color so admired by lobbyists. Besides, the country was not in much of a mood for conservation. The lawgivers were generally in accord with Joe Cannon's dictum of "not one cent for scenery." There were still plenty of old-timers around whose faces purpled at the thought of paying for a hunting or fishing license to support their sports. Hardly anyone went camping. And as for walking—well, a citizen might take a reasonable dosage of that, say one mile a week for exercise's sake; but more was barely respectable, something that an Indian or a hobo or other unreliable American did.

The nation just wasn't ready to grant foot travelers a secure right-of-way, though eager to pour enormous sums into automobile highways.

The hiker burns up a good deal of shoe leather on the trails but very little petroleum. The backpacker carries his shelter and food with him and is fairly independent of motels and restaurants. It is not to these outdoorsmen that Chambers of Commerce sing their hymns. In a community of, say, one thousand and five persons, five may be walkers but one thousand will be riders. As Brooks Atkinson, *The New York Times* critic-at-large and an ardent knapsacker, remarked, it has become easier to distinguish virtue from vice now that the automobile has "completely separated the walkers from the riders." (Mr. Atkinson wittily allows us to interpret his mot as we will.)

Although the Hoch Bill was defeated, it was the germ of future efforts. The population explosion was making convincing noises that the trail could only be saved through legislation and—let's face it—big money. Meantime, the generation that had served in the Second World War was out camping, boating, bird watching, fishing, hunting, beer guzzling on lonely roads, climbing mountains, and even walking in unprecedented numbers. And their children—Oh, dear God, how many of them there were, all shiny-faced, taller, bratty, and better looking—were doing the same. Not since the magic year of 1890, when the Census Bureau proclaimed that America was completely settled and no longer had a frontier, had so many Americans found values in nature. By 1960 conservation was occasionally being spelled with a capital C. By 1965 it was one of the thoughts of the thinking man. Now it has become a mote in the eye of the spoiler.

But Conservation, capital C, has always had champions in the United States, from Thoreau in the early 1800s through Ralph Waldo Emerson, George Catlin, Carl Schurz, John Muir, John Burroughs, Theodore Roosevelt, Aldo Leopold, Joseph Wood Krutch, Sigurd Olson, David Brower, and a galaxy of others to this moment. Drawback has been that conservation has not so much produced money as it has saved it, and provided enjoyment of the kind that money can't buy. If it had been food additives or sulphuric acid, conservation would be traded on Wall Street today. There is, nonetheless, a whopping pile of loot to be garnered from conservation.

So widespread have been pollution and destruction, mishandling and waste of natural resources—air, grass, trees, oil, coal, minerals, water, marshlands, beaches, and even desert—that to put things back into joint will take even more time, money, and brains than it did to disjoint them. The smarties are beginning to look into this angle, and when they have the arithmetic of it figured out—Wow! It's entirely possible that whole new industries will have to be created which in turn will require cleaning up, to say nothing of government subsidies and tax advantages. What a pool for the fishers in troubled waters!

In May 1964, Senator Gaylord Nelson of Wisconsin wrote a bill to "facilitate and promote federal, state, local, and private cooperation and assistance for the promotion of the (Appalachian) Trail." Since no action was taken by that year's Congress, he reintroduced it in 1965 and hearings were held. Nineteen sixty-six was a busy year: eight trail bills were dropped in the hopper by members of the House of Representatives,[5] Sen. Nelson again authored a proposal for a nationwide system of footpaths, and an Administration-backed bill to much the same purpose was entered by Senator Henry M. Jackson of Washington and the late Representative Mendel Rivers of South Carolina. Early 1967 saw Representatives Donald

[5] Representatives John G. Dow, New York; Philip J. Philbin, Massachusetts; Roy A. Taylor, North Carolina; N. Neiman Craley, Jr., Pennsylvania; John J. Duncan, Tennessee; Leo W. O'Brien, New York; Henry Helstoski, New Jersey; and James H. Quillen, Tennessee.

Fraser of Minnesota and Melvin Price of Illinois proposing trail legislation while a revised version of the Administration bill was sent up for approval by Representative Roy A. Taylor of North Carolina and Sen. Jackson. The next year the Administration bill was rewritten and passed both Houses. But this only reports the bare facts of executive and congressional interest in hiking. All this time there had been anxious onlookers and offers of assistance. The Appalachian Trail Conference's legislative committee, consisting of Dr. Walter S. Boardman, chairman, and Grant Conway, Edward B. Garvey, John Oliphant, and Frank Wallick, was frequently consulted by the lawmakers.

Tenacity was rewarded on October 2, 1968: President Lyndon Johnson signed the National Trails System Act, Public Law 90-543, to preserve and foster two national scenic trails, the Appalachian Trail and the Pacific Crest Trail. The latter trail, running from the Mexican border through California, Oregon, and Washington to Canada, where it connects with the Canadian Centennial Trail to Vancouver, British Columbia, needs more pathway, notably in southern California where land prices are already inflated beyond reason, to complete its approximately 2,350-mile length.

The Secretary of the Interior was appointed to administer the Appalachian and Pacific Crest Trails in consultation with the Secretary of Agriculture. (National parks and the Bureau of Land Management are under the Interior Department while national forests are managed by the Agriculture Department.) Motorized travel, including that by jeeps, cycles, tote goats, and all-terrain vehicles (ATVs), is prohibited to the general public on the footpaths. The act provides up to $5,000,000 for land acquisition for the Appalachian National Scenic Trail, though only 25 acres per mile (an average width of 200 feet, which is downright skimpy) can be procured by condemnation. Up to half a million dollars is provided for land purchases for the Pacific Crest National Scenic Trail—a pathetically inadequate sum.

Upon passage of the federal act, three states—Massachusetts in 1969, Maryland in 1970, and Virginia in 1971—moved officially to protect the Appalachian Trail within their borders. The laws of Massachusetts and Maryland now authorize acquisition of land, rights-of-way, and easements along the trail, and construction of shelters, sanitary facilities, and footbridges. Virginia's Scenic Trails Bill does not provide funds, but it is that "all important first step," as one hiking enthusiast who worked for enactment put it.

A lead role is being played by the Appalachian Trail Conference in identification and description of the trail and in coordinating efforts between the federal, state, and local governments and landowners.

The trail has been surveyed from the air and listed in the *Federal Register*[6] as an entity under government protection and a handsome contribution to the national inventory. But full protection is slow years away (which is why Massachusetts, Maryland, and Virginia took the bit in their teeth). A vast amount of paper work—enough to cover Mount Oglethorpe more completely than chicken feathers now do— is in prospect, not to mention the expenditure of sufficient physical energy to move a mountain.

Trail statistics are like a lot of the trails themselves—pretty sketchy. By a trail is meant here a marked land path, usually narrow—no wider than it has to be—for the public use of persons afoot or riding animals and packstock. I've read figures that the country has 225,000 miles of land trails. Maybe so, but most of the total lies along mining, lumbering, ranch, and fire roads. No matter how rustic they might be, and usually they are simply dismal, vehicle roads are not footpaths. Neither, for that matter, are highways called trails, such as the Hiawatha Trail, the Apache Trail, the Rip Van Winkle Trail, and similar exercises in imagination designed to beguile the tourist and soothe the native's bump of local history and legend.

While the United States is the fourth largest nation in both area and number of human beings, it can claim less than two dozen individual trails of about 100 or more miles in length. Canada has only two marked hiking trails that exceed 100 miles and both were blazed in the 1960s—the Bruce Trail in Ontario, running 439 miles west and north from the Brock Monument at Queenston below Niagara Falls to Tobermory on Georgian Bay, and the 135-mile Centennial Trail from Vancouver east to E. C. Manning Provincial Park in British Columbia.

A few states have no trails. Mammoth Texas has less than 200 miles of foot trail and its famous Cavalcade, with horses, saddles, and *caballeros* dripping silver, minces along highways escorted by whining patrol cars and enveloped in a fog of exhaust fumes and Early Times.

We do plenty for the car driver but mighty little for the pedestrian. According to the Bureau of Public Roads, at least 80,798 miles of vehicular arteries were built in 1967, yet the bureau had no idea of how many miles of sidewalks or trails were gained. In recent years it has become commonplace to see new housing developments rising without sidewalks.

If dedicated private citizens had not created the Appalachian Trail Conference and the hiking clubs there would be no Appalachian Trail

[6] As of February 9, 1971. Eighty-five maps and seven pages of narrative description were required.

today. That is made abundantly evident by the fate overtaking the
California Riding and Hiking Trail. A few years ago work was begun
on a trail to thread the state's picturesque desert, mountain, and
coastal areas for a distance of 3,000 miles. Over 1,000 miles were
actually completed and marked with metal placards painted orange
and blue showing a man afoot exchanging greetings with a rider on
horseback. But interest was succeeded by disinterest; even the influential Sierra Club displayed no inclination to boost the project.
Finally the state legislature refused further financial support. Save
where it was incorporated into national forest trails, the R & H Trail
no longer is kept up, and most of its redwood signposts lie in fragments (redwood splinters beautifully with a single blow of an ax).
The grandly conceived path seems as dead as the California grizzly
which, like a mortuary token, sadly graces the state flag.

But the Appalachian Trail journeys onward. In itself a pioneer, it
has become a part of the American scene, native as hoe cake and
do-it-yourself. To endlessly skirt the stony cliffs, to ford unnumbered
streams, to walk in the shadow of ancient trees, and to pause on
mountaintops—these are only the physical substance of the Appalachian Trail.

Although walking every one of its 2,000 miles may be justifiably
considered as something of an athletic feat, particularly in an era
which has sought to live with a minimum of physical effort, this is
not the only challenge of the trail. Neither is it a primary reason for
its existence.

Perhaps no one has expressed its true meaning, the basis of its
fascination, and the motives that brought it into being better than
did an early worker on the trail who said of it:

"Conceived on a continental scale, it traverses regions of such varied
charm, presents so endless a series of delights to the senses and stim-
uli to the imagination, as to rank high among the inspirational assets
of a materialistic age.

"Remote for detachment, narrow for chosen company, winding for
leisure, lonely for contemplation, it beckons not merely north and
south but upward to the body, mind, and soul of man."

The words were by Harold Allen, may the earth rest lightly over
him.

The Botanical Garden

When Hernando De Soto and his company of adventurers probed
the Appalachians over 400 years ago they came upon a treasure that

was greater than the gold they sought—and sought so single-mindedly and vainly.

In Georgia, the invaders saw wild roses blooming "just like those in Spain." They gorged on plums in Tennessee as juicy as the ones ripening in the warm sun of the Estremadura, the poverty-ridden province from which most of them hailed, and with their pikestaffs cracked black walnuts that were "much better" than the walnut which grew back home. In actual fact, nearly all the plants were different. Botanists were one day to find that not a single native species of tree is common to both Europe and America. And where Old World forests may brag two or three dozen species of trees, this silva numbered more than a dozen times a dozen.

Though none suspected it at the time, the conquistadors were traveling in the corridors of the greatest hardwood forest in the earth's temperate zones. All about them was the treasure they failed to perceive.

Unlike rare metals and gems, it was renewable and capable of providing endless bounty in the form of lumber, shade, streams of sparkling water, flowers, nuts, fruits, and pharmaceutical products. (There is not a drug store on the globe but which stocks medicines made from the herbs of this forest.) It was, and it still is, in spite of reckless, even contemptuous, treatment, a magnificent botanical garden.

Not once in its 2,000 miles does the Appalachian Trail leave the confines of this garden. Only where asphalt, concrete, and buildings cover the land does the garden—for the moment—fail to prosper. But let the buildings crumple into ruin, let the roadway fall into disuse and from the cracks and between the boards and bricks its seeds will germinate and plants rise. Within several decades all will have surrendered to a virile botanical embrace.

When North America was still largely uncharted wilderness, European mapmakers gave this silva a name: The Great Forest of America. Later, the name would be forgotten as the intricate pattern of woodland Indian culture and the mute plants and animals was shattered, like a glass of crystal abused by unappreciative hands. Today, the forest is known more for its parts, rather than as a whole. We speak of the Green Mountain Forest, the Cherokee Forest, the George Washington Forest, and others.

Francis Parkman, the nineteenth century historian, described the Great Forest of America as a vast kingdom of trees which "shadowed the fertile soil, covering the land as the grass covers the garden lawn, sweeping over hill and hollow in endless undulation, burying mountains in verdure, and mantling brooks and rivers from the light of day."[7] Trees overlaid nearly all of the country from ocean strand westward to Arkansas and north to Minnesota, Manitoba, and southeastern Canada. The forest's boundaries were the Atlantic on the east, the open prairies and grasslands of the West, the swamps of Georgia and the Gulf Coast to the south, and in the north the horizon-filling stands of spruce commonly known as the North Woods. The Great Forest sprawled over one-third of the United States.

Half of the Great Forest's original one million-plus square miles is now taken up by farms and fields (the word "fields" means "felled" woods), cities, highways, factories, mines, airports, reservoirs, and the backwaters of a plethora of hydroelectric dams. And cemeteries and trash dumps. The remainder has largely become a managed forest— 95 percent is second, third, and fourth growth trees and subject to constant, if generally supervised, cutting. To the unknowing, rushing through it to the throb of gasoline engines, this remnant may seem impressive. Some of it is. But it is merely a pale shadow of that which once graced the land. The height of the trees has been reduced to 50 percent or less of what it was when nature was still unblessed by European civilization, while their trunks are certainly no more than a third of their forefathers' girths.

Only a small portion is virgin, and most of that is on summits where terrain makes logging difficult. But few trees grow tall on mountain peaks; there, maturity finds them stunted, if hardy, from exposure to cold and the buffeting of winds. It is in sheltered valleys, on gentle slopes, and well-watered lowlands that trees find encouragement to swell their boles and stretch their canopies.

But for all of that, the hiker on the Appalachian Trail will come upon tracts which are miniature copies of the original. In parts of the Great Smoky Mountains and Shenandoah national parks, in Connecticut's Cathedral Pines and elsewhere are stands—seldom large and nearly always remote—of botanic nobility. These rare groves provide insight into the past. It is an awesome past which only rarely has been permitted to flourish into the present.

To walk through one of these green mansions is a compelling experience, such as might be found within an ancient cathedral of Christendom. Mighty columns soar to the vault, where their boughs intertwine as if they were hands clasped in prayer—the very inspiration of the Gothic arch. Like candles, slender beams of amber sunlight flicker in the medieval dimness. From the greenery comes a wafting of soft incense. Birds and bats flutter about distant niches.

---

[7] The secondary title of Parkman's voluminous *France and England in North America* is, significantly, *A History of the American Forest*.

The traveler's footsteps slow and then halt on the mosaic of last year's leaves. He waits, listening in the hush for an unseen organ to crash into the *Te Deum*.

This is the forest primeval, the climax forest, a state which takes hundreds of years of striving to achieve. An equilibrium in the total ecology has been reached. Unless some calamity occurs, as fire, plague, or human interference, the forest will perpetuate itself with little change. From the raw materials of rock, air, water, sunlight, and time, Nature has created a masterpiece.

Here, because of the shadows thrown by mighty trees, nurslings succeed only when an oldster topples from a murrain of bark or leaves, spears and tridents of lightning, spell of abnormal freezing, or violent storm. Every year the mature trees fling their seed to the winds and to the loam to ensure dominance of their kind. Long ago, captains of sailing ships plowing the waves out of sight of the American mainland would jot entries in their logs that decks were awash with brimstone: the power of Beelzebub was manifest. But the manifestation was an amazing example of generative, not destructive, power. The "brimstone" was yellow pollen borne on air currents which had stirred the stands of white pine scattered from northern Georgia to Newfoundland.

The white pine was one of the paragons of the Great Forest. Its wood helped to fire the American Revolution. Its tapering trunk rose string-straight for 150 to 200 feet; some even pushed to 250 feet. European eyes blinked to see stands of millions of these glorious spires, of a height and species of conifer undreamed of heretofore.

England's expanding navy saw in these long, flexible sticks the solution to its masting problem. Vessels, increasing in size, needed more wind power. Longer masts could hold more canvas and stretch higher for a breeze. In short order, white pine masts and spars from the Great Forest were soughing and swaying with the winds of the seven seas.

At first, 100 pounds sterling were paid for each great log landed in Britain. But not many years were to pass before the Crown virtually appropriated for itself the white pine stands of its northern colonies. Prison terms and heavy fines were meted out to illegal axmen.

The White Pine Acts, as they were called, blew up a gale of hard feeling among the colonists, who wanted the trees for their own clippers, for trading abroad, and for constructing homes and furniture. The wood is light, soft, and typically creamy white with few blemishes. It saws like butter and warps or swells but little. A first rate mast would fetch a useful sum, $500 or even twice that in today's money; on moonless nights many were rafted to foreign ships loitering nervously in colonial harbors. On a few occasions settlers donned Indian disguise (as if rehearsing for the Boston Tea Party) and chopped down trees in the King's Woods to demonstrate their pique.

The white pine became a symbol of colonial resentment. The ensign of America's infant navy, whose first fleet was assembled in 1775 to intercept a pair of British munitions ships, bore a pine and the inscription "An Appeal to Heaven." But the victorious citizens of a new nation were reckless with their forest patrimony, supposing it inexhaustible. By the 1920s, less than a century and a half later, the monumental stands of white pine were mostly a memory.

In Great Smoky Mountains National Park, botanists have counted 130 species of native trees, more than in all Europe. All but a few are hardwoods. On the park's list are the names of over 1,300 native flowering plants, about 2,000 species of fungi, nearly 350 mosses and liverworts, and 230 lichens. A hardwood forest provides wildlife with a greater quantity and variety of food than a conifer forest, and this riotous diversity of vegetation supports 50-some kinds of native mammals, from flying squirrels and the tree-climbing gray fox to bears, and 200 species of birds, from the tufted titmouse to the wild turkey. Visiting naturalists from many nations have expressed amazement at the flora and fauna of this relatively small preserve of 800 square miles. One fourth of the park is virgin—the largest such area east of the Rockies to escape the attention of the timber engineers. It is a microcosm of the Great Forest at its hospitable best.

Near Darjeeling, India, in the Himalayan foothills where Nepal, Sikkim, Bhutan, and East Pakistan rub frontiers, and again along the course of the great Yangtze River in Middle China and in the Manchurian highlands and central Korea, are woods remarkably like that of the Great Forest of America. Although on opposite sides of the world, trees such as ash, choke cherry, hornbeam, basswood, chestnut, and many others are common to all; so are wild flowers, as columbine, trillium, and jack-in-the-pulpit, magic herbs like ginseng, and even such mischievous vines as poison ivy.

In the 1860s, Asa Gray of Harvard set the pulses of naturalists racing by the news that he had identified 92 families and 155 genera of trees and flowers as matched pairs in northeastern Asia and northeastern United States. Foresters believe that our eastern woodland, as well as the sadly depleted Asiatic forests, had a common parent in the forest of northern India, though ages of separation have wrought some changes in all the species. The whiskey-drinking mountaineer of Dixie and the tea-drinking hillman of Hindustan would probably find much that is familiar were they to swap surroundings.

Ninety million years ago the mother forest was in full development. Humankind had not yet been admitted to the Garden of Eden and its plants bloomed luxuriantly and grew hugely. Fostered by periods when climates favored and land masses were in different positions than now, the forest branched out and crept northeastward into the then warm polar belt near the roof of the world. As the Arctic turned to ice, it moved southward into Europe and the United States in front of the glaciers. Travel time consumed perhaps 20 to 30 million years. The silva did not migrate as individual plants, but all at once, as a complete ecology. When continents shifted the forest was broken into widely scattered parts.

By far the greatest of the several remnants is the Great Forest. The Appalachians are at once its backbone and its stronghold. Were it not for the difficulties their steep slopes present to the farmer and the logger, it is safe to say they would be at least as sparse of trees as are the level lands spreading from their base.

Dwellers in the Great Forest—and that includes the majority of the people of the United States plus millions of Canadians, whose national flag bears the autumn-red leaf of a hardwood tree, the maple —are usually astonished to learn they live in a silva which has few counterparts. Most of its trees are not only broadleafed (as opposed to the needle leaves of pines) but deciduous. Trees which are deciduous lose their foliage in the fall: this is the "why" of the word fall. Evergreens discard their leaves gradually the year around, managing to look verdant, if a little monotonous, in all seasons. The word deciduous, itself, is from the Latin meaning "to fall off." Antlers of deer are deciduous, as are trees with leaves that drop off within a brief period of time, generally a few days, either at maturity or seasonally. *The New Yorker* magazine once ran a cartoon showing a couple picnicking beneath a tree whose leafy mass, like a dark cloud, is descending all at once.

"Look out, Janet! It's deciduous!" cries the man as they stare upward in alarm.

Deciduous hardwoods shed leaves in autumn, remain unclad in winter, and break out in new dress in the spring. Indian Summer owes much of its elegance to this habit, while winter is drear because of it. Putting on and taking off of foliage in splendid seasonal bursts of color are characteristics of the Great Forest.

This forest's four seasons with their extremes of weather, ranging from the biting severity of winter to summer's sultry languor, encourage the growth of more kinds of flora—approximately 190 species of native trees alone, 175 of which are deciduous—than any other forest on the planet, excepting only the tropical hardwood forest of the Amazon Basin.

As we have seen, this is a silva par excellence of hardwoods, the forester's term for a broadleafed tree. Broadleafed means just that: leaves are flat and wide, neither scaly nor stiletto-shaped as are those of the other great class of trees, the softwoods.

Virtually all softwoods are evergreens and all are coniferous, or cone-bearing. They are pine and the piney relatives, such as spruce, fir, hemlock, and larch, or tamarack. Some softwoods, though not many, are harder of lumber than certain hardwoods.

Man has existed in the Great Forest for perhaps 20,000 years. And for more than half of that period he has had a constant companion in the form of an almost unique wild plant.

This plant—today recognized as the oldest living thing—covers over 100 acres near Losh Run, a half-dozen miles north of the Appalachian Trail crossing at Duncannon, Pennsylvania. The low evergreen shrub, a species of box huckleberry, first attracted attention in 1790. Not until 1918, however, was it made the subject of extensive study.

Investigators found its small, oval, serrate leaves and edible dark blue berries to be uniform in shape throughout; moreover, tests showed it to be self-sterile, incapable of producing offspring. They concluded the patch is a single plant that is steadily enlarging.

Owing to the physical geography of its mountainous site, the *Gaylussacia brachycera* is 1¼ miles long, though limited to a width of a few hundred feet. Measurements indicate that its rhizomes or underground stem-roots which send up leafy shoots, are elongating at the rate of six inches yearly. So scientists believe this box huckleberry has been occupied in attaining its present length for over 12,000 years!

Dr. Edgar T. Wherry, Professor of Botany, Emeritus, University of Pennsylvania, states that "whether one terms this entity a colony, a patch, a clone, a plant, or an individual strain of protoplasm is immaterial; it is a 'living thing' of great antiquity."[8]

G. brachycera is also ranked with the rarest of wild plants, for only a few specimens have been discovered—all in the southern Appalachian region.

Many of the trees of the Great Forest have uses in which they

[8] Quoted from a letter by Dr. Wherry printed in *American Forests*, December 1968.

excel, and are not only used at home but exported by the shipload. Hickory smokes meat, is shaped into the shock-resisting handles of striking tools as axes and hammers, and provided spokes for the wheels of the pioneers' Conestoga wagons. American holly becomes piano keys and the resilient ash is worked into oars. The policeman's club is osage-orange. Tupelo makes wear-resisting factory floors. Furniture that defies time and knocks is manufactured of red maple. Black gum, which will not split even under assault by wedge and sledge, is favored for wooden machinery parts; the mountain ladies of the South select its twigs for "chaw sticks" to brush snuff, or pulverized tobacco, behind the lips—a tingly practice known as "dipping snuff" as opposed to the rarer "sniffing snuff." Flowering dogwood has long been used by weavers for shuttles. Thread seldom snaps on its smooth surface, and the closely-knit wood withstands great centrifugal force. Each spring this little tree heralds the new growing season with outsized immaculate white bracts; each October it enriches the autumn palette with small scarlet fruits which, it is said, sate the appetites of 93 kinds of birds.

And there is the tulip tree, a lordly tower of light, easily worked timber popular with cabinet makers since Puritan times. George Washington, who knew an aristocrat when he saw one, planted the tree on his Mount Vernon estate. Two of these *Liriodendron tulipifera,* now pushing above the 120-foot mark, are the tallest plants at this national shrine. The tulip tree (often, and erroneously, called the yellow poplar) has an unusual leaf which is most unlikely to be mistaken for any other species: it does not come to a point, but ends with a broad edge rather like a spade. The tree's bouquets of tuliplike flowers, each an exotic composition in pale green and orange, remind the onlooker of the Tahitian paintings of Gauguin.

Oliver Wendell Holmes, the elder, was a noted tree fancier of the last century. His particular fancy was the American elm, with its classic vaselike silhouette and almost feminine grace.

He would drive long distances in his one-horse buggy to spend a leisure hour with a choice *Ulmus americana* celebrated for "size of trunk, spread of limbs, and muscular development." In *The Autocrat of the Breakfast Table* he refers fondly to "my tree wives," whose dimensions he would take with the delight of a pasha in his seraglio. "I have worn a tape almost out on the rough barks of our old New England elms," Dr. Holmes confessed. He didn't wonder if before the tape "the proudest tree of them all quails and shrinks into itself."

Under the knowing gaze of such a distinguished connoisseur of elms it would not be hard to imagine the object of his affections quaking a little under its jade frock of leaves and jangling its samaras, or winged seeds, like bits of costume jewelry.

Of the world's 18 elm species, *U. americana* is held to be the loveliest on reaching maturity. When its days as a stately lawn tree are over the strong, beautifully cross-grained wood is sought after for furniture and flooring. Sadly, those days are now numbered—it is being ruined by the Dutch elm disease. The disease entered the United States about 1926 as a fungus in a shipment of Carpathian elm burls which were to be sliced into veneering. D.E.D. is carried from tree to tree by two kinds of beetles and produces great masses of spores which crowd into the small vessels within the tender spring shoots, literally choking the tree to death. In recent years whole cities have lost their considerable populations of elms. Springfield, Massachusetts, is no longer the "City of Elms."

White oak, *Quercus alba,* has played a stirring role in American history. Its timber launched swift windjammers by the thousands to convey a new nation's produce to foreign shores. Good oak was resistant to the shock of minor bottomings and could absorb the stresses of hard naval duty without failure. For hundreds of years the sea power of many nations rested on oaken hulls. Britain seized Canada from the French partly in order to deny her ships the oak planking and pine masting of the Great Forest.

Prodigious amounts of oak were swallowed up by rival fleets. During the Revolutionary War, Massachusetts alone sent out more than 1,600 privately manned vessels to prey on British commerce. As another example, some 500 choice white oaks were hewn in Delaware in the 1920s to help reconstruct just one man-of-war, the U.S. Frigate *Constitution.* When an English cannonball bounced screaming off the *Constitution's* staunch oak side in the War of 1812 she fought on to glory as "Old Ironsides." Her mainmast, three feet square and 112 feet in length, had been originally a white pine tree, but all the highest pines having been chopped down in the century that followed her triumphs at sea, a Douglas fir from Washington State was substituted when she was rebuilt.

The days of sail predated the widespread use of copper sheathing or closely spaced nailheads to thwart the borings of the toredo, the ravenous shipworm, below the saltwater line. The best wooden vessels lasted only a few years. Whole forests of *Quercus alba* lie on the bottom of the oceans.

If white oak and white pine built America's sea arms of commerce and war, the discovery of a precious herb was responsible for the birth of the enormously profitable China trade.

About 1715, Father Joseph François Lafitau, of the Society of Jesus, saw ginseng growing near Montreal. A fellow missionary serving in China had wondered in a letter if the manlike root, so much in demand by the subjects of the Celestial Kingdom to prolong and gladden life, might also grow in the American colonies. And the hunch panned out, for the Great Forest was kin to the groves of the Yangtze River Valley, until now the principal bower of this strange plant. Ginseng's pronged root resembles human form, with trunk, "arms," and "legs." Chinese believe that such an herb can treat an ailment of any part of the body. *Jin-tsang*, the "image of a man!"

The Jesuit's find was nothing less than a bonanza. Indians and white settlers alike rushed to the woods to collect sacks of the root to dry and then send on a voyage which in those days logged some 17,000 miles. Fast clippers from the Atlantic coast exchanged the root for tea, silk, porcelain, ginger, camphor, and coins of silver and gold. The American merchant marine tripled in size. In 1862, the peak year for ginseng shipments, 622,761 pounds were transported; about 100,000 pounds are still delivered yearly to Hong Kong, Macao, Bangkok, Seoul, Taiwan—and Honolulu.

Not only Chinese, but numbers of Manchurians, Koreans, Hindus, Siamese, and Japanese believe that ginseng juice is better than any goat serum invented for toning up a man's system. Western medicine has twice investigated the herb, and both times has concluded—regretfully—that it is harmless. But, so potent is imagination, an Oriental swallowing a tonic of ginseng becomes scrutable in no time at all. Ten thousand dollars was paid by a Chinese emperor for a single perfectly shaped root. Many have sold for their weight in gold. The late Syngman Rhee is said to have consumed quantities of ginseng; he was a man of marked vigor.

Ginseng is extoled in the latest Chinese medical books as the most valuable of plant remedies. While its use as a recreational drug is not overlooked, greater stress is laid on its ability to moderate the course of various ills and act as an all-around disease preventative. Most botanical medicines prescribed today by Western doctors are alleged to have their origin in Chinese practice. China's pharmacopeia includes about 1,500 drugs of vegetable origin; many are unknown outside the Far East.

"Sang" digging remains a source of cash in the Appalachian region. Although over 100 wild herbs of commercial importance are regularly gathered by hill people, it is "sang" that year-in, year-out fluctuates least in price and is in constant demand.

In 1972, pickers were receiving up to $50 a pound for the dried root. The plant isn't easy to find, being but 7 to 18 inches tall with a single slender stalk from which stems three branches bearing three large and two small palmate leaves each. In the fall *Panax quinquefolius,* as it is called, flaunts a cluster of small crimson berries, but at any season is mightily inconspicuous in the understory of the forest. With reason the Cherokee Indians, who named the botanical "Little Man, Most Powerful Magician," believed it could make itself invisible. Cherokees employed ginseng to relieve sundry *female* complaints.

The Chinese market for ginseng is seemingly insatiable. Coming improvement of business relations between the United States and the Colossus of the East will almost certainly result in something of a boom in *P. quinquefolius.*

And that means better times for those hardy Americans who still make their livelihood in Appalachia's backwoods.

There is no mechanical substitute for a tree. In addition to providing food and abode for birds and wildlife, trees offer shade and shield the earth from the sun's fire. Roots bind the soil, staking it down to prevent gullying and washing away. The spongy floor of a live forest holds tremendous reservoirs of fresh water; these are the founts of rivers. Insects tumble from branches into streams to feed hungry trout and catfish. Harmful noise, loud, incessant, startling, or irritating, is absorbed and muffled. Dust is held down and ruinous winds are tamed by trees—the taller the trees the better—to a mere whimper, a tenth or less of their force. Plants purify the air by breathing in carbon dioxide and returning oxygen. (Man and his combustion machinery do the reverse.)

Besides adding to the vital supply of free floating oxygen, plants moisten and cool the air. They accomplish this feat by breathing out vast quantities of water through the stomatal openings of their leaves. A mature apple tree, for instance, will lift three to four gallons of water every hour of daylight into the atmosphere during its greenleaf season; the transpiration of a great elm with perhaps eight million leaves might be 30 times that amount. One large, well-watered tree can produce cooling equivalent to over one million Btu.'s[9] or 200 times that of the average room air conditioner. And the power source of the tree air conditioner is free—the sun.

When I walked in the Berkshires, miles of Massachusetts were running a temperature. The air quaked with heat. At first I looked about uneasily for the roll of smoke and the red lick of flames, but there was no fire. Every leaf of each hardwood tree was a sieve of ragged

[9] Btu, the abbreviation for British thermal unit, is the amount of heat required to raise the temperature of one pound of water by one degree Fahrenheit.

Photo by Elmer L. Onstott

Showing "bear fence" installed at Silers Bald Lean-to in the Great Smokies.

APPALACHIAN TRAIL

NATIONAL SCENIC TRAIL

FOOT TRAVEL ONLY

PURSUANT TO EXISTING LAW AND REGULATION, THE TRAIL
BEHIND THIS SIGN IS CLOSED TO ALL FORMS OF MOTORIZED
VEHICULAR USE UNLESS OTHERWISE EXPRESSLY AUTHORIZED
IN WRITING BY A UNITED STATES FOREST SERVICE
DISTRICT RANGER OR FOREST SUPERVISOR.

Photo by Robert Winslow

Sign along the trail.

holes eaten by a silent army. The caterpillar of the gypsy moth was traveling.

In 1869, the gypsy moth was brought over from Europe by a French scientist who thought it might spin as good a silk as the mulberry silkworm. It paused not for naturalization papers but winged straight from the laboratory to the groves.

There were places in the Berkshires where little foliage was left to whisper secrets to the wind. Except for a strange pitter-patter, it was as still and ominous as the parlor of an undertaker's. From overhead a rain of debris was falling; bits of chewed leaves and twigs littered the Appalachian Trail.

Although the trunks crawled with caterpillars—to touch the bark was to feel the shuddering of furry larvae tufted with brown and yellow hairs—there were no birds. Deer, foxes, squirrels, moles, and serpents were absent, too. They had fled for their lives from a forest that was being cannibalized.

And there was little shade for the hiker. Sun poured through the skeleton of the woods and he felt the feverish turf crackle under his boots. Springs and creeks had withered to basins of caked mud and trenches of hot gravel. "100,000 Acres Face Defoliation" said a black headline in the Pittsfield *Berkshire Eagle*. "We're sick about it," Douglas K. Poland, of the Massachusetts Department of Natural Resources, was quoted as saying. The hiker felt sick, too, as he walked between trees that were fast becoming grave markers. The forest was ceasing to function.

Just below the bark, that spongy wrapper protecting the trunk and branches of a tree, is a glistening girdle, wet to the touch and from one to several cells thick. This paper-thin layer, called the cambium growth tissue, sheaths the wood of the tree from roots to twigs. It and the root tips and hairs, twig ends, buds, leaves, and flowers are the only living parts of a tree.

A tree weighing tons sustains life with a relatively few pounds of living cells. Imagine, if you will, those cells being flooded with a radiopaque dye and an X-ray photograph taken. The living part of the tree would show up on the film as a diaphanous veil, like a wisp of smoke enveloping a Grecian pillar and the lofty roof it supports.

All the rest of the tree is dead—the greatest mass being the heartwood, of which a new layer, or ring, is formed each year.

When a tree comes of age it is said to be mature. At this point it has started to slow down in annual growth, though continuing to increase in size throughout its life. A misconception is being foisted

on the public today by those who want to increase for their own benefit the already heavy over-cutting and leave to future generations the
problem of nursing the public forests to vigorous adulthood.

They suggest, not always subtly, that after a tree reaches maturity
its wood begins to decay or is impaired in quality.

This is not true.

As long as a tree lives and is not infected by disease or damaged by
storm or other natural calamity its lumber is sound. Many redwoods
are being leveled that are 2,000 years old; timber is sawed that was
created before Jesus was born. And after two millenniums of death,
that wood is as fragrant and supple as his memory.

The real death of a tree begins when it is attacked by a malignant
outside force.

Nonetheless, limited timbering enriches the life of every person.
Fields must be kept open for row crops and dairy animals. And there
are scores of thousands of uses for wood and conversion products,
from matchsticks to rayon to the pulpwood that makes a prayer book
or the *Congressional Record,* though a complete list has never been
compiled.

It is written that Gautama Buddha received the heavenly light as
he sat in meditation beneath a pipal tree, the *Ficus religiosa.*

"The forest," Buddha said (among other pronouncements), "is a
peculiar organism of unlimited kindness and benevolence that makes
no demands for its sustenance and extends generously the products of
its life activity; it provides protection to all beings, offering shade
even to the axman who destroys it."

Having said this Buddha glanced upward and smiled. The sun
fondled the pipal tree and its leaves stirred dreamily in the gentle
breeze. In its cool shadow was serenity.

Vanishing American

American chestnut trees are almost extinct. Blame for this condition
must be laid to *Endothia parasitica,* or chestnut blight. Its dismal toll
is owing in part to an uncanny ability to propagate in wet weather
as well as in dry. To state what has been said about another denizen
of the forests, chestnut blight is smarter than the average blight. The
United States Department of Agriculture declares flatly that it is the
"most destructive forest disease known."

Endothia parasitica reproduces itself through two kinds of fruiting
pustules, blister-like growths the size of pinheads. In dry weather, the

perithecia pustule creates two-celled spores which are shot into the atmosphere as passengers in a peculiar explosive mechanism—transparent, thin-walled sacks that pop out of the pustule's opening, rise above the trees, and then burst like balloons. The spores, no larger than dust particles, are now on their own. After launching, they may sail for scores of miles, wafted by breezes. Most of the Lilliputian seeds drift into oblivion, but Nature in her prodigality assures that one or two in every million lodges in the bark of chestnut trees, there to renew its destructive life.

When moisture dampens the bark, the dry-weather pustule closes shop and the wet-weather pustule opens for business. In place of airborne spores that would be downed by rain, an entirely different type of spore is spawned. The *pycnidia* pustule produces unicells which, linked like tiny sausages, ooze out in long tendrils resembling curling ribbons of toothpaste.

Being sticky, the curls adhere to insects, birds, and other animals, and are transported until brushed off against some unfortunate chestnut.

Impelled by its sexual virtuosity, the blight has raged furiously throughout the natural range of the American chestnut—roughly the eastern third of the United States from the Canadian border south nearly to the Gulf of Mexico. Within 50 years after the disease was discovered in this country, it had annihilated more than nine million acres of valuable chestnut trees. This would make up an area the size of Connecticut, Massachusetts, and Rhode Island put together.

The parasite apparently arrived at these shores as a stowaway on Asiatic chestnut nursery stock. It was first recognized in 1904 when American chestnuts in New York City's Zoological Park began dying. Its potency was soon felt elsewhere. From New York the canker spread into New England, then swept to the Mississippi River. By 1950 the forests of the southern Appalachians, where every fourth large tree was chestnut, were a shambles.

A disaster of such magnitude calls for action. The virulence was used as an effective argument for plant inspection at ports of entry. In 1912, a quarantine law was passed to protect American plants from destruction by invaders against which they had no natural immunity. *Endothia parasitica* is native to China, Korea, Japan, and Taiwan; however, Asiatic chestnuts are highly blight-resistant, particularly the Chinese species. Resistance seems dependent upon the abundance and solubility of tannin secreted in the bark. On both counts the tannin of the American tree is inadequate. Like the Indian who was beset by European smallpox, so has the native chestnut been over-whelmed by an unwanted import.

One way to kill a tree, and more certain than an assault by fire, lightning, or storm, is to girdle it. The thin and delicate growth layer, or cambium, is easily severed by drawing a knife through it laterally. With its lifeline cut, the tree speedily dies. This is, in effect, what the blight does to chestnut trees.

Visible on the bark as a mass of fungus, yellowish brown to orange in color, the blight penetrates to the growth layer. Living cells are de-stroyed as the attack spreads and, like a noose, encircles the bole. Leaves shrivel and hang limply, bark loosens and drops off and sap-wood sloughs away. Within eight years the chestnut is in ruin. The trunk may stand some 25 more years, lifeless limbs raised in mute supplication while it bleaches in the rain and the sun. Roots wither and relax their grip in the earth. The trunk sways unsteadily in the wind, loses its balance, and crashes. Decay continues. Soon the oldest part of the tree—its inner core of timber—disintegrates, and the log is left hollow. Insects, molds, and the elements renew their assault, now from within as earlier from without. The decaying tree, cell by cell, returns to the soil that was its womb.

Such is the story of the death of a tree—a death enormously hastened by *Endothia parasitica*.

These vanishing Americans were very grand trees. Imposing, broad, heavily leafed canopies crowned them royalty whose shade was largess for man and beast. A mature specimen would soar 80 feet or more. Numerous chestnuts were ten feet through the bole, although three or four feet was more usual. (A tree's diameter is measured 4½ feet above the ground.) In Francis Cove, near Waynesville, North Carolina, a forest ranger taped one boasting 17 feet in diameter. A bevy of wood nymphs could have frolicked at the foot of such a titan. Longfellow opened his poem, "The Village Blacksmith," with

> Under the spreading chestnut tree
> The village smithy stands

Most of today's citizens have never witnessed a blacksmith at his proud, sweaty trade, let alone a large chestnut *en gloria*, its leafy crown adorned with thousands of creamy-white blossoms.

In the interests of strict reporting, it must be noted—regretfully—that the tree which inspired Henry Wadsworth Longfellow was a large horse chestnut growing near his Cambridge, Massachusetts, home. The horse chestnut (*Aesculus hippocastanum*) is a trans-planted native of Asia. Worse, it is not even a chestnut, but a member of the buckeye family. It produces nuts so inedible and puckery that their dried powder has been mixed with bookbinder's paste to repel such nasty vermin as the bookworm.

Those few large American chestnuts remaining are nearly all on the Pacific coast, where they were planted by early settlers who carried seedlings with them from the East. The national champion makes its home in Oregon City, Oregon, where its circumference of 15½ feet, height of 90 and spread of 64 are much admired. These trees have escaped the unwelcome attention of *Endothia parasitica* simply because so far they have been out of its nomadic range.

An army of people, particularly the mountaineers of the South, made a living from the chestnut for generations. There are those who see in the tree's passing an example of Divine Wrath. Grandpa Ben Yancey, who farms in the Great Smokies, shakes his gray beard somberly when the subject is brought up. "The big city folks," he says, "come in here when times in the hills was hard and bought up all the timber land they could and cut down all the trees. They wouldn't even let our young-uns gather the fallen nuts no more. And we let them git away with hit. Then the awful blight descended. I reckon hit's the Lord's way of teaching folks a lesson. Some was too greedy and others didn't do nothing to stop what they knowed was wrong."

Chestnut wood is easily worked for fence posts, mine props, cross-ties, piles, slack cooperage, cordwood, pulpwood, and lumber. It makes excellent furniture and as a core material for paneling is without peer. For a number of years the leather tanning industry subsisted by salvaging tannin from dead chestnuts, but now has turned to a species of oak for the vital extract. So scornful of decay is the wood that split-rail "worm" or "snake" fences fashioned from it over a century ago still guard fields in mountain regions of the Virginias, Tennessee, Georgia, and the Carolinas. Unlike maple and oak, the fibers of chestnut do not interlock, hence split for the length of the log at a single stroke of maul against wedge. From one log 10 to 15 long fence rails can be separated. About the time of the Civil War a General Brisbin estimated that the country had over two billion dollars in rail fences, and chestnut was the favorite wood. Foresters often termed it the finest of America's hardwoods.

Castanea dentata is the tree's scientific name. The words pay tribute to the toothsome nut it bears at maturity.

Nuts are bright brown, a distinctive color which, not surprisingly, has come to be known as chestnut. The horse with a coat that matches the color is called a chestnut. Jokes or stories whose pith is yawningly familiar are "chestnuts"—last year's nuts have often been passed off for new crop.

Chestnuts were an important food for hog, bear, wild turkey, deer, squirrel—and human. Rich stuffing for fowl and pork was concocted from the boiled nuts. Roasted, they were a hearthside snack for hill people, and as much favored as popcorn. In city streets vendors hawked them piping hot from glowing braziers—their customers can testify that chestnuts may be hotter than potatoes. Food specialty shops sold them expensively as marrons glacés, a delicacy achieved by boiling the skinned nuts in sugar syrup flavored with vanilla. But raw or boiled or roasted the creamy meat had a delicious flavor.

About 20 million pounds of European chestnuts are imported yearly for livestock feed and flour for thickening gravies and soups. Now that source is declining as the blight has infiltrated France, Italy, Switzerland, and Yugoslavia.

The European chestnut may not survive, for it seems only slightly more blight-resistant than its New World cousin. The loss will be poignant. In the old countries *Castanea sativa,* the European species, is regarded with affection. Many stalwarts are esteemed as "pets," but pets which endure the ravages of time and circumstance while they shade and delight generation after generation of men.

On a slope of fire-breathing Mount Etna in Sicily is the Tree of a Hundred Horses, a chestnut credited with the fantastic trunk circumference of 204 feet—a girth far exceeding that of any other known tree. Its exact reach into antiquity has yet to be determined but almost certainly invading Greek and Roman legionnaires knew it well. The chestnut acquired its title centuries ago when, it is said, Joan the Mad, Queen of Aragon, and her large retinue took cover under its leafy boughs from a storm. Though severely damaged by volcanic action, the tree still struggles for existence.

Despite grim efforts here and abroad, no remedy has been found to aid the trees or even to much retard the infection, as fatal to them as smallpox was to another aborigine. Not one single diseased American chestnut has ever been saved by the tree doctor. A hiker in the backwoods of the Southern Hills, which was the last area to be infected, will come on stands of the trees—whitened hulks on the shores of moonlit time. Here and there a solitary trunk looms, defiantly erect though bereft of life, crown, and raiment.

For most of the 1900s the Department of Agriculture has been tussling with the blight. Groves of seedlings have been pampered in selected locations.

Hybridization with parasite-resistant Asiatic types is being tried with a small measure of success—there are foresters who express cautious optimism. Meantime, the victim of an onslaught unprecedented in recorded botanical history persists in sprouting. As the canker does not proliferate below ground, shoots spring up around the stump of their departed ancestor. Now, since the old trees, their prime hunting grounds, are gone, there are fewer blight spores hitch-hiking rides from passing animals or air currents, and so frequently the new arrivals grow to small tree size, even bearing a hatful of nuts before they, too, are stricken and laid low. The American chestnut, mourned the late John Kieran, has become a Peter Pan, destined never to grow up.

If the original species is to survive its own version of the Black Death, however, it will have to summon unexpected reserves from within its fibers. We have no way of knowing whether these reserves exist; yet, by sheer endurance through continuing propagation, the tree might develop immunity to *Endothia parasitica*.

And if it succeeds, the American chestnut may reclaim its throne as king of the Appalachian hardwoods.

The Oases

Scattered along the route of the Appalachian Trail are 270-some shelters. These oases for backpackers are spotted at varying intervals; few are farther than 12 miles apart—a fair day's march for most hikers. It is not that a dozen miles are many, but the mileage is apt to be spiced with almost constant climb and descent. Often the grade is steep and the footway rough and overgrown.

Scarcely a year passes without new additions to the shelter chain. A large number were put up in the 1930s when the great trail was being completed. Many were built by the Civilian Conservation Corps (the CCC), a body of youths hired in the Depression to work on conservation projects at the field hand's traditional wage of one dollar a day, room and board. Some were erected by state and federal forests and parks, still others by walking clubs, and a few by private individuals eager to advance the sport of hiking. One was constructed by a logging company interested in buffing its image. (As a breed, hikers tend to be ardent conservationists.)

For the most part they are of the type known as lean-tos: small, low, three-sided sheds of boards, logs, cement blocks, or fieldstone, and roofed, but open in front. Capacity ranges from four to eight persons. A handful, such as the sturdy quartet of native rock put up in Shenandoah National Park by the late United States Senator Harry

Byrd of Virginia and called Byrd Nests (what else?), have space for more. But several lean-tos can contain in good conscience no more than two hikers; there is even one, whose location eludes memory though I overnighted under its pervious roof, that would be taxed to accommodate a set of Siamese twins.

Despite their rather cramped proportions, the shelters have been known to quarter platoons of wayfarers on a stormy evening. During one fierce downpour, a humble lean-to in New Jersey provided cover for 27 birds of passage; it was perching room only. On such occasions, sleep comes sketchily, if at all. Tall stories and strong coffee fill the hours of darkness. As incense rises from reeking boots and sodden garments, prayer is offered that the morrow shall come and the sun shall shine again.

While all the shelters boast fireplaces of a primitive sort, these are usually found outside where danger to the building from a blaze is lessened. A number of New England shelters are furnished indoors with cast iron stoves. Generally there is firewood, which the user is expected to replenish before leaving, since the next hiker may arrive in rain and be unable to collect dry wood. Nonetheless—so damp may become the Appalachians—the presence of a woodpile, however ample, is no guarantee of a fire.[10] From a week of rain and near-saturation humidity, the dryest sticks and logs become as if green again, though all the while they have been nestling inside the shelter. And, after much difficulty, if flames are ignited, the wood may weep with moisture and quench the spark. It is amazing what bitterness a reluctant fire can kindle in the human breast. Seldom does it refine the vocabulary.

Thus it is that many backpackers tote a mountaineering stove which burns gasoline, butane, or solid, jellied, or liquid alcohol.

A goodly proportion of the structures flaunt breezy gaps where siding has sprung or chinking has fallen away. Leaky roofs are no novelty. Flooring may be tamped earth, but generally is a wooden platform. A few lean-tos have floors of peeled saplings laid side-by-side, and are uncommonly well ventilated with fissures of every degree. Some archaeologist of a future date will make his reputation probing beneath these pole floors for the artifacts of our peculiar culture.

Often there is a sleeping frame of wire netting; wooden bunks are sheer luxury. No bedding is furnished. Now and then an ax or broom or shovel will thoughtfully occupy a corner. They have a way of disappearing, but a shovel is rarely necessary and a leafy branch will

---

[10] A small (2⅝ oz.) can of Sterno (jellied alcohol) makes a good fire starter and may be used to heat prepared foods.

sweep the shelter. An ax can be very useful, but so far I've managed without one by collecting small dead tree limbs for my cooking fires.

There may be a plank table suffering from the weather and the atavistic urges of a certain type of visitor to leave an engraved account of his visitation. One or two smoke-blackened gallon tin cans fitted with baling wire handles usually dangle from nails driven in the wall. These do for boiling water, laundering, and sponge bathing. A very few shelters, notably those in eastern Vermont along the stretch of trail maintained by the volunteer efforts of Mr. Ben Rolston, are stocked with an array of elderly, yet serviceable, cooking utensils, and surplus copies of the quarterly *The Long Trail News* should any hiker want for inspirational reading.

In Great Smoky Mountains National Park, where black bears have turned brazen owing to feeding and teasing by visitors (practices that lead to dangerous familiarity but whose prohibition is as difficult to enforce as the Volstead Act was once and the ban on Mexican *yerba* is now), the lean-tos are fronted with heavy wire grills. They allow entrance to light, air, and hikers, but not bears. In vain may Bruin show his strong yellow teeth, rattle the grill, whine pleadingly, or march back and forth as militantly as a Women's Libber wearing long pants with a zipper—a superior cunning occupies the cage.

Some campsites in the park are impaled with "bear poles," tall masts with crossarms suggestive of television antennae. The arms suspend packs beyond the stretchy reach of temptation. Adult black bears are as uninhibited tree climbers as their raccoon cousins, yet no matter how they paw and scramble, cannot master the slippery metal poles.[11] At other sites, Park Superintendent Keith Neilson is having installed separate bear-proof caches for food.

In that region also are lean-tos with perimeters ringed by barbed wire like military outposts. These enclosures are called—with the same direct logic—"bear fences," and are crossed on wooden stiles. One might not suppose that a stile, which is merely a set of steps going up one side of the wire and down the other, would thwart a brute so laden with thinking cells as Old Ephraim. But it does, probably because he fears becoming wedged in the narrow passageway.

Mutilated trail signs are not always the work of malicious persons, but sometimes evidence pure and simple that a bear will travel far to find a scratching post to its liking. Foresters stud the markers with spikes and "bob wire." But the bear maddened from ticks, fleas, and mange will scratch on a Devil's Walking Stick tree.

The great majority of shelters have a spring or stream of good

[11] Adult grizzlies (the grizzly isn't found in the Appalachians) seldom climb trees. Their claws, unlike the long hooks of the black bear, are stubby.

drinking water handy. But a few are dry camps, having been erected where landowners permit them (not always the location of choice) or on a waterless mountaintop for the sake of the view. Some front torrents where pounding waters tremble the earth and chill the air; some overlook blue lakes to whose boggy shores come whitetailed deer and moose to browse at dusk; others lie in shadowy hollows in which only the crowns of the trees receive sunlight; a few are moored in dismal swamps where the spirit sighs while the body rests.

I haven't seen all the shelters on the Appalachian Trail. Several I walked past unseeingly in my preoccupied way. Others were bursting with Boy Scouts when I came up; none except a self-sacrificing scoutmaster dares to overnight amidst a troop—the pace is dizzying and who can relax inside a drum that is being incessantly beaten? At others I ate my lunch, took a siesta, or found an hour's refuge from rain. Some I visited briefly, dropping down side trails to stand looking them over for a minute or two. In the same way I sometimes park my car in a small town in order to walk its main street and then, my bump of curiosity reduced to a freckle, take up the journey again.

Vermont has the most heavily sheltered portion of the Appalachian Trail. From the Massachusetts line north to Sherburne Pass the Appalachian Trail uses the footpath of the Long Trail.[12] This 95-mile segment has 25 shelters. Thirteen are lean-tos, nine are cabins (a cabin in hiking parlance is an enclosed structure with a door), and three are lodges (larger cabins).

In the weather-stung White Mountains of New Hampshire are, in addition to a string of shelters, nine rest houses or "huts" that accommodate hikers for a fee. They are maintained by the Appalachian Mountain Club, of Boston, Massachusetts, which, having been established in 1876, is the oldest mountaineering group in the country. Each hut provides hot meals family style, snacks, and trail lunches—good and plentiful food is one of the attractions—and dormitories for men and women. All are heavily patronized. Their existence makes it possible to walk the Appalachian Trail from Lonesome Lake Hut near U.S. Route 3 in Franconia Notch to Carter Notch Hut without the necessity of carrying food or sleeping bag.

The principal camp in Pinkham Notch on N.H. Highway 16 is open

[12] The Long Trail extends from Massachusetts to Canada for 262 miles through the Green Mountains of Vermont. It was conceived in 1910 by James P. Taylor, associate principle of the Vermont Academy, and completed in 1930. By 1973 about 600 persons had hiked its full length. The Green Mountain Club, based at Rutland, Vermont, is in charge of the Long Trail. The trail guidebook (some thousands of which are sold annually) is a model of conciseness and readability.

year round, while the other units, with capacities of from 36 to 96 guests, generally open in June and shut down in early September. During the rest of the year, hut entranceways are left open to serve as refuge for stormbound ski, snowshoe, and hiking parties. By springtime they are often disgustingly befouled. Despite abuse, the AMC declines, in the true spirit of the mountains, to completely seal its huts. The chain is unique in the Western Hemisphere, though similar to European hut systems.

For the most part, huts are staffed by college men who take turns at cooking, cleaning up, and backpacking in provisions. On hut duty the good-natured staffers usually wear conventional slacks, sports shirts, and the stiff-soled collegiate moccasins that Indians never wore. When backpacking on the rugged trails, however, the costume undergoes a remarkable change. It begins with a garish headband to keep hair and sweat from the eyes and ends in black lug-soled thumpers handmade by Peter Limmer of Intervale, New Hampshire, and considered by some to be the best hiking boots turned out in the United States. Between headband and boots, however, is not much: socks, a shirt with buttons and sleeves removed for greater ventilation, and short shorts made by ruthlessly hacking off the legs of an old pair of jeans. In those cases (frequent on the evidence) where inseams have split, the tattered shorts become a sort of breech clout modernized with a fly. The abbreviated garments are held in great esteem by their proud owners, and in eyes-averted awe by "goofers." No "goofer," as the persons who stop at the huts are called (the term long ago lost its derogatory implications), would dare wear them; a Texan couldn't!

Hut boys are not excessively salaried, though they do get a discount on the price of their Limmer boots. Twenty-six dollars a week and lodging are standard, plus, of course, the opportunity to live in the high mountains for a season.

The work is coveted by athletic fellows. How many jobs are left today that afford a male the singular masculine satisfaction of using his muscles?

Other young men are hired by the Appalachian Mountain Club and the Dartmouth Outing Club to work at trail clearing. Sherman Adams, later to become a congressman, governor of New Hampshire and administrative assistant to President Eisenhower, labored in the summer of 1920 on one of these trail crews. From midnight to midnight on May 31, Mr. Adams and William P. Fowler hiked 83 miles on roads and trails, including 5,600 feet of climbing and 6,500 feet of descent, from Hanover to Dartmouth's Skyline Farm Cabin in Little-town. Their record still stands.

Walking marathons are common in the White Mountains. A few years ago Christopher Goetz claimed the AMC hut traverse record from Lonesome Lake to Carter Notch—51.76 rugged miles in 16 hours 41 minutes. Heeding Napoleon's dictum, Mr. Goetz fortified himself with several pounds of broiled beefsteak on the way.

On the Appalachian Trail are a dozen locked cabins which may be rented by hikers. Those in northern Virginia, Maryland, and southern Pennsylvania are operated by the Potomac Appalachian Trail Club, 1718 N Street, N.W., Washington, D.C. 20036 (an old brick dwelling in the Georgian style), while the cabins in eastern Vermont and western New Hampshire are the property of the Dartmouth Outing Club, Robinson Hall, Dartmouth College, Hanover, New Hampshire 03755. They are equipped with all necessary items—inside wood stove for cooking, kitchen and eating utensils, bunks and mattresses—but no food, firewood, or sleeping bags. Because reservations must be made in advance of occupancy, long-distance hikers seldom stop over at these private shelters.

Along the route of the trail in Maine are a number of sporting camps—a form of "hostelry peculiar to Maine," with cabins, rental boats, and communal dining hall—where vacationers, hunters, fisher-men, canoeists, and hikers may find food and shelter deep in the woods. The best raspberry pie I ever tasted was assembled by the caretaker of a Pleasant Pond lodge. As we washed down the pie with coffee, a moose wandered by the dining hall to feed on aquatic plants in the lake. Pleasant Pond was made famous by John Burroughs in "A Taste of Maine Birch," a chapter of his *Sharp Eyes and Other Papers.*

No charge is made, nor is permission required, for use of the Appalachian Trail lean-tos. Like the trail itself, they are open to all travelers afoot. The concept proceeds from the caravansaries of the Arabian lands and the trail lairs and *tambos* of the Indians of North and South America.

Its chain of shelters is one of the glories of the Appalachian Trail. Aside from the national parks, few of the western trails have shelters, and none that I know of which are maintained by private persons or trail clubs for the free use of anyone.

Routine housekeeping is performed by the users, who are expected to tidy camp before departure, and to burn or properly dispose of litter and garbage. The vandal, of course, constitutes a threat to every work of man in the United States. Since he scarcely exists today in Latin America or Europe (as distinct from the conduct of rioters at sporting events and occasional armed revolutionaries) it is not amiss to suggest that he is a by-product of civic behavior as practiced between the Forty-ninth Parallel and the Rio Grande.

Professor Roy Buchanan of the University of Vermont, who for decades headed the Long Trail Patrol to construct and maintain shelters, exclaimed after a particularly harrowing season of repairing damage: "I wish we could find these vandals. If we could have a conference with them, we could find out how they want the camps maintained. At last they have shown us that they don't want any glass or sash in the window openings. There seems to be a feeling against stoves and bunks, although we aren't sure about that yet. Of course, bunks are for burning so they may be tolerated for a while. We know that toilets are to be tipped over and later used for kindling." Prof. Buchanan went on to suggest Disposalls for the vandals, but on reflection vetoed his proposal because "their boneheads would only jam the machines."

The traveler in Scandinavia will come upon a telephone booth on a country road five miles from nowhere and it will be spotless. Every page of the directory will be in place. There will be neither scribbled obscenities on the walls nor excrement underfoot. The stroller in the plazas of a thousand towns from Mexico to Chile can rest on benches whose seats are intact and gaze on plashing fountains where naked babies may play but every passerby will respect as basins of holy water not to be defiled with sputum, cigaret butts, or nameless trash. Statuary from Finland to Vatican City will greet each dawn as blithely as the day before, every part of every statue in place in the very image of man as The Maker created him. The insomniac may wander nightly at will among the sacred ruins of Athens and Rome; he will find little evidence of scabrous visitations (within this century) nor will he leave any. At two in the morning he may light a candle in the ancient Gothic treasure that is the cathedral at Rheims, and its doors will not be locked, though almost every house of worship in the United States is as tightly shut as a bank vault at sundown, and often all day long.

Tacked to the wall of Stony Brook Lean-to in Vermont is the notice:

READ AND HEED

"This is a Green Mountain Club camp built, paid for, and maintained by it for your use and the use of all who want to get into the woods and onto the mountains.

"Some people spell use ABUSE. We hope you are not one!

"Stoves are heavy to lug in, so if you must throw the lids or legs at a visiting porky, put them back in the morning. A stout club works better anyway, so you don't have to use the stove. That has other uses.

"It's nice to come into camp and find a little dry wood, especially if it's raining. Also, it saves chopping up the floor to start the fire. Small dry wood, twigs, and branches make good firewood, even better than the tables, doors or bunks, and there is more of it.

"Porkies love dirty camps. It's right smart business to keep a clean camp unless, of course you love porkies.

"Don't shoot the roof. It's doing the best it can and besides you might hit your pal up there stargazing.

"Carry an old newspaper. It has lots of uses including starting fires. Then we won't have to replace this sign."

A rule of trail etiquette is first-come, first-sheltered. The first comers are enjoined to welcome—and in the friendly fashion that comes hard to cankerous individuals—late arrivals to the limit of the shelter's capacity. Should you be a solitary male and the later arrivals are Girls Scouts, you will find yourself in an untenable position, unfair as it may seem. I can only suggest that you bear the mistrustful glances of the shepherdess and the sheep's eyes of her flock as manfully as you may.

Most hikers are convivial. Indeed, one of the joys of the sport is meeting the many who show warm consideration and hospitality. I have found warm friends at shelters.

Hikers leaving the trail often stow leftover food on joists out of reach of rodents and the elements. Thanks to such thoughtfulness, I have on occasion dined well: canned fruit, beans, and meat; dried eggs, milk, and potatoes; tea, coffee, and sugar.

When supplies are running low, no provender is spurned. Once I was greeted by an abandoned tin of smoked mussels, and consumed them gladly to the last withered bivalve.

I found the shelters to be ports of call on clear nights and Grand Hotels on rainy ones. In all seasons they are home to wood mice, which prance merrily on the beams, emitting squeaks of love and fury to punctuate the darkness.

Now and again an owl wings soundlessly into the shelter. From its perch on the rafters, the gray ghost of the witching hours stares unblinkingly at the hiker in his sleeping bag.

Ah, but then the mice are still!

The Provident Packer

At times the Appalachian Trail leaves a perfectly good course to attack some knoll or other protuberance whose ascent offers neither view nor attraction that seems in any way different—no matter how intently one gazes—from every other protuberance in the vicinity. The protuberance was not in the way; for ages it had stood blamelessly off to the side, content to be merely one geologic bump among hundreds of like size, shape, and namelessness.

Now, unaccountably, the great trail shies to the right, yaws painfully up one flank of the protuberance, and tacks crookedly down the other. Then it shies left to get back onto what, after all, is the logical track. The suspicion arises that the digression was plotted by a hiking club leader to whom the obstacle, not the walk, is the reason for going into the woods.

It was while straining on such an obstacle that the sound of cloth ripping brought me to a halt. With a surge of panic I felt of territory to the south. As I did so, a passing breeze told me the chilling fact: my pants had failed in a vital area.

Fortunately—the month being June—I was hardly at the mercy of the elements. And I was alone, so it was not modesty, but only mild sunburn, that brought a blush to my cheeks.

Next day, patched with adhesive tape and treading gingerly, I came to a road. I put out a thumb. A bread salesman with a hangover and two new jokes drove me to the town of Franklin, North Carolina. The clock had struck noon when I got off in the business center. Shop girls and stenographers formed chattering clusters on the sidewalk; across the busy street was a clothier's.

The curb was high and when I stepped down the sound that I had heard before was heard again. My patchwork had sprung. From behind me came the muffled shriek of a young woman, followed by a gale of hilarity. There was a rush of air to my rear and a rush of blood to my face. I did not look back.

A hundred yards of fast, breezy walking brought me to refuge and the toughest britches that ever I have owned. They were constructed of brown canvas, heavy as the sails of a clipper rounding the Horn. Evidently they had been designed to blunt the attack of a bull alligator in the coastal swamps. In them I felt equal to any outdoor crisis. Nothing more reduces the male to absurdity than does an accident to his trousers.

The jolly experience taught me to take two pairs of pants on long-distance hikes: one of medium weight, the other a light weave for emergency use or when I would leave the trail to wash clothing at the coin laundry. Both pants are wash-and-wear. Hiking shorts may substitute for the second pair. Whatever the combination, the two together weigh less than the single pair of disaster-proof canvas. And if one should split its stitches, the second will be summoned to the breech.

My wet weather gear includes a rain parka, a pair of rain chaps, and leather waterproofing compound.

For a long time I carried a rain poncho. Made of rubberized nylon, this blanket-like cape, with a slit in the middle for one's head, surpasses the conventional raincoat in several ways: first, since it is worn over the backpack, the hiker's necessaries are covered as well as himself; secondly, it may be used as a tarp (admittedly skimpy) or as a ground sheet (ample); thirdly, being sleeveless, it is a bit less bulky and folds neatly. This would seem to be the ideal wet weather garment for the backpacker but, unhappily, the poncho has drawbacks.

In storms where forest cover is sparse, as above timberline, on exposed ridges, through fields, and along roads, the poncho is sure to flap and snap like a pterodactyl. Its owner will get a brisk soaking, and if the hood and poncho are separate pieces and not closely attachable, more water will trickle icily through the neck opening and down the spine. The poncho has another minus: since it can't be worn under the pack (because the shoulder harness bunches the fabric in such manner that one's arms are left unprotected) it must be taken off each time some item is needed from the pack. This is guaranteed to bring out the Anglo-Saxon in the vocabulary. Besides, the garment when wet tends to cling together in folds, refusing to drape properly.

Owing to these drawbacks, and because my latest packsack is made of waterproof material and doesn't need extra protection, I now use a rain parka. Like other parkas, it is an elongated jacket with an integral hood. There are two flap pockets (few ponchos have even one pocket) and it weighs 12 ounces as compared to my old poncho's 17.

Fancy rain parkas are on the market, but mine is see-through vinyl plastic and cost about $2. The first rain parka that I owned was fabricated from coated nylon and lightened my wallet by $12. It gave out on the third wearing. Friction from the packframe rubbed away the waterproof coating inside its shoulders and back. To date, my vinyl parka has withstood the abrasion of a half-dozen trips in the rain, and looks as if it might resist a few more.

Chaps are by no means so essential as the rain parka, but can be welcome allies when wind flails the falling drops in every direction. They do for the legs what the parka does for the rest of the body. I like to don them on early morning tramps when heavy dew or the aftermath of a night rain may result in soaked trousers. My chaps are of coated nylon. They consist of two separate pant legs with wide bottoms allowing them to be pulled on over boots, and are held up by tapes that fasten to the belt loops of my trousers. The chaps total four ounces, but have shed a ton of water; they fold into a letter envelope-sized packet.

Since the parka and chaps are made of water-impervious materials, very little body water and condensation can escape from under their plastic embrace. The body loses water continuously, about one and a half pints a day through drying out of the skin, and greater amounts when hot and sweating. Rain garments steam up in short order. This unpleasantness has given rise to a perennial campfire debate: is it better to be wet from the inside out or from outside in?

While a warm summer shower is a benediction, a heavy downpour, especially if accompanied by cold and blowing air, is a curse. Then it is far better to be wet from the inside out: perspiration and condensation will total much less than anything but a sprinkle. Unless the air is warm and stays balmy—and mountain temperatures are notoriously treacherous—prolonged wetting of clothing and skin will lower body heat. Chilblain is as much to be avoided as a rattler's fangs.

For comfort and safety, a body temperature of 99 degrees must be maintained at all times. A fall of only a degree or two brings on shivering. This is nature's way of exercising the muscles to generate warmth, but it also draws on the body's stored energy and is tiring. Shivering is sign positive of overexposure. At 96-92 degrees the brain numbs (thinking and shivering don't go together); violent shivering sets in at 91-90 degrees. Unconsciousness occurs at 86-78 degrees—and hypothermia claims another victim.

The United States Forest Service ran tests on four cans filled with 110°F. water and placed out in a rainstorm. Four hours later their temperatures were taken with these startling results:

The first can, wrapped in cotton fabric, fell to 60 degrees, while number two, without any covering at all, registered 72 degrees! (The wicking action of cotton had produced super-cooling.) Number three, protected with woolen cloth, showed 83 degrees (wool does not wick). Number four, sheathed in wool *and* a layer of lightweight plastic, came off best, at 96 degrees. (Plastic is wind and waterproof.) The moral is plain: keep dry.

Greatest consideration must be given the feet, for they are what the backpacker marches on—even though Napoleon insisted it was the stomach.

Ravages of the trail are best met by boots with lug soles and leather uppers. A composition rubber sole molded with numerous projections, of the type commonly called Vibram after Vitale Bramani, the Italian manufacturer and mountain climber, will make the walker more sure-footed.

In slippery weather the lugs (also called cleats or grips) give traction on rock, logs, and mud slicks and, of course, even better purchase when the trail is dry. The sole, itself, is moisture proof. My boots, which stand six inches high, also have hard toes and reinforced heel counters. When I insert a pair of felt-on-leather insoles to cushion the feet, they weigh a trifle over four pounds.

Boots, which are high shoes as contrasted to oxfords or low-cuts, are preferred for trail work since their ankle covering makes them less likely to be invaded by sand, gravel, sticks, leaves, mud, water, and snow. At the same time they offer more protection against the attacks of gnats, mosquitoes, thorns, vesicant plants, and serpents. The fact that they give extra support to the ankle is important to the beginner; the dedicated walker quickly develops sturdy ankles and muscular calves.

Leather is the preferred upper for nearly every state of weather. It is warmer than canvas and, unlike rubber or vinyl, has pores through which it may breathe. Shoes that cannot do this become damp inside: perspiration is trapped. On freezing days this dampness, by drawing off warmth, can lead to frostbite; under almost any condition the feet have the feeling of being smothered. Yet on miry paths most hikers would willingly swap for footgear wet only from the inside out.

For persistently juicy travel, one would be wise to substitute the type of boots generally known as shoepacs. These have ankle-high rubber bottoms with leather uppers and manage to combine some foot ventilation with a practical degree of water resistance. Hikers in Maine, where flooding beaver dams may swamp the trails, often use shoepacs. Wearing them is not unlike wearing rubbers.

No such critters as completely waterproof leather shoes exist, though one reads advertisements to the contrary. Walk in such, as I have, for a few hours in a soaker; thereafter they will ship as much water as less boastful brogues. The chemicals with which the pores of the leather have been stoppered will wash away.

I have acquired the habit, and I think a provident one, of packing waterproofer. This goes on the leather with a dauber or one's fingers. Despite the promise of its name, waterproofer is a temporary thing, for an hour's rain is usually enough to dissolve the protective coating. But if the coating is not renewed, the leather dries out, stiffens, chafes the feet, and absorbs water like a thirsty sponge. I carry two fluid ounces of silicone base waterproofing compound—sufficient for several modest applications—in a plastic bottle.

On a trip to Maine over 100 years ago, Henry David Thoreau resorted to *buttering* his boots. He also thoughtfully added an ulster of India rubber to his 60-pound pack before taking to its wet woods.

Prolonged walking in sodden footgear can result in sore, painfully tender feet. When you feel water squishing among your toes like nibbling minnows, stop! Remove the shoes, empty them, and wring out socks. If rain persists or the way leads through puddles and dripping thickets, I put the same socks back on as in short order they'll be sopping again. Otherwise I treat my feet to a fresh pair; the wet ones can be stowed in a plastic sack till opportunity is found to dry them. One does encounter hikers whose packs—Oh, Ye Gods of Rumblebellypore!—are festooned with drying hosen secured by clothespins. At close range these ambulatory laundries are gamy affairs.

When I took up hiking for sport, my feet were barely equal to the trudgery. For hundreds of miles I wore three pairs of socks at a time: light socks next to my flinching epidermis and over them two pairs of wool. In addition, my boots were fitted with insoles. Alack, this padding was not enough: weeks of walking a few miles daily would be required to toughen city-soft feet. And the fact that I began with a pack about twice as heavy as was necessary—a discovery which literally forced itself upon me—caused my extremities to protest all the more. As the soles of my feet thickened, I was bemused to find my foot size increasing by one-half size in length and a corresponding amount in breadth. Some enlargement was to be expected; what I hadn't foreseen was that my chest would expand two inches in the same period. But mountain trails demand deep breathing and Nature, seeking to fit the body to its tasks, works prodigies when given the chance. (No wonder that aspiring Hollywood starlets sign up for courses in respiration.)

With several socks plus insoles my feet were wadded into my boots like the charge in a Kentucky musket. They were cramped and uneasy, though not so restricted that any deformity might result. I'd luckily heeded advice to buy hiking boots one-half to one size larger than street shoes, and so there was room for all this padding.

Nowadays, having become less tender of foot, I wear but one pair of socks (mediumweight wool) and keep two changes of the same in my pack.

A doctor taught me how to treat blistered feet, that plague of many hikers. Paint each blister with an antiseptic such as iodine or Merthiolate. If it has not burst—and it is unwise, not to say potentially infectious, to punish a blister by walking till it bursts—sterilize the point of a large needle in the blue flame of a match[13] and cautiously puncture the bubble from the side in one or two places to release the accumulation of watery fluid. Pierce only the graying, distended skin, not the flesh! With a clean finger gently press out any remaining fluid. Coat again with antiseptic. Using a small scissors (your wife's manicure scissors will work better for this than your knife), cut a piece of adhesive felt to completely cover the now-deflated blister. Press on firmly. The felt ("moleskin" is a brand found in every dime store) will adhere for days, protecting the sore from contamination and further abrasion until it heals.

Both moleskin and ordinary adhesive tape effectively protect spots on toes, heels, soles, and ankles that are rubbing and becoming tender. Band-Aids, however excellent for covering small wounds on other parts of the body, if applied to the feet tend to work loose rather quickly, especially when wet. Next to gum and candy wrappers, the most common item of litter seen on the more heavily traveled footpaths is discarded used Band-Aids.

Wool socks are the choice of most long-distance walkers. Not only do they offer resilient cushioning, but wool feels and actually is warmer when wet than other fibers, whether natural or the planned offspring of a laboratory. Wool makes the only fabric that dries from within—from the inside out.

It does not transfer water, or wick, as do cotton and nylon. Expose the cuff of a cotton shirt to rain and presently the entire garment is wet. Ford a stream wearing wool pants and they will wet only to the waterline. As added virtues, wool is extremely warm for its thickness,

---

[13] Fire instantly cremates any germs. The blue, or inner, cone of flame is sootless and will not deposit a layer of possibly unhygienic black carbon on the needle, unlike the yellow, or outer cone.

resists matting (this makes it ideal for socks), and provides warmth even when soaked. Another bonus is that flying sparks from a camp-fire won't burn holes in wool garments as readily as in synthetics.

As a chronic tenderfoot I appreciate the extra buffering that insoles furnish. Felt-on-leather insoles for mild temperatures, or lambs-wool-on-leather insoles for freezing weather, are the most serviceable, yet hard to find. Insoles of plastic mesh are good; however, they are de-signed more to ventilate the feet than to cushion them. Those made from polyfoam are sold everywhere, but are thin and wrinkle under-foot when wet. A fair set may be fashioned by slicing Japanese rub-ber thongs in half with a sharp knife; each thong becomes a pair of hiker's helpers.

Repeated trial by the ordeal of wet feet has caused many hikers to regard a walk in the wet woods with the mixed feelings of John Heywood's cat which "would eate fish and would not wet her feete."

It would be instructive to know what the Indian, that student of nature *cum laude*, does when skies glower and paths become rivers. The old-time Indian had lean-tos handy on important trails and must have used them. The modern Indian, I have observed, loses little time in finding an overhanging rock or cave; mostly he stays home and talks about the weather.

It is the buck with chipped antlers, they say, that has the greatest following of does; but when Sol radiates tongues of fire or Jack Frost puffs his cheeks, as they do in the ancient woodcuts, nothing takes the place of thatch on the roof. Suitable cover is a necessity for pates which have become trophy pieces. Where the route leaves the shade of trees to bisect a meadow or some burning tract of rocks, I clap on a tennis cap; it works, and there is a certain charm in its shape-less ambiguity, for its usefulness is beyond impairment. But my stock-ing cap is the covering that I would least care to leave behind. Knit from nonscratchy orlon yarn, it increases baggage by a mere ounce and a half. It wards off chill and was indispensable on the occasion that I came down with Asiatic flu on a walk. More heat is lost through the head than any other part of the body; as HQ of the corpus it receives the greatest circulation of blood. At 40°F. an uncovered head may lose up to half of the body's total heat production. From this fact has come the saying, "If your feet are cold, put on your hat."

As my walks are usually undertaken in summer, I find a short-sleeved pullover to be ample uniform above the waist for most day-light hours. During insect time, a long-sleeved shirt buttoning at the neck is helpful. At dawn and again at dusk my down jacket is pressed into service. A nylon shell parka, though unlined, is a fair windbreaker; it weighs little and seems to be in use at least once every day. Its hood, which rolls into the collar, gives additional head covering. Combinations of these garments enable me to cope with considerable variations in temperature and humidity.

Every item assumes importance when borne on the back. Neither poundage nor bulk can be ignored. Strength and space are limited. "A knapsack may prove to be anything from a cheerful companion to the burden of Atlas," observed Charles Coleman Stoddard.[14]

To Colin Fletcher, who conquered the Grand Canyon of the Colorado by walking the crumbling Tonto Trail, it is his "house on my back," and he lists its furnishings by ounces and fractions of an ounce.[15]

Among the most basic pieces of equipment is the sleeping bag. It has all but totally supplanted the rig of woolen blankets and a square of canvas, that burdensome bedroll of Teddy Roosevelt's day.

I alternate between two sleeping bags. My cold-weather bag is a mummy type crammed with goose down that, with a removable liner, approaches 4½ pounds; for most summer nights, however, a rectangular ("envelope" style) dacron-filled bag weighing three pounds keeps me warm enough. Each compresses into a roll about sixteen inches long by nine inches in diameter. (Down is warmer and more compressible than dacron.)

Owing to its confining shape, a mummy bag holds more body heat than the rectangular sleeper. Its tapering contours put one in mind of the successes enjoyed by the undertakers of Gizeh. While the mummy suits, as it were, most people, its cocoon design brings on claustrophobia in others. The hiker who thrashes Somnus will forego its intimacy for the more roomy rectangular bag.

Though "weariness can snore upon the flint," I much prefer a pillow to Shakespeare's truism. For a while I used an inflatable pillow, but my head lay uneasily upon its shifting atmospheric surface. Then I bought a small cushion, shaped like a Polish sausage and stuffed with foam shreds. On this I lolled content as if in the lap of Diana, goddess of the wood. But its bulk, plus the pound of filler, prompted me to abandon it when I came upon the obvious solution: any clothing which is not at the moment being worn is stowed in a drawstring

[14] Charles Coleman Stoddard, *Shanks' Mare* (New York: George H. Doran Company, 1924).
[15] See *The Complete Walker* by Colin Fletcher (New York: Knopf, 1968). Good talk on backpacking and gear.

sack; when filled it's fifteen inches in length and seven in diameter—this becomes my pillow.

Since its contents are necessaries and the sack, itself, is their shepherd, this improvised headrest adds neither weight nor bulk to my pack.

My first backpack, a canvas bag on a metal tube frame, came from the sporting goods department of a large mail-order house whose agents may have angled bass or gunned quail but most certainly never—judging from the product they advertised—packed on a foot trail. It was a disaster.

The bag was poorly sewn and by the fourth day a side pocket hung limply from its stitches. Next day rain fell, only moderately, but it was sufficient to soak the untreated canvas and increase weight by a pound or two until it dried. A weld joining the tubing gave way as I leapt across a mountain rivulet. With a length of cord I tied the frame together and struggled on to the first gap in the hills served by a road. There I left the trail long enough to buy a backpack which could meet the stresses of hiking.

The backpack which travels with me now has a waterproof nylon bag (coated inside with a plastic that resists chafing) and rainflaps covering the zippers on its side pockets. The bag is secured to a sturdy, but very lightweight, frame which is fitted with padded shoulder straps and a waist strap that transfers much of the weight of the load from the shoulders to the hips. The "recurved" alloy frame—shaped like an elongated S—curves a little at top and bottom to snug into the small of the back and over hips and shoulders. The curves bring the pack closer to the body, enabling the carrier to walk upright rather than hunched forward to counterbalance the weight.

A belief generally held is that the waterproof packbag, unlike the nonwaterproof type, will condense moisture. I have used two coated nylon packbags in temperatures ranging from zero to 110 degrees and under the extremes of humidity, from bone-dry Death Valley to the heavy, prolonged rains of Vermont. Neither bag ever showed any wetness within. Yet mountain downpours have soaked every one of the three nonwaterproof bags that I have owned. Not only did their contents dampen considerably, but the pack became heftier, too. Even one pint of water will increase weight by one pound.

For condensation to occur two factors must be present: water vapor and cooling that will condense the vapor to liquid. The liquid will form on the coolest surface. But the packbag and its gear are normally at the same temperature as the air and the necessary contrast is absent, no matter how much vapor may be around.

An item of importance is a tent. Some stretches of trail lack shelters while existing ones are often occupied. After trying out various kinds of tents, I've settled on the plastic variety for summer use.

This is a seven to nine-foot long tube of polyethylene that may be strung on a line between two trees or large bushes. Stakes are not required for the base automatically assumes the width of one's sleeping bag, though in windy weather a rock placed inside each of the tent's four corners will aid in keeping the sides flat. It is most economical, folds into a small packet, weighs from 13½ to 20 ounces and shrugs off the heaviest rains. Bits of sharp rock and broken twigs readily puncture it, but any tears are easily mended with adhesive tape. Drawbacks are that it lacks insect netting, cannot be completely closed for fear of suffocation, and "sweats," collects moisture on the inside, somewhat more than a tent of porous cloth. Unpitched, the tent may be utilized as a sleeping bag cover or as a ground cloth. It keeps bedding from absorbing moisture and soiling on contact with earth or the floorboards of a shelter. Occasionally lean-tos are swabbed with creosote or other compounds to make them resistant to rot and, hopefully, distasteful to wood-greedy porcupines. For whatever inane reason, it is customary for the treatment to be administered in mid-hiking season and the noisome stain lingers stickily for weeks to entrap hikers as surely as flypaper catches flies.

I have distinguished several schools of culinary thought among backpackers. Dominating are what might be called the desiccated and the canned. Adherents of the first rely extensively on packaged edibles which have been relieved of moisture content by the food engineers. Lacking water, these products of factory diuresis require the addition of liquid, while considerable mixing, stirring, simmering, and sautéing are frequently part of the preparation process; by the same token, they are almost as lightweight as today's food technology can make them. The canned contingent depends upon the tins of meats, stews, soups, and fruit to be found in every grocery.

While there seems little doubt this school has the best of it as far as preparation is concerned—at the most only heating is necessary—its members do have to bear a heavy burden between meals: water makes up to three-fourths or more of many foods, and the canneries, having long ago discovered water to be the cheapest, as well as the heaviest, ingredient, are not sparing at the spigot.

There are a few Spartan backpackers who subsist almost exclusively on such alimentary trivia as yerba maté and peach pits. I would term them the antigourmet faction, and have marveled how they survive the demands of the trail; yet somehow they do, free of the vice of gluttony and bright-eyed if not always bushy-tailed.

As for myself, after brief periods of membership in both the desiccated and canned schools, I joined the amorphous or in-between faction, whose daily fare reflects a compromise with pocketbook, weight, and availability. Into my packsack go dried potatoes, rice, and macaroni, tins of lunch meats and sardines, cheeses and smoked sausages that keep without refrigeration. These are articles stocked by all self-respecting food shops.

I like hot meals for both lunch and supper. This is not always possible, for rain often interferes, but nearly always one hot meal a day is managed.

Appended is a list of my equipment for summer walking. Suppliers and brand names (where pertinent) and most costs and weights are also given. Trail foods "my style" are briefly discussed.

Starting a week's hike on a warm, sunny day, my backpack will tip the beam at about 28½ or 29½ pounds, depending chiefly upon which sleeping bag is chosen. These figures include one quart of water, which by itself weighs 2.1 pounds, but none of the gear listed under ITEMS FREQUENTLY TAKEN. Neither do they include clothing and shoes actually being worn nor miscellany carried on the person.

About 90 different pieces of equipment and clothing, not counting food, may make up my load. From 70 to 75 of these articles are usually carried in my packbag. As food is consumed, the burden lessens at the rate of about 1½ pounds daily. And that spare tire which I carry about my middle deflates, too.

Equipment

ITEM	COST	LB.	OZ.
Backpack (*Camp Trails* "Skyline" waterproof nylon packbag mounted on their "Summit Cruiser" magnesium alloy packframe; waist strap included)	$ 45.00	3	3
Sleeping Bag (*Alp Sport* "Nordic" goose-down-filled mummy shape with tie-in nylon liner; stuff sack of waterproof nylon included)	97.50	4	8
2 nylon straps to secure sleeping bag to packframe below the packbag.	1.00	0	1

Note: The hiker can spend as much as $60 for a backpack and $130 for a sleeping bag, though very adequate gear is procurable for far less through outfitters such

ITEM	COST	LB.	OZ.
as Recreational Equipment, Inc., 1525 11th Avenue, Seattle, Washington 98122.			
I have successfully used a *Herter's* G-88 dacron polyester-filled rectangular shape sleeping bag ($13.97—3 lb.), carrying it in an *Eddie Bauer* waterproof nylon stuff sack 17½" x 8½" ($2.50—1½ oz.). Dacron filling is less warm than down and on cold nights I would go to bed wearing pants, jacket, socks, and stocking cap.			
Tent (*Rec. Equip.* "Instant One-Man Tent," a polyethylene tube 9' long by 3.2' in diameter (5' flat). Long enough to accommodate both the hiker and his pack. Can be pitched between two trees or used simply as a sleeping bag cover or ground cloth.	$ 2.50	1	3½
Note: Also on the market is a polyethylene "Instant Two-Man Tent" that weighs 2½ lb. and sells for $4.50.			
Forty feet of ³⁄₃₂" red braided nylon avalanche cord (*Rec. Equip.*) to pitch tent or hang up pack.	0.80	0	1½
Water bottle with attached cap, plastic, 28-oz. capacity (*Ski Hut*)	0.75	0	2
Collapsible water bottle, plastic, 4½-qt. capacity (*Rec. Equip.*) for use in camp to avoid numerous trips to the spring, which all too often is far, far down the mountainside.	0.40	0	2½
Note: (1) One quart of water weighs about 2 lb. 1½ oz.; (2) A discarded 1-qt. "Clorox" bottle weighs 1¾ oz. and makes a serviceable canteen.			
Rain parka, plastic (*Rec. Equip.*)	1.50	0	12
Rain chaps, coated nylon (*Holubar*)	4.50	0	4
Shell parka, nylon (*Rec. Equip.*)	6.95	0	10
Down jacket (*Eddie Bauer*)	28.50	1	4
Stocking cap, orlon knit (*Wigwam*)	1.00	0	1½
Pullover, short sleeve nylon knit	4.95	0	6
Shirt, long sleeve wash-and-wear	3.95	0	9½
3 pairs wool work socks, medium weight (*Sears* or *Penney's*)	3.00	0	7½
Leather belt (*L. L. Bean*)	2.00	0	4
2 pairs drawers	3.00	0	7½
Bandanna (handkerchief)	0.25	0	1
Cap	2.50	0	2½
Pants, brown color, wash-and-wear	6.95	1	2½
Spare pants, lightweight wash-and-wear or	5.95	0	12

Item	Cost	Lb.	Oz.
Walking shorts	$ 5.95	0	8
Clothing not being worn is stowed in a waterproof nylon drawstring sack 12½" x 7½" (*Eddie Bauer*). This does double duty as a pillow.	2.25	0	1
Boots, lug-soled	30.00	3	15
1 pair felt-on-leather insoles (*L. L. Bean*)	1.35	0	3½

Note: Though now wearing my sixth set of trail boots, manufactured by as many firms, I have yet to own a really satisfactory pair. Experience has taught me, however, that a boot intended for extensive use on rough trails should have doubled or hardened toes (to prevent collapse of the leather, a matter that leads to blisters on *top* of the feet), reinforced heel counters and steel sole shank to help the boot keep its shape under twisting and soaking, a bellows tongue (it does not have to be padded) which extends well above the uppermost lacing, heavy nylon laces (leather laces deteriorate rapidly when wet) and thick soles of tough, slip-resistant material such as rubber or neoprene (a synthetic rubber). "Vibram" deep cleated lug soles are excellent, but few hikers realize they come in more than one thickness: the thin "Vibram Montagna" is the one affixed to most hiking boots, and it will not last much longer than 1,000 miles of walking; the heavy thick "Vibram Montagna," which gives more mileage and foot support, is the preferred sole. This type of sole should be attached not merely by gluing but also with brass screws to avoid separation.

Mess kit (in drawstring sack): *Sterno* cooking pot (1¼ qt. capacity) with cover, aluminum soup spoon (a fork is unnecessary), *Thermos* plastic cup, two-cent box of strike-anywhere matches, G.I. miniature can opener, salt and pepper in discarded plastic medicine vials. Total	3.40	0	9½

Medical and repair kit (in aluminum container with screw-on lid) consisting of tubes of burn salve and toothache remedy, a plastic bottle of Merthiolate antiseptic, aspirin, and codeine tablets, adhesive tape, bandage, 6 Band-Aids,

Item	Cost	Lb.	Oz.
Dr. Scholl's Moleskin for blisters and tender spots on the feet, Halazone water purification pills, scissors, scalpel, magnifying glass, small glass mirror, plastic vial of 24 small strike-anywhere matches, one foot of 2″ wide fabric repair tape (*Rec. Equip.*), safety pins, needles, 1 bobbin of thread, buttons, 2 wristwatch pins, 1 #PR-4 flashlight bulb, 2 dimes for pay phones.			
Total	$ 9.25	0	9
Miscellany (carried on the person, in pockets of the packbag, or in a waterproof nylon drawstring sack):			
Safety razor (with screw-on handle sawed to half-length) and blades	1.00	0	1½
Toothbrush	0.50	0	½
Skin lotion in small plastic bottle	—	0	1
Washcloth, lightweight	0.15	0	¾
Half a bar of soap	—	0	1¾
Sunglasses with case and lens cloth	4.95	0	1¾
Mallory pocket flashlight with 2 "AA" pen-size long-life alkaline batteries	2.00	0	3¼
Taylor compass	2.50	0	¾
Pocket knife, single blade (*L. L. Bean*)	4.00	0	½
Ballpoint pen	0.50	0	1¼
Pencil and small notebook	0.30	0	1½
Comb and nail file	0.75	0	½
Whistle, plastic (distress signal)	0.30	0	½
Standard candle, about 5″ long (burns over two hours in still air)	0.05	0	1
Boot waterproofing compound	1.00	0	3
Insect repellent	1.00	0	1½
Wallet	—	0	3½
Wristwatch, waterproof	25.00	0	2
Several each plastic sacks and heavy rubber bands	—	0	1
Paperback book (after entertainment its pages help to kindle fires, clean cooking utensils and you-name-it)	—	0	6
Highway and trail maps and guidebook pages	—	0	6
Grand Totals	$313.20	24 lb.	3 to 7 oz.

ITEMS FREQUENTLY TAKEN: mosquito head net (2 oz.), camera with two rolls of film, lens tissue, and lens brush (1 lb. 3½ oz.), Bleuet butane gas stove with disposable fuel cartridge good for about three hours of flame, or sufficient for one week's food preparation "my style" (1½ lb.). One full butane cartridge for this burner weighs 10½ ounces.

NOTE: Plastic bags are used liberally to enclose certain foods and items that might leak (antiseptic, bug dope), need protection against the weather (wallet, matches, maps), are soiled or wet (clothing, washcloth), or require wrapping (soap, razor, candle).

Food for one week: Basic breakfast—seven cups of a mixture of oatmeal, concentrated protein cereal, wheat germ or raisins, sugar, salt, and dried milk in a heavy plastic sack (1 lb. 3 oz.).

Basic lunch—three cans sardines (14½ oz.), two cans Vienna sausage (12½ oz.), two cans potted meat (7 oz.), five cups dehydrated potatoes in a plastic sack (10¾ oz.), two packets dried green pea soup (8 ¾ oz.). Total 3 lb. 5½ oz.

Basic supper—3½ cups of cornmeal carried in a heavy plastic sack (1 lb. 4½ oz.).

Additional food—hardtack (12 oz.) one-half pound of margarine as sold in its aluminum or plastic tub (9 oz.), roll of hard salami sausage—holds without refrigeration (1 lb.), one ounce instant coffee —enough for 20 to 25 cups—in an aluminum container with a plastic lid (1½ oz.), two ounces fruit juice crystals—makes about 10 cups of juice—in a similar aluminum container (2½ oz.), 14 each small rolls of hard candy and sacks of peanuts (1 lb. 8½ oz.). Total 4 lb. 1½ oz.

Food is stored in a drawstring sack weighing 1½ oz. Counting the various containers and wrappers, one week's supply of food totals 10 pounds.

I don't bother with cooking the oatmeal mixture for breakfast. Water—hot or cold—is stirred into a cup of it and the result is eaten forthwith. It has a nutlike taste lacking in the usual boiled porridge. In Scotland oatmeal that is mixed with water and eaten raw is called brose.

For the midday meal I often prepare a cup of dehydrated flaked potatoes (which doubles in bulk when added to water), then add the contents of a can of sardines or Vienna sausage. Or I might settle for soup and potted meat with hardtack.

The evening meal consists of one-half cup of cornmeal, which thickens to 2½ cups of mush after simmering a few minutes with 2½ cups of water. I stir in a few thin slices of salami as it cooks, then add a good dollop of margarine as it's taken from the fire.

With the above foods, my appetite can be readily assuaged and meals need, at the most, no more preparation than cooking in water.

Besides, every fourth to fifth day on the Appalachian Trail one usually passes a country store or filling station selling something to eat or arrives at a road leading to a nearby community where provisions can be purchased.

On such occasions I seize the opportunity to enjoy fresh milk, ice cream, fruit, pastry, and so on. I may return to the woods with a few eggs to simmer in water till soft or hard-cooked or hot dogs to broil over the embers. And in my pack may be tucked onions, bell peppers, tomatoes, carrots, or other garden truck for a salad of green growing things. Not infrequently there is room for a bottle of Liebfraumilch or a couple of cans of beer.

Foodstuffs like macaroni, rice, cornmeal, and dehydrated potatoes are not to be spurned. In contrast to the specially designed trail foods, they are sold everywhere and are quickly and easily prepared. They also substitute nicely for store bread, which for the most part is voluminous and crushable owing to water and air—lots of air. The cooking directions which follow specify the amounts of these foods that can be readily cooked in a one-quart (four-cup) pot and that will furnish the principle part of a meal for one hungry adult.

MACARONI. To cook dry macaroni (spaghetti, fusili, noodles, etc., are only varying shapes of macaroni, which is the generic name) break the strands into pieces from one and a half to two inches in length. Gradually add one cup of them (about three ounces) to two cups of boiling water in which has been dissolved one-half teaspoon of salt. (The reason for cooking with salt is that many foods, especially bland foods, need it to improve their normally flat taste; salt develops flavor.) Stir until the water resumes boiling and each piece of macaroni is separate from its fellows, since otherwise the result may be wallpaper paste. Simmer, and when the *pasta,* as Italians call this favored food, no longer has a starchy, uncooked taste, but is still firm to the bite, it is done. This usually takes from 10 to 18 minutes. The one cup of macaroni will have become two cups. Drain but do not rinse. Add a little margarine and stir until it is melted and every strand of macaroni glistens. Stir lightly, using a lifting motion to separate the strands. A pinch or two of dried orégano or parsley flakes, onion or garlic powder (fresh minced garlic is even better), black or red pepper, and a bit of cheese or sausage cut into small pieces or tuna fish may be added for interest. Good macaroni is made from very nutritious high-protein hard wheat—look for the word "durum" or "semolina" on the package.

If fuel is short or rain interferes, when the water resumes boiling after the addition of the macaroni the pot may be covered tightly, removed from the fire and kept in a warm place or wrapped in a shirt or even put in the sleeping bag for a few minutes. The macaroni will finish cooking by itself. This method is known as "fireless cooking." It was a method much practiced during the Great Depression. Then a family with more debts than income frequently constructed a "fireless cooker," an insulated box in which the pot of stew or beans could reach savory fulfillment without the services of Consolidated Edison or Cleveland Cliffs.

It should be noted that macaroni can be prepared with considerably less water and heat than directions generally indicate if the cook takes extra care to prevent the pieces of *pasta* from sticking to each other or to the vessel.

RICE. Rice is also cooked by dribbling into boiling water and stirring till the water returns to a boil. Thereafter cover and simmer till done—from 15 to 25 minutes. One-half cup (about three and a half ounces) of rice cooked with one cup of water and one-quarter teaspoon of salt will expand to almost two cups. The amount of water used is critical: too much and the rice will turn out soggy; too little and it will be undercooked and hard, failing to swell up as proper rice should. If the cover fits too loosely, steam will escape, prolonging cooking time and making it necessary to add more water. Extra liquid will also be required if the rice is exceptionally starchy from age or dried out from long residence on the grocery shelf.

Quick-cooking or "minute" rice will prepare if merely stirred into cold water, which is useful to the backpacker when a rainy day moistens the fire, but it is far more bulky and expensive than ordinary dry white rice and, I think, not so tasty, whether served hot or cold. Brown rice is more flavorful and nutritious than either; however, it takes twice as long to cook as white rice.

Rice will profit from seasoning: add one tablespoon margarine, a little pepper, and a chicken bouillon cube (or bouillon granules) to the water in which it is simmered. To make Spanish rice, also include a thread of saffron[16] and a spoonful of mixed vegetable flakes. For *arroz con pollo* add canned chicken to the Spanish rice.

CORNMEAL. Whether of the white or yellow variety (the yellow has more vitamin A), cornmeal is another cereal obtainable almost everywhere. Like the others it furnishes both the bulk and the

---

[16] Saffron, which is the stigma of crocus flowers, provides the yellow color and characteristic iodinelike fragrance of Spanish rice. (It also provides the yellow dye of the robes worn by Buddhist monks.) Owing to the hand labor involved in gathering saffron, it is one of the most expensive of all food seasoning agents —yet a 50-cent vial, the barest fraction of an ounce, will season many pounds of rice.

calories necessary to satisfy hunger. To prepare, stir one-half cup cornmeal and one-half teaspoon salt into one-half cup cold water in your drinking cup. Now bring two cups of water to a boil in the pot and then slowly add the cornmeal mixture. Barely simmer for 5 to 10 minutes, stirring often from the bottom. One-half cup (about three ounces) of cornmeal makes two and a half cups. (By mixing the meal with cold water before adding to boiling water the risk of its sticking to the bottom is reduced.) Cornmeal will be enhanced if subjected to seasoning akin to that suggested for macaroni.

Just before finishing the length of the Appalachian Trail, I chanced upon a concoction that I dubbed Idiot's Delight. The recipe, which I wish I had known about long before, will feed two idiots to satiety at one meal. To make, mix one packet of dried pea soup in four cups of cold water until thoroughly blended and free of lumps. Bring to a bubble. Now mix one cup cornmeal and one teaspoon salt in a cup of cold water and slowly add this mixture to the simmering pea soup, along with one or two cloves of chopped garlic, a good dash of pepper (red pepper preferred for its tang) and one 7-oz. can of tuna fish. Cook over low heat, stirring often and adding more water if necessary. On serving, add a generous tablespoon of margarine to each portion of the thick gruel.

POTATOES. One cup of dehydrated potato flakes (about two and a half ounces) when stirred into one and a half cups of liquid (water or water mixed with milk powder) and one-half teaspoon salt, makes two cups of mashed potatoes. The liquid used may be either hot or cold, though cold mashed potatoes have never made any gourmet's list, and probably never will. Margarine, pepper, onion, carrot, and parsley flakes and small amounts of meat, fish, or cheese—all will contribute to making a tasty trail meal of a pot o' spuds.

Altitude has a pronounced effect on cooking time when liquids are involved. While water at sea level boils at 212°F., at 5,000 feet it boils at 203°F. (one degree lower for each 550 feet of rise), and food which is prepared in water takes up to twice as long to cook. The cooking times given in this chapter will do for altitudes to 3,000 feet, which is close to being the median elevation of the Appalachian Trail. Above 3,000 feet do not be surprised to find yourself spending more time at the cooking fire. And that cup of cocoa or coffee will not be quite so piping hot, either.

As important as the quality of eats for the trail traveler is the purity of the water he drinks. While brooks, springs, and seeps in the

Photo by Elmer L. Onstott

Tulip tree (yellow poplar) blossom, near Groseclose, Virginia.

Photo by Eric Ryback

Deer seen along the trail in Virginia.

higher and remoter reaches of the Appalachians are frequently pristine and invigorating as Vichy water, this is not always the case in populated areas. In fact, from the trail paralleling the Potomac I have observed raw sewage trickling into this river which flows bravely onward to become the principal source of drinking water for the District of Columbia. Before being piped into the Halls of State, however, the fluid is screened for subversive particles, aerated to repair its taste, and disinfected by bell, book, and candle.

Disinfecting is suggested for the water the Appalachian walker ingests or even uses merely to brush his teeth. Questionable water is generally rendered harmless by boiling from five to ten minutes.

An easier, if slightly less dependable, treatment, is chlorination. One may use ordinary household bleach liquid that contains 5.25% to 6% sodium hypochlorite; Clorox and Purex are two widely sold brands available in grocery stores. They are potent germicides. To one quart of water add one drop of bleach, stir or shake well and allow to stand for a half-hour before drinking. If the water is cloudy or otherwise suspect, add three drops.

Another method employs ordinary medicine cabinet tincture of iodine—two or three drops to each quart of clear water and eight to ten drops for cloudy water. Mix and allow to stand a half-hour.[17] Iodine-releasing compounds are preferred in tropical areas—Panama and Vietnam, for example—because they destroy some waterborne bacteria which resist chlorine.

Water purification tablets, obtainable in many pharmacies and and sporting goods shops, are handier to use than solutions on the trail. Most commonly encountered brand is Halazone, which has a chlorine base. The small 100-tablet size bottle costs about 85 cents. Recommended dosage is two tablets per quart of water, followed by a wait of a half-hour.

In Pennsylvania one is urged not to quaff at old coal mine sites. The water may be heavily mineralized; sulfur and iron are notable cathartics. Germicides will not mitigate their action.

A friend who walked on the northern end of the trail in Pennsylvania wrote me a week later as follows: "My hiking pardner, Bill, and I got so damn thirsty crossing St. Anthonys Wilderness that we drank from a spring near an ancient mine dump. The water didn't smell and was clear as gin. But it turned out to be a cocktail with the

[17] The chlorine and iodine solution dosages given are those recommended by the United States Department of Defense. See the pamphlet *Emergency Sanitation at Home—A Family Handbook* (Washington: Government Printing Office, 1961).

kick of an Arkansas mule. We spent the next three days beating one another to the bushes.

"P.S.—I now hold the unofficial world record for the 100-yard dash of four and six-tenths seconds."

Vipers

At midmorning, sun filtered through the tree canopy to float in warm yellow pools on the floor of Tennessee's Cherokee National Forest. Rain had fallen during the night, and leaves still glistened wetly in the green shadows.

A circle of light fell on a somber object that seemed out of place on the footpath. My heart thumped; there, in its coils, lay a large snake. Gripping my walking stick, I quietly advanced to within several feet.

Except for a forked tongue that darted in and out, testing the languid air for scent, the beast was motionless. I could make out an arrow-shaped head with vertical pupils. It was a pit viper—poisonous.

On touching the head with the tip of my stick, it jerked back; a tremor rippled through the coil. The rattlesnake's heavy body swelled and broadened. It rose slightly and swayed as I slowly moved the tip in short arcs. Cat eyes stared malevolently.

I lightly tapped its snout. The serpent convulsed, sprang backward, and rewound, all in less time than the telling. Its tail, girdled with horny segments, stood erectly and vibrated: the sound of castanets was heard in the forest.

Picking out a seat on a nearby stump, I removed my backpack. The grim clicking persisted. Once it faltered, but when I stamped the ground, resumed with vigor.

A half-hour passed; it was time to go.

I walked over to the snake—it stabbed tentatively in my direction; I lashed out furiously—it bit at the stick in agony. Soon the animal was dead.

The timber rattler had a brownish black torso with camouflage blotches. It was almost four feet long and thick as my wrist. Nine gray rattles ringed the short tail. The end of the stick was spattered with venom that dried to a varnish.

That afternoon, where the path entered a wildlife management area, I met a game warden nailing a No Hunting sign to a basswood tree.

"Reckon you're hiking the Appalachian Trail," he said, looking me over. I pleaded guilty to the charge.

"Seen any snakes?"

I admitted sighting a timber rattlesnake.

"Swatted it dead, I reckon?"

I hesitated; my mind heard the rattling and saw the thrashing of a dying wild creature; I was not pleased with myself.

"No," I lied.

The warden gaped. "Why," he said, and his voice was aggrieved, "you ought've killed that snake. Now it's up there on the mountain just waiting to bite somebody, maybe a ginseng picker."

But I knew well, even if I didn't say so, that men bite, too.

The Traveler

It was blistering—100 degrees in the shade, and there was mighty little of that at sun high of a June day—as I came down off Bald Mountain to (as the Russians begin their novels) the village of ———— on the frolicking ———— River.

The Appalachian Trail followed the road through the village. It led past a tiny country store, a shanty from which every fleck of paint—if indeed it ever boasted paint—had long since vanished. No sign announced its commercial function, but nailed to the front was a metal strip proclaiming the satisfaction to be obtained from chewing a certain brand of tobacco. Another rectangle bore a thermometer and the advice to drink a cola beverage when thirsty. I was thirsty.

Stepping onto the porch, I opened the screen door. At first I couldn't see; then my eyes made the adjustment from glare to gloom. In mid-room was profiled an old man—he must have been 90 or more —sitting upright, knees crossed, hands clasped in lap, in an old-fashioned, high-backed spool chair. He wore a black suit, perfectly pressed and brushed, a starched white shirt and dark tie, and black shoes that gleamed with polish.

For a long moment I thought he was dead—that I had come upon a corpse that had just given up its spirit. Then the still form stirred. The handsome head, crowned by snow-white hair, slowly turned and I stared into faded blue eyes.

"Good afternoon," he said.

I replied that I was walking the trail, and yearned for a cold drink, no matter whether soft or hard. I suppose that I was being facetious; "hard" beverages are sold publicly in few settlements of the Bible belt.

"Yearn no more," he said, nodding gravely at the cooler. I fished out a bottle of pop, deliciously dripping with ice water, and glanced about the store.

A dusty showcase paraded cartons of bubble gum and candy bars. Unpainted shelves held crackers and a dozen cans each of peaches, sardines, and corned beef. Chief item of merchandise was tobacco: numerous brands of cigarettes crowded the counter, and as many more of chewing tobacco. But snuff obviously was first choice of his customers. There were tins, bottles, and boxes of snuff; I counted over 20 kinds. A heady miasma floated over the display.

We exchanged a few more sentences. The old gentleman's words were chosen with care and were spare as his bony frame. His regard was blandly courteous, with nothing in it either of curiosity or of the usual shopkeeper's attentiveness.

I drank a second bottle of pop. He dropped my coins into his suitcoat pocket.

"Good traveling to you," he said.

Outside on the porch, I shouldered my pack and turned for a last look at the thermometer. The red spirit level had risen.

"It's up to 101," I said, poking my head through the doorway.

The thin visage was again in profile, eyes fixed on the far wall. There was no reply. I closed the door.

My feet took me along the dusty road in the hush of midday. I thought of him sitting quietly in the hot room, waiting patiently. Despite his attire, he had seemed cool: the internal fire must have been banked low. He was traveling, too.

I shivered a little; for a moment the day lost its heat.

Still, the old man was going in style: erect, elegant, grammatical. Few men go like that. It was really something to envy.

Double Negative

To the strict grammarian—and who is stricter?—the dialect of southern Appalachian mountain people seems to beg for correction. There is, however, small chance of success in this matter, for the hillman has learned that most changes are not to his advantage. He is all too well acquainted with the federal crackdown on backyard distilling, the blight that wiped out millions of acres of the finest wild chestnut trees so important to local economy, and now the attack on tobacco, the only cash crop of many a hollow and creek bottom. No, sir, change is not welcome in these parts.

On the other hand, by a linguistic student the speech of the hills is regarded with a positive affection: here is an English sublanguage not much affected by anything that has happened in this century and spurning the hucksterisms of the electronic media as alien corn. A full poke of grammatical eccentricities are, he knows, a modest price to pay for the enjoyment of a unique tongue; one, moreover, without whose lively assistance it would be difficult to imagine such caricatures of the work-shy backwoodsman as Snuffy Smith and of American Boy-ism as Lil Abner.

Leaving off the obvious exaggerations, parodies, and ironies of the comic strip artists, it is the everyday tongue of several million dwellers in the hills of the two Virginias, both Carolinas, Tennessee, Alabama, and Georgia.

The region is lofty, forested, and steeply inclined. Barely 300 miles wide and 500 miles long, it is an oblong thicket of the fiercest conservatism, where every change is resisted and every government mistrusted. Among America's diverse social groupings, the people of this oblong are the most independent and hanker least to be like others. The Appalachians are not ant hills.

Their dialect, as dialects do, spills over into the flatlands on either side, and beyond; many mountaineers have regretfully left their job-poor homeland, and their talk now is heard in the streets of Chicago, Detroit, and Wilmington, Delaware, and lately as far afield as Boise and Flagstaff.

This sublanguage sprouted on the American frontier of the eighteenth and nineteenth centuries, the frontier of Andrew Jackson and Colonel John (Nolichucky Jack) Sevier. Elizabethan English was its base, the syntax homespun, and the pronunciation often pure anarchy. Its singular expressions were born of experience, sacred and profane. "Root, hog, or die," they said, and those who didn't did.

An expanding colonial population was primarily reponsible for the push westward from the seaboard into the coves and onto the high meadows of the smoky Blue Ridge. But peppering the border stew were religious groups such as the Scotch-Irish Covenanters[18] seeking haven. Then there were those, and they were not few, who hungered for uncrowded paths and as free a life as any white man could know without turning Indian.

[18] These were Scots who made a Covenant with The Lord to defend Reformed Presbyterianism. When English Anglicans and Puritans responded with the "killing time," numbers of Covenanters fled to Ireland, later emigrating to the North American colonies. Many found their way into the hills of Virginia and North Carolina. From sojourn in Ireland, and not through ancestry, came the sobriquet "Scotch-Irish," for while Scots and Irish are both Celtic people, they seldom mingle blood except in argument.

European life, with its land expropriations, self-perpetuating aristocracy, and callousness, prompted multitudes to pass into voluntary exile. Even well into the nineteenth century several hundred Englishmen were executed yearly by the state. In 1819, Sir T. F. Buxton listed 223 crimes for which the death sentence was provided. America, itself, was not free of the blood lust, but its wilderness offered escape from an oppressive society.

It became the fashion for longing Europeans to romanticize the Indian as one who lived in a new Eden. It was a sylvan Eden where every tree showered nuts and fruits, even shillings and dollars when shaken hard, and where the numbers of wild animals obviated poaching, one of the Old Country's capital offenses. In truth, the North American Indian of the forest often enjoyed the blessings of abundance with a minimum of government and a maximum of leisure and personal liberty. And this aboriginal man was generous to a fault: it was a day when the European, made hard by class arrogance or deprivation, was stingy beyond belief and could, as the saying goes, squeeze an orange till the pip squeaks. Dr. Carl Gustav Jung, the Swiss clergyman's son who became one of the three founders of modern psychiatry, was to say that he saw something of the Indian in every American.

Still, as the emigrants arrived they set up governments not much modeled on the Indian democracies, but more like the only ones they had known, restrictive and pettifogging; it took the Revolutionary War to bring the first important changes.

Down where the land leveled out, plantations sprang up on Indian properties frequently obtained by dubious transaction and complete with harsh social distinctions, bondage for poor white laborers, slavery for imported Africans, and a nostrum of cultural mythology.[19] In brief, a Pandora's Box of inequities that aped the Old World autocratic formula, put a premium on docility, and left a threatening legacy to future generations of Americans.

But in the Appalachians every man was his own master. He thought freely, spoke freely, acted freely. If he would not be a slave neither would he own one. No wonder the most hilly state of them

[19] A culture whose notions of chivalry were borrowed from the romantic novels of Sir Walter Scott according to the southern writer, Mark Twain. "Sir Walter had so large a hand in making southern character," said Twain in a peevish mood, "that he is in great measure responsible for the War (Between the States)." In adversity the Scots-born Scott proved as brave as any hero of his turgid novels. Although a leg was crippled by infantile paralysis, he learned to walk 30 miles a day. And when through no fault of his own financial failure struck at age 56, he refused to walk the easy path of bankruptcy, scribbled on desperately, and died with his debt of 127,000 pounds sterling almost paid off.

all, West Virginia, took for its motto *Montani Semper Liberi:* Mountaineers Will Always Be Freemen. It is safe to say that a number of the counties of high Appalachia have not even to this day one single resident descended from a slave.

No treasure trove to fatten the pot buried under the doorsill was revealed by the mountains—or rather, if it was, then like those later discoveries, coal, iron, and petroleum, it left mostly black grit between the native's teeth and stench in the air. Men who came seeking an easy life soon retreated or passed through to the broad river valleys of the western country. Those who stayed did so because here at least was the untrammeled life: four parts forest to one part field, self-sufficient and thoroughly rural, it suited them. Customs, manners, and speech that are much the same today as generations ago, developed along distinctive lines. They persist as the hillman's vital link with the past and demonstrate the kinship of common memories and shared hopes. Above all, is the hope that the freedom of the hills will forever be his.

Every hillman knows every other hillman, however far from native branch and slick. Not in person, of course, but always by his talk—talk which is both language and attitude, and which has been shaped by an isolation far more enduring than in the northern tier of the Appalachians. It must be understood, too, that whereas New England's mountaineers are nearly all of Anglo-Saxon stock, in the South they are of Anglo-Saxon and Celtic derivation. Here, English surnames such as Hall and White are set off by Welsh ones like Hughes, Williams, and Jones and Scottish patronymics beginning with Mc. There were numerous German-speaking settlers in Pennsylvania and some of them moved below the Mason-Dixon Line, whereupon they took the English of the Anglo-Celt as their tongue.

Outside influences, including contact with citified people and books (the Holy Bible excepted), have been minimal since pioneer days in the southern uplands. Gaps in the mountain chain are few; a jumbled terrain is not easily penetrated. Besides, the hard economy never attracted the literati. Even now, it is difficult to find a serious magazine in the smaller towns, nor is a copy of a daily newspaper always obtainable. The young clerk in a crossroads Tennessee drugstore told me why: "I reckon," he said, "we-uns don't read much."

As the decades unreeled, localisms appeared and Celticisms entered the sentence structure. But the basic Elizabethan character of the speech did not change. Nor has it ever become so soft and drawling as the idiom of the lowlands. Now almost romantically archaic, it has a pungency unknown to the rest of English-speaking North America.

Fight, for instance, comes out as "fit," while cucumber becomes "cowcumber." This is pure Middle English as pronounced in the reign of the first Queen Elizabeth, a remarkably well-spoken monarch. Other holdovers are "ast" for asked, "jine" for join, "git" for get, "arter" for after, "pizen" for poison, "bile" for boil, "obleege" for oblige, and "fitten" for fitting. "Surround" is much used in its ancient sense of going around, or bypassing, rather than the modern meaning of enclose or encircle. The word it is uttered as "hit," as in "hit was good." "Hit" is simply the Anglo-Saxon neuter of "he"; Good Queen Bess said "hit."

Typical is the casual verbalization of nouns. "I was just funning," explains the practical joker. "Never mind that scrich-owling," I overheard a red-faced man in overalls admonish his woman who was carrying-on how he'd shamed her by some contrary act.

Having gone that far, of course, it is easy to go farther and perform like service for other parts of speech. Grand Ole Opry's Cousin Jody, an elderly baggy-pants comic, showed what can be done with even new-fangled words when he discounted a modern trend in the hillbilly, or country, beat. "Some of these young'uns," he said, "try to play it pretty *cooliefied*. I don't dance much to their music."[20]

Obsolete expressions are common as kindling sticks. "I'd give a pretty penny to learn what happened" is a sample. I have heard that shortened to "I'd give a pretty." The language of the hills tends to be succinct, shying from verbosity while shunning the drab. It is rich and racy, but with a thoroughly homey flavor. A gossip is a "bone-carrier," and a reserved person is said to be "offish." "Likker" is also "giggle-soup"; the dentist is a "tooth-doctor"; The Great Beyond is referred to as "Yonder." When you least need them, here come the *po*-leece.

"A little piece" is a little way and "a far piece" involves more distance; "the far furrin world" is overseas. "Sookie" or "sook cow" is the way one calls cows from the pasture; the "milk gap" is the enclosure where the lacteal fluid is coaxed forth. A "slue" is a lot but a small amount is a "smidgen."

When a thing is very good it may be "right good." The employment of "right" as an intensive adverb was current, according to *Fowler's Modern English Usage,* when the American colonies were founded and was "preserved by the emigrants but forgotten by those they left behind." The one who says "right glad" or "right soon" has

[20] As reported by Larry L. King in "The Grand Ole Opry," *Harper's,* July 1968.

his authorization from the translators of the Psalmist in the Bible: "Then Israel should be right glad" and "O hear me and that right soon."

At the square dance, the participants whirl to the fiddle's tune while the caller chants in singsong

'Possum up a 'simmon tree,
A-shakin 'simmons down,
Grab your partner by the hand
And swing her twice around.

"An old broom knows where the trash is" is a common saying. Others are "It takes a lean horse for a long race," "Give a weed an inch and it will take a yard," "Every cow needs a tail in fly time," "It's a poor dog that won't wag his own tail," and "Fine as fur in the North."

Vocabulary might be limited, but the words are energetic. Emphatic past tenses abound like "hurted," "knowed," and "blowed"—didn't the Bard himself use "blowed" for blown? Some nouns are echoed for strength: "granny-woman," "neighbor-people," "preacher-man," "ham-meat," "rifle-gun," "hound-dog," and "jail-house."

Regularly heard are verbs with Middle English endings, as in "he 'throwen' the ball." But a person taken with a fit "turns fitified"—and that's pure native, as is the remedy for the fitified: "Shave the hair from the armpits, put the hair in a hole in a tree, and stop up the hole."

The "pully-bone" is a wishbone and a "poke" is, among other things, a paper bag. The privy is the "necessary" or "johnny house." A "fish worm" is an earthworm, a "whistle pig" a ground hog, and a bear a "b'ar." A "polecat"—you hear?—is only a skunk under another name.

While to the flatlander more than one of us together are "you-all," to the highlander the word is "you-uns"[21] Whatever he owns is "his'n"—otherwise it is "her'n." And "The War Amongst Us" is how he sometimes refers to the Civil War.

Before the advent of grammatical rules—and grammar as a subject has been studied for little more than a hundred and fifty years—the double negative was in good standing among English speakers. In the Romance languages it still is the rule. The argument that one negative cancels out another, so that two negatives make a positive, is more suited to mathematics than to linguistics. Given the usual exceptions, the contrary is likely to be true where the meaning is at

[21] The insistence on making a vocal plural of you is not confined to the South. "Yous" is general in the Pennsylvania Dutch country and frequently encountered in the Midwest. "Youse" is the choice of Brooklyn.

all clear.[22] It is stronger to say "Clay doesn't take no snuff" than "Clay doesn't take snuff." The first statement could not possibly be construed to mean that Clay masticates the cured leaves of *Nicotiana tabacum*.

Nonetheless, schoolma'rm English frowns on the compound negative as being a vulgarism, reflecting a lack of formal education. Hill people are fairly unaware of this attitude, or if they are, pay it no-never-mind and persist in speaking as folks did in Will Shakespeare's time, innocently or artfully, with many an embellishment of their own.

Your mountaineer uses double negatives as a matter of fact; triple negatives are wielded with almost equal abandon. Moments of stress may see quadruplets and quintuplets birthed on the spot.

"I ain't never had no money" is not only a frank admission of a condition embarrassingly familiar to many of us, but also a fair specimen of the triple negative.

I encountered a septuplet once on State Street in Bristol, Tennessee, or was it Bristol, Virginia? State Street is the dividing line. The berry-picking season was in full swing and everyone from upcountry was in town shopping for mason jars and sugar.

"That rascal Leroy hasn't never done no good for nobody notime nowhere nohow," was what I heard.

It was a rare find, and has rung in my ears ever since. Samuel Johnson would have admired it.

When next you hear "receipt" employed for a recipe, and one negative in hot pursuit of a second or a third, kindly remember that this usage is Standard English as spoken once upon a time by every good man and true.

And for that matter, still is.

Appalachian Rain

Storm had been threatening for hours, and in the steamy quiet were building mountains of thunderheads more massive than the Blue Ridge peaks below. At six o'clock, long before sundown, the ceiling closed in and rain began. There would be no campfire tonight.

Paris Walters sighed deeply from his corner of the forest lean-to at Wiggins Spring on the Appalachian Trail.

"I was brought up all over the South," he said, "and never saw

---

[22] The contemporary double negative, in which a word is de-emphasized, as for example when "important" becomes "not unimportant," has yet to penetrate the hills.

country so wet as this. For several years I've been trying to hike straight through the 70 miles in the Pedlar District, but rain always washes me out. Last September I was stuck in the lean-to at Johns Hollow near the James River for four days while upstairs leaked like a bum faucet. When it finally quit, the trail was a mess of mud, my time was up, and I went home to Delaware."

Paris blew up his air pillow and gave it a thump. A mouse squeaked beneath the wood plank floor on which we had laid our sleeping bags.

Thunder rolled and flashes lit the Virginia woods. A tree, executed by electricity, split and smoked on the hillside. The family of fat muskrats living at the spring a few steps away followed our example and retired early. Most sensible thing to do when a hard storm lashes the trail is to find cover and zip into the sack; it's apt to be too soggy and chilly to do much else. One usually awakens to find the sun ushering in a newly scrubbed day.

But this storm hung on. Rain was still hammering the roof at midnight. Dawn crept in by inches. Trees tossed their fraying canopies against a dismal sky as the wind ripped away boughs and flung them to earth. A flying limb whacked the lean-to with an explosive report. The ground was littered with green leaves and ran with freshets. Paris yelped indignantly when a gust whirled through the shelter's open front and sprayed his possessions.

"We may achieve climate," said O. Henry, "but weather is thrust upon us."

I brought out my Bleuet stove, a European job which burned butane. Sitting up in our sleeping bags, Paris and I drank coffee and watched the elemental carryings-on. I opened my book, but the weak light made reading impossible. It is better to doze than curse the gloom, and we settled back, now and then starting awake to inform one another that he had snored most vilely.

By midafternoon the gale was emitting only random howls. We shrugged into our harnesses, draped ourselves in coated nylon ponchos, and set forth. The ponchos came alive in the gusts and flapped wildly against our legs. A backpacker in his poncho does not present a fashionable appearance—it smacks somehow more of Sam's Surplus than of Abercrombie & Fitch. There is strong resemblance to the Arab robed in his bedsheet djellabah and carrying the camel's load.

We splashed through the brown ooze to a crossroads where a general store dripped forlornly in the scud. Our systems were repaired with jelly glasses of peach wine, a local product reputed to cure dampness. Like things cure like: it is an ancient principle of medicine. The cure completed to our satisfaction, Paris bribed the proprietor's son to drive us to town in his hopped-up sedan. There we sheltered for a day while Nature purged herself and the trail dried.

Moisture is a commodity the Appalachians possess in abundance. The romantic haze that gives the Blue Ridge its adjective is the product of great humidity and plant transpiration. "Mountain smoke," as it's called by hill people, is responsible for the naming of the Great Smokies. A veil of mist enlaces the countryside, softening the crags with a bluish glow, and painting a dark line on the crests.

During spring and summer every green growing thing transpires: a modest bush may cast off a gallon of water daily. In polygamous association of two atoms of hydrogen to each atom of oxygen, the molecules of fluid dance heavenward to swirl with others in visibly growing clouds. Afternoon heat followed by cooling mountain drafts induce a watery climax punctuated by electrical discharges, the exclamation points of the gods. Where paths meander in rhododendron slicks and over rocky domes, the walker picks his way through drifts of fog. Droplets, sparkling like diamond chips, collect on hair and clothing. In berry time the black bears will be out carding the bushes with widespread claws—the fruit is all the sweeter for the dew. As the silent billows unfold, ranges are glimpsed as goblinbook hills, spectres in indigo from somewhere north of the moon.

When hardwood trees shed their foliage and transpiration slows, the view changes dramatically. There are winy fall days when one can see across the Valley of Virginia. There are winter days when the air is crystalline. But vapor will cause nearby mountains to seem farther off than they actually are, and one mile may be misjudged as two or three. An opposite effect is given by the dry, thin air of the trans-Missouri country, where faraway objects appear closer.

Because of such misleading phenomena, treasure seekers and homesteaders from the Appalachian region who flocked to the West in the last century sometimes estimated distances and water availability in a fatal manner. So accustomed to streams, ponds, and frequent rain were the emigrants that they could barely comprehend a land where waterholes might be 40 miles apart. Many journeyed on foot. It seemed to them that the next range of ochre hills would surely harbor a brook or a spring to wet their mouths and cool their feet. But the hills were many miles distant and the water did not run.

On the 130-mile length of the Camino del Diablo (The Devil's Road) Trail on the Arizona-Mexico frontier are buried the earthly remains of from 500 to 1,500 souls—the number is unknown—who perished of thirst while trekking to California during the '49 gold fever. They found the Sonoran Desert deceitful, for thronging the sides of its arroyos are tesota, mesquite, and paloverde trees, some up to four stories tall. It would seem that surface water is plentiful—the reality is that for only a few hours each year does water lie handily on the land. When rain halts, the streams as quickly cease to flow. Giant organ pipe and saguaro cacti are equipped with shallow root systems to instantly absorb moisture before it disappears; the roots of desert trees may probe down 50 feet through porous sand and gravel to hidden pockets of water. In the blaze of the desert, the human need is one gallon a day if resting in the shade, and two or more if moving about. The crackling aridity is as desiccating to human flesh as the heat.

Later parties on the Devil's Road, when not also plagued by parched throats and the screaming urge to push on to the next well, would pause to dig shallow graves for the fallen. On these sites would be placed stones, their arrangement enumerating the nameless dead. Some corpses never were found. Unfortunates would stagger from the thorny pathway in delirium and, expiring, become food for buzzards and ravens. Coyotes gnawed and scattered the bones.

There, on a flat only a few miles from the lifesaving oasis of Quitobaquito, I came upon a mass grave whose stones spelled out the numerals "16." At the sight I thought to check my canteen. It was leaking! The gasket that lined the screw cap had split; with each step a drop of precious liquid escaped. It is humbling to think one's life may depend on such trivia as a penny gasket.

The Sonoran Desert is a territory whose dried parts receive less than two inches of rain a year. Ten inches would be accounted a deluge, and would send the snakes racing to high ground. In contrast, the Appalachian country is bountifully endowed as are few places on earth. On the heights of the southern end of the French Broad Valley in North Carolina more than 100 inches of precipitation have been measured in a single year. Forty to sixty inches are common throughout much of the mountain system. Some of this comes from snow, frost, hail, and dew, but the greater portion descends as rain.

There is less moisture, of course, on the flatlands to either side. But compare the 40-odd inches of annual precipitation at Atlanta, Asheville, Boston, New York, and Quebec with the 18 inches of San Francisco and the 25 inches or less of Paris, London, and Berlin (it takes a lot of California's "liquid sunshine" or English drizzle to deliver an inch of water) and the 12 inches of Denver or the 8 inches of ever-thirsty Los Angeles.

One reason the New York metropolis has periodically had to ration water is that it has succeeded in blocking nature from renewing its supplies.

Most of the area is covered with buildings and paving; this combination forces rain and snow melt to be channeled into storm sewers, then wastefully voided into the salty Atlantic. Were less of the ground sealed over, it could absorb more of the moisture and store it under the surface in aquifers. Pumps then would draw from these natural cisterns. At present, one million acres of land is being superimposed each year in the United States with roads, parking lots, homes, and businesses.

Still, a positive excess of moisture often falls to defy and overcome any works of man.

After savaging the Gulf Coast in August 1969, Hurricane Camille sailed north along the Appalachian Mountains. The witch's 190 to 200 mile an hour winds dropped quickly to ordinary storm levels as they broke against the forests and the obstructions of the land, but her clouds, writhing like Medusa's locks, pushed upward to great altitudes. On the night of the tenth, the bottom dropped out of the sky over the Appalachian Trail where it crosses Tye River Gap in central Virginia: 32 inches of water descended in five hours—a world's record. Slopes of The Priest and Three Ridges, whose apexes overlook the gap 3,000 feet below, were heavily scarred by landslides; the Tye River bed was so choked with dirt, boulders, trees, boards, and broken farm implements that teams of bulldozers labored most of the next spring and summer to clear it. Houses, people, and livestock were swept away and drowned. On Davis Creek, a tributary of the Tye, an entire clan—all 16 of the bloodline together with 8 cousins—was wiped out.

The walker soon learns that when clouds marshal over the eastern mountains they are less likely to march on than to unload their cargo. Lofty elevations, where the Appalachian Trail winds, host far more downpours than lower places. While the traveler on the skyline is being drenched and stabbed at by forks of high energy direct current, the farmer on the valley floor may be mowing in golden sunlight.

Another seminal fact becomes evident: water is wetter in the woods. This statement may seem too happily alliterative to be entirely factual, but it's one with which no plant chemist would quarrel. A jot of firsthand experience shows it to be true. Few of us, however, are chemists and so a slightly scientific explanation may be in order.

Rain striking the leaves and bark of trees dissolves a certain amount of plant matter such as tannin. These compounds break down surface tension, that physical tendency of liquids to resist dispersion. (Detergents do likewise.) Thus the water becomes more penetrating. It has acquired, in short, extra wetting power: two drops can do the work of three. As a practical matter, this means that clothing and footgear are rapidly soaked.

Seven hours of hard rain on an autumn day in Vermont demonstrated the fallibility of my guaranteed waterproof wristwatch. It died when water entered the works. Now I wear a skindiver's watch.

Yet another juicy fact discomfits the hiker. Long after rain has ceased he will continue to enjoy its blessings, even unto excess. Trees drip for hours. Drops collect on leaves and in the chalices of flowers and to touch a branch is to flick the cold water handle in the shower stall and release a cataract down one's neck; the slightest brush against shrub or clump of grass dampens the journey. It is dismaying to take a bath fully clothed and familiarity lessens not the contempt.

Morning dew can be a nuisance, but it does provide excuse to dawdle over coffee at the campfire and not to begin travel until the sun is well up over the forest and drawing the moisture back into the atmosphere. I know how the freshness of early morning beckons the trail disciple; I also know how much dryer may be the walk that starts at seven o'clock instead of at five or six.

"Rain rarely improves a hike," remarked Albert Field, a New York science teacher, upon completing the 2,000-mile trail. Mr. Field learned to take wet weather in stride and didn't bother to count the times the rain came down during his 164 days of hiking. One who did was an experienced backpacker from the West Coast. In a letter fraught with pain he wrote the Appalachian Trail Conference that "it once rained ten days straight" while he was walking from the southern terminus to the Shenandoah. After 29 days and 725 miles he called it finis and returned to less damp country.[23]

The walker needs equipment—boots well lathered with "waterproofing" compound, raingear that covers from head to below the

[23] *Appalachian Trailway News,* May 1967.

knees—or better, to ankles—and perhaps a small tent if backpacking, plus a tolerant, even combative, spirit to cope with rain which is generous, persistent, super-wet, and lingering—the rain that anoints the Appalachian Mountains.

Snaykes

A forgotten book, its pages now mottled with time, once cautioned its readers that "venomous Snaykes and treacherous Indians" abound in the Great Forest of America.

The name of this work does not rise to the surface; what clings to the barb of memory are Snaykes and other Wordes. Their spelling has the flavor of the Elizabethan Age before Dr. Johnson came along to set it right.

Certainly the adventurer in the Great Forest of that era, when printing was an innocent craft still, did well to keep his musket dry and mind where he put his feet. "I was constantly afraid of snakes," wrote André Michaux in the diary he kept while botanizing in the wilds of the Appalachians.

Then a wood mantled the Atlantic Coast inland to beyond the Mississippi "as the grass covered the garden lawn." Since the beachhead at Plymouth Rock, it has been cut and recut, halved in height and extent, burned, and plundered. Even its proud name of the Great Forest of America, given by English travelers, has been lost. It is known only by its remains; today one speaks of the Pisgah or the Jefferson or the Green Mountain Forest.

The Indian of the Great Forest has been reduced as well. His "treacherous" conduct in defending his homeland has been treated with cures to fit the offense.

Yet "venomous Snaykes" still abound. They are fewer now than in the less populous colonial period—an increase in human beings makes for a decrease in Snaykes. Mankind has not left off chastising the Serpent for its deceit as recorded in the Book of Genesis.

So heeded has been the ancient curse that the blacksnakes, the kingsnakes, and others receive the same vengeful heel as the poisonous brotherhood. Yet these snakes are harmless to man. It is the rodent that spoils so much grain which could tell us of their skill; no rat trap invented is more efficient. For all their secret ways it may be they out-mouse the barn cat, which is so punctual at milking time, though often nooning on rooftops instead of watching mice. It has been said that the farmer who kills one of these snakes has torn up a five dollar bill.

Walkers in the Appalachians will see more blacksnakes than any other large species. I have come on many stretched across the trail, drowsing in the shadows of a summer day. As they are slow to take alarm, I am satisfied that it was not a blacksnake which tempted Adam's wife.

More than one kind of snake is black, but the largest and perhaps the commonest is the black rat snake, *Elaphe obsoleta obsoleta*. This is the blacksnake of the Appalachian Mountains. It is as much at home in the altitudes as it is at sea level, and so ranges a considerable territory. At maturity it is typically plain black with a white or cream chin and throat, thick-bodied, 3½ to 6 feet in length, and an agile climber. A few have been taken that were 8 feet long. No larger harmless snake is found in eastern North America save the indigo of the extreme south.

The blacksnake "glides and glitters and slides" and is apt to show temper if cornered or handled.

It may rear upward, hiss, and strike boldly. The bites are no more serious to a man than so many scratches. When excited, the tip of its tail vibrates like a coloratura's larnyx. It lacks "rings," however, and so in itself is noiseless, though in dry brush the agitation can produce a whir similar to a locust's.

I have picked up several on the end of my walking stick. At first they show curiosity, twining upon themselves, flicking black tongues, and looking about. But in short order they turn restless, eye the ground in longing, and try to slip away. If the stick is not lowered the snake will glide to the ground by way of one's arm and leg. The sensation is mildly electric.

While an asset to any farmer's granary, the black rat snake seldom makes a gentle pet, remaining feral and unreliable in temper. It has been descried peering from the hollows of rough-barked trees where it sometimes makes a home. Hill people commonly call it the mountain, or pilot, blacksnake.

The name of "pilot" comes from its supposed habit of guiding rattlesnakes to their prey. Origin of this addition to the folklore of reptiles is attributed to Cotton Mather, an eighteenth-century divine and authority on witchcraft in Boston. The Reverend Mather described how a timber rattler sank its fangs in the wooden tongue of his buggy. When the tongue began to swell from the poison, Mather hurried to save the buggy by uncoupling it.[24] Crafty rattlers bit his cherry tree and the poor robins that ate its fruit were gulped as they fell lifeless. Anno Domini 1714 was not a very good year in Old

[24] Mather's tale has made its rounds. A hill farmer in West Virginia counted his blessings when his hay wagon was similarly attacked, for presently there were two wagons where only one had stood before.

Boston town. (In his 65 years of life, Mather left fewer thoughts unsaid than probably any American before or since. He mounted the pulpit at age 17, married three times, delivered countless sermons of great length and vivacity, and penned an estimated 470—470!—books, none of them conscious fiction, although a number are of interest to psychopathologists. The truth is stranger than even Mather's natural history, for he was one of the strangest men ever to live in the Appalachian region.)

Explorers in the Great Forest marveled to come upon a serpent that danced an evil jig to the tune of a musical tail. The story caused jeering among the solid types back home, but painful experience made the truth evident. Soon Englishmen were talking of the "rattlesnake" while Spaniards spoke of the "cascabel," or jingle bell.

The jingling of the cascabel is a sound to which—then as now—the walker in the Great Forest becomes quickly attuned. On hearing its notes he is apt to raise his hair and spring into a jig of his own.

Only the rattler is equipped with rings on its tail to give the alarm. It is an instrument of displeasure unique in the animal kingdom. The rattlesnake is native to the Americas and unknown to other lands; some 30 species have been found from southern Canada to northern Argentina. Seven kinds are recognized in the United States east of the Mississippi.[25] They are the timber, canebrake, diamondback, massasauga or "swamp rattler," and three types of pygmy rattlesnakes. All live in low country, but the timber rattler flourishes in the highlands as well. It is, in fact, the only rattler that will be seen coiled on Appalachian mountain trails.

This heavy-bodied creature ranges the woods of eastern United States and southernmost Ontario; the "timber" in its name comes from a preference for forested terrain.[26] It usually measures three to five feet from appetite end to alarm (one captive was taped at six feet two inches). Basic coloring is brown to black or even lavender—and sometimes a startling yellow, like a traffic caution sign. Dark V-shaped crossbands have caused it to be termed the banded rattler and often to be mistaken for the diamondback. No matter what its tinge—and black is the commonest—a sullen and defiant attitude leaves no doubt as to identity. While it is said not to be aggressive toward humans, even when attacked, it is slow to retreat and may boldly hold ground. Zoologists know it as *Crotalus horridus horridus*

[25] Not among them, fortunately, is *Crotalus durissus terrificus* of South America. The scientific Latin name echoes its reputation as the deadliest rattler. Not every person lives out the day on which he feels its sting.

[26] The timber rattler is not to be found in the West, although several western rattlers are mistakenly called that by those who cannot think of another name.

—clearly a beast to reckon with. (The redundancy of the name shows what can be done with a little Latin.)

The rattlesnake pit is a southern Appalachian institution. It is typically an adjunct to a family-operated grocery or filling station in the countryside. The snakemaster may be the owner, his wife, an elder son, a fearless daughter, or a diffident attendant. Off to one side, apart from cases of soft drinks and tangled coils of air and water hoses, is a pit formed of concrete. The sides are vertical and smooth: no captive will scale this arena to lash the audience as once did a troop of gladiators in the Circus at Rome. There is a fence to keep customers from inadvertently thickening the plot.

The snakemaster appears, flicking his pant leg with a bamboo cane. He offers a few remarks on the hellish nature of rattlers, and proves them by stirring in the pit with his cane. Eight or nine snakes contort into fighting posture. Tongues quiver from broad, flattened heads; ever-open eyes, pupils elliptical in daylight like felines and foxes, stare coldly. Tails cock upright and blur in motion. A noisy clattering rises from the enclosure.

From his pocket, the snakemaster draws a toy balloon. He inflates it, ties the neck, and sets it loose. As the balloon floats down, a pair of rattlers unwind; their bodies stretch up against the walls to resemble arrows standing on end. They strike—for a moment, no longer than the flash of a stroboscope, jaws gape and twin fangs spurt droplets of yellowish venom. Onlookers start nervously as the balloon pops and flutters onto the floor of the pit. The rattlers subside while the snakemaster collects 25-cent pieces. A faint musky odor, like a cantaloupe's, lingers in the air.

Unless clipped by a mowing machine or the man with a hoe, the rattler's short, blunt tail is fitted with horny segments, or loosely interlocking rings, which click as the tail is shaken from side-to-side. When mildly disturbed, a single click or two may be all that is produced. Anger or anxiety gives rise to a passionate clatter averaging 48 cycles a second. This is double the cycling of television frames and nearly that of alternating current.

I have never heard a rattlesnake hiss, but Laurence M. Klauber the herpetologist, author of *Rattlesnakes: Their Habits, Life Histories, and Influence on Mankind,* states that the hiss is its secondary warning, often uttered at the same time as the rattle.

Rattling is not automatic, but controlled, and indicates only that the snake is alarmed—and only to that extent would the warning precede a bite. The rattler about to strike a sparrow is not so foolish as to give away its intentions. And the individual that is stepped on will not think first to buzz and second to bite.

These snakes start life with a button on the tail, and add a ring with each change of skin. Rings often break off. The individual with 15 of them is seldom encountered, no matter how old it may be. Contrary to popular belief, the number of rings flaunted is (unlike a dowager's) no accurate index to age; it does indicate whether meals have been regular, since a well-fed snake discards its skin frequently. This may be two or several times a year—or none if times are hard. Whether shedding occurs because a snake is hidebound and outgrows the skin or merely outwears it in friction with the ground is matter for dispute. The new skin, which is bright and shiny, develops fully before the old, thin sheath is snagged on bushes and pulled off inside out.

Rattlers are pit vipers, and between cat-eye and nostril on each side of their broad heads is the loreal depression, or "pit." This is a temperature-sensing organ that enables the rattler both to detect warm-blooded prey in dark places and to more accurately direct its strike.[27] (If you are close enough to see the pits you are too close.)

Snakes breathe through their nostrils but smell (and perhaps taste) by means of their tongues. In the roof of a snake's mouth are two cavities termed Jacobson's organs. The tips of its long, bifurcated tongue touch these organs for analysis of minute odor particles gathered out of the air or from the ground or any interesting object.

The Appalachian Trail winds through snake country for most of its route. Only in northern New England does the possibility of sighting a poisonous reptile become remote. In addition to the rattler, one other species bearing venom will be met with in the mountains—the copperhead.[28]

I have met more copperheads on the trail than I have rattlers. The

---

[27] Vipers are of two kinds, pit vipers and pitless vipers. The pitless viper is called the true viper or adder. All the New World vipers are pit vipers. Western Europe and Africa have only pitless vipers while Eurasia has both.

The Sidewinder missile, which guides itself to target by means of a heat-sensitive device that picks up the hot exhaust of enemy aircraft, is named after the desert-dwelling sidewinder rattlesnake of notorious repute.

[28] Four dangerous species of snakes exist in the United States, the other two being the cottonmouth, or water moccasin, and the coral.

The natural abode of the cottonmouth and the coral is the flatlands, and no farther north in the Appalachian region than the Dismal Swamp of the southern Virginia coast. The cottonmouth, rattler, and copperhead are pit vipers; the coral, which is related to the cobras, is at once the smallest, the least likely to bite, and the most virulent. Five or six others, such as the crown snake of the Southeast, also subdue quarry with venom. Their bite, however, offers little danger to humans.

Canada's only poisonous snake is the rattler.

crevices of the low walls of piled rock bordering the Blue Ridge Parkway are favorite lurking places. Indian summer days find them basking on warm rocks and old stumps.

Copperhead identification is simple and unmistakable: the top of the head is richly copper or brown in hue—no other snake on the continent is so colored. The body is marked in an hourglass pattern. Its business end has the flat arrowhead, or wedge-shape, of the pit viper. Although lacking the rattler's rings, the tail vibrates in the presence of danger, making a buzz if among fallen leaves, as if to toll:

> the knell that summons thee to heaven or to hell

The secretions of the copperhead are, however, only a fraction as potent as the rattler's. It is the least poisonous of pit vipers. Besides, it is a lesser snake, usually growing to but 2½ feet, with 4½ feet the record. As a general rule, the smaller the snake the smaller the injection. Nearly 2,900 Americans are bitten by copperheads in an average year; rarely is a death reported.

Unlike the rattler, which is partial to dry, grassy, or brushy situations, caves and ledges, the copperhead prefers to hunt in damp places near springs and along watercourses. The rattler generally avoids human dwellings, but swarms of the more gregarious copperheads live snugly in the fissures of stone wells and quarries and beneath the floors and within the loose board walls of cabins, barns, and sheds. Numbers flourish in old cellars and outhouses of such populous cities as Baltimore and Washington, D.C.

Normally the copperhead is pacific, almost lethargic, and quick to run away. Yet it has a feisty reputation—one well deserved, I think. More than one has made vigorous feints in my direction from 20 or 30 feet off—hopelessly out of range. As if knowing that its poison is not so lethal as those of its relatives in viperhood, the copperhead may hit the same target repeatedly, striking with the manic rhythm of a boxer punching the bag. It may well be the fastest snake in the East, perhaps quicker on the draw than the rattler.

Of the three subspecies of copperheads in the United States, only the Northern copperhead, *Agkistrodon contortix mokeson*, lives along the Appalachian Trail. Its markings distinguish it as the most handsome of the lot.

No other family of snakes boasts the rapid-fire action of vipers: an uncoiling, jab, and recoiling so rapid, silent, and painless of fang that many a victim could not believe his bad luck till he saw the wounds and the bane began to heat his veins. The strike—given in one study as consuming the twelfth part of a second, but doubtless varying according to temperature, species, and mood—is not the streak of lightning it has been compared to; high-speed photography shows the average man's punch to be faster. But it is fast enough. In contrast, the strike of cobras and their ilk is sufficiently slow (barely one sixth as quick) that an alert and agile person may dodge it, and live to dodge another day. Snake charmers performing in the bazaars of the Orient often pat a cobra on the head in the middle of its thrust.

Snakes ordinarily strike no more than one-third to one-half of their length: however, an incensed rattler may go all out, so to speak, lunging a distance equal to or a little exceeding its length and actually leaving the ground in so doing.

I read one account of a rattler "about 30 inches long" that sprang clear across a 5½ foot wide trail. It was not rattling and "what made it jump none of us knew," said the writer, adding that it "looked like a loosely coiled rope being tossed across."[29] Of course, jumping isn't striking.

The celebrated viperine armament consists of twin glistening white fangs (which could be compared to pearls if only their owners were more desirable) up to an inch or more in length, curved and pointed like scimitars. These modified teeth are hinged and folded against the roof of the mouth, but swing down before and retract after each strike in unison. They are hollow, pumping and injecting serum exactly like hypodermic needles, which they in fact are. Jaws open 180° to bite. Two drops of rattler toxin are enough to cause a severe reaction in an adult person; four drops can kill.

Corals and related cobra types literally grind venom into the flesh. On biting, the coral does not immediately withdraw, but holds fast, gnawing in order to effect the toxic transfer. The poison is exuded through short, rigid fangs. Delivering venom is the only use of fangs. The teeth of nonpoisonous species may assist in holding struggling prey. No snake chews food, but swallows it whole and alive.

In the mountains it is unwritten law that every rattler and copperhead be executed on the spot. Inoffensive snakes are likely to meet with similar fate from gunshot, caning, or stoning. There probably is no hill family living south of the Mason-Dixon Line that has not had one of its members punctured by a pit viper. News of snakes is a

[29] Fred Rynerson, *Exploring and Mining for Gems and Gold in the West* (Healdsburg, Calif.: Naturegraph Company, 1967).

topic as absorbing as Holy Writ and the raids of revenue agents. Between friends meeting on the road it generally takes precedence in the order of business to be discussed.

"Hey there, Clyde, what do you say? Have you come across any snakes lately?"

"Hel-l-l yes, Horace. I got two copperheads sneaking round the spring house last week, but another of the rascals got away."

"I'm always sorry to hear of any snakes getting away, Clyde. It's happened to me and I know it is something that can't always be helped. Did you see the yellow rattler hide that Old Man Jenks has nailed to his gate?"

"How many snakes did you kill?" is the standard question put to the trail walker by mountain men. An overalled farmer tilling tobacco on a North Carolina hillside showed me a hand and ankle scarred from bites by copperheads. He was still astonished at the reply he received on asking the famous Mrs. Emma (Walking Grandma) Gatewood if she had killed many snakes with her umbrella.

"Now why should I kill a snake?" Walking Grandma retorted. "None has ever tried to kill me!" And with that she had marched off, on her way to finish the Appalachian Trail for the third time.

Nearly all attacks by snakes on humans take place in the warm months after they have left their winter dens and are "running." A "running" snake is one that has his mind on perpetuation of the species. He is exceptionally active and quick to take offense. Irritability is also pronounced during the brief period when old skin is being exchanged for new and eyesight is obscured in the process.

Pit vipers will strike from any position, coiled or not, whether on land or water or even under water. All are able swimmers and may be spied coiled and floating on still ponds.

Deliberately aggressive individuals are not unknown, but the timber rattler for the most part is mild-mannered and not likely to make a pass at a man unless it feels threatened, as by footsteps or hands near or on it. Your woodsman crosses fallen trees with eyes open, since snakes may lurk in ambush for mice and toads in the shadows. And the fellow who crawls under deadfalls without a pause to reconnoiter, is tempting Providence. Those who approach rattlers too closely are bitten not for food—no venomous snake has been known to eat human flesh—but in self-defense.

It is rarely that one hears of a snake entering a sleeping bag. The warmth of the sleeper would be attractive to a cold snake.

Ben Lilly, the compulsive hunter from Alabama, who spent most of the nights of his long life sleeping in the open on the ground, had a recipe for handling such occurrences. He would wait motionlessly till the rattler settled itself and was fast asleep. Then, giving one mighty bound, Ben Lilly would leap from his blankets.

I can testify to how soundly the rattler can sleep. Snakes are normally sensitive to ground tremors, fearing any encounter with larger animals that may trample or otherwise harm them. Deer, burros, and pigs will sometimes go out of their way to jump on rattlers. When walking overgrown trails, a good method of warning off Brother Buzztail is to thump the ground with a stick. But don't count on it! I have come upon rattlers wound up like clock springs in the middle of the way and so slumberous that they came to life only after I stamped about like an Apache in a Left Bank boîte.

A snake's eyes do not shut; though always wide open, they see nothing when the snake is sleeping.

The individual who appoints himself snake-killer should exercise his duties with caution. While vacationing at Skyland Lodge in the Shenandoah years ago, an elderly man and his daughter saw a timber rattler alongside the footpath. The daughter felt the chill that most daughters of Eve feel at sight of the serpent, but failed to dissuade her father from trying to kill the now alarmed and rattling animal. Picking up a dead branch, he struck with all his might. The branch was rotten. It snapped and he fell onto the pulsing coils. The old gentleman was a lifelong teetotaler; on this occasion he forgot his pledge—it was a day when whiskey was the remedy for snakebite. That evening his maker called. Awestruck guests said the end came peacefully, but whether it owed most to the bite of the rattler, the dosage of high proof "mountain dew," or the excitement is a moot point.

> But beware the false footstep—the stumble that brings
> A deadlier lash than the overseer swings.
> Bret Harte, "The Copperhead"

In any event, the walker in meadow or woods is seen by far more snakes than he sees. "They are simply content to let you pass, or they silently crawl away," says James Oliver, Curator of Reptiles at the Bronx Zoo. Seeing snakes requires a more sober grip on the faculties than commonly supposed.

Being cold-blooded, they are dependent for body warmth and cooling upon outside sources, chiefly sun and shade, warm and cool ground, dry or humid sites. They are unable to cope with extremes of temperature. One hundred degrees Fahrenheit at ground level will prove fatal to most snakes within a few minutes. On hot days they keep to the shade, out of the direct rays of the sun, and on chilly days bask in sunny locations protected from wind; cold winters find them hibernating below frost level from late fall to spring. Biologists call this behavioral temperature control.

They are most active when the spirit level is registering between 75°F. and 85°F.; 80°F. is just right. When it sinks below 55°F. or rises above 100°F., terrestrial snakes go underground. So scientists say—but scientific observations are usually made under controlled conditions. The snake in the grass might respond differently from the snake in the zoo. I have seen three or four snakes abroad when the temperature was in the neighborhood of 45°F., not far from freezing. Admittedly, a 45°F. snake is torpid and a sluggard compared to the one with 80°F. blood racing beneath its scales. But I shouldn't care to test its reaction if stepped on.

Snakes spend much of their time underground or in niches where radiation hardly penetrates. They will certainly be around after the atom bomb or some biologic weapon has removed man to the very periphery of life.

No doubt Nature will carry on, and very well, too, without our presence—or even "that lovely creature called 'I'." From the point of view of a snake that would be Eden.

It is possible for snakes to go months without food, outwardly indifferent to hunger as a yogi. Yet when food is abundant they may turn as greedy as Crassus. Zoo keepers have remarked on the capacity of their charges in swallowing prey, one after the other, for almost as long as the supply holds out. A captive kingsnake 38 inches long engulfed an 8-inch brown snake, a 15-inch glass lizard and a 40-inch cornsnake, all in one day! A hog is no glutton alongside a famished snake, whose elastic throat and digestive plumbing easily accommodate animals greater in length or diameter than their own bodies. Klauber once fed 30 tree frogs to a "moderate-sized two-striped garter snake" which tucked them away "as rapidly as they were handed in." Keeping in mind that a "moderate-sized two-striped garter snake" will measure two or two and a half feet in length and each tree frog about one to two inches, it would seem here was a serpent that not for long would have to endure its moderate description.

Fasting for long periods is no hardship. Metabolism is low and most snakes pass rather indolent lives. Since they are cold-blooded, food goes almost solely for nourishment, very little being spent for body heating. In contrast, warm-blooded creatures must expend considerable fuel to maintain temperature.

Ways of killing vary. The racer corners a mouse or rabbit in its burrow and with a loop of the body presses down till it is suffocated. The black rat snake constricts birds and rodents in its strong coils, applying pressure to stop the victim's breathing. The small and gentle green, or "grass," snake gulps spiders and insects, while the larger garter, or "garden," snake gobbles slugs, earthworms, and salamanders. (Green and garter snakes are common in the mountains.)

Pit vipers administer the quietus with poison, but are not above a constricting squeeze now and again, or simply bolting a live and kicking frog.

To see a rattler killing a rat is instructive, if not edifying. The snake jabs and recoils. The rat jumps straight up and falls back in convulsions. Death follows in a few seconds. It is probably so numbed by the massive injection that no pain is felt. After a short wait to make certain the rat is dead and harmless, the rattler unwinds and approaches to begin its meal. Eating is accomplished by swallowing the victim whole, usually head first.

A belief, fixed as gospel among hill people, is that hogs are immune to copperhead and rattler venoms. Bitten swine ordinarily evince no symptoms other than squeals of rage at what for most animals would be a terminal experience, and go on to slash the snake to ribbons with their hooves. The hog's thick layer of fat with its scanty network of blood vessels retards circulation of the toxin. But a hog that is struck in an artery will drop dead.

Other things being equal, the fat man stands a better chance against a poisonous dose than does the stringbean lacking a protective girdle of lard. Jack Sprat's wife will forever have more in the pinch than Jack.

Having neither eardrums nor middle ears, snakes apparently cannot hear airborne noise. Though ranking among the most high-strung of creatures, gunfire and piercing bugle calls near them produce not the least reaction. Sonic booms leave a snake unperturbed. The cobra hears not the charmer's flute—it sways to follow his moving torso. Rattlers do not hear their rattles; the lively tattoo expresses anxiety or rage and the warning is incidental.

That a rattler may sound the tocsin in a tetanic spasm is attested to by the naturalist Arnoldo Krumm-Heller in his learned monograph for *Kosmos* entitled "Die Feinde der Klapperschlange." In Mexico he saw a spider on a branch observing a rattlesnake that appeared to be dozing on the ground below.

"Suddenly it darted all the way down on its thread, bit the snake on the head, and then climbed as rapidly as before up to the branch. The snake for a while remained quiet, but then became very restless, writhing from side to side and rattling with all its might until it became paralyzed from the quick action of the poison injected by the spider. The rattling of this snake grew gradually weaker, its movements much slower and in less than a minute it was dead."[30]

Other spiders may kill small snakes by first trapping them in their webs, then stinging. Hawks, owls, wild turkeys, and many birds are not averse to dining on snake flesh; neither are other snakes, fish, cats, swine, coyotes, and some people. The handsomely pigmented kingsnakes are unaffected by the bite of rattlers, which they often kill and devour, the venom adding a peppery fillip to the repast. Given a whiff of kingsnake scent, zoo rattlers snap into the fighting coil.

Although rattlers do not prey on their own kind they can be killed by injections of their own venom. (Cobras seem immune to snake poisons.) Freak two-headed snakes in captivity have been known to attack each other, thus dooming their collective self. One head to a family is quite enough.

Never having been invited to a collation of snake, I cannot vouch for its taste. A friend who attended the annual Rattlesnake Roundup & Barbecue in Okeene, Oklahoma, swears that the meat of grilled rattler is white and sweet—rather like veal or shrimp—and tender. It is as easy to peel, he said, and "almost as boneless as a banana." He ate his *klapperschlange* on a bun with lettuce, tomato, and red pepper sauce.

The reptile has a negative emotional impact greater than that of any other creature. Vice, heresy, pernicious wisdom, envy, the demonic impulse—all are imputed to it. No wonder that morbid fear of serpents is a common affliction. It has an uncommonly long name. Ophidiophobia, say the doctors, is what ails the snake-shy.

The first American Navy jack depicted a rattlesnake, very handsomely ringed, and the legend DONT TREAD ON ME; it became a famous banner of the War for Independence and has been reproduced on a postage stamp. As early as 1751 infuriated colonists had suggested turning loose live rattlers on oppressive British officials. When the Revolution succeeded, Benjamin Franklin in 1782 commissioned a medal to signalize the triumph. It showed Liberty fending a raging lion (King George III) while an infant (the new Republic) strangles two snakes dispatched to kill him (the British armies defeated at Saratoga and Yorktown). Franklin pointedly sent the medal to all the crowned heads of Europe.

During the Civil War northerners referred to their own kind who

[30] *Kosmos*, v. 7, p. 417 (1910) as cited in *Animal Wonder World: A Chronicle of the Unusual in Nature*, by Frank W. Lane, copyright 1951, Sheridan House, New York.

sympathized with the Confederacy as "copperheads." Southerners who found good in the Union cause were "snakes" (types unspecified) to their neighbors.

Serpent worship was probably as universal as the plague in olden times. Vestiges of it persist today in corners of Appalachia, where religious oddities enjoy considerable tolerance.

In the 1940s newspaper accounts told of ecstatic rites at the Dolley Pond Church of God with Signs Following. The little Tennessee congregation held aloft live snakes, the sinuous bodies flowing through their hands like streams of healing water. Had not the Gospel according to Mark 16:17–18 promised "signs shall follow them that believe . . . they shall take up serpents . . . they shall lay hands upon the sick, and they shall get well?" In 1955, Evangelist George Went Hensley of Grasshopper Valley was bitten by a rattler he was handling, sickened, refused medical attention, and died.

"On Springfield Mountain" probably is the earliest of the original American lays, and is sung by folk singers to this day. It commemorates the "fatal axsident" of Timothy Mirick, 23, on August 7, 1761, at Wilbraham, Massachusetts.

> One Friday morning he did go
> Into the meadow for to mow
> A round or two and he did feel
> A pisin sarpent at his heel.

"Within two or three ours," continues the ballad, the bite of the "Ratel Snake" laid Timothy Mirick "dead as a stone upon the ground."

Should you publicly accuse a citizen of these United States of being a "snake" or a "viper" you may find yourself charged with libel if the incautious word was committed to writing, or slander if cast to the air. The courts have held that the allegation must be proved literally by the one who uttered it—the moral judgment factor is not taken into account. It has so far been impossible, even for the most circumlocutory lawyer, to convince judge and jury that any human being has, per se, the physical form of a snake; both are vertebrates, but apart from such generalities proof begins to falter. Nonetheless, if it can be shown that the plaintiff is an individual whose reputation, like Hitler's, is already so miserable that it is incapable of being damaged further, the epithet dropper will come home free of penalty.

In national parks, such as Shenandoah and Great Smoky Mountains, which are legal sanctuaries for all wild things, the wanton killing of an animal is punishable by a fine of up to $500 or up to six months in the lockup. The law is not enforced in the case of per-ilous snakes.

Copperheads and rattlers are fond of mice, birds, and frogs. Because of constant appetite for large insects and rodents, snakes play an unquestioned part in man's economy. They add their bit to stream pollution control by eating dead and diseased fish. All are predatory and exclusively carnivorous. There is not a vegetarian in the lot: the farmer's corn is safe from snakes.

Economic justification of the toxic species is seldom advanced—as if one can fairly use such a term as "economic" in judging wild-life. On certain islands, including Iceland, New Zealand, Bermuda, and Ireland, there are no snakes; other localities, as Alaska, Mada-gascar, Puerto Rico, and Cuba, have no venomous types. Hawaii was a paradise without snakes before a few imported specimens escaped from their owners (and they may yet be exterminated through natural causes). These places appear to get along well without snakes. The many roles the animals fill in Nature's scheme have yet to be fathomed; the mystery is no reason for their indiscriminate slaughter.

The late J. Frank Dobie, who gave up wrangling cows in Texas for corralling words, said in *Rattlesnakes*[31] that he himself had slain "hundreds of rattlesnakes," but "the next one I meet I think I shall tell how much I appreciate him. There are legions of morons driving around in automobiles over the country more dangerous and less interesting. Why should I pick on rattlesnakes?"

Snake oil seems outlandish now, yet until the early 1940s was peddled at fairs and on street corners by itinerant "medicine men" and for millenia has been considered a treatment for rheumatism, sore throat, and toothache. After all, who has ever seen a snake bothered with stiff joints, difficulty in swallowing, or caries? Medical science is taking a long look (the pun is unintentional) at snakes. Venom is being researched for use in cancer, hemophilia, polio, nerve disorders, and inhibiting tissue rejection. The caduceus, or Hermes' wand of two snakes intertwined on a winged staff, is the symbol of medicine today—and now you know why the doctor's bill stings.

Because a rattler is dead does not mean it has lost its cussedness. The jaws of a completely severed head can snap shut on the finger or toe of an unwary person, injecting the venom it failed to deliver when alive. Reptilian muscles retain the power of reflex for some time after death. The reflex is mindless, but dangerous as mindless things often are.

Venom is not produced as freely as saliva. The provident snake

[31] J. Frank Dobie, *Rattlesnakes* (Boston: Little Brown and Company, 1965).

conserves its ammunition: supply is limited and after several strikes may run dry, not to be renewed for hours or perhaps a day.

Rattlers in a hurry have been timed crawling at three miles an hour, which may sometimes be faster than a man could walk over rough terrain. An adult, however, can easily outrun any snake. So far as is known, rattlers do not migrate, but live in the neighborhood of their birth. They are born about two months after mating, ready to hunt with poison glands and tiny fangs. Snaklings receive neither affection nor training from their parents and shift for themselves from the moment of birth.

For reasons of His own the Almighty has provided the male snake with not one, but two sets of generative organs. As befits a dignified reptile, he employs only one at a time. To distinguish a male from a female is not a matter for the timid. There already is an easy way, but what it is snakes aren't telling.

The Rev. Cotton Mather was not the only American colonial whose observations of reptiles owed little to the scientific method. John Brickell in his *The Natural History of North Carolina,* printed in 1737, has left us another observation to ponder.

He says (first taking a deep breath) that "Tortoises are mortal Enemys to the Rattlesnakes, killing them wherever they meet, which they do by catching the Snake a little below the Neck, and so draw his head into their Shell, which makes the Snake beat his tail, and twist about with all the strength and violence imaginable to get away, but the Terebin soon dispatches him by pressing him to Death between his Shells, and there leaves him."

The full story of Appalachia's pit vipers is too long to detail here, though they have been responsible for many sudden conversions to Christianity. In passing it should be mentioned that the titles of largest snake and most venomous rattler in North America are held by the eastern diamondback.[32] It also is the largest of all rattlers and perhaps the heaviest of all poisonous snakes, though the king cobra of Asia grows much longer. Diamondbacks have very thick bodies and commonly are 5 feet in length. Oldsters attaining 8 feet have been taken; an 11-footer with a body "larger than a man's thigh" was once reported killed in Florida. This diamond-patterned snake makes its home in flat country and has a liking for bushy tangles and palmetto scrub—it will not be encountered in the highlands.

The South is snake territory, *per se.* Of the estimated 6,500 to 7,000 people lashed by venomous snakes each year in the nation, 37 percent

---

[32] The western diamondback ("coontail rattler") of the arid Southwest is more numerous, more irascible, and bites more people.

are from the nine states of the southern Appalachians and the District of Columbia. Every twelve months in North Carolina alone some 800 persons feel the viper's needle. Statistics often are dreary things, but there is a certain dread fascination in those dealing with the involvement of serpents with mankind.

Georgia counts over 500 cases annually; Virginia, West Virginia, South Carolina, and Alabama about 200 each; Kentucky almost 150; Tennessee approximately 75; and Maryland 40. The nation's capital averages 5 cases.

In contrast, the northern Appalachian states have relatively small incidence of snakebite—less than 150 cases a year, or only two percent of the nationwide total. Pennsylvania records about 75, New York 35, New Jersey 25, Connecticut 4, Massachusetts 2, New Hampshire 1, Vermont 1 in three years, and Maine none in recent years.

It is, sadly, no "Texas brag" that the Lone Star State reports 1,400 casualties yearly. Florida, Arkansas, and Louisiana each register over 300; Mississippi, Missouri, Oklahoma, and California more than 200 each; Arizona and Kansas 100 each.

While Texas has the greatest number of victims, it is North Carolina that, in proportion to population, has the distinction of being the state in which you are most likely to be fanged. Arkansas comes second in this regard, then Texas, followed by Georgia, West Virginia, Mississippi, and Louisiana.

The United States Public Health Service notes that 15 people die of snakebite in the average year. The rattler accounts for perhaps a dozen fatalities, and the cottonmouth and the coral one or two apiece. Death from copperhead bite is rare.

Rattlers injure approximately 3,000 humans each year—more than any of the three other toxic snakes. Close behind is the copperhead with 2,900 victims. The cottonmouth is blamed for 750 and the coral for about 20.

Agricultural workers are most likely to be stung. Remarkably few hunters and fishermen are attacked—about 350 a year. No figures have been compiled on hikers, but almost certainly they would be low. The hiker watches his feet.

Dr. Clifford C. Snyder, a Salt Lake City surgeon, is an authority on the treatment of snakebite. He advises the stricken person to contact a man of medicine without delay and meantime to keep his cool. Uncontrolled fright may lead to shock; individuals nibbled by innocuous grass snakes have keeled over from panic. In any event, almost no one stung by a copperhead dies and only one of every 250 American rattlesnake victims becomes a candidate for the undertaker, though most are pretty sick for a few hours and frequently for days. According to statistics, the person who is bitten by a black widow spider is six times more likely to depart this life than if wounded by a rattler.

Dr. Snyder's next suggestion is to make a flat tourniquet from belt, handkerchief, shirt sleeve, or even adhesive tape and place it between the heart and the wound, preferably a couple of inches above the fang marks. (It's assumed that a bite of the face will not be followed by a tourniquet on the neck!) The tourniquet should be tied so loosely that a finger can easily be inserted between it and the flesh. It may be left in place for an hour without harm—providing it is loose. The band should be loosened slowly as otherwise a surging uptake of venom may result; this could be worse than no tourniquet at all.

Apply antiseptic to the bites and with a knife or scalpel (first sterilizing the blade in flame) carefully make a single tiny, very shallow incision at each puncture. Cut up and down, rather than crosswise, in order to avoid severing a vein, artery, or nerve. And cut only through skin and fat; do not slice into muscle, tendon, or bone. Fangs seldom penetrate below the subcutaneous tissues, but it is better not to cut than to cut improperly, especially if fingers or toes are involved. With thumb and forefinger gently press out the venom. Continue pressing for at least an hour, or till medical help is at hand.

The ordinary snakebite kit doesn't get high marks from Dr. Snyder. He believes that knowing fingers will do a better—and gentler—job of squeezing out venom than any suction device, and with less damage to flesh.

But he does think highly of the antivenin kit. This contains a hypodermic needle and serum to neutralize the poison. The serum is readily available in dry form that will keep for five years without refrigeration. Antivenin is not an inoculation, but an actual cure.

Mouth suction, except for emergency cases where the bite is in a difficult location, is discouraged today since the human mouth is so germ-laden that were it to clamp on a rattler the snake might well expire from infection more virulent than its poison. The procedure is, however, fairly free of peril to the person applying the suction. It is an excellent way of determining one's true friends, especially if the bite is on an undistinguished part of the anatomy.

Most important monition of all is to not move around after a bite: the slower the progress of the harmful substance, the easier it can be handled by the body. Since exertion increases flow of blood and lymph, it must be kept to a minimum whether or not assistance is forthcoming. When snake-poisoned, the Indian of the Great Forest would promptly wrap up in his blanket and lie immobile for the passage of two or three

Photo by Art Smith

Towpath along the old C & O Canal, Maryland.
Timber rattlesnake (*Crotalus horridus horridus*) on trail near
    Hawksbill Gap, Shenandoah National Park, Virginia.

Photo by Garnett W. Martin

Photo by Elmer L. Ons

Footbridge over Laurel Fork, Tennessee.

suns. The method should be seriously considered today by the walker who finds himself bitten and miles from a phone.

Reptilian venoms defy exact analysis, but contain similar elements of destruction in varying proportions and intensity. Coral poison is chiefly neurotoxic, affecting the nervous system to bring on paralysis of heart and lungs; that of rattlers, cottonmouths, and copperheads is mainly hemotoxic and hemorrhagic, and breaks down the blood.

Severe burning pain immediately follows the jab of a pit viper, though occasionally all that is felt is a numbness spreading from the site of the bite. (A coral's bite may not produce any symptoms till hours have passed.) The majority of bites are on the ankle. If a fang injects its toxin into a vein there will be instant circulation, and all may be over within moments; however, such bites are very rare.

Now and then no distress is experienced. In this happy event, the snake for some reason probably did not release any poison or, what is more probable, was a nontoxic and harmless species.

Viperine poison dissolves red blood corpuscles, inhibiting coagulation, and breaks down blood vessels, especially the thread-like capillaries. The now watery blood oozes through the surrounding tissues and the victim, with blood trickling from nostrils and discoloring patches of flesh, appears to have suffered a severe beating. Nausea, faintness, a profuse cold perspiration, drooling, and bloody diarrhea are common. In addition there may be such swelling as to choke off flow of blood at the site of the bite, making gangrene and loss of flesh a possibility. While few deaths occur nationwide, a number of persons every year suffer permanent disfigurement, crippling, or even amputation of a limb. Much of this results from mistreatment of the bite, as deep cutting, failure to sterilize the cutting instrument or to use an antiseptic on the wounds, and too tight a tourniquet.

In the case of poisonous snakes, familiarity does not breed contempt.

If there be any reason for avoiding their strike, consider the warning by Roger Conant, Curator of Reptiles at the Philadelphia Zoological Garden, that "Snakebite can be an extremely serious thing. If complications develop you may be hospitalized for weeks and the experience may cost you a thousand dollars or more."[33] That was written in 1958; hospital costs have since trebled. The person who is treated for snakebite may find that he is being held for ransom.

Whiskey no longer is regarded as the antidote to snakenip, though some have asked who could want a better. While it quiets the mind,

[33] Roger Conant, *A Field Guide to Reptiles and Amphibians of the United States and Canada East of the 100th Meridian*, page 26 (Boston: Houghton Mifflin Company, 1958).

liquor is quicker—it sets the heart to stronger pumping and so speeds the "slumbering venom."

Adam Brotherhood is a taxi driver in a Maryland community near the Appalachian Trail. I am giving only his first and middle names, not his family name. But he'll remember me if you see him because I was the bearer of unwelcome tidings.

Adam was saddened to learn that whiskey has lost its position as the sovereign cure.

"I wish you hadn't told me that," he said. "I always carry a jug in the trunk behind the spare tire and whenever I run over a snake I stop and take a little just to be on the safe side. Up till now it has worked right good."

Damascus

Not many inhabited places know the tread of the solitary Appalachian Trail, but the main artery of Damascus—all one-half mile of it—is the trail itself. Leaving the green slopes of Cherokee National Forest, the hiker crosses J.E.B. Stuart Highway (U.S. 58), then Norfolk and Western Railway's two strips of rust, and enters Laurel Avenue. A bridge leapfrogs squalling Beaverdam Creek.

At Ramsey's 5 & 10 the walker turns left for a block to pick up his mail in general delivery. Postmaster Paschal Grindstaff epitomizes the quiet friendliness of this corner of Virginia: he has been known to patiently hold letters and packages of food and equipment marked "Trail Hiker" for week after week till one day the hiker, detained for whatever reason, showed up to claim them.

On the creek back of the post office is weathered, tin-sided Wilkinson Mill. It shut down in 1951, but many people prefer that the meal for their corn cakes be ground in the old-fashioned way between stones slowly turned by water wheels. Several mills in the area, including one in a nearby village with the mind-boggling name of Mouth of Wilson, still grind grain to order.

Wilkinson Mill stands on the site of Mock's Mill, by which name Damascus was known till 1890. Henry Mock came from North Carolina to build his grist and saw mill in 1823. He begat 30 children, triggering this population explosion with the cooperation of three wives. Having outlasted 12 of his offspring and two of his partners in matrimony, he died abed, on a goose feather mattress, at the age of 97. His business dealings were said to be not always pleasing to his neighbors; of course, with all those dependents, the old gentleman couldn't afford any unprofitable dealing.

In 1886, General John D. Imboden bought land from Mock, platted it and called it Damascus. The ex-Confederate general was a promoter and explained rather grandly that the new community was "destined to become as famous as its ancient namesake" in Syria.[34] American town founders were once fond of borrowing names from venerable locales. Hardly a name of Biblical import does not boast a counterpart somewhere, as witness Zion, Bethlehem, Antioch, Palestine, Baghdad —the list would cover a page. (For reasons that defy conjecture, there are Sodoms in Arkansas, Connecticut, Maine, and North Carolina, and two in New York, but not a single Gomorrah.)

Gen. Imboden had cause to dream, for iron, manganese, and coal had been uncovered in the neighborhood; it was just the combination to make another steel city like Pittsburgh or Birmingham. But the iron deposits turned out to be on the surface only and the manganese ore not so "rich and unlimited" as was hoped.

Damascus, however, was strategically located in the heart of a splendid hardwood forest of oak, tulip tree, and chestnut which had never known the ax. Rails were laid into town in 1901 and the next 25 years saw over 3½ billion board feet of lumber on their way out of town. In 1912, more trees were felled in the vicinity of Damascus than in the entire state of Pennsylvania. Reforestation is underway now, but few trees have grown to cutting size. It takes long years for a plundered silva to recover.

Damascus basks restfully in a break of the Blue Ridge known as the Damascus Water Gap. It enlivens the junction of two cold and bold mountain torrents, Beaverdam and Laurel creeks, and three major mountain ridges, Iron and Holston mountains to the south and Feathercamp Ridge on the north.

Pack on his back, the Appalachian traveler strides the tree-shaded street, a low-keyed medley of small shops and neat white-painted dwellings. When he enters the Owl Cafe to order a hamburger and coke, the constable slips on to the next stool to drink coffee. Acting as municipal greeter, the lawman invites the hiker to sign the Trail Register in Town Hall. Its pages bear the signatures of many personalities walking the trail.

Mrs. Emma (Walking Grandma) Gatewood has been here. In her sixty-seventh year this mother of 11 hiked the trail's 2,000 miles in 146 days, thereby becoming the first woman ever to do so in one continuous trip. Two years later in 1957—guess what?—Walking Grandma did it again. Once more she took to the footpath, but after a few hundred miles of averaging her usual 14 or 15 miles daily announced to her flabbergasted kinfolk that she was going to hang up her tennis shoes.

[34] Louise Fortune Hall, A History of Damascus, 1793–1950 (Abingdon, Va.: John Anderson Press).

The next summer, however, she laced them back on and in 1964, at age 77, completed the Appalachian Trail for a third time.

Sneakers are not considered heavy-duty footwear and how Mrs. Gatewood's feet ever survived the punishing rocks that sprinkle the trail to bedevil even walkers shod with lug-soled thumpers—that is her secret. She doesn't carry a water canteen—another secret. But then, Grandma is a small, slight woman who flits from peak to peak, flourishing umbrella to combat rain and reptiles. She wears a skirt: no smarty-pants jeans for her. Afghan shawl serves as blanket if caught out by sunset.

The Ohio woman doesn't have much truck with ponchos, tents, and sleeping bags—"all that heavy gear." For a while she packed a ladies' dainty .22 caliber pistol but, never having come upon a varmint worth using it on, now leaves the weapon at home. Seldom does Grandma burden herself with food; mountain folk are glad to whomp up another serving of victuals and to invite her to tarry the night. While preferring the "company room" for slumber, Grandma isn't a bit finicky: hayloft will do nicely. In return, she gives freely of her sociable self. Accounts of her exploits, delivered in brisk style with bright blue eyes snapping to underscore vital opinions, would keep any family boiling in excitement through the long hours of darkness.

A few years ago, Mrs. Gatewood was invited to participate in centennial observance of Oregon statehood by joining a trek on the old Oregon Trail. Setting out from Independence, Missouri, the caravan of wagons creaked over the Great Plains, Walking Grandma marching alongside. Nebraska, Wyoming, Idaho, and Oregon had to be crossed. The slow pace of the pioneers galled, and finally could be endured no longer. Grandma took off for Beulah Land, as the old-timers called Oregon, on her own. At the environs of Portland, the band assembled to toot welcome to an advance scout; Grandma reached trail's end two weeks ahead of the rest of the party.

At age 84 she still hikes, "but not on a large scale." Current plans include walking the newly completed Buckeye Trail, stretching 500 miles from Cincinnati to Mentor Headlands State Park on Lake Erie in her home state. Neither Mrs. Gatewood's husband nor her children are trail enthusiasts. Perhaps from among her 20-some grandchildren will come one to fill her size seven tennis shoes.

The Appalachian traveler adds his name to the Trail Register and steps out into Damascus's sunny afternoon. Down the street past Palmer Mullins Dollar Store and Jim Greer's Insurance Agency. Mr. Greer is a walker, too; among his trail keepsakes is a pair of Grandma Gatewood's worn-out tennis shoes.

Should he be so fortunate as to visit Damascus on a Saturday, the hiker will find the people from up-country on their weekly visit to town. He will see grandmothers peeping shyly from poke bonnets and dressed in long skirts from an era when all skirts were maxi. On the sidewalks are men in new blue overalls and others wearing the garish outsize ties and double-breasted suits with wide lapels that were hall-marks of the 1940s and now, though faded and patched, are in vogue again. They are folks to whom prosperity is a foreigner but who have a greeting for the stranger. Schoolboys bicycle by, shouting hello; storekeepers wave from doorways; old men shift plugs of home grown tobacco and grin.

Around the corner is the Minute-ette Food Market and Anderson's General Garage. Guy Anderson was a glider pilot in the Second World War and has a hard-luck fame for on his first mission was shot down over Holland and taken prisoner by the Germans. This is the road to Shady Valley; four miles south it tunnels through Backbone Rock, a short, but high and narrow ridge with sheer walls. Onto the "backbone" leads a footway; below is a national forest campground through which murmurs a trout stream.

Back on Laurel Avenue, now pausing at Mt. Rogers Handicrafts. (Not-far-off Mount Rogers, 5,729 feet, and White Top, 5,520 feet, are the Old Dominion's highest elevations.) Owner Harry Thompson, re-tired Air Force flier, explains that his sales outlet is a beginning attempt to support native crafts—in wood, wool, cotton, leather, metal, painting, and other exercises of ingenuity. "People here don't want to leave the mountains," he remarks. "We're encouraging crafts that will enable them to stay and make a decent living."

In the years to come it is hoped that development of two new areas will provide customers for the hearthside arts. Mount Rogers State Park, 6,000 acres big, and Mount Rogers National Recreation Area, a 154,000-acre chunk of land, most of it within Jefferson National Forest, have begun to attract visitors from afar. Annual visitations may soon reach the one-million mark.

Some citizens even envision Damascus, now an unhurried country trading center, as becoming another Gatlinburg, Tennessee. As the expensive, crowded, neon-lighted "Gateway to the Great Smokies," Gatlinburg has its charms—mostly commercial.

Now the traveler passes the City Shoe Shop (repairs for tired boots here) and First Baptist Church with its new tower—alas, a conven-tional spire has replaced what was one of the nation's most distinctive steeples, an aluminum cap, shaped like the business end of an artillery shell and aimed directly at heaven. On by the large brick home of Mrs. W. F. Keebler, who takes overnight lodgers; next over the bridge spanning Laurel Creek and its orchestra of frogs, then past Poff Jewelry and Smithey's General Store. At the intersection is the Appalachian Trail signboard. Follow its black arrow straight ahead, up the hill and under the trees. In the near distance is conical Cuckoo Peak; once there you may look back for what the guidebook describes as "a fine view of Damascus."

And so it is.

But hurry. Forces are at work to turn Damascus from its pleasant ways into a noisy tourist trap. There is no end of Gatlinburgs in America; there are too few Damascuses.

As It Was in the Beginning

Mother Earth had to go several times into prolonged creative spasms before producing the Appalachian Mountains as they are today.

Her efforts took place at the time of the Elemental Mysteries, as set down in the opening chapter of Genesis.

It was perhaps one billion years ago, on the Fifth Day, when fractures appeared in the then flat country which is now hilly eastern North America. From the earth's womb issued streams of glowing lava, both the aa and the pahoehoe, and clouds of superheated vapor and fetid compounds of sulphur and the odorless but deadly oxides of carbon. Lateral pressures crumpled the surface, forcing it to buckle and heave upward. From the raging core of the earth vomited the material of volcanoes; its broken crust formed the more common mountains of blocks, sheets, and fragments of rock.

For ages the land stood on end, lapped on either side by seas in which primitive animals dumbly stirred and contended.

But ever so gradually—and this doubtless took millions of years— the range subsided. Its stony masses, under ceaseless attack by gravity, running water, wind, frost, and lichens, were ground down and washed into the seas. Again the land lay flat. Once more it slowly rose and fell, and yet again as geologic epochs marched in dreamlike procession.

Then, some 60 million years ago, the earth smoked and convulsed and labored anew in this region.

When the dust of nativity settled, the Appalachians had been recreated. A new range had risen on the remains of the old; the wreckage of the Ancient Appalachians was folded up into the New Appalachians.

Standing regally, two to three times present height, they rivaled the Sierras, Alps, and Caucasuses in elevation. The foothills were cloaked in a splendid hardwood forest, newly arrived from India. Pinnacles glittered in the sun, veined with glaciers from which poured icy rivers to nourish the plants and swarming mammalian life below timberline.

Yet no sooner had they risen than erosion began to undo them.

By the Sixth Day, when man arrived out of the mists, the New Appalachians had become elderly. Its crags now only hinted at their former strength. But if the grandeur that is the Rockies and the Andes was long past, what remained was a range that, with its numberless round hills draped in flowering trees, affords some of the most pleasant scenery to be found anywhere. The Appalachians' aging contours present an aspect of serenity and pastoral bounty.

"What man has attempted in music, in painting, in architecture," noted Dr. Ferdinand Lane, "Nature, upon a grander scale, has achieved in mountains."[35]

But in contrast to most mountains, the individual Appalachians are small. In 1631, a Walter Neal described them as "rocky hills as thick as molehills in a meadow, and clothed with infinite thick woods." Neal's "molehills" make for many a climb and a dip in a single day's journey afoot.

On mountains of greater hulk, the walker frequently travels a dozen miles in either continuous ascent or descent. Here he may go up and down a dozen hills to cover the same distance. To traverse the Great Smokies on the Appalachian Trail, for example, the hiker must cross over about 30 prominent summits and ridges in 68 miles. But just to walk *around* Mount Rainier in Washington will take him 90 miles on the encircling Wonderland Trail.

All too often in the Appalachians, it seems, deep ravines separate the heights. Merely to look up one of these steeps constricts the throat and brings on a taste of raw cotton. Southern hillmen swear this accounts for the numerous (if you know where to look, a problem that also is the concern of the United States Treasury's Alcohol Tax Unit) clandestine lubrication stands, or "Rocks of Moses," to refresh and sustain the traveler on his wearisome path. Hikers who have tramped the tall mountains of the West find a similar challenge in these hills. The Appalachians start from sea level to 1,500 feet, while the Rockies and Sierras generally rise from plains that are a mile or more high. Eastern and western mountains alike commonly jut several thousand feet above their bases.

If the Appalachian traveler labors upward bathed in his own dew, he sometimes finds downgrades so near the perpendicular that his

[35] Ferdinand C. Lane, *The Story of Mountains* (Garden City, N.Y.: Country Life Press, 1950).

struggles to keep from tumbling head over bootlaces make for a passage equally moist. I asked an old mountain man which he preferred, to climb uphill or downhill? "Going down when I'm a-going up, but going up when I'm a-going down" was his answer. It was the perfect solution.

Principal ingredients of the Appalachians are Precambrian granites and other igneous rocks together with sediments laid down in the Paleozoic Era. All rock, of course, is originally igneous in character: formed into magma by the fires of inner Earth in ways that are still mysterious, and then spewed to the surface to become its hard sheathing.

Sedimentary rocks result when igneous matter is broken up into soil, later to be compacted or stratified.

Every state and province corrugated by the Appalachians benefits not only from the copious rainfall the highlands generate and the incomparable timber and recreational values, but from its rocks and the minerals therein. Quebec owns the most extensive deposits of asbestos on the planet while neighboring Vermont leads the United States in mining of this noncombustible. Vermont also quarries huge quantities of granite (near Barre is the world's largest granite pit) and fine grades of marble—untold numbers of Americans rest beneath its grave markers.

Alabama, Pennsylvania, and Quebec have been enriched by iron ore; Maine digs for beryllium, mica, and the rare metal cesium; North Carolina profits from government stockpiling of mica while kaolin found at Burningtown near Franklin was once exported to England to become Wedgwood china. Nova Scotia supplies berite, Virginia mines titanium and zinc, West Virginia has an important cash crop in limestone, New York produces talc and from Georgia comes bauxite, manganese, and three-quarters of the republic's supply of porcelain clay.

A federal government report lists these minerals, among others, prospected in the vicinity of Grandfather Mountain near Linville, North Carolina: copper, lead, iron, garnet, mica, zircon, feldspar, uranium, talc, asbestos, and gold.[36] Every locality claims its measure of mountain wealth. Certainly everyone knows of Appalachia's coal —the fuel compressed from the giant jungle plants of carboniferous times. Nova Scotia's underwater seams provide 37 percent of Canada's coal; Pennsylvania leads in anthracite production.

For all the vicissitudes suffered by the rocky warpings saluted as

[36] *Geological Survey Bulletin 1121–D,* United States Government Printing Office, Washington, D.C., 1962.

the Appalachians by Don Hernando De Soto,[37] it is kin to all mountains everywhere in the ways in which it was formed and is now being worn away. The Andes, Himalayas, and Rockies are much less ancient and far taller, but eventually they, too, will be honed down: Everest will become a pygmy.

It's estimated the Appalachians occupy about as much surface as does the whole state of California. Since land surface, like water surface, is measured only horizontally, such figures completely ignore the ups and downs of terrain. If mountains were pressed level, the surfaces would spread over a vast area. Calculations made in Switzerland show their Alps, if flattened, would widen that small country by 150 miles. The hillman who holds a deed to 80 acres may actually farm 120 acres. His problem is to keep from falling off them. Planting the fields is easier: "we-uns do that with a shotgun."

Meantime, the Appalachians are about 1,500 miles in length, generally 80 to 100 miles wide in the northern part and 300 to 350 miles wide in the southern, with 6,684-foot Mount Mitchell the supreme promontory. In fact, Mitchell is the highest elevation in the United States east of South Dakota's Black Hills.

Lowest point is the zero elevation of the Atlantic Ocean where it washes the foot of the ranges in Canada; the least elevation in the United States is the surface of the Hudson River—about 50 feet. The extremes of elevation on the Appalachian Trail are, respectively, 6,642-foot Clingmans Dome on the Tennessee-North Carolina line in the Great Smokies, and the bear den, 115.4 feet above sea level, at the Trailside Museum in Bear Mountain State Park in New York.

Taking the exact height of a mountain is no easy chore, involving several instruments and a nice knowledge of physics and mathematics —and sometimes the agility of a human fly.

At that, the various calculations are all subject to a degree of error. It was a simpler, if less exact, matter in the early days of mountain exploration when a thermometer was dunked into a pot of boiling water at the summit. Water comes to a boil at progressively lower temperatures as altitude increases and atmospheric pressure upon the surface of the water correspondingly decreases. At sea level it boils at 212 degrees Fahrenheit, but if transported high enough water will boil just above the point where it would solidify into ice.

Unfortunately for topographers, many peaks are unclimbable; besides, atmospheric pressure is not always constant since it fluctuates

[37] The name came from the Apalachee, an Indian tribe that harassed the ill-fated De Soto expedition as it crossed northern Florida and entered Georgia in 1539. By custom, Apalachee is usually spelled with a single "p" and Appalachian with two. The tribe has long since disappeared and there is none left to lament this orthographic injustice.

with the weather. A common aviation accident is the collision of plane with mountain during an overcast when the craft's aneroid altimeter, which measures height above sea level by atmospheric pressure, gives a traitorous reading.

On a day in 1794, André Michaux hoisted himself to the top of Grandfather Mountain (5,964 feet) in North Carolina and believed that he had surmounted the loftiest of the Appalachians. Grandfather is craggy, often shrouded in murky, mysterious clouds, and looks like a mountain should. Exulting, the French naturalist shouted to the winds "Vive l'Amérique et la République Française! Vive la liberté!" He also sang the Marseillaise. Michaux's journal does not say whether he stumbled on a "Rock of Moses" at the summit, but the suspicion lingers that something besides water was bubbling there. Altogether it was an exciting, if mistaken, moment.

The highest single Appalachian elevations in each of the five provinces and 17 eastern states are:

CANADA
New Brunswick—Mount Carleton (2,690')
Newfoundland—Lewis Hills (2,673')
Nova Scotia—North Barren (1,747')
Prince Edward Island—hills to 450'
Quebec—Mont Jacques Cartier (4,350')

UNITED STATES
Alabama—Cheaha Mountain (2,407')
Connecticut—south slope of Mount Frissell (2,380').
    The peak of this mountain is in Massachusetts.
Georgia—Brasstown Bald (4,784')
Kentucky—Big Black Mountain (4,139')
Maine—Mount Katahdin (5,267')
Maryland—Backbone Mountain (3,360')
Massachusetts—Mount Greylock (3,491')
New Hampshire—Mount Washington (6,288')
New Jersey—High Point (1,803')
New York—Slide Mountain (4,180')
North Carolina—Mount Mitchell (6,684')
Pennsylvania—Mount Davis (3,213')
South Carolina—Sassafras Mountain (3,560')
Tennessee—Clingmans Dome (6,643')
Vermont—Mount Mansfield (4,393')
Virginia—Mount Rogers (5,729')
West Virginia—Spruce Knob (4,862')

There is marked similarity between the Appalachians and the Urals of the Soviet Union, which run close to 1,600 miles from the Arctic Ocean down into Kazakhstan and from 60 to 70 miles wide in the north to 250 in the south. Except as they approach the Arctic, the Urals are thickly wooded. Average crest is little more than 3,000 feet; most elevated peak is Gora Naroda at 6,212 feet. Like the Appalachians, these hills are hoary and bowed with years, having also come into being at the start of the Cenozoic Era; now they, too, are wasting away, apparently at a comparable rate. And, again like the Appalachians, which for centuries were the dividing line between East and West in North America, so too do the Urals (the "Earth Girdle") divide Russia into East and West, a crustal scar conjoining Europe to Asia.

As a convenience, long-distance hikers bisect the Appalachian Trail into southern and northern sections of almost equal length. The great Susquehanna River in Pennsylvania is the approximate mid-point. For years a bronze plaque on Center Point Knob, a few miles south of the river near the village of Allen, informed the traveler that he had sweated half the length of the trail: he had only 1,000 miles to walk in either direction! Then spoilers prized the plaque from the boulder to which it was proudly bolted, and it seems to have joined the list of things permanently "lost."

Geographers, however, often separate the Appalachian chain of mountains into three main links, or divisions—Southern, Central, and Northern. Two rivers draining the country in quite different directions comprise the boundaries: the Kanawha, whose waters find the Gulf of Mexico by devious ways, and the Hudson, emptying directly into the Atlantic Ocean. All Appalachian streams south of the Kanawha reach the Gulf; north of it they seek the Atlantic.

In central Alabama, the Southern division begins in a succession of low hills, but quickly mounts to more imposing heights in Georgia, Tennessee, North Carolina, and southwestern Virginia. Here are the Appalachian's highest peaks; south of Roanoke are over 60 peaks topping 6,000 feet and 288 more that exceed 5,000 feet.[38] This region

[38] "South, Beyond 6000" is an achievement attainable by those who have climbed on foot 40 selected peaks of over 6,000 feet in the southern Appalachians of North Carolina and Tennessee. Information on the requirements can be secured from either Hugh M. Thompson, Jr., of the Tennessee Eastman Recreation Club Hiking Club, P.O. Box 511, Kingsport, Tennessee 37662, or the Carolina Mountain Club, P.O. Box 68, Asheville, North Carolina 28801.

In the northern Appalachians the ambitious hiker may become a member of the "Four Thousand Footer Club of the White Mountains" by clambering to the summits of 46 selected peaks exceeding 4,000 feet in height. If, after this accomplishment his feet yearn for further conquests, he may propel them to the tops of

also has the wettest weather east of the Pacific coast. Kentucky and the Virginias present decline in altitude, but the Shenandoah looms impressively with escarpments springing smartly from the plains.

At the Kanawha River in West Virginia the Middle division begins. It furrows the sky through Maryland, Pennsylvania, and New Jersey to the Valley of the Hudson in New York. The mountains are not acclaimed for height, generally lifting but 2,000 feet above the sea. New Jersey, whose most prominent summit is 1,803 feet, shows the least elevation.

The Northern division advances from the Hudson River—as picturesque as the Rhine, though similarly under siege by churning factories and poisonous wastes—through Connecticut, Massachusetts, Vermont, New Hampshire, Maine, and into Canada. In upper New England the land planes boldly upward into 70 eminences over 4,000 feet. Ten of these surpass 5,000 feet, while one, Mount Washington in New Hampshire, passes the 6,000-foot mark. The peaks become scattered in Maine, yet imposing in their isolation, including several beautiful cones that suggest Central American volcanoes and mile-high Katahdin with its 46 adjoining peaks and ridges, one of the largest *massifs* of granite on the planet. Surging into Quebec, the mountains close ranks in the Notre Dame and Chic-Chocs (pronounced—and frequently spelled—Shickshocks) ranges, where Mont Jacques Cartier overlooks the fjordlike reaches of the St. Lawrence from 4,350 feet. They spread into the maritime provinces of New Brunswick, Nova Scotia, and Prince Edward Island, then form the Long Range of Newfoundland. There, on the wintry shores of the North Atlantic, the Appalachians expire.

A common misapprehension, one repeated even by a popular encyclopedia, is that the Adirondacks are a branch of the Appalachians. In reality, this cluster of about 100 peaks in northeastern New York, with Mount Marcy at 5,344 feet standing tallest in the state, belongs to the Laurentian Highlands of the Canadian Shield. With its base of exposed Archaean rock, the shield is the oldest uplifted part of the continent.

But if the Adirondacks can't properly be counted as Appalachian,

---

12 selected Maine and five selected Vermont peaks (a total of 63 peaks rising 4,000 feet or more) and be welcomed into the "New England Four Thousand Footer Club." Membership eligibility for both clubs is passed upon by the Four Thousand Footer Committee, Appalachian Mountain Club, 5 Joy Street, Boston, Massachusetts 02108.

The Appalachian Trail surmounts many of the peaks listed by the South, Beyond 6000 and Four Thousand Footer organizations.

the Ozark and Ouachita mountains can. These two groups of rather modest crests, whose most noted elevations are reached by 2,753-foot Magazine Mountain in Arkansas and 2,950-foot Rich Mountain in Oklahoma, rise close to each other in the western Mississippi Valley. Geologists consider them to be Appalachian outposts, in spite of the fact they are upwards of 200 miles distant from the main range. Through thousands of years, the Mississippi River washed down much of the intervening country.

Except for confusing jumbles of transverse ridges in the Deep South, notably the Great Smokies, the Appalachian system is tidily arranged in parallel ridges with northerly and southerly axes. Two of its most striking features are the Blue Ridge and the Great Appalachian Valley.

The Blue Ridge, a succession of ranges on the eastern front of the system, extends from Dahlonega, Georgia, to Carlisle, Pennsylvania. In Maryland and Pennsylvania, where it presents a long, level silhouette, it is customarily referred to as South Mountain. The Blue Ridge is distinguished for its base of the most antique of rocks that went into the making of the Appalachians, its array of masterful peaks, and its raiment of the greatest variety of flowering plants of any region in the earth's temperate climes. Shenandoah and Great Smoky Mountains National Parks together with several national forests are on the Blue Ridge. So also are 574 miles of a picturesque ribbon of roadway, fringed with split-rail fences, peppered with overlooks, camp and picnic grounds, and restricted to low speeds and noncommercial vehicles. From Front Royal, Virginia, the Skyline Drive winds 105.4 miles amid the heights of the Shenandoah, then is followed by 469-mile Blue Ridge Parkway, which presently ends at Cherokee, North Carolina. Parkway plans call for its extension to Kennesaw Mountain Battlefield Park, some 25 miles northwest of Atlanta, Georgia.

The Great Appalachian Valley is a fertile corridor from Alabama to Quebec that gives continuity to the system. In Alabama and Georgia it is generally known as the Coosa Valley, but it is also known as the Tennessee Valley in Tennessee, the Shenandoah Valley in Virginia, the Lebanon and Cumberland Valleys in Maryland and Pennsylvania, the Kittatinny Valley in New Jersey, and the Hudson River Valley and the Champlain Trough in New York and Quebec. It ends at the St. Lawrence. Whereas south of New York it divides the ranges into two longitudinal portions, in the north it swings west to separate the Appalachians from the Adirondacks and the Laurentian High-lands.

In Canada, the Appalachians little hindered expansion to the interior of the continent, for they were detoured by the wide, sea-level, 2,350-mile St. Lawrence Waterway linking the ocean to the Great Lakes region. The Waterway became the route of French fur traders, priests bearing the Sermon on the Mount, and explorers chartered by the Bourbon kings. But elsewhere on the seaboard, from Maine to Georgia, they constituted a wall in which there were few chinks. Several likely water gaps existed, but shoals, floods, and tricky currents were hazards not to be overcome by bravado alone. It wasn't till the nineteenth century that the Erie Canal, which has been in use ever since, was dug 363 miles across New York State to connect the Hudson with the Great Lakes.

Other artificial channels were excavated alongside the James River in Virginia and the Potomac River on the Maryland border. These tame watercourses did much to open the middle United States to settlement.

Nor were there many land gaps. Even the least altitudinous of them called for considerable straining by men and stock. Early roads were primitive winding corridors of boulders and ruts "deep enough to bury a mule." Difficult grades exhausted horses and wore out wagon shoes; uncounted loads of freight and wagons stuffed with the meager household goods of families bound for new lands ended up scattered and broken at the foot of precipices.

Congress in 1806 authorized the construction of the National Road (now U.S. Highway 40) through Maryland, Pennsylvania, and West Virginia to Ohio and beyond. Travelers grumbled that the roadbed itself was a formidable obstacle and the tolls excessive. In Ohio there was a tollgate about every ten miles by 1837. An ordinary passenger buggy was charged 16 cents for ten miles, while a stagecoach paid 25 cents and 3 cents were collected on a horse that was led. Those were times when dinners cost 20 cents and a shot of whiskey was poured for 3 cents. But this turnpike, however crude in its formative years, did provide access to virgin territory. Long before 1852, when it reached Vandalia, Illinois, 609 miles from Cumberland, Maryland, it had become the chief artery of Western migration. An account of the "greatest wagon road in the nation" was penned by Charles Fenno Hoffman, editor and novelist, in 1833. He saw "numbers" of pedestrians trudging the pike. "They generally have a tow-cloth knapsack, or light leathern valise, hung across their backs, and are often very decently dressed in a blue coat, gray trousers, and round hat. They travel about 40 miles a day." The horse-drawn wagons, observed Hoffman, "go about 20 miles a day."[39]

To this date the Appalachians restrain overland traffic. Between New Brunswick and Georgia barely a score of good roads pierce the hills to link the coast with the heartland. "Thank God it's hard to build a mountain road," said a Virginia friend, reflecting a new point of view regarding the arteries of mechanical transportation.

Historians have remarked on the tremendous effect the Appalachians exerted on the development of the United States. As late as 1783 only about 25,000 white Americans were thought to be living west of the mountains. The densely forested ridges acted as a barrier that confined the British colonies to a seaside house of 13 rooms. Energies of the inhabitants (as restless a lot as later Americans) were restricted to their own hearths. If they found common cause in the prosperity of the house, the colonists also discovered affinity in grievances. The rent was rising and His Royal Landlord was viewed as a grasping, impolitic fellow who favored the interests of his stay-at-home subjects over those of his enterprising colonials. There have been "great Imprudencies on both sides," said Benjamin Franklin on February 5, 1775.

Were it not for the confining Appalachians, America's Revolution would have erupted much later than it did, if at all, for the obstinacy of King George III and his Parliament was to change in a few years. At any rate, a good argument could be made that the loss of the first British Empire would have been greatly postponed. When it did occur, the shock was poignant but was met with a very stiff upper lip. On surrendering arms to victorious Revolutionary troops at Yorktown, the bands of defeated British regiments played—with admirable detachment—"The World Turned Upside Down."

But the history witnessed by the Appalachians is already beyond human understanding in terms of time. What is to come—for it is quite likely the old hills have a few million years left in them—is equally unimaginable.

Goethe spoke of "mountain masses grandly dumb—I question neither whence nor why they come." Yet he was only expressing the reverent wonder of the Psalmist when he chanted

I will lift up mine eyes unto the hills.

[39] Charles Fenno Hoffman, *A Winter in the West* (New York, 1835).

Balds

The Appalachians of the South are keepers of a natural mystery that defies solution.

Stretching from northern Georgia through North Carolina and Tennessee into southern Virginia are about 85 mountains known as balds. Their summits are without trees in spite of being well below timberline, which is around 7,000 feet in those latitudes. As a contrast, North Carolina's Mount Mitchell—the apogee of the Appalachians—is densely wooded at 6,684 feet.

Although trees mantle every slope of the balds, upon reaching a more or less irregular line just below their crowns they inexplicably cease to grow. This gives a bald the appearance of a tonsured monk.

Actually, balds are thatched either by grasses (grass balds) or shrubs (heath balds, some of which can get pretty shrubby), hence are not entirely exposed to an unblushing Nature. Andrews Bald in the Great Smokies is much admired by botanists for its bog in which flourish the sundews, protein-hungry plants that ensnare and devour insects.[40] A few balds are as small as one-quarter acre in nakedness, others large as 100 acres; biggest is the 1,000-acre expanse on Roan Mountain (not all balds bear the title of "bald"[41]) straddling the North Carolina-Tennessee border.

A few balds exist also in Wyoming, Nevada, and the South Island of New Zealand.

Why is a bald?

Pat answers are lacking. To date, no combination of botanical or geological reasoning has made sense of the riddle. Scientists admit the barren eminences have them checkmated—for the present. Being stubborn by training and disposition, they haven't given up their quest for an explanation.

Even the Cherokee, the red men who once dominated this haunting land, were baffled by the balds. They named them *Udawagunta* and, as if that wasn't alarming enough, would solemnly warn wide-eyed small fry that the *Udawagunta* harbored one *Ulagu*, a hornet-like ogre who was mighty partial to making a one-dish meal of runaway children. Scary thoughts of *Ulagu* kept youngsters from straying.

[40] Andrews Bald (5,860 feet) is accessible by 2½ miles of walking along the wide Forney Ridge Trail, which intersects the Appalachian Trail four-tenths of a mile south of Clingmans Dome.

[41] The "Rocky Top, Tennessee" of the country song ("corn won't grow on Rocky Top—that's why folks git their corn from a jar") is undoubtedly a bald.

Ours is a pragmatic culture, and the question arises: what use are balds?

Tangles of blackberry, raspberry, and huckleberry find nourishment in the soil of numerous balds—and there, too, gourmands browse on hands and knees for the tiny, but delectable, wild strawberry. Many a bold mountaineer distills tonsil-tingling cordials from fermented berry juice, thus incidentally providing well-paid, invigorating outdoor employment for Uncle Sam's revenue agents. His women folk turn berries into pies that would win a vote of approval from Julia Child.

Whitetailed deer forage and wild turkeys cluck anxiously to their broods as they search for grasshoppers. Bears doze in the noonday sun. A herd of half-savage razorback hogs may idle about, grunting and gossiping. All balds serve as lookouts for carnivorous birds. Heat reflects from their open tops and hawks and vultures spiral lazily on the thermals of rising air.

The view is three dimensional and one realizes why Indians habitually spoke of six, rather than four, directions: east and west, north and south, up and down.

Georgia's three highest elevations are balds. Brasstown Bald peaks the list at 4,784 proud feet. Number two is Rabun Bald—4,717 feet. Blood Mountain ranks third with 4,461 feet.

Struggling up Blood Mountain's forested inclines and onto its heath-grown dome, the walker will be refreshed with what the guidebooks are fond of terming a "splendid panoramic view." This is the most altitudinous point of the Appalachian Trail on its 78-mile run through the state from Springer Mountain to Bly Gap. Anvilheads, milky as chalk, toss and growl in bright blue space. Jostling on the horizon are verdant hills clothed in precious hardwoods and furrowed with purling runnels of sweet water. Toward the end of spring, catawba rhododendron, which English gardeners think the fairest evergreen shrub to come out of North America, puts on a tropical extravaganza of great clusters of bell-shaped lilac pink flowers that exhale a perfume to dizzy the senses, much as it must have those of our first parents in the Garden of Paradise.

Over 300 walking miles north is 6,285-foot Roan Mountain, tallest of the balds. On its summit, as they have for a century, thousands of visitors arrive in mid-June—most by car but some afoot and a few with knapsacks—to wander at cloud level on the Appalachian Trail among massive concentrations of blooming rhododendron, the "most beautiful plant."

Here is the southern wilderness at its mountainous best: the vista that belongs so uniquely to the balds.

Things That Go Bump

Near Harpers Ferry in West Virginia, where the Appalachian Trail rises to overlook two broad rippling rivers, my nose warned me of a pungent happening. In minutes I came to a glade where a tiny mountain tent was pitched. On a stump well apart sat the tent's owner, wearing the air of a man whose life has become sackcloth and ashes. The night before he had been awakened by an animal bumping against the tent wall. He struck at the wall with his hand, and then discovered what sort of animal it was.

Choking, he erupted from the tent. A small, thickset form with a pair of white stripes on its furry black back was hopping across the moonlighted ground. Now, though a dozen hours had passed, the vapor that an alarmed skunk ejects from twin glands under its tail still hung heavily in the air. The hiker wanted only to fold his befouled tent and silently steal away. But how? The telltale smell, like a bad reputation, would follow him wherever he went.

Not knowing if it would work, but recalling advice gleaned somehow, I suggested he bury the tent in earth—better, in charcoal—for a day or two to absorb the musk, which even a skunk thinks so disagreeable that if any gets on its fur during the salvo it wallows in dirt to cleanse itself.

Later I received a letter from the hiker. He had washed his tent in the Potomac River, and after drying put it in a bag of charcoal brought out from town.

A night and a day in the charcoal de-skunked it, he said, adding that otherwise he would not have risked going on with the tent among civilized men "lest I suffer the fate that befell John Brown in Harpers Ferry; a little skunk is a dangerous thing."

Chemical warfare experts know how to handle noxious fumes— charcoal is an important ingredient of gas masks. It is highly absorbent. Even spoiled fish odors vanish from the camper's food chest if a few lumps of the black charred substance are placed inside and the lid closed tightly for several hours. A crude form of charcoal is easily made by smothering embers of hardwood with earth before they are consumed by fire. I have since learned that a few hours in hot sunlight or washing in ammonia or chloride of lime solution (household bleach) will remove skunk musk from clothing. Tomato juice or vinegar does the same for the skin. Bonnie, my fastidious Shetland sheepdog, came home one night rubbing bleary eyes with her paws and obviously ashamed of a high odor that could have come from only one source. I hurriedly mixed vinegar and water together and washed her eyes and fur. The next morning Bonnie reeked more of garlic than of skunk—I had grabbed the bottle of salad vinegar.

Despite his bad smell, the skunk is not a bad fellow. He may contract rabies, but this is hardly his fault; such a nice creature as the milk cow may also be infected with the virus, and overnight become less than a benefactor to humanity. In the hill country, a skunk suspected of being loaded with rabies, making of him a double-barreled instrument, is called a hydrophobia skunk or simply 'phoby skunk.

Stinky's fare of bugs, mice, and carrion ranks him as a useful predator. Yellow jackets, grasshoppers, snakes, worms, shrews, fruit, garbage and bird, turtle, and chicken eggs are on his list of good things. He will enter a shelter in search of food.

While Stinky may be the fastest gun in the East when he perceives his life to be in peril, against the great horned owl and the gray fox he usually loses. Both pounce from the air before he can draw. The American gray fox, strictly a New World citizen, is the only fox on earth that ascends trees, and is so good at it that he is often referred to as a cat—the "swamp cat" from his usual habitat in remote, dank places. Hunters have found him 40 or 50 feet in the air prowling the branches for nesting birds. Other skunk enemies are bobcats, badgers, coyotes, and dogs.

But they must take Stinky with his brushy tail down, for he is fearless and does not give ground, knowing well that in fair fight no animal can withstand his singular weapon. Anklets of skunk fur were worn by Indian braves to show they would not retreat. Meeting Stinky on the pathway, it will be you who circles around.

Ross Allen, head of the Reptile Institute at Silver Springs, Florida, once challenged a skunk and it "let me have it right in the eyes." After freshening up in a nearby swamp, Allen skinned the skunk and "went upwind to cook it. The meat was delicious."

For all his self-assurance in public, rare among wild animals, Stinky is no bully, and is amiable save when crossed. Then—provided there is time—he faces his aggressor and stamps the ground with forefeet.

If this stiff little dance doesn't bring a truce, his long tail is hoisted. The third, and final, warning, is when the tail's white tip spreads like a fan. One foot closer and his body whips into a semicircle, head and rear now both pointing forward, and from the one end issues a hiss and from the other a phosphorescent spray, like an arcing tracer bullet, aimed at the face. Sometimes he just does a handstand and shoots over his own head. *Mephitis* (Latin for vile exhalation from the earth, the term by which the skunk is known to science) can fire a half-dozen rounds 10 or 12 feet with marksmanship. A few hours are needed to recharge, but meantime he can bite.

It is said that no European before Columbus ever smelled a skunk, but this is only technically true, for while the skunk is an immemorial citizen of the New World, across the Atlantic lives the civet, or polecat, a cousin that defends itself with jets of the same Mephistophelean quality. Only the atomizer, not its fragrance, was new. Chemists have a name for the spray: mercaptan, a yellowish, oily sulphide that can burn the skin and cause temporary blindness, loss of voice, and nausea.[42]

From "things that go bump in the night, Good Lord, deliver us!" goes the old Scottish prayer. When darkness and fog creep through the hollows, the catalog of nocturnal mischief is opened. Backpackers know of other cheeky animals roving the eastern hardwood forests.

I lay in a lean-to on a black night, sleepily listening to the pitter, patter of little feet, when the feet suddenly pattered across my upturned face. They felt light as raindrops. I sprang into the air like the bolt from a crossbow. Squeaking in terror, the mouse fled among the rafters.

The shelter without a family of wood mice in residence is rare as ambition in Eden. Few creatures have so many enemies—from the bloodthirsty quarter-ounce shrew to the quarter-ton bear; self-preservation cautions them to lay low in daytime. As the curtains of dusk are drawn, mice leave their nests, and from then till day are in a flurry, scampering on the beams, racing across the tract of cleared ground in front, inspecting every nook for the eleventh time for possible nourishment, twittering and romping with others of the clan. Their comings and goings are the hiker's lullaby. The patter of mice feet is a rustic sound, easier to take than the blat of trucks through Richmond or Baltimore.

The mouse, *Mus,* is not a rat, *Rattus,* but a distinct species of rodent, smaller and with less formidable dentition. The common

---

[42] A trace of synthetic mercaptan is added to bottled LP gas to provide a warning signal in the event of leakage.

(gray, brown, or Norway) rat, was a stranger to the Americas till arrival in the holds of ships.

Mice are found everywhere, but the common rat prefers people-congested areas where it may scavenge to its heart's content. Though it is a member of "noble and ancient family," I've never seen a common rat on the Appalachian Trail.

A hungry mouse is not a serious contender for the hiker's food supply. Elfin three to four-inch long bodies are fueled via pygmy appetites. Still, their foraging can result in spilled and tainted food and often a chewed packbag. The giveaway is a persistent rustling. A mouse will worry a box of cereal the night long and perhaps only nibble at the grains. But it may be doing more than this. One gray morning I discovered my packbag had been converted during the night to a home for mice, and spent an hour in housemoving.

When lodged in a lean-to or the occasional closed cabin, I hang up my food from a rafter, avoiding any crossmember that could be used as a runway by mice. Sound judgment dictates keeping vittles separated from pack during the hours of darkness—or daylight, for that matter, if they are to be left unattended more than a very few moments. If there is a raid, let the oatmeal take the brunt, not the packbag, which is fairly costly and an item neither easy to repair nor to replace.

Not only mice, but others of the clan *Rodentia* will gnaw a packbag to get at the food their keen nostrils detect.

Once I left my pack leaning against a tree while I scouted for water; minutes later a side pocket hung in shreds and the salted peanuts it had carried were bulging the cheeks of a red squirrel. The impudent mite set up a rancorous chatter of protest at my return.

Another time a raccoon as big as a Husky dog sashayed into camp in broad daylight. After a short pause to size me up, he began rummaging in my belongings while I stared, dumfounded at his bold contempt for a fellow mortal who was many times heavier and infinitely more predatory than himself.

My indignant yell sent him loping. But he went only as far as the nearby creek, for I saw him there later, examining the shallows for crayfish.

Parts of New Jersey and New York near the Big Town are home to regiments of raccoons. They fit in neatly with suburban living: well-fed suburbanites don't regard them as table fare, while the omnivorous creatures thrive on the well-filled garbage buckets.

I recall a particular night in New York's Harriman section of

Palisades Interstate Park. From fire-out to first light at Letterrock Shelter a troop of masked burglars scurried determinedly, each in turn visiting the couple bedded down in the lean-to and the solitary sleepers under the sky. Shouts of "scat" and the thud of hurled boots rang among the trees. Though my pack was hung on a branch ten feet off the ground, something was attracting the raccoons to me, as well. I didn't know it then, but a lump of cheese had fallen unseen —but not unsmelled—on the ground beneath my sleeping bag.

I'll not soon forget awakening scarcely able to breathe from a heavy, furry weight pressing against my chest. A strangled cry burst from my throat.

Next day the talk around the breakfast fire was of the great raccoon raid. One hiker was missing a loaf of seeded rye and a package of Bircher Muesli; another was minus his unwashed socks. An Explorer Scout had been taken for his considerable stock of Tootsie Rolls. Everyone had lost sleep.

"But whatever was that horrible noise about two o'clock?" the lady hiker asked. "It sounded like—like I don't know what!" She shuddered and her husband patted her hand soothingly.

All present had heard it; their blood had almost congealed. None could think of what it might have been. Murder? Something escaped from the Bronx Zoo? Big Foot?

I didn't reply—but thought it just the very noise that would be emitted by a hiker whose chest is sat upon by a big boar coon in the middle of the night.

Another night prowler of no mean appetite is the porcupine. This chunky vegetarian stuffs itself with inner bark, juicy leaves, maple sap and, yes, wild flowers and pond lillies. Living in a garden, he expends more energy eating than in searching. There probably is no such critter as an underweight porcupine. And he dotes on anything salty.

Favorite snacks are plywood with its tasty glue and planking on which salted food or dishwater has been spilled. Urine-salted lumber stands high in his regard. In New England, one may meet him in trail privies earnestly chomping on the seat. A pair of sweat-salted boots—*Boots pré-salé*—is reckoned gourmet fare. If some hikers have risen to find themselves without a seat to sit on, others have awakened to find themselves without a sole to stand on, and obliged to take the homeward path with the sorry remains of Porky's midnight meal tied to their feet by strips torn from their underwear.

Porcupines are at home in the trees; curved claws on all four feet help to grip rain-wet trunks. Theirs is a redoubtable defense, the only example of its kind among North American fauna. The wise woodsman never touches a live porcupine with his hands; it is a walking cactus. Concealed in the salt-and-pepper coat are sharp, hollow spines of varying length—an average of over 100 to the square inch. At the slightest hostile touch, the animal humps its back, puffs its coarse fur, and diligently flails its muscular tail, nailing scores of spines into the offending object, be it walking staff or nose of a curious dog. Some of the more loosely attached quills may fly off, but, despite legend, the porkie can no more throw them than a milk snake can milk a nanny goat.

Quills are tipped with minute reversing barbs that lie flat when entering the flesh, but open when the quill is pulled to extract it. The dog that annoys a quill-pig generally gets the worst of the encounter. Unless his owner is there to withdraw the spines, a distressing experience for both, he may die miserably from infection, hemorrhage, or insanity as the points gradually work their way deeper to pierce an artery or vital organ.

A veterinarian will administer anesthesia to a quilled dog before attempting extraction. In the field, the procedure is to wrap the maddened dog in a blanket, leaving only its head exposed, and place a stout stick between its jaws to keep from being bitten. The quills are then pulled, smartly, one-by-one. After this the quivering pet will probably run a fever. It should be given plenty of fresh water and consolation by its owner.

Fishers, large members of the weasel family, are the porcupines' foremost enemy, attacking fiercely without apparent harm to themselves. Bears, wolverines, and mountain lions prey on the slow-moving animal—but only when famished and then with caution, since they lack the fisher's strange immunity to injury from the cruel points. Assault is directed to the underside, which, unlike the rest of the body, is not protected with quills.

I heard of a trapper into whose arm a two-inch spine was driven so deeply he was unable to remove it. The spine disappeared and a few weeks later came out at the ball of his foot.

Since its armament procures considerable immunity to attack, the thorny beast has a better chance than most wild animals of reaching old age—in his case, about 20 years.

At maturity he will be about 3½ feet in length, of which 6 to 9 inches are tail. Weight may run to 40 pounds, but 15 is average. The animal is anything but aggressive. When captured he quickly becomes a gentle and phlegmatic pet, never raising spiny hackles unless startled. But, for all his points, personality is minimal and decidedly lower case. His ways, like those of many guileless dullards, are surprisingly insistent.

When Porky comes calling in the moonlight, snuffling as he maunders at his customary waddle, I rap the floor of the lean-to with my walking stick. The tattoo echoes from the ring of trees outside the lean-to's open front.

There is a long pause during which not another snuffle is heard. As the minutes tick away I burrow deeper in my sleeping bag. I can visualize Porky now: having retreated to the shadows, he regards the building with an obtuse, if greedy, eye (his only expression). The porcupine has a strangely quick pulse for so sluggish a creature —280 to 320 beats a minute. I wonder if my thumping has further elevated his pulse.

Soon the piggish intonations are heard again. I sit up and address the blackness in a mixture of Old Norse and Early Anglo-Saxon. The short, frank words are alarming, and the porcupine clumsily withdraws, clicking his teeth and breathing hard.

I subside, and dream of stumbling on a lost mine of Appalachian garnets. Precious red crystals blink as I gloatingly carry them by the handful to the sunlight. A sudden grunt shatters the vision—Porky is inside the lean-to. His chisel-like incisors are abusing a post that runs from sill to roof. This is no prissy diner; his lips smack audibly. Sybarite!

My hand reaches stealthily into the ditty bag alongside. It comes out holding a Chinese salute. Porky looks my way in dim puzzlement as I strike a match. He is an untidy looking fellow, lumpish and bristly, rather like a large bird's nest. I let the match burn a moment, savoring the anticipation of a worthy deed.

Now! Lighting the fuse, I toss the salute onto the floor. I open my mouth and press hands against my ears.

In the confined space, the big firecracker explodes with a lightning-like flash and a stunning roar.

Porky panics, squealing. He makes for the bushes at a run, or what passes for a run with such a slowpoke. He won't be back before tomorrow night.

Porcupines are protected by law in numerous areas as survival food for persons lost in the wilds. Vermont, however, encourages you to do them in as a public service since their large numbers damage so many trees and trail shelters, ski chalets and summer cabins. They are easily killed with a stick; a smart rap on the snout usually induces Porky to give up his spiky ghost. I am reluctant to levy capital punishment on an inoffensive animal whose natural ways are sometimes at variance with mankind's schemes. But I wouldn't let myself go hungry for long if there were surplus porcupines about.

Their meat is dark, tasty and tender as young pork. The liver, I am told, is particularly good.

One Anonymous (wisely anonymous) put the matter in dietary perspective when he wrote in a Massachusetts trail register that

> Porkies may not be a dainty dish
>   to set before a king,
> But for a really hungry man
>   they're just the very thing.

After a porcupine has been dispatched, it can be picked up by a paw and the quills and hair singed off in a hot fire to facilitate handling. Inside the forelegs are small kernellike glands that, in common with various other game animals, must be removed or the flesh will have a strong taste; it is easier simply to cut off the forelegs. An incision is made from vent to ribs and the viscera removed. The blood is dumped out and the cavity wiped clean with dry grass or piece of cloth. Next, skin the carcass and sever the head. Porky is a lazy cuss, normally obese, and most of his thick layer of fat should be cut away. The body is disjointed and the pieces broiled over the coals.

In porcupine territory—to avoid the disjointing of his boots— the prudent wayfarer will hang up his footgear every night.

And he will hang his food high at all times everywhere on the trail.

The Curious Crotalus

It wasn't a loud sound, just insistent. There was a buzz like a bee makes that is trapped in a jar. The sound started and kept on.

I was walking, but my mind was drifting. That part that heard the sound was not communicating with the part that was adrift. So I walked on, thumbs hooked under the web straps of my backpack.

"Stop, Charley!" my hiking partner, Bob Haag, shouted from behind me. I stopped, waking up. Looking carefully at the bushes and the rocks we inched forward. A dozen paces off the pathway a rattler was shaking its tail. It was barely the length of my forearm and not very thick and not at all impressive.

No doubt the snake first became aware of us from our footsteps since before we could have come into view (snake eyesight is mediocre, anyway) it set to ringing its patented alarm.

When preparing to flee or defend itself, a snake will often disgorge an undigested meal; this specimen was ridding itself of a mouse it had begun to swallow. We stood motionless. When some moments passed without further footfalls, it broke off buzzing and slowly unwound. The mouse lay dead on the ground.

But then, instead of beating a retreat as per textbook, the rattler turned our way.

Its tongue, a black flame, darted to pick up scent. Obviously this rattler was bent on determining the cause of the disturbance that had ruined luncheon. The air was running at a tangent, however, and our scent was not easy to follow. For two or three minutes it crawled, now to the right, then tacking to the left, now back again. But always it slithered nearer. Then it came directly at me.

When the rattler was several feet away and closing in, Bob craned to see better and inadvertently moved one leg. As his shoe scraped the gravel the creature whipped into the S-coil of the defensive stance. The triangular Argus-eyed head pointed unblinkingly in Bob's direction. The buzz of danger was heard again.

If Bob hadn't moved, I probably would have done so only seconds later. I had decided to let the rattler approach to a safe 2 or 2½ feet —just beyond the extreme range of strike for its length—before putting it off with my walking stick.

Now I rapped the nose, an action that turned its attention back to me. It did not lunge at the offensive stick. I stroked the throat and long muscles shuddered under the glistening skin. Still it refused to bite. And there we left the animal: a cryptic coil with a nervous tongue at one end and a busy tambourine at the other.

What would the rattler have done if it had touched my body? Would it have struck? Or tried to climb my leg? Or would it have fled as a wise small serpent should?

We discussed the incident[43] afterward with a ranger whose hobby was snakes. Rattlers are unpredictable, he said, by which he meant they are individuals in a reptilian world inhabited largely by conformists. He cited one of his charges that would advance on him seemingly with malicious intent every time that it was freed from its cage. And he had heard of another that became quite tame and rattled only at strangers. It was wont to curl up nearby in the friendly O-coil, or spiral, of repose. When master moved to another chair, the pet would presently stick out its tongue and, leisurely

---

[43] Other instance of rattlers tracking humans are described by Frederick Kent Truslow and Frederick G. Vosburgh in "Threatened Glories of Everglades National Park," *National Geographic* (October 1967), pp. 543–44, and James A. Oliver in *Snakes in Fact and Fiction* (New York: Macmillan, 1958), p. 70.

unwinding, follow the familiar scent to again take up its sociable position.

Yes, the ranger said, you can bet that rattlers are unpredictable —but the human reaction is not. Being tracked by an individual of the genus *Crotalus* will always be an unnerving experience.

And we all agreed to that.

A Hiker's Pay

To the keenest walker come days when he feels unequal to the self-appointed task. In a complicated world, that task is primitively simple: move legs up and down X times to proceed from point A to point B. Normally it is accepted with gusto.

Yet today, for no apparent reason, penance is being exacted: footing is uncertain and seems forbiddingly steep; large rocks have mysteriously weighted the hiker's pack and jab nastily at his backside. He no longer walks alone in the woods nor with chosen company; unwanted twin companions have joined him. Ahead, stepping arrogantly, is Futility; alongside, jostling rudely on the slender footway, trudges Exasperation. In short, the wind is in his face.

It was on such a day when, traveling northward on the Appalachian Trail, I arrived at the base of a craggy mountain in the Southern Highlands. The sky was brassy, signaling one of those brooding, sultry afternoons when even the copperhead, its mercurial temper stilled, lies inert in a hollow log, and only the hiker crawls through the solitary glades.

Climb began easily enough by zigzags which, although adding length to a mountain journey, lessen its angle of ascent. In the homey jargon of hill people, this ages-old device is known as rickracking. But presently the trail straightened out and the incline stiffened. My pace—already dragging in the heat—slowed to a tortoise's measure. Forsaking its springy bed of leaves and grass, the path entered the rocky bottom of a dry gulch.

I found myself laboring in a trench with earthen walls that shut off light and air. Rivulets of sweat dripped from face, neck, and body, staining clothing and pack with gray rings of salt. Broken quartz jabbed underfoot. My tongue tasted of raw wool but there was no stream to wet it. My heart thumped and my breath came in gasps.

I longed for that state of profound abstraction which frequently sustains the long-distance walker—a state when time and toil cease to be counted as obstacles are surmounted mechanically while the mind ebbs like the tide. Instead, every minute slowly added another

link to an endless chain; each step upward strained will and liga-
ments. The metal frame of my pack had broken the day before and
it chafed a saddle sore. I plodded miserably on.

Suddenly, gusts of wind funneled down the gulch. Branches
rattled like prayer sticks in an Oriental shrine. Flowering rhododendron crowded the banks; now, on each freshening draft, the plants
cast loose thousands of huge blooms. They fluttered to my feet,
leaving a supernal fragrance on the mile-high air. The last few hundred yards to the summit were spread with an inches-thick carpet
of rose-colored petals.

A hiker had received his pay.

Blood Mountain

On top of Blood Mountain is a low stone hut of two small rooms
put together in the thirties by the Civilian Conservation Corps, a
long since defunct federal agency staffed by Army officers and
founded to give both them and jobless young men useful outdoor
work during the Great Depression. From that time, the shelter has
been haven from storm and night for thousands of walkers.

Sole furnishing is a wooden table which still serves despite the
assaults of two generations of soup spillers and initial carvers. In
the corners are nests of dried grass and leaves, the lingering attempts
of travelers to soften their beds on the rough planked floor.

I was glad to see the hut. It was set in a thick heath of flowering
rhododendron—what the southern mountaineer calls a "laurel slick."*
The afternoon was young; there was time to rest and yet do more
miles. I lifted the latch and the door opened with protesting creaks.
Rain, not oil, was the lubricant of its rusting hinges. With a grunt of
relief I backed up to the table and dropped my pack.

At this a commotion erupted in the back room: first a sort of
frantic scratching, then a thr-r-r-rump, like a log dropped onto wet
ground.

I rushed witlessly through the connecting doorway with no idea
as to what had disturbed the peace. The room was empty. Nothing
was to be seen through the open, shutterless window save forested
peaks above which drifted white clouds and black vultures. But the
air was pungent with a zoo smell of manure and silage and the
unidentifiable.

Wondering, I brewed coffee, then stretched out on the table and

* To the dweller in the hills rhododendron is "laurel" and laurel is "ivy." A
dense stand of either in an exposed location, as on a summit, is a "slick." A
"hell" is the same thing in a cove, usually alongside a stream.

dozed. Later, sleepily bumbling down the switchbacks to Neels Gap, I came to a tourist facility—hotel, restaurant, and curio shop —operated by the State of Georgia. Through an archway in the courtyard runs the Appalachian Trail. It is very picturesque, mentioned in guidebooks, and a pity that more footpaths don't have arches to run under.

When I told the hotel manager of the peculiar noises, he smacked his hand on the guest register and chortled.

"Why," he said, "that must have been the 'Bear of Blood Mountain.' He lives in the hut's back room, but zips away when anyone gets near. Reckon he was sound asleep when you walked in. Lots of hikers tell me about him; usually they just see his big fat rear going away fast. He's like most of our Georgia black bears—shy, right shy."

And right smelly, I could have added.

Crabby

On another Georgia mountain I was to encounter a black bear with a markedly different personality—one not at all shy. As to being smelly, in the manner of most self-respecting bears, I cannot testify, since for a time I stopped breathing.

Facing up to a bear when one is alone in the woods armed with only a walking stick is not the same as meeting him at the zoo or from a car while touring the Blue Ridge Parkway. The quid pro quo has become uncertain.

I first became acutely aware of this when, ascending a hogback near Bly Gap on the Georgia–North Carolina border, a low growl pulled me up short. Several feet to my right hulked a black bear. A fist-size patch of hair was missing from its left rump. Was gunshot the cause? A bear that has been wounded, even if only by a nick on its hide, may turn ugly.

I stood stock still. The beast shuffled up the ridge. On either hand the slopes fell away so abruptly that no large animal could cross the mountain without using the trail. Perhaps when the bear was well out of sight I could resume my journey. A short while before, a signpost had been passed which indicated there was a lean-to and spring on the far side of the summit.

Crabby (for that is how he struck me) moved slowly. His manner was not reassuring. There was a redness in his eye and his shaggy head rolled heavily from side to side.

A hundred yards away, Crabby swung around and faced in my

direction. Hackles were raised as he growled and ripped at a clump of bushes.

He appeared to be working up to a charge. Could he be she? The sow with cubs is dangerous. Had I come between a mother and her youngsters?

My heart beat rapidly; it was one time that I regretted not having a hiking companion.

The book on ursine protocol has yet to be written, but I felt that my status had become persona non grata. In studied deliberation which I hoped Crabby would translate into nonchalance, I backed down trail until the bear could no longer be heard or seen, then halted in a grove of pines.

It was discouraging to note how far from base were their lowest branches. I despaired of shinning up one of those soaring trunks should it become necessary. Black bears are famous climbers, but do not always elect to pursue their quarry up a tree.

A forest ranger to whom I talked afterward told me that in his opinion (as proven by similar experiences of his own) I need not have doubted my agility under stress. A desperate man, adrenal glands pumping at full gauge, would squirrel up such a tree. Any difficulty, he added, would come only in dismounting: the higher the tree, the farther one would wind up from the bear—and the ground. Every timber topper knows that descent is more hazardous than ascent.

Uneasy moments crawled by while I watched the trail and waited for the big black to go on its business, whatever that might be.

A rasping noise was heard. I jerked about to stare at a hairy tan muzzle poking through a raspberry entanglement just behind me. I was the business! A deep throaty rumble seemed to say "Git!" And that I did, though not quite at a gallop, for the same reason one doesn't run from a hostile dog.

But I strode briskly, gentlemen, briskly.

Downtrail I went with thumbs hooked under the harness, ready to jettison my pack. I kept looking behind, but didn't glimpse Crabby. Flight stopped a mile beyond in a sag. Facing warily uphill I considered the situation. The day had been sultry and my canteen, filled at a rivulet long before, was almost empty. Gray rain clouds swarmed overhead; nightfall wasn't far off. Should I continue my retreat and try again in the morning, or wait here for an hour and then go forward cautiously? Neither choice was attractive.

As I stood indecisively, there was a flurry on the footpath and a rabbit pelted by. A Good God woodpecker followed, winging low. Squeals and grunts parted the air as a quartet of razorbacks bolted past. The wild swine were lean-bodied and long-legged; yellow tusks gleamed like lancets. I was content they failed to see me. But a disturbing thought intruded: bears are fond of pig meat! Was Crabby coming my way after all?

There was silence while the wilderness pondered the question. A minute ticked by gloomily. Then another.

As if in answer, a faint sound floated down from the heights and expired in the greenery. Profound quiet again enveloped the mountain.

The distance stirred hesitantly and then began to drone. The drone swelled into a babble that strove to become articulate. It resolved into many voices. A discordant chorus approached on tramping feet.

As I gaped, down the trail stampeded 27 Boy Scouts from Atlanta herded by a pair of harassed scoutmasters. The racket of a troop of adolescents on the march is impressive. Filing abreast of me, the caravan halted.

"Say, Mister," a Scout asked plaintively, "have you seen any game? This is our fourth day out and none of us has seen so much as a 'possum."

I knew the answer to that, and to tell the truth I was glad. In all the hubbub, one evil-minded black bear was even now fleeing Georgia and scampering along the rising ground to the safety of North Carolina.

That was for sure, gentlemen, that was for darn sure.

Overnight in the Pisgah

Sam Gilliam and his young brother, Ernie, made camp in a pine clearing of the Pisgah National Forest.

First off, Ernie filled their canteens at the spring and brought back water for tea in a billy can. Sam busied himself collecting an armload of dead and fallen limbs—squaw wood—and arranged a ring of stones on a patch of barren ground. A pyramid of dry twigs and sticks was artfully erected in the center of the ring. Into the hollow base of the pyramid Sam thrust a piece of wax paper and lit it.

Several matches later the pyramid caught onto the idea that it was combustible and burst into flame. As the fire mounted it was fed with branches no thicker than the little finger. Larger pieces were laid on, then the whispering, small-popping blaze was spanned with a stiff wire bent into a U-shape that was about a foot and a half long. The ends of the wire rested on stones. Onto this improvised but level grill went the billy.

While the icy water warmed and began to bubble, Sam and Ernie put up their tent. It was an ultralightweight backpacker's model with waterproof roof and floor. Including aluminum poles and stakes it weighed only four pounds, but had room enough for a man and his kid brother—providing the kid brother didn't squirm around too much in his sleep. Of course, the peak was only waist high, so neither occupant could stand inside. Like all their major items of equipment, the tent was brand new.

Sam enjoyed spending part of every summer hiking and camping on the Appalachian Trail, each year in a different locality. Until this trip, which he was sharing with his eleven-year-old brother, he had settled for old Army equipment bought at the surplus stores. Most of it was good equipment, tougher and better than anything Daniel Boone and Davy Crockett had used on their pathfinding in these same mountains, but heavy and cumbersome.

This year, however, Sam had exchanged his teaching job at the county grade school for one at a high school on the coast. He had opened an account at the bank, but a good share of his savings had gone for the tent and deluxe backpacking items for himself and his brother that he could hardly wait to try out.

The brothers unrolled air mattresses, put their mouths to the nozzles and puffed away. Critically, Sam kneaded the inflated pads. "Yours is blown up so hard it'll sleep like a rock," he cautioned Ernie. "Better let some of the air out."

Sam pulled his sleeping bag from its tight-fitting carrying sack, or stuff sack, and stood admiring it. The bag had cost an unholy sum, but was very light and astonishingly warm. Now he shook and fluffed it and laid it on his mattress. Sleeping bag and mattress were slipped into the tent as one unit. Ernie, watching closely, duplicated Sam's movements.

The water was singing in the billy now and Sam dropped in a couple of tea bags. A packet of quick-cooking beans was emptied into a two-quart pot, followed by water and a generous helping of onion flakes. When after a few minutes the beans were swollen and tender, the contents of a tin of corned beef were added. Steaming fragrantly, the mulligan was ladled into drinking cups and eaten with spoons.

"A fork is just something that takes up room in a pack," Sam

Photo courtesy Elmer L. Onstott

Elmer Onstott crossing log footbridge, Stratton Pond, Vermont.

Photo by Albert Fie

April on Big Bald, North Carolina.
Pink rhododendron.

Photo by Elmer L. Onstott

said judiciously between mouthfuls. "And unless it's stowed right, it's liable to prong you in the back almost as bad as one of those tidewater mosquitoes. A jackknife and a spoon are all the eating tools needed in the woods. Lots of fellows I know carry a hunting knife, but what are you going to hunt with a knife these days? A good jackknife will clean fish or skin out game quite as well if it comes to that, and it fits in your pocket."

Ernie nodded. Sam was pretty near right in most things. Personally, Ernie would have preferred a hunting knife to his old Barlow because—well, because it looked more adventuresome.

Supper tucked away, the utensils were scoured with handfuls of leaves, given a final rinsing in boiling water, then dried sterile over the embers. For a time Sam and Ernie sat, backs to a log, quietly contemplative as the glowing fragments sparked and the day faded.

A pair of grouse, wings beating noisily, pursued insects in and out of the lofty evergreens at the far side of the clearing. A boar coon came by and peered inquisitively until they pointed in his direction, whereupon he melted into the sundown. There was a sudden apparition overhead, and Ernie gasped to see a great horned owl rushing soundlessly amid the murky aisles of the forest.

With a yawn, Sam got to his feet and scratched where red wool shirt itched his bare skin. "Time to lay us down to sleep," he said. "But before we roost, Ernie, let's hang up our packs and food."

Sam weighted a stout cord with a rock and flipped it up and over a tree limb about 15 feet from the ground. There was no snagging —the maneuver worked perfectly on the first try.

Ernie whistled and clapped his hands together. Sam made a courtly bow in his direction.

The loose end of the cord was tied to both packs and Sam pulled until the packs were a dozen feet in the air yet still well below the limb. Discarding the rock, he knotted the cord to a sapling.

"Reason we're hanging up our things," Sam explained, "is to disappoint any bear that comes prowling. The packs are high enough off the ground and far enough away from the tree trunk so he can't reach 'em no matter how much he stretches or climbs. And the limb we picked isn't strong enough for even a yearling cub to trust his weight on."

"Then why," questioned Ernie, "did you leave two, three feet of cord between the limb and our packs?"

"That's to keep a raccoon or a squirrel or maybe a mouse from crawling down to the goodies. Talking about goodies, we want to be mighty sure we don't take any into the tent with us—some bears will enter a tent if they smell sweets. Right?"

"Right on," Ernie agreed.

It was sometime after midnight when Sam was awakened by a frantic whisper:

"Sam! Wake up, Sam! There's a bear shinning up the pack tree."

With a groan, Sam turned over. "Don't worry about it, Ernie," he said. "No bear is going to get our packs."

His older brother's calmness was reassuring, but Ernie kept looking through the tent flap and watching the black bear as it clung to the tree trunk with three paws while the fourth paw tried vainly to hook the dangling packs with its claws. This bear was the first that Ernie had seen outside a zoo.

A full moon was riding above the forest, silhouetting every move the big animal made. It gave off a heady odor, like a barnyard reeking under a hot sun, and panted from the strain of holding to the trunk while repeatedly swiping at the packs.

Ernie's eyes grew big as the bear clawed higher up the trunk and swung a front leg over the limb supporting the packs. Its free paw hooked outward. There was a tearing sound and food spilled to the ground. The bear scrambled backwards down the tree.

"Sam," yelled Ernie, "that bear's got our food!"

Sam jumped to his feet, striking the tent roof with his head. The tough nylon cloth recoiled and knocked him flat. He crawled out of the tent on hands and knees and began to shout angrily at the bear.

The beast turned his way in mild annoyance. Oatmeal had whitened its muzzle and it looked like a bandit with little eyes staring from a black mask. Sam picked up stones from the fireplace and began chunking them. The bear retreated, growling through a package of bacon clamped in its jaws. When a stone rapped its flank it hurriedly took off.

Sam and Ernie stood for a minute together, listening to the bear's feet drumming the ground as it made tracks through the forest.

"I guess that's the last we'll see of that fellow," Sam said. "When a bear slinks away he might be back, but if he runs like a two-alarm fire he usually is gone for good."

They assessed the damage—one packbag bore a foot-long rip, but it could be patched. The bacon was lost. What was left of the box of oatmeal Sam threw into the fireplace with an expression of disgust.

Before returning to bed, the packs were hoisted—this time so far out on the limb that it quivered from the weight.

Sun was flooding the peaks when the brothers awoke. In the dim light of the conifers they groped for kindling to start a fire. Birds were tuning up and the song and the tantalizing aroma of brewing coffee raised their spirits. Sam was joking about the raid when Ernie interrupted:

"Look! Sam, there's another bear! Isn't he the same one that came around last night?"

Sam whirled, coffee sloshing from his cup. He was dumfounded to see the bear enter their tent.

The walls bulged as the animal rummaged. Goose feathers from a torn sleeping bag sailed out the door. There was a loud pop followed by the hiss of escaping air: a sleeping mattress had been bitten. Smacks were heard as the bear slapped at the noisy object. With a cry of bitter rage, Sam grabbed a stick of firewood and charged.

Wondering at the fuss outside, Bruin poked his head through the flap. Sam held the stick high with both hands and slammed down on its muzzle as hard as he could. Again he slammed down, and the bear, shaking its head and clapping a paw to its snout, galloped into the shelter of the trees.

When Sam had cooled off he took a seat on the log.

"I never saw such a darn pesky bear," he told Ernie. "He must be one of those Great Smoky Mountain Park bears that tourists spoil by feeding and become so ornery the rangers trap and release them miles outside the park. I'd never mess with a bear, but that rascal made me so mad I couldn't stop myself."

Ernie looked at his older brother. His brown eyes were troubled.

"Sam," he said in a small voice, "you remember what you said about not taking food to bed in wild country? Well, there was some sugar candy in my jacket pocket that I forgot about; I guess that's why the bear went into our tent, following up the scent." Ernie choked.

Sam's mouth opened as if to say something, then shut. After a long pause he cleared his throat and spoke.

"Forget it, Ernie. This was your first overnight hike and you're entitled to a mistake. Now, I'm an old hand, and an old hand should gauge a bear's reach better than I did last night when hanging our packs."

"Besides"—and here Sam gave a rueful wink—"it isn't every day the teacher gets a lesson, is it?"

Fat Man in a Fur Coat

The story related in the previous chapter was told to me by Sam Gilliam when our trails crossed at the stone shelter on Mollies Ridge in the Smokies. The brothers' experience with a bear (or were there two bears?) is duplicated a hundred times each year, wherever men are a little careless and bears a little bold.

When white settlers first pushed deep into the Appalachians they found the black bear in great numbers. As an animal of the forest it thrived in the primeval stronghold. It was a ferocious brute. Unprovoked sorties against Indian and European, indiscriminately, were common. Some Indians classed the bear with man on the hierarchial list; a few tribes thought it was superior. Others believed the animal to be a reincarnation of the Indian.

Certainly the bear was cunning and self-centered and immensely strong. Its front and rear paws have evolved into different shapes, and when it rises on hind legs it looks like a man—a fat man in a fur coat. From prehistoric times the bear had been Two-Legs' most formidable antagonist. The hunter who dared the fearful risk shared its flesh with his neighbors, for thus was something of its vital powers imparted to the tribe. But "your damned saltpetre digged out of the bowels of the earth" and most treacherously converted into gunpowder was to change all that: the long rifle instilled a fear of human beings in the bear. And fearful he remains to this day. The black bear that fails to backpedal or detour on scenting man is a rarity.

Let the wind blow ever so faintly from you toward the bear and he glides away soundlessly as the vagrant air that brought the bad news. But come upon him without warning, and he may be seized with panic; then he rushes headlong through shrubbery, snapping branches, dislodging loose stones and bounding over fallen trees. The rout ends only when he is safely up the mountain or perhaps over the one after that.

The people-spoiled bears of the national and regional parks in the United States and Canada, however, do not always guide their conduct by the rule of retreat. They are the bruins usually involved in those publicized incidents where man comes off second best. Fortunately, they comprise only a small part of the total bear population. Often as not the man is to blame.

While on patrol, a park ranger came upon this arresting tableau: a car, driver's door open, parked in mid-highway. Beefy gentleman, camera dangling from neck and jaws clamped on a cigar, engaged in pushing a black bear into the driver's seat. Gentleman's wife in other front seat. Tourist types. Bear seems cross—probably only self-conscious. What a photo for the gang back home—bear taking wife for a drive! Did you get a nice hug, dear? Hey, man, when did you start wearing a fur coat?

The tableau was broken up by the ranger. Summarily relieved of his role, the principal actor huffed off into the woods and was not seen thereafter. The producer received a dressing down.

The black bear, *Ursus americanus*, ranges the continent. From 160,000 to 180,000 of his species are distributed among 30 states. Canada's total is unknown, but may be several times greater. The black is the only bear that calls the Atlantic seaboard home.

Grizzly, coastal brown, and polar are larger bears and inhabit the Far West and North or Arctic.[44] The coastal brown and polar are only variations of the grizzly, which itself is descended from the European brown bear.

No American bear has so accommodated to man as has the black bear. Grizzlies are much more prone to react violently and resentfully to the human presence. For their valor and intransigence they may yet be exterminated as they have been in California, which still proudly shows the grizzly on its state flag. Today not one grizzly lives east of the Rockies. There remains only the black, and he has become shy and prudent. His timidity has been his salvation.

In western areas are to be found many black bears that are not black but sport furs of brown and, less frequently, cinnamon, chocolate, cream, or blond (albino) color. Coats of blue gray, orange, and even yellow with dark stripes have been seen in Alaska. But your eastern species has little to do with color phases: Ethiopian is its hue.

From 25,000 to 30,000 black bears still roam the Appalachian forests from the Canadian line to Georgia, avoiding the haunts of men for the most part and making out as best they can in the face of a civilization that has been ruthlessly intolerant of wildlife. By choice, the black bear is a daytime animal; under man-pressure, however, it has become a successful moonlighter.

Among the Appalachian states, Maryland only has run out of bears. Connecticut may have 10, New Jersey 15, and Massachusetts 50. Kentucky, where "D BOONE KILT A BAR," has an estimated 20

---

[44] From having been common in 18 states, grizzlies now exist in merely 6, Alaska harboring 11,000 and Idaho, Montana, Wyoming, and Colorado sharing about 850, most of them living in national parks. Washington may have several left in the North Cascades. Possibly 12,000 polar (snow or ice) bears rove the frozen wastes of Canada, Greenland, Norway, and the Soviet Union. The coastal brown bear of British Columbia and southern Alaska, also known as the Kodiak, Peninsula, and Alaskan brown, is not plentiful, having long been the quarry of trophy hunters. Growing to more than nine feet in length and three-quarters of a ton in weight, the coastal brown is the largest of all bears and the largest land-dwelling flesh-eater left on the planet.

b'ars. South Carolina reckons 40 and Alabama 200. Tennessee, historically famous for numerous and scrappy *ursi*, these days can count only 400 of the much (and often illegally) hunted beasts. West Virginia tallies 575 and North Carolina 1,000. New Hampshire is host to 1,100 while Virginia claims 1,500. Vermont and Pennsylvania are credited with 2,000 each. Georgia lists 3,000 and New York 4,000. Great Smoky Mountains National Park, which straddles the boundary of Tennessee and North Carolina, enumerates 300; Shenandoah National Park in Virginia has 60. It's Maine the bears most fancy, for 10,000 to 15,000 are on the roster there. In ursine preference, the Pine Tree State is outranked nationally only by Alaska, Washington, and California.

The Appalachian regions of Canada (principally the ranges of Newfoundland and the Gaspé Peninsula) may be home for 20,000 or more bruins, but a count has never been made.

Bear facts are not easy to come by, and these statistics, although gathered from official sources, are admittedly the result of guesswork to which the adjective of educated may be applied more or less happily. Bears do not wait on census takers.

Sadistic and thoughtless hunters have never been lacking to shoot anything that presents a good target, and great numbers of these splendid beasts have been murdered—not for hide, fat, and flesh, but solely from the lust for blood.

"I was wrathy to kill a bear," said Davy Crockett, relating his adventures on the Appalachian frontier. And he and his fellows killed hundreds of thousands of bears in the eighteenth and nineteenth centuries; seldom did they say why. Many bears were drilled just because they were there, provided by inscrutable Providence as large practice targets.

In mid-1959, a black bear appeared in the wooded countryside between Baltimore and the District of Columbia, and for two weeks was hunted round the clock by police. At last the weary and frightened animal was cornered by a suicide posse—some say a "mob" —of over 100 of Baltimore's finest. The bear was butted three times by a squad car and then shot. The *Washington Post* in an editorial wondered that the men in blue hadn't used a "small atomic bomb" as then "surely the triumph would have been sweeter."

Why was the bear chased? Why was it killed? The animal was no "outlaw"—it hadn't threatened any human. The answer must be that this bear was killed because it was a bear.

If bears could voice their collective opinion of mankind, it would doubtless be "people are no damned good"—so conjectures John Hunt in *A World Full of Animals.*

Bears' one marked physical weakness is a thin-boned skull which can be smashed with a hard blow. Pliny the Elder recorded that bears were often slain in the Roman arena by a blow on the head from the gladiator's fist.

American frontiersmen sometimes killed marauding bears with axes. Ben Lilly gave many the quietus with long homemade knives sharpened on both edges and tempered in melted mountain lion grease.

Bears scrap among themselves, of course, and the grizzly on his range is likely to attack a black on sight. But apart from the ravages of old age and disease, the adult bear in this era can count man as his only serious enemy.

Few are the animals so rash as to challenge Bruin.

The Florida winter quarters of Ringling Brothers Circus in 1956 was the scene of such a folly. A Maine black bear and an African lion were being trained for an act when the lion sprang on its partner. Blackie reared, the big cat bounced off and was swatted with a forepaw. One swat and the fight was over; with a shoulder nearly torn off, the lion had to be destroyed.

Perhaps the balmy air of Florida is to blame, for another large animal there was found guilty of the same error in judgment. A boat-man on Lake Okeechobee reported seeing a bull alligator assault and pull under a swimming black bear. In short order the bear surfaced—alone—and proceeded on its course. Since the alligator didn't reappear, the presumption is that it was in no condition to do so.

The black bear is fond of water and is a good, if ponderous, swimmer. Once under way, however, he navigates in a straight line and, like wooden Juggernaut, turns aside for no object, whether man, canoe, moose, or log. Up and over he goes. This robotistic behavior is hazardous and mystifying. It suggests that the lords of Olympus may be, after all, as capricious as the Greeks believed they were.

When the craving is upon them, bears will come down off the mountain to raid cornfields and beehives. Cobs are eaten together with their corn and bees with their honey. In Pennsylvania, the State Game Commission reimburses farmers for lost bees, honey, hives, and frames. Claims total several thousand dollars a year. The Commission feels the price is little enough to pay, for "he is a noble bear, worthy to roam in the wilds of Penn's Woods."

Owing to his famous sweet tooth, he is one of the very few wild creatures plagued with cavities. Bruin in need of a dentist is a mean customer.

Bears that take to killing cattle customarily dispatch beeves with one or two powerful blows to the neck or sheep with a single crushing bite to the neck. These often are old bears that, crippled or losing their teeth, can no longer forage.

Hill farmers keep their domestic swine inside high fences—bears have a weakness for side meat. As a result of eating raw pork, they may contract trichinosis, a malady the housewife also risks if she tastes her uncooked breakfast sausage for seasoning.

Black bear cubs are born in the winter den, and the half-light falls upon a toy: blind, toothless, with undeveloped ears, almost legless, barely covered with fuzz, eight inches in length, and weighing possibly eight ounces. The newborn bear has been described as having the appearance of a piglet and the size of a rat.

The sow's first procreative effort (females mate every other year) results in a single cub; thereafter, twins are the general rule.

Triplets are not uncommon, but larger litters are exceptional. Nursing cubs may emit a curious humming sound, like bees droning. Youngsters are weaned at seven or eight months, and receive training, discipline, and love from mother for as long as they remain together. She teaches them what insects are savory, how to catch crickets, butterflies, frogs, mice, woodchucks, rabbits, and beaver, the art of fishing, and where to find edible fruits, grasses, herbs, seeds, nuts, and roots. In campgrounds she escorts them from garbage can to garbage can, and the more the leavings, the more the rounds are made. They are taught to scamper up a tree on command and to stay put till she signals that danger is past. Disobedience and antisocial behavior merit a smart cuff—or two or three. An hour later she may be fondling her two roughnecks, cradling them against her hairy breast and crooning.

When the cubs are well-developed, at 15 to 16 months of age, Mother spanks them up a tree for the last time, and then ambles off with some male suitor for a fortnight or two of June romance, never to return. The cubs are now on their own. For the next year the twins may adventure together, still as brotherly as Romulus and Remus. But on nearing maturity, they drift apart and become members of the solitary world of the adult black bear. At 3½ years they are ready to breed, yet continue to grow for another year or two.

A full-grown black may tip the beam at from 200 to 400 pounds; 500 are unusual, but 600 pounds are not unknown. Davy Crockett's biggest bear weighed 617 pounds. Not many females reach the

300-pound mark. The male will measure between four and six feet from caninelike muzzle to tiny stub tail and about three feet tall at the highest point of his back. When he stands on hind legs, man-fashion, and stretches, he may be ten feet tall!

Vision from his small eyes is nothing to excite the admiration of an oculist, but it is probably as good as a man's. Hearing is not of the keenest. Bruin's sense of smell, however, would make him a quick fortune were he in the perfumery business rather than the ursine business. He has a nose for smells that please—and those that spell danger.

Most famous black bear is Smokey. As a badly burned orphan cub he was rescued from a New Mexico wildfire in 1950 and placed in the National Zoological Park in Washington, D.C. Smokey was christened after the symbolic figure in the Forest Service's extremely successful nationwide fire prevention program. His coat is the brown phase. But so far there have been no offspring of Smokey Bear to try on the old man's ranger hat for size—Smokey has been reluctant to mate. Canada and Mexico also participate in the Smokey Bear antifire campaign. Mexicans know Smokey as *Simon el Oso* (Simon the Bear).

"The beast that walks like a man," was one of the names admiringly given the bear by Indians.[45] Normally he shuffles along at two to three miles an hour, a pace customary to humankind, but can shift up to 25 or 30 in a jiffy. He will stand erectly to see over obstacles or to trade blows with a rival. Although the "tame" park bear may seem a nursery darling, the omnivorous beggar is anything but 'umble, and when no tidbit is forthcoming has been known to remind the tourist of his duty with a vigorous cuffing. The person who thinks to hand a bear only part of the food he visibly holds will discover that Bruin takes the rest by force.

Along with other traits, the bear may be comical, appealingly clumsy, droll, curious, devoted. To see him long and luxuriously scratching against a rough-barked tree, eyes glazed in ursine bliss, or

---

[45] Anthropomorphism, the ascription of human characteristics to things not human, such as God and His beasts, is an error to which movie makers, pet lovers, and very amateur bird watchers are especially prone. The error is deplored, and sometimes over-deplored, by animal behaviorists. (When the car salesman speaks of your trade-in as "Old Betsy" and pats its chassis he is cunningly indulging in the rankest anthropomorphism.) But there is another side to the coin: the insensitive attitude of many scientists—and others—towards living organisms. This is mechanomorphism. The mechanomorphist is a mortician of the spirit.

perhaps draped on a log, limp as a rag rug and groggy from prolonged siesta, or with his broad-beamed rear upended as he rummages in a campground garbage bucket for toothsome leavings, is to observe Nature's leading clown.

A few are amenable to instruction and are drafted for a career in the sawdust ring; the fat man in a fur coat pedals unicycles and performs ridiculous stunts only bipeds have mastered. In captivity the black bear may achieve up to 27 years of age; in the wild, his span is 12 to 15 years, somewhat exceeding that of the domestic dog. A pack of bears is a sloth, but the term has fallen into disuse.

Favorable comment has always been forthcoming on Mother Bear's fierce solicitude for her offspring, though isolated instances of abandonment in danger are on record. While she is a "sow," he is a "boar;"[46] he regards Teddy as an egregious nuisance and is apt to knock him galley-west, for which reason she undertakes all the early upbringing. Woe unto boar, cougar or man who gets between sow and cub.

Mating black bears are conspicuously affectionate, and have many times been observed upright on two legs exchanging pawings, wrestling holds, and other carryings-on. The young cub, which is the end product of this impetuous behavior, has feet remarkably like a human baby's—soft and pink on the bottom and with the usual five toes. When fretful, he complains in a voice that puts one in mind of Junior noisily teething in his crib. When his teeth are all in they number forty-two.

Ordinarily, bears have little to say to each other or to the world at large, but no animal is more vocal in times of stress. The squalling of an angry male can be heard a mile away. Bears injured by gunfire sometimes cry aloud, sob, and lament in such manner as to smite the hunter with remorse and the feeling that he has perpetrated a monstrous crime. When skinned out, the bear's carcass resembles a man's. The sight is unnerving and might be compared to the shock felt at suddenly encountering Grandpa minus his long underwear; it has caused many a would-be Natty Bumpo to take the pledge and consign his rifle to the garret.

As a truly feral animal, resisting the give-and-take of domesticity, black bears make poor pets. When not whining for food or companionship, the cubs are into mischief. Beady black eyes miss nothing,

---

[46] In spite of the swinish nomenclature, bears are not pigs, but members of the *Miacinae* subfamily of raccoons, coatis, pandas, jackals, foxes, wolves, coyotes, and dogs. Indians called the raccoon "Little Cousin of the Bear"—an acute observation. Female dogs have nursed motherless cubs in zoos.

and they are endowed with curiosity enough to kill all the cats of Siam. In spite of endearing antics, youngsters have the instincts of a vandal. Sharp, nonretractile black claws are capable of real damage. Older bears become short-tempered—and potbellied. Great strength and unpredictable behavior make them less than reliable members of the household.

This unpredictability may owe something to their diet. Persons who have raised cubs report they are what they eat. After a feed of pancakes and syrup they gambol good-naturedly. A meal of flesh brings out a latent belligerency: the fur flies as they thump each other and bawl in fits of temper. Game officials have noted that bears having access to a steady meat supply are pugnacious, while the same animals subsisting primarily on roots, berries, and other vegetation are markedly pacific.

Blackie owns a thundering appetite. Like a hog or a man, he'll eat anything: standing grain, watermelon pickles, carrion, shoo-fly pie, ants, Liederkranz, cartons of freeze-dried food—and never mind reconstituting same. His digestive apparatus is equal to almost any strain. Stubborn wrappings of plastic and foil may provoke impatient grumbling (even as a higher order of being), but little hinder a sagamore capable of opening a can with his long white teeth or simply clouting it into submission.

The inebriated black bear is not unheard of.

In the fall of 1969, several bears in western Massachusetts were observed in a condition described as "falling down drunk" and State Game Director James H. Shepard charitably closed the bear hunting season. The animals had been munching frostbitten apples and the ferment turned to hard cider in their stomachs. It would be unsporting, said Mr. Shepard, to shoot a boozy bruin.

In Canada, a black bear raided a woodsman's cache of dried apple chips with a less happy result. After cramming down 20 pounds of the fruit, the animal waddled to a nearby stream to slake its thirst. The desiccated food swelled, and the bear was discovered later "split from stem to stern."

Food may cause any bear to abandon its native caution; the trail-wise will take pains to keep supplies beyond its greedy reach.

When camped on the ground or in a tent, I put all my food into a cloth bag and string it up from the end of a high tree branch. Snacks (even chewing gum) are not taken to bed at night—a practice that has resulted in many injuries, and worse. Once Bruin's attention is riveted on the menu, he resents distraction, while the person awakened by his rummaging is apt to thrash about mightily.

"Hold still there," snarls Bruin. "All I want are those lemon drops that seem to have wound up around your feet; I can smell them. How delicious!"

Meanwhile, the shuddering wretch in the sleeping bag fumbles to open the zipper (difficult enough to do quickly under ideal circumstances) and fly his cocoon. Naturally, he doesn't savvy a word the bear is snarling.

Another way to collect a furbearing bedfellow is to anoint the sleeping rig with a few drops of oily juice from a tin of sardines; this method will succeed where all else has come to naught.

Because food driblets also attract insects and dirt, it's smart to remove them pronto from any piece of camping equipment.

I've had bears prowl my camp at night, but they seem to know the tent is off limits when I'm in residence. On occasion they have sniffed at me—always at my head from behind—as I lay in sleeping bag under open sky. Since they fade away promptly after one sniff, I can only suppose that some odor repells them—my hair tonic, no doubt.

Bruin, himself, is no rose garden. His body odor is pronounced as that of an aging dog just come in out of the rain.

For a bear to enter a tent, lean-to, or cabin when people are within is highly irregular conduct. Recently, however, bears have been invading shelters after dark in Great Smoky Mountains National Park, seeking artificial food they have come to relish in this most-visited park, with its garbage dumps and tourist handouts. A nighttime experience of that sort may be described as adrenal.

Still, the solitary traveler in the woods is in almost no danger from the black bear. Leave him alone and he'll do the same; all animals respect the man who respects them and shows no fear. A bear's main interests are food and comfort, not terrorizing backpackers.[47]

Of course, he is a great bluffer—with other bears as well as with human beings. Bears will rear, show their teeth, huff and puff, slap the ground as if it were a drum, maul the shrubbery, bellow like a steam locomotive, snort, and make false lunges. The bear from whose company I shrank in a previous chapter probably only wanted to be fed. Odds were he was one of those deported campground prowlers that associate people with food and have lost their dread of man; his growl of "Git!" may really have been "Gimme!" Several hillmen, one of them a preacher, told me later that I could easily have driven Mister Crabby away by swatting him on his tender muzzle with a

[47] Robert Franklin Leslie in *High Trails West* tells of entering a shelter during a storm and finding a pair of wet blacks already in occupancy. For two days, until the weather cleared, Leslie and a hiking companion lodged with the bears. Though the animals would rub companionably against them, the men resisted their urge to run fingers through the thick, glossy coal black fur. And they were careful to eat only during those hours the bears were away meal-hunting.

tree branch. I thought it significant that the ecclesiastic, who presumably would have the least to lose should such an encounter turn out fatefully, did not prescribe entreaty to the Almighty as the remedy. Be that as it may, swatting is medicine that any bear, as a naturally expert boxer, might administer in kind.

Up in Maine they tell of an Indian who caught a young bear by the hind leg in a trap. Wishing to preserve its hide from an unsightly bullet hole, he thought to kill it with a heavy club cut from a maple sapling.

As he advanced, the bear rose to its hind legs and looked him steadily in the eye. The trapper swung and Bruin countered with a blow that sent the club crashing into the brush. A roundhouse followed that would have lofted the aborigine into the Happy Hunting Ground had he not dropped to the earth just out of reach, leaving only his stocking cap in the animal's claws.

Bears never should be teased, and there are times when they must be left strictly alone—especially sows with cubs, bears in the mating season (early summer) when skirmishes with other males for female lagniappe leave them ornery, the occasional specimen that is obviously in ill health, and while feeding.

A shelter has plenty of human scent to repel bears that have not become accustomed to people, but this is seldom the case in a remote forest clearing. Before occupying such a spot, urine might be sprinkled on the perimeter to create an olfactory "Keep Away—Humans Here" warning. I am told this method works, though naturally less productive at a dry camp, but haven't tried it and so pass it on *cum grano salis*.

Most important measure in keeping bears from camp is to burn thoroughly all table leavings and discarded containers, including cans, and carry out the trash (and its lingering food odors) in plastic litterbags whenever possible. Burying garbage is useless; bears will root it out and double the mess for the next camper. Better to just pitch it over a cliff than to leave it at a good site. Bruin has a palate to be tickled, and is all too ready to abandon Nature's simple fare for man's sophisticated offal.

Bears that have been hunted put two and two together upon sniffing burnt gunpowder. My pack includes a few large firecrackers, and before bedding down in bear country I may break one of them apart and burn it in a tin can or piece of foil. The smell, similar to that issuing from the mouth of a rifle, lingers pungently for hours.

The blast and glare of a bursting firecracker are also alarming, for Bruin has little relish for thunder, gunfire, and other loud sounds.

Concerted yelling by several persons or the racket made by beating on a cooking pot are on his list of abominations.

A flashlight, however, is of uncertain value except to spot him at night since, like many animals, Bruin is not intimidated by a quiet light or even a light that blinks frantically as it may.

Tear gas is not effective as he has no tear ducts; the chemical spray Mace, so effective against two-legged baddies, doesn't bother him much, either. The postman's dog repellent, a stinging aerosol stream of capsaicin, only arouses his dander.

Bears will usually leave the vicinity of a barking dog—or of a person who is barking like a dog—in a hurry. It is not that they cannot handle Rover; the dog hasn't been whelped that can lick even a half-grown bear. Indeed, pet dogs sometimes are singled out for deadly attack, for there is an ancient enmity between bears and dogs.

Southern hunters who chase bears employ two kinds of hounds: "hold dogs" and "ketch dogs." A hold dog will loudly track a bear for as long as it retreats, but maintains a prudent distance. Ketch dogs, and there are very few of this gumptious breed, will bite at a bear, keeping him occupied till their master arrives with his arsenal. Even Lloyds of London wouldn't write insurance on a ketch dog.

But an inborn fear of the canine is part of the ursine makeup. In bygone ages, wolf packs were probably the bears' chief foe; a dozen or two hungry wolves could harry even a monster bear to the point of exhaustion and kill him when he collapsed. Today the bear that has been hunted connects barking with guns and men.

When making my way through blackberry entanglements or abandoned orchards, I may whistle (snatches of *John Brown's Body* or *Sweet Georgia Brown*) and rap the path with my walking cane. The discordant sounds let the Fat Man, who could be gorging on fruit, know that I'm approaching. Startled bears have been known to charge or flee in the wrong direction, trampling the hapless walker underfoot.

Height of a person has a relationship to the black bear's fear, says Dr. C. H. D. Clarke, Chief of Ontario's Fish and Wildlife Branch.

To get down on hands or knees or to lie prostrate in its sight may trigger an attack. A man upright—even a child—is taller than a walking bear. While an adult who runs from a black bear is ordinarily quite safe, the child who does so may be pursued and killed. Dr. Clarke cites observations and experiments to back up his contentions.

If directly confronted by Bruin—in what John Muir termed the "awfully strenuous interview"—the lone traveler is recommended to stand quietly, neither advancing nor threatening. Make human noises (a soothing tone is advised), slowly back away if necessary, and remember that while a black bear can outrun, outclimb, and outbox any man alive, he seldom tries it.

Routine Question

I had paused on the Appalachian Trail where it crosses State Route 22, consulting the guidebook and wondering if I could make the eight miles up past Quaker Hill to Webatuck Lean-to before sunset, when a car coasted to a stop alongside.

The car bore the emblem of the New York State Police and was manned by two uniformed troopers.

"This is a routine check," said the young trooper in the right-hand seat. "Where are you going?"

I told him I was hiking—no, not hitchhiking, but trail hiking. Walking the Appalachian Trail. In the woods and the hills.

"Are you traveling by yourself?"

"Yes," I said.

"Why are you by yourself?"

"None of the girls I know would come with me," I confessed, smiling.

The young trooper did not smile back. The older trooper sat behind the steering wheel and gazed at nothing. Both wore sunglasses.

"We'd like to look at some identification," the young trooper said.

I shrugged out of my backpack, laid it on the grass, and removed my wallet from the flap pocket. Straightening up, I picked out a loose card and handed it over.

He studied it for a minute, inspecting both sides. "This card is out-of-date," he said.

I looked at the date on the card. Sure enough, it was. I hadn't paid my Green Mountain Club dues for the new year.

"It's out-of-date," he repeated. From the tone of his voice it was hard to say whether he was being accusatory or merely enjoying a small triumph of percipience.

"Is there anything wrong with that?" I asked.

"No-o-o, but it's not current. We'd like to see more identification."

I gave the trooper a plastic card case that opened accordion-fashion. It contained two insurance cards, three credit cards, a Federal Recreation Area Permit card, several photographs, and a couple more trail membership cards (current).

He scanned each in turn, then returned the case, dangling.

"You got a driver's license?"

"Yes—but I'm not driving a car at the moment. I'm hiking."

The other pair of sunglasses turned my way. Two faces, their mouths pulled down at the corners, regarded me coldly.

I thought of a detective from my police reporting days on a newspaper. He would sometimes regard me like that until the day I asked him not to.

"Otto," I had said, "don't look at me like that."

"Like what?"

"Like the way you're looking at me now."

"What's the matter with the way I'm looking at you now?"

"You know what," I said.

"All right," Otto conceded. After that he looked at me normally, the way a man might look at another when he has no good reason to look through him, the way it is taught in police academies.

Otto was practicing. He was really a good fellow, if hell on evil-doers, but frequently his professional manner slopped over, as it is apt to do with life insurance salesmen, United States senators, and large businessmen in small towns.

After a silence the young trooper spoke up.

"This is just a routine check," he said. "We want to know what a person is doing when we see him standing alone out in the country."

"If he's like me," I said, "he's probably out hiking."

My cheeks were beginning to flush; I could feel anger rising. I knew now that this cop, like Otto the detective, was practicing.

"May I ask you a question, Officer?"

He waited impassively behind the dark glasses.

"What is the motto of New York State?" I asked.

"Is that a question?"

"Yes."

The trooper behind the wheel opened his mouth for the first time.

"What do you want to know that for?"

"I'm a tourist," I said, "and it's a thing I ought to know. I just thought an official of New York State might be able to tell me."

For a long hard moment the dark glasses stared. Then the older trooper reached to the dash and whirled the knob of the patrol car's radio receiver. Background static exploded from a mutter to a crackling roar.

The young trooper closed the window vent on his side and sat looking forward through the windshield.

The car lurched from the shoulder onto the pavement. On its roof the red light began to flash; I did not hear a siren. The car sped southward, rounded a curve, and poured out of sight.

I put my wallet back in the pack and slipped my arms through the pack straps. The trail led east and north up a lane across which tree shadows were lengthening.

What is the motto of your state?

It was a fair quesion, Officer. I suppose I'll never know now.

Furor Canis

I had come down off Jug End[48] on the Appalachian Trail and was walking the dirt road that leads to Massachusetts Highway 41. It was eight-thirty in the morning. As I neared the intersection, two dogs roared in my direction from the lawn of a house. One was a black mongrel, the other a German short-haired pointer with yellow eyes. Their owner, a swarthy man in his middle thirties, stood on the porch watching.

"They don't bite," he called cheerily.

This announcement was barely concluded when the black dog bounded at me from the front while the pointer attacked from the rear and slashed my left leg behind the knee. The needle-sharp teeth felt like knives.

"It bit me," I cried, and brandished a piece of deadwood snatched from the ground. The dogs backed off and retreated across the highway to their master. I showed him where my trousers were ripped by the fangs.

"Hell, man, only your pants are torn," he scoffed.

"No," I said, "I've been bitten."

"Well, I'm a doctor," he said. "Come into the house and I'll give it a look."

I stepped onto the lawn. Then I paused. "If you are really a doctor," I said, "you might show me your credentials."

"Don't be an ass," he said, "I am a doctor. Come along."

At that moment, the German dog padded by with flattened ears and began to circle me. Something inside my system began to churn. I pointed at the animal, then at the man.

"It was once the custom," I said, "for a dog biting a person to have its head removed for rabies examination by the Public Health Service. If you're really the doctor you claim to be, you might initiate the matter."

The man's face took on a fine puce color. "Get off my property,"

---

[48] A plunging stretch of pathway for which the hackneyed designation of "Suicide Leap" would not be excessively descriptive.

Beyond Highway 41, the Appalachian Trail turns into Bow Wow Road, a name that in other circumstances I would have found pleasantly waggish.

he shouted. "Get off, you're trespassing. Get off or I'll sick both dogs on you."

An open two-seater sports car thrummed south along the highway toward Sheffield, the nearest town. It bore two young women with long hair streaming brightly in the wind. I waved and it stopped.

"Girls," I said, "a dog has bitten me. Would you drive me to the nearest police station so that I can get first aid and report what has happened?"

From his lawn the man called out to the girls. "I'm a doctor. That man is insane. Don't you let him get in your car."

The pair, who had seemed willing to help, now looked fearful. Their car pulled slowly away. In a shaking voice one girl called over her shoulder: "Just down the road is a house with a phone."

I limped to a large white house where Franklin Curtiss, an attorney, answered the doorbell. He brought me to his bathroom. There I removed my trousers, washed the bleeding wound, and painted it with antiseptic. His wife made us coffee. Then Mr. Curtiss drove me to Sheffield where I was bandaged by Dr. Percie Roberts.

Dr. Roberts, unlike the bluffer, is a real doctor, an M.D. He loves dogs and raises them as a hobby. He also is realistic about dogs. "Always carry a heavy stick when walking in the country," was his advice.

Professional advice.

As luck would have it, on descending Jug End my walking stick of the moment, cut from a black cherry sapling growing wild in the Berkshire hills, had slipped from my hand and clattered down the precipice. I hadn't bothered to search it out. An hour later I would have been glad to buy one.

The dog that chewed me was placed under observation for signs of rabies. At the end of the ten-day waiting period I was far north on the trail, but the report of negative—telephoned to me from the Sheffield Township Office—brought a sigh of relief. My journey had been delayed several days and I was out of pocket for a pair of britches and medical attention.

But that big minus sign on the report insured that my health was intact. Only scars are left.

Shortly after this experience, I wrote to the National Communicable Disease Center at Lawrenceville, Georgia, for information on rabies. The Center replied that while national data is not compiled on how many people are set upon by animals, wild or domestic, an estimated 30,000 do receive antirabies injections in the United States each year following bites or clawings. In most of these cases, the animal runs off after the attack and cannot be examined for disease. Owing to their number and attachment to humans, dogs are the usual agents of transmission, but cats, rats, skunks, raccoons, squirrels, bats, foxes, cattle, and other warm-blooded creatures also may be infected and pass on the virus.

A course of immunization consists of daily injections for 14 days. Treatment may be extremely painful with severe neurological side effects and is capable of reducing strong men to childish sobbing. But it is undergone just the same, for rabies leaves no survivors once its symptoms appear. Actually, one human has been known to survive. A Willshire, Ohio, boy, bitten in the thumb by a sick bat in 1970, came down with the disease in spite of the full course of injections. Round-the-clock care which anticipated and treated every symptom as it developed apparently was responsible for this seeming miracle.

The disease breaks out after an incubation period of roughly two to four weeks from a rabid bite.

Symptoms include feelings of impending doom, catching of the breath, abundant salivation, and spasms of the throat muscles. The violent contractions cause the victim to dread swallowing anything, even water, lest he strangle—hence another name for rabies is hydrophobia, or fear of water. Sometimes there are fits of delirium and aggressiveness during which confinement in a strait jacket may be necessary. Death ends two to seven days of unholy torment, though a few suffer for weeks.

Thanks, however, to animal control measures and prompt treatment, not many Americans die—fewer than five persons annually in recent years.

The immunization method was developed by Louis Pasteur in 1884. A photograph has been preserved of a group of Russian peasants glassy-eyed from terror just arrived on the transcontinental train in Paris to beg Pasteur to save them after they had been bitten by rabid animals.

A dog shows the terminal stage of rabies in either the "furious" or the "dumb" form. The "furious" is that of the classic mad dog with slobbering and foaming mouth, rages, and biting. In the "dumb" form the dog is listless, slinks away from people, and has a slack jaw with mouth held open. Any wild animal that is acting strangely or seems to have lost its usual fear of man should be avoided.

If an animal is killed after an assault its head should be packed in ice and sent to a government laboratory where the brain tissues will be tested for the so-called Negri bodies that reveal the presence of rabies.

Since the brain is necessary for a correct diagnosis the animal should not be shot in the head.

Letter carriers get my sympathy. Dogs inflict them with 10,000 bites a year, says the Post Office Department in an official release. After a few rounds as a perambulating toothing ring, your friendly courier is likely to become morose. He would find grim consolation upon reading the Old Testament, for all but two of its thirty references to dogs are derogatory.

I imagine that bill collectors could recite a mournful litany; his dog may be the debtor's first line of defense.

Few things are more bothersome to the wayfarer than the dog on mischief bent. One learns to keep eyes peeled on a stroll, for Man's Best Friend may be less than friendly. A few are mean as that bottomless pit.

Reason for all this snarling, snapping annoyance very frequently lies at the master's doorstep. Either M.B.F. is an uncontrollable or vicious animal that should receive merciful release, or has never received training. Then again, it might belong to a psychotic who imparts to the animal his own brand of confusion. The dog can become antisocial, frustrated, or uncertain of temper. Veterinarians know that pets kept by neurotics may incur nervous breakdowns and have to be put on sedatives; the same blue capsule does for both.

There is a dark side to being a pet, and there are crimes against them that have no witnesses. Karl Menninger the psychiatrist from Topeka writes of the thin-lipped heroine of business, mannishly dressed, who acquires a large male dog and then treats the dumb brute in private as she would never dare treat a man. In short, she treats it as M.B.F.

"A trained dog is a happy dog," declares Willy Necker, one of the country's foremost canine experts. Seldom does the working dog—hunting hound, packdog, or stock herder—create trouble; this seems to be the province of idle, aimless dogs. That they get away with it is a matter owing much to public indifference, or perhaps a belief that the dog which bites a stranger cannot be all bad.

While dogs are apt to bark at any stranger who is afoot, their unkindest cadenzas are reserved for the man carrying a pack. I suppose the hunched-up profile is alarming, what John Hillaby the veteran English walker calls "the *Rigoletto* syndrome." Then, too, the ambulatory person, as a member of a rare species, rates higher as an object of curiosity than the riding person. At least he rates higher with the dogs. He is more accessible to canine investigation, certainly. And there is no doubt that because of the walker's physical exertion the man scent is pronounced. Perhaps it is more feral. The chief sense of dogs is their ability to smell, an ability reckoned by science to be fifty times that of people.

When M.B.F. approaches in full cry, the hiker's best course usually is to press on unhurriedly, ignoring this show of insolence to a member of the highest, or Primate, order. Hostilities have been pronounced—unilaterally, it is true, but any hesitation will be construed as weakness.

Seldom can a truce be reached by signaling the bellicose party with amicable word or gesture, for then he suspects you are buffaloed or else plotting countertreachery. Only the young, unworldly dog is taken in by that kind of bone; the older dog vocalizes his disdain.

Very effective is a string of "Nos!" uttered loudly and sternly as the animal approaches. The effect is heightened if at the same time the open palm of the hand, with wrist down and fingers held up, is presented in the gesture used to repel something distasteful.

If threats persist, a smartly tossed pebble or two will urge M.B.F. to withdraw at the double, or at least to maintain a safe distance. Most dogs know the sting of a missile and scuttle out of range when arm is raised to cast the sling. Dogs running in packs are not so easily handled, for a mob is braver than any of its individuals, but will generally disperse when faced with determined resistance, backed by a shower of stones.

In dealing with a pack or a large guard dog, it may be necessary to withdraw slowly, guarding the rear and flanks as best as is possible until one's back is secure against a tree or building. Preserve the cool and remain in control of the situation: a display of great excitement may only provoke the dogs to mindless behavior.

Walkers and bicyclists of the Gay Nineties armed themselves with rubber syringes loaded with solutions of ammonia or asafetida; a squirt of either would send a wolf ululating to the tall timber. (The Nineties were years distinguished not solely for gaiety, but for practicality.) Personally, I'd settle for an aerosol can charged with the inflammatory sauce brewed from the pungent *chilipequín* peppers grown in the border counties of South Texas.

As M.B.F. opens jaws wide to bite, the can would be aimed and a generous spray of sauce released to drench his incisors; as the scamp turns howling to flee, a parting shot, directed to the most obvious target, would speed departure. *Similia similibus curantur.*

A similar, if far milder, repellent is now carried by mailmen. This bite-back product is called "Halt!" It comes in two petit sizes: the ¾-ouncer (good for about 15 short squirts) with a gross weight of 1¾ ounces and the 1½-ouncer with a gross weight of 2½ ounces. Firing range is up to 10 feet. The smaller can is 1 inch in diameter, the larger 1⁵⁄₁₆ inch in diameter. Both are 4¾ inches long and fitted with a plastic pocket clip.[49] I tried "Halt!" on a dog. The dog was not attacking, just making a confounded nuisance of itself.

It was one of those curs that worry the heels and then suddenly clamp on. I let it have it between the eyes from point-blank distance. The liquid spurted not as a mist but as a visible stream making it Tommy-gun easy to correct for aim. The dog retreated several yards, shaking its head. Its expression switched from slyness to puzzlement. There were no dramatics, no sound effects, and no indication that anything hurtful had occurred. Then the dog drifted away. The lack of histrionics was a little disappointing, but there was no doubt that the animal had undergone a change of mind.

The manufacturer claims that "no harm has been observed in the many hundreds of dogs exposed to this material under scientific conditions" and that "no ill effects have been found in humans accidentally exposed in the course of development work."

Obviously the repellent must be employed with discretion, for the pet owner who feels his pet has been needlessly abused may retaliate energetically. This is particularly true if the trail you are following crosses his land.

"Halt!" should not be directed against bears. Not only does it appear to have negligible effect on the critters but, to quote the manufacturer, "the tests we have run show that 'Halt!' tends to aggravate bears more than repel them." The future in aggravated bears is pretty slim.

Despite their formidable teeth and powerful jaws, dogs have weak necks. A hard kick on the back of the neck can fracture it, rendering the dog instantly helpless or, indeed, dead. Should an arm or hand be seized, push it further between the jaws, pressing the head up and back until the dog chokes or the vertebra snaps. Dogs are vulnerable in the nose, as well. A solid blow with stick, rock, or fist on this tender part will usually cause a dog to run away or even bleed to death.

The walker alone is more likely to be molested than if traveling in company. Least subject to harassment, curiously enough, is the person

---

[49] If the hiker is unable to buy "Halt!" locally he can write to the manufacturer, Animal Repellents, Inc., Box 168, Griffin, Georgia 30223.

accompanied by his own dog. The pet diverts attention to itself, for normal canines are more interested in strange members of their kind than in strange humans. At the same time, so I have found on walks with my sheltie, the pet is almost never subject to harm when it is with its master.

According to tradition as old as the republic, the person who points out the shortcomings of dogs, even ill-bred, contumacious, unpacific dogs, is expected to wax maudlin and recant at the end. "If you pick up a starving dog and make him prosperous, he will not bite you," said Mark Twain in *Pudd'nhead Wilson.* "This is the principal difference between a dog and a man." Twain, of course, was right.

And it was Erle Stanley Gardner, God bless him, who gave it as his considered opinion that "if a man will live his life so he can be really worthy of a good dog's affection, he doesn't need to look much further for a worthwhile ambition."[50]

But what of the man who does not, or will not, train or restrain his dog? To judge a man by his dog may be as fair a way as any.

This I would resent—were I a dog.

The Worst Weather in America

Timberline!

To the mountaineer, timberline is more than just a word meaning the altitude above which trees will not grow because of a conspiracy of wind and cold, thin air and thinner soil.

Nearing timberline the trees become gradually less tall—and finally dwarfed with contorted trunks and limbs streaming like weathercocks in the draft. There follows the familiar, yet always dramatic, passage when at one moment the climber is still among the trees and at the next is above them. The world of plants gives way to a desert of stone where tiny pools of rainwater reflect every mood of the sky. Little vegetation breaks the force of the wind: this is the domain of sun and storm, of oceans of light which suddenly vanish behind clouds hurling snake tongues of flame.

There is a mystique to open heights. The alpinist lives for those hours when his own unaided efforts put him atop a peak from which he can look out as far as the day after tomorrow. Above tree line he feels the surge of emotion that was Praxiteles on confronting a block of virgin marble from Olympus.

Timberline spells adventure. In this connection, however, the hiker

[50] Erle Stanley Gardner, *Gypsy Days on the Delta* (New York: William Morrow & Company, 1967).

would do well to keep in mind a famous explorer's definition of adventure as "accident or mistake in judgment" which luck or foresight "may" keep from turning out badly.

Just below timberline on the trails of the Presidential Range of the White Mountains in New Hampshire stand yellow and black signs which warn the hiker:

STOP

THE AREA AHEAD HAS THE WORST WEATHER IN AMERICA.

MANY HAVE DIED THERE FROM EXPOSURE, EVEN IN THE SUMMER.

TURN BACK NOW IF THE WEATHER IS BAD.

The Presidentials, so-called because of their summits named for early presidents of the United States—Mounts Madison (5,363'), Monroe (5,385'), Jefferson (5,715'), Adams (5,798'), and Washington, first among his peers at 6,288 feet—are crisscrossed not alone by the Appalachian Trail, but by more than 60 other trails. Here is not only the nation's greatest network of footpaths, but the most heavily traveled, winter as well as summer. Yet for all their heavy usage (the Boston and New York metropolises are within easy driving distance), the narrow walks rank with the most perpendicular and rock-strewn in the land. And the weather is downright unpredictable. It is "Damn weather, sir," and seldom improves; a day that begins in a temper is likely to turn very rude. The fairest morning may within an hour become a shrieking arctic blackness into which hail is discharged like shrapnel.

On a wonderfully sunny August 15 I first poked my nose above timberline in the Presidentials. My shirt was soaked with sweat as I stopped to blow on the crest of Mount Madison. Then, glad to be descending, I walked down its western flank to the Appalachian Mountain Club's Madison Hut and ordered coffee.

My watch read two o'clock when I left the refreshment room. I stood blinking in the strong light before taking up my pack. A breeze had sprung up and the wire cables that anchored the hut to the mountain were beginning to sing.

The sky was serenely azure and I set out confidently on the six miles to Mount Washington. But I didn't get to Washington that afternoon—or the next. An hour later the day was colored ominously gray and drops of ice water were being squeezed from low-sailing clouds. The footpath was typical of the White Mountains—shakily paved with rocks, now becoming slick from rain. I struggled awkwardly to keep from being knocked over by heavy gusts.

Two miles beyond Madison Hut I reached Edmands Col where

the White Mountain National Forest people have put up a refuge. Starkly utilitarian, it consists of half a large galvanized iron tube (the corrugated sort used for culverts) bolted to a thick slab of concrete. The emergency shelter resembles nothing so much as a stream-lined sarcophagus—I wouldn't have been surprised to see the letters RIP. An entranceway that makes a right angle turn to keep the elements at bay gives admittance to a cavern perhaps ten feet in length. Though only midafternoon, darkness was enveloping the col and through the small window seeped a grimy trickle of light. The temperature had dropped to freezing, wind roared at hurricane strength (above 72 miles an hour), and .50-caliber hail lambasted the refuge. It was marvelously clammy within. But no matter, here was safety!

Snug inside the refuge were Bill and Mike Murphy, father and son, of Lawrence, Massachusetts, who had arrived minutes before the storm broke. The Murphys were on their first backpacking trip. We agreed they had undertaken a tough assignment for a novice hike!

Next day continued squally, though the rain let up before noon. Together we took the side trail to Gray Knob Camp, a rustic two-story cabin below timberline.[51] The following morning the Murphys and I made the top of Mount Washington, and that day—all day, for a change—was clear.

There are seldom more than 61 days a year in the Presidentials which fit this cheerful category.

The second time that I stood on Washington was in fog on a July twentieth. At nine o'clock the billows abruptly parted in a rush of cold air and dazzling sunlight. A map was snapped from the hands of a Boy Scout leader; he and his charges watched helplessly as it danced aloft and then flapped out of sight into gaping Tuckerman Ravine. I waited two hours at the pleasantly unpretentious Summit House, a long low wooden hotel, souvenir shop, and cafeteria owned by the State of New Hampshire. Several times I dashed out to check the instruments on view to the public in the two-story meteorological observatory. As I fretted, vainly hoping for a break in the weather, the anemometer stepped up from 25–35 miles an hour to a gale of 45–55 miles an hour. Though the mercury trembled at 40 degrees, the gusts lowered the chill factor close to zero. I put on a second wool shirt under my parka, clapped on stocking cap, added woolen gloves and sunglasses (as much to deflect the blast as the actinic glare), and

[51] Gray Knob Camp, together with nearby Crag Camp, is open to walkers at a charge of one dollar a night for each person. The Camps are maintained by the Randolph (New Hampshire) Mountain Club.

staggered off across the tormented plateau, heading for Crawford Notch. There were 12 miles to go, five above timberline.

I met a score of hikers above timberline that day. Sad to tell, a few were attired only in shorts, cotton T-shirts, and light nylon jackets. Their eyes were teary and inflamed, their teeth chattered a polar litany, and their legs had turned as blue as their prayers. With miles to walk—and few can average better than 1½ miles an hour on these rough grades—any worsening of the weather would have put them in danger.

The wind wailed its dirge all day, but it was only a solo that it sang.

A "Small Killer of Fools" is the title of a notice in the Mount Washington weather station, and it declares that "as mountains go Mount Washington is a pygmy, but contempt of it can be the first step on the trail to disaster. That this mountain has some of the world's worst weather is no idle boast. A matter of minutes can change the summit's aspect from one of shirtsleeve comfort to one where survival, if you are still in your shirtsleeves, becomes a race with time. Why has this diminutive hill accounted for so many lives? Mostly because it is so accessible and familiarity breeds the contempt mentioned before. A mountain sporting a road, a railroad, and a summit population cannot, after all, be very formidable. Well, there are more than 50 ex-people who would now be willing to dispute this if they could, and for each of these there is a score of near-misses, still able to vocalize, either through luck, the efforts of rescuers, or the grace of God."

The notice goes on to attribute a third of the area's fatalities to exposure, from which "hundreds have had very narrow escapes. This form of fatality is closer to suicide than accident. Inadequate clothing is almost invariably the cause of these tragedies."

Overexertion and heart failure are blamed for 15 percent of the deaths, while falls account for a similar number. Not many days of the summer pass without someone's bones cracking from a misstep in the Presidentials. Even veteran hikers and Himalayan climbers make the casualty list.

Anyone accustomed to the splendidly brushed and graded trails of Shenandoah and Great Smoky Mountains National Parks will find quite another sort of pathway in the White Mountains.

At times he will find himself stretched on a cliff face like a lizard, and realize that he is taking lessons—however unwillingly—in elementary rock climbing. Rock climbers, who are a breed apart, exult in the problems posed by terrain where a miscue—to use theatrical terms—means curtains. Hikers are normally less appreciative òf these delights.

To Mount Washington goes the distinction of having been crowned with the first mountain weather observatory in the world. Since that date, in 1870, a low of minus 58°F. has been recorded, but never has the temperature exceeded 71°F. The yearly average is 27°F. Annual precipitation has been about 71 inches; snowfall usually is 178 inches (ten inches of new snow equal one inch of rain) and there is no month in which snow does not whiten the summit, however briefly. It is a bit of northern Labrador in climate, flora, and fauna. Five states and Canada can be seen from the top; on a clear night the lights of Montreal, largest Canadian city, glow on the horizon.

The weather shack, which houses a staff of five meteorologists year-round, is known as "the strongest frame building in the United States." Ten-inch railroad trestle timbers provide frame for seven-layered walls; the base of the 22' × 44' structure is fastened to long bolts that extend downward at least five feet into solid rock and concrete. After all, the strongest natural wind ever measured anywhere on this planet—231 miles an hour—buffeted the gauge here on April 12, 1934. The typhoons of the Pacific and 1969's devastating Hurricane Camille have reached, but have not been known to surpass, 200 miles an hour. Mount Washington is one of the world's most dangerous peaks; the weathermen, who take eight observations daily, have dubbed it "Misery Hill."

The plateaus (locally called "lawns") presided over by Mount Washington are not uncommonly combed by summer tempests of 80 miles an hour. Average wind velocity is 37 miles an hour!

In winter the tantrums may simply become more intense. On occasion over 3,000 miles of wind—more than the airline distance from Boston to Los Angeles—have swept the summit in a single 24-hour period.

An altitude of 6,288 feet makes this the tallest mountain in the northeastern part of the continent, ranking twelfth in stature among all the Appalachians—yet only a piddling 396 feet less than the champion 6,684-foot Mount Mitchell in North Carolina. (More high crags are on the North Carolina–Tennessee border than anywhere in the United States east of the Missouri River.) But compare Mount Washington's altitude with Pikes Peak (14,110'), Mount McKinley (20,320'), Mont Blanc (15,781'), or Fujiyama (12,389').

Still, in the entire Appalachian system only the higher peaks of the northern ranges—the White Mountains of New Hampshire and Maine, the Green Mountains of Vermont, and the Notre Dame Mountains of Quebec—truly thrust above timberline, which in that clime girdles the hills at about 4,000 feet. The estimated tree line of the Southern Highlands is at 7,000 feet. None of the peaks of the South reach to this height, and most are well-forested. The many balds of Dixie, "bald" because their tops remain treeless even though they are far under the line where trees fail to thrive, constitute a botanical conundrum; however, their exposed domes are rather minute in area— nothing like the sterile expanses encountered above the Forty-third Parallel—and thus seldom trap even the unwary with capricious weather.

The tempestuous climate of Mount Washington is generated by air currents that rove inland not only from the nearby Atlantic Ocean, but from the Great Lakes, the far-off Gulf of Mexico, and the Arctic ice cap, to meet and dispute above the White Mountains. The pot is always at a simmer here; when these vectors mix it comes to a boil.

White Mountain people have a saying: "If you don't like the weather, wait a minute."

U.S. Supreme Court Justice William O. Douglas, one of America's most experienced hikers, discovered for himself just how fickle that weather can be, even in late June.

Following supper at an AMC hut he strolled off, intending "to explore some of the nearby botanical wonders. I wore no hat or jacket and felt comfortable enough. Suddenly, the wind came up. It arrived like gunshot. In a few minutes it was blowing a gale. The temperature dropped fast, and before I could walk a hundred yards I was blue with cold. There were moments on the half-mile hike back to the hut when I questioned whether I would be able to reach it. The experience taught me the awful threat Mount Washington holds for incautious hikers."[52]

Walkers who find themselves in Judge Douglas's predicament, but who cannot quickly reach shelter, should get below tree line with all haste. Here will be found incredibly dense thickets of *Krummholz*, or elfinwood—hardy alpine shrubbery that grows to a man's height and baffles the wind. *Krummholz* will pull the teeth of a 100-mile-an-hour hurricane, braking it to a five or ten mile-an-hour mumble. The elements have made timberline plants cretins in growth but heroes of resistance.

Appalachian Mountain Club's *White Mountain Guide*, the shirtpocket bible of the range, urges the foot traveler to "carry a compass.

[52] William O. Douglas, "The Friendly Huts of the White Mountains," *National Geographic Magazine* (August 1961).

If lost in a cloud (Author's note: on Mount Washington there is normally some fog 304 days of the year), remember on which side of the mountain you stand. If you are experiencing difficulty from the weather, abandon your climb. Storms increase in violence with great rapidity toward the summit. . . . Since *the worst is yet to come,* turn back without shame before it is too late." Among the White Mountains, Washington has accounted for the most tragedies—29 known fatalities since records have been kept. The Indians generally gave it a wide berth.

Situated as they are, with their ridges trending north and south, the Appalachians actually channel weather between the tropics and the North Pole. Quite the opposite is the case in Asia. There the Himalayas, sprawling east and west, hinder the interchange of winds from warm and frigid climes. As a result, the Indian subcontinent languishes in some of the most torrid weather on the globe while Siberia shivers in the coldest.

Though the Appalachian states lie within the Temperate Zone, their summers wax exceedingly hot, in a word intemperate. The diplomats of at least one foreign power receive extra pay as recompense for enduring the steamy equatorial climate of a number of posts in the good old U.S.A.

A glance at the world map shows the extreme limits of the Appalachian Trail to fall in latitudes that we, with our European orientation, think of as southerly. Springer Mountain in Georgia corresponds roughly to sinful Tangier on the tip of northwest Africa, while Mount Katahdin in Maine stands no closer to Santa's workshop than does the opera house in Milan, Italy. The halfway point in Pennsylvania lines up with Madrid, Spain. Nearly all the prominent cities of the South, so rich in classical architecture, lie south of Athens, Greece.

Mount Washington was first ascended in 1642 by Darby Field accompanied by two Indians. In 1861, the Carriage Road, eight miles long, was opened to convey horse-drawn coaches.

The three-mile Cog Railway (the cogs grab the roadbed) was completed on the opposite, or western, slope in 1869 with grades ranging up to 37.4 percent. The Carriage Road, now an auto toll road, and the railway are very much alive today, both reputedly earning handsome profits for their owners.

Many trails lead to the top, but hikers often walk the Carriage Road or the railway track. No charge is made to travelers afoot, though the track must not be used when trains are in operation. Someone has counted the steps that will bring the hiker from the base of the Carriage Road at Glen House in Pinkham Notch to Summit

House: 16,925! The uphill speed record was set in 1972 by Ronald Cormier—1 hour, 9 minutes, 16 seconds. Edgar Welch holds the downhill record of 45 minutes.

It is likely that the name of "white" was affixed to the White Mountains by the Algonquins (and later the English) because of the large masses of whitish rock visible above the green mantle of plant life as well as the snow which lies like frosting for much of the year. But the name, given for whatever reason, certainly owes nothing to imagination. Imagine, however, the spectacle displayed twenty thousand years ago when, geologists believe, the pinnacle of Mount Washington was the only point of land in the vicinity that protruded above the white frozen ocean of the three million square miles of continental icecap which covered North America!

How the weather must have misbehaved then!

Katahdin

From Katahdin Stream campground at the base of Mount Katahdin there are five point two trail miles and 4,168 vertical feet to the top. Tree line is halfway and then the path enters a field of boulders strewn on the mountainside like Aztec altars fallen down temple stairs. White blazes point up into the tangle.

On this slope, called the Hunt Spur, iron rungs project from rock faces to give holds for hand and foot.

I was lifting onto an enormous boulder when awkwardness brought impasse. The first of a series of rungs had been started on the wrong foot and now a knee, injured two years before, refused to deliver leverage for the highest grip. Retreat was to risk a bad tumble.

Though I lay not uncomfortably, face down and one leg suspended in space, I was, in a phrase, hung up. Still, all I really had to do was rest quietly in the sunshine until someone appeared to offer a hand. It was early Sunday morning in September and soon Old Katahdin would be swarming with New Englanders.

I recalled the lively narrative of Major John Wesley Powell, one-armed veteran of the Civil War, who was sent by the Smithsonian Institution to explore Colorado River canyons. In a moment of forgetfulness, while maneuvering on a cliff, Powell put out his only hand to grasp an overhang and then, lacking the aid of a second limb, trembled to discover that "I can get up no farther and cannot step back." If he let go he would fall six or seven stories down the precipice.

The major had begun to weaken with the effort of holding on when his companion, Bradley, managed to come out above him by another route. With astonishing presence of mind, Bradley whipped off his drawers and lowered them over the cliff. "I let go with my hand," said Powell, "and seize the dangling legs."

Why did Bradley proffer his drawers to the major rather than his britches? Had the poor guy lost them in some earlier misadventure, or was it because in that modest era drawers were usually one-piece unionsuits, providing cover from whiskers to hocks, and the longest garment a man might own? Well, Powell, who was a gentleman as well as the chief of expedition, didn't press Bradley for an explanation—at least he made no comment on the choice in his diary.

It was something to think about as the Indian Summer sun beat down and Katahdin's granite, pink beneath its greenish gray mantle of lichen, blushed warmly.

"Hey, Mister," a voice piped.

I looked down to see a little blond girl standing on a rung. A diminutive pack was on her back; its flap was open and within could be seen a soft drink and a sandwich in a plastic bag.

"Child," I asked, "will you be my Bradley?"

Round blue eyes regarded me gravely. "I'll have to ask my Daddy."

"Where is Daddy?"

"His shoestring busted; he's coming now."

Up he came. The resemblance between daughter and parent was manifest.

I explained how I had gotten hung up. When I said "Ready," he pushed on my bum leg and I scrambled to my feet.

Child flew up the stone walls like a wren among the columns of Canterbury Cathedral, while two men (no longer in the first flush of youth) straggled in the rear. When Daddy called for a rest we flung ourselves down, panting, on the rocks. But Child was breathing easily. She perched on a ledge and thoughtfully nibbled a Hershey bar.

When our hearts had slackened to a moderate thumping, Daddy and I put our packs back on and followed Child upward and through The Gateway.

Here we stepped onto The Tableland. A broad, tilted plateau sandpapered by the continental glacier, it extends south and west for a mile and north for three more. The steep part was behind us, but the target was Baxter Peak, a mound that shimmered rosily on the eastern brink of the plateau. Among Katahdin's pinnacles, it stands highest at just 13 feet under a mile in height. On a few days of the year the peak is probably the first point in the United States to be touched by the new day's sun[53]—a not inappropriate illuming of the generosity of its donor, late Maine Governor Percival P. Baxter.[54]

Less than two miles of walking remained.

Near the trail whispered Thoreau Spring. (The chanticleer of Walden Pond improved a day in 1846 by scrabbling up Katahdin.) Icy water trickled between plants that crouched like gnomes against the stony ground. There were alpine varieties of azalea, bilberry, bearberry, and others. Two of the commonest plants bore the names *Arenaria groenlandica* and *Dispensia laponica:* Katahdin is an arctic mountain, and Greenland and Labrador are floral analogues.

Streaks of paint on ragged outcrops led across the Venusian landscape and ended at a tall cairn. I added a pebble from Springer Mountain, Georgia, to the pile. Two thousand miles of continuous pathway had come to an end; there were no more white blazes.

The Appalachian Trail expired on Baxter Peak.

❊   ❊   ❊   ❊   ❊

On a plaque I read the words by which Gov. Baxter had expressed the spirit of this mountain:

Man is Born to Die, His Works are Short-Lived
Buildings Crumble, Monuments Decay, Wealth Vanishes
But Katahdin in All its Glory
Forever Shall Remain the Mountain of the People of Maine.

Slipping out of my harness, I sat and rested on the rim of the Great Basin. Circular walls dropped to a sea of spruce far below; the trees flowed out of the Basin through its pass and lapped in green waves at the horizon. Light flashed from a hundred cerulean ponds.

The rim from which I gazed is called The Knife-Edge, and for a mile beyond Baxter, past South Peak and onto the rounded dome of Pamola, can be walked. But this is a stroll for the light of foot,

[53] Owing to the fact that the place of rising of the sun varies from north of east in the summer to south of east in the winter, several other places in Maine rotate with Katahdin the honor of receiving the earliest sunrise. These include Cadillac Mountain, Mars Hill, and West Quoddy Head Lighthouse. See "Where (in these United States) Does the Sun Shine First?" by Blanton C. Wiggin, *Yankee* (Jan. 1972), pp. 58–63.

[54] When the state legislature refused time and again to acquire Katahdin from lumbering interests (most of Maine is the fief of giant paper companies), Gov. Baxter reached deep into his own pocket to buy the land—it took him more than 30 years—and then gave it to the people.

Baxter State Park, containing 201,018 acres, by statute "forever shall be held in its natural wild state." The alpine paradise has seven campgrounds and is intersected by a gravel road and 84 miles of footpaths which are well-trod in the mid-May to mid-October season. Nine trails lead to Baxter Peak.

Photo by Elmer L. Onstott

Cross on Mt. Washington marks place where a hiker, caught in a storm, spent his last moments.

ATTENTION

TRY THIS TRAIL <u>ONLY</u> IF YOU ARE IN TOP PHYSICAL CONDITION,

WELL CLOTHED AND CARRYING EXTRA CLOTHING AND FOOD

MANY HAVE DIED ABOVE TIMBERLINE FROM EXPOSURE

TURN BACK AT THE FIRST SIGN OF BAD WEATHER

WHITE MOUNTAIN NATIONAL FORES

Photo by Chuck Ebers

Sign in White Mountain National Forest.

not of head: the rim is a mere several feet in width and falls away for 1,500 feet on either side in a jumble of fractured granite. Here is no path to be caught on by storm.

To the west lay The Klondike, a rarely visited region owing its name to Joe Francis, the famous Penobscot Indian, because it reminded him of the Canadian Klondike. It is one of the nation's few sizable areas that has never rung to the logger's ax. It's the only one I know that is so flat—and flatlands are first to be timbered. But the way into The Klondike is roadless and difficult and therein has been its saving.

The day's clarity was blemished by a distant haze, like the faint cloud in a bottle of souring wine. Though the Atlantic couldn't be seen foaming against the Maine coast 90 miles away, one could make out a squall line hovering over the water. Later in the day, puffs of cumulus appeared over Katahdin. In their shadows the air became chill with autumn's promise of winter. The wind rose and fell with little moans.

A throng of weekend hikers, strung out on the trail like a procession, came into view, approaching the crest of the monolith revered by the Indians as *Ket-adene*—the "greatest mountain." If their faces showed the strain of the climb, they also glowed with the expectancy of the pilgrim nearing the shrine.

The Reason Why

I know a man who once walked from Louisville, Kentucky, to Cedar Keys, Florida, more or less along the route of John Muir's celebrated thousand-mile walk to the Gulf of Mexico. Whereas Muir made a botanizing expedition, with the notes he jotted later becoming a book,[55] this man wished to take a long walk for his own satisfaction only. He admired Muir and thought it would be enjoyable to trace the famous naturalist's footsteps while stretching his legs.

When Muir took his solo walk in 1867, the people he met nearly always treated him with kindness and hospitality. This was as true in the Deep South as it was in the North, although the bitter Civil War had ended just two years before, the southern countryside swarmed with brigands and appeared on the verge of anarchy, and a regiment from Muir's own state of Wisconsin had been on Sherman's town-burning, hog-sticking, skirt-raising march through

[55] John Muir, *A Thousand-Mile Walk to the Gulf* (Boston: Houghton-Mifflin, 1916).

Georgia. Plant study was virtually a new science then, and people nudged one another at seeing the intent young naturalist peer into the throats of wild flowers with a "spy glass." Muir had little trouble gathering all the strange herbs his tote bag could hold.

Now, as this man followed Muir's track down dusty roads and through villages, people would ask why he walked. When he replied that it was for his own pleasure, they reacted as to a hateful thing. Hardly anyone seemed to believe him.

When he said (a little lamely, for it sounded like an excuse) that he was on foot because Muir had been on foot, people frowned and asked why he didn't use a car—or even a motorcycle. Certainly the driver is more efficient at covering territory than the pedestrian. It was clear that his explanations were unsatisfactory.

Thus he discovered that an unconvincing answer is no answer at all. Truth is usually beside the point if it does not fit into daily experience or familiar ideas. "For men," as Pope observed, "never approve any other's sense, but as it squares with their own." The man knew then what must be done: he would copy a page, as it were, from Muir's notebook. At a small college on the route he visited the department of natural history and came away with a plant press and a book on herbs that fitted handily in the pockets of his jacket. In the press he arranged several fine specimens of pennyroyal culled from the roadside.

Thereafter, when the customary question was raised, out would come the press with its pennyroyals squeezed flat and exuding a strong minty smell. He was collecting plants, he told everyone. Where there had been dislike, now there was warmth. People smiled and shook his hand. They invited him into their homes. By the time he reached the Gulf whole platoons of chickens had been marched to the chopping stump, rolled in cornmeal, and fried crackling brown in his honor. He had the memory of happy hours spent in woodsheds over tin cups of homemade bourbon.

Another thing also happened. Before obtaining the plant press this man hadn't known lady's slippers from Jimson weed. But now his interest in an unknown subject was stimulated. Today he is an expert botanist, and women's clubs 200 miles distant beg him to lecture in the springtime on the topic "Fragrant Flowers of the Field."

The third day of my own hike on the Appalachian Trail in Georgia I met a young man cutting trees and splitting them into fence posts. This is work followed by many hillmen who have no love for supervision and will labor only for their own account. It is as ill-paid as are most healthy and solitary occupations. At my approach the post-splitter shut down his chain saw, seated himself comfortably on a log, and lit a cigarette.

"How much do they pay you for walking the trail?" he asked politely. By "they" was meant the federal government. He had noted other strangers on the trail and had come to believe that walking was a new activity of mysterious Washington, D.C. Maybe he could get on. It might be easier than wrestling trees.

Unfortunately, walking as an end in itself results in no salable product. People who make money from walking are those who make it unnecessary. In fact, the greatest fortunes in history have gone to the Fords, the Firestones, the Rockefellers and the others who have exploited the feeling that the proper way to travel is on one's back-side. Only pennies have been made in the other direction.

I was sorry that my answer disappointed the post-splitter. That he didn't believe me was plain. There was a small flash of resentment in his good-bye. I suppose he is at his trade yet, now and again glancing up the footpath in hope of meeting the employer of those who walk the trails. He is young, and the wait will probably be lengthy.

The conviction that the hiker is paid in hard coin for what he wants to do is not uncommon. It owes much to the specious idea that whatever is worth doing should be well worth one's while. Few Americans accept the notion that walking may be a pleasure, much less a hobby. The effort involved is far too strenuous and resists such easy substitutes as words, slogans, and machinery. It has been for-gotten that the human being's natural method of locomotion is shanks' mare.

Like the man who followed Muir's route, in time I, too, concocted a story that would please. If he could pass for a plant collector, I could be a tester of trail footgear. So it is that I became an indepen-dent, unpaid party of one to judge the qualities, good or bad, of hik-ing boots. And I still am. None of many pairs of boots have quite suited me and the vital testing continues apace.

It has been a very satisfactory answer.

Appalachian Hiker

By Edward B. Garvey*

Started at SPRINGER MOUNTAIN on April 4, 1970
Finished at MT. KATAHDIN on October 7, 1970

On April 4, 1970, I found myself sitting beside the bronze marker at the southern terminus of the Appalachian Trail on Springer Mountain. As I sat there soaking up the warm Georgia sunshine, I wondered if I would really make it to Katahdin. My thoughts went back some forty-three years.

In 1926 in the little town of Farmington in southern Minnesota two events took place that certainly had some bearing on my hiking activities. One was the announcement by the high school principal that a Boy Scout troop was about to be formed. This coincided with the fact that on November 13, 1926, I would be twelve years of age, then the minimum age for becoming a Scout. I became a charter member of that Boy Scout troop. One of those who assisted the high school principal in the formation of the troop was a seventeen-year-old high school junior named Kenneth E. Parr. Oddly enough, when on October 7, 1970, I completed my 2,000-mile hike at Mt. Katahdin and hiked back to Katahdin Stream Campground, this same Kenneth E. Parr, now sixty years of age, was on hand to meet me.

The skills acquired in years of scouting were later to prove useful. I drifted away from scouting and hiking for a fifteen-year period. My wife and I and three children moved to Falls Church, Virginia, in 1949. In 1951 I learned of the Appalachian Trail and of the Washington, D.C.-based Potomac Appalachian Trail Club (PATC) which maintained some 300 miles of hiking trails in the Pennsylvania–Maryland–Virginia area. They also issued high quality maps of the hiking

* Adapted from *Appalachian Hiker: Adventure of a Lifetime,* published by Appalachian Books, Oakton, Virginia 22124. Copyright 1971 by Edward B. Garvey.

trails, primarily the Appalachian Trail, in those states. I promptly purchased a complete set of the fourteen maps then available.

I joined PATC in October, 1952. One of the first publications I received from that organization was the January–March, 1953, issue of the *PATC Bulletin*. It contained an article describing the 2,000-mile hike of the entire Appalachian Trail by PATC member George Frederick Miller, age seventy-two. This article captured my imagination. Quite possibly this is when I first entertained vague thoughts of someday hiking the entire trail myself. Sixteen years later when plans for my own hike became rather definite, I went to my stack of *PATC Bulletins* and from near the bottom of the pile pulled the one on Miller's hike. One of the features of his hike was a preprinted log form he had used for pertinent information on each day of the hike, and I borrowed this idea.

In 1953 I volunteered to become an overseer for a three-mile section of the trail in Maryland which was some seventy miles from my home. As an overseer, I made from three to five trips a year to my section of the trail to remove any fallen logs or trees, to cut out summer growth, and to see that the trail was properly identified by white paint blazes, by the four-inch diamond-shaped Appalachian Trail Conference metal marker, and by wooden directional signs.

In 1960 I spent the night at the Indian Run Shelter in Shenandoah National Park and chanced to meet Lochlen Gregory and Owen Allen on their ninety-nine-day hike from Georgia to Maine. In the next few years I was to meet on the trail a number of through hikers: Ray Baker in 1964, Elmer Onstott and Everett and Nell Skinner in 1968, and Jeff Hancock and Eric Ryback in 1969. Eventually, I met and talked with over half of the small fraternity of some forty people who had hiked the entire trail through 1969. In October of 1969 I retired. With retirement my long-held dream of hiking the entire Appalachian Trail became feasible. True, I had a wife to consider; moreover, the two youngest of our five children were still of school age. There was the possibility that my wife would take a dim view of her husband being on the Appalachian Trail for over five months. Married men reading this book will appreciate my predicament. I sent up a few tentative smoke signals. No outward reaction. I sent up more and stronger signals. Still no reaction. I interpreted this as calm acceptance of the inevitable and proceeded to make definite plans.

There are two ways to plan a hike of this magnitude. One way is to tell no one of your plans. Then, if you decide you have had enough after a few days or a few weeks, no one is the wiser and no embarrassing explanations are necessary. The other way is to tell everyone of your plans. Then you have no choice: unless death or injury intervenes you must complete the entire hike. I chose the latter method. Notice of my hike appeared in the January, 1970, issue of *Appalachian Trailway News*. Shortly before my hike began I gave a talk to members of PATC on my plans and preparations. I was now totally committed.

I reached the summit of Springer at 12:00 noon on a beautiful spring day. I signed the register and noted that Branley C. Owen of Brevard, North Carolina, had signed the register on April 2, two days ahead of me. He had indicated on the register sheet that he was hiking all the way to Maine. I thought it quite possible that I might catch up with Owen somewhere along the trail, but this was not to be. Owen broke all existing records for speed, arriving at Mt. Katahdin in Maine on June 12, 1970, a mere 117 days ahead of me.

The great majority of through hikers start in Georgia rather than in Maine. There is a reason for this, especially if the hiker plans to begin his hike in the early spring. Spring comes early in Georgia but very late in Maine. There is frequently snow on the ground in Maine until June 1. Even after the snow melts, the ground is soggy until well into the summer. In addition, the mosquitoes, the flies, and the no-see-ums make life miserable for the hiker until around the first of August. Early spring in the Southern Appalachians is extremely beautiful. As the hiker walks north he is walking in eternal spring. A hiker who begins his hike in Georgia around April 1 will see and enjoy more of the spring season than ever before in his life. As I review my daily notes for those delightful April and May days with the entries describing the flowers—trillium, bluets, spring beauties, rhododendron, and azalea—I get the urge to revisit that beautiful area. For those planning to hike the entire trail in the five or six months that should be allowed, I recommended the south-to-north route. In that way you can enjoy the best of both seasons, spring in the Southern Appalachians, autumn in Maine.

An equally important decision is whether you will hike alone or with a companion. The Appalachian Trail Conference's Publication No. 15 in its Chapter 13, "Precautions," has three pages of do's and don'ts for the hiker. The final paragraph of that chapter consists of a single italicized sentence as follows: "*Above all, and as a final monition, do not travel alone.*"

After reading all of the warnings against solo hiking you may wonder why it is that so many of the fifty-seven through hikers have hiked alone. If safety were the only factor to be considered, there would be no solo hikes. Danger is always present in mountain hiking; danger of bad falls when bones can be broken or severe cuts sustained. A heart attack, a stroke, or a sudden severe illness could occur. There is some danger of a poisonous snakebite or attack by a vicious or rabid animal. All of these things could occur, whether you are alone or in the company of others; but the possibility of getting help is greatly increased if you have one or more companions. So, why solo hike? The answer is that it is very difficult to find someone who is free to hike, who wishes to or is able to hike at the same speed you wish to hike, and who has a personality compatible with yours. It is one thing to hike with a companion for a few days. It is a different matter to hike with the same person for five or six months.

I had planned to do most of my hiking with Maurice A. (Gus) Crews of Bethesda, Maryland. We took two conditioning hikes in February and March, 1970. On the second of these hikes Gus developed an infection. His doctor advised against his taking the long hike. Despite this, it seemed that I would have plenty of companionship because in announcing my plans in the January, 1970, issue of *Appalachian Trailway News,* I said I would welcome company for a few days or a few weeks. I received about twelve or fifteen inquiries, but for various reasons I hiked with only one person of that group, and then only for part of one day. One of these, Tom Herring of Mobile, Alabama, did not receive his equipment in time to begin on April 4. He started later but finished ahead of me in Maine. I traveled alone for about two-thirds of the entire hike. Sometimes I met friends by prior arrangement and hiked with them for as long as two weeks. Sometimes I met people on the trail who were hiking north, and I joined them for short periods of time. And yet, even though I am naturally a gregarious individual, I also enjoyed those days when I had only my own company. No one, unless he is a total recluse, can live his life exactly as he pleases. Each day of a man's life is a series of compromises with members of his family, his co-workers, his boss, his neighbors, and others. It was pleasant, therefore, to have some days on which all the options were mine: the time of arising and the time of going to bed, the choice of food to be eaten at each meal, the speed at which to hike, and the side trails chosen to explore.

Someday a solo hiker on the trail will die or be killed; and when that happens, the event will receive nationwide newspaper coverage. But in that same year some sixty thousand people (the yearly average) will be killed in automobile accidents.

During the course of my hike, I walked 2,028 miles on the Appalachian Trail and another 157 miles to shelters, springs, small towns, and other points off the trail. Each day was a new experience—different scenery, different vegetation, different people (when I chanced to meet people), and each night marked a different place to sleep. I am thankful that I have copious notes on each day's activities. I had committed myself to an ambitious schedule of trail and shelter inspection. The voluminous notekeeping became a chore at times; but I stuck to it religiously. Much of my writing was done on 5½-by-8½-inch printed log forms. I completed these forms with ballpoint pen.

In addition to the log form I kept a diary in a 4-by-6-inch bound book. I used two such books during the hike and devoted one or two pages for writing up each day's activities. Frequently, the material in my diary—written as events took place—is more accurate, more spontaneous, and more colorful than any words I could call to mind as I wrote this story. I have used verbatim sentences, paragraphs, and at times almost whole pages from my diary. Whenever you find quoted material you may assume it is from my diary.

Georgia

FRIDAY, APRIL 3, 1970. My wife Mary, my eleven-year-old son Kevin, and I arrived in Gainesville, Georgia, at the tail end of an Easter-week vacation to the Florida Everglades.

From Gainesville my family and I drove to nearby Amicalola Falls State Park where Bob Harrell, a reporter from the *Atlanta Journal and Constitution,* was waiting for me. I talked with him for about an hour; I discussed the plans for my hike, the things I was carrying, the inspection duties I intended to perform. At the park I also met Major Garnett Martin of Denver, Colorado. He had hiked the entire trail in 1964 and had returned to revisit various points of the trail. Later in the evening I was privileged to view some of his excellent 35-mm slides, taken on his 1964 hike.

SATURDAY, APRIL 4. Up at six. A quick hot shower (my last for some time); a ham-and-pancake breakfast; and shortly thereafter we headed over rough mountain roads for Nimblewill Gap. At the gap I met my hiking companion, Elmer Schwengel of Kansas City, for the first time. He planned to hike with me for the first several hundred miles. After picture taking and good-byes to my wife and son and others, Schwengel and I started hiking up toward Springer Mountain.

It was a beautiful spring day, warm and sunny, with the temperature reaching 67° F. at noon. Here I experienced my first disappointment.

It became painfully obvious that Schwengel was not in proper physical condition to hike at anywhere near the pace necessary if I were to reach Maine before snowfall. After about thirty minutes I reluctantly pushed on ahead, hoping he would catch up with me either at the summit of Springer Mountain (2.3 miles) or at the first lean-to, which was 1.6 miles north of Springer.

I reached the Big Stamp Gap Lean-to at 1 P.M., ate lunch there with the Morrises, the Engels, and other members of the Georgia Appalachian Trail Club, made the first of my 238 lean-to and shelter inspections, and had the misfortune to drop my little 16-mm Minolta camera in the spring. By 1:45 P.M. Schwengel had not shown up. I left a note for him at the lean-to urging that he not give up his hike but that he continue it at a pace he could manage. I never did see him again nor have I ever heard from him. I learned later that he discontinued his hike and returned to Kansas City. I felt badly about going ahead without him, but I had warned all would-be fellow hikers in early March that I would be hiking at a rate of about fourteen miles a day.

After leaving Big Stamp, I pushed on steadily toward Hawk Mountain Lean-to, 8.0 miles further north, reaching it shortly after six. I barely had time to make camp and cook my evening meal before darkness set in. The afternoon's hike had taken me along beautiful streams bordered by rhododendron, laurel, and hemlock. I was fascinated by the mica particles imbedded in the soil. They looked like thousands of jewels sparkling in the bright afternoon sun. At the lean-to I was entertained in a most unusual way. A scant fifty yards away the U.S. Army was conducting helicopter maneuvers. The choppers would zoom across the mountain, land quickly near the lean-to, soldiers would rush out, and the chopper would take off and zoom away. These maneuvers continued until darkness. I had hiked 12.2 miles this day despite the late start. Sleep came quickly that first night, as it did for most of the 158 nights I spent on the trail.

SUNDAY, APRIL 5. Breakfast eaten and ready to hike by 7:10, except that I had to spend a full hour catching up on my paper work. Joined by twenty-year-old Jim Meredith of Charlottesville, Virginia, who would hike with me for a week. Leisurely hike of 9.1 miles to Gooch Gap Lean-to. Reached it at 2:00 P.M. Hiked a mile beyond lean-to to the residence of Mr. and Mrs. Homer Gooch and had a forty-five minute visit. Was given four eggs. The Gooches had befriended Everett and Nell Skinner when the Skinners temporarily lost one of

their two dogs on their 1968 hike. Back at the lean-to I tried out my
one-pint plastic shaker, mixing powdered milk, water, and instant
pudding. Worked fine. Instant puddings in various flavors became one
of my most frequent desserts.

MONDAY, APRIL 6. Cooked the four eggs at breakfast time, ate two
of them poached, the other two hard-boiled for lunch. This was one
of few times I had fresh eggs on the trip; I should have cooked them
more often. Have been hiking during these past two days on Foot
Travel Only trails, these trails being (hopefully, at least) protected
by forest service signs designed to exclude two-wheeled and four-
wheeled vehicles. During hunting season the signs are taken down
and hidden by the violators, who then claim they saw no signs. To
combat this, the forest service erects heavy wood posts. These posts
are cut down with chain saws and vehicles obtain entrance. The
forest service retaliates with more wooden posts, and this time drives
one-inch thick steel rods through the posts and into the ground. And
so the battle goes—each side trying to think of new ways to outwit
the other.

I left the trail at Woody Gap and hitched a ride to and from the
village of Suches where I talked to Postmaster Lloyd Gooch and
visited the grocery store. Mr. Gooch has been lending a helping hand
to Appalachian Trail hikers for many years, frequently helping them
pack and mail unneeded items home. Back on the trail I hiked north
to Jarrard Gap and walked the 1.5 miles west to Lake Winfield Scott
Recreation Area where I slept on the stone floor of a picnic pavilion.

TUESDAY, APRIL 7. Up at 6:00 and by 6:40 I am hiking on a road
toward the Appalachian Trail. Should have reached it in thirty minutes, but kept hiking, hiking, hiking. Finally realized I have taken the
wrong blue-blazed trail at Lake Winfield Scott. I intersected the
Appalachian Trail at Slaughter Gap instead of at Jarrard Gap where
I had left it the day before. Made good time to the lean-to at Tesnatee
Gap, which I reached at noon. Found a note there from Meredith.
He had left an hour or so before I arrived. No water at lean-to but
a passerby gave me a ride to a stream two miles away and then drove
me back. On my way again, not desiring to stay at Tesnatee which
is cold, windy, and directly beside the highway. Realize I can't make
it to the next shelter, so stop at a forest service campsite 5.3 miles
north of Tesnatee Gap and make camp in the open, gambling it won't
rain. "Heated water. Had sponge bath. Washed T-shirt. Shaved. Feel

like a new man. Hiked 16.5 miles today. Paper work 1¼ hours. Trail very pretty. Am enjoying the day-by-day advance of spring."

WEDNESDAY, APRIL 8. "Was awakened 5 A.M. by owl hooting nearby. Stars like crystals. Big Dipper had swung around from northeast to due west. Very still except for owl, who departed after ten or twelve hoots. Watched stars slowly grow dimmer and sky brighter. Bright enough to see at 5:45 and I arose. Had a quick cold cereal breakfast. Temperature 38° F. at 6:00. Very still. Reached Cold Springs Gap at 8:00 and scared up full-grown black bear thirty feet downtrail just south of gap. Saw two deer at Chattahoochee Gap. Beautiful views of Brasstown Bald with its imposing tower."

I reached Rocky Knob Lean-to at 11:00 and found Meredith and a second man from New York who hoped to hike the entire trail. He had hiked the almost fifty miles from Springer to Rocky Knob without realizing that the white paint blazes signified the Appalachian Trail. He (as well as Meredith) was hiking without guidebooks.

Meredith and I went on ahead and arrived at Tray Mountain Lean-to at 4:45. Saw three deer north of Unicoi Gap. Never did see the man from New York again, or learn how far he progressed on the trail.

THURSDAY, APRIL 9. In morning I backtracked south on Appalachian Trail to Tray Gap for a meeting with U.S. Forest Service officers. At 10:00 I was met by Paul Sweetland, assistant regional engineer from Atlanta, by James Milner, engineer from the Gainesville office, and by Neil Hunt, a reporter from the *Gainesville Daily Times.* We hiked north to Tray Mountain Lean-to where I packed my gear, then the four of us walked in leisurely fashion north to Addis Gap Lean-to. The forest service had money budgeted for a prototype trail and for one shelter. We stopped many times during the hike to discuss trail design and construction and the location and design of shelters. I made a resolution to return to Georgia after the prototype trail was completed and hike that section again. We reached Addis Gap Lean-to at 3:30, and shortly thereafter the three men left. This lean-to has been extensively modernized as compared to other Georgia lean-tos. Went to sleep with the pleasant sound of the stream gurgling outside.

FRIDAY AND SATURDAY, APRIL 10 AND 11. Two pleasant days in which Meredith and I hiked about ten miles each day. Stayed at Plumorchard Gap Lean-to on the tenth and at the new Standing Indian Lean-to in North Carolina on the eleventh. Crossed over into North

Carolina at Bly Gap at 8:30 A.M. April 11. Dropped my camera in spring for second time. This finished it as far as getting any decent pictures was concerned.

A few comments about the trail in Georgia. The footway was in excellent condition and the paint blazing was excellent. There was an almost complete lack of signs. Litter on the Georgia trail quite high —twenty-five to thirty cans per day and perhaps forty to fifty pieces of other litter.

There are no tables, shelves, fireplaces, toilets, or direction signs at most shelters. Trail throughout Georgia extremely beautiful. This was tremendous chestnut area before the blight. Even now one could walk for hundreds of yards stepping from one fallen chestnut tree to another. Even in early April the spring flowers were in bloom. I enjoyed Georgia immensely. My principal regret was that I was too early for the displays of wild azalea, mountain laurel, and rhododendron.

North Carolina, Nantahala National Forest

From Bly Gap we walked to Deep Gap and spent forty-five fruit-less minutes looking for a nonexistent shelter described in the guidebook as being located near the forest service recreation area there. Finally concluded that the shelter had burned or been torn down and we began hiking north. In thirty minutes we came upon a new shelter which turned out to be the Standing Indian Lean-to. Extremely nice wood floor, nice location, swift flowing stream twenty feet in front of lean-to. We washed clothes, bathed, aired our sleeping bags, cooked a leisurely evening meal, and generally enjoyed life on a beautiful warm spring day.

SUNDAY, APRIL 12. Meredith and I parted company at Mooney Gap. He planned to walk to the nearest primary road and hitch a ride back to Charlottesville, Virginia. During the week he hiked with me he subsisted almost entirely on short-grain whole rice—one-half cup each day. The last several days of our hike he had accepted some raisins from me. He was losing weight. I was sorry to see him go; he was a good outdoorsman and pitched in willingly on my litter-pickup campaign. Began raining in early afternoon. Stopped at a fire tower and visited with the guard, which was a mistake. The fellow was rabid on the subjects of politics and religion and would talk about nothing else. I was glad to get away. Reached Big Spring Gap Lean-to at 3:00 after 14.0 miles of hiking.

MONDAY, APRIL 13. Left shelter early. Raining slightly. Quite foggy.

Had difficulty following trail. Lost it twice, and after one hour and forty minutes I found myself back at the shelter from which I had started! Started out again and made it to Wallace Gap (U.S. Route 64) at 10:30 and immediately caught ride on a logging truck carrying twenty-five tons of hardwood timber. We roared—and I do mean roared—the full seventeen miles into Franklin, North Carolina. The trucker informed me that his outfit was logging near the Appalachian Trail but that they were cutting no timber within three hundred feet of the trail itself. I was surprised that he would stop that big rig on a curve on a narrow highway, but he recognized the Appalachian Trail patch on my shirt sleeve. At Franklin I visited the U.S. Forest Service office and met District Ranger Duke Barr. Had a hearty lunch with Barr, then a quick trip to local newspaper office for a picture, after which Barr drove me back to the Appalachian Trail. "Began hiking 2:30 and made the 6.9 miles to Siler Bald Lean-to in three hours for 2.3 mph. Picked up trash for first four miles until my bag got full. Had given first bag to Barr. Another 6.9 miles of beautiful country. Cold and windy at Siler Bald Lean-to. Cooked some potato soup, ate a huge bowl of it, and drank hot coffee. Wrote my notes till darkness. Crawled in bed 7:45. Rained hard around 9:00 or 10:00. Slept well."

TUESDAY, APRIL 14. This was one of those ideal hiking days. Got an early start (up at 5:30, on trail 6:10). Temperature a cool 38°F. at 6:00. High of 55°F. at noon. Was hiking in the four-to-five-thousand-foot range most of day. Trail took me over two impressive "balds," Wayah Bald (5,336 feet) and Wesser Bald (4,627 feet). There were towers on top of each that afforded magnificent views. Ate lunch at the delightful Cold Springs Trail Shelter—a thirty-year-old shelter built by the Civilian Conservation Corps of ten and twelve-inch chestnut logs. This shelter is fenced in, located in a rhododendron glade with clear cold water coming from a walled spring with pipe. Reached the Wesser Creek Trail Shelter at 4:10. Had made 18.2 miles—my best so far. Saw no one during the day except the fire tower guard at Wesser Bald. I visited with him for half an hour and prevailed upon him to carry out my two full trash bags. Went to sleep to the subdued roar of Wesser Creek some forty feet in front of lean-to.

WEDNESDAY, APRIL 15. Quickly hiked for three miles, almost all downgrade, reaching first U.S. Route 19, then the Nantahala River, and finally the little village of Wesser, elevation 1,723 feet. En route I hiked past a number of small mountain homes; four or five of them had tiny little boxwood nurseries in their yards. I had eaten but the scantiest of breakfasts and looked forward to a substantial meal at the restaurant in Wesser, only to find that it would not open until May 15. Grocery store was open even at this early hour of 7:15; I bought a few supplies and sat around the potbellied stove visiting with Larce Mashburn, the store manager, while I slowly ate a quart of ice cream.

Wesser provides a dividing point between the fifty-five miles of the Nantahalas nearest Georgia and the twenty-five miles nearest the Smokies. The fifty-five miles I had already hiked were indeed beautiful —high elevations, spectacular views, well-maintained trail with frequent clearly-painted wooden signs. Litter on this fifty-five miles of trail was heavy; and I was distressed to find each day some ten to twelve aerial survey panels still on the ground, almost two years after the aerial photography of the trail had been completed. These panels are made of white plastic, about two feet wide and perhaps fifteen to twenty feet long, and were placed on the trail as an aid to those who were flying and photographing the trail. Although many trail clubs had worked like beavers to put the panels in place, some had been rather derelict in removing them.

North Carolina, Cheoah Region

This twenty-five-mile section of the trail proved to be the most strenuous in the entire trail for me. From Wesser at 1,723 feet, I climbed in 4.9 miles to the top of Swim Bald with an elevation of 4,720 feet, descended to Sassafras Gap, and then clambered up to the top of Cheoah Bald at 5,062 feet. The entire day was spent in climbing straight up the sides of many knobs, mountains, and balds, and straight down the other side. There were no switchbacks or attempts to provide a graded trail as had been the case during my previous four days of hiking. Although the steepness of the trail literally begged for serious erosion, there was almost none. Neither was there much litter. The absence of both erosion and litter was due, I think, to the brutally steep grades which discourage all but the very hardy few from hiking in that area. There are Appalachian Trail enthusiasts who argue that there should be some areas like the Cheoahs that are so physically demanding that all but a few will be excluded. I personally do not share that view. I believe that the Appalachian Trail, even at more moderate grades, is strenuous enough and that blue-blazed side trails should be provided for those who want the maximum in solitude and physical exertion.

Blue-blazed trails are not used in the Cheoahs, and I was unable to locate most of the sources of water described in the guidebook. The trail to Sassafras Gap Trail Shelter was identified by neither sign nor blue-blazed trail. I was lucky to find the shelter. Had intended staying there overnight but changed my mind after seeing it. It was located in an uninviting spot directly beside a dirt road that provided auto-mobile access, and there was the inevitable accumulation of litter.

Here's how I discovered the high insulating qualities of a full pack. At Wesser I had planned to buy a pint of ice cream, but finding none of that size, I bought a larger size which I thought was a quart. Upon opening it I discovered I had purchased a half-gallon package. Even with my tremendous capacity for ice cream this was too much, espe-cially with those steep climbs to Swim and Cheoah balds directly ahead on the trail. Therefore, I ate one quart and put the remainder in a plastic bag. I prevailed upon Larce Mashburn to put the plastic bag in his freezer until it was frozen hard. I then transferred the plastic sack with the now frozen ice cream to the middle of my pack, where it was protected by a cloth sack containing my extra clothes. Even though the temperature reached 80° F., the ice cream stayed firm. I nibbled at it on three different occasions and finished the last of it at Sassafras Gap, a full four hours after I had left the store.

Realizing I could not reach Cable Gap Lean-to, I stopped hiking at 6:00 and made camp in the open near a spring 2.57 miles north of Stekoah Gap. Quoting again from my diary: "By 7:40 P.M. I had made all sleeping preparations, cooked evening meal, boiled four eggs for use on Thursday, and cleaned utensils. Climbed into bed at eight, staring up at half-moon directly overhead. Experienced incredible feeling of well-being. Pleasantly exhausted, well-fed, warm in my sleeping bag. A beautiful moonlit night. Air pleasantly cool. Lay on my back and remembered experiences of the day and of the trip so far. Good night's sleep. Never got very cold."

THURSDAY, APRIL 16. I reached North Carolina Highway 28 at 1:30 and within a few minutes caught a ride into the village of Fontana Dam. Picked up mail at the general delivery window, enjoyed a second lunch at the delightful cafeteria, and weighed myself on an accurate scale. Was shocked to learn I had lost eleven pounds in the first twelve days of my hike. Had my clothes laundered, bought gro-ceries, obtained a room in the lodge. Had a late Swiss steak dinner at cafeteria, but had to eat cautiously as my stomach was not used to so much rich food. I talked with Mr. and Mrs. Monroe Wetmore, members of the Connecticut Chapter of the Appalachian Mountain Club. Back in my room, I brought all my records up to date, wrote some letters, and collapsed into bed between white sheets at midnight.

Great Smoky Mountains National Park

FRIDAY, APRIL 17. Up at 6:15 next morning, breakfast with the Wetmores, then back to my room where I repacked all the groceries I had purchased.

The Wetmores picked me up at 11:30 and drove me out to the trail intersection on Highway 28. It was raining steadily. I donned my rain parka and rain chaps, the first time for the chaps. Took them off shortly as they were insufferably hot. Didn't wear them again until I reached Maine. Birch Spring Trail Shelter at 4:30. Dark, damp, and dripping. Shelter located in a low spot. Was muddy, with much litter. A most depressing place to spend the night. During the night mice jumped on my head several times, and I chased two of them out of my pack at 4 A.M. I carry a stout nylon cord attached to the top crossbar of my packframe. The cord has a loop in its free end. Just before going to bed I fasten the loop over any convenient nail in the shelter and let the pack swing free. This is usually effective in keeping mice out, except they were smarter at Birch Spring. These mice climbed along the rafters overhead and then dropped down onto the pack. To provide protection from bears, the shelters in the Great Smoky Mountains National Park are equipped with a sturdy steel fence across the open side. I fastened the steel door securely, but learned later that this precaution was probably needless as mid-April was too early for the bears to be active at the higher elevations of the park.

SATURDAY, APRIL 18. A clear, pleasant day. Shelters are frequent in the Smokies. This slowed my hiking progress as it was necessary for me to visit and inspect shelters. I trudged into Derrick Knob Trail Shelter at 6:00; found eight people already there and cooking fires burning.

Had observed serious erosion during the day—especially on north side of Thunderhead Mountain where the trail is already a small gully some three feet wide and two feet deep. The side trail to Old Spence Field Trail Shelter is horrible—gullied to a depth of five feet.

SUNDAY, APRIL 19. A most pleasant day. Up early. On the trail at 6:05. Just east of crest of Silers Bald I met Gus Crews, my friend from Bethesda, Maryland. We had arranged to meet the next day at Newfound Gap, but he surprised me. We hiked together as far as Mt. Buckley. Gus returned to his car and tent at Indian Creek Campground. I proceeded to Clingmans Dome (6,643 feet), highest point on the Appalachian Trail. There were scores of people at the observation tower, and they looked at me and my pack as though I were a man from Mars. Walked over snow and ice on the north side of Clingmans Dome. Trail very badly eroded all the way to Mt. Collins Trail Shelter—gullies two to three feet deep. "Reached the Mt. Collins Trail Shelter at 3:30 and met Lionel Edney and LeRoy Fox, longtime members of the Smoky Mountains Hiking Club. They had all the makings for a steak supper. We had a delightful meal and visited around a blazing balsam fire. They left at 8:00. Shortly after, a torrential rain set in, with high winds. The rain on the metal roof was a continuous roar. Fire burned brightly for an hour. Lay in bed watching fire and musing over the events of another full and very pleasant day."

MONDAY, APRIL 20. On trail at 6:20. After a two-inch rain the trail was a mess; the name Appalachian Creek would have been more suitable than Appalachian Trail. Reached Newfound Gap (U.S. Route 441) at 8:30 and met Gus. I repacked my gear, and included some supplies from home that Gus had brought in his car. We ate lunch at Ice Water Spring Trail Shelter. A little later we left the Appalachian Trail and began hiking the Boulevard Trail toward Mt. Le Conte (6,593 feet). Reached there at 3:30. I had been wanting to visit this place for fourteen years. Had huge supper at lodge with six other guests. Other guests slept in cabins; Gus and I slept in the open trailside shelter about four hundred yards from the lodge.

TUESDAY, APRIL 21. Up at 6:15, and to the lodge for a delicious sausage-and-egg breakfast. Began hiking under cloudy skies, but at eight the skies cleared, making for beautiful views. Gus and I parted company at junction of the Boulevard Trail and the Appalachian Trail. He returned to his car at Newfound Gap and I proceeded northward. Met eight people on trail; walked with group of four to the Tri-Corner Knob Trail Shelter. Reached shelter at 5:30 P.M. Had hiked nineteen miles and I was bushed. It was turning very cold and prospects of finding wood for a cooking fire did not look too promising. At this point John Burton and three sixteen-year-old boys from Boston came to my rescue. They had hiked in the last mile or so with me, and Burton offered me his propane stove to cook my meal. Not only that, but Burton and his boys began stripping boughs from a large balsam tree that had blown down in a recent storm. They tossed a supply of balsam boughs on the wire bunk I was to use. Worked on my notes until darkness, then put on all the clothes I had and climbed into my lightweight sleeping bag. Even though the temperature was near freezing, I was warm and enjoyed my best sleep of the trip.

WEDNESDAY, APRIL 22. A pleasant day; my last one in the Smokies. Made eighteen miles. The pleasantly warm temperatures at five to six thousand feet became unpleasantly hot at three thousand feet. Temperature in the eighties at Davenport Gap. Gus Crews met me in his car and we drove to Cosby, Tennessee, for a fried chicken dinner. Then we went over to the very nice AAA-approved Indian Creek Campground. Showered and shaved. Gus slept in his tent and battled a hard rain. I spread my ground cloth and foam mattress on the clean concrete floor of the laundry room and slept well.

It was with regret that I said good-bye to the Great Smoky Mountains National Park and to the seventy miles of the trail that lie within its borders. I was distressed at the amount of erosion on the trails in the Smokies. The trails have moderate grades, but even moderate grades cannot sustain such heavy human and horse traffic as these are receiving. There are miles of the trail where erosion had bitten down twenty-four to thirty inches, and there were a number of places where it was much deeper than that. Except for the erosion factor, the maintenance of the trail was excellent.

The shelters in the Smokies are different from those I found elsewhere on the trail. The typical Smoky shelter is 24' x 18', stone, metal roof, with a bear-proof fence across the open side. There is one small thirty-six-inch inside fireplace. The shelter has six double-deck wire bunks (capacity twelve persons) with floor space providing additional sleeping room. There is a toilet at each shelter, but no table. There are no garbage facilities. Hikers are urged by signs to pick up and carry out all trash. The shelters have no shelf spaces. All walls are stone, straight up and down with not even a fireplace mantel on which to put articles. When several parties occupy one shelter it can become a four or five-hour job for all of them to get to the fireplace to cook a meal.

Tennessee–North Carolina

With the Smokies behind me I headed toward the Virginia state line and Damascus, Virginia, 192 miles to the north. I looked forward to this section for several reasons. It was over trails not previously hiked through the big bald country of eastern Tennessee and western

North Carolina. Second, at the end of the section I would be in my home state of Virginia with over one-fifth of the 2,000-mile trail behind me. Spring was coming on rapidly now. Each day the trees were slowly becoming obscured. Spring flowers were out in profusion— violets, irises, trillium, dogwood, bluets, and mayapples, to name the most common. Birds were becoming more frequent, and I could hear, see, and smell the many unmistakable signs of spring.

THURSDAY, APRIL 23. Up at 5:30. Gus drove me to the starting point. Warm day. Hiked in T-shirt. Reached Groundhog Creek Lean-to at 10:00 and found a table there, only the fourth table in 240 miles of hiking. Reached the Max Patch Road and hiked on it for 3.8 miles. Joined Gus and his car at Lemon Gap where I repacked my Kelty for the hike into Walnut Mountain Lean-to. We reached the lean-to at 4:30 to find it already occupied by two young ladies, Patricia Wenner of Williamsport, Pennsylvania, and Ann Longanbach of Columbus, Ohio. They were seniors at Wittenburg College in Ohio, had completed all the requirements for their degrees, and had three months before commencement exercises in June. What was more logical than that they talk their folks into driving them to Fontana Dam, and begin hiking the Appalachian Trail north? They had hiked through the Smokies. They planned to leave the trail at Hot Springs, North Carolina, and hitchhike to Cosby, Tennessee, to attend the annual ramp festival. And what is a ramp? It is a luxuriant leafy plant that grows in the mountains of the Southern Appalachians. It has an underground bulb like an onion. It is said to combine the potency of onion and of garlic and it is highly prized for seasoning by the people of the hills.

FRIDAY, APRIL 24. "Up at 5:30. I built the fire and the girls cooked dehydrated eggs, bacon bars, and oatmeal. On my way at 6:40. Very pretty country. Small farms tucked away here and there. Began raining around 9:00; rained hard, much wind, but I kept hiking in my T-shirt, choosing not to use rain parka. Made the 3.44 miles from Garenflo Gap to Deer Park Mountain Lean-to in one hour and ten minutes, reaching lean-to at 11:00." Ate lunch and made my lean-to inspection. Rain stopped at noon and I proceeded on to Hot Springs, North Carolina, meeting Gus Crews who had hiked in to meet me. We reached the town at 1:00 P.M., and I began to experience the first of many days of extreme discomfort due to diarrhea or dysentery. I suspected that I had drunk impure water, not too surprising when you consider that I was drinking water from a half-dozen or more unprotected water sources each day. I fought the dysentery business for almost ten days. At one point I was almost ready to return home temporarily until I could shake the ailment. "Dr." Crews gave me a supply of lomotil pills which his doctor had prescribed for situations like this. I took the pills faithfully but they proved ineffectual. Gus and I camped three nights at the U.S. Forest Service Rocky Bluff Recreation Area three miles south of Hot Springs.

SATURDAY, APRIL 25. By prearrangement we met Stanley A. Murray, chairman of the Appalachian Trail Conference, and hiked with him from Hot Springs to Allen Gap, about eleven miles. Gus had recently been appointed chairman of the conference's Trails Standards Committee, and I was about to assume the chairmanship of the Shelters Committee. Therefore, we had many things to discuss with Murray. Near the end of our hike with Stan Murray he confided to me that he had been somewhat apprehensive about hiking with me. He had done very little hiking recently, and he was aware that I had three weeks of conditioning. His fears were groundless. I was walking slowly and gingerly, with frequent unscheduled stops; I would have had difficulty outwalking a ten-year-old Cub Scout.

SUNDAY, APRIL 26. Gus drove me over to the Catholic church, and I attended Mass for the first time since the beginning of my hike. Learned that the church had a small guest house on the premises which they make available to hikers. Ate a big breakfast at Henderson Grill. Afterwards Gus drove me back to Allen Gap. Hiked a mere ten miles for the day, all of it in a steady rain.

MONDAY, APRIL 27. Packed Gus's tent and said good-bye to the Rocky Bluff Recreation Area. Picked up mail at post office, telephoned my wife (our thirty-second wedding anniversary—and I did remember!). Gus then drove me out to Camp Creek Bald Fire Tower, and I began hiking the thirteen miles to Devil Fork Gap. Pleasant day for hiking, but witnessed one very depressing sight. The new Jerry Cabin Lean-to, an attractive stone-and-concrete affair, had been built beside a road which was used by both vehicles and horses. The amount of litter inside and immediately outside this new lean-to was unbelievable. I estimated twenty bushels of trash including three rotting bed mattresses and much discarded food. The flies were so thick I was forced to walk down the trail to complete my notes. In two thousand miles of hiking this was the most litter-strewn lean-to I saw. Lesson: *Do not build lean-tos near roads!*

TUESDAY, APRIL 28. A short hiking day. Bothered with diarrhea all day. Rained hard throughout the morning. Hiked only 7.8 miles to Sams Gap where Gus met me and we decided that was enough for the day. Trillium, mayapple, and dogwood blooming in profusion. Filled my litter bag in the first five miles: twenty cans and twenty-five pieces of other junk.

WEDNESDAY, APRIL 29. Hiked 15.8 miles from Sams Gap to the No Business Lean-to. Reached summit of 5,516-foot Big Bald after first meeting two men who were digging ramps. They were plants I had been seeing for over a week; they looked like oversized lilies with ridged leaves.

THURSDAY, APRIL 30. Hiked from No Business Lean-to to Cherry Gap Lean-to today, 22.4 miles—but only 7.4 miles with full pack. Am recovering from the diarrhea. Hiked without shirt during much of day, quite warm, refreshing breeze. "Reached Cherry Gap Lean-to 6:30. Had delightful supper cooked over wood fire. Most pleasant day. Writing this at 8:10. Birds singing as daylight fades. Water on fire steaming for my evening shave. Feel in excellent shape. Now for 6,285-foot Roan Mountain tomorrow."

In building the wood fire I found the charred remains of an envelope with enough writing still legible to convince me that Ann Longanbach and Pat Wenner were somewhere ahead.

FRIDAY, MAY 1. Apple orchards in bloom at four thousand feet on Iron Mountain. A 17.1-mile day over the top of Roan and my last day of hiking with Gus Crews. Reached Hughes Gap, elevation 4,040 feet, at 1:15. It was marked by a huge roadside garbage dump. Was sorely tempted to leave my full sack of trash there but resisted the temptation and carried it all the way up to top of Roan where I deposited it in a forest service trash can. Reached top of Roan and Gus's car at 3 P.M. Spent forty-five minutes sorting all the stuff to be sent home and repacking my food. Then I began the short hike down to Carvers Gap. Reached the gap at 5:00. Coming down Roan I saw a patch of snow, my first since the Smokies, and hopefully the last I will see on this trip.

SATURDAY, MAY 2. Hiked through big bald country; climbed over summits of five balds with elevations exceeding fifty-four hundred feet. Came to home of Pink Winters (mentioned in guidebook) about 1 P.M. Was promptly invited in for dinner: meat loaf, hot biscuits, homemade apple butter, the works! Left at 2:30 and hiked to U.S. Route 19E where I caught a ride into Elk Park, North Carolina.

Checked in at Trivett House; $4.00 for lodging and breakfast. Bought half a gallon of ice cream, ate half, put the remainder in the Trivett freezer, and finished it off before going to bed.

SUNDAY, MAY 3. Ate 7:00 A.M. breakfast with Trivetts. Hiked the 1.5 miles back to the Appalachian Trail as I was unable to catch a ride. Began hiking north from U.S. 19E and lost the trail twice in the first mile and a half. I was forced to obtain directions from landowners on both occasions. Had rained all night and occasionally during the day; my feet and legs were thoroughly soaked. Even in the rain I could appreciate the breathtaking beauty of Laurel Fork Gorge. Reached the Laurel Fork Lean-to at 7:30 after a nineteen-mile hike and was lucky to find it. The lean-to is marked by neither a sign nor a blue-blazed trail. I wonder how many hikers have missed that lean-to?

Saw my first rhododendron in bloom at the lower elevations in the gorge. Regretfully left a full sack of litter at Moreland Gap Lean-to. Had no place else to leave it. Picked up no more the rest of the day. Disposing of litter is a real problem.

MONDAY, MAY 4. Resumed my hike down the Laurel Fork Gorge. Extremely beautiful. Enjoyed the rustic footbridges, the high sheer cliffs, the roar of the water. Reached Tennessee Highway 67 at 8:15 and the post office in Hampton, Tennessee, at 8:45. Repaired to restaurant next door, had second breakfast, and brought my notes up to date. Hiked back to trail and reached South Pierce Lean-to at 1:30.

Around 3 P.M. I photographed a flying squirrel. He was lying in the middle of the trail and hopped awkwardly to a nearby tree. Upon reaching the tree, he shot upward like a rocket. When I shook the tree slightly, he spread his "wings" and soared into space, landing some distance away.

Reached Vanderventer Lean-to at 7:30. Spent a half hour locating water on a faintly blazed trail that had no sign. Barely had time to cook supper before darkness set in. Vanderventer Lean-to commands a spectacular view of the Watauga Valley. I only wish the water supply was closer.

I began practicing a going-to-sleep routine early in my hike and continued it throughout my trip to Maine. Sleep generally came quickly after a hard day's hike, but in the few minutes before it did come I would recall the name of the lean-to or other spot where I had spent each night of my hike and I would associate the shelter name with the date and day of the week that I stayed there. In all, I was to spend 158 days on the trail; and even as I write this 8 months after completing the hike, I can still recall all the essential facts for each of those 158 days.

TUESDAY, MAY 5. Overslept. Had hot breakfast for a change, much coffee. Even shaved! "The view this morning from Vanderventer Lean-to really something. Looking down steep east slope, all the mountaintops dancing in bright sunlight. Valley area obscured with white, snowlike clouds."

A perfect day for hiking. Temperature 45° F. at 7:00 A.M., a comfortable 68° F. at noon. Walked through two large areas dominated by violets and mayapples. In another area observed large number of shagbark hickory trees. Saw a few clumps of those delightful bluets. Saw a chipmunk today—one of the very few I saw on the entire trip. Seems strange when they are so numerous in Shenandoah National Park. At Tennessee Highway 91 talked to landowner briefly. He mentioned two men hiking a day ahead of me. Reached Rich Knob Lean-to at 4:20 and in fireplace I found a piece of plastic tape with the one word "Humanities" on it. I knew then that the two "men" hiking a day ahead of me were none other than Pat and Ann. "Humanities" was the clue because they had used this particular tape in repackaging all their dehydrated food.

Scared up numerous grouse hens nesting near trail. Found a nest with a clutch of fifteen eggs. "This was the most time I have spent at a lean-to in quite a while, so I did some extra cooking. Had creamed tuna and rice which was perfect. Got the sauce just right. I also used some of the rice and cooked it with mincemeat. Made excellent dessert. Found three one-gallon tins here with handles, so heated lots of water, washed dishes, and shaved—twice today! Writing this at almost 8:40 P.M. Big owl hooting nearby. Birds singing gently . . . fire dying down . . . a real good day."

WEDNESDAY, MAY 6. Up as early as I could see, and on the trail by 6:30. Reached Abingdon Gap Lean-to, 8.1 miles, at 10:25. Another beautiful day. Temperature 60° F. at noon with a nice breeze. Reached Damascus at 3:00 having hiked 18.7 miles. Good time for me. Signed the Appalachian Trail register at the town hall. I saw two heavy packs and asked the state trooper about them. He told me the packs belonged to two girls who had arrived about thirty minutes before. He asked if I knew the girls. When I replied that I did, he asked me what type of girls they were. I was disturbed by his question: partly at the question itself, but more so at the manner in which it was asked. It was as though the trooper had already formed his own opinion. I told him the young ladies were two of the nicest I had ever met and that a man would be proud to introduce them as wife or daughter. However, I don't think he was convinced. Perhaps his opinion would have been different had he seen them three months later: one was in Japan on a church-sponsored two-year teaching assignment and the other was doing professional social work in Pennsylvania.

Damascus is a small town. The trail goes through its center and the people generally are friendly to hikers. I made arrangements to stay overnight at the home of Mrs. Keebler, who has been providing lodging for Appalachian Trail hikers for years. Cost of overnight lodging: $3.00. I met Pat and Ann shortly after leaving the town hall. They had arranged to sleep in the backyard of Mrs. Hall, a member of the Mt. Rogers Appalachian Trail Club.

Southwestern Virginia, Jefferson National Forest

THURSDAY, MAY 7. Breakfast at Carney's restaurant where I was joined by my longtime friend, Keith Argow, administrator of the forest service's new Mt. Rogers National Recreation Area. Argow was new in the region, having been assigned to the office at Marion, Virginia, only two months previously. He made arrangements to hike with me that day as he wanted to see the condition of the trail and the shelters. Pat and Ann hiked with us. Two things were disturbing: (1) the Appalachian Trail was obviously being used for sanctioned motorcycle races, and (2) there was a great amount of litter left by crews surveying for the new scenic highway to be built through the Mt. Rogers National Recreation Area. The litter we picked up, almost a hundred pieces on a twelve-mile stretch of trail; but Argow was still wrestling with the motorcycle problem when I left. Having crossed into Virginia I would now be hiking for days in the Jefferson National Forest. The two shelters we visited were most inviting: immaculately clean, equipped with tables, fireplaces, toilets, and good signs. I was to find the shelters in the 240-mile stretch of trail in the Jefferson to be among the best of my entire hike.

FRIDAY, MAY 8. Breakfast at Argows and then over to the U.S. Forest Service office where we discussed many aspects of the Appalachian Trail but dwelt most heavily on the problem of identifying water. I was told that the Atlanta, Georgia, office of General Counsel of the U.S. Department of Agriculture had issued a ruling with respect to identification of water sources. The ruling, in effect, would prohibit the forest service from erecting signs reading WATER or even SPRING. It was feared that such signs would mislead hikers into believing that the water so identified would be safe, drinkable water whereas no state board of health could give a "safe" rating to an unprotected spring or stream. In the same legal decision it was ruled that a sign containing the word STREAM could be safely erected as this could not be interpreted as a guarantee of the water supply. A fine point of law, perhaps, but in response to it the Forest Service had removed most of the SPRING and WATER signs. Since the new STREAM signs had not yet been erected, the hiker was in somewhat of a dilemma as to location of water. In the Shenandoah National Park, the Park Service solves the problem nicely by erecting a sign at each spring reading essentially as follows: UNPROTECTED WATER SUPPLY—RECOMMEND BOILING OR USE OF PURIFICATION TABLETS.

Argow dropped me off at the intersection of the Appalachian Trail and the Skulls Gap Road. (That name, Skulls Gap, has always fascinated me; I wonder about its origin.) I repacked my groceries at the side of the road, burned all the excess wrappings, and began hiking at 12:30. Reached the pleasant Cherry Tree Shelter at 3:30; found Ann and Pat already there. Saw one of the rather rare pileated woodpeckers at the lean-to. Am still seeing the mayapples coming out of the ground; they look like little unopened umbrellas as they first emerge. With each day of growth the umbrella opens up a bit more, and in a week or so it is fully open. Fascinating little plant. It has a single flower, and later in the season it puts forth a single, small, egg-shaped apple. The apple is edible but I never got a chance to eat one as the animals always beat me to them.

SATURDAY, MAY 9. Up at 5:30 and built a fire. Had hot breakfast with the girls, then said good-bye. They planned to hike only the seven miles to Raccoon Branch Shelter, whereas I planned to hike the twenty miles to Killinger Creek Lean-to. Much of the trail between Cherry Tree and Raccoon Branch shelters had been relocated, and the new trail substituted some delightful woods walking for the uninspiring road walking that I had hiked in 1968. Reached the first shelter before noon and ate lunch there; then pushed on towards Killinger. Thought I never would make that last four miles to the second shelter. During the afternoon, in the little village of Teas, Virginia, I had learned that two young men with packs had been seen hiking in the direction of Killinger Creek Lean-to. I half expected to have company for the night, but I was not prepared for the company I found. Nearing the shelter I was dismayed to see six or seven cars in the nearby parking lot. I found a big Saturday night picnic supper in progress. A group of truckers and their families were having a farewell party for one of their friends. Two girls advanced toward me with a huge plate of hot baked beans, salad, potato chips, and a hamburger. And who were these two maidens feeding a hungry stranger? None other than Ann and Pat! The truckers and their families had two cooking fires going, and there was plenty of food and drink for all. Shortly after darkness the truckers and their wives and children cleaned up the shelter site spick-and-span and departed. A wonderful group.

Ann and Pat then told me how they had arrived at Killinger ahead of me. After I had left Cherry Tree Lean-to that morning, they packed their gear and also began hiking the trail. However, when they reached the highway, they hitched a ride into Sugar Grove, bought a few groceries, and then hitched a ride to a point near Killinger. They were the two young "men" who had been seen hiking near Sugar Grove. To cap off the day's events, the girls produced a package of popcorn they had purchased in Sugar Grove. We cranked up their gasoline stove and popped a large panful of the delicious stuff for a late evening snack.

SUNDAY, MAY 10. We had a big breakfast of food left for us by the picnickers: chili sauce, hard-boiled eggs, bread, and coffee. I again said good-bye to the girls and left the shelter at 7:30. Saw two deer close to the shelter. Reached U.S. Route 11 at 9:20 and promptly caught a ride directly to the church in Marion. I was an hour early, so I sat on the church steps and brought my notes up to date, a never-ending job. After church and a lunch at a nearby diner, I caught a ride with Father Fahey, the priest who had just offered Mass. He let me off two miles west of Groseclose, Virginia, on U.S. 11, the same point at which I had discontinued hiking some three hours earlier. The newly relocated trail seemed to evaporate at this point, so I pounded the pavement the two miles into Groseclose, where I knew the trail had previously gone. When I arrived at the little store in Groseclose, I found Ann and Pat holding up a hitchhiking sign reading WYTHEVILLE. Pat's pack was broken. We enjoyed some ice cream at the store; I telephoned my wife. It was the second Sunday of May, Mother's Day.

I said good-bye to the girls for the umpteenth time and began hiking at 2:30. I visited briefly with Rev. Atwell, who for years has furnished shelter and food to Appalachian Trail hikers. I would be one of the last hikers to visit him now that the trail was being relocated. The trail led past a small mountain home where a huge and vicious German shepherd dog was chained to an old outbuilding. No one seemed to be at home. The dog made repeated lunges at me, but was brought up short at the end of each lunge by the big chain. I studied both the dog chain and the wooden door frame and hoped that neither would fail before I got out of that area.

This was not my first encounter with dogs, nor would it be my last. They plagued me from North Carolina to Maine. During my hike people would invariably question me about the danger from bears and snakes, but danger from domestic dogs is much more serious. When approaching domestic dog territory I armed myself with a stout cudgel. If dogs advanced, I would also pick up several stones or just go through the motion of picking up a stone. This discouraged many of them. Nevertheless, I felt many times that there should be some other weapon (short of a double-barreled shotgun) that would discourage dogs who seemed to be enraged at the sight of a hiker with a pack on his back.

MONDAY, MAY 11. Hiked all day along the top of Walker Mountain. Apparently water sources are not too plentiful on the mountain because the forest service has installed concrete cisterns at the four shelters in this area. Water from the shelter roof drains off into the underground cistern; the water is then available from a spigot. Forest service officials are somewhat apologetic about these cisterns because untreated water in cisterns will not receive approval from state boards of health. From a practical standpoint the cisterns permit shelters to be erected at convenient spacings along the trail.

At 10:45 I reached U.S. Route 21 and stopped for a snack. I began hiking again at 12:00. It was almost all road walking for the next ten miles to the Turkey Gap Shelter. On the way I scared up a wild turkey. I arrived at the shelter at 4:30; 17.8 miles for the day. This is another cistern shelter, so I boiled the water. I saw mayapples in bloom today for first time. I am still finding aerial survey panels littering the landscape, four to six per day.

I find that I am eating large quantities of Mounds candy bars. I seem to have a tremendous craving for sweets.

TUESDAY, MAY 12. On trail at 6:10, one of my earliest starts. Reached High Rock Lean-to at 9:30. Climbed the fire tower and drank in the views. Pleased to see so many examples of Soil Conservation Service (my former employer) work in the valley farms below: contour strip cropping and farm ponds, to name two. Reached the little settlement of Crandon at 11:30 and spent an hour at the excellent grocery store eating two pints of ice cream and visiting with Mrs. Bernard. After Crandon, it was road walking all the way to Wapiti Lean-to—too much road. At 3 P.M. I was overtaken by Wayne Kelly, district forest ranger for the Blacksburg, Virginia, Ranger District. By prearrangement, he brought me two big sandwiches and a bottle of wine. Talked with Kelly until 5:15. I ate both sandwiches and later cooked a chicken-and-rice supper which I washed down with the wine. Coffee and instant pudding for dessert. Never had it so good.

From my diary: "Stoked up fire around 9:00, put on my pajamas, and watched fire die down. Whippoorwill perched near shelter and serenaded me. It then got real curious and fluttered down to within three or four feet of the fire. I guess the heat and smoke frightened him, as he flew away and serenaded me from a safer point. They have entertained me at many shelters all the way from Georgia."

WEDNESDAY, MAY 13. I was awakened at 5:30 by a sharp blast from Mr. Whippoorwill. Scared up a deer at 7:00. If yesterday could be called "Trillium Day," then today could be called "Wild Azalea Day." They are in full bloom—the air is enlivened with their delicate scent. Made the 15.5 miles into the town of Pearisburg by 1:00 P.M. Had reached Angels Rest, the prominent peak overlooking Pearisburg at twelve, and enjoyed both the views and the rhododendrons that crown Angels Rest. On the highway (U.S. Route 460) at the outskirts of Pearisburg a young man drove up beside me in his car. He inquired politely as to how far I was going. When I told him he said something like this: "Sir, I admire you. I would love, dearly love, to do something like you're doing! But I'll never do it. I'm trapped. I'm a manufacturer's salesman. I've got a wife and three children. I'm making mortgage payments on a $32,000 home. By the time I get out from under all of my obligations I'll be too old to do something like you're doing." I felt sorry for the young man and became increasingly aware of my own good fortune in being able to enjoy six months of adventure on the Appalachian Trail.

I proceeded to the post office in Pearisburg. As soon as I opened the door and walked in, a mail clerk looked up from his work and said, "You're late! We've been expecting you for three or four days!" I learned early in my hike that post office employees in towns along the trail have developed a strong empathy for the long-distance hiker. If a letter is sent in care of general delivery and if the envelope bears those magic words HIKING APPALACHIAN TRAIL, the post office employees will make every effort to see that the hiker receives his mail.

They will hold letters long after the ten days or so prescribed in postal regulations. They know the next towns north or south where Appalachian Trail hikers might be apt to pick up mail, and they will forward letters even without instructions if they learn that a hiker has passed by their post office without getting his mail. In my case, they had several letters for me, including one from my fifteen-year-old nephew, Shannon Garvey of San Diego, California, asking if he could hike with me after school was out. I wrote back to Shannon with a warm invitation to join me in early June.

THURSDAY, MAY 14. A wild, wild day! Up at 5:00, on my way at 7:30. Hiked a good mile; had forgotten the guidebook. Dashed back. Forty minutes lost. Couldn't follow blazes in Pearisburg streets. Motorist stopped and gave me directions. Turned off U.S. 460 and blundered ahead on the old trail. Back to U.S. 460. A state trooper helped me out. This time found the new trail. Rough going, especially climbing the second very steep mountain in the hot sun. First day I have been bothered by insects to any degree. Had to wear kerchief around my head and ears. Chugged into Interior at 6:30; reached Bailey Gap Lean-to at 7:45. Quickly made bed, put water on dehydrated food, and dashed to spring with upper part of my body clad in a paper-thin T-shirt. Trail to spring horrible. No sign. No blue blazes. No trail. Finally found the water; and promptly got lost.

"Took an east-west compass bearing trying to pick up the Appalachian Trail. No luck. What a predicament. My open pack back at the lean-to contained all of my gear including matches and flashlight. There was nothing I could do except bed down, bare arms and all, pull leaves over me for warmth, and grit through eight hours of misery. Slept but little. Watched the moon slowly sink. Luckily it stayed clear, no rain."

FRIDAY, MAY 15. From my diary: "Up at 6:00, collected my water bottles, shook leaves and dirt out of my clothes. Took a south reading on compass and climbed to the top of the mountain and found a dirt road. Followed it north for ten minutes and hit the Appalachian Trail. Turned left, hit the lean-to from the north side in ten minutes. All my stuff OK. Promptly cooked supper (now breakfast)! Ate a huge meal, then brought all my notes up to date. Leaving lean-to at 9:00; not an early start."

Rest of day uneventful. Ate hot lunch at the beautiful War Branch Lean-to with its rushing stream. Would have loved to tarry there the rest of the day. Pushed on to the not-so-beautiful Big Pond Lean-to. Water supply here is a stagnant-looking pond, which at this time of year is covered with pollen. Most uninviting. Luckily, on my way in to the lean-to I met a forest service employee, Bane Burton, who gave me a quart of good water. Cooked a light supper. This day most unusual in that I had three hot meals. In bed at 8:45 and to sleep immediately. First sleep in two days!

SATURDAY, MAY 16. A cool, rainy, foggy day. Reached Virginia Highway 42 at 7:40. Grocery store closed. Began hiking Sinking Creek Mountain at 8:40. Reached the excellent Niday Lean-to with its big apple tree at 3 P.M.; 16.2 miles for the day. Visibility about thirty yards most of day. Big event of the evening meal was that I finally finished the last portion of the dehydrated chicken and rice packages that I had found at Addis Gap Lean-to in Georgia. Carried that last package over five hundred miles. Stupid! Cooked huge meal. An hour later I was hungry again and cooked a snack of grits. Resolve that when I reach U.S. Route 11 near Roanoke, I will stop at the pancake house and fill up. It is amazing how much food I eat, and how often my thoughts dwell on food.

SUNDAY, MAY 17. On trail at 6:25 and made the six miles to Trout Creek Lean-to in one hour, fifty-five minutes. Mostly road walking. Cool and overcast. Enjoyed the new trail relocation south of Dragons Tooth. Reached Dragons Tooth at eleven and began hiking through deep pink rhododendron. First I had seen in several days and the biggest display to date. Reached home of J. L. Hodges around noon and was invited in for huge Sunday dinner. Hodges, a retired railroad man, collects hives of wild bees and sells wild bee honey. He is also an expert woodworker and showed me the huge grandfather clock case that he had built.

I had heard about two shelters north of Virginia Highway 311, but no one in the area seems to know anything about them, including four hikers I met at the highway who had just returned from that area. Fifteen minutes later, I noticed clear blue blazes leading to the right. I followed these for 250 yards and found a huge thirty-two-foot-long shelter, apparently little used. I was the only occupant.

MONDAY, MAY 18. "On trail 6:20. Cool. 48° F. at 10:00. Delightful day for hiking. New trail location a big improvement. Reached power line at 1:15 and took a thirty minute sunbath. Walked through acres of poison ivy and jewelweed. Delightful views all day. Trail is right on cliff edges."

Reached U.S. 11 at 4:20 and proceeded to the Travelton Pancake

House for a big sausage-and-buckwheat-pancake feast. Called Tom Campbell in Roanoke. Campbell is a longtime member of the Roanoke Appalachian Trail Club and has been vice-chairman of the Appalachian Trail Conference for many years. Tom picked me up at the pancake house, drove me to the grocery store where I laid in a huge supply of groceries. We then went to his home. Had delightful visit with Tom and his wife Charlene. Weighed myself and found that I was down to 138 pounds stripped, 143 dressed, some 15 pounds below my normal weight. I had used all my food so my pack weighed 26 pounds, the lightest it was to weigh the entire trip. The next day it weighed 35 pounds.

TUESDAY, MAY 19. The Campbells were slightly horrified but mostly amused to find that the bed which they had provided for me had not been slept in. When staying at private homes throughout my trip, particularly for one-night stands, I rarely used a bed. Since I was sleeping on the wood floors of shelters almost every night, it was no inconvenience or hardship to me to spread my sleeping gear on the floor of a private home.

At 3 P.M. Tom deposited me at the point where I had stopped my hike the day before. Hiked the 4.7 miles to Fullhardt Knob Lean-to. Reached there 5 P.M. Knowing I would have a short hike to the lean-to, I had purchased a nineteen-ounce can of Bounty Beef Stew plus a can of crushed pineapple. Consuming these two items for supper reduced my pack weight by thirty ounces. This is the last of the cistern shelters. The water comes out of the spigot clear and cold, but I boiled it to be on the safe side.

During the past several days I had noticed that the tree foliage was completely closing in on me. Gone for another season were the winter views. And now an incident from diary: "At 6:10 P.M. I was startled by loud flapping of wings. Two big buzzards were headed straight for all my food on the table when they detected life in the silent figure writing notes. They frantically changed course at a point twenty-five feet above my head."

WEDNESDAY, MAY 20. Awakened at 5:20 by my wristwatch alarm. On trail 6:05. I loved these early starts and felt very smug when I could perform my early morning chores and be on my way by 6:00 or shortly thereafter. The small alarm on my watch was not too loud, especially if I left the watch on my wrist and if that wrist happened to be inside the sleeping bag when the alarm went off. Therefore I hit upon the idea of putting my watch in my metal cup and putting the cup inside the metal cooking pot. The noise resulting from that combination rivaled a conventional alarm clock.

From Fullhardt Knob north, I walked through miles of deep pink rhododendron. Absolutely gorgeous.

THURSDAY, MAY 21. On trail 6:25; late for me. Saw wild turkey. Picked my first wild strawberries. Arrived Cove Creek Lean-to at 10:25, exactly four hours after I started. Had hot coffee and more substantial lunch than usual. Pushed hard from 12:15 to 4:30: up, up, up. On arriving at Cornelius Creek Lean-to I found Bob Wilson and Malcomb Edwards. Edwards is from the forest service office in Roanoke. He took picture of me as I came off the trail, bare from waist up, red handkerchief over my head to ward off gnats, black hat, guidebook in one hand, trash sack in the other. It should be a dilly! During these proceedings, Ann Longanbach and Pat Wenner popped in. After Edwards and Wilson left, Pat and Ann recounted their exploits since I left them at Groseclose. It had been a fabulous ten days during which time Pat bought a used '67 Dodge camper in Roanoke and drove all the way to Harrisburg, Pennsylvania, for a job interview. They were now headed back to Roanoke.

About 7:00, as they were leaving, Newton Sikes arrived. He is U.S. National Park Service ranger for the northern Virginia section of the Blue Ridge Parkway. We visited until 8:15.

A very full day. Have had trouble with gnats last two or three days. Expect I will be wearing my red kerchief for next two or three months.

Not all of my days were as full as May 21 but I had many like that. From what you have read you might suppose that Ann and Pat were to meet me at various points during the rest of my hike, but it was not to be. I walked out from the shelter that night to wave good-bye as they headed for Roanoke. I was not to see them again.

FRIDAY, MAY 22. Another busy day. Hiked only twelve miles today. Climbed over Apple Orchard Mountain (4,244 feet) and reached Thunder Hill Shelter at 9:00. Scared up two wild turkeys and located a towhee nest while hiking. Tremendous wild azalea display extending for a mile north of the Thunder Hill Lean-to. Reached Marble Spring Lean-to at 1:20. Last two miles marked by heavy nettle and poison ivy growth. I was joined at 5 P.M. by Charlie Burroughs and Gus Crews, who had driven down from Maryland.

It was a mild, pleasant evening with a light breeze. We kept a few

Photo by Robert Winslow

Tom McKone and springtime.

Photo by Max Bende

Autumn foliage in the Shenandoah National Park.

coals in the fire all night. Were entertained, then annoyed, by a whip-poorwill who kept calling off and on from lights-out to dawn.

SATURDAY, MAY 23. Up early; had hot coffee, bacon and eggs on the table before 6:00. Hiked with Charlie while Gus ferried the car north. Reached Matts Creek Lean-to at 9:00 after a pleasant walk through flowering rhododendron. Reached U.S. Route 501 and the historic James River at 10:00. The James marks the dividing line between the Jefferson National Forest and the George Washington National Forest.

Southwestern Virginia, George Washington National Forest

I took some of the heavier gear out of my pack and transferred it to the car, then began the ten grueling miles to the Punchbowl Spring Lean-to. Elevation at the James River is 600 feet and I climbed to 3,372 feet at Bluff Mountain. At 3:30 I was startled by a buzzing sound. I heard it in midstride and my reaction was immediate—I jumped away from the sound! It was a timber rattler, eight rattles, an inch and a half in diameter and about four feet long. I went back and studied him, and he rattled again. Close call.

Reached Punchbowl Spring Lean-to at 5:30; eighteen miles for the day. This shelter has a dam and a small pond in front of it. The bull-frogs, tree toads, and insects made a continuous din.

SUNDAY, MAY 24. Although we hiked 17.7 miles from Punchbowl Spring Lean-to, to Wiggins Spring Lean-to, the day was more notable for eating than hiking. Charlie Burroughs had brought with him several freeze-dried goodies, and what better place to try them out? We started off at breakfast with ham à la king over toast, plus cereal and coffee. At Wiggins Spring we began with an appetizer of creamed tuna over rice and finished with a pork chop dinner complete with green beans, applesauce, and hashed brown potatoes. Fruitcake and coffee for dessert. Let no one offer me sympathy for roughing it on the Appalachian Trail!

MONDAY, MAY 25. This was my last day of hiking for almost two weeks. Hiked the twelve miles from Wiggins Spring to the Crabtree Farm Road with Burroughs. Gus Crews waited with his car at this very rough road. We changed clothes and proceeded to Charlottes-ville, Virginia, via the little settlements of Tyro and Massies Mill—or what was left of them. Both settlements were almost wiped off the map by Hurricane Camille in August, 1969. Our efforts to buy strawberries were to no avail because all the strawberry beds had also been washed out by Camille.

Arrived home 8:30 P.M. and ate another supper to top off the big meal I had eaten at Charlottesville. I weighed 140 pounds, 13 pounds under my normal weight but 2 pounds heavier than at Roanoke. And so the first leg of my long hike is finished. My daily log No. 52 shows that I hiked 713 miles on the Appalachian Trail and 60 other miles.

The twelve days I was off the trail were much more strenuous in many ways than fifty-two days I had spent on the trail. I ate like mad all the time I was home. I gained a pound a day and when I resumed hiking my weight was back to normal. During this period at home I was bothered by severe leg cramps at night, and at the end of each day I had badly swollen ankles. It seemed that after fifty-two days of strenuous hiking, my body rebelled at the sudden inactivity.

FRIDAY, MAY 29. Up at 5:30 after 3½ hours sleep and drove 100 miles to Shippensburg, Pennsylvania, to attend 9 A.M. meeting of the Executive Committee of the Appalachian National Scenic Trail Advisory Council. I left at 4:00, returning by car to Falls Church for the annual banquet of the Falls Church Bowling League. Both my wife and I are avid duckpin bowlers.

Early the next day, May 30, my wife and I drove back to Shippensburg to attend the final two days of the ATC meetings.

SUNDAY, MAY 31. I gave a twenty-minute talk on my hike.

From June 1 to 5, I relaxed a bit and made plans for resumption of my hike. My nephew Shannon Garvey arrived by plane from San Diego, California, on June 5.

SATURDAY, JUNE 6. Left home at 1 P.M. in my 1961 Volkswagen camper with Shannon and my longtime friend Ed Hanlon of nearby Oakton, Virginia. We began hiking at 5:30 P.M. We stopped very briefly at The Priest Lean-to, just long enough for me to make my inspection, then pushed on north; we hoped to reach Harpers Creek Lean-to, 7.8 miles from our starting point. The evening was overcast, and I was doubtful if we could make that last mile. Therefore, when landowner W. D. Fitzgerald hailed us (after first calling off his dog), I explained our predicament; and he offered to let us use the wood floor of his apple packing shed. He invited us into his home, and we cooked an evening snack on his stove and visited with the family.

SUNDAY, JUNE 7. Up at 5:30 and invited into the Fitzgerald home at 6:00 for hot coffee. By the time we reached Maupin Field Lean-to, both Shannon and Ed Hanlon were quite tired, and understandably so. They had hiked fourteen miles since 5 P.M. the previous day, and were not conditioned for such strenuous exercise. I therefore proceeded on alone while they walked out to the Blue Ridge Parkway and hitched a ride to where the Volkswagen was parked.

MONDAY, JUNE 8. Shannon and I began hiking at Humpback Rocks at 9:00. Scared up a hen grouse with chicks which were already big enough to fly. We met Hanlon near Rockfish Gap and hiked together for an hour and then ate lunch. Shannon and I then pushed on north, meeting Hanlon at Sawmill Run Parking Overlook. Had planned to stay overnight at the nearby shelter, but Ed had already checked it out and reported that its water supply was inadequate. We drove north to Dundo Hollow Campground. "Closed." Drove still farther north to Doyle River Cabin, one of the PATC locked cabins. I had a key and a reservation for the following night, but we gambled that no one would be using it. Did our cooking over my two-burner Coleman stove. We were bothered during our evening meal and until bedtime by a persistent raccoon who we judged had received handouts from previous cabin users. He was not easily discouraged.

Shenandoah National Park

TUESDAY, JUNE 9. Began hiking from Sawmill Run at 7:00. Reached Sawmill Run Shelter within minutes. Shannon cleaned out the spring while I made the shelter inspection. Made excellent time hiking the ten miles to Blackrock Gap Shelter and then pushed north, reaching the Doyle River Cabin parking area at 3:00. Had hiked sixteen miles to this point. I packed camping gear the 0.3 mile to cabin while Ed Hanlon and Shannon drove to Waynesboro for supplies. Sat at table on spacious stone porch at Doyle River, brought my notes up to date, and enjoyed beautiful view to the south. And from my diary: "Legs and ankles OK since I resumed hiking. No more cramps and my ankles have stopped swelling. My right foot is a mess; am losing toenail on second toe, may lose big toenail, have a numb feeling in right big toe, and a huge callus on the second toe of each foot (bigger on right). Biggest problem, however, is sore rear end, chafing.

Can't figure why I should suffer so much from that area now when it gave me so little trouble in first seven weeks. Ed and Shannon returned at 6:00. Delicious supper of hamburgers, onions, lettuce salad, coffee, wine. Visited by raccoon, deer, and jumping mouse. Another mild pleasant evening. Half-moon trying to shine through the trees in the clearing in front of the cabin."

The reference to chafing is the first I find in my notes on this problem. It was to bother me during much of the hot weather season. In talking with other hikers I was to find that chafing is a common source of discomfort in long-distance hiking, probably second only to ill-fitting shoes. Chafing can occur on any part of the body where skin rubs against skin or even where clothes or equipment rub against skin. I had always naively assumed that Mentholatum was a cure-all for chapped skin, dry skin, or chafed skin. I found that it was not the answer for constant chafing. Later I learned that medicated powder (I used Ammens) or cornstarch provides effective relief.

WEDNESDAY, JUNE 10. Left Doyle River Cabin at 7:00. Reached Ivy Creek Shelter at 9:20 and Pinefield Shelter at 10:45. Saw two deer, eight rabbits, and a grouse with chicks. Picked strawberries for third straight day; excellent patch at Powells Gap. Met Ed Hanlon at Smith Roach Gap, repacked our gear, and the three of us began the hike to High Top Shelter. Reached there 3:30 P.M. after a day's walk of seventeen miles.

THURSDAY, JUNE 11. Reached Swift Run Gap (U.S. Route 33) at 7:30 and reached South River Shelter at 9:15. Hiked through much mountain laurel in bloom. Saw three deer and grouse with chicks, now an almost everyday occurrence. Reached the locked Pocosin Cabin at 11:00 with its big never-dry spring. This is the first PATC cabin that I ever used (1951) and one of my favorites. After a quick lunch we drove to nearby Big Meadows, showered, laundered our clothes, and were interviewed and photographed by Hugh and Aggie Crandall, seasonal employees of the park service. I phoned home and learned that my sixteen-year-old daughter Sharon, her friend Liz Sorgen, and my eleven-year-old son Kevin were headed for Pocosin Cabin. They arrived at 5:30. My nephew Shannon was most happy to see them as he was a little homesick anyway and welcomed companionship from those his own age. We had a glorious evening. First, a big supper. As darkness set in, we lit the Coleman lantern, and the four young people played cards and visited. Ed and I sat in the clearing a short distance from the cabin and drank in the view. The mountainside was bathed in bright moonlight, and the valley to the east was dotted with blinking lights. One of those perfect evenings that we have relived in our thoughts many times since.

FRIDAY, JUNE 12. Shannon and I began hiking at 8:45. Reached Milam Gap at 11:30. Met Ed Hanlon and Kevin where Sharon had dropped them off. Sharon and Liz Sorgen had driven back to Falls Church. The four of us hiked into Lewis Spring Shelter for lunch. Reached Hawksbill Gap Shelter at 5:30. Three people already there, but there was room for us. Has been fair and warm throughout the day; in the evening rain fell.

SATURDAY, JUNE 13. Up at 5:30. The four of us ate quietly while the other three occupants of the shelter slept. Then we began hiking north. Reached Shavers Hollow Shelter at 11:00, and shortly thereafter the huge stone shelter known as Byrd Nest No. 3 (named after former United States Senator Harry F. Byrd). About 3 P.M. we arrived at Panorama (U.S. Route 211). Had a snack at the coffee shop and learned that a fellow looking remarkably like me had been seen hiking toward Pass Mountain Shelter looking for his brother and his son. This would have to be my brother Jerry from San Diego (Shannon's father). Shannon and I pushed on rapidly and overtook my brother near the Pass Mountain Shelter. We all drove to the Elk Wallow Picnic Grounds for supper. Afterward Ed Hanlon packed his gear in my camper and headed for home. I hated to see him go. It had been a pleasant week hiking with him and having the Volkswagen handy.

Yesterday was the last day of school, and it seemed that all boys of Boy Scout age had immediately headed for the Shenandoah National Park. Previously we had seen only a handful of people on the trail during the day, but now we saw scores. There were forty or more Scouts camped in little green tents in the area around the Elk Wallow Shelter.

SUNDAY, JUNE 14. Up at 6:00 and drove into Luray to attend Mass. Had huge breakfast at Brown's restaurant. Then back to the park, and Shannon and I began hiking north from Beahms Gap. Jerry and my son Kevin returned to Falls Church. We pushed on north on a cool, cloudy, windy day. Stopped briefly at Range View Cabin, then on to Gravelly Springs Shelter. Saw more deer and grouse and caught, photographed, and released a grouse chick.

Reached Gravelly Springs at 5:30 to find that the shelter (bunks for six) already held eight Boy Scouts and their leaders from Dayton, Ohio. Another twenty to thirty people were camping in the vicinity.

Shenandoah Park is popular in the summertime! Shannon cooked supper while I worked on my notes. We slept on the ground underneath the roof overhang of the shelter. It rained during the night, and we kept inching further into the shelter. Togetherness! It's wonderful!

MONDAY, JUNE 15. Cool, cloudy day with intermittent rain in afternoon. Reached Indian Run Shelter at 10:15 and pushed on to Mosby Shelter, arriving there at 2:00.

Enjoyed wild strawberries, wild cherries, and mulberries on trail. Reached little town of Linden at 4:00 and enjoyed a pint of ice cream. Reached Manassas Gap Shelter at 6:30 having hiked 22 miles for the day. This shelter, maintained by the Potomac Appalachian Trail Club, has always been one of my favorites (only fifty-five miles from my home), and it was in excellent condition. It has an excellent spring, three tables, three fireplaces, and is equipped with broom, saw, grass whip, food storage box, and register board. It is located on private land; and in April, 1971, the landowner gave notice that his land and the shelter would be barred to the public as of May 1, 1971. A severe loss to the club and to hikers generally.

Northern Virginia

TUESDAY, JUNE 16. Reached Yellow Rose Shelter at 9:15. At 11:15 reached Ashby Gap (U.S. Route 50) and had snack at George Frye's store. The Yellow Rose Shelter was also closed to the public early in 1971. More and more of the trail is being forced onto Virginia Highway 601 in this area, and we walked for miles on hard-topped 601. Reached Three Springs Shelter at 3:30. Hikers going north from Three Springs marvel at the huge ant hills beside the trail. Most of them are round, being about four or five feet in diameter and thirty inches high. The biggest was rectangular, fourteen feet long, six feet wide, and three to three and a half feet high.

WEDNESDAY, JUNE 17. We were joined by Allan Levander, a seventeen-year-old of Charleston, South Carolina, and then to our surprise, by sixteen-year-old Maurice Gordon of Falls Church. I was surprised to see Gordon as he had planned to hike all the trail from Maine to Georgia. He said he had started with a 70-pound pack at Mt. Katahdin on June 14, and had twisted his knee badly at the top of the mountain. This forced him to discontinue his hike and fly home. He was now carrying a much lighter pack and testing his knee.

Reached Keys Gap Shelter 4:30. Big supper and plenty of time to work on my notes. Enjoyed company of the three young men.

THURSDAY, JUNE 18. Awakened at 3:30 by heavy wind and rain. Shelter roof leaked, and we hurriedly moved our sleeping bags to the driest part. Shannon and I left the shelter at 6:15. Skies cleared as we approached the Potomac River. We were able to obtain beautiful views from several points on Loudoun Heights. The views here command the Shenandoah and the Potomac rivers and their confluence, with the town of Harpers Ferry nestled between the two rivers. This is one of the more spectacular views on the entire trail. In addition to the rivers, three arteries of transportation are also visible: the Baltimore and Ohio Railroad, the old Chesapeake and Ohio Canal, and U.S. Route 340. Upon reaching the highway, we left the trail and walked into Harpers Ferry. The town and surrounding area is now part of the Harpers Ferry National Historical Park and many of the old buildings have been restored.

I visited the park service office and talked to Ben Davis, the superintendent. He very graciously made available to me a desk and a typewriter. Maurice Gordon arrived at noon and informed me that his knee was still acting up. My nephew Shannon had also decided that Harpers Ferry was as far as he wished to hike, and it was agreed that both of them would go back to Falls Church the next morning.

FRIDAY, JUNE 19. Up at 5:15, said good-bye to Maurice and Shannon, and was on my way at 5:50. I would now be hiking alone, for the most part, all the way to the New Jersey–New York state line. I was sorry that Shannon discontinued his hike so soon, but he was having foot troubles.

At 7:00 I crossed the Potomac River and entered Maryland. At 7:30 I reached Weverton Shelter on the C & O Canal and had a second breakfast cooked by a group of Boy Scouts from Steubenville, Ohio.

Visited for forty-five minutes with Howard DeGrange, superintendent of the Gathland State Park in Maryland. DeGrange told me of four local yokels who made frequent nightly visits to the nearby Crampton Gap Shelter to harass hikers. Since it was not on state property DeGrange was powerless to take the type of action he would have loved to have taken. I visited Crampton Gap Shelter and warned fourteen-year-old Mike Harris of Garrett Park, Maryland, and his two companions of the nightly visitors. They were somewhat apprehensive and wanted me to stay overnight. I would have liked to have stayed, but this was one of many instances when I had committed myself to be at a certain shelter, so I reluctantly pushed on. Reached Rocky Run Shelter at 4:00 having hiked seventeen miles for the day.

SATURDAY, JUNE 20. Reached Wolfe Shelter at 4:20. Saw 18 people on the trail today, 31 yesterday. Shortly after I arrived at Wolfe Shelter a group of eleven people from New Jersey and New York arrived. After darkness set in, they built a huge fire at a point about thirty yards from the shelter. This disturbed me—not only from the standpoint of conserving the small firewood supply but also because this was on private land and landowners become justifiably alarmed when hiking groups build large fires. I walked over to the group and asked them to cut down the size of the fire. They immediately did so. Since that time this shelter also has been closed to the hiking public by the landowner.

Pennsylvania

SUNDAY, JUNE 21. A horrible day weather-wise. Hard steady rain most of day. It was still raining when I went to bed. Visited four shelters—Devils Racecourse, Mackie Run, Antietam, Tumbling Run. Found groups of people in each, twenty-five in all. Had tentatively planned to stay at Tumbling Run; but it was partially occupied, not in the best of shape, and the locked PATC Hermitage Cabin was only 0.6 mile beyond. I gambled that the Hermitage would not be occupied on a Sunday night and it proved not to be. The Hermitage, which has a dark interior on even a bright day, was particularly dark and gloomy on this rainy night.

MONDAY, JUNE 22. The following is from my diary: "Reached Quarry Gap Shelter 6:30 P.M., cooked an excellent supper: soup, Lipton's Chicken Dinner with six ounces canned chicken added, instant pudding. All done and eaten by 7:45. Washed dishes, cut kindling for breakfast. Then to work on notes. Cooling down, 60 degrees at 9:00. Quarry Gap is a delightful place to camp—bubbling stream, three tables, rhododendron in bloom around the shelter. As I wrote a whippoorwill fluttered down five feet from where I sat, sang his piercing call for a full three minutes, then fluttered off a short way and resumed his calling.

TUESDAY, JUNE 23. Clear, pleasant day. At noon I reached the pride and joy of the PATC locked-cabin system, the beautiful Michener Cabin, built carefully and expertly by the loving hands of many PATC members. I had checked on occupancy and learned that a Ken Lehman of Harrisburg, Pennsylvania, had the cabin reserved for part of the week. Which part? I heated up huge quantities of hot water, washed clothes, bathed, and shaved. Found a 12½-ounce can of tuna in the cupboard and had a monstrous dinner of creamed tuna and instant potatoes. At 6:00, who should show up but Ken Lehman with his bride of three days! They were on their honeymoon. I hastily packed my gear and departed. Michener Cabin is becoming steeped with matrimonial tradition. Bill and Beth Oscanyan had been married here.

I went on to Toms Run Shelters. Arrived at dark, 9 P.M. Five young men were occupying the two small shelters. Room for one more—me! Picked my first blueberries of the season today.

WEDNESDAY, JUNE 24. Fair weather until 6 P.M., then overcast and windy. Reached Pine Grove Furnace Cabin at 7:00 and Pine Grove Furnace State Park at 8:45. This marks the end of the PATC territory, through which I have been hiking since June 8 for 225 miles.

I reached the Tagg Run Shelters at 12:00 and had a very difficult time finding the spring. No sign and no blue blazes. Reached Pennsylvania Highway 34 at 1:30 and hitchhiked into Mt. Holly Springs. Picked up mail, bought groceries, and ate a meal. Caught ride back to Appalachian Trail and resumed hiking at 4:30. Decided later that it was poor planning on my part to have gone into Mt. Holly Springs as the next day the trail passed directly in front of a combination post office and grocery store in the little town of Allen, Pennsylvania.

I pushed on very hard after 4:30 and figured I would reach Dark Hollow Shelter by 8:00 P.M. at the latest; but when I reached Center Point Knob, a mile beyond the shelter, I knew that something had gone wrong. I learned later that the Dark Hollow Shelter had been abandoned. Hiked along the crest of White Rocks. A beautiful place, but I had neither the time nor the inclination to enjoy it properly. Finally quit hiking at 9:00 and made my bed on the windward side of the ridge. Ate a cold supper and was in bed at 9:30. Hiked 22.7 miles. Saw deer on six occasions. About half the hiking today was on roads.

Let me comment on those strange creatures, the seventeen-year locusts: On June 16 we crossed the "locust barrier" at U.S. Route 50. South of that point, I had neither seen nor heard the locusts. North of U.S. 50 I was to hear their shrill singing for hours on end, whenever the temperature rose above a certain point. Along the trail I had seen thousands of neat three-eighths-inch round holes from which the locusts had emerged after a seventeen-year stay underground. Of late, I had been seeing dead locust bodies littering the trail. A strange cycle of nature.

THURSDAY, JUNE 25. Up at 5:20 and on the trail at 5:40 without breakfast. Reached road in twenty minutes and hiked into the town of Allen, almost all the way on hard-surfaced roads. Picked black raspberries (the first of year) and a half-pint of cherries on the way. Cooked breakfast on my Primus stove in the little cemetery across from the combination store-post office. Left Allen at 10:00 and hiked on roads almost the entire day. Ate my fill of cherries and black raspberries. Crossed U.S. Route 11 in early afternoon. Lost trail twice during the day; not too well-blazed, very few signs. Hiked sixteen miles, warm and humid. Again having trouble with chafing.

FRIDAY, JUNE 26. Dark, gloomy day; it rained hard during the night. Hiked the twelve miles into Duncannon; reached there 2 P.M. after a brief stop at the Thelma Marks Memorial Shelter at 10:00. Harry Baker of the volunteer fire department offered me the use of the recreation room quarters overnight, and I gratefully accepted his offer. Fabulous setup; toilet facilities with water so steaming hot I could and did make coffee and tea with the tap water. A water cooler, tables to write on, a couch to sleep on, a TV if I wanted to use it. Had the whole building to myself. I stayed up until 1:30 A.M. catching up on my correspondence. Several of the firemen had apologized for the condition of the rest room. It was a bit littered, so as my contribution I made the place spick-and-span.

SATURDAY, JUNE 27. Left the firehouse at 6:30. Overcast, rain threatened most of day. Walked Clarks Ferry Bridge over the Susquehanna River, then crossed U.S. Route 22 and the railroad tracks, then ascended the steep ravine. Came to Clarks Valley Shelter at 4:00; fourteen miles for the day. This is the first concrete block shelter I have seen since Tennessee. Yesterday, and again today, I saw the perforated four-inch metal ATC markers. I have read that these were used in the early years of the trail, but I don't recall ever having seen them before. Picked about one quart of black raspberries.

SUNDAY, JUNE 28. A clear, cool, delightful day. There are no shelters for the twenty-eight-mile stretch between Clarks Valley Shelter and Applebee Shelter. No shelters to inspect and none to sleep in. Hiked through St. Anthonys Wilderness, one of the most beautiful areas on entire trail. It is somewhat comparable to Laurel Fork Gorge in Tennessee. The trail follows an old stagecoach road. Within the quiet fastness of the wilderness the hiker sees the remains of the once-thriving town of Rausch Gap. The old town well, the little cemetery, the railroad beds, and the remains of the trestles are still visible. I ate lunch at a pretty spot beside rushing Rausch Creek.

I heard no more seventeen-year locusts, so think I have passed through the locust country. I now weigh 143 pounds stripped, 10 pounds under my normal weight.

MONDAY, JUNE 29. Hiked with Hank Finerfrock of New Cumberland, Pennsylvania, and a friend of his, fourteen-year-old Greg Grissinger. Hank's daughter Jan, his wife Doris, and her mother had a hot lunch all laid out at Applebee Shelter when we arrived. Such conveniences on the Appalachian Trail! After the Finerfrocks left, Greg and I hiked to the nearby Lundgren Cabin, a locked cabin belonging to the Blue Mountain Eagle Climbing Club of Reading, Pennsylvania. Club members had spent hundreds of hours renovating the cabin, and it was a delightful spot in which to spend the night.

TUESDAY, JUNE 30. Up at 6:00, stoked the fire, and had a huge breakfast of grilled cheese sandwiches, fresh milk, canned cherries, pie, and coffee. Not bad for a trail breakfast! Pleasant day, mostly clear. Had a leisurely fourteen-mile hike to Neys Shelter. A group of fifteen boys was already at the shelter when we arrived, but left shortly. Several times we saw deer walking inquiringly around the camp. Had a late snack of freshly popped corn.

WEDNESDAY, JULY 1. A leisurely seven-mile hike to Port Clinton interrupted midway by my second encounter with a rattlesnake. Greg Grissinger was walking in front of me when suddenly he jumped backward. Three feet ahead of him on the trail was a four-foot rattlesnake with eight rattles. The snake was not coiled and had given no warning. It appeared indifferent to our presence, and we walked to one side of it and passed on.

I stopped at the Port Clinton Hotel for a sandwich and to sign the Appalachian Trail register kept by Mr. and Mrs. Royle Carbaugh who operate the hotel.

THURSDAY, JULY 2. Repacked groceries and weighed my pack, forty-three pounds with my two canteens full of white wine, my heaviest weight so far. A hot, humid, overcast day. At 6:45 I reached the big 28′ × 32′ cabin owned by John Rarick, a member of the Blue Mountain Eagle Climbing Club. Cooked over a propane stove and had propane lighting for the evening. Pretty luxurious for a hiker. Rarick and his wife arrived about 9:45 P.M. He brought me a package of breakfast pastries. He also brought half a bushel of old bread and rolls for the many raccoons in the area. They left at 11:30. To bed at 1:00 A.M.

FRIDAY, JULY 3. Overcast and foggy all day. Missed all the views on what is probably the most scenic part of the trail in Pennsylvania.

SATURDAY, JULY 4. Another hot, humid day. Reached Outerbridge Shelter at 9:00. It is a very attractive shelter, but it was disfigured by thirty to forty bushels of trash in an open pit forty yards in front of shelter. Met four boys at the shelter who were camping there, not hiking.

I walked through a concentration of sassafras trees today, the biggest such trees I had ever seen. Reached a paved road at Little Gap. Hitched ride into Danielsville and obtained a room ($4.00) at the Mountain View Hotel. Showered, shaved, and washed clothes. Have been hiking with wet feet for three days because of the hot, humid weather. It felt wonderful to get into clean clothes.

SUNDAY, JULY 5. Left hotel 6:15. A forty-five minute walk back to the trail at Little Gap. Arrived at Smith Gap at 10:30 and met Tom Miller of Bethlehem, Pennsylvania, and his group of twenty horsemen.

Although I had seen evidence in a number of places that horses had used the trail, the encounter at Smith Gap was the only time I actually saw them. The issue of horses using the Appalachian Trail is a thorny one. Horsemen, as well as bicyclists and motorcycle enthusiasts, have precious few places to pursue their hobbies. To all of these groups the well-maintained Appalachian Trail looks inviting. The National Trails System Act, Public Law 90-543, prohibits the use of the trail by motorized vehicles and discourages, but does not actually prohibit, its use by horses. The matter is one that must be handled through regulation as the states and the federal government acquire rights to the lands over which the trail passes.

As I left Smith Gap I experienced a strange feeling. It was as though I was back in Georgia and the time was early April. The sun shown brightly through the trees where there should have been shade! Here, for a five-mile stretch, the leaves had been stripped from the trees by gypsy moths. The forest was too bright; very few birds were in evidence. I experienced an eerie feeling. It made me think of Rachel Carson's *Silent Spring*.

MONDAY, JULY 6. I was now hiking the last few miles in Pennsylvania and approaching the Delaware River and the spectacular Delaware Water Gap. As I stood at the various viewpoints looking down on the river, it reminded me of the view of the Potomac River and Harpers Ferry. At the post office I picked up a mountain of mail—fifteen letters and four packages.

One of the packages contained a new Kelty pack—I had ordered it to replace my old Kelty, which had taken quite a beating when the luggage rack tore loose from my car on the way to Georgia in March.

I also received three pounds of fruit cake, a heavier pair of hiking shoes sent from home, and the New York–New Jersey guidebook. I tied my various boxes together and began walking over the bridge to New Jersey.

On this date, July 6, I had completed my hike through seven states. Seven states still remained. I had hiked 1,156 miles and had 872 more to go. I was pleased that my trip had been so successful to date.

New Jersey–New York

TUESDAY, JULY 7. Today I hiked a side trail to the summit of Mt. Tammany. The views of the Delaware Water Gap from various vantage points on Mt. Tammany are spectacular. It seems a shame that the Appalachian Trail is not routed over this very interesting spot. During the previous three months I had struggled over scores of steep mountains. When I reached the top there was nothing to see; often the top was completely wooded. I wondered why trail planners had gone to such pains to put the trail over those mountains when there are no vistas for the hiker, while here in New Jersey the trail comes within a mile of one of the most spectacular water gaps in the eastern United States, and the trail skirts the mountaintop from which there are marvelous views.

Shortly thereafter I met another lone hiker, also with pack. It was Casey Kays of Hackettstown, New Jersey, a never-give-up conservationist whom I had wanted to meet for years. A factory worker, Casey was the first person to call public attention to the plans of utility companies to use Sunfish Pond as the upper reservoir of a pumped storage plant for generating electricity. For over five years he fought, writing and mailing thousands of letters, conducting hikes so that the public could see the now famous pond, and testifying at hearings.

I was distressed to note that the Sunfish Pond area seems to be suffering from wall-to-wall camping and wall-to-wall littering.

I had an unusual experience about two miles north of the pond.

Approaching me from the north were two people walking single file. The first person was a young man, barefoot, wearing only a pair of dungarees. However, when I drew abreast—and I choose that word carefully—I saw the second person was a very curvaceous young lady; and she was not wearing dungarees—or anything else! She seemed a little new at the nudist game and somewhat ill at ease. As I came within speaking distance, she giggled and said, "Nice day, hunh?" I smiled and replied with an enthusiastic, "Indeed it is!" After passing these two, I heard a baby cry. Looking to my left I saw a baby being comforted by a large, naked young man. I spoke to him, and he returned my greeting. Beyond him were another eight or ten young adults, all nude. Shortly thereafter I met Harry Nees who had hiked in from the north end of the section to meet me. When I related my experience he shook his head sadly and said, "It just isn't right. I've maintained this section of the trail for fifteen years and have never seen anything more exciting than an occasional deer. Now you come up here from Virginia and the first day out you hit the jackpot!"

The day had been noteworthy in other respects. I met seventy-five people on the trail, a very high figure. I had picked up 15 cans and some 120 other pieces of litter, a very heavy day. I had learned to identify a new plant, Indian pipe. I had seen deer on three occasions. And I had passed through another large area being defoliated by the caterpillars of the gypsy moth.

WEDNESDAY, JULY 8. Warm day. Made fairly good time, but blueberries slowed me down! Saw deer on three occasions, including one spotted fawn. Some striking views in this area, quite a few natural lakes. Reached Stokes Lean-to at 6:45. It was fully occupied by a Boy Scout troop. They were kind enough to furnish me a tarp and helped me erect it.

THURSDAY, JULY 9. This was the heaviest litter-pickup day to date: 15 cans, 160 other pieces of junk. Litter pickup in New Jersey is killing me!

FRIDAY, JULY 10. It rained during the night and then intermittently throughout the day, with torrential rains around 8:00 A.M. I became soaking wet and remained that way most of the day. At 12:30 I reached Unionville, New York, and searched for a restaurant. I was directed to a small place well back from the highway. It was fittingly named Side Road Pantry. What a find! I love homemade pies; and as I approached the Pantry I had an inkling of what I would find when I saw a lady coming out with an armful of freshly baked pies. Inside was a large table completely covered with hot pies that had been set out to cool. All of the bread and rolls served to customers with their meals was homemade and of top quality.

After leaving Unionville, it began to rain again. Much of the trail was along country roads. From the High Point No. 1 Lean-to, it is forty-five miles to the next shelter in New York, so I knew I would have no shelter to sleep in that day or the next. It was approaching 6:00 P.M., and I had hiked twenty miles. So as I neared the community of Maple Grange, New Jersey, I asked and received permission from dairy farmer Lynn Presher to use his machine shed for the night. Not only that, but he permitted me to use the boiling hot water of the dairy room. This machine shed was much more inviting than some of the shelters I had slept in. It was a pleasure to have steaming hot water for coffee, for shaving, and for washing dishes!

SATURDAY, JULY 11. I was awakened at 5:10 A.M. by a cow that thrust her head through a hole in the machine shed wall and bawled impatiently at me. It was time for milking; and ten minutes later Bill Presher, Lynn's brother, flicked on the barn lights. The cows ambled in, and the milking process began. I had begun making preparations for breakfast, but Bill invited me to his home. I accepted with alacrity. Much bacon, two eggs, and fresh banana nut bread. Began hiking at 6:30; at 8:15 I spotted a tent directly beside the trail. I hailed the occupant, Gary Rutherford, a bearded twenty-seven-year-old civil engineer from Pen Argyl, Pennsylvania. He packed his gear, and we began hiking together. He expressed a desire to hike with me all the way to Katahdin. We ate lunch on the Warwick Turnpike, even finding a fruit stand a hundred yards down the pike. The Appalachian Trail does offer surprises now and then.

At 3:30 we reached Cascade Lake and went for a brief but delightful swim, my first of the year. Pushed on steadily for several miles, high above beautiful Greenwood Lake. At 5:30 we left the Appalachian Trail and hiked on the blue-blazed Mountain Spring Trail to the resort village of Greenwood Lake, New York. We ate our evening meal and stayed overnight at Murphy's Hotel and Bar.

During the afternoon we had passed from New Jersey into New York. Eight states behind me; six more to go! Picked my first blackberries of the season. I am still seeing rhododendron in bloom and still seeing and smelling wild azalea.

SUNDAY, JULY 12. A clear, warm, and very humid day. Up at 6:00, went to eight o'clock Mass, and began hiking at 9:30. A hard climb up a mountain; we reached the top at 10:00, dripping with sweat. Made poor mileage; many road crossings, met numerous groups of people with whom we stopped and visited. Hiked over miles of those big glacial conglomerate rock formations. The trail is steep in many places. Beautiful views of the New York lake area.

At 6:30 we crossed New York Route 17, near the New York State Thruway. By prearrangement we met Harry Nees at that point, and he whisked us to his lovely home near Garrison, New York, with its magnificent view of the Hudson River Storm King area.

MONDAY, JULY 13. Up at 5:30. Worked on notes and correspondence until the others arose. Had an out-of-this-world breakfast and lunch cooked by Harry's good Danish-born wife, Kirsten. After lunch Harry drove us back to the Appalachian Trail at Route 17. Gary and I hiked but eight miles for the day, our progress slowed by the need to inspect three shelters. Our hiking was entirely within the Harriman section of Palisades Interstate Park. The first six miles, from Route 17 to Lake Tiorati Circle, was on the very first section of the Appalachian Trail to be completed. That section had been opened on Sunday, October 7, 1923.

We reached the Letterrock Lean-to at 7:00 and found it occupied by a church group from New York City comprised of twenty boys. They cooked a hot dog and a hamburger for Gary and me. With that and our coffee and fruitcake we made out famously. As darkness enveloped the area, we were plagued with no-see-ums. Gary erected his two-man tent. The boys in the twelve to fourteen-year-old class played a little rough. The firecrackers, name-calling, and an occasional rock banging on the tin roof of the shelter, plus the hungry no-see-ums, made sleep difficult.

Litter was again heavy: ten cans and eighty other pieces. We did not attempt to clean up around Island Pond as the area was saturated.

During the time I hiked with Gary (to Pittsfield, Massachusetts) I lived well as far as coffee was concerned. He carried a small coffee pot in which he brewed real coffee over his gasoline stove. We both loved good fresh coffee; and he brewed it often, even at lunchtime. His coffee pot was small, but we overcame that difficulty by brewing extremely strong coffee, then removing the percolator basket and adding water. The diluted mixture was still strong enough, and by diluting the coffee there were two full cups for each of us.

TUESDAY, JULY 14. We began hiking at 8:00, but lost a full hour because we hiked in the wrong direction—the second time I had done that! Met part of the group that had stayed at Letterrock Lean-to. They had noticed us starting out in the wrong direction, but were reluctant to challenge anyone who had hiked all the way from Georgia. I had the feeling that the group would not have given me a very high rating as a woodsman!

Made slow time, encountered some extremely steep climbs. The views looking down on the New York lakes were superb. Somehow we missed the one shelter in this section, the West Mountain Lean-to. The lean-to is 0.6 miles off the Appalachian Trail, and we observed no sign indicating its location.

We reached the summit of Bear Mountain at 11:30 and then proceeded down the steep litter-strewn trail toward Bear Mountain Inn. During the day we picked up 10 cans and 150 other pieces of litter. There seemed to be thousands of people milling about the playground, the concessions, and the sites adjacent to the inn and the museum. We had difficulty finding the trail through this congested area. We reached Bear Mountain Bridge and paid the five-cent toll for crossing by foot—the only toll or admission I paid in 2,000 miles of hiking. I'm not complaining about the five cents. I would have paid many times that amount to cross a bridge over the Kennebec, in Maine, if there had been one.

WEDNESDAY, JULY 15. We hiked only five miles. It was a warm, overcast, humid day and mosquitoes and deerflies were troublesome. Gary was wearing shorts and he did not have enough hands to keep the insects off.

All through the Southern Appalachians I had seen wild azaleas or flame azaleas as they are also called. They were of two colors, orange and pink. When I resumed hiking on June 6, I still saw a few of the fading azalea bushes at higher elevations; each time I recorded them as the "last azaleas" of the season. When I reached New Jersey, I was informed by Casey Kays that I would see a different type of azalea all through New Jersey and New York—smooth azaleas, he called them, and they would have white flowers. He was right; we saw and smelled them on a number of days. On July 14 I saw the biggest azalea bushes of my trip, several of them standing ten feet high.

THURSDAY, JULY 16. Began hiking at 8:15. A muggy, buggy day. Several times we passed near swamps and the mosquitoes and the deerflies were ferocious. Hard rains from 11:00 to 1:00. I was drenched from head to foot. Water squishing out of my shoes at every step.

We hiked through interesting country with grown-over fields enclosed by rock fences. These fields are not being farmed anymore. It must have been extremely difficult trying to make a living from this rocky land. Mosquitoes much of the day. I used bug repellent and wore a kerchief over my head and neck. We reached Torrey Memorial Lean-to at 6:00.

FRIDAY, JULY 17. We met veteran hiker Charlie Konopa of Green Bay, Wisconsin, near the village of Holmes. Konopa is also hiking the entire trail, but he has been doing it in bits and pieces. When we met him he was using his camper as a base and was hiking with a day pack. We stopped at Holmes for groceries and refreshments, and went on to Pawling, New York. I telephoned the town police that evening and they guided Charlie to the pavilion in a recreation area where Gary and I had obtained permission to camp. Charlie visited with us until 10:00 P.M. We slept on the concrete floor, a happy choice as the pavilion was free of mosquitoes and we were protected from the drenching dew which settled that night. We had hiked twenty miles; we had seen two deer, several woodchucks, and three more of those ugly aerial survey panels littering the landscape.

SATURDAY, JULY 18. We began hiking at 6:00 through the quiet streets of Pawling. At 6:45 we reached New York Route 22 and stopped for a ham-and-egg breakfast at Charlie Konopa's camper. In midmorning we plunged into the Pawling Nature Preserve Tract. It was extremely buggy and a veritable grass jungle near its northern end. We emerged about 10:45 and moments later reached the Girl Scout Camp of Sacajawea. The leaders, Barbara and Chuck Chase, invited us in. I spoke briefly about my hike to a group of the girls. Then we were treated to a huge turkey sandwich, fruit, coffee, and doughnuts. Around one o'clock we reached the side trail leading to the Webatuck Lean-to and then spent a full thirty minutes trying unsuccessfully to find it.

Gary and I climbed steadily up Schaghticoke Mountain, signed the register at the New York–Connecticut line (9 states and 1,315 miles behind me!), and then proceeded down the steep trail to reach Thayer Brook at 6:00.

Connecticut–Massachusetts

SUNDAY, JULY 19. We walked slowly and carefully down the steep slope on Mt. Algo, and then left the trail to walk into the village of

Kent. I went to 9:30 Mass after I visited the church basement to change clothes, shave, and trim my shaggy hair.

We hiked but thirteen miles today yet encountered three lean-tos: Chase Mountain, Macedonia Brook, and Mountain Brook. We reached the last one at 7:15 P.M. and spent the night there.

MONDAY, JULY 20. We began hiking at 6:25. A moderately warm, clear day with low humidity and a light breeze. Ideal for hiking. We lost the trail twice during the morning. At one point, after locating the trail, we elected not to use it as it was an uninviting looking poison-ivy jungle. We took the longer way, via a dirt road. We reached the town of Cornwall Bridge at 9:45 and bought groceries and a half-gallon of ice cream.

We hiked up Dark Entry Ravine, an incredibly beautiful place that ranks with St. Anthonys Wilderness in Pennsylvania and Laurel Fork Gorge in Tennessee for single-day hiking beauty. We walked slowly, admiring the brook, the falls, and the cascades. Later in the day we hiked through another beautiful area, Cathedral Pines. Near sundown we encountered two lean-tos barely a mile apart, the Mohawk and then Bunker Hill, where we stayed overnight.

TUESDAY, JULY 21. We took off at 6:45 and pushed on to new Limestone Spring Lean-to—reached it at 5:00 P.M.

WEDNESDAY, JULY 22. After breakfast, while I worked on my notes, Gary performed a major operation. First with scissors, then with razor, he removed his luxuriant big black beard! We left the lean-to at 8:10. Stopped for some minutes to enjoy striking view of the Taconic Range. On reaching U.S. Route 44 later in the morning, Gary and I were met by Robert Tabor, a member of the ATC Board of Managers from Charleston, West Virginia, and Allerton Eddy of nearby Twin Lakes, Connecticut. After buying groceries in Salisbury and spending two hours at the Eddy home on Twin Lakes, we returned to the trail. We picked blueberries until our tongues and lips were blue. Relaxed that night and all the next day at the AMC Riga locked cabin.

THURSDAY, JULY 23. A gorgeous day, a high of 70° F., clear. A day for relaxing. This was one of only three days on the trail that I did not hike at least a few miles. I read all of my mail, wrote letters, and brought my notes up to date. I washed clothes, shaved, and prevailed upon Gary to cut my hair.

For all practical purposes I had now hiked through Connecticut;

Massachusetts was but two hundred yards away. Connecticut surprised me. I really don't know what I expected but I did not expect the trail to be so rugged or so beautiful. We had hiked in splendid ravines, through wooded areas, up and down steep mountain trails, and we saw some spectacular views.

FRIDAY, JULY 24. Massachusetts: six days and eighty-four miles. We left at 8:30, and within minutes were walking along beautiful Sages Ravine. We picked a quart of blueberries on top of Race Mountain. At 1:00 P.M. we reached the summit of Mt. Everett, and I noticed a man with a camera standing on the first landing of the fire tower. He asked if I was the fellow hiking the entire Appalachian Trail; when I said I was, he began grinding away furiously with his movie camera. He seemed so intense about his photography and took so many pictures from so many angles that I finally asked him if he would mind telling me who he was and who he represented. He introduced himself as Tex Griffin, a free-lance photographer from Bronxville, New York. He had heard I was hiking the entire trail, was captivated with the idea, and decided to document parts of it with both color movies and color slides. He was to meet me again in Vermont, in New Hampshire, and at the end of my hike on Mt. Katahdin. In all, he made about five hundred color slides of my hike.

SATURDAY, JULY 25. Gary, Sam Steen, and I began hiking at 8:45. The temperature was about 90° F. much of the day; there was a brief shower at 3:00. We did considerable road walking through the pretty Massachusetts countryside. We crossed the Housatonic River for the umpteenth time. Water was scarce; the brooks and springs were running dry. We made it all the way to Benedict Pond, fifteen miles, by 4:00 P.M.

SUNDAY, JULY 26. I went to 7:00 A.M. Mass; then in two cars we proceeded to our starting point at Benedict Pond. The Arthur Koerbers of Pittsfield, Massachusetts, hiked with us part of the day. At Mt. Wilcox Lean-to we met George Wright, a hiker from New York City, who asked if he might join us. George was on his first extended hike and carried a guitar. He sang professionally when opportunity presented and sang for fun at other times. He was a traveling troubadour, and his singing was to enliven our evenings.

Although it was a clear day with the temperature about 80° F. in the woods, it sounded as though a light rain was falling. This sound was caused by the hordes of gypsy moth caterpillars defoliating the trees. The insect droppings and the particles of leaves pattered down just like rain. We were to be very conscious of this sound for the next two days.

MONDAY, JULY 27. Hiked a scant eight miles. We met George Wright and learned that he had made out famously after we left him on Sunday afternoon. He had sung at a night club for his meals and money; one of the patrons took him to his home for the night and then brought him back to the Appalachian Trail. At 12:00 we reached the home of Mrs. Fred Hutchinson at Washington Town Hall. Mrs. Hutchinson is the grand old lady of the Appalachian Trail. She treated us to a delightful lunch with homemade bread and pie. After lunch, she read us excerpts from a lengthy paper she had written about some of the many hikers she and her late husband had befriended over a forty-year period.

TUESDAY, JULY 28. George Wright and I stopped on Warner Hill and in twenty minutes picked all the berries we could eat from a single eight-foot highbush blueberry. That afternoon we hiked through some interesting beech groves and later some white birch groves. We reached Cheshire, Massachusetts, at 5:30, having hiked nineteen miles for the day.

WEDNESDAY, JULY 29. My pack weighed forty-two pounds, including my new supply of groceries. I reached the Kitchen Brook Lean-to at 10:30 and had an early lunch. During the morning I had encountered several families of blueberry pickers on the mountaintops. I reached Bascom Lodge atop Mt. Greylock at noon.

I was horrified to see forty or more wrapped sandwiches on the floor of the front porch. The sandwiches had been discarded by boys from a nearby camp. The attendant picked them up and threw them in the trash can. He said it happened every day!

I learned that George Wright had conducted a songfest the previous night at Bascom Lodge and was somewhere ahead of me on the trail. I arrived at Wilbur Clearing Lean-to, one of four lean-tos in Massachusetts and the only really good one. It is a 15′ × 20′ shelter with a five-foot overhang in front. It has a very ingenious wood storage area underneath its rear overhang. I judged it would sleep ten or twelve boys comfortably. It was about to have its capacity tested by the thirty-five boys and their leaders who arrived at the same time I did.

I had now hiked 1,451 miles and had all but completed my hike through Massachusetts. I was surprised and pleased with the beauty of the western part of Massachusetts, but there is too much road walking, and the paint blazing, the shelter situation, and the wooden direction signs all need improvement.

Vermont

THURSDAY, JULY 30. A long day. The first few miles of the trail have been rerouted away from roads within the past year. Big improvement. Visited Seth Warner Shelter. Saw deer on two occasions, the first in a week. Scared a woodchuck up a tree.

At 4:30 I met Clifford Smith and his wife Margaret who left Mt. Katahdin June 14 headed for Georgia. They do not have a guidebook, only road maps. They buy food for seven to eight days because they don't know where the next store is.

FRIDAY, JULY 31. Hiked only seven miles today, but much of it was up, up, up to the Glastenbury Shelter at an elevation of 3,500 feet.

There were two young men at the shelter. At eight o'clock George Wright and Craig Bumgarner arrived. George played his guitar and sang, and seventeen-year-old Marty Gil chimed in with a harmonica.

SATURDAY, AUGUST 1. Breakfast was a congested affair with ten men firing up stoves and packing gear in one shelter. Intermittent rain all day. Reached Stratton Pond at 5:45. There are four shelters on this one pond, and all but one were filled as it was Saturday night. Craig, George, and I moved into Vondell Shelter, joining a couple who had arrived earlier.

SUNDAY, AUGUST 2. A turnabout in the weather. Sunny, low humidity, light breeze: ideal for hiking. Made a scant fourteen miles from Vondell Shelter to Bromley Camp. My progress was slowed by the need to inspect nine shelters in this stretch. This was the heaviest concentration of shelters since I began my hike in Georgia.

Today I had passed the 1,500-mile mark in my hike. In honor of the occasion George sat on the top bunk, played his guitar, and sang a folk song made famous by the Peter, Paul, and Mary trio, "500 Miles from Home."

MONDAY, AUGUST 3. Overslept; the alarm device on my wrist watch stopped working.

I did some shopping in Manchester Center and was given a ride back to the trail by Joe Gumberger, a college student and seasonal employee of the forest service. He, like scores of people I met on my hike, harbored a secret desire to hike the entire Appalachian Trail.

My litter pickup has dropped markedly in New England. Apparently, the big spring litter-pickup drives have been effective.

Called it a day on reaching Peru Peak Shelter. My diary reads: "Delightful evening. Cool. 64° F. at 7:00. Got cooler. Nice big shelter. Good fire going. George began singing, and a minute later I was asleep. Was awakened later by George clubbing a porcupine about two feet from my head."

Porcupines do a great deal of damage along some parts of the trail, especially in Vermont. They chew on wooden toilets, tables, and even shelter floors. One toilet had three walls completely eaten away. The newer toilets are of metal, and the tables are covered with galvanized steel.

TUESDAY, AUGUST 4. Ideal cool hiking day. Visited five shelters, four of which I rated excellent and one very good. Trail led through beautiful woods, ponds, and streams, and was in good shape, easy to follow.

George and I reached Little Rock Pond Shelter at 4:00. Took a swim—delightful. Hard to describe the beauty of this place—crystal-clear pond, conifers and white birch trees along the shore. Took a walk around the pond and when I returned George was singing at the shore. Sat and listened for almost an hour. I was sorry to see such a perfect day come to an end.

I am afraid I have heard and seen the last of the towhees for this trip. I have enjoyed their company since the first day in Georgia. The Vermont border seems to mark the northernmost point of towhee territory. Their place has been taken by the white-throated sparrow whose high-pitched plaintive five-note song we now hear frequently.

WEDNESDAY, AUGUST 5. Wakened at 3:30 by an owl hooting on far side of pond. Four notes, and then the same four notes immediately repeated. The sound traveled clearly across the water. All of us were up at 5:30. Another fine day. We reached Vermont Highway 140 at 11:00 and found Craig Bumgarner waiting for us. He was discontinuing his hike at that point.

At 7:00, after hiking nineteen miles, we reached the Governor Clement Shelter. There were three separate groups at the shelter, twenty people in all, including Ken Lesenko and Jim Burdick. The latter two were as happy as kids at their first Christmas. This was their first hike on the Appalachian Trail. They had been uncertain of their ability; they had had rough going the first couple of days; but now they had found that they could hike fifteen or more miles a day, get into camp early, and not be too tired. After all were in bed, George got out his guitar and began singing. He had a big audience that night, and the group was captivated.

THURSDAY, AUGUST 6. A leisurely day. After two hours of hiking we reached the new Tamarack Shelter. I was very interested in the design of this shelter and that of its older counterpart, the Glastenbury Shelter seventy miles to the south. They were unique among the 238 shelters inspected. Each had a wooden sleeping platform four or five feet above the ground with room for six to eight people. This sleeping platform provided a spacious area underneath for either an immense amount of gear or four additional people. The Tamarack Shelter was a big high structure with a wide front overhang to provide protection from the elements. George and I hiked on to Sherburne Pass (U.S. Route 4) where the Long Trail Lodge is located. Later, George sang here during the ski season under the name "Peregrine."

FRIDAY, AUGUST 7. Spent the day visiting friends.

SATURDAY, AUGUST 8. I made plans to attend five o'clock Mass at the little interdenominational church in Killington. It was a folk Mass; I recognized one of the guitarists—George Wright! Whether it was a night club, a lonely shelter on the Appalachian Trail, or a church— there was George with his trusty guitar and his pleasant voice.

SUNDAY, AUGUST 9. I reached the Gulf Lean-to at 4:30. I had not planned to spend the night there, but it looked too inviting to pass up. The weight of my pack when I left Killington was 35 pounds; my weight was 159. I was satisfied with both. That was the first shelter I had slept in alone since Pennsylvania.

MONDAY, AUGUST 10. Up at 5:30, on trail at 6:05—my quickest getaway in weeks. The reason: a cold cereal breakfast. I reached the unlocked Dartmouth Outing Club's Happy Hill Cabin at 5:30 P.M. and made a revolting discovery. No water! Both the spring and the brook were dry. I had no water with me, but I did have a scant pint of wine. I ate an uncooked meal and washed it down with the wine. It was the only time during my trip when I had to go without water overnight.

TUESDAY, AUGUST 11. Left the cabin at 5:50 without breakfast. Reached the Connecticut River at 8 A.M. Another milestone—twelve states now behind me and almost 1,600 miles. I reached downtown Hanover, New Hampshire, at 8:15 and picked up a pile of mail.

WEDNESDAY, AUGUST 12. Arrived at the unlocked DOC Harris Cabin at noon and ate lunch there. Diary reads: "Reached Goose Pond about 4:00 P.M. Then my troubles began—lost the trail twice in the next two miles—then upon reaching Clark Pond I lost much time trying to find shelter. Blazes have been obliterated—trail being relocated. Reached shelter at 6:00—had a delightful swim—then a light supper. Worked on notes—started a brisk wood fire at 8:30—and had another swim 8:45. This was even more delightful. There was still some daylight. The fire was illuminating the interior of the shelter and an almost full moon was coming up over the white birch trees. A truly wonderful sight. A joy to be alive. A little mosquito problem but not bad. Crawled into sleeping bag. Applied insect repellent to face and neck—and had no trouble. Not a ripple on the lake. End of a wonderful day."

THURSDAY, AUGUST 13. Up at 5:30 for brisk and invigorating swim. Temperature 60° F., but no wind. Day dawning clear. Pond is so beautiful, a little vapor hanging above the water and drifting slowly southward.

I found a note at the Mt. Cube Lean-to from Everett and Nell Skinner of Bristol, Vermont. Said they would come back later. They did return after 5:00 P.M. with the makings for a huge steak dinner. They had hiked the entire trail in 1968, and I had met them in the Shenandoah National Park in Virginia. I had fun eating and visiting with them and comparing notes on our hiking experiences.

FRIDAY, AUGUST 14. Had one of my favorite breakfasts: sausage, buckwheat pancakes, and Vermont maple syrup, all supplied by the Skinners.

I had planned to stay at the Wachipauka Lean-to, but decided against it as the shelter was 0.8 mile off the Appalachian Trail and had no water. Instead, I camped at an attractive spot on the shore of Wachipauka Pond. I went for a swim immediately upon reaching camp. A breezy night—minimum trouble with mosquitoes.

SATURDAY, AUGUST 15. Began hiking 6:45. Reached Glencliff, New Hampshire, Post Office at 8:20 and picked up mail. On the post office scales my pack now weighed forty-six pounds. That was disturbing because the elevation at Glencliff is 1,540 feet while the top of Mt.

Moosilauke has an elevation of 4,810 feet. Reached summit of Moosi-lauke at 4 P.M.—tremendous viewpoint, but day quite hazy. Made slow progress to Beaver Brook Shelter. Trail very steep and eroded. I used the wooden ladders and steel cables provided at the steepest points. Reached shelter at 7 P.M.

SUNDAY, AUGUST 16. Had a hot hard climb to the tops of the two Kinsmans. Reached Kinsman Pond Shelter after an unimpressive eleven miles for the day.

MONDAY, AUGUST 17. A long hard climb from Franconia Notch to the top of Mt. Lafayette. The elevation of the highway in the Notch is 1,420 feet; the elevation of Mt. Lafayette is 5,249 feet. The temperature on Lafayette was 58° F. at 5 P.M. I reached Garfield Pond Shelter at 7:00. It was an overcast, windy, chilly night, and thirty-three members of a Boy Scout troop were already in residence. I had met sixty-five people on the trail and in shelters that day. Just before reaching the shelter, I crossed the outlet stream of Garfield Pond and took a copious drink. Moments later I saw a sign on the shelter warning that the water was not safe and should be boiled. Great! The shelter was pretty well saturated with boys; but one of the Scout leaders let me use a tent that was all set up and ready to sleep in. I should state at this point that the two Boy Scout laws of courtesy and kindness were certainly observed, as far as I was concerned, by all of the Scout organizations that I met during my trip.

TUESDAY, AUGUST 18. Up at 5:30. Temperature 46° F. and windy. I reached Zealand Falls Hut at 6:00 P.M., in time to get washed up before the evening meal was served. After supper, Doug Teschner and Chris Hawkins, two of the hut boys, built a fire in the sauna. At the appropriate time we stripped naked and walked gingerly into the smoky, unlighted sweat room. We absorbed much heat and steam and no little smoke from the fire below us. After we were sweating profusely we went outside and immersed ourselves in an ice-cold pool in the mountain stream. We repeated the operation once, then toweled off, put on clean clothes, and returned to the hut. Quite an experience, and for some reason the cold water is not the shock one would imagine.

WEDNESDAY, AUGUST 19. Left the hut at 7:50. There was a full moon still showing in the morning sky. A beautiful day—excellent visibility. Enjoyed the easy walk down the gentle grade of the old railroad bed.

Reached Ethan Pond Shelter at 10:00. Some twenty girls from a private camp were staying there. Very nice shelter. It has a stated capacity of ten, but I was assured that seventeen girls had slept there the previous night.

THURSDAY, AUGUST 20. Sam Steen arrived from Kingston, New York, and will hike with me for the next five days.

It took us 4½ hours to walk approximately 4½ miles. The trail was very steep, rocky, and eroded. Weather foggy—no views. I saw some of the water bars (used to divert runoff water from the trail) which had been installed by Appalachian Mountain Club crews but concluded it was a losing battle.

We carried full canteens because we had heard that the spring at the Nauman Shelters was dry. We arrived at the shelters at 6:15. The spring was almost dry, its iron pipe discharging water a drop at a time. Even so, two boys had spent several hours capturing 2½ gallons. We had enough water for supper, but we borrowed breakfast water from the two boys. Shortly after dark, a young man and his girl friend arrived—no water, no stove. They used Sam's stove and all of our breakfast water to cook an evening meal. It began to rain very hard at one o'clock and continued most of the night.

FRIDAY, AUGUST 21. Delayed getting up until 6:30 because it was so very dark and still raining slightly. Visited the spring and found that water was now coming out in a steady stream. The long dry spell in the White Mountains had been broken. Began hiking at 8:00. Reached the big Mizpah Spring Hut at 9:30 and stopped for hot coffee and coffee cake. Reached Lakes-of-the-Clouds Hut at 12:30 and ate lunch there. We left the hut at 1:45 and the sky cleared—good views thereafter. We hiked above tree line most of the day, frequently above 5,000 feet, and went over Mt. Washington whose elevation exceeds 6,000 feet. From my diary: "Reached Thunderstorm Junction about 6:00. Decided to try for Craig Camp. Reached there 6:45—delightful arrangement—custodian, propane gas, running cold water, utensils—all for $1. Cooked a good supper. Sam and I and the custodian are the only occupants." I had passed the 1,700-mile mark—my hike was 85 percent completed!

SATURDAY, AUGUST 22. Up at 5:30 and used the three-burner propane stove to make coffee and pancakes. Clear day, 44° F. at 6 A.M. We reached the Madison Hut at 9:15 and stayed for coffee. We climbed over Mt. Madison, elevation 5,363 feet, and began the long, slow hike to the Pinkham Notch Camp and New Hampshire Highway 16. I had difficulty keeping my balance on top of Mt. Madison because of the strong wind. Both Sam and I were suffering from sore knees caused by the constant pounding from rock hopping day after day. We met twelve groups of people in eight miles—sixty-eight people in all—most of them heading for Madison Hut. We worried about some of these groups, family groups with small children who, late in the day, were beginning the eight-mile uphill climb to the hut. We lost the trail shortly before reaching Pinkham Notch and came out on the highway. We reached the hut at 5:00 P.M. and weighed my pack on one of the spring scales provided at each hut for that purpose. It weighed forty pounds.

SUNDAY, AUGUST 23. Because of the rain we spent the day in the lobby at Pinkham Notch Camp. Pinkham took on the atmosphere of an airport waiting room on a day when all planes are grounded. It had poured during the night; there was intermittent rain much of the day and low visibility, and it was a Sunday with many weekenders who had to get back home for the Monday–Friday work week. All day wet bedraggled hikers came down out of the mountains, took showers, made long-distance phone calls, waited for rides, and killed time.

MONDAY, AUGUST 24. Up at 5:30, breakfast, and over to Pinkham Notch Camp to obtain the weather report. It was posted at 8:00; it looked favorable, and we began hiking at 8:30. We reached the gondola lift at 11:00 and had our first lunch there. The temperature was 55° F. The climb to the summit of Wildcat Mountain was sticky, the descent into Carter Notch even more so. Trails were wet and slippery from the long rain. Ate a second lunch at Carter Notch Hut. Made the tough climb to Carter Dome, then South Carter, Middle Carter, North Carter—all of these mountains have elevations in the 4,500–4,800-foot range. Then we made a steep and treacherous descent, and daylight was beginning to fade as we reached the Imp Shelter at 7:45. Both Sam and I were beat. We had hiked thirteen miles of some of the roughest up-and-down climbing that I experienced. It was cool and windy at the shelter. We cooked a quick meal over Sam's Primus propane gas stove. I cooked a whole package of Lipton's Green Pea Soup, to which we added a can of sausages. It tasted good!

We congratulated ourselves on *not* having hiked on Sunday. Not only would it have been sloppy and dangerous to have hiked in the rain and fog (it was dangerous enough as it was), but we would have missed so many fine views. The White Mountain trails are characterized by the three R's—Rocks, Roots, and eRosion. At Imp Shelter, the trail to the trash pit and toilet is almost straight up and down on an eroded trail.

TUESDAY, AUGUST 25. Sam cooked a hot breakfast (his propane stove is a jewel) including a ham-and-scrambled-egg mix. We left at 7:30 and made the very steep ascent of Mt. Moriah. Reached the summit at 9:00 (4,047 feet). Our knees were sore as boils; it hurt to walk. Arrived at Rattle River Shelter 11:35. Ate a hearty lunch, finishing up a lot of food I had carried for miles. The temporary end of my hike is just an hour away. My knees need the rest! My shoes are a mess— worn down into the subsole, right heel coming off.

We reached U.S. Route 2 (near Gorham, New Hampshire) at 2 P.M. Caught a ride to Sam's car at Pinkham, showered, shaved, changed clothes, and began driving.

WEDNESDAY, AUGUST 26. Spent the day traveling to my home in Falls Church, Virginia.

THURSDAY, AUGUST 27 TO WEDNESDAY, SEPTEMBER 9. This two-week period was spent at home. It was devoted to preparations for, participation in, and recuperation from my daughter Kathleen's wedding on September 5. On the tenth I met Tex and Jean Griffin in Brooklyn.

FRIDAY, SEPTEMBER 11. After a big breakfast, Tex Griffin and I took off in his VW for Gorham, New Hampshire. I began hiking at three o'clock.

For the last three hundred miles of my hike I wore Bean's Maine Hunting Shoes, nine inches high. I wore heavier shirts and slacks. And my unlined four-ounce windbreaker had been replaced by a twenty-five-ounce Holubar parka.

I reached the Gentian Pond Shelter at 6:30, ate a cold supper, and worked on my notes until darkness.

SATURDAY, SEPTEMBER 12. A clear, beautiful day. Steam hovered over Gentian Pond. I left the shelter at 7:45 and reached Carlo Col Shelter at 12:20. Both at the Gentian Pond Shelter and later atop Mt. Success, I could smell the fumes of the paper factory at Gorham. I took a nasty spill at 11:00 A.M. while climbing a rocky slab. My feet slipped out from under me, and I skidded downward. I had mittens on, but suffered a small cut on my left wrist.

Had fine views while hiking—could see Mt. Washington clearly—

the Carriage Road—the smoke from the Cog Railway—and once the train itself etched clearly on the skyline. Could see and faintly smell fumes of the paper mill at Gorham even from the top of the West Peak of Mt. Goose Eye. I passed from New Hampshire into Maine at noon. Thirteen states and 1,749 miles behind me.

Maine

SUNDAY, SEPTEMBER 13. I spent all day hiking 8.1 miles, but they were among the toughest and most spectacular miles on the entire trail—from Full Goose Shelter through the famous boulder-filled Mahoosuc Notch, then a hard climb to the summit of Mahoosuc Arm, on past Speck Pond, and then the steep climb up Old Speck (4,180 feet). Finally, there was the steep descent into Grafton Notch.

I left Full Goose Shelter at 7:00. Clear day, temperatures 44° F. at 7:00 A.M.—only 60° F. at 1:00 P.M. Reached Mahoosuc Notch at 8:00 and spent an hour and twenty-five minutes carefully threading my way over, under, and between the giant boulders. Climbed and hiked steadily until 1:30 when I reached Speck Pond. Went for a brief dip; the temperature of the water was 54° F.

Had beautiful views all day. I walked to the observation tower on Old Speck and then down into the notch and on to Grafton Notch Lean-to, which I reached at 5:20.

MONDAY, SEPTEMBER 14. Clear, cool, excellent visibility. Temperature 50° F. at noon. Enjoyed spectacular views from Table Rock, the West and East peaks of Baldpate, and along Frye Brook. Hiked in T-shirt most of day despite low temperature. Poorest time I've made in months, but it was a fine day and I had promised myself a few of these leisurely walks. Reached Frye Brook Lean-to at 4:30—made pudding, put prunes to soak, gathered firewood, and then to my diary. Hope I can get all paper work finished tonight and get an early start tomorrow. Went to sleep to sound of brook and light from campfire. Glad I took it easy.

TUESDAY, SEPTEMBER 15. Made eighteen miles today from Frye Brook Lean-to, to Elephant Mountain Lean-to. "Up at 6:10, awakened by alarm watch. Hot breakfast. On trail at 7:10. Intermittent rain. Wore rain parka all day, and rain chaps most of day. Pleasant hiking—not strenuous. Went by three ponds—beautiful.

"From 11:15 to 11:30 a chipping sparrow preceded me on the trail, alighting every few yards and sometimes flying into a tree and letting me pass only to again fly ahead and resume the game. I counted 90 landings in the last 5 minutes. Estimated he made over 200 landings in about 1,200 yards.

"Went through interesting forest area predominantly balsam—some places all covered with moss—fairylike appearance like some of the Disney movie scenes. Maine is pretty, but it is a wilderness.

"Made slower time in P.M. Reached the lean-to at 4:30. Cold—42° F. For my evening meal I cooked my old reliable, creamed tuna over rice. But this time I added an extra flourish; I put in basil leaves, krauterbutter, salt, pepper, the rest of my minced onion, and—when the meal was ready to eat—I garnished it with Lipton Garnish for Beef Stroganoff!"

Watched fire. Crawled into bed at 7:40. It began raining hard and rained all night.

WEDNESDAY, SEPTEMBER 16. Hiked only eleven miles—from Elephant Mountain Lean-to, to Sabbath Day Pond Lean-to. The all-night rain stopped at 6:45 A.M. Overcast most of day. Had tough hiking. Woods were wet and slippery. Foggy, visibility fifty yards. I know I missed some first-rate views. Temperature never got above 50° F. It was somewhat eerie on top of the various Bemis mountains; the cairns and blazes would not be too easy to see in the best of conditions and the fog made them doubly difficult to see. I was glad to get down into the timber.

Wore my rain chaps all day; they worked well. My shoes were wet, and my feet cold. The leather uppers of my Bean boots got saturated, and water oozed down to my feet.

I reached Sabbath Day Pond Lean-to at 2:45. Laid in wood and built a fire. Was pleased that I was able to get a fire going immediately with the woods so wet.

THURSDAY, SEPTEMBER 17. Hiked twelve miles to Piazza Rock Lean-to with four hours off for a trip to Rangeley, Maine. At 9:15 I was eating a second breakfast of hot cakes and coffee in Doc Grant's restaurant. Picked up mail, shopped for groceries, and bought a pair of after-ski boots. At 1 P.M. Postmaster Earl Frasier picked me up and gave me a ride back to the trail. He does this for any through hiker.

Reached Piazza Rock Lean-to at 3:30. Took off my boots and wet socks and donned new wool socks and the fleece-lined after-ski boots. Gad, but they felt good. I explored the Piazza Rock, a big tablelike rock jutting out into space. Built a big fire, washed socks, wrote letters by firelight, crawled into my sleeping bag early, and watched the fire die down.

FRIDAY, SEPTEMBER 18. Took four bad spills in an hour. My Bean shoes have very little traction. Cut my left elbow and reopened cut on left wrist.

Overcast entire day, but visibility on Saddleback Mountain and The Horns was perhaps eight miles; on Saddleback Junior visibility was only fifty yards! Reached Spaulding Mountain Lean-to 5:20. Cooked huge meal—creamed tuna over potatoes and hot, fresh applesauce cooked in brown sugar and cinnamon. I had picked the apples along the way. I hiked sixteen miles and collected only eight pieces of litter. The trail was extremely clean all through Maine.

SATURDAY, SEPTEMBER 19. Up at 5:50 and tried a new breakfast combination: Grape-nuts mixed with the remains of the apples I had cooked the night before. With hot coffee, it made a delicious breakfast. Left shelter at 7:40.

SUNDAY, SEPTEMBER 20. Began hiking at 11:00 on a beautiful autumn day. Before me lay one of the grandest mountain ranges in Maine, the Bigelows. I met ten people on the trail in the first seven miles. Reached the two Horns Pond Lean-tos at 2:45, and the Avery Lean-to at 5:30. I missed the company of the very tame snowshoe rabbits who had visited us when I stayed overnight here in September, 1967. I did have the company of a Canada jay who made countless trips to the fireplace six feet in front of me to eat the shoestring potatoes a previous camper had discarded.

I enjoyed splendid views throughout the day, both looking up toward the impressive Bigelow Range from below and later, looking down on the valley from the top of those same mountains. I had seen blueberries, clintonia, and bunchberry—all with fruit. I had also taken another spill, and for the fourth time completely ripped open the cut on my left wrist.

MONDAY, SEPTEMBER 21. I made a leisurely traverse of the Bigelows, hiking only eleven miles the entire day. It was clear and sunny; the temperature was 70° F. at noon and was still 70° F. at 4 P.M. I saw seven spruce grouse in three groups and marveled that this sluggish bird has not become extinct. On top of Avery Peak I saw a sign reading: MT. KATAHDIN, 184 MILES.

Reached the south end of the Bigelow crest at 12:00. Sunny, mild

Photo by Jeffrey M. Hancock

Mrs. Genevieve L. Hutchinson.

Photo by Elmer L. Ons

Clark Pond, New Hampshire.

breeze. Ate snack in T-shirt. Admired the colors in the trees. Watched and listened to three ravens doing aerial acrobatics below me. Saw moose tracks on trail. Reached Jerome Brook Lean-to at 3:30. Quite warm—even had a few mosquitoes! Worked on my notes first thing. Finished 5:45. Raining slightly; lucky me, got to shelter again before the rain. For supper I opened an unmarked (label removed) can of food I had picked up at Poplar Ridge Lean-to. It turned out to be chicken spread, and that dictated the menu for supper. I made a half-batch of Lipton's Chicken Stroganoff and mixed in the whole can of spread. Completely filled one of my three-cup saucepans— delicious and filling. Very very still except for an occasional car on the road a hundred yards away.

TUESDAY, SEPTEMBER 22. It rained all night. I left the shelter at 6:15 wearing my rain chaps and a T-shirt. Reached West Carry Pond Camps at 7:40 and had a big breakfast with Mr. and Mrs. Elwyn Storey. I was one of the last paying guests, as this well-known Maine sporting camp was due to close permanently on September 30 after seventy-five years of operation. Reached the East Carry Pond Lean-to at 12:30. The lean-to is in a beautiful spot, seven yards from the lake-shore. Left the shelter at 1:00 P.M. and made steady progress. Temperature reached 75° F. at 4:00 P.M. I was bothered by mosquitoes and no-see-ums. Reached the new Pierce Pond Lean-to at 4:10. It is an absolutely delightful place. At 6:45 the pond was perfectly calm; the sun had set; the trees and the mountains were mirrored in the pond.

Washed clothes, shaved, had a swim, and felt wonderful. It was a warm evening. I went to bed at 7:30 on top of my sleeping bag.

WEDNESDAY, SEPTEMBER 23. Up at 5:30, left the shelter 6:30, and hiked the three miles to the Kennebec River in one hour. I judged the river to be about a hundred and fifty yards wide. I stripped down to my underwear, put my boots back on to protect my feet, obtained an eight-foot pole, and began wading across. The water reached my crotch, then my waist, and one-third of the way across the water was chest high. I am a strong swimmer and could have swum across easily enough without a pack, although I would have ended up far down-stream. With a forty-pound pack it was a different story. I returned to shore, dressed, poured the water out of my boots, and backtracked on the Appalachian Trail for three miles. At that point, I left the trail and began walking south on a dirt road toward Bingham, Maine. I had hiked for six miles when I was given a ride by a French-Canadian logger. He could speak little English but he looked at my pack and said two words that sounded like "Oppolockian Trail?" I nodded.

He gave me a ride all the way to Bingham, which was perhaps ten or twelve miles farther south. At 11:40 I walked into the Thompson Restaurant in Bingham, had a good lunch, and was given a ride back north to Caratunk by Emmons Casey and a companion whom I had met at the restaurant. At 1:15 I walked down to the east bank of the Kennebec where the Appalachian Trail resumes its course on dry land.

I stopped for half an hour at the combination grocery store and post office in Caratunk. Picked up mail and had a pint of ice cream. Pushed on toward Pleasant Pond Mountain Lean-to, walking on hard-surfaced road almost all the way.

It turned out to be a very pleasant day in spite of the initial disappointment of not getting across the Kennebec quickly. I had hiked only nine miles on the Appalachian Trail but had hiked another eight miles on dirt roads.

THURSDAY, SEPTEMBER 24. Reached Joes Hole Brook Lean-to at 10:35. Later, along Moxie Pond, I saw a small animal swimming. I picked a spot where I thought the animal would emerge from the water and waited. I was surprised to see that it was a mink. He had swum a good two hundred yards across the south end of the pond; it seemed like a long swim for such a small animal.

Reached Breakneck Ridge Lean-to at 5:45. Had to work fast to make camp, cook my meal, and shave before darkness set in. All paper work deferred until next day. I had hiked twenty miles on another one of those beautiful fall days.

FRIDAY, SEPTEMBER 25. Left shelter at 8:05. Intermittent rain all day. Passed through the little community of Blanchard and reached Monson, Maine, at noon.

I picked up a good deal of mail in Monson, including two packages of food that I had mailed to myself from Gorham. I laundered all my clothes in the laundromat and bought ten dollars worth of groceries. I used the restaurant as an office for reading my mail and writing letters. I ate my evening meal there and then received a ride to the home of Esmond Richardson, who lives a couple of miles outside of town. I guess it would be proper to state that Richardson lives on the fringes of the wilderness. I base this on the fact that in his garden a week before he had shot a 100-pound bear, and also on the fact that he had recently seen a moose in his yard. To me, that spells wilderness! Repacked my groceries in Richardson's kitchen, all the while having a pleasant conversation with him.

SATURDAY, SEPTEMBER 26. After a delicious bacon-and-egg breakfast cooked over a wood range stove I was off on the last leg of my journey. Monson was the last resupply point I would have. It was 118 miles from Monson to Mt. Katahdin. I was carrying the heaviest supply of food of the entire trip, and I judged my pack weighed between fifty-two and fifty-four pounds. From Monson to Baxter State Park the Appalachian Trail goes through an almost roadless wilderness. I would be traveling through some beautiful lake country, and the heaviest concentration of moose in the state.

SUNDAY, SEPTEMBER 27. Up at six. Raining. I donned my rain chaps and rain parka and wore them all day. Slippery walking. Woods almost in full color. Took the 0.3-mile side trip to Little Wilson Falls. My company for the night at Long Pond Stream Lean-to was twenty-two-year-old Sandy Thomson of West Hartford, Connecticut. He had been on the trail for eleven days and was almost out of food. Sandy writes poetry, and I was to see samples of it in the shelters farther north.

MONDAY, SEPTEMBER 28. Rose at six. The temperature of 38° F. was the coldest since April. I made a hot breakfast and would continue to have hot breakfasts the rest of the trip. The day was clear, but the woods were saturated after three days of rain. I left the shelter at 7:35 and the first order of business was to ford the Long Pond Stream, which was a torrent after the rain. At the far side of the stream I took off my shoes and socks and removed some of the water. Auspicious start!

It was treacherous hiking. I wore all my raingear. Ate lunch at Cloud Pond Lean-to. Had made only four miles. Pushed on slowly, using walking stick to keep from slipping. One of the hardest days I've had, footway rough and up and down all the way. Beautiful views from various summits. Autumn color at, or almost at, peak. Particularly good views of Boarstone Mountain and Bodfish Intervale as I climbed. Also many views of Long Pond.

Reached Chairback Gap Lean-to at 4:50. Used stove to cook supper and then cleaned up. In bed by seven—temperature in low forties. Night clear—no moon.

TUESDAY, SEPTEMBER 29. It was 9 A.M. before I left the lean-to for

I had spent a full hour on my notes and additional time sewing up the webbing on my packframe. Clear weather and trail reasonably dry. A pleasure to hike without wearing raingear. Reached the Chairback Mountain Camps at 10:30. They were closed, but the big mess hall had been left unlocked. Ate lunch there. Beautiful setting for a private camp. Reached the Pleasant River, took off shoes and socks and waded across the ice-cold stream. A few minutes later I left the trail to visit The Hermitage area and to admire the virgin white pines towering 80 to 100 feet. This area now belongs to The Nature Conservancy. I pushed on steadily, often walking on roads. It rained slightly several times. Reached the White Brook Lean-to at 2:45. Found a bounteous supply of wood nearby so I decided to cook Appalachian Trail Mix (two parts whole rice, one part barley, one part lentils). I cooked it a full hour, adding one-half can of Spam. I was very pleased with the result. Before going to bed I had a final snack of popcorn from a supply I had found at Cloud Pond Lean-to.

It began raining steadily at six, and it was already so dark I could barely see. The fire was burning merrily; this helped to dispel the gloom.

WEDNESDAY, SEPTEMBER 30. "A long day. It began at 1:05 A.M. when I looked at my watch. Moments later, I heard an animal in front of the shelter. It sounded like a moose. Flashed my light, but could see only eyes floating about seven feet high in the air! Mr. Moose then came to within four feet of the shelter. There my light brought him clearly into view. Gad, but he was big! He watched me four or five seconds then meandered down toward the brook, twigs and branches snapping underfoot. Now I'd seen my moose, but certainly not in the manner I had expected. It began raining. Arose at 5:30, lit a candle, got fire going immediately with birch bark. Heated up Appalachian Trail Mix left over from last night. With a dish of cereal this made a hearty breakfast. Left shelter 6:55.

"Didn't put on rain chaps—a mistake. It poured, and I went through a lot of overgrown trail. Soaked from hips down, including feet. Reached White Cap Mountain Lean-to at 10:45. Had hot chocolate and hot coffee along with other stuff. Gasoline stove surely appreciated on cold wet raw days. Reached top of White Cap Mountain (3,707 feet), but didn't hike to tower because of rain and overcast. Slogged away until I reached East Branch Tote Road Lean-to at 6:30 P.M. Raining, dark. Put on dry clothes. How these warm pajamas and after-ski shoes are appreciated! Would be hell to sit around for hours in cold wet rubber boots. Hiked a miserable 14.5

miles today. Sixty-four more miles to Mt. Katahdin. Surely hope weather clears."

THURSDAY, OCTOBER 1. Up at 6:30—another dark, cloudy day with early morning rain. After breakfast I had to face up to the dismal task of taking off my warm dry clothes and after-ski boots and putting on trousers, two pairs of socks, and rubber boots that were wet and cold from yesterday.

Made good time and at 9:15 reached the Kokadjo-B Pond Road, where I left the Appalachian Trail and hiked three miles to the Yoke Ponds Camps operated by Keith Skillin and his wife Cody. Had lunch and got into a long discussion with Skillin on the use of the Appalachian Trail shelters by groups of undesirable people. Skillin feels very strongly that some way must be found to police the shelters on the trail. Bob Wing, a logger I had met at Pleasant Pond, had been just as emphatic on the same subject.

After lunch Game Warden Charles Howe of Greenville and a companion arrived. Their mission: to find and destroy a sick moose cow that had been seen staggering around for several days in a nearby area. I asked for permission to accompany them, and we paddled by canoe to the spot where the moose had last been seen. We found her tracks everywhere, found where she had lain down in the high grass for long periods of time; but we were unable to find her. Back to the camp kitchen for coffee and some more of Cody Skillin's homemade bread; then I hastily got my gear together and hiked the six miles to Cooper Brook Falls Lean-to. For supper I used the last of my Lipton's Potato Soup, mixed in tuna, flour, rice, and milk, seasoned it well, and produced an excellent stew. Wrote my notes by candlelight.

FRIDAY, OCTOBER 2. Hiked an enjoyable eleven miles today.

Left shelter at eight—looked longingly at the nice swimming hole at Cooper Brook Falls, but 38° F. is too cold! Reached remains of the old Antlers Camps on Lower Joe Mary Lake and ate lunch on the edge of the lake. Wonderful spot for a camp. Temperature 50° F. at noon, and sunny. Heard loons on lake. Reached Potaywadjo Spring Lean-to at 2:45. Found all the wood I needed from a single small dead tree. Made a huge batch of Appalachian Trail Mix. Beautiful gushing spring at shelter, water temperature 42° F.

SATURDAY, OCTOBER 3. Up at six. Leisurely breakfast. On trail at eight. Dark in woods. Reached Mahar Campground at 9:30. Saw a deer—first one in Maine. Steady drizzle but rain parka too warm. Kept on chaps and took off parka. Ate hearty lunch topped off with hot popcorn. Two men drove up in a jeep—first people I had seen on the trail in six days.

Saw my second deer, then one of those great big owls which are frequently heard but seldom seen. Began raining hard, then harder. Reached Wadleigh Pond Lean-to at three. Had hiked a scant twelve miles. Found two medium-size potatoes, boiled them, and cooked three freeze-dried hamburgers given to me some three hundred miles back on the trail. Cleaned all my gear, and then enjoyed the luxury of warm pajamas, dry socks, and fleece-lined after-ski boots. Had seven days of rain in the last nine and have worn raingear for nine straight days! During the night it rained in torrents; shelter area a veritable lake with a river running directly underneath the sleeping platform. I was thankful for that good aluminum roof. Slept rather well despite the cloudburst.

SUNDAY, OCTOBER 4. Up at 6:15. It had stopped raining about 1:30 A.M. Sun shining, hard to believe! Left shelter at 8:15. Streams of water everywhere. Took off boots and socks and forded Pollywog Stream. Water high—well above knees. Reached Nahmakanta Lake Camps at 9:45. The custodians, John and Audrey Richards, cooked me a second breakfast and told me that yesterday's storm had raised the lake level three feet and almost washed the boats and canoes away. Left there 10:30 and reached the outlet dam of Rainbow Lake at 1:00. Got my first glimpse of Katahdin. A few white clouds drifted around its summit. Magnificent sight. Reached Rainbow Lake Lean-to at 1:45—extremely beautiful campsite with a big spring down by the lake shore. Built fire, heated water. Aired all my clothing and sleeping gear. Watched a family of six ducks on the lake. Went to bed at the very late hour of 7:15 with a good fire blazing merrily in the stone fireplace directly in front of the shelter.

MONDAY, OCTOBER 5. Up at 6:15. Reached Hurd Brook Lean-to after some beautiful views of Katahdin from the top of Rainbow Ledges. I had a quick lunch and laid in a supply of firewood. There was a twenty-bushel open trash dump at the rear of shelter, similar to trash dumps I had seen throughout my hike. I examined the dump carefully to ascertain if it consisted of hiker trash or trash left by others, i.e., picnickers, hunting parties, fishermen. I concluded that no more than five percent of the trash was hiker trash. Hikers do not carry in their packs such articles as 32-ounce cans of fruit juice, gallon cans of Coleman Fuel, 16-ounce cans of beer, and quart glass jars of Pream, just to name a few of the articles I saw in the trash dump. I am convinced that we are winning the battle of litter on the trail. The matter of litter at the trailside shelters is a much more serious problem.

TUESDAY, OCTOBER 6. Up at six, temperature 37° F. Got wood fire going, cooked hot oatmeal (the last I had), cooked the last of my rice, used the last of my brown sugar, and finished the can of cinnamon that I had carried all the way from Georgia. My food is about gone.

Began the nine-mile hike along the east bank of Nesowadnehunk Stream. It would be hard to imagine a more perfect early autumn day. It had rained for days: the stream was high—scores and scores of cascades and small waterfalls, and two big ones. The fall color was at its absolute maximum. The air was clean. The woods had that fresh smell which comes after long rains. It was a hiker's paradise.

WEDNESDAY, OCTOBER 7. Up at 5:20 with Tex Griffin to begin the 5.2 miles to Baxter Peak, the northern terminal of the Appalachian Trail. These 5.2 miles involve a climb of 4,156 feet over rough footway. It was a bright sunny day. Nature seemed to be rewarding me after all those rainy days of the previous two weeks.

We reached the summit at 12:15. The hike was finished. It had been exciting to climb those 5.2 miles to the summit. It was drudgery going down. The trip I had planned for a whole year was finished, and the goal that I had hiked over 2,000 miles to reach was now behind me. I had not anticipated any emotional letdown, but it was there.

The long trip was now officially over—and what a trip it had been! I would be months and years getting all the pieces into place, writing up observations and recommendations for consideration by the Appalachian Trail Conference Board of Managers, conducting correspondence with a host of new friends, and writing articles on various aspects of my hike. The recollection of places I had been, of experiences I'd had, and of the people I'd met would influence the rest of my life.

There and Back

By Bradley W. Greuling

Started at SPRINGER MOUNTAIN on June 19, 1970
Finished at DELAWARE WATER GAP on October 12, 1970

Hiking started for me with a very cold and windy ascent of Mt. Jefferson from Dolly Copp Campgrounds in New Hampshire one autumn day with mom and brothers Bill and Bruce. In the next few years we climbed and reclimbed Mt. Washington, Mt. Jefferson, the Carter Range, and Indian Head. I saw campgrounds change from pit toilets to "flushies" and then become commercial areas. In 1963 the family camped in Baxter State Park in Maine, near Mt. Katahdin. Perhaps this is when I first thought of making an Appalachian Trail hike. In the next few years, during vacations, we climbed Katahdin and the peaks in the Presidential Range. When I was 16 my brother Bruce and I hiked from Mt. Bigelow, Maine, to Dolly Copp, New Hampshire, in 13 days. Little did I know then that two years later I would be walking the entire 2,000 miles of the Appalachian Trail!

In 1970 all the stars were in the right place, and I had the money ($200), the time, the ambition (and the lack of experience) needed for the big trek. How did it begin? The conversation went something like this:

"What are we going to do this year about vacation?"

"Why not go hiking?"

"Where?"

"Well, we've been north. Perhaps we should go south."

"This would be a good time for you and your brother to do the whole trail."

So it was decided. The next few months were full of activity. How do you learn all there is to know about camping? We went through many books. A friend gave me Colin Fletcher's *The Complete Walker*. Fletcher's books contain a wealth of information—for the wealthy. I avidly read and enjoyed his books, and got many ideas of what was needed for an extended trip, but it seemed that everything he used was the best and the lightest. I saw that it would be easy to buy hundreds of dollars worth of stuff that would be both useless and cumbersome. I decided that three things should be of the best quality: pack, boots, and sleeping bag. Everything else could be found at home or in local grocery stores, I thought. We sent for all the catalogs, and it was fun to read the manufacturer's blurbs but my advice is: consult your pocketbook!

After much soul-searching and weighing, my equipment consisted of: (a) plane ticket to Atlanta, Georgia; (b) Minolta camera, no flash, two rolls Kodak 35-mm color film for slides; (c) nylon tarp from Eastern Mountain Sports; (d) plastic groundsheet made from a drop cloth used by painters; (e) nylon line and rawhide thongs for rigging tarp; (f) Ridgeline pack and frame with tie-down pockets on sides and front; (g) Dacron 2½-pound sleeping bag for the South, and an army surplus mummy bag for the North. (I would never take anything but the down mummy bag again); (h) red stuff sack for sleeping bag, the red for visibility; (i) army-type bayonet (*no good!*); (j) metal quart canteen (*no good!* I discarded it for a plastic disk canteen which weighed less and did not flavor the water); (k) quart saucepan; (l) Boy Scout mess kit and metal spoon; (m) red plastic poncho, which proved very durable.

Clothing consisted of one pair long pants, one pair leather shorts, three T-shirts, three pairs cotton knit underwear, and three pairs of wool and Orlon blend socks (they wear better than all-wool), a wool army shirt donated by my brother Bill, and a pair of bathing trunks which became my favorite gear. (I sent my leather shorts home.)

My boots were Ann & Hope specials, double-stitched and lined. They were made in England and were a really good buy. Other equipment included a Mallory flashlight and 2 extra batteries; first-aid kit containing adhesive tape, Band-Aids, moleskin, snakebite kit, water purification tablets, vitamin pills, Off for bugs; spool of nylon thread and 2 needles; large and small safety pins; fishing kit; shaving gear; soap and washcloth; Basta toothbrush with toothpaste self-contained; 2 pipes and tobacco; metal mirror; and magnesium safe matches.

Freeze-dried foods came from the only place near enough for us to visit often, Eastern Mountain Sports in Boston. I think we bought their complete stock of trail cookies. Trail cookies should be made the emblem of hikers, rampant on a smoked sausage and cheese cross! In hot weather it was necessary to spend the extra money and buy dehydrated meats. Wilson bacon bars and meat bars were especially good. Snacks were an important part of every day. Space sticks were handy but expensive. I had a craving for chocolate and Tropical chocolate was good. Hard candy was good, but it got sticky if there was much moisture in the air and it attracted animals, especially mice. Smoked sausage and beef jerky of the Slim Jim type are good if you like the flavor. Vegetables were an important item in my diet. Dehydrated corn and beans were good and instant potatoes were light, filling, and cheap. On the last half of the trail I made bread from Bisquick because I really missed bread of some kind.

A good pack of the Kelty type is necessary for a through hiker because this bit of metal and cloth will be his house for months. It will be dragged, bumped, scraped, dropped, and generally abused until you wonder how it can possibly hold together. Many times during my trip I wished I had traded my pack for my brother's Kelty. A pack should be kept well-organized, and the Kelty divided bag helps do this.

Your bed is the next most important item. If your sleeping bag has a zipper you can open it up if it gets too warm. Of course you can also sleep on top of your bag if the bugs permit it.

In a local department store, for about $15 I purchased a pair of serviceable boots which I thought compared favorably with $50 name-brand hiking boots. I prefer boots with tops that go above the ankle. They are a little heavy, but will spare your ankles when you are on rocky terrain. I still have the boots I wore on my hike, and they have had to be resoled only once. I think boots should have leather linings, and the soles should not be too stiff. When my boots were repaired the shoeshop put on smooth soles. Several times when it rained I thought I was going to slide off cliffs because of those smooth soles. It was almost impossible to walk on wet rocks with them, and it made walking on roots and branches a hazard.

I started with an army bayonet. Why anything so big? Simply because it made me feel better. I'm a bit of a coward, and the bayonet gave me a feeling of security. It also served as an emergency can opener, fork, and spoon—and if it ever had been necessary, I could have chopped down some fair-sized trees with it. After all this rationalization, I must admit that the bayonet was a big mistake and too heavy, and I threw it away after two weeks. My Swiss army knife was all I ever needed.

The most important part of any hiker's equipment is knowing how to use what he takes along. I decided not to worry about my equipment; I figured that if anything got lost or broken I could fix it or do without, or if necessary, find my way to civilization. None of my equipment was new; everything had been used before except the Mallory flashlight, which proved unreliable due to the dampness in the South. I finally sent it home, and in my next package mom sent a small standard flashlight.

More by luck than anything else we all arrived in Atlanta within an hour of each other. Dr. Bortle, his son Donald, Bruce, mother, and I, all went on the same plane from Warwick, Rhode Island. Cindy Moses arrived next from Pennington, New Jersey, and finally Sharon Hainsworth arrived from Rochester, New York. We took a bus to the general vicinity of Amicalola Falls State Park, and then all seven of us, with several hundred pounds of equipment, rode in a panel truck to the jumping-off point. What a group we were! Bruce with his knickers; Dr. Bortle with his huge pack; Donny, who only came to our waists; Sharon who had never hiked before; Cindy, so petite, complete, and collected; mom, who was the only one in our family who knew what was really going on; and me, in my leather shorts! We took pictures of Amicalola Falls, and began what for me was the experience of a lifetime. After checking in with the ranger, our driver took us to where the trail started toward the top of Springer Mountain. Camp was set up and we had supper. Mother brought out a bottle of wine and we all had a "we made it" drink and went to bed in happy anticipation of the next day.

Packs were put on with groans the next morning, and away we went. We made it to the top of Springer Mountain that afternoon. None of us had realized what it would be like to hike 19 miles with a pack. We were so tired we didn't even wake up for the things that go bump in the night. However, as the days progressed we made it to Woody Gap, where Dr. Bortle and Donny left for Florida. I had assumed that my brother was going to hike the whole trail with me, but at the final moment he told me that he had to work all summer, and he left with the others. I was miserable. Here I was in the middle of nowhere, with no one to rely on but myself. What was I going to do?

I found that the best remedy for homesickness was to walk faster. When I walked fast enough I was so busy watching for trail blazes that I didn't have time to get very lonesome. The guidebooks helped, too, for when I was lonesome I could always count the miles I had to walk to get home. I also found that it gave me great peace of mind to know that a telephone call home was only 28.62 miles away. The maps and the guidebooks weren't always available or accurate, however, and the directions were not always correct. I learned to *follow the blazes*.

One result of being alone was that I could "go back to nature," meaning that I didn't have to shave, wash my clothes, or use deodorant, or do any of the civilized things. So I didn't—for a while, anyway. However, after about two weeks I discovered that cleanliness and organization were an important part of being able to walk 20 miles a day.

I arrived at Fontana Village on July 7 and made the first of over $60 worth of collect telephone calls home. Poor mom! My food package hadn't arrived at the post office. I had about $2 so I went to a grocery store. Another customer in the store asked me if the pack outside was mine and then asked the usual questions. Where was I going? Where had I come from? How long had I been hiking? We talked for a while and he pressed $2 into my hand. "That's just because I wish I were you," he said. With this extra money I was able to have steak and fresh milk for supper.

There was a large picnic area on the south side of the Fontana Dam, and I found this to be a good place to stay. The latrines had hot and cold running water, and the maintenance men were helpful and pleasant. I left my pack there for long periods of time and didn't worry about it because the men told me they would look after it. Eventually my food package came. As it was planned for two people, there was plenty of food, but all of the smoked meat had spoiled and I had to throw it away.

A standard two-weeks' supply of food in my package from home would contain 2 lb. mixed dried fruit; 2 smoked sausage sticks (about 6 lb.); 2 doz. Slim Jims; 2 doz. jerky strips; 2 doz. space sticks; 1 lb. hard candy; some semisweet chocolate bars; 3 large pkg. Wyler's lemonade mix (I never had enough!); 14 orange gelatin drinks; 16–18 tea bags; 15 instant oatmeal packages (my breakfast mainstay, with wheat germ); 7 or 8 dried ham and egg omelets; 7 or 8 pkg. dried scrambled eggs; 1 pt. powdered milk; instant cocoa; 4 smoked cheese sticks (about 2 lb.); 1 pt. sugar; 7 Wilson bacon bars; 7 Wilson meat bars; 10 pkg. assorted soups; 10 dehydrated dinners—the rice and macaroni were great with meat bars, ham and beans (large size), shrimp creole (my favorite meal), beef Stroganoff (very good!), pilaf, and dried peas; chicken and beef cubes for soup and flavoring; dehydrated potatoes; instant rice; freeze-dried vegetables (Richmoor); freeze-dried fruit (pineapple tidbits and spiced apple slices); 4 pkg. trail cookies; 1 pkg. Bisquick.

The dried fruit, especially the freeze-dried, was better than candy. Sloppy Joe sauce packages were invaluable for adding variety and flavor. The only special supplies I got were the freeze-dried meat, cookies, vegetables, and the large-sized complete dinners. Everything

else came from grocery stores. Each day's supply was repackaged in
Baggies. Although I thought the food was fairly complete nutritionally, there was never enough bulk. I was usually hungry and on the
lookout for anything edible. That was part of the fun—trying not to
miss a wild berry bush or an apple tree. I was always looking for
something to nibble on while walking. The candy, space sticks, and
meat bars were tasty, but in areas where there wasn't much water
they created a thirst problem. I made a big mistake on one shipment:
I had my mother send standard navy C rations, with just a few supplements. Those two weeks were desperate! I can't imagine how these
rations could keep a flea alive, if that flea had to go anywhere. Incidentally, in deciding on whether to mail food, buy it on the way,
or combine these methods, I decided on mail shipments because I
felt that if I carried money to buy food I would worry about losing
it more than I wanted to. Also, I thought better meals could be
planned by buying where a larger variety of food was available.

After leaving Fontana I was in the Smokies and there seemed to
be a different flavor to the trip. This is where I began to find berries,
apples, and assorted fruits to eat. I also began to experiment with
other food I found along the way. A fairly common animal, and easy
to catch, was the turtle. However, having tried it, I can tell you that
it was difficult to open the shell and the meat was rather tough and
stringy. However, with greens, it made a good soup.

On one of the balds in the Smokies I met some campers on horses.
They told me I could eat the little red berries of a certain tree and
they tasted somewhat like apples. Speaking of apples, I found them
to be good either ripe or green if sliced and boiled with sugar. There
were many apple trees along the way, and apples became a major
source of food for me. Blackberries were abundant, too. I sampled
one of the rattlesnakes I killed, and it did taste a bit like chicken,
as my mother had told me long ago. While I was still with the horsemen, we saw a day-old fawn lying by the side of the trail. Deer were
abundant in both the Smokies and in the Shenandoah–Blue Ridge
area. I was coming around a shelter on my second day in the Smokies
when I met my first full-grown bear. Surprise! We both jumped high
in the air and took off in opposite directions.

My food package hadn't arrived when I reached Damascus, Virginia. The postmaster was very helpful and told me about a camping area four miles down the road. I called mom and explained that
I had no food, and then went to the campground. It was raining so
I put up the tarp and then went scouting for something to eat. There

were no berry bushes, so I settled for a package of soup. Next morning, as I was thinking about the sad state of my affairs, a dog walked up and I started playing with it. Soon the dog's owners, Bob and Donna Shirley, arrived and invited me to their trailer for coffee. I thought it was the best I had ever tasted. The package had not arrived when I went back to the post office, so I called home again. Mom told me not to worry, that the package probably would come the next day, and that she would telegraph emergency money. (In the three days I waited for the package, I made four phone calls home.)

The Shirleys went home that afternoon. It was raining so I stayed under the tarp. About six o'clock I heard a car stop but I didn't bother to look outside. Suddenly two men stuck their faces in the opening near my feet and asked if they could come in. They said their car window wouldn't close. As soon as they crawled in I knew they had been drinking. They asked the usual questions: Where had I been? Where was I going? Then they asked if an outfit like mine cost a lot of money. I told them it didn't, and took out my knife as if to make some repairs, but really to give myself some security. Their eyes got big and they made some excuses and backed out, got into their car, and drove away. I went to the latrine, and while I was there I heard what sounded like the same car again. Sure enough, the two men were coming out of my tent. I shouted for the men to put my stuff back, and banged on a trailer that was parked nearby. One of the men threw my Minolta camera inside the tent. Then the people in the trailer came out and the robbers fled. I took inventory. I had lost my knife, and all of my paper money. I had only the change that had been in my pocket.

Shook up, I went to town, where I found that my food package had arrived. What a joy it was to open it! Extra socks, clean white shirts, and other surprises were included—letters, cartoons, and thoughts of home, for example. This was the only time during the trip that my supply line failed me. I had started with infinite faith in the U.S. postal system, and for the most part my faith was justified. However, I did learn one thing from this experience: a hiker having food mailed from home should have enough for a few extra days in case the package is delayed.

Back at the camping area I spent much of the night with my eyes open, and was almost running when I left at daybreak. It's too bad that some of the camping places are so accessible to town toughs. I was upset by the recent events, but as usual, a long day's hike lifted my spirits and I felt good again. I looked forward to reaching Delaware Water Gap, New Jersey, and a visit from mom and the Moses family who lived in nearby Pennington. All I had to do to get there was go through Virginia, Pennsylvania, and Maryland. It was a long way to Roanoke, but finally I was there, only to be stopped four times by the police and asked to empty my pack each time. I got a haircut, fast!

The Shenandoahs were absolutely beautiful. One night, after dark, I was greeted by a cheery hello as I came up to a shelter and it was in this way that I met Chaplain A. C. Anderson and his son Hugh of Bethesda, Maryland. The next day was one of the very few days that I didn't hike. I spent most of the morning talking with Chaplain Anderson. When they left he said he and Hugh would meet me at the Patterson Shelter near Harpers Ferry. We figured it to be a five days' walk, but it took me only four days, probably because I was looking forward to being with someone who was interesting. Sure enough, on the fifth day they arrived, and Hugh hiked with me the next day. They were two of the nicest people I met on my trip.

I had not been able to obtain maps for the next section, but at a shelter I met a Commander Brown and he was kind enough to lend me his U.S. Geological Survey quadrangles. I made bread that night, and it disappeared in about 10 seconds. To make bread I mixed Bisquick in a pan, added some raisins, put the cover on, cooked it lightly on one side, then turned the whole thing over. I had found bread easy to make, and filling. After burning my first 10 tries, I was able to make delicious golden loaves. Sometimes I added a little sugar and some sliced apples.

Pennsylvania was something. The trail crossed a wide valley on roads, then went to the top of a long ridge and stayed on the ridge, more or less, all the way to Delaware Water Gap, where I left the trail to visit friends in Pennington. Mother met me there, and offered to drive me to Maine so I could walk the rest of the trail from north to south—otherwise I would be getting to Maine about snow time.

Things had changed at Katahdin. There was a barrier across the road and a guard who wouldn't let me into the park until morning. I tried to explain that I was a through hiker but it was no use, so I slept in a nearby field that night and hitched a ride to Katahdin Stream Campground the next morning. I left my pack at the ranger's cabin and practically ran up and down the mountain. From the campground it was 13 miles south to the first shelter at Hurd Brook, and I arrived there at about 7:00 p.m. Including the climb of Katahdin, I had hiked 23 miles. The next day, on Rainbow Ledges, I met a mother bear and her two cubs. They were browsing and I got close enough to take some pictures before they ran.

It felt good to be in New England, where I knew the trails. I spent three days in one shelter because of sickness—apparently caused by bad water. I went to town to see a doctor, and he told me there might have been a dead animal upstream. This was the only time I was sick during the three and a half months of hiking. New Hampshire was easy and familiar hiking for me. I ran most of the time, as I didn't have to worry about losing my way. I met a girl who let me use her room in Bennington, Vermont, to take a bath. I gave her a guidebook in exchange, as she and her boyfriend were going to hike the Long Trail. In Springfield, Massachusetts, I stopped at my grandparents' home for supplies and my guitar, and I must have been quite a sight thereafter, with my guitar and a pack on my back!

I was at a shelter near Route 4 in Connecticut when a man and his young daughter arrived. She had lost some clothing from her pack about two days before. I told her I would try to find it, and we agreed to meet near a little restaurant on Route 7. They were traveling by car so I left my pack with them and started out at a trot. I had 30 miles to go. I found the clothing without any trouble as someone had hung it in a tree. I arrived at the meeting place that evening at about 5:00 P.M. and the man and his daughter arrived soon afterward. They couldn't understand how it was possible for me to cover so many miles in such a short time, but after so much hiking I could have run 50 miles without too much trouble.

I was on the home stretch now, with only a few days of hiking left. I thought mother would like to finish the hike with me, and we made it to Delaware Water Gap in one and a half days of clear weather. I met many wonderful people on the trail, and there were many pleasant interludes. I want to thank everyone who helped make the trip possible. What are some of the things I remember now that the trip is over? I remember awakening at daybreak on a mountaintop and watching the world transform itself into miles of rolling forest-covered hills. I remember having my faith in humanity renewed. I remember asking myself "why?" about things I couldn't understand, and I remember not being able to answer in words, but knowing the answers, just the same.

A Mountain Every Morning: Margaret and Bump Smith's Hike

By Margaret Smith and Wilma Servisky

Started at MT. KATAHDIN on June 13, 1970
Finished at SPRINGER MOUNTAIN on November 9, 1970

You're out of your minds!
You tried it once and couldn't do it.
Bump with a serious back problem—Margaret, high blood pressure and one kidney. *Insanity!*
You'll be back in a week.
Over 40 and quitting your job? You'll never get another one.
You'll never make it!
On June 13, 1970, as my husband and I stood on the summit of Mt. Katahdin, some of the gloom-and-doom prophecies that met our decision to walk the Appalachian Trail came back to me. Our climb to Baxter Peak, the official starting point, seemed a quarter of an inch compared to our 2,000-mile goal. However, the prophecy most vivid in my mind was my husband's cockeyed grin and flat statement, "Hell with 'em. We can do it." He stood now, looking first at me and then at the box that should have contained a registry sheet but was empty. Crazy? Maybe, but happy because we were doing it, at last. After all the planning and preparation, after the unsuccessful attempt two years before that had ended only a hundred miles down the trail in Monson, after the waiting and saving and dreaming—this time we were going all the way.

Our 19-year-old son, Steve, and his girl friend, Cathie, had come up over the Chimney Trail and across the Knife-Edge to meet us on Baxter Peak. The four of us went down the mountain together and made camp in a lean-to at Katahdin Stream Campground. It was a beautiful place with the stream clear and talkative and the air tingly cold on the thirteenth of June.

We had hiked perhaps 10 miles, considerably less than the daily mileage necessary to reach Georgia before winter. However, tomorrow would be different. Today was a holiday, an excitement to be shared with Cathie and Steve, for after the next morning we didn't expect to see them for at least four months. Tomorrow and the days to come would belong to Bump and me and the trail. Warmed by the fire, filled with beef stew and biscuits and coffee, it was easy to discount our first ill-fated try at walking the Appalachian Trail. Steve, who had been hiking with us on that first attempt, jokingly began to talk about my arthritic knee. "This time I'm not praying for rain to drown the mosquitoes," I told him. "If I keep dry, I'll be all right."

"All the same, I hope you have lots of fly dope in those packs." That would be the extent to which Steve would voice his concern. He was eager for us to make the journey, having been directly responsible for our "walking" life-style which at this point encompassed three years of hiking on Jacob Buck Mountain near our home, exploring the woods for many miles around us, and walking often to our jobs in the neighboring town. His concern for us would not be voluble, but it was there.

"Those packs have everything, boy," Bump told him. "From fly dope to high blood-pressure pills to feather beds. And speaking of beds—" He yawned loudly.

I couldn't sleep. Long after the others had succumbed to the combination of clean crisp air and full stomachs and warm sleeping bags, I listened to the small animal noises that came softly out of the night. The embers of the fire spit and crackled. By the flickering light I made a final entry in my log: *We've begun. This time we're going all the way.*

Morning in Baxter State Park was incredibly beautiful. The sharp sense of beginning, plus Cathie and Steve's leave-taking and the glory of the Sunday morning made an ache in my heart. We sat at the foot of Katahdin, eating and talking, our voices hushed. The feeling was almost one of reverence. I knew that for me there never would be a church or a sacrament that could evoke what I felt here, in open air near the stream and the surrounding woods, in the presence of this mountain. I could only guess at the others' feelings. We weren't an articulate family when it came to our emotions. Finally the time for good-byes approached. The weight of all the things we would leave unsaid was heavy. We cleared the planked table in busy silence and stowed the utensils in our packs.

"Cathie, you keep Steve out of trouble while we're gone," Bump said. "You'll be at the university, too, so keep his nose to the grindstone!"

They raised hands in half-salute, and were gone, and we put on our packs. Across the Nesowadnehunk Road, a few yards into the woods, I reached for the camera slung over my shoulder. A great bull moose, his antlers bigger than any we had ever seen, stood just a few feet off the trail. I got one shot and was making adjustments for a second when Bump prodded my elbow. "Better move before he gets wind of us." I hung back, watching. For all his seeming ungainliness, the moose was handsome. He had stopped feeding when we approached and now began slowly moving his head from side to side.

"Look," I whispered. "Isn't he something!"

Bump turned, scowling. "You'll think so if he starts after you with his head down."

"Okay, okay. I'm coming."

Along Little Niagara Falls in Nesowadnehunk Stream the nip of early morning warmed into noonday heat. Little Niagara gradually matured to become Big Niagara and we felt the purity and peace of the sun-splotched water and trees. We hiked at a steady pace for nearly 14 miles. The air grew hotter, and thicker with blackflies and mosquitoes. The fly dope helped, but not enough. When we hit Abol Bridge Campsite we were ready for a break. Off came our new boots and socks. We sat on the riverbank with our tired feet in the water, watching the pulpwood float down the Penobscot toward the Great Northern Paper Mill. Lunch was what it would often be: peanut butter and jam carried in plastic tubes, bread when we were close enough to civilization to buy it, biscuits made in a frying pan when we weren't, and water.

Out of Abol the trail took us a quarter of a mile along the highway, then back into woods where we had hiked on other occasions. Moving through them produced the same ease I felt among good friends. Having learned to pace ourselves on other hikes, we walked steadily and spoke little. Six miles farther along we came to Hurd Brook Lean-to, our home for the night. As soon as we stopped hiking we suffered from relentless mosquito raids. Burrowing into my sleeping bag, I managed to keep out the sound of their endless buzzing, but I still heard Bump's grumbling and swatting. On the heels of one particularly vehement growl and whack Bump said, "Margaret, here's company."

I saw two boys, probably 15 years old, standing uneasily by the lean-to's open face. "Hi. We're Scouts," one of them offered. "Been cleaning up this section of the trail."

"Great. Bunk in when you're ready," Bump said, waving to the vacant floor space. "Just don't bring any mosquitoes with you."

"We can take care of the mosquitoes," the second boy answered, and in moments they had a smudge pot going in a bucket they had found. "Hot coals smothered with ferns. Green leaves will work, but ferns are better. We'll set it on tinfoil," one of the boys explained. So the problem of bedding down with mosquitoes was alleviated. However, sleeping with a smudge pot burning had its side effects. In the morning our eyes felt as if someone had buttoned them shut.

After a companionable breakfast with the Scouts, we left them. A few miles of walking through fierce flies and heat brought us to the fishing lodge on Rainbow Lake. Sweaty and thirsty, we gratefully slid out of our packs and sank to the ground. The lake was spread before us like a fluffed blue blanket. Its softwood edging was mostly spruce and fir, shafts of green splitting blue water and blue sky.

I shook my head. "We'll never see anything more beautiful."

"Maybe not," Bump said, "but we're prejudiced."

Agreed. To be Mainiac by birth and by confirmation presupposed bias, yet I honestly could not imagine anything to surpass this magnificence.

Bump got to his feet. "Boy, I'm dry." We weren't carrying water on the Maine stretch. We depended on the lakes and streams, but there hadn't been a trickle of water all the way from Hurd Brook. A man emerged from the lodge and started toward us. "How would you like a good cold bottle of pop?" I could have hugged him!

The man, a guide, told us that the next lean-to was in poor condition from rough usage, and when we arrived we understood what he meant. The area was crowded with tents and boisterous fishermen. They shouted greetings and insisted that there was "always room for a coupla more," but we declined. The liquor-laden plank between two trees suggested a late and rowdy evening, and we needed rest.

The Nahmakanta Lake Camps were four or five miles farther along. We hiked on through mosquitoes, blackflies, deerflies, and heat, only to find the camps filled. Now what? Tramp miles to the next lean-to? We were hungry and tired. Throw a tarp over a tree limb? The couple operating the camps ended our indecision by offering us all they had—an old icehouse. It had an open front and a sawdust floor but to us it looked good and we were grateful. No fires were allowed so we ate freeze-dried bacon and instant chocolate pudding, and then collapsed into our sleeping bags. Even the mosquitoes left us for dead.

At 5:30 we were up and on the move, going without breakfast until we could build a fire. By 10:30 we had hiked up hill and down for 3.5 miles while rounding Wadleigh Mountain, slogged knee-deep through a brook with icy water, and stumbled onto another lean-to, also occupied by fishermen. As they headed out for the day's fishing, they offered us the use of their stove. "Help yourselves—anything at all!" We promised we would, and I, with my eye on their apple turnovers, meant every word of it. The sticky heat, our swelling hands, the bugs, the soggy boots and jeans—all of this was forgotten during a hot breakfast that was topped off with the turnovers. With a last hungry glance at the fishermen's food, we hauled on our packs. We had gone only a few steps when I turned and dashed back to the lean-to, then ran to catch up with Bump with a can of tomato soup in each hand. "They *wanted* us to help ourselves," I told him, a little sheepishly.

Eight miles brought us to a shelter at the south end of Nahmakanta Lake, occupied by two more fishermen. Hot! And we would need a smudge, for the air was filled with mosquitoes. The midges (no-see-ums) weren't doing badly either. The two men were preparing supper. Their supplies were ample and fresh, and we needed no urging to join them. They served us fried potatoes, onions, hot dogs, and ice-cold lemonade. What a treat! As we ate I marveled at the willingness of everyone we had met to share what they had with us. At the same time I couldn't help wondering how we would be received as we moved farther and farther away from our home territory.

From Nahmakanta Lake to Antlers to Joe Mary Lake to Cooper Brook was 18 miles. We felt every one of them. Much of the land was flat and swampy, the heat intense, and the blackflies and mosquitoes nearly unbearable. At Antlers Camps we ate the tomato soup with gusto. Some yards beyond I photographed a moose wallowing in swamp muck. With so many insects around, the idea of a mud bath was appealing. Farther along the trail we stopped to rest by one of the Joe Mary lakes. We were sitting in a thick stand of poplar enjoying the leaf-riffling breeze when it began to rain, or so we thought at first. Then we realized the plopping noises were being made by falling caterpillars. They fell like fat green raindrops, and it was a phenomenon I neither understood nor appreciated. At Cooper Brook we found the two fishing rods and four cans of baked beans we had cached last summer. The cans had frozen and bulged completely out of shape so we dared not eat the contents. The fishing rods, however, with grubs for bait, provided a few trout for supper. The day's heat still festered, heavy now with an impending thunderstorm. We cleaned our few dishes and holed up for the night. Eighteen miles of trail was a long haul.

The storm that crackled and thundered throughout the night had spent itself and there were only spasmodic grumbles and splatters of rain by morning. At the end of a 10-mile walk to the East Branch Tote Road Lean-to we were cooler than we had been for days, and with our $15 Sears Roebuck rain suits already ripped and useless we were also considerably wetter. In order to dry our clothing and cook we needed a fire. With the woods drenched and the fireplace torn down by bear, building a fire became quite a challenge. We managed to fix the fireplace and cut green poles for a grate. Eventually, after a good deal of searching for dry wood, and using toilet tissue for kindling, we managed to start a fire. Dry and fed at last, we were relaxing when three fishermen stopped by the lean-to. After swapping stories with Bump, they gave him a can of worms and headed on down the brook. Bump, worms, and fishing rod disappeared into the drizzle. An hour later he returned with 13 rainbow trout. Thirteen! My insatiable appetite took command and when we had finished picking the bones and licking our fingers, Bump made a tally. He had eaten three of the trout. I had eaten ten! Upon leaving next morning, exclaiming once more at the good fortune of having had worms for bait, we walked smack into a sign that commanded: FLY FISHING ONLY! I'm sure my face was properly contrite, but my stomach was smiling from ear to ear.

The terrain began to grow hilly. The sky remained overcast, the weather damp. We felt the eight miles to White Cap Mountain Lean-to had earned us lunch and a rest. While our boots dried, I prepared macaroni, freeze-dried meatballs, and instant beef gravy mix. Our utensils were limited. We had one kettle and used its cover as a frying pan, one 2-cup measuring cup, one plastic bowl, one tin measuring cup and one teaspoon apiece, one large community fork and one large community spoon. Meal preparation required a little juggling and a lot of patience. I finally slopped the whole mess together and filled Bump's bowl. "There. Spaghetti and meatballs to rival the finest Italian restaurant!" He lifted his skeptic's eyebrow. "If you say so." Then he tasted. "Well! Not bad." From him, this was real praise, and he was right—it wasn't bad.

White Cap Mountain, with an elevation of 3,707 feet, was steep, strewn with blowdowns, and fingered with narrow icy streams. What a climb! It was six o'clock when we came down the mountainside to

White Brook. We looked back to see vapor rising from the streams like white smoke. The exhilaration of the climb and the wild beauty all around us seemed like confirmation of the rightness of our decision to take to the trail.

We were just settling in at White Brook Lean-to when someone shouted, "Hello!" It was a young man and woman from Tennessee, hiking part of the Maine trail. They were packing a tent and when it was up we all sat around the fire drinking coffee. The woman had been severely bitten by blackflies. Ugly swellings showed the poisonous effect the tiny black insects have on some people. She said nothing she had used had relieved the itching and burning caused by the bites. Bump dug into our first-aid kit and offered her a small can of salve. "Try this." She began smoothing it on her face and arms and legs. "What is it?"

"Bag balm."

She stopped rubbing. "*Bag* balm. What's that?"

"It's used on cows' udders," Bump replied.

I didn't know whether she was going to laugh or cry! "We use it a lot," I said reassuringly. "It's the most healing thing there is."

"Sure," Bump chuckled. "Wouldn't be without it."

"*Bag* balm," she exclaimed, laughing now, and repeating in her easy Southern way, "*Bag* balm! Of all things!"

When her husband finally stopped laughing he gave us a few tips. He said wood was scarce through the Smokies. We should carry a stove. In hiking some sections of the Appalachian Trail beyond Maine and New Hampshire, he and his wife had found springs to be as much as a mile off the trail. We would need a canteen. Before we slept, we had shared many experiences. They were fine people. I wondered later if they were as intrigued with our Maine dialect as we were with their Southern one.

That night another storm thrashed about us. There was lightning, and split seconds later, jolting crashes of thunder. Wind and rain lashed the lean-to. I lay quietly in my sleeping bag, remembering other nights at home when I would wake abruptly, my mind unwilling to let go of a moment and a place like this one, held over from some vivid dream I had been having about the Appalachian Trail. How badly we had wanted it! Now we were here. I remained still, ostensibly asleep, listening to the roar of White Brook. Because of the sensitivity born of years of marriage and a common bed, I wasn't surprised when Bump spoke. "Storm keeping you awake?"

"No. Just thinking."

"Worried?"

"No. It's just that it's difficult to realize we're here, really doing it. Can you think of any place you'd rather be right now?"

"Yes. In that sleeping bag with you. I'm cold."

"That isn't what I meant," I said, laughing.

"I'm exactly where I've wanted to be for the past four years. Now go to sleep, Maggie. You and I have a mountain to climb in the morning."

After breakfast we said good-bye to the couple from Tennessee and faced the West Branch of the Pleasant River. It was almost 100 feet wide, swift running, high and icy with melted snow from mountain streams. I knelt by the water's edge and dipped my fingers. *Cold!* Bump looked back at me, grinning. "You coming?" Cringing, I waded in behind him. Halfway across, waist-deep, I muttered, *"Pleasant River, indeed!"* Soaked to the waist and squishing with each step we kept going and crossed without mishap. The air was warm and we dried as we walked, like clothes hung on a line. After a time even our boots lost their sogginess.

We met a lone fisherman, rod on his shoulder, a dog at his heels. After opening howdyes came the usual exchange about the variety and ferocity of the insects. This man said he had them whipped, and introduced us to a small plastic bottle of Repel. "Made right here in Maine in the university laboratory," he said, letting us try it. We thanked him and moved on, soon discovering that he was right. It was better than anything we had tried, discouraging all the pests save an occasional deerfly.

The trail was green with fern and spruce and fir and pine. The stillness of the sun-splashed shade was broken only by the rushing brooks and chittering squirrels and the birds. God's country. At noon we came to the first Chairback. We began the climb in weather that was perfect for walking. Part way up we came upon a huge moose. He was standing on a bank near the trail, munching on the fir. His stance was as majestic as the mountainside itself. I grabbed my camera and a flashbulb! I hoped for one good shot, but he swung his head and Bump bellowed, "He's coming! Give him the right-of-way!" I did—quickly. The moose galloped up the trail, his great strides taking the steepness easily. "I wish I could have ridden up on his back," I said.

"Just be glad you didn't ride on his antlers," Bump retorted.

We went up and up and *up* and finally, at the top of a last 150 feet of sheer ledge, we came to a lean-to. Weak-kneed and thirsty, the first thing we saw was a sign: SPRING—150 FEET. The arrow pointed straight down! I groaned. "We must have come right past it!"

"Okay," Bump said, sliding to the ground, "what do you want to die of—thirst or exhaustion?" That did it. We broke up in laughter and then fetched water and made ready for the night. Perched on top of the bluff, the lean-to was raked mercilessly by the wind. The only tree cover was short stubby spruce. Firewood was scarce. Our space blanket, and indispensible 40-by-60-inch sheet of tinfoil and insulation, was used as a windbreak across the open front of the lean-to. Bump chinked many of the holes between the logs with moss. There was a register, and I wondered if the scarcity of names was testimony to Chairback's ruggedness.

Early in the morning we signed the register and left. It was too cold to linger. On the aptly named Barren Mountain we came to a fire tower. It was unmanned, but I had heard that these towers were sometimes stocked with food for emergencies. After I convinced Bump that my desperate need of a chocolate bar constituted an emergency, he climbed the tower and investigated. There was nothing, but until he peered out from the top, shaking his head, I could almost taste that candy bar.

Approximately 4,200 feet in elevation, the Barren Ledges were so terribly steep and slippery that we came down by sitting, sliding, and half-falling. We finally reached a reasonable trail and came out of the woods at Long Pond Stream, which we crossed on a narrow log just inches above white water. After climbing a steep bank we reached the lean-to. The day's hike had been only 11 miles, but it seemed twice that long. An old stove lid served us as a grate, and our meal was hot and hearty. There were no other hikers. We were alone in the wilderness and civilization seemed pleasantly distant.

On Monday morning, June 22, we followed an old jeep road to a small settlement called Bodfish Farm. Yankee economics were in evidence at the gate—one dollar admittance to come through and fish the brooks. No charge for hikers, though. Beyond Bodfish we had three or four miles of dirt road from which we could look back and admire the austere grandeur of Boarstone Mountain. Then we were walking on a paved road, passing an old railroad station, and farther on, crossing a sturdy bridge over Little Wilson Stream. A jeep road led through the woods to Little Wilson Campsite, and here we took a break. People were camping in the area and within moments of our arrival we were having coffee with a family from Bangor, a city not 20 miles from where we lived. It would have been a most pleasant interval had it not been for the little girl with the chocolate-covered cherries. A whole box! She played happily about, popping one chocolate after another into her mouth. My salivary glands began to work overtime, and I made a concerted effort to keep my eyes away from the child and her treasure until we left.

Just past the campsite there was a deep shady brook. We crossed it slowly, jumping from rock to rock, trying to keep our feet dry. I was poised in midstream, waiting for Bump to make his next move, when he said, "I saw the gleam in your eye back there."

"I couldn't *help* it," I said. "If I don't have a piece of candy soon, I'll probably *die!*"

"I was afraid you were going to smack that kid and take her chocolates!"

I started laughing so hard that I slipped off my stone perch into the water. *"Darn* you! Now look what you made me do."

"I don't know if I can keep you out of trouble all the way to Georgia or not," Bump said, reaching out a hand. He pulled me ashore, wet and still laughing, and we headed for the Old Stage Road. The lean-to in which we found our night's lodging was in the worst condition of any we had seen. It was without a floor and full of bugs. After we had eaten and made the lean-to as habitable as possible, we explored the area. Near the spring we unearthed an old quart bottle. Its twisted neck suggested hand blowing. Realizing its potential value, I stowed it in my pack. We tried to imagine what it was like, perhaps a hundred years ago, to live and work here. We discovered no further traces of those remote lives, and somehow I wasn't sorry.

About a mile down the road next morning we met two girls and a boy, pleasant young people about Steve's age. They were from Colorado. We talked briefly, knowing that another mile would put us in Monson. We were eager to measure the impact of civilization after our 10-day absence. Our top priority when we arrived in town was a call to Steve. How good it was to hear his voice! As we talked, it was decided that he would drive to Monson and bring us some of the things we had discovered we needed.

We located a rooming house, then hurried to the nearest restaurant. Oh, the aroma! We ordered steaks, mashed potatoes, vegetables, salads, pie and coffee, and ate like starved children. Fortunately, since Monson is one of the two places in Maine where Appalachian Trail hikers can get supplies without leaving the trail, the people were not unaccustomed to sights such as we presented. We wore our trail clothes—dirty shirts, slept-in jeans, high boots—for we had no other clothing. We had been thoroughly chewed by various bugs and the bites looked bad. My hair was dirty and untidy. Bump was unshaven.

Lingering over coffee, we speculated about the way people might look at us farther along, in places where we would have to leave the trail to procure supplies. Would they dismiss us at a glance as "hippies"? Would they be repulsed by what showed on the surface? I hoped not. I hoped they would look beneath the trail dirt and find the people there. Bump said this hope I had for finding humanity in human beings was an incurable disease.

Sated at last, we turned to our errands. Our one change of clothing was washed and dried in a laundromat instead of a brook and a branch. We bought food, including plenty of chocolate bars. I ate three of them as we walked back to the rooming house. For $5 we had a room, a bed with a real mattress and clean sheets, and a bathtub. Luxury! Ready for the tub, I was horrified to see that I looked very much like a scarecrow. We knew we were losing weight, but I was unprepared for this. I had lost 10 pounds, at least! We luxuriated in hot bath and shampoos, but when we took a nap we found the bed too soft. Later we had another huge meal while we waited for Steve.

Steve greeted us by saying we looked absolutely awful. We sat in the restaurant over steaming mugs of coffee, checking what he had brought from home and deciding what we would send back. He had our windbreakers to replace the insulated sweat shirts which had proved too warm. Bump planned to exchange his sleeping bag for a blanket, which weighed less, and he made certain that Steve had brought his coffee mug. He claimed coffee just didn't taste right in anything else. In addition to fresh foods we purchased two bottles of Repel, a can of water repellent that hopefully would waterproof our packs, and a can of Raid that we hoped would keep deerflies out of our hair. All in all, we were in good condition for traveling. We spent the remainder of the evening catching up on hometown news. When Steve was ready to go, Bump asked, "When we telephoned, did you think someone would have to come after us—like the last time?" Steve shook his head. "No way. This time you're going to make it."

Yes, I thought, we would make it or drop in the attempt. There was more at stake than the challenge of the trail. The original idea had been an outgrowth of many things: enjoyment of the healthy walking pattern of living we had developed, a deep feeling for the outdoors and all it had held; the desire to see a part of the country that was one of the last strongholds against bulldozing "progress." Probably strongest of all was our need to escape the hectic crazy complexity that living seemed to have become. All these things shaped our decision. There would be no turning back.

Sometime very early in the morning I was awake again. Although in the midst of ease and comfort, I was uneasy and uncomfortable as I remembered our journey of two summers ago. Four of us had started —Bump and I, Steve, and our nephew Ken. Pushing too hard, and striving for too much mileage had been our mistake. The blackflies, mosquitoes, deerflies and no-see-ums had been then, as now, a savage torment. It had rained on 9 successive days of the 14 we were on the trail. Arthritis had settled into my left knee, making walking painful. Steve had developed an infection in one eye. The boys' good-natured antics, while providing welcome comedy relief, hadn't always disguised the fact that occasionally they wished they were back home pursuing other interests. It took us two weeks to go from Katahdin to Monson, and when we arrived there we all knew we were finished. We had telephoned Bump's sister and her husband to come and get us. We went home to face the "I told you sos" and the "knew you'd never make its." But even in the death of that hike a determination to try again was being born, and here we were. I rolled over carefully in what had to be Monson's downiest feather bed and ran through a mental checklist of our equipment. It was the same as it had been on the first trip, minus anything we had learned wasn't vitally necessary. Our prize investment was Gerry packs with aluminum frames; the packs' four-zippered compartments were utilized to the fullest. In the bottom ones we carried our bedrolls wrapped in plastic, mine was a 2½-pound down sleeping bag; Bump's was now a lightweight blanket. Our clothing included a change of underwear plus a pair of thermal long johns; two extra pairs of socks, one nylon, one wool; a T-shirt for me, a flannel shirt for Bump. He had one extra pair of long pants and a pair of shorts; I had one pair of each with no extras.

In another section of the pack I had a Cutter first-aid kit plus bag balm and Ben Gay, a small bottle of Johnson's baby oil, $30 worth of blood-pressure pills, a snakebite kit, a tiny sewing kit, and film for my Argus Instamatic camera. Bump's comparable section was filled with the space blanket, book matches, a watertight container of wooden matches, toothbrushes and paste, our one washcloth and all-purpose bar of Ivory soap, toilet tissue, fish hooks and line, insect repellent and a length of nylon rope. We had small flashlights. Bump had the tarp, his hunting knife and cigarettes; I, my logbook and personal feminine appurtenances. We divided our few utensils and the food between us on a "space available" basis.

It was still dark outside when I began reviewing some of the "we can get by without its," and Bump began to toss and turn. It was amazing how the human body adapts itself, I thought, as I shifted on the fluffy mattress. How quickly our backs had adjusted to their log and bough beds on the trail! Air mattresses and shorty pads had been on our "rejected" list, along with other items such as tents, stoves, swimsuits, and pajamas. And shaving equipment, I suddenly remembered, as Bump rolled over and his whiskers scraped my arm.

Nudging him, I asked, "How come you didn't bring a razor?"

"Because I'm gonna raise a beard. Besides, you didn't bring any hair curlers, did you?"

"I'm gonna raise pigtails."

He yawned, rolling over again at the same time I did. We both sort of slid downhill and collided in the feather bed. I stopped worrying about the things we had left behind.

At daybreak on June 24 we put our nemesis behind us. We hiked on and off the highway, in and out of the woods, through Blanchard, across the Piscataquis River, then back into the woods again. The walking was good, with very little climbing. We had covered 17 miles between Monson and Moxie Bald Mountain by the time we stopped. The area around the lean-to was littered with garbage and the evidence of a recent bear killing. Inside the shelter there was perhaps 50 pounds of salt in a box, left over from curing hides. It wasn't a pleasant place to curl up for the night, but we were tired. With miles of trail behind us and a mountain ahead, we were in no position to be choosy. At dusk, having performed our usual chores, we were settling in when I heard a strange sound. "What's that noise?" I whispered.

"What noise?"

"That *swishing*."

"I don't hear a swishing."

We were near the edge of a pond, and I said, "It sounds like someone swimming. If you won't get up and look, I *will*."

"All right." He didn't budge.

"All right, *what?*"

"All right, go look if you want to." *My hero.* I crawled out of my sleeping bag and tiptoed outside, just in time. In the mirrored stillness of the water I saw a giant moose. For several moments he remained perfectly motionless. Then, apparently refreshed by his evening swim, he moved into the night. It was a rare moment for me. As I returned to my bed, Bump said sleepily, "See any water-skiers?"

"I saw a moose, and it could have been a *bear!*"

He chuckled. "Wasn't, was it?"

No argument could jar that kind of logic. I gave up.

The next morning we faced Moxie Bald Mountain. Over 2,600 feet high, it was a good climb in the bracing air. From this point on the trail was brand new to us. It required strict attention to blazes. As we neared the mountaintop a forest warden hailed us, inviting us into his cabin. While the coffee brewed, we relaxed. Sunshine spilled over the treetops into the clearing, flooding the cabin and the hillside, which was pink-topped with wild onion. Reluctantly we left the ranger and hiked on, stopping for lunch at Joes Hole Brook Lean-to, then forging up Pleasant Pond Mountain. This was the second real climb of the day and it made us appreciate the lean-to we found at Pleasant Pond. It was a clean solid structure with a handy spring and ample firewood. Our routine was now well established and we were soon ready for night. The closing of a day by quiet water edged with pine and hemlock was a special time. The air was clean, good to breathe, and the stillness was uncluttered by human noise. The only sounds came from the trees, the lapping water, and an occasional animal cry. We began to hear one animal sound that gradually became louder and more insistent. Sitting very still, we located the source. It was a baby fox. He peeked in the lean-to—then, still crying, scampered away.

I said, "I hope his mother finds him."

Bump laughed. "Don't worry, Maggie. Most youngsters are pretty resourceful—ours included," he added, reading my mind.

We broke camp early and headed for Caratunk, a small town with a country store and post office. We mailed postcards, bought supplies, ate Italian sandwiches, and learned the whereabouts of a ranger who could tell us how to cross the Kennebec River. We were told that the river was being dragged for the body of a man killed in a log drive. The ranger located a man to take us across the river, and for $5 we were transported in an aluminum rowboat across the Kennebec. I was glad when we reached the opposite shore and could put the dead logger's river behind us.

Pierce Pond was one of the loveliest places we had seen. We would have enjoyed staying in the new lean-to but there was half a day's hiking time left. We had to be satisfied with sitting on the bank, eating peanut butter and jam sandwiches, and dangling our feet in the cool clear water. We made East Carry Pond by nightfall. A pleasant evening and restful night turned into a dismal morning. We woke to the sound of rain drumming on the roof. I rolled over in my sleeping bag and asked Bump what time it was.

"I don't know. My watch broke."

I thought about that for a while. It was a peculiar feeling, lying there in the half-dark as the rain beat down around us, not knowing what time it was. Time, as measured by a watch, had governed most of our lives, but here on the trail that sort of time had no real meaning.

Finally there was an easing in the downpour so we ate a hurried cold breakfast and moved out. The trees and grasses were gleamingly wet and dripping. Every branch we jostled gave us an additional shower. After a few miles we looked and felt as if we had been swimming. The slashing rain eventually tapered off to dripping and drizzling. When we reached the lean-to at Jerome Brook we stopped for the day.

Inside the lean-to we discovered packs but no people. It was a little eerie, but we began to concentrate on our most desperate need of the moment—a fire. How wet and cold we were! My teeth chattered furiously as we searched for dry wood, bits of bark, twigs—anything that would burn. At last the tiny carefully nurtured flame caught and began to blaze. We were sitting almost on top of it, warming ourselves, when we heard a thrashing in the brush. We looked through the mist to see a rather large woman carrying a little red lantern emerging from the bushes. Behind her came another woman, slipping and sliding across the log bridge. Here was the answer to the unattended packs.

The women were teachers from Maryland who spent their vacations exploring the Appalachian Trail. They were tremendously excited to learn that we planned to go the entire trail. The four of us shared the warmth of the fire and the shelter of the lean-to. We couldn't have asked for more pleasant company. In the morning Miss Willis, whom I would always picture peering out of the bushes clutching her little red lantern, cooked breakfast for us. She and her friend were carrying fresh eggs, something we hadn't seen for some time. The fireplace grate was uneven and the eggs persistently slid into a heap on one side of the pan. Trying to be helpful, Bump attempted to straighten the grate and burned his fingers. I admired his efforts at self-control and solicitously dug out the bag balm for him, then dug into my eggs. They were delicious, and I could have eaten a dozen of them.

We left Jerome Brook to head into the Bigelow Range. The low country we had been traveling was mossy and thick with wide-bladed swale grass. The peaks ahead, reaching high above tree line, were rocky and bare. On Bigelow we were to pick up freeze-dried and dehydrated foods sent from home. We found the ranger in whose care the supplies were to have been sent, only to discover that they hadn't arrived. We were traveling faster than we had anticipated. We asked the ranger to send the supplies on to Sugarloaf when they did arrive.

Miss Willis had told us Bigelow Mountain would be the longest 11 miles of the trail we would find, and she certainly knew her mileage. It was the roughest going we had encountered. On Myron H. Avery Peak, at an elevation of 4,088 feet, we came to a sign: 95 MILES TO MAINE–NEW HAMPSHIRE LINE. I promptly sat down.

Bump grinned. "Quitting?"

"Resting," I retorted, glaring at him.

"Come on," he laughed, pulling me to my feet. "I'll buy you a Coke and a Baby Ruth at the very next roadside stand we hit." A bottomless source of inspiration, my husband.

We made it over Bigelow by suppertime. It was the most exhausting day yet. That evening we were joined at our cozy retreat by a Boy Scout troop. "Ah, the solitude of the Maine Wilderness," Bump sighed, but I knew he enjoyed having the youngsters around.

By noon the next day we had put the last of the Bigelows behind us. On the way out of the woods we skirted beaver swamps, then walked along Stratton Brook Flowage where I got some good pictures of another bull moose, a much more amiable subject than the last one we had encountered. This moose seemed to enjoy posing. We trudged on to a gas station where the attendant, after hearing our story, offered us a vehicle and a driver to take us to Stratton. It was a kindness that saved us a six-mile walk. The driver waited while we bought supplies and tried, unsuccessfully, to find Bump a new sleeping bag. His blanket wasn't doing the job. Driving back, the fellow offered to trade his own sleeping bag for Bump's blanket, and invited us to have supper with him. He was taking care of a chalet on Sugarloaf for the summer. The chalet was beautiful with open wooden beams and walls of glass, and it seemed to grow out of the mountainside. We dined in splendor on baked beans and ham, with our interesting new friend and a magnificent old mountain for company. We went on to a lean-to for the night; in the morning there would be another mountain.

The night was showery; the morning foggy. Sugarloaf gave us fairly easy climbing, but afforded no view from the peak. Our supplies hadn't arrived. We had lunch and trekked down through the dismal grayness of the fog and began to climb Spaulding Mountain. We were thoroughly soaked by the time we reached Spaulding Mountain Lean-to. We had been at the shelter just long enough to build a roaring fire, change, and hang up our wet clothing when we were joined

Photo courtesy Margaret Smith

Margaret and Bump Smith starting their hike.

Photo by James R. Wo

One of the Chairback Ponds in Maine.

by another hiker, a lone man who obviously was happy to find the lean-to inhabited.

"That fire feels just great. You don't know how glad I am to find someone here. I've lost my guidebook and was getting worried."

"Afraid we can't help there," Bump said. "We don't have a guidebook, either."

"You don't? Lose yours, too?"

"No. Just didn't bring any."

"Well—maps, then. You must have maps."

"No."

"Compass?"

Bump shook his head.

"How far are you planning to go?"

"Springer Mountain."

"Springer Mountain, Georgia? That's the whole trail! How can you go the whole Appalachian Trail without guidebooks or maps—or a compass?"

"Well, we're depending on markers and on meeting people who'll give us tips," Bump explained.

The clean woodsy smell of the night, laced with the aroma of frying hot dogs and boiling coffee, was heady as wine. We ate with our backs to the fire's warmth, lulled and contented. Suddenly Bump said he smelled something burning that shouldn't be burning, and we discovered that Bump's boots, set by the fire to dry, were not only dry but had shrunk, and the toe of one boot was burned completely through.

"What'll you do?" the man asked. "You can't walk to Georgia barefoot!"

"He'll think of something," I said, and Bump was already setting margarine to melt over the fire. He soaked the boots in margarine for some time, and finally pushed stones in to stretch them and left them overnight. In the morning they were wearable again.

The morning sun was blistering by the time we began our assault on Poplar Ridge. There was none of nature's gentleness here. The ridge was long and steep and grueling and seemed to fight us every step of the way. We fought back, sweating our way across. There were sighs of relief when we spotted the tin roof of a lean-to gleaming in the late afternoon sun. As we dropped our packs and mopped perspiration from our faces, I gasped, "That was a *ridge?*"

"You must be out of shape," Bump said, flopping on the ground.

Later we spread our sleeping gear to air on the roof and collected wood and water. Eating, we did battle with a horde of insects we could not identify. They seemed especially fond of white surfaces and persisted in alighting on our dishes. When we crawled into our dark-colored bedrolls the little beasts left us alone.

The Saddlebacks were tough, and again we were moving through heavy fog that cheated us of any view of the surrounding country. Most of the approaches were thick with what we had come to call "moose muck." It smeared our boots and legs like salve, making walking difficult. Around noon we reached Piazza Rock Lean-to. Water, wood, a fire, and food. Our routine was quickly executed now without discussion or direction. When Bump returned to the site with an armload of wood his free hand was filled with daisies and buttercups and Indian paintbrush. "This *is* July 2, isn't it?"

"Oh, Bump, they're beautiful! Thank you." I poured water into my coffee cup and arranged the flowers. "I didn't think you'd remember."

He laughed. "Not remember 20 years in double harness? Fat chance!"

I passed him my last treasured Milky Way. "Happy anniversary!"

"Thank you," he said. Then, grinning, "Don't worry. We'll share it."

Another hiking couple stopped by the lean-to and we were able to record a special moment. Dirty, shaggy-haired, Bump's beard scraggly, both of us with moose muck all over, we had our picture taken. Deciding we had ample reason for celebration and goofing off, we spent the rest of the afternoon lazying around, happy just to be alive.

In the morning we passed a beaver flowage which contained quite a few six-packs of beer, probably set to cool by some fishermen. We came to the road and found a ride into Rangeley. After writing a few postcards and buying groceries we went back to the trail. At a lean-to beside Sabbath Day Pond we had hamburgers and potatoes. Delicious! Afterward, all conditions were right for my first full-scale bath on the trail.

We awoke to a rainy Fourth of July. No fire crackers. No Roman candles. Just drizzle. "No traveling today," Bump decreed. Around midmorning a lady fisherman materialized at our lean-to. She lived in the only cottage on the pond and invited us to a lunch of sandwiches plus cucumbers and radishes straight from the garden. I don't think anyone could have appreciated that lunch more than we did. Fresh fruit and vegetables are not practical backpacking items. On our way back to the lean-to we passed an old abandoned cabin that had a fine woodpile. We "borrowed" a few chunks and they produced a marvelous crackling fire by which we finished out a very satisfactory Fourth of July.

The next day, in fair weather, we went over Bemis and Elephant mountains. The day was gone by the time we had covered perhaps

12 miles. It didn't seem enough as we settled into Elephant Mountain Lean-to. We told ourselves that tomorrow would be better, and it was. Stopping only for peanut butter and crackers at noon, we were at Frye Brook Lean-to by suppertime with 20 miles between us and breakfast. What a tremendous feeling, snuggling into a sleeping bag near a dying fire with a full stomach and the satisfaction of a good day's hike!

The good weather stayed with us the next morning as we geared up to head for Grafton Notch, Old Speck Mountain, and ultimately, the Maine–New Hampshire line. Following Frye Brook was like walking in a great gorge. It was shady, cool, and green—refreshingly different from the ledges and blueberry bushes of the Baldpates. We were still in the mountains, though, and soon we were climbing the East Peak of Baldpate, topping off at over 3,800 feet. The view stretched over many miles and let us appreciate the great beauty of the mountains we were crossing. We were at Grafton Notch Lean-to before noon and Bump wanted to go on and take Old Speck, the third highest mountain in the state at over 4,000 feet. I was for saving it until morning. As in many of our compromises on the trail, we did it his way. The approach to Old Speck was rocky and made for slow going. When we were perhaps halfway up we came to an empty shack. It looked to me like a good place for an early supper and bedtime. We got in plenty of wood, built a nice fire, and cooked Kraft macaroni and cheese. We were quite comfortable when two people came down the mountain and told us of the fantastic view from the huge fire tower on the peak. I shot a quick glance at Bump. Sure enough, it wasn't bedtime yet. When we reached the summit at nine o'clock there was nothing to admire except the thickening darkness. The great roofless fire tower was fine for daylight viewing but useless for shelter.

"*Now* what?" I asked.

"Might as well go on down and see what's on the other side of the mountain."

"I *know* what's on the other side. Dark, just like here!"

"Got a flashlight, haven't you?"

"Well, yes, but where's the trail? Where are the blazes?"

The dependable white trail blazes we had followed all the way from Katahdin seemed to have disappeared. All we could depend on now were the two small flashlights and instinct. My instinct said to bear in one direction; Bump's said to go in the other. We stumbled around in the dark, arguing.

Bump said, "This way seems to be the most traveled."

"That doesn't make it the right trail. I think we should take the other one."

"Those lights way off there must be a city—maybe Gorham. We have to hit that."

"You don't know if those lights are Gorham or not. They're miles and miles off."

Silence. Then he said, "I'm going this way. Are you coming?" End of discussion. For better or worse, two flashlight beams bobbling along Old Speck's night-blackened backside. We went down through the darkness, picking our way along, hoping we had the right trail. Finally, after nearly two hours, we knew we were on the right trail when we reached Speck Pond Shelter. We were thankful, and Bump even had the grace not to say "I told you so." The lean-to was spilling over with Boy Scouts whose counselor wanted to move them out to make room for us but we were so happy just to know where we were that we gratefully spread our bedrolls on the ground.

The next morning we came to Mahoosuc Notch. The Appalachian Trail is one thing; Mahoosuc Notch is something else. Forsaken by the sun, it is almost a mile of snow, ice, sheer ledges, caves, and moss-covered rocks. Walking in Mahoosuc Notch isn't something you expect your feet to do by themselves. We clambered, slipped, clung, slipped again, and eventually emerged into the sunshine. Some time later we reached the Maine–New Hampshire state line. Hallelujah! That porcupine-chewed sign, surrounded by bright blue-topped little spruce, was a most welcome sight. It was July 9 and we had been on the trail 27 days and had traveled 279 miles. I wanted to cheer, and we did. I persuaded Bump to pose by the sign and it was a fine shot: the gnawed wooden signpost and Bump beside it, grinning through his whiskers and wearing Steve's University of Maine beanie, which served time as a pot holder. Now Maine, and home, were really behind us.

Our next stop was Carlo Col Shelter, which was floorless and dirty. The sole compensating factor was the hiker we met. A young fellow, doing parts of the trail, he was extremely proud of his fine expensive boots. He eyed our rather ordinary leathers. "Where'd you get your boots?"

"Sears, Roebuck."

"Like 'em?"

"No complaints so far."

He looked admiringly at his feet, then shook his head. "You'll never make it across the Presidential Range in 'em. You should have something like mine here. Best boots money can buy."

"Don't doubt it," Bump said, "but I think we'll manage."

I had been watching the boy with interest, mainly because it was the first time I'd ever seen anyone smoking marijuana. When he took off his socks I saw that almost every toe sported a Band-Aid. I hoped that the tarp muffled my laughter. Best boots, ha!

Next day put us on the Peabody Brook Trail, with Gentian Pond Shelter our noon stop. Here we met an interesting man who told us that his stay at this shelter was a yearly one, something that he and his father, now dead, had done for a long time. He spent a good deal of his vacation in cleaning up the trail in this area and I imagine other hikers appreciated his efforts as we did. From Gentian Pond we hiked along Peabody Brook to the Androscoggin River and the highway. After a lot of walking and thumbing, we got a lift into Gorham. First we called Steve, asking him to hold up on the dehydrated food. The initial shipment had never caught up with us, and having survived without it this far, we decided we could manage at least until we reached the Blue Ridge Mountains.

I invested in a new pair of shorts; my present pair had virtually no seat left. Then we tended to our appetites. It felt strange to be in a fine restaurant. We were a little disconcerted by the lifted eyebrows of some of the other diners, but we feasted, drank glass after glass of milk, and gorged ourselves on hot fudge sundaes. In a final splurge, we hired a lady cabby to drive us back to the trail. We found the shelter full of kids, and sleep was a scarce commodity that night. They were drinking beer and shouting and having a high old time. Wherever the trail might take us tomorrow, it couldn't be far enough from the city limits to suit me.

We left the shelter early, bleary-eyed and irritable. The trail was good, but we were tired. We stopped to chat with a man who was building a house with stones taken from Rattle River. We stopped again while I cut through the hems of my new shorts. They were binding against my newfound thigh muscles. We stopped a third time to admire the sign that read: APPALACHIAN TRAIL—A FOOTPATH RUNNING FROM MAINE TO GEORGIA. We stopped again for water and to eat. In short, it was hard to keep going. Lack of sleep made hiking a real chore. We were in the White Mountain National Forest now, and at Imp Shelter we decided to call it a day. The shelter was a good one, but full of Boy Scouts. We made camp under our tarp again. Our campsite was next to a brook and camped on the other side were a man and several 8- to 10-year-old boys. As usual, the youngsters had gravitated to Bump for conversation and foolishness. One little guy, maybe two-and-half-feet tall, piped up. "Boy, are you going to have a rough day tomorrow!" Bump asked why. "Because today we hiked through miles of ferns and goldenrod taller'n my head!" The last thing we saw before going to sleep was the little guy and his pals "making water" on their campfire to put it out.

During the night we had a thunderstorm, mild compared to some we had experienced, but enough to freshen the forest. We moved out toward Carter Notch and Wildcat Mountain. At Carter Notch Hut we met the boy with the boots again. Though he stayed with us all the way up Wildcat, we talked little. Serious hiking precludes chatter. I did notice, though, that even with expensive boots the boy seemed to fall down a lot.

On the Carter–Moriah Trail we had thunder, lightning, and beating rain. On the summit we stood beneath a leaky fire tower for protection until the shower slackened, then walked on to a ski lodge where we stopped for hot chocolate. After a hearty supper at the foot of Wildcat we headed for Mt. Madison and soon lost the trail. It was late and the weather was threatening again. There was nothing to do but make camp and try again in the morning. We put up the tarp by a small stream and tried to make ourselves comfortable. We're not lost, I told myself, just temporarily misplaced. Sometime before daybreak I awoke to the sound of rushing water. Worse than the sound was the *feeling!* Water seemed to be coursing all around us!

"Bump!" I shouted. "Wake up!"

Our innocuous gurgling brook had swelled to overflowing and was drenching us, soaking our sleeping bags and creeping into our clothing. Suddenly, it was just too much. "Bump, *do* something," I cried, on the verge of tears.

"What shall I do? Build you a castle?"

I decided I might as well laugh as cry. We pulled the jumbled mess of our equipment up onto higher ground and tried to get a fire going. Wet. Soggy. Cold! At *last*, a fire, hot coffee, and oatmeal. Simple comforts, but all we asked at the moment. With daylight, after finding no signs and no blazes, we climbed about six miles up the mountainside and finally met some people who set us straight. Not only were we on the wrong trail; we were on the wrong mountain! The man and woman gave us their map and pointed us back down the mountain to the road and the spot where the sign, perhaps now hanging in some souvenir-happy citizen's recreation room, should have been. They probably wondered what kind of people would start out to walk a couple of thousand miles without maps. I was beginning to wonder, myself.

We walked a swinging bridge across a brook toward Mt. Madison and faced 3,500 feet of water-slicked ledge, with scarcely a toehold to be found and nothing to grasp but slippery roots. Twice during our upward struggle we stopped to pull off our packs and stand under the space blanket, at the mercy of thunderstorms that were accompanied by crackling lightning and punishing hail. I thought of the sign we had seen earlier, warning against traveling in these mountains in bad weather. Particularly haunting was one terse statement: MANY HAVE DIED ABOVE TIMBERLINE.

When we reached the summit we were wet through and chilled to the bone and another storm was close on our heels; we felt it might have been December 25 instead of July 12. Finding shelter, warmth, and hot food at the Madison Huts represented all the security in the world. Bunks and blankets were furnished. Men slept on one side of the hut, women on the other. We could have purchased paper sheets and pillowcases as well, but decided there was no sense in starting to be fancy now. We learned a lot from the other hikers, including "Moose," who was a jolly man full of stories, and the most interesting person I had met so far on the hike. He had once attempted to do the whole trail with a friend, but the friend inconsiderately broke his leg, thus ending the venture. When Bump and I mentioned our confusion concerning the trail blazes since we had left Maine, he explained that through New Hampshire and Vermont we would have orange and black blazes, compliments of the Dartmouth College Outing Club. Orange and black were Dartmouth's colors. No wonder we couldn't find a white blaze!

In the morning we paid $14 for the supper, lodging, and breakfast for two. Reasonable, but not something we could afford to do often. We were in the Presidential Range, following a cairn-marked trail over crests draped with fog. We knew we had more than 20 miles of hiking above tree line as we crossed the flanks of Mts. Adams, Jefferson, and Clay. It was cold and there was no wood for fires. We stopped only once, to change into long pants. Though it isn't part of the trail, we climbed to the top of Mt. Washington. Rising 6,288 feet, it is New Hampshire's highest point and we couldn't pass it by. We saw the Cog Railway and the weather observatory on the summit. Best of all, from the highest telephone in the northeastern United States, we called home!

We followed Crawford Path to the Lakes of the Clouds. No other name could so aptly describe it! At one unnerving spot on the path we peered down into some 5,000 feet of sheer space. As far as we could see in every direction there were mountains and more mountains. We passed up the accommodations of Mizpah Spring Hut on Mt. Clinton and trudged on to Nauman Shelters. Here we shared the space with four young men whose appearance neatly fit our ideas of "hippies." During the evening they sat cross-legged in a circle, passing around a pipe with a small bowl and a long stem. A marijuana peace pipe, they told Bump. Long after we had retired for the night, they sat there talking and laughing. The happier they got, the edgier I got.

"Relax," Bump whispered, crawling into bed after his nightly sojourn. "Guess what I just read."

Oh, oh. Little niceties carved on outhouse walls. "I don't think I want to hear it."

"Love," he said. "In great big capital letters."

"Groovy, dad," I told him. "Very reassuring."

Real reassurance came with the morning. It was a brisk sunny day just made to be greeted with enthusiasm. From Webster Cliffs we looked down on the highway, running like a zipper along the back of a billowing green dress; then we hiked Zealand Ridge and the Ethan Pond Trail. Whitewall Mountain was rough, with loose rocks that rolled under our feet. After about 18 miles we camped outside Galehead Hut. That evening we met a teacher from Massachusetts who had a two-man mountain tent to sell. It had a rain fly and was waterproof and practically new. To me it looked like a palace. Bump told the man we didn't have enough money with us to buy it.

"Try it for the night," he said. "If you like it, send me a check later."

Bless him! In the morning he took our tarp to send home for us and we packed the tent, shook his hand, and set out. Still in the Presidential Range, our mountains for the day were Garfield and Lafayette, with other less formidable heights in between. Fog was settling in and other hikers were few as we started up Mt. Lafayette. On the mountain's top, at over 5,000 feet, there was fog so dense we could barely see the cairns, and they were the only way the trail was marked. Great gusts of wind were so strong that we were nearly plucked from the ground. It was frightening, and I had a new reason to be grateful for my 35-pound pack.

It was still miserably foggy and raining hard when we made it down to Liberty Spring. The shelter was already overflowing with campers, and the roof was leaking to boot. Several hut boys, who had been packing in lumber for reconstruction, were staying here. One of them came to our rescue, letting us change our soaked clothing in his tent. He insisted that I use his sleeping bag because the wind had torn my impromptu plastic pack cover and rain had seeped into my bedroll. Then he loaned us his Coleman stove so we could make hot chocolate. In the morning the boys offered to take us to town to buy the small Svea stove we had decided would be worth carrying. Terrific people, these kids. During the ride they delved into the "whys and wherefores" of our journey. We tried to explain how we felt about the wilderness, about wanting to see it and live in it before it was polluted and superhighwayed out of existence.

"You know," said one boy, "I have the same feeling sometimes. Guess that's why I like this job. How were you able to get so much time off? You teachers?"

"No," Bump said. "My wife has five months leave without pay. I had to quit my job."

Their admiration was obvious. "You quit your job to do the trail? That's terrific!"

"It probably won't be so great next winter when we're eating snowballs," Bump said dryly. The boys were impressed, nonetheless. We had sort of kicked the establishment in the teeth to "do our thing."

Before we left, the boys told us about Ross Morgan, the hutmaster at Lonesome Lake. "There's a man who knows the woods by heart. You tell him we said he'd better treat you right!" When we reached Lonesome Lake Hut that night we found Ross to be a good and helpful person. He made a place for us to dry our wet clothes, and in a kitchen hung with big shiny pots, he gave us beef stew and refused to let us pay for it. We had a happy evening, singing and spinning yarns with him and the hut boys. Next day, after a breakfast of sourdough blueberry pancakes, we headed out toward Fishin' Jimmy Trail. In the clear warm weather we climbed many mountains, with only grouse and some baby raccoons for company. Despite our enjoyment of the friendly people we had been meeting, it was good to have a day all to ourselves. We spent the night at Lost River Reservation and in the morning we cooked breakfast on our new stove. It was a tiny thing that fit easily into Bump's cupped hands. Supposedly, if he held it that way long enough the warmth from his hand would make the fuel bubble up into a little basin where it could be ignited. Then when a detachable key was turned, more fuel was supposed to keep feeding the flame. It was a great theory, but it didn't work for us. Bump decided it wasn't getting enough heat from his hands. He poured a little Coleman fuel onto the ground, lit it, and held the stove over the flame. Presto! Fuel puddled up in the basin. He lit this fuel and let it burn a while, then attached the key and turned it, and we had a micro-mini-one-burner gas stove. We turned the three metal prongs to the outside, set a pot of water on top, dumped in the coffee and let it brew. The stove was so light and compact it was going to be a real boon in wet weather.

We went along Beaver Brook, then up and down the steep Mt. Blue, then over Moosilauke. Finally we reached the town of Glencliff, where my smoldering passion for candy flared up again. The next day we met some weekend hikers, the Hadleys from Hanover, New Hampshire, and the Nicksons from Woodstock, Vermont. Both couples, after hearing our story, said we need only to call them if we wanted a night's lodging when we reached their area. We maneuvered over the precipitous reaches of Mt. Cube and, finding no fresh water, we apprehensively sipped from potholes in the rocks. We were still alive the next morning so we decided there had been no ill effects and shrugged into our packs, which by now felt more natural on than off. Somewhere along the way we lost the trail. Eventually we blundered into Hanover and hailed a policeman. He gave us a lift to Dartmouth College, where we hoped to get a guidebook, as getting lost was too time-consuming. A director of the college, Mr. John Rand, gave us a guidebook of the Long Trail, which coincides with the Appalachian Trail through much of Vermont. We called home and talked with Steve, bought groceries, then called the Hadleys. They took us in as if they had known us forever and made our last night in New Hampshire a thoroughly memorable one.

On July 21 we crossed the Connecticut River into Vermont. Our first stop was at Happy Hill Cabin, which belonged to the Dartmouth Outing Club. Students who were at the cabin doing repair work took us in, fed us chicken and rice, bedded us down, and started our new day with heaps of raspberry pancakes. Farther on, near Woodstock, we came to the highway and called the Nicksons. They took us to their little farm and fixed us a Chinese dinner. Mrs. Nickson insisted on preparing a specialty for each of us—anything we wanted. For me, a tossed salad; for Bump, pecan pie. In the morning Mr. Nickson made cornbread with meal ground from their own corn, and the coffee was from fresh-ground coffee beans. We began the day well fortified.

We started for Gulf Lean-to with the best of everything—good weather, easy hiking, and the warmth and hospitality of some wonderful people. The valleys were deep and green. There was the sleek beauty of Morgan horses behind white pasture fences, and enduring stone walls that seemed to speak of quiet patience and serenity. We journeyed through hot days, spending our nights in stone lean-tos with bunks made of chicken wire. From Stony Brook to Gifford Woods State Park to Pico Peak we had a long dry stretch. We went up Deer Leap Trail, where we heard the deer blowing, and at Pico Camp we found water and a magnificent view of Killington Peak. We walked extra miles for supplies, and spent the night at Clarendon Lodge, a lovely place situated in the middle of a cow pasture. We were on the Long Trail now, 261 miles of hiker's trail extending the length of Vermont from the Massachusetts state line to the Canadian border. We walked a footbridge to a shelter on a tiny island but the shelter was filled with Girl Scouts, so we backtracked to Tye Lean-to on the edge of the same little pond. Here my freshly laundered underwear, hung by the fire to dry, was burned to an ash and my bare feet were jabbed by porcupine quills strewn along the outhouse path.

Hiking through the heat we reached Mad Tom Shelter where we met some people from New Jersey who asked us to telephone them if we made it as far as the Delaware Water Gap. We went on through Vermont's Green Mountains. We went up Bromley through oppressive tension-building heat which finally cut loose in a cooling thunderstorm. We were kept awake at Caughnawaga Shelter by fighting porcupines. On Glastenbury Mountain a tall Texan named Ted Field teased us about our "R-less" Maine accent. We met Ed Garvey, who was hiking from Georgia to Maine. He advised us of water shortages from New York south. At Congdon Camp we met goateed, guitar-playing George Wright, who was singing for his supper from Georgia to Maine.

On July 31, our forty-fourth day on the trail, we entered Massachusetts and reached a shelter in a cool and quiet pine grove at sunset. It was a time and a place for retrospection. We had traveled through three states, had been on the trail 44 days, and had hiked more than 550 miles. We had been chewed by blackflies, jabbed by mosquitoes, stung by horseflies; we had been sticky and smelly with sweat, and dry with thirst; lost; footsore; our hands had swelled and our backs had been weary; we had been pummeled with hail; starved for fresh fruit and beefsteak and candy bars—yet right now we probably were healthier and more relaxed than we had been at any time in the last 10 years.

Our basic diet of oatmeal, peanut butter, and Kraft dinners, although not very appealing aesthetically, seemed to be providing enough protein and vitamins. Although we had been wet and chilled at times, we had developed no colds. We had used water from unreliable sources without harm. Our feet were toughened and our shoulders strengthened. Though our hands still swelled, sometimes quite a bit on extremely hot days, they produced no real discomfort. Bump, still smoking two packs of Camels a day, was feeling their effect less and less. The insects that had put us through purgatory at first had now lost their punch. We were winning. The dream was one-fourth reality.

We gave a full day and night to Mt. Greylock. Parts of the trail were narrow, almost like tunnels through the hardwood and spruce. How human the trees seemed! Old and gnarled, or youthfully supple; thickset, slender, balding, hirsute; some raucous in the wind, some whispering; many prolific with seed; a few diseased, waiting quietly for death. Such places always stirred an echo of Thoreau: *It is not their bones or hide or tallow that I love most . . . but the living spirit of the tree . . . it is as immortal as I am.*

The view from Greylock's summit held us. To the west, ridges plunged into ravines; to the east there were wide ribbons of hills; deep valleys reached north and south. In our immediate vicinity there was a huge fenced-in stone monument, with an eternal light on top, honoring the Massachusetts war dead. Here, too, was Bascom Lodge, an old building, big and rambling, faced with stone and weathered shingles. Here, for a brief moment, we lived in style of a sort, eating chicken cacciatore and sleeping in actual beds. Consensus: for us, style was not only too expensive, but it didn't seem to fit us, either. By 6:30 the next morning, we were on the trail again. Coming off Greylock we were hailed by two hikers camped in a blueberry field near the trail. They had seen us at the lodge and were waiting for us. We gathered round and toasted each other with wine, which was heady fare so early in the morning.

At the next shelter we overtook Jay Smith, whose name we had seen in the registers. He had left Katahdin a week before we did and the blackflies had nearly eaten him alive. Now he was taking his time, trying to get healed. How we could sympathize! Farther along the trail we met a Mr. Herring, 66 years old, hiking alone from Georgia to Maine. Stalwart folk, these backpackers!

Next day, after going through Dalton, we ran onto more of the bushes, six to eight feet in height, that we had thought would bear juicy pears. We now saw that they were highbush blueberries, the likes of which we had never seen! We picked and ate our fill. On a steeply descending section of trail Bump tripped over a rock. Down he went and down he stayed. His pack probably weighed 45 to 50 pounds and it held him flat. Looking like a derailed train, he glowered at me. "For @!#*! Help me *up!*"

"I will if you stop raving," I said, trying not to laugh.

"Dammit, Margaret, it's not funny!"

"You'd think it was if you could see yourself." I giggled until finally he began to laugh, too.

"OK, it's funny," he agreed. "Now get me out of this."

"And you were going to keep me out of trouble," I said, pulling at his pack.

We had magnificent weather, clear and warm, through the Berkshires of western Massachusetts. I began to catch myself singing bits and pieces of *Mountain Greenery*. One nice day we had lunch with Mrs. Hutchinson, a kind lady who spends her summers in a circa 1811 farmhouse near the trail, often feeding Appalachian Trail hikers. We camped overnight by beautiful Finerty Pond, but later learned that it was a public water supply and definitely taboo as a camping spot. We crossed Mt. Wilcox and went down and across the Housatonic River. We had several 20-mile days, took coffee and cookies with an artist from Greece, and climbed up and down, mostly up, over Jacobs Ladder Highway. On Bump's birthday, August 6, we were in Connecticut. Bear Mountain was our first climb that day. At the top I saluted my 42-year-old husband. "Happy Birthday to the Old Man of the Mountain!" I shouted. He was beginning to look the part, slightly stooped against the weight of his pack, one big hand clenched around his moosewood walking stick, his gray whiskers shaping into a beard. Jokingly, I said, "You don't look a day over a hundred."

"For that *you* get to start the stove and make the coffee tomorrow morning."

"Oh, I didn't mean it," I said, with mock contrition. "You'd pass for fifty easy."

"I *feel* about twenty," he roared, "so you'd better look out!"

Speed being the better part of discretion, I moved right along down the mountain. Later, in Salisbury, I bought him a birthday present— six Three Musketeers candy bars, his favorite, and a pound of brown sugar. A little sweetening never hurts.

We went through the hushed majesty of Cathedral Pines, with the sun slanting on a quiet needled carpet. It was like being in a church that had no need of doors or statues or preaching. We went over mountains and more mountains, not terribly high, but there. We reached Red Mountain Lean-to and a dry spring. We were hot, thirsty, and tired during the two-mile backtrack to a brook, but our faith was renewed when a man from New York gave us his 2½-gallon collapsible plastic water jug. We reached Cornwall and had a long telephone conversation with Steve. Then we went up to Coltsfoot Mountain and through Dark Entry Ravine, with its clean pure water splashing over ledges and its stands of pine. We went along the ever-changing Housatonic, its docile expanses and its rapids edged with maple and oak. In Macedonia Brook State Park the beech and hemlock and thick hardwood groves threaded with streams might have been Long-fellow's forest primeval. All along the way the generosity of strangers spurred new appreciation of such simple things as water and fresh fruit and friendly smiles.

On August 10 we crossed the New York state line and headed for Rattlesnake Den and Schaghticoke Mountain. We had expected to find these mountains crawling with snakes. So far, to our great pleasure, we had seen none. We attributed their absence to the intense heat and aridity, figuring that animals with better sense than ours were moving to the valleys and water. Passing an Explorer Science Boy Scout camp, we were invited in for a grand tour and lunch. Experiments on rats were being conducted; there was a pervasive etherish odor about the place. The extreme heat didn't help, either, and from the look on Bump's face, I expected to see him slide to the floor in a dead faint at any moment! We camped that night by privately owned Quaker Lake, near a game preserve, and listened to the sporadic snorting and blowing of deer.

Long hot days followed. Some days were spent predominantly on highways; others were a mixture of tough climbing and easy walking in the rolling farm country. At Pawling, we bought supplies and tele-phoned home; then we went on past green fields with Black Angus cattle in them. A big grayish-black bull snake, rearing out of a ditch in front of us, kept me marching in the rear flank thereafter. A stretch of beautiful countryside was being scraped and bulldozed into a high-way. Progress? I wondered. We took one afternoon off to accept an invitation from a fellow camper who was also a writer, piling into his Volkswagen bus and riding to Peekskill, a little old-fashioned town where *Hello, Dolly* had been filmed. That evening I did a little tailor-ing, cutting the legs off my jeans and using the salvaged cloth to patch my worn-out shorts. Now I had two pairs of shorts instead of none; a whole new wardrobe!

By August 14, when we had been on the trail two months, we were leaving the shelters very early in an effort to beat the heat. One morning we walked across the Bear Mountain Bridge over the Hudson

River. At the other end of the bridge we were confronted by a rather cranky looking fellow. "You just cross the bridge?" he asked testily.

"How do you think we got here?" Bump wanted to know.

The man scowled. "Ten cents."

Right.

At the entrance to Bear Mountain State Park we were confronted again by the long arm of authority. "Can't go in yet. Isn't nine o'clock."

Turnstiles and stop watches. Life measured in dimes and minute hands. *Do you know,* I wanted to shout, *that we have walked through hundreds of miles of timelessness? Do you know there is another life out there where you have mountains for breakfast and trees for friends and nine o'clock means nothing?* Instead of shouting I bit my tongue and kept the peace.

"We'll go around, then," Bump said, and we did. Farther on we came down into the park. There were no signs or blazes, and we were not sure of just where we were. There was a tourist area, a huge parking lot, an inn and souvenir stand, and a small police station.

"We'll go in and ask where the trail is," Bump decided.

I looked at him for a long moment. "Are you going to leave your pack outside?"

He shook his head. "Wouldn't want them to think I have something to hide."

In we went. There seemed to be policemen all over the place. We explained our problem and the desk sergeant answered our question. "You're on the Appalachian Trail right now," he said pleasantly.

"Good enough," Bump said, turning to leave. "Thanks a lot."

The sergeant's voice stopped us cold. "You come all this way without weapons?"

Bump laughed, slapping his hip. "No, sir. Got my hunting knife right here."

The sergeant looked steadily at us and finally nodded. "Okay." As we left, I tried not to think about the loaded .38-caliber revolver in Bump's pack.

During the day we saw several deer moving gracefully through the shade of the trees, and several people lolling about, some clothed, some not. At one spot there was a young fellow, naked as a jay, sitting on a rock. Bump coughed and the boy scrambled out of sight, reappearing with his trousers on. Some of the other nudists sat about, apparently nonplussed by our presence, chatting, offering small talk.

The next day we went off the trail to Monroe, resupplied, and came back again to heat that wouldn't quit and ridges that I thought would never end. On August 17 we left New York State behind, and I was glad. On Bearfort Mountain in New Jersey we had a wild thunderstorm, followed by refreshing cool air and the discovery of crunchy apples growing near our campsite. At High Point State Park we met a young couple with an infant who had driven up to spend an afternoon in the park. They made sandwiches for us, and bologna was a marvelous change from the peanut butter we had been eating for what seemed like 50 out of the 49 days we had been on the trail. When they left they gave us their leftovers—tomatoes, cupcakes, soda pop. We shared an extra sandwich and a Coke with David Shariff, a high school student who had hiked up from Harpers Ferry and planned to leave the trail at High Point and take a bus home. David had topographical maps covering the area he had traveled and he offered them to us. Through Pennsylvania and Maryland we would know where we were!

We moved due south along Kittatinny Mountain. We were on the ridge crest most of the time and our feet, in boots with the soles worn thin, were beginning to complain. The weather remained indulgent, though, helping us make good time. I experienced a moment's disillusionment at one of the familiar Appalachian Trail signs. This one read: MAINE 927 MILES—SPRINGER MOUNTAIN, GEORGIA 1,673 MILES.

"No matter how you add it," I said, "it comes up 2,600. That's almost 600 extra miles!"

"Well, there's been a mistake somewhere, so don't get your fluffer down," Bump said.

"All right," I said wearily. "But I'm going to set it down temporarily pretty soon. My feet are sore." They surely were and Bump's were, too. We would have to get new boots soon.

On August 20 we had 20-odd miles of rocky climbing over Rattlesnake Mountain and Mt. Mohican. We passed Sunfish Pond where the area was strewn with scantily clad people in variegated clusters of blacks and whites, to all appearances stoned on something. We went down through a deep ravine and finally, late in the afternoon, came to the Delaware Water Gap. This must be where the word breathtaking was coined. We were struck by the beauty of it, with the Delaware River, blue and sandy-beached, gently curving between the steep rocky walls of mountains rising over a thousand feet on either side.

On the opposite shore was Pennsylvania and the little village of Delaware Water Gap. Near the bridge we stopped at a ranger station and telephoned the Gourmleys, the couple we had met in Vermont. They were full of congratulations, and although over a hundred miles away, were determined to drive from Trenton and take us out for a meal. We waited, chatting with the ranger and his wife, drinking iced tea and listening to stories about the wild doings of some of the colony we had seen around Sunfish Pond. When the Gourmleys arrived they took us to an all-night restaurant in Stroudsburg.

It was nearly three o'clock in the morning when we got back to the Gap. Our benefactors dropped us at the Bridgeview Rooming House because it was on the trail. Like everything else in the village, it was buttoned up tight. We sat on the front porch and watched the early light grow into day. Around six o'clock a very nice Mrs. Jones discovered us and we rented a room. After naps, real soak-in-the-tub baths, and shampoos, we had breakfast and then took a bus to Stroudsburg to purchase new shoes. Having exhausted $400 in traveler's checks we went into a bank to cash the personal check Steve had sent us. The teller's eyes went slowly from Bump to me and back to Bump. His expression said, "You've got to be kidding!" When we tried to explain the situation we were promptly referred to another man who put us on hold and disappeared. There we sat, bearded and pigtailed, a little ragged around the edges and more than a little out of place in the stuffily plush surroundings. Bump said, "Maybe it would have been simpler just to rob the place."

"I think that's exactly what they expected us to do!"

Finally another man arrived. More discussion. Identification? Bump's driver's license had expired back in Connecticut. Eyebrows raised at me. Illogical, I suppose, but I was becoming annoyed. "I walk," I said. "Don't need a license for that. Yet."

The man scratched his balding head. "Well, I don't know—"

"Listen," Bump said, "couldn't you just call our bank in Bucksport, Maine?"

"No," he interrupted, holding up a hand. "No, I think we'll do it. We'll cash it." Benevolent smile.

Bump nodded, "Thank you. Thank you very much."

I kept quiet, which was an exorbitant price for me to pay even for new boots! We went shopping and the salesman, although he didn't have the boots we wanted, did have a friend who worked for the *Pocono Tribune*. The result was an account of our trip and our picture taken for the newspaper. We finally found boots in an army surplus store. They were like the old ones, leather moccasin-toe hunting boots. I also bought a T-shirt to replace the stained and rotted one I was wearing.

Back at the rooming house we were surprised to see Tex, our friend from Glastenbury Mountain. Teasing still, his first crack was, "Hey,

Maggie, say *dipper* for me!" He was camped on Mt. Minsi and had heard about us at the restaurant where we had eaten earlier. We had a good visit and promised to stop by his campsite. After supper we started for Tex's camp. The higher up Minsi we went, the more fantastic the view became. This was leisure hiking at its best. When we finally came to Tex's campsite, a snug little bower on the mountain, we found him stretched out on his bedroll fast asleep. We didn't have the heart to wake him. Returning to the village, we crawled into bed for a long night's rest. Tomorrow's mountain was waiting.

We climbed up and out of the Delaware Water Gap onto Blue Mountain and went on to Wind Gap. Here we found a fine spring and an ideal campsite. While we were scouting for the best place for our tent, we came upon a small grave with fresh flowers on it. The words *Hi Punkin* were written on a piece of broken slate. Suddenly everything seemed very still. The power of imagination! We looked slowly around us. Off to one side was a fireplace with an open can of meat on the grate. On the other side there was a tarp, with boughs beneath it. I looked at Bump. Puzzled, he shrugged his shoulders. "We might as well eat."

I couldn't shake the feeling that someone was watching me. Just as I was finishing my sandwich I noticed the sneakers, a huge pair neatly placed beside the tarp. They must have been size 12, at least. That did it for me. We picked up and moved on, and eventually were forced to set up camp near a highway, where the distant buzz of traffic disturbed the stillness of the night.

In Pennsylvania we had rocky climbing with rain and rocky climbing with heat, and rocky climbing with high humidity. The rocks plus the new boots equaled tender feet, but the knowledge that we were halfway to our goal gave us new determination and kept us going. At the Allentown Hiking Club Shelter we found the spring dry and discovered that we had lost the key to our stove. At a highway diner the lady in charge asked if we were Mr. and Mrs. Smith. We confessed that we were. She said that about an hour earlier two boys had been looking for us. One had been a redhead; the other had light-colored long hair. Steve and Ken! We realized the boys must be hitchhiking, and a truck driver on a neighboring stool volunteered to drive to the intersection and look for them. When he returned shaking his head, the woman's husband drove farther down the highway. Kind gestures, but to no avail. The boys were gone. We could only hope that we would see them when we reached the next town.

At Dans Spring we tented, preferring the tent to the wire bunks in the shelters along this stretch of trail. Babying our sore feet with shorter days and longer nights, we limped into Port Clinton on August 27. We called home and verified the fact that Steve and a friend had hitchhiked to Pennsylvania hoping to see us. We asked around in the village but no one had seen them. Disappointed, we bought supplies and pushed on.

At Neys Shelter we had lunch and an informative chat with Mr. Ney. Probably in his late seventies, he said he hiked up to this shelter almost every day. His family's homestead had been here, but the land had been sold to the state and was now used as a game propagation and hunting area. He told us that long ago, before Ox Spring had its present concrete housing, a young ox had stumbled into the deep spring and drowned, hence the name. He also talked about snakes. Years ago rattlesnake meat was cured, he said, and the residual fat and oil used as a medicine for earache. Timber rattlers and copperheads were now hunted for sport. "And don't let anybody tell you snakes don't climb trees! One day I watched a great big feller haul himself right up a tree and into a hole, slick as you please." I shuddered, just thinking about it.

Later that same day when we saw our first timber rattler, I didn't shudder—I froze. We heard him rattling and halted in midstep. There he was, a monstrous thing, as thick as my forearm and perhaps six or seven feet long. Crossing in front of us, he seemed to reach from one side of the road to the other! When we began to breathe again, Bump said, "Like Maine moose, aren't they? Just give them the right-of-way." They could have it and welcome, as far as I was concerned.

We came to Rausch Gap and then to an abandoned village where building foundations and wells had apparently been buried long ago by rock slides. There must have been a recent windstorm as well, for the surrounding vegetation was bent to the ground and many of the trees had been violently uprooted and flattened. All told, the place had an eerie chilling effect on us, and we didn't dawdle.

Stony Mountain was appropriately christened. We decided there must be more rocky terrain in Pennsylvania than in all the other states combined. We were through Clarks Creek Valley and coming up to the Earl Shaffer Shelter when we heard gunfire. Thinking we were being shot at, Bump yelled. Two boys appeared, guns in hand. They had been target shooting. They asked if there was anything they could do for us.

"Sure is," Bump said. "Got a pair of pliers you don't need?"

They were happy to oblige. Within moments they presented us

with the needle-nosed pliers they used for tinkering on their Volkswagen and we had a new key for our stove. We dined rather well on beef Stroganoff and Kool-Aid while a storm built up around us. We opted for the shelter, but it leaked like the proverbial sieve. We were awake most of the night, watching the lightning strike and dodging raindrops.

At dawn it was clearing, cool, and breezy. We went along the beautiful Susquehanna River using a small branch with leaves on it to brush away the hundreds of webs spun across the trail by spiders. We picked up supplies in the village of Duncannon and went on past Cove Mountain and Conodoguinet Creek into the Cumberland Valley. At a fruit and vegetable stand near Churchtown the proprietor insisted that we help ourselves to anything we wanted. We gratefully loaded up on plums. At a dairy bar the kids laughed at Bump's ragged pants, but we ignored them as we stuffed ourselves with ice cream and milk shakes. Unable to find Dark Hollow Shelter, we camped beside a peaceful brook. Over breakfast Bump complained about the coffee-soaked edges of his mustache. I fished out my all-purpose sewing scissors. A little dull, but they would do.

He inched backward. "Don't know if it bothers me *that* much."

"Only take a minute," I said, starting to snip.

"Ouch! That pulls!"

"Sit still and be quiet."

Snip, snip. Again the *ouch*.

"There. See? Told you it wouldn't take long."

"Good thing it didn't." He gingerly put his fingers to it. "You're a beautician by trade. Do you make all of your customers yell?"

"Of course not," I said, "but I don't do many mustaches."

As we were leaving I noticed a funny little stick attached to a tree trunk. As I watched, it began to move! Obviously it was some kind of living thing, one with which we were totally unfamiliar. We began to keep an eye out for these little sticks and saw many more of them. Our cool weather, good for walking, was heating up again. We passed South Mountain, Piney Mountain, and Pine Grove Furnace Park. The Pine Grove furnace was constructed of stone and had been used at one time for smelting lead. As usual, we were most aware of the trees in the park. What was there about a stand of mature pine that made me feel so good? Tall and straight, enduring the passage of years with quiet strength, they were like men grown old with time's buffeting, somehow stronger and more resolute for the experience. Walking in the woods was conducive to such introspection. On this point my husband and I were in complete accord. The only time he glanced at me as if I'd been in the sun too long was when I compared the personality of a particular tree with the personality of some person we'd known.

On September 5 we were still following the ridge of South Mountain when we entered the state of Maryland. About noontime we stopped at a fish and game installation and were invited to lunch. The men were very kind and helpful, but their Southern accent was so heavy I had difficulty in understanding them. Bump managed, though, and assimilated enough information so that farther on, confronted by a roadside telephone and a PLEASE CALL FOR CLEARANCE sign, we knew we were passing Camp David. Should we have elected not to dial the prescribed numbers and check in, there was a possibility that we would be picked up and interrogated. We called.

Just beyond Greenbrier Park we met Tom and Ruta Rose and accepted a kind invitation to stay at their farm for the night. How gratifying it was to meet such friendly and helpful people, who accepted us as we were, for what we were. We had barbecued steaks with all the trimmings. *Ohhh!* And melon. I knew I was being piggish, but I couldn't stop eating the melon. You have a new appreciation for the flavor and just plain *goodness* of a food when you haven't tasted it for a long time. Tom, a science professor at Hood College in Frederick, telephoned a fellow teacher, a hiker who had walked many sections of the trail. The teacher turned out to be none other than Miss Willis, the lady with the little red lantern at Jerome Brook back in Maine! How nice it was to see her again! She brought us maps, told us where to look for the springs, and advised us to take an 8- to 10-day supply of freeze-dried foods for our hike through the Smokies.

In the morning the Roses took snapshots they would send to Steve. It wasn't long after we were back on the trail that my stomach started giving me the business. Too much melon? In Washington Monument State Park we stopped to talk with another couple and their children. They wanted to feed us, but for once I couldn't eat a thing. Incredible! We thanked them, and as we were leaving Bump shook the fellow's hand. They were a black family and the man looked at Bump with surprise. He said, "You're the first white man to shake my hand in seven or eight years!" It was a sad commentary and I could think of no adequate response. Perhaps there was none.

After five or six more miles I was feeling nauseous and light-headed. We had stopped along the trail to rest when we heard a terrible squawking racket. Buzzards! We watched them, two black, red-wattled, scrawny-necked buzzards fighting in the top of a tree.

Holding my stomach, I asked, "Do you think they know something I don't?"

Bump laughed. "The winner gets to pick your bones!" I quickly became ambulatory. A few more miles put us in Gathland State Park and we decided to stop. It was a small park, clean and well kept. I was too miserable to enjoy it properly, so I eased myself into bed. Next day the park ranger urged us to stay, offering us the softest piece of ground he had. He also wanted to take me to a hospital, but I assured him I wasn't that ill. After we had left the park we realized we were being followed. A basset hound, long ears flopping, was trailing along behind us. We told him to go back, but nothing doing. It began to look as if we had been adopted.

Through the morning I had intermittent nausea and sporadic attacks of diarrhea. Oh, how I cursed my greediness! At last we were in sight of the Potomac. It was dirty and edged with campers. In Sandy Hook the basset took an abrupt left turn and trotted off down the street. I watched him go, hoping he was as sure of his destination as he seemed to be.

We climbed high to cross the bridge, then skirted Harpers Ferry. My head continued its spinning spells. Along a narrow path I saw and felt it all at once—*a copperhead was striking my boot at about ankle height!*

I yelled, and then Bump had a pole and was beating the snake. At last it was dead. The copperhead had a strong odor; to us it smelled like cucumber. Bump notched the copperhead's length on his walking stick and then tossed the lifeless snake into the bushes. The episode didn't help my nausea any, but we kept pushing along the ridge, having determined from earlier signs that we were traversing the Virginia–West Virginia boundary. At Keys Gap we stopped. I was too sick to travel farther. After settling me in, Bump left to find medicine. He was gone for a long time. Between dashes to the outhouse I flopped on my sleeping bag, gagging, fighting nausea, my head whirling. What if Bump got lost? What if he didn't get back? My head went round and round. After what seemed like hours, I heard him coming. He had some Pepto-Bismol, which I began taking immediately. We holed up the next day and night, and by the following morning I felt able to travel. A little woozy, but ready to go. Crossing a highway, we saw some men working on the road and Bump asked if they had a tape measure. It was a peculiar request, but one of the men pulled a steel tape measure out of his pocket and passed it over.

Bump measured his walking stick to the notch he had put on it to indicate the copperhead's length. 38¾ inches. "Thanks a lot," Bump said. He handed the tape back and we continued walking. They must have thought we were crazy.

We had warm weather and good trail. In the distance we caught glimpses of the famed Skyline Drive winding through the beautiful Blue Ridge Mountains. In the Shenandoah National Park the trail provided spectacular views. The mountains were distantly blue and always hazy. At Panorama we awarded our rather dubious patronage to a fancy restaurant where we had an elegant meal, punctuated by a few surreptitious glances and some openly disdainful stares from the other patrons. We used the telephone to call our respective mothers and left for the woods.

On September 13 we were at the Hawksbill Gap Shelter; we had been on the trail three months and still had 400 miles of trail through Virginia, not to mention many more miles through Tennessee, North Carolina, and Georgia. Water was becoming an increasingly scarce commodity and our funds were running low but we both felt we would overcome these inconveniences somehow. As we were leaving one waterless shelter, two hippies drove seven miles out of their way to take us to a store. Kindness comes in many guises and the trick is simply to accept it as offered.

Our plastic tubes had worn out; we now carried a mixture of peanut butter and jam in a margarine container. A couple of good swipes across a slice of bread, which was then topped with another slice, and a cup of Carnation instant milk provided some protein and was filling. We planned to hike off the trail and find a phone and call Jack Stewart at the University of Virginia. Steve was to have sent money and freeze-dried and dehydrated foods to Jack with instructions to hold it for us. It was one hike we didn't have to make. We fell to talking with some people from Alabama who were headed for Bar Harbor, Maine. They asked us if we had had enough of the trail. Did we want a ride home? They would drive us right to our own front door in Millvale. *Get thee behind me,* I thought. It was a temptation, but a small one. We thanked them and shook our heads. Well, what could they do to help? We told them about Jack Stewart and the food, and they took us to a telephone, gave Bump change to make the call, and waited for us. Bump came back shaking his head. "Mr. Stewart isn't in. I left word we'd call again from Rockfish Gap."

Money was going to be tight. On the drive back to our campsite the man from Alabama said, "If you need money I can let you have a hundred dollars."

Bump looked at him in surprise. "You don't know us. You might never get it back."

"Wouldn't be the first hundred dollars I ever gave away."

Such kindness made up for the occasional turned-up noses we had encountered. "Thank you. Thank you very much, but we'll manage. Really, we will," I said.

We went on and on. It was hot! A bandanna around my forehead kept some of the perspiration out of my eyes. We climbed, sweat-soaked. On Loft Mountain, we enjoyed baked potatoes, hamburgers, and salad with some wonderful people from Long Island. We passed up a lean-to that was already full and set up our tent near a spring. We tried to encourage a smoldering fire with a little gasoline and the result was a whooshing backfire that destroyed the container in which we carried our fuel.

Farther along, warned that there was no water at a shelter ahead, we hiked beyond it and at a ranger's recommendation set up camp in a NO CAMPING area which for some reason was called Dundo Campgrounds. Wary of bear, we hung our packs on the NO TENTING, NO CAMPING sign. It created an impression of rebellion as false as the name "campgrounds" was when it was used for a place where no camping was allowed. I kept a watch for bear, but didn't even see a track. There were a lot of deer, but they were paunchy and unhealthy looking. The food of park deer must differ greatly from the food of wild deer.

The next day we tramped on the highway and the heat was like a heavy pressure. Water was nil. As we plodded on our thirst became a real threat. We attempted to hail passing motorists but the only one who even slowed down shouted something unintelligible and hastily sped away. There was nothing to do but keep moving.

When I saw the water, I thought it must be a mirage. It was running from the piece of pipe sticking out of the roadside bank. We drank by turns, then filled our jug. A little later on night forced us off the road and into a rocky pasture. The accommodations weren't the best, but at least there was a vacancy. To have our breakfast served to us at a small restaurant in Rockfish Gap was a rare treat. Afterward we telephoned Jack Stewart and he brought our food and cash and took us to lunch. Just before entering the woods again we came upon a group of workingmen who were booted to the knees as a protection against snakes. They told us the section we were heading into

hadn't been cleared since hurricane Camille. One man looked pity-
ingly at us. "I wouldn't put my hound dog through where you're
going!"

It can't be that bad, I thought, but it was, with fallen trees, brush,
tangles of vines, and briers that grabbed our legs. And so hot! We
pitched the tent under the humid breath of a fast-approaching thunderstorm. We got the rain fly up just in time, and sat cross-legged
eating canned sardines while the storm snapped and stabbed at us.
Bump paused between sardines and looked at me. "Aren't we stupid?
Sitting here like two idiots when we could be home in a nice dry living room watching TV."

"So which is better?" I asked him. "Here or there?"

Indecision. Then, "Here."

After a night of rain the air was cooler next morning. Humpback
Mountain was a climb of over 3,000 feet, and we crossed others nearly
as high. After a night at Harpers Creek we went down to the Tye
River and over the bridge. Evidence of Camille's destruction could
still be seen in the tumble of boulders and the marks of floodwater
high up in the birches. Our food was running low as we climbed The
Priest, some 4,000 feet of mountain. We clambered over the ridges
of several other mountains and finally bedded down, only to arise
and start another day hungry and discouraged. We didn't know
where we would find the next store; we were only sure that we would
find a great many more mountains. In a picnic area we met a family
from Maryland who invited us to eat with them and told us where
to find a store about four miles off the trail. We went to the store
and restocked. When the owner of the store drove us back to the trail
we found a plastic bag full of shrimp packed in crushed ice. A postcard addressed TO THE HIKERS was attached. It told us the shrimp
were a gift from some people from West Virginia. It seemed that
whenever we were down, someone came along and gave us a boost.

It was hot again, and the mountains seemed to rise higher and become more demanding. One blistering afternoon, when we had been
without water for a long time, we came to a lean-to with a brook
running by it. Into the cool beautiful water we went! It was pure enjoyment. The lean-to was tucked into a stand of hemlock, and the
trees seemed like old friends from home. As we drifted into sleep,
listening to the splashing chatter of the brook, I remembered a line
from one of Loren Eiseley's books: *If there is magic on this planet,
it is contained in water.* At that moment I believed it.

On September 23 it was so hot that we had to force ourselves to
move. We crossed the James River and walked an extra mile or so

into the town of Snowden. I had developed a craving for candied orange slices comparable to the craving of an expectant mother. Bump bought some Elmer's glue to repair the loosening sole of his boot. At midday we stopped to rest at a shelter; the heat was taking its toll. Only the skink lizards had energy enough to skitter about. While I washed a few clothes, Bump whittled some fine shavings and mixed them with glue. With this mixture he fixed his ailing boot and placed it under the leg of a heavy picnic table to help set the glue.

We went through mountain laurel and stands of small fir and spruce; we went over great knolls filled with clutching briers and dotted with white rocks. Always about us was the bluish haze of distant mountains. We hiked through sun-scorched days that ebbed into magnificent sunsets and evenings cool enough to send us searching for dried laurel limbs for a fire. Shirts that clung damply to our bodies in the afternoon were dried stiff and white with salt by morning.

A man on a bread truck drove us to a store, then loaded us down with bread and rolls and doughnuts. Bonanza! Afterward we went down through ravines that were choked with weeds and vines. Everything was parched; I knew that in the event of a brush fire we would never make it out. At Fullhardt Knob we enjoyed the luxury of an artesian well, and found grapes to munch. Following the road one rainy morning we came to a truck stop near Troutville and went in for a cup of coffee. Perched on stools in the truckers' side of the place, we gave our order. The waitress frowned at Bump. "Are you driving a truck?"

"No, ma'am. I'm packing a pack."

Grinning, she directed us to the other side of the restaurant—the fancy side. We would have been more comfortable having our coffee with the truck drivers. The rain was still coming down and, unsure of shelters for the next 30 or 40 miles, we decided to splurge and stay in the motel. We enjoyed the hot showers, the big double beds, and walking barefoot on the thick carpet, but we didn't even turn the TV on. Later in the day we rode to a store with one of the truckers and bought food and a pint of Coleman fuel. That amount of fuel would last about six days.

There had been a distinct change in the weather when we left the motel and walked into the mountains. The air was chilly, nippy. We would need long pants soon. These were beautiful mountains, with huge rocks and views of trees, farms, factories, mills. From the top of Tinker Mountain we looked out over a lovely lake that, judging from the unnatural perfection of its edges, must have been man-made. We seemed to wind around and around it, first on one side, then on the other. Coming down off Catawba Mountain, on a stretch of shelf-like ledge, we watched a small plane. It circled, tipping its wings. We waved, feeling a communion with the pilot, and inexplicably, with the whole world.

We followed paths around giant pointed rocks and skirted wide crevices that looked eerily bottomless. The weather really was becoming cold and it felt good. Through the Skyline Drive area most of the shelter floors were of concrete and we had avoided them like the plague. Now we were finding wooden floors again, in lean-tos with steeply-pitched tin roofs and wide overhangs. At Niday Shelter, named for a family who had homesteaded here in 1865, we drew water from the same spring the Nidays had used and walked among gnarled trees from which they had gathered apples. We hiked along the same ridge that the Nidays' six children must have walked to school some hundred years ago. Here, at least, the land had not changed much.

In the little town of Huffman a kind lady in a store gave me a huge pair of long pants and a dozen eggs, all the while telling us of the copperheads that descended into the valley. She mentioned their cucumber odor, which we knew about from our experience at Harpers Ferry. A man told us our next lean-to would be dry, and advised us to stop at his uncle's place for water. We stopped as he advised at the Taylors' little farm, snugged against the foot of a mountain. They gave us a pair of pants for Bump, hot coffee, and 2½ gallons of cold water. We took turns carrying the water up the mountain.

On the first day of October we talked for a time with a slightly inebriated gentleman who was accompanied by his hound dog Maggie. I didn't tell him that was my nickname, too. With a thick tongue he explained the intricacies of making moonshine and said we weren't far from the spot where he once ran a still. He said I looked like an Indian, and I told him I was one. I tan quickly and by now my face and arms were a deep nut-brown. I suppose the coloring, coupled with rather high cheekbones and long black braids, fitted his image of an Indian, especially when viewed through rum-shot eyes across a campfire. Sometimes I wished I could lay claim to more than my one-eighth American blood, but in doing so now I seemed to have made the man uneasy; I wondered if he expected me to let fly with a tomahawk. In any event, he soon whistled for Maggie and moved unsteadily into the deepening shadows and was gone. A pity, I thought, that we so often see only stereotypes instead of individuals.

The mornings were cool but they warmed up nicely. The leaves displayed colorful hints of autumn. In Pearisburg I bought new boots, and we each got a pair of light gloves. Bump invested in insulated underwear and I settled for long pants that fit. I had found that extremely loose-fitting clothes were as uncomfortable as clothes that were too tight. Tired of drinking from a tin cup, I bought a china coffee mug. Bump had carried his coffee mug all the way from Maine without breaking it; with any luck at all I thought I might make it the rest of the way to Georgia. Guided by a card left in a lean-to by Ed Garvey, we went to Mary Finley's rooming house in Pearisburg. The lady was just leaving for the beauty shop when we arrived. "Go right in and make yourselves at home," she urged us. Price? Two dollars each. Mr. Garvey had known what he was recommending when he said it was a clean and economical place.

In the morning we climbed Pearis Mountain and went on to Sugar Run Gap and Sugar Run Mountain. It was a comparatively easy day except that my feet were sensitive because of the new boots. The weather was cool, and the trail went by black walnut trees and yellow birches. At Dismal Creek Lean-to that night we were awakened by the cold, and what a frosty morning! At a store in the next settlement we were told it had been cold enough for ice to form. They gave us hot coffee and told us that the Dismal Creek Lean-to hadn't been used for months because the area was so thickly infested with snakes. We hadn't seen any snakes, but perhaps they had been all around us? I had a case of belated shivers. It was 20 miles to Turkey Gap Shelter. On Walker Mountain, at 3,900 feet, the lookout tower offered spectacular views and great opportunities for picture taking. We spent one night at Walker Mountain Lean-to and another at Killinger Creek, with the day in between being incredibly mountainous. We stopped at a village called Teas for groceries. Back on trail we headed for Cherry Tree Lean-to. There had been a little false advertising here—the tree beside the lean-to was a crab apple.

In Damascus, a small town sitting in a bowl in the mountains, we located a good rooming house, thanks to another card Ed Garvey had posted in a lean-to. The cost at Mrs. Keebler's was $2.50 per couple per night. At the post office we picked up lots of mail that had finally caught up with us. It was good to hear from so many relatives and friends. We decided to make a two-day stop and lazied around, taking full advantage of the bathtub and the bed, rereading our mail, and even watching a little television. The next day my diehard Yankee husband got his shoes resoled and we did our shopping. On both days we ate almost constantly, although since my melon fiasco I had been trying to control myself. Before we went to sleep that night we got into a discussion of "what we should have had" and "what we should have done." Hindsight is an amazing faculty.

"We should have had a double sleeping bag," Bump said. "Think of the lost body heat."

I agreed. "But who would have carried it?"

"I would, of course," he said generously. "At least half the time anyway."

"We should have had good raingear," I said. "Something light but durable, not tearing on every little twig. And waterproof pack covers."

"Right. And we really should have had the tent and stove to start with. We made out okay, but they would have been nice."

"How about maps?" I asked. "They would have been nice, too."

Bump pooh-poohed that. "Now, how many times have we been lost?"

"Plenty!" I exclaimed. "As soon as we left Maine—"

"Oh, it hasn't been that bad. Those topographical maps are fine, but you'd need a mule train to carry them."

"I'd like to stop at a shelter or come to a road and have some idea of how far it is to a store—and know what direction to take!"

"And miss all that adventure?"

"Some adventure!"

"Seriously, though—a better arrangement for money is what we really should have had. But all in all, we haven't done too badly, have we?"

"No." I twisted in the bedclothes, wondering if I would have to relearn sharing a bed with my husband. "But we've been lucky," I said, remembering that we had suffered no snakebites, no sprains, no broken bones. Would we continue to be lucky? Growing sleepy I rolled over, taking my share of the blankets with me and making Bump complain. "We have about four hundred more miles of mountains, including the Smokies," I said. The Smokies. I fell asleep to dream of those mountains.

On October 10 we went up Holston Mountain and hiked the mountain crest in the Cherokee National Forest and the state of Tennessee. Each time we crossed a state line it seemed like a momentous occasion. Nearing Double Springs Gap Lean-to at dusk, we saw a big bonfire. As we came closer we could see three men, all wearing sidearms. What now? We went ahead to the lean-to and in five minutes Bump had become fast friends with Elmer Jones and his two boys. They were in the mountains gathering ginseng roots, which they told us could be sold for $50 a pound. The pistols were for protection from snakes.

The Jones boys gave us their leftover supper beans and treated us to candy. We all sat around the fire and talked awhile. Checking out the lean-to I found a dirt floor with wall-to-wall chicken wire about a foot above the ground, and several fleeing mice. Could we sleep in here with the Joneses? Thinking of the snakes outside, I decided we should try. From experience we knew that the custom in wire-bed sleeping is for every other sleeper to reverse his direction, so that there is a head, then feet, then a head, and so on. This seems to keep the whole precarious business somewhat stabilized. We rolled out our sleeping bags. The Joneses had burlap bags. Not wanting to sleep near the wall because of the rats and mice, I ended up with my head between two pairs of feet, Bump's and Elmer's. It was impossible to get upwind of everybody. Oh, well, I thought. You can't have everything. It was a night of snoring and scratching sounds; one person rolling over jiggled four others; mice scampered indiscriminately across the lot of us. I slept with my head tucked into the sleeping bag and the first thing I saw when I emerged in the morning was a tiny mouse sitting on Elmer's shoulder. Hiking surely makes strange bedfellows.

We joined Elmer and his boys for a breakfast of Spam and eggs, then moved out. We followed the crest of Holston Mountain for a long time, then there was Locust Knob, Iron Mountain, and Turkeypen Gap. We spent a night on a mountaintop overlooking Watauga Lake. The moon was full and we stood on a huge rock near our lean-to and looked down on the sleeping village. The scene, the smell of the night, and the sharp fleeting sense of being a part of everything that ever had been or ever would be brought quick stinging tears to my eyes.

We had rough climbing on the steep ascent to Iron Mountain, then we went along the crest and down the south slope and caught a ride to a store with a forest ranger. We passed the time of day with a man whose front porch was almost on the trail; he raised pigs, feared copperheads, and gave us water. In Laurel Fork a gas station proprietor gave us free Cokes. "Mister," he said to Bump, "you got one helluva woman!"

In Laurel Gorge we came to what must be the most beautiful spot in all of Tennessee. Laurel Fork Lean-to was in a shady gorge with abundant rhododendron and mountain laurel and a stream that plunged and splashed over rocks. During the night we heard a bobcat howling in the distance. Sunlight streamed into the gorge in the

morning, highlighting the leaves, playing on the water. It was a place
I would like to come back to in early summer to see it alive with
blossoms.

We had tough going as we scrambled up White Rocks Mountain.
It was an appropriate monument for the end of our fourth month on
the trail. We stopped at a little country store for candy bars and were
warned that it was dangerous to hike in the Roan Mountain area,
particularly Grassy Ridge, when it was foggy. We went up and down,
into gaps and over tote roads. Occasionally, as in the past, one of us
would stay at a blaze while the other went ahead to search for the
next one. We put up the tent in an apple orchard which was fine
until the middle of the night when it began to rain and the wind blew
so hard I thought it would tear up the tent and us with it. We rolled
up our bags, pulled down the tent, and ran to a rickety apple shed
for shelter. As soon as we were inside we got our stove going and then
sat on crates under the space blanket and dozed fitfully for the rest
of the night.

By daybreak the rain had stopped and we left for the highway. The
first town we hit was a perfect picture of the Old West. It proved to
be Elk Park, North Carolina, so evidently we had crossed the state
line somewhere. We located a good rooming house, run by an elderly
couple named Trivitt. That evening the Trivitts left for church and
Bump went to the store. I was happy not to move and stayed behind,
sitting in the parlor with a gentleman roomer, watching television.
The man was busy doing something with leather and gimp, and for
a very welcome change I was busy doing absolutely nothing. When
Bump returned a conversation started. It seldom takes Bump long
to get acquainted. He expressed interest in the man's work and he
produced a sample of the finished product—a handsome leather
wallet.

"Beautiful. Where in the world did you learn to do that?"

"In the pen," the man replied.

The rest of the conversation was lost to me as I pondered the potential danger of having sat alone with a man who had been imprisoned in a penitentiary for who knows what. I watched him working diligently as he talked with Bump, and soon I was disgusted with
my own foolishness. There sat a man, a person—not a rioting mob of
hardened criminals. Before we retired Bump had been given a fine
handworked wallet.

Bacon, eggs, hot biscuits—*mmm!* After breakfast we started toward
the fog-shrouded Roan Mountain area we had been warned about.
It didn't look too bad, and we didn't want to waste a day, but what
climbing! First the Hump, up 5,587 feet into wind and fast-moving

clouds; then Bradley Gap, 4,960; Yellow Mountain Gap, 4,682; Grassy Ridge, 6,189. When we finally stopped for the night we knew we had been somewhere!

Grassy Ridge Lean-to was cold and wet. There was a good spring, but we could find very little wood. Everything was damp from the fog, which was so thick I half-expected to hear squawking sea gulls. We spent a miserably cold night, and in the morning we were still fogged in, with the wind cold and our scanty wood supply wet. We managed a feeble fire and put up the space blanket for protection from the wind, but still we couldn't get warm. The fog made it difficult to see the trail, but we were too miserable to stay where we were. We decided that anything was preferable to sitting around freezing so we started out, scarcely able to see our hands before us. The wind was fierce, driving the fog. We walked through the famous Roan Mountain rhododendron gardens but could see nothing but a big sign. After 17 miles of ups and downs we stopped at Cherry Gap. It was cold and there was not a cherry tree in sight but at least our equipment was reasonably dry and there was plenty of wood. We kept a fire going all night.

It was 22 miles to No Business Knob Lean-to and by the time we reached it we had crossed ridges, knobs, slopes with herds of saddle horses, and barbed-wire fences that ran right to the mountaintops. I swapped my T-shirt, which was full of holes, for a better one that had been abandoned and hung on the wall of the lean-to. We crossed more mountains, many in the 5,000-foot category. The weather was cold but we saw beautiful leaves of many colors as we hiked. A kind-hearted farmer took us to a store and offered to let us stay in his barn. We accepted gratefully, sharing the barn with his white-faced Herefords. We put up the tent inside the barn, banked it with bales of hay, and sat toasty warm eating honey buns and canned black-eyed peas.

The Pisgah National Forest, with its hills and gaps and mountain folk, was hiking country that reminded me of the book *Christy*. In Devil Fork Gap we were invited into a shanty by a woman and her brother, both chewing tobacco, both eager to do something for us. The woman took a box of raisins from a meagerly stocked shelf and insisted that we take them. She then pressed two pot holders into my hand. Impoverished as they were, these people's need to give was greater than their need to possess.

We passed Flint Creek Gap, Gravel Knob, and Big Butt. It rained but we were dry and warm in a cozy lean-to with an inside fireplace.

Photos by Elmer L. Onstott

Laurel Fork Gorge, Tennessee.

Copperhead snake near Pine Grove Furnace, Pennsylvania.

Photo courtesy Elmer L. Ons

Elmer Onstott in White Mountains. Photo made with self-timer.

Then came Bald Mountain, Bearwallow Gap, and more rain. At Allen Gap we found a store and selected supplies to the beat of country and western music. Paying, Bump said to the cashier, "You've sure got some pretty mountains in North Carolina."

"What's the matter with the mountains in Tennessee?" she asked pleasantly.

"Not a thing. Why?"

"Well, that's where you are right now."

We had been crisscrossing between the states of North Carolina and Tennessee. Outside, I gave Bump the elbow. "Next time you hand out a compliment find out what country you're in first!"

Buzzard Roost Ridge, Deep Gap, Spring Mountain, all dismal with rain. Dry out, eat, sleep, get up and do it again. In a Hot Springs hardware store we talked with a man who raised tobacco. He showed us a picture of himself with his prizewinning crop, and gave us some tobacco leaves to send home. Glancing at the cigarette in Bump's hand, he said, "You wouldn't smoke it if you knew what was in it."

Through the gap, over Bluff Mountain; climb, climb, climb. Higher and higher. On the way up the mountain to a lean-to we saw packs hanging in a tree. When we reached the lean-to we found a man and his two young sons. They were the owners of the packs and had left their gear behind in order to make it up the mountain. They must have overestimated their physical condition or pushed too hard, or both, because they were totally exhausted and had decided to cancel the rest of their trip and take a bus home to Indiana.

For a couple of days we seemed to climb steadily through autumn foliage that surpassed anything a painter could ever put on canvas. At long last, on October 24, we were in the Great Smoky Mountains National Park. We stopped at the Davenport Gap Lean-to, the first in the park. Across the front of the lean-to there was heavy chain link fencing with a gate that could be kept closed and bolted. It was put there to keep bear out of the shelter. Garbage was not supposed to be carelessly tossed aside here, as we had seen it in some places. Such precautions led us to believe that bear were as prevalent in the Smokies as moose had been in Maine. Surely we would see a bear, at least I hoped so.

As the lean-tos would be close together through the Smokies, and as we could expect the cold weather to have a numbing effect on snakes, we decided we no longer needed the tent. In any case, with its waterproofing worn off, our once reliable home on the trail had become pretty much deadweight. When the men with whom we were sharing the lean-to offered to pack our tent out to a post office and send it home for us, we let it go.

The Great Smoky Mountains National Park, with crests of 6,000 feet and more, has been etched by the waters and winds of centuries. We passed Rocky Face Mountain, Camel Hump Knob, and Mt. Guyot— a 15-mile stretch and uphill all the way. Tri-Corner Knob Lean-to was built into a soggy bank and oozed dampness. We were sharing the lean-to with a man from Ohio who was obviously at home in his surroundings, and a couple from New York, who just as obviously were not. Bump and the Ohioan went after wood and came back dragging a fir tree. Bump put it against the bank and jumped on it to break it into usable lengths. Wanting to be a part of the scene, the New Yorker offered his services. Unable to resist some fun, Bump pulled the tree down a little too far, so it would bend instead of break. The New Yorker gave a great arm-swinging leap onto the fir—and bounced off like a big rubber ball. When he regained his balance and his composure he laughed almost as hard as the rest of us did. The New Yorker had seen Bump start a fire in our little gasoline stove and insisted that he give it a try. He dumped about half of the fuel from the stove on the ground and with studied nonchalance tossed a lighted match on it. *KaWHOOM!* Backward off his log he went, scattering a pile of pots and pans. It was like the Keystone Cops turned loose in the woods!

We went over Mt. Sequoyah and Eagle Rocks and through gaps and around the sides of mountains. Unlike the Blue Ridge with its profusion of side trails and fire roads, there was but one path to follow here. We went through spruce and fir and colorful hardwoods and around the starkly treeless Charlies Bunion. Newfound Gap was a popular tourist stop, and near the gap we came upon a nature study group. Some of the members eyed us as if we were new and strange specimens.

We had long since learned that the best assurance of a quiet uncrowded spot was to find a place that couldn't be reached by automobile. People who won't go to a place if they can't drive to it don't know what they are missing. Roadside picnic areas are sometimes nice and drive-in campgrounds are sometimes fine, but they both often attract people who bring a noisy transistorized world with them. To turn your back on the macadamized beehives and go into the forest, to walk the quiet footpaths and hear nothing but bird songs and animal sounds, to see the colors, the shapes of trees and mountain streams, is to evoke a sense of life that is often forgotten in the business of living. The serenity of the forest can rejuvenate the body and restore the soul.

On Mt. Collins we stopped at a lean-to nestled in a fir grove. It was so much like Maine that I felt a nostalgic longing for home. Three miles beyond the lean-to we came to Clingmans Dome, which at 6,642 feet is the highest point on the Appalachian Trail. Everything was shrouded in fog. How disappointing it was to have come so far and climbed so high to see so little! We moved on, across Mt. Buckley, through Double Springs Gap, across knobs and narrow ridges and balds. At Derrick Knob Lean-to we squeezed in with 24 college students. The next morning we climbed Thunderhead, which we had been told was terribly difficult. It was steep and strangely gullied, but not nearly as tough as we expected. Somewhere along the trail from Maine our perspective on mountains had changed.

At Russell Field we stopped for a quick lunch. Since entering the Smokies we had been eating such things as dehydrated eggs and beef stew, and freeze-dried steaks and chops. They were tasteless but filling. They also saved space and were easy on the back and shoulders. At the lean-to we talked with a young man for several minutes before we realized he was one of the camp counselors we had met back at Speck Pond Shelter in Maine. Like Bump, he was bearded now, and his hair was long. It was good to see a friend. The camaraderie among hikers meeting again is heartwarming.

On October 28 we left the crest of the Great Smokies. How it did rain at the lean-to at Birch Spring Gap! We passed the evening in the lean-to talking with other hikers. There was no letup in the rain the next morning, but knowing we were within six or eight miles of Fontana Village and real food, we struck out in the downpour. Late in the forenoon, very wet, we crossed over Fontana Dam. The dam was almost 500 feet high, and at that time was the highest of over 40 dams in the Tennessee Valley. It was an impressive sight, the only thing it lacked was a little sunshine. A man who worked for the TVA gave us a lift to the village. We rented a little cabin, then went to the cafeteria where we met a reporter who wanted a story and pictures for his paper. We told him OK, but we had to eat first. He waited patiently, even when we went back for seconds.

We picked up some welcome mail, but there was no check. It was still raining when we made our way to the cabin. It contained a tiny kitchen-living room, a bedroom, and a bathroom with a tub. *Ahhh!* How marvelous it was to be wet and warm and soapsudsy instead of wet and cold and shivering. We had all manner of good things to eat, mail to read, a bed to crawl into. What did it matter if rain drummed on the roof? Tomorrow we might have problems, but to-night we had none.

There were about 1,850 miles of trail behind us now and we slept easily under any circumstances except concrete floors. On logs, boughs, boards, chicken wire, the ground; alone in the forest or jammed in a shelter like cordwood with a dozen other people; in stifling heat, sky-ripping thunderstorms, or foggy chilling cold, we slept. This soft bed wrapped us in comfort and we slept as though tomorrow would never come—but of course it did, and with it, more rain. Rain, *rain*. There was still no money at the post office so we asked that it be forwarded to Suches, Georgia, when it did come. The cabin cost $13; there was an additional cash outlay for supplies, and more for breakfast. We had really splurged, eating like mad, filling our packs with all the food and every last candy bar we could carry. We left Fontana with $3, and laughed like fools in the spattering rain because there was no place to spend it in the woods.

Entering the Nantahala National Forest I remembered reading somewhere that Nantahala was an Indian word meaning *Land-of-Noon-Day-Sun.* How I wished we might see a little sun at noonday—or any time. It was miserable to be wet all the time. We went up and down over the steep Yellow Creek Mountains, and even though we had covered only about five miles when we reached Cable Gap Lean-to at noon, we called it enough, and got under cover to dry out and stay dry for a while. Sometime in the night the rain finally quit. We left before daylight, but were slowed in our attempt to recoup yesterday's lost mileage by the steepness of the Cheoah Mountains.

On November 1 the weather turned cold as we went over Swim Bald, Tyre Top, and Flint Ridge, then crossed the Nantahala River bridge and went south along Wesser Creek. In the distance we could see an elusive fire tower that appeared, disappeared, and reappeared as we zigzagged from one mountain to another. At last we zeroed in and climbed Wesser Bald's 4,627 feet to the tower. Then we climbed the tower to take pictures. It was a clear day and we could see far out over the Nantahala Mountains, their thick spruce and fir interspersed with the strange balds. We climbed down from the fire tower to follow the crest to Tellico Gap and on to a lean-to. Rain dimmed the autumn beauty of the walnut and maple trees. We walked across a half-dozen balds and wondered about their origin. The rain stopped and we kept going over Sheep Knob to Panther Gap, to Swinging Lick Gap, to Winding Stair Gap, to Rocky Cove Knob, to Buck Knob. I found these names intriguing and tried to imagine how each place had earned its name. At Rock Gap Lean-to it rained again. Besides being wet it was cold and the temperature was still dropping. There was very little wood and fire building was discouragingly difficult. We shivered as we blew on the fire with smoke in our eyes; we were hungry and longed to be *warm*. Eventually, after several false starts, we had a blazing fire. What had been dismal and wet became warm and cheery. Reluctant to let the fire die, we tended it spasmodically through the night. In the morning we were glad we had made the effort. It was *cold!* As we walked along that morning we plucked icicles from ledges and sucked them. The day was clear and it warmed up a little. We made about 20 miles, climbing Big Pinnacle, Albert Mountain, the Ridgepoles and Little Bald. Below Standing Indian there were banks of clouds that made the other mountaintops look like islands in the sea. The lean-to and its nearby brook were all ours. It was cold, but there was plenty of dry wood, so we settled in comfortably. Tomorrow we would be in Georgia.

In the night I had a dreamlike sensation of discomfort, of cold. I fought my way up through layers of sleep, and saw *snow*. Snow everywhere! It actually was *snowing!* I poked Bump, and he reared up, the snow flying off the foot of his sleeping bag. "What——?" he began, but the "what" was grimly obvious. We were caught in a blizzard.

Our boots were frozen stiff. Our hands felt the same way. The thin cotton of our gloves and our pants gave us little protection from the snow and cold. Bump built up the fire, piled on wood, and set our boots close to the fire to thaw out. We covered ourselves with the space blanket, but the wind was blowing hard and driving all the heat out into the snowy darkness. Our boots thawed enough so we could get them on. My shoes had been too close to the fire and the laces had burned. With numbed fingers Bump replaced them with pieces of our clothesline. I cooked some oatmeal and we ate, standing over the fire with snow blowing all around us.

We were afraid that if we stayed we would surely freeze to death, so we threw the dirty dishes into our packs and started hiking. We were at an elevation of some 6,000 feet. If we could work our way down we might be able to walk out of the storm. It was almost daylight now but we could see very little. We crept along, hair and eyelashes caked with snow, boots like chunks of ice. The soles on Bump's boots were worn smooth and he kept slipping and half-falling. I was terrified, afraid he would fall and injure his already weakened back. We had said we would finish the trail or drop trying. I began to get angry. In frustration I shouted to Bump, "If we die I'll come back and haunt this damn Standing Indian!"

For hours it seemed that we barely moved over the slippery snow-covered trail. However, we gradually made our way down out of the wind and the blinding snow, and off the mountain. Finally, a long way off, we could see buildings and smoke curling into the frosty air. Half-frozen, we moved toward that smoke. It was a farmhouse, and when we reached it we met Willard and Elva Rogers, who get our vote for being the best people in the world. Willard took off our packs; we couldn't. Elva took care of our wet jackets and boots and huddled us around the stove. They listened to our story and told us we were to stay with them until we could buy warmer clothing. We agreed wholeheartedly with this idea, but we had no money. We started making phone calls, but no one was home—not Steve, not Bump's parents or his sister, not my mother—*no one!* Then Bump remembered Howard Bridges, a friend who had said, "If you run into trouble, just call." Howard was at home. "No problem. I'll wire the money. It's as good as there."

We were in Titus, which was a very small place. The nearest town was Hiawassee, and Mr. Rogers said he would drive us over in the morning. The Rogers fed us a hearty supper, and bedded us down with an electric blanket! I was too weary to think about the extremes of our fortunes. It was enough that we were under cover, warm, dry, and fed.

We awoke with itchy peeling feet, a result of the chilblain we had suffered. We ate a breakfast of squirrel and hot biscuits and eggs. Sitting around the table with the Rogers and their little boy and girl, Keith and Brenda Jean, we felt like part of the family. Later Willard drove us to Hiawassee. We got our money, bought hooded sweat shirts, heavy woolen pants, and rubber pacs. The weather was a little better, but it was still frosty. We needed little coaxing when the Rogers urged us to stay another night. I had heard about Southern hospitality, but these people had taken us in and cared for us just as if we were a part of the family. We would never forget them.

In the morning we left, almost regretfully, but still had miles to travel. We went through Park Gap and over Mule Mountain; over the ridge from Hellhole Mountain to Dismal Mountain. How appropriately named they were! When we came down off Rocky Mountain into Unicoi Gap our legs were cruelly chafed and our feet were blistered. The rubber pacs hadn't worked out too well.

At the highway we started thumbing. It was almost dark when a college student picked us up and drove us back to the Rogers' home.

They greeted us warmly, glad to see the bad pennies turning up again. We called Steve and told him our estimated time of arrival at Springer Mountain. He said he would be there to pick us up. We had another nice evening talking with Elva and Willard Rogers and playing with the children. When we left the next morning we wore our old beat-up boots, leaving the parboiling pacs behind. Again we went over the mountains and through the gaps. On November 7 the deer season opened and there were hunters by the thicketful. We stopped at one lean-to that was on a road. Swathed in moonlight it was *The Highwayman* incarnate. Having left Bump snoring to make a midnight trip to the outhouse, I headed back and heard him call, "Helloo?" Thinking I'd be funny, I falsettoed, "Hel-l-o-o-o." Entering the lean-to, I faced the barrel of his revolver. *"Dammit,* Margaret! I could have *shot* you!"

I gave him a small dose of his own logic, "Didn't, did you?"

Blue Mountain and Blood Mountain were steep, rugged, and high. We didn't have many more miles to go—we were really going to make it! At Woody Gap we hitched a ride to Suches. It was Sunday and we were lucky to find a store open. We talked with the storekeeper and answered the usual questions, and as in all small friendly places, other folks joined in the conversation. One of the several people who came into the store while we were there was the postmaster. Bump asked him if there was any chance of getting our mail on Sunday. "Sure thing!" he said, and in a few minutes we had the check and our other mail. Right behind that piece of good fortune came a man and his two sons, all packing .45s. "You're staying with us tonight," the man said firmly. Mr. Stanford was from Atlanta and was up here hunting. He drove us to his summer home and told us to help ourselves, that he and the boys would be at their hunting camp up the road. There we stood in a lovely fully-stocked cottage, marveling for the umpteenth time at the goodness of some of the people we had met. We had homemade beef stew for supper, watched a little television, and slept in a comfortable bed. Next morning, after a breakfast of bacon and eggs, Cary and Buddy Stanford drove us back to the trail.

There was a clear sky and the air was brisk. The mountain green was enriched with autumn bronze and red and yellow. Climbing, we began to see dugouts and foxholes. Finally we were stopped by a man in uniform and learned that we were in a Green Berets' training area. We kept walking, too near the end of our journey to stop for anything now. I was busy unwrapping a candy bar when I almost stepped on a snake. I yelped and Bump swung his walking stick. The snake slithered away. We went on up a mountain, along a ridge, down again, crossed a road and had another mountain to climb. But this mountain was different—it was the last one! It was Springer Mountain. On the summit we dropped our packs in a sudden tumble of feelings—triumph, exhilaration, fulfillment, gratitude, regret. I was between a smile and a tear as I looked at the sign: SOUTHERN TERMINUS OF THE APPALACHIAN TRAIL. A MOUNTAIN FOOTPATH EXTEND-ING 2,000 MILES TO MT. KATAHDIN IN MAINE. We signed the register: *Bump and Margaret Smith. 1:20 P.M. November 9, 1970.* One hundred and fifty days, with mountains every morning. Bump put his arm around my shoulder and grinned. I grinned back at him. "Yes, we did it. We made it all the way."

The 2,000-Mile Classroom

By Art Smith

Started at SPRINGER MOUNTAIN on February 17, 1971
Finished at MT. KATAHDIN on July 8, 1971

As a young boy my summers were divided between the New Jersey seashore and camp in the mountains of Vermont and New Hampshire. One August, at camp, a trip to climb Mt. Washington was announced and I signed up out of curiosity. Although I was tired, damp, and cold the whole time, that trip still sticks in my mind as the most exciting hike of my life. Among other things, I discovered the Appalachian Trail that day.

I spent my school years at a private boarding school only a few miles from the Kittatinny Ridge in New Jersey. Most of the boys there found relief from the disciplined life in athletic competition, but I was not very good at sports and sought my escape in other ways. Long walks in the surrounding woods in the fall and spring and constant skiing in winter served as my release. During these years I developed a real love for the woods.

College life changed all of this, for now only summers and vacations could be devoted to the woods and mountains. In the summer of 1970 I took a job as a counselor at the camp in Vermont that I had attended years before as a child. That summer I devoted all of my free time to exploring the White Mountains, which were just across the Connecticut River. Sometimes I would lead groups of campers along those high ridges, just as I had been led along them more than 10 years before. It was hard to return to the university that fall, as I wanted to be out walking the ridge crests more than I wanted to be in a classroom. In January of 1971 I returned from a skiing trip to Vermont to prepare for final exams. I knew I didn't want to start another semester of school, and it was then that I, along with a long-time friend, Lee Hudgins, thought of an end-to-end hike of the Appalachian Trail as an alternative to spending another semester in college. With only four weeks before the start of a new semester, we had to find quick solutions to the problems confronting us. Neither of us wanted to quit school altogether, for this would mean not only being financially cut off from home, but also being drafted. We were attending the University of South Carolina, and we knew of several programs that granted credit for independent study projects. We decided to try to sell the idea of a trail hike as a mode of education. After several days of going from office to office to tell our story, we finally got the idea approved by the University Without Walls. When we had the backing of the university our parents readily agreed to finance the venture.

Somehow I struggled through exams, but my mind was far away. The end of exams signaled the start of a hectic two weeks of putting the trip together. The biggest problem was that of equipment. Although we both had equipment from past trips, this hike would be much longer and colder than anything we had experienced. We didn't have time to order by mail, so we went to New York to buy equipment. On the way south we stopped in Washington, D.C., and purchased a set of maps and guidebooks from the Appalachian Trail Conference. We also tried to find out what kind of weather we could expect through the southern Appalachians in winter. However, the weather turned out to be far worse than the predictions we got.

Although we planned to buy our food along the way, there were a few items that we packaged and left for mailing to post offices near the trail. Included in these packages were vitamin and protein pills, guidebooks, maps, and a few goodies like nuts and candy. As the trip progressed I discovered that I could not always find what I wanted in the small towns along the way, so whenever I found a store with the exact food and film I wanted, I would buy an extra quantity and mail some of it ahead. During the second half of the trip I also called home and had food and clothing sent to me. By using these different methods I was rarely without an abundance of food. However, I now think that the best way to stay well-fed on an end-to-end hike would be to use food caches buried near road crossings. I felt that I wasted a lot of time on long road walks and hitches into towns, only to find a poor selection of food when I got there. This was particularly true from Pennsylvania south.

The equipment I carried changed with the seasons. The starting equipment included a large Camp Trails Skyline packframe and nylon Camp Trails packbag, a large Gerry Himalayan sleeping bag (54 oz. of down), a Gerry Yearound two-man tent, a Svea 123 stove, a pot, pan, and cup from a Boy Scout mess kit, a Gerry shortie pad, a Coast Guard waterproof flashlight, and a Nikonos II (Nikon brand) camera with a Sekonic light meter in a waterproof case and ten 36-frame rolls of Kodachrome-X film. My clothing included two pairs of long underwear (one tight fitting nylon, one fishnet type), one pair of jeans and one pair of shorts, two T-shirts, a ski parka, a Gerry rain parka, leather ski mittens, a wool ski cap, and four pairs of socks (two cotton, two wool). On my feet I wore high insulated Dunham boots, and on my head a leather hat with a wide brim. I also carried a pair of sunglasses to protect against snow blindness. Equipment carried in the pack pockets included a small compass, 6-by-8-inch notebook, Bic pen, Swiss army knife, tablespoon, half a bar of yellow soap, metal mirror, brush and comb, cut-off toothbrush, roll of toilet paper, waterproof match container and a metal match (for emergency), box of wooden kitchen matches in two plastic bags, pocket watch, two one-liter plastic canteens, plastic fuel container (1 qt.) and small funnel, 30 feet of 550-pound-test cord, Cutter snakebite kit, and a first-aid kit containing iodine, Halazone pills, roll of cotton gauze, Band-Aids, aspirin, 2½-inch Ace bandage, surgical needle and cord, and ChapStick. I used two plastic garbage bags to protect my sleeping bag from rain.

From past experience I knew that these were the basic things I would need, and with the exception of the first-aid kit, every item was put to good use. As in all backpacking trips there were other things I could have used, but they would have added extra weight. The more I've hiked, the lighter my pack has become. This trip was no exception. At Springer Mountain my pack, with a week's supply of food, weighed about 45 pounds. At the Maine line it weighed only 30 pounds with the same amount of food. Of course the change in season allowed me to discard many items that had been necessary in winter. The key to comfort in backpacking is lightness. After months of hiking I could feel the difference when my pack was just a few ounces lighter or heavier. Ounces can make the difference between climbing a mountain with relative ease, and straining all the way to the top.

Although everyone who hikes the Appalachian Trail covers the same ground, no two trips are the same. Not only does the time of year and the weather play an important role; the preparedness of the hiker in terms of conditioning, food, equipment, and knowledge of the environment also make a difference. My hike was intended as a laboratory for studying these things, as well as for personal pleasure and satisfaction.

By February 15 we were set to go. We were to receive school credit in three general fields: English, psychology, and education. The basic living on the trail, and writing about it, would cover these fields. However, we both wanted to examine specific topics in more detail. Lee was interested in the people we would meet; that is, how they lived and how they would accept us. As it turned out, we met very few people for the first few weeks, and this was the main reason Lee left the trip when he did. My in-depth study was to concern itself with why anyone would want to make a trip of this magnitude, and also with the psychological changes that took place during the trip. I could not imagine what 2,000 miles and four to five months in the mountains would be like, with only myself, Lee, and the animals as companions, and I was curious as to how it would all work out. However, most of all, I wanted to experience the trail and all it had to offer.

Lee and I began the trip with rather fixed ideas as to what lay before us, but we soon found things to be quite different from what we had imagined. At 3:00 P.M. on February 17, 1971, we arrived at Amicalola Falls State Park in Georgia to begin our adventure. Within hours our 40-pound packs felt too heavy, and it wasn't until about noon of the next day that we reached Springer Mountain and the start of the Appalachian Trail. It was soon obvious that five months of sitting around school was not the best way to get in shape for such a trip. An unusually warm spell put our cold-weather clothing into our packs, and this extra weight helped change the hike from a romantic adventure into a struggle with simple exhaustion. On our first day on the Appalachian Trail we covered less than 10 miles. Completely exhausted, we stopped at a shelter. An army helicopter buzzed us just as the sun set—I guess they were curious as to why anyone would be out there in the woods at that time of year.

After about three days I began to adjust to this new way of life. At the start of the hike we were on a diet of organic foods—oatmeal, rice, noodles, nuts, dried fruit, dehydrated vegetable broth and tea —but this diet proved to be unsatisfactory. I carried protein pills and vitamins to supplement my diet, but I still found myself constantly hungry and lacking in energy. At the small town of Suches, Georgia, we stocked up on Spam, instant soup, and lots of candy. I had attempted to organize the contents of my pack by repackaging all the food into plastic snap-top containers, but this idea didn't work out, partly because it was hard to ration one meal, from, say, a quart container of rice. Packing meals in plastic bags was a tedious process, but it told me exactly how much food I had.

The people of Suches assured us that the warm weather would soon change, and it did. That night we pitched our tent near the top of Blood Mountain, the highest point on the Appalachian Trail in Georgia. The next day I wrote in my log: "Very cold and windy last night. I didn't sleep. I was waiting for the tent to blow down, but it held. This morning everything was frozen—including the water in the canteens and the tent zipper. A thin layer of snow covers everything, but the view is fantastic, and that makes it all OK." My feelings that morning told me why I was there. The air was so crisp and fresh, and there were beautiful views in every direction. I ran around up there like a little child, wanting to take it all in at once, not knowing in which direction to look first. It gave me a feeling of indescribable exhilaration and joy.

The remainder of the trip through Georgia taught me that this was not just a long hiking trip, but a new way of life. On past hikes when the weather got bad I always had known that dry clothes and warmth were only as far away as a parked car—never more than a few days away. It was different now. Wet clothes took a long time to dry in near-freezing weather. Sprained joints and muscles had to be nursed back to strength.

We were moving awfully slow. The views we had from mountaintops on a few clear days provided enough inspiration to keep us pushing on, but our goal of reaching Katahdin seemed more and more impossible. We had been hiking for two weeks and were only a little way into North Carolina. One cold rainy day during the first week in March we were low on food and decided to hitch a ride to Franklin, North Carolina, in search of a store. By the time we got to the store it was late in the day and the rain had changed to snow. It was not very difficult to decide to stay in Franklin and get a dry bed and a hot meal. Between the inadequate food and the bad weather, the trip hadn't been very pleasant so far, but something happened in Franklin that made me want to go on. Someone suggested that we visit Rev. Rufus Morgan, as he knew a lot about the trail. We had seen his name in the guidebook as the author of some of the trail descriptions. Rev. Morgan might be called the Grandfather of the Appalachian Trail in the southern Appalachians. He had watched the trail come to life in that section, and despite his age and his partial blindness, he still hiked parts of it. As we sat in front of the fire in his home, he told me that it had been his lifetime dream to hike the entire trail, and that he envied us for having the opportunity to do it at our age.

Any thought I might have had of quitting the trail vanished with this visit. I was not about to be discouraged now by a little bad weather or unsuitable food, when I had the opportunity to fulfill my "lifetime dream" at the healthy age of 21. That night I telephoned a professor at school and he reassured me that we need not worry about the time factor. Now we had the whole spring and summer to do the trail. We realized that if we were to go back to the trail some reorganizing was necessary, and we were practically a new expedition when we set out from Franklin. Food now consisted of Quaker instant oatmeal, dried fruit, and Tang for breakfast; cheese, bread, and bouillon for lunch; and Lipton dried soups with extra rice and noodles for dinner. I also carried extra dried fruit and candy to eat along the trail for energy. Although a few inches of snow covered the trail, I was more confident now. The food had a little more life, and so did I.

When we were crossing Wayah Bald a heavy snow started to fall. We made it to a shelter which became our home for the next 36 hours. Sitting in that shelter, catching up on my writing and watching the snow fall, I sensed what was on Lee's mind. He had wanted to meet the people of the mountains and see how they lived. So far we had met very few people, and had spent most of our time being cold and wet in the woods. I finally told him I was willing to do the trip alone if he wanted to go back to the university. As a matter of fact, I was kind of hoping I could be alone in the mountains. In some ways I thought it might be easier alone, as I would be able to set my own pace, lingering where I pleased. So at the Nantahala River, Lee and I parted with a handshake.

I was now almost as detached from the civilized world as the animals whose woods I shared. I soon found that being alone was enjoyable. Although the weather was very cold and the trail rough, the freedom I felt was exhilarating. Watching the sunrise from Cheoah Bald as I overlooked the Smokies was one of the most memorable occasions of the whole trip. In the clear cold air I could almost precisely outline the trail as it followed the crest line through the Smokies.

Clear weather soon gave way to poor weather. At Fontana Dam a light rain was falling from very low clouds. Higher up this rain would obviously be snow, but I decided to go on anyway. Soon the snow began to fall heavily. Having gone less than 200 miles in three weeks, I had decided that I must travel at least 15 miles a day. However, Mother Nature had different ideas. By the time I got up Shuckstack Mountain there was at least a foot of snow on the ground, with drifts that were more than knee-deep. The snow was sticking to the trees, and I couldn't see the blazes. I was not even sure I was on the trail. As the afternoon wore on it became a frightening experience. It got darker and I was thinking of putting up my tent and waiting out the storm when a very welcome shelter appeared through the fog. As I dined with the shelter mice I realized that the experience probably wouldn't be fatal, even under these severe conditions. I had plenty of food, a stove with fuel for cooking, a good tent for shelter, and a warm sleeping bag. There was nothing to fear as long as I didn't panic. That was the last time on the trip that I felt any fear of being alone.

During the next two days a warm sun melted most of the snow, making for wet and heavy footing. My shoes had lost all resistance to water under the constant soaking and drying. With thick wool socks this wetness was only a minor discomfort, but a discomfort nevertheless. At Newfound Gap, the halfway point in the Great Smoky Mountains National Park, friends from school met me. It was a welcome interlude, but I was anxious to go on. For the rest of the trail in the Smokies I had good clear weather, and for the first time I began to find my pace. Soon I crossed Davenport Gap and was on my way to Hot Springs, North Carolina. Many old-time Appalachian mountain folk live along the trail here. With my long hair and growing beard I was somewhat cautious about meeting them. However, the people turned out to be different from what I had expected. Several times I was invited into small homes for a simple meal, and in one instance, I was offered some pure mountain moonshine! That 'shine sure warms a hiker on a cold day!

In Hot Springs I found a motel and got a good night's rest. Snow was starting to fall as I left the next morning, and I trudged through the white stuff all the way to Erwin, Tennessee. Walking in the morning was pleasant, but as the afternoon wore on I would become tired and wet and disgusted with the weather. My brother, on vacation from school, met me in Erwin. He intended to hike with me to Virginia, but once again Mother Nature had other plans. On our first day out it began to snow. After sitting in a shelter for one whole day while the snow fell, we finally decided to try to go over Roan Mountain. The snow proved to be much deeper than we had anticipated, and it was almost sunset when we reached the summit. Cold, and pressed for time by the approaching darkness, we hurried on in search of the abandoned cabin mentioned in the guidebook. When we found it by flashlight it was just a shell with no floor, but at least we were sheltered from the wind and possible snow.

Warm weather followed for the next week, quickly melting the snow and putting spring in the air. I was glad to have the snow behind me—at least I thought it was behind me. On the morning of April 6 I awoke on Big Walker Mountain in Virginia to a light chilly rain. Not long afterward the rain turned to snow. My clothes, having been soaked by the rain, now froze as the temperature fell. By 12:30, when I reached High Rock Lean-to, my hands were so stiff from the cold that I had difficulty in undressing. Finally, though, I crawled into my sleeping bag and from it I watched as snow fell for the next 21 hours.

When the snow let up I decided to try to make my way down the mountain. This was the worst time of the entire trip. With the snow knee-deep, and many trees blown down, it was almost impossible to keep on the trail. I was disheartened when I trudged into the small town of Crandon. However, parked next to the only store in town, I spotted a car with Vermont license plates and a number of small dogs inside. I knew instantly who the car belonged to, and my spirits lifted. Two days earlier I had met Everett and Nell Skinner on the trail. They had hiked the entire trail a few years before and were now visiting people they had met on their trip. I was soon sitting in a warm house, laughing about my recent experiences. It was wonderful to be with people who really understood what I was doing. Throughout the rest of my trip I often remembered this meeting with the Skinners.

After Lee left the trail I set up a check-in system. Figuring on hiking 15 miles a day, and allowing an extra day a week for snow, I would select a point from which I would call home or school and tell someone that I was safe. If I didn't call in by the agreed-upon time a search was to be organized. To reach Pearisburg, Virginia, by a certain time I pressed on through the snow and arrived two hours before the deadline. However, when I arrived I learned that someone had already sounded the alarm that I was missing. Luckily, the search had not yet begun so I was able to call it off.

After Easter Sunday I had unusually warm weather. Having forgotten how taxing a hot day on a long open ridge could be, I carried only one cup of water on the 10-mile section of Sinking Creek Mountain. The trail was rugged because of winter blowdowns, and I was soon out of water. The afternoon seemed endless. When I reached Niday Lean-to I felt like the men I had seen in movies about the Sahara Desert—my mouth and lips were swollen and dry, and I was exhausted.

By this time I had found a diet that was nourishing, good tasting, easily divided into meal-sized portions, and light in weight. Breakfast included Quaker instant oatmeal with dried fruit, tea, and Start orange drink. The oatmeal came in small individual packets making it easy to know how many breakfasts I had with me. I found that two packets made a good nourishing hot meal. I would also make a cup of tea and flavor it with Start. On very cold mornings I would prepare all of this from my sleeping bag by just boiling a pot of water on the Svea stove. A variety of Start flavors kept me from getting too bored with the same thing every morning. The best thing I found for lunch was cheese and bread (whole wheat, if possible), and Kool-Aid. Usually I used sliced American cheese, making two sandwiches with two slices of cheese in each sandwich. For dinner I needed something very filling, but light enough to carry. The freeze-dried foods put up especially for backpackers were out of the question because they weren't always available, and also because of their high price. I found that Lipton made an instant dinner that I thought was better than the specialized trail food, and which weighed only about six ounces for a large portion. Called Main Dishes, they were made with a number of different meats, but I found that most stores carried only the beef and the chicken Stroganoff. Although I got pretty sick of this as a steady diet, it was easy to prepare and each night's portion was individually wrapped. I usually ate a piece of bread with my dinner and had some tea or Kool-Aid. The constant walking kept me hungry all of the time, and in order to satisfy my craving for food I carried a variety of goodies. Candy bars, Swee-Tarts, and Canada mints were my favorites. Raisins and dried apricots were also eaten throughout the day.

On April 22 I reached Rockfish Gap, Virginia, the beginning of the Shenandoah National Park. Here I exchanged my winter gear for spring-summer gear. For my tent I substituted a 6-by-8-foot plastic-coated nylon tarp. The tent had served me well on cold snowy nights when I couldn't reach a shelter. I was glad I had carried it, but now it was just extra weight. As the ground was no longer frozen, I exchanged my foam pad for a plastic groundsheet of about 4 by 8 feet, cut from an old tube tent. The most notable changes, however, came in clothing. In place of long underwear I now had two pairs of jockey briefs. The mittens, ski cap, and ski parka were also sent home. For warmth in the evening I had a heavy cotton turtleneck jersey which I could also wear under the rain parka. A few times, in cold rain, I wished the jersey was wool, but in general the cotton was good enough. By this time my boots were well-worn, and in Charlottesville I bought a pair of Redwing Irish Setter boots. They weighed much less than the boots I had been wearing, and they made my feet feel light as feathers, but they didn't give enough protection against the rocks of Pennsylvania. The days were getting longer so I didn't need a big heavy flashlight. I changed to the small Mallory, and found it a great piece of equipment. It was small enough to keep in my sleeping bag at night, so I always knew where it was. Because of the saving in weight I wished I had carried a Mallory from the start.

The only animals I had seen in winter were deer and skunk. Skunk were common visitors at night and before long I would keep right on sleeping as they prowled for food. With the coming of Spring more animals appeared. I came upon a sleepy rattlesnake and scared myself as well as the snake. In the Shenandoah National Park deer were everywhere, as were birds of many kinds, and a few bear passed me, hardly acknowledging my presence. The Shenandoah National Park was the turning point of my trip. After all the unpleasant weather I had come through, hiking in the mild spring days was wonderful. Now I could concentrate on the natural beauty around me, and on my work for school, without worrying about soggy boots and gray clouds. I really felt free. Mileage was no longer a worry. Fifteen miles a day was quite easy to do, and many times I slowed down in order to enjoy the hike more. In Pennsylvania I toyed briefly with the idea of waiting until the following year to do the remainder of the trail, but after that bit of wavering I never again doubted that I would reach Katahdin that summer.

It seemed like it rained all the way from northern Virginia to the Delaware Water Gap, and with all the rain, and the less spectacular scenery, I hurried through Pennsylvania. Although I still enjoyed the walking, I sometimes became depressed at the end of the day while sitting and thinking about my friends at school. It was at these times that my notebook served me well. It became my speechless friend whenever I felt lonely—I would write what I was thinking, and thus get it off my chest and feel a little better.

At the Delaware Water Gap my brother met me with a new pair of Voyageur Whitney boots. By wearing a pair of tight silk dress socks under heavy Ragg socks, I was able to avoid blisters while breaking them in. The wool would slide against the silk, rather than against my skin. These boots proved to be the best I'd ever owned. Not only did they take me all the way to Maine; I'm still using them after about 1,200 miles.

I was now anxious to get to the New England I knew so well. In New Jersey and New York whole mornings of walking would pass swiftly while I daydreamed about some other place. Soon I was in the mountains surrounding the Housatonic River in Connecticut—I had reached New England. One day while walking next to the river just south of Cornwall Bridge I saw two wild turkeys in the grass ahead. Wild turkeys usually flee at the sight of a man, but these two held their ground as I approached. It was obvious that they were protecting a nest, so I got my camera ready and slowly approached, talking quietly to the big birds. For a few moments I thought they were going to let me get my pictures, but when I got about 10 feet from the nest they both came at me in a frantic rage. Those birds weren't fooling around. A comic chase followed. I would get far enough ahead so I could turn and strike at one of them with my stick before he bit me in the leg. Then I would run a little farther and we would do it all over again. This went on for about 200 yards before they finally decided I was far enough away from the nest. The next time I see a wild turkey that doesn't run I intend to approach more cautiously.

With warm weather and long days I settled into a regular schedule. Arising at first light I would prepare and eat breakfast, usually while still in my sleeping bag. On nice days I would be walking within an hour of the time I awoke. On days when the weather was bad I would stall by drinking several cups of tea. Over breakfast I would review the trail ahead in the guidebook and on a map, and set a goal of about 15 or 20 miles for the day. This goal would be what looked like a good place to sleep that night, considering the availability of water and shelter. I carried very little water on most days, so it was important to have water where I slept.

Mornings were the best time to walk. With a good night's rest, the freshness of early morning in the woods made hiking a joy. I would usually set a brisk pace for the first few hours. Becoming hungry by 11:00 or 12:00 o'clock, I would look for a place to eat lunch. Lunchtime was my big rest period of the day, so I always ate at a good scenic spot. After stopping an hour or so for lunch I found it hard to get back to the morning's brisk pace, and I usually spent the afternoon wandering along the trail, stopping to enjoy anything that caught my fancy. By 3:00 or 4:00 o'clock I would start thinking about a place to sleep. About half the time I would not stop at the place I had decided upon that morning. Unless I was in a hurry for some reason, I would stop at the first suitable place I reached after 4:00 o'clock. About half the time I slept in shelters because of the convenience, but I preferred to sleep under the stars. I prepared dinner at six, afterward relaxing and writing of the day's events in my notebook. Before turning in I would hang my pack so animals couldn't get at it, and make sure I had enough water for breakfast. A short length of cord, permanently tied to my packframe, was used to hang the pack. I kept my watch and flashlight in my sleeping bag at night. I rarely used either of them, but it was nice to know they were there.

I tried to get into a town or to a store every four or five days, but at times it was necessary to go for as long as eight days without re-supplying. If it was late in the day when I reached a town, and if there was a motel convenient, I would check in for a hot shower and a meal. In the winter I had done this about once a week, as it allowed my boots to dry out completely and gave me a chance to catch up on my paperwork. As I got farther north and the weather got warmer I stayed in motels less and less. In Vermont, New Hampshire, and Maine I found myself actually avoiding motels, preferring cold mountain streams to hot tiled showers.

On June 4 I arrived in Vermont. It was good to be back in the woods I knew and loved so much. Each day was exciting as I traveled through Vermont and New Hampshire, and reaching the Green Mountains was like being reunited with an old friend. A lot of people were out on the trail now, and many of them offered food and assistance. In Hanover, New Hampshire, I made my last equipment changes. Finding the mud from the melting snow sometimes coming over the tops of my boots, I bought a pair of Alp gaiters. I found that they were also useful in keeping my socks from getting wet in the early morning dew, and in keeping pine needles and leaves from sticking to my socks and falling into my boots. Except in very hot weather I wore the gaiters all the time.

Late spring is blackfly season in the northern woods and I tried a variety of insect repellents in an attempt to find relief from the little flies. Woodsman's Fly Dope worked best on blackflies for me, and Off worked best on mosquitoes. I also bought an army surplus mosquito head net which protected me while I slept. By the time I got to Maine I had so much Woodsman's Fly Dope on my hair that the bugs left me alone.

Soon I was touring the high ridges of the White Mountains, my favorite part of the trail. A clear day on one of those long ridges is an awesome thing. One's perception of distance and time becomes warped. A peak that appears to be only a short distance away turns out to be a two-mile trek as you walk to it. Looking across the notches one can almost see the glacier that cut its way through so long ago. Excited by the grandeur of the country, I forgot to be tired. I would soar over the peaks, absorbing everything as I went. Nowhere but in these mountains have I been able to see so clearly how small man is, compared to the world he lives in. A humbling experience indeed!

Arriving at Lakes-of-the-Clouds Hut near Mt. Washington, I found myself in the middle of an Appalachian Mountain Club leadership class. For four months I had spoken to no more than three or four people at a time, and now I was confronted with 90 people eager to hear my story. Trying to converse with a lot of people all at once was hard, especially when questions were being fired at me, and at dinner I found that my fingers cramped when I tried to cut the pork chops. I had been eating with a spoon for so long that my knife and fork muscles had deteriorated! It was all quite embarrassing, and the moment dinner was over I retreated to the top of Mt. Monroe to survey the scene from afar. In my notebook I wrote: "The most striking thing in the hut is the confusion. Everyone is trying to help everyone else. No one is left alone to complete his own individual task. I guess there is always confusion in numbers of people, but you don't realize it until you are away from people long enough to learn the peace that accompanies solitude."

The next day I crossed the peaks that had started my hiking career more than 10 years before, and soon I was in the rugged Mahoosucs in Maine. With the end of the trail so close, I sometimes wanted to race ahead as fast as possible, and at other times I wanted to slow down so that I could experience this way of life for as long as possible. Maine in July provided a perfect finish for a trip that had begun in such poor weather. As I got closer to Katahdin I met more and more people heading south, some with the hope of reaching Georgia. I wondered if the trail seemed as infinite to them as it had to me when I started. At least they were starting in better weather.

The wildlife in Maine was more impressive than anywhere else on the trail. Every day I would get a good look at a beaver at work, or a porcupine waddling to safety. On the Fourth of July I saw my first moose, a large bull dining in a beaver pond. At these times I wished I had a telephoto lens for my camera. My 35-mm wide-angle lens was excellent for panoramic shots, but left much to be desired in photographing animals. Incidentally, the camera and lens worked flawlessly throughout the trip, even with the beating it took. I had no problem with the manual focus, and most of the approximately 1,000 slides I took came out very sharp.

My brother and I made the ascent of Katahdin together on the morning of July 8. As we approached the summit Mark produced a half-gallon of imported champagne, and in the fog and wind on Baxter Peak we dined on raisins and champagne. It was over, and I had finished the trail, but the real work was still to come. There were many pictures to edit and notes to organize. A lot of people, professors and friends, were anxious to hear my story. I really felt that the hike had been educational, and that I had learned things that I could not have learned in any other way. Being alone for the amount of time it takes to walk the trail from Georgia to Maine demands that a person examine himself, his relation to others, and his relation to the universe. Life on the trail teaches us that man is no more than a highly intelligent animal who has not been out of the woods very long in relation to the length of time the world has existed, and that the earth itself is no more than a speck of dust in the universe. The trail causes the hiker to live somewhat like the caveman did, and in doing so he rediscovers the warmth of fire and the need for shelter. The hiker gains some understanding of how Indians lived with their environment instead of fighting it. The trail shows one aspect of American history in the abandoned settlements, and the hiker can understand at least some of the hardships the early settlers encountered. It is one thing to be aware, in a general way, that the settlers had a hard time; it is something else to experience some of the same hardships, as a hiker does on a long hike. The Appalachian Trail should be preserved in a wild state, as much as possible. In the eastern part of the United States it provides one of the few chances to see the natural woods.

Someday I hope to walk the trail from end to end again. I will do it differently the next time—not because I didn't like the way I did it the first time, but because I will be looking for different things. First of all, I would set no time limit for the completion of my hike. This would allow me time to linger as long as I liked anywhere along the way. One could spend years exploring everything the trail has to offer. I would do the trail from north to south, and thus see it from a different perspective. The longer you stay on the trail, the more you feel a part of the natural world, and this feeling of oneness with nature is what I would strive for on another end-to-end hike. If a hiker is concerned mostly with just seeing the sights along the trail, I think the best way to do it would be in sections. Each part of the trail is different from the other parts, and any one part is different in the different seasons. In order to see the whole trail, then, one would have to walk each geographical section in each of the four seasons. However, hiking the trail in this way would rob the hiker of the feeling that the trek is a way of life, perhaps all of life—and this is one of the really great feelings that a long hike can give.

My advice to anyone thinking of hiking the whole trail would be, first of all, to have good dependable equipment. Obviously, a pack-frame that breaks when you're 10 miles from a road is going to make for an unpleasant trip. Food planning is essential, for without good food, hiking can be an unpleasant task. Second, have confidence in yourself and what you have set out to do. If the hiker doesn't have confidence that he will reach his goal, he becomes too preoccupied with merely getting to the end of his hike. Relax and enjoy the trail; if you do this, the end will come all too soon. Learn how to take care of the environment. I met many people who didn't know what kind of wood to burn, or where to wash their dishes. Enjoy the trail, but leave no reminder that you were there. Third, remember that there is always something new to be discovered. The magic and beauty of nature is a joyful thing. I was constantly amazed at the new sensations I discovered in the woods. In a world of great engineering feats with steel and concrete, we tend to forget that Mother Nature has performed feats that are even more amazing.

I would like to thank the people who made my trip possible—my parents, and Drs. Lindstrand, Buford, and Lodziak of the University of South Carolina, and all of the people, too numerous to name, who helped me along the way.

Georgia to Maine on the Appalachian Trail

By Thomas McKone

Started at SPRINGER MOUNTAIN on April 1, 1971
Finished at MT. KATAHDIN on August 5, 1971

Fitful gusts of wind swept across the summit during the night, shaking the forest to its roots and flapping the sides of the tent so violently I thought they would collapse. Toward dawn the wind subsided and as the sun rose on Springer Mountain on the morning of April 1, 1971, Bob Winslow and I broke the first of many camps we would make on our way to Maine. We were not yet in condition and laboriously plodded along the overgrown woods roads with 35-pound packs on our backs and sweat on our brows. Sometimes the trail slabbed the side of a mountain instead of going over the top, and during those first days we loved to see "slab" in the guidebook trail descriptions. We agreed that it was the most beautiful word in the English language.

There were still patches of snow beneath the laurel and rhododendron bushes, but the days were warm and sunny. An ice storm had hit the area the previous week, leaving much of the trail in shambles. Climbing through the fallen trees with full packs was an extra strain on our city-soft muscles. We hiked 10 miles the first day and spent the night at the Hawk Mountain Lean-to. After dark I walked out to a nearby field and strolled around in the moonlight, playing the harmonica and singing and whistling, and listening to the music echo off the next mountain. Four deer came to the edge of the field, then ran back to the protection of the woods. Storm clouds began to move in, gradually covering the moon and stars. I walked back to the lean-to and went to sleep. I had not been sleeping long when I heard Bob ask, "What are you doing in my pack?"

"I'm not in your pack. I was sleeping."

"Well, somebody's in my pack."

I fumbled for the flashlight. A moment later the beam was shining on a black-and-white animal that had its paws in the open zipper of Bob's pack. I thought it was a raccoon and reached out to push him away, but just before I touched him I realized that it was a skunk. I yelled, then Bob and I both yelled. The skunk, hardly disturbed, waddled out of the lean-to. He visited us twice more that night, each time leaving the air as fresh as it was before he came; he must have realized that we were more afraid of him than he was of us.

Mice scampered around all night, and ate a hole through a nylon sack to get at some peanuts. After that experience we hung our food out of reach of the various animals that were interested in it and slept more peacefully. The mice continued to scamper around the lean-tos, and sometimes ran over us, but at least they didn't get any more of our food. With the appetites we had developed, we were not willing to share our food with any nocturnal visitors. The next night we stayed at Gooch Gap Lean-to. Like many of the lean-tos in Georgia and North Carolina, it had a Bible in it. After supper I read aloud the account of creation in Genesis, including the line about God making "little creatures that crawl upon the face of the earth." We laughed at the line, but we also refrained from swearing at the mice that night.

On our third day on the trail we climbed Blood Mountain, which at 4,461 feet is the highest point on the Appalachian Trail in Georgia. The mountain gets its name from an Indian legend to the effect that the Cherokees and Creeks once fought such a horrible battle there that the mountain ran with blood. Now Blood Mountain runs only with the sweat of hikers.

There was some snow beneath evergreen bushes and behind rocks, but when the temperature reached 74 degrees on the summit we thought that Spring had come. On our way down the mountain, when Lucy Rogers of Newton, Massachusetts, showed us how to make snow cones by putting snow in a cup and flavoring it with Tang, we thought it would be a one-day treat. Two days later, however, we had more snow than we could eat in a lifetime. That was the day we crossed into North Carolina, and it was the worst day we had in our four months on the trail. The day started calmly; then in turn it rained, sleeted, and hailed. The cold forced us to keep our coats on under our ponchos and the temperature difference between our bodies and the outside air caused moisture to condense inside our ponchos and soak our clothing. However, we were less wet, and warmer, than we would have been if we had walked without our ponchos. After we had gone about 10 miles the sky began to clear. We stopped for lunch by a side trail that led to a shelter and discussed the situation. We could go to the nearby shelter and build a fire and dry our clothes, or we could continue hiking and let our clothing dry as we walked. The next shelter was 10 miles away, but it looked like the weather was going to be good. We decided to hike another four or five miles and camp out. Half an hour later the sun went behind clouds and we never saw it again that day. We should have gone back to the last shelter, but we had already developed an aversion to hiking in the wrong direction. We continued on, not knowing that the weather would soon get worse. It began to sleet, then to snow. We had expected cold weather during the first part of April, but not snow; we were not outfitted for winter camping. We had a floorless tent, no axe, no pads to put under our sleeping bags, no mittens, no scarves; we would have to keep going until we reached the next shelter. The snow continued to fall as we climbed our first 5,000-foot mountain; the wind howled through the naked forest and snow beat against our rosy faces. We grew tired and began to dread each footstep, but we had gone halfway to the next shelter, so nothing would be gained by turning back. We dug towels out of our packs and wrapped them around our necks for scarves, and put socks on our hands for mittens. The snow piled up quickly and tramping through it exhausted us. We were so weak that we decided not to take breaks, fearing that we would not be able to start again.

Late in the afternoon the wet snow began sticking to the trees and covering the blazes. The snow also obscured the trail, and at times a white blanket covered even the rocks and bushes. Visibility was very poor. With only a few minutes of daylight remaining, we came to a clearing which was the junction of six or seven woods roads. We knew one of these roads led to a shelter, but the guidebook description was too ambiguous to be of any help. Guessing that the shelter was on the Appalachian Trail rather than on a side trail, we found the road with white blazes and followed it into the forest. Earlier in the day we had seen bootprints in the snow, so we expected to find someone at the shelter. With our last reserves of energy we called into the white blindness for help, but our Maydays got no answer. The last bit of twilight was fading, and still there was no sign of the shelter. There were only white trees against a white sky, white ground, and white air—a terror of whiteness. Suddenly fatigue overcame me and I wanted to sleep, nothing mattered except sleep. Then we heard a sound that was almost lost in the louder sound of the wind in the trees, and the next moment a shelter appeared through the snow.

The two hikers in the shelter were Bill Finucane, of Bucksport, Tennessee, and a man named Arnold from Washington, D.C. Like us, they had been surprised by the storm, but they had reached the shelter before it got too bad. I was hungry, but too tired to eat. Putting on all the dry clothes I had, I got into my sleeping bag. Since lunchtime we had walked six hours through mountainous terrain without taking a break, and much of the time we had been in the snowstorm with high winds. Somewhere in the midst of that storm we had crossed into North Carolina.

Bill Finucane was tall, slim, and long-legged. Nicknamed the Tennessee Ridge Runner, he was probably the strongest and fastest walker we met on the Appalachian Trail. In the 18 weeks we were on the trail we met only two or three people who could out-hike us with full packs on. Bill was one of them. I don't mean to say that we were fast hikers, or that Bill rushed. Most people seem to think that because we walked 2,000 miles, we walked fast. We walked no faster than most people, but we were not slowed down very much by hills or mountains, and we didn't need many rest breaks. Once we were in condition, we could walk all day without tiring. Although we could have hiked 30 or 40 miles a day in some areas, we never did more than 27 miles. Our average was 15 or 16 miles. Speed was never one of our goals. Bill was not particularly interested in speed either, but he had a helluva stride. We appeased our 2,000-miler pride by telling ourselves that he could out-hike us because we were not in shape yet, but the Tennessee Ridge Runner was not in shape, either.

Arnold taught conservation law at George Washington University. He hoped to be the first person to hike all of the Appalachian Trail in winter. He told us he began hiking only after Labor Day and stopped before Memorial Day. At the time I thought he was crazy, but after hiking through New England in summer I changed my mind.

The morning after the snowstorm we sat in our sleeping bags and watched the snow melt. The storm had left about six inches of snow where we were, and more in the higher mountains. Arnold took a side trail to the highway and started back to Washington. Bill stayed with us. By lunch the sun had melted almost half of the snow, so the three of us decided to hike eight miles to the lean-to at Carter Gap. The first day after bad weather is always enjoyable, and now our worst day on the trail was followed by one of our best. During the afternoon, with the sun shining brightly, we went over Standing Indian (5,498 feet). The snow averaged three or four inches, but there were drifts up to our knees.

At the end of seven days we had gone 92 miles. We had estimated that we would do only 75 or 80 miles the first week, so we were quite content with the 92 miles. For several days I wore only one pair of socks; I had never gotten blisters wearing one pair of socks on day hikes, and I wanted to see if I could do without a second pair on a long hike. My feet were fine when we were doing 10 or 12 miles a day, but as soon as we increased our mileage I got no less than 10 blisters, including 2 on my heels that were larger than any I had ever seen. Deciding that the one-sock experiment was a failure, I began wearing a pair of Wick-Dry socks under my wool socks. During the next four months of hiking I had a total of only three blisters, all small.

The section from Wesser to Fontana has the reputation of being one of the most challenging parts of the Appalachian Trail, so we split the 25 miles up into three days of walking. We entered the area in the middle of one day, completed 13 miles the next day, and hiked the final five miles and went on into the Smokies on the third day. The trail was all up and down; however, because of the way we divided it up, we didn't find it too bad. A scarcity of water was the only difficulty we encountered.

We left Fontana Village with heavy stomachs and overflowing packs. We had stuffed ourselves with the sort of food we couldn't get on the trail, and loaded our packs in a rather futile effort to carry enough food to satisfy our ravishing appetites. One bad thing about towns, as every bloated hiker knows, is that they are always in gaps or valleys. Every time a hiker resupplies at a grocery store, or gorges himself in some small country restaurant, he starts off again by going uphill. At Fontana Dam the Appalachian Trail crossed the Little Tennessee River and entered the Great Smoky Mountains National Park. From the dam the trail climbed steeply until it reached the crest of the ridge, then wove along that ridge for the next 70 miles, with not more than two or three difficult climbs. In many places, the ridge fell off sharply on either side, and since there were no leaves on the trees yet, we often had fine views on both sides. We had been hiking for 12 days and were getting into good condition, and most of the park trail was well-graded and rather easy.

On our first night in the Smokies we shared the Birch Spring Lean-to with four people from North Carolina and Georgia. This lean-to was large enough for 12 people, and had a heavy wire fence across the front to protect the occupants from bears. Someone said that a bear had been seen there two nights before, but our only visitor was a deer. In fact, we didn't see any bears in the Smokies; we were told that it was too early for them to be so high in the mountains.

Clingmans Dome, with an elevation of 6,643 feet, is the highest point on the Appalachian Trail. Until recently, Clingmans Dome was thought to be the second highest mountain in the eastern United States, but the May, 1970, U.S. Geologic Survey showed Mt. Craig, which like Mt. Mitchell is in the Black Mountains of North Carolina, to be 6,647 feet, or four feet higher than Clingmans Dome.

Clingmans Dome was the first summit we shared with tourists. A paved road brings people to within a short walk of the top. In one hour we saw more people than we had seen in two weeks on the trail. People in high heels, skirts, and dress shoes seemed like an awful insult to the mountain, to the trail, and to hikers. In our opinion the tourists had cheated themselves, for we felt that no one could really appreciate a mountain if he had not climbed it.

We arrived at a shelter late in the afternoon and were relieved to find only three people there—Scott and Judy from New York, and a girl from Michigan named Linda, who was hiking alone in the Smokies for a week. Like Lucy Rogers, whom we had met in Georgia, Linda found solitary hiking lonely and discouraging. She was the last lone female backpacker we met until we reached Maine. Soon after we set down our packs and removed our boots, a couple from Michigan, Bruce and Liz, arrived. Although most of the sheltermates we had along the trail were companionable, we occasionally had to put up with a misfit. I described Scott in my journal: "For company in our shelter tonight we are fortunate enough (?) to have a 22-year-old, know-it-all backpacker-hiker-camper-walker-thinker-philosopher-psy-chologist-sociologist-writer-mathematician-critic-of-all-trades who be-sides knowing everything, understands everything, has an answer to everything, and believes nothing he reads unless he wrote it himself."

After suppers were finished and the sun had set, Scott, Judy, and Bill engaged in a long and noisy argument on religious and social matters with Bruce and Liz. Linda and Bob were in their sleeping bags trying to sleep. When I finished writing in my journal the five were still at it, so I mentioned that they were breaking shelter etiquette and disrupting the social order, which earlier in their argument they had all agreed was necessary. Bruce and Liz acknowledged that it was late and got into their sleeping bags. Scott, Judy, and Bill continued to talk, at first in quieter tones, but then in normal voices again.

A little later one of them said something about having nothing against the Asian (Vietnamese) people. In the middle of the sentence I interrupted him with "Well, what have you got against *us* people?" Again I reminded them of how inconsiderate they were being, and for the first time in five hours of nonstop talking, Scott had no comeback. After a few private whispers, they got into their sleeping bags. The following day we ran into Bruce and Liz at Newfound Gap and they asked where I got those rules about shelter etiquette. I told them I had made up the rules because I wanted to get some sleep.

Bill Finucane had intended to hike to northern Virginia, but now he decided to leave the trail as spontaneously as he had started it. He was good company, and I was glad to have met him, but I was relieved when he was gone. He liked to hike longer days than we did, and he did not like to stop as often to look at views or flowers. Traveling in a twosome is difficult enough, but traveling in a threesome is impossible, to my way of thinking. Often, when one person wants to stop, the others want to go on, and when this is repeated often enough, company becomes a burden. Hikers can hike separately and meet at the end of the day, but this is not always comfortable, either. Going it alone may be the best way to make the hike. There are always people on the trail, so a hiker can have company when he chooses, whether it is for an evening or a week or two. As Bob and I discovered, being with the same person 24 hours a day for several weeks is extremely difficult, even for the best of friends.

April 17 was our last day in the Smokies and the first day we didn't see snow or ice. As Bob observed, we had been seeing juncos (snowbirds) and robins on the same mountainside. That day we caught up to Jim Wolf, also on his way to Maine. Jim had left Springer Mountain on March 23 and planned to reach Katahdin about Labor Day. He had started planning his hike a year ahead of time, and had figured his stops, pickups, and stay-overs much more precisely than we had. Jim wore a brimmed hat, carried a camera and binoculars, and had an "office" on the front of his shoulder strap. Two days before, someone had asked him if he were Colin Fletcher!

After the Smokies we moved into the Pisgah and Cherokee National Forests. The beauty of these forests was inferior to that of the Smokies, but they were still nice. Here we began a month of solitude. For the next 500 miles we had the Appalachian Trail almost completely to ourselves. After spending the night with Jim Wolf at a lean-to, we shared shelters with hikers only two more times before reaching the

Shenandoah National Park, and in that whole time we met only a handful of people on the trail.

Coming from the south, the first town the Appalachian Trail passes through is Hot Springs, North Carolina, population 721. Hot Springs actually has hot springs, and was once famous as a health resort. The springs are still warm (110° F.), and are still open, but they are not as popular as they once were. The town used to be called Warm Springs, but the name was changed in 1888. The townpeople seemed to be very proud of the fact that the Hot Springs area was one of the largest producers of burley tobacco in the country. Life in Hot Springs, and in almost all the areas we passed through on the Appalachian Trail, was much slower than life in cities. After we bought our groceries we sat in front of the store, eating lunch and repackaging our food. The owner of the store came out to sit with us, and so did the man in the hardware store across the street. The four of us sat there in the center of Hot Springs, North Carolina, just passing the time of day, as though there was nothing in the world more important to do.

Two days after we left Hot Springs, high in a remote section of the southern Appalachians, we passed the graves of two Civil War soldiers, William Shelton, Co. E, 2 N.C. Inf., and David Shelton, Co. C, 3 N.C. Mtd. Inf. Since we were in the South, and since their military identification included N.C. for North Carolina, I assumed that these men were in the Confederate army, but later I learned that although they lived in North Carolina, the men were in the Union army. They were killed by Confederate soldiers when they came home to visit their families while the war was still in progress. Millard Hair, a 13-year-old boy who was with them, was killed and buried, too. However, since he was not in the army, the government didn't give him a marker. The Shelton tombstones were erected in the early part of this century by two local preachers, Rev. Frederick Webb and Rev. Monroe Shelton. They obtained the gravestones from the government, but did the work themselves. That afternoon we walked across the farms of two Shelton families. We talked with one of the Mrs. Sheltons, who told us that the soldiers buried on the mountain were distant ancestors of hers. As in many backwoods communities, one or two family names dominate the census lists. Most of the people in this area, she told us, were either Sheltons or Hensleys.

On April 22 we completed our third 100-mile section of the trail. It was our second consecutive rainy day. We had read that many

2,000-milers encountered weeks of rain in April or May, and we were pessimistically anticipating that we were about to get ours. We were right. For the next 2½ weeks we had rain almost every day. Fortunately, it usually came in the form of showers, and the sky was clear for a part of each day.

There was supposed to be a spring about a hundred feet off the trail on the way up Big Bald. I kept my eyes open and spotted a very green area with several kinds of plants and mosses. I bushwacked over and found a beautiful little spring. The water was shallow and clear, and the bottom was covered with small pebbles. Rhododendron grew nearby. Moss covered many of the rocks, and it also covered a fallen tree which lay across the stream just below the spring. Bob identified the pleasant aroma that filled the air as coming from wild peppermint. I could not get the scent out of my mind. When we left I wanted to take it with me and regretted that, although I could preserve a sound with a tape recorder and a scene with a camera, there was no way I could preserve the smell of the wild peppermint. The best I could do was to put a few leaves in my pocket and keep them until they lost their aroma.

When we reached the summit of Big Bald I forgot all about the peppermint. The trees stopped well below the summit, so the top of the mountain was a huge field. Southern balds are actually too far south to be above timberline at 5,000 or 6,000 feet. Some of the summits were cleared by man, but what made the old balds remains a mystery. Big Bald rises to 5,516 feet and is much higher than any of the neighboring peaks. It provides a 360-degree panoramic view. We sat on the grassy summit for three or four hours, gazing at the valleys and the smaller mountains below us, and at the larger mountains in the distance. What a place it would be to watch the sun rise and set, and see the stars shine! For the man with an eye for the stars, the summit of Big Bald might be as close to heaven as anywhere on earth.

As we sat on top of Big Bald we watched clouds form and disappear. The entire sky was blue (we saw a complete hemisphere) but the air mass coming from the northwest was moist and clouds formed when the air reached the cooler temperatures over Big Bald. After going over the mountain, the air mass would descend to lower warmer altitudes and the clouds would dissipate. The process was exact. We knew precisely where to look to see clouds form, where they would reach their greatest size, where they would begin to disperse, and where they would disappear completely.

The next morning it rained as we were walking down a beautiful

Photo by Robert Winslow

Tom McKone and friends in Massachusetts.

Photo courtesy Robert Win

Robert Winslow and Tom McKone on Dartmouth campus,
Hanover, New Hampshire.

ridge from No Business Knob. The ridge was supposed to offer spectacular views, but the visibility that day was only a hundred yards. During the rest of the rainy spell we made weather forecasts by reading the guidebook. When the guidebook mentioned spectacular views, we predicted it would rain. After the rainy spell we became more scientific weathermen and began forecasting according to clouds, weather patterns, and "how it felt." In New England I often gave weather forecasts to hikers and did quite well. One night on the Long Trail, just after I had completed my Appalachian Trail hike, I told a shelter full of people that I could predict the weather fairly well because I had been in the open for four months. As a demonstration, I predicted that it would rain the next day. In the morning the sky was blue, and I felt a little foolish. However, the sky soon turned dark, and it began to sprinkle. It rained all that day and into the next. For once I was glad to see rain; my honor as a weather prophet was at stake. I would have hated to leave those hikers with the impression that someone who had hiked all the way from Georgia to Maine didn't know what he was talking about!

A weekend Naturalist Rally was in progress near Erwin, Tennessee, when we passed through. As we hiked up the dirt road on Unaka Mountain (5,180 feet), a string of cars on their way to the outing passed us. One of the cars stopped and the driver told us he was Charles L. Johnson of WEMB radio in Erwin. He asked us some questions and taped two interviews to use on WEMB in connection with the Naturalist Rally. I was slightly taken aback when, in one of the interviews, Mr. Johnson called us "strange characters with beards." However, later on, when I looked at a picture Bob took of me on Unaka Mountain, I was surprised that Mr. Johnson had stopped at all. It had been laundry day, which meant that we had semiclean socks, T-shirts, fishnet shirts, and underwear hanging on our packs. We always tried to look respectable, but without Amy Vanderbilt to guide us, we occasionally forgot the rules. A new etiquette manual is in order, for there is a subculture in America in which it is perfectly proper to carry your dirty underwear wherever you go.

The next day we went over Baldtown Mountain, Roan Mountain (6,150 feet), and several other nice balds. Roan Mountain is famous for its rhododendron gardens, but we passed by too early in the season to see them in bloom. Coming down the north side of the mountain we saw more patches of snow and ice, and the trail was muddy. To avoid stepping in mud I sometimes stepped on rocks four or five inches in diameter and some of these sank so deep that most of my boot disappeared with them. The day after we went over Roan Mountain we went over two more large bald mountains—Big Yellow and Hump. On Hump Mountain we encountered the strongest winds I have ever known. A great portion of Hump was bald and afforded no protection at all. Each time we lifted a foot to go forward we would be blown sideways and end up making twice as much progress to the side as we did forward. Eventually, however, we reached the summit, and after lunch we left North Carolina for the last time and headed into Tennessee.

We stayed at a lean-to high in Laurel Fork Gorge, and during the night we had torrential rains, brilliant flashes of lightning, and tremendous crashes of thunder. The storm was right on top of us. In the morning everything was peaceful, and the violent storm of the night before seemed like a bad dream. After breakfast we continued through Laurel Fork Gorge and passed near Watauga Dam and Watauga Lake. From there we followed the top of a ridge and had good views all afternoon. On our last night in Tennessee, from the rock behind the Vanderventer Lean-to, we watched the shadows of the mountains crawl over the valleys. The lights of civilization came on one by one until it seemed as if there was a field of stars on the earth below us as well as in the heavens above us. It was the best view we had yet had from a lean-to.

Damascus stands in the area which was once known as Mocks Mill, after a man named Mock who came from North Carolina and built a home and mill. There in the undeveloped Virginia wilderness Mock raised three families, having three wives and 33 children. In 1890, Gen. John D. Imboden, a pioneer in the coal, iron, and lumber industries of southwestern Virginia, came to Mocks Mill to promote a town. He named it after Damascus, the ancient capital of Syria, "because of the confluence of beautiful mountain streams there." On our way into town we went across a Mock farm. A young man in a jeep, presumably one of Mock's many descendants, waved to us.

The Appalachian Trail goes down the main street of Damascus, passing the town hall, post office, grocery stores, laundromat, and ice-cream stand. Our first stop was the post office. The postmaster and two other postal employees were delighted to see two Georgia-to-Maine hikers. They had us sign the register they keep for long-distance hikers, and showed us a file folder full of newspaper clippings about Appalachian Trail hikers and letters and postcards they had received from some of the hikers who had been through Damascus. After the post office, we made our regular visits to the laundromat and supermarket, and finished our morning in town with a stop at the ice-cream stand.

A few days earlier two hikers had told us that Virginia forests were closed because of fire danger, and signs posted outside of Damascus confirmed their warning. We didn't stop because of the signs; we hiked on, perhaps going a little faster than usual when we crossed roads. Since neither of us smoked, the only adjustment we made was to have no campfires. As always, we were extremely careful with our stove, so all in all we felt that we were not a fire hazard.

On the morning of May 3, two or three days out of Damascus, we were surprised when we awoke to find an inch of snow on the ground. If it had rained during the night we would have heard it, and hence wouldn't have been surprised in the morning, but the snow came on "cat's-feet" and never made a sound. Most of the snow melted within a few hours, but a few patches remained until the next day. It was the last snow we saw until we reached Mt. Washington in New Hampshire. The following night was one of the coldest we experienced on the trail. When we awoke in the morning the water bag was frozen to the floor of the shelter and there were chunks of ice in the water. Spring seemed to be late in coming. It was the first week of May, yet the trees in the mountains were bare. It was only when we went down into a valley that we saw signs of spring.

The first day the Virginia forests were officially reopened we met a ranger sitting in his truck on a secondary road. He told us he was driving past the next shelter, the Wapiti Shelter, and offered to give us a ride. We explained that we were walking the entire Appalachian Trail, therefore we couldn't take a ride. However, keeping our ponchos, we let him take our packs. He told us that several years ago this area had been stocked with elk and that a hunting season on them had been opened. (The name of the shelter we were headed for, Wapiti, means "elk.") However, the area was not suited for elk, and the animals had been destructive to crops on nearby farms. Although all of the elk had not been accounted for, the rangers were fairly certain that all of them had either been taken by hunters or had died.

In some ways rainy days are good for walking. They are often very good days for thinking and for getting things in our heads straightened out. When it is raining it is very easy to get into the rhythm of walking and let the mind wander. There are few distractions, no views, fewer animals, no sunny springs, no dry places to sit, and over-all, nothing to do except walk and think. On rainy days our mileage was good, and it helped make up for the lower mileage we had on sunny days when various distractions slowed us up. Several successive days of rain, however, are hard to take. After the first two days, the weather becomes monotonous and discouraging. On May 6 the rain was especially hard and was accompanied by a strong wind. The wind blew our ponchos around so much we got soaked to our waists. Every-thing around us was wet. There was nothing we could do but walk—and after several days of rain, walking bored us to death. The longer it rained, the muddier the trail became. The treads on the boots I had bought in North Carolina were almost worn off, and when we came to a series of steep descents I kept falling on the muddy trail, often sliding for quite a distance on the seat of my pants. Soon I was a human mud pie. When we reached a road near Pearisburg we didn't discuss whether or not we would go into town—the only ques-tion was where we would stay. We were directed to Mary Finley's boardinghouse, and for two nights we slept on the convertible sofa bed in her parlor at the anti-inflationary rate of $2 each per night. We forgot about the trail, and spent our time in Miss Finley's parlor and in the Pearisburg Public Library. We ate our meals in restau-rants and washed our clothes at the laundromat.

It was in Pearisburg that I realized that I had been making a mis-take by not living each day for itself instead of constantly thinking about the length of the hike and how far it was to Maine. The more backpacking I have done, the more I have come to understand that the hiker's reward is not in reaching his destination, but in the jour-ney itself. I think the best way to hike is probably the way Averill and Takaro, who were a few weeks ahead of us, were hiking. They had no specific goal, but were just following the Appalachian Trail for the length of time they had to spend. They put their destination in registers as "seven weeks north." If our society were not so goal-oriented, this would be the way most of us would hike. If we hiked without a deadline and destination, there would be no pressure to move on when we found a place where we would like to spend some time. Every 2,000-miler faces the dilemma of wanting to slow down in a favorite area but at the same time wanting to get to the other end of the trail as soon as possible.

When we returned to the trail after our stop in Pearisburg we were refreshed and in good spirits. Except for a few warm days in Georgia and the Smokies, May 10 was our first springlike day. That night we stayed at the Niday Shelter. It was on the site of the homestead where the Niday family had settled about 1865. The shelter was clean and new, with a grassy area in front of it and a clear cool spring nearby. In the yard there was a huge apple tree, the largest I have ever seen. The tree, planted by the Nidays a hundred or more years ago and still bearing fruit, was in bloom when we were there. The next morning, May 11, was the first time it had been warm enough for us to get out of our sleeping bags for breakfast. For the first 40 days we had eaten breakfast while still in our sleeping bags, with our coats on.

Through the southwestern part of Virginia we met no hikers to tell us what the trail ahead was like, and the guidebook for this section was out of print at the time. We never knew what to expect. Although this sometimes caused problems, it also made many of our discoveries more enjoyable. When we reached the top of Cove Mountain we had one of these pleasant surprises. The top of the mountain was made up of huge rocks resting in bizarre positions—many were on end, reaching high into the air. Without a second thought we put down our packs and started climbing on these rocks. We later learned that the place was called Dragons Tooth, after the highest of the vertical rocks. Just after Cove Mountain the trail went along the top of the cliffs of Tinker Ridge. One huge slab of rock extended beyond the face of the cliff, hanging in the air with nothing underneath except the trees far below.

As we approached the road to Snowden we spotted a red pack on the trail ahead, and knew we were going to meet more backpackers. We caught up with this group quickly and when we overtook them it was easy to see why. Al and Melinda Boyers of Raleigh, North Carolina, were accompanied by their three children—a third grader, a first grader, and one in nursery school. They were all very friendly and we enjoyed talking with them. It was the first backpacking trip for the children, and they seemed to be enjoying it and doing well—except for the smallest who sometimes had to be carried. All the way from Georgia to Maine, when we had to go off the trail to pick up supplies, we met people who went out of their way to help us. Now Al Boyers offered to drive us to Snowden. This side trip should have been a short one, but as it turned out, Snowden was one of those towns that you can drive through without even knowing you have reached it. The town consisted of four buildings: three houses set back from the road behind many trees and almost impossible to see, and a small store with a post office in it. The store was closed because it was Saturday. The Boyerses drove us 10 miles to Glasgow,

waited for us to do our errands, and then drove us back to the trail.
A few weeks later we learned that Al Boyers had written to our parents and gave them an "unbiased account" of how we were. He wrote
that we "smiled freely, looked good, and smelled bad, liked to talk,
and could walk fast with long strides," and he predicted that we
would achieve our objective of completing the trail.

The next day we hiked a rough trail of some 20 miles from the
Brown Mountain Creek Lean-to to The Priest Lean-to. That afternoon
painters had painted the ceiling and half of the floor of the Priest
Mountain Lean-to. They had not intended to paint any of the floor,
but I suspect they were really foresters, not painters. Fortunately it
was a clear night and we did not need shelter. Except for rainy nights,
we did not stay in lean-tos much, anyway. We usually camped near a
lean-to because that was where the best campsites and water sources
were, and if the weather changed the lean-to roof would be available.
We carried a two-man tent which we used in a few emergencies, but
we hated sleeping under such claustrophobic conditions. Most nights,
whether we slept outside or in a lean-to, we would be in the woods, so
we seldom had a good view of the stars. Our nights in the woods made
us treasure a clear night in the open when we had one. An astounding
number of stars were visible when there was no moon and you were
far from civilization. It was almost like a different sky; there were so
many stars that some of the common constellations were hard to
pick out. The sky out here was not like the one we saw in urban and
suburban areas; here it was filled with stars all the way to the edges
of the sky. The Milky Way stretched from horizon to horizon, and
was so distinct that it looked like a cloud. Meteors fell and quickly
burned out in a streak of light as they raced toward the earth. When
sleeping under the stars I liked to wake up every couple of hours to
see how much the sky had changed, and what stars were rising and
setting. Some nights the moon rose. If it was only a crescent, the moon
added to the show, but if it was any larger it made it impossible to
see so many stars.

One evening at dinner we sat through an invasion of whippoorwills.
First we heard one in the distance, then he came closer. Others followed. Without being able to see any of them, we could hear whippoorwills on three sides of us. Then one landed near the fireplace,
25 feet away. Another flew into the tree beside us and a third flew
into a tree behind the shelter. We could see and hear all three of

them at once, and we could hear many others in the distance. One or two whippoorwills were delightful to listen to, but a flock of them could almost drive you crazy.

When we reached Rockfish Gap we had been on the trail for 50 days. For seven weeks and a day we had been living peacefully in the woods. Our visits to towns had been brief. We had become more accustomed to the quiet and calm than we realized, and Rockfish Gap gave us a severe shock. The trail came out near the parking lot of a Holiday Inn, crossed a busy highway with all of the usual travel facilities, and then went through an area where an interstate highway was being built. Civilization was with us again—motels, hotels, restaurants, gas stations, highways, construction, cars zipping by, trucks rumbling, dust flying, horns honking, everyone hustling and bustling. As quickly as we could we went to Waynesboro, picked up our mail, bought our food, and hurried back to the tranquility of the woods.

The stretch from Rockfish Gap to the northern end of the Shenandoah National Park was the easiest 100 miles of the Appalachian Trail. The trail was well-graded and cleared, and such easy walking that we never noticed whether we were going uphill or downhill. We would complete our daily quota of 15 miles by 11:30 or 12:00 and spend the afternoon on a nature trail, horseback riding, bathing, writing, or talking with people we met. This section, and the areas north and south of it, was no challenge. As far as we were concerned there were no mountains from a few days south of the park to Connecticut—an opinion which upset many sweaty hikers who thought there were. Although the low fertile mountains in the Shenandoah National Park were pretty, and abounded in flowers and wildlife, the trail was overcivilized and overcrowded. The park was packed with tourists, and the excessive crisscrossing of the Appalachian Trail by the Skyline Drive gave the tourists access to all parts of the trail. In 104 miles the trail crossed the parkway 25 times. No backwoods hiking here—just a pleasant stroll through the crowded woods. We saw more deer in the park than anywhere else on the trail. Since hunting was prohibited, the deer were rather tame and often allowed people to come quite close to them. Bob almost got one to eat out of his hand.

One morning I started ahead of Bob. (We often hiked separately and met at lunchtime or suppertime.) About 15 minutes after I left camp I heard a rustling noise, then saw a large black bear in the bushes 75 or 80 feet ahead of me. He walked out onto the trail, turned abruptly, and ran the other way. The trail curved and he was soon out of sight. The only other bears I saw along the trail were in the zoo at Bear Mountain State Park in New York.

Because of construction at Swift Run Gap, the trail followed the Skyline Drive for almost a mile. While I was walking this section two drivers stopped, at different times, to ask me questions. The first asked directions to the Appalachian Trail, which we were on. The second asked where he could get a permit to hike the Appalachian Trail. At the time this question seemed absurd, but considering how overused the trail is in summer, it may not be as farfetched as it sounds. A permit system has already been started in the Smokies.

That day we finished hiking at the South River Shelter before noon. Bob took a hike and I planned to spend the afternoon alone, writing. It was a Saturday and the shelter was only a half-mile from the Skyline Drive, so I should have known better. Shortly after lunch I started getting visitors. Before supper a dozen people had arrived to stay for the night, and another two dozen had stopped by on their hikes in from the road. I met several interesting people, but did not catch up on my journal and letter writing.

We had made camp at Byrd Shelter No. 3 when a woman came up the trail from the Skyline Drive with a box on her shoulder and an armful of pots. She told us that her husband and four friends were hiking on the Appalachian Trail, and she had come ahead in the car to make supper for them. We spent a pleasant evening with the Greists and their hiking companions. They invited us to dinner and Mrs. Greist proved to be an excellent cook. It was the best meal we had on the trail. Over the years Ned Greist had hiked all of the Appalachian Trail, with the exception of one 50-mile stretch, from Katahdin to this point. He had also hiked Vermont's 260-mile Long Trail, had climbed all 46 of the 4,000-foot peaks in the White Mountains, all 46 of the 4,000-foot peaks in the Adirondacks, all 3,500-footers in the Catskills, all 4,000-footers in New England, and the 100 highest mountains in New England. He had been at it for 40 years. During the same period he had raised five children and saw them through college, had been a scoutmaster for many years, and was active in the Appalachian Mountain Club.

Immediately north of the Shenandoah National Park several landowners had closed the trail across their land, so for 20 or 25 miles we had to walk on roads. We spent 28 days in Virginia—then in one 25-mile day we left that state, hiked through the easternmost tip of

West Virginia, and crossed the Potomac River into Maryland. West Virginia was the only state in which we didn't spend at least one night. Incidentally, West Virginia, with some 20 miles, has less of the Appalachian Trail in it than any of the other 13 states through which the trail passes.

We spent our first night in Maryland at the Weverton Shelter, a converted bathhouse located on the northern bank of the Potomac between the river and the C&O Canal. Camping by a river was totally different from camping in the mountains. Our conversation turned to Mark Twain and Huckleberry Finn, and our minds kept drifting downriver with them. We wondered how anyone living on the bank of a river could resist building a raft and going with the current. As Huck said, "Other places do seem so cramped up and smothery, but a raft don't. You feel mighty free and easy and comfortable on a raft."

The Chesapeake and Ohio Canal is now a national monument. It extends 184.5 miles from Washington, D.C. to Cumberland, Maryland. The first 22 or 23 miles out of Washington are navigable, but open only to boats without motors. The towpath, where the mules once walked to pull the barges, runs parallel to the canal for the entire 184.5 miles. It is wide, flat, and smooth, and open to bicyclists and walkers. Along the way there are a number of hiker-biker stops with water and picnic tables. In 1954, United States Supreme Court Justice William O. Douglas, with others, made a walk along the towpath to help save the C&O Canal. The effort succeeded. Justice Douglas made the walk in response to a newspaper editorial proposing the construction of a scenic highway through the area. He invited newspapermen and others to take the hike with him and, by showing them the natural beauty which would be destroyed, convinced them that a scenic highway would not be as valuable as other uses to which the canal and the towpath could be put. The Appalachian Trail follows the towpath for only a short distance.

We hiked the 38 miles of the Appalachian Trail in Maryland during the Memorial Day weekend. On Friday and Saturday the trail was crowded, but showers reduced the crowds for the remainder of the weekend. Near Hagerstown, Maryland, the Appalachian Trail has its own footbridge over Interstate 70. This bridge is similar in construction to the regular concrete bridges over highways. Just as other bridges have the names of the streets or routes that cross over them, so this bridge has a large green-and-white sign that says: APPALACHIAN TRAIL. We stood on the bridge for several minutes watching the cars race by below us. They were covering as much distance in an hour as we covered in four or five days. We spent the night at the Pine Knob Shelter with several people from Hagerstown. Like many others we met on the trail, these people assumed that we lived in either Georgia or Maine and went to college in the other state.

On a topographical map the Appalachian Trail in Pennsylvania looks easy. According to the map there is not a single difficult climb, and only relatively small changes in elevation. Moreover, the trail usually follows the tops of long low ridges. When actually walking the trail in Pennsylvania, however, the hiker finds that the path is not as simple as it looks on the map. It is never really flat; in fact, it is more like an obstacle course across miles and miles of loose jagged rocks. When someone asks me what part of the Appalachian Trail I liked least, I usually mention Pennsylvania, noting how low the mountains were, how dry it was, and how I got shinsplints from walking on hard surfaces and sore ankles from the uneven rocky trail. These were the unpleasant aspects of our hike through the state, however, and in looking back through my journal, I find that interesting things happened there, too. We encountered a great deal of small wildlife in Pennsylvania, including an abundance of snakes. During my four months on the Appalachian Trail I saw 32 snakes, and most of them were in Pennsylvania. Of these, only two were poisonous—both copperheads; 12 were garter snakes, one was a puff adder, and a half-dozen were blacksnakes. The rest were either grass snakes or snakes I couldn't identify. I was disappointed because I didn't see any rattlesnakes, but I did get a good look at both copperheads. One of them was actually between my boots when I noticed it.

June 5 was county snake-hunt day. All the local people who liked to catch snakes were out for the annual competition. The judges tallied all varieties of snakes, but the serious hunters brought back only poisonous ones. One hunter we met had three copperheads which he had captured without going off the Appalachian Trail. He showed us where he had been bitten on other hunts, and told us about a friend who had lost the use of his hand because of a snakebite. He then reached his bare arm into his bag and pulled out one of the copperheads. Despite the danger and the bites he had received in the past, he continued to hunt snakes and said that at the end of the day he would be working in the snake pits in town. Most of the hunters we met carried two sticks: one had a hook for pulling snakes out of holes and crevices; the other had a leather loop which could be put around the snake's head and tightened by a cord which extended to the upper part of the pole. Each hunter wore high boots and had a cloth sack in which to carry the snakes he caught.

One morning we met a young woodchuck who had taken it upon himself to guard the Appalachian Trail from all human intruders. We found him sitting in the middle of the trail. He let us come close enough to photograph him, then he ran 100 feet down the trail. When we caught up with him, he ran another 100 feet and waited. Now his Spartan blood was in a rage and he made his stand. This time, when we reached him, he charged toward Bob. We both started laughing. This little woodchuck was no larger than a boot, yet he seemed ready to fight the two of us to protect his section of the Appalachian Trail. Actually, he was only trying to get back to his den, so eventually we stepped aside and let him run back down the trail to where we had first seen him.

Occasionally we met wild dogs in the woods. To call them "wild" is misleading; they are more appropriately called "homeless." We never encountered a pack of these dogs, and the individual homeless dogs we met were timid. The only animals that gave us any trouble were hostile domestic dogs. In rural areas we often met small packs of these dogs. I never had to strike any of them with my walking stick, but having the stick gave me assurance and helped keep the bolder dogs a little farther away. One of the common questions we were asked was what we carried for protection, and many people seemed to think we should have been carrying a gun. City people, and even some rural people, think it is safer to spend a night in the city than in the woods. What they really fear is the darkness and the unknown, for there are far more dangerous "animals" in any large city than there are in all the woods of North America.

On June 3 we crossed the Cumberland Valley. This was not the longest day I spent on the trail, but it was my best day for mileage. I did 14 miles by 11:00 A.M. and 27 miles for the day.

All morning on June 6 we wondered how close we were to Castleman and Weirich. We had been following them since Georgia—more than two months and over 1,000 miles. We knew we were close to them. We had never met either John Castleman or Dan Weirich, nor had we seen a picture of them. However, we had been hearing about them from postmasters and store clerks all along the trail, so we knew a great deal about them and could easily identify them. As we approached Applebee Shelter we saw Dan returning from the spring.

He glanced up and saw us coming, but of course he didn't know us. From the register entries we knew that John was now hiking in moccasins, and that he had sore feet. As we came to the shelter I said, "How are your sore feet, John?" Bob turned to Dan and said, "Hi, Dan." We then rattled off their life histories and an account of their adventures along the trail. They just sat and stared at us! After they got over the initial shock, the four of us had plenty of trail experiences to share, and we talked for many hours into the night.

By modern backpacking standards, Castleman and Weirich were the two most unorthodox long-distance hikers we met. Actually, there was nothing truly unorthodox about their methods and equipment except that they were old-fashioned. They had decided to hike the trail on the spur of the moment, with little time or money for preparation, planning, or equipment. Although they did have packframes, they used canvas packbags and carried regular kitchen pots. I don't think they had any lightweight equipment at all, and I know they had no maps or guidebooks; they simply copied information from the guidebooks of hikers they met along the way. These two hikers proved, better than anyone else I met, that very little money is needed to hike the Appalachian Trail, or just to take to the woods for that matter.

When we left the next morning, John and Dan were getting ready to bake bread. Through the central part of their hike, they baked in the morning, starting hiking late, and quit early to bake again. However, the baking was just an excuse: after 1,000 miles they were tired of walking. They continued getting slower and slower, until they finally split up in New York. After they separated, John and Dan got back into the swing of steady hiking.

At Dans Pulpit in Pennsylvania we spent an hour reading the register. Many registers, especially when the entries were written under difficult conditions, contain some unique trail-made humor. This register was filled more with complaints than with humor, but the entries were still amusing. Most of the accounts were written by out-of-shape day-hikers who thought they were going to die. One man complained that the guidebook did not warn readers that the trail was not fit for older people. Another wrote: "You should have been honest and put in the guidebook that this trail is treacherous and should not be traveled." A third hiker gave an elaborate account of how he had started out with a group of over 100 hikers; then he told of the disasters that had overtaken all of the others. He concluded by saying that only he and his dog had made it through alive.

We spent our last night in Pennsylvania at the Kirkridge Shelter.

The shelter was on a ridge with a good view of the valley below. Mosquitoes were out in full force and we built a smoky fire for protection as we didn't have any insect repellent. During the night we had the unpleasant choice of leaving the sleeping bags open and enduring the mosquitoes or leaving the bags closed and roasting. We had lightened our packs by a few ounces by waiting to buy insect repellent until we actually needed it—a mistake we would not make again.

As the southern Appalachians were never covered by glaciation, they lack the glacial ponds that are so numerous on the northern part of the trail. Sunfish Pond in New Jersey was one of the first natural lakes we came to; it was also the first opportunity we had to swim in anything larger than a stream. From this point on, the farther north we went the more abundant the natural bodies of water became. In Maine we sometimes passed half a dozen ponds in a day. At Sunfish Pond I started the day with an early morning swim. Although there were at least 60 people camped nearby, only a few were awake. As I stroked across the smooth surface of the water, I could see no one and could hear no man-made sound except for someone chopping wood in the distance. For a few moments I was back in the days of the pioneers, for my ideal was to travel on more than just one level of consciousness; the Appalachian Trail can lead to more places than one would think. On my best days I traveled the Appalachian Trail as Thoreau traveled the Old Marlborough Road:

> If the fancy unfurled
> You leave your abode,
> You may go round the world
> By the Old Marlborough Road.

On our second day in New Jersey, after a morning rain, I slipped on a wet rock and fell directly on the end of my spine. The lower part of my back hurt for only an hour or two but my spine remained sore and tender. After about 10 days the pain flared up and the bottom of my spine started to hurt intensely. I was reluctant to go to a doctor because I was afraid he would tell me to stop hiking. However, the pain persisted and I finally decided to leave the trail the next morning and seek aid. To my surprise, the pain disappeared that night, and I never had any spine trouble again.

Considering all that our bodies went through, we had very few health problems and never had to stop because of an injury or illness. Except for blisters in the beginning and my injured spine, neither of us had any aches or pains that lasted more than two or three days. Occasionally we would get sore ankles, a sore leg, or a sore foot, and periodically, sore hips from the weight of the packs. However, we never had anything serious or anything that lasted long. We were each sick one day in the beginning of the hike, and I had diarrhea three times, but most of the time we felt exceptionally healthy. Minor aches and pains are taken in stride when you are in good condition, and active and happy.

We had hardly entered the Garden State before we left it. We entered the Empire State at Unionville. As we walked through town we watched the storm clouds brewing and knew we were in for a rainy night. There were no lean-tos in the area, and we avoided using our tent whenever possible. Under these circumstances the large barns of the neighboring farms looked especially attractive. We approached one of the farmers and after a little good-natured bargaining we won a luxuriously soft night on Mr. Cosh's piles of hay by simply promising that we wouldn't set up our stove or make a fire inside the barn.

The next day was rainy and we had to walk several miles on hard-top roads. Late in the afternoon we lost the trail for the second time that day. As we walked along a dirt road we came to the New Jersey state line again. We were supposed to have left that state for good, so we turned around and went back. Shortly before dark we found the overgrown entrance to the trail. Back in the woods we made a lean-to with our tent. It kept us reasonably dry through the night's showers, but we had no room for our packs inside. There were no large trees from which to hang them, so we simply leaned the packs back to back and covered them with a poncho. Except for the interruptions caused by two persistent raccoons who kept trying to get into the packs, we slept very well.

Although New York and New Jersey were the most populated areas through which the Appalachian Trail passed, the walk through these states was more pleasant than I had anticipated it would be. I had expected to weave in and out of shipping centers and along freeways for 158 miles, but we found that most of the trail was in the woods. Even the occasional stretches on roads had a rural flavor. I didn't know there were as many wooded areas in the whole state of New Jersey as we saw just in the northwest corner.

Bear Mountain State Park, by the Hudson River, is a playground where frustrated New Yorkers go to recreate on Sunday afternoons. It was also the most atrocious place the trail took us: noise, herds of people, outlandish prices, extreme apathy and self-centeredness. We made the best of the situation and followed a nature trail through the park. We stopped by the statue of that great exponent of the open road, Walt Whitman, and passed the bear den which, at 115.4 feet above sea level, is the lowest point on the trail. The only bargain I got at Bear Mountain State Park was on a set of scales where I learned both my weight and my fortune for a penny. After 2½ months on the trail my weight was down to 147 pounds, some 22 pounds less than it had been on Springer Mountain. By the time I reached Katahdin I had lost 30 pounds.

One evening I couldn't find the water source near the lean-to so I took the canteens and went down a dirt road to a boys' camp. At the camp I met a middle-aged counselor who directed me to their pump. We talked about backpacking for 10 minutes, then for some reason he started talking about the Vietnam War, social problems, racism, poverty. He did all the talking; I had nothing to say and had no interest in the conversation. That night I wrote in my journal: "Those were problems of another world. Now I live in a new world. At college I could have talked about those things all night, but they are meaningless to me now. If he wanted to talk about the dry spring up the road, the terrain or trail conditions, or about how healthy and pleasant it is to be living close to nature, I would have had plenty to say. This episode made me realize for the first time why Thoreau did not vote, and why he would not attend a political or social gathering, although he might attend a meeting to save endangered species of pine."

On our last night in New York we camped on the rifle range of a Boy Scout camp. We had received permission to sleep there from the ranger's wife, and she told us that the ranger probably would come over to visit us when he got home. When we saw a man coming over the hill, we figured it was the ranger. However, it turned out to be Ned Greist, whom we had met in the Shenandoah National Park. Ned was dropping off Tom Kern, whom we had also met in Virginia, for a few days of hiking.

The next morning the sky was clear and it promised to be a beautiful day. Ned fixed fresh eggs and hot chocolate for us. By 6:30 we were on the trail, with only 2½ hours of hiking to the Connecticut state line on top of Schaghticoke Mountain. I am a native New Englander, and after traveling for three months on foreign soil, so to speak, I relished this return to my own land. We reached the Chase Mountain Lean-to shortly after noon and met the Winslows there. We had lunch with them, then Bob went home to Avon for a day. I stayed on the trail, and the next day, June 20, my family and a friend drove out from Hartford and I met them in Macedonia Brook State Park for a picnic. That afternoon the Winslows brought Bob back to the trail. After a couple of hours at the picnic grounds, Bob headed up to the lean-to and his family started back to Avon. Later my own family left for Hartford. As I walked through the darkening woods I felt a little lonely. When I reached the lean-to, being very conscious of the weight of my freshly loaded pack, I introduced myself as Colin Fletcher—"because I don't know of anyone else who is crazy enough to carry such a heavy pack." One of the people sitting by the campfire went along with it: "Well hello, Colin Fletcher. I'm Sam Prentiss." Soon I felt good again. I had my pack, I was at a lean-to with a white Appalachian Trail blaze on the trail beside it, and I was sitting by a campfire with good people. I wondered why I would ever want to go back to the city.

The next day we hiked 12.5 miles with Sam and his son, Bard, over St. Johns Ledges, Calebs Peak, and along the bank of the Housatonic River. Northwestern Connecticut and southwestern Massachusetts are noted for an abundance of beautiful ravines. At Dean Ravine we came to a section of the Appalachian Trail that we had hiked the previous fall. There was much more vegetation now, and it was like walking a different trail. It occurred to me that with every change in the season, and even on each new day, we did indeed walk a different trail—even if we covered exactly the same ground. There is really no need to go far away for variety. If we look closely there is as much to see in one mile of trail as there was in 2,000 miles.

Bear Mountain (2,316 feet), which is only a few miles south of Massachusetts, is the highest peak in Connecticut. Although we enjoyed sleeping on mountaintops, wind and lack of shelter prevented us from doing it very often. In fact, Bear Mountain was the first summit we had camped on since Springer Mountain in Georgia. After breakfast we descended through Sages Ravine and entered Massachusetts, our eleventh state on the trail. After going through the ravine, we went over Race Mountain (2,365 feet) and Mt. Everett (2,602 feet), then had lunch at Guilder Pond.

Late that afternoon I left the trail to make a telephone call. Bob waited by a road, and while I was gone he met Eric Agar, a 15-year-old who lived on a nearby farm. Eric gave us permission to sleep in one of his family's fields. The field was covered with deep wet grass, so we set up camp near the road where the grass was shortest. A row of trees sheltered us from the road. Soon a green truck pulled in. The driver jumped out, and without saying a word to us, dumped several gallons of gasoline on a large pile of tree trunks and branches nearby and lit a fire. We were stunned by his reckless and inconsiderate action. We were especially surprised because Eric had made a point of telling us not to have a fire. After lighting the fire, the man leaned against his truck and watched the blaze with childish fascination. We returned to our dinner, but kept an eye open for the fire-happy fellow's next move. A little later he asked if we would watch the fire for him. Although I told him we didn't want to do it, he got in his truck and left anyway. The flames were very high and the fire smoked heavily. People driving along the road slowed down to look, and we were afraid people would think the fire was ours, and that it would give them a bad impression of backpackers.

An hour later another green truck, similar to the first one, drove up and stopped. This man looked concerned, and asked us if we had a permit for the fire. Bob and I thought he was joking, but he wasn't. He told us he was with the Dutch Elm Patrol, and said he had received complaints about the fire. After hearing our story he decided that the man who had started the fire was actually one of his own employees who had not been scheduled to work that night. He told us that the grass was wet enough to contain the fire, and that it wouldn't be dangerous for us to sleep there.

Sam Prentiss came by while we were eating lunch—and told us that on the previous afternoon he had passed Washington Town Hall and Mrs. Hutchinson had asked if he had seen us on the trail. He said a newspaper article about us was hanging on her dining room wall. When we arrived at Mrs. Hutchinson's house we found her dozing on a couch on the porch—or the veranda, as she would call it. We stood there for a moment, afraid to wake her up, and wondering what to do. She solved the problem by opening her eyes and very calmly saying, "Oh, it's you," even though she had never seen either of us before, except in the newspaper photograph. Mrs. Hutchinson was a very active and interesting woman. At 88 she had so much life and energy—that she made a younger person feel ashamed that he was ever tired. She lived in a beautiful old house that had been built during the Revolutionary War period. It was called the Country House because around 1811 it had been used as a tavern with that name. We camped behind the Country House for two nights, and on our second evening Mrs. Hutchinson's daughter and son-in-law, Mr. and Mrs. Allen, who lived across the road in a more modern home, invited us over for hot showers and to wash our clothes in their washing machine. The two homes stand with the old Washington Town Hall on top of one of the Berkshire hills, but regardless of altitude, this was one of the high points of our journey along the Appalachian Trail.

On both mornings Mrs. Hutchinson invited us in for breakfast and afterward read us Robert Frost's poems. She had known Frost for 20 or 30 years, both through a poetry society she belonged to and as a neighbor in Amherst. She had several volumes of Frost's poems that had been autographed by the poet. When they were living in Amherst, Mrs. Allen went to Frost to ask his advice on how to read his poem, "Death of the Hired Man," which she was going to read in an oratory contest. Frost told her that each person had to decide how to read it himself, but he did say he regretted that a time limit would force her to leave out sections of the poem. "Everything I put in there I put in for a reason," he told her.

Mrs. Hutchinson had kept a diary for each of the 51 years she had lived or summered in the Berkshires, and all 51 volumes were in a bookcase in the Allens' home. She had also kept a guest book since before the trail was routed by her home, and had entertained many of the 2,000-milers as guests or visitors.

After our day with Mrs. Hutchinson we hiked an easy 10 miles to Dalton. Frost's poems were running through our heads, and when we went through a grove of white birches, we had to swing them. I was 21 years old, yet had never swung a birch. Despite my many years of schooling, this was a part of my education that was lacking. How could I have understood the poem, "Birches," before? Any literature student who has not spent some time in rural New England can hardly be expected to understand Frost or any other New England writer. In school you can analyze Frost, but only when you are in rural New England can you understand him.

Back on the trail we again met the Bad-Off Appalachian Jug Band, a good-hearted group we had first encountered a few days before at Benedict Pond. Mike, Ed, Wes, Pete, and Mark had several instruments, including kazoos, harmonicas, mouth harps, and a recorder, and with these instruments they made some of the strangest sounds ever heard on any trail. The band was not very concerned with campings dos and don'ts and simply took things as they came. One of their outstanding characteristics was their lack of organization. Now, at this camp, no one cleaned the pots or put the food away. In the morning they were missing eight chocolate bars, wrappers and all. During the night I had seen a raccoon making trips up and down a tree to the picnic table, but not until morning, when I heard about the missing candy bars, did I understand the reason for the raccoon's trips. The one member of the group who had already eaten his two bars had a good laugh, and the others learned something about camping.

We reached the top of Mt. Greylock (3,491 feet) early in the morning. In every direction it was totally undercast with morning fog and our only view was of the clear blue sky above. Many of the trails on Mt. Greylock were so wet they could best be described as mudways or mushways. This was a preview of the Appalachian Trail in Maine. The worst parts of the mudways were usually made passable by log walks; some of these walkways were made with long logs laid lengthwise along the trail, but usually they were made with short logs laid parallel across the trail.

Soon after Greylock we went through Blackinton, then entered Vermont. From the Massachusetts state line to Sherburne Pass we followed about 95 miles of the Long Trail before the two trails separated with the Long Trail continuing through Vermont to Canada, and the Appalachian Trail turning east toward New Hampshire and Maine. One of the many hikers we met on the Long Trail was a quiet youth named Russ. He was a slow walker, was afraid of nonexistent bears, and said he preferred going from town to town rather than staying in the woods. I could never figure out why he was in the woods in the first place. Russ told me repeatedly that he could not believe how much I ate. He said that the most amazing thing he had seen on his whole trip was my appetite. As a matter of fact, on the trail I did eat about three times what I normally ate, but with the energy I burned up, even that was not enough. Whenever Bob and I were not hiking, we were eating. Two days after picking up food we would usually have to start rationing ourselves in order to make the food last until the next pickup. On the northern half of the trail, where stores were more common, we sometimes ate a full week's supply of food in three days and then had to load up again.

On the night of July 3 the temperature dropped to 40° F. in a nearby town, so we figured it was probably in the thirties in the mountains. (We had already broken two thermometers and no longer carried one.) Our sleeping bags were comfortable to about 10° F., so we kept warm. The next day we crossed four peaks: Bromley Mountain (3,260 feet), Styles Peak (3,394 feet), and Peru Peak (3,429 feet), and Baker Peak (2,850 feet). Rock-topped Baker Peak offered very interesting views of Otter Creek Valley, and the views from the observation tower on Bromley Mountain were good. The ski lift was running on Bromley, bringing people to the summit for $3.50 per person.

We passed Little Rock Pond the next morning. If we had known how beautiful it was we would have walked an extra six miles the day before and camped there. The pond was small, clear, and clean. It was surrounded by forest, and there was an impressive rock cliff on the west, and a rocky mountain above that. An ideal Walden Pond, if you could chase all the people away. After a boat ride and a visit with some campers, we hiked on to Sunnyside Camp. (On the Long Trail a "camp" is a four-sided closed shelter which usually has a stove and bunks.) The next day I had a long conversation with a farmer who had motioned from his tractor for me to wait for him. He started the conversation by asking, "How come everyone has red packs?" After talking about the trail for a while, he started quoting me all sorts of farm prices for the past 15 years. He told me he had 660 acres, most of which he didn't need. Even though he had had many good offers, he refused to sell because "neighbors only mean trouble."

A half-mile after Sherburne Pass the Appalachian Trail and the Long Trail separated. At this junction we stood only 166 miles from Canada by the Long Trail, but still 490 miles from Katahdin by the Appalachian Trail. When we came to the first register after Sherburne Pass we were surprised to find that Dan Weirich, the 2,000-miler whom we had passed in Pennsylvania, was the last person to sign it. Apparently he had passed us while we were off the trail for supplies.

Bob's camera broke for the third time the day we went through Gifford Woods State Park, and we went to the ranger's office so Bob could call his parents and make arrangements for another one. While Bob was on the telephone I talked with the ranger about backpackers who had stopped there in recent years, and the conversation turned to hippies. The ranger was about 55 or 60, with short hair and no beard or sideburns, so he was far from what anyone would call a hippie. He told me that the park commission had sent out a warning to state parks to the effect that 200,000 hippies would invade Vermont during the summer. "When one of the hippies came in I waited for him to do something wicked. From the warning, I thought they were supposed to come in dancing on their heads, but they just walked in like anyone else. I've had a hundred longhairs in here and they're very nice people. In my report to Montpelier, under the section on hippies, I said they had been 100 percent perfect, and that I hoped I got a lot more of them."

Late in the afternoon of one of our last days in Vermont we met

Arthur Wood of South Woodstock. Mr. Wood had never met Bob or me before, but his daughter worked with Bob's mother. He took us out for supper, then to his house for the night. Arthur's brother Clyde, who lived across the road, was a beekeeper. He also trained chipmunks. At various times he had worked with 23 chipmunks that he called "educated." The chipmunks lived behind his house in the natural state, and he had constructed an elaborate trap to catch any cats or raccoons, that tried to interfere with his "students."

The next morning we met our first Maine-to-Georgia hiker, Jim Rutter. When we shook hands with him, Katahdin and Springer Mountain met. We had no golden spike to drive, but we did have much to talk about. Bob and I had less than 500 miles to go, but Jim still had over 1,500 miles of hiking before he reached his journey's end.

Later in the day we picked up food and mail in West Hartford, and before supper we were in New Hampshire with 12 states behind us and only New Hampshire and Maine ahead. As we approached the main street of Hanover, another fellow 2,000-miler, Jim Ross, greeted us. Jim passed us while we were off the trail at Mr. Wood's house. Long-legged and fast-walking, he had left Springer Mountain on April 26. Jim's family was driving up from Massachusetts to meet him and to drop off his sister, Andrea, who was going to hike with him for about 50 miles—from Hanover to Glencliff. Jim's family invited us out to dinner and we dined with them on the patio of the expensive Hanover Inn. Bob and I had on dungaree shorts, dirty wrinkled shirts, and hiking boots, and our legs were dirty. However, despite our appearance, we were happy and in excellent physical condition. Several of the clean well-dressed obese diners, who could not see beyond our clothes, gave us indignant looks. Two nights later, when we stayed with a Dartmouth Outing Club trail crew, they were overjoyed to hear that we had eaten at the Hanover Inn while wearing hiking clothes. One of them told us he had once been asked to leave the inn because, although he was wearing a sports jacket, did not have a tie.

Three days after leaving Hanover, Bob and I split up. Being with the same person almost every hour of the day is very tiring, no matter who the person is. Since we were not getting along well there was really no reason to continue hiking together. I climbed Mt. Moosilauke, my first 4,000-foot peak in the White Mountains, with a new feeling of independence. For weeks I had been hearing about how rough the ascent of Mt. Moosilauke was. When I got there I discovered that going north, it was the *descent* that was steep. Several places had ladders or steel cables to help the hiker. The following day I climbed South Kinsman (4,363 feet) in the rain. The climb was hard but interesting. I had to use my hands constantly. Sometimes I threw my walking stick ahead because I needed both hands to climb. As always, I was intrigued with the clouds and how quickly they moved and changed. I went into a cloud halfway up the mountain, and when I reached the summit I found myself in a thunderstorm. Fearing the lightning, I hurried along the trail to the woods.

I arrived at the Appalachian Mountain Club's Lonesome Lake Hut in pouring rain and found only two hut boys there. Although 13 people had made reservations and paid, no one else came, except for a third hut boy. Since the AMC huts are inaccessible by automobile, supplies are carried in on hut boys' backs. Getting one of these jobs is hard, just as the work is, but a hut boy holds a respected position in the White Mountains. The hut boys take pride in how much weight they can pack in to a hut and how fast they can do it. The hut boy who arrived after I did was carrying 122 pounds. His record load was 130. The four hut boys at Lonesome Lake were all trying to get up to 130 pounds before the end of the summer. They told me that the boys in another hut had set their goal at 150 pounds. The all-time record, they said, was 180 pounds.

The next morning I went down through Franconia Notch, then up across the shoulder of Mt. Liberty and followed the Franconia Ridge Trail over Little Haystack Mountain (4,560 feet), Mt. Lincoln (5,108 feet), and up to Mt. Lafayette (5,249 feet). Much of the walk from Little Haystack Mountain to Mt. Lafayette is well above tree line and has some of the best views in the White Mountains. Little Haystack Mountain, although it rises to 4,560 feet, is not included in the AMC list of 4,000-foot White Mountain peaks. To be on the list, a peak must rise 200 feet above the ridge from any neighboring 4,000-foot peak, and this stipulation disqualifies several mountains. As I followed the Appalachian Trail through New Hampshire I climbed 19 of the recognized 4,000-footers, including all of the ones the trail goes over, and a few on side trails.

On the Franconia Ridge Trail, I met Steve Gorman of Long Island, New York, who was hiking the Appalachian Trail from Maine to Georgia. As far as I know, Steve and Jim Rutter were the only Maine-to-Georgia hikers I met who made it to Georgia. In New Hampshire and Maine I met over 20 people who said they were going all the way to Springer Mountain. However, I could tell that not more than four or five of them had any chance of making it. Most of these people had the money, the time, and the equipment to complete the trip, but they lacked the determination. One morning at 10:30 I met three young men who were just finishing breakfast. The trio thought they were going to Georgia and told me so, but I knew they would never make it. I had already climbed three mountains that morning; if they were determined to go to Georgia, they would have been doing the same. Another day I met three women who were physical education teachers and they told me they were going all the way to Georgia, but they were not hiking that day because it was raining. A backpacker who does not hike in the rain would never get out of Maine.

One late afternoon I reached Crawford Notch after going over South Twin Mountain and Mt. Guyot. From the notch I had a 2,000-foot view-filled climb up the Webster Cliff Trail to Mt. Webster (3,910 feet). Coming down Mt. Webster I started to slip occasionally. Although I still felt strong and alert, I knew that this slipping was a sign of fatigue. Soon my feet started to feel sore every time I put them down. When I reached the Nauman Shelter I realized why I was tired. I had walked 19 or 20 miles—nothing exceptional in most areas, but a good day's hike in the White Mountains.

The next day was July 17. The weather was beautiful and I spent most of the day above tree line, following the old original trail to the summit of Mt. Washington. First I went to the summit of Mt. Clinton (4,310 feet), then across the shoulder of Mt. Pleasant (4,761 feet), over the summit of Mt. Franklin (5,004 feet), across the shoulder of Mt. Monroe (5,385 feet), and finally to the summit of Mt. Washington, which at 6,288 feet is the highest mountain in the northeastern part of the United States. Walking above tree line on a clear day is one of the most extraordinary and fulfilling experiences I have known. There is a feeling up there on the rock-strewn summits that is as close to perfection as a feeling can be. In bad weather these treeless summits are a danger and sometimes a killer; but in good weather they are a giver of life. We climb mountains more for our mental health than for the physical exercise. From tiny alpine and subalpine plants to miles of aged rocks and broad flat tablelands and piked peaks, to scattered cumulus clouds and brisk winds and blue skies, to the welcoming and friendly valleys below, to the beckoning summits in the distance, and most of all to the sacred mountains themselves, everything fills us with exhilaration and wonder.

The Appalachian Trail misses the summit of Mt. Washington by 0.2 mile, but a short side trail leads to the top. The summit is in clouds 60 percent of the time, so I was pleasantly surprised when I found it clear. After Mt. Lafayette and other spectacular summits, the summit of Mt. Washington is a letdown. It is too wide to get a panoramic view in all directions at once, and the buildings further limit and break up the view. Also, Mt. Washington is located in a less interesting place than many other mountains. It is on the edge of the White Mountains and in one direction the view is of lower, flatter land. The summit buildings, besides being obstructions to the view, are so commercialized as to be disgraceful. The weather station is the only respectable enterprise on the summit. Meteorologists have been living there the whole year around for many years in order to record weather conditions. As the White Mountain National Forest's signs warn, the area has some of the worst, fastest changing, and most unpredictable weather in the world. The highest surface wind speed ever recorded in the world—231 miles per hour—was recorded on Mt. Washington. The average wind speed on the summit is 35 miles per hour. The highest temperature ever recorded at the station is 71° F. The lowest temperature recorded there is −49° F. The average temperature is 27° F. The record snowfall is 97.8 inches (just over 8 feet) in about one day. Although record snowfalls occur in winter, it is not uncommon for some snow to fall during the summer months.

I have read that more people have died on Mt. Washington than on any other mountain in the world. Most of these deaths were caused by underestimating the weather possibilities. The hiker in the valley below often does not realize that the valley weather bears little relation to the weather on Mt. Washington. If an ascending hiker finds that the weather is bad, he should turn around and go back down; conditions are only going to get worse the higher he goes. The stubborn hiker who refuses to do this may pay with his life, or endanger the lives of others who go to search for him. It is no disgrace to turn back because of bad weather on Mt. Washington, Mt. Katahdin, or any other mountain.

Most of the people at the Madison Huts were out for the weekend and were staying at the huts each night, so they carried only day packs. My bulging pack stood out. Someone asked where I had come from, and as soon as "Georgia" was out of my mouth, several people looked up. Soon I had a large audience and held, as one person called it, a "press conference." The Madison Huts are in the col between Mt. Madison and Mt. Adams, and are well above timberline. From the inside of one of the huts we could see the shoulder of Mt. Adams and a bright orange tent that was pitched less than 100 yards away. Suddenly a dark cloud came up over the side of the mountain and within a few minutes we could see neither the shoulder of Mt. Adams nor the tent. In three or four minutes visibility had been reduced from good to zero. From the safety of the hut this was an amazing scene to watch—but outside in the storm it would have been a frightening experience for most people. As we looked on in amazement, two hut boys with huge packs appeared out of the dense fog and calmly walked in. Who knows the trail better than the hut boy who walks it all summer long with a heavy load on his back? No other hiker has to watch and plan each step as carefully as he does.

After having eaten with the hut crew at Lonesome Lake, I was disappointed with the breakfast at the Madison Huts. At Lonesome Lake I had a satisfying breakfast—a quart of orange juice, a quart of fresh whole milk, hot cereal, pancakes, eggs, bacon, toast, and hot cocoa. At the Madison Huts they served me only a glass of juice, hot cereal, a bun, and hot cocoa. When they cleared the tables I thought they were preparing for the second course, but when it didn't come I realized that at Lonesome Lake I had been served *a hut boy's breakfast* but at the Madison Huts I was getting only a *hiker's breakfast.*

At Pinkham Notch I met my family and went with them to their campsite at Moose Brook State Park. The following morning my father dropped me off at Pinkham Notch at 6:30 so I could hike the 19.9 miles to the Gorham–Shelburne Road (U.S. Route 2) and meet him there that evening. The guidebook said that three days should be allowed to traverse this section. I allowed myself 12 hours, and told my father I would meet him at 6:30, but carrying only a day pack I was able to make it in only 8 hours. After the first two hours I did not push, and late in the afternoon I even loafed. That day I went over six 4,000-foot peaks and 12 peaks in all, including Wildcat E (4,041 feet) and Wildcat Mountain (4,397 feet). From both of these summits I had excellent views of the Presidential Range. The morning was exceptionally clear; there was no haze and not a cloud in the sky. Visibility on Mt. Washington that morning was said to have been 100 miles. Beyond Carter Notch I went through the Carters—Carter Dome, South Carter, Middle Carter, and North Carter. When I was on Middle Carter it began to get cloudy, and after Mt. Moriah it began to rain. When my family met me at U.S. Route 2, my mother was surprised that I was wearing my poncho since it had been clear that morning. I told her that I was used to mountain weather and was prepared for almost anything.

After a day of rest, I got back on the trail at U.S. Route 2 and entered the Mahoosucs. As I left North Road I met Jim Ross again. We hiked together and just after lunch we found ourselves shaking hands on the Maine–New Hampshire state line. Maine was no longer a dream—it had become a reality. Except to backpackers and hikers the Mahoosucs are an unknown mountain range, for the only way in is on foot. I had never even heard of the Mahoosucs before beginning my hike on the Appalachian Trail, but once on the trail, even as far south as North Carolina, I started hearing stories about the steep cliffs, the snow and ice in summer, and the mile of trail that takes many hours to traverse.

The Mahoosuc Range has several difficult ascents and descents, but what gives it uniqueness is the Mahoosuc Notch. The trail descends steeply into the notch, then goes between impregnable rock walls for almost a mile before coming out at the other end. The walls on both sides are almost vertical. There are no significant changes in elevation on the floor of the pass, but the area is covered with huge boulders which make normal walking impossible. Often the trail climbs over these rocks, and several times it goes through gaps beneath them. I went through Mahoosuc Notch during the third week of July, yet snow and ice remained in some of these chilly forever-shaded passageways. I could have avoided climbing under some of the boulders by going over them, as I could see others had done, but climbing under them was a new experience which added variety and adventure to the hike. To get through some of these passages I had to take off my pack and push it ahead of me. Once I tried to save a few seconds by leaving it on, and then lost several minutes trying to get myself unstuck.

Maine proved to be a very wet state. It showered almost daily. There were few level campsites. The cleared areas near lean-tos were about the only places where a tent could be pitched. The sleeping platforms in many of the lean-tos in Maine were made of two-inch logs, and these bumpy little logs made the worst bed I have ever tried to sleep on. They made me feel like I was really roughing it in the wilderness!

In both Georgia and Maine the Appalachian Trail went through some lumbered areas and sometimes followed dirt logging roads. In addition to being ugly, newly lumbered areas often obscured the trail. Trees with blazes on them were sometimes cut down. Places where the trail left the road and entered the woods were obscured by piles of branches, gravel, and rocks. After following the unblazed trails of New Hampshire I was out of the habit of watching for blazes. This, together with the disruption of the trail by logging, caused me to lose the route several times. I made a conscious effort to reprogram myself to the valuable habit of watching for blazes. Losing the trail occasionally is almost inevitable, but the hiker who is watching for blazes knows very quickly when he has strayed, and hence loses less time in finding the trail again.

I had looked forward to the quiet and solitude of the Maine woods. I had anticipated experiencing "perfect natural silence," but I never did find it. Chain saws were the worst offenders. I could hear them for hours at a time, although I seldom saw the workers who were using them. Occasionally I saw or heard lumber trucks or tractors, and sometimes I heard the drone of an airplane, but even when these reminders of civilization were completely absent, the wind and rain insured that I never found total silence.

I reached the 1,800-mile mark at Sabbath Day Pond Lean-to. This shelter was in a beautiful location on a small isolated pond which had an excellent triple echo. Two loons made quite a racket during the night, but they were more interesting and amusing than disturbing. Near the pond I found moose tracks, but did not see my first moose until several days later.

Many of the Maine peaks were engulfed in clouds a great deal of the time. In the southern Appalachians I had walked in mountain fogs on many mornings, but here I walked in fog on summit after summit for days at a time. I went over Saddleback (4,116 feet) and The Horn (4,023 feet), both in the clouds. The next day I went over Spaulding Mountain (3,988 feet), Mt. Sugarloaf (4,237 feet), and West Peak of Bigelow (4,150 feet)—all enveloped in clouds.

When I arrived at the Myron H. Avery Memorial Lean-to, between the main peaks of Bigelow, I found a group from a boys' camp already there. It was beginning to rain, and when I walked up to the lean-to the boys asked me where I was going to stay. I said I was going to stay in the lean-to. There was not enough room, they said, and suggested that I go back three miles to The Horns Pond Lean-tos. I told them that there was enough room in a lean-to for as many people as came, and besides, I never hiked south. I had never refused anyone room in a lean-to, and with this one exception, no one ever tried to refuse me. I stayed, but made no friends. Between Georgia and Maine I met several well-organized and happy Scout groups, but only one such camp group. Most of the group from the boys' camps were on a required overnight hike. Usually the leaders knew little or nothing about camping and sometimes hated it; the trips were not well-organized, and the routes were too strenuous for the children taking the hikes. I felt that such an experience could only lead to a lasting dislike of the outdoors; many of these middle-class city kids would never again voluntarily set foot in the woods.

The next morning I climbed Myron H. Avery Peak (4,088 feet), but missed seeing Katahdin because of clouds. At West Carry Pond I met two men who were surveying beside a dirt road. One of them asked how I would like a Coke. "A Coke?" (Tom Dickson later told me that I sounded like I didn't believe there was such a thing in the Maine Woods.) He directed me to his camp on West Carry Pond, where Mrs. Dickson invited me inside—wet boots and all. I sat with Mrs. Dickson and Mrs. Storey and had soda and cookies until Mr. Dickson and Mr. Storey joined us. They had met several 2,000-milers, including Branley C. Owen. They were the only people I met who had seen Owen stop; it seems he couldn't turn down a soda, either. Tom Dickson had been born in Scotland, but his family had brought him to Maine when he was still an infant. He had been summering at the Carry Ponds since 1927. Back in the thirties he had been a supervisor of the Civilian Conservation Corps camp at Flagstaff Lake when the CCCers built several trail lean-tos in the area, as well as part of the original Appalachian Trail in Maine.

Every hiker has his own story of how he crossed the Kennebec. The river is about 1,000 feet wide and has no bridge, and from the south, no ferry service unless it is arranged in advance. Each morning, usually at about 9:00, a dam upriver is opened and logs are floated down. Southbound hikers I met had used various methods of crossing. Some had hired a boat or canoe in Caratunk and had been ferried across, but most of them had forded the river. Some hikers waded across bareboot and said that method worked well; some went barefoot and cut and bruised their feet. Some wore boots and suggested wearing them; others wore boots and said it was better *not* to wear them. Most suggested using a walking stick or pole. Some used a rubber raft for their packs; one made a log raft. Few people agreed on what time the logs started coming down the river, or whether the water level rose.

I got into a long conversation with a southbound hiker and reached the Kennebec later than I had planned. Just as I got to the river one of the fishermen on the other side hollered that the water was coming up, and I was surprised to see all 10 or 12 fishermen get out of the water immediately. Hoping that I was not too late, I started into the river. I was wearing my boots, socks, shirt, and shorts. The current was quite strong. When I was about 50 feet out into the river I decided to turn back, and when I reached the shore I was glad I did.

Looking out across the river I saw scores of logs where there had been only a few of them two minutes before. I decided that the Kennebec would have to wait until another day. I climbed up on the bank, found a good campsite, and spent the day reading and watching the cars on the highway across the river.

The next morning I had a leisurely breakfast and watched two hikers ford the Kennebec from the other side. They inched across the river, pulling and pushing an air mattress they were using as a raft for their packs. When I had welcomed them to the southern shore I started across myself. This time I wore only my boots, without socks, and my shorts. I carried my pack on my back as usual, except that I put the sleeping bag *above* the packbag instead of below it. I made my crossing about 100 yards upstream from where the Appalachian Trail comes down to the river. Rapids extended two-thirds of the way across, so I only had to worry about the depth of the water for the last third of the crossing. The current was strong and the bottom was covered with small, slippery rocks. Each time I took a step I made sure I had found secure footing before I put my full weight down. My walking stick served as a third leg and helped me keep my balance. Most of the time the water was only up to my knees; in the deepest places it rose to the lower edge of my shorts. The surging current reminded me of how easily I could be washed downstream, but overall, the crossing was easier than I had expected.

At the general store in Caratunk I was surprised to learn that Jim Ross had been there only an hour before. I wondered why I had not seen him cross the river, but when I reached Moxie Bald Lean-to in midafternoon I found Jim there and learned that he had crossed 300 yards downstream from my camp.

The next morning I hiked into Monson with Jim. He set the pace and I got to Monson quite a bit sooner than I would have if I had been walking by myself. We were in Monson at about 11:15, with 16 miles behind us. Monson is a friendly town some 1,912 miles from Springer Mountain or 116 miles from Katahdin, depending on your point of view. For Jim and me it was a major landmark—our last food and mail pickup on the Appalachian Trail.

Monson has one of the best inexpensive restaurants along the Appalachian Trail. Hikers rave about it when writing in the registers or when you meet them on the trail. Jim and I ate there, or rather, we *overate* there. We started with a full dinner, then had lunch, then several desserts. The waitress was shocked with each new order. The table was intended for four, but was not large enough for the two of us, even when we stacked the empty plates and dishes. Eventually the waitress had to take some of the empties away before she could bring our next order. Jim and I camped outside of Monson that night and the next morning he left before I did. That was the last time I saw him on the trail.

Late the following afternoon I went over White Cap Mountain. Hoping to get a glimpse of Katahdin I took a side trail to the summit, where there was a fire tower. It was hazy, so I still didn't have my first view of Katahdin. I also missed seeing the celebrated moose who "lives" on the trail on White Cap Mountain, the moose that *everyone* sees. Two days later, however, I finally did see my first moose. I was walking along an open road and heard a sound behind a clump of bushes 100 feet ahead. As I walked closer, taking care to be quiet, I saw a brown back in the bushes and knew it was a moose. Looking like an awkward and malformed horse, she started trotting down the road away from me. I had assumed she would run off quickly, as most deer would, but she stopped a short distance down the road, turned her head, and looked at me over her shoulder. Then she stood politely while I got out my camera and took a picture. After that she ambled off into the woods.

By the end of the day I was over the 2,000-mile mark—some 2,003 miles, by my calculation. I spent the night at Rainbow Lake Lean-to, where I met two friends of Mark and Pete of the Bad-Off Appalachian Jug Band. They were waiting to meet Mark and hike to Katahdin with him. They told me some elaborate stories about the wolf they had seen the night before, but long ago I had learned that only inexperienced backpackers tell wolf stories, and only even more inexperienced backpackers believe them.

August 4 was another rainy day. It was not until late in the afternoon of this last day before climbing Katahdin that I got a view of the mountain—first with its summit in the clouds, then from Katahdin Stream Campground with the summit clear.

The next morning was beautiful. I had a leisurely breakfast and started for Baxter Peak at 8:30. As I walked through the woods I savored each beautiful moment. By the time I reached timberline I was bubbling over with a joy that I had felt only once or twice in my life. The sky was perfectly blue except for some snow-white cumulus clouds in the distance. Above me were some huge granite boulders, and beyond them I could see a point that I thought was the summit of Katahdin and the end of my long journey. As I got closer I realized by looking at the neighboring 4,000-foot peaks that I was not high enough, but I could see no higher peak ahead of me. I continued to be puzzled until I reached the crest of the ridge. Then I was amazed to see that the summit was still a mile or more away across a broad flat tableland. The summit of Katahdin had been hidden by the ridge. In the excitement of the last few days I had neglected to look at my maps and no one had described the top of the mountain to me.

More than any other kind of mountain, I love rocky primitive summits; not the gentle forest-protected peaks, but the ones that soar to the heavens. Katahdin is as near to perfection as a mountain can get. As I neared the summit I recognized the brown weather-beaten sign that marked the northern terminus of the "endless" footpath through the Appalachian Mountains, an endless path to which I had found an end. Four people were on the summit when I got there. Although I knew it was the end, I cried in an incredulous tone, "Is this the end of the Appalachian Trail?" Without waiting for a response, I rather compulsively started telling them my story, "I've hiked the whole Appalachian Trail from Springer Mountain. I left Georgia on April 1, and. . . ."

I stayed on the summit of Katahdin for a long time. I couldn't think of anywhere else to go or anything else to do, but Pamola[1] finally drove me off. Perhaps too many people had climbed Katahdin that day and he was angry. The clouds moved in and darkness hovered over our heads. Raindrops fell and the wind howled. From my experience with mountaintops I knew that Katahdin would soon be engulfed in clouds. I discovered that my hands were numb. I had spent too much time in the heavens and it was time to return to earth. I could not hike the Appalachian Trail forever. For four months I had lived a whole life, and a great one, but when we reach the end of one trail, it is time to look for the beginning of the next one. There is not so much life in what we did yesterday, or in what someone else did, as in what we do today.

[1] "To the Indians, Pamola was the deity of the mountain. In awe of Pamola's wrath, the Indians never ventured too near Katahdin. Those who accompanied Charles Turner Jr. in 1804 told him how Pamola had destroyed a party of Indians who had previously ventured into the fastness of Katahdin."—Myron H. Avery, in KATAHDIN SECTION, GUIDE TO THE APPALACHIAN TRAIL IN MAINE.

For the Simple Joy of It

—Or How to Travel in at Least 13 Different Directions at Once

By Robert Winslow

Started at SPRINGER MOUNTAIN on April 1, 1971
Finished at MT. KATAHDIN on August 8, 1971

In a joyous and carefree time a decade ago, when I ran cross-country in high school and Kennedy, King, and Khrushchev were still alive, I held the brash and boyish notion that I could walk forever and not be tired. But in those years around the ball fields, swimming pools, tennis and basketball courts, it didn't rain continuously for a week—not in the sheltered world of northern Westchester. Packless and blind with youthful vigor, I can remember literally running up the mountains I climbed each summer in the Adirondacks. It was not until the spring and summer of 1971, when I backpacked the 2,000 miles of the Appalachian Trail, that my childish conceit was tempered.

Neither Tom McKone nor I are really sure anymore as to how it all began, but in the fall of 1970 the idea grew. Tom was the one who took the initiative and wrote to the Appalachian Trail Conference for information. After looking over the literature we received, there was no doubt in our minds as to how we were going to spend the summer. When we told people what we were planning to do, we got two reactions—either "Wow, that really is great! I wish I had the time to do something like that" or "What in the world would you ever want to do that for, and what kind of a gun will you carry?" There just doesn't seem to be any middle ground here—either you love the idea or you hate it.

We read and reread Colin Fletcher's, *The Complete Walker.* We ordered the guidebooks and maps for the entire trail (the guidebook

Photo courtesy Robert Winslow

Robert Winslow near Duncannon,
Pennsylvania.

Photo by Robert Winslow

Tom McKone on McAfee Knob, near Catawba, Virginia.

for south and central Virginia was out of print and unavailable at that time, but we obtained a mileage sheet for the section and a small map of the Jefferson National Forest). We figured out our mail stops, guessing that we would average 100 miles a week in most areas, planning to do more than that through Pennsylvania, New Jersey, and New York, and less in other sections. We didn't plan any mail pickups for the 300-mile section in Virginia for which we had no maps or guidebooks.

At these mail stops we would receive welcome letters from family and friends, and pick up the supply package which had been air-mailed to us from home. Tom and I had made up and addressed these packages before leaving. Each package weighed over five pounds, and a typical box contained two 2-pound boxes of Familia, five to eight packages of Maggi soups, paper for our separate journals, one to four rolls of film, a plastic bag or two, perhaps a package of freeze-dried vegetables, coin envelopes for mailing film home (I now use Kodak mailers), larger envelopes for mailing journals home, and usually a few surprise goodies dropped in by our families.

When we arrived in a town we would go to the post office first. Then, if there was one, we would go to the laundromat. Wearing as few clothes as possible, we would do our laundry, read letters, write postcards, prepare envelopes to be sent home, and talk with the ladies. Then we would go back to the post office to mail home whatever it was we were mailing home, and finally go to the grocery store to buy our next week's supply of food.

We ate lunch while we were repacking our food in plastic bags and bottles. For me, this lunch usually consisted of a pint of chocolate ice cream, two apples, two Hostess Twinkies, a 15-cent apple pie, and a quart of chocolate milk. Unfortunately, most towns lie in valleys or gaps and this meant a climb when we were leaving them. With an overflowing pack weighing 40 to 43 pounds and a bloated stomach it could be quite a struggle.

We usually spent two hours in a town. During that time we met many of the townsfolk. Our impression of the South changed. The people seemed interested and impressed by what we were doing and were unhurried enough to stand around and talk with us. We found them to be genuinely open and friendly. This was especially true of Damascus, Virginia, and Hot Springs, North Carolina. Holmes, New York, was also a very friendly town.

With the help of Steve St. Onge of Clapp and Treat Inc., a local sporting goods outfitter, and armed with Colin Fletcher's advice, Tom and I were able to work out a surprisingly good equipment and supply list. The only unnecessary items we took with us were a Gerry Pioneer tent and air pollution equipment.

The air pollution equipment was mostly my fault, I guess. I thought it would be exciting to do some sort of scientific research along the way. It was one of those things that seems like a good idea at the time. We wrote letters to a number of agencies and institutions asking for ideas. Somehow or other, the National Field Service Office, Department of Education and Information, Office of Air Pollution Control, got wind of us and our intentions. They contacted Dr. Donald L. McClenahan of the Atmospheric Sciences Research Center of the State University of New York at Albany. After several meetings and telephone conversations with Dr. McClenahan, Austin Hogan (also of ASRC), and Ted Rich of Environment One, it was agreed that we would carry a small lightweight compact condensation nuclei counter designed and built by Mr. Rich especially for our use. We were to send our readings back to Mr. Hogan, who was tabulating air pollution data from all over the world.

If taking these readings had been our main objective in hiking the trail we might have gone about it with a little more enthusiasm, but the extra weight and the time lost in stopping to take periodic readings became an inconvenience, especially when it was raining or when we had a lot of miles to make. However, we did conscientiously take readings well up into Virginia. I am presently writing a thesis on this data for the University of Hartford. The instrument we carried, weighing 3 lb. 12 oz., is still the lightest and most compact piece of air pollution equipment in the world. Someday it will find its way into a museum. Presently it is in my closet. I use it now and then for demonstration purposes, and I take readings with it during temperature inversions over Hartford.

Regarding my list of equipment and supplies: it must be remembered that we all have different tastes, and what I find suitable might not be suitable for someone else. A hiker should also remember that his *attitudes* and his *hiking experience* are just as important as the equipment he carries. The lightest most modern equipment in the world will not carry you from one place to another; *you* must still do the walking.

Clothes

BOOTS. I wore a pair of Herman Survivor boots ($31, 4 lb. 14 oz.) from Georgia to Connecticut. When I arrived in Connecticut the soles were coming off. Tom had started out with an identical pair of boots, but his soles came loose after 100 miles. He got them re-soled a number of times during the trip. Down South I had swollen ankles for over 400 miles, but I don't know whether the boots caused this or not. It was extremely painful to walk, and to try to bring the swelling down and ease the pain, I padded the inside of my boots with foam rubber, laced the 10-inch-high boots only halfway up, and slept with something under my feet at night to keep them propped up. Eventually the swelling went down and the pain stopped but I cannot say with any certainty what caused the swelling in the first place or why it disappeared. Upon arriving in Connecticut I bought a pair of German-made Bass boots ($32.50, 3 lb. 12 oz.). These boots broke in very well and I didn't get even one blister from them. How-ever, I found the Vibram soles on these boots to be extremely slip-pery on wet rocks. The boot was very comfortable and offered good ankle support. The main reason I chose this boot was because I thought it would break in easier on the trail than other hiking boots of similar quality.

I now own a pair of L. L. Bean Maine hunting shoes ($22, 2 lb. 15 oz.) and they have become one of the joys of my winter life. I would wear these boots if I walked through the state of Maine again. I think the chain tread soles on these boots hold better on wet rocks than Vibram soles do. The Bean shoes are also waterproof, which is a joy when slogging through the swamps. (I had rain just about every day while in Maine, so perhaps I am a bit biased. My boots never dried out once, all the way from the Kennebec River to Mt. Katahdin.) Where the terrain is rocky, however, leave the Bean shoes at home. I have the steel-shanked innersoles ($2.50) in mine and find them warm and comfortable. Anyone undertaking a long hike should start out in a comfortable pair of boots that are broken in. Also have a similar broken-in pair at home so they can be shipped to you in case your first pair starts to disintegrate. If you are walking the entire Appalachian Trail the chances are good that they *will* disintegrate.

SOCKS. I carried six pairs of socks with me: three pairs of wool Ragg socks ($2.50, 3½ oz.) and three pairs of single layer Wick-Dry inner socks ($1, 1½ oz.). I had surprisingly few blisters. In the begin-ning I had two or three, but I kept them covered with moleskin and they rapidly hardened into calluses. I changed socks once a day and washed them about once a week (watch the dryers—my Wick-Drys shrunk and melted in a dryer in Damascus). Along the way my orig-inal six pairs of socks wore out and I received replacements in the mail. What a joy it is to put on brand-new clean socks! Six pairs of socks do involve some extra weight, but the ecstasy of a dry pair of socks is worth it! On the Appalachian Trail, dry feet are happy feet. I tried to save one set of socks for evenings around the camp-site. I sometimes put the socks I was going to wear the next day into my sleeping bag the night before. There is perhaps something Freudian about this particular action; if so, I have not yet figured it out.

In the evening, weather and location permitting, it is a good idea to hang out to air and dry on available nails or tree limbs not only socks, but all of your clothes and your sleeping bag as well. If you wash clothes in the evening, chances are they will still be damp in the morning. To dry clothes, lash them to your pack; they will dry while you are walking. The sight (and smell) of such a mobile clothesline can be extraordinary, and some day, without you even knowing it, perhaps it might save you from having a moose, bear, or backpacker run over you from behind.

PANTS. I carried one pair of long corduroy pants. My original pair were from Sears, but the zipper on these ripped soon after I began the hike and I bought a new pair in Pearisburg, Virginia. I do not remember the price and I tore off all labels to save weight (I really did). The pants weighed about 1½ pounds. They were warm, loose fitting, comfortable, and did not chafe when I was walking. I wore the long pants only in the evenings or on very cold days. The rest of the time, through all sorts of weather, I wore a pair of loose fitting shorts made from a pair of army and navy store pants with the legs cut off. They weighed only five ounces, and lasted the entire trip. Jim Ross wore gym shorts, which is an excellent idea, although they do not have pockets. Wearing shorts while backpacking is the only way to travel. Not only are they comfortable, cool, and offer free leg movement, but the girls at the Dairy Queen in Pearisburg will whistle at you. Really.

SHIRTS. I carried four shirts. Perhaps I could have done without some of them, but I found each to be ideal for one use or another. I carried a fishnet by Scandinavian Knitters ($4, 6 oz.); a long-sleeved thermal undershirt, half-cotton, half-polyester by Healthknit ($6, 6 oz.); a short-sleeved cotton shirt of unknown origin weighing 5 ounces; and a long-sleeved, half-wool, half-polyester Sears shirt of unknown price weighing 12 ounces. Except in extremely hot weather I wore the fishnet while walking. Sometimes I wore the short-sleeved shirt over it on summer days. This shirt had one breast pocket with a flap that buttoned down. This pocket was very handy for carrying all kinds of things (especially edible things). The long-sleeved Sears shirt was nothing short of incredible. I wore this shirt a good deal of the time while on the trail and it stood up amazingly well. When I got back home it looked as good as new. I still wear it to school and get compliments on how smart it looks. There are two breast pockets with buttoned flaps. Occasionally I still carry snacks in these pockets and more than once my pet raccoon has tried unsuccessfully to chew her way into them. The long-sleeved thermal shirt was reserved for wearing around camp in the evenings. I dyed it blue to hide the dirt. It was a great pleasure to put on a clean dry warm shirt after a long day.

JACKET. I bought a winter jacket in a department store during the spring sales for $12 (it was later reduced to $8). It weighed 1 lb. 6 oz. without the belt (I used parachute cord) and was hip length with four delightfully convenient pockets with flaps and snaps to close them. The nylon shell of the jacket was filled with a polyester padding. It did not stuff very well so I carried it lashed to the outside of my pack. It was always warm, served as an excellent windbreak, and had a hood with drawstrings concealed in a zippered pocket inside the neck. It served as pillow or as padding for my bed at night. I now own a down jacket made by North Face ($39.50, 24 oz.) and for the price I consider it the best jacket available today. It is incredibly warm and stuffs into a small bag.

JOCKEY BRIEFS. I carried two pairs (2 oz. each) and sometimes wore neither of them. BANDANNA: I carried two, one wrapped around a piece of air pollution equipment to protect it, and the other in my pocket. DICKIE: In the South I carried a 2-ounce turtleneck dickie as neither my jacket nor any of my shirts provided protection around my neck. The dickie proved ideal. If it got too warm while I was walking, I could take it off without breaking stride and shove it into a pocket. When I stopped for a break I could pull it out and slip it on to stay warm. It was black in color—to hide the dirt, catch the sun's rays, and look sexy. I mailed it home when the weather got warmer. EAR BAND: Instead of a hat I carried an ear band (1 oz.) that I had worn when skiing. It kept my head and ears warm while providing ventilation. Whether I was walking or sitting it could easily be put on or taken off to control body temperature.

PONCHO. When it is cold I think the most convenient protection from rain is with a cover for your pack and a poncho for yourself.

Tom and I carried Camp Trails ponchos ($21, 13 oz.). The two ponchos would make a small shelter when snapped together. You get damp from condensation when wearing a poncho, and if the weather was warm I didn't wear mine.

Equipment

PACKFRAME. The Kelty frame ($27) proved comfortable and durable. The end buttons finally wore off and the backband had started to rot by the end of the trip. We wore Camp Trails padded hip belts ($6). My first one lasted about 1,400 miles. Since we wore the belts the bottom backband on the pack was unnecessary and we removed it. PACKBAG: We carried the Gerry CWD (Controlled Weight Distribution) Traveler Sack ($22). Sack, frame, and belt weighed a total of 3 lb. 12 oz. The principles behind the CWD design are noble. The load rides higher, and items are more easily accessible. However, three of the four zippers on my pack either ripped or lost teeth or both, and I had to lash my compartments closed with parachute cord. I now own a Kelty BB5 and find it suitable, but not ideal. Locking wires and clevis pins are normally used to hold packs to frames. These wires sometimes catch on things and bend out of shape. We turned the pins around and fastened them on the inside with split rings that had a habit of breaking our fingernails when we put them on or took them off. The pack was fastened to the frame with four pins on each side. We used 1½-inch pins for the middle two; for the top and bottom we used pins 1⅝-inches long and fitted a lash stud over each one. With these studs it was easy to lash my jacket and laundry to the pack, and made it easier to lash on the groundsheet when it was used as a rain cover. Red is the best color for a packbag for photographs.

CORD. I carried about 50 feet of parachute cord. A 12-foot length was tied around the top of my pack, and was used to secure my jacket and to lash down the groundsheet-pack cover when it was raining. One length of about 25 feet was strung between trees when erecting a shelter, and was also used for hanging out laundry. The belts on my pants and jacket were also made of parachute cord. The ends should be melted a bit after cutting to keep them from unraveling. The cost for 100 feet of line was $1.87 (about 4 oz.). Parachute cord will hold up to 600 pounds.

SLEEPING BAG. I carried a Sierra Designs #100 ($80, 2 lb.

14 oz.). It, along with the North Face Superlight, is one of the best bags for the Appalachian Trail. It is light and stuffs into a small bag. If not washed for a while the down will shift. I washed it with Ivory soap in a big industrial 50-cent washing machine in warm (not hot) water. We washed our bags once while on the trail and it helped tremendously. Several times when we hit a town, I would tumble mine in a dryer at the laundromat, always making sure that the dryer was at the coolest possible setting. The bag was a mummy with a 70-inch zipper, velcro closing at the top, and drawstring hood. If you are ever bored in a laundromat, take out your sleeping bag and show it to the ladies. One woman in Erwin, Tennessee, thought mine was a parachute. GROUNDSHEET: Tom and I cut a 6-by-8-foot tarp in half, giving us each a 3-by-8-foot section. This served as a ground-sheet, and as a rain cover for the pack when needed. The 6-by-8 sheet was made of 1.9 Rip-Stop nylon, and had eight grommets ($9.95, 14 oz.).

STOVE. Our Svea 123 ($9.95) worked beautifully and averaged 500 miles to a quart of gas. GAS BOTTLE: Our gas bottle by Sigg ($2.98, 3 oz. empty) was made of spun aluminum, was red, and had a leak-proof gasket. I carried it every whichway in my pack and it never leaked.

POTS. Sigg Tourist pots ($9.95) built to go with the Svea stove, proved ideal. We didn't carry the small pot as it was not needed. Inside the pots we carried an aluminum funnel (19 cents, ¼ oz.), and a small dish towel (2 oz.). The weight of the pots plus the empty Svea stove was 1 lb. 14 oz. SPOON: I carried one large spoon from a camp cook kit (2 oz.). Drill holes in it if you are worried about the weight. CUP: I carried a 12-ounce plastic cup that I bought in a department store for 20 cents. It clipped nicely onto a belt loop in my pants. Eventually, it broke and I bought a large "dishwasher safe" plastic measuring cup holding 16 ounces. This turned out to be a good idea. I ate all my meals out of the cup. The larger the cup the easier it is to eat, and more importantly, if you happen upon a communal supper at a campsite, chances are you will get a larger serving than most people. (RULE: hunger over humility, always.) Be nice about it, do some dishes later, tell a few stories, give them a package of soup if you can afford it, but grab what you can.

KNIFE. I carried a sheath knife tied to the top right-hand side of my pack. It was at just the right height so I could reach up and grab it. Of course, I did not use it much, as it proved to be impractical and was extra weight, but it looked cool as hell riding up there on the outside of my pack. Occasionally I would throw the knife at a stump. This is a terrible thing to do to a knife, but I couldn't resist. It was perfectly balanced and a joy to hold in the hand. Being able to consistently stick it in a tree (already dead ones, mind you) from 10 yards away did wonders for my primitive barbaric ego. The knife was made by Solingen of West Germany ($2.95, 4½ oz.). It had a comfortable sure-grip bone handle with metal rivets and a metal edge on the sheath. This metal edge is important. I once saw a hiker in the Adirondacks fall on his sheath knife, which he was carrying on his belt, and stab his leg severely. A good sharp penknife is all you really need.

CANTEEN. A one-quart Austrian poly canteen with attached stopper and screw cap, carried on its side in my pack, never leaked once (85 cents, 3½ oz.). WATER BAGS: The Gerry water bags (three for $1.75, 1½ oz.) are extremely convenient. They take up almost no room in the pack and hold six quarts of water. This means that with one trip to the spring you are set with enough water for dinner, breakfast, and dishes. The cap pours easily. The bag is double thick, but will eventually break. POLY-SQUEEZE TUBES: Peanut butter traveled in my Gerry squeeze tube (three for $1.25, 1 oz. each). I found it very handy. PLASTIC JARS: I used two widemouthed Austrian poly jars, one pint each (25 cents, 1¾ oz.) for carrying such things as jelly and honey. They never leaked.

TENT. We brought along a Gerry Pioneer tent that we used once or twice. In my opinion, a tent is largely unnecessary on the Appalachian Trail, and impractical for an end-to-ender to carry. We dumped ours in Connecticut and should have done so earlier. If there aren't any shelters or barns around, a resourceful backpacker should be able to rig up some sort of shelter with a groundsheet and poncho. If for some reason this is impossible, just keep walking. Incidentally, I would not recommend sleeping in the abandoned sporting camps in Maine. I met several people who had tried it, and they came away infested with bugs.

CAMERA. My Practina FX was a single-lens reflex that took good pictures, was cheap (under $100) heavy (2 lb. 2 oz.), had no meter system whatsoever, and broke down all the time. The final tragedy occurred in Vermont (everything seems to break down in Vermont) when the shutter jammed open and I unwound a roll of 36 exposures past the open lens. I made an emergency phone call home, and a few days later my parents met me in Hanover, New Hampshire, bringing a borrowed Argus C-3. Thank God, and just before the White Mountains, too! I did not carry a light meter; from experience I was able to judge the proper exposures with a fair amount of accuracy. Before leaving to hike the Appalachian Trail I bought 27 rolls of Ektachrome and Kodachrome film (36 exposures each) and placed rolls in the supply boxes we would pick up along the way. I carried my camera in a cloth pouch with a plastic bag sewn inside. The pouch's neck had double nylon drawstrings which I hung over the top left-hand corner of my packframe. In the pouch I also carried a pen and a memo book. The camera never fell from the frame, and was convenient to grab for quick shots. As far as taking pictures is concerned, I will not advise. I am a madman with a camera in my hands. If you see something you like, take a picture of it. It's that simple, it's that complex.

FLASHLIGHT. Tom and I carried one small Mallory flashlight ($1.95, 3 oz. with batteries). The connections seemed poor, the switch was loose, and the flashlight was generally not as reliable as it might have been. In Vermont we met a couple from Ossining, New York, and they gave us their two flashlights. (Someone not familiar with backpacking or the Appalachian Trail might be surprised at this, but they should not be. The Appalachian Trail is a real world with real people—sometimes real weird people—doing real things. The Appalachian Trail brings us closer to Nature, to ourselves, and therefore to each other. No matter how crowded a shelter might be, there is always room enough and food enough for one more. The belief that man is inherently evil is sheer folly.) The flashlights that were given to us are called Lectra Light and are virtually the same size and weight as the Mallory, but are much sturdier. Carrying a few small candles is a good idea. Don't waste your flashlight batteries, you might really need them sometime. I kept my flashlight handy at night; I was always curious as to what kind of animal had just crawled over me.

JUNK BAG. In a plastic bag, which I thought of as the junk bag, I carried the following: (a) four or five pieces of parachute cord; (b) about six books of matches; (c) a 35-mm film can with two GI ¼-oz. can openers, two split-ring pack fasteners, a flashlight bulb, rubber bands, and a safety pin (1 oz.); (d) a 35-mm film can holding 20 feet of fishline, two split-shot sinkers, two hooks, three dry flies, and one screw eye (¼ oz.); (e) a bottle of salt tablets; (f) one or two spare alkaline batteries for the flashlight; (g) a small compass; (h) four Versa Ties. They work on the same principle as Visklamps, but are cheaper and lighter ($1 for a package of 12, 2 oz.); and (i) one and a half feet of Rip-Stop tape (50 cents/yd. ¼ oz.).

FIRST AID. In the first-aid bag was a small tube of ointment, Band-Aids, gauze, small scissors, needle and thread, moleskin, a Cutter snakebite kit, water purification tablets, and a match safe with matches (about 6 oz.). INSECT REPELLENT: We tried the Cutter repellent first, and the little dab just didn't seem to do ya. Next we tried Off, and that worked better, but was much heavier and took up more room. I found that fly dope worked well when applied liberally. After a while you get to like the smell.

SOAP. I carried half a bar of Ivory soap in a small plastic bag. TOWEL: A light hand towel sufficed for the entire trip. TOILET PAPER: Never carry a full roll of toilet paper. Take out the cardboard center and roll on paper for a few days. A day or two before you are going to run out, borrow some from a hiker who is carrying too much, or if you come across a well-supplied outhouse or bathroom, roll some of the paper onto your roll. Always carry your toilet paper where you can get at it in a hurry.

WALKING STICK. For almost the entire length of the trail I carried a walking stick. It really wasn't necessary, but it helped when crossing streams (not to mention rivers), going over barbed-wire fences, keeping dogs away, propping up the pack, poking snakes, and chasing away mice. I found mine to be a great burden in the White Mountains where I had to use both my hands to climb sometimes, but I couldn't throw it away—not after carrying it for so long.

MEMO BOOK. I carried a spiral-bound 4-by-6-inch memo book. In it I wrote addresses, grocery lists, film exposure data, poems, and notes on each day's hike. These notes were expanded later in my journal. I carried the memo book in the camera pouch which was slung over the top left-hand corner of my packframe. JOURNAL: For my journal, I folded typing paper in half and bound these pages in a transparent plastic binder with a "backbone" at the fold, the kind used as a cover for term papers at school. Since the pages were folded in half I cut the binder down to the appropriate size. Before leaving I bought a packet of 100 sheets of 8½-by-11-inch typing paper. Folded in half this gave me 400 sides measuring 5½ by 8½ inches. Since the trail is 2,000 miles long, this allowed me five miles per side.

In this way I figured out how many sheets of paper to put in each supply box. If the distance between mail stops was 100 miles, I would allot 20 sides of the 5½ by 8½ size. The farther north we got, the less time I seemed to have for writing. There was always someone in camp to talk to, or some other excuse for not writing, so toward the end of the hike I was just writing small bits in my memo book each day. PEN: I carried a Bic pen in my camera pouch. TREE BOOK: I brought along a *Master Tree Finder* (50 cents, 1½ oz.). Again not essential.

MONEY AND IDENTIFICATION. My money and identification cards were carried in a small plastic bag which I kept readily accessible. Eventually the plastic bag ripped and in Vermont I bought a leather pouch to replace it. The pouch looked just like the kind old-time prospectors carried their gold in. I took traveler's checks. The only time I needed my identification cards was when a policeman made me empty my entire pack by the side of the road as I was hitchhiking home from Mt. Katahdin. WATCH: We carried a watch mainly because we had to take air pollution readings at certain times. Not essential, but convenient.

Food

I lost only five pounds during the entire 130 days of the hike, and as I write this, more than five months after its completion, I still have not gained those five pounds back. I was sick to my stomach the first day on the trail, probably due to nerves. I was in incredibly good health for the remainder of the journey. I believe that I ate about three times as much food as I normally eat. To save weight and space I carried all food in plastic bags and jars.

BREAKFAST. (a) One and a half cups of Tang, which will not dissolve in some water, but so what. (Also, on occasion, I had hot Tang. Tang mixed with a cup of snow makes a delicious snow cone.) I used one small jar a week; (b) two Unicap M vitamin pills. My father sent them to me and I took them faithfully; (c) four or five ounces of Familia, with one spoonful of powdered milk. I used two pounds of Familia a week; (d) a candy bar or piece of jerky.

LUNCH. Three to four sandwiches made with whole wheat or oatmeal bread and either honey and margarine, or peanut butter and jelly. Each week I used three loaves of bread (squashed down to one-third their actual size), 12 ounces of honey and a small tube of margarine, or 8 ounces of peanut butter and 24 ounces of preserves. I ate gorp at lunchtime and all the time. My ingredients for a week's supply were as follows: 15 oz. raisins, 6–8 oz. peanuts, 16 oz. M&M's candy. Sometimes I added semisweet chocolate chips, or toasted sunflower seeds, or BacOs chips. All of this was mixed into one glorious, delicious, nutritious bag. (I still carry gorp as part of my lunch when I go to school or work.) A candy bar or part of a candy bar finished off lunch and helped me get back on the trail.

SNACKS. On the Appalachian Trail I was always hungry and I carried snacks in my pockets. Some people don't like the taste of Space Food Sticks, but I like them. Three boxes usually got me through a week. They will not melt, are chewy, easy to carry, inexpensive, and are supposed to be nutritious. How nutritious they are I am not really sure, but I always ate one before starting up a mountain. It gave me a psychological boost, if nothing else. Kendall mint cake (mint-flavored sugar) is about the yummiest candy bar around, and is also the most expensive and the most difficult to find. Baker's chocolate is good, and is also expensive. I allotted myself one of these Baker's chocolate bars a day. When carrying Hershey bars I would eat two or three a day. Smoky Bac-o chips by Richmoor (55 cents, 5 oz.) are a delicious protein supplement. I ate them plain, and put them in my Familia, soups, rice, or gorp. Freeze-dried pineapple chunks are nothing short of mind-blowing.

DINNER. Each supply box contained a large variety of Maggi soups. On a cold damp bone-chilling night there is nothing quite as good as oxtail soup to warm you up. Although I am not quite sure why, I always broke up crusts of bread and put them in my soup. Sometimes my family would send me a Wilson meat bar and I would crumble part of one bar into my soup. I usually had cheese with me and ate a few cheese sandwiches at dinnertime with the soup. Gorp and a candy bar rounded off the meal. Our dinners were the only meal Tom and I shared. Since we had different tastes and appetites, we bought our food separately. Sometimes when we ran out of soup we bought instant mashed potatoes or a box of macaroni and cheese. Occasionally we would get a package of freeze-dried food from home.

I walked the last 350 miles of the trail with Mark Zangara of Bronx, New York, who was hiking from Connecticut to Mt. Katahdin. Several other hikers walked with Mark and me from time to time through

New Hampshire and Maine: Peter Newman, also from the Bronx and walking from Connecticut to Gorham; Jim Bruce, from Rochester, New York, also walking from Connecticut to Mt. Katahdin; and Jim Ross, of Lexington, Massachusetts, hiking the entire trail. In the evenings we usually cooked brown rice over an open fire, but we occasionally used the Svea. It performed flawlessly, sometimes running continuously for over an hour. Into the brown rice we threw such things as freeze-dried vegetables, powdered soups, bouillon cubes, canned salmon, Dinty Moore beef stew, mashed potatoes, onions, Smoky Bac-o chips, or almost anything else we had in the way of food. It was a horribly delicious mess.

The Appalachian Trail can be divided roughly into three sections: Springer Mountain to the Shenandoahs; the Shenandoahs to Connecticut; and Connecticut to Mt. Katahdin in Maine. The southern, or first third of the hike, was characterized by high mountains, smooth trails with few rocks, many ascents and descents, beautiful clear cool mountain spring water that ran around your heart like velvet, snow, and the slow magical procession of Spring up the sides of the mountains. The southern section of the Appalachian Trail is incredibly beautiful as it passes mostly through national forests and affords many unbroken miles of woodland walking. The height of the mountains down South is impressive; several times we descended into a gap, and found that the gap itself was still well over 4,000 feet in elevation.

A ranger in Virginia told us that spring was about three weeks late that year. I believe it, as juncos and snow followed us well into Virginia, and into the month of May. Our big snowstorm occurred the day we crossed the Georgia–North Carolina line. We walked 20 miles that day, the last 8 or 9 of which we climbed through a blinding snowstorm. As night fell we had to brush the snow off the trees to find the white blazes, but eventually we reached Standing Indian Lean-to. As we traversed Standing Indian the next day there were four to eight inches of snow on the ground, with drifts up to our knees. On May 3, in southern Virginia, we awoke to a light dusting of snow. The first time it was warm enough to have breakfast out of our sleeping bags was May 11, at the Niday Lean-to. Tom and I met only four other backpackers from the Smokies to the Shenandoahs, a distance of over 500 miles.

A typical day on the trail went something like this: I awoke about sunrise, sat up and slipped on my jacket, which I had been using as a pillow. Then I would slide my pants down inside the bag to warm them up. We usually suspended our packs so they were safe from mice, but could be retrieved without getting out of our sleeping bags. With the pack propped beside me, I would eat breakfast while sitting in my sleeping bag. The night before I had made sure that there was a full quart of water in my water bottle. First I had a cup and a half of Tang and two vitamin pills; then four or five ounces of Familia with a dash of powdered milk. Familia is extremely chewy and a lot of repacking could be done between spoonfuls. Reading the guidebook was also a common practice at this time. Either Tom or I would do it each morning. We usually had our stops planned a few days in advance. Many times we would figure out how many miles we had to go to our next mail pickup, then find the closest campsite to that town, and work our schedule back from there. We took into consideration such things as the type of terrain we would be going over, and how much time we might want to spend at points of interest along the way. These early morning reading sessions were primarily a review of the day's topographical features, with special attention being given to water sources and possible spots to eat lunch.

After breakfast I washed my cup and spoon, put on my socks and pants, and finally emerged from the sleeping bag to greet the morning. Then I would pack the rest of my gear, stuff my pockets with candy, gorp, or jerky, make sure I had enough water, lace up my boots, stuff the sleeping bag, check to make sure I had left nothing behind, and hit the proverbial trail. The entire routine, from waking up to leaving camp, took about an hour. As a rule Tom was more organized than I was and left a few minutes before I did. This arrangement proved ideal, as we both enjoyed walking alone, stopping to rest or take pictures when we wanted to, and generally traveling at our own pace. I loved the early morning. It was a great time of the day to be out walking. The entire world seemed fresh and beautiful and alive. Many times during the day, as the miles drifted by beneath my boots, I would make up songs, or poems, or just little nonsense jingles like:

> While hiking on the Appalachian Trail,
> I met a man who looked very frail.
> "Sir," I inquired, "do you need a stretcher?"
> "No," he replied, "I'm Colin Fletcher."

At the beginning of the trip we stopped every hour or so for a 10- to 15-minute rest and water break. Later, when we were in better shape, and especially if it was raining, we would walk for three or four hours without stopping. Lunch usually took about an hour. It was a great time to just sit and rest and watch butterflies and clouds drift by, or to converse with the trees and towhees. We usually, but by no means always, arrived at where we planned to camp by six o'clock. Upon reaching camp we would get about five quarts of water —enough for dinner, breakfast and dishes—go to the toilet, take off pants and socks, change shirts, hang clothes out to air, and then slide into our sleeping bags. We propped our packs up alongside, and placed pots, stove, water, and food between us. We snacked, read guidebooks, snacked, checked maps, snacked, wrote in our journals, and snacked until dinnertime. After dinner, which had been cooked and eaten without leaving the warmth of our sleeping bags, we would emerge for a few brief moments to hang up our packs, pay a brief visit to the great outdoors, and then scamper back into our sleeping bags. We might read or do some writing by candlelight. Finally, sometime between eight and nine o'clock, we would go to sleep. The night, although peaceful, was never very quiet. Whippoorwills dropped down to within 10 feet of us and called out, peepers sang by the spring, and ruffed grouse drummed in the underbrush. Fireflies danced with the moon and stars overhead. We were not alone, and I was not lonely. I cannot remember having a bad night's sleep on the Appalachian Trail.

The Shenandoah to Connecticut section was easy and rather uninteresting. The trail running through the Shenandoah National Park was the easiest on the entire Appalachian Trail. It had no rocks or roots and was evenly graded, with few steep ascents or descents. Tom and I usually got an early start and had our day's hiking done by early afternoon. A few times we finished by lunchtime. After the Shenandoahs there was some road walking and then the very rocky trail in Pennsylvania. There were no mountains or long climbs in this section. Tom and I hurried ahead, doing 460 miles in 23 days. Once we hiked 17.5 miles by 12:30.

The trail from Connecticut to Katahdin was much rockier and much more crowded than the trail in the South. It was warmer now too, and we would not dive into our bags as soon as we hit camp. It was fun sitting around camp at night, meeting new people, swapping stories, and getting free food. However, at times the trail did get too crowded, and it was a relief to find an empty shelter.

After Glencliff, New Hampshire, (and Tom's decision to go on ahead) came the White Mountains. Jim Ross and I were socked in for an entire day on the summit of Mt. Moosilauke, and we spent two nights in the emergency shelter built by the Dartmouth Outing

Club as a storm howled around us and visibility was reduced to only a few feet. The trail through the White Mountains is fantastically beautiful and exhilarating. The section of the trail between Mt. Lincoln and Mt. Lafayette is my favorite. As I came to the summit of Mt. Washington I noticed one man taking a photograph of me, while another man was shooting motion pictures of me as I walked along. Mt. Washington is reputed to have the worst weather in America, and I have heard that over 50 people have died while hiking on this mountain. There is a large cafeteria on the summit, where we thought the prices charged were exorbitant. Mark, Pete, Jim Ross, and I stayed there for two hours, watching the people. Eventually we returned to the safer saner world of mountains and sky.

Seven words about the unbelievable boulder-strewn Mahoosuc Notch: *don't plan to make time through it.* However, of all the incredible things on the Appalachian Trail, the Kennebec River takes the cake; it really does. Mark and I camped on its banks the evening before our crossing and watched the logs float by. That night we shared our camp with two porcupines, one moose, and a million mosquitoes. We had learned from southbound hikers that the logs started coming down the river "about nine o'clock." Just before the logs come, the water is at its lowest level for the day, and this is the easiest time to wade across. The best place is in the rapids a quarter of a mile upstream from the Appalachian Trail. We wore our boots and used our walking sticks as a third leg against the swift current. We "tripoded" our way across, if you can visualize what that means. The water came up as high as my crotch, the current was strong, and the rocky bottom was very slippery. No logs came down, thank goodness. It took Mark and me 20 or 30 minutes to cross that two-tenths of a mile. By 6:30 A.M. we were on the other side. Fording the Kennebec River has to be one of the most exciting—if not *the* most exciting—experience on the Appalachian Trail. I was glad it was necessary to ford the river, and I hope no ferry service or footbridge will ever mar the river's banks. In my opinion, hikers who have crossed the Kennebec by other means have cheated themselves of an incredible experience. Mark and I ate breakfast at Howard Mitchell's General Store in Caratunk and sat around for a couple of hours listening to the local Yankees tell stories. It began to rain, and would continue to do so fairly steadily for the next seven days.

Katahdin is without a doubt the most beautiful mountain on the entire trail, and the day I climbed it was one of the most memorable of my journey. The Appalachian Trail passes through Katahdin

Stream Campground, which lies at the base of the mountain, 5.2 miles from the summit. There is a climb of 4,163 feet. Along the trail we had heard that it was necessary to have reservations to stay in the campground, and that camping was not permitted in the park outside the campground. We had been told by hikers coming south that it was impossible to find a place to stay, and that if we showed up at the campground the rangers would throw us out. Mark, Jim Bruce, and myself were not enthusiastic about being hassled at the campground, or for that matter even staying in it, so we didn't. The day before we climbed Katahdin we did our laundry and swam in the nearby Nesowadnehunk Stream. Then we stretched out naked on some boulders (we heard only two ladies scream all afternoon) and soaked up the first sun we had seen in over a week.

We camped that night a few miles south of Daicey Pond. In the middle of the night I awoke. The moon was almost full, the stars shone like diamonds. Almost automatically, since one of my hobbies is astronomy, I looked for an aurora borealis, but there wasn't any. Jim was moving around. I sat up and poked him, "What do you think?" He shrugged his shoulders and we lay back down. A minute later he was jabbing me in the leg, "Let's go." We woke Mark and got ready. It was 2:30 A.M. We had to jump from rock to rock to cross a stream in order to get back on the trail. It then took us over two hours by flashlight to get through the swamps to the campground. We talked some about the stars, Francis Marion, and how crazy we were, but most of the time we walked in silence.

No one was awake at the campground. We left our packs leaning against the flagpole outside the ranger station with a note saying we would pick them up that afternoon. I tied my jacket around my waist. Carrying sandwiches that had been made the night before, candy bars, water, and my camera, all in a stuff bag, we turned toward Katahdin just at dawn. After half a mile we no longer needed our flashlights. We ate peanut butter and jelly sandwiches by a stream, and if I felt a little sleepy here, I was wide awake once we got above timberline. After a brief rest at Thoreau Spring I scrambled ahead, and then quite suddenly I was on the summit.

I had always known that I would reach Baxter Peak and the end of the Appalachian Trail, but it was tough to comprehend, just as death is tough to comprehend. I wished that the Appalachian Trail would continue on. I did not want it to end. But why? Walking 2,000 miles from Georgia to Maine, fording rivers, climbing mountains, walking through rain and mud, carrying a 32- to 40-pound pack, watching clouds, and listening to the early morning symphony of bird and wind songs might be considered senseless acts—at least they serve no practical purpose. But back down there to the south someplace, hidden in the trees, winding through the hills, and wandering over the horizon, was the Appalachian Trail, and at the other end, 2,000 miles away, was Springer Mountain, Georgia, and in between lay a path of unforgettable experiences and wonderful beautiful people. This may sound foolish, but I walked the trail for the simple joy of it, and if I gained anything it was the reaffirmation and the strengthening of my belief that despite all the hate, greed, and mixed-up priorities there are on this earth, it is still a fantastically beautiful planet that we live on. There is a constant poetry that flows through all of Nature, and if we open our eyes a bit, we can see miracles. It is an incredibly exciting world; I love it for what it is and I am glad to belong to it.

A friend of mine, who is an astronomer, once told me that he had figured out that it was possible for us to travel through space in at least thirteen different directions at the same time. Through this timeless universe we are all relatively transient individuals. The Appalachian Trail had been my home for 130 days and at that moment on Katahdin it seemed like a lifetime to me. Everything that had occurred in my life prior to this hike seemed like it had happened in another incarnation. Standing alone on the highest point in Maine, a monadnock, an ancient granite monolith sculptured by glaciers ages ago, with timberline 2,000 feet straight down, I knew what it was like to be tired at the end of a day, but I also knew that I would sleep soundly because of it. In a few minutes Mark and Jim would join me. It was 7:45 in the morning of another incredible day.

To the Truest Mountain

By Brian Winchester

Started at SPRINGER MOUNTAIN on April 28, 1971
Finished at MT. KATAHDIN on August 31, 1971

Thunder echoed through the hills occasionally as the night gave way to a pale gray. I was in my tent halfway up Frosty Mountain on the approach trail to Springer Mountain and my first lessons in mountain living were already over. Yesterday, a few hours before dark, I'd arrived at the base of Amicalola Falls through the kindness of a fellow who had driven six miles out of his way to help a starry-eyed hiker. There had been a bounce in my step as I began to ascend the bluff over which the falls tumbled, but in five minutes the bounce was gone, replaced by aching legs and laboring lungs.

"Well, you knew it wouldn't be easy at first. You've got to shape up, and that's going to take a little while." The conversation ended when I realized I was talking to myself, but in the silence that followed my mind was filled with doubts and worries. Now that I was actually on the trail, my ideas of the physical hardships to be endured had undergone some changes. I'd recognized that the initial weeks would be exhausting. The mountains weren't about to give themselves easily to a dreamer or a romantic, not unless he had strong legs. However, that had been an intellectual concept; now I knew it on a physical level. It was going to be harder than I had thought.

Forty-five minutes later the uneasy thoughts were gone; there was only the water spiraling and crashing down to the rocky stream 500 feet below. The last 150 feet of the trail had been extremely steep, and wooden steps had been built for a part of the way to assist hikers. Unfortunately, I had somehow managed to stray from the beaten path and didn't notice the steps until I was looking down on them from the top. I turned and continued along the path, pondering the fact that the long-awaited beginning was already over.

Not many miles later I came upon a fellow hiker encamped against

1549

the mountain beside a small spring. As the day was almost done, I settled down to share some words and his fire. His name was Glad, and he too had hopes of trekking to Mt. Katahdin. In anticipation of rain I strung up my tube tent, which was the only storm protection I had. I'd felt that anything more sophisticated was self-indulgent; after all, I was supposed to be roughing it. Also, the tube tent had cost only $1.50, and most important of all, it weighed a mere 18 ounces. After seeing the tube tent, Glad diplomatically mentioned that his tent could easily sleep two. However, I was bound to give the tube tent a try, and I must admit that I was still a bit distrustful of friendly strangers—a trait of the city dweller that is curiously lacking among trail folk. The rain began, and we retreated to our respective sleeping bags and tents. I sealed off both ends of the tube with clothespins, leaving enough of an opening to prevent suffocation. The rain was spattering solidly against the plastic, and I was still dry and comfy. In silent self-congratulation, I dropped off to sleep.

Lightning was cracking close-by when I awoke to find my tent billowing and flapping before sheets of rain. Clothespins were obviously not designed to hold the tube tents shut during mountain gales. Small streams of water were trickling down inside. I managed to secure the opening above my head, but I could not close the opening at my feet without turning around inside, which was an impossible feat. Assuming a fetal position to keep my feet dry, and with one hand half-heartedly holding the plastic above my head, I went back to sleep.

By morning the rain had stopped but the clouds and a lingering morning mist still hung close to the ground. The trees, the earth, the fallen leaves—all had the freshness and cleanness which is the aftermath of a heavy storm. We had a breakfast of oatmeal, nuts, dates, and raisins, and then broke camp. The four miles to the summit of Springer Mountain (3,782 feet) seemed dreadfully long. Every time the trail started zigzagging up a slope I found myself wondering if I really wanted to walk 2,000 miles through these mountains. However, I quickly learned that these doubts occurred only when I was going uphill. On level ground or descending I became engrossed with the surrounding majesty (or sometimes the height of the next mountain). Periodically Glad and I wound our way through thickets of laurel and patches of scrub pine, but the land was mostly covered by deciduous hardwoods sending forth their spring growth. On top of Springer Mountain we signed the register. Glad had pushed himself so hard that he was trembling with fatigue. We were both anxious to go on, but Glad had no choice but to give his tired frame a rest. Feeling a little guilty at deserting my new friend, I started down the mountain. I never saw Glad again.

Sunset found me camped just below the summit of Hawk Mountain with a group of soldiers who were to be the target of a ranger foray sometime in the predawn hours (this part of the Chattahoochee National Forest is used as a ranger training area by the U. S. Army). The soldiers smothered me with kindness and questions. How could I enjoy hiking through country like this with that big pack on my back? And so on. Every 10 minutes one of the soldiers would come over and ask me if I'd like to have some of his C-rations to carry with me, or at least to eat now, or could I use some of these nifty fuel tablets? After a few minutes of reflection from the summit tower (the weather was now sharp and clear, leaving a panoramic, thought-provoking view from the tower), I crawled into my feather-filled army surplus bag on one of the soldier's not-yet-surplus canvas cots.

You don't appreciate the racket that guns make until they startle you out of a sound sleep. I asked if the rangers were attacking. No, I was told, the rangers were lost. The Hawk Mountain soldiers had built a large fire so the rangers could locate them in the darkness, but the rangers couldn't even find the fire, so some of the soldiers were firing their guns to help them.

I got an early start, and the day proved to be full of lessons. First of all, I learned that you do not nonchalantly toss your roll of toilet paper aside if you are on a hill with any appreciable slope. You may be rewarded with the spectacle of this precious article gleefully tumbling down the hillside, unrolling all the way. Since it is the only roll you have, you are then faced with the sorry task of rolling it back up again. Contrary to popular opinion, backpackers do not prefer leaves.

The second lesson was a little more serious. Throughout the day the trail was continuously passing springs or following brooks, but when I was ready to make camp no water could be found. I traveled without guidebooks to save weight and money, and so I had no idea of the distance between water sources. I didn't have enough water to cook with, so I trudged on for another five miles until I discovered a seeping pool partway up Blood Mountain. After that experience I was more water-conscious, with a greater awareness of how much water I had in my one-quart plastic canteen and where I'd seen the last spring. As it turned out the supper wasn't worth the extra five miles. The menu that evening consisted of seven ounces of pinto beans and a protein concentrate, and after knocking the pot of beans over I was too tired to start anew. I went to bed hungry.

Before beginning the walk I had worked out a cheap lightweight diet which I hoped would be healthy and supply all of the ingredients needed to make me a strong hiker. In the morning I had dates or honey, which were chockful of natural sugars that the body could assimilate quickly. Such a breakfast would theoretically chase away all signs of just-woke-up lethargy, and I would be equal to the challenge of the mountains. Until time for the evening meal I periodically munched on handfuls of gorp, made of nuts and raisins and anything else I could scrounge. The calorie content of the nuts was high, and the constant nibbling insured that a little something was always in my stomach. On the first night after going through a town my evening meal included cheese. Otherwise my nightly meal usually consisted of a choice between pinto beans, red kidney beans, black-eyed peas, or garbanzos. The beans were rather filling, and they provided carbohydrates, but those were their only redeeming features. They took more than half an hour to cook, even when they had been soaking from the day before, and when they were finally ready they were so unappetizing that I really didn't care whether I ate or not. Last but not least, they worked ghastly changes in my digestive system so that during the day I had to take frequent "rest stops," and during the night I was denied uninterrupted sleep.

Since this diet was deficient in protein, I carried a protein supplement. It was palatable enough with milk and sugar, but when mixed with water only it became a nasty mess. It wasn't that it tasted bad —it had no taste whatsoever. Its consistency was like that of muddy water, or mud if I added less water. If I tried to eat it slowly, every swallow became progressively more difficult, and my agony was prolonged. If I tried to gulp it quickly to end the ordeal, I simply gagged. The solution, I found, was not to eat it at all.

At Tesnatee Gap, 38 miles into the trip, I met a number of people heading for Maine: Jim Ross, Ed McInery, and two couples. We gladly used each other as an excuse to stop and rest, discussing such things as the merits of moleskin and how blisters were such a bother. I learned that violets were an excellent source of vitamins A and C, and thereafter dutifully ate a handful every day. I even tried adding violets to the beans that evening, but they didn't help.

Every day brought forth a greater profusion of plant and animal life along the trail. Towhees could be heard and sometimes seen rummaging among the dead leaves, kicking them backwards with their feet to unearth what they could. Juncos hopped about, nuthatches scurried down tree trunks headfirst, and scarlet tanagers kept a wary distance. Wild flowers were becoming plentiful; purple and dogtooth violets, delicate irises, and an occasional trillium. Vast colonies of mayapples sometimes carpeted the forest floor. Flowering dogwoods could be spotted from afar, their splash of white in sharp contrast to the general bleakness of a distant hill. Deer would bound off through the brush at the sound or scent of my coming, and then turn to have a better look before running any farther. Icy springs bubbled up through mossy rocks and tree roots, providing a habitat for dark cray-fish and squirmy brown salamanders. In the ethereal minutes between light and dark the elusive wood thrush would lilt his melancholy song. If the morning was especially damp, mottled dew-dropped toadstools would push from under every fallen leaf, and red newts would venture into the open. When I woke up on such a morning my sleeping bag would be covered with dew.

The Titus Post Office was my first scheduled mail stop. I expected to pick up a new can of protein concentrate (*yechh!*) and catch up on all of the gossip from my hometown. I left Jim and Ed at Plum-orchard Gap. We were more or less hiking together now, or rather, camping together, for we often walked alone at our own particular gaits. I discovered that Titus contained nothing but hog farms now, having lost its post office back in 1952. I hitched on to Hiawassee, where Titus mail was held. A retired marine corps colonel gave me a ride, and after we had talked awhile, he kindly invited me to stay at his home that night and pick up my mail the next morning.

In the morning my mail had not arrived, and in checking through the National zip Code Directory I discovered that Titus was not the only mail stop I had planned to use that didn't have a post office. To have some idea of the distance to towns and major highways where I could get supplies, I carried segments of state road maps which showed the Appalachian Trail. I'd mistakenly assumed that any town big enough to be on a state road map was big enough to have a post office. It was now necessary to reorganize my list of mail towns, but I decided it wasn't worth spending another day to do it just then, so I picked up some spaghetti and cheese to substitute for the evening beans, and returned to the trail.

Shortly after noon on May 3 I reached Bly Gap and crossed the North Carolina–Georgia line. A viciously cold wind funneled through the open sag, making it uncomfortable to linger, but it was a moment I wanted to imprint upon my mind. Huddled down in the lee of an old gnarled conifer, I tried to take it all in. The mountains stretched interminably in all directions, bluish-brown, impervious to the cold. The valleys were wild, unbroken except for a few sporadic dirt roads and a handful of homesteads.

That night it got even colder. I sheltered in the forest service lean-to on Standing Indian (5,498 feet) but there was no way to keep comfortably warm. I tried sleeping with all my clothes on inside the bag, and then I tried putting them all underneath me, but still the coldness crept in. In the manufacture of my sleeping bag the army had saved money by decreasing the amount of feathers sewn into the bottom part of the bag, reasoning perhaps that the sleeper would be on a cot or an Ensolite pad. I had neither, and the warmth my body produced was soon sucked out through the bottom part of the bag. Cold as I was, I couldn't justify building a fire on the wooden floor of the lean-to, although I must admit that the thought occurred to me. If I went outside to build a fire I would become vulnerable to the frigid wind. To compound my problems a mouse kept making its way into my pack, which was hanging from the ceiling, and scratching about inside. I was in no mood to respect the needs of my fellow creatures, and every time I left my sleeping bag to scare him away my disposition got worse. Once he made the mistake of stopping on top of the pack to look back at me, and with a savage cry I slapped him far out into the darkness. Still he came back. Finally, in defeat, I took my bag of food and stuffed it down into the foot of my sleeping bag.

At the very first hint of morning light I broke camp. The air was crisp and still; the only sound was the crunching of frozen earth beneath my boots. Jim and Ed were at Silers Bald Lean-to, our planned rendezvous. Jim had thumbed from Franklin that morning after replenishing his supplies, and had brought back potatoes and T-bone steaks for a reunion feast. The trail was beginning to work its wonders on all of us. Things that we had taken for granted in our everyday lives were now assuming a profound importance. The delight that we had from eating a blueberry pie or taking a hot bath is not easily put into words. Sometimes just the thought of these things was enough to revive our drooping spirits. There were other more important changes. The facades, the roles, the symptoms of the social machine began to slough off one by one. You came to value other people solely for their company and the joy of sharing experiences. Because friendship or a smile was all that you had to give, you learned to give them freely. And you learned to accept them from others. For me, at least, life became richer.

Soon we were deep into the Nantahala Mountains. For one whole day storms raged over adjacent peaks, somehow sparing the ones we were momentarily passing over. I had actually begun to believe that we might make it to a shelter without going through more than a few light sprinkles when the granddaddy of all storms settled over the next peak we had to cross, Wesser Bald, and just waited to give us our due. As we began to ascend to the bald, the sprinkle turned into a serious rain, and as we sloshed higher the rain became a torrent. When we were halfway up, the fire warden came sliding down the muddy road in his jeep. He knew better than to be on the mountain in weather like this. It seemed almost an anticlimax when we crossed the bald and none of us were struck down. We began to descend steeply into the Nantahala Gorge, and the sharpness of the incline, combined with the rain, made the footing very treacherous. If you got off-balance for any reason or if you stepped carelessly on a pile of leaves, your feet would shoot out from under you. The weight of your pack made even the simplest fall a bone-jarring experience. Spring came earlier to the gorge, and the farther we descended, the greater the array of flowers and the thicker the leaves on the trees. At times the trail tunneled through dark dripping stands of mountain laurel, their boughs interlocking just a few feet above our heads, and every few minutes we would come upon a fern-lined rill cascading down the mountainside. The gorge was no less beautiful for all of this windy wetness.

On May 7 I hiked my first day on hardened feet, free from Band-Aids and blisters. Before crossing the Nantahala River the trail wandered through a few miles of Appalachia, complete with rustic shacks, hogpens, decaying chicken coops, and a local dialect that we couldn't understand. Jim almost trod on a rattler that afternoon. I had stepped aside to let Jim lead the way for a while, and five feet farther up the path a 40-inch rattlesnake lay stretched out. The rattler was practically indistinguishable from the leaves, and Jim was almost on top of it before he let out a mighty yell and made an even mightier leap backwards. I had not seen the snake until that moment, and it was rather uncanny that I had picked precisely that spot to let Jim go ahead. The rattler was unmoved by the excitement; he continued to bask in the sun while we debated what to do. I was willing to knock him well away from the trail where he wouldn't hurt anyone, but Jim had a hankering for the rattles, so finally we compromised. Jim would get the rattles and we all would dine on filet of snake that evening. I picked up a sharp rock and hit the snake right behind the triangular head. Somehow the snake bent with the blow and whipped, rattles buzzing, into a coiled ready-to-strike position. Apparently he was unharmed. My second rock gashed a large hole in his side, but there didn't seem to be any fatal damage. I was beginning to regret our decision not to let him go when Jim picked up a tree limb about seven feet long and hit the snake with all his strength. The limb came down with terrific velocity, yet the snake was quick enough to strike it as it crashed down. We cut off and buried the mangled head. Then we put the rest of the snake into a plastic bag and continued on our way. At Sassafras Gap Lean-to we dressed and spit-roasted our kill over an open fire. The flavor was a delectable blend of chicken and fish, and there was not enough flesh to satisfy us all.

We left Ed in Fontana Village to have his boots repaired, and Jim and I continued on into the Great Smoky Mountains National Park. In the craggy wilds we had walked through before reaching the park, the trail had been blazed without recourse to switchbacks or slabbings. The original trailblazers evidently had subscribed to the idea that the logical way to get from one peak to another was to go straight down the first one and straight up the second. Now, however, the footway was carefully graded and switchbacked, and low-hanging branches had been cleared away. The park was a land of rolling ridges and sheer thousand-foot precipices. Peaceful grassy meadows and lofty balds served as counterpoints to the mountain hardwoods. At higher elevations thickets of mountain laurel or rhododendron often gave way to cool, dark, dense stands of balsam fir. Astride a rocky perch shortly before sunrise you probably would be met with the spectacle of islandlike peaks jutting up from the cloud-enshrouded lowlands. Spring beauties and bloodroots were often underfoot; red squirrels and chipmunks chattered their alarm at our approach. It was that time of year for grouse, and every now and then a hopeful male would commence his drumming, sounding like some ancient motor coming to life. This was not an isolated wilderness. On the contrary, people were everywhere. The shelters were invariably full by the time we trekked in, but it was such a merry affair that nobody really minded the close quarters. Usually, that is. On a cloudy Tuesday we reached a shelter occupied by a group of girls and their middle-aged leader from a Methodist college in Tennessee. There was only one sleeping space left, and since Jim had been ahead of me he had first claim to it. The middle-aged leader solemnly informed us that neither of us would be permitted to sleep in the open space. Why? Because we would be sleeping next to one of the girls. Well, I'll admit we were a bit unkempt, but underneath the ragged exterior we were nice guys, really. Jim thought it was all rather funny, and I was too tired to hassle about it, so we slept on the floor.

All through the Smokies I was plagued with a recurring dizziness and light-headedness. The feeling usually struck me when I was exerting myself, and it took all the joy out of the day. At the time I thought it was due to some dietary deficiency, perhaps salt, but I've since come to believe that I was just exhausted. I was pushing myself too hard, and was physically and spiritually degraded because of it. At one point I was feeling so incredibly lousy that I began to think seriously of quitting. However, I was miles from the nearest road at the time, and by late afternoon, when the opportunity to quit the trail presented itself as I reached U. S. 441, my spirits were higher and I no longer wanted to give up.

Our first supply stop after the Smokies was Hot Springs, North Carolina, and by that time my body seemed to have adjusted to the new way of life. I found that if my pace was slow and rhythmical I could go up moderately steep slopes without constantly having to stop and rest. I became winded, but only to a certain degree, and as I became accustomed to being slightly out of breath I could disregard the clamors of my body and focus more attention on the world about me. I had started eating cold instant oatmeal in the morning, just adding *cold* water, and mixing in a generous supply of brown sugar and gorp. I thought this made an ideal breakfast. It was filling and nutritious, and no time was wasted in heating water. I could eat, pack, and start out in a short time. During the day I still relied on nuts and raisins, plus an occasional instant breakfast which, when mixed with brown sugar and icy spring water, tasted just like a milk shake. This part of my diet remained essentially the same for the rest of the journey. The evening meal of cheese and spaghetti was eventually replaced by various freeze-dried concoctions. I was supplementing my regular food with a variety of wild greens, having learned which ones were edible from the local folk. Wild lettuce and ramps (wild leeks) were eaten fresh from the earth. Ramps tasted especially good with cheese; with a cup of tea it made a meal that was quite acceptable. Lamb's-quarters and poke greens tasted similar to spinach after boiling, though I had to be careful to pick poke only from young plants, for this plant became cathartic with age.

As the days grew warmer I wore only a baggy pair of cutoff corduroy shorts. They were much cooler than long pants, and did not limit the freedom of my legs. This was particularly important in rainy weather, when long pants had an annoying habit of binding at the knees. This increased the possibility of a fall as it prevented an instantaneous reaction when I slipped. Shorts were something of a disadvantage when hiking through brambly areas, but I soon became adept at weaving through such spots without appreciably shortening my stride.

In between laundromats I rinsed socks and shirts with water from the handiest brook. My sleeping bag was stuffed in a large plastic bag and lashed to the packframe above the packbag, and the wet clothes were simply tucked under the lashings. Pots and cups could be scoured with sand or soil, provided I washed them as soon as I finished. Chunks of moss were also good for washing pots, being easy to grip and having a gritty underside. As for washing myself: as soon as I reached the evening campsite I went to the runoff stream below the spring and scrubbed myself with a washrag as best I could. This kept me reasonably clean. At any rate, it was the best I could do, for although springs were common, bath-sized creeks were rare and terribly cold. This daily bathing also helped keep my sleeping bag clean.

As I headed north the isolated bumpy peaks began to melt into long knobby ridgelines with sparsely settled valleys on either side. Pastures and barbed-wire fences began to dot the countryside, usually at the lower elevations. Stiles over the barbed wire were sometimes provided by the landowner, but often I had to drop my pack over the fence and then crawl under or through the wire. It seemed that this inevitably took place in plain sight of a contentedly masticating bull, and I began to feel a trifle self-conscious about my red pack.

At the Nolichucky River both Jim and I picked up supplies, but as I had mail to pick up in Erwin we separated soon afterward. Rides were not easily thumbed that day, and almost four hours had gone by before I finally made it back to the Appalachian Trail. The ascent out of the Nolichucky River Gorge was tediously long and hot until I took a brief shower under the falling waters of a chilly brooklet. Thereafter, whenever my spirits began to wilt, I had only to dip my head into a spring to feel revived and refreshed. The night promised to be clear so I continued past Curly Maple Gap Lean-to, which had garbage strewn all about, and finally chose a grassy bald as my campsite. A cool wind sprang up just after sunset, dispersing a bothersome swarm of blackflies. Unlike northern blackflies, these critters rarely bit, but they did crawl all over you and get into your eyes.

On May 18 I got lost for the first time. After a panoramic vista of the Nolichucky River from the crest of Unaka Mountain, the trail descended on a forest service fire road. I had been following the road for five miles and had become used to seeing only three or four blazes per mile. Exhilarated with such a fine morning and a trail that was going downhill, I opened my stride and began a-truckin' down the road, whistling and singing and just generally feeling good. An hour later I suddenly realized that I hadn't seen a blaze for a long time. No longer singing or whistling or feeling good, I gingerly continued down the road. A hundred yards along I saw a white blotch on a tree that might have been a careless blaze. If it wasn't a blaze I would have to trudge all the way back up the mountain— therefore I rationalized that it *had* to be a blaze. Half an hour later I knew that I was off the trail but I walked on, figuring that there would be some way to get back on the Appalachian Trail without retracing my steps. At last I came upon a farmer working in his field and stopped to ask directions. The farmer looked me over for a second. "Well, yore goin' the wrong way, son. The Appalachian Trail's back on top a the mountain thar." I explained that I didn't want to backtrack, so he gave me directions on how to reach Iron Mountain Gap, where the trail intersected the road. Two hours later I was back on the trail.

On May 19 I lost my way for a second time. After a brief respite in a little country store which was located off the trail, I spotted a blaze on a telephone pole across a field. To save myself five minutes I headed for the telephone pole. The blazes continued down the road for another mile and then stopped. A little belatedly I realized that these old blazes had been painted over with wood stain, but to me they had looked just like the regular blazes, a bit weather-bleached. I was on an old trail that had been abandoned. Retracing my steps, I had little difficulty in finding the point where the trail branched off, but my problems were not yet over. Farther up the road there was a conspicuous double blaze, warning of a change in the trail's direction, but I couldn't find any blazes to indicate where the trail went from there. I wasted the better part of an hour cautiously checking out all of the local woods trails, but they were blaze-less. I had no alternative but to continue down the road. I did so, and after half a mile or so the blazes suddenly reappeared.

The next morning found me descending into the sheer rocky chasm etched by Laurel Fork. From the bottom, the craggy walls of the canyon sometimes stretched upward for a thousand feet, barren except for a few scraggly pines and a handful of tenacious rhododendrons now triumphantly in bloom. Upheavals of a bygone age had left faults and slippages in the exposed strata, all to be viewed with wonder by the passing hiker. As each side of the stream in turn became impassable, the footway crossed the churning water on rickety log bridges to search its way through the outcroppings of the opposite wall. The trail continued downstream until it came to a magnificent waterfall, and then crawled back up out of the gorge to the ridgeline. Late that afternoon the weather turned stormy. Once again lightning crackled all about me, somehow renewing the strength in my tired legs.

Well before dawn the next morning a pair of whippoorwills fluttered playfully about in front of the lean-to, then settled down to give a raucous welcome to the morning sun. The fact that sunrise was still an hour away did not deter them; neither did my shouts for silence. I finally got up and fixed a pot of tea, only to have the whippoorwills depart to hoot elsewhere. Ten yards from the back side of the shelter a rocky brink overlooked Wilbur Lake and its valley community. I perched on a granite boulder, sipped my cup of tea, and watched the sleepy town come to life.

The ridgetop proved to be such easy walking that I covered 16 miles by midday. I had planned to cross into Virginia and reach Damascus the following day, but after making such good time I decided to push on and perhaps make the 17.5 miles by nightfall. Whenever my body began to get weary I conjured up a mental picture of strawberry pie with whipped cream and was filled with vim and vigor again. As the day drew to a close I began to feel a little apprehensive. I had not begun my descent into the valley yet; the trail still wound through the quiet woods. A woodchuck scrambled up a tree for a few feet and then froze; it seemed like strange behavior for a creature that usually scurried off through the underbrush. I had an excellent opportunity to take him for dinner, but I still hoped to have dinner in town. At last I broke out onto a hilly pasture and stopped, entranced. The whole village lay before me. The sun was low on the horizon, but still bright enough to bathe the green hillsides with a golden aura. The sky was a darkening blue, scattered with fleecy clouds. Truly, it looked more like a painting than a scene from life.

To my surprise I caught up with Jim shortly after Damascus, but as his pace was increasing and mine was easing up, it was only a few days before we parted for the last time. At Monster Rock Lean-to the cistern was dry. Springs were rarely to be found on these summit ridges, and some of the lean-tos had rainwater cisterns to store the runoff from the metal roofs. A small puddle of greenish water in the concrete catch basin was teeming with little squiggly creatures. I had only a third of a quart of decent water left, so I decided to boil some of the puddle water for tea, being careful to fish out the mosquito larvae, tadpoles, and any other visible squirmies first. Somewhat to my surprise the tea tasted the same as usual, although it was a mite darker.

I spent the next night in a cow pasture, after asking the owner's permission. In trying to get away from the mosquitoes I crawled into my sleeping bag and covered my face with Cutter's insect repellent. The mosquitoes persisted in whining about my head all night, searching for an un-Cuttered spot. They would land for the briefest second, and then take off again. If I opened my eyes I could see them dancing above me in the moonlight, and I could always hear them. It would have been a hellish night without my bug dope.

Taking a gorp break on an overhanging rocky ledge, I startled a wild nanny goat out of her lair somewhere in the ledges below. She nimbly leaped from rock to rock, but didn't go far away. After a while she began to approach closer, keeping a watchful eye on me and scrambling away at my slightest movement. I scattered some nuts and raisins on the rocks below as encouragement, then tried to sit perfectly still. The blackflies loved that; they walked all over me with nary a swat. I could see that the nanny was full with milk, and figured that she probably had her kids hidden on the lower ledge. That would explain her reluctance to leave the area. After half an hour she finally dared to come within five feet of me, blowing the dirt away with curious snorts as she gobbled up the nuts and raisins. Her tannish-brown coat was sleek and short, her horns delicately arched and embossed with intricate convolutions. Most remarkable of all, her eyes were a brilliant golden-green, and they almost made her look intelligent.

I reached Pearisburg well before dark that evening but it was too late to get my mail so I had to spend the night in town. As was often the case, the people I talked with wanted to hear my story, and I was more than happy to talk with someone other than myself. After talking awhile, folks sometimes offered hospitality. This was truly appreciated, but the real value of these roadside encounters was that when you went your separate ways you were no longer total strangers, and sometimes you had become good friends. In one Virginia town the sheriff invited me to spend the night in jail, even though it was against the law if you weren't a felon. It just goes to show that people are people, no matter what their uniform. Sometimes it's difficult to reach through the outer shell, and sometimes you don't want to, but there's always someone there.

At the beginning of the trip, in rainy weather, I used a nylon parka treated with Scotch-gard, but the waterproofing soon wore off so I took to borrowing Jim's extra plastic poncho. Coming down off Pearis Mountain there were loose rocks in the footway and I took a fall, sliding some 20 feet downslope in a pile of scree. That was probably when the poncho fell out of its niche between the sleeping bag and the pack, where I kept it on rainy days for easy access. Its absence

went unnoticed until the end of the day, and I couldn't find a replacement in town. With no effective protection, I gambled that any
rain I encountered would be either warm or short-lived. However,
when the rains did come they were unseasonably cold. I was soaked
to the skin when I reached the shelter, but I managed a fire and was
soon in my one change of dry clothes. The next morning, as was my
habit in such weather, I donned the wet clothes and placed the dry
ones safely inside my pack before heading out. Around midday I made
the mistake of taking too long a rest at a lean-to and became chilled.
This necessitated changing into my dry clothes to get warm. Although the wood on the ground was oozing water and I carried no
ax, I finally had a fire after an hour or so. My hastily gathered hearth-
stones had a disturbing habit of exploding, sending embers and stony
shrapnel into the lean-to, and into my spaghetti. I took a short nap
while my nylon socks hung above the fire and awoke to find them
partly melted, and smoke billowed into the lean-to and into my eyes.
However, in spite of all this, the fire was very welcome.

The rain continued to come down, and I had to make a choice. I
could stay at the lean-to, using up more of my dwindling food supplies, or I could strike out for Webbs Mill, which was 26 wet slippery
miles away. There was another lean-to a few miles this side of Webbs
Mill, but if I was unsuccessful in my fire-making I would have to
search out accommodations in the settlement. My stomach won the
argument, so off I went, wrapped up in all the clothing I had except
a shirt and a pair of long pants. I walked with my arms folded and
with each hand grasping a shoulder strap. In this way my hands were
covered and I conserved body heat. For the first six hours I was not
too uncomfortable. I stayed reasonably warm as long as I kept moving, and after a while I knew better than to stop except for the briefest rest. Occasionally the rain was replaced by a fine mist and icy
drops of water from the trees, but always there were drafts of frigid
air to suck the warmth from my body. I began to shiver. I could only
guess how far I'd come, but it probably wasn't more than 17 or 18
miles. That meant I still had at least 8 miles to go. The trail crept
along an exposed crest edged by cliffs and rocky bluffs. The footway
was littered with loose rocks and fallen branches, and as I became
more fatigued my tendency to stumble increased. With a few miles
to go, I slipped on a lichen-covered slab of rock, twisting my foot and
pulling some tendons in my right leg.

After what seemed like an eternity of hobbling I reached the
lean-to, only to find it occupied by three marines with an impressive
array of handguns, automatic rifles, and machine guns. They had

Photo by Robert Winslow

Sign in the Shenandoah.

Photo by James R. Wolf

Well-camouflaged rattlesnake in St. Anthonys Wilderness,
Pennsylvania.

been trying to start a fire for a couple of hours, and had finally given up. I didn't think I could do any better, so I just kept on limping. The marines had told me that there were no stores or motels in Webbs Mill, only farmhouses. I decided I would knock on the first door I came to, and keep knocking throughout the town until I found a place to sleep. I'd reached the point where I needed a helping hand, and for once I was not going to be too proud to ask for it.

A young man opened the first door. Dripping and bedraggled, I asked him if I could possibly stay the night. The poor fellow didn't have the heart to turn me away. He told me to come in and warm up, and when his parents got home I could ask them about staying. His folks proved to be just as kindhearted as their son, and they soon had me feeling right at home. The next day it was still raining, and I was invited to stay until the weather cleared.

May 31 dawned sunny and bright, and after a hearty breakfast I left the Walker house. I was anxious to be traveling again, but a little sad at leaving such a happy place. The streams were still swollen, and it seemed like I spent half the day putting on or taking off shoes and socks. A number of times I almost lost my footing because of the swift current or the slippery rocks. My injured leg had healed somewhat during my stay with the Walkers, but it really wasn't ready for steady hiking. After a few hours I was limping along at a fraction of my normal speed.

After Tinker Ridge the Appalachian Trail began to go more or less parallel to the Blue Ridge Parkway. The hardwoods now had a full complement of leaves, and the laurel and azaleas were all abloom. Jewelweed and nettles completely dominated the ground cover of some mountainsides. On first contact with a nettle there was some pain, but it was nothing compared with the excruciating itching that followed a few minutes later. There was a nonstinging variety of nettle which was similar to the stinging breed; the only difference was that one of them was just the slightest shade darker. I slowly and painfully learned to tell them apart. Jewelweed sap was supposed to be helpful in relieving itches, but it didn't relieve mine. In open sunny areas wild strawberries could be found, but as a rule they were too small to be worth more than a minute's picking. Mulberries were more worthwhile.

My equipment had been holding up fairly well, but after 657 miles the lower backband on my packframe began to rip. I had a Kelty packbag and packframe, and with the exception of the backbands, the equipment held up well and was generally worth the price. I thumbed a ride to Glasgow to order a replacement which I would pick up farther along the trail. I asked the postmaster where I could find the cheapest, most filling meal in town and he invited me to share his son's birthday supper. The day was still young, and I could have made many miles before nightfall, but I had decided some time ago to stop sacrificing chances to form new friendships simply to cram a few extra miles into the day. Lost time can be made up, but the opportunity to make a friend cannot.

I stayed at Punchbowl Spring Lean-to on my first night out of Glasgow. Next to the lean-to was a pond just brimming over with frogs and salamanders and other assorted amphibians. As dusk approached a dreadful cacophony began. I detected at least four different frog calls: green frogs, of which 10 went into the evening pot; bullfrogs; peepers; and a mysterious frog that I never did see. The pond probably had a few hundred of each, all trying to outdo the others with their calls.

The days began to turn hot and sultry; afternoon thundershowers became a regular thing. Although I now had a poncho, I rarely used it during these brief summer storms, for the cool rains were a blessing. On June 9 I entered the Shenandoah National Park. Here, as in the Smokies, the trail was graded and well-maintained. The woods in the park actually seemed richer and fuller than the woods I had just passed through, and there appeared to be more animal life. Chipmunks sounded their danger cry as I drew near, to be followed by a mass of panic scurryings underfoot if I tried to locate the sound. Presently, if I sat quietly, they would reemerge from their burrows to watch me from some mossy stump, or quickly tiring of this, continue their hectic running about. Occasionally a lame-winged grouse hen would flush in front of me, trying to distract my attention while her chicks found cover in the underbrush. Once I came upon a doe and her tiny fawn crossing a grassy meadow. The fawn was hardly larger than a Chihuahua dog. They were completely unworried by my presence as I approached. However, as I began to pass them and my pack became visible, the mother sneezed in alarm and both began to leap away. I turned in surprise at their sudden flight, and with my pack once again hidden behind me, they both immediately stopped, the mother stamping the ground with her forefoot as if to show her anger at being frightened for no cause.

The shelters still had the normal complement of mice. No matter what I did with my pack the little varmints still managed to get in and chew through the plastic food bags, filling their tummies with gorp or cheese (they never touched the protein supplement). The only solution I found was to sleep with my pack very close to my head. If I slept lightly enough I could hear the mice when they commenced their gnawing and chase them away before much damage was done. One disadvantage of this method was that I was startled out of a sound sleep by the pitter-patter of tiny feet scamping across my stomach. One night when I was particularly tired a very daring fellow decided to have a better view of the shelter from the back of my head. I was in that curious state of being halfway between wakefulness and sleep, and it was 15 or 20 seconds before I could summon the energy to shake my head.

I shared supper one evening with some vacationing Alabamians, and slept quite comfortably under a flowering black locust tree. Throughout the night the blossoms dripped just the slightest spray of nectar. The night was clear and it took me awhile to puzzle out the origin of these gentle sprinkles. In the early morning hours a skunk sniffed about my pack, but finally decided there were better pickings elsewhere and left.

At Elk Wallow Shelter, while sharing the lean-to with some 16 Boy Scouts, I saw my second bear of the journey. The forest service sign, ENJOY THEM AT A DISTANCE, was covered with graffiti—TELL THEM THAT, and HE MUST BE A KOSHER BEAR, HE LIKES RYE BREAD—so we were all expecting a visit. Sure enough, just before dark the bear came lumbering in. All the Boy Scouts started to yell and dash about in search of their flashcubes. The poor bear took one look and solemnly retreated into the quiet woods.

Dogs are the most dangerous animals an Appalachian hiker is likely to run across. After a few encounters I learned to react instantly to any canine approach that was not cautious and friendly. On one occasion my reaction was almost too slow. I had left the park when I spotted two dogs farther down the road. As I came nearer they both slunk underneath a parked car with their tails tucked, and although I kept an eye on the car while passing it, I made the mistake of turning my back too soon. Then everything happened at once. As soon as I turned away the larger black dog, a female, streaked out from under the car and headed straight for my back. I sensed the approach, and in one movement I turned and leaped aside, gave a fierce shout, and raised my right arm as if I had something to throw. For a second she flinched, and in that second I quickly unfastened the waist belt to my pack so I could bend over and pick up a fist-sized rock. Immediately she rushed again and I flung the rock with a mean speed, catching her painfully on the front shoulder. With a yelp she retreated and stopped a couple of yards away, trying to decide whether to rush me again. By that time I was armed with more rocks. I bounced one off the pavement beside her as a warning, then started backing down the road until I was a safe distance away.

That evening at Mosby Shelter I found half a bottle of wine thoughtfully corked with a candle and set aside in the corner. It was a bit too dry for my liking, but it helped to perk up the evening stew. I had gathered a number of what I thought were wild scallions to add to the stew, but they were rather strong, and I eventually fished them all out. Later I learned that they were really wild garlic, not wild scallions.

The remaining 50 miles to the Maryland state line entailed a lot of walking on hard-surfaced roads due to trail relocations. Vandals had been roaming about, and some of the landowners became fed up and retracted permission for the Appalachian Trail to cross their land. Some of the relocations had not been marked very well yet, and I was often worried as to whether I was on the right road.

After crossing the Potomac River into Maryland the trail followed the old towpath beside the river. There was a dead pond between the Appalachian Trail and the railroad tracks which had an interesting array of turtles and bump-on-a-log frogs, and no doubt it had also given birth to the bloodthirsty swarm of mosquitoes that trailed me until I left the river. If you looked closely amongst the submerged tires and the silt-covered beer cans you could even see a few minnows.

Before leaving Maryland I came across an old lady of the mountain. She was living in a sag between two hills and witnessing her faith to anyone who cared to listen. She had just finished putting up some 30 jars of strawberry preserves, and she kindly gave one of them to me. I didn't have any bread and I didn't want to tote the jar, so I fetched my spoon and ate it there. She was a treasure-house of mountain lore, and she walked me about the sag for an hour or so, pointing out various herbs and wild greens. Pennyroyal was a ground-growing aromatic that was useful in clearing up sinus headaches. The inner bark of the slippery elm could be chewed or brewed to relieve sore throat. If your mouth got bored you could playfully mumble on a sprig of sweet birch or sassafras, both of which made excellent toothpicks. And, of course, the dried bark of the sassafras root made delicious tea.

On June 21 I had completed 975 miles of the Appalachian Trail, with some 1,036 miles to go. I left Whiskey Spring in high spirits, planning to cross the Cumberland Valley that day and perhaps make it all the way to Duncannon. I had spent the previous night with a fine group of Boy Scouts, out to get their 100-mile patches. Their curiosity was insatiable, and it seemed like I spent the whole night answering their questions and telling my tales. I really enjoyed their company, and I'm sure my ego swelled a bit. They appeared to have more common sense than some troops of Scouts I'd met—a tribute to their scoutmasters, I suppose. Speaking of common sense, I shall never forget the troop of Scouts who washed their clothes in the only spring in the area while their scoutmaster was off hiking somewhere. The water came to the surface in a succession of four very slow-moving pools, and the boys did their laundry in the uppermost pool. It wasn't until morning that water untainted by the taste of soap could be taken from the spring.

Crossing the Cumberland Valley took longer than I expected. The countryside was fertile and covered with farms, and it was a welcome change to be walking under an open sky in such a flat land. Slowly the Blue Mountain Range 10 miles across the valley began to grow; slowly the mountains behind me sank into the distant haze. As midday drew near the temperature rose and I began to wish for the cooling canopy of a forest. The sole of my right boot was flapping about as I walked, and every six or seven miles I would borrow tape from a gas station attendant or a farmer and make temporary repairs. Nearing a river I came upon some children at a black cherry tree heavily laden with fruit. The children were gathering the cherries for a pie, but there was enough for all, so I shed my pack and began picking.

I reached Duncannon and the Susquehanna River the following day and hitched down to Marysville where a kind old cobbler reglued and tacked the soles of my boots. Back in Duncannon I met a southbound hiker who wanted to stay in town that night, so we shared a motel room and split the cost. He had just recently begun his hike, and was going south on the trail until his money ran out. Eventually he would return to his job of stretching hides in a local tannery.

In Schuylkill County the trail passed through an old mining community which had been abandoned since the turn of the century. A hundred years earlier it had been a living town. The Civil War was over, and the young men who had survived the war had come home to join their fathers and younger brothers at the coal face. New railroad tracks had been laid to hurry the coal to the growing industrial centers of the East. However, as time progressed, the mine became less and less productive. The fathers passed away, and one by one the younger brothers picked up their belongings and left the community. Some went west, some went to the richer mines upstate. In the end, when no one remained, the forest patiently began to reclaim what it had lost. Now all that was left were the stone foundations of a few houses, the graded mound upon which the railroad tracks had been laid, and the village cemetery.

While eating Polish sausage in a tavern at Swatara Gap, I was befriended by a Dutch-accented farmer named George Motter. As a neighborly gesture, he offered to treat me to a barbecue that evening. I didn't want to quit hiking so early in the day, so he said he could bring his family up and meet me where the Appalachian Trail crossed the highway some 10 miles farther on. How could I say no?

The footway became rockier, and the rocks were such a conglomeration of shapes and sizes that it was often impossible to walk at a steady gait. Missteps were common, but my ankles soon became flexible enough to bend painlessly as far as my boots would allow. Sturdy uppers are essential for this kind of walking as they absorb what otherwise might be bone-breaking stresses. There were areas of large jagged rocks that were completely devoid of trees and plants, housing only a variety of snakes and lizards. Even with a 40-pound pack it was not too difficult to leap from rock to rock, but it was a slow ungraceful process at best, and the shrubs on either side of the trail were now well into their summer growth and their branches snatched at my legs and sometimes obscured my view of the treacherous footway.

The trail began to enter the domain of the gypsy moth, a pest introduced from Europe in the nineteenth century. I saw hillsides and valleys stripped of their greenery by the voracious caterpillars. In the course of a day's hiking I stepped on hundreds of them, but there were always thousands more to take their place. Dark masses of cocoons clung to the fissured bark of the barren leafless trees. In a few weeks the adult moths would emerge to lay their eggs, and the life cycle would begin anew. The tufted larvae showed a preference first for certain hardwoods, then for conifers. Eventually they gnawed on the laurel and grasses when nothing else was left, and after that they began to starve to death. This summer had been the last chance to survive for some of the trees. Having been weakened by the plagues of previous summers, they needed their leaves to transfer the sun's energy into food reserves, to be drawn upon in winter. Now they were again denuded and weakened further, and for some of the trees the coming winter would be their last one.

After crossing the Lehigh River there was a 17-mile stretch of trail to Wind Gap with no springs or brooks that I could find. The day was sweaty and humid, but by taking only small sips from my precious quart of water I managed to reach the small settlement of Wind Gap without suffering any great discomfort. I was drenching myself under a garden hose, when I heard the sound of distant bells. Could it be possible? *Yes!* I caught a glimpse of it as it passed between two houses, and sprinted to intersect it. You guessed it—an ice cream truck!

That evening at Kirkridge Shelter my Svea stove caught on fire. Having filled it with too much gasoline, the pressure inside the tank became dangerously high when the stove heated up. The safety valve released the excess gasoline vapor and it immediately caught fire. This minimized the chance of an explosion, but when the stove began to spew forth a two-foot flame I forgot all about the safety valve and slapped the stove out of the lean-to to avoid what I thought would be the inevitable blowup. As the stove began to roll down the hill it suddenly occurred to me that I might start a forest fire. Dashing down the hill after the stove, I threw a large rock in its path and began to scoop handfuls of dirt over it to smother the flame. Finally the flame went out—not because of my frantic efforts, but because the fuel had been used up.

The following day, July 1, I crossed the Delaware River into New Jersey. As if I'd passed through some invisible boundary, the hillsides became fresher and greener. It was a pleasant change from the scraggly worn forests of Pennsylvania. Although New Jersey had its own areas of gypsy moth infestation, somehow they didn't seem quite so serious. In the southern Kittatinny Mountains the summit ridges were often clad in a fine green grass. There was a sprinkling of hardwood trees but the ridge crest was open enough to leave sweeping vistas of the valleys on either side. Although the terrain was rather gentle on top of these ridges, there were often sheer sides that effectively isolated the hiker from the valley below. To rock-climbers, however, these vertical faces were a delight. I came upon a number of climbers testing their skill and equipment against the mountain, and once I even stopped hiking for a day and joined them.

Mountain ponds dotted the land, and water, or rather the lack of it, was no longer a worry. At Sunfish Pond I took a quick skinny-dip to cool off, and then became so enthralled with the quiet beauty of the place that I decided to stay for the day. At first I shared the pond only with a few other hikers, including a fellow who sat and played his recorder to a frog at the water's edges, with neither of them moving for over an hour. In the afternoon the number of people camping on the lake steadily increased. After a crimson sunset a few drinking parties began on the far shore, with shouts and laughter echoing across the moonlit water.

After leaving the lush Kittatinny Mountains the trail began to head eastward, winding through the lowlands on potholed country roads, then reentering the forest to cross hilly untillable ridges. Lean-tos were few and far between, and sometimes I had no choice but to sleep by the roadside. On the night of July 4 I fell sick with a fever and a splitting headache. In the morning I felt well enough to hike, but a few hours of relatively easy walking found me completely drained of energy. My head felt like it was spinning with a sickening velocity, and it was simply impossible for me to go any farther. I stopped for a breather at a Jewish youth camp filled with a spirited group of friendly people. I ended up sleeping on their land, and felt better in the morning. I started off down the road, but my condition worsened with every hot humid mile. I began to realize that my body would need complete rest if it were to overcome the intruding organisms. That night I camped on a mosquito-ridden mountain close to a highway, resolved not to stir a foot until I had mastered my illness. The night was filled with nausea and diarrhea, aches and chills. In the morning I gathered my remaining strength and headed for Greenwood Lake, the nearest town, in search of medical attention. I walked for what seemed like an endless time, although the town was only a couple of miles down the highway. I finally reached the office of the only doctor in town, only to learn that it was his day off. A few minutes later the doctor's nurse came by to pick up something. She found me sitting on the doorstep trying to decide what to do next. I looked absolutely terrible, she said, and she advised me to go to the general hospital at Warwick. At the hospital they gave me a shot of penicillin. I returned to Greenwood Lake and the following day I saw the doctor and he prescribed more medicine. Evidently I had picked up a virus of some sort, and if I hadn't sought medical aid the virus might have caused severe complications. The owner of a small grocery store told me I was welcome to camp in his backyard until my strength returned. My body slowly began to restore itself with the many hours of sleep and fine home cooking I had, and I began to feel restless to be back on the trail.

On July 11 I left Greenwood Lake and in 10 days passed through the remainder of New York, Connecticut, and Massachusetts. I met Roger and Don King, two brothers who had hiked northward from the Shenandoah Valley; both were tall and long-legged, and they rambled along at a fast pace. We covered about the same distance each day, but I usually reached camp two or three hours behind the King brothers. Making a common camp soon became a habit. As we walked northward the long ridges vanished, to be replaced by a series of loftier peaks—a hint of the great mountains to come. Paper birch had become one of the dominant lowland hardwoods, accompanied by an assortment of oaks, elms, maples, and other birches. At higher elevations these trees gave way to a variety of evergreens, and sometimes to dense swampy stands of spruce where a carelessly placed foot usually resulted in a boot covered with oozy mud. Huckleberries and shadberries (sometimes known as Juneberries) could be easily gathered on the mountainsides, and thickets of luscious red raspberries were abundant in areas where there was no shading canopy overhead.

Occasionally the trail would come upon dark hemlock-enshrouded ravines which gathered the water off the mountain in gurgling brooks. These places were precious, for they gave the hiker some idea of the ageless primeval forest that must have covered the land long ago. I would catch myself trying to step quietly, unconsciously striving to make my passage through these shadowy ancient regions as silent and respectful as possible. In places like these I could easily imagine that the mountain did indeed have a sentient spirit.

On entering Vermont and the Green Mountains the footway became increasingly wet and boggy. Many of the mountain streams drained out of higher marshy ponds and the water was stained tea-brown by tannin. Often these ponds were the backwaters of beaver dams long since abandoned by the builders, but some of the ponds were still inhabited, as evidenced by freshly girdled trees and the sounds of a beaver's tail smacking the water. Once a frolicsome trio of weasels romped across the path in front of me, playfully nipping and leaping at each other. Upon noticing me they stopped and made a few inquisitive beeps and then joyfully continued their chase through the woods.

Porkies would often waddle in to visit the lean-tos after dark. They were fond of nibbling on anything that contained the slightest trace of salt, which was just about anything that had been touched by a human hand. Broom handles and outhouses were especially favored. So were pack straps, if your pack was not carefully strung aloft. The porcupines' greatest nuisance value, however, was that their nightly gnawing was so incredibly noisy. Each bite made a sound not unlike the breaking of a pencil. They could be easily frightened away, but their craving for salt brought them back a few minutes later.

Mosquitoes were still occasionally bothersome, more often while camping than while hiking. For some reason, just being in a three-sided lean-to drastically reduced the number of mosquitoes homing in to take a bite, and I seemed to be virtually mosquitoproof as long as a fire was blazing in front of the lean-to. During the day, deer-flies were much more irritating than mosquitoes. They would buzz in endless circles about my head, then get entangled in my hair and make a terrible racket trying to free themselves. Every now and then one would penetrate and get in a piercing bite, but rarely did they descend to the bare and vulnerable shoulders a few inches below.

On July 27 we reached Killington Peak. At 4,241 feet it was the highest point the trail would cross in Vermont. From the top of Killington I caught my first glimpse of New Hampshire's famous (or infamous) White Mountains, where freezing storms have been known to spring up suddenly in the middle of summer. Although they were only 60 miles from where I sat, the Appalachian Trail would wind for 100 miles before reaching them. A bitter wind was whipping over the summit, but the sunset was so awe-inspiring that I barely felt the cold. The whole sky was radiant with a clear sharp redness, and the clarity of the air somehow lent a clarity to my perception of the physical world surrounding me. As the sun sank below the distant peaks it was too brilliant to look at—I could only steal glances— yet I kept looking back, hypnotized by the beauty and the power of it all. Then, suddenly, the glowing orb was gone, and there was nothing left but a fading blush of pink above the far horizon.

The next day was an anniversary for me. I had been on the trail three months. Upon reaching Sherburne Pass we all hitchhiked down to Rutland for what we considered a fitting three-month anniversary celebration meal—pancakes. After a brief nap in the town park to let our meal settle, we returned and started following the trail east-ward, leaving the Green Mountains and the Long Trail and venturing across the highlands toward New Hampshire. At Hanover we re-plenished our supplies, and I replaced the lower backband on my packframe for the second time. It had worn through in exactly the same way again. Continuing our approach to the White Moun-tains, we were forced to take refuge from driving rains at Mt. Cube Lean-to. We passed the day with an improvised chess set. A grid was marked on the wooden sleeping platform by using a lump of charcoal, and wood chips, metal fragments, and a variety of pebbles were used as pieces.

A couple of days later we struck out for Great Bear Cabin at the base of Moosilauke (originally known as Moosehillock). There we would be in a better position to take advantage of any improvement in the weather. The descent of Mt. Cube in all its wetness turned out to be somewhat hazardous. Often the trail dropped over smooth rock faces at inclines of 30 or 40 degrees, and after all the rain the footing was uncertain. The only safe way to descend was to squat close to the rock and shuffle/slide your way down, hoping you could control the speed of your descent. On the steeper inclines of 60 degrees or more, steel cables had been placed to help the hiker remain perpendicular to the slope and thus retain a certain amount of balance.

At Great Bear Cabin we were honored with a visit from an audacious old gent who, according to entries in the cabin register, made a pastime of dropping in to mooch meals from travelers. He was living in a rest home a few miles away on a regulated and probably dreary diet. Immediately upon entering the cabin he wanted to know what we had to eat. Roger and Don, who had their food supplies spread all over the table, politely offered him a peanut butter and jelly sandwich. I discreetly stashed my cheese and chocolate under a sweater. In between gulps the old man rambled on, cursing the war days he remembered as well as our general appearance (I was a "wild man from Borneo"). On discovering that he could beg nothing more, he left us. He was a rather colorful old character, but he wasn't the least bit interested in getting to know us—all he wanted was our food.

In the morning it was still overcast but the rain had stopped and the cloud cover seemed to be lifting. We decided to push on. After a long tedious trek the trail joined the Carriage Road along the spine of the mountain. It was bordered on either side by thickets of knotted century-worn evergreens. As we clambered our way upslope we noticed that the evergreens were becoming markedly dwarfed and misshapen, their gnarly limbs hugging close to the weathered rocks. Near the summit all that survived of the thickets were a few hardy specimens no more than three or four inches high, although their branches covered a radius of two or three feet.

The summit was clouded and windy, and after spending a few minutes getting warm in the emergency shelter we began our descent. Due to the heavy rains the trail, meandering along a breathtaking ravine, consisted of a series of pools and runnels. When confronted with a submerged footway I generally did my best to keep my feet dry by leaping from stone to bank to root, or simply straddling the water. Roger, who had plenty of dry socks, plodded straight through the boggy areas. In the long run we got equally wet.

The next morning was beautifully clear and chilly and from Eliza

Brook we began the climb up the craggy Kinsman peaks. Nearing the top the climbing became steeper and rockier and our hands became sore from scrabbling for holds on the sharp rocks. We were on the leeward and sunward side of the mountain, and looking up we could see the morning clouds catapulting over the summit to be torn into thousands of wispy fragments of vapor upon meeting the sun's rays. The view from the top was magnificent. To the west was Killington Peak and the Green Mountains and directly to the northeast were the towering barren peaks of Mt. Lincoln and Mt. Lafayette with their sheer faces glinting in the sunlight wherever they were moistened by seeps or springs.

The following day we traversed the Franconia Ridge in winds that gusted up to what we estimated to be 60 miles an hour. The peaks were all above timberline, so that there was virtually no protection from the numbing fog-laden blasts. When the misty cover broke momentarily, we would glimpse the next wall of clouds hurtling up out of Franconia Notch with terrific velocity. Then we would be engulfed once again, with visibility instantly shrinking to 20 or 30 feet. It was necessary to lean well into the wind to maintain any semblance of balance, and any abrupt decrease in wind speed usually sent us reeling forward, a potentially dangerous situation if we were on a downward sloping incline. To make it a little more exciting, some of the downward sloping inclines had thousand-foot precipices on either side. In the midst of this tempest we met a wrinkled old Czechoslovakian woman carefully picking her steps over the jagged slabs. She looked at least 75 years old, yet she had come from Mt. Katahdin and hoped to reach Springer Mountain!

My first view of Mt. Washington without its cap of clouds was from Mt. Jackson on a bright moonlit night. I was sleeping with some 14 other exhausted hikers when the movements of a restless sleeper awakened me. Rubbing the sleep from my eyes, I was astounded by the brilliance of the moonlight outside the shelter. The restless hiker was Harry Latimer, who had hiked the trail from Virginia. He put on his clothes and disappeared, returning in a little while to breathlessly tell me of the view from Mt. Jackson. His excitement was contagious and I left my cozy sleeping bag for the frigid night air, anxious to see for myself. There was enough light to illuminate every single rock and tree, but perception of depth and angles was distorted. More than once I stepped on what I thought was a flat rock, only to discover it had an appreciable degree of slope. I stopped on a stony ledge a short distance below Mt. Jackson's summit, and from that vantage point I could plainly see Mt. Washington and the three preceding peaks—Mt. Pleasant, Mt. Franklin, and Mt. Monroe. Harry had not exaggerated. In the pale blueness the mighty mountains looked subdued, perhaps even gentle. It was hard to believe that they had claimed so many lives.

According to Indian legend, Mt. Washington was the dwelling place of the all-powerful quick-to-anger Manitou, and any mortal who dared trespass upon his sacred territory would meet a swift and horrible death. A New Englander named Darby Fields is given credit for being the first white man to attain the summit of the "White Hill." He made his climb in the summer of 1642. History doesn't tell us whether he was searching for the legendary carbuncle, which the Indians claimed was hidden in the crags, or just climbing for the sake of climbing. In the centuries that followed, many others braved the perilous mountain and returned unscathed by the wrath of Manitou. It was on a sunny Sunday 329 years after Darby Fields that I trod the summit of the White Hill. Throughout the morning, as I worked my way over the stony tops of Mt. Franklin and Mt. Monroe, whistles from the Cog Railway had shattered the silence. When I reached the top of Mt. Washington there must have been at least 200 people pushing their way in and out of the observatory and cafeteria, and another 50 crawling over the mountainside in search of souvenir rocks. In all my dreamings and expectations of Mt. Washington, I never once thought it would be like this.

That night, as Roger and Don had temporarily moved ahead, I camped alone in the sag between Mt. Adams and Mt. Madison, sheltered from a rising wind by the stunted trees. In the morning the weather was still clear, but the winds had increased to hurricane strength. Approaching the peak of Mt. Madison the gusts were so incredibly strong that I was instantly blown off-balance whenever I tried to walk erect. I was determined to reach the top, however, and after about a hundred yards of pulling myself up by my hands, I gained the summit.

I entered Maine on August 11, catching up with Roger and Don at Carlo Col Shelter. There were 16 people at the shelter when I arrived, and since the night promised to be rainy, I slept in my tube tent. By now I had the use of a tube tent down to a fine art, and could comfortably weather the strongest storm in it. Other latecomers who were tentless stayed awake most of the night, huddling together under blankets beside the fire.

Mahoosuc Notch was a rather narrow chasm with exceedingly steep walls. The bottom of the chasm was filled with an almost impassable jumble of boulders and rocks. A number of times the blazed trail squirmed its way underneath the monstrous boulders rather than attempting to go over them, and sometimes the underground passage-ways were so tight that packs had to be removed and pushed through. On one occasion, when Roger sat down on a rock to rest, he leaned back and unfastened his pack. Unfortunately, there was a pack-sized hole behind him, and as soon as he let go of his shoulder straps the pack went clunking down into the darkness. We finally managed to stifle our laughter—although Roger really wasn't laughing too hard —and with a few suppressed chuckles descended into the hole to retrieve the pack. It had bounced down 10 or 15 feet before coming to rest on the ice at the bottom of the cavern.

The next day, Friday the thirteenth, we descended to Grafton Notch and Maine Highway 26. This was the destination of the King brothers, after over 1,000 miles of hiking. Their parents had driven up to meet them, bringing a picnic that included chocolate cake, homemade butterscotch pudding, and other delectables. We parted after passing a pleasant afternoon. For over a month we had camped and walked and joked together, and now I was alone again. It was a sad feeling. They put the picnic leftovers in my pack, and I looked forward to sharing them with whatever hungry hikers I came upon, but when I reached the next shelter it was empty.

More than any other state through which I had passed, Maine gave me the feeling of being a true wilderness area relatively untouched by civilization. There were times when I saw neither hiker nor high-way for a whole day, with the only mark of man being a faintly worn footpath over mossy rocks. Maine was also a very wet state, with the trail often skirting or plodding through root-filled swamps of cedar and spruce. The boggy soil was sometimes carpeted with a six-inch layer of spongy green sphagnum moss which oozed dark water with every step. Red-veined pitcher plants sat on top of the moss, waiting patiently to entrap any wayward insect that happened along. A marshy pond or a clear rock-bottomed lake mirrored prac-tically every mountain. These ponds and lakes provided excellent swimming, although you had to keep moving if you were to avoid the leeches.

Approaching Sabbath Day Pond in the late afternoon I was startled by weird tremulous laughter. The sound was so uncannily human that I turned to see who was behind me. I thought that a couple of nuts were hiding in the woods and making strange noises at passing hikers. As the source of the sound moved above me I realized, with a chill running down my spine, that it was the call of some airborne creature—some kind of bird, I hoped. I was relieved when I learned later that the weird sounds had been made by a couple of loons.

That evening I shared an uncomfortable lean-to with two scout-masters and a number of Scouts. As was the case in most of the lean-tos in Maine, the sleeping platform was made of bumpy saplings nailed side by side. In the early morning hours I was awakened from a restless sleep by the sound of something clop-clopping its way down the trail. As I rubbed the sleep from my eyes an immense gangly moose appeared in front of the lean-to. I involuntarily let out a cry of "moose!"—frightening the young bull away and scaring every-one in the lean-to half out of their bags.

After picking up supplies in Rangeley I stayed with a Connecticut family and a southbound hiker and her dog on the shore of Moose-lookmeguntic Lake. We stayed awake the entire night on the lake-side dock, watching meteors and listening to the loons. The Horn, the Saddleback Mountains, Spaulding Mountain, and Mt. Sugarloaf were slowly conquered, bringing me closer to Katahdin. The Bige-lows proved to be a rugged scenic range of sharply pointed peaks which were covered with ripening wild cranberries and not-so-edible crowberries. The damp sags between the peaks were densely forested, and in one such area I came upon an agile pine marten, scolding me from his refuge among the branches. Spruce grouse often perched silently on a rock or a low limb, undisturbed by my passing.

The well-furnished lean-to and view at Pierce Pond were so in-spiring that I was moved to make more than my usually scanty entry in the lean-to register: "8/21/71. Words fail to describe my wonder. In 1,900 miles I have never seen so beautiful a lean-to. A large can of peaches, the rocking chair, and the view before me combine to make this the long-distance hiker's dream—and I almost trudged on to the Kennebec, just to have 3.4 more miles out of the way! Some-day I'll learn to walk *with* the woods instead of against them. BRIAN WINCHESTER, Georgia→Maine."

In the morning I was up and walking by 5:30. I reached the Ken-nebec River in a little less than an hour. Although the water was swift, it was relatively shallow and capable of being forded. The crossing had to be made in the early morning, for between 8:00 and 9:00 A.M. the dam upstream was opened to float pulpwood to the paper mills downriver. When that happened the depth of the water suddenly increased a couple of feet. The river was silent, dark, and deep where it intersected the Appalachian Trail, and I spent an hour looking for the best place to ford it. Finally I decided on a spot a few hundred yards downstream. After selecting a stout pole to help me keep my balance, I waded into the water. It was 7:16 A.M.

The rocks were slippery and the current strong. A number of times my feet were almost swept out from under me by the force of the water, and only my staff prevented it. The crossing was a slow process of cautiously raising one foot, carefully sliding it over the bottom and replanting it between the slimy rocks, and then repeating the whole procedure with the other foot. As I ventured toward mid-stream the water became deeper and deeper and colder and colder. Finally it rippled only a few inches below my waist. For a moment the current felt stronger, but my anxious glance upriver revealed no mass of logs or wall of water coming down on me. I couldn't help but be somewhat amused at my helplessness, for it had taken me 15 minutes to work my way this far into the river, and if the water were to rise suddenly there was no way I could save my pack—it would be a chore even to save myself. I gave a big sigh of relief when I finally reached the shore. After wringing out my socks, I continued on my way.

At Monson I replenished my supplies for the final time and crossed the last paved highway I would see for over 100 miles. The end of the day found me well into the Barren–Chairback Range, jury-rigging a spare upper backband to strengthen the lower band, which had given way for the third time. From the top of Barren Mountain I had a broad view of Bodfish Valley and the lake-dotted lowlands to the east. The valley was untenanted except for three rustic home-steads, and somehow they didn't detract from the air of wildness— they seemed a part of it. If I had stood on the same mountain 50 or 100 years earlier it probably would have looked pretty much the same. At Chairback Mountain Camps, which were deserted, I took a day off and used one of the camp's rowboats to go fishing in the lake. I didn't catch a thing, but I did have an excellent look at a moose grazing on waterweeds.

From the top of White Cap Mountain I caught the haziest glimpse of Katahdin. My journey was nearing its end. For the remaining 70 miles after White Cap Mountain the trail went along old tote roads and through flat woodlands, occasionally short-cutting across boggy swamps. In one such swamp the Appalachian Trail took a sharp obscure right turn after crossing a sluggish stream. Many hikers, communing with nature or perhaps staring dully at their muddy boots —both common behavioral characteristics of hikers—did not notice the sudden turn and continued to plod straight ahead into a sapling-studded marsh. This false trail ended abruptly after about a hundred yards. At this point the average hiker seemed to be struck with a nagging suspicion that something was amiss and retraced his footsteps to the original turnoff. Evidently I was not the average hiker, for when I was confronted with the path's end, I floundered on for an additional 50 yards into the marsh, still searching for that elusive blaze. It was undoubtedly through the efforts of such pathfinders as myself that the marshy dead-end trail had been established in the first place.

On August 28, my four-month anniversary of trail walking, I sheltered in an abandoned logging camp to escape the last squalls of a dying hurricane. All the cabins were broken and decaying except one, which had windows intact, a cast-iron wood stove with a boxful of firewood, and a couple of bunk beds with damp mattresses. With a little bit of work it would have made a fine home for some ex-hiker. The lake abounded with fish and freshwater mussels, and I gathered and boiled three dozen of the latter for my evening meal.

During the next two days I caught no glimpse of Katahdin, for either we both were enshrouded in mist and rain or I was traveling through woods so deep that no view at all was possible. It was only after I reached Daicey Pond, some seven miles from the summit, that the weather cleared enough to give me an open view of Katahdin. Without a doubt it was the truest mountain I'd met in all the miles I'd walked. Compared with Katahdin, the other mountains seemed like mere glorified hills. Only the very summit of Katahdin was clouded, and those churning summit clouds were a spectacle in themselves. As the sun set they turned from amber to red and on into deeper hues. For what seemed like an endless time I sat and watched as the enveloping darkness crept in. A chilling evening wind sprang up, and still later the moon rose to illuminate the now-cloudless naked summit. A loon wailed from the far shore. Tomorrow I would climb Katahdin. Tomorrow my journey would be over.

On Equipment

PACK AND PACKFRAME.   I used a Kelty Mountaineer packframe and a B4 packbag. The frame proved to be equal to the rough treatment it received throughout the trip. The waist belt was not a single piece, as it is in some packs; rather it was a combination of a lower backband attached to the packframe and a pair of straps that fastened in front. With this arrangement the waist belt could be easily tightened, loosened, or released while hiking. I generally wore the waist belt quite tight, although not tight enough to impair circulation. I loosened it for steep ascents and wore it tighter than normal while descending. The waist straps were unpadded, and this led to some chafing early in the hike. However, as in everything else, my body adjusted. The fabric of the packbag was a durable tightly woven water-repellent nylon. Only during heavy prolonged rains did any appreciable amount of moisture soak through to wet such things as matches, toilet paper, and dry clothes. My solution for this was to stow *everything* in plastic bags. This waterproofed the items I was carrying, and also isolated them and made for easier access. It also eliminated the need for a rain cover for my pack, thereby saving some four ounces and $5. It should be remembered that a good poncho not only protects the hiker from the rain, but also affords partial or full protection for the pack, depending on the size of the poncho.

SLEEPING GEAR.   My sleeping bag was an army surplus featherfilled mummy bag. In no way except for cost ($39, unused) was this bag preferable to a down bag. The weight was a disheartening 6 lb. 10 oz. The bag, miserably inadequate for temperatures any colder than 35° F., was carried in a large plastic bag *above* the packbag, rather than below it, which is the method more commonly used. The reason for this arrangement was to avoid puncturing the plastic covering on rocks and twigs when the pack was set down. On especially dewy mornings I found that the sleeping bag gained a pound or two through water absorption. It also lost some of its compressibility and did not stuff into the plastic bag as easily as usual. In a situation like this the sleeping bag would retain the moisture because the plastic stuff bag was airtight. Perhaps, to avoid this dilemma, both the hiker and the sleeping bag should habitually nap in the morning sun until the dew has completely lifted.

My groundsheet consisted of a piece of 6-mm polyethylene plastic folded longitudinally to make an effective thickness of 12mm and a folded size of 6½ by 3¾ feet. The weight was 1 lb. 6 oz. and the cost under a dollar. A close examination at the end of the journey failed to reveal a single puncture or rip in the sheet, so perhaps an effective thickness of 6 to 8mm, would have been adequate. If so, I lugged an unnecessary 12 ounces for 2,000 miles. The theory behind the doubled sheet was that if I was surprised by a light rain I could remain dry by slipping between the two sheets. Unfortunately, if the sprinkle turned into a downpour the groundsheet no longer gave enough protection, so I had to erect my tube tent anyhow, getting considerably wetter than if I'd set it up when I felt the first few drops. However, the double-layered groundsheet did give me more plastic for such uses as keeping rain from coming in the open side of a lean-to. When breaking camp it is a good idea to fold and roll the groundsheet so the sleeping surface does not touch the side that has been next to the ground. This keeps the sleeping side, and your sleeping bag, relatively clean.

A polyethylene tube tent can *comfortably* shelter a hiker from the strongest rains (below timberline) provided it is properly erected. First of all, the line supporting the tent should be taut and close to the ground. If the line is loose, the ends of the tube tent tend to travel toward the midpoint of the line. If the line is strung rather close to the ground, the tent will offer less wind resistance, and the sleeper will have more room. Heavy objects, usually rocks, can be placed inside the tent at each corner to hold down the floor and keep the sides tight. Clothespins can be used for sealing off the ends, but only if the tent is secure enough not to flap about in the wind. After being used a few times the bottom of the tube may start to show small punctures and tears, but this presents no real problem if the groundsheet is laid *inside* the tent. Any water in the tent, whether from holes in the tent floor, condensation, or water coming in through the tube ends, will hopefully flow down beneath the groundsheet and the sleeper will remain dry. The groundsheet should be large enough to extend a few inches up each side of the tent. The ends of the groundsheet, at each end of the tube, should be elevated from the tube floor by placing small objects under each end. Since the floor of the tent tends to accumulate small holes, it is obviously wise to use the same area of the tube for your floor each time.

CLOTHES AND FOOTWEAR.   My wardrobe consisted of 1 pr. loose corduroy shorts; 1 pr. loose corduroy longs; 2 pr. cotton underpants; 2 light cotton shirts, long sleeve and short sleeve; light wool cardigan; heavy woolen turtleneck sweater; 2 pr. light socks, silk or cotton; 2 pr. heavy socks, wool reinforced by nylon; Sears work boots; gymnastic slippers; ski cap; bandanna and/or washrag. Theoretically, the truly self-sufficient hiker has no need for clothes, trusting only to his body's natural ability to endure the elements. However, for those individuals who have not yet reached this level of self-sufficiency, there is the adventurous prospect of making clothes out of natural materials. Animal skins are excellent for this. The beginner may have to restrict himself to small mammals and birds until his hunting ability improves, but this is not a hopeless prospect. For example, lean-tos invariably have healthy mice populations that are not presently being harvested. With a little imagination these costumes could become quite colorful, and they most assuredly would add excitement to a hike, especially during the hunting season.

If you should decide to buy your hiking clothes, you must make choices concerning weight, cost, durability, and comfort, and these matters will be decided differently by each individual. I preferred to travel as light as possible, and this meant having only one change of clothes. By using one set of clothes for hiking and the other set for the evening camp and emergencies it was possible to keep the latter set relatively clean. Not only is this change of garments appreciated by your shelter mates—it prevents your sleeping bag from acquiring the rather forceful aroma of your hiking clothes.

Comparatively little clothing is needed while walking, for the activity tends to keep you warm, and at night you will have your sleeping bag for warmth. Therefore your principal need for warm clothing is during chilly moments in camp, or when you are taking a break during the day. When you turn in for the evening your extra clothes can be placed underneath your sleeping bag for insulation or stuffed back into their plastic bag for use as a pillow. If your sleeping bag doesn't adequately cover your whole head, you will lose a surprising amount of heat through this unprotected area. A ski cap is the answer, and if it can be folded down to cover your ears and nose, so much the better. Hiking through the rain without clothes may seem like a gloriously dashing idea, but when the rain is cold and the storm seems unending, a poncho is more practical. A plastic poncho will do as well as one made of waterproof nylon provided care is taken not to rip it.

The boots I chose (Sears work boots, $15) seemed to endure the rigors of the trail as well or better than many of the more expensive hiking boots I saw. My first pair, which was extremely easy to break in, showed no serious signs of wear until I was in mid-Pennsylvania, about 1,000 miles into the journey. At that point the front part of the right sole began to come loose. If tacked and reglued the boots might have lasted the rest of the hike, but as the soles were beginning to be too thin for comfortable hiking on sharp-edged rocks, I replaced them after another 200 miles. The replacements were similar to the first pair, and I was not disappointed with them.

Having a pair of comfortable slippers or moccasins to change into after a day's hike can be a blessing, especially during the early part of your hike when your feet are being hardened to their new role. I found gymnastic slippers to be ideal. They were light in weight (5

oz.) and cheap ($2.50). In some respects they were superior to moc-
casins, for they could be folded and tucked away, and could be run
through a washing machine with no ill effects. Their drawback was
that they offered very little protection from sharp rocks and tree
roots and it was necessary to watch your step rather closely when
wearing them.

COOKWARE.   The maxim concerning cookware is: *avoid dupli-
cation.* That means having one lightweight aluminum pot big enough
to cook any conceivable meal. Mine had a 2½-quart volume, with a
lid which could be used as a frying pan. I also carried a knife with
a three-inch blade, a Sierra cup, a spoon, no fork. Some hikers argue
that a large knife offers a measure of protection from wild animals,
which includes some people, but a spray can of dog repellent or
Mace might serve this purpose more effectively, with less risk to the
user. If an occasion arises when a fork seems necessary, it can be
whittled from a forked twig.

Cooking over an open fire has some advantages, but I decided to
carry a small gasoline stove. With a stove I had a dependable and
convenient source of heat, with no worry about such things as gathering firewood in the pouring rain, starting the fire under rainy or other
adverse conditions, violating fire regulations in national parks and
forests and on privately owned land, and leaving fire scars in the
woodlands through which I passed. All in all I was quite satisfied
with the Svea 123 I carried. Since the Svea required prewarming, it
was sometimes a little slow to start in cooler temperatures. This was
easily remedied, however, by burning a piece of scrap paper under
the stove, or by priming it with some gas from the fuel canister. Fuel
could be obtained from any service station that had white gasoline.
Amoco was one such company; there may be others. This gasoline
worked every bit as well as the more expensive lantern and stove
fuel. I found that 1½ pints of gasoline, carried in a 5-ounce tin alloy
container, lasted from 9 to 12 days. Hikers who fix hot breakfasts
and lunches will use more fuel, of course.

SUMMARY.   The following is a list of equipment I now consider
important for an extended hike. Bear in mind that this list has been
revised since I completed the Appalachian Trail, and will vary somewhat from the equipment that I actually did take. BASIC NECESSITIES:
pack and packframe; down-filled mummy-type sleeping bag; polyethylene groundsheet with an area, after being folded in half, of 6½
by 3½ feet and an effective thickness of no less than 6mm; plastic

tube tent with six clothespins and a 20-foot length of one-eighth inch nylon line. CLOTHES: see preceding discussion. COOKGEAR: Svea 123 white gasoline stove with cleaning needle and valve key. Two ounces can be saved by discarding the cover/cup included with the stove; 2½-qt. aluminum pot; 1½-pt. metal fuel container; small plastic funnel for filling stove; small knife and whetstone; metal spoon; metal cup; 1-qt. plastic canteen; large-mouthed plastic jar, 1-pt. capacity, for such things as jam, honey, or extra water; army surplus can opener. FOR CLEANLINESS AND GOOD HEALTH: small 3-oz. block of all-purpose soap; toothbrush and small vial of salt for brushing teeth; toilet paper; salt tablets; deodorant and comb (optional); a 1-oz. vial of Cutter's insect repellent lasted the whole trip; Cutter's snakebite kit. The following can be carried together in one small plastic bag: assorted Band-Aids; sterile gauze; moleskin; aspirin; Halazone tablets; small tube antibiotic ointment; glacier cream; scissors and tweezers; a few inches of surgical tape; small metal mirror. MISCELLANEA: plastic bags and small plastic vials for waterproofing everything else listed; rubber bands, twice as many as you think you'll need; assorted lengths of nylon line (can be used to close the larger plastic bags); a few inches of strong wire for repairs; nylon-reinforced tape, at least 12 inches, and wide enough to be used for patching; needles, *nylon* thread, buttons, safety pins; razor blade; matches, including an emergency supply of the water/windproof type carried in an airtight container; small candle (some may prefer a flashlight, and this is wise if you expect to be doing any hiking after dark. For around camp, however, my personal opinion is that a flashlight is more trouble than it's worth; compass; flies and imitation worms, hooks, fishline; notebook and pen; maps; identification and travelers checks; small Bible.

ONE LAST POINT: if you are to be hiking in any but the mildest of climates, you probably will have a slight cold and chapped lips for the first week or so. If you take good care of yourself, this should pass away without developing into anything serious. If the symptoms should get worse, seek medical aid.

From Springer's Peak in Spring I Sprang

By James R. Wolf

Started at SPRINGER MOUNTAIN on March 23, 1971

Finished at MT. KATAHDIN on September 10, 1971

How many months of planning are needed to prepare for a hike on the Appalachian Trail? Night after night I would pore over maps of the route, study catalogs of equipment, write ahead for information or accommodations, or take care of any of the other chores that had to be done. It was a labor of love; looking forward to imagined pleasures was itself among the greatest rewards of the venture.

Perhaps I carried things to an extreme, devoting several hundred hours to the project. I did so with two objectives in mind. First, I wanted to work out a detailed itinerary to provide a scientific basis for dealing with all the logistical problems of food, mail, and so on. My second aim was to cram myself full of natural history in order to be better prepared to appreciate the flora and fauna.

The Appalachian Trail Conference guidebooks are the indispensable primary sources of information. They have their limitations, though. With few exceptions, their maps give no hint of the lay of the land. They are frequently deficient or obsolete in identifying the location of stores, post offices, public accommodations, and sources of water. Often they fail to reflect recent changes in the route of the trail. And so the compulsive planner will try to supplement them in any way he can.

Fortunately I had access to the comprehensive collections of topographical maps in the Carnegie and University of Pittsburgh libraries. On newer quadrangles, the Appalachian Trail might be clearly marked; but often I would be bewildered trying to trace

1585

the route from the guidebook description. Nevertheless, as best I could, I transcribed data for the entire 2,000 miles in sufficient detail to record every indicated contour change of fifty feet or more. This information was subsequently typed on index cards or, in some cases, directly in the guidebooks (and ultimately edited by actual experience on the trail).

There were other important sources of information about the route. These included maps and brochures from the supervisors of the national forests and parks and the reports of relocations printed regularly in *Appalachian Trailway News*, the publication of the Appalachian Trail Conference. Ben Rolston of the Green Mountain Club was especially helpful in sending me the latest data for Vermont, hot off the press.

With all the ups and downs recorded, it became apparent that the Appalachian Trail was far more strenuous than I had ever imagined, even after reading numerous printed accounts. With an average climb of 200 feet per mile, it would clearly require more than the four months I had originally estimated.

The next step was to develop curves of equivalent effort, plotting distance against vertical climb. From prior experience supplemented by several autumn shakedown hikes I settled on about 12 miles as a feasible average daily distance, but with substantial variations in especially easy or especially difficult country. It wasn't always possible to follow these estimates because whenever possible I wanted to spend the night at a lean-to or at least at a reliable source of water. So inevitably there would be some very hard days and some delightfully short ones. It took some juggling, but finally the itinerary was worked out. (And ultimately I followed it quite closely, though owing mostly to bad weather I ended up stretching the trip one week.)

I planned on resupplying at intervals of four or five days to minimize the burden of food and fuel. Some people carry up to two weeks' food, and this simplifies the logistics considerably; but I'm not Atlas and my pack was heavy enough as it was.

Having tentatively selected resupply points, I had the opportunity to check out most of them in advance on two automobile reconnaissance trips—one to New York, and one to Georgia. I wrote ahead to a number of places in New England and was assured that packages would be held for me at the places I had selected. I tried to avoid arranging pickups at post offices because I might be coming by on a weekend.

The pieces were fitting into place and now I prepared index cards, some 60 of them, each containing a list of precisely those items that had to be sent ahead or that would have to be purchased at specific points along the way. The supplies to be used as far as Rockfish Gap in Virginia had to be ordered and packed. I would drop them off while driving down to Georgia to begin the hike. For the rest of the trip, I prepared detailed orders with instructions about shipping dates, markings, etc. and left them with two suppliers—the Mountain Trail Shop of Murrysville, Pennsylvania, and Recreational Equipment of Seattle, Washington, both of whom were letter-perfect in their deliveries.

Though the planning of food and fuel was the most complex item of logistics, there were a host of equipment decisions to be made as well. Ultimately I decided upon the following, among other things:

ITEM	SOURCE	COMMENT
Pack	Kelty	Model B4 (uncompartmented) Mountaineer, Large, with extra large sewn-on pocket; also with rain cover. Sturdy;but belt slipped, lower back band didn't stay in place, buttons at bottom of frame fell out.
Trail guide pocket	Moor and Mountain	Colin Fletcher's "office." Indispensable for a solo hiker.
Tent	Gerry	Pioneer, 27 ounces. Excellent for the weight. Mosquito netting a blessing.
Sleeping bag	Recreational Equipment	Bivouac, 36 ounces. Excellent for the weight. Too hot with temperature above 65°.
Foam pad	Gerry	Shortie, 18 ounces. Covered. Practical design with snap-on stuff bag for pillow.
Stove	Bleuet	24 ounces including one full butane cartridge. Base and windscreen unnecessary. Foolproof. Not recommended unless hiker is willing to work out logistics with suppliers. Special ICC label required to ship fuel.
Pots		Aluminum saucepans, nesting 1½ pint and 4 pint capacity. Sierra cup. No frying pan.
Water bag	Gerry	Extremely strong and lightweight (1½ ounces). Very valuable.
Boots	Peter Limmer	Heavy, but indestructible. Custom-made. Must be ordered at least six months in advance.
Socks		Various. Most satisfactory were thin nylon (not olefin) inners and bulky washable thermal outers.
Rain suit	Recreational Equipment	Satisfactory in cool weather.

ITEM	SOURCE	COMMENT
Camera	Rollei 35	Expensive, but excellent quality. Lightest weight 35 mm camera.
Binoculars	Burton	9 x 35. For bird watchers.
Flashlight		Eveready Captain. Uses two C cells. Satisfactory.
Knife	Recreational Equipment	Swiss Army Craftsman, with scissors, tweezers, and can opener. Excellent choice.
Pen		Fisher Space Pen. A sturdy and reliable ballpoint. Outstanding.

In selecting equipment and making my plans, I took advice wherever I could get it—from books, from my friends, and from those who knew the Appalachian Trail. Colin Fletcher's *The Complete Walker* is the best text I know, though I've never cared for his ideas about using a walking stick. From Gus Crews I received an advance copy of the Mileage Fact Sheet summarizing the location of shelters, roads, and supply points. I picked up a number of helpful tips from Ed Garvey at the May, 1970, convention of the Appalachian Trail Conference while he was taking a break in his Georgia-to-Maine trek; at the same meeting I took in the inspiring account of the Skinners' "journey of a lifetime."

Not all the advice was so welcome. One Forest Service official —and I don't blame him at all—cautioned that "It is not uncommon for downed planes to remain lost for many months despite intensive searching. Don't you have a friend who would hike with you?" Another gentleman wrote: "Unless you are an experienced hiker, I would not plan to do the whole trail. My recommendation is to try some one- to three-day hikes that will help you understand the problems involved. That will save you plenty of grief." That's not bad advice, either, but it rather irritated me at the time.

Despite the often-tedious work involved, despite the occasional sour notes of discouragement, these months of planning were extremely happy ones, and when I set out on the trail, I knew where I was going. I was confident that I could, if I but would, make it all the way to Katahdin.

Just making it to Katahdin was not enough, though. Here was an incomparable chance to open my eyes and ears to the sights and sounds of nature, and I wanted to make the most of it. I tried to read everything available on edible and poisonous plants. If you're already an advanced botanist, or if you carry a five-foot shelf of references with you, then no doubt you can vary your diet with a wide range of tasty wild foods. It's a tricky business, though, and as a result I proceeded with caution.

Most reference books, even the field guides, are too heavy to carry along the trail. I tried to abstract critical information on index cards, but in practice this worked out poorly. However, I did discover a pair of superb booklets, less than two ounces each, that deserve a place in the pack. These are the *Flower Finder* (spring flowers only) and the *Master Tree Finder* published by the Nature Study Guild (see BIBLIOGRAPHY). Other candidates are some of the Golden Nature Guides; I usually carried the one on non-flowering plants.

It is not possible to translate a few weeks of study into an encyclopedic knowledge of Appalachian plants and animals. However, even though my new knowledge barely scratched the surface, that was reward enough for the study involved.

Physical conditioning played little part in my preparation for the hike. In fact, according to my performance on a standard treadmill test immediately before my departure for Georgia, my condition was slightly below average for persons of my age. (After the hike I took precisely the same test, taking 24 minutes instead of 16 minutes to reach a pulse rate of 172; this put me easily in the excellent category. I had also shed 25 pounds on a diet of about 4,000 calories per day!)

Inevitably there was a final flurry of chores and farewells. Though I could cut off the phone and the delivery of the morning newspaper, bills would continue to roll in. On this score, my mind was eased because my mother "volunteered" to handle all my mail for me and no one was ever more reliable or efficient. I also arranged to phone her frequently, and she was prepared—and perhaps half expecting—to sound the alarm for me if I failed to call at the appointed hour.

All the loose ends finally came together on that cold day in March when it was time to head south. I was in a daze as I walked out of my warm office for the last time. Hundreds of pleasant hours had been invested, and hundreds of dollars, and now there was no turning back. The adventure was about to begin.

A Bird Watcher's Journal

MARCH 23, 1971 (TUESDAY). "Can you imagine? He's walking all the way to Maine from Georgia. A real crackpot, that's what he is."

I smiled as my hitch-hiking rider described a young man he had come across the day before on the Appalachian Trail. He was a bit sheepish when he learned that I was a similar crackpot.

He more than made up for his gaffe, though, by driving us—Brooke, Paul, and myself—high up into the mountains to Nimblewill Gap, just a couple of miles from Springer Mountain, the southern terminus of the trail.

At 1:45 P.M. we were left without wheels, alone to our own devices. A prettier day we couldn't have ordered; a sky that was almost cloudless, good visibility everywhere, and a comfortable 47°F.

On the wooded summit of Springer we found the first of the white blazes that would mark my way to Maine. I was now officially on the Appalachian Trail. A neat sign promised me 2,000 miles of grandeur and adventure.

It was still early when we set up camp at the dirt-floored Big Stamp Gap Lean-to. The fire was pretty, but did little to keep us warm. We talked a bit about the hundred miles or so we would be hiking together before my companions had to return to school. It was cold, though, so we gave up talking shortly after sundown, and turned in.

MARCH 24. Suddenly I was startled by Brooke's thrashing and shouting. He had been attacked in the middle of the night; or so it had seemed to him. The problem was the spicy sausage he had carelessly left in his unsuspended pack. A raccoon, having sniffed it, came to investigate. He might have been a more successful thief if he hadn't tromped over Brooke's sleeping bag to get at the food. We frightened the intruder away and managed to get back to sleep.

At least I did, since I was wearing a set of down-filled long johns and a heavy down parka inside my bag. This extra clothing was needed because the night was a chiller. At 7:30 A.M. it was 22°F. and it might have been colder during the night. My plastic one-liter water bottle was frozen solid, though fortunately it didn't crack.

We were on the trail about 9:45 and found the morning's hike to Three Forks enjoyably scenic. Though winter's greys and browns prevailed, and there were no wild flowers or young plants to be seen, the landscape was relieved by occasional strokes of green—large white pines and hemlocks, abundant rhododendron and mountain laurel, and American holly. Hugging the ground were hardy patches of the galax, its burnished red leaves conspicuous amidst the drabness.

After pausing an hour for lunch, we ascended to a double set of waterfalls just off the trail. It was a really sensational cascade, not more than 30 feet or so in height, but in a bower of conifers and rhododendron. There wasn't a single beer can to be seen. If every day had treats like this, it would be easy to keep going.

The view from Hawk Mountain rewarded us for our 1,000 feet of climbing. Among the summits we could see we picked out Blood Mountain ahead of us and Springer to the south, a lovely view under the crisp blue sky. Near the fire tower was a patch of planted daffodils that reminded us that Spring was on its way.

The Hawk Mountain Lean-to, our home for the night, was also without bunks, but it was much better sheltered than Big Stamp Gap Lean-to, and we were able to get a pretty good night's sleep.

MARCH 25. Today was the day of the blizzard. It started as we were beginning to get up, and it never quit. By lunchtime there were two inches of snow and by the time we reached Gooch Gap Lean-to over six inches had fallen.

Not far from Hawk Mountain we came to a fairly roomy old structure that provided a roof, so we rested while we had the chance. There were some sparrows around, but my binoculars fogged up and I never got a really good look. I saw a red cap and figured they were chippies—there seemed to be some white beneath the crown. But Brooke said he saw a black spot on the breast and this would mean tree sparrows. Oh, the frustrations of being a bird watcher!

At Cooper Gap the boys suggested we continue along the road to Gooch Gap, as the snow was getting deep. I didn't want to depart from the Appalachian Trail, though, and so we trudged on in the woods. The nastiest part of it was that we got thoroughly wet —my trousers got pretty soaked even through the rain pants, and above the waist I sweated right through my shirt. Fortunately, my boots were treated with a heavy coat of Sno-seal and kept my socks and feet reasonably dry.

It was so foul at Gooch Gap that we rigged our tents inside the shelter. Not that it was so cold, but we needed protection from the wind that was blowing snow right in on top of us. Paul and Brooke were losing their enthusiasm. With the rotten weather, I was not sure I blamed them. If the next day wasn't better, we might have to alter our plans and leave the trail at Woody Gap.

MARCH 26. It had stopped snowing by the time we got up. At a random point near the lean-to it measured 7½ inches. During the day it was frequently 12 inches and in occasional drifts it was up to our knees.

The only thing good you could say for the weather was that it wasn't raining or snowing, but a mist persisted all day long. You could see from one blaze to the next, but not much farther than that. It was 36°F. when we started, dropped a couple of degrees during the day, and was 36° again in the evening. All in all, it was a very gloomy and depressing situation.

We got a fairly early start, at about 9:15. Everything I had worn Thursday was wet. It particularly bothered me that my down jacket was damp because that would lessen its insulating properties.

Our aim for the morning was to reach Woody Gap, 3.7 miles away. It was tough going up Ramrock Mountain, especially with the thin crust on the surface of the snow. Brooke and Paul set a fast pace and it helped me to be able to follow in their path. It was noon when we reached Woody Gap, shrouded in the fog and with big snowbanks pushed up by the plows.

Brooke told me he and Paul had had enough. When I suggested that they go down the hill to Suches and hitchhike to Lake Winfield Scott, he said I had misunderstood; he and Paul had decided to call it quits and go back north instead of hiking with me to Fontana Dam. I guess Paul had meant it when he said that yesterday had been the worst day of his life. I was unprepared for this sudden breakup of our expedition. Coupled with the snow, the cold, and the mist, it was very demoralizing.

I was too tired to do much debating. They agreed to come back and meet me after picking up the car.

The outhouse across the highway was the only shelter around and I took full advantage of it. I ate peanut butter and bread, some gorp, and a package of beef jerky, and was ready to go again.

The next stretch was really rough. The trail was well marked and nicely graded, but the snow was deeper than ever and now I was making my own path. The rise up Big Cedar Mountain was only 600 feet but it took me over an hour to walk the mile. From there down to Miller Gap wasn't much easier. It was nearly 3:00 P.M. when I reached Miller Gap and it seemed foolhardy to try to keep going the remaining 3.3 miles to Lake Winfield Scott through this wilderness. Prudence won out and I trudged down half a mile to the highway, which had just been plowed.

I got a couple of offers of rides, but turned them down. It seemed to me that it was sporting and fair to make detours where weather demanded it, so long as the continuous walk was not interrupted.

Just as I reached the Lake Winfield Scott Recreation Area, Brooke and Paul drove up. It was good to be reunited. We rented a frigid cabin and settled down for the night. I had left some supplies here and so we were able to have a feast of corned beef hash instead of the freeze-dried foods we had been eating for the last couple of days. It was a welcome change.

MARCH 27. The weather was beautiful—warm, clear sky, and hills covered with a glistening snowy cover. However, a different kind of misfortune was ahead.

I was off the Appalachian Trail and had to take a side trail to get back on it. According to the guidebook, this side trail was clearly marked with blue blazes. After bidding farewell to Brooke and Paul, I set out, following the directions of the park manager as I understood them. He told me to take a left fork—but before reaching the point he had in mind I came to another intersection and I incorrectly made my left turn here. After about a quarter of a mile the road dead-ended and continued as an old logging grade.

Instead of doing the sensible thing and retracing my steps, I assured myself that I must be headed in the right direction. So what if there were no blazes; they would start higher up on the mountain. So what if the route was overgrown instead of being passable by automobile; it just meant that the guidebook was out of date and needed to be revised.

When I had climbed to about 3,800 feet—where I had expected to reach the Appalachian Trail—there was a clearing. Here my path petered out completely. I had certainly expected to find blazes here, but there weren't any. It was disconcerting. Still, I felt that if I contoured a bit to the south I would soon find the Appalachian Trail. After a couple of hundred yards I reached a rocky crest and discovered that I had climbed the wrong mountain! This was Slaughter Mountain, separated from Blood Mountain and the Appalachian Trail by what seemed to be an uncrossably deep chasm. With a topographical map, I might have been able to find my way over to the trail. Rather than play such a reckless game, I decided to head back down to Lake Winfield Scott. I was chagrined, but at least I would be safe.

So at the end of the day I was right back where I had started. The only solace was the pleasure of finding a magnificent pileated woodpecker high on the mountain. But this was no way to make it to Maine.

MARCH 28. My camp for the night was beneath a roofed picnic site. Early in the morning I was aroused by the chorus of cardinals along with Carolina chickadees, titmice, and loud blue jays.

This time I started out for Jarrard Gap, which is only 2.3 miles from the point where I had left the Appalachian Trail on Friday. And just as the guidebook says, this approach trail is an automobile road and it is blue blazed.

It was an uneventful though long walk up to the gap and then to the summit of Blood Mountain, the highest point on the Appalachian Trail in Georgia. Near the top of Blood Mountain the weather suddenly changed for the worse, with ominous grey clouds springing up in the west and soon covering the sky. It was good to know that the Blood Mountain Shelter, a completely enclosed two-room stone hut, was just a few hundred yards ahead.

The sanguinary place names here are reminders of Indian legend. Supposedly the Creeks and the Cherokees fought here before the white man came and the battle was so fierce that the streams ran red with blood. Another story has it that the Cherokees buried all their gold in a cave on Slaughter Mountain before they were forced to move to Oklahoma. It is said that the gold is still there, waiting to be found by some lucky adventurer.

Ever since Jarrard Gap I had been looking forward to catching up with a hiker who had left fresh Vibram prints in the snow. He was headed north and from accounts given to me by passing Boy Scouts, he was a through hiker headed for Katahdin. By his beard and long hair, they said, ye shall know him.

His name was Marty, and he was at the Blood Mountain Shelter when I arrived. We had all afternoon to relax and compare notes. I was stunned by his casual approach to the trail. He had done absolutely no planning, made no provision for picking up supplies, and was generally uninformed. He didn't even know where the trail started, and so picked it up at Woody Gap instead of Springer Mountain. I asked Marty how he would feel when he got to Katahdin, after 2,000 miles, and then remembered that there was a 20-mile stretch in Georgia that he hadn't walked. What difference would it make, he replied; he was not on an "ego trip," but simply wanted the enjoyment of a pleasant hike in unspoiled country. I wondered if it were possible to walk for weeks and weeks, day after day, without trying to prove something to yourself—that you

Photo courtesy James R. Wolf

James Wolf near Siler Bald Lean-to, North Carolina.

Photo by Eric Ryb

Storm in northern Virginia.

were strong in spirit and body. I hadn't thought of it in just that way before, but my venture was an ego trip as Marty aptly described it.

We had company as the day wore on. It's not often I can say something nice about the Boy Scouts, but three or four of them had climbed the mountain with large plastic garbage bags which they filled to the brim with litter and then carried off. They deserved the merit badges they would earn for this service.

Toward evening we were joined by some students from a nearby college who serenaded us with singing and recorder music. I pulled out my little sopranino recorder and tried to join in, but I had a hard time finding the right key and the right notes and soon decided just to listen and enjoy.

It had been a warm day and during the night we had a steady rain. By morning, almost as if by magic, the snow had completely disappeared except for a few tiny patches.

MARCH 29. This seemed to be the beginning of spring. It was bright and comfortably warm, though windy. For the first time on this trip I became conscious of new life. A couple of kinds of plants had produced young leaves that were up about an inch above the ground.

There weren't many birds, but there were a few good ones. A single junco on the summit of Blood Mountain was no surprise, but a red-tailed hawk soaring about was a good find. Later on there were single chickadees and vultures. The real spectacular, however, was a *coot* which I flushed from the hardwood forest on the side of Levelland Mountain just south of Neels Gap. What would a marsh bird like that be doing so far away from its normal aquatic habitat? Yet there could be no doubt; the coot's grey color, white bill, plump body, and trailing white wing edges were distinctive. What other surprises did the spring migration have in store for me?

Aside from the wind, which was not really strong but enough to cause a little chill, it was good walking. The trail was a bit wet, but there was not a trace of snow on it. There were interesting sights —a large balanced rock at Flatrock Gap and the view of Georgia's highest peak, Brasstown Bald, from Levelland Mountain. From Neels Gap to Tesnatee Gap the Appalachian Trail was completely wild, often following a ridge line not more than ten yards wide.

The Tesnatee Gap Lean-to was only a few yards from the recently built Richard Russell Scenic Highway, so during the night there were occasional automobile noises that added nothing to our enjoyment of the woods. There were four of us, including Marty and two of the students we had met on top of Blood Mountain. Things were a bit crowded and confused, but by 8:00 P.M., we had finished cooking and eating and hit the sack to rest up for a 12-mile hike the next day, the longest so far for me.

MARCH 30. Many new sights and sounds. The first was the wind roaring through Tesnatee Gap last night. Fortunately the wind had dropped off by 7 A.M. when I began to get up. It took me an hour and a half to get some Tang, cold cereal, and cocoa under my belt and to get packed and moving. It was especially hard with the thermometer reading 28°F.

Just as I left camp I got a good look at a couple of juncos. Next a lizard scampered across the path so fast that I had only the briefest glimpse.

Approaching Poor Mountain I flushed a large rufous bird from the trail ahead. Leaving its perch, it flew through the woods gracefully and silently with a deep arc of the wing—with quite a slow beat. Most likely a great horned owl. Next a couple of blackbirds, probably redwings, flew overhead. Some crows cawed in the valley below.

Wide Gap was a particularly pretty spot. There were mountains all around, in every direction, a fine panorama in early spring before the foliage blocked the view. Nearby a few chickadees were singing "fee-bee fee-bay" and chattering "chickadeedeedee."

At Low Gap, I paused near the spring to inspect and photograph the spiny-edged leaves of the spotted wintergreen. I was so completely absorbed that I failed to see a skunk wander up until he was just a few feet away. He ignored me and ambled over for his drink of water, confident that I would leave him alone. He was right, of course, though I did take his picture from a respectful distance.

There were a number of things to nibble. I tried what appeared to be young dandelion leaves and found them a bit bitter, but not unpalatable. Another new plant had a basal rosette of untoothed leaves that were very tender and mild. And there was a member of the mint family—always easy to recognize because of the square stem—with hairy purplish leaves that made a good cool chew.

Approaching Chattahoochee Gap, a rufous bird flew across my path. At first I thought it might have been a thrush, but as I got closer I could see the heavy bill of a sparrow. The large size and heavy streakings left no doubt that this was a fox sparrow, though it was exceptionally late for this northern species to be sticking around.

Chattahoochee Spring, the source of the river that flows through Atlanta, was a short but strenuous walk off the Appalachian Trail. It was not particularly scenic, but at least the river's water was good to drink here.

To complete the day, there were three white-tailed deer that bounded off gracefully from the little draw behind the Rocky Knob Lean-to as I approached.

Marty fascinated me with his macrobiotic diet and occult beliefs. Really far out. Every night was an adventure for him as he traveled to the far ends of the earth in his sleep, attached to his body by a slim silver thread. He seemed to be especially fond of visiting his brother in Akron on these nightly journeys. He found special inspiration in the Book of Revelation, which a wise cell-mate guru had expounded to him while he was locked up in a Wyoming jail for hitch-hiking.

MARCH 31. Every day's tale was a bit different. Today it wasn't so much the coming of spring as it was the experience of leaving all companions behind. Marty was going to try to reach Addis Gap while I would head only for Tray Mountain.

Rocky Knob had the best setting of any of the shelters so far and it was warmed by the bright morning sun. It was 36°F. when we got up around 7:30 and it looked like a beautiful day coming.

More birds. I heard a song that I knew to be a vireo—many inquisitive phrases—but I couldn't be sure of the species. I saw them briefly, three of them, but they were quickly off to the north before I got the glasses on them. Next I met some Carolina wrens hopping about from rock to tree stump along the trail as it descended steeply to Unicoi Gap. In the gap, near the piles of roadside litter, I spotted a song sparrow.

At Unicoi Gap I found a forester posting some Appalachian Trail distance signs and the handsome new Appalachian National Scenic Trail emblem. We got to talking and he offered me a ride to Indian Grave Gap. I declined, but said I wouldn't mind if he took my pack. Our routes were about the same for most of the day and three times we followed this routine—first over Rocky Mountain and down to the Indian Grave Gap Road where I stopped for lunch. He was waiting for me there and pulled out a Thermos jug of coffee and some of his wife's delicious home-baked peanut butter cookies. Next up the road to Indian Grave Gap itself, and finally to the old goat cheese factory site on the Tray Mountain Road. Going without a pack for four hilly miles made the day quite a bit more enjoyable.

Not only that, but Loyd Payne was an interesting man. Though he hadn't gone to college, he had put his son through the University of Georgia. The son was employed as a forester right there on the Chattahoochee. From many years with the U.S.F.S., Loyd certainly knew the woods. He identified the trees for me—a maple, a birch (here, taste the bark), cherry, sourwood, hickory (see how tough the bark is), white oak (note the whitish bark and the leaves that stayed on during the winter), dogwood (look how finely the bark is segmented and how the branches stick straight out), a young ash, and several pines.

After leaving Mr. Payne, the birds kept me company—a crow overhead, a robin, some nuthatches, and a male hairy woodpecker. Though I had heard woodpecker chirps before, I couldn't distinguish the hairy from the downy by ear. However, when I got a good view of the bill, I could tell one from the other easily.

The air was pleasantly warm and the sky a clear blue when I reached the summit of Tray Mountain. It was just a trifle lower than Blood Mountain. Landmarks such as Brasstown Bald and Yonah Mountain stood out clearly and gave me an opportunity to check out my compass for magnetic deviation. To the north the view was very fine, with Standing Indian and the intervening route along the Blue Ridge easily discernible. In the other direction, I thought I made out Springer Mountain in the far distance behind many other peaks. I spent half an hour or so enjoying the panorama before proceeding to the nearby shelter.

Here was the first trail register I had come across. It included the name of Art Smith, headed for Maine, who had been here on February 25—*brrr!* Tonight I was the only visitor. It took me the better part of an hour to get a campfire burning well and it wasn't worth the effort.

APRIL 1 (THURSDAY). One warbler didn't make a spring, but it was a fine way to begin an April. Actually, morning began with my startling a ruffed grouse from in front of the lean-to. I didn't even have my glasses on, but saw and heard the whoosh as he flew away. The juncos were back again—every lean-to seems to have them—and they cleaned up some crumbs I had left the night before.

One nice feature of this shelter was the table built at one end. It made a convenient place for cooking.

A woodpecker was tapping somewhere near the trail. A titmouse called out "Peter-Peter-Peter." There was another song that I didn't recognize, not unpleasant and with a little gurgle. High up in the trees I traced this to a male bluebird. A couple of others were nearby. I can't imagine a more beautiful bird, except perhaps the scarlet tanager or the wood duck. Then very briefly I spotted a single solitary vireo—undoubtedly the species I had heard yesterday—easily recognizable by the yellow on its flanks.

The warbler that greeted April, not surprisingly, was a black-and-white that methodically probed for insects on the bark of the tree trunks at Steeltrap Gap. The warbler migration was on.

I paused briefly on the Swag of the Blue Ridge, disappointed that there were no good views. Continuing up Kelly Knob, I chanced upon a woodchuck in the middle of the trail a couple of hundred feet away. Sensing danger, he quickly lumbered off to the safety of his burrow beneath some nearby ledges. In the same area a dainty little spring azure butterfly fluttered about, a token of the changing season.

Reaching the highway at Dicks Creek Gap, I hitchhiked without difficulty to the Blue Ridge Motel near Hiawassee, where I enjoyed a warm shower and a soft bed. My clothes were a bit stale after nine days, so it was good to be able to stick them in the washer and dryer before turning in for the night.

APRIL 2. This was to be an easy day, so I took plenty of time getting started. My pack was heavier again, loaded with food supplies I had dropped off in advance.

A cold front had passed through during the night, bringing a bit of rain in the wee small hours. It remained overcast in the morning, but turned clear (though cool) later in the day.

Spring was more advanced at the lower elevations near Hiawassee. I had to wait for quite a while to get a lift back to the trail, but this gave me time to appreciate the growth along the roadside. There were some low square-stemmed plants bearing spikes of small blue orchidlike blossoms. It was a member of the mint family, gill-over-the-ground.

There were more interesting things on the Appalachian Trail north of Dicks Creek Gap: British soldier lichens, for instance—tiny staves of light green tipped with scarlet caps. As I stopped for lunch by the small stream, I noticed some yellow birches for the first time. The common fern here was the evergreen Christmas fern, easy to recognize by the "ears" on the leaflets. But there were also some polypody among the rocks. The birds included the solitary vireo, nuthatches, chickadees, a titmouse, a couple of pileated woodpeckers, and a little downy woodpecker at Bull Gap.

There was a mystery awaiting me at Plumorchard Lean-to. Marty's orange pack was neatly propped against the wall of the shelter, along with his boots, but he wasn't anywhere around, and his sleeping bag was missing. Puzzled by his absence, I thought he might have become lost somewhere nearby and played my recorder shrilly to give him the location of the shelter. He didn't show up, so I wrote a note describing the situation so the forest service could look for him.

APRIL 3. Next to the day of foul weather around Woody Gap, this was the most tiring day of the trip so far. It wasn't so many miles, but there was an awful lot of climbing, some of it quite steep.

I continued to be fortunate with the weather; the rule seemed to be clear skies and afternoon temperatures of about 60°F. Occasionally there would be a good view. For days now the Appalachian Trail had been circling around Brasstown Bald and it had become a familiar beacon.

I came to Bly Gap on the border between Georgia and North Carolina, and besides the vista, there was the thrill of reaching the first state line. It was a choice place to stop for lunch.

All day long I kept encountering ruffed grouse, including one that sat on the trail about 30 yards ahead of me while I got a good look. Perhaps the fact that I was now hiking above the 4,000-foot contour line accounted for their abundance. The elevation might also have been responsible for the yellow-bellied sapsucker which I saw for the first time. Another treat was a brown thrasher right on the trail. I had no trouble recognizing it by sight, but was unfamiliar with the peculiar hissing sound it made when it flew off and perched in the nearby brush.

The Standing Indian Lean-to was supposed to be half a mile from Deep Gap, but it seemed considerably farther to me. It was the best shelter yet because it had a wooden sleeping platform instead of the dirt floors of the shelters in Georgia. Just 20 feet away was a good stream of cold clear water. It must have been a popular place during the warmer months, but that night—even though it was Saturday— I had it all to myself.

APRIL 4. This was to be a long day, so I was on the trail by 8:00 A.M. Immediately the hike started with the climb of Standing Indian Mountain which, at 5,498 feet, was the highest point reached so far.

I heard a sweet, fairly slow staccato song which I traced to a junco.

I hadn't realized it had this song in addition to the familiar little trill. During the day, the same song recurred several times. Then at nightfall, at the shelter, three more of these quite tame little grey birds squabbled over the bread crumbs I threw to them just a few feet away. For the moment, they were my closest friends.

The only new thing in the bird kingdom was very localized atop Standing Indian. Near the summit were three blue jays. I suspected they were migrating and flew from one high point to the next, resting occasionally when their flight path crossed a tall ridge.

Two red squirrels on Standing Indian put on a good show for me. These noisy little critters chatter away excitedly with a combination of metallic chirps, buzzy notes, and rasping squawks. This performance went on for several minutes, with a twitch of the tail with every note, and the little animal quivering all the while.

Although the summit of Standing Indian Mountain was not on the Appalachian Trail, the side trail to the top was short and justified the effort. From an outcrop there was a grand view to the south. Tray, Blood and Slaughter mountains, and Brasstown Bald were some of the peaks that I could pick out with the help of my compass.

Leaving the spruce woods of Standing Indian behind, I headed on to Beech Gap for lunch. There didn't seem to be any large beeches around; they probably were cut long ago.

The trail passed a watershed used for research by the Forest Service. There was an unattractive 200-acre clear-cut area over most of the watershed. A sign told how great clear-cutting was for you. The precipitous scramble up the rocks on the south side of Albert Mountain was a bit of a feat with a heavy pack. There were some route-finding problems on the north side, but I got straightened out and found Big Spring Gap Lean-to at about 6:30.

It had been a long tough day. My feet were beginning to hurt, as if I were straining some muscles or tendons in the balls of my feet. Another problem was the chafing of my legs by my trousers. And since I hadn't brought a wide-brimmed hat, I was suffering a bit from sunburned ears.

APRIL 5. Though the trees were still barren, new signs of spring appeared every day. Aside from the cultivated daffodils on Hawk Mountain in Georgia, I had not seen any flowers along the trail. Now the trailing arbutus was beginning to blossom. Like the galax, with which it was often found, it had large leathery evergreen leaves that hugged the ground. The pretty flower consisted of a tube that opened up to five white, slightly purplish, petals. The other occasional sign of spring was the delicate pussy willow with its furry buds. There were some on Albert Mountain and a few more along the trail now.

The character of the Appalachian Trail had changed. Instead of following the narrow crest of the Blue Ridge, it now snaked about at lower elevations and didn't provide opportunities for vistas. To compensate, though, there was a delightful dell where I rested by a brook amid luxuriant rhododendron, mossy logs, and towering hemlocks. While listening to the drumming of a ruffed grouse from some courting ground in the woods, I was startled by four hikers—the first people I had seen since leaving Dicks Creek Gap three days before. We chatted awhile and I asked them to tell the Forest Service about Marty's disappearance when they returned to civilization.

At noon I reached the Rock Gap Lean-to where I had left a box of supplies two weeks earlier. It was still there, unopened and untouched by the raccoons and squirrels. Scribbled on it were notes of encouragement and good wishes from some members of the Georgia Appalachian Trail Club and the MIT Outing Club. They had camped at the shelter in the interim. Their friendly sentiments really cheered me.

Across Wallace Gap, in the afternoon, I met my first serious southbound hiker, a lawyer from Washington, D.C., who was active in the conservation movement. Arnold had been hiking pieces of the Appalachian Trail for 20 years and on this trip was headed from Fontana to Tesnatee Gap.

He solved the mystery of Marty's disappearance for me. Finding his pack a burden, Marty had set out from Plumorchard with nothing but his sleeping bag. Moving at a rapid pace, he had reached the Wesser Creek Trail Shelter near Nantahala Gorge. By that time, having walked over 50 miles in sneakers in a couple of days, his feet were covered with blisters. He hadn't eaten for 24 hours and was going to leave the trail and go home to Connecticut. As for his pack, he was just going to abandon it. Arnold thought he would catch up with the hikers I had met in the morning and said he would see that the Forest Service didn't go out on an unnecessary search for Marty.

I had to get the moleskin out, as blisters were starting to develop on the inner edges of my heels. The moleskin seemed to take care of that problem. The sunburn on my ears was a more troublesome matter.

I had company at the Siler Bald Lean-to—a well-equipped family of four from Dayton, Ohio, who were hiking from Wallace Gap to Fontana.

APRIL 6. Winter came back today; not a blizzard like a couple of weeks ago, but enough cold and snow to be uncomfortable. Fortunately, I didn't have an especially ambitious hike planned for the day.

Nature observation was poor. The juncos were out in the morning to see if we would throw them anything, but for the rest of the day—only two chickadees, one nuthatch, one crow far down in the valley, and a woodpecker. There was also a bird which flew overhead at treetop level, calling out with a note repeated about 13 times. From its size and slightly undulating flight, I think it was probably a sapsucker.

There was also a little mouselike mammal, probably a shrew, that scampered off across the snow before I could get a good look. As I climbed the Wayah Bald Tower Road, a two-inch brown centipede was vividly silhouetted against the white ground. Was it unusual for a centipede to be out on a such a day?

Near a sign which advised of a scenic vista ahead, I missed the Appalachian Trail cut-off and so continued to the top of Wayah Bald by the longer, but more gradual, road. There are some tourist facilities near the summit. I found a covered porch which served as shelter for lunch. Before I started on, it stopped snowing—about six inches covered the ground. It was still foggy, though, so I missed the fine panorama that you're supposed to see on a clear day.

My friends from Dayton were waiting for me at the Cold Springs Trail Shelter. The guidebook said it was for four but fortunately there was plenty of room for a fifth. Young Bob was a skilled fire builder and had a good blaze going. With the temperature hovering around 36° F., the campfire was really appreciated. We didn't stay up to socialize, though. As soon as we had some hot grub we were happy to snuggle into our sleeping bags.

APRIL 7. This was the day I took a trip to spring. Starting at around 5,000 feet, it was downhill all day to Wesser on the Nantahala River at 1,700 feet.

It had snowed some more overnight. Despite the 28°F. reading and the dreary skies, I managed to bestir myself and get on the trail a bit after nine o'clock. Before long, however, the cloud cover began to break up. The sun's rays probing through the grey overcast gave me a chance to take some dramatic pictures of the valleys far below. There was little bird life—a chickadee, a ruffed grouse, and a bird that sounded like a squeaky door. It turned out to be a blue jay which called its usual scream as it flew off.

Wesser Bald was particularly exciting because here I could get my first view of the Smokies—very grand even though still distant. Clingmans Dome stood out and Mt. Le Conte peeked up from the far side of the range over Newfound Gap. Everything above the 4,000-foot line was covered with white.

The trail then descended along Wesser Creek. By the headwaters I first discovered patches of ramps, whose large parallel-veined leaves make them conspicuous. I dug down to get a few of the small, sweet tubers. I refrained from gorging myself though, because I didn't want my breath to smell of onions for the next week.

Spring really became evident below 3,000 feet. The tulip trees' cup-shaped blossoms were opening. Curiously, there didn't seem to be flowers except on quite mature trees. Small buckeyes were develop-ing; their distinctive compound leaves, still bronze in color, were bursting out of their buds. And now there were more wild flowers, too—the showy (and toxic) bloodroot and the more delicate rue anemone.

I finally hit the dirt road. Dogs barked at me about four separate times in the two miles to U.S. Route 19. Surprisingly, the only birds in this stretch were seven juncos. However, I was interested to see a little white-footed mouse scamper off into a farmer's field.

Upon reaching the highway I was able to use a phone in a private home to call Mr. McCraw, the manager of Nantahala Lodge a few miles to the east. Mr. Mac came right out to pick me up and drove me over to the lodge where I spent the night in comfort. It was a friendly place, with a fine view of the Smokies, and the food was, as they claim, the best in the Nantahalas. It certainly beat freeze-dried beef stew. The roast beef, carrots, green beans, corn, and salad were as tasty as I had been anticipating they would be for the past several days.

A few chores, such as laundry and packing the supplies I had left in advance at the lodge, and telephone calls back to civilization, and then to bed.

APRIL 8. The grapefruit, hotcakes, and bacon for breakfast were de-licious. I would need something hearty to carry me over the next stretch, which some through hikers had found to be the hardest on the entire Appalachian Trail.

Mr. McCraw gave me a lift down to Gasaway's store, near the bridge over the Nantahala River. I was able to get some baby powder (for my chafed legs) and some cigars and started on my way at 10:00 A.M.

Along the river I found a single cardinal and a song sparrow. The folks from Dayton, who caught up with me after a bit, saw a king-fisher.

All sorts of leafy plants now covered the ground. Dandelions were in flower. There were mullein and dock, little white violets, and some golden buttercups. The plant with compound leaves and spikes of snapdragonlike flowers was the wood vetch, according to my *Flower Finder*. Others were the blue and gold asterlike robins-plantain and a dainty yellow violet.

The trail passed a one-acre pond at about the 2,200-foot elevation. I thought it should be a good place for ducks, though I didn't see any at first. Just as I was thinking this, a single duck took off and flew overhead, probably a female mallard, but I couldn't be sure.

Above the pond was an abandoned field, the richest bird habitat so far. There were 18 crows, another cardinal, three flickers, two towhees, a redwing, and a couple of sparrows that I chased about for some time before finally identifying as white-throats. To add to the butterfly list, there was a tiger swallowtail.

In five miles the trail ascended from 1,700 feet to about 4,700 feet. Most of the way was pretty easy, with gentle grades. There was only one bad spot, The Jump-Up, where the trail went from 3,500 to 4,000 feet in about two-tenths of a mile. Even here there was no need for rock-climbing; it was just a very steep dirt trail. Still, it was good to reach Swim Bald and to have a short descent, for a change, to Sassafras Gap. There was a lean-to nearby, but if I stopped I would have a long hike the following day. It was only 4:30 in the afternoon, so I decided to fill my water bottle and go on.

This meant climbing another 650 feet, sometimes steeply, to the top of Cheoah Bald. With young Bob from Dayton I took the short side trail to the viewpoint. The close-up view of the Smokies was very fine, but even more exciting was the large bird soaring in circles immediately below us, not more than 100 yards away. We watched quietly as it soared off west along the ridge on absolutely flat wings. How it could travel, so quickly and without effort! Through my binoculars I could make out an extensive white patch at the base of the tail and think it must have been an immature golden eagle, though I can't exclude the possibility that it was a young bald eagle. In the distance it joined another speck in the sky and the two vanished together. This was the wildness I'd been seeking; such sights repaid the hard work with interest.

The descent, quite steep with much of the trail covered with snow, was very perilous going. At places where the trail slabbed a knob, there was virtually no footway—perhaps six inches between the hillside and a tree or laurel bush. It was still light when I reached Locust Cove Gap at around 6:45. Finding a fairly level spot in the gap I set up my tent for the first time on the trip. I walked off a couple of hundred yards to fill my water bag, and then cooked in the twilight before retiring at the end of a very satisfying day.

APRIL 9. It was good that I had continued beyond the last shelter and camped out because the hike to Cable Gap took a full day. The route continued to be very steep, both up and down, and the trail surface left much to be desired. It was often rough and rocky and in one stretch wandered through a stream bed. For most of the day I averaged less than one mile per hour. Only after Wauchecha Bald did my pace pick up.

I went down to Stekoah Gap and then over to Sweetwater Gap for lunch. Here it was quite breezy. There were numerous young beeches, most of them sending up two or three trunks from a single root system. I understand that they can withstand strong winds better than other kinds of trees, so someday this may be a fine beech gap. The usual variety of birds put in their appearance, including a pileated woodpecker that flew overhead while I lay on my back resting after lunch. There were also a number of butterflies, but the most common was the mourning cloak with its light-edged brown wings.

During the afternoon I spotted a fast-moving lizard, probably a five-lined skink; it had a conspicuous chocolate stripe, neatly bordered by fine cream stripes above and below, along its sides.

After half a dozen ridges and gaps, it was a relief to cross Wauchecha Bald. The trail then descended to Cody Gap and some streams. Nearby were spring beauties, lovely low plants whose little white petals were gaily marked with lavender stripes.

Once the trail hit the road it was smooth going and I made good time for the last few miles. The Cable Gap Shelter was the first one with bunks. They were made of wire and very comfortable. As I lay there relaxing, a full moon climbed over the hillside into the starry sky.

APRIL 10. It was an easy walk over the Yellow Creek Range and then down to the highway overlooking Fontana Reservoir. In the lowlands, flowers again became more common. The yellow violets were particularly abundant, almost forming mats.

I had left a box of food with the helpful TVA officers at the Fontana Dam Visitor Center and spent about an hour having lunch and transferring the goodies to my pack. The first barn swallows of the season swooped by as I crossed the dam. Just beyond was a register, with one other Katahdin entry: "John Castleman/Dan Weirich" on March 30.

This was the Great Smoky Mountains National Park and the trail was in pretty good shape. Nevertheless, it was a long grind up to Shuckstack. Near the crest there was a splendid view back over the parallel ridges crossed in the last couple of days—Cheoah Bald high in the distance, Wauchecha Bald and the Yellow Creek Mountains closer in.

There were two other parties at the Birch Spring Trail Shelter. One was a group of boys from Toledo, starting to hike the length of the park to Davenport Gap.

We had some excitement about 10:00 P.M. when one of the kids returned from the latrine (the first of its kind I'd seen) and shrieked, "Open the gate!" Running into the shelter, and still trembling, he told of a bear a hundred feet tall in the creek outside. We looked out, but no one else saw the beast—was it just imagination? There certainly were bears around. The Park Service had built fences on the open side of the lean-tos. As a result, the bears wandered around freely while the campers slept in cages.

APRIL 11. A beautiful Easter Sunday. The hike through the Smokies really began when the crest was reached at Doe Knob. This stretch has apparently all been logged and at the higher elevations (about 5,000 feet) the forest cover was mostly young yellow birch. There were few views—none spectacular until Mt. Squires.

It was a poor birding day. However, juncos were abundant—there were about 20, including good numbers in the evening around Spence Field. The most noteworthy bird was the robin, which likes the grassy areas. There was one at the Mollies Ridge Trail Shelter and another at Spence Field. Just about the only other birds were a couple of titmice, a solitary vireo, and a turkey vulture.

Flowers continued to be in short supply. Only the spring beauties and the tiny four-petaled bluets were at all common. There was some trailing arbutus around, but it didn't seem to be in blossom yet this high up.

There were a number of steep climbs. From the last one, up Mt. Squires, there was another fine vista to the south over Fontana Reservoir and the Cheoah section. With my binoculars I picked out a distant mountain which was probably Standing Indian; the gorge to its west could only be Deep Gap, I thought.

Emerging from the birch forest, the trail reached the open crest at Spence Field. Here there were just grasses and shrubs and the full rounded masses of Thunderhead and the Smokies ahead. It was a beautiful spot.

In addition to the boys from Toledo, I met a two-man party from Georgia at the New Spence Field Trail Shelter. One of them was among the GATC members who had written notes on my package at Rock Gap. I asked him to relay my appreciation to the others.

APRIL 12. Bird-watching was good. Blue jays scolded about the shelter early in the morning. A number of towhees seemed to like the cover of the laurel thickets in Spence Field. As I was studying them, a redwing flew over. It was a record day for juncos—31 of them. There were chickadees, solitary vireos, nuthatches, and titmice, and I was quite sure I'd heard a raven.

Butterflies were on the scarce side. Tiger swallowtails were completely absent. There was a mourning cloak, though.

The park was crowded. During the day I passed about 30 hikers headed the other way in about eight parties. Still there was room at the Silers Bald Trail Shelter. Besides the group from Toledo, I met a party from Roanoke who welcomed me with a warming shot of bourbon and orange mix. They told me of some of the problems on the trail in their area—the long dry stretch over Tinker Mountain and a couple of miles where the blazes have been covered with green paint.

APRIL 13. The interesting thing about this day was the fir-spruce forest, apparently virgin, that I entered just past Double Springs Gap. Not that I had much opportunity to enjoy these dark and rich woods. I was in a hurry to reach Newfound Gap.

Near the summit of Silers Bald, some campers had set up tents on the grassy slopes overlooking the ranges of mountains to the south and east. A more exhilarating campsite would be hard to imagine.

Silers Bald produced a couple of towhees and a white-throated sparrow. Not much farther on, a raven circled beneath me on the Tennessee side of the crest. There was a difference in the chickadee's song. At these elevations, I heard the black-capped chickadee singing a high note followed by one or two short ones instead of the fee-bee fee-bay of the almost identical Carolina. Similarly, the red-breasted nuthatch had replaced the white-breasted that I had been seeing earlier.

The real novelties, which are associated with the spruce-fir forest, were a couple of golden-crowned kinglets flitting about and a brown creeper climbing up the dead trunk of a conifer in search of insects. In the fire-scorched area west of Mt. Buckley, a field sparrow was perched in the new scrub growth.

People weren't the only mammals—on Jenkins Knob there were two white-tailed deer and a red squirrel.

My lunch stop was at the Clingmans Dome Observation Tower, which was overrun by tourists. They didn't get much of a view, though, because of a heavy haze. The next five miles were rough going. There was still some snow on the ground from last week's storm (up here 24 inches of new snow had been recorded) and the Appalachian Trail was a channel for the run-off. The path was eroded and rocky and I suppose it would have been more sensible, or at least easier, to follow the road instead.

At the Indian Gap parking area I chatted briefly with some folks from New Jersey, and when I reached Newfound Gap they were there also. The driver wondered whether, by any chance, I was Colin Fletcher! I had the pocket "office" and Sierra cup that Fletcher recommends, but I don't use a walking stick. The conversation gave me a chance to bum a lift down to the Rippling Waters Motel in Cherokee, where I stayed for the night. I had a hot shower and steak dinner, followed by a needed trip to the laundromat next door.

I had left one of my packages here and did some organizing of my gear before going to bed. One item I picked up was the guidebook for the remainder of the Appalachian Trail in North Carolina and Tennessee. The volume covering the southernmost part of the trail was sent home; this was tangible evidence of the progress I'd been making.

APRIL 14. I decided to take a chance that the worst of the cold weather was over and mailed my down pants and heavy yellow parka home. This reduced my load by about three pounds.

It was afternoon when I left the motel. A car gave me a lift to the park boundary, but I stood there for hours as station wagons of tourists streamed by without stopping. Finally I flagged down a park ranger. He gave me a lift to Newfound Gap, where I thanked him and light heartedly set out again. The trail sign advised me that Mt. Katahdin was now only 1,823 miles away.

Some segments of the trail were covered with ice. Where this surface was combined with a substantial grade, the going was treacherous. I took a couple of falls and scraped my wrist, and was grateful not to have any more serious bruises.

The rocky crag of Charlies Bunion was dramatic under the darkening skies, but I was chilled by a cold wind and hurrying to reach the False Gap Shelter before the sun went down, so I couldn't relax and enjoy the scenery. Pressing on after taking a couple of pictures, I arrived at the shelter around 6:30, having made 6.4 miles over hard terrain in the good time of 3.5 hours.

APRIL 15. This was a soft day for a change. Only nine miles to go, so I could afford to sleep in while my Toledo friends headed on for a 16-mile day. The register showed that Art Smith had been here on March 15 and Castleman on April 2.

A hairy woodpecker tapped away nearby as I packed and got ready to hit the trail. The clear prolonged joyful song of a winter wren rang out through the morning air from some hidden sanctum. Later on I traced an unfamiliar song, something like a Carolina chickadee's but with gurgling in place of the lower notes, to a brown creeper.

With fair skies and mild temperature, and with no reason to rush, it was a very pleasant day. I took a long lunch stop at Bradleys View, just enjoying the out-of-doors. To the west I could follow the route of the Appalachian Trail for miles.

At the Tri-Corner Knob Trail Shelter I was received with great hospitality. A group of four Explorer Scouts and their leader, learning that I was an end-to-ender, invited me to join their feast of ham and trimmings. My compliments to the chef: it was a real treat. Their adult member "Doc," a kindly gentleman with neat grey beard, was the general practitioner in a small town in Ohio. With a warm welcome from folks like this, solo hiking wasn't entirely lonely.

APRIL 16. The virgin forest, the land of the kinglet and the winter wren, continued a bit farther to Hell Ridge. Descending to 5,000 feet (from 6,360 on the side of Mt. Guyot), both the woods and the birds changed. There were towhees and vireos again, and a flicker rose from the ground and flew off along the trail. Along with yellow violets and ramps, and oceans of spring beauties, there were patches of the peculiar brown-mottled foliage of fawn lilies (though only an isolated plant or two was blooming as yet). Past Cosby Knob there were masses of dog hobble whose finely toothed evergreen leaves seemed to be blotched with raspberry juice stains. In one particularly nice shaded area beneath tall hemlocks, the hillside was covered with the trailing stems of the partridgeberry. A few berries had been left by the wildlife; they were insipid, but not distasteful.

On the final climb up Sunup Knob, the comma butterfly put in its first appearance. Its orange wings were blotched with black spots in a nondescript pattern; it was the raggedy edges of the wings that were peculiar and so distinctive. Nearby was another new sight— the first large shrub to be in flower. Actually, if I'm not mistaken, the reddish bloom was the blossoming of a young red maple tree.

It was a long descent to the Davenport Gap Trail Shelter, which was at 2,000 feet. However, because it was downhill, I covered the 14.7 miles in less than ten hours. Southbound, the same distance would have involved climbing 5,400 feet. As it was, I was free to rest frequently and take some pictures. One shot was of a yellow birch which was spreading massive roots along and down the sides of a decaying giant nurse tree, probably an ancient hemlock.

APRIL 17. I spent my last night with my friends from Toledo, who were heading home. They surprised me early in the morning by gathering around my bunk and singing a hearty "Happy Birthday." They even had a frosted pastry with a candle for me to blow out.

The lean-to was in a forest of tall tulip trees. Bloodroots and rue anemone were common here. I pulled up one of the former to examine, but not taste, the juicy toxic red root. Nearby there were the first fiddleheads of the trip, probably young Christmas ferns.

With the descent to lower elevations, the nature of the forest changed. There was much scrub and white pine; more shrubs were starting to put out leaves, and the mountain sweetbells were decorated with their long rows of droopy small white urn-shaped blossoms.

Continuing past Davenport Gap, where I was serenaded by two or three solitary vireos, there were more treats—blossoming shadbush, a single jack-in-the-pulpit, a black-throated green warbler singing high in a flowering maple above State Line Branch, and some yellow and white trilliums. One of these plants was an exceptional find—the mottled trillium, exactly like the one pictured in the Forest Service pamphlet on endangered flowers in the Southern Appalachians. There were violets and phlox and more.

The black and tiger swallowtails were common at the lower elevations—in fact just past Interstate 40, I saw both of them, along with some bees, feeding on the nectar of the flowers of a single redbud tree.

The banks of the Big Pigeon River were decorated with patches of yellow green, the new foliage of the tulip trees. Along with the redbuds and some tinges of scarlet on the maples, this brightened the otherwise drab scene.

If further evidence of spring were needed, I found it on the trail at the beginning of the climb up Snowbird Mountain. A chipmunk, enjoying the 70°F. weather, was out in the woods on chipmunk business.

As I was leaving my long lunch spot at Painter Creek, two hikers approached and in the best "Dr. Livingstone, I presume" style asked if I was Jim Wolf. They were Tom McKone and Bob Winslow from Connecticut, also headed for Mt. Katahdin. They had left Springer Mountain on April 1 and had been closing the gap ever since.

I continued the long and steady climb of Snowbird Mountain, well-graded all the way. What irony that during the entire day I didn't encounter a single junco (which is what a "snowbird" is) after having seen so many in the Smokies. The summit was adorned by some sort of radio beacon station that sits in a large clearing. It was a worthwhile view along the state boundary, with Mt. Guyot and the Smokies one way and the Appalachian Trail route over Max Patch the other. As I sat there relaxing, a flash of steel blue sped across the mountain. I'm quite sure it was a falcon. Because of the size and the absence of rufous markings, I think it must have been a pigeon hawk.

Tom and Bob rejoined me at the Groundhog Creek Lean-to, where the wire bunks were coming apart pretty badly. We spent the evening comparing notes about our experiences, techniques, and anticipations.

APRIL 18. Tom and Bob have an interesting project. With a three-pound sampler they carry, they are making air pollution measurements along the Appalachian Trail. The device determines light transmission, which can be converted to particulate matter concentrations. The cleanest air they've encountered yet was in a cloud on Silers Bald in the Smokies, where the reading was almost down to natural background levels.

The day wasn't much scenically. Nearly four miles were on a dirt road passing some uninteresting rural dwellings. Crossing Harmon Den Mountain I noticed mayapples for the first time—some already with little umbrellas, others with what looked like little yellow clenched fists just breaking through the ground. Farther on I had lunch before reaching the dirt road. It was a good place for birds—downy woodpecker, sapsucker, and hermit thrush. The thrush, which must be migrating, gave me a good view of its reddish tail as it flew from one tree to another.

I stopped to chat with two men who were picking fresh greens. They were particularly interested in a plant growing on a wet hillside which they called branch lettuce (I think it's saxifrage). The young leaves, green or reddish, are about two inches long and toothed and grow out horizontally from the root. The leaves were very crisp and tasty. For a satisfying salad, the men advised serving branch lettuce and ramps soaked in hot grease—it sounded good.

Leaving the road, the trail passed through a small clearing. Here there was a carpet of blue specks which turned out, on study, to be gill-over-the-ground (ground ivy). There was also a conspicuous yellow composite, with deeply cleft leaves, which keyed out as golden ragwort.

There was no one else at the Walnut Mountain Lean-to. Tom and

Bob had pushed on and were camping somewhere ahead. However, for company there were hundreds of little flies that were a nuisance; a couple of them bit feebly.

It was a long way down to the spring so I took my water bag and filled it with several quarts. I was finished with supper and the diary by dark (7:30 these days) and had a chance to play the recorder before turning in.

APRIL 19. The warmest day of the trip (up to 80°F.) and more delights of spring.

Spring beauties were abundant. The ones at the lean-to were tightly closed when I noticed them early in the morning. Only later, after the sun had been out a while, did they open up; then they cover the hillsides with white. When I stopped to photograph them on the far side of Bluff Mountain, there were 100 blossoms to the square foot—millions in an acre!

Approaching Garenflo Gap, I recognized a cardinal's song and a little farther on thought I caught a glimpse of a gnatcatcher. Nearby the lacy foliage that I had been seeing in recent days put up some flowers that proved to be squirrel corn. Their sweet fragrance attracted a huge bumblebee.

Two members of the rose family, the lovely wild strawberry and the cinquefoil, added some color to Garenflo Gap. The dogwoods were just starting to open. I stopped for lunch and while resting tried to imitate the song of a Carolina chickadee on my recorder. It seemed a lousy rendition, but pronto three chickadees appeared, quite upset. Farther on, there continued to be good displays of violets, trailing arbutus, and a small cream-colored bellwort.

Reaching Hot Springs, I signed the register at the Ranger Station —Art Smith had been there on March 19. Then on to the Alpine Motor Court where I picked up my mail and another box of supplies and checked in for the night. I even watched television—oh, how decadent can I be!

APRIL 20. It was afternoon before I got going. Before leaving town I stopped at a hardware store that had a scale. My pack weighed 44 pounds, including a quart of water and a three days' supply of food. That weight didn't include my binoculars and camera. It was quite a load, heavier than I had thought. On the good side, I figured I'd lost about five pounds; I still had plenty to spare.

Just across the French Broad River I got a picture of the brilliant scarlet fire pink growing out of the crack in a rock, and along the trail up Rich Mountain there was a single wild iris.

It was another long trudge upward—over 2,000 feet up Rich Mountain. I took the short side trail to the summit and visited the ranger there.

Reaching Spring Mountain Lean-to around six o'clock, I had plenty of time to make camp, eat, and wash dishes before it became dark. Instead of going to sleep, I indulged one of my weaknesses and picked up the Pirates–Braves game from Atlanta.

While listening to the game, I heard an animal noise. I tried to track it down, and after much searching with the flashlight, I finally spotted a large toad on the dirt floor beneath the wire bunks.

APRIL 21. My luck with the weather finally failed. Hardly had I left the lean-to before it started to rain. I tried to keep dry in my rain suit, but it didn't breathe at all and I found it much more comfortable walking in shorts with bare legs. I reached Allen Gap in a couple of hours and took shelter for a long lunch stop at the service station there. The proprietress asked whether I had seen something in the Smokies. "Fires," I thought she said—no, "briers," maybe. Finally she spelled it: "b-e-a-r-s."

Not long after leaving Allen Gap the rain tapered off and the rest of the day's walking was better. Altogether I only hiked a bit over eight miles, to the Little Laurel Lean-to. I loafed for a while and had dinner before a terrific thunderstorm hit with a heavy downpour. The metal roof had numerous leaks, but one bunk was reasonably dry and I was happy to be in a lean-to instead of my little tent in such weather.

APRIL 22. The morning's weather was cool and foggy. The blazes were visible only about 100 feet away, but the trailway was well worn. The moisture blown off the trees by the wind was like a light rain.

My first hour on the trail was a good one despite the weather, 1,100 feet up and 1.3 miles. With a good grade it was possible to move pretty well.

On the relocated section near the summit of Camp Creek Bald there were extensive patches of fawn lily. Only an occasional yellow blossom was out now, but in a couple of weeks it would be quite spectacular.

There was a new lean-to at Chestnut Log Gap at the site of the burned Jerry Cabin. Unfortunately, jeeps and motorcycles could drive up here and the place was an incredible mess. Though only two years old, it was completely surrounded by beer and pop cans and other litter. The walls and roof were covered by explicit graffiti, and the wire bunks had been vandalized to the point of being unusable. I couldn't find the water supply, but it didn't matter as I had been carrying a quart of water all morning.

Among the noteworthy flowers were both Dutchman's-breeches (at Chestnut Log Gap) and squirrel corn (at Flint Gap). There were more blossoming sweetbells and at places the ground was covered with fallen flowers of the red maple.

The skies were clear at Big Butt, but the views were not very photogenic. The Tennessee countryside was over 3,000 feet below —so far that it seemed indistinct. A hawk took off at my approach. My guess is that it was a Cooper's, but I can't be sure.

A little later I paused at the graves of David and William Shelton who, though southerners, fought with the Union in the Civil War. They returned home while the war was still going on and were ambushed by some rebel soldiers sent to punish them for their treason. The gravesite was desecrated by beer cans and shotgun shells. I carted off the litter and took a picture which I hoped would express the solitude of the place.

I went on to the Locust Ridge Lean-to. It was nicely located, though the spring didn't produce much water.

APRIL 23. This day marked a month on the trail. I had averaged about ten miles a day. Spring had come a long way, though the trees hadn't yet started to turn green.

Once again the weather was lousy. There was a pretty good thunderstorm in progress when I got up, so I took plenty of time, hoping it would taper off. I even made a little campfire for some psychic, if not much physical, warmth.

Just as I was about to shove off, two long-distance hikers pulled in. Bruce Balderston and Gary Wiesendanger were from New York. They had started from Springer Mountain on April 2 and expected to arrive at Katahdin around August 24. We chatted briefly while they stripped off their wet clothes. I soon headed off in the rain so I could make my destination at Sams Gap without rushing. We would have more time to talk when they caught up with me again.

At Devil Fork Gap, I asked permission to sit out of the rain on the farmer's porch. He cordially invited me to come inside, where I spent a warm and comfortable 20 minutes while he extolled the virtues of branch lettuce and hot grease.

Following the farmer's advice I found some tasty branch lettuce

along some of the rivulets on the way to Sugarloaf Gap. Soon afterwards it stopped raining, and I had a leisurely lunch. It was only
42°F., though, so I pulled out my stove and drank my fill of hot
tea and cocoa before moving on.

The trail was steep in parts, often muddy though not too difficult
to negotiate. At the higher elevations there were thin patches of
new snow. Among the plants were more ramps, some trilliums nodding on little stalks, and the deep purple spring larkspur.

Upon reaching Sams Gap, after crossing or ducking under at least
a dozen rusty barbed wire fences, I had to walk another mile or
more to a service station where I had left my next box. Fortunately
I was able to get a room for the night at the nearby Little Creek
Cafe, with the unexpected bonus of a bath.

APRIL 24. After the gloomy weather of the past three days, blue
skies and scenic vistas were a welcome change. I was lucky enough
to have someone give me a lift and so was able to get on the trail
by 8:30 A.M.

Big Bald, the highest peak since the Smokies, dominated the day.
Soon after leaving Sams Gap I passed a field with mayapples, Indian
paintbrush, golden ragwort, some colorful dandelions, and one of the
yellow mustards. Farther up was gill-over-the-ground and spearmint.
And then, at the crest of the hill, I suddenly looked out over a green
pasture to the barren slopes of Big Bald. Both tiger and black swallowtails fluttered about the meadow and off to one side the shadbush
splashed the hillside with white. The fences in the foreground added
to the photographer's delight.

The summit was still four miles away. First there was a short
descent to Street Gap, and shortly after that I came across a hairy
caterpillar. It wore Pittsburgh colors—a row of golden spots on each
side on a background of black. For the next couple of miles there
were ramps everywhere. Here I met a couple of men wearing specially designed aprons with large deep pockets which they were
filling with fresh (and fragrant) ramps. Though they were now
city dwellers, they returned to the mountains each spring to get these
tasty morsels.

The summit of Big Bald, grassy with only an occasional hawthorn,
had a first-rate view. Among the mountains to be seen to the east
was Mt. Mitchell, the highest peak in the eastern United States.
Ahead and behind me I could follow the route of the Appalachian
Trail from the Smokies to Roan Mountain. And to the northwest
there were still more summits. No one seems to know how to account for the absence of trees on these southern balds; if today

was typical, though, I'd venture that the fierce cold wind has something to do with it.

I pitched my tent in a grove of white pine and hemlock trees near Spivey Gap. As a special treat I added some fairy spuds (spring beauty tubers) to my mushroom soup. Despite Euell Gibbons' raves, I hardly thought they were worth the effort.

APRIL 25. Part of my problem with bird identification was uncertainty about the songs of the black-throated green warbler and the ovenbird. I was just about certain I'd been hearing both of them regularly, but never seemed to be able to catch the bird in the act.

There were some good observations, though. Just after the first climb of the day, the trail crossed a road and dropped down into some open tulip-poplar woods. I saw something move, something brownish that blended well into its background, and was pleased to discover when I got my binoculars that it was a good-sized turkey. Then on the side of No Business Knob there were black-and-white and black-throated blue warblers. In the evening, the whippoorwill, repeatedly singing its name with hardly a pause, was added to the bird list.

I had my lunch at No Business Knob Lean-to and was idly studying the flowers—pleased to discover the uncommon magenta fringed polygala—when the silence was shattered by the arrival of two intruders on motorcycles. It seemed foolish to try to act tough since there were two of them and one of me. I did point out to them that the FOOT TRAVEL ONLY sign was there for a reason. I hoped they got the message.

During the afternoon there was the exceptionally steep descent to the Nolichucky River—about 1,500 feet down—and then up nearly as much on the other side. At the lower elevations the redbuds were very conspicuous and there were a few shadbush in bloom. Near the river there was an occasional silverbell in full flower and here, too, fresh leaves were appearing on the maples and oaks.

The Curley Maple Gap Lean-to, my first in the Cherokee National Forest, was a concrete block affair with six wire bunks. All but one of the bunks were in bad shape and the grounds were pretty badly littered. There was nothing rustic about the design, but it may be practical. The next day would be a long one, then some breathers. Now that daylight saving time had started, I'd be able to keep going longer.

APRIL 26. There were wood thrushes today. One was good enough to hop by 30 feet in front of the shelter while I was having break-fast. There were plenty of ovenbirds, too. Several of them were in the classic pose on the ground of a well-wooded slope, but I saw some in the trees as well. They sounded to me as if they tried to count to ten on a single breath and got louder as their breath ran out. Even the afternoon had some birding interest. At Beauty Spot, a bald on the lower slopes of Unaka Mountain, there were lots of robins, towhees, and juncos. One of the juncos—normal in every other way—was peculiar in that it had a completely white head. Incidentally, the place is a beautiful spot indeed and I'm sure it must have a great view in clear weather, but unfortunately it was drizzling when I was there.

Returning to the woods after several miles of walking along the Unaka Mountain Road, I discovered the large maroon blossoms of the red trillium or wake-robin.

The Cherry Gap Lean-to was already occupied by a party of four young men, accompanied by three barking hounds. They were "moss-pullers" who range the forests stripping the dead logs of their thick blanket of green moss. It's a profitable enterprise because they can sell the moss (for resale to florists) for $20 a hundredweight. They claim that they are permitted to take as much as they want, provided they leave the trees within 200 feet of the trail undisturbed.

When I arrived, they had a hen that was walking around the shelter aimlessly. The next time I saw it, it was plucked and ready to roast.

APRIL 27. The moss-pullers believe you have to scare the wildcats and other horrible critters away, so they had a Coleman lantern going all night. I got up late in the morning; by then they had already collected a couple of hundred pounds of moss.

It was a short and easy day. The shadbush were never common, but there were enough about to give some occasional color to the landscape. The white cut-leaved toothwort, easily recognized as a member of the mustard family by its small symmetrical four-petaled flower, had appeared in the woods along with the bloodroot, spring beauties, Dutchman's breeches, fawn lilies, and red trillium.

There was a gap in the string of lean-tos, forcing me to rely on my tent. The only sure source of water was at an old homestead site marked by a pile of stones and about a dozen ancient maples. It was an excellent spot to camp. Among its other attractions were patches of ramps, some of which were used to fortify my soup.

Radio predictions were for rain; the thunder had started in the distance and the wind was strong.

APRIL 28. Bad weather came overnight with a vengeance. Thunderstorms began around 11:00 P.M. and lasted almost until dawn. Sometimes it was a downpour, sometimes just a steady rain. Though lightning never struck closer than a mile or so away, it was terrifying enough.

Considering that the tent was completely open at each end, it was remarkable that I wasn't drenched. The walls were completely waterproof. My only problem was that the rain blew through the opening at the foot, slowly making a puddle beneath the lower part of my sleeping bag. I had carelessly left my long pants and wool shirt there for padding, so they became soaked. To keep something dry, I hugged a pair of long johns and my down jacket all night and was grateful to have them in the cool morning. Needless to say, I didn't get much sleep.

It was a bother packing so much wet gear, but in due course I was off again. Just a mile farther along the trail was an abandoned cabin, mentioned in the guidebook, where I might have spent the night. It had a sound roof and walls and, though filthy with broken glass, it would have been a dry shelter.

After a bit of steep climbing, the trail crossed Little Rock Knob and descended to Hughes Gap. Here I had hidden a cache of food in a hollow tree stump. Finding it in perfect order, I stopped for lunch and devoured some of the special treats right on the spot: a can of sliced pineapple and a beer, which was timely because of the shortage of water along that stretch of trail.

The grey clouds of the morning suddenly passed by and with a great rushing of wind the skies became completely clear. It was ideal weather for drying out my sleeping bag and clothing. By the time I set out again a couple of hours later, I was able to proceed in my trousers instead of immodestly in my long red underwear.

A new bird was seen at Hughes Gap—a veery on its migration north. The tawny hue and faint breast spots make this thrush easy to distinguish. Most common during the day were juncos, ovenbirds, and towhees. But with my return to the spruce forest around the 6,000-foot heights of Roan Mountain I once again encountered the golden-crowned kinglet, red-breasted nuthatch, and raven.

Getting up Roan Mountain was something else again—two and a half miles of steep ascent. Beartown Mountain, which I climbed first, had incredible numbers of ramps. Near its summit there was an outcrop with a spectacular view back to Big Bald and Unaka with distant peaks—perhaps even Snowbird—in between. That was only the first of several good vistas. From the bald on the Roan (where the azalea hadn't yet started to blossom), the Black Mountains and Mt. Mitchell were prominent. Then, after descending to Carvers Gap (often sinking to my knees in the ooze on the old carriage road), I reached a particularly photogenic stretch looking ahead along the main ridge to the graceful heights of Big Yellow Bald and Hump Mountain. My camera worked overtime.

The trail passed through some alder thickets and then arrived at the Grassy Ridge Lean-to. It was in good shape, solidly built, with the wire bunks in excellent condition, and with abundant water. I had company—a couple from Virginia who were headed south for a few days. They had met Tom McKone and Bob Winslow at the Laurel Fork and were expecting to find me.

The shelter was extremely high, around 5,850 feet, so it was quite cold after the sun went down. However, with so little sleep the night before, and having climbed over 4,000 feet in a single day for the first time, I was able to rest well.

APRIL 29. Groping one's way across the balds on Yellow and Hump could be tricky in foggy weather, but the day I crossed it was beautiful. The views were superb. The wildness and the solitude made for a special enchantment. Unlike Big Bald and Beauty Spot, these summits were unscarred by roads; and they were unlittered. Unlike Spence Field and Silers Bald, you could pause and think your own thoughts here without the distracting presence of so many others.

Starting with Watauga Lake and the Iron Mountains to the north, the panorama included Virginia's highest peaks (Mt. Rogers and White Top), the rugged and ancient Grandfather Mountain massif, the Black Mountains, the Roan, and the Unakas.

I crossed Big Yellow during the morning, passing through some stands of quite mature beech near Bradley Gap and then some hawthorn-covered hillsides along the way. In the thickets near Yellow Mountain Gap I came across my first catbird of the season along with another brown thrasher, veery, and white-throated sparrow. Just beyond the gap, a broad-winged hawk left its perch at the edge of the cleared field, circled effortlessly to gain some altitude, and flew off in the distance.

A sea of spring beauties covered the ground on top of Hump Mountain. Leaving the woods behind, the trail reached the pastures at

Bradley Gap. Vesper sparrows flew about in search of seeds. Barn swallows swooped across the ridge, finding the gale-force winds no obstacle at all. It was a grand place to stop for lunch. The only disappointment was the spring, which was surrounded by old cow manure. I had to use the water anyway, so I dosed it pretty heavily with Halazone.

After crossing the balds of Hump Mountain, I started the long descent to the highway. Near the road, a couple of vicious-looking black dogs raced out and barked at me—they were just bluffing, though. Reaching the highway I got a lift to Elk Park where I picked up another package and some mail. Among other things was a St. Christopher's medal, which was to keep me out of trouble for the rest of my trip.

A Mrs. Trivett was happy to put me up here. She was a good cook and along with her other boarders I enjoyed her chicken dinner. According to her scale, I was now down to 161 pounds. I'd lost 14 pounds. After a shower I shaved my ten-day beard, and ran my clothes through the washing machine. I was refreshed and ready to go again.

APRIL 30. This area marked a new chapter in the hike. The walk was now along rural roads instead of on the high ridge tops. The difference in birds was astounding. After devoting the morning to shopping and writing letters, I got a ride back to the Appalachian Trail. My pack was a little lighter, as I'd sent my leather gloves, long johns, and rain suit home. From now on, I would be using a poncho.

There had been a relocation near Elk Park and I lost the trail completely. For a while I followed some blazes that had been blacked out. When they disappeared I headed off cross-country in a generally westerly direction. Fortunately, I soon met some men who were able to steer me the right way.

There were a couple of shorebirds at the edge of a little water hole. One, bobbing up and down continuously, was easy to identify as the spotted sandpiper. The other, much warier, was a solitary sandpiper. Down one hollow and up the next, where a house wren gurgled happily from its perch on a fence post. Farther on, I watched two kingbirds fly off with a nervous twitter at my approach. Next I flushed a green heron from a little pasture brook. Altogether there were 26 species, including numbers of chipping sparrows, robins and cardinals, and a meadowlark.

The Moreland Gap Lean-to was clean, with good wire bunks. It was only 6:00 when I arrived, so I had a chance to read a bit of *Time* while fixing dinner and getting ready for bed.

MAY 1 (SATURDAY). Hurray, hurray, the first of May. While I was having breakfast, an ovenbird strutted in front of the shelter in search of food. Hopping up on a two-inch rock close-by, he blared out his crescendo song as I enjoyed the performance.

The morning's walk was commonplace except for the picturesque cabin site called the Knutt Place. Crossing over a knoll here, I came across wood thrushes in the open meadow; they quickly flew back into the forest when I approached. There were also a couple of titmice, one of which was singing some husky unfamiliar figures.

Waterfalls were the highlights of the afternoon. The first, Coon Den Falls I believe, consisted of a water chute through a narrow notch arcing down to a rock apron whence it cascaded into a series of small pools. The Appalachian Trail then crossed the Dennis Cove Road and followed the gorge down to the impressive 50-foot falls of the Laurel Fork. The area didn't have much protection. Some men with rifles had driven close to the falls and were tossing tin cans into the stream and pumping shots at them for "target practice."

It was a pretty season. The leaves were starting to come out. There were more flowers: the creamy little merrybells, chickweed, and the long-tubed violet wild sweet william. Christmas fern fiddleheads were common in the gorge. In the mammal line, I noted a couple of deer and a rabbit.

I spent the night at the South Pierce Lean-to, where I met Gary and Bruce again. Each of us did his own thing, theirs on an open fire and mine on the butane stove; then we shared our experiences before turning in.

MAY 2. This Sunday ended with a dramatic race with a thunderstorm. I lost and was caught hiking in a heavy rain for the first time. Had I not got such a late start, around ten o'clock, it could have been avoided.

The first stretch along Iron Mountain was easy. If it hadn't been so overcast, the views over Watauga Lake would have been very pretty. Descending to the river, I passed some flowering azalea. Services were in progress at the Horseshoe Bend Baptist Church. The beautiful baritone, singing to the accompaniment of a guitar, almost prompted me to join the worship inside.

The birding by the river was very good. There were both rough-winged and barn swallows and some goldfinches. Among the others observed during the day were blue jays, scarlet tanagers, solitary vireos, and a black-and-white warbler.

Off and on during the morning there were sprinkles, but in the early afternoon the weather deteriorated and the rains came. It was particularly uncomfortable, with lightning striking nearby, to find myself scampering across an exposed knife-edge ridge. Perhaps I should have stopped to let the storm pass, but I chose to hurry on as the lean-to was only a mile away. I reached the shelter just as the shower ended. Had it continued, I would have been able to collect all the water I needed from the roof. Instead I was forced to descend far down the ridge, three-tenths of a mile each way along a blue-blazed trail, to fill my plastic water bag.

The view eastward from the Vanderventer Lean-to was spectacular. From my perch on the outcrop behind the shelter, I looked over five or six arms of Watauga Lake and beyond, on the southern horizon, were the imposing heights of Roan Mountain.

MAY 3. A cold night and a cold day. Sleeping with Duofold top, sweater, down jacket, and wind parka, I was just barely warm enough in my bag. In the morning it was snowing and foggy as I set out. The trail was easy, though, with gentle rises and dips along the crest of Iron Mountain. It was too cold to dawdle studying flowers or looking at birds, so I moved right along.

The snow had left lacy tracings on the cobwebs low in the shrubbery. These, and the delicate icicles on each needle of an occasional white pine, were graceful ornaments.

Several towhees put on a show chasing one another and scrounging about in the leaves on the ground near the Iron Mountain Lean-to. Among them a wood thrush hopped about, robinlike, looking for food. Two brilliantly crowned pileated woodpeckers, the first in weeks, sounded their flickerlike calls and tapped away high in the trees before flying off.

Following the trail along Cross Mountain, I came to a farmhouse where I had left one of my packages in March. I was cordially invited in for a cup of coffee and a piece of homemade cherry pie. Considering how miserable the weather was, my hosts wondered if I might care to spend the night with them. They didn't have to ask twice. Nothing could have been nicer just then than a warm place to rest and kind folks to be with.

Other end-to-end hikers had been there before; Grandma Gatewood and Walter Boardman were mentioned. Only in the last couple of years, though, had there been much traffic on the trail.

A hearty home-cooked meal of Brunswick stew, with candied

yams, home-packed pickles, fresh milk, pie, and coffee hit the spot. So did the soft bed. Outside the cold wind whistled.

MAY 4. The TV was filled with news reports of the record cold. The puddles were covered by thin sheets of ice. A big breakfast and then back on the trail under cloudless skies.

Almost as soon as I reached the national forest land again I added two more birds to the trip list—a great crested flycatcher and a chestnut-sided warbler. I'd been counting black-throated blue warblers for some time on the basis of hearing their ascending buzzy songs, so it was reassuring to see one. The same with the solitary vireo which I continued to see only occasionally, but counted all the time.

High on Holston Mountain, where the trail skirts a green meadow overlooking White Top in the distance, a brilliant bluebird allowed me to get quite close. And then, after a brief pause at the McQueens Knob Fire Tower, I headed on and eventually reached the sign welcoming me to the Jefferson National Forest. I had finally made it to Virginia! To greet me a pileated woodpecker flew across the trail, followed immediately by another and then still another. Altogether there were 25 species that day, including another new one, the rose-breasted grosbeak, at the outskirts of Damascus.

The day's hike covered more than 21 miles, the best mileage so far, and I made it in less than 11 hours. I had a reunion with Gary and Bruce, who were also staying at Mrs. Wright's hiker-haven in Damascus. My mail included a birthday present—a good Sony AM-FM transistor radio to replace the weak one I'd been carrying.

MAY 5. This was a day devoted completely to loafing and eating. Laundry, a bit of shopping, and letter-writing were the principal items on the agenda. Damascus had house sparrows, robins, blue jays, catbirds, cardinals, and chimney swifts.

MAY 6. Midday thunderstorms caused me to push back my departure until nearly 2 P.M. That gave me a leisurely morning to have a haircut, the first since leaving Springer Mountain. I spent some time chatting with Postmaster Grindstaff, a friendly man who keeps a trail register and a folder of letters from Appalachian Trail hikers. He told me the story of Uncle Nick, whose grave I had passed on a remote section of the trail a couple of days before. Nick was a hermit, with good reason. He had gone West and made his fortune. While headed back to Virginia on the train, some bandits conked him over the head and robbed him of the whole wad (just like in the movies!). Losing all faith in humankind, he headed for the woods, where he spent the rest of his days. Occasionally a hunter would pass his way and one, thinking he was being helpful, killed a big rattler near Nick's place. Instead of being grateful, the old man was sorely grieved because the snake had been his pet and closest companion!

Leaving Damascus, which deserved its reputation as the friendliest town on the Appalachian Trail, I headed into *terra incognita*. The guidebook for the next 300 miles was out of print and I would have to rely on the blazes and the exhaustive notes which I had made from topographic maps. The Jefferson National Forest had a brochure which showed the route, but it was not very detailed. Because of the lack of reliable information on water sources I picked up another one-quart Oasis canteen. Another addition to the pack was a tube of ointment that actually shrinks hemorrhoidal tissues.

An interesting bird observation was a worm-eating warbler looking about under dead leaves for tasty morsels. Its trilling song, which reminded me of rolling dice, first attracted my attention. It seemed unconcerned as I observed its distinct head stripings through my binoculars.

The Sandy Flats Lean-to wasn't marked by any sign on the Appalachian Trail. From my notes I knew just about where it should be and so had no trouble recognizing the blue-blazed trail that leads to the shelter. There were no bunks—just a wooden floor as in the Nantahalas. But it was clean and dry, with a good water supply close at hand.

MAY 7. It rained steadily all last night and continued with showers, sometimes pretty good ones, throughout most of the day. Reaching the Straight Branch Lean-to for lunch, I was surprised to find Gary and Bruce lying on their sleeping bags. They had been caught in the thunderstorm yesterday morning and Gary had picked up a virus. No doubt the crippling load of ten days' rations they had carried out of Damascus was an added stress.

Towhees and ovenbirds were especially common. The black-and-white and two black-throated warblers were also frequent. There were cowbirds near Sandy Flats, ruffed grouse along the trail, a white-throated sparrow, and at the Cherry Tree Lean-to, where I spent the night, a veery.

With the higher elevation, the spring beauties had reappeared. There was plenty of trailing arbutus lower down, but it seemed to have passed the blossoming stage. The trees above 4,000 feet were still barren. It would be a while before spring arrived.

MAY 8. I was awakened last night by thunder and lightning, one bolt cracking down right by the shelter. It was scary. There were more storms during the night. To avoid the water dripping through the leaky roof, I set up my tent inside the shelter. It was still dreary in the morning and my clothes, wet from yesterday, had not dried out.

The relocated trail to Virginia Highway 16 was longer than I had expected. Slabbing through the upper reaches of a watershed, it crossed several small streams which were swollen by the rain. Even without the high water, their cascades would have made them quite lovely.

A family of five passed me headed in the other direction. Their plan was to hike the entire Appalachian Trail in bits and pieces over weekends, a project they expect to take five years!

The rhododendron thickets along the streams were good places to find warblers—black-throated blue, black-throated green, and the Canada gaily singing its chirrupy song. I liked the birds of the woods—these and the juncos, titmice, tanagers, grosbeaks, and more; but it was nice, too, to pass through rural sections where species such as the barn swallow, mockingbird, bluebird, meadowlark, and starling made their home. All of these were along the trail near Teas.

It was disappointing to find that the country store at Teas was out of business. However, I had the luck to find a Good Samaritan who drove me to the grocery store at Sugar Grove and then put me up for the night.

MAY 9. After wading through swollen streams near Teas, I followed the trail through some abandoned strip mines. The eroding mud reminded me of the Badlands of South Dakota. From this treeless vantage point, apparently a hunting ground for the broadwinged hawk, I could look back to Mt. Rogers in the distance.

I counted 35 species of birds, including a Baltimore oriole, a phoebe at the Killinger Creek Lean-to, and a flicker. It was good country for violets—white, yellow, and blue (common and bird's-foot). The bellwort family was represented by large and small varieties. The wake-robin was still in bloom, too.

MAY 10. The weather was nice for a change, but the 15-mile hike, with over 3,200 feet of climbing, left little time to enjoy it.

The Great Valley provided excellent birding. Killdeer were in

Photo by James R. Wolf

Deer at Blackrock Gap Shelter, Shenandoah National Park.

Photo by Albert Fiel

Black bear near Silers Bald Lean-to, Great Smoky Mountains
  National Park.

Cloudland Rhododendron Gardens, Roan Mountain, North
  Carolina.

Photo by Elmer L. Onstot

the fields just a stone's throw from the interstate highway. Farther on, along a dirt road bordered by hedgerows, I had good views of bobwhite and a white-crowned sparrow. But the best of all was the orchard oriole, an addition to my life list and a bird I had been trying to find for years. It was the dull orange male, much drabber than his Baltimore cousin, and was in some low bushes.

Brushy Mountain was memorable for the good stands of fringed polygala beneath the scrub pine. Along with it were long-spurred violets. There was cinquefoil and wild sweet william and higher up, on Walker Mountain, there were chickweed, toothwort, and still some blossoming bloodroot.

From the fire tower on Walker, I could see the route of the trail for miles along the crest. Ravens and vultures soared along the ridge, suspended in air by the strong updrafts. At the register in the nearby shelter I found the familiar names of Smith, Castleman, Weirich, and Winslow—all apparently outpacing me.

The remaining seven miles to Monster Rock Lean-to took me nearly four hours, until almost 8:00 P.M. The ridge kept on going and it was not nearly so flat as I had imagined. I kept thinking the lean-to must be just over the next rise, but there was always another. Taking water from the leaf-filled catchment basin, I fixed dinner and wearily turned in.

MAY 11. About 18 miles today, but most of it was easy going on a Forest Service road. Along this stretch were yellow rocket or winter cress, wild geranium, and blossoming sweetbells.

After leaving the road at Turkey Gap, the Appalachian Trail continued on the crest, which remained relatively flat. I found it tough going, rocky at places and with excessive deadfall which had to be circled or stepped over. I'm sure it must be good country for game, but all I saw were one deer and one woodchuck.

The low point of the day was my arrival at the High Rock Lean-to, where I was unable to find any water. Fortunately I had nearly a quart left from my stop at Turkey Gap—enough on tight rations for dinner, with a bit left over for the morning. A whippoorwill serenaded me as I cooked and got ready for bed. I guess the high point of the day was that breakfast of hotcakes and sausage at the Big Walker Lookout.

MAY 12. My luck with the weather held. There were forecasts of rain and the skies had been cloudy, but the only severe shower came and went while I was safely inside the grocery store at Crandon.

This country store was spotless and well-stocked. With hardly any breakfast at High Rock, I gorged myself on milk and doughnuts while waiting out the rain. The shopkeeper welcomes hikers and carries on a regular correspondence with some end-to-enders who have traveled through on the Appalachian Trail.

After resting during the afternoon at the Wapiti Lean-to, I headed up to the wildlife cabin campsite on Flat Top Mountain. Being uncertain about the water supply there, I lugged a couple of quarts up with me. It was like carrying coals to Newcastle.

Along one switchback I noticed a snail crawling across a large tree stump. I'd seen many snail shells, but this was the first living one I'd seen. I waited until it obligingly moved to a lighter place where I could take its portrait.

I had a good list of birds: raven, towhee, ovenbird, rose-breasted grosbeak, wood thrush, wood pewee, crow, grackle, turkey vulture, barn swallow, redwing, chimney swift, starling, house sparrow, blue jay, song sparrow, tufted titmouse, catbird, redstart, flicker, goldfinch, cardinal, chipping sparrow, kingbird, Baltimore oriole, indigo bunting, meadowlark, white-throated sparrow, great crested flycatcher, downy woodpecker, green heron, solitary vireo, and Carolina chickadee.

MAY 13. The best thing about this day was that Pearisburg lay as a pot of gold at the end of the rainbow.

From 10 P.M. to 4 A.M. it had poured without let-up, 1.29 inches at Roanoke and probably about the same where I was. Again the foot of my tent got drenched, as did the clothes I had stuffed in plastic bags to use as leg cushions. Fortunately I had left some clothing in my pack in the sturdy latrine and they remained dry.

I wanted to get to Pearisburg before the post office closed. After following some Forest Service roads for a while, I passed a new lean-to still under construction and stopped there for lunch.

Soon there was a hard shower that soaked me completely. With the temperature up to 65°F. I found it was best to walk in shorts. The wetness underfoot was not only uncomfortable, but treacherous as well. I took a nasty spill on a wet rock and bruised my knee slightly; had I fallen a bit differently, I might have been seriously injured.

The crest of Pearis Mountain was a vast mayapple farm. There were also some good views over the New River and toward Peters Mountain. The descent from an outcrop called Angels Rest was devilish. It started as a slick and precipitous mud slide, though farther down there were switchbacks that make the grade more negotiable.

I checked into a motel and picked up a box of supplies at the post office, then spent the evening doing laundry and packing.

MAY 14. Setting out after lunch, with fair and mild weather, I had to follow U.S. Route 460 for a couple of miles in order to get across the New River (which is the first westward-flowing stream outside of the Tennessee River watershed). It was a relief to get away from the big trucks and back to the trail again.

An unhappy feature along here was that in the lowlands near the highway, the hiker has to walk through great patches of poison ivy. This was the first poison ivy I'd seen and I was glad I was wearing long pants.

There were compensations, though—the grey squirrel that was startled by my approach and scampered off, a few blossoms on the mayapples, and the bracken fern fiddleheads that I nibbled on Hemlock Ridge.

It was 7:30 when I arrived at a good campsite near a spring on the crest of the mountain. This late arrival barely left me time to set up my tent and fix dinner before it got dark.

MAY 15. All afternoon and evening it rained steadily. This was the first time I had had to hike for hours in the rain, but there was little choice since the Bailey Gap Lean-to, my destination, was the nearest shelter.

I managed to get over Peters Mountain Bald, a delightful grassy area with good views back along the ridge, while it was still dry. There were a number of very rocky stretches and lots of fallen trees to scramble over.

A small swamp at the upper reaches of Pine Creek might have been a good spot to study birds if the weather hadn't been so dreadful. Pine Creek was full of water, making its cascades and small falls particularly pretty. The trail descended steeply along the creek's banks, and the moss-covered rocks were a constant peril.

The only thing to do on such a day was to keep moving. I was wearing too much: string vest, wool shirt, wind parka, poncho, long pants, and rain chaps. They protected me from the outside, but I got just as wet from perspiration.

At the shelter I learned that Bob Winslow and Tom McKone were already a week ahead of me and that Gary Wiesendanger and Bruce Balderston (who must have overtaken me while I was in Pearisburg) had made a stop here earlier in the day when it was, in their words, "raining like hell." There was no spring nearby, but I had carried some water up the hill with me and easily collected an additional supply from the water running off the roof.

MAY 16. From Bailey Gap I followed the forest road for several miles through the fog along the top of Big Mountain. While I was dropping down to War Branch, the weather tried to clear. I had lunch at the fine shelter there and filled my canteen, water bottle, and empty cereal jar—about 90 ounces of water—because I was unsure whether there would be any other springs or streams for the remainder of the day.

The valleys, such as the Johns Creek Valley a bit farther on, were all green and had good displays of dogwood and some azalea. But 2,000 feet higher, along the 4,000-foot mountains, the trees were still leafless.

There were showers and thundershowers during the remainder of the afternoon and I was happy to reach the springless Big Pond Lean-to. It turned out that there was a seep in the jeep road bank on top of Johns Creek Mountain, so I was able to drink up again and still have plenty of water for the night.

MAY 17. The weather was fine, and a good thing, too, because I wouldn't want to be hiking on Sinking Creek Mountain during the rain.

The descent to Sinking Creek Valley had some of the best trail so far—a gentle downward slope, good surface, and well cleared. Along the roads in the valley itself were Carolina wrens, indigo buntings, brown thrashers, both orioles, a single yellow warbler, and a number of others. One disappointment was that Duncan's Store was closed, but I was probably overstocked anyway.

I stopped for lunch at the stream on the side of Sinking Creek Mountain, the last water until the Niday Lean-to. The mountain was unique in that the crest was a narrow rocky ridge, often with abrupt outcrops on either side. Fallen trees blocking the trail continued to be a nuisance, but the walk was worthwhile because of the excellent views. Parallel ridges, five or six of them, extended far out to the southeast. Farther north, on the route of the Appalachian Trail, was the prominent high peak of McAfee Knob. I observed the red spurred blossoms of the columbine around the outcrops along with the white flowers of chickweed, trillium, and violet. (But there was also poison ivy, the first I'd seen on the ridges.)

The shelter was excellent. Tacked on the wall was an account of the Niday family who had settled here so long ago. Some of the trees they planted were still standing and bearing fruit.

MAY 18. It was fast going, mostly along roads, to a lunch stop at the Trout Creek Lean-to. Along the way I plunged across three fords. There were some good birds, such as the black-throated green warbler, spotted sandpiper, and green heron. The best discovery, though, was a white-eyed vireo singing in an oak tree along Trout Creek. Another interesting one was a hawk which circled upward over the farmlands, most probably a red-shouldered.

The next stretch of trail was a bit of a disaster. After crossing Pickles Branch, I came upon blazes that had been painted over in green —just as a hiker had told me back in the Smokies. I tried to follow them anyway, but they disappeared. Retracing my steps half a mile, I still couldn't find any alternate route. Eventually I had to follow a private road out to the blacktop and then detour several miles to pick up the Appalachian Trail again on the far side of the Dragons Tooth.

Back on the Appalachian Trail, I crossed a knoll (more fences here) and then carefully tiptoed my way on a log over swollen Catawba Creek. After three miles along the crest of Catawba Mountain, I pulled up at Buck Sweeney's Mountain Top Inn on Virginia Highway 311. For hours I ate hamburgers and ice cream before getting into my sleeping bag, outside near the road, and trying to get some sleep.

MAY 19. This was a different day in many ways. It was the hottest day of the trip so far. It was a shorter hike than the recent ones. There was lots of poison ivy to wade through in my shorts. And, enjoyably, I had the company of Bruce and Gary.

They had spent a day off the trail with friends in Roanoke, and we met as I was finishing my breakfast at Sweeney's. We set off on the Forest Service road, pausing soon to inspect a couple of small milk snakes.

The hike up McAfee Knob was worthwhile, especially with a camera. At the cliffs on top a shelf of caprock projects far out, making a pedestal for dramatic pictures.

The wild flowers included dwarf iris, wild geranium, and bird's-foot violet, but I was most conscious of the poison ivy that was common all along Tinker Mountain. I hoped that washing with laundry soap at the end of the day would prevent a bad case. With the temperature over 85°F., it was simply too hot to wear long pants.

We made camp at the stream in Lamberts Meadow, the only reliable source of water in the 20-mile Tinker stretch. A can of spaghetti and meatballs purchased at Buck Sweeney's was a welcome change from freeze-dried foods.

MAY 20. Aside from some rocky places, the trail was pretty good—very little blowdown and hardly any poison ivy.

Right along the trail there were a number of pink lady's slippers or moccasin flowers, large red-pouched members of the orchid family. With spring coming so fast now, it was hard to keep track of all the flowers. Among the most conspicuous was the turkeybeard, a yucca with a tall spike of creamy blossoms. Just a few inches from the ground were the little yellow six-petaled blooms of the star grass. The common fern was the bracken, almost all of them fully developed.

Descending to U.S. Route 11, I caught up once again with my friends, probably for the last time. They were busily stuffing their packs with enormous quantities of food. They had hardly left before a thunderstorm struck. Rotten luck for them, but it didn't bother me since I was spending the night at the Howard Johnson's Motel.

One reason I stayed here was the chance to use the motel's guest laundry. I picked up another box of supplies, and after cleaning up, enjoyed a huge dinner.

MAY 21. This day had a lot going for it—a short hike on good trail in fine weather. The trail followed roads for about three miles and then headed up to Fullhardt Knob on the Blue Ridge. I was happy to see that the pathway was smooth dirt and gently graded for the entire distance. The walking was much more pleasant than it had been on a number of the recent ridgetops.

The Fullhardt Knob Lean-to was a nice place to stop for lunch and enjoy the luxury of a sunbath. There were flowers all about—wild geraniums, spiderwort ranging from indigo to magenta in color, and some blue violets (palmate, probably). There were also downy yellow violets and patches of chickweed. The real floral treat of the day occurred later on, though, when the Appalachian Trail again descended into the valley. There, along Curry Creek, the Catawba rhododendron was in bloom—many purple blossoms completely developed, others partially or wholly in bud.

The one sour note was pack trouble. The metal brace that held the left shoulder strap to the bottom of the frame broke. Fortunately, I was able to make satisfactory repairs with an extra boot lace.

The Wilson Creek Shelter had a nice location by a mountain stream, but the lean-to itself was a depressing place. Over half of the front side was closed in, and it was musty and dirty inside, so I bedded down outside under the stars.

MAY 22. Having descended a thousand feet to Wilson Creek, I then had to climb back up to the Blue Ridge. For most of the day, the Appalachian Trail remained on the ridge, crisscrossing the parkway. There were good views, especially at the overlooks opposite Peaks of Otter.

As this was Saturday, there were other hikers. First I passed a troop of Boy Scouts marching along in near-military formation. About noon I ran into half a dozen members of the Old Dominion Appalachian Trail Club from Richmond and spent a pleasant lunch hour with them. They gave me some helpful trail information, cautioning me particularly about the excessive growth on Tar Jacket Ridge. Arriving at the Cove Creek Lean-to, I found the area occupied by a group of young people from Roanoke holding a training session. They operate an emergency service for youth—counseling on drug, family, and draft problems and the like—and seemed quite serious about their responsibilities.

I started out with two quarts of water and that was sufficient, but for 15 miles (from near Wilson Creek all the way to Cove Creek) there were no springs or streams within easy reach of the trail.

In the afternoon, one of the brackets attaching the neck strap to the frame of my binoculars broke. That finished bird-watching, but not bird-listening, for the day. Even without the glasses, though, I could study the grey squirrels. And there was a woodchuck, too, headed south on the Appalachian Trail. He let me get within about 100 feet of him before turning tail and taking off.

MAY 23. This was an anniversary of sorts—two months on the trail and still going strong. Aside from that it was a rather pointless day. I couldn't figure out why the Appalachian Trail had to go all the way back down to the valley at Cove Creek, which was below 1,000 feet in elevation. Today's climb back up the Blue Ridge was completely devoid of views—just a long trudge uphill.

I had stayed up until almost midnight with the Roanoke group, enjoying particularly the company of a Washington & Lee junior who said he would like to hike the Appalachian Trail, so it was a late start in the morning.

Well up the mountain were patches of large-flowered trillium, now turned pink with age. The ferns were past fiddlehead stage, with the maidenhair and interrupted being most obvious. My first fresh mushroom of the trip was a brown gilled affair, about 1½ inches across, but I didn't take time to try to identify it.

Jury-rigging my binoculars, I was once again prepared for the birds. The first was a Louisiana water thrush which wandered about the campground tables near my sleeping bag close to Cove Creek. The other good find was a Swainson's thrush on Floyd Mountain, eye ring very distinctly visible. And it was like old times to have a friendly junco again at the Cornelius Creek Lean-to. The juncos had been missing for the past week, but now I was high enough to find them again.

The lean-to was particularly clean, with a good stream nearby. It was a clear night, cool and just right for sleeping.

MAY 24. This was an unexciting day. The principal point of interest was my stop at the Bedford Air Force Station to pick up another package. The timing was good, as the snack bar was open for lunch; I was also able to get a shower and shave.

Much of the trail here passed through scrubby second or third growth forest. Scrub pine and blackjack oak were typical. However, the red oak woods along the crest of the Blue Ridge were more mature and attractive. At the higher elevations, around 4,000 feet, the oaks were still leafless.

Poison ivy was thick along the trail at High Cock Knob. I wore long pants, washed with laundry soap, and hoped for the best. The few blisters from the poison ivy on Tinker Mountain didn't seem to be spreading.

The juncos commonly build their nests on the ground in the low growth along the trail. One of the birds flew up at my approach, revealing its cup-shaped abode with several eggs. As I paused to get a good look and a picture, the junco stayed close-by, calling to me several times with some annoyance.

The vireos were now represented by the red-eyed as well as the solitary and I was finding it impossible to distinguish them by voice alone. The female ruffed grouse put on a touching performance, crying piteously in order to attract my attention and lead me away from her nest. A new bird was a sharp-shinned hawk on Apple Orchard

Mountain. I was able to observe the hawk in flight long enough to make out the definite notch in its tail.

At Petites Gap the lousewort or wood-betony was in blossom. In the early spring I had frequently seen its distinctive deeply cut narrow leaves, then a rich red, without recognizing the plant. Now, with its bunches of yellow flowers, I was able to identify it easily.

MAY 25. From the Marble Spring Lean-to, I followed the trail over Hickory Stand and down to Matts Creek. The shelter here had a particularly attractive setting, with the creek rushing past it through a natural rocky flume.

Crossing the James River, I left the Appalachian Trail to follow the road to the post office and store at Snowden. I loafed a couple of hours, guzzling beer with ice cream and buying a few groceries, before returning to the trail via the Hercules slate quarry access road.

It was still quite early when I reached the Johns Hollow Lean-to. It was my first lean-to in the George Washington National Forest and seemed to employ the same wood-floor design that was used in the Jefferson. It was located in a grove of hemlocks (with some tulip trees, hickories, and redbuds) by a stream of ice water.

This was a colorful time of year, with the mountain laurel adding its showy blossoms to those of the rhododendron and azalea.

MAY 26. There was a steady hour-and-a-half climb to ascend some 1,500 feet to the ridge at Little Rocky Row. Here there were splendid views of the Blue Ridge across the James River. Apple Orchard Mountain was the prominent feature, easily identified by its radar domes.

Big Rocky Row, where I paused for lunch, had no view. What it did have, though, was tiny golden spiders which invaded my pack by the dozens.

Heading up Bluff Mountain I ran into a new species—a timber rattlesnake. It was a bit unsettling because the high-pitched rattling didn't start until I was abreast of it. When I first saw it, the snake was stretched out, head uphill, among the leaves and brush about five feet above the trail. As I stood there staring at it, figuring that it must measure between four and five feet long, it coiled and stared right back. The rattling continued until I was at least 100 feet away.

I had planned to stop for a breather at the Punchbowl Spring Lean-to, but I passed by without seeing it. This gave me a bit of a problem because I had started out with a single quart of water, which was now all gone. Not being able to replenish at Punchbowl meant another four miles and a couple of thirsty hours. Eventually I reached a refreshing brook just beyond the remnant of a lovely virgin forest.

Northern fence lizards, brown with chevron-shaped markings on the back, had become common. So had the horse gentians, hairy plants with purplish irregular flowers.

Some of the birds I'd been seeing fairly regularly were the white-breasted nuthatch, great crested flycatcher, scarlet tanager, tufted tit-mouse, phoebe (at shelters), and Carolina chickadee. The most common, though, were towhee, ovenbird, wood thrush, and wood pewee. The unusual ones today were the rough-winged swallows and the spotted sandpiper at the spillway below the Lynchburg Reservoir Dam.

It was 7:30 when I finally made camp at Swapping Camp Creek. The radio predicted a rainless night, so I didn't bother setting up a tent.

MAY 27. A visit to the outhouse at the Brown Mountain Creek Lean-to afforded me a chance to examine a phoebe's nest, with a clutch of eggs, on the beam above the door. Along the creek the poison ivy was bad and so unavoidable that I had to change to long pants.

In the morning I identified a square-stemmed plant with spikes of purplish flowers as self-heal, according to my *Flower Finder*.

The picnic area along U.S. Route 60 was a good place for lunch. From there it was once again a long climb to the 4,000-foot ridges. The trees at the higher elevation were finally starting to show some life—mouse-eared red leaves on the oaks and stout leafstalks bursting their buds on the hickories.

From Cole Mountain, the trail dropped down to a dirt road at Hog Camp Gap. A half mile away was the Wiggins Spring Lean-to, with its excellent percolating spring. I spent the night there beneath the yellow birches and sugar maples. A "camper" was parked nearby and I chatted a while with its owner. He described the Camille flood of 1969 for me. Thirty inches of rain fell in a single night, with particularly devastating effects in the Tye Valley where whole families were lost as their homes were washed away.

MAY 28. The forecast had been for pleasant clear weather, but around midnight it started to rain. I dawdled a bit, but seeing no sign of improvement in the weather I headed off at 9:45 wearing poncho and rain chaps.

After getting back up to the Appalachian Trail, the first task was to cross Tar Jacket Ridge. This meant following an indistinct path through scrub growth for a mile and a half. It wouldn't have been easy to follow the blazes painted on the rocks at any time, but this morning it was particularly hard because it was not only raining but foggy besides. I made my way carefully, taking frequent compass and altimeter readings and checking them out with my topographic map notes. Some of the blazes were obscured by young cherry trees and other scrub growth, but I managed pretty well and only lost the trail one time.

It was comforting to get back on well-marked trail, actually a dirt road, past Salt Log Gap. With the temperature in the 40s, it was much too cold to stop. I did put my pack down briefly at Lovingston Spring, but just long enough to spread some peanut butter on several slices of bread and wolf them down along with a few handfuls of gorp. That was lunch.

There was more rain, a little higher though, in the afternoon. The fog made it tricky to follow the route at a couple of places on the descent to Fish Hatchery Road.

It was a relief to reach the lean-to near the summit of The Priest at about five o'clock. As quickly as I could, I got out of my wet clothes and into my few remaining dry things—string vest, T-shirt, Duofold top, and wool sweater. After getting water from the nearby first-rate spring, I crawled into the sack and for about an hour did nothing but lie there. Eventually, I started fixing dinner, especially savoring the hot tea laced with Start. The Bleuet stove worked like magic; I couldn't imagine having to try to cook on a wood fire in such weather.

MAY 29. It must have been one of the wettest Mays on record. It started raining quite hard around midnight and forced me to move back against the rear wall of the shelter. By morning it was only drizzling, but the visibility was poor. Able to spot blazes for only about 75 feet, I passed by the side trail to the viewpoint at the summit of The Priest.

The fury of Camille was evident on the lower slopes of The Priest, where the trail crossed a couple of mountain streams. The water had carried away sediment and vegetation alike, leaving nothing but bare bedrock in the water course. Mighty tree trunks were strewn along the banks, dropped carelessly by the dying flood. The old route of the Appalachian Trail was now a deep gully. The trail had been re-routed for a few hundred yards along a rough footpath through the woods.

In the Tye Valley I found a haven in a vacant garagelike structure marked SNACK BAR. With the weather so miserable (raining again), this was just what I needed—a dry place to get warm and have a real meal. Best of all, there was a small electric heater which I used to dry my clothes. It took all afternoon, but I managed to get everything pretty dry—though in the process one pair of wool socks was scorched.

It became clear that I could not make it to my original destination at Maupin Field. The rain became increasingly heavy, and was a steady downpour by midafternoon. I finally had to move on—weather or not—to reach the Harpers Creek Lean-to before dark. Arriving there after an hour's climb, I found the creek swollen but managed to ford it without difficulty.

Though the shelters in the George Washington National Forest left something to be desired (they ought to have registers and brooms), they were at least waterproof, and that was the important thing right then.

MAY 30. Harpers Creek was awesome in the morning. The water was so high I thought I might be trapped on the shelter side, but with a stout stick I managed to get across, completely soaking boots and socks in the process.

From there it was a continuous nonstop 2,000-foot ascent in the fog to the top of Three Ridges, with a few fragrant spicebush-lined streams to cross on the way. Though it wasn't raining, the wet trees dripped copiously in the breeze.

After a stop at the Maupin Field Lean-to for lunch, I soon emerged from the woods and out into fog-shrouded moors along the Blue Ridge Parkway. Though I knew where the road was, I was apprehensive because there didn't seem to be any blazes to mark the trail. Groping along blindly I soon reached the Three Ridges Overlook. A parkway ranger happened to be there and gave me a lift to Rockfish Gap, where I checked in at the Holiday Inn and picked up the last of my boxes of supplies: film and film mailer, powdered milk, Start, Familia, peanut butter, jerky, cheese (squeeze package), lemonade, salt tablets, Tea Kettle chicken chunks and beef almondine, Armour corned beef hash, Mountain House chili with beans, butane cartridge, and notebook. The only other supplies I would have to pick up would be bread, sugar, gorp (raisins, M&M's, nuts), cigarettes, and cigars.

The lead story in the Charlottesville paper was headlined "Soaking Rains Surprise Area." The ranger said the storm had dumped between four and five inches of rain. Would it ever stop?

The day had a joyful end with an unexpected visit from my close friends Dan and Carol Berger and their boys. They were on a Memorial Day excursion to Monticello and gambled that they might be able to find me. Celebrating with a steak dinner, we talked on into the evening about events in Pittsburgh and experiences on the Appalachian Trail. However briefly and vicariously, I was back home.

MAY 31. The Waynesboro paper was filled with news of the six-inch rainfall over the past three days, but the skies were now beautiful and it remained nice all day.

Dan and Carol drove me back to the Three Ridges Overlook. We stopped along the way for a breakfast of steak and eggs on their charcoal grill. The whole crew joined me for a little way on the Appalachian Trail and then, after fond farewells, turned back to continue their drive to Monticello.

After crossing Devils Knob I paused to study the birds—singing chestnut-sided warblers, towhees, and catbirds—in the brushy areas near the trail. A bit farther on, on the rocky outcrops high on Humpback Mountain, I looked southward at Three Ridges and The Priest with an understanding and appreciation that can only be earned by a struggle along the trail.

There were stretches between the Humpback Rocks' parking area and Rockfish Gap that were densely overgrown. It was a real jungle in places. I was happy to get through it and back to the hard-surfaced road where I encountered lots of birds—indigo bunting, robin, flicker, bluebird, goldfinch, mourning dove, and cardinal among others.

JUNE 1 (TUESDAY). Crossing Rockfish Gap was like crossing the Rubicon into the lands of civilization, so this was a big day.

The first seven miles were on private lands. In the cleared fields there were dense patches of sheep sorrel. Each plant had long spikes covered with tiny inconspicuous blossoms; from a distance they form a solid russet block. There were also fences to cross, and a couple of times I had to stop to remove ticks.

After Jarmans Gap the Appalachian Trail entered Shenandoah National Park. The path was beautiful here—a wide flat footway, well graded and surfaced with a thin layer of crushed stone. I spent the night at the Sawmill Run Shelter with four girls from Baltimore who were finishing a traverse of the park. This was the first shelter in a long time to have built-in bunks.

JUNE 2. The trail continued in splendid shape, with easy grades. Unfortunately, there were no vistas.

Now that the trees were in leaf I was able to identify them better.

There were black gums, along with chestnut oaks and red maples, at Sawmill Run. Striped maples were common in the new growth along the trail. There was also a new amphibian, a leopard frog—two prominent ridges and spots along the back and a vivid yellow-green patch beneath the eyes.

Upon arrival at Blackrock Gap Shelter, I found it occupied by a young couple—students who had hitchhiked out from Norfolk to spend a few days camping. They were on a vegetarian diet. While we were having dinner, a deer came out of the woods and browsed within 50 feet of us, warily keeping an eye and ear cocked in our direction. We remained quiet as she went about her business, pausing below the spring for a drink and then continuing on her way.

JUNE 3. During breakfast our deer friend returned to browse near the spring. Posing motionless in a shaft of sunlight about 25 feet away, it allowed me to photograph it.

I continued on to the Dundo Picnic Grounds for lunch. The drinking fountains were not operating and I was soon dry. Fortunately some kind folks parked at a Skyline Drive crossing let me have a can of pop from their cooler.

The azalea and laurel continued in good flower and for the past few days there had been good numbers of buttercups. Waterleaf blossoms occasionally formed large mats of pale violet.

It looked as if there never was a warbler wave. Ovenbirds remained abundant, but other species were uncommon. There were single black-and-white and chestnut-sideds that day, and a male Blackburnian high in a leafy tree, but the warbler numbers generally were disappointing.

The Pinefield Shelter—with more red maple, black birch, and white oak than pitch pine—was quite close to the Skyline Drive. A couple of college students, whose camper was parked by the road, gave me their leftover corned beef hash and pears.

A shower came along after I had arrived at Pinefield. There was even a bit of hail and it continued to thunder ominously as the evening wore on.

JUNE 4. A long day, with a lot of climbing, but it didn't turn out to be too rugged because of the gentleness of the grades.

The forest was generally quite young as much of this land consisted of open fields before the park was established during the Depression. The average height of the canopy was only about thirty feet, much less than in the national forests farther south.

Flattop Mountain had quite a bit of poison ivy. Generally the trail was wide enough to allow me to walk around it, but occasionally I had to step over the stuff. Keeping my eyes glued to the ground took much of the joy out of hiking.

Road construction at Swift Run Gap had disrupted the trail. The markings were poor and I missed a turn, but a ranger helpfully directed me back to the trail.

Arriving at South River Shelter, I found it occupied by a single hiker from Washington who was spending a few days in the park. Though he was on the brown rice-and-raisin diet, he mixed some chicken soup in with his rice so I took it that his diet was a matter of economy rather than philosophy.

Bruce Balderston was here three days ago, by himself. I wondered what had happened to Gary and hoped everything was OK with him.

JUNE 5. I woke up quite early and took the usual couple of hours to get going. There was no way to avoid making something of a racket and I was sure the noise disturbed my cabin mate.

Even though it was Saturday there were only a few people on the trail. I met just one backpacker out for the weekend and a couple of families out for a walk of a mile or so. There was little evidence that many people were interested in walking or getting away from their cars.

Near the South River Fire Road some rue anemone was still in flower —very surprising since it had been weeks since I had last seen it. Other flowers included a single columbine, some golden ragwort, common violet, spiderwort, trillium (very wilted), cinquefoil, wild strawberry, and wild geranium. The interrupted fern was also extremely conspicuous.

During the afternoon I passed the highest point on the Appalachian Trail in the park at Hazel Top Mountain, over 3,800 feet. The hickories and oaks had their leaves, though some were still small. I had the feeling that this was the last gasp of spring and from here on it would be summer.

Arriving at the Big Meadows Lodge in an afternoon shower, the first order of business was drying out. Then I had a fine turkey dinner. Afterwards, it was over to the washing machines. I threw my down sleeping bag in, since it was pretty gamey by now; unfortunately the down remained matted and wet even after several cycles in the dryer.

It was a bit hard writing coherently after consuming a half bottle of wine with my good dinner—soft living following a day in the rough.

JUNE 6. I picked up a box of supplies, organized my gear, ate lunch, and set out again. Shortly I came across a clump of yellow lady's slippers and a little farther on, near Hawksbill, an old jack-in-the-pulpit.

I paced my afternoon hike so I would arrive at Skyland as the dining room opened at 6 P.M. In the words of Robert Frost, words that crossed my mind every day, this would then leave me 3.5 more "miles to go before I sleep." I had promises to keep.

Later, while I was relaxing at the Shavers Hollow Shelter, a curious raccoon came along and began sniffing hopefully at my pack. Shouting and shining my flashlight at him didn't seem to bother him at all, though he ambled off as I got out of my bunk and started over in his direction. It wasn't until one of the other hikers at the shelter lobbed a rock at him that he decided to search elsewhere for his dinner.

Mammals were fairly common, though this was the first raccoon I'd seen. Chipmunks were all over the place. I also took note of a rabbit, a grey squirrel, a woodchuck, and two deer.

Towhees were by far the most common bird, but every day I saw several ovenbirds, wood thrushes, wood pewees, titmice, and red-eyed vireos as well. Blue jays, catbirds, robins, rose-breasted grosbeaks, and ravens were other regulars. I had now reached black-capped chickadee country, though there still might be Carolinas at the lower elevations farther north. Fortunately their songs were easy to distinguish.

JUNE 7. Most of the day's hike was over familiar terrain, covering eight miles north of Panorama that I had walked as part of a shakedown trip last Thanksgiving. In June there were no persimmons to eat, but in November you couldn't enjoy the beautiful azaleas. Every season has its own rewards.

A thunderstorm struck as I approached Byrd Nest No. 3 and I was drenched. A group of hikers at the shelter had a pot of vegetable soup on the fire and generously offered me a cup. Warmed and wearing a dry T-shirt I continued after the rain had tapered off a bit.

A party of three experienced hikers from Baltimore were at the Elk Wallow Shelter when I arrived. While we were having dinner a deer approached to browse. One of the hikers, a comely cellist, quietly walked over to the deer and was able to pet it. Never have I seen one so tame.

Apparently a bear came around the shelter every night, and I was not too happy about having a bottom bunk. The register was filled with comments about hanging packs high. One hiker, perhaps the one whose macadamia nuts were swiped, suggested that the camp bears be "exported."

I was puzzled by the large soaring bird, definitely not a vulture (though I saw one of them, too), observed from The Pinnacle. It certainly seemed to be an osprey, but I can't imagine what an osprey would be doing so far away from water at this time of year.

JUNE 8. Notwithstanding some worry over the bear (who never did put in an appearance), I had my best night's rest in a long time. After a brief stop at the Elk Wallow Wayside, where I bought a few supplies and had coffee and doughnuts, I continued along the first-rate footpath. In fact it was so good that I had been misled, after hiking here last year, into thinking that I would be able to make the same kind of progress along the Appalachian Trail generally. There were some good views, too, especially on South Marshall and North Marshall.

The azaleas, upon closer examination with my magnifying glass, seemed to be two species—both with pink blossoms—the early azalea and the pinxter flower. A tiger swallowtail posed patiently for me against a background of pink petals. The other common butterflies continued to be the black swallowtail and the mourning cloak, but that day there was a new one—creamy with a single gold line across the wings perpendicular to the body—that I was unable to identify.

There was no way to keep up with all the blossoming plants—false Solomon's seal, mapleleaf viburnum and milkweed, for instance.

Two hikers at the Indian Run Shelter, where I spent the night, told me that there was a northbound end-to-ender a day ahead of me. Unless someone had passed me along the way, I couldn't imagine who it might be.

JUNE 9. Leaving the park behind, the trail descended to Chester Gap. Much of the next stretch, over High Knob, passed through patches of poison ivy. However, there was sweet with the bitter: the wild strawberries, bright red and tasty, were ripe.

From the Mosby Shelter register I learned that the end-to-end hiker ahead of me was Jim Ross of Massachusetts who must be traveling at a very speedy clip. Closer to my pace were a couple of box turtles I passed along the trail during the afternoon.

After stopping at Linden (with visits to the grocery and post office), I soon came to the hand-lettered sign announcing that the Manassas Gap Shelter was closed. Hikers were instructed to follow the highway. Fortunately, I had enough water to set up camp at the Trico Fire Tower. The lack of a spring was no problem, but the bugs were a nuisance that necessitated setting up my tent.

The variety of habitats made for a good day of birding—with mockingbird, red-tailed and broad-winged hawk, pileated woodpecker, and bobwhite among the 32 species. Ferns were abundant (there were now fruiting cinnamon ferns, as at Compton Spring yesterday), but mushrooms were virtually absent. There was a flat-topped brown one, possibly a rooting collybia, at the Mosby Shelter, but that was just about all.

JUNE 10. After climbing the tower to admire the good view to the north along the Blue Ridge I set out for a day of hiking almost entirely on roads—dirt to Ashby Gap and blacktop from there on. Apparently a single landowner had barricaded the Appalachian Trail on his property, perhaps for good reason, thus blocking off several miles of woodland path and making the Yellow Rose Shelter inaccessible.

There was no water until Ashby Gap, where I filled a canteen and had a beer and cheeseburger at George's Snack Bar. There was little of interest on the road up to the classified installation on Mt. Weather, so I kept my recorder out and tooted as I walked.

Finally the trail returned to the woods and soon reached the Three Springs Shelter with its plentiful supply of cool water. The problem here was the insect life. The big bees had drilled one-half inch circular holes into the lean-to crossbeam and into the bottom of one of the planks of the table. Besides that, there was a hornet's nest. Still it's a nice place, on the site of an old farmhouse. And how the squirrels must relish the nuts in the fall!

Though I noted one of the smaller flycatchers today, this was one group that had always baffled me and I still couldn't tell them apart. I must have been hearing their calls regularly, without recognizing them. On the other hand, knowing the chickadees' songs enabled me to identify several as Carolinas—a couple at a nest in a tulip tree which was also occupied by a downy woodpecker. A new bird was that aeronautical wizard, the ruby-throated hummingbird, which buzzed about the Three Springs Shelter.

JUNE 11. The day had several birding events. First was a yellow-breasted chat in the thick tangles of wild roses, poison ivy, and other vines a little way from Three Springs. Not much farther on, where the Appalachian Trail blazes had been blacked out and the trail closed, I had a quick glimpse of the black-billed cuckoo. Late in the day I stumbled across a female ruffed grouse who put on the usual crying act to lure me away from her chicks, which were now old enough to fly off under their own wing power.

The first mile before the trail closure passed some enormous ant hills—one was about twelve feet long, eight feet wide, and three feet high. Who can say how many ants it might contain?

Finally, leaving the road again after Snickers Gap, the trail followed a looping route for a short distance into West Virginia. The feature of this stretch was the Devils Racecourse, an inclined river of boulders. I had no idea what its geological history might be.

Pausing at the Wilson Gap Shelter (where I couldn't find the spring) I was surprised that after lying down for just a few minutes my pulse ran a slow 64. I was getting into pretty good shape. I'd been taking it easy all along, very rarely running a pulse over 120.

The combination of weekend and proximity to Megalopolis brought about the inevitable crowd at the Keys Gap Shelter. When I arrived there was just one other hiker, an avid fisherman headed south for a couple of weeks, but after dinner a horde of Boy Scouts, poorly equipped and poorly led, noisily tramped in.

JUNE 12. The night was a disaster. The boys were absolutely undisciplined and kept chattering away until after midnight. Most of them piled on the platform bunk, overcrowding it. The night was warm, far too hot for my sleeping bag. And to top everything off, the biting bugs were out in good numbers and had a feast.

Unable to sleep, I was up early and on the trail by the (for me) incredibly early hour of 7:00. The quick start gave me time to make an unplanned detour to Harpers Ferry (actually to Bolivar) where I picked up some groceries and had a haircut. A happy event was crossing the Potomac, finally finishing the endless hike through Virginia.

The hike to Crampton Gap followed a particularly nice section of trail. For a couple of miles the Appalachian Trail used the Chesapeake & Ohio Canal towpath. On one side were the riffles of the river while on the other side kingfishers rattled away in flight over the still ponds of the canal. A high canopy, untouched for decades, towered overhead. Continuing on good trail, with a pause at the Weverton Cliffs viewpoint, I headed on to the camping area at Gathland State Park. My neighbor, a Vietnam veteran who had hiked the Appalachian Trail from Maine to Pennsylvania many years ago and was now on a weekend trip with his two stepsons, was good company for the evening.

JUNE 13. The trail in Maryland continued to be delightful, with a wide and usually good footpath through rich woods. Between Dahlgren Road and the entrance to Washington Monument State Park I couldn't avoid the poison ivy. As soon as I got to the park I washed my bare legs with laundry soap.

By then it was raining, throwing a monkey wrench into the picnic plans I had made months before. My brother and sister-in-law, with their daughters, met me here with all sorts of goodies. Because of the weather I suggested that we drive down the mountain to a place where we could dine in comfort. We packed a lot of socializing into four hours, at the same time having lunch, stopping at a laundromat, and reorganizing my gear. I left a few things behind (string vest, sweater, and wool cap) and picked up a mosquito head net and light wool shirt. The most important item of logistics was the substitution of boots. Leaving off the pair I had been wearing (to be resoled) I picked up my other pair for use on the next stretch.

The weather was much better and it was still fairly light as I crossed I-70 and walked up the hill to the Pine Knob Shelter. To satisfy a craving, I had asked Mim to bring me some delicatessen corned beef, rye bread, and kosher dill pickle, so supper was something very special. I had the shelter to myself (except for a domestic cat prowling around) but the noise of the nearby highway was a steady drone.

The past several days had seen a complete absence of azalea and rhododendron. However, the laurel was in blossom. Crown vetch bloomed along the roadsides and rattlesnake weed was common along the trail. Blueberries were starting to form, but of course they were all green.

JUNE 14. There were several viewpoints over the Great Valley. I walked out to Black Rock Cliffs and took a picture, but the haze was a problem. The trail continued over a rocky, poison ivy-covered stretch and then headed down to a road where I had expected to find the Wolfe Shelter, but when I got there I learned that it no longer existed.

The common grackle was the most numerous bird of the day. I only saw them a couple of times, but they congregated in loose flocks of 20 or more and in that way add up very quickly. Towhees, wood pewees, wood thrushes, red-eyed vireos, and ovenbirds were still abundant. Cardinals, blue jays, crows, cowbirds, and great crested flycatchers were some of the others regularly included in an average day's list of 20 or so species. Today's best find was a red-bellied woodpecker near the ruins of the old Bagtown Hotel, though a pileated woodpecker was also noteworthy.

About 4:30 the thunder began and soon I was drenched. I hurried on to Pen Mar where I planned to spend the night and buy groceries.

Pen Mar was a disappointment, as there didn't seem to be either a store or lodging. As a result I had to keep going in the rain for another two miles, to the Mackie Run Shelter. Because I had hiked here before, I knew that the crossing of rampaging Falls Creek could be avoided by a detour to a bridge downstream.

There were four girls from Pittsburgh and a couple from Washington at the lean-to, but they cheerfully made room for me, stretching the capacity of the shelter to its limit. My planning had broken down and I was without any hot meals. I cadged some dried soup vegetables and brewed a big bowl of soup to go with some cheese, peanut butter, and rye bread. I had enough food left to reach Caledonia tomorrow. I hoped it would stop raining before then.

JUNE 15. My left foot was giving me real problems. It was not so much the spot just back of the big toe, which my orthopedist brother diagnosed as early arthritis, but rather the tender area on the edge behind the little toe which hurt whenever it pressed against my boot. The condition had been aggravated by new boots and by long mileages (almost 19 miles the day before).

This was a day for fast walking, whether my foot hurt or not. It was a damp and cold day, the kind when any stop was uncomfortable. There were some nice stretches, but for about five miles I followed roads, and some of the woodland paths were rocky.

Reaching U.S. Route 30, I walked half a mile east and got a room at the Manor House. It had a restaurant and bar, but no dryer. Wet and damp clothes were spread about the room with the hope that they would get dry enough to wear by morning.

JUNE 16. "What is so rare as a day in June?" Not that the weather was so great; it was cool and overcast, but merely being dry was an improvement over the last two days. The fine thing was that this was the easiest hike in ages—less than ten fairly gentle miles.

There was still a problem of food supplies. By waiting around Caledonia State Park until the swimming pool concession opened, I got lunch and still had enough food to reach the grocery at **Pine Grove Furnace**.

Finally getting on my way, I headed up Chinquapin Hill and was delighted to find some chinquapin shrubs along with the numerous chestnuts. The chinquapins have slightly smaller leaves, with less pronounced teeth. From my manual I learned to look at the undersides of the leaves and with my magnifying glass I could distinctly make out the fine hairs on the chinquapins.

For the most part the trail was in good shape, though there was a rocky stretch past Quarry Gap. Low blueberry bushes were abundant beneath the canopy of chestnut oaks. The laurel was showy, much of it just coming into bloom.

Birch Run had two small shelters—one occupied by a couple from near Pittsburgh and the other by me. Dinner was just some peanut butter sandwiches, the remainder of the soup vegetables, and a box of Cracker Jack from Caledonia. But, along with some gorp, it was enough to keep me from being hungry.

JUNE 17. Eighty-six days on the trail now—at least half of the time I had allowed for the whole hike, and almost half the total distance.

I had covered the part of the trail from the Arendtsville Road to Pine Grove Furnace during last year's meeting of the Appalachian Trail Conference at Shippensburg, so this section was familiar. I noted an indigo bunting singing from the very same tree near Dead Woman Hollow Road where I had seen one last year.

The only hitch in the day was my discovery from some other hikers that the Pine Grove Furnace grocery wasn't open. They also told me that a few days ago some hikers camping at Tagg Run had been beaten up pretty badly.

To deal with the food crisis I detoured to the office at Camp Michaux, a summer church camp, and explained my plight. They couldn't have been more helpful, and allowed me to purchase a few needed items.

Though the grocery was closed, the swimming area concession at Pine Grove Furnace was operating, so I was able to buy hamburgers and ice cream. Best of all, I could get cigarettes and a cigar. My only regret was that I didn't have the time to stick around and go swimming.

I saw another red-bellied woodpecker near Toms Run Shelter. Some of the other birds were the house wren, phoebe, mourning dove, brown thrasher, chestnut-sided warbler, flicker, mockingbird, chipping sparrow, and barn swallow. The most interesting, perhaps, was the Louisiana water thrush—actually two of them—bobbing about along the stream below Pine Grove Furnace.

Ramon and Cathy, the couple who had given me the soup vegetables, were also spending the night at Tagg Run. After hearing about the campers who had been assaulted here, I was happy to have company. Tagg Run Shelter was grossly polluted and the spring didn't look too great.

JUNE 18. This was a grueling day, as I knew it would be. Besides the distance, over 21 miles, there were a couple of difficult rocky stretches.

Setting out a bit after eight o'clock, I ran into my first problem inside the triangle of paved roads at Hunters Run. There was some poor blazing here and I ended up on Pennsylvania Highway 34, off the trail. With the PATC map, it was easy to pick up the route again. On the way I observed some purple martins.

A few miles farther along the trail headed up Rocky Ridge, well-named, with massive boulders on top. The Appalachian Trail goes through, over, and around these boulders. With a pack the rock-climbing is too strenuous to be any fun.

After a lunch break at Whiskey Spring, I again lost the trail, missing the turn from the road in spite of watching carefully for it. This time I had to travel two miles on a road before intersecting the Appalachian Trail again. As a result I missed, and some day will have to return to, Seven Bench Hill.

There was a steep ascent to Center Point Knob, followed by about a mile of third-class climbing on the boulders of White Rocks Ridge. This would be a great place for a day's outing, but it was an ordeal with a pack. However, there were splendid views of the Cumberland Valley.

By the time I reached the sycamore tree by Yellow Breeches Creek it was already five o'clock and there were still over eight miles to go. My next surprise was to find the grocery store at Churchtown out of business. I couldn't buy supplies, but I did get hamburgers and a milk shake at a road stand.

Arriving at the Quality Motel on U.S. Route 11 after dark, I found a postcard from Tom McKone and Bob Winslow. They were 15 days ahead of me and about to overtake John Castleman and Dan Weirich. I was pleased to learn that they were doing well and appreciated their good wishes.

Among the less commonly seen birds that day were three downy woodpeckers and a black-throated green warbler. The open country of the Cumberland Valley produced bobwhites, song and field sparrows, goldfinches, pheasants, meadowlarks, chimney swifts, barn swallows, starlings, and a sparrow hawk being mobbed by a kingbird.

JUNE 19. One trouble with the long summer days was that they were giving me blisters. It was a bit surprising, after walking a thousand miles, to find that both of my heels were very tender.

Because of a relocation of the Appalachian Trail, I followed a circuitous route to pick up the trail a bit farther north. Where the route follows Conodoguinet Creek through dense groves of poison ivy, I ran into a work party from the Mountain Club of Maryland busily engaged in pruning the shrubs and cutting the undergrowth. I was glad to have the opportunity to thank them personally for their work.

Some of the interesting things found in the valley were huge lavender thistles and blossoming yellow honeysuckles. Again I noted kingbirds harassing a much larger victim, this time a crow. A Baltimore oriole was the first I had seen in over a month.

By not paying attention I missed the turn along the road atop Ironstone Ridge and had to backtrack a few hundred yards. The climbs over Blue Mountain and up Cove Mountain were routine, but the remaining six miles turned out to be tough. The trail slabs at an even contour, but the path was covered with rocks and stones. Finally I reached the spectacular viewpoint at Hawk Rock overlooking the Susquehanna River. The Promised Land, the second half of the Appalachian Trail, lay just beyond.

Arriving at Duncannon at 8:45 P.M., I was just in time to get into a small supermarket before it closed. I bought enough food to carry me to Port Clinton. After a pizza and beer at the hotel I headed out to do my laundry. There just wasn't any time to be wasted.

JUNE 20. This was a benighted day in more ways than one. Not having gone to bed until after midnight, and still having to organize my grocery purchases, I got a late start. It wasn't until about 11:30 that I finally crossed the Susquehanna. I was now more than a thousand miles from Springer Mountain.

There was an exceedingly steep short stretch of climbing to reach the shelf near the Susquehanna Shelter. Here I made the mistake of changing into shorts. In the brief moments it took to change, the mosquitoes tore into me to the point that I could think of nothing but the irritation of their bites. A worse problem was the poison ivy. I thought I had avoided it, but I was wrong. I got a pretty good case on the back of my right leg, especially in the bend of the knee.

Early in the afternoon I came to a spring, the last one near the trail before my evening destination, the Clarks Valley Shelter. While bending over to get a cup of water, my transistor radio (on which I was listening to the Sunday afternoon ball game) slipped out and fell into the water. I grabbed it quickly, but it seemed to be a total loss.

There were some boulders to be crossed at Shikellamy Rocks, but the trail was generally fairly good. The view from Table Rock over several mountains to the south and westward toward the Susquehanna Water Gap was especially rewarding.

Reaching the side trail to Clarks Valley Shelter at 8:15, I found that the blue blazes had been painted out! What to do? I headed on down to the road hoping there would be some place to get water as I had less than a pint left. According to the guidebook, there was a spring a quarter mile along the trail in the next section, and I found it without difficulty.

The bugs were bad and, despite the warm weather, I was forced to pitch a tent to get some protection from the mosquitoes. I was bitten badly enough in this process to make the chore of fixing dinner a hard one; concentration was necessary to avoid starting a forest fire with my stove. My can of lasagna was followed with a couple of Pop-Tarts, and then bed.

For the first time in many weeks I didn't write my diary the same day—I was too tired and uncomfortable. Yet for all of my exhaustion I got very little sleep—mostly because of the heat and the rocks.

With so much going wrong, there was one happy event—the addition of the cliff swallow (at the Susquehanna crossing) to the bird list.

JUNE 21. The abandoned old stage road through St. Anthonys Wilderness was a pleasant walk. Chestnut oaks, red maples, and black birch shaded the trail. There was little undergrowth and no poison ivy. Gnats and mosquitoes were pesky, though.

It was good weather and terrain for snakes. A rattler coiled and noisily warned me. I ventured close enough to take a picture and went on, soon coming upon a five-foot black rat snake. Occasionally there was a box turtle. Chipmunks were common and there were a couple of deer.

Ovenbirds were out in record numbers. I counted 22 of them,

even more than the towhees. The chickadees for the past several days had been black-cappeds. An occasional black-throated green was just about the only warbler seen in the woods, though at the end of the day I heard (and then attracted by "squeaking") a yellowthroat in the bushes along Trout Run.

The foundations of the structures in the long-abandoned village of Yellow Springs were easily seen. It was a delightful spot, a good place to pause and read in the register the comments of other hikers who had passed by.

I was invited to share a room at the Mountain View Motel with a hiker, his wife, and infant son who had come from Port Clinton. It was an unattractive lodging, but I was happy to have it anyway since it was by no means clear where I might find a campsite with water in the vicinity.

JUNE 22. The poison ivy had spread up and down my leg. It was still in the early stage and I expected that the next few days would be pretty uncomfortable ones. I hoped to be able to hike without wearing long pants.

After crossing Swatara Creek and climbing Blue Mountain, the trail followed the crest with moderate ups and downs. Occasionally there were nice views to the south, especially at the Mahlon Boyer Memorial which had been generously donated to the Blue Mountain Eagle Climbing Club and dedicated just a week before I passed.

It was 6 P.M. when I arrived at the Applebee Shelter. This was the start of one of my shakedown hikes last fall and it was a reassuring feeling to be back on familiar terrain. After a refreshing pause at Pilger Ruh, an historic spring, I headed on and soon passed the mile-long rocky stretch overlooking the Kessel. Finally reaching the site of the old Hertlein Shelter, where there was an excellent brook, I laid my sleeping bag out under the hemlocks and the stars. It was a clear night, with almost no bugs, but there was a noisy if invisible whippoorwill nearby.

Besides the poison ivy, I had developed a line of hard round welts on my backside and on the inside of my left knee. The day before I had felt stings at exactly these places while descending Second Mountain. My diagnosis was that I had been brushed by some toxic-haired caterpillars.

My radio showed some signs of returning to life; it picked up a couple of nearby stations.

JUNE 23. On a familiar trail, I covered the 17 miles to Port Clinton in ten hours. Shortly after my lunch stop at Pine Spring (the only shady spot in the six miles of road in the State Game Lands) I met another rattlesnake. This one was unhurriedly making its way across the road and soon disappeared into the thick brush.

Auburn Lookout was worth a stop to enjoy the view of the hills and winding streams to the north. From there it was a very steep descent to the Schuylkill River and Port Clinton, where I camped at a large pavilion. Just across the road was a swimming hole. "Swimming" may be an exaggeration because the river was only a couple of feet deep, but the water was clear and hopefully unpolluted. Anyway, the dip was refreshing.

I had dinner at the Port Clinton Hotel, where I met septuagenarian Jack Froehlich. Currently hiking from Harpers Ferry to Connecticut, he had only a few segments to do before completing the entire Appalachian Trail. We shared our memories; he seemed particularly fond of Bly Gap on the Georgia–North Carolina border. Well-fed and having signed the bound hikers' register, I returned to the pavilion for the night.

Towhees were exceptionally abundant; I counted at least 69. The scrub growth along the gamelands road must be ideal for them. Other birds noted in the same habitat were several yellowthroats and a single yellow-billed cuckoo.

JUNE 24. Caterpillars were everywhere. They were voracious eaters and what went in one end came out the other. The falling droplets made a steady patter in the woods that sounded like a light rain. The flocks of grackles must have had a feast.

Picking up a box of supplies and mailing a few items home to lighten my load (including my Duofold shirt and my bird and tree books), I was ready to set out again.

The hike started out with a steep ascent of about 1,000 feet and then dropped down to cross Furnace Creek near the ruins of Windsor Furnace. I cheated a teensy bit by following the road instead of the adjacent rocky trail up to Pulpit Rock, which had a good viewpoint. The next two miles involved a great deal of rock-hopping and rough path, causing me to curse the benighted souls who had relocated the Appalachian Trail to follow this route. The added four miles were at least partially justified, though, by the panoramic scene from the Pinnacle.

Late in the afternoon, at Eckville, I got caught in a shower that sent me looking for cover. Unfortunately, I found a small canvas-covered picnic area in front of a private residence. It was unoccupied, so I had dinner while it rained and grew dark, and ended up by making camp right there.

JUNE 25. The night was unpleasant. It was hot and there were many bugs on the attack. I got an early start, climbing Blue Mountain through the lands of the Hawk Mountain Sanctuary. At the crest the Appalachian Trail turned east to the outstanding overlook called Dan's Pulpit, where the Blue Mountain Eagle people had installed the best register I'd come across. Comments, mundane and philosophical, told the story of a year of hikers. Many names were familiar; their owners had become my friends—Art Smith, Dan Weirich, John Castleman—in addition to others such as Tom McKone and Bob Winslow, whom I'd met. Katahdin-bound Harry Latimer, who had started hiking weeks ago at Harpers Ferry, reported that he was having trouble with his boots. The most frequent gripe concerned the rockiness of the trail east of here. Typical comments at Dans Pulpit: "these rocks are a-getting me down"; "vegetarian power!"; "overestimated ability and underestimated time; tonite we stay in a motel (oh the good life) and maybe find a girl (?)"

There was a nice tavern where the Appalachian Trail crossed U.S. Route 309. After stopping for a sort of early dinner—beer and hamburgers—I continued on along the rocky trail. One of the worst stretches was the area near a transmission tower where the poison ivy was thick. The Cliffs was a knife-edge of rock along the crest of the mountain but it only lasted a couple of hundred yards and was easy boulder-hopping. I climbed to the top of Baer Rocks and intend to return some day because it must be a superb place to watch the autumn hawk migration. I went on to Bake Oven Knob, crossed a terrible rock slide, and finally arrived at the Bake Oven Knob Shelter. The lower spring, quite far down the hillside, provided a bit of water. I shared the lean-to with a young college graduate who worked as a carpenter in the winter and took trips in the summer. It was Consciousness III.

The poison ivy remained pretty well stabilized on my leg, though there were isolated blisters on my arms as well. The yellow antihistamine pills I'd been taking seemed to be a big help—there had been very little itching.

JUNE 26. A heavy thunderstorm came and went during the night. As the dawn broke a whippoorwill serenaded us, leaving us no choice but to get up.

It was easy going in the morning, with only one rocky stretch near

Bake Oven Knob Shelter. Some of the trail went through scrubby areas where the first ripe huckleberries of the season were ready for plucking. After lunch at Outerbridge Shelter, I exchanged trail intelligence with some southbound hikers, then descended to an industrialized area of the Lehigh Valley.

With a pint of ice cream under my belt, I made my way slowly up the steep trail through a talus field unlike anything I'd seen in the East. It was a jumble of large rocks, fortunately stable and well blazed. It was just a matter of going slowly and carefully and eventually I reached the top. I took several pictures along the way, not to record the beauty of the scene but as a reminder of the filth being spewed from the stack of a factory below.

Then there were about four miles of game lands gravel road, easy walking but without shade. Along this stretch I suddenly came across two red foxes. They hadn't observed my approach until I was about 50 feet away, when they bounded off gracefully into the scrubby cover.

It would have been very easy to miss the next spring, as there was only a tiny sign with obscure carved letters. I had been warned in advance, though, and knew where to look. Because I would have to make camp that night away from water, I loaded up with all I could carry.

Passing Little Gap, a miserably buggy spot, I continued a bit farther until I came to a little clearing under pine trees a few feet off the trail. It was remarkably flat and free of rocks, though the insects were still bad. With the mosquito netting on my tent, I could at least get away from the bugs at night.

JUNE 27. The day's walk was on a narrow path with rocks—though not boulders—all the way to Wind Gap. Each ankle twisted once, but the Limmer boots kept them from real damage. Poison ivy was sporadic; only around Hahns Lookout was it unavoidable.

Leaving the campsite after breakfast with almost a quart of water, I had no difficulty reaching Smith Gap. The gushing piped spring near there was certainly a welcome one, though it required a side trip of 0.6 miles each way down the mountain and back up.

That afternoon I had a Sunday doubleheader to absorb my attention—a split with the Pirates beating the Phillies in the weird nightcap, by 10-9, on a pinch hit homer by the Great One, Roberto Clemente.

I was glad to reach Wind Gap, get a shower, have dinner, and do my laundry before turning in for the night. It was a nice town, and I received a good welcome at the Gateway Motel.

JUNE 28. I had thought Wolf Rocks would be something special, but when I got there early in the afternoon it was too hazy for a view. Right below the rocks, though, the foliage of mountain ashes forms bold geometrical designs that I tried to capture on film.

When I was walking I often pondered the question of why anyone would want to hike the whole Appalachian Trail. That day's theory was that the long-distance hiker hikes because there is a *specific goal* attainable by great effort. Most of us have day-to-day activities that are frustrating because they lack clear objectives and rarely result in a feeling of accomplishment. Work with a large organization involves compromises, with an individual providing "input" instead of being able to take decisive action of his own. If the results of his action are ever seen it is only after a long time.

The fire tower on Mt. Minsi had a good view back along the snaking crest of Blue Mountain. The descent to Delaware Water Gap was punctuated by stops to admire the vista of the river below. There were some possible campsites, but I was completely out of food. I continued to town where I lodged at the Deer's Head. Speaking of deer, there was one in the middle of the road right on the outskirts of town.

Lately the blue jay had joined the list of common birds. So had the ruffed grouse, but in a special way. I usually saw a hen sometime during the day, but since she was accompanied by several chicks, the total count was fairly high. Delaware Water Gap was a particularly fine place to find turkey vultures, with about a dozen gliding on the thermal updrafts rising from the river.

JUNE 29. Delaware Water Gap was a memorable place to experience a thunderstorm. The bass rumble of the thunder echoed in the narrow canyon, back and forth, until it finally vanished somewhere in New Jersey.

There was a great deal of mail waiting for me, including back issues of *Time* and the New Jersey–New York trail guide. There was also a box of supplies: butane, powdered milk, Campsite beef stew, and so on.

The walk up Dunnfield Creek on the east side of the river was lovely—tall hemlocks, enchanting little waterfalls, and a Louisiana water thrush running about on the stones in search of aquatic insects. The real gem was just a bit farther on—Sunfish Pond, the first natural pond that I had encountered. There were probably 25 people, mostly students, camped around the water.

The gypsy moth caterpillar had been a scourge in the Mt. Mohican area, with the forest stripped bare over vast areas. It was a depressing sight. The infestation was severe at my campsite near Camp Mohican Road, but fortunately the tent kept the caterpillars on the outside.

JUNE 30. The defoliation was incredible. Having finished with the trees, the caterpillars were working on the blueberries. Even the laurel was not completely immune. Perhaps the Catfish Fire Tower area was the worst, and I took some pictures in the vicinity, including a particularly dense mass of the critters.

The laurel was just about finished blooming and the forests, without leaves and flowers, were unattractive. The most obvious impact upon the bird life was the scarcity of the wood thrush, and the absence of red-eyed vireos.

The trail had a few rocky stretches, though it was still an improvement over the eastern part of Pennsylvania. The 85°F. weather made the going harder, especially in the absence of shade and wind. I had a good long drink at Rattlesnake Spring and then nursed two quarts of water the remaining 11 miles to the Stokes Lean-to.

The day's bird list included the ovenbird, towhee, chipping sparrow, white-breasted nuthatch, crow, blue jay, robin, field sparrow, black-capped chickadee, flicker, turkey vulture, Baltimore oriole, cardinal, grackle, redwing, wood pewee, great crested flycatcher, grouse, phoebe, catbird, kingbird, yellowthroat, indigo bunting, brown thrasher, wood thrush, house wren, and a shakily identified great horned owl. Just about all the familiar woodland species were here except the red-eyed vireo, downy woodpecker, scarlet tanager, tufted titmouse, and mourning dove.

JULY 1 (THURSDAY). This buggy season wasn't so great for camping. I had tried to sleep in my clothes and head net on top of my sleeping bag, but with mosquitoes constantly buzzing about, I was miserable. I finally got up in the middle of the night and set up my tent. The timing was good because a thundershower followed immediately, blessedly cooling things off.

The morning hike was uninteresting. Though there were views from the ridge, the thick haze obscured everything. I hurried to reach Worthington's Bakery at Culvers Gap, a store praised by other Appalachian Trail hikers. I found the fresh pastry almost worth walking 1,200 miles for.

During the afternoon I spent a couple of hours at the Sunrise Mountain pavilion waiting in vain for a thunderstorm to pass. When I finally left, it was still raining. I stopped at the High Point Lean-to, a few miles short of my original destination for the day. Aside from the lack of a spring or pump close-by, the lean-to was an excellent campsite. It was a handsome stone structure, and had just been completely reroofed. The dirt floor was covered with a layer of fresh straw.

JULY 2. I was on the trail fairly early. Following the woodland paths along Kittatinny Ridge, I came upon several two-inch reddish salamanders, red efts. I suspected yesterday's rain was responsible for bringing them out. Also of interest was the snake, patterned and colored like a young copperhead, that skittered off into the rock pile near the High Point Monument where the Appalachian Trail leaves the ridge.

After lunch at the next lean-to, which was sadly littered, I reached the lowlands and many miles of walking on rural roads. It was actually a pleasant change of scenery. For example, I passed an ancient cemetery near Mt. Salem where, in the shade of magnificent sugar maples, I read the tombstones of another era—a time when people bore such intriguing names as Temperance Fountain.

My principal purchase at the store in Unionville was a new pair of cotton pants, a full size smaller than my pre-trip 36s. After a sandwich and piece of pie at the good restaurant I continued to Liberty Corners, traversing the pastoral Wallkill Valley en route. A friendly homeowner filled my canteens for me and gave me some directions for finding the trail, which was obscurely marked at this point.

As soon as I hit the woods on Pochuck Mountain, the bugs attacked. Putting on my old long pants and head net helped, but my arms were chewed up pretty badly. Reaching the top after ascending quite a steep pitch, I started looking for a campsite, but the rockiness of the terrain and the prevalence of the mosquitoes pushed me on. I quickly signed a register, noting that it was too buggy to write more. Bruce Balderston, I learned, had been here on June 23. Finally, a mile farther on, I found a fairly flat space without rocks where I could rig my tent between a couple of trees. The only problem was that the ground cover included poison ivy, which

Photo by James R. Wolf

Young woodchuck near The Pinnacle, Eckville, Pennsylvania.

Photo by Garnett W. Mar

Lehigh Gap and Lehigh River Bridge from trail in Pennsylvania.

would certainly contaminate the tent and the poncho that I was using as a ground cloth.

A black-billed cuckoo uttered its croaking three-noted call from the tangled growth on the ridge near the High Point Monument. The lowlands had redwings in abundance, also barn swallows and goldfinches. At one point there were at least five killdeer, one of which walked the road ahead of me for at least a quarter of a mile, presumably trying to lure me away from her nest. Though its presence at this time of year was unusual, I can think of no alternative to my identification of a yellow-legged shorebird with solid wings as a yellowlegs, probably the greater.

JULY 3. The guidebook proved unreliable. I expected to reach a spring early in the morning, but when I reached the general vicinity there was no marking. I may have found the spring anyway—covered with planks—but the water smelled foul and I didn't drink it. A bit farther on I was able to fill my canteens at a private home. A more serious problem was the disappearance of blazes east of Wawayanda Mountain. Inquiring at a nearby house, I was told that "everyone" lost the route here. I was directed to follow Barry Road (not "Barrett" as in the guide) several hundred yards north to intersect the trail again.

However, today's hike did have some rewards. There was a red-headed woodpecker perched in a sycamore tree in the Vernon Valley. It was a clear day, so I could make out the unending crest of the Kittatinny, all the way from far south of Culvers Gap to the High Point Monument and beyond, from a rocky outcrop on top of Wawayanda Mountain. A red-tailed hawk circled about as I was enjoying the view.

By prior arrangement I was planning to spend the night at a religious center, the Kutz Camp, on Bowen Road. Rabbi Smith welcomed me cordially and invited me to plunge into the barbecue dinner of burgers, corn, and watermelon which was just being served. Several of the staff members were interested in my trip and offered me a ride to Middletown where they were headed, on their night off, to see a movie. I went along and did some grocery shopping and laundry while they enjoyed the show.

JULY 4. Although the guidebook continued to be misleading, I managed to follow the trail during the morning without undue difficulty. I interrupted my walk to take a dip at the sandy beach along little Cascade Lake. The lightweight plastic bathing suit that

I usually wore only when my laundry was in the washing machine held up well.

The trail above the western shore of Greenwood Lake provided some good views of the blue waters, spotted with tiny white boats, far below. But the going was much tougher than I had expected. For the most part the ridge consisted of solid rock, broken though by fissures every few feet. It was constantly up and down. At a couple of points there were steep climbs up the escarpment, and this continued at Eastern Pinnacles and Cat Rocks north of New York Route 17A. The scampering about was exhausting and it required considerable effort to balance my pack.

The big concern during the afternoon was water. I had left Kutz with about two quarts. Of the streams on the trail above Greenwood Lake, one was dry and the other was a putrid trickle. There was supposedly a spring, but other hikers told me they hadn't been able to find it. They advised me to get water from some people who live on the highway at Mt. Peter. The poor folks must have had to put up with a parade of hikers. They seemed used to it and pleasantly let me use their outside faucet.

With enough water for the night I set up camp on a splendid flat shelf halfway down the slopes of Bellvale Mountain. The bugs disappeared after dark and I went to sleep under the stars to the accompaniment of some festive fireworks.

JULY 5. After a few minutes on the trail, I descended to a private campground where hordes of folks, bumper to bumper, were enjoying their holiday "in the country." I picked up drinking water and ate some ice cream before moving on.

With the weather continuing to be fine for the third consecutive day, I enjoyed the views around Mombasha High Point (with the Kittatinny still visible from one spot) before going down to Bramertown Road. I left the trail here briefly to have lunch beneath a weeping willow on the grassy bank of Lake Mombasha.

The hiking continued with frequent steep climbs up and down rocky cliffs. It took an hour and a quarter to cover the 1.8 miles over Arden Mountain and down the Agony Grind. East of New York Route 17, in Harriman Park, there were more interesting rock formations—notably a narrow defile called the Lemon Squeezer which can only be squeezed through by removing your pack.

I could have stayed at the Brien Lean-to, with a fine view over Island Pond, but wanted to make more progress for the day. The pump described in the guide was broken, so I had to use pond water.

I threw in some Halazone to be safe; very rarely would I bother to take this precaution.

My camp for the night was on Surebridge Mountain. It took a bit of scouting to find a suitable place, flat and without rocks, but eventually I got settled. The shortening of the days was already noticeable. Stopping at 7:30 was about right, as it left about 1½ hours before darkness. In the trees nearby, I observed a black-and-white warbler, a bird which had been very uncommon of late.

JULY 6. Notwithstanding the high prices, I couldn't resist the opportunity to fill up on hot dogs, milk, and ice cream at the refreshment stand at Lake Tiorati Circle.

Just beyond the summit of Black Mountain I ran into a smoldering fire. At first I thought there were only a couple of burning spots and I attempted to stomp them out. But as I continued along the trail, it became clear that acres of scorched ground were still smoking. I came across some blazing laurel and beat out the flames, getting a hot foot in the process, but there was more fire farther on. Fortunately the smoke was blowing uphill and away from the trail, so I didn't have to pass through it. At first I didn't know whether the fire was being fought, but later I met some park personnel who told me the fire had been burning three days—probably started by a hiker's cigarette. For the rest of the day, from West and Bear mountains, the rising grey smoke was visible.

With good weather it might be inspiring to get your first view of the Hudson River from West Mountain, but the day I passed it was overcast. Bear Mountain, though, was memorable. Much of the climb consisted of near-vertical rock slabs—exceptionally steep for unroped climbing with a pack.

At the top of Bear Mountain the tower was locked because of the lateness of the hour. Fortunately, there was a drinking fountain. Water had been a bit tight, with two quarts being nursed from Tiorati Circle. I also had another problem—finding the trail again. I assumed that the Appalachian Trail went to the highest point because the guide talked about crossing the summit. In fact, the trail veered off just before the top, and it took me a long time to find it again.

Finally I reached Bear Mountain Inn. Oh, how great a shave and shower felt! Dinner at the Inn was my best meal since Nantahala Lodge, if not the best on the entire Appalachian Trail.

JULY 7. I had been looking forward to a brief visit with my parents, who drove over from Westchester to spend the morning with me. They brought all the mail that had accumulated, along with various supplies I needed for the next stretch of trail. These included the Connecticut–Massachusetts guidebook and my resoled boots. Unaccountably, the itinerary I had worked out for the Appalachian Trail east of the Hudson (a list of planned overnight stops, with the intervening distances and estimated climbs) was missing.

It would have been only a short trip home to get the itinerary but I wanted to keep moving, so set out again after a big lunch. I passed the lowest point on the Appalachian Trail (115.4 feet above sea level) and headed on to the Bear Mountain Bridge. It cost me 10¢ to go east; a southbound hiker could save the dime. I shared the vista of the scenic Hudson with a lone herring gull gliding far overhead.

There was a new route on the east side of the river. It involved extra climbing, but from the top of the high ridge there was a magnificent view of the Hudson with West Point in the background. A few miles farther along I stopped off at a private pond, Lake Celeste, where some ladies emptied their water jugs to fill my canteens. I was sorry I couldn't accept their invitation to take a swim, but felt I didn't have the time to spare. It was 7:30 when I arrived at Indian Lake Lean-to. It was unattractive and badly littered, but at least it was a place to stay.

It was hard getting to sleep because of the heat. When I finally dozed off, I was awakened by an animal scrounging around beneath the platform of the shelter. The culprit, only a few feet away, was a skunk. I tried to tell him in a firm voice that he should leave, but I wasn't bold enough to do more. In the morning I discovered that the attraction was an opened can of luncheon meat that some hiker had left.

JULY 8. From the top of Candlewood Hill there was a good view westward to the Hudson and what seemed to be the Indian Point reactor near Peekskill. From this vantage point the vast extent of caterpillar damage was apparent. There was hardly any green to be seen anywhere. The summit ledge was bugfree—a welcome change from the woodlands—so I had a small lunch. With my peanut butter I had some whole wheat Ry-King (red box) that I thought was particularly good.

Some other impressions of the day: impressive stone fences marking the site of an abandoned settlement at Wicopee Road; the lack of water at the Torrey Lean-to; the fascinating Monte Rosa Inn (where the whole Rosa family pitches in to cook big Italian dinners). My visit with an elderly couple tending their garden near the Farmers Mill Lean-to was particularly poignant. Within the past two weeks the gypsy moth caterpillars had stripped their trees, including the needles of some handsome white pines, depriving their home of charm and shade alike. They sent me on my way with filled canteens; it was a good thing, since there was no water at the lean-to.

It had been the hottest day of the year, 96°F. in New York City, 88°F. on the Appalachian Trail. After walking nearly 19 miles in such weather, I was happy to call it a day.

The birding highlight was a yellow-throated vireo. Hearing a burry voice I looked upward into a maple expecting to see a scarlet tanager and found the vireo instead. Some other species were grackles (two flocks, in caterpillar-infested areas), flicker, Baltimore oriole, yellowthroat, hairy woodpecker, great crested flycatcher, and turkey vulture.

JULY 9. Another scorcher (up to 89°F.) but it was easy trail, nearly all on roads. The caterpillar problem seemed less severe, and on the roads the bugs weren't bad.

Having used up all of my water, I was happy to be able to fill my canteens at a private home. During the day I carried more water than I actually needed, but with most of the springs dry it seemed like good insurance.

Kelly's grocery in Holmes, clean and friendly, was a delightful oasis. They kept a register, and all of the northbound through hikers except John Castleman had signed. After a little shopping, and some drinks and ice cream, I was on my way. The next stop was the park in Pawling, where I was again invited to take a swim and camp for the night. It was tempting, but if I stopped I wouldn't be able to make it to Kent the next night. I took advantage of their facilities for a shave and shower, though, and was refreshed, if only briefly.

It was getting late as I passed Dapplemere, the late Governor Dewey's lovely estate. By the time I left the paved road it was near sunset and I hurriedly set up camp at the first possible site, using a tree and the rusty door of an abandoned jalopy as supports for my tent cords. The bugs were bad, but I found refuge in head net and long pants. Since I had eaten a lot at Kelly's, my dinner was light: just some sardines with Ry-King, cooked vegetables, and a pastry.

The most notable bird was the tufted titmouse, which I had last observed in Pennsylvania. Though the species has been extending its range gradually northward in recent years, this must still be about the very limit of its occurrence. A bluebird was another good find.

Others listed were phoebe, towhee, cardinal, white-breasted nuthatch, blue jay, wood thrush, robin, catbird, crow, mourning dove, black-capped chickadee, redwing, ovenbird, wood pewee, song sparrow, house wren, field sparrow, downy woodpecker, kingbird, rose-breasted grosbeak, chipping sparrow, house sparrow, ruffed grouse, scarlet tanager, starling, chimney swift, cowbird, and red-eyed vireo.

JULY 10. The first two miles of the day's hike were especially buggy. The briefest pause served as an opportunity for the pesky deerflies to close in for a bite. My elbows and the back of my neck seemed to be favored targets. The trail had been rerouted to traverse the Pawling Nature Reserve. In a different time of the year it could be very nice, but the insects and the extensive stretches of brambles and other plants overgrowing the trail certainly diminished my enjoyment.

The folks at the Explorer Scout Science Camp insisted that I have a thick ham sandwich from their kitchen before going on my way. Another gustatory treat was a new wild food—the peppery buds of the day lily.

Some white birches were growing on the slopes of Schaghticoke Mountain, beckoning me on to New England. There is an Appalachian Trail register in a rural mail box right at the Connecticut line. Bruce Balderston had complained about the bugs when he was here; Harry Latimer was unhappy to find no water at Farmers Mill; John Castleman was simply tired.

Continuing on down the mountain past Rattlesnake Den (no snakes, though) the trail reached Thayer Brook and a fine campsite. Then it went over Mt. Algo and the one hard part of the day; the descent to Kent was *very* steep.

Crossing the Housatonic, where a black duck rose and speedily flew off, I went on into town where I was surprised to find that neither food nor lodging of any kind was available. I explained my plight to the parson's wife, who generously gave me a ride several miles to the Valley View Motel.

Both tiger and black swallowtails were still in evidence. Others were the great spangled fritillary, the mourning cloak, the monarch (first one), the red-spotted purple, and one of the sulphurs. I was seeing an occasional woodchuck, lots of rabbits, chipmunks everywhere, and a few grey squirrels.

I picked up another case of poison ivy—a few blisters on my ankle.

JULY 11. The folks at the Valley View fed me some delicious blueberry pancakes and let me have a couple of hot dogs to take along for dinner. Then a departing guest drove me back to the Appalachian

Trail, several miles out of his way. When you needed help badly enough, people seemed willing to assist.

The boys from Kent School have traditionally painted initials and class numerals on the glacial boulders above the highway. In this age of ecology, maybe they'll give up the practice.

During a light rain I took shelter and had lunch at the Chase Mountain Lean-to. Previous hikers had left supplies and I helped myself to some soup and powdered milk, the latter neatly packaged and labeled in what seemed to be the familiar penmanship of Bob Winslow. At Cobble Mountain there was a fine view westward into New York; then the trail descended steeply over wet rocks to the Macedonia Lean-to. More goodies here: a big plastic bag filled with gorp, from which I took a generous ration. Though neither Chase nor Macedonia had any water, I was able to replenish my supply from the pump at Four Corners.

The descent from St. Johns Ledges was precipitous, some 600 feet of drop in four-tenths of a mile. The rock was quite exposed, much of it without nubbins for fingers and toes and too steep for good balance. I finally reached River Road and the Mountain Brook Lean-to, where the wire bunks were so bad as to be unusable. Still, there was water and the bugs were scarce, so I didn't complain.

JULY 12. For several miles the trail followed a level unused dirt road along the banks of the winding swift Housatonic. Beneath a great hemlock, with the rustling leaves of a white oak and the ripple of the waters, I mused on the tranquility of it all.

It was ironic that here, on one of the easiest stretches of the Appalachian Trail, I tripped on an embedded rock and landed, literally, flat on my face. The fall bruised my right cheekbone, but fortunately there was no damage to my glasses.

Another problem was a relocation, inconspicuously marked, extending the route farther along the Housatonic. I followed the guidebook and lost the blazes, but a gal on horseback rode by and assured me that I could pick up the trail again by continuing straight ahead.

Reaching Cornwall Bridge, I was surprised to find that it had a post office and even a bank. It also had a fine store where I purchased lunch and groceries. On Mondays they close at 1:00 in the afternoon and I had just made it with half an hour to spare.

A part of Dark Entry Ravine, above the relocated section, was a hemlock-shaded ravine with delightful waterfalls and pools. There was little water at this time of year, but in spring this must be a jewel. A little farther on was a large, rather spongy bolete with a brownish cap and yellowish flesh, the first pored mushroom I'd seen on the trip; not edulis though, or I would have collected it for dinner.

Cathedral Pines was a beautiful grove of enormous, probably virgin, hemlocks and white pine. In this quiet sanctuary, the black-throated green warbler made its home.

It was a good thing I detoured off the trail at the Pinnacle in the Mohawk Mountain ski area to get some water, because the next pump, at the picnic area near Connecticut Highway 4, didn't have a handle. Camping at the new shelter near the highway, I found I wasn't alone. While I was warming up my can of spaghetti and meatballs, a raccoon sauntered up to within four feet of me and started sniffing at my pack. I shouted at him, but it made no impression. He finally backed off when I tried to take his picture.

JULY 13. The morning was a series of gentle rises and falls. A veery and a Canada warbler, harbingers of the northern birdlife to come, were about the only sights of special interest. I had to take water from some questionable brooks and was much relieved to get a better supply from the spring that was still trickling at the Pine Knoll Lean-to.

The scenic highlight of the day came in the afternoon at Deans Ravine, another deep hemlock-lined gorge. The stream, when there is water, leaps down a hundred-foot waterfall and then cascades through a line of small pools. There were some kids camped at the lean-to here; a couple of them were using hammocks. It looked like a comfortable arrangement if it didn't rain. The long sweet song of the winter wren rang out from some hidden niche among the leaves and mossy logs, but ventriloquist that he is, I never was able to find him.

Following a section strewn with poison ivy, the trail crossed Barrack Mountain, steep on both the ascent and descent. Fortunately, the rocks tended either to form a staircase with reasonably sized steps or were sloped gently enough to permit balance climbing.

My walk into Falls Village took me past the Blass homestead—a nice brick house on two or three acres with plenty of room for a kid to practice throwing a baseball. It was already 6:30 and instead of pushing on to Limestone Spring I decided to stay overnight at the Inn, where I had a steak dinner and nursed a beer or two while watching the All-Star game.

JULY 14. Today marked the return to higher mountains, the highest elevation in fact since Shenandoah National Park. As I emerged from the woods into an open field on the side of Prospect Mountain, the

Taconics suddenly spread out ahead, with the summits of Bear, Race, and Everett mountains luring me on. The plodding over hill and dale was over; the exhilaration of the heights began again.

Salisbury was especially meaningful for me as I had spent a summer there as a boy of 11 and had never been back since. Compelled by remembrances of things past, I detoured through the village before the long climb up Lions Head. Now lying far below was the expanse of Lake Wonoskopomuc, my childhood swimming hole.

The view from Bear Mountain, elevation 2,300 feet, was even grander because the hills to the south rose only to around 1,500 feet; there was a feeling of great height. In the other direction was the impressive summit of Mt. Everett, only a few miles away in Massachusetts.

Sages Ravine was another charming canyon. Even with the small flow of water, I couldn't resist pausing to admire some of the graceful little waterfalls. Here I picked up another long-missing friend, the black-throated blue warbler, before proceeding to Bear Rock Stream where I camped beneath the stars and the hemlocks. Still one more old-timer, the slate-colored junco (last seen near Skyland in Shenandoah Park), was waiting to greet me as I arrived.

JULY 15. Hardly had I left camp when there was another treat, a brown creeper spiraling its way up a dead tree trunk. Then it was over Race Mountain and Mt. Everett, with good views east over the Housatonic Valley and north toward Mt. Greylock. My lunch stop was at a picnic area on Mt. Everett, where about 20 sixth-graders from a nearby camp peppered me with questions about my trip, and in exchange left me with a juicy orange.

A relocation, of which I was unaware, apparently made the descent to Jug End Road considerably easier than the former route. One problem, though, was that it necessitated a much longer walk on the road to reach Jug End Resort, where I was spending the night. There was another hiker at the roadside picnic area. On his trip from Sherburne Pass, he had met Bruce, who had told him to be on the lookout for "the lawyer."

Jug End Resort, where I was greeted warmly, was a *gemütlich* sort of a place. The desk clerk, holding parcels and mail for me, had been expecting me and didn't seem taken aback by the sight and smell of a hiker. I hastened to take a shower and shave and even had time for a quick dip in the pool.

Dinner, an outdoor clambake, would have been more pleasant if it had not been interrupted by the heaviest cloudburst I'd encountered since Sunrise Mountain in New Jersey. With the lightning striking less than a mile away, I was grateful to have good shelter.

My mail included a copy of my itinerary. It showed that I was four days behind my original schedule. My present pace would put me on Katahdin on September 7 instead of September 3. There were also index cards with my typed notes of distances, elevations, and other key information. A particularly welcome note from my friends in Pittsburgh urged me to call upon *their* friends who live right on the Appalachian Trail in Dalton, 50 miles north. While doing my laundry for the first time in 12 days, I caught up with my correspondence. A letter to Dalton was one of the major items.

JULY 16. One of the staffers gave me a lift to Great Barrington for a quick haircut and then drove me back to the trail. Covering about three miles an hour on the roads crossing the Housatonic Valley, I had gone nearly five miles before stopping for lunch.

The first climb went through some buggy woods to reach Homes Road. There something very peculiar had happened. The blazes had been painted black, but there were white wooden arrows that seemed to point along the old route. There didn't seem to be any other markers, so I took the old trail, using the arrows as a guide. It was all very confusing and probably wrong, but eventually there were white blazes again. For a stretch I wasn't sure whether I was following them northbound or southbound, but eventually they headed up the cliffs on East Mountain and I knew I was headed in the right direction.

I didn't like the looks of the weather and was particularly unhappy because I would have to cross open ledges. I hurried as much as the steep climb allowed. As I reached the top there was a tiny trace of rain.

It was a different story later in the day, though. My destination was Benedict Pond Campground. As I was headed up the ridge north of Massachusetts Highway 23, the deluge came. Just at that point there was a large unoccupied canvas tent, and I sought shelter in it. While the storm raged outside, I ate a filling Campsite beef stew and wrote in my diary. The only annoyance was poison ivy—a few scattered blisters, but nothing serious.

The interesting birds of the day were those of the valley: tree swallows, barn swallows, a purple finch, catbirds, and goldfinches, among others.

JULY 17. Serendipity was the order of the day. It began at the picnic grounds near lovely Benedict Pond where I met a couple who improved my diet by giving me a hard-boiled egg, an orange, and some cherries.

Having solved the minor route-finding problems on Mt. Wilcox, I enjoyed these goodies with my lunch. Unfortunately, though, I had forgotten to pick up my cap when I set off on the trail again. This meant that the deerflies had more area on which to be a nuisance.

It was a disappointment to find that the Tyringham general store was closed on Saturday afternoons. The good people of the village came to the rescue; a lad drove me a few miles to Lee where I shopped at the supermarket.

Continuing on my way, I came across a perfectly good sailor-type white hat that fit me well, giving me good head protection if not the full visor I preferred.

Sensing more rain, I stopped at a house on Goose Pond and asked to wait out the shower on the porch. The folks were most hospitable, inviting me in for beer and chips and showing off the talents of Mr. B., their young Brittany spaniel.

I resumed my walk when the rain tapered off. The good weather didn't last long, though, and soon I was drenched by a new shower. Lightning was striking not far away. The trees provided some protection from the rain, though I was completely exposed when crossing the bridge over the Massachusetts Turnpike.

Just beyond the turnpike was a little white cabin that turned out to be part of an abandoned tourist court. It was in a state of general disrepair, but still had a good roof and a bed with a serviceable double mattress. It took all of two seconds to decide to spend the night there, and not much longer to shed drenched clothes and switch into my dry long pants and wool shirt.

I had a good dinner and spent the evening listening to Brandenburg concerti on WQXR.

It had been a good day for birding, too, with a white-throated sparrow, yellow-bellied sapsucker, and ruby-throated hummingbird especially worthy of note. Others were scarlet tanager, wood pewee, towhee, blue jay, kingbird, redwing, robin, goldfinch, song sparrow, grackle, yellowthroat, black-capped chickadee, white-breasted nuthatch, red-eyed vireo, black-throated blue warbler, black-throated green warbler, ruffed grouse, chipping sparrow, crow, house sparrow, flicker, and wood thrush. Ovenbird numbers have been reduced of late, with none at all the last couple of days.

JULY 18. The hamlet of Washington Town Hall, Massachusetts, is the home of grandmotherly Mrs. Fred Hutchinson, whose avocation is looking after the needs of Appalachian Trail hikers. Everyone you meet on the trail reminds you to be sure to pay her a visit. Arriving in midday, I was immediately invited in for milk and homemade cookies. As soon as you've caught your breath, Mrs. Hutchinson begins a thorough cross-examination of your background, interests, and experiences. If she were to write an article about the trail, based on her interviews, it would be worth reading.

By coincidence, another end-to-ender came by at the same time— blond Jim Rutter, who was headed north to south. We posed while Mrs. Hutchinson took our pictures, and signed a log that had almost every familiar name. Bob Winslow and Tom McKone had spent a happy night here, but I couldn't spare the time and after some trail talk with Jim Rutter I thanked my gracious hostess and went on my way.

One reason for rushing off quickly was my eagerness to reach Dalton. After writing ahead from Jug End, I had been able to reach Don and Maureen by phone. They were as warm and helpful as I knew they would be when I first talked with them.

It wasn't so much the bed and board (though Maureen's pork chops rated four stars) as the relaxing hours when we shared our common interests of sailing and photography. There's no denying the loneliness of a long solo walk, a loneliness that makes you cherish the brief moments that tie you to home. So, adopting me for the evening, Don and Maureen and their son Tim made my visit a success and a pleasant memory.

JULY 19. My weight was now about 156, some 20 pounds less than it was in March. My pack weighed about 34 pounds without water and with hardly any food, and not counting camera, binoculars, and long pants.

Maureen volunteered to take care of a couple of chores which would otherwise have required my leaving the trail. The critical one was taking my glasses to an optometrist in Pittsfield; the wire frame had snapped and needed to be replaced. (In the meantime I used my sunglasses). She was also going to have my leather camera case restitched so that I could again wear it conveniently on my belt. Best of all, she took my pack, which she would return to me on top of Mt. Greylock; until then I would be happily unburdened.

After I'd passed through the dark woods of the Crane estate, it started to rain. Soon it was a downpour which kept up until late afternoon. In a few minutes I was drenched to the skin. Being without the pack, I was able to move fast, pausing only occasionally to check landmarks in the guidebook. My nourishment was peanuts and

Pop-Tarts, gulped without missing a stride. Aside from the brambles near Anthony and Gore ponds, the trail was in good shape and I arrived at Cheshire—some 10.5 miles from my starting point—in four hours.

I stopped at the post office long enough to pick up some mail and then headed for the laundromat. With only the poncho between me and an arrest for indecent exposure, everything else went into the dryer for a couple of cycles. By then the rain had let up and I was able to buy my groceries and walk to Mrs. Bickford's tourist home.

JULY 20. The climb from Cheshire, 950 feet above sea level, to the 3,500-foot summit of Mt. Greylock was a lark, since I was walking without pack.

The upper parts of Saddle Ball and Greylock are characterized by stunted fir growth. Here birders scout for the Bicknell's thrush. Search as I would, though, the birds wouldn't cooperate and I had to pass on without being able to add a new species to my life list.

There was a long stop for burgers at Bascom Lodge on the summit. For the rest of the day—now with my pack and repaired glasses and camera case—it was nearly all downhill. I'm sure views from Greylock and Mt. Williams are fine under blue skies, but they were washed out that day by the heavy overcast.

Though my hopes of finding Bicknell's thrush were frustrated, there were compensations. On the outskirts of Cheshire, I encountered the well-groomed cedar waxwing for the first time on my hike. It was a good day for juncos, black-throated blue warblers, and yellowthroats. The sure sign that I'd reached the northern woods was the abundance of the white-throated sparrow languidly whistling "Peabody, Peabody, Peabody" and the hermit thrush, more often heard than seen, its flutelike triplet notes spiraling upward. By contrast, there were two cardinals near the roadside in Blackinton, a location that must be at the extreme limit of this southern bird's range.

JULY 21. The hiking was much tougher than I had anticipated. The relocation in southern Vermont goes over mountains instead of following the old level route. Fortunately I got an early start from Mrs. Stevens' tourist home, where I had spent the night.

The forests had changed their character in the last couple of weeks. Arching over the fern-covered ground were white and yellow birches, beeches, sugar and striped maples. The oaks seem to have disappeared. The streams all had running water, and it was a relief not to have to worry about finding something to drink. The bug situation was much better and the poison ivy didn't appear to grow above the 1,000-foot contour line.

There was a good variety of warblers: ovenbird, black-throated blue, black-throated green, yellowthroat, Canada, and chestnut-sided; and now the red-eyed vireo seemed to outnumber the long-time leader, the towhee.

Two parties were already camped at Congdon when I arrived, but there was still a bunk for me. Lipton's beef stroganoff was a tasty dinner dish. Afterwards, I joined the others around the warm camp-fire and we talked on into the night.

JULY 22. In order to make a side trip to Bennington, I got an early start. Some of my kitchen gear had been left outside on a table and had attracted some animal—a raccoon? a porcupine? Whatever it was had taken a fancy to my plastic water bottle and had chewed holes in the bottom. It also had eaten the cap off one of my half-ounce detergent bottles, but I had three others, so this didn't matter.

I reached the highway and a driver gave me a lift to town. I picked up the freeze-dried dinners, jerky, Wyler's lemonade, and so on that had been mailed ahead and made a few purchases, including mailers for my Kodachrome-X film and a new Duofold top. With the chilly weather, I was worried about exposure in the event that some of my clothes got wet. A cab took me back to the trail.

There was supposed to be another relocation to Glastenbury Mountain, but I was happy that it hadn't been completed yet. It will be longer, with more climbing. The trail followed Bolles Brook on a dirt road for several miles—a pretty, clean stream with such birds, uncommon or absent of late, as the rose-breasted grosbeak, indigo bunting, and ruby-throated hummingbird.

Just before leaving the roadway I made a rest stop and while reviewing my trail notes inadvertently brushed away a bee. It stung me before buzzing off. This was the start of an unpleasant evening with my right hand gradually puffing up for several hours. I immediately took an antihistamine pill and a salt tablet and after dinner a couple of aspirins. It wasn't until my entire hand had blown up, except for the fingers, that the swelling finally stabilized.

I wasn't alone at the Glastenbury Shelter. Some 20 Boy Scouts were camped there already. Most of them were in tents though, so I found room inside the shelter.

JULY 23. My overriding concern was my hand—the swelling reached into my knuckles and a couple of inches into my wrist. It was not especially painful, but it was a constant low-grade irritation.

Because of the haze, there was nothing to be seen from the Glastenbury Fire Tower. The trail then descended, with a few ups and downs, to Caughnawaga Shelter where I stopped for lunch and a sunbath. I couldn't find the new shelter that was supposed to be nearby. The next stretch had much more climbing than I had expected; it was quite rocky, and often overgrown. Passing a beaver pond it was buggy as well. The common wood sorrel, whose fine-lined petals are reminiscent of spring beauties, added a colorful touch to the scene.

The Story Spring Shelter was the first Forest Service lean-to I had seen since the similar ones in Virginia. It was sturdy, clean, attractively located, and with an elevated wooden sleeping platform; I wished all of the shelters came up to this standard. A couple of lovesick kids from Missouri, on their way from Pinkham to Greylock, told me of a relocation around Moose Mountain in New Hampshire. It should make the route easier, which would be a good thing because my schedule called for a hard day in that section.

Though it was already 7:00 P.M. when I arrived at placid Stratton Pond, there was still time for a dip in the brisk waters before dinner. It was a popular place; though I had Willis Ross Camp to myself, both lean-tos were occupied and there were a couple of parties in tents. I was accustomed to the hippies bearing big bottles of red wine, but this was the first time I had met one with a violin. I encouraged him to fiddle away at the setting sun as I recorded his silhouette and the still waters on film.

JULY 24. It was too bad there was such a haze. The beauty of both Stratton Pond and Bourn Pond was obscured. Later in the day there was still nothing to be seen from the Prospect Rock Overlook. The trail was rough in spots and occasionally a bit mucky, but there was very little climbing.   Shortly after checking in to the Kandahar on Vermont Highway 11, I was joined by three other hikers who had been gradually closing the gap behind me. One of them was Brian Winchester of Miami, who started at Springer on April 28; with him were the King brothers, Roger and Donald, who had been keeping the same pace since they started in the Shenandoah.

When I was in Bennington I learned that Brooke's dad was going to be attending the Orvis fly-casting school that weekend in Manchester. We made arrangements to get together. Along with some of his friends, one of whom loaned me a jacket for dinner, we went out to a fancy place. What a change of pace! Paté, onion soup, duckling Montmorency (with black cherries), and profiteroles–not exactly trail fare. Brooke had driven my car back to Philadelphia after he left the trail in Georgia, and apparently it was still in good shape.

JULY 25. Back on the Appalachian Trail there was the long ascent of Bromley Mountain. A handful of people had taken the chair lift to the summit, but the threat of rain made it a poor day for sight-seeing. The trail both up and down Bromley passed through heavily overgrown areas. Wearing my track shorts, my legs were often wet, but that was probably less uncomfortable than soaked trousers. Fortunately the brush wasn't thorny.

Shortly after the steep climb of Styles Peak, I met a strong young long-haired hiker, Steve Gorman, now on his forty-third day from Katahdin to Georgia. We compared notes for a few minutes before going on our way.

The narrow rocky ridgeline of Baker Peak should afford a splendid view across the deep valley to the west and along the main ridge north to Killington, but because of the haze you could barely see the massive hulk of Dorset Peak less than ten miles away.

There had been sapsuckers and redstarts of late. A female ruffed grouse with chicks, a winter wren, and on the top of Bromley about five chimney swifts were among the interesting bird observations. I was particularly happy to hear, though I didn't see, the blackpoll warbler. The spruce forests of Vermont are about its southern breeding limit; its soft song of repeated notes on the same pitch, with a crescendo followed by a diminuendo, can hardly be confused. What had happened to the towhees? All of a sudden they had disappeared. I hadn't seen or heard any at all during the last three days.

This was not a peaceful evening in the wilderness, as the Lost Pond Shelter was overrun with over 20 Boy Scouts and a half-dozen vulgar loud-mouthed leaders from Connecticut. Fortunately, they went to sleep at a sensible hour.

JULY 26. I was up early for one of the last 14+ mile days, though it turned out that I made such good time that the early rising wasn't necessary. It was pleasant going, especially the climb along the banks of Little Branch. Here, at one pool in the pretty stream, its rocky ledges covered by verdant moss, I watched a young man hook a small brook trout—too bad it got away.

Continuing beneath the high canopy, the trail soon reached Little Rock Pond. I didn't circle the water to reach the famous shelter on an islet, which many hikers feel is the most beautiful camp on the entire Appalachian Trail. Instead I stopped for lunch at the Lula Tye Shelter on the Appalachian Trail side of the pond. Though it was still hazy, the air was an ideal 79°F. and I plunged in for a good swim. The water was warm and clear enough to see my toes perfectly at a four-foot depth.

It wouldn't do to eat the fruits of the woods around here indiscriminately, for that showy golden mushroom with the scaly top was the toxic fly amanita, and the inviting blue berries clustered on a stalk above the large leaves of a lily are clintonia, also reputedly poisonous.

Aside from the mosquitoes on White Rocks Mountain, there was nothing else noteworthy before Sunnyside Camp. It was a well-built, new cabin with a good spring nearby, but the setting had little to recommend it. There were two pairs of hikers here, but it was not crowded.

I couldn't remember seeing any deer in a long time—perhaps back in New Jersey. Toads were common; around Peru Peak the ground was covered with miniature brown amphibians (immature toads?). No rattlesnakes since Pennsylvania, but there had been quite a few garter snakes.

JULY 27. Last night was not a good night for sleeping. My cabinmates snored loudly. There were a few mosquitoes about. But mostly it was just too warm and humid. Then in the middle of the night the thundershowers began, continuing on and off until early morning.

Because this was to be the easiest day in weeks I was in no hurry to get started. I waited until the last shower had passed before heading north. In fact, by the time I had reached Clarendon Gorge there was enough clear sky to warrant a swim in the pool above the rapids. It was great.

Shortly afterwards, Roger and Donald King strode up and I walked on to the Clarendon Lodge with them. There, joined by Brian Winchester, we had lunch and talked about our experiences. Brian had some of the same problems in finding water and following the route that I had had. He was doing the trail without guidebooks, because of their expense, and seemed to take every day as it came. He didn't seem to be aware that the Appalachian Trail crossed the Kennebec River. What was he going to do when he got there? For that matter what was I going to do? Brian praised the fine art of cadging food from campers, an art that every through hiker learns and practices, though perhaps not with his skill.

Along the way to the Governor Clement Shelter, I stopped for some raspberries, which had been ripe and tasty the past few days. My rations were low and supper consisted of three packages of jerky and two packages of freeze-dried peas, plus two Pop-Tarts and a little crispbread and peanut butter. There was plenty of crispbread, but I had to save peanut butter for the next day's lunch. Not as skilled as Brian, all I managed to scrounge from the other campers was a bit of spice cake and some marshmallows.

JULY 28. The wire bunks and cooler weather made for a good night's sleep. I made a leisurely start and a slow and steady walk up to the new Tamarack Shelter. While I was having lunch, high in the conifer forest, a dark dusky butterfly with a broad white band arcing from the front to the rear edge of the wing flew by lazily and alighted on the fireplace. Just like birds, the butterflies have their own favored habitats and this one, the white admiral, breeds in these northern woods.

After dropping my pack at Cooper Lodge, I took the short side trail to the top of Killington where I found myself in the company of scads of tourists who had come up in the gondola. I can't blame them (though it would be better if people left the tops of mountains alone) for the view was simply stupendous. For a hundred miles there were mountains in every direction—the Adirondacks to the northwest, the Green Mountains south to Glastenbury and north to Mansfield, and even the White Mountains far off to the northeast. It was hard to break away.

Long Trail Lodge was a friendly place. They were holding mail and a box of supplies for me. It was a busy evening—shower and shave, a fine turkey dinner with fresh-baked banana bread, letter writing, and laundry.

There had been a few towhees again, but now the ovenbirds seemed to have vanished or at least stopped singing. There were plenty of juncos, white-throated sparrows, black-capped chickadees, and red-eyed vireos. Today had a redstart and a myrtle warbler to go along with the black-throated green and black-throated blue. I had a glimpse of a red-breasted nuthatch in its favored conifer haunts.

JULY 29. It took me all morning to get organized, so it was after lunch when I started. Soon I reached Maine Junction, where the Appalachian Trail heads east and leaves the Long Trail.

A downpour caught me at Kent Pond and for a few hundred yards I walked on a road with fields on one side and the pond on the other, while the rains pelted me and the winds stormed. There was some thunder around, but luckily not nearby. I was relieved to get to the comparative shelter of a canopy of trees.

It was wet going all the way to dreary Stony Brook Lean-to. The shelter had a dirt floor, but it was more like mud that night. Fortunately, there was a metal bed frame that I was able to use—how it got there I can't imagine. With dry clothes, and a dry bed to lie on, I was pretty comfortable. The beef stew was passably fair, though not really filling.

A college dropout, who looked like the Dutch Boy on the paint can, and his girl friend and her Irish setter were congenial company.

JULY 30. To my surprise it was 7:30 when I woke up after ten hours sleep. It meant a later start than I had intended. It had rained some more during the night and there was still a drizzle. The radio station in Burlington was predicting showers for the day. The upshot was a forced march, with no birding and few rests, and those brief. The binoculars and camera were both packed away.

I paused for lunch at the Gulf Lean-to, which would have been a fine place to spend the night. Its stream of clear cool water, bending around a graceful curve, was picturesque as well as refreshing.

The Dartmouth Outing Club section of the Appalachian Trail began at Vermont Highway 12. I headed up the bank, following the distinctive orange-and-black blazes. Ouch! The single-strand wire fence that I crossed was electrified and gave me a nasty shock. No warning signs around anywhere. That was no way for DOC to welcome strangers.

My destination was a spot a mile past Barnard Brook Road. It was described in the guidebook as a good campsite. The guide didn't mention water, so I filled my canteen and poured a couple of quarts into my flexible water bag. Right after that, though, I came to a little clearing with a locked shack and a porch covered by a tin roof. Though a half-mile or so short of my destination, it seemed too good to pass up. So I set up camp and had dinner.

JULY 31. The rain didn't come until 5 A.M. and by then I had slept almost eight hours anyway. I headed over to the little porch and sat comfortably in my sleeping bag fixing breakfast.

Two or three miles farther along the trail I passed a farmhouse and as usual was barked at. I waved at a towheaded kid in the front window and the door opened and I was asked if I'd like to rest. I went in and joined the whole family, hikers themselves, for a great second breakfast with plenty of fresh-brewed coffee and toast with strawberry jam.

Back on the trail it began to rain. It rained hard without letup for three hours straight. Under these foul circumstances, I met yet another solo hiker headed south, bearded Peter Dunning from Dallas, a free-lance writer who was carrying a Pentax and a Leica and writing up his trip for national conservation magazines. Dunning started in Georgia in April and after reaching Rockfish Gap in June left the trail and traveled up to Katahdin to do the remainder from north to south. I couldn't see the logic, because now he had relatively little to look forward to; it was the anticipation of the White Mountains and Maine that kept me going.

The rain brought out red efts yesterday and today. Last night I observed a bat flying over the campsite in the twilight. There was much that I couldn't identify—but among the flowers were bee balm and black-eyed susans, and one of the mushrooms seemed to be the sheathed amanitopsis.

A visit to the general store in West Hartford gave me a chance to pick up some supplies, including a needed bottle of Kaopectate.

The weather for the rest of the day was much better. I spent the night at the Happy Hill Cabin, which was unlocked, and occupied by six boys from a summer camp who were spending a week on the Appalachian Trail.

AUGUST 1 (SUNDAY). At 2 A.M. we were awakened by the racket of trail bikes and much shouting of joy for having arrived at a difficult destination. It was three kids on two cycles and—to give the devil his due—when they found us sleeping in the cabin they rode off into the night and didn't bother us any more.

Even though it was Sunday, the supermarket in Norwich was open, so I stocked up with more food and bought a new visored cap. Then on to Hanover, New Hampshire, the next-to-last state, where I washed my clothes at the laundromat. I weighed my pack and found it to be a staggering 45 pounds. Though that included nearly 10 pounds of food and water, it was still too heavy a load. Right in the middle of town, a nighthawk and a flight of chimney swifts were busily hunting insects overhead.

A relocation of the trail east of Hanover had added a series of uninteresting ups and downs that were an annoyance in the 86°F. weather; the old way, along the road, would have been shorter and easier. Eventually after passing through a bothersome buggy section, I reached my destination, the DOC Harris Cabin. It was a mansion, with a large fireplace, several tables in the middle, and a corner filled with mattresses. There was no one else around and I made myself at home, cooking up a big batch of spaghetti before turning in.

AUGUST 2. More poor weather. It was raining as I got up and from time to time during the day there was a little drizzle or sprinkle, but no cloudbursts.

The bugs continued to be a problem. The deerflies were back, and I squooshed large numbers of them. But one that I swatted turned out to be a yellow jacket that stung me on the chin. I had a Benzedrine pill that one of Brooke's dad's sympathetic friends, herself allergic, had given me a week ago and I immediately swallowed it. At the same time I fished out my metal mirror and tweezers and made a stab at finding the stinger. In any event, there was almost no more swelling and no more pain.

Although the relocation had shortened the trail a bit, there was still as much climbing as ever. The modest rise along the flank of Moose Mountain, the climb up to Holts Ledges and on through the Dartmouth ski slopes, and the ascent of Smarts Mountain add up to 3,900 feet of climb—more than any day since the Roan in North Carolina. Yet, perhaps because of the Benzedrine pill, I made good time even on the slanting wet bedrock of Smarts and covered about 14 miles in less than nine hours.

The shelter was a small log affair with a recently installed floor. On a clear day, the unobstructed view to the south must be very worthwhile, but that day it was so misty that I got only a brief glimpse of the distant hills through breaks in the clouds. The shelter was still very welcome, as it had become blustery. The smell of rain was in the air.

I shared the lean-to with a lone hiker, a young high school student just setting out for a couple of weeks of adventure on the Appalachian Trail. The poor kid wasn't able to keep his dinner down. I was not surprised because I'd found some of the trail packets pretty unsettling myself. The freeze-dried dishes I'd been making might not be fit for a gourmet, but at least they went down and stayed down.

We enjoyed a visit from the fire warden. He manned the tower on Smarts during the summer and then goofed off for the rest of the year, enjoying himself with such escapades as a two-week ascent of El Capitan. It sounded like a pretty good routine.

AUGUST 3. Again it rained, starting about 1:00 A.M. and continuing for the rest of the night. The only way to keep dry was by hugging the rear wall of the shelter as the wind blew the raindrops deep into the lean-to.

The hike down Smarts Mountain in the mist wasn't much of a problem, but then it started to rain again. I kept going, though I took advantage of an abandoned barn at Quinttown and the DOC Mt. Cube Lean-to for rest stops.

The summit of Mt. Cube consisted of sloping and slippery rock ledges. While traversing this mile-long stretch, the heavens opened up and it wasn't a good place to be. A bit farther on there was a primitive emergency shelter where I took refuge. Figuring on being able to dry my clothes in the evening, I pulled a dry T-shirt and my heavy woolen shirt out of the pack and managed to get reasonably comfortable in them before moving on again. The descent, over steep and wet rock, was treacherous. It took extreme caution. A handline that had been placed at one particularly bad point was a welcome aid.

It was a relief to reach the highway. Though there was more light rain, the problem for the rest of the day was primarily mosquitoes and deerflies. Wouldn't they ever go away?

Chick Soloway, the director of Camp Walt Whitman, and his wife Ann put me up for the night. One of my friends from Pittsburgh had been one of their counselors for several years and I had long been looking forward to this stopover. I enjoyed having a *warm* shower, some real food, a chance to dry my clothes, an opportunity to listen to the thrushes' songs on the phonograph (I wanted to make sure that it was the hermit thrush song that I'd been hearing so often), and some pleasant conversation in a friendly atmosphere.

AUGUST 4. After breakfast, Chick urged me to take any supplies I might need—so I picked up some peanut butter, a loaf of bread, raisins, and packages of broth. Best of all, the campcraft counselor, Pat, gave me Appalachian Mountain Club maps of the area (much better than the maps in the Appalachian Trail guidebook) and then offered to take my pack (with just the slightest hint on my part) around to Great Bear Cabin in his car.

Despite a late start, I made good progress during the day because I was traveling very light—not even a canteen or guidebook, although I did take my wind parka and poncho.

The rattle of kingfishers disturbed the wilderness silence of Wachipauka Pond. As a duck, probably a black duck, flushed near the shore and flew off to the far side of the water, an osprey silently rose from a dead snag, wheeled about close enough for me to see the dark line on the side of its head with my bare eyes, and quietly disappeared.

After helping myself to generous portions of raspberries and black-berries along an abandoned railroad right of way, I soon reached the post office in Glencliff, where several items were waiting for me—including long johns and a warm jacket as well as food.

From near Glencliff the climb was continuous from 900 feet eleva-tion to 4,800 feet, probably the longest steady climb so far on the whole trip. My pace was good—from Great Bear (where I picked up my pack) at 1,700 feet to the cabin at 4,800 feet in about 3.25 hours, with a couple of rest stops along the way. In only a few places was there any rock, so not much exertion was needed.

I was happy to have the new warm clothes to put on for the last mile on the ridgetop of Moosilauke, much of it above tree line. It wasn't especially cold, but the wind was very strong. The cairns were easy to follow, although it was misty. The two-room DOC cabin, painted with brilliant orange stripes, was a welcome sight and a snug refuge.

The howling wind and the bleak outlook were awesome. It sug-gested what the White Mountains might be like. I guessed there would be more people around the other peaks; my only company that night was a friendly snowshoe rabbit.

AUGUST 5. My advance planning led me astray; I had thought this would be an easy day and so made no attempt to get an early start. Clouds were wafting over Moosilauke and I spent quite a while on the summit among the ruins of the old hotel, taking an occasional picture when the sky opened.

I had no idea just how tough the Beaver Brook Trail was going to be. Slabbing around Mt. Blue was a pain of boulder-hopping. Then there was a long descent to 1,850 feet with the drop concen-trated in about two miles of very steep going on eroded footway, rocks, and exposed roots. Every step had to be taken with care and even so I fell a couple of times. It took nearly 3.5 hours to go about 3.5 miles downhill. Along the way I met a number of hikers—a couple out for the day, a group of Girl Scouts, two ladies doing the entire Appalachian Trail in sections (last year Maine, this year the rest of New England), and John Seymour. John was the first prospective end-to-ender I'd met who was my senior. He used a big walking stick (I didn't—it's impossible if you're carrying binocu-lars around your neck). He also carried a heavy pack. He had started walking at Cape Cod, hiked all the way up to Katahdin, and from there he had been following the Appalachian Trail at a clip of 100 miles a week.

After a detour to the Lost River Gorge—for a hamburger, fries, milk shake, cake, and ice cream—I realized I would have to push. There was considerably more climbing than I had anticipated, probably because the present route was a relocation not shown on the USGS quadrangles. The recent rains had left some stretches very quagmiry.

Mt. Wolf didn't have much to commend it except the name. It was a wide plateau on top, with bumps glorified as the South and East Peaks.

It was becoming dark when I finally reached the Eliza Brook Shelter at 7:45. It was a clean log affair with a good raised floor for sleeping. There was a rushing stream just outside and a full moon beamed directly into the lean-to. The Apollo 14 astronauts were out there, too, heading home for splashdown on Saturday. To my surprise there was no one else at the shelter; the Kings had signed in the night before.

AUGUST 6. Not so many miles, but they were tough ones—5,000 feet of climbing, probably more than on any other day on the whole 2,000-mile trip. I'm glad I got a fairly early start (8:30), but even so I was always rushing, with a shortened lunch hour and brief rests and walking as fast as I safely could.

The climb up South Kinsman was the hardest section, with several steep pitches on slab rock which, fortunately, was dry. Along the way the trail followed along the lovely cascades and pools of Eliza Brook and then passed Harrington Pond where I was disappointed not to find any waterfowl.

Despite the haze, I enjoyed the views of Moosilauke and the Franconia Ridge from the summit of South Kinsman. After lunch at Kinsman Junction, the descent was steep. At one point there was a welcome ladder. Slabbing the Cannon Balls was a real bother because there were some unexpected ups and downs and more boulders, roots, and mucky spots. I hadn't stopped to take off my Duofold top, so by the time I reached the Lonesome Lake AMC Hut I was soaked.

Past the stream of cars on the highway through Franconia Notch, then a long, long climb up to Liberty Spring. Starting at 4:30 and already tired, it was tough to climb another 2,500 feet. However, though steep, the trail had a good dirt base and didn't require using hands and worrying about balance as on Kinsman. When I arrived at a little past seven all of the tent platforms were taken, but the AMC resident found a spot where I was able to pitch my Pioneer and have dinner by the light of the setting sun.

AUGUST 7. This hiking above tree line, with views of range after range of distant peaks, was what I'd walked almost 2,000 miles to see. And the weather had held for me to enjoy it.

The skies were overcast in the morning. When I left the shelter of the forest on Little Haystack, racing clouds enveloped me and cloaked the trail in mist. Being Saturday, there were lots of hikers, some just wearing shorts and obviously very chilly. By the time I had crossed Mt. Lincoln to reach Mt. Lafayette, the clouds were lifting and I could relax and enjoy my lunch in comfort with a view from my mile-high perch. It was easy to recognize where I'd been; I could see Moosilauke, Mt. Wolf, Kinsman, and the Franconia Ridge itself. Some features, like Franconia Notch, were unique and unmistakable. The terrain to the northeast was still unfamiliar, though, and I couldn't identify the peaks in the Presidentials.

The remainder of the day's hike was tough, just about all of it on a terrible rock-strewn footway, with especially steep descents from both Lafayette and Garfield. The AMC didn't use blazes and sometimes you just had to have faith that you were going the right way.

There were few birds: mostly juncos and an occasional blue jay, golden-crowned kinglet, black-capped chickadee, and white-throated sparrow. In the col before Garfield I stumbled onto a grouse chick. The nearby hen with a red stripe above the eye and heavily barred breast was a spruce grouse, a new bird for my life list.

My rushing got me to Galehead in time for a feast of roast pork, corn, mashed potatoes, salad, fresh-baked bread, wonderful chocolate-chip cookies, and even some beer that the hut boys had carried up. One of the other guests was kind enough to give me three good cigars, enough to hold me awhile.

AUGUST 8. Sleeping in the dormitory was uncomfortable both because of the snoring and the heat. Around midnight I took my bag out to the porch where it was cooler and finally got some rest. Setting out in the morning after a filling French toast breakfast, I ran into another end-to-end hiker, the last of a group of four who had started out a month ago at Katahdin. I wondered whether he would stick it out by himself.

The vista from South Twin was magnificent, and for once the skies were sparkling clear. To the south there were peaks of all sizes and shapes as far as the eye could see, interrupted only occasionally by a deep glacial notch, with the impressive mass of Mt. Carrigain especially prominent. To the west Franconia Ridge walked the skyline, with the distant blue summit of Moosilauke peeking up proudly behind it. Now, finally, there were the Presidentials to the northeast, the bare rounded heights of Mt. Washington inviting me to hurry over.

My lunch stop on Guyot was shortened when the bumblebees became too intimate. Having been stung twice, I had developed a bit of a phobia.

The trail, generally in better shape the rest of the day, had more rewards—especially the grand overlook above Zealand Notch. There are some problems though; it was a bit difficult finding the way down to the Zealand Falls Hut, and the distance to the Ethan Pond Shelter seemed so much greater than indicated by the guidebook that for a time I worried that I might have passed it.

The lean-to was filled, but the occupants invited me to join them for their beef stew dinner. It was a timely treat; otherwise I would have had to make do with some bouillon, a bit of jerky, peanut butter sandwiches, cereal, and a single package of freeze-dried peas.

Again there were spruce grouse; also winter wrens and a black-and-white warbler. From here on, I was going to have to be careful with my chickadees because near Ethan Pond I found not only black-capped, but the more northern boreal as well. Except for the cap, they are quite similar by sight, but the chickadee chatter of the boreal has rather a raspy flavor.

AUGUST 9. Ethan Pond was in a lovely setting, with a backdrop of Whitewall Mountain, Zealand Ridge, and South Twin Mountain progressively farther off.

Descending to Crawford Notch I passed a couple of members of an AMC trail crew carrying loads in excess of 100 pounds high on their backs on sturdy wood frames. They were on their way to Ethan Pond to build tent platforms. They guessed I might be traveling from Georgia to Maine, they said, because my Kelty pack had a frayed and worn look and I appeared "comfortable" with it.

I was becoming almost as adept as Winchester at getting food. In Crawford Notch I stopped for lunch by the bridge across the peaceful shaded Saco River. I got to talking with a group of kids from a camp in Massachusetts and wound up with a nourishing roast beef sandwich.

The upper parts of Mt. Webster and Mt. Jackson had considerable third-class rock-climbing, and the trail around Jackson had some mucky spots, so all in all it was pretty slow going. In fact it took nine hours to cover less than ten miles.

Despite the modern design, I thought Mizpah Spring Hut was quite an attractive place. The sleeping arrangements were much better than at Galehead, with only six to a room.

AUGUST 10. Hut living was pretty royal. I had a good night's sleep and a big breakfast of pancakes. The weather continued to be dry and comfortable.

It was a short and leisurely hike, with enough time even to stop and play yodels and other tunes on my recorder. The only misfortune was the haze that made good views impossible. For much of the day fog obscured the summit of Mt. Washington.

Most of the plants of the tundra were unfamiliar to me. In addition to the plentiful heaths, there were abundant cranberries and tiny blueberries to be tasted.

The weather forecast for the next day called for a 40 percent chance of afternoon thundershowers. It seemed to make sense to try to do a little more walking right then in order to decrease the risk of getting caught by bad weather. So instead of relaxing at Lakes-of-the-Clouds Hut, I left my pack and scrambled quickly along the manicured trail up Mt. Washington.

At the summit there were lots of people who had arrived by cog railway and car. I didn't stick around, except to buy some cigarettes and cigars at outrageous prices. I could barely make out the Carter Range to the east, and the summits of Jefferson, Adams, and Madison to the west, beyond the deep chasm of the Great Gulf. I'd have to come back as a tourist on a clear day. I arrived back at Lakes-of-the-Clouds, by way of a side trail, just in time for goulash.

Birds were quite scarce at these altitudes. The total for the day was seven juncos, five white-throated sparrows, two boreal chickadees, a female spruce grouse with two chicks, a Canada warbler, and a single raven soaring high on Mt. Washington.

AUGUST 11. The forecast was 70 per cent chance of thundershowers, but in the morning it just seemed foggy—no views, but not too threatening.

The first shelter was over four miles away—a windowless emergency quonset hut at Edmands Col. I hurried to get there and arrived in what seemed to be improving weather. There were a couple of parties of Pittsburghers having lunch and I stopped for a bite myself.

After 45 minutes, I started out again for the 2.5 miles to Madison

Hut. I had taken only a few steps when some drops of rain spotted my jacket. I figured that the weather might be bad all afternoon and that my best chance of reaching Madison lay in starting out right away and hurrying. Another party of five had left just ahead of me and I expected to be able to overtake them.

A couple of hundred yards from Edmands Col the rain intensified and I put on my poncho and chaps and pushed onward, hardly able to see one yellow-topped cairn from the last. The guidebook said that "On these heights dangerous winds and low temperatures are likely to occur with little warning at any season of the year." That was exactly what happened. Quickly the winds picked up and the rain turned to small hail. There was no lightning or thunder, so I headed on. Water collected in little rivulets and the lichen-covered stones were treacherous.

In a few minutes I began to hear thunder. It was comforting to catch up with the other group of hikers and I continued to ascend with them.

The next mile was quite exposed going up the flank of Mt. Adams. The storm got worse, with the lightning striking a mile or two away. The wind must have reached 50 miles per hour in gusts.

There were a number of hikers at Madison Hut when I arrived. They welcomed me with hot coffee. I had a good supply of dry apparel, but for trousers I had to use my long johns under track shorts, comfortable though perhaps not very elegant.

It was a lazy afternoon of talk with the other hikers. Among them was John Nutter, the AMC Director of Environmental Education, who had met Art Smith and Jim Rutter earlier in the year. While I was chatting with John about the stresses on the tundra resulting from the ever-increasing use (including increased Appalachian Trail use), a radio call came in with word that a girl had been hit by lightning on the far side of Edmands Col. John and two of the hut boys set out as a rescue party. They returned several hours later with a report that apparently the victim had been able to get off the mountain under her own steam.

Dinner wasn't much of a success because the hut boy carrying supplies had hurt himself and had to return to the valley. Because the weather had forced a camp group of 25 boys to turn back, the place was nearly empty. It was quiet enough to become acquainted with all the young staff members and the guests.

AUGUST 12. It was a foggy morning, with a strong biting wind. The idea of climbing an exposed summit in these conditions didn't appeal to me and I debated whether to bypass Mt. Madison completely by taking the slabbing Parapet Trail.

At breakfast John Nutter told of the rescue trip the day before. When they reached Edmands Col they had found two camp groups holed up there for the night. With incredible lack of foresight, one group had been hiking with just shorts and T-shirts. With the turn in the weather, they were frightfully exposed and one of the kids had developed a severe case of hypothermia (inability to maintain body temperature). The boy might have died, as many others have in these mountains, had it not been for another party at the quonset hut, this one under the leadership of a medical student who knew exactly what to do. Her group shared their food and clothing with the shivering boys, and one of her charges crawled into a sleeping bag with the very sick kid and warmed him up with his own body's heat until the patient was out of danger. John was as impressed by the superb leadership in the one case as by the appalling lack of qualifications in the other, and was going to communicate his observations to the respective camp directors.

I was apprehensive about climbing, but eventually wandered out. It turned out to be not so bad, with the cairns marking the way clearly at all times. The wind was strong, though hardly comparable to the blasts of yesterday's storm. The clouds lifted and I was able to look out at the Great Gulf and the lower slopes of Mt. Washington, at the Carter Range, and at the Mahoosucs (Maine at last!). The dark overcast provided a dramatic backdrop for photographs, but with occasional distant rumbles of thunder I was hardly in a mood for dallying; I wanted to reach the sanctuary of tree line far below.

Back in the woods it was mostly easy going, with time to poke along and study a bolete here, a hobblebush there. However, aside from kinglets and chickadees, there just didn't seem to be any birds.

The Pinkham Notch Camp was much more businesslike than the other huts—they wouldn't serve seconds on dessert. I picked up the supplies they were holding for me, including my Maine Appalachian Trail guidebook. In the evening I did my laundry, and with a shower before dinner, I was a new man.

AUGUST 13. The hut boys gave me a lift to Gorham after breakfast. Besides picking up a box of food and fuel, I had a haircut. The groceries I bought ran to $12.00 and weighed a ton.

Back at Pinkham I packed and left behind most of the food and some of my spare clothing. John Nutter drove into Gorham on

Sundays and he generously volunteered to meet me on the trail as I passed by. For a couple of days I would be traveling light.

The first mile, especially the view of Mt. Washington behind the reflecting waters of Lost Pond, was very nice. The ascent to the top of the Wildcat gondola lift was something else again—steep almost all the way and with a couple of pitches of interesting rock-climbing. Along with the tourists, I stopped for a hot dog, coffee, and a jelly doughnut, and then asked for a glass of water. They wouldn't give me any. I guess you could be dying of thirst and they'd only serve you if you shelled out the silver.

The trail finally reached the escarpment above Carter Notch and then descended steeply to the hut. With only about 20 guests, it made for a social evening.

AUGUST 14. From my experience in the White Mountains I knew this was going to be a long day, so I got a fast start around 8:00 after filling up on bacon, eggs, and muffins. I needed to cover nearly 13 miles, with some 3,800 feet of climbing, so I kept up a steady pace. After walking an hour or so, I would stop for a cigarette break, usually where I could enjoy the view or get some water.

There continued to be many hikers around, especially on the Carter–Moriah Trail. I passed one guy who had climbed several miles in his bare feet!

There should have been excellent vistas from several peaks, especially the view of Mt. Washington from Carter Dome, but the haze eliminated most of the contrast and I gave up on picture taking.

Despite the fact that it was Saturday, there was only one other hiker at the Rattle River Shelter (a good Forest Service one) when I arrived at around 7:00 P.M. A particularly bold mouse was a permanent resident—he tried to nibble some chocolate from a candy bar while I shouted at him from less than ten feet away.

The Rattle River, just below the lean-to, had scoured a channel through a bed of rounded rocks and after sliding along a smooth gentle slope it slipped into a lovely five-foot deep pool. I took an icy but refreshing bath before fixing my supper of Lipton beef stroganoff followed by the inevitable Pop-Tarts. With the days becoming shorter, it was getting dark as I lit my cigar and did the dishes.

While having lunch on Middle Carter, I was rewarded by the appearance of a female accipiter—from its size and habitat almost certainly a goshawk—which flew nearly directly overhead and off to the north, disappearing into the thick forest on the next ridge.

The variety of birds was better than it had been lately, with black-throated green warbler, blackpoll warbler, winter wren, white-throated sparrow, raven, redstart, boreal chickadee, junco, wood pewee, and hairy woodpecker.

AUGUST 15. The trail down to U.S. Route 2 was delightful and took no time at all. A little beyond, past the bridge over the Androscoggin River (lots of barn swallows here), John Nutter drove up with the 15 pounds of food and clothing.

The Peabody Brook Trail started off gently through handsome forests of hemlock, white oak, and beech, but then ascended at a pretty good clip all the way to Dream Lake.

The Gentian Pond Shelter wasn't the best—a dirt floor covered with hemlock needles, with cracks between the logs in the walls. On a clear day the view of the Moriahs beyond the Androscoggin Valley would be quite appealing.

I was joined by two counselors and three campers from Camp Pemigewasset. They offered me an "extra" steak they had packed in. Despite my feeble demurrer, they insisted and I accepted their hospitality. I couldn't remember my last steak—but this one, cooked over a wood fire and tender and full of juices, was surely the best.

Besides several of yesterday's birds, there were blue jay, Canada warbler, myrtle warbler, crow, Swainson's thrush (in the valley), black-capped chickadee, and catbird.

AUGUST 16. Georgia to Maine accomplished! But what a greeting Maine gives the hiker—the Mahoosucs are rough!

The first mountain of the day, Mt. Success, was not especially steep, though it did involve nearly 2,000 feet of climbing. From the cool and breezy summit, there was a fine view back to the Carters and Presidentials. A couple of miles beyond, on a nondescript section of trail, I reached the Maine state line and a worn Maine Appalachian Trail Club sign which said it was 279 miles to Katahdin.

I had to detour to the Carlo Col Shelter, a quarter mile off the trail, to fill my canteen. This was the only running water of the day. Mt. Carlo wasn't too bad, but after that the fun really began. Goose Eye was a real killer, with numerous steep rock pitches—on some of them a belay might be welcome. To compound the difficulty, there were no blazes. Once I needlessly climbed a tough pitch. Another time I failed to see the rocky route and ended up on a path that had been hacked through by other hikers—it was obviously not the Appalachian Trail. For a couple of minutes I was worried about losing my way.

Goose Eye's problems weren't limited to the rocky sections of the first two of its three peaks. In the relatively flat portions the trail was mucky and I sank to my ankles. Fortunately, I had set out to do less than ten miles, so I was able to make camp at a one-mile-per-hour pace despite the difficulties.

Full Goose Shelter was a new Forest Service lean-to that would sleep a small army. Though I had the shelter to myself, I had met other hikers during the day. Among them were a couple of strong brothers, laden with 50-pound packs, who had covered all of Maine in only 18 days and were hoping to make Springer about November 1.

The large numbers of spruce grouse were noteworthy, as were the hermit thrush and a red-breasted nuthatch on Mt. Carlo.

AUGUST 17. Mile for mile, this was probably my hardest day's hike on the Appalachian Trail. It started with a steep climb of Fulling Mill Mountain, and then a steeper descent into the Mahoosuc Notch.

Someone had aptly written "Hellhole" on the AMC sign pointing to the notch. I had heard that it was rough, but didn't have a clear picture of what was involved. The notch was hemmed in by the very sheer rock cliffs of Mahoosuc and Fulling Mill mountains. In the narrow ravine was a maze of boulders. For a mile the trail wandered in and out among them. There was no single spot that was excessively difficult, but put together it was taxing. There were chimneys, laybacks, and crevasse jumps. Four times it was necessary to remove my pack and drag it through a tight spot where the route passed under the rocks. Beneath some of the especially well-shaded boulders, there was still solid ice in the middle of August.

After a pause for lunch beside a little pond near the bottom of the notch, it was again steep up to Mahoosuc Arm. Finally reaching the top after several stretches of solid rock with good friction climbing, there were good, though hazy, views back to Mt. Washington, the Carters, and Goose Eye.

Speck Pond, the highest body of water in Maine, is beautiful. I had to push on, though, with a final ascent over some barren and windy sections to the abandoned fire tower at the summit of Old Speck. Going down was tough, too, especially when the trail dropped 2,700 feet in 1.7 miles. The first half-mile was especially bad. Every step had to be planned and executed carefully from one rock to the

Photo by Robert Winslow

Hiker coming up Katahdin. Lakes can be seen far below.

Photo by Garnett W. Martin

Autumn colors near Yoke Ponds, Maine.

next. From the old warden's cabin it was much easier and I completed the entire descent in 1.5 hours, pretty fair time I think.

The Grafton Notch Lean-to, close to the highway, was filled, but it seemed like a good night to sleep out under the stars anyway.

AUGUST 18. I got up early and started on the trail by 7:30. Though Baldpate wasn't as high as Old Speck, it was steep and had three distinct rises. The true summit, the East Peak, was a great rounded block of rock which the guidebook warned should be climbed with extreme care. It turned out, though, to be ideal for friction climbing —no need to use hands at all. It was a good place for lunch: for views there were several lakes to the north, Elephant Mountain to the east behind the radio dome and radio telescopes of Andover, and Goose Eye and Old Speck to the south and west.

Fryé Brook, near the base of the mountain, was one of the outstanding spots on the entire Appalachian Trail for me. The waters had carved a deep flume with absolutely vertical walls about 25 feet apart and some 40 feet deep, the brook below spilling abruptly over angular ledges and cascading through a series of pools. Downstream the forceful current shot freely off the edge of a cliff and arched gracefully down to a deep pool, 50 feet below, where four young boys frolicked in the foam. I couldn't resist the opportunity to take a dip in one of the pools nearer the lean-to—my bonus for getting an early start.

Later on, I found beauty and solitude at Surplus Pond—the rattle of the kingfisher, the gradual fall of the evening sun behind a notch in the hills to the west.

My supplies from Gorham were working out just about right—I sure ate a lot. I'd had to ration Pop-Tarts a little bit, sometimes one instead of two at a meal, and I found I wanted about 4 oz. instead of 3 oz. of Familia for breakfast. Lunch included at least 4 oz. of peanut butter as well as jerky and a Pop-Tart. Gorp went at the rate of 3 to 4 oz. per day. All in all it amounted to about 4,000 calories.

Still headed north with the birds, I'd finally reached the land of the ruby-crowned kinglet. The ones observed on the climb of Baldpate definitely lacked the golden-crowned's conspicuous head patch. Others for the day included junco, white-throated sparrow, boreal chickadee, black-throated blue warbler, winter wren, kingfisher, and a single raven soaring on the high mountain.

AUGUST 19. Much of the walk during the morning passed through logged areas, now overgrown with shrubs and grasses to a height of five or six feet. When this growth was covered with dew, it was impossible to avoid the discomfort of getting wet. However, the birds found such habitats attractive, so maybe I shouldn't be too critical.

In a more wooded section near Mountain Brook I came across a porcupine on the trail. Upon my approach, it immediately headed for a nearby tree and started a slow painful climb up to safety, quills spreading fearsomely as a token of defense. Though the lighting was poor in the deep woods, I ventured close enough to snap a picture before continuing on my way. Nearby I became aware of an unfamiliar fern with chest-high dark green fronds, tapered at both ends that fit perfectly my Golden Nature Guide's description of the ostrich fern.

While I was having lunch at the Squirrel Rock Lean-to, I was joined by Harry Latimer. He had been stalled for several days in the White Mountains by that dreary rainy period of a couple of weeks ago. Apparently I had passed him while he was off the trail in Gorham. It was incredible that he had started out to do over 1,000 miles of the Appalachian Trail without ever having done any backpacking at all beforehand. He had read everything on the subject he could get his hands on, though, and had only one real problem—he had gone through three or four pairs of boots. We spent about an hour comparing notes and gossiping about the friends we'd made on the trip. He was big on peanut butter—carried about three pounds of it! He also had big sacks of Lipton dinners, with all of the ingredients dumped in together.

Harry moved faster than I did, so I told him to go ahead while I poked along to study a bird, or to take a picture of a fruiting hobblebush laden with red berries, or whatever.

Upon reaching the road I walked a couple of miles to Sunset Camps where I had a reservation. Somewhat on the run-down side, the camps had a lovely setting on Lower Richardson Lake, and the owners were very friendly. I wasn't able to call home, as there was no phone, but they were holding mail and supplies for me.

Solitary vireos seen in the morning were the first observed in a long time. At Squirrel Rock there was a hummingbird, always a welcome visitor.

AUGUST 20. Mr. Gammon drove me back to the trail, stopping along the way at the South Arm Campground store where I picked up some bread, doughnuts, film, batteries, cigarettes, and cigars.

Along the climb of Elephant Mountain, a small cluster of evening grosbeaks feeding on wild cherries attracted my attention. It wasn't the only new species: the camp robber, the gray jay, was waiting for me at the next lean-to.

In the afternoon the trail descended over the four separate summits of Bemis Mountain—the third being quite open. There should have been fine views of the Rangeley Lakes to the north, but the dense haze restricted visibility to barely five miles.

When I reached Bemis Stream it was after 6:00, but there didn't seem to be any particularly good campsite there. Farther on, the trail was often mucky and never level. I finally found a fairly flat spot a little way before reaching Maine Highway 17, within easy reach of the water of Four Ponds Stream, and set up the tent. I was glad to have a Tea Kettle chicken with rice because it meant that dinner could be prepared quickly—just boil and add water— and there would be no dishes to wash.

I ran into a couple on the trail, out for a day hike, who recognized me from an earlier meeting near the Kutz Camp almost two months before. We chatted away like old friends and they promised to call my parents and assure them that I was on schedule.

AUGUST 21. It was good to find that I could still make miles when the trail was easy enough. And for a change there were no mountains to climb, no boulders to hop.

Aside from a glimpse of what seemed to be a pine warbler, the walk to pristine Sabbath Day Pond was uneventful. Fifty yards from shore, a loon swam away, disappearing for long dives and popping up again at unexpected places. A robin, regular but not common lately, appeared in the woods nearby.

A five-mile walk along a fire road, with a steady gradual descent, must be about the easiest stretch on the entire Appalachian Trail. It took me only about an hour and a half.

The afternoon hike circled a large beaver pond with inundated dead trees. No wood ducks, though there were a kingfisher, a downy woodpecker, and some cedar waxwings. The waxwings were at the top of the bare snags, perhaps after some insects to go with their diet of berries. It was a rather surprising location for them, I thought.

The weather was kind, with the rain holding off until after I arrived at the Piazza Rock Lean-to. As it was Saturday, I was surprised to find only one other hiker, a University of Massachusetts student named Mike Combs. Mike had just started that day and

was headed for Katahdin. At these Maine lean-tos you were supposed to sleep on a platform made of logs. I was glad I had a foam
rubber pad.

There was a chipmunk in the morning at the Piazza Rock Lean-to.
I had seen very few of them lately, though there were lots of red
squirrels. The snake that I'd seen a few times was most likely the
northern brown snake—dark brown above, lighter below, and with
some dark chocolate-colored or black spots on the upper surface.

AUGUST 22. Piazza Rock was worth a visit. It was a huge flat-topped
boulder about 50 feet long and with a trapezoidal cross section of
400 square feet. It jutted out, apparently unsuspended, like a grey
corvette with a deep keel.

There were good views from the extensive heaths above timberline on Saddleback. Ahead were the prominent summits of Sugarloaf, Spaulding, and Abraham. To the southwest the gap between
Blue and Elephant mountains was clearly visible, and I thought I
could see Baldpate fuzzily through the haze. The expanses of Rangeley and Mooselookmeguntic (what a name!) lakes were far below,
to the northwest.

Detouring to the spring on Saddleback I found a flicker. More
interesting was a bird some 100 yards off that caught my eye. It
had the bold head markings, red tail, and hovering behavior of a
sparrow hawk. I saw the same bird or others like it two more times.
There was also a pair of ravens soaring and croaking.

Blueberries were growing in profusion on the open summits. I
stopped several times to grab a handful.

After an afternoon of ups and downs, with bothersome deadfall
at places, I found Mike Combs at the Poplar Ridge Lean-to. The
weather repeated the performance of the day before. It was turning
grey as I hustled along and during dinner there were a couple of good
showers.

AUGUST 23. It rained on and off all night and our plans to get
up early came to naught. We lay in our bags watching the downpour and it was clear that we couldn't reach our original destination,
the Mt. Sugarloaf Lean-to.

After the rain tapered off, Mike and I hiked together on the descent to Orbeton Stream. With the wet rocks, it would have been
easy to slip and fall, but we took it slow and had no mishaps.

Because of the weather, there was no time for lunch—just some
gorp and jerky along the way. There were no views, of course, but

one interesting sight was beds of Indian pipes—70 in one clump. Pointing to the fly amanita, Mike referred to it as the "pizza mushroom"—a name I had never heard—because of its large round colorful cap.

Harry Latimer was waiting for us at the Spaulding Mountain Lean-to. He had holed up there all day instead of tackling Sugarloaf in the bad weather. There was a brief shower in the afternoon, and in the evening it was 42°F. and windy. Harry entertained us with anecdotes about the hikers he'd met. We snickered a bit about the tale of one fellow from Ohio who gave up, after the rocky going of the White Mountains got him down, caustically muttering that there was dirt on the ground where he came from.

AUGUST 24. I set out on the wet trail when the rain slowed up a bit. I had to reach Bigelow because I was out of food, except for some remnants of Ry-Krisp and peanut butter.

The bare summit of Sugarloaf was covered with clouds. With winds of 40 miles per hour or more, and the temperature at 40°F., it was chilly. However, with my wool shirt, polyester jacket, and wind parka (drenched from contact with the wet spruces and firs), I remained reasonably comfortable.

While pausing for lunch at the Sugarloaf gondola station, the overcast began to break up. The bold contours of the Bigelow Range across the valley were an inspiring sight.

My original plan was to pick up a box of supplies that had been left for me at the Bigelow gas station. It was too late to reach the next lean-to, though, so I decided to spend the night in Kingfield. For 70¢ I got a lift into town with the mail carrier and was able to get a room, shave, and shower at the old Herbert Hotel, and do my laundry.

A growing problem was the crossing of the Kennebec. For over a year I'd been trying to take care of this and thought I had lined up someone to ferry me across, only to learn recently that this gentleman was no longer available. At his suggestion, I called Mr. Harold Smith in Caratunk and Mr. Smith volunteered to come and meet me at a prearranged spot at 5 P.M. Saturday. So at least that worry seemed resolved.

AUGUST 25. Despite the climbing, some 3,600 feet, this was one of the very finest days. The skies were perfectly clear, the temperature around 60°F., few bugs, interesting birds, and rewarding views.

The mail carrier dropped me off on his morning run. I dawdled along looking at one thing and another—a bolete here, the sensitive fern there, and the forest of maples, beech, birch, and both the quaking and large-toothed aspen. An ovenbird was perched in the young second growth, close enough to make out its orange crown clearly. It was the first one I'd seen in a long time; perhaps the bird's apparent scarcity was because they had stopped singing.

Stratton Brook Pond meandered about in a photogenic setting beneath the mountains. A great blue heron slowly flapped its black-edged wings and flew off to the cover of the rushes farther away. A female rose-breasted grosbeak landed at the tip of a spruce and clicked her characteristic metallic note. It seemed that there was a warbling vireo as well as red-eyes. Among the other birds of the day were myrtle, black-throated green, black-throated blue, and pine warblers, redstart, black-capped and boreal chickadees, blue and grey jays, white-throated sparrow, junco, winter wren, red-breasted nuthatch, golden-crowned kinglet, flicker, and hairy woodpecker.

A fearless grey jay had staked out The Horns Pond Lean-to as its territory. I put out some raisins and nuts a few feet away. The raisins vanished almost immediately and although the jay took only a few pecks at the nuts, it no doubt returned to finish them later. A comma butterfly, raggedy wings edged with black, fluttered about without apparent purpose.

The panorama from South Horn was spectacular. With visibility of at least 70 miles, I picked out Old Speck to the west and might have seen White Cap, just before Katahdin, to the east. Sugarloaf and Saddleback were prominent to the south, and lakes to the north. Without the hordes of people I had encountered on Killington, or the chilling winds of Sugarloaf, it was a very special and precious spot and I was reluctant to leave it.

The view from the West Peak of Bigelow would have been comparable, except that it had begun to cloud up late in the day. I camped at the Avery Memorial Lean-to, along with three other hikers.

AUGUST 26. The fine eastern peak of Bigelow was a worthy monument to the long-time chairman of the Appalachian Trail Conference, Myron Avery. I read the inscription which recalled his diligence and leadership in making the trail a reality, and was grateful not only to him but to all the others who were inspired by his dreams.

It was a bit hazy, so I didn't stay long. After making a deep dip, the trail followed the long summit ridge of Little Bigelow—a rocky footway with lots of ups and downs. One section of the steep descent consists of about 500 feet of large boulders which can only be negotiated by climbing carefully from one to the next.

After skirting Flagstaff Lake, unattractive with its waters drawn down, I climbed over the berried ridge (white baneberries as well as raspberries) to the Jerome Brook Lean-to. The Bolducs, proprietors of Sugarloaf Ski Specialists, were waiting for me with great quantities of supplies. Outdoor people themselves, they thought nothing of driving all the way from Kingfield to meet hikers passing through at some remote road crossing.

I was not keen about the lean-to's split pole platform. There was an excellent register, though, with most of the familiar northbound and southbound names. Excerpts: "You can get lost on this stretch easier than you can in Boston"; "Started at Katahdin, never hiked before, planned on going all the way to Georgia. Boy, was I dumb!" Bruce Balderston, here on August 9, left a note for me: "You're almost there. Keep up the good work! I hope it doesn't rain on you the way it did on me. I got rain on seven of the first nine days."

AUGUST 27. At dawn I was awakened by a skunk which had been attracted by the gravy I had spilled from last night's steak pie dinner. Finished with that, he rummaged around beneath the sleeping platform. Climbing back on the low wall at the entrance of the lean-to, he paused with his white bushy tail pointed directly at me. I asked him softly to leave, and eventually he did.

I took a cabin at East Carry Pond Camps just before it began to rain. Clean sheets and the coziness of a good wood-burning stove were worth the $5.00. During the day I had recorded the wood pewee (for only the second time in Maine), brown creeper, solitary vireo, black-and-white warbler, and hermit thrush along with most of the regulars (no juncos, though). The real birding treat was still in store, a female goldeneye on the waters of East Carry Pond opposite the little boat landing.

AUGUST 28. This was a day when I very nearly just stayed put. And why not? The cabin at East Carry Pond was comfortable and warm. The weather was dreadful—rain for over 12 hours already, and the forecast was for it to continue for another 24. There was also the concern about being stranded on the west bank of the Kennebec River. What if the water was too rough for Mr. Smith, or what if he didn't show up? However, the alternatives seemed just as bad; not hiking would upset plans for the ferry and would set me back in my schedule.

I wanted to stop at the East Carry Pond Lean-to because the folks at the camps said there were a couple of hikers, of opposite genders, who had stopped for water yesterday before heading to the lean-to for the night. I wanted to tell these hikers about my ferry arrangements in case they were headed for the river.

It was a most inopportune moment when I walked around the edge of the shelter and came upon them. I don't know who was more surprised. It was clear that they had reached the goal of their hike and didn't need transportation across the Kennebec.

I headed on in the frequently heavy rain. There was no problem in following the blazes, but the footway was wet, and at one place it was a veritable stream bed.

After a detour along blue-blazed trails to enable me to cross Pierce Pond Stream on the dam, instead of by fording, I eventually found myself at the Kennebec. It was quite an impressive sight. No signs of life on either side, just a very choppy swift-flowing stream with vast numbers of six-foot logs floating down to the mills of Waterville and Augusta.

I crossed the outlet of Pierce Pond Stream with some difficulty and reached the area where Mr. Smith had instructed me to wait. I wrapped my bright orange plastic ground cloth around some bushes near the bank to mark the spot and then set up my tent for shelter from the rain. While changing into dry clothes I thought I heard voices and looked out to see some people taking a dip on the far side of the river. I crawled out and tried shouting to them, "Please tell Mr. Harold Smith in Caratunk that his canoe passenger is here." Before we could get farther, though, the rains started heavily again and I beat a retreat into the tent.

I soon heard a whistle and saw that the folks I had called to were back, this time with a canoe. They set out across the river and made it across against the current. They hadn't understood me, but suspected that I needed help, possibly as the result of capsizing a canoe. Grateful to them for coming to my aid, I rapidly loaded my pack and other gear and we shoved off. In midstream I asked if they had done much canoeing, and they said no, they hadn't! That wasn't too comforting as we were taking waves nearly broadside and running into and being run into by logs. We made it across safely, though, and I was happily over the long-feared Kennebec.

My new friends, vacationers from New Jersey, gave me a lift to Mr. Smith's. We arrived just as he was setting out after me. I spent the night at the home of the Smiths, hospitable folk, where I shared their traditional New England Saturday evening dinner of franks and beans and laid out my wet clothes to dry.

AUGUST 29. My plan was to resume hiking at the place where I had been ferried across, but Mr. Smith just about goosed me into wading the river "for sentimental reasons." We drove to the Appalachian Trail crossing and he cut me a stout pole. There was a good ford about 150 yards downstream; wading across was a snap with the water low. I couldn't believe the contrast from yesterday, for now the water was flat, with only a few logs drifting idly along.

Wearing my boots, it took only about ten minutes to reach the other side of the river, with the water hardly coming up to my knees. I was just as happy not to have my pack—especially since my camera, binoculars, and Accutron watch shouldn't get dunked. Once across, I walked the Appalachian Trail back to the point where I had left it yesterday and then returned to ford the river again to the east bank; now my 2,000-mile hike hadn't been interrupted even by a 200-yard stretch of water. Had it been any day but Sunday, I wouldn't have been able to cross because the high water to float the logs downstream started at 9 A.M. However, on the Sabbath, even the river rested. (The general store stayed open, though, so I enjoyed some ice cream before setting out again.)

It took only 2.5 hours to cover 5.5 miles along roads, climbing nearly 1,000 feet along the way, to the Pleasant Pond Mountain Lean-to. After lunch it was over the mountain and down through open areas covered by raspberry bushes (yummy) and alders.

Crossing the inlet stream of scenic Moxie Pond was a problem as the water was high. Rather than try to keep dry at the risk of falling in, I forded through the knee-deep water and got boots and feet wet again. There was an alternative—crossing 100 feet of water on two taut wires, one for hands and one for feet. I tried it for a couple of steps, but soon decided it was impossible for me with my pack on.

I arrived at Joes Hole Brook Lean-to a bit after 6:15, which was about as late as it was comfortable to hike; there was just enough time left to cook and do the dishes in the fading dusk. The register had lots of complaints about bugs in early July, but they were not bad any more.

The interesting birds were a herring gull above the Kennebec, cedar waxwings, chipping sparrows, crows, and a flock of 37 grackles near Pleasant Pond, flickers, a hairy woodpecker, and a veery on

Pleasant Pond Mountain, loons and a kingfisher at Moxie Pond, and another female goldeneye in the slough across the road.

AUGUST 30. The morning climb up Moxie Bald Mountain was easy enough. I was disappointed, though, because it was still impossible to see Katahdin through the haze.

I found Harry Latimer and Mike Combs loafing about the lean-to on the far side of the mountain. They had been way ahead of me for a while, but lost a full day on Saturday while the storm raged.

We all headed on to Breakneck Ridge Lean-to at our own pace. When I had gone about halfway it began to rain and for about an hour or so I had to put up with being wet. It wasn't only the rain from the sky, but also the moisture from the thickets along the trail. Much of the area had been lumbered and was covered with dense growths of alder, raspberry, and head-high flowers and grasses. The ground was soggy and my boots were full of water; they were causing me some concern because the soles were starting to separate from the uppers.

AUGUST 31. This really marked the beginning of the end. Monson was the last outpost of civilization before Baxter Park.

It was a magnificent day, cool and with an absolutely clear and cloudless sky. What a shame that I couldn't be on a mountain to enjoy a view.

Though I had a package waiting for me at Yoke Ponds, I left Monson with about 12 pounds of food, including five boxes of Pop-Tarts. My pack was stuffed and really groaning with all the food and gear crammed into it. It was particularly hard to carry because of the problems I had with the belt. The original Kelty belt kept slipping, so I replaced it with a belt I picked up at a sporting goods store in Salisbury, Connecticut. This worked fine for a while, but now my weight was down to 150 pounds and I couldn't pull the belt tight enough so the pack would ride on my hips and keep the weight off my shoulders. To make things worse, the lower back band had torn clean through a few days before, so the metal frame often rode directly on bone.

I spent a few hours with Mike and Harry before they set out again. There were chores to be taken care of—shopping, mail, and laundry —before putting up for the night at Mrs. French's tourist home.

The real distinction of Monson is the Kahvila (the Finnish word for coffee house) restaurant. I kept returning for more to eat; the fresh-baked blueberry pie was the greatest.

SEPTEMBER 1 (WEDNESDAY). Another day of perfect weather, though without any vantage point. Still I was certainly not complaining, especially as this was one of the last nights I would be camping out.

The Kahvila served me Finnish coffee bread and blueberry muffins (so full of berries that the insides were all blue) to go with the bacon and eggs. Then back on the trail. After a couple of miles on a road, the route consisted of a pleasant stroll along an old stage road through an open hardwood forest. An attractive lean-to, with a new flat wood floor, made a good spot for lunch.

The next point of interest was Savage's Mills on Little Wilson Stream. Though the settlement was abandoned over 100 years ago, the slate foundations of the old dam remained. Growing on top of it, in a bed of moss, were some small hemlocks that had taken root in the thin layer of accumulated soil.

I took time to make the short side trip to Little Wilson Falls. Sitting at the lip of the falls, one looks straight down about 100 feet into a cramped gorge bounded by sheer and absolutely smooth cliffs of slate. It was a sight I wouldn't want to have missed.

There was no one else at the Little Wilson Campsite, a pretty spot at the base of a wide cascade. The no-see-ums were bad, though, and after eating a Wilson beef stew I retreated into my tent for the night.

Vase-shaped chanterelles were colorful dabs on the forest floor along the trail. There were a number of noteworthy birds. It had been ages since I had seen (though perhaps I'd been hearing) a white-breasted nuthatch and a wood thrush; I saw both of them well. Some others were chipping sparrow, phoebe, golden-crowned kinglet, winter wren, brown creeper, and kingfisher.

SEPTEMBER 2. Less than a 100 miles to go! It was a fast road walk during the morning, with good birding along the way. By lunch I had already recorded flicker, blue jay, Nashville warbler (I believed I'd been seeing a few of these lately), raven, black-capped chickadee, solitary vireo, cedar waxwing, goldfinch, black-throated green and black-and-white warblers, myrtle warbler, redstart, downy woodpecker, and at least four yellow-bellied sapsuckers. During the afternoon I added a large hawk, probably a goshawk, flying over Barren Ledges, and listed the junco and boreal chickadee as well.

I had lunch at the Long Pond Stream Lean-to. After a bit of tricky rock hopping the steep climb of Barren Mountain began. Reaching the crest, I was rewarded by a vast panorama of mountains, lakes, and streams. The pointed peaks of Bigelow, 50 miles away, towered over the lowlands to the west; but Katahdin, eclipsed by White Cap to the northeast, still eluded me.

There was a party of four giggling kids at Cloud Pond when I arrived. Along with them was a young vegetarian hiker from Virginia, headed south, who had made a hard 22 miles from White Cap Mountain Lean-to in one day; I was a bit concerned about making that distance in two days! The shelter was a small one, with a dirt floor, and things were a bit cramped.

SEPTEMBER 3. According to the topographic map, there shouldn't have been much climbing, but the trail across the Chairback Range was very rough, with lots of small ups and downs and little drops where I had to place my feet carefully. Blowdowns were an added nuisance.

A blue-blazed trail afforded an opportunity to cut four miles off the hike. I resisted the impulse to take it and wrote in the Chairback Gap Lean-to register that hikers who took that blue-blazed trail were going to Hell; it had been put there by the Devil to tempt weak souls.

I still hadn't seen Katahdin. I couldn't even see White Cap, just a few miles away. Closer at hand, though, there were some special treats—patches of pitcher plants along a boggy section near Third Mountain and then a cow moose that ambled out of a beaver pond just past East Chairback Pond.

A hummingbird paid me a visit before I headed on to The Hermitage, located on a bluff overlooking the West Branch of the Pleasant River. The cabins, locked but with good covered porches, were situated beneath a forest of ancient white pines. The tract was in good hands, under the ownership and loving care of The Nature Conservancy.

Some of the leaves of the sugar maples had started to turn brilliant red.

SEPTEMBER 4. "It was the best of times, it was the worst of times." It was the best of times because Katahdin was so near, only about 75 miles away. Also because with the climbing of White Cap, I'd finished the last mountain before Baxter Peak. However, for a change, I was suffering from various ailments.

The main problem was a lack of sleep. With six of us at Cloud Pond, I hadn't slept well, and the next night the flies kept attacking me. I was also suffering from stomach cramps that made walking uncomfortable, and I had a few pimples on my face that could develop into boils, and a scratch on my palm where I fell on a root— if I had hit the ground a quarter of an inch nearer I would have gotten a nasty puncture.

The first few miles were largely on a road, with just a bit of climbing before my lunch stop at the White Brook Lean-to. Continuing gently uphill a bit farther, in woods brightened by the golden leaves of the yellow birch, I eventually came to the steep trail up White Cap. Although it rises 1,000 feet in six-tenths of a mile, it was mostly a dirt footway and I made it up in the good time of about 50 minutes. They say you shouldn't miss the fire tower on the summit, but it was so hazy that I didn't bother with the quarter-mile side trip.

I had company again at the White Cap Mountain Lean-to, the same two boys and two girls I had met at Cloud Pond. It was a better shelter here, larger and with a plank floor instead of dirt.

SEPTEMBER 5. I was sick. Something in the water or food hadn't agreed with me. A teaspoonful of paregoric in the morning didn't solve the problem. On top of this, it was a day of maximum exertion— not much climbing, but over 20 miles at the pace of a forced march.

Along with my companions, I was up early and managed to cover over eight miles before lunch. This stretch had a number of boggy areas, so the absence of rain for the past several days undoubtedly was a blessing. I just made it in time, however, because around noon there was a heavy shower. It would have been nice to wait it out at the lean-to, but I couldn't afford the time and continued on my way. The rain jacket I had picked up in Monson kept me reasonably dry.

It would have been easier to reach Yoke Ponds by crossing Little Boardman Mountain, but I hadn't known that the trail was blue-blazed all the way and feared getting lost. Instead, I left the Appalachian Trail on B Pond Road and walked three miles each way to pick up my box of food.

By the time I got to Cooper Brook Falls I was really dragging. The lean-to was at a scenic location just below a long series of cascades and beside a pool that looked inviting for swimming. Just in front of the shelter, I watched a red-tailed hermit thrush exploring for some morsels while farther away a kingfisher flew above the roaring stream.

SEPTEMBER 6. Still sick, but after a good night's sleep and with an easy day of hiking for a change, things seemed a little bit better.

The hiking was uneventful—a stop for lunch at the abandoned Antlers Camp on the shores of Lower Joe Mary Lake and then an easy climb over Potaywadjo Ridge. There were some big hemlocks and lots of mushrooms, including chanterelles and small scarlet ones. There were some dead waters to be crossed on logs, but no mishaps. Still there had been no sign of Katahdin.

In the forest of beeches, firs, and red maples along Cooper Brook I studied what must have been a parula warbler, its bright yellow throat crossed by a band of orange-grey wash. The chilling wolflike cry of the loon at Lower Joe Mary Lake, appropriate to the wilderness all around, was another memorable experience.

It was hardly 3 P.M. when I arrived at the Potaywadjo Spring Lean-to, which I shared with my four young friends.

SEPTEMBER 7. A short detour took me to the edge of Pemadumcook Lake. Because of the haze and overcast there was still no view of Katahdin. The birds were interesting, though—spotted sandpipers, herring gull, grackles, and a kingfisher.

Just beyond my lunch spot at Nahmakanta Lake Lean-to—its only distinction a patch of good blackberries and raspberries now past their prime—was a swampy section. Here I was forced to cross some foot-deep dead water by crawling on hands and knees across the downed logs.

On a warmer day I might have stopped for a swim at a pretty sandy beach on the shores of Nahmakanta Lake. I kept going, though, to reach the Nahmakanta Lake Camps where I hoped to get accommodations.

The camps had a beautiful setting, looking out over miles of water. Although there were signs of life—the grass neatly cut and laundry hanging out to dry—the place was completely deserted. I rested in the shade of the tall trees for a while. Finally, when no one showed up, I made myself comfortable on the porch of a new cabin just under construction. If it rained I could get inside, otherwise the porch would be fine. It was probably my grooviest campsite on the whole trip.

I was lucky that there had been only one shower on the way from Monson. Wet clothes *and* wet bogs wouldn't have been any fun.

SEPTEMBER 8. A big day! I finally saw The Mountain! The end of my hike was literally in sight. What a happy prospect!

I was up early enough to watch the soft-glowing sunrise over misty Nahmakanta Lake. Again I heard the cry of the loon, and saw two of the birds diving near shore. Around the camps, juncos, sapsuckers, blue jays, black-capped chickadees, and a brown creeper were feeding.

The trail along Rainbow Lake was much harder than the maps suggested, with a number of small rises and dips, a rough footway, and some boggy areas. After a stop for lunch at a decrepit lean-to, I continued to the end of the lake and took a refreshing dip in the brisk water before heading up Rainbow Ledges.

There was a climb of about 500 feet and then a short detour to a viewpoint. There it was! Mt. Katahdin. A magnificent mountain hulk, with a precipitous escarpment jutting down thousands of feet below the summit. It looked enormous. It had to be close because in the other direction I could just barely make out Pemadumcook Lake. White Cap and Chairback were lost in the haze.

My feeling was that this was my last long hike. Condemnation to walk the Appalachian Trail every day would be a punishment fit for Greek mythology. My future hikes were going to be nice easy ones— five or six miles a day, time to sleep late and to take unhurried swims, time to read Victorian novels along the way.

SEPTEMBER 9. It rained during the night and was cloudy in the morning. The footway from Hurd Brook to Abol Bridge was rough. At the bridge I stopped at the store with a pent-up longing for ice cream, but they didn't have any, so I had to settle for some pop, beer, and pastry instead. I got enough food for the next couple of days and a can of beer for my summit celebration.

The trail here was very scenic, first along the Penobscot West Branch and then even more so along Nesowadnehunk Stream. By the time I reached Little Niagara Falls, the skies had cleared and I enjoyed a beautiful picture-postcard view of the mountains as seen behind the spruce-lined banks of the cascading stream. There was still one more obstacle—the swamp, perhaps the worst on the whole trail, near the end of the day's hike. However, since all of the bad spots were bridged with logs, I made it across uneventfully.

One thing of interest along the Penobscot West Branch was the appearance of white and red oaks. There had been few oaks of any kind in northern New England.

Arriving at the Katahdin Stream Campground I had a reunion with Mike Combs and Harry Latimer. Both had climbed Mt. Katahdin that day and were now finished with their adventures. "We made it, we really made it," Harry kept saying, somewhat in disbelief, joyful and proud, and yet with a tone of regret that the months of freedom were coming to a close. Though it had been foggy at the summit, the skies had cleared while he was still high on the mountain on his descent and he had been able to make out landmarks along the winding trail back as far as the Bigelows.

SEPTEMBER 10. A great day in every way. It was early to bed, early to rise, with a bright blue sky on that Friday morning. Harry and Mike were going to be around all day, so I left my things at the shelter and took only food and warm clothing up the mountain.

After about a mile of ascending very gradually on excellent footpath, the trail became steeper, with lots of roots and rocks to sidestep. From around the 3,000-foot contour to the 4,500-foot level the route followed the narrow and precipitous Hunt Spur. Especially in the lower portions this was a real challenge, with difficult boulders to get through, over, and around. At about four spots iron bars have been driven into the granite to provide handholds. They were needed, too, particularly if you were carrying a pack.

A few miles away across a valley is The Owl, which rises high overhead but gradually falls behind as you gain altitude. Emerging from the woods and out on the exposed rock of the ridge, I looked out on the whole world to the south and west. In the far distance, two weeks of walking away, were the distinctive pinnacles of Bigelow, with what seemed to be Sugarloaf nearby.

There were lakes all about, with Pemadumcook one of the more prominent; it was huge. I could easily see White Cap behind the Boardmans; and from the summit a bit of the Chairback Range stuck up over the White Cap massif.

After the strenuous climb up Hunt Spur, the trail reached The Gateway, where I suddenly got my first view of the summit only 1.5 miles off. From this point on it was an easy rise over alpine tundra covered with low blueberries. I made a stop at Thoreau Spring in the midst of this treeless expanse and then continued to the summit.

It was an emotional moment when I reached the goal I had been heading toward for 171 days. As I got near the sign, I started to choke up, and when finally there, having thrown my pack down, I enjoyed a bit of a cry.

Katahdin was so magnificent. There was an enormous deep cirque on the north side, with Chimney Pond at its base. Around this, the well-named Knife-Edge circled to meet the South Peak and then over to Baxter. To the northwest were the lower summits of the Katahdin Range.

For celebration I had the can of beer carried from Abol Bridge, along with my usual fare of peanut butter and crackers. There were swarms of people, so I had no problem getting my picture taken with the sign that marked the northern terminus of the Appalachian Trail—2,025 miles from Springer Mountain.

The excitement of the day wasn't over yet, though. On the way down Hunt Spur a magnificent hawk soared almost directly overhead. As it circled to gain altitude I could clearly make out a brilliant white rump patch and, considering size and shape and all, believe it must have been a marsh hawk, a final addition to my list of birds for the hike. I like to think that this mighty raptor had made his own trip along the Appalachian Trail in the spring, and now, headed south for warmer winter climes, paused to greet a fellow traveler upon his safe arrival.

Harry and Mike were waiting to welcome me at Katahdin Stream. I celebrated by shaving, washing, and putting on clean clothes. After dinner and a pleasant evening of talk with these friends, the 2,000-mile adventure drew to its close. For years to come I will recall this time, these companions, this mountain—a mountain that is not only the end of a hike but a pinnacle in the path of my life.

Five Moons Have Passed

From Springer's peak in early spring I sprang
Before the birds began to sing. I found—
No vernal leaf, nor blooming rue, nor tang
Of fragrant allspice—I found but slumbering ground.

I walked through woods; crossed balds 'neath azure sky;
Passed Shenandoah, Susquehanna, Schagh-
ticoke and Housatonic, Greylock high,
Its firs and spruces shrouded by the fog.

I'd hike each tiresome day to dusk from dawn
O'er rocky cliffs, through boggy tundra sod.
By lakes of loons the lonesome trail led on.
Five moons to Maine, two thousand miles, I'd trod.

Near fall on Baxter's Peak I fell with pride.
For joy I sang. But deep inside I cried.

Appalachian Trail Hike

By Ned Smith

Started at SPRINGER MOUNTAIN on May 1, 1971
Finished at MT. KATAHDIN on September 30, 1971

SATURDAY, MAY 1, 1971. *Near Hawk Mountain Lean-to, Georgia.* The first day of my new undertaking started at 4:30 A.M. I didn't want to get out of bed to face the beginning of the trip, but it was too late to turn back. I was nervous and had a tight feeling in my stomach. My girl friend (now my wife) was 20 minutes late in picking me up. Not a good omen. We met four friends for breakfast before starting the two-hour drive from Atlanta to Nimblewill Gap and the approach trail to Springer Mountain. All the way I worried about what I might have forgotten, or that I would get blisters on my feet, or that some unexpected disaster would occur to stop the walk before it had begun.

My friends walked with me today and will go back to Atlanta tomorrow. We started up the approach trail at 10:00 A.M.—and I do mean "up." After the first 10 yards I was puffing hard. After the first 100 yards I thought I would die. My pack was the heaviest I had ever carried and my leg muscles hurt with each step.

It was two miles to Springer Mountain from Nimblewill Gap and by the time we reached the register my legs had loosened up and I was feeling pretty good. I felt confident about my chances of going all the way. As the day wore on and I became tired my confidence slipped, and now I will promise only one day's journey at a time. My legs are dead. My feet are sore. I've gone 12 miles today and I'm not up to it. I must watch the trail markings more closely. I have missed the trail twice already. The shelter was occupied so we camped a few hundred yards away at the edge of a grassy meadow. Tomorrow my friends go back to the city and I am on my own!

Those were my notes for the first day of a trip that would take me over 2,000 miles in five months. It is difficult to set down on paper or to say in words why or how I came to make this hike. At the time I was 34 years old and a graduate of Georgia Tech in Mechanical Engineering in 1964. There were several reasons why I quit an interesting and rewarding job as a data processing manager to take this trip. I had hiked most of the trail in Georgia the summer before on weekend trips with friends, and it was always hard to head for home on Sunday afternoon with more trail still ahead of me. Articles in the *Appalachian Trailway News* about private landowners closing the right-of-way made me uneasy about the future of the trail as a continuous footpath. Commercial interests were pushing closer and closer to the wilderness areas that border the trail. In Georgia the national forest near Standing Indian was being heavily logged. I wanted to enjoy natural areas without the intrusion of chain saws. Finally and probably most significant was the simple desire to meet and withstand the physical and mental challenge of a 2,000-mile walk in the woods, to see the country somewhat as the pioneers had seen it even though my journey was backed by the products of modern technology.

I began making plans for the trip in January, 1971. The Appalachian Trail Conference supplied me with guidebooks that covered most of the trail. The Jefferson National Forest and George Washington National Forest had maps of the areas not covered by the guidebooks. Road maps that showed the approximate location of the Appalachian Trail were furnished by the Gulf Oil Company Travel Service. I used these maps to find towns that were near the trail. With these references, using an average speed of 15 miles a day (10 miles per day for the first week) I made a day-by-day itinerary. Each day ended at a water source. In actual practice I rarely used these exact locations, since I averaged about 17.5 miles a day. Also, many springs that I picked from the guidebooks as stopping places did not have a flat camping spot nearby. When this happened I would fill my water bag with enough water for supper and walk on to a suitable campsite. On long summer days when the weather was good I would cook supper near a spring around five o'clock and then walk on a few more miles to make camp just before dusk. I had to pitch my tent in the middle of the trail by flashlight a few times because I was caught without a flat spot nearby when darkness came. However, I tried not to travel after dark.

At intervals of six or seven days and at some convenient place where a paved highway (not an expressway or interstate highway) crossed the trail, I located a town or motel within hitchhiking distance to use as a resupply point. Towns that are big enough to have a Laundromat and rooms for rent, but small enough to be able to walk from store to store, are ideal. I wrote to the post office or to a motel (listed in the trail guides) in these towns and asked if they would hold a box of supplies for me until I arrived. Post offices are required to hold packages for 30 days only on written request, so I wanted to make sure the local postmaster would stretch the rules for me. I mailed all of my food packages before I left to be sure that each one would be in place. If you have friends who will mail packages to you at regular intervals, you don't have to go through all of this letter writing, but you do stand a chance of missing a package if it is delayed for some reason. Post offices are closed on weekends, so mailing to motels or private individuals gives more flexibility to your schedule.

For several reasons I bought all of my food at one time before the trip started. For one thing, I was able to save some money by buying at a discount supermarket. Freeze-dried food and high-energy breakfast cereal are not available in small towns. Finally, I wanted to be sure that every item on my menu would be available when I got there. When you are on foot it is hard to chase around looking for things.

I met several people walking the trail who had done very little planning. They just "got their bag together" and started out, buying food as they went along. It can be done that way, but I'm the kind of guy who likes to know where his next meal is coming from before I start out. These food stops also gave me a chance to wash clothes and take a hot shower. I originally allotted a half-day for these stops, but I found that it took quite a bit of time to get the package from the post office, do additional food shopping (I will tell how my menu changed later), and then transfer the food to special containers for my pack. I also enjoyed the break from the daily grind of walking. When the trip started, it never occurred to me that I would be bored. I thought the constantly changing terrain would hold my interest. However, after six weeks of walking, eating, sleeping, walk, eat, sleep, and so on, I was very anxious to take breaks and go into towns. I began going a few extra miles each day so that I could have a full day off for rest and relaxation. Boredom was especially bad when the weather was rotten, and it seemed to be rotten more than half the time. If it rained for five minutes it seemed like it continued raining for three days. In southern Virginia it rained at least once a day for 14 days. During that time I didn't see another hiker. That was as close as I ever came to quitting. The woods were depressing in the rain, my clothes were always wet and cold, fires were hard to start, and it was difficult to break camp without getting everything wet before I got it into my pack. On top of everything else, some landowners had painted over the blazes and I got lost several times.

Modern lightweight backpacking gear is what makes a trip of this distance a pleasure rather than a strenuous ordeal. I carried a Camp Trails Skyline bag on a Skyline Cruiser frame. This is the smaller pack made by Camp Trails but I found it adequate in all respects. A full week's supplies bulged out the top a little but caused no problems. It was supposed to be waterproof but I had to use a pack rain cover. No pack is mouseproof, though. Every time I neglected to suspend my pack at night or lash it to a tree trunk, mice got into my food. Also, I learned not to leave sealed containers out of my pack when I hung it up. Raccoons would carry off plastic boxes to examine them at their leisure. The frame of welded aluminum was sturdy enough under normal conditions but I managed to break mine by falling down a ravine. In Vermont I was attempting to supplement my diet with a few apples when I came in contact with an electric fence that I thought was dead! The little dance I did getting away from the wire sent me rolling down a slope and into a tree. I was quite lucky that the frame was the only thing damaged—and the apples weren't even ripe! I also used a Camp Trails padded hip belt. I feel that this item made a large contribution to the success of my trip. I wouldn't go backpacking again without one.

I assembled my cooking kit from several sources. I used a 1½-quart pot from a dime store for boiling water for tea. I drilled a hole through the handle so that I could unscrew it from the pot for easy storage. A one-quart Teflon-lined saucepan was used for cooking stew. I removed the handle from this pot completely, and used aluminum pot tongs to pick it up. I also had a one-quart covered pot from a Boy Scout cooking kit that I originally used to boil rice. It also did duty as a Dutch oven to bake biscuits. When I stopped eating both those items it became a mixing bowl for pudding.

For drinking I splurged and carried two cups. One was a green plastic measuring cup that came in a Boy Scout kit. The other was my regular coffee cup from home; I took it because I didn't like drinking from the green cup, and it brought a touch of home that I was glad to have when my spirits were low. I carried a soup spoon and a fork. The fork turned out to be unnecessary gear but I used it some for mixing powdered milk and pudding.

All of these items nested together quite well. I carried a Scotch Brite scouring pad and bar soap to wash dishes. I didn't scour the outside of the pots and pans so I had to carry them in a cloth pot bag to keep the soot out of my pack. This method saves a lot of time in pot-washing, and the fire-blackened bottoms make the contents of the pans heat quicker. Another useful item was a backpacker's grill. Since I often camped in primitive areas where there was no fireplace, the grill was very handy.

I started out with a Svea 123 stove, but it overheated and blew out the filler-cap safety valve the first time I tried to use it. The safety valve couldn't be reset, so I sent the stove home and never really needed it until I got to the White Mountains where stoves are required for environmental reasons. When the wood was damp, as it often was, I used fire ribbon to start my cookfire. I also had a length of rubber tubing with a four-inch copper tube on one end. Blowing through this encouraged the wettest wood to burn. It was one of the handiest items I carried although it failed the Backpackers Weight Test because I used copper instead of aluminum tubing.

I carried a Sven saw. It is lighter than an ax and produced firewood with less effort. Actually, I didn't need it most of the time. A good cookfire can be made with branches that have fallen to the ground and are easily broken by hand. I considered sending the saw home because I wasn't using it, but sometimes the only wood available was fir, which doesn't break readily, or the large dead limbs that other campers had been unable to break up.

I carried a tent because I planned to cover a certain number of miles each day rather than to go from shelter to shelter. None of the sporting goods catalogs I looked at had a light one-man tent so I made my own from coated nylon with nylon netting at both ends. It had a floor and a storm door. The front was 36 inches high and 36 inches wide. The foot was 18 inches by 18 inches. It weighed 24 ounces including six skewer-type tent pins. I used my walking staff to support the front end and any stick that was handy to prop up the back end. Because it could be sealed all around, I felt quite secure from insects, snakes, mice, and other small animals which might try to crawl in bed with me to get warm. Condensation did accumulate on the inside whenever it rained but it was a minor problem. The saving in weight over a double-wall tent offset that inconvenience.

I used a sleeping bag with 1½ pounds of down and a cotton sheet on the trip from Georgia to New Hampshire. At Pinkham Notch in the White Mountains I was told that I would probably see snow before I reached Katahdin so I sent my light bag home and bought a sleeping bag with 2½ pounds of down. This served me quite well for the rest of the trip. Another important piece of sleeping gear was my polyester foam mat, called a Kampamat. I am sold on its comfort and insulating properties. It rolled up small enough to go in the same stuff sack with my sleeping bag. For a ground cloth I used a space blanket. I could have used a cheaper ground cloth but I thought I might need the space blanket's insulation qualities in an emergency. A plastic air pillow cut from a cheap air mattress completed my sleeping equipment.

I carried a Mallory pocket flashlight. One set of alkaline batteries lasted for over four months. The shape of the case makes it easy to hold this flashlight in your teeth, leaving both hands free for work. A spare bulb came in handy when the original one suddenly quit. Actually I didn't use the light very much because I went to bed at sundown. It was useful, though, for seeing what was making that strange noise on the other side of the shelter.

I chose a Konica C-35 camera. It is a compact 35-mm camera with a built-in light meter, wide-angle lens, and range-finder focusing. Light and small, it fit in a side pocket of my pack where I could reach over my shoulder and get it quickly. I used high speed Ektachrome film with excellent results.

Other equipment included such items as a stenographer's note pad, wooden matches in a plastic pill bottle, a Swiss army knife with small scissors, a Silva compass, a safety razor, first-aid and snakebite kit, toilet paper, sewing materials, Off insect repellent spray, nail clippers, rubber bands, wash cloth and small towel, tooth brush and paste, and comb. As for medicine: after my illness, mentioned later, my family doctor, Dr. Wilson, gave me various pills for upset stomach, pain, and diarrhea. Luckily I never needed these pills, but I met quite a few trail walkers who needed the diarrhea pills badly.

A Jonas Watten water bag was one of my most useful items. It held up to four quarts of water and had a handle and a tap for easy use. It was light in weight and could be rolled up when not in use. I got it from Holubar in Boulder, Colorado. As for my compass, I wish I had carried a wrist compass to check directions on overcast days. I had to stop and take off my pack to get at the compass I carried. A length of nylon line was used as a clothesline, for hanging my pack, and as replacement shoelaces.

I ended the trip with only one more item of clothing than I started with, even though the average temperature had gone from 75° F. in July to 35° F. in September. The extra item was a wool shirt which I had mailed from home. I could have used a wool ski hat but I didn't think of it until it was too late.

My clothing included two pairs each of undershorts, thin inner socks, and heavy outer socks, one pair of Levi's, one long-sleeved denim shirt, two bandannas, two handkerchiefs, leather gloves, and a bathing suit I wore only when my other clothes were in the washing machine. I wore Bean's hiking shorts, and had to get a new pair halfway through the trip. I needed a replacement for my fishnet undershirt, too. It was red so it wouldn't show the dirt too badly. I carried a lightweight rain parka and chaps. This raingear kept the water out but I was still wet from perspiration. I think the raingear was necessary, though, as it kept me from becoming chilled. A down jac-shirt from Bean's was a very comforting item to have on cold rainy nights, even in summer.

After two months of hiking and getting my clothes wet and not being able to get them dry again, I developed a system which I followed for the rest of the trip. I would walk in hiking shorts and T-shirt, which always became wet with rain or sweat. When I reached camp I would take a sponge bath and change to dry socks, Levi's, and a denim shirt. The next day the wet shorts and T-shirt would go back on again. This way I always had a dry change of clothes for camp. The wet things were cold to put on in the morning but they would warm up quickly after a few minutes of hiking. Before this trip I had always hiked in some kind of long pants. Now I'm sold on wearing shorts. They are comfortable even in cold weather if you keep moving. Your legs are free to swing. The hut boys in the White Mountains wear cutoff jeans. Some have cut out the crotch of their shorts to make a kind of skirt. One boy had taken the style to its natural conclusion and was wearing a short pleated skirt. These fellows carry tremendous loads up very steep slopes so there is no point in calling them "sissy" for their choice of dress, and my experience confirms their judgment.

I wore three kinds of boots on the trip. I tried a high-top hunting boot with a Vibram sole first. After several weeks of wet weather the leather was so limp that I felt I wasn't getting enough ankle support. My arches also became very sore so perhaps there was no arch support, either. These boots were supposed to be waterproof but weren't after three days. The next pair were Raichle hiking boots. I liked these best of all. The feature I liked most was the lace hooks all the way to the toe. When I made camp each night I would remove the laces and use them to hang my water bag and backpack. The boots were then like bedroom slippers that could be kicked off while changing clothes or walking on the clean floor of some shelters. Raichles are not waterproofed so they get wet quickly—but they also dry out quickly. When the Vibram soles on these hiking boots wore down, I switched to a pair of Sears boots. The Raichles went home to be resoled. The crepe soles on the Sears boots lasted about four weeks on the rocky trail in Pennsylvania and New York. The waterproofing lasted two days.

There was some sort of mixup at home about getting Vibram replacement soles for Raichle boots and I was told that the old soles had more tread than the new. The Sears boots were in sad shape so I had the Raichles sent back to me with the original soles still on. I finished the trip with worn boots but I tried several places to get the soles replaced. Most shoe repair shops did not have Vibram soles and if they did have the soles, they refused to work on my boots ahead of their other customers, even when I explained the nature of my trip and told about the expense of staying in town more than the one day I had planned. They were the only people I met on the whole trip who were not willing to do what they could to help me out. In any event, I needed two sets of Vibram soles to walk the whole Appalachian Trail.

Food, of course, is the important item, both from a nutritional and a pack-weight standpoint. I started the trip with this menu: Breakfast —Familia (a dry cereal) mixed with powdered milk, pitted prunes, Russian tea. Lunch—biscuit, nutrient soup, peanut butter. Dinner— Wilson's Campsite beef or chicken stew, rice, peanut butter. The peanut butter was removed from the heavy glass jars and placed in Gerry poly-squeeze tubes. The stew comes in tin cans so each week I had to open the cans and place the contents in plastic bags. I made a biscuit each night by using my one-quart pot and lid as a Dutch oven.

As the hike wore on I began to feel tired and listless, and I thought my diet needed a change. Breakfast remained the same but lunch was changed completely. Instead of a biscuit and soup, I had a quarter of a pound of Cheddar cheese and two Slim Jims (dried sausage). For supper I substituted egg noodles for the rice and added Jell-O Instant Pudding. I also bought all the Hershey bars I could carry from each store I passed. This menu may sound rather monotonous for eating every day for five months but it wasn't. I was always eager for dinner and each item tasted great, especially the chocolate bars and the Jell-O Instant Pudding. The Russian tea with its sweet clove taste always revived my spirits after a cold wet day on the trail. It was made as follows: 2½ cups Tang, 1 cup sugar, 1 cup instant tea with lemon, ¾ tsp. cinnamon, ½ tsp. ground cloves. One batch lasted about one week.

SUNDAY, MAY 2. *Gooch Gap, Georgia.* Started off at 8:00 A.M. Felt exciting to be on my own. Several steep climbs to Hightower Gap. I wish I had a tape recorder to catch thoughts as they occur. I haven't described my surroundings very much, as my thoughts are mostly directed inward.

Met Pete Dunning at Hightower Gap. He is having trouble with his legs. Wonder if he will make it all the way? (I met Pete again in Massachusetts. He walked to the south end of the Shenandoah National Park and then had flown to Maine and started south. He actually finished several days ahead of me.)

Spring is just starting here. You can see the difference in the leaf cover from the balds to the valleys. Stopped for lunch and a nap. Awoke with lump in my stomach and nausea. As I walked on, I began to feel feverish. Felt worse after several steep climbs. Got to Gooch Gap and road. Stopped to take a nap before continuing on for three more miles. Couldn't sleep. Put up tent to spend night here. Cold; climbed into sleeping bag for warmth. Still couldn't sleep. Got up and vomited. Decided I had better try to get out. First truck that passed would not stop. Walked about a mile to a farmhouse to get help.

The farmer called a friend who drove me to a clinic in Dahlonega, Georgia. I telephoned my friends in Atlanta to come and get me. I was really embarrassed to have to come home after only one day on the trail. The sickness disappeared the next day and I felt fine. It was decided that I had suffered a reaction to a typhoid shot I had taken the day before I started out. So let this be a lesson to you hikers: get your shots (typhoid and tetanus) well before you leave home in order to avoid a similar setback.

I spent my time until the next weekend replanning the first week of the trip so I would have less distance to cover each day. This added three days to the trip and ruined the resupply schedule I had set up. I had to write letters to all the people who were holding food packages to tell them that I would be several days late. The next Saturday my hiking friends and I were once again on the road to northern Georgia and the spot where I had left the trail.

SATURDAY, MAY 8. *Two miles south of Blood Mountain, Georgia.* Today was a good day. We covered seven miles and I was glad to stop. In some places the trail is covered with petals from blooming dogwood. Last year's hickory nuts lay along the path. Walking was easy. Had to go on past the spring where I had planned to camp because there were no flat spots to set up our tents. Found a straight lightweight poplar branch to use as a walking stick. Plan to carry it all the way to Katahdin. (This was the first of three sticks I had. I fell and broke the first one and left the second in a friend's car. The third lasted from southern Virginia to Katahdin.)

SUNDAY, MAY 9. *Bull Gap, Georgia.* Alone at last. I was rather apprehensive when I parted with my friends at Neels Gap but now my confidence has grown. I have found water, built a good fire, and cooked a filling and tasty meal. I'm lying on a foam rubber pad sipping a cup of hot Russian tea. What more can I ask for? The hiking was fairly easy today. This is the first time I have been on Blood Mountain when I was able to see more than 50 feet. The view today was impressive. We could see Black Mountain Fire Tower, which we passed yesterday. It was hard to believe that we had walked so far over such rough looking country. Tonight will be my first night alone. I hope the "things that go bump in the night" will not disturb me. My biscuit should be through baking by now. Success! It was a delicate golden brown.

I passed through an area that had been burned over. Trees are still standing but all small green plants are gone. Dead leaves and branches have been burned off and the ground is naked. Erosion will be a problem here when spring rains come. In one place the trail itself served as a firebreak and stopped the spread of the flames.

MONDAY, MAY 10. *Low Gap, Georgia.* Morning started off fine. Two deer came near my tent at 5:00 A.M. I'm amazed that all this stuff (tent, cooking utensils, clothes, sleeping bag) fits into my pack. It feels like it's all there but I keep wondering if I've forgotten anything. Walked 4.6 miles in two hours. Very good time but fatigue mounts. I ate the same food for lunch that I had eaten just before I became ill last week. Could hardly get it down and felt somewhat out of sorts afterward. Don't know if the stuff really doesn't agree with me, or if it's all in my mind. Went on five more miles to my camp. There is plenty of daylight to go farther but my legs and feet are very tired. It's been a gray dull day since 9:00 A.M. This has not helped my spirits. Now (5:00 P.M.) the sun has broken through and I welcome its warmth. The only animals I have seen so far have been birds. They wake me in the morning and cheer me on my way. The variety of songs they sing is quite wonderful.

After supper my spirits rose greatly. I went to bed at 9:30 P.M. No sooner had I gotten situated in the sleeping bag than an owl two or three trees away went "screeeeeech, hoo-hoo-hoo"! That brought me upright and set the mood for the rest of the night. Deer came through camp around midnight snorting and stamping their feet. At least I think they were deer; I couldn't see in the dark. Sounded like a pony blowing its nose. Then whippoorwills started calling and this went on until 2:00 A.M.

TUESDAY, MAY 11. *Tray Mountain Recreation Area, Georgia.* When man has left this world and his cities have crumbled back to dust, one monument will outlive him to mark his stay—the ring and tab from a snap-top can. They are everywhere. Most people have become more aware of littering so they remember to take the cans out with them but the rings are thrown on the ground.

Today started well. Got breakfast ready and the rain came. Not hard but heavy enough to make me scurry to get my gear into the tent and my rain parka on. I ate leaning over my cup of cereal to keep the water out. Rain stopped about the time I got everything packed. How do you fold a tent in the rain without getting the inside wet? The first four miles were on fire roads which was easy walking but dull skies kept my spirits low. I wondered if I really wanted to do this all summer.

Skies lightened and spirits rose. Covered six miles before lunch. Something about the food I am eating for lunch still makes me nauseated. Disturbing. Did another eight miles after lunch. The trail is very pretty here. By the time I made camp I had sore feet and was unable to walk in a straight line. Supper is done and here comes another hiker. He has walked 19 miles today. WOW!

WEDNESDAY, MAY 12. *Addis Gap Lean-to, Georgia.* Rain, rain, rain. Rained several times last night. Tent was snug so there was no problem. Awoke to fog and a slight drizzle. Not wet enough to put on raingear but wet enough to get clothes damp. Reached top of Tray Mountain and the rain became stronger. Put on rain parka. No place to stop for lunch because of the constant sprinkle. Went on to my destination for the night, Addis Gap. Covered 7.2 miles before 12:30. Rain stopped and I gathered firewood. Had to use fire ribbon to get it going. Dried all of my clothes except jeans and cooked supper before it began to rain again, heavily. Covered fire with fresh logs and hope it will stay alive. Pack is half-empty now but doesn't seem to be any lighter.

FRIDAY, MAY 14. *Standing Indian Lean-to, North Carolina.* Couldn't write last night. I was too busy getting wood, starting a fire, and drying clothes. It rained all day. Everything was sopping wet and cold. I got to Plumorchard Gap Lean-to and took off all my clothes, dried off with a damp towel, and crawled into my sleeping bag for an hour's nap. Then I went about my business. Today the sun broke through for the first time in five days. It sure makes a difference in my outlook. Passed over the Georgia state line into North Carolina. That means I've covered about 80 miles. Five men from the Tennessee Eastman Club are staying with me in the shelter tonight. It's good to talk and laugh with someone. They tell me there are several people a day or two ahead of me who are also going to Maine. This must be the year for it.

SUNDAY, MAY 16. *Siler Bald Lean-to, North Carolina.* Is everybody working hard out there? I just finished an excellent meal topped off with a bottle of imported Italian wine that I had cooled in an icy spring. I met my friends at Wallace Gap today and got my next week's supplies, and the bottle of wine. Sure was good to see familiar faces, especially that little redhead.

The pack sure seems heavy again with the new supply of food. I thought I was getting used to the weight but I guess the load was just getting lighter. All of the food, except for breakfast, has lasted longer than I expected. I may have to get instant oatmeal to supplement that meal. Once again I couldn't write yesterday because of the weather. It rained steadily all day. My extra clothes had not dried from the last rain. All wood was dripping wet so I used my gas stove for supper. It overheated and shut down just after the stew had cooked. I tried for three hours to start a fire with fire ribbon and gasoline but without success. I was very cold and miserable. I have been told by another trail hiker, Dave Goad, that there is a motel and Laundromat in Fontana Village so I will stop there. I need to wash clothes and bathe.

MONDAY, MAY 17. *Wesser Creek Lean-to, North Carolina.* Today was the longest yet. I covered 17 miles. I'm tired and my feet are still aching. I'm not up to a 15-mile day yet. I do feel better about my overall condition, though. The first climb of the day was four miles long and I took it in stride. Reached my planned destination at 1:30 and decided to go on so I would have a shorter day tomorrow in the Yellow Creek area. The views from Wayah Bald to the south and Wesser Bald to the north were magnificent. I could see where the trail ahead follows the Smokies and it looks formidable. However, when I look back and see where I've been I'm amazed that I covered that rough-looking country. My spirits are higher now that the sun is shining and I'm not so exhausted. Got some new harmonica music with my supplies yesterday. Really good.

TUESDAY, MAY 18. *Sassafras Gap Lean-to, North Carolina.* Today I had the worst climb of the trip so far. This section from Wesser to Fontana Village has the reputation of being the most strenuous on the whole Appalachian Trail. You climb from 1,650 feet at Wesser to 5,062 feet in only seven miles of trail. I reached the shelter at 2:30 and took a nap. I'm still tired. There is very little water along this steep ascent. I used all of my water for lunch about halfway up the mountain and I was really dry and exhausted when I stumbled across a small deep pool almost at the top of the mountain. I should not get into that situation again. This lean-to is not very clean. It is on a fire road and car campers have used it. There are papers and cans everywhere. From the rim of Nantahala Gorge I can look back to the fire tower I passed yesterday afternoon. It doesn't look too far away. In the other direction lie the Great Smokies, and I can see the ridge I will cross through the park. That is still two days away.

WEDNESDAY, MAY 19. *Cable Gap Lean-to, North Carolina.* I hiked directly over the top of every knob in southern North Carolina today, or so it seemed. It was the most physically grueling thing I have ever done. Fourteen miles of that stuff. Up a thousand feet, down a thousand feet. The path was so steep that going down was almost as hard as going up. At least going up you had a closer look at where to put your feet. The views were beautiful, though. I stopped often to rest so I had many chances to look around. The trees on the mountains have more leaves now. The valleys are lush. Tomorrow—Fontana Village and a chance to wash clothes and get a hot shower.

SUNDAY, MAY 23. I haven't kept my notes for several days. The first day in the Smokies I arrived late at my campsite and it was almost dark before I finished baking and eating. The second night I was with a group of hikers and I sat around the fire talking until bedtime. Two things were uppermost in my mind: the temperature and my feet. It has been quite cold here for the past three days. As soon as I stop walking I put on my jacket and build a fire. I sleep in my clothes at night so I'm warm enough not to lose sleep. I've been late in getting started each morning because I am reluctant to leave my warm nest. My feet are killing me. No blisters, just sore. It feels like my arches are breaking down. After only five miles they are tender and aching. It takes all the enjoyment out of the scenery. Strangely enough, my feet feel best while climbing. On the level or going down it's murder. I hope they toughen up.

MONDAY, MAY 24. *Somewhere in the Great Smokies.* My feet still hurt and the weather is still cold. I'm camped with two other guys in the middle of a fire road. It's the only flat spot around. The wind is howling over the ridge like an express train. This is the best part of the day (if I didn't have to write these darn notes). Cooking is done and I can relax and think of nothing. I covered over 15 miles today. Something must be done about my feet. Each step is an effort. If I have time tomorrow, I'll try to whittle some arch supports. I can walk like this all day, and I will, but it takes all the fun out of it. It rained a little this morning. Just enough to get everything wet and cold. I'm depressed. I am ahead of schedule, however, and I think I planned a short hike for the day after tomorrow. If so, I'll rest and make those supports. The country has changed to very steep ridges covered with balsam forests. The trail runs along the crest and is the easiest walking I've had. I wonder how my feet will hold up when the trail gets rough and my pack weight suddenly increases 30 percent as it will tomorrow night?

TUESDAY, MAY 25. *One mile past north end of Great Smoky Mountains National Park.* I think my fortunes have changed! I carved one arch support at lunch today and I think it helped. I picked up letters from home and my next box of supplies from Mr. William Hochstetler, just as planned. I'm in a small valley where it is warm and a small brook gurgles at my doorstep. A truly idyllic spot. I've had a good meal and read my letters several times. Even though it rained hard this morning and I had to have a cold breakfast standing in the middle of the trail, everything has dried out nicely and my fire is burning brightly. Tomorrow I hike only six miles so I will have time to lay around and mend clothes and get extra sleep. I feel buoyed up.

WEDNESDAY, MAY 26. *Groundhog Creek Lean-to, North Carolina.* Today was a short day. Went about nine miles, four miles climbing up from the Pigeon River gorge. I sewed the pockets of my jacket, hung up a clothesline and dried my sweat-soaked duds, carved one more arch support, and greased my boots. (I never found a waterproofing that worked more than 24 hours, so I gave it up for the rest of the trip.) I'm not sure the arch support I have is working. My feet are still tired no matter how far I walk. I think of many things as I walk along but I can't recall them when I start to write. I opened my saltshaker to dry it out and forgot to close it when I threw it back in my pack. Lost half the salt. I'll have to ask someone I meet if they can give me some salt. This lean-to has a table in front of it. Quite a luxury to be able to sit and eat properly. Didn't sleep very well last night. Think it was the cigar I smoked just before bedtime. Tomorrow I have to go over 15 miles. Hope my feet can take it.

THURSDAY, MAY 27. *Seven miles south of Hot Springs, North Carolina.* This was the best day for traveling so far. I went 16.1 miles in less than eight hours. Feet are tired but not painfully so. Walked four miles on a dirt road before lunch. Discovered that my new arch support is too high. I did some adjusting at lunch.

Saw a blacksnake and two families of grouse. When the grouse hen sees you, she starts running back and forth. If this doesn't scare you away, the chicks scatter while the hen spreads her tail and neck feathers and comes forward hissing. When she thinks the chicks are safely hidden the hen flies off, presumably to return when the danger has passed to collect her brood. The chicks can't tell a leg from a tree trunk so I always have a few little ones running between my feet, trying to escape.

Have you ever thought about the allocation of work as related to the increasing refinement of civilization? Technology has shifted labor from the food-gathering process to a convenience-oriented industry. For instance, you work at your job to earn money to spend as you see fit—some for shelter, some for transportation, some for recreation, some for food, and so on. If you have performed your tasks and amassed enough money, you may eat an almost infinite variety of food prepared conveniently at any time you choose. In my low state of technology on this hike I have a certain set of duties to perform in order to enjoy even a limited menu. I must find water, gather wood, start a fire, and cook the meal. If I neglect these duties or am unable to carry out any of them, I don't eat.

FRIDAY, MAY 28. *Spring Mountain Lean-to, North Carolina–Tennessee line.* This is an old log lean-to built in 1938, the year of my birth. It has a good tin roof and I'm glad. It rained a little last night and then a little more as I started walking. The sun broke through around 10:00 A.M. for a few minutes, then it became foggy again. Now the rain on this tin roof sounds like the sky is falling. I was able to get a fire started before the rain became heavy and I've had a good hot meal. Everything is a little damp because of the fog but it will be warm in the sleeping bag.

I stopped in Hot Springs for lunch today. Had typical café fare: meat, two vegetables, salad, rolls, and a drink for $1.25. The vegetables were candied yams and buttered corn. Hot Springs was quite a resort town when health spas were in fashion. Now it is a typical small town in Appalachia. Men over 40 standing on street corners talking and watching the more affluent citizens drive by. I guess to them I'm affluent. All I own is on my back, but I can afford to be unemployed for the summer.

I don't see how anyone can walk this trail and buy food as he goes along. I went into a store looking for salt and biscuit mix. There was little variety, no instant things, and everything was in the large size.

Photo courtesy Ned Smith

Ned Smith in camp at Low Gap, Georgia.

Photo by Chuck Eberso

Blacksnake.

The salt was in five-pound sacks, and what hiker needs 100 marshmallows or a pound of mustard? The box of Bisquick I bought will last me for three weeks.

My feet are better. At every rest break I take off my boots and whittle some more on my arch supports. There must be some optimum shape that will do more good than harm. Dogs from houses along the trail are giving me a hard time. Making friends with them takes too much time and I'm afraid that if I hit one of them with my walking stick some farmer will shoot me, so we maintain an armed truce. They bark and follow closely and I talk friendly but keep my stick at the ready and walk backwards. If they get too bold I swing at them and that usually ends the encounter. So far the score is DOGS 0, ME 0. And that's the way I want to keep it. (I forgot to mention that I was bitten by a dog on the second day of my hike, when I was sick and went off the trail for help. I was bitten when I turned away from the dog to knock on a farmer's door.)

TUESDAY, JUNE 1. *Motel in Erwin, Tennessee.* The fog stayed and the rain kept coming. The temperature dropped and in my already wet clothes I got very cold. I was going to stay in the open the night of May 29 but I thought I had better cut my distance by three miles to stay in a dry shelter, under a roof. However, it seems the trail has been relocated since my guidebook was printed so there was no shelter. I pressed on to my original destination with the intention of putting up my tent and eating a cold supper. Luckily, when I got there I found that a new shelter had been built.

I tried to build a fire with wood that had been rained on for two days but the fire ribbon just burned a few twigs. I was cold and shivering, and my fingers were stiff. I felt desperate. The wind was howling and mist was blowing into the shelter. The second time I tried the fire ribbon did the trick and I had a roaring fire in no time. Had a good warm meal and dried most of my clothes. In the fog dry things don't stay dry.

The next morning was more of the same. I lay in my sleeping bag until 8:00 hoping the skies would clear, but no luck. I finally got up, packed, and headed down the trail. I hadn't gone more than 100 yards when I realized I didn't have my canteen. I thought I remembered where I'd left it hanging on a tree yesterday. Nothing for it but to go back and get it. I went back about half a mile and found my canteen lying in the path. I hadn't left it hanging in a tree after all. It had fallen from my pack without me noticing. The rain stopped about noon but the sun didn't come out. I was now two hours or four miles behind schedule. I made camp around 5:00 P.M. and managed to build a fire. The skies started clearing and by nightfall I could see the moon.

To catch up on my notes: May 31 was ideal. Clear blue sky, warm sun, and cool breezes. This is the kind of a day that makes my hike worthwhile. I stopped in a high pasture and soaked up the sun while I ate chocolate bars. The view from Big Bald was superb. In the far distance I could see Beech Mountain, where we ski. It will be getting closer next week.

WEDNESDAY, JUNE 2. *One mile past Beauty Spot Bald, North Carolina–Tennessee line.* Mostly uphill and road walking today. It started getting cloudy right after I left the motel and it began to sprinkle before I got out of Erwin. When I was hitching a ride back to the trail an old man picked me up. He proceeded to tell me that I was going in the wrong direction to get to Virginia, and then he told me how many people had been murdered around here lately. With that happy thought I thanked him for the ride and started off in the rain.

The trail was not too steep and the rain ended around noon. I hit a gravel fire road at about that time. Road walking is hard on my feet. The surface is hard and the pebbles on it roll around like ball bearings. When the trail follows a road it is usually not well marked. The through hiker needs more blazes to reassure him that the trail has not left the road. I've had a lot of trouble when the trail leaves a road because the exit into the woods is not plainly marked. My pack was much heavier because I restocked in Erwin and brought a lot of extra things for a picnic supper tonight. Egg salad, spring onions, hot dogs and buns, cucumbers, and mustard.

THURSDAY, JUNE 3. *Half a mile past Little Rock Knob Cliffs, North Carolina–Tennessee line.* Today was a hard one. Much road walking, steep ascents, and the bugs are beginning to bite. The woods here contain mostly maples. I remember them from my childhood in Cleveland and it's good to see them again. Lots of beech, too. I did something tonight I plan to do more of as time goes on. I stopped for dinner near a spring, in a low place, an hour earlier than usual. I ate my supper, then packed up and went on two or three more miles to a high place to sleep. Walking after 7:00 P.M. is easier because it is cool, and the woods are very pretty as the sun goes down. It also allows me to slow down during the day.

FRIDAY, JUNE 4. *Hump Mountain, North Carolina.* I'm not over the Hump, I'm on it. From where I sit at 5,587 feet every direction is down. It ought to be. I've been climbing all day. I've gone over five peaks today, all over 5,400 feet, with deep gaps between. It's a good thing I was three miles ahead of schedule when I started this morning because I'm back even with my schedule now. The first four miles took three hours. I usually cover over six miles in that time. It went like that all day and my legs and feet feel it. The Hump is a bald mountain with a meadow on its top. It's rather hazy now so I can't see more than 10 miles in any direction. I'm hoping for a beautiful sunset and a grand sunrise tomorrow. If the haze lifts I could see Beech Mountain from here. I don't think I will be able to see the ski slopes, but I should be able to see the mountain for several days. I've seen the last of the fir trees until I get to New England. As to getting there, I feel sure I can make it now, barring an accident. I wasn't so sure two weeks ago.

A jet is going overhead. That is the most common sound of civilization I hear. Lately I've also heard farm noises from the valleys below. I haven't seen any hikers for several days, or talked with anyone since Erwin. When I meet someone after a long spell I tend to get excited and giggle at my own jokes. A small plane just flew over and dipped its wings to me as I took the plane's picture.

SATURDAY, JUNE 5. *Laurel Fork Gorge, Tennessee.* It has been a long but beautiful day. It started badly, though. My grand sunrise was hidden by thick fog. I packed up and went down below the clouds to start a wonderful day. First I went through an apple and peach orchard, then through the woods to a back road, then up a pasture to another road. The walking was hard but the sight of rolling farmland was inspiring.

At one point, as I walked down a gravel road, I saw a small but neat white farmhouse with a red tin roof. In front were two large maple trees with an old tire swinging from a low branch on one of the trees. Beside the house was a small vegetable garden. In the large backyard a small boy in shorts was running through the grass holding a butterfly net high above his head, shouting for his mother to look. She was up to her knees in a small brook at the bottom of the yard pulling weeds from the bank. An even smaller toddler was sitting on a footbridge dangling his feet in the water and watching his mother work. I stopped and watched this scene for several minutes, hoping one of them would turn and see me and wave and thereby include me in their world.

I had supper by a rushing stream, and bathed in a small cold waterfall. After that I walked on to Laurel Fork Gorge, where I'm camped at the base of a 40-foot waterfall which comes over the sheer wall of the gorge. Plenty of mosquitoes, too.

SUNDAY, JUNE 6. *Vanderventer Lean-to, Tennessee.* Today was extremely rough. I seemed to be going up and down all day. It took me an hour to walk three miles out of the gorge, then four hours to walk five miles up and down the next section. I think they routed the trail here just to see how high you can go—and then when you get up there you can't see anything because of all the trees. One small section between Wilbur Lake and Watauga Dam seemed to cover more distance vertically than it did horizontally. I was going to walk after supper but I was too tired.

MONDAY, JUNE 7. *Thirteen miles south of Damascus, Virginia.* Easy walking today. Once you are on the ridge the trail is pretty level. Any climbing only lasts a few minutes. The mountains are not so high and the views show pleasant farmland. I think I like to see neat fields better than wilderness.

TUESDAY, JUNE 8. *Damascus, Virginia.* Just 13 miles downhill today. Nothing tiring about it but I still feel lethargic. Maybe my diet needs a change. All my body fat has been used—I've lost over 15 pounds— so maybe I need more calories.

THURSDAY, JUNE 10. *One mile north of Skulls Gap, Virginia.* Two things happened today that I really don't believe. First, the bathroom scales at Mrs. Vann McQueen's lodging house said my pack weighed 50 pounds. I don't think my skinny little body can lift 50 pounds. I'm now using egg noodles instead of rice in my stew. I'm also using an instant pudding that requires milk, which means I pack a box of dried milk. Second, according to the map of the Jefferson National Forest, I've walked nine miles in 3½ hours. I've come 16.2 miles with no trouble so the walking must be easy, but all day I've felt rather lethargic. Almost weak. Just before supper I took a nap and awoke feeling nauseated. I took one of Dr. Wilson's little pills and felt fine at once. Maybe my nausea was caused by all that rich food and cookies and milk in Damascus. I was trying to build up an energy reserve but I guess that's not the way to do it. You can't get a steak in those small cafés. It's cool and windy tonight. Might have some rain. My tent is pitched right in the middle of the trail. Hope no one is walking after dark. Tiny black bugs are eating me alive.

FRIDAY, JUNE 11. *Eight miles farther than yesterday.* I got so far ahead yesterday that I loafed along today. Slept an hour later than usual. Got to my lunch stop at 10:30 A.M. so I napped until noon. The ridge here is so level you can walk almost three miles an hour. Stopped and made camp at 3:00 P.M. Took another nap. I've only had one day off in the past month so I think I deserve the rest.

I don't have a guidebook for the next 300 miles so it's difficult to plan ahead. I just stop for supper at the first spring I come to after 4:30 P.M. and carry enough water for the other meals. I still feel listless. Maybe this slowing up will help.

SATURDAY, JUNE 12. *I don't know where I am.* The distances marked on my map seem to be wrong. I think I'm about six miles behind schedule now, and the rain has slowed me even more. I came out of the hills to cross a river at Teas. There used to be two stores here, but both are closed now. Rain started as I crossed the river at 3:30. As I started up into the hills again I came to a strip mine. The mine has left a wasteland, just mud and gravel everywhere. Sure looks bad. I crawled into my sleeping bag early tonight because there is no dry place to sit. I'm going to walk a full day tomorrow and forget about the map.

SUNDAY, JUNE 13. *Under a big maple tree in Virginia.* Today was wildlife day. I saw one woodchuck, one turkey, two grouse, and two deer. These are the first deer I've seen. Unfortunately, it had been raining so I had my camera zipped in one of the pockets on my pack. I fumbled over my shoulder trying to unzip the pocket while the doe looked at me suspiciously. She finally walked into the brush before I could get the camera out. The turkey looked like a small ostrich galloping through the woods trying to find a space big enough for a takeoff. I keep thinking I hear thunder but it's only another jet. Looks like it is going to rain again tonight. The sun had better come out tomorrow, as I don't have any fire ribbon left.

MONDAY, JUNE 14. *Monster Rock Lean-to, Virginia.* I should be farther along but I stopped to be in the movies. It rained heavily last night, and my tent is not quite watertight at the seams so I got a little wet. I packed while rain dripped from the trees. What ever happened to those days when it rained at night, but dawned on a bright new day? I haven't seen one yet. If it rains for five minutes it rains for three days and takes another day to clear up. As soon as I started up the mountain it started raining again. Hardest rain I've seen on the trip. It was even difficult to see the trail for a while. At a highway crossing I met a man, Tex Griffin, who was pointing a movie camera at me. He asked if I was Ned Smith. I said I was and he started shooting. We did scenes of me walking along the trail and at a scenic overlook. He says he'll try to catch me again in northern Virginia, then in New Hampshire, and finally at Katahdin. I may be "discovered."

TUESDAY, JUNE 15. *High Rock Lean-to, Virginia.* This trail is the worst I've seen. The land is almost level on the ridge but the trail is overgrown with weeds, briers, and small saplings. It is also covered with dead limbs and fallen trees. The surface is loose boulders. My ankles are sore from trying to walk on rocks that tilt when you put your full weight on them. I passed a trail crew today. Maybe they can fix things up. There were six men, one with a chain saw and five with bush hooks. They all wore baseball shin guards to keep from cutting their legs off with the bush hooks.

I started my fire today with dry wood I had carried in my pack from last night's lean-to. The lean-tos along here have a supply of cut firewood and an ax to split it with. Some thoughtful soul had also stored a few logs in the lean-to out of the rain. The grouse chicks are on their own now. I scared up several coveys today without a guarding hen.

WEDNESDAY, JUNE 16. *By the road six miles south of Pearisburg, Virginia.* It rained again. This means it has rained at least twice every day for the past six days without any sunshine between to dry things out. I was all set for cold stew tonight because I am out of fire ribbon, but by using the dry wood from my pack I got a fire started. I had hot stew and Russian tea after all.

I saw another turkey today. He flew out on the road behind me and strutted around as though I wasn't there. They sure are big birds! I ate lunch sitting beside the road while the rain poured down. I made a kind of tent out of my rain parka and leaned over my cup to keep the rain out. It's not very comfortable but it's real cozy under there.

THURSDAY, JUNE 17. *Pearisburg, Virginia.* If I had gone two miles farther last night I would have come to a new shelter that's not on the map. The workmen's tools were still there. It's still misty but there is no rain. Maybe this is the "clearing up" day. When the trail is in the woods in this area it is almost impassible because of blowdowns and brush. Try walking for two hours through wet brush up to your waist! You feel like you've been swimming with your clothes

on. It's better to wear shorts so only your bare legs get wet. In that
way you will keep your long pants dry to change into at night. I must
be in better shape now because all this wet weather has not damp-
ened my spirits as it did before. Because of the map I was late in
meeting Bill Sandberg for my food package. Bill is a friend of mine
from Charlotte, North Carolina. He travels in this area and agreed
to meet me on the trail. It was really good to see a familiar face. He
took me to a motel, to a Laundromat, and to a grocery store—and to
a steak dinner! I'll see him again next week for another package of
food.

I've switched hiking boots. The old ones were comfortable but so
soft I don't think they gave me much ankle support. The new ones
are regular hiking boots with hook laces all the way to the toe. They
feel a little tighter but I'm sure they will form to my feet. Bill will
bring my old boots back next week in case the new ones don't work
out. Got a new supply of fire ribbon and my down jacket, both welcome items. I passed the 500-mile mark a day or two ago. Only 1,500
miles more to go!

FRIDAY, JUNE 18. *Bailey Gap Lean-to, Virginia.* Well, I got lost
today and must admit it wasn't the map's fault. It wasn't my fault,
either. I left the motel in Pearisburg and headed for the blazes Bill
and I had scouted out yesterday. I kept cursing the local club because
the blazes were so old and so far apart. I missed the trail twice and
had to ask for directions. Each time people assured me that the trail
went such and such a way and sure enough, I would find a blaze farther down the path. When I got to Kimballton, Virginia, I lost the
way again and stopped at the general store to ask the way. The elderly lady behind the counter said, "Why son, you're six miles off the
trail. They relocated it five years ago—but don't feel badly, you're
the twelfth person to go wrong this year. Someone near Pearisburg
keeps sending them this way." She told me that if I kept to the old
marks and followed the hard-surfaced road I would run into the new
trail in about six miles. I followed her instructions and found the trail
again.

For some reason road walking gets me down. I think it's because
I can see where I am going so far ahead. It takes the sense of expectancy out of hiking. After I got on the right track again it was a three-
mile climb out of the valley to this lean-to. Water is a quarter of a
mile away on another path. I said good-bye to a faithful old friend
tonight—my trusty poplar walking stick. He gave me his last full

measure of service tonight after 500 miles of duty. I cut him up and cooked my stew with him, then scattered his ashes in the forest where he grew. I was genuinely sorry to see him go. I was understandably attached to his familiar grip. I've bought a slick new rake handle to take his place. The new stick is stronger and has a shiny finish, but I'll still miss the old one.

SATURDAY, JUNE 19. *Big Pond Lean-to, Virginia.* I had a sunny morning for the first time in nine days. It clouded up some as the day wore on but it was generally a pleasant day. I hear thunder now so I expect rain this evening. The woods are still wet from previous rains. Firewood hisses and makes smoke as it burns.

I met two girls on the trail today. They had a minimum of equipment—knapsacks with sleeping bags tied underneath—and weren't sure where they were going. They said they were hitchhiking around Virginia looking for tall mountains. I pointed out that there weren't any around here and recommended North Carolina. They agreed, and I walked on. Incidently, they had come only one mile from the shelter where they stayed last night and were already having lunch. They were the first hikers I have seen in over two weeks. Not much hiking activity around here, and I can see why with all the road walking and trouble with private landowners.

SUNDAY, JUNE 20. *Niday Shelter, Virginia.* I came through country where the trail was barricaded last summer. Saw several hand painted KEEP OFF signs. The path has been rerouted up the ridge about two miles.

I find there is a bat living in each shelter I've been in lately. Maybe it's the local mascot. Walking should have been easy today since 12 miles lay on a ridge with little change in elevation. However, once again the poor condition of the footpath made progress a struggle. High brush and dead limbs and blowdowns constantly blocked the way.

I awoke to sunshine this morning but it soon changed to clouds. No rain today, though. That makes 10 out of 11 sunless days recently. A farmer I talked to said it was the strangest season he had ever seen. Maybe there's a dark cloud following me from Georgia. I guess I should be grateful for having cool days for walking, but the constant cloud cover sure gets me down. I'm not wearing my arch supports with my new boots. My feet seem OK but I'm keeping the arch supports in my pack just in case. Scared up two turkeys and one deer today. I had just a brief glance at the deer as it raced away. I couldn't tell whether it was a doe or a buck and I don't see how a hunter could, either.

MONDAY, JUNE 21. *Catawba Mountain, Virginia.* Today was not my day. It was clear at 6:30 A.M. when I got up but it was cloudy by 7:00. And it stayed that way until 5:00 P.M. No rain, though. I thought I heard mouse sounds last night. When I turned on my flashlight I found the inside of the shelter covered with some kind of insect. There was one about every square foot. They had spheroid bodies about an inch long with legs like a grasshopper's and two long antennae. They were hopping around and fighting. I couldn't shoo them away so I pulled the sleeping bag hood over my head and went back to sleep. Later, when the real mouse came out, the insects were gone.

Made a typical valley crossing today. First the footpath joins a logging track which turns into a graded forest service road which becomes a secondary road which joins the highway running down the center of the valley. My first mishap occurred as I was going up the other side of the valley. The farm road I was on forded a stream several times. I made the first ford OK but not the second. The rock I stepped on tilted and down I went. Both feet and the seat of my pants got soaked and my right wrist was slightly twisted. It's still a little stiff. That's a good way to break an arm or sprain an ankle, and I was lucky not to do either. At the next ford I didn't try to stay dry. I just waded through.

A few hours later I got lost. A friendly landowner had painted over the blazes with green paint. I saw a few of the painted-over signs but not enough to tell where the trail left the field and entered the woods. I walked about four extra miles but I missed a steep climb so maybe it worked out even. It's hard to put down landowners for closing the trail. It's their land and I can understand their reluctance to have strangers using their property as a thoroughfare, especially if the land is abused by the hikers.

I saw something very disheartening this afternoon—logging operations along the trail. The crews had even gone over the Appalachian Trail itself with a bulldozer to make a drainage ditch. Blazed trees were knocked down and broken trees and limbs blocked the path. I thought it was a firebreak until I saw the fresh stumps. I guess it is private land and the dollar rules. This is the second such area I've covered. It looks like it's a good thing I'm taking this trip now. The trail may soon be plowed under all the way.

TUESDAY, JUNE 22. *Roanoke, Virginia.* It rained last night. One of those light showers that is good for sleeping. I awoke to clouds and it began to rain again around 9:00 A.M. Once again the terrain is easy but heavy spring growth and blowdowns made progress difficult. I had carried two gallons of water from a restaurant last night, and this morning, 200 yards from my campsite I found a spring. I didn't have to carry all that water after all! That discovery was the ominous beginning to one of the worst days I've had on the Appalachian Trail. I guess the depressing effect of continuous wet weather has finally gotten to me. The foliage was wet and every time I bumped into a branch I got a cold shower. I was drenched after only a few minutes.

That's the way it went all day. I got to some overlooking cliffs around lunchtime but the view was marred by low clouds. At 5:00 P.M. I got to the place I had planned to make camp but there was no water, so I had to keep going—and keep going, and keep going. I was cussing the map for giving incorrect distances, the local club for not clearing the path, and myself for coming on this damn trip. Finally I came off the mountain where I-81 crosses U.S. Route 220 at 7:30 P.M. and spent the night at a motel.

WEDNESDAY, JUNE 23. *Wilson Creek Lean-to, Virginia.* Started the day with a big store-bought breakfast: two eggs, two biscuits, a four-ounce steak, three hot cakes, and coffee. I was going to bounce back and show the world that I was not beaten. Instead, I got lost. Once again the trail had been relocated and the old blazes had not been removed, so I spent the morning taking false turns and knocking on doors to get directions. I finally got back to the relocated trail after three hours of horsing around. I got to a lean-to at 11:15. It was too early for lunch but I was so depressed that I took off my pack and stopped anyway. I had just sat down to write a few lines when a fellow came down the trail from the other direction. He was looking for a horse that had run away. We talked for a while and then it began to rain. It rained hard for two hours. When you're walking and it starts to rain, it's no problem to quickly put on your raingear and keep going, but when you're in a dry lean-to it's hard to suit up and go out into the rain. So I didn't. I stayed till 2:00 P.M. when the rain stopped and then I walked on. I've eaten supper and I'm going to walk on so I won't have so far to go tomorrow to meet Bill with my next food package.

FRIDAY, JUNE 25. *Cornelius Creek Lean-to, Virginia.* Well, I forgot my new walking stick in Bill's car. When Bill left me and I put on my pack I didn't take two steps before I knew that I'd left the walking stick in his trunk. I walked for 45 minutes and then I couldn't stand not having a stick any longer. I felt off-balance and empty-handed. Mainly I felt defenseless. That stick was my weapon against snakes —if I ever see a poisonous one—and my defense against dogs. I stopped right there and cut a new one. It is not as sturdy as the stick I just lost but it has character. (This stick went all the way to Katahdin.) I put in a good day of walking. It was all uphill this afternoon on a well-graded trail. I ran out of water about 1½ hours before reaching camp. I'll have to start filling my extra canteen all the time now. It was a very pleasant day for a change.

MONDAY, JUNE 28. *Wiggins Spring Lean-to, Virginia.* I haven't written for three days. On June 26 I was at a shelter with 30 Boy Scouts and 4 hippies. The hippies were smoking short little cigarettes and talking strangely. The next night I walked late and didn't have enough light for writing. I should be walking tonight—this place is near a road and picnickers have thrown garbage everywhere—but I'm too tired. I have been walking uphill for at least 12 miles from 1,000 feet by Lynchburg Reservoir to 4,059 feet at Bald Knob. The Appalachian Trail here in the George Washington National Forest is in much better shape than it was in the Jefferson National Forest. Still, there isn't much water and there aren't any side trails to springs lower on the slope. I carried three quarts of water with me and still ran out before I reached the good spring here.

On another topic: I want to go home! I'm not sure why, but lately I've been bored stiff. The past two days have been sunny but hot, so maybe it's the weather that's bothering me. If I wouldn't lose face with my friends at home and be ashamed of myself, I'd quit right now. I hope I get over this feeling soon. It makes it hard to hike when I'm not very interested in it.

I wonder if the gnat buzzing in my ear is the same one that's been there all day. If so, it has flown almost 15 miles sideways—not to mention the up-and-down distance. Even if it has indeed performed that great feat, I'd still squash him if I could get hold of him. I had a few wild strawberries a week ago and today I had blueberries and black raspberries. A few on each bush are ripe now. In a week I should have all I can eat.

TUESDAY, JUNE 29. *The Priest Lean-to, Virginia.* It's been a good day and I'm in much better spirits. I climbed to 4,072 feet and stayed near that height most of the day. I had bats in my lean-to last night. Two of them were playing tag from wall to wall. I could feel the wind from their wings as they flew by. I'd rather have bats than mice.

I carried three quarts of water up from last night's lean-to to 4,001 feet because no streams were marked on the map. Sure enough, there were two large springs at the top of the mountain. Better safe than thirsty, though. A thunderstorm is coming up. Thunder is rolling nearby, the wind is blowing through the treetops, and the fog is so thick you can't see very far.

The rain has started and I've moved my things to the back of the lean-to. My fire is going out. When I stopped for lunch I picked some wild strawberries. I'll have them for breakfast if I can get the caps off the tiny berries. Spray is getting on my notebook, making it hard to write with a ball-point pen. I'm thankful the rain waited until I was through cooking.

My right knee has swollen. It is not painful but the joint is stiff. I can't remember doing anything to hurt it. I met three hikers late today. As I approach Shenandoah National Park the activity seems to be increasing. Did you know that black raspberries are red before they are black, and that blueberries are red before they are blue?

WEDNESDAY, JUNE 30. *Maupin Field Lean-to, Virginia.* I had bats again last night. They don't seem to bother anything. I'm dead beat again tonight. Had another long climb from 1,000 feet to over 3,900 feet. These climbs seem to take all the energy out of me. I ran out of chocolate bars yesterday. Maybe that's the trouble. Ran into a crew painting the shelters today. The man in charge has been with the forest service for 42 years and he will retire at the end of July. He was part of the crew that built the Appalachian Trail through the George Washington National Forest back in the early 1930s. I talked with him for 45 minutes. It seems very easy to start a conversation these days, in spite of my grubby appearance. I just smile and say "howdy" or "morning" and they all seem eager to talk. The first question I am asked is always, "Have you seen any snakes?" I say "none" and we go on from there. Everyone wishes me luck but not many want to come along—and I don't blame them.

THURSDAY, JULY 1. *Five miles south of Shenandoah.* This part of the Appalachian Trail is very dry. I've run out of water twice this week. The only water is at shelters with sometimes one or two streams between.

The mice ran me out of the shelter last night. I had my bed all made and it wasn't even full dark yet when two mice began to investigate my belongings. They were so bold that when I held out a small stick, one of them came up to see if it was something to eat. He didn't become alarmed until I pinned his tail to the floor with the stick. Afterward I pulled out my tent and set it up by flashlight several yards from the shelter. I know when to get out!

At that point in my trip I stopped keeping a diary. Each night in the Shenandoah National Park I had company at the shelter and it was much more enjoyable to talk than to write. When I left the park I was five days behind in my notes and it just seemed too difficult to try to catch up. Looking back, I can also see a trend toward simplification, or perhaps laziness, in my daily routine. I had reduced my cooking chores to a one-pot operation. I eliminated any nonessential work to make more time for just plain sitting around. Since writing was a chore to me, I stopped it. Now I'm sorry I stopped for I'll never have a day-to-day record of the events of the rest of the trip.

I continued the hike in spite of my growing boredom and tiredness. I decided that I was walking too slow. I found that if I moved out at a steady purposeful gait I felt better at nightfall. Just moping along made me feel rotten at the end of the day. Also, when I reached the halfway point at the Susquehanna River, I began to feel better. From there on I had less trail before me than I had behind me, and this gave me a great psychological boost.

As I went north from the Shenandoah National Park, the path became more rocky. The terrain was easier through Pennsylvania, New Jersey, and New York, but the uneven and rocky surface of the trail kept me from going any faster. Some general impressions:

PENNSYLVANIA. Rocky and dry. When the guidebook says that a certain spring may be dry in summer months, believe it. Several times I had to go off the trail a mile or more for water when springs near shelters were dry.

NEW JERSEY. I was surprised at the remoteness of the Appalachian Trail in this state. I had thought that I would be walking through someone's backyard all of the time, but that wasn't the case. True, there was lots of road-walking here but it was on pleasant back roads. At one point on the heights above Greenwood Lake I could see one or two of the tallest buildings in New York City, but I was still in wilderness surroundings.

At the Delaware Water Gap I met a group of boys from a YMCA camp who had set out to walk 100 miles. We stayed together through five days of rain and two days of sunshine to the Bear Mountain Bridge over the Hudson River. They were the only people I met who made the same distance I did each day. The boys were from Brooklyn and for some of them this was their first hike. We didn't walk together because our paces were so different, but we did camp together each night. It was great to have such pleasant company around the campfire.

NEW YORK. Pleasant walks along grass-covered abandoned farm roads. And many more hikers.

CONNECTICUT AND MASSACHUSETTS. Surprisingly rugged country. As I went farther north I noticed that the vegetation on hilltops was becoming sparser and smaller. The tree line was coming down.

VERMONT AND THE LONG TRAIL. An excellent trail over increasingly rough country. Vermont hikers are well organized and the condition of the trails and shelters reflects it. Litter barrels are placed at road crossings. The trail is patrolled weekly to keep the path clear and clean. Two problems here, and at other places farther south, were vandalism of the shelters and live-in campers. Several times I discovered small groups living in the shelters for extended periods. Vermonters were trying to stop this practice by closing shelters that are accessible by road and having permanent caretakers circulating between two or three camps.

NEW HAMPSHIRE, THE WHITE MOUNTAINS. This was by far the most spectacular and strenuous portion of my trip. Up to this point I had been able to make 17 miles a day without much trouble. I could only make 10 miles a day in the White Mountains. I took advantage of the hut system whenever possible. These huts furnish two large meals and a bunk for $11. That seemed expensive after spending $20 a week for the rest of the trip, but it was well worth it. Primitive campsites are available—like those everywhere else along the Appalachian Trail —but you must have a stove for cooking. I used three shelters and four huts in my passage through this area.

MAINE, THE BEST OF ALL. Mahoosuc Notch is a ravine between two large mountains. Large boulders have fallen from the mountain and filled the ravine. I didn't find it difficult or strenuous; it just takes a lot of time. I thought it was fun to find my way through the tumbled mass of rocks, and then pull the pack through after me. At the very bottom are ice caves. I thought Maine had the best system of shelters of any section of the trail. They were built of logs, with aluminum roofs. Most of them were located in remote areas with no access roads. Because of this there was very little litter or vandalism.

The last five days from White Cap Mountain to Katahdin were the most pleasant of the whole trip. I found this trail easy to walk, the days were clear and cool, and the leaves were just changing to autumn colors. I even saw three moose. And maybe I felt good simply because I knew these were the last days of the journey.

I had mixed emotions as I neared the end of my hike. I felt much closer to God and His creation and took a deep joy in this closeness. I was glad to be done with my labors and able to return to my friends with my goal attained, yet I knew I would miss the straightforward demands of that simple life.

The end of my hike on top of Katahdin came at noon. I wish Georgia had such a spectacular ending to the trail for hikers going south. By nightfall I was in Bangor, Maine, and the next morning I was on a jet headed home. The sky was clear and I could follow the trail from Katahdin to the White Mountains. I covered with my eyes in 30 minutes what had taken me almost three weeks to walk.

Physically, I guess it was good that I finished the trail when I did. My knees were starting to hurt from days of coming down the steep slopes of New Hampshire and Maine. My feet were covered with tough calluses. I had lost almost 20 pounds. I felt good, but my friends said I looked very thin. My calves and thighs bulged with muscles but my shoulders had disappeared. I guess it just takes a frame to hang the pack on and legs to move it along. Even with the muscled legs, I couldn't get up from a deep knee bend. I think my legs were so muscle-bound from constant walking that they weren't good for anything else. To wrap it all up, I'm very glad I hiked the whole trail. The tired feet, the cold wet clothes, and the screaming boredom were simply the price I paid for a rich experience.

Suggestions for End-to-Enders

By Gene G. Fiducia

Started at SPRINGER MOUNTAIN on May 24, 1971
Finished at MT. KATAHDIN on October 10, 1971

I had lived on an island on the southern Jersey coast most of my life and knew very little about backpacking, and previous to my hiking it, I had never even heard of the Appalachian Trail. However, I have always been willing to explore new places and try new ideas, so when Elmer Boyd came to me with the idea of walking the trail, I was willing to give it a try. Actually, Elmer got the whole thing moving. He had the knowledge of backpacking that I lacked. Since he was in Nebraska and I was in New Jersey at the time, we had to work things out individually and then combine our ideas when he arrived home two weeks before we left for Springer Mountain.

Our two major concerns were equipment and food. After reading Colin Fletcher's *Complete Walker*, we had a good idea of the equipment we needed, and we decided to have our food sent to us at post offices along the way. The Mileage Fact Sheet put out by the Appalachian Trail Conference was very helpful in planning our food pickups. It lists lean-tos, grocery stores, lodgings, and post offices, and shows their mileages along the trail, and distances if they are off the trail. Elmer and I made a basic list of types of food with quantities for approximately 10 days, and left the list with Elmer's father so he could send food packages to us, in care of general delivery, as we requested them. The Mileage Fact Sheet indicated grocery stores along the way where we could supplement the food sent in our packages. Taking into account the terrain ahead, as described in our guidebooks, we would decide where to have our next food package sent and then call Elmer's home. If we needed additional food or equipment, all we had to do was make another telephone call and the extra supplies would be sent with our regular food packages. We never worried about the packages not being there when we called for them. The post offices are very good about holding packages for hikers; it is only necessary to indicate on the package that it is to be picked up by an Appalachian Trail hiker.

My pack and frame were by Camp Trails, and I thought they were as good as any I saw on the trail. The packbag was completely water-proof and needed no rain cover. It had tie-down flaps over the pockets instead of the usual zippers. I thought the tie-down flaps were more leakproof, and the ties could be replaced much easier than zippers. Then, too, the ties couldn't stick or rust as was possible with zippers. The only problem I had with the pack was that after every hundred miles or so the backband would tear and need replacing. Finally I had it reinforced with leather and it lasted for the remainder of my hike. Other hikers I talked with had this same problem, no matter what kind of pack they carried.

A hiker's most important piece of equipment is his boots. Never having hiked before, I made the mistake of buying a pair of army-type boots with 9-inch tops. The tops were too high, and they in-jured my Achilles tendons. After a few days I could hardly walk. I was in considerable pain during the first two weeks and 111 miles of the hike, and in Franklin, North Carolina, I bought a pair of Red Wing boots with 6-inch tops. After this change of boots and a short rest the pain disappeared and my miles hiked per week doubled. My enjoyment of the hike increased a hundred percent, too. The Red Wing boots lasted approximately 1,400 miles to Pico Peak, Vermont. I then bought a pair of Dunham boots. They were comfortable, but the soles came off after a while. If I were to hike the trail again I would invest in one pair of good boots, and then buy another cheap but comfortable pair. When the good boots needed repair, I would have the cheaper boots mailed to me and wear them while the good boots were sent home. When the good boots had been repaired, I would start wearing them again, and so on. This system would save time and money, as it is hard to get repairs on the trail, especially without losing time.

My clothing for the trail was simple: walking shorts, T-shirt, long-sleeved shirt, long pants, three pairs of socks and a lightweight but warm jacket. A poncho was carried for protection against the rain and was also used as a ground cloth. After a thousand miles or so it was necessary to replace some of my clothing, and it was sent with the food packages. Even before that the clothing needed mending, so I carried a small sewing kit. I considered the sleeping bag as a part of my clothing. It protected me after everything else had failed to do so. Since the sleeping bag is so important, it should be chosen with care. I think the best bag for the Appalachian Trail is a mummy type with 2¼ pounds of down. This weight gives enough protection for most people unless travel in the winter months is planned, yet it is not overly warm for summer nights. The mummy shape helps keep the warmth in the bag, where it counts. Although many people think a mummy bag might be too confining, you get used to it and appreciate the additional warmth. My sleeping bag was of this type, and on only a few summer nights was it too warm. Toward the end of October I started wearing long underwear so I would be warm enough to sleep.

Another important decision a through hiker has to make is when and where to start his hike. I would say that the best place to start is the southern terminus of the trail, and the best time is from the beginning of April to the middle of May. By starting at this time the trail can be hiked in favorable temperatures without too much fear of snow. When I say favorable temperatures, I do not mean that the weather will be perfect all the time. Rain is a big problem. Sometimes it rained for days, and this slowed us and prevented us from picking up food packages on time. Elmer and I started on May 24, which was a little late. We worried about hitting snow in Maine but luckily we had only rain and a few extremely cold nights toward the end of our journey. We finished on October 10 at Mt. Katahdin and were glad that the snows had not arrived yet. We did not carry a tent, so we tried to make it to a lean-to every night. Sometimes this was not possible, and on those occasions we found what shelter we could under huge boulders and in abandoned shacks. It is a good idea to check weather reports when possible, and also to try to figure out what the weather is going to be by studying the sky. It is amazing how good a weatherman a hiker becomes after a few weeks on the trail. We wore as few clothes as possible when walking in the rain. As long as we kept moving we were warm enough, and when we stopped we had dry clothes to put on.

I had many great experiences on my hike, and I hope the reader will also someday enjoy the natural beauty and adventures that are waiting on a long hike on the Appalachian Trail.

The Long Green Tunnel

By James Leitzell

Started at SPRINGER MOUNTAIN on June 17, 1971
Finished in NEW HAMPSHIRE on October 17, 1971

My Appalachian Trail hike fulfilled an ambition of many years duration. A half-year of intermittent preparation went into the expedition and the walk itself lasted four months. It was one of the signal events of my life. Certainly I have done nothing more physically demanding; its emotional and mental demands were at least as great.

Since boyhood I have been interested in hiking and camping. Growing up in the inner city—Chicago's Near North Side—I joined the Boy Scouts solely to participate in camping and hiking. We camped on weekends in Cook County's forest preserves. In the summer we went to the forests and lakes of northern Wisconsin, Michigan, and Minnesota. There we lived beneath the spruce and birch trees, took long portaging canoe trips, and hiked trails deep in the northern forest. There was little in the way of mountains, but everything else was there—woods, lakes, streams, and solitude.

At 18 I saw and climbed my first real mountain. I had set off from Chicago on a motorcycle to tour the nation. Initially I rode west across the cornfields of Illinois and Iowa, across the Great Plains, and arrived at the Black Hills of South Dakota. The first thing I did when I arrived was to hike up Mt. Mitchell. It was an easy walk, but for a city boy who had never before seen a mountain, it was high adventure. Since that day I have been a confirmed mountain climbing enthusiast.

My motorcycle tour continued for six months. Each time I came to an interesting mountain I stopped and tried to climb it. I obtained an ancient Bergans rucksack and, lashing my tattered kapok sleeping bag beneath it, took a number of short trips into the Sierra Nevadas and the Rockies. The equipment was crude, cumbersome, and heavy,

1741

but these sojourns into the backcountry opened a new world to me. By carrying the necessities of life on my back I could leave virtually every trace of civilized man behind in a day or two of hiking.

Tired of roaming, I enlisted in the Marine Corps. For the next three years I spent most of my time running up and down mountains in California and the Far East with the Fleet Marine Force. When off duty I climbed in the San Bernardino Mountains and the Sierras.

My first long backpacking trip took place in the spring of 1959. Using heavy but sturdy USMC camping equipment, I hiked for two weeks in the high mountains of the Sequoia–Kings Canyon National Park. It was early in the season and snow lay deep on the ground at higher elevations. However, I could walk on top of the frozen crust early and late in the day. Not another hiker was there, and I reveled in the solitude. Midway through the trip I encountered, to my surprise, an occupied cabin in Kern Canyon. Bill Jones, an almost legendary backcountry park ranger, had come in early to enjoy a few weeks of quiet preseason solitude. He was as startled to see me as I was to see him, but we soon became friends and I stayed two nights with him. He had a new Kelty pack and a Trailwise down-filled sleeping bag. I had never seen lightweight hiking equipment before and could hardly believe how little it weighed. The first thing I did upon returning to civilization was to order a Kelty pack for myself. Twelve years later this same pack rode my back the length of the Appalachian Trail.

After military service I enrolled at Colorado University in Boulder. The area offers a great variety of climbing possibilities, ranging from easy scrambles to difficult rock, ice, and snow ascents. I climbed on weekends and during the summer, but school and work consumed so much time that I was able to get to the mountains less frequently than I wanted. I decided that upon graduation I would take a summer-long trek in the High Sierras as a sort of compensation for all the hiking and climbing I had missed. My plan was to start at the southern end of the range, near Lake Isabella, hike its length, then continue in the Cascades to the Oregon border and perhaps beyond. For food I would fish, and when staples ran low I would drop down to the nearest settled valley to resupply.

Unfortunately for the trip, I fell in love and was married near the end of my senior year. My bride enjoyed hiking and wanted to go on the expedition with me. However, she was unable to keep up the 10- to 15-mile daily pace that I had envisaged. Even at a slower pace more suited to her strength, she became weary and bored with the trip. We made camp in a high alpine valley where wild flowers were blooming in profusion and waterfalls tumbled from cliffs on every hand. We camped there until we had used up our food and then returned to civilization. I was frustrated by the premature ending of the journey and vowed that some day the trip or its equivalent would be made.

For the next two years we lived in New Hampshire, where I studied graduate mathematics. Often we hiked in the White Mountains, and I became aware of the existence of the Appalachian Trail for the first time. During our second summer we lived in the heart of the mountains at the tiny community of Dundee. Formerly this was a farming settlement on the side of a high mountain valley near North Conway. Agriculture became unprofitable after World War I, and the properties were bought up by some friends of ours in 1940. They have preserved the old buildings, which date from the early 1800s, in their original state, and every summer a succession of scholarly friends comes to visit and partake of the mountains. The intellectual atmosphere has led them to fondly dub the establishment Dundee University. Much labor is needed to keep the fields mown, the trails clear, and the buildings in good repair. Each summer they hire a young couple to live in one of the old cabins and help out, and that summer we were the hired help.

I devoted my spare time to climbing the "four-thousand footers" in New Hampshire. There are 46 mountains in the state whose summits rise more than 4,000 feet above sea level, and for years the Appalachian Mountain Club (AMC) has contained a select sub-club consisting of those who have climbed them all. By summer's end I had hiked to the tops of all the designated peaks. In so doing, I had of necessity hiked virtually all of the Appalachian Trail between Mt. Moosilauke and the Mahoosuc Range. Actually I avoided the Appalachian Trail, taking pains in particular to camp near it as infrequently as possible. Even then, when backpacking was barely beginning its explosive growth in popularity, the Appalachian Trail in New Hampshire was heavily traveled. The side trails, by way of contrast, were lightly used. Often one could hike an entire day on the side trails and not meet anyone, and frequently it was possible to spend a night alone in a shelter. Of course, I rarely had the need to camp out because the secluded forest setting of the little sugar house at Dundee could hardly be improved upon for solitude.

One July weekend I met a young man and his wife at the old Garfield Pond Shelter. They had started walking at Mt. Katahdin six weeks earlier and were attempting to walk the entire Appalachian Trail. The young woman was neither strong nor athletic, so their pace had been slow. Given my experience with husband-and-wife backpacking in the Sierras, I was quite sympathetic with the man's frustration. At the rate they were going they could not possibly finish the hike in one season. We spent the night together, talking about their experiences as we lay around the campfire. After combating the frigid waters of the Kennebec River, the stinging bites of the black-flies, and the difficulties of AMC trails, the girl was ready to throw in the sponge. She had decided to drop out after they finished the New Hampshire section. Her husband would continue at his own pace, and she would provide logistical support the rest of the way to Georgia. The idea of hiking the Appalachian Trail from end to end had not previously occurred to me; it struck me as an intriguing idea, a challenge to be met someday when the opportunity arose.

The notion remained dormant for several years until 1968, when the time at last seemed ripe. I was applying for admission to medical school and, having had excellent college grades, admission test scores, and interviews, assumed that I would be accepted to begin work in the autumn. At the time I held a mathematics lectureship in Oklahoma, and my teaching duties would be completed early in June. The medical schools I was interested in did not start classwork until late in September, so three and a half months would be available to walk the trail. It would have to be a fast trip, but others had done it in less time, so why not me? Planning began in January with purchase of the Appalachian Trail Conference (ATC) guidebooks and overhaul of my backpacking equipment. Two months later I received the crushing news that the medical schools had turned me down.

A period of profound depression followed. In retrospect it was easy to see that I had made many naive mistakes during the application process. I felt reasonably sure that, profiting from experience, a second round of applications would gain a place in a med school class. However, the initial failure traumatized my ego, and it was slow to regain its usual self-esteem. I therefore wanted to obtain every possible advantage the next time around. In particular, this meant that the application forms should be submitted as early as possible, i.e., in late summer. This in turn necessitated considerable correspondence during the summer. It would be impossible to manage this from the mountains, so my summer hiking plans were reluctantly canceled.

Experience and attention to detail bore fruit, as five of seven schools sent acceptances the second time around. I chose to go to Utah, in large measure because of the superb hiking, climbing, and skiing opportunities in the Wasatch and Uintah mountains. The school there also offers unusually flexible scheduling of the third- and fourth-year ward work. Indeed, it is possible to take all of one's vacation from the last three years in a single continuous block of time. During my freshman year I was too busy with classes, work, and recreation to think much about an Appalachian Trail hike. At the beginning of the second year, I made the decision to go ahead with it. Exams would be finished in the middle of June, and it was possible to defer beginning the third-year clerkships until late in October. Allowing a week for travel to and from the trail, there would be four months in which to complete the hike. This was less time than I would like to have had, but was the most that could be managed.

For several reasons this might be the last opportunity I would have to make the hike, and it seemed to me that it was now or never. With seven years of time-consuming medical school, internship, and residency to look forward to, followed by the intense, hyperactive life of a practicing surgeon, it was unlikely that it would be feasible for me to take off for such a long period of time again until much later in life. At that time I might be physically unable to hike—or no longer have the desire to do so. Further, there had been an exponentially increasing number of backpackers the last 10 years. Already large areas of the Sierra Nevadas were intolerably crowded by hikers during the summer. I had not been East in five years, but the Appalachian Trail could hardly be much better off. I thought that at the very best it must be disgustingly crowded in some areas, such as the national parks and New England. As bad as the existing situation might be, one could safely assume that it would be immeasurably worse in a few years.

Preparations

The first decision to make was whether to hike from north to south or from south to north. In favor of the north-to-south approach was the avoidance of southern heat during the summer and of northern cold in the autumn. Against this choice was the fact that one would be in Maine and New Hampshire at the height of the midge and blackfly season. In favor of hiking northbound was having the sun at one's back, seeing the rhododendrons and azaleas in bloom, and finishing on top of an impressive alpine summit, rather than a wooded hilltop. Against the south-to-north route was the very real possibility of encountering nasty early winter weather in Maine. My instinctive preference was to travel northward, and in the end this is what I decided to do.

Exams would last through June 16, and I would have to be ready to begin ward clerkships on October 24. Assuming one day for travel to Springer Mountain and a week for the return trip from Maine, stopping en route to visit my mother in Chicago, and finding a place to live in Salt Lake City upon return, there were four months available for the hike. Including approach trails, the total distance was around 2,025 miles. If I averaged 18½ miles a day, I would finish in 110 days. If the average was only 16½ miles a day, then 120 days would be required. I figured that I could walk 20 miles a day under average conditions. Making the assumption of an occasional day off, I aimed for a 110-day hike. This left a cushion of 10 days. I would have preferred to have five months for the trip, since I felt the pace I was committed to was a bit hurried. The anticipated daily mileage was not the problem; rather it was the impossibility of making layovers when the mood struck me.

Jaunts in the White Mountains had convinced me of the need for shelter from rain every night of the trip. I did not want the weight or nuisance of a tent, so I planned to rely primarily on the lean-tos. For protection in those sections where shelters were scarce or awkwardly spaced, I would carry a lightweight tarpaulin. Although I had no definite plans to utilize public accommodations, the possibility was left open. On occasion, a hot bath and soft bed might prove to be a welcome luxury. Having a number of friends who reside near the trail in New England, I also planned on several overnight visits.

Over the years I had accumulated a plethora of hiking and climbing equipment. Not much of it had been purchased with the idea of long-distance hiking in mind, but to minimize expense I tried to use it when possible. The first and by far the most important item was boots. My criteria for boot selection were comfort, light weight, durability, and modest cost. I settled on a pair of Bean's Ruff-Out Mountain Climbers with Vibram soles. Although not wholly suited to my taste, they were a better approximation than anything else. As backups, I had a comfortable pair of Marine boondockers. Since I am very easy on shoes, I thought one pair might suffice for the entire trip and did not worry much about replacements.

My 12-year-old Kelty pack had tumbled out of an airplane, fallen from a motorcycle, and been mauled by a bear, but it was still in reasonably good condition, and I thought it would hold up. I had a Bauer Snowline mummy bag that I knew from experience would keep me warm to 25° F. Sometimes it might be colder than that in Maine, but I felt that I would rather tolerate a few uncomfortable nights than carry anything heavier. I debated between using an Ensolite pad and a shorty air mattress, opting for the latter because it is more durable and easier to pack. A 3-by-7-foot coated nylon sheet would serve as a groundcloth, and an 8-by-8-foot coated nylon tarp would be the emergency shelter. My cookset consisted of a pair of nested aluminum kettles and a steel frying-pan lid. I would also carry a plastic cup, a spoon, a pocketknife, some aluminum foil, and an S.O.S pad. For brewing tea at midday and cooking when it was difficult or impractical to start a wood fire, I would carry a small Primus stove and a quart bottle of fuel.

For rain and wind protection I had a durable below-the-knee USMC sentry's raincoat and a Stetson hat. I planned to hike in cutoff Levi's, reinforced at the seat. Blue denim work shirts would protect my upper body from the pack's chafing, from the sun, and from insects. For camp use I would carry a pair of long Levi's, a second shirt, and a down-filled jacket from Bauer. When the weather turned cold in the fall I would add long johns, mittens, and a woolen shirt. For inner socks I like to use a pair of lightweight nylon socks. For outer socks, the inexpensive and durable Penney's work socks have proved quite satisfactory. Nature provided me with a swimsuit, and a couple of bandannas completed the clothing list.

My first-aid kit consisted of Band-Aids, iodine, gauze rolls, gauze four-by-fours, adhesive tape, an elastic bandage, a snakebite kit, two scalpel blades, a hemostat, a pair of forceps, a pair of scissors, and two nylon sutures with attached needles. I carried insect repellent, several waterproof packets of matches, a small compass (which I never used), a safety razor, a small bar of soap, a bit of detergent, and an abbreviated sewing kit. Leaving my Accutron at home, I carried a five-dollar Pocket Ben. Onionskin paper, envelopes, small notebooks, and pens, all in waterproof bags, served for letters and journals. I have never needed a flashlight when backpacking, so I did not plan to carry one. Not being interested in photography, I carried no camera. I would have carried books for recreational reading, but doubted if there would be much time for it.

I thought it would be interesting to study the changes in resting and exertional blood pressure, heart rate, and respiratory rate as my physical condition (presumably) improved. The kit included a blood pressure cuff and a stethoscope. My imagination conjured up a variety of other experiments that could be conducted on a long-distance hiker, but most of these would have required too much equipment and time. I wanted to keep my studies simple and use a minimum of equipment.

Food was naturally a major consideration. For a weekend trip one can take almost anything along. The total amount is so small that even the heaviest foods do not weigh one down. Most foods will keep for a couple of days without refrigeration, and one does not have to concern himself with nutritional aspects. For a more extended outing, say 10 days, it is important to pay close attention to both weight and perishability, but nutrition is still not a very important consideration. So long as one consumes plenty of fluid and calories, the body has ample reserves of vitamins, minerals, amino acids, and lipids for making up any deficiencies in the diet. However, when one plans to be on the trail for four months, vigorously exercising almost every day, it is essential that one's diet contain all the nutrients that the body demands. Otherwise, the hiker would soon exhaust his body reserves and become weak, lethargic, and susceptible to infection. Being an impoverished medical student, cost was another factor to be considered.

Hikers' diets tend to err on the side of too much carbohydrate and too little fat and protein. I wanted to insure an adequate intake of the latter substances, as well as of essential vitamins and minerals. The lightweight freeze-dried backpacking foods are very expensive for the amount of nutrition they furnish. Further, I find them extraordinarily unappetizing. Canned foods are obviously unacceptable on the basis of weight and bulk. Fresh foods would not be available much of the time, and they have the additional drawbacks of perishability, heaviness, and bulk. As on previous hikes, I planned to rely primarily on dehydrated foods that are readily available. For variety they would be supplemented with produce and meats when I found a grocery or restaurant near the trail.

Breakfast would consist of a variety of cereals—oatmeal, Cream of Wheat, chopped wheat, and granola—a different kind each week. Raw sugar, dried milk, and dried fruits would dress up the cereal. Eggs would add animal protein and fat to the meal whenever they were available. One can buy a dozen eggs in the afternoon, hard-boil them at night, and then eat them the next three or four mornings. Usually they will keep three days, even in warm weather, and often longer. I eat a number of small snacks during the day, rather than one large lunch. For these I planned to carry bread, preferably wheat or rye, and either dried or fresh, depending upon availability. Peanut butter, honey, preserves, butter, cheese, and hard salami would be used to make sandwiches. Candy and chocolate would satisfy my sweet tooth.

Supper would be the day's main meal. It would consist of meat or fish, dehydrated soup, brown rice or barley, and powdered milk. Jerky would be the meat mainstay, and an occasional tin of tuna or salmon would satisfy my desire for fish. The jerky would be prepared by my wife and mailed to me. There would be fresh meat whenever I chanced on a grocery or café. Coffee and tea would satisfy my addictions for caffeine and theophylline, respectively. I hoped to pick fresh berries for snacks, but would not rely on them. The guidebooks suggested little in the way of fishing possibilities, so I left my fishing equipment at home. Whenever possible I would purchase fresh fruit and vegetables, bread, eggs, and butter at stores near the trail.

When I first began to think about hiking the Appalachian Trail, I thought that the ideal logistical support would be to have someone drive up to meet me every week or two with food and other supplies. Initially my wife was amenable to taking a job in the East for the summer so that she could fetch supplies and walk short sections of the trail with me. This was fine with her as long as the trip was only a theoretical possibility. When the plan became definite, she changed her mind and decided against uprooting herself for the summer, so I had to devise another means of support. Using Appalachian Trail Conference maps and a post office directory, I divided the trail into 13 segments of approximately 150 miles apiece, in such a way that there was a post office near the trail at the beginning of each section. A package of food and supplies would be mailed to each post office a month or so prior to my anticipated arrival. Periodically I would write back to Salt Lake City with instructions as to what should be included in subsequent packets. This entailed a long time lag between discovering a need and receiving the desired item in the mail, so I tried to anticipate needs as accurately as possible before beginning the hike. Those needs that could not wait a month to be satisfied would have to be taken care of from local sources.

Since grocery stores are scarce along the trail and there was no way of knowing in advance what they stocked, I wanted the mail packages to contain almost all of the food that would be required. I made the assumption that near every post office there would be a grocery where I could buy eggs, butter, bread, meat, and produce. All the cereal, dried fruit, dried milk, dried soups, nuts, rice, chocolate, peanut butter, coffee, tea, and jerky would be in the mailed packets. It turned out that by buying these foods in bulk and shipping them the cost was no greater than if they had been purchased piecemeal along the way. Matches, soap, S.O.S pads, washrags, maps, and guidebooks would also be in each package, and fresh socks, shirts, and jeans would be in every second or third parcel. Cold weather clothing would be included in the shipment destined for Gorham, New Hampshire, and the spare boots would be sent to a pickup point to be determined when I learned how well the first pair held up.

Most of the planning and preparation was done during the two months immediately before the hike was to start. Medical school and other activities kept me so busy that there was time to do only the bare minimum of planning. I read the general descriptions of the trail in the guidebooks, glanced at the maps, and made crude estimations of each section's difficulties. For easy and less interesting sections (e.g., Shenandoah, New York, and New Jersey) I assumed a faster rate of travel; for harder and more interesting sections (e.g., southwestern Virginia and New Hampshire) I planned a slower rate. For each of the sections I then allotted a number of days according to its difficulty and distance. Once on a section, I would study the guidebook and plan the details of daily mileages and overnight stopping points. My preference would have been to travel with no schedule whatsoever, going just as far and as fast as I felt like going on any given day, and stopping whenever the mood struck me and staying for as long as I wanted to, but my limited time forced me to exert some control so I would finish in the time available.

Our marriage had suffered increasing difficulties as the school year advanced. Among other differences, the Appalachian Trail hike was becoming a bone of contention. My wife's argument was that I would not go off on such a silly expedition and leave her for four months if I really loved her. The basic conflicts ran much deeper, and it became obvious that the marriage could soon end only in divorce. The situation deteriorated very rapidly as the semester neared its end, and the divorce occurred abruptly in May. My wife had promised to mail the packages, and even in divorce agreed to honor her commitment, but early in June, just as final exams were about to begin, she informed me that she had decided not to help out with the logistics. She refused even to post previously prepared packages, so while in the middle of trying to study and write exams, I had to revise my supply system extensively. I made the best estimates I could as to when various supplies would be needed, wrapped all 12 packages, addressed and stamped them, and left them with a classmate, together with a schedule of mailing dates. All he would have to do was take a package to the post office every week or 10 days. Unfortunately, there was no feedback in this supply system, but it was the best I could devise at the time. After final exams there was a free week prior to National Board Examinations. I packed and stored my belongings, finished preparations for the hike, and flew to Chicago for a few days to get away from everything and study in peace. The exams were on June 15 and 16. Like the tests which our medical school faculty is fond of subjecting us to, they require no more than the most elementary reasoning. Again, like medical school tests, there is no substitute for knowing the currently accepted "facts." The emotional trauma of the separation and divorce and my preoccupation with preparing for the hike had caused my academic performance to take a nose dive during the winter and spring. Merely passing the exams posed no particular problem. It was an insult to my ego to write them at a mediocre level but there was no avoiding this inevitable consequence. One cannot perform well intellectually when he is emotionally upset, and in the final analysis, climbing, skiing, music making, and Appalachian Trail hiking were much more important to me than receiving high grades.

I spent my last evening before the trip playing chamber music with some other friends. We usually play string quartets, but this time an excellent pianist had accepted our invitation, and we played the Schumann piano quintet and the two Mozart piano quartets.

The First 500 Miles

The great adventure began on June 17, a warm clear day. A neighbor drove me to the airport for the early morning flight to Chicago. The lightly loaded 727 took off to the south, climbed out over the city, and made a sweeping turn to the east above the snowcapped peaks of the Wasatch Front. With a touch of sadness I bid farewell to the familiar mountains which I would neither see nor stand upon for four months.

There was a two-hour wait between planes in Chicago, but the time passed quickly and soon it was time to board a Northwest Airlines flight for Atlanta. As the plane passed between towering thunderheads over the southern Appalachians, I kept peering down and wondering if any part of the Appalachian Trail was concealed in the dense green forest 30,000 feet below.

An air-conditioned bus carried me 60 miles northward to the little town of Jasper. As it jolted along the narrow winding Georgia roads, the southernmost ramparts of the Appalachians appeared on the horizon, first as small hills, then as large hills, and finally as rolling mountains. After innumerable stops the bus deposited me in Jasper. No taxi was to be found, but the town constable said his son might be willing to drive me to Amicalola Falls State Park for a price. A short session of bargaining resulted in agreement on $3 for the ride.

I climbed into a hopped-up 1957 Ford sedan with the boy and his two teenaged friends, and we commenced a high-speed chase along winding mountain roads to Amicalola Falls. The unmuffled engine roared and the tires screeched as we tore around the curves. All the while the boys tried to bait me about the wild animals I would encounter up in the mountains. I assured them that I was accustomed to living in the woods and could handle any bears or snakes that the eastern mountains might harbor. Then we all shook hands and they raced off back down the highway toward Jasper.

After a day filled with crowds and noise, I stood alone in the gathering darkness. It was eight o'clock and barely an hour of daylight remained. Rain was beginning to sprinkle down. The guidebook indicated that there was a shelter only two miles up the trail. This could easily be reached before nightfall, so I pulled on my pack and entered the moist dense forest. It felt good to be there. For five years I had not been in an eastern deciduous forest. The dry sparsely vegetated intermountain region has a beauty of its own, but one never gets over missing the eastern forests.

As the last iota of light disappeared from the woods I came to the stone foundation of what had once been a shelter. About this time the skies opened and a deluge began. Since there is a complete string of shelters from Georgia northward through and beyond the Great Smokies, I was carrying no emergency tarpaulin. It would arrive in the first supply package. Having no flashlight, it was impossible to return down the trail to the shelter of the park buildings. The only alternative was to stay put for the night. I wrapped up in my raincoat, hunkered down beneath a massive oak, pulled the Stetson over my face, and prepared for an uncomfortable night. The rain poured down, lightning flashed in every quadrant, and the hills reverberated to the thunder. As the night wore on, rainwater slowly worked its way inside around my neck and wrists. By morning I was soaked through. Surprisingly, although I was cold and stiff, I did not feel too bad. As I set off up Frosty Mountain in the drizzle and fog, I reflected that the worst had happened in terms of sleeping discomfort and I had come through it without difficulty. In the future it should be possible to reach shelter of some sort every night and avoid further drenchings.

Two hours of easy ascent brought me to the summit of Springer Mountain and the southern terminus of the Appalachian Trail. The mountaintop was solidly closed in by forest and fog. A dozen hikers lay scattered around beneath tarps, all sleeping soundly. The register contained the names of many hikers who had announced their intention of walking the entire Appalachian Trail. They came from all over the country—alone, in pairs, in threes and fours, young and old, male and female. Most of them had started in April and May. There was a sprinkling of entries dated from early June, and a last belated entry by a Californian who had started the preceding day. He indicated his intention of completing the hike in no more than 75 days. An image of a Westerner who had never hiked in the Appalachians came to mind. He would have thought how easy it must be to hike in those flat eastern mountains and what a simple matter it would be to average 30 miles per day. I chuckled as I thought of the rude surprise he was in for and wondered how long it would be until I overtook him.

The rain stopped as I started off along the trail, but the woods remained wet all morning. The forest was exclusively deciduous, in contrast to the pines that dominate the Georgia lowlands. The ground beneath the trees was carpeted with a verdant growth of annuals and perennial bushes. I was disappointed by the lack of views, the woods being densely wrapped across all the mountaintops. The forest was lush and odoriferous, however, and the path was soft underfoot, so I tripped happily along, the themes from the Mozart quartets playing in my mind. I stopped frequently to examine now a flower, now an interesting plant, now a tree, now a gold and black caterpillar, now an abandoned and crumbling graveyard. It was good to be on the trail at last, after so many years of waiting.

I had had no opportunity to condition my body so I wanted to hold down mileage for the first part of my trip. Thus at noon I stopped for the day at the Hawk Mountain Lean-to, even though I was not tired, having covered only 13 miles. The sun came out, and I spread my things to dry. (I had not brought a pack rain cover as I thought that waterproof stuff bags would keep my equipment dry. However, when it is constantly raining water manages to seep in through the most minute openings. A day later I fashioned a pack cover from a heavy, plastic garbage-can liner liberated from the forest service. It lasted two weeks, and then I made another one, and in this way managed to maintain a dry pack throughout the hike.) The afternoon was enlivened by two Boy Scouts from Nashville who stopped in to wait out a thundershower. They planned to walk as far as the Smokies, and being anxious to get there, they pressed on when the sun reappeared. The rest of the day I was alone—straightening out equipment, writing, and roughing out my itinerary for Georgia. Birds kept up a chorus of song, and as I worked I savored the sights and smells of the woods. When the evening began, I became lonely and depressed. I had some second thoughts about continuing with the hike, but after a good night's rest the doubts evaporated. Indeed, I had no more second thoughts about the trip the rest of the way.

The second day out I swung into high gear, covering 20 miles. Already I was passing numerous hikers who had either given up or radically reduced the scope of their trips. Four kids had taken six days to cover the first 20 miles. Their feet were badly blistered, and they had decided to quit. One of a group of Scouts en route to the Smokies suffered an asthmatic attack, and they had all decided to go home. I passed my two Scout friends from the first day. They were limping painfully along because of blisters, and looked about ready to throw in the towel.

After two full days on the trail I had not seen a single view. Blood Mountain was reputed to have an excellent outlook. (Its name stems from a legendary Creek–Cherokee battle of such ferocity that the mountainside ran red with blood. Ever since, so the story goes, the ground plants have been stained a dusky red by the blood in the soil. And they do have a reddish tint!) As I approached Blood Mountain's summit near dusk, clouds rolled in from the east and the mountaintop was immersed in fog for the rest of the night. I had company on this second night on the trail. He was a gentle charming hippie from Atlanta. He had little interest in material possessions and consequently worked only at an occasional odd job to provide funds for rent and groceries. Frequently he went into the mountains for a few days of meditation, carrying a sack full of homegrown vegetables and a blanket. With great difficulty we built a fire from damp rhododendron twigs and sat next to it, alternately blowing to keep the blaze alive and rapping about meditation, mountains, foods, gardening, and Oriental medicine. Eventually we tired of talk and simply sat together staring into the flames.

The next morning while descending Levelland Mountain towards Tesnatee Gap I overtook a heavyset man sitting beside the trail. He had curly black hair and wore a sweat-soaked gray T-shirt and shorts reinforced at the seat. The biggest, most heavily laden Kelty pack I had ever seen rested against a tree. Not only was it stuffed to overflowing, but there were canteens, mess gear, and clothing dangling from its sides, back, and bottom. When he walked, it rattled and clanked as if he was wearing a suit of armor. The pack must have weighed 70 pounds, and given the fellow's abundant adipose tissue, it seemed small wonder that he was soaked with perspiration and exhausted. He turned out to be the Californian who had started on the trail a day ahead of me. Dave Odell had already revised his estimate of how long the hike would take to 80 days. He said, "Just

Photos by Garnett W. Martin

Sign in Sassafras Gap, North Carolina.
Trillium with single seed pod, Mt. Wolf, New Hampshire.

Photo by Albert Field

Nolichucky River, Tennessee.

wait. Once I get in shape, I'll really begin to move out. I'll clip along at 30 miles a day." I surmised that he might have to revise his estimate upward again, and by a considerable number of days.

We walked down to the gap together, had lunch at the pretty little log shelter there, and continued on to Rocky Knob for the night. He had hiked in the California mountains as a Boy Scout, and during the preceding summer had hiked the John Muir Trail in its entirety. He was planning to hike the entire Pacific Crest Trail during the summer of 1972. The Appalachian Trail hike was to serve as a warm-up for that trip. His concept of this hike as a mere prelude, rather than an outstanding trip in its own right, nettled me. It is not that I disparage the western mountains. Indeed, I prefer hiking and climbing there, but the Appalachians are fine mountains, and they deserve consideration and respect as such.

My feet had begun to ache the very first day. There were no blisters, and indeed I only developed a couple of insignificant ones on the entire trip, but the constant pounding made the soles of my feet burn and throb. The pain usually began early in the afternoon and intensified as the afternoon wore on. Removing my boots and socks in camp lessened the hurt, but my feet continued to ache until late at night. Bathing them in a pool or walking around barefoot on the cool damp earth was soothing. After a few days my feet toughened up and the pain was markedly reduced. Thereafter, it recurred daily after 15 miles or so, but only when walking more than 20 miles in a day was it strong enough to be a nuisance.

The Appalachian Trail in Georgia was not especially interesting. Most of the forest was rather undistinguished second growth, although there were occasional stands of massive oaks. The trail was close to civilization. Frequently it followed an old logging road or a currently used gravel road. Numerous highways crossed it, and sometimes one encountered that lowest form of trail life, motorcyclists. The trail was buried in the forest. Only rarely were there outlooks, and when I came to one it always seemed to be obscured by clouds. I found it extremely frustrating not to be able to see where the trail had been and where it was going.

Suddenly the trail broke out of the woods into Bly Gap at the North Carolina border. The little gap was open and grassy. The meadow was full of yellow, red, and white wild flowers, and there was a clear view down into the valleys to the north and south. A brisk cool breeze whipped through the notch, chasing puffy white cumulus clouds overhead. Court House Bald loomed ahead, and for the first time it seemed as if the trail was about to enter some real mountains. A steep scrambling climb brought me to the summit of the mountain. It was the first good ascent on the trail and it was exhilarating to exercise my heart, lungs, and climbing muscles. The mountaintop was covered with blooming mountain laurel and flame azalea. Now and then I walked through dark, cool tunnels cut in rhododendron thickets, but few rhododendrons had been in bloom. On the next summit—Standing Indian (which looks more like an Indian lying flat on his back)—they were in full bloom. This summit is broad and open. One looks across an expanse of orange azaleas, white laurel, and pink rhododendrons; then one descends through the thickets of flowering bushes, inhaling the flowers' fragrant odors all the while. This flowering peak alone justified my decision to walk northbound.

After six days on the trail I was at Albert Mountain, having traversed 105 miles. On the summit there is a fire tower that commands an outstanding panoramic view. This was my first 360-degree outlook on the trail, and I spent an hour perched high on the tower enjoying it in the afternoon, and again just before sunset. Standing Indian was the dominant feature on the skyline. The valleys below were full of mist and seemed remote and mysterious. The sun threaded its way down to the horizon amid broken clouds and finally set in a dusky red haze. I climbed down from the tower as the night grew dark and sat around a campfire munching cookies with some Floridians who had camped there. A strong breeze fanned the flames, eliminating the usual need to constantly fuss with the fire. (The wood is so damp in these parts that building a fire is a bit of a project to begin with, and then one cannot leave it for a moment lest the flame go out.) My company was an older couple and their son. He had earned an MFA in painting and sent out 700 letters of application to college faculties. From these 700 letters he had received *one* invitation for an interview and *no* job offers. He supported himself by driving a school bus in Michigan.

Dave and I were seeing a great deal of one another along the trail. We had not formally teamed up, but our paces were approximately the same. I walked faster but I also took longer breaks, so the net result was that we usually came to the same shelter at night. He seemed rather lazy and lethargic whenever I was behind, but as soon as I passed he came alive. He would pour on the coal and quickly catch up, even if he had given me an advantage of several miles by sleeping late. The constant association began to irritate me because I prefer to travel alone. A single night at a shelter with someone was fine, but more than that made me feel that my independence was being encroached upon. I was neither strong enough nor ambitious enough to speed up my pace and outdistance him, so I decided to drop back and let him go a day's distance ahead.

At noon we stopped for lunch at the Siler Bald Lean-to. After eating, Dave hastened on and I remained behind. It seemed sinful and a waste of time to stop so early in the day, especially when I felt strong and the weather was good, so it was with difficulty that I restrained myself from setting off for the next shelter. There were interesting people at the shelter, however, and talking with them passed the time. Two Pennsylvania hikers, wearing light day packs, rested and ate their sandwiches. Each day they walked short distances from gap to gap. Their wives drove them up to the trail each morning and at night met them and fetched them back to the valley. The two couples shared a large trailer, and each week they moved it to a convenient location for the forthcoming week of hiking. Sometimes the men had to camp overnight on the trail because there was no convenient access point, but in general they had their hot showers, home cooked meals, and warm conjugal beds each night. They planned to hike the southern half of the trail this summer and the northern half the following summer. I thought it would be wonderful to be able to do the hike in such comfort. There is no way to make hauling a heavy pack along every mile of the trail pleasant. On the other hand, they were missing a great deal by not camping out in the hills each night. When I think back about the hike, the best memories are usually those of the camps, whether alone or with company.

The physiological studies never began. During the frantic weeks prior to departure I had no time to perform base-line measurements. During the first week on the trail I had concentrated solely on hiking, camping, and shaking down my equipment. The studies never entered my mind at that time, and when I thought about them at last, they filled me with boredom and distaste. I wanted nothing to remind me of the preceding two years of basic science study, of medicine, or of medical school. For four months I would exclude all of it from my mind, living solely for the here and now—free of the petty pomp and circumstance, the material preoccupation, the obsessive compulsiveness of my peers and mentors. The medical instruments I started with were mailed home at the very first opportunity.

At the Wesser Creek Lean-to I camped with an amusing young fellow known to me only as Tom. He was a tall skinny blond boy, gregarious and friendly as a puppy. He had set off into the mountains four days earlier from the town of Franklin, some 15 miles away. Armed with a machete, he had laboriously hacked his way cross-country through the tangled underbrush. After three days of cutting (and perhaps three miles of forward progress), he intersected the Appalachian Trail. Only too happy to sheath his knife, he turned north along it and reached the shelter, where he was recuperating for a day. While I bathed in a bathtub-sized pool in the stream and beat my clothes clean on a rock, he collected strawberries and baked a pie for us. While we ate, he showed me his amazing collection of gear. Besides the machete, he had a hundred-foot climbing rope, a hatchet, a sheath knife, a heavy winter coat, three sets of clothing, bath towels, and two antivenin kits. Needless to say, this was his first attempt at backpacking. He was a fast learner though, and the next day he mailed the irrelevant equipment home from Wesser. He continued north toward the Smokies but fell behind and I saw no more of him.

The Yellow Creek–Wauchecha–Cheoah section, which extends for 25 miles southeast from the Great Smokies, is reputed to be one of the ruggedest sections on the trail. To my surprise I found it rather easy. Perhaps this was because the dire warnings about its difficulty had psyched me up for it; perhaps it was because I was still holding back in order to let Dave move out well ahead. In any event, I loafed through it in two easy days, camping at each of its two shelters. The weather was very warm, water was scarce, and insects were bothersome. The trail constantly went steeply up and down, and there were no viewpoints worth mentioning, but for two days I did not meet a soul. This was a pleasant contrast to the first week on the trail, when dozens of hikers were encountered almost every day. It did my soul good to be completely alone with my thoughts for 48 hours; it was the first such opportunity since the preceding summer.

One of the things that I most missed on this initial part of the trail was scenic views. Most of my hiking has been either in the West or in the White Mountains of New Hampshire where virtually every mountaintop is above timberline, affording sweeping unobstructed outlooks. The ATC guidebooks kept promising marvelous outlooks, whetting my appetite with such phrases as "superb views . . . a magnificent outlook . . . one of the most outstanding panoramas on the entire Appalachian Trail." However, when one came to the promised viewpoint it would either be overgrown, socked in with fog, or a mere peephole.

After 10 days in the woods Fontana Village seemed a strange place. It swarmed with people, and cars prowled every foot of pavement. A swimming pool's loudspeaker blared popular music, and tourists stared at me as if I were some sort of freak. To my relief the first package of supplies was waiting at the post office. I had worried about whether it would arrive, because on numerous occasions in the past the postal service has lost mail important to me. Most of the food I needed for the next leg of the journey was in the parcel. This was fortunate because the village store had a poor selection of exorbitantly priced foods, most of which were unsuited for backpacking.

As I sat on a lawn reorganizing my pack, people kept walking up, staring, and asking streams of questions. It became a nuisance to answer the repetitive queries again and again. A typical dialogue might begin, "Oh, are you hiking?" I would reply in the affirmative.

"How far are you going?"

"To Mt. Katahdin."

"Oh, that's nice. Where is that?"

"In Maine."

"Really! You mean you're going to walk all the way there from here?"

"That is correct."

"Oh, how will you ever do it? Isn't that an awfully long way?"

"Yes, about 2,000 miles."

"My goodness! Don't you get tired?"

"Sometimes."

"Well what do you do for food—eat roots and berries and all that?"

"No, food is mailed to me and I buy some in stores."

"Well, where do you stay at night?"

"In the shelters along the trail."

"That sounds like so much fun! But don't you get terribly lonely?"

"Not at all."

And so it would go until my interrogator ran out of inquiries. The most commonly asked question was, "How many snakes have you seen?" When I reported that I had seen only a few, people were inevitably disappointed, so after a few weeks I adopted the stock reply, "I quit counting at 50 back in North Carolina somewhere."

After a very few days I developed the habit of not telling people that I planned to hike the entire trail. Instead I would say that I was going as far as the next logical stopping point. In Georgia I told people that I was going as far as the Smokies; north of the Smokies I would say that I was going to the Virginia state line; and so on. A hiker out for a week is not as unusual as one out for four months, and the number of questions is correspondingly reduced. Sometimes I told people that I was from Utah, but this would usually initiate a long chain of questions concerning why I was back East. The more knowledgeable would also pester me with inquiries about the Mormons. I soon adopted the policy of naming some local city as my home. This policy was not wholly successful in the South, because, whereas my drawl fooled Yankees, it did not pass muster with the natives. Once into the Shenandoah National Park and beyond, however, it worked beautifully. I leveled with some people, usually those I camped with and those few on the trail who appeared to be intelligent and knowledgeable about hiking; it was more trouble to keep a consistent lie going all evening than it was to answer the stock questions.

As I ascended into the Smokies from Fontana Lake, the scattered cumulus clouds abruptly built up into towering anvil formations, a cool wind whistled down from the heavens, lightning flashed, and thunder roared. Soon a drenching rain began to fall. There was lightning on every side and the crash of thunder was well-nigh continuous. Given the heat of exertion, there was little point in donning my raincoat; perspiration would have soaked me almost as quickly and thoroughly as the rain. In a twinkling I was soaked. The lightning came closer and closer. Given all the trees surrounding me, I figured that there was little chance of being struck by a bolt. Nevertheless, I could not help becoming nervous when a large oak 25 yards away was splintered. The storm passed as quickly as it had arisen. I wrung out my dripping clothing, and the heat generated during the remainder of the climb virtually completed the drying process. Unfortunately, just before reaching the Mollies Ridge Lean-to, my destination for the afternoon, a second shower soaked my clothes again. This was the pattern in the Smokies. Every day it rained, and I was rarely dry except in the sleeping bag at night. Several times I tried the raincoat, but leakage and sweat soon soaked me anyway. As the raincoat was hot and awkward to wear I usually walked along in sodden shirt and shorts, my boots squishing with every step.

I walked the Great Smokies during the week prior to the Fourth of July weekend. This usually is a relatively slack time for tourists, and the constant drenching rains apparently also helped to keep people away, and as a result the shelters were uncrowded. As I was building a fire at the Mollies Ridge Lean-to a tall and muscular young man with shoulder-length blond hair strolled in. He wore a loose yellow silk shirt, flowing purple satin trousers, and a sturdy homemade pair of sandals. Since he was fasting, his pack consisted only of a bedroll. For a man with such an impressive appearance, he was surprisingly nervous and insecure. Fidgety and ill at ease, he talked incessantly in a rambling monotone. It was his belief that fertilizers poison the soil, hence the crops that grow thereon, hence the men that eat the crops, thereby causing all disease. Fasting mobilizes the body fat where the poisons are stored, thereby curing all disease. After describing his theory of disease and therapy in considerable detail, he launched into a diatribe against traditional medicine. This done, he relaxed a bit and described his unhappy childhood, miserable marriage and divorce, and subsequent difficulty in holding a job. With all of this out of his system, he turned out to be a rather pleasant fellow, and we had a companionable evening protected from the rain by the sturdy rock shelter.

Next day the sun came out for several hours as I walked across the open meadows of Spence Field and climbed over Thunderhead. Picking strawberries and snoozing in the lush grass beneath the warming sun was a delicious experience. Descending the north side of Thunderhead, I came on a young couple brewing tea. They happily greeted me and invited me to join them. As we sipped our brew, they told me about their harrowing experience of the preceding night. They had been asleep in their tent at Spence Field when a bear ripped the tent open and hauled off their packs. The bear then tore the packs open and destroyed much of the hikers' food, thoroughly unsettling their nerves and upsetting their hiking plans. It turned out that they were South Africans. He had built a yacht himself, and they sailed the seven seas in it for three years before he sold it in Florida. He was working as an engineer in Tennessee until he could save enough money to build another boat, when they would resume their life upon the sea.

The trail climbed into spruce woods for the first time, and the rain resumed. In the Smokies the higher summits are covered with sweet-smelling balsams. Walking among them in the fog and drizzle, one feels as if the rest of the world has ceased to exist. His sphere of consciousness shrinks down to a small patch of firs immersed in the enclosing mist. Infrequently someone appears, like a specter, from the murk. The travelers meet, exchange a subdued greeting, then each disappears into the gloom. It is easy to imagine that they are the last souls left alive on earth, wandering alone in the cloudy netherworld.

I walked out into Newfound Gap and the spell was broken. The only road over the Great Smokies goes through this pass. Despite the fog and rain, the road was packed with slow-moving vehicles and the parking lot was full. It was a bedlam of people and automobiles. The clouds lifted a little, and I could see down into the valleys. I took off my pack and sat down on a stone retaining wall to rest and admire the view. As I relaxed, streams of tourists came up, impolitely stared, snapped my picture, and asked inane questions. One little boy, pointing with outstretched finger, asked his mother, "Is that a real mountain climber?" She replied, "Yes, it is. But don't be afraid. He won't hurt you if you don't tease him."

Soon surfeited with humanity, I climbed back up the trail into the woods. It continued to rain as I hiked the eastern half of the park. By this time I was habituated to wetness, and the constant deluge no longer bothered me. Several times I met long files of Boy Scouts, but they were invariably southbound, and there was no need to joust with them for space in a shelter.

I spent my fourth and last night in the Smokies at the Cosby Knob Lean-to. At first only a young couple from Connecticut was there with me. They were naive tenderfeet who had never been in the mountains before, but they were well equipped with the finest of backpacking gear, having carefully researched the subject in Colin Fletcher's books before setting out. A thunderstorm blew up, and just as the first drops began to fall a trio of Tennessee mountain boys came running in. They quickly settled themselves in and soon the air was filled with the aroma of frying ham, biscuits, coffee, and the musical twang of their speech. The rain poured down in sheets, and the sky was green and dark. The raindrops striking the tin roof created such a din that conversation was virtually impossible. Abruptly two more young couples came tumbling in from the storm. Like the first pair, they were properly equipped with the latest in expensive new hiking gear; they too had studied their Colin Fletcher carefully. Indeed, one had actually brought his copy of Fletcher along for ready reference.

Unfortunately, the book gave few hints on how to deal with mischievous mountain boys. The lads quickly recognized that they had six perfect foils in an ideal setting. They launched into a long series of bear tales, describing in detail how the bears had been known to maul hikers in their quest for food, how they delighted in running up on top of the shelters' roofs at night, and how, when provoked, the bears sometimes even tore down the protective fences across the fronts of the shelters. The storm was an effective setting for the stories, and soon the six tenderfeet were reduced to a state of nervous terror. They tied their packs from the rafters, locked and relocked the gate, and armed themselves with sheath knives and flashlights. Then they settled down in their sleeping bags to await the onslaught of the dreaded bears.

Sure enough, a bear arrived on the scene shortly after darkness fell. He came sniffing around the front of the shelter, and one of the alert guards instantly spotted him and raised an alarm. A chorus of shrieks filled the air, flashlight beams bracketed the animal, and a deafening clatter of spoons on aluminum plates arose. Not the least disturbed, the bear continued to nose around the fence several minutes and then ambled off. For the rest of the night a branch falling in the forest or a pebble surreptitiously lobbed against the chain link fence produced an anxious alert.

Taking my leave of this amusing group in the morning, I set out into the rain and soon left the park behind. It rained all day. Once out of the park walking became more difficult. In the park the trails are broad and smooth, and the brush is kept down. Outside, the trails are neither so well built nor so well maintained. One constantly wades through wet brush and weeds. No waterproofing works for long, and even if it did, water would run down one's legs and soak the boots from within. The effect of the dripping foliage slapping against one's body is cumulative. An hour of it is not bad, but a day of this sort of travel can be extremely depressing. I was only too happy to reach the first shelter north of the park, a venerable log structure at Groundhog Creek.

A grizzled man and handsome boy were huddled inside the shelter, choking on clouds of blue smoke that the wind blew directly into their faces from the campfire. Wet socks and shirts dangled from the rafters, drying in the warm smoke. They introduced themselves as Herb and Dwight. It was immediately apparent that they were intelligent and erudite people, despite their scruffy appearance. Herb turned out to be a university mathematician, out on a two-week hike with his son. We had mutual friends and gossiped about them during the gloomy evening.

After the almost constant rain in the Smokies, a few days of clear warm weather came as a welcome change. The fortress-like stone shelters with their chain link barricades gave way to rustic little log shelters which were erected by the Civilian Conservation Corps (CCC) during the 1930s. No crowds of hikers were here; only an occasional stroller. The trails were for the most part smooth and graded, the shelters evenly spaced, and one could effortlessly reel off from 18 to 20 miles a day. The berries were at last beginning to ripen. For the next month I feasted daily on blueberries, raspberries, and strawberries. Despite their impressive heights and forests, the Great Smokies had depressed me. Probably it was the combination of dreary weather and crowds. In any event, my spirits rose immediately upon departing the park, and they remained elevated for the next 10 days as I hiked to the Virginia state line.

My favorite shelters along the trail were the weathered old CCC structures. They had been carefully and lovingly built with natural materials obtained from the surrounding forests. Hand-hewn log walls rose on stone foundations. Only the corrugated iron roofs that were hauled in piece by piece on man or mule backs were foreign to the environment. No concrete foundations, cinder blocks, or prefab-ricated plywood walls airlifted in by helicopter deface these lean-tos. Although of a common conception, each is unique, having its own distinctive personality and charm. The men working for the CCC gave careful attention to the sites of their shelters. All have lovely woodland settings, ample water, and sometimes fine views as well. Fireplaces and other camp accoutrements are thoughtfully placed for maximum convenience. Whenever I came to one it seemed as if I was saying hello to an old friend. Such was the case with the Deer Park Mountain Lean-to, which is located a few miles from Hot Springs, North Carolina. I came to it in midafternoon of July 3, having hiked 20 miles that day. One reaches it by walking a quarter-mile on a side trail, first down a little grade through hardwoods, then across a rill in a dark, damp rhododendron thicket, and then uphill to a small knoll, on top of which stands the shelter. The logs are weathered and gray, and there is room inside for just four side-by-side wire bunks. The four-foot overhang of the roof in front protects the stone fireplace and half of the split-log picnic table from rain. There is no view, but the woods are open and airy. One feels se-cluded, but not at all hemmed in. My first chore upon arriving at this shelter (or any shelter) was to police the area. The sight of litter at a camp was as abhorrent to me as it would have been in my own home. This particular shelter, like most of those in North Carolina, was relatively clean. Only a few minutes were needed to pick up the trash. Then I unpacked, hung my sleeping bag up to air in the sun, and arranged my other equipment in a convenient manner. There was a small pool in the creek, in which I was able to bathe and wash my clothing. (I tried to take a bath every day and usually succeeded —if not in camp, then someplace along the trail.) Bath time over, I collected wood—enough for cooking, a campfire, and a small cache for the shelter. Then I looked in the register to see who had been there before me, tallied the day's mileage, planned the next day's walk, and wrote journal entries and letters for an hour or two. By this time the sun was setting, and I was ready to prepare supper. After eating I sat cross-legged upon the picnic table, watching the light fade from the sky and listening to the forest and its inhabitants. When darkness fell I sat in the shelter before the fire, tending it until midnight or thereabouts; then I went to bed and instantly fell alsleep.

For the next few days the trail was often located on private land. There is a crazy patchwork of land holdings in these hills, resulting in a plethora of boundary fences crossing the trail. Some are split rail, but the majority are of barbed wire. At each one I had to un-buckle the pack, toss it over, scramble between the wires myself, then heave the pack up on my back again. After doing this the tenth time in a morning, one becomes rather irritated. For the most part the trail stays in woods, but frequently it goes by little farms where one sees cabins, chicken coops, hog sties, kitchen gardens, and pastures. Each farm also has its hillside tobacco patch, and sometimes one sees a farmer tilling with a mule. (The hillsides are so steep that a tractor would tip over.) The farmers are guaranteed a good price for their tobacco leaf by the government, and frequently it is their best cash crop, the mainstay of their economy. The people are shy, but when approached with a smile they are happy to take a break from their work and chat awhile.

For 10 days I had been behind Dave. I fell back one day's hike initially, but had closed the gap a little each day since then. I was not consciously attempting to catch up, but traveling at my own pace it seemed that I went just a bit faster. People along the trail kept telling me about the big fellow with the enormous pack who was a day ahead, then half a day ahead, then just a couple of hours ahead. My feelings about the prospect of overtaking him were ambivalent; on the one hand, I did not want to catch up because to do so implied that I would have constant company again. On the other hand, I did not want to slow down artificially, and I was anxious to see how he was getting along. Finally, late one afternoon, I stumbled into Sams Gap, exhausted after a long and difficult day, and found Dave encamped on the porch of an abandoned house. His hair was growing long and lank, his clothing was becoming ragged and torn, and his unshaven stubble was blossoming into a full black beard. He stared in disbelief at the apparition that strode up to the porch—I had told him that I planned only to hike to the Smokies when we were together in Georgia—and then hurried out to greet me. We had a joyous reunion, reminiscing about the good and bad of the hike thus far, comparing notes about mutual acquaintances along the way, and discussing the trail that lay ahead. His knees were sore and swollen, and walking had become excruciatingly painful for him. However, he was a very determined person and had plugged right along at virtually the same rate as when he had been in good shape. I examined his knees and there were no abnormalities other than inflammation. I could only suggest that he rest them a day or two and reduce the stress his knees were subjected to by lightening his load and reducing his daily mileage. My advice fell on deaf ears; he was not about to slow down the least bit so long as he was capable of walking.

The day that I picked up my second parcel of supplies was one of the most difficult and unpleasant days of the trip. Dave and I camped the preceding night at a shelter three miles south of Erwin, Tennessee. I shaved, trimmed my hair, and donned clean clothes in order to present as favorable an appearance as possible for hitchhiking. Dave, on the other hand, made no attempt to clean up. We could not catch a ride, even after half an hour of thumbing on a busy road. I began to feel that he was the cause of our lack of success, reasoning that his wild and unkempt appearance was frightening off the motorists. Finally we split up and tried hitching independently, and we soon caught rides. Before getting my ride I had walked a mile on the hot asphalt, and my feet were burning from the heat. I felt that the townsfolk were staring at me with suspicion and disdain, and this added to my mounting irritation. The fact that the supplies had arrived intact at the post office was some solace, and quickly catching a ride back to the trail after doing my errands was another. Dave was still in town, so I set off up the trail alone.

At first the trail led along a brook in a cool grove of hemlocks. It was so dark and the trees were so impressive that I was reminded of the Muir Woods near San Francisco. Soon the trail began climbing, and hiking became hot and dusty work. I was ready to camp when I reached a shelter at two o'clock, but it was a dirty, dreary, and unpleasant place, so I decided to push on. Reaching the ridge crest, the trail followed the Unaka Mountain Road for a number of miles. The hard gravel added further insult to my tired and aching feet. To add to my discomfort, the pack's weight had increased by 20 pounds in Erwin. The afternoon was showery, and I became anxious to find a campsite with some sort of shelter. At sunset I came to a deserted picnic ground in a ridgetop meadow. It had a beautiful view, so I stopped and made camp. The tarp thrown across a picnic table would provide shelter if necessary. It seemed an ideal spot until the first midge bit me. Soon swarms of the minute insects were nipping every exposed part of my skin. The constant sharp pains soon became intolerable; the only solution was to get into the woods for the night. However, I did not want to camp without shelter and the next lean-to was three miles away, with only half an hour of light remaining. I hastily threw the pack's contents together and set off down the trail. Fortunately it was smooth and rockfree, so I did not stumble and fall in the gathering darkness. As the last iota of light disappeared from the forest I came to the shelter. I was soaked in perspiration from the exertion, I was nauseous and near prostration, and pulsing flashes of burning pain emanated from my feet. I lit a candle, prepared my bed, and then walked back and forth in the darkness for 20 minutes to cool down. The nausea passed, but the foot pain rapidly increased.

It was so severe, throbbing in knifelike thrusts into my ankles and legs, and so prolonged, that I could sleep hardly a wink all night.

In the morning my feet were swollen and extremely sore. Nevertheless I arose at sunup and pushed on. At first I was so distracted by the pain that I hardly noticed my surroundings; then I saw that the woods were open and parklike, that there were several good views, and that the day was bright and clear. The pain subsided to tolerable levels and I made good progress. In midafternoon I came to Hughes Gap, at the base of Roan Mountain, and sat down to rest.

Roan Mountain was a steep and slippery climb, and the air was hot and humid. The summit was covered over with a forest of birches and spruces, the last to be seen on the Appalachian Trail until New England. I descended the mountain and climbed again along the Grassy Ridge. A scant quarter of a mile from the lean-to a sudden shower drenched and chilled me. I arrived there with aching, swollen feet and soaked clothing. To my delight, there were two campers in the shelter. They had managed to preserve their fire from the deluge, and it was blazing cheerily. A change to dry clothing and a hot meal quickly served up by my companions resolved the chill.

Ernie and Warren, my companions in the shelter, were a television producer and his college-age son from Long Island. They had started out from Springer Mountain in May, planning to hike the entire trail, but soon realized that they had neither the time nor the ambition to complete the expedition. They had therefore proceeded at a leisurely pace, carrying packs laden with luxuries, living comfortably and eating superbly as they traveled. When I staggered into the shelter they were in the midst of baking a wild strawberry pie, on which we all feasted when it was finished. In the morning their meal consisted of bacon, fried eggs, pancakes with butter and syrup, and more berries. I admired their elegant style and regretted that I did not have the extra month which would have permitted me to travel in similar relaxation.

My feet felt better the next morning, but I decided it would be wise to rest them by taking a day off. I had hiked every day for three weeks, averaging 17 miles a day. This put me slightly ahead of schedule. The Grassy Ridge Shelter is in a beautiful location. The lean-to was situated high on a ridge just below timberline, surrounded by dwarfed balsams, beeches, birches, and rhododendrons. It is completely enclosed by the trees, but a walk of a few rods to the south brings one to meadows that in July are replete with ripe strawberries. The open ridge crest affords views of mountain ridges and valleys, and the beflowered grass makes a soft bed for sunbathing and sleeping. It was a warm clear day, ideal for lounging around camp, writing letters, making repairs to pack and clothing, and snoozing.

Early in the afternoon Dave limped in, his knees hurting even worse than they had two days earlier. He had planned to walk farther that afternoon, but was seduced by the loveliness of the location and decided to stay for the night. Clouds obscured the sky and lightning flashed on the horizon as evening came. The storm approached very slowly, and it was still far away when we went to sleep. Sometime after midnight we were awakened by a violent crash of thunder and a tremendous roar of rain on the shelter's tin roof. We felt very secure in our warm sleeping bags inside the sturdy little lean-to, despite the raging storm just a few feet away. Notwithstanding the commotion outside, I soon fell asleep again and slept deeply until morning.

Dave and I were together on the trail for the next 10 days. Sometimes I lagged behind, and sometimes Dave fell back, but at day's end we usually arrived at the shelter within a few minutes of one another. His knees continued to be swollen and painful; my feet, injured initially by the excessive punishment inflicted on Unaka Mountain, remained sore. Indeed, their condition gradually deteriorated. We both limped in pain as we hiked, a pair of walking wounded. In addition to his knees, Dave's pack was causing him concern. His Kelty was new at the start of the hike, but its backbands, shoulder straps, and waist belt were wearing out and beginning to tear. Soon they ripped completely through and had to be replaced. My Kelty, on the other hand, was holding up well. In spite of the fact that it was 12 years old and had been used over many miles of hiking, it showed few signs of wear. Apparently the difference was that Dave subjected his pack to much more stress as he walked.

One afternoon we were walking through farmers' meadows on the Walnut Mountain ridge when we came to a large tree laden with ripe red cherries. The urge to climb the tree and feast on the fresh fruit was irresistible. As we perched on limbs filling our kettles with juicy cherries, a thundershower came rolling along the mountain from the south. We barely had time to clamber down from the tree and scurry 50 yards down the slope to find refuge in an opensided hay barn before the storm struck. The rain reverberated on the barn's roof while we lay on the soft hay inside and munched our cherries. When the storm showed no sign of relenting, we collected runoff water from the eaves for cooking, cleared a large bare spot on the floor in which to ignite our stoves, and made soft beds in the hay for sleeping. It was as soft and comfortable a place to sleep as I had on the entire trip.

I fell behind Dave the next day in the Laurel Fork Valley. The valley was deep and heavily forested. During World War I most of it was lumbered; old railroad grades and cuts still persist, but now the second growth has developed into a forest of fair-sized trees. The Laurel Fork itself has cut sheer-walled little canyons in the layered sedimentary rocks, and there is one spectacular waterfall—a broad, high series of cascades, which weave and intertwine across the broad extent of the rock wall like an elaborate tapestry. I planned to catch up with Dave at the South Pierce Lean-to, but as I started the two-mile climb from the highway to the lean-to, I passed a man attempting to nail a plywood ceiling beneath his porch roof. For a lone man it was awkward to simultaneously position the four-by-eight sheets and nail them up, so I offered to give him a hand. After a moment of deliberation, he accepted. Being in no great hurry, we first sat in rockers on the porch and sipped coffee. J. C. Ranshaw and his wife Kathleen live in a comfortable brick house that they have constructed themselves on their 60-acre section of mountainside forest. They have worked on it for four years and have lived in it for three. Now it is virtually complete; only finishing touches remain. The Appalachian Trail ascends a gravel road to the home, skirts its yard, and then plunges into the woods behind on a foot trail. Nearby is a garden patch and a number of beehives. Pigs roam in the forest and eat the Ranshaws' table scraps, and a large family of cats lives in and around the sheds. Through canning, freezing, and curing, they maintain virtual self-sufficiency with regard to food. After we had fitted and nailed a few sheets of plywood, the Ranshaws invited me inside to a meal of ham hocks, peas, beans, potatoes, corn, onions, cornbread, apple pie, preserves, honey, and coffee. The only items on the table that had been purchased in a store were the meal for the cornbread, butter, salt, and coffee. As I was preparing to move on following the repast, a storm blew up the valley and another drenching rain began. I was kindly invited to stay for the night. What luxury —a hot shower and a soft bed with clean sheets! In the morning we finished the ceiling, and Kathleen cooked a breakfast of ham, eggs, biscuits, and gravy. Soon I was on my way again, carrying a lunch she had prepared for me and a bottle of sourwood honey from their hives.

The last 40 miles in Tennessee were relatively dull. One walks along level mountaintops on trails badly overgrown with weeds. Only an infrequent ascent or descent interrupts the monotony of pushing through weeds that are waist-high, wet, and prickly. Views are rare, and few hikers choose to spend their time on this uninteresting section. Twice I camped at shelters, and each time the spring was a quarter of a mile down the mountainside. A tiresome hike was required whenever water was needed.

I spent one night in a shelter with a physician and his wife, who was a nurse. They were from a small town in Alabama. I had not planned to stop at that particular shelter, but it was a good opportunity to learn about medical practice in a semi-rural setting from an authority. Neither of them had much expertise in camping. Their attempts to build a fire with damp wood had met with scant success. I walked out in the woods, collected a bit of dry tinder, and then built a crackling fire, to their amazement and my amusement. They spent the evening answering my questions about rural practice.

Damascus was the first town on the trail in Virginia. The Appalachian Trail follows the main street right through the center of town. Apparently its residents are accustomed to hikers, for they let me off with no more than perfunctory stares. It was with relief that I returned to the woods. The first few days in Virginia, in the Jefferson National Forest, were very pleasant. The trails were plainly marked and well maintained, and the ascents and descents evenly graded. I had been unable to sleep comfortably on the wire mesh bunks in the shelters in North Carolina and Tennessee. The forest service lean-tos in Virginia, with their plain wooden floors, afforded far more comfortable sleeping as far as I was concerned.

The condition of the shelters is inversely related to their accessibility to motorized vehicles. Those that are within a few rods of an access road are invariably filthy vandalized slums. Those more removed tend to be clean and well preserved. Sometimes I came to one of the despoiled shelters with the intention of camping there, only to be so disgusted by the squalor that I pushed on to the next one. One of the better shelters in this section is at Raccoon Branch, some 25 miles north of Damascus. Motor vehicles cannot approach within three miles, and the shelter itself is a quarter of a mile off the Appalachian Trail on a side path. It is situated in a sunny little clearing amidst oaks. No one had visited the shelter in 10 days. The most recent campers were a pair who had started from Springer Mountain with the intention of hiking the whole trail. They decided after a month to hike only as far as New York, rather than continuing to Mt. Katahdin. In contrast to the majority of trail users, they had had the courtesy to leave a little cache of dry wood. I found that only one shelter in three contains a supply of dry wood. It is not that good hikers fail to do this; rather that too many ignoramuses wander into a shelter on a pleasant day, see the cut wood, and use it instead of gathering their own. Occasionally they even rip the sides from the shelters for fuel, and in one instance I saw a charred hole in the floor of a lean-to, where some thoughtless individual had built his camp-fire on a rainy day.

Virginia Highway 16 crosses the Appalachian Trail on Brushy Mountain. This was the first familiar place I encountered on the trip. Once, several years earlier, I drove this road during a meandering trip to the East Coast. Seeing the Appalachian Trail marker at the trail crossing, I had stopped to investigate. I took a half-mile stroll along the trail and then picked up the litter at the crossing. It filled two cardboard fruit boxes at that time. Pausing now at the same place to recall the memory, I estimated that the current collection of trash would easily fill 25 boxes. It is discouraging in the extreme to witness such clear testimony of the exponential increase in slovenliness in our country.

Later that day the trail descended briefly from the mountains to cross the Holston River valley near the village of Groseclose. The trail follows paved roads as it crosses the settled valley. At the farm where the trail regains the woods, I met an old man leaning on his gate. He had suffered a series of heart attacks, and recently had also been afflicted with a stroke. He was moderately aphasic, but we managed to communicate fairly well while sitting together on the stoop of his house. He told stories from his past and talked about the disposition of his farm and belongings after his death. He seemed to be in the process of making his peace with the world, recognizing that he had little time left. He suggested that rather than going on seven miles to the next shelter, I should spend the night in an old farmhouse which belonged to his wife. It was barely a mile farther along the trail, and being worn out from a long day's hike, I was happy to accept the offer. The little house was not in use, but it was completely furnished, clean, and well maintained. I found the interior confining, however, and camped on the porch. A tiny brook burbled merrily a scant five yards from the home; its banks were lined with bushes laden with ripe black raspberries. A cupboard contained beer. The berries and brew were refreshing supplements to my habitual food.

Next day a hot six-mile climb brought me to the southern tip of Walker Mountain. An abandoned fire tower stands here. It was in good condition, with intact windows and a bed and cupboard inside. I was sorely tempted to stop in the airy tower, but I had hiked only six miles. I was anxious to put in a full day because the weather was good and the long flat summit of Walker Mountain promised easy walking and excellent progress. I compromised between my urge to lie around all day and my desire to move on by sunbathing for an hour on the tower's catwalk.

The trail follows a level ridge for nearly 30 miles, and I ripped off 20 of them in the afternoon. It was easy hiking in rather pleasant woods. Shelters were present every few miles, but there were no springs. Water was available only in cisterns, which are filled by run-off rain from the shelters' roofs. Some of them had run dry and others had regulating devices that metered out no more than a quart of water in an hour, so the best one could hope for was drinking water. After a long hot day on the trail I found it exceedingly unpleasant not to be able to take even a sponge bath.

Dave and I spent the night at Turkey Gap, each having no more than a quart of water for drinking, cooking, and washing. The next day was swelteringly hot. Much of the walking was on valley roads. The temperature and humidity were both in the eighties. I was constantly soaked with perspiration, and my feet ached from the pounding on hot pavement. The camp at Wapiti Lean-to was ample compensation for much of the discomfort, however. The neat log lean-to is on a wooded bank two rods above a gravel forest service road. Trees conceal it from the sight of passing motorists, and no sign points it out. It is hence surprisingly well maintained, despite its proximity to the road. An excellent spring nearby allowed me to rinse off a two-day accumulation of grime and dried sweat. We lolled in the lean-to after supper, smugly watching the Sunday picnickers driving home. They were quite oblivious to the existence of our shelter. Next morning a brushy ridge walk in driving rain brought us to the town of Pearisburg, where supplies awaited both of us in the post office. This marked the quarter-way point in the trip. A bit more than 500 miles had been traversed in one month's time. I had no particular sense of accomplishment: there were still 1,500 miles to go, and as far as I was concerned, there was hardly any difference between 1,500 miles and 2,000 miles.

The Second 500 Miles

Small areas on my big toes became inflamed after the Unaka Mountain Road walk. This inflammation gradually worsened during the next 10 days. The boots exerted some pressure on my toes, and apparently this was sufficient to initiate the pathological process. By the time we reached Pearisburg a small but ugly suppurating sore had developed on one toe. The pain was sufficient to make me limp. It was only midday, but the next shelter was 20 miles away, and I thought that a night in public lodgings was in order.

A friendly clerk at the post office suggested that we stay with Mary Finley, an elderly lady who lets rooms in her home to hikers and other transients. For a nominal sum she provided us a clean comfortable room.

The afternoon was spent in getting ready for the next leg of the journey. Both of us collected our parcels from the post office. Dave's included the spare parts for his Kelty; soon it was repaired and as good as new. We did our laundry, scrubbed our filthy bodies and hair, and then sat in the porch swing studying maps and guidebooks. My foot was still sore and swollen, and I could hardly walk. I decided to stay with Mary another day. Dave was up bright and early and left by sunup. I rested in the porch swing most of the day, keeping my leg elevated and immobile. I wrote letters and caught up with the preceding month's news. I did everything I could think of that needed doing to my equipment, and talked with Miss Mary, as the townsfolk call her, for several hours. However, I couldn't help becoming restive and anxious to be on my way again.

The foot had ceased aching while I rested, but the moment my boots pressed the sores in the morning a stabbing pain began. I set off at six, limping badly. The pain made walking almost intolerable, but my urge to go on was stronger than the pain's message to stop. I staggered through town, passed a factory that had an obnoxious smell, and took to the woods again. Prior to 1970 the trail followed a woods road along the New River to the Stony Creek valley. Then it led along a road for 10 miles up the valley. It has since been rerouted along the ridge of Peters Mountain, which forms the northern wall of the valley. I walked along the woods road looking for the turnoff to the new route. After a little while I came to forks in the road which had no mark indicating which way to turn. Choosing the left path, I came to a decrepit farmhouse and asked directions. A deaf old man told me to follow the other path.

After an hour of limping along, I realized that the turnoff must lie somewhere behind me. Sitting down with a map, I decided that it must have been two miles back. I considered retracing my steps, but that would have added four miles to the planned 20-mile walk. Twenty miles was a full day's work even with healthy feet. I could have retreated to Pearisburg and set off again the next day, but my ego would not permit such an ignominious advance to the rear. I continued along the old route, following first the river and then the valley. It turned out to be an interesting detour. Most Appalachian Trail hiking is along remote ridgetops. It was a change to follow a large river for several miles and then walk near a picturesque rapids-filled stream. Its bed consists of very large boulders, and there are water cascades in every direction as it wends its way around and over the rocks. Despite my aching feet, the hot pavement, and the occasional whizzing auto, it was an enjoyable day.

Because of the foot it took until almost dark to finish the 20 miles to Bailey Gap Lean-to. In the morning my foot was extremely sore—inflamed, swollen, and oozing pus—so I decided to lay over another day. It was certainly not the best place to kill a day: water was a good quarter of a mile away, the shelter was not in an overly attractive place, and there was little to do to pass the time. Most of the time on the trip I could have filled a day with activities that I had had no time to get around to, but all of my chores had been done during the enforced rest in Pearisburg. However, there was no alternative to resting; if I pushed on, the foot might become so infected that I would not be able to walk. I spent the day sleeping and sunbathing. In the afternoon a flock of wild turkeys came to visit. I sat very quietly and watched them for nearly half an hour. I tired of maintaining the same position, and my movement scared them. They flew off into the woods. A few minutes later Mark Baldwin, a young man from Alexandria, hiked in from the north. He had graduated from high school in June, and this solo walk from the Shenandoah National Park to Pearisburg was to be his last fling before enlisting in the navy. He gave me a bottle of benzoic acid, which was of great help in doctoring my feet. He also contributed odds and ends of food that were left over from his trip. They were lightweight delicacies, and therefore a welcome addition to my already heavily laden pack.

After the second day of rest my foot was better, but a second problem had developed that was at least as bothersome as the foot had ever been. Apparently I came in contact with poison ivy, for my legs, thighs, abdomen, and posterior parts broke out in giant hives while I was laying over at the shelter. Soon the blisters began to rupture, and slow seepage from them kept my clothing and sleeping bag wet for the next week. The discomfort was so great that for seven days I could hardly sleep. I averaged about three hours of sleep a night, and walking in the daytime was as much of an agony as trying to find a comfortable position at night.

The section from Pearisburg to Rockfish Gap, some 220 miles, was a horror. The going was rugged—numerous climbs and descents, rough trails, dense weeds for miles on end, almost constant rain—but the main reason I found it so difficult was my continued ill health.

My foot improved with time, but it was still a source of concern even when I was entering Shenandoah National Park. The poison ivy attack made me miserable most of this stretch, and numerous minor cuts and bruises added to my discomfort. The weeds were so thick that I had to wear long pants to protect my thighs. The pants were constantly soaked and muddy, and the stiff wet denim chafed my legs, causing painful chapping and open sores. If I donned shorts to remove the irritation caused by the long pants, then prickly weeds caused almost intolerable itching. In addition to these woes, I slipped and fell one night in camp, landing so heavily on my hip that I thought it must surely have broken. The pain was sudden and severe, and I went into mild shock. Despite immediately lying down inside my sleeping bag, I lost consciousness for a few moments. There was no broken bone, but my entire buttock was very tender for several days.

During the first month there was rain two days out of every three. This is not to say that it rained all day every day, but once a shower had passed through an area, the woods remained wet for hours afterwards. Fog alone was capable of wetting the brush and consequently soaking one's clothing. If the days had been dry, I could have camped out anywhere at night, using the tarpaulin for shelter. However, the constant wetness during the day made it almost mandatory to find a sheltered place at night in which to dry out and warm up. As a result, I was preoccupied with weather and the accessibility of shelters. Sometimes there was no shelter within 10 miles of the optimal stopping point. When this was the case I agonized over whether to hike a very short or very long distance for the day, or whether to hike the right distance and hope that something would turn up.

Ascending towards McAfee Knob from Catawba Mountain, I knew there was no shelter within my range of endurance. There was a number of vacation homes along the locked fire road leading to the knob, and as it was Sunday afternoon, the chances of finding an unoccupied one and using its porch seemed good. However, the cottages and grounds were plastered with KEEP OUT signs. The overt hostility expressed by the placards spooked me and I decided to hike on up to the knob and take my chances. The open cliffs gave a marvelous view of the valleys and ridges north of Roanoke. Small airplanes passed by frequently at an elevation that was lower than that of the cliffs; from the city airport they are in the midst of their climb-out as they cross the ridge before McAfee Knob. I would have slept out on the rocks and watched the airplanes if the weather had looked promising, but rain was in the air. I went looking for a cave, and intuition led me through a narrow cleft between two tall boulders. I found myself in a natural amphitheater about 10 feet across. One of its walls had fractured and the two fragments had slid several feet apart, forming a cave six feet wide, four feet high, ten feet long, and open at both ends. There was a thick carpet of dry oak leaves on the floor, and it was snug and weatherproof. An infrequently used fireplace indicated that others had found the nook. I built a fire and roofed it over with large flat rocks. Soon the rain began, and I retired to the cave, from which I could reach out and tend the fire. Pots collected runoff water for cooking. Sitting in the cozy cave on a soft cushion of leaves, watching the fire and its shadows dancing on the walls of the grotto, hearing the rain rustle on the ground, I felt justifiably smug. A good fairy may have been watching out for me that day.

The rain stopped while I slept, but naturally the woods were soaked all morning. Tinker Ridge is 20 miles long and shaped like a huge "L" opening towards the city of Roanoke. The summit has several minor bumps, McAfee Knob being one of them, but it is essentially level. However, the trail is for the most part primitive and rough. The four miles along a fire road to the first cliffs had been easy, but the 16 miles that remained for the next day afforded one of the hardest day's hikes on the entire trip. I did not get off the mountain until it was almost dark, and I was exhausted. Fortunately, the trail crosses Interstate 81 a scant mile from the mountain, and there are several good motels close to the crossing. I had hoped to be able to hike three miles to the next shelter, but darkness and fatigue directed my steps to the nearest motel. The third hot shower of the hike was immensely refreshing, and the novelty of television, which I do not have even at home, kept me up until one in the morning.

Climbing back up into the mountains from Roanoke, the first changes of color in the forest foliage were visible. It was only July 27, but the leaves of a few of the ground plants which had already borne their fruit were turning yellow. As the days passed, some of the weeds that stood chest- and even head-high, blocking and obscuring the trail, began to wither. This gave rise to hopes that they would soon die off in their entirety and therefore lessen the difficulty of travel. However, I was to be well north of the weedy sections before this happened.

From Roanoke to the Shenandoah National Park, the Appalachian Trail roughly parallels the Blue Ridge Parkway. Now it follows near at hand for several miles, now it swings away on a 10- or 15-mile detour, but it always returns to the road, which provides a continuity to the hiking. It is a stable reference point that recalls the existence of the outside world in an unobtrusive manner. One afternoon I was wading along through some high weeds close to the parkway. The rolled-up legs on my shorts had come down, and I was absent-mindedly looking down as I rolled them back up. Suddenly I became aware of a long black cylinder, chevroned with golden markings, lying on the trail between my legs. I instinctively recoiled and found myself face to face with a fat timber rattlesnake. We glared at one another for a few seconds as I briefly considered the matter and decided against killing it for food. A truce mutually agreed upon, it turned and silently glided off into the undergrowth, and I continued on my way.

As I walked this tiresome section, I was learning to recognize and accept my limitations in the realm of strength and endurance. I was anxious to finish the section because travel had been difficult for weeks and I thought that once the Shenandoah National Park was reached, the hiking would become easier. I thus had a tendency to push as hard as possible. At night I studied maps and planned big mileage for the next day, based upon the very limited information appearing on the charts. Often my ambitious plans were thwarted. The distance I could cover turned out to be primarily a function of the ruggedness of terrain and my physical status, rather than my desires. It made no difference that I might think I should be able to walk 20 miles in a given day. If the trail was rough and my reserves of strength low, I had to settle for the 15 miles that was feasible. If I insisted on hiking on in an exhausted condition for the last five miles, I would be weak and lackadaisical the next day, and progress would be correspondingly poor.

At the James River a third of the mileage was behind me, as well as a third of the days. I spent the night at the nearby Matts Creek Lean-to. I was tired, wet, and sore after a day of rain. It was one of the prettier lean-to locations, being deep down in a valley and looking out over a tumbling brook. A long shallow pool lies before the shelter, and a hanging rope allows one to swing back and forth from one bank to the other. When there was an all-day rain, as on this day, I usually did not bother to build a fire. The Primus stove was adequate for cooking, and I didn't like to spend the time necessary to build and maintain a fire under wet conditions. It was the end of July and already the evenings were noticeably shortening. I was hard-pressed for sufficient daylight in which to finish camp chores. I began to use candles for reading and writing in the evening.

In four days I would be out of the southwestern Virginia wilderness and into the park. I could hardly wait. Rain and weeds were my constant companions in the George Washington National Forest, but it did encompass some very pretty terrain. I enjoyed the long ascents and descents, the lonesome woods, and the open summits of the balds. One afternoon I dropped down to the dirt road passing through Hog Camp Gap and encountered an old man with two boys in a small car. They were looking for Wiggins Spring, where there is a shelter. I told them it was a short distance down the road, and they offered to drive me there. The man had lived his entire life in this area of the mountains, but had never been to the spring. Armed with a bottle of Old Crow, he had persuaded his grandsons to drive him there. As we drove down the winding dirt road he offered me several swallows of his bourbon. When we arrived at the camp and he had seen the spring, he insisted on filling my cup with whiskey before driving off.

A troop of Scouts from Lynchburg was camped around the shelter. The boys slept in hammocks covered with orange tube tents, and their four leaders shared the shelter. The men made room for me inside and invited me to share their fire and dinner. Whenever the fire needed wood or pots required washing, one of the scoutmasters summoned a Scout, who would scurry off to accomplish his mission calling out, "Yes, sir!" Camping with a dozen willing servants is certainly one way to go about it. They were a playful, laughing bunch. In the morning two of them set out to finish the hike ahead of the others. Each unwittingly carried a large stone at the bottom of his pack, lovingly placed there the previous night by his fellow hikers. I would love to have been present when they discovered that each had been carrying an extra 10 pounds up and down the mountains.

The remote Tye River valley and the high mountains that bound it —The Priest and Three Ridges—were two of the most scenic locales in the South. There is a climb of 3,000 feet from the Appalachian Trail crossing of the river to the peaks. The mountains ring the valley from north to south, leaving an opening only to the east, where the river exits. Except for the banks of the river, the valley is heavily forested and sparsely inhabited. The trail briefly emerges from the forest into the inhabited fringe along the stream, then quickly plunges back into the woods. Rather than camp at the established Harpers Creek Lean-to, I spent the night nearby in a rude shelter that the Lynchburg Scouts told me about. It consisted of a sheet of plastic lashed on top of a framework of poles. It was low, affording barely enough headroom to sit up, but before it there was a large, deep pool. Diving six feet down to the bottom of the pool and swimming a few strokes was a refreshing change of pace after a warm day of hiking.

From Harpers Creek to Rockfish Gap, the southern gateway to the park, there are 24 strenuous miles. I was so anxious to finish the section that I hiked it in one day. I knew in advance that it was too much for me, but I could not wait another day to leave the George Washington National Forest. All day I concentrated on staying in motion, paying little attention to the surroundings, in order to accomplish my objective before nightfall. Exhausted and footsore, I reached the gap with an hour of daylight remaining and took a room in a motel. A new freeway was in the process of construction through the gap. Giant earthmoving machines roared up and down the mountain, trailing red dust, until darkness fell. A steady stream of tourist autos poured over the notch and raced along the parkway. The place teemed with vacationers, and the motels did a thriving business. The activity and crowds were a source of pleasure for me. I felt as if I had come out of the wilderness, both literally and figuratively speaking. The preceding two weeks had been difficult and wearing, and now the crowds of motorists presaged actively maintained trails and relatively smooth sailing for the next six weeks.

Shenandoah National Park is an altogether different world from southwestern Virginia. The trails are broad, smooth, evenly graded, and beautifully maintained. Although the highways, campgrounds and other public places teemed with vacationers, the trail was crowded only on a few sections. Quite a number of campers were at the shelters, but most of them had walked only a short distance from their cars. The real hikers at the shelters made up a distinct minority. As I progressed through the park, southbound hikers kept warning me about the difficult ascents facing me a few miles to the north. However, the threatened hard climbs never materialized. I would start up a hill expecting the worst, but soon I would be at the summit wondering whether this was the mountain that had been mentioned. I can honestly state that I never worked up a sweat in the Shenandoah National Park, despite warm weather and moving along at a brisk clip whenever I walked. It would have been child's play to travel 25 miles a day, but I held myself down to 15 or 20 miles in order to have plenty of time to enjoy the forests, the mountains, the views into the Shenandoah Valley, and the small minority of people on the trail whom I felt inclined to rap with. All in all, it was a much-needed vacation following the discomforts and difficulties of the preceding weeks.

At the Hawksbill Gap Shelter, midway through the park, I camped with a Boy Scout troop from Virginia Beach. The kids were naval dependents, and the leaders were navy men or civilian employees from the Norfolk Navy Yard. When I arrived in midafternoon, the shelter and its environs were bestrewed with packs and sleeping bags, but the place was deserted save for one man. Dave Barnett was a 12-year navy man, a CPO electronics technician, and a corpsman to boot. He had come along on the troop's 50-mile hike in large measure because of the latter skill. He conducted sick call morning and night, treating a variety of cuts, burns, insect bites, poison ivy attacks, and sprained ankles. We spent a quiet afternoon together, talking as I bathed in an icy creek and performed my chores. He was raised on the Maine coast and grew up hiking in the New Hampshire and Maine mountains. He had served in Vietnam as a forward observer, and was aboard the Forrestal during its tragic fire.

As evening approached, the shouting Scouts returned from a swimming hole. A detail soon prepared supper. They invited me to join them at the meal, which I was glad to do. All the bunks in the shelter were spoken for, but Dave had brought his Gerry tent along and invited me to share it with him. The generous troop fed me a second time in the morning, and then I was on my way.

By laying over to rest my foot I had fallen two days behind Dave Odell, my erstwhile hiking companion. He lost a day somewhere, for when I entered the park his lead had narrowed to one day. Most of the hikers I met had either spoken with him or heard about him. Their reaction was typically one of awe, "The guy is actually walking the whole trail." The few who learned that I too was hiking the entire trail must have had their minds blown by the experience of meeting two "end-to-enders" in as many days. The Scouts from Virginia Beach had shared a camp with him the night before I encountered them. They coined the not altogether inaccurate apellation of "gorilla man" for him. He had lost his excess fat during the first two weeks of the trek and was now a very solid, muscular person. With his powerful upper body, massive pack, huge long-armed body, thick stubby legs, and long dark hair, it was not difficult to understand why the Scouts had conjured up the name.

At the Pass Mountain Shelter I spent a night with an interesting group of campers. Two men who had recently graduated from George Washington University entertained me with stories about their trips in the Canadian Rockies and the White Mountains. Both possessed exceptionally fine beards and wiry hair which stood out from their heads in Afro style. Both were vegetarians as well, and they fed me a delicious meat-free stew concocted from soybean grits, tomatoes, and herbs. In the morning they served up their own granola, which was superior to the commercial preparations I had been eating. Two muscular high school football players joined us in the shelter, and a silent young man armed with three cameras set up his tent near at hand.

An elderly couple pompously strutted into camp wearing Gerry packs. They erected their Gerry tent and sat down on their Gerry sleeping bags to eat supper, which consisted of anchovies, caviar, cocktail crackers, wine, steak, and Pepperidge Farm cookies. The athletes had brought along a rumor that scavenging bears were at the shelter, so I hung my pack up from a tree and showed the others how to do the same. The arrogant older man declined my advice and hung his food from an obviously vulnerable limb. In the morning, he was dismayed to find that the bear had pulled down his food bag and consumed the bacon, eggs, English muffins, and marmalade it contained.

There was another interesting group the next night at the Indian Run Shelter, the northernmost one in the park. A troop of young Scouts was starting a 50-mile hike with their leader, Reverend John. They were an extremely noisy and raucous bunch, totally ignorant of camp etiquette but friendly and amusing withal. Four youths from Pittsburgh were also present. Either group was vocal enough, but somehow the two disparate groups served as catalysts for the aggressive instincts in each other. All evening they tried to outdo one another— talking, arguing, exchanging insults, pitting their checkers and chess champions against each other. People kept producing popcorn, roasted apples, and sassafras tea. The fire blazed and candles illuminated the interior of the shelter. It was a noisy party, lasting far into the night. All the while Reverend John did his subtle thing. This handsome, black-haired, Baptist minister's consuming passion was to persuade people to "speak out for Jesus." He played a cool game, slipping in a comment here and a remark there, never coming on so strong as to cause his quarry to feel threatened, all the while insidiously laying a snare for his unsuspecting prey. I had little doubt that he would draw it taut towards the end of the trip, and it would contain several innocent little souls. I thought the man was possessed by a devil. He seemed to believe that his worth in the eyes of God depended not so much upon living the tenets of his faith as upon tallying up souls on his personal scorecard.

In the morning I walked the remaining miles to the park's northern boundary and thumbed rides to and from Front Royal to pick up the next package of supplies. The last 50 miles in Virginia were mostly along secondary roads lined by farms and resort cabins. Formerly the trail paralleled the roads along the mountain crests, but many landowners had recently closed their land to the trail. Local people told me that it was a calculated effort to force relocation of the trail away from their property, so that when land is eventually purchased for the Appalachian Trail easement it will become a permanent feature of other people's backyards, not their own. Given the many stories I heard about abuse of the trail and adjacent structures in recent years, I could not help sympathizing with these efforts to preserve their land from depredations of some hikers. On the other hand, my feet were made sore by pounding along on hot rocky roads for mile after mile. Numerous prominent NO TRESPASSING signs lined the way. I found them extremely irritating and tended to take them as personal insults. The land closings also resulted in the closure of several shelters that I had planned to use. As a consequence, my hiking and camping plans were annoyingly disrupted for a few days.

It was very dry, too. Closings made several springs inaccessible, and others that I had counted on contained no water. One warm afternoon I came to the Wilson Gap Lean-to with only a pint of water to last seven miles to the next spring. The shelter's spring was dry, as I expected. I decided to drink all of my water with lunch as a pot of tea rather than dole it out in sips during the afternoon. When the tea had steeped, I looked for the leather glove that I carried for handling pots. It was nowhere to be found, so I used my handkerchief to remove the hot lid. Floating on the tea in a greasy, brown layer of scum was the errant glove. It had stuck to the bottom of the kettle lid and then fallen in and steeped along with the tea. Since I was quite dehydrated and there was no prospect of finding water for another three hours of hiking, I had to drink the repulsive brew. After scooping off the scum and adding copious amounts of sugar and Tang to mask its flavor, I gulped down the glove-leather tea.

After the first two weeks on the trail I developed a well-nigh insatiable desire for food. No matter how much I consumed, I was always hungry. I could pass neither restaurant nor grocery without going inside to purchase something to eat. If I had just eaten and someone offered to share his meal with me, I was only too happy to eat again. After a long month in Virginia, I arrived at the Maryland state line near Harpers Ferry. The first thing I did was to find a café and order breakfast. After devouring an enormous meal, I did a little sight-seeing and then walked on a few miles to Crampton Gap. As the morning progressed I started to feel weak and nauseous. By the time I came to the shelter at the gap, I was vomiting almost continuously, had abdominal cramps, and suffered frequent diarrhea. The illness was apparently caused by the restaurant meal. I lay prostrated in the shelter all afternoon and most of the night, and was weak and tired easily for the next week. It was the only time I suffered ill effects from either food or water on the trip.

On the fifty-seventh day I crossed the Mason–Dixon line and entered Yankeeland. Hiking in southern Pennsylvania was disappointing. The trail was unpleasantly close to civilization much of the time: roads, resorts, garbage dumps, public camps, and state parks abounded along the way. Even in the woods one rarely escaped the sounds of automobiles and barking dogs, and litter was a constant feature of the landscape. The shelters were attractive and prettily located, but they suffered from proximity to roads, with consequent overuse and abuse. The woods near these lean-tos were ravaged and trampled, the grounds littered with trash, and the shelters themselves dilapidated.

I spent my first night in the state at Raccoon Run, where a pair of tiny log shelters are situated. A trio of unfriendly kids from New York City already occupied one of the shelters, so I took up quarters in the other. What a contrast these raucous, suspicious, and hostile youths were to the quiet, shy, and friendly mountaineers of the southern states! As darkness was falling, two carloads of local teenagers roared into the camp from an adjacent road. They obviously had planned to have a party and were irked at finding the place already taken. There was a strained standoff for half an hour. We all sat quietly guarding our shelters, ignoring them as much as possible, while they milled around their autos drinking and shouting, ignoring us in turn. When they had demonstrated that they had only come to have a few drinks and really had no intention of staying any longer, they piled back into their vehicles and raced off. The mutual threat had given the campers a common bond, and we became acquainted. I built up the fire that the New Yorkers had unsuccessfully fussed over for the last hour, and we sat down to smoke together. I did not get off, however, so I went to bed. As I was falling asleep a brace of couples drove up. Finding the shelters occupied, they quietly left. One more group of nocturnal visitors disturbed our slumbers. Two motorcyclists arrived on the scene late at night, but they left immediately upon finding us there.

The walk along South Mountain between Caledonia State Park and Pine Grove Furnace State Park was the most enjoyable section in southern Pennsylvania. It was a warm weekend day, but few hikers were about. There were few roads and no garbage dumps near the trail. The forest was sunny and open. There was a northern feeling to my surroundings. Not that these were true northern woods, not by any stretch of the imagination. Rather, they gave a subtle suggestion

of the North—the pines interspersed with hardwoods seemed to intimate that the trail would soon wend its way beneath the spruces and
birches of New England. The date was August 14. There were now
definite changes in the color of the trees' foliage. Scattered leaves had
turned yellow and red, and an occasional sapling was cloaked entirely
in scarlet. I met a weekend group of hikers, members of the Blue
Mountain Eagle Climbing Club. They were interested in my expedition and invited me to look them up when I neared their homes in
eastern Pennsylvania. However, when I arrived in that area I had no
crucial needs and did not wish to break the chain of my thoughts by
dropping down into civilization, so I passed up their kind invitation.
Like the trees and the changing forest colors, these people were of
the North. It raised my spirits immeasurably to realize that I was
once again on native turf, nearing the halfway point of the trip, with
autumn only a short month away.

The crossing of the broad Cumberland Valley was one of the most
exhilarating times of the trip. After two months of hiking along rough
woods trails, it was a delight to walk almost the entire day on smooth
macadam roads. I put my legs in high gear, and walking rapidly became an automatic activity. Freed of the chores of watching the trail
surface, fending off weeds and brush, and scrambling over and under
and around obstacles, I could look about and think without distraction. I enjoyed the fertile well-maintained farms, the traditional two-
story farmhouses, and the friendly people. Stopping for vegetables at
the Musser Farm fruit stand, I discovered that the proprietors were
distant relatives of my grandmother, whose family stemmed from this
area of the state. They loaded me down with a large sackful of garden-
fresh vegetables and refused payment. It was a 24-mile day, one of
the longer ones. My feet were sore when I reached the Thelma Marks
Memorial Shelter, which was a few miles from the town of Duncannon
on the bank of the Susquehanna River. Trail relocations made the
precise position of the halfway point of the hike uncertain, but it was
within a few miles of the lean-to, one way or the other. From this
point on the trip would be downhill: I could start counting down
both the miles and the days.

Two young men shared the evening there with me. One, Wes Bob-
bitt, was to enter college in the fall. He was the son of a pathologist
at the University of Virginia and had not hiked prior to this summer.
Early in June he had purchased a fine new backpacking outfit, filled
the knapsack with freeze-dried foods, and set off along the Appalachian Trail in Virginia. The other lad was also a Virginian—a lanky
blond boy who had grown up in Boston and had hiked in the White

Mountains. Deetle Lamont now lived near Washington. He had also set off on a sojourn of undefined length in the mountains. The two had met in northern Virginia and teamed up.

An entry from my journal that day describes one aspect of solo long-distance hiking: "I have suffered much loneliness on this trip. After several days devoid of contact with mankind, one develops a positive craving for company of any sort. A brief encounter on the trail or in a town gives one a psychological boost which lasts for an hour or two afterwards. Then one settles gradually, inevitably, back into his loneliness and depression. Increasingly I miss the familiar, stable things in my life—close friends, casual friends, acquaintances, my cats, musical evenings, my own bed, my own apartment. At particular moments, I miss particular people acutely, e.g., tonight I wish that I could visit with Kurt and Emily Fiedler. Sometimes I even miss the bleak, unfriendly medical center and the frustrating, harassed life of a medical student."

The Third 500 Miles

Descending into Duncannon with a pack full of rubbish collected at the Thelma Marks Memorial Shelter, I found the post office and my food package. A bag of powdered milk had ruptured, and the gritty powder had distributed itself through the parcel. It trickled from cracks in the box in fine streams onto the floor, to the disgust of the postal clerk who handed it to me. My field boots were in the package. The original Bean boots were worn, but it looked as if they would last another 500 miles or so. I considered mailing the field boots to a post office farther along the trail, but there was no accurate way of predicting when the first pair would give out. The replacements had a new set of soles, so I threw away my Bean shoes and donned the field shoes. My feet were still giving me trouble. The sore would not heal completely, and a similar lesion had developed on the other foot. They hurt constantly and occasionally suppurated. The new boots were slightly more comfortable, and they pressed more lightly on the sore areas, so it seemed advantageous to wear them. There was also a replacement pair of cutoff jeans in the parcel. The originals had so many holes by now that I did not wear them in town for fear of arrest on charges of indecent exposure.

At the post office I was informed that Dave had been there the previous afternoon. This meant that he was only half a day ahead of me. I could not understand why he was moving so slowly. He had built up a 2½-day lead at the Shenandoah National Park's northern gateway. There was an imminent prospect of overtaking him a third time and this was bad news because despite my occasional loneliness and depression, I wanted to hike alone. Once we were in contact, the earlier pattern of catch-up would undoubtedly resume, and we would start spending too many nights together. I calculated that he would probably do the 14 miles to the Clarks Valley Shelter that day. I considered stopping at the Earl Shaffer Shelter after only eight miles to avoid contact, but the shelter was in such bad condition that I pressed right on. To my surprise the Clarks Valley Shelter was in ruins. I could not decide if the destruction had been due to natural forces or the hand of man. Fortunately there was no rain, so I camped close-by.

Next afternoon I caught up with Dave. He was slowly and painfully limping along. The muscles in his legs were cramped as hard as rocks. He could not recall any reason for his leg problem, which had flared up a few days earlier. It amazed me that he could walk at all. I admired his determination; I would have been unable to continue if afflicted with half the pain he seemed to be suffering. His packframe had disintegrated in Maryland and at Duncannon he had received a brand new one from Kelty. His boots were rapidly wearing out. They looked as if the next hundred miles would do them in. Despite everything, I was very happy to see him. It seemed as if our lives had begun on the trail together, as if the trail was our whole existence and the only conceivable future. I knew that sometime I would walk out the end of the long green tunnel but that moment seemed an eternity away. Judged from this perspective we were the oldest of friends.

We came to Swatara Gap that afternoon. A busy highway and railroad ran through the gap beside the dirty, foam-flecked Swatara Creek. The guidebook suggests camping at a site which is near the bridge, but it was exposed to public view, strewn with wrecked cars and other debris, and close to stagnant water that formed the breeding grounds for clouds of mosquitoes. We retraced our steps to the Mountain View Motel in the gap and took a room.

The eastern Pennsylvania ridges were a joy to traverse. Objectively, I do not understand why. They are long, low, and level, with relief only at the infrequent gaps cut by a river. The woods are pleasant, but hardly exceptional. Hikers were personable and friendly for the most part, but far too numerous. Water was scarce, which necessitated careful planning and conservation, and the shelters were spaced at awkward intervals for through hiking. The trail surface alternated between gravel road, forest road, rocky path, and jumbled rock pile. For the most part it was exceptionally rocky and consequently very hard on the feet. Once I had driven along the freeway beneath Blue

Suspension bridge over Mill Creek, Georgia. *Photo by Garnett W. Martin*
Sign at Carvers Gap, Tennessee—North Carolina line. *Photo by Elmer L. Onstott*

Photo by Art Smith

Shenandoah sunset.

Mountain, the long ridge which the Appalachian Trail follows most of the distance between the Susquehanna and Delaware rivers. Looking up at its level crest, I had decided this would be a simple section to hike. However, because the trail was so stony, it turned out to be as difficult as most of the other sections. I probably felt so good because the halfway point in the trail had been passed, and because I could feel the imminence of autumn, my favorite season. Fall promised cool weather which would be a blessed relief for my sore feet, diminution of the crowds on the trail, and, in particular, the approach of journey's end.

I could feel that my body was running down. I had lost a considerable amount of weight (15 pounds from an already lean 160) and my feet were chronically sore. One day in eastern Pennsylvania I took a half-day off. Earlier in the trip this would have rejuvenated me, but now it had no restorative effect whatsoever. Next morning I was as tired as if I had walked all day. The Kelty was slowly disintegrating, too. The frame was bent in several places, and I worried about it breaking apart. The backbands wore out, and I replaced them with parachute cord woven into a rectangular backrest. The waist strap was accidentally burnt in a fire, and this too was replaced with nylon parachute shrouds.

There being no shelter located conveniently for us, Dave and I stopped for a night in Port Clinton on the Schuylkill River. I haggled with the hotel proprietress until she dropped the ante to $7 for the two of us. We spent the evening touring the little town's shops and drinking in the hotel bar. The townsfolk enjoyed talking with the strange looking pair of visitors as much as we enjoyed talking with them. They described their way of life, their likes and dislikes, and their joys and sorrows. A busy six-lane highway stands just a few feet from the hotel and shops. Cars and trucks roar through the hamlet at 60 miles an hour night and day. One cannot escape the racket any place in town; one simply endures it. What a shame it is that we subvert the quality of our lives to the mindless convenience of the internal combustion engine.

Throughout the course of the hike I read the trail-side registers with curiosity and frequently with amusement. On occasion there are entries of remarkable wit and clarity, but my chief interest in reading them was to follow the hikers ahead of me, finding out which ones were still hiking and what progress they were making. Hikers kept dropping out, one by one, until only a hard core remained. The attrition was virtually complete at the New Jersey line; few if any dropped out after that point. The dozen remaining hikers seemed like old friends by now. I had read their comments for two months and had very definite impressions of what sort of person each one was. I even imagined what they looked like. I wished that I could overtake them to compare my impressions with the reality, but there was little likelihood of doing this. They had all started much earlier in the season, and even though Dave and I traveled faster than the majority of them, their lead was too great to overcome. I expected to meet a few southbound hikers and was disappointed not to have met a one thus far. I figured that a few early birds would have started in May and June. In three months some should have traveled the 900 miles to eastern Pennsylvania. I was ready to believe that there were no southbound hikers this year.

Lehigh Gap was another spot of historical significance for me. My grandfather initially practiced in the town of Portland, which is a mile south of the gap, after graduation from medical school. I could see the town from the ridge but made no attempt to visit it. He left it after only a few years to set up a practice in Wisconsin. Now, 50 years later, there is probably not a soul in town who remembers him. I sat on the ridge trying to imagine what it was like when he lived there, wondering whether he had ever climbed up to the perch where I rested.

A few miles farther along I overtook my young acquaintance Deetle Lamont. He told me that he had made up his mind to hike all the way to Mt. Katahdin rather than begin college in the fall as he had planned. He and Wes had parted ways, and Deetle had hitchhiked around from Duncannon to Port Clinton, which explained how he happened to be ahead of me. He was sitting exhaustedly on a log with a newfound hiking companion when I walked up. We rapped for a while; then I moved on. They immediately sprang up and set off in pursuit. They stayed close behind me the rest of the afternoon. I kept myself in high gear until they finally ran out of energy and fell back. I could never understand why, when I overtook young men (and even middle-aged ones) on the trail, they invariably interpreted my desire to pass them as a challenge and began to race. I had no particular desire to race with anyone; that was the opposite of the reason I had started on my hike. I wanted only to be allowed to amble along at my own pace, but I quickly learned that to do so was to invite company for hours and even days. The best solution was to burn along at high speed for several hours until the other hikers had been run into the ground, so to speak. Then they had to stop and rest while I continued and quickly left them behind. Even though I was beginning to become worn out physically, my condition after two months on the trail was so superior to that of the vast majority of hikers that it was easy to employ this tactic successfully.

Dave and I traveled together the length of this section—between the Susquehanna and Delaware rivers. At times I became annoyed at having no opportunity to spend a night alone, but on the whole it was good to have a companion. Only another through hiker could understand one's peculiar thoughts, needs, and way of life. The walkers going only a short distance had scarcely any conception of where we were mentally. The two of us and the handful of others far ahead formed an exclusive fraternity, and only the most sensitive among the weekend trampers could sense the estrangement between them and us.

We spent our last night in Pennsylvania camped at Wind Gap. Arriving there an hour before Dave, I found a grassy plot beneath a pair of low-branching trees. It was situated on a bank 20 yards above the busy freeway through the gap. I collected wood, built a fireplace, and obtained water at a nearby trailer court. A frigid wind blasted through the gap from the northwest and I built a low stone wall to serve as a windbreak for sleeping. Dave appeared on the scene and we cooked and ate. Then we sat by the fire bundled in our down jackets. The sky was clear and the stars were near at hand. The autos and trucks roared past all night, but somehow their noise and flashing lights were not at all obnoxious. Indeed, they seemed friendly and comforting. Snuggled into the sleeping bag behind the rock wall, I slept deeply and refreshingly.

It had become my habit to light the Primus stove first thing in the morning and drink my first cup of coffee while comfortable and warm in the sleeping bag. Usually breakfast consisted of cold food, but when it included cooked cereal, the stove sufficed for that, too. Two or three times during the day I might stop and use the stove to warm water for tea or coffee. Evening cooking usually took place over a campfire, but the stove was useful at night when weather conditions made a fire impractical. The stove was certainly worth its weight in convenience, as was the quart bottle of fuel. I began the trip using Coleman fuel, then switched to white gas when I learned that the Amoco stations sell an unleaded petrol from their pumps. Amoco stations became scarce in the North, and I discovered that ordinary leaded gasoline worked beautifully. Once a week I cleaned the burner orifice, and no plugging occurred at any time. One quart of fuel sufficed for a week or 10 days.

After a stop in Delaware Water Gap for the next package of supplies, I tramped up to Sunfish Pond for my first camp in New Jersey. It is a lovely treelined lake approximately a quarter of a mile in diameter. Unfortunately, it was surrounded by campers. The number of campers, their trash, and their noise spoiled the beauty of the place for me. I walked most of the way around the pond to avoid the beer-and-radio campers. The most isolated campsite I could find was next to a pair of longhairs who had been encamped there all summer. Given the extreme crowding, I thought it selfish for them to squat there so long. It turned out that their camp was a hangout for all the heads and freaks at the pond. As the evening came on, they started drifting in by twos and threes, until there were at least twenty of them milling around the fire. Hash and marijuana circulated freely. I found it appalling that they needed drugs to get it on up in the mountains. Several were obnoxiously loud, and one in particular kept shouting from the bank to his chum across the lake, "Hey, George! Fuck you!" George invariably replied in kind. The pair of long-haired campers prepared a big pot of stew. We all partook freely of it, crowding around the fire for a bit of warmth in the chilly evening. Eventually the stoned crowd tripped merrily home to their individual camps. I was glad to have spent my evening with them, but could not quell my disgust at their kind of "wilderness life."

While camped at Sunfish Pond I met my first southbound through hiker. He was Steve Gorman, a tall slender blond boy from Long Island. He looked tired and pale. He had suffered considerable sickness and had had to take several weeks off to recuperate. His overall rate of progress had been rather slow, but he was young and very determined, and he was regaining his health. We shared a campfire and briefed one another on salient features of the miles ahead.

New Jersey afforded uninteresting travel for the most part. The first two days, spent atop the ridges of Kittatinny Mountain, were rather enjoyable but bland. The alternation of woods and open grassy areas with rock outcroppings made for pleasant walking, but the numerous hikers and the ever-present red-brown cloud on the eastern horizon were depressing. To avoid crowds, I picked a lonely ridgetop site for my camp one night, but the threat of rain forced me to seek the security of a shelter in High Point State Park the next night.

As I policed the garbage-strewn ground around this lean-to, a band of giggling young girls with two liberated leaders entered the clearing. They were New York City children from a nearby camp and had just completed a two-mile hike. A truck was to bring their food and bedding later. They soon left to go swimming, and to my relief, I saw no more of them until morning. Rain began in the evening and continued all night. In the morning one of the leaders and two girls straggled in to collect the equipment they had left behind. The trio was soaking wet, with chattering teeth and blue lips. They were wrapped in sodden wool blankets. Rather than return to the shelter, they had decided to sleep on the lawn near the park headquarters. When the rain began, the leaders had insisted that the children stick it out in the rain with only a blanket apiece for shelter. After six hours of drenching rain they retreated to the porch of a ranger cabin, but the damage had already been done.

I had a premonition that the continuing rain might be due to a hurricane. If it was to be a three-day rain, I would have to hike regardless of the weather. If it was only a local storm it would be more sensible to wait it out. I slept late, testing this possibility. Around nine o'clock two teenagers appeared at the shelter and confirmed my suspicion. The ranger had told them that tropical storm Doria was approaching the northern coast. Several days of rain were expected. My hopes of waiting out the storm were dashed, so I started out. It was wet, cold, and miserable. Fortunately the woods soon gave way to country roads. At least I would not have to wade through wet weeds and slip along on a muddy trail. I had been walking on the road only twenty minutes when a car pulled up beside me. Its driver leaned out the window and called, "Hey, Jim!" To my amazement, it was Barney Kinahan, a Yonkers hiker I had met on Iron Mountain in Tennessee. He had been helping Dave get his boots resoled by acting as messenger boy between trail and boot repair shop. He had just delivered the resoled boots to Dave at the park headquarters and was now on his way home. Dave had told him that I was close at hand, so when he chanced on a dripping figure trudging along the road, he knew it must be me. I hopped into the car with him, and we reminisced for a few minutes. However, I couldn't afford to sit there and become chilled, so I soon hopped back out into the downpour and continued on my way.

An hour later, thoroughly soaked by this time despite my raincoat, I heard a voice call out from behind, "Hey! Come in out of the rain for awhile." I paused. "Yes, you! Turn right around and come back here!" I turned but did not move toward the speaker. "Come on now! I have hot coffee and soup waiting for you inside." Convinced at last, I trotted back to his house and dropped my pack on the porch. Raleigh Johnson, my host, was an outdoors-minded man who used to live in Newark. Fed up with the urban scene, he had purchased a country home several years earlier and now commutes to work from it. My two young acquaintances from earlier in the morning were sprawled inside, drying out before a crackling fire. One had slipped and suffered a nasty fall on the muddy trail. Raleigh had seen him limping dispiritedly along the road. When he hailed them, they were only too glad to go inside and have a hot drink. Once within they came to their senses and decided to cancel the remainder of their trip. I sipped coffee and soup for an hour, but failing to come to my senses, I then insisted on going back out into the storm despite Raleigh's protests. He was as kind and generous a person as I met on my hike.

The remainder of the day was unremitting misery, but finally it came to an end. I found a motel and rented a room. The storm raged violently all night, but by morning it had blown itself out. The sun shone for brief moments between low fast-moving clouds. The state was flooded, highlands and lowlands alike. Every stream had overflowed its banks, and every low-lying area had become a shallow lake. Not a mile passed without two or three places where I had to ford water from knee- to thigh-deep and from 50 to 100 yards wide. I soon gave up any attempt to keep my boots dry, and wore them as I waded through the water. Once in a while I stopped and poured the water out of them when the squishing became intolerable. At one place the trail led through a little marsh, then alongside a stream for half a mile. There was a road which essentially paralleled the trail. I knew that the trail must be flooded and considered bypassing it on the road, but finally waded through the marsh, forded the thigh-deep stream, and then sank ankle-deep with every step in gray, gooey mud for a hundred yards before coming to the road that I should have followed in the first place.

I was on the verge of tears with rage and frustration and threw myself down on the pavement to rest. An auto whizzed past barely a foot from my head. It screeched to a halt, backed up, and a raucous Bronx voice expressed its opinion about the suicidal folly of anyone who would lie in the middle of the road. I was so angry that, despite the man's obvious good intentions, I suggested that he go commit an unnatural act with himself. Insulted and furious, the poor fellow roared off. I sat up and saw a filthy old man ambling toward me from an adjacent shack. His clothes were shabby and as dirty as his face, and he smiled through broken, jagged teeth and babbled some senseless gibberish. He seemed to want to know what I was doing, so I explained my mission in elementary language. Apparently satisfied, he grinningly wandered back to his shack.

It began to rain again, so I hitched a ride down to the resort town of Greenwood Lake and took a room in a tourist home. Next morning one of the brightest moments of the trip occurred. As I was eating breakfast in a diner, the Sunday morning delivery of the *New York Times* was made to an adjacent cigar store. I bought a copy, then sat in the café devouring its contents for the next two hours, to the amusement of the proprietor. Reading the *Times* on Sunday morning is an addictive pleasure that I have never lost the desire to indulge in.

The morning of indulgence precluded hiking more than 13 miles that day. I made camp at Island Pond, a fair-sized lake in the woods of Palisades Interstate Park. True to its name, there is a small island in the center of the pond. Numerous rock outcroppings on the shore make fine diving points. Swimming is officially prohibited, but the crowds of picnickers that had walked in a mere 200 yards from the nearest road paid little heed to the prohibition. Nor did I, for diving in the deep cool water was a pleasure I rarely had been able to enjoy along the trail. The shelter was nicely located on a rise overlooking the lake, but it was vandalized and decrepit. Two large oil drums were overflowing with garbage, and much more was scattered around on the ground. As darkness approached, all the picnickers left. I picked up the filth and piled it by the garbage cans. Dave walked in about the time the camp was clean. We had not seen one another for five days and had a good evening together, reminiscing about the mobs in Jersey and the miseries attendant upon the downpour of Doria.

At three in the morning four teenage boys from Brooklyn arrived at the shelter, having walked in from the highway by flashlight. Incessantly shouting in the loud grating accent characteristic of their borough, they lay down in their sleeping bags. When one of them had the gall to turn on a portable television set, I lost my temper and yelled at them to knock off the noise. Surprisingly enough, the racket ceased instantaneously. There was not another peep from them until morning.

Continuing the next day through nice woods cluttered by hordes of hikers, almost all of them conversing in the harsh and nasal New York City accent, Dave and I climbed up and down several small mountains and then came to Bear Mountain State Park. After looking at the Hudson River through the haze from the summit of Bear Mountain itself (at first I thought it was a lake), we descended to the roadside area of the park, which includes an inn, play areas, a beach and boating lake, a zoo, a swimming pool, and several museums. Thousands of city dwellers crowded the premises. We were hungry and investigated the cafeteria. The prices were outrageous and the quantities of food minute, so we walked upstairs to the buffet. It was being served in a good restaurant for $3.50, which was not much more than the cost of a couple of sandwiches and a drink in the cafeteria below. The hostess was reluctant to seat us because of our long hair, beards, and ragged clothing, but I explained that we were walking the Appalachian Trail and had nothing better to wear. She relented and let us sit down in a corner well-removed from the respectable patrons. Two hours later, after four heaping platefuls apiece, our appetites were satiated, and we bloatedly departed.

Surprisingly enough, neither of us became sick after this gorging, although hiking was a bit of an effort for the rest of the afternoon. We strolled through the zoo, looking at the moth-eaten coats and listless eyes of the caged animals, then crossed the Hudson on the Bear Mountain Bridge. In terms of elevation this was a low point on the trip, but emotionally it was a high point. As we walked across far above the river, with excursion steamers trailing broad wakes on the muddy water below, I was filled with joy. I felt that a major milestone was being passed. The essential change was that at this point the boring, crowded central portion of the trail was left behind. We camped at another ghetto shelter. It took hours to pick up the rubbish, flatten the cans, and incinerate the burnables. Once the camp was clean, it was not at all a bad place.

My body's slow debilitation had continued during the preceding month. I had not taken a day off since the stop near Pearisburg, six weeks earlier. I had been hiking up to 25 miles a day, attempting to put the bad sections behind as rapidly as possible and get ahead of schedule. I succeeded in this, but paid a heavy price. My feet were sore and swollen, my knees constantly ached, my back was sore, and my kit was in need of repairs. Most of all, I was sick of trudging along day after day, through rain and shine, with neither rest nor diversion from the hiking. Dave too was running down. He was thin and haggard, and his legs hurt constantly. One morning, to my surprise, he was still in bed at 7:00 A.M. At the first rattle of my stove he heaved over like a giant flounder and moaned, but made no attempt to rise. To my drowsy "good morning" he growled, "What's good about it? I feel lousy. I'm sick to my stomach." As I cooked and packed, he made no effort to get under way. However, he soon began to feel better, so I departed. I expected to see him later in the day, but we were not to meet again for six weeks.

Some of my relatives live near Danbury, Connecticut, which is about 30 miles from the trail's southern entrance into the state. Next day I called them up, and a cousin drove to meet me in Kent, a little town just inside the state border. For two days I lounged around my aunt's house, napping and reading all day by the swimming pool, wining and dining with my cousins and their spouses in the evening. It was good to visit friends I had not seen in almost a decade, but the rest did little to rejuvenate my tired body. I regained 2 of the 15 pounds I had lost, but was as tired upon departure as I had been upon arrival.

My cousin took me back to the Appalachian Trail on the Saturday morning of Labor Day weekend. I spent the three-day holiday traversing the 50-odd Connecticut miles of the trail. It was warm and humid all weekend, with daytime temperatures in the 80s. I sweated profusely for the first time since leaving the South. The warm weather was appropriate for the last long weekend of the summer. Even though autumn would not officially begin for another three weeks, this was, practically speaking, the beginning of fall. On Tuesday the school children would return to school. The college students would drift back to the campuses as September passed, until by the end of the month all of them would have returned to classes. Now there would be no more Scouts and family groups on the trail, and soon there would be no more young people. Only a handful of diehards would remain. I was looking forward to lonesome tranquility in the autumnal forest.

Campgrounds, roads, and resorts near the trail teemed with people, but the trail itself was not heavily populated. Partly because of inconvenient shelter spacing and partly because of my desire to avoid crowds, I camped out alone at night. Twice I found isolated, sheltered campsites in hemlock groves bisected by little brooks. Pools in the streams permitted me to bathe away the day's accumulation of sweat. The fallen hemlock needles made soft mattresses for sitting and sleeping. Among the big trees it was cool and restful, a refreshing relief from the heat of the day.

Walking down a primitive road which follows the west bank of the Housatonic River, I was offered a ride, but declined. An hour later I met the same family picnicking in a pine grove by the stream. They invited me to stop for lunch, which I was happy to do. The children played in the shallow waters of the stream while we sat together talking, sipping wine, and eating. The woman was a handsome, black-haired lady of middle age; her man was a cheerful, intelligent, and youthful person well into his 60s. His father was a doctor, but he was restless and left home at an early age to roam the world. He had been many places and seen many things. Finally, at a relatively late age, he settled down to a young wife and sired his children. Largely self-educated, he could converse intelligently on virtually any topic. He was the sort of man who would have succeeded at whatever he set his mind to. I took my leave of this remarkably sweet and loving couple thoroughly inebriated by their company and the wine.

One night I camped at a shelter with a slender, bespectacled, college man from England. Failing to gain admission to a British university, he had worked his way across the Atlantic on a freighter and entered an American college. After working all summer as a clerk in a boys' camp, he decided to try his hand at what he had observed the campers doing all summer, namely hiking and camping. His funds were very limited, so his equipment was makeshift. His pack consisted of a cardboard box which he carried before him in his arms. A soft-drink can, a throwaway pie tin, and a spoon comprised his mess kit. After three days on the trail, his clothing and tennis shoes were in shreds. His cheap sleeping bag dangled from his shoulders by a piece of cord. My initial impression was "how ridiculous," but after spending the night with him, my contempt turned to admiration. He was an unusually plucky young man, making the best of his limitations of mind, body, and finances.

Upon entering Connecticut the woods became familiar and companionable. I no longer felt as if I was a stranger in them, as I had on the central portion of the trail (but not in the South). Small stands of pine and hemlock were intermixed with white birch, beech, and maple. It felt good to stroll through a forest with the pale trunks of birches interspersed among their darker cousins. The leaves on all the trees were beginning to show color changes now. Despite the warm days and nights, autumn was definitely in the air. I passed the two-thirds mark, both in time and distance. It was another milestone.

As the Labor Day weekend drew to its close a thousand tiny rivulets of people streamed down the hillsides, gradually merging into huge streams of humanity returning to the cities. Now there was an emptiness to the hills. The only signs that hordes of people had recently been in them were the litter and the trampled ground where they had set up their camps.

Massachusetts was much like Connecticut, but better. The mountains were higher. Their summits were crowned with spruce, the first I had encountered since the afternoon on Roan Mountain in Tennessee. The crowds were gone: only an infrequent southbound long-distance hiker was to be seen. The nights grew longer and colder, and fewer leaves remained green. I camped out in this little state most of the time, not so much for the sake of avoiding people as for camping in the prettiest locations. One exception was the Kitchen Brook Lean-to on the south flank of Mt. Greylock. I came to it in early afternoon and found the place so attractive that I decided to stop for the day. It is another of the old log CCC shelters, situated on a slope in a cheerful forest of birch, beech, maple, and pine. A few rods from the shelter a brook flows in broad thin sheets of water over mossy green granite slabs, its course punctuated by small crystal-clear pools. A fresh supply of hemlock boughs was scattered on the shelter's floor. I thatched them together into a soft mattress. Then I bathed in one of the pools, sunbathed on a granite slab, and sat and meditated until it began to grow dark. I had not had an afternoon alone in such a pleasant setting for weeks. Indeed, I had not enjoyed a camp so much since the Raccoon Branch Shelter, far behind in southwestern Virginia.

The first day in Massachusetts I noticed that water was entering my right boot at an unusually rapid rate whenever I stepped into a stream or mudhole. Inspection revealed a one-centimeter crack in the vintage leather close to the sole. I decided I would replace them in Hanover, some 200 miles farther along the trail. Two days later I noticed that the crack had extended itself to an eight-centimeter tear, and the other boot had developed a similar crack. It was obviously necessary to obtain replacements immediately. I walked through Cheshire the same morning and thumbed a ride to a shopping center in Pittsfield. My ride was with a homely but friendly girl who clerked at the K-Mart in the shopping plaza. She recommended their boot department highly, so I went there first. I wanted a cheap, sturdy pair of work boots that would last as far as Katahdin. My choice was an ankle-high pair of moccasins with corrugated rubber soles costing all of $10.95. They turned out to be admirably suited for the job at hand. Despite the aspersions frequently cast upon them by Appalachian Mountain Club hikers in New England, they are one of the best pairs of boots I have ever owned. At the end of the trip they were in excellent condition; I still use them for less demanding climbs in the Wasatch Range.

Despite the fact that I had paused two full days in Connecticut, Dave was only half a day ahead of me entering Vermont. I was irked by his close proximity, fearing that I would catch up again and we would be traveling together. Earlier I had felt guilty about my distaste for hiking with another person and my consequent inhospitality, but thinking it over while I walked in southern New England, I came to the conclusion that my guilt was unjustified. I had planned this hike for years as a solo venture, never once considering the possibility of a companion. There was no reason on earth why I should change my mind midway in the course of the expedition and dilute the experience by accepting a traveling companion. The fact that Dave and I had started out at the same time and happened to walk at essentially the same pace made frequent contact between us a foregone conclusion. There was nothing for it but to make the best of the situation. However, this was my hike, my own private thing, and it would be finished alone so far as I could manage it.

The Vermont section had an inauspicious beginning. I stopped at the southernmost shelter in the state after an agreeable day of travel in Massachusetts. For virtually all of its course in Vermont, the Appalachian Trail follows the famed Long Trail. Shelters are frequent and well maintained. Two Boston men were already at the shelter. Both were around 25 years of age, both bore modest paunches, and both steadily nipped at a communal bottle of white wine. They drove a moving van for a living and took little trips into the mountains between runs. A quiet boy joined us, and we were all having a convivial time before the blazing fire, cooking and passing the bottle, when an older man jauntily swaggered into the camp. He wore corduroy knickers, a heavy pair of rough-out mountain boots, and a little Tyrolean hat. A new Kelty graced his back, and his right hand bore a carved walking staff. He might well have stepped directly out of the pages of a backpacking mail-order catalog. He immediately launched into a pretentious description of his three-day 20-mile hike, discussing it with as much enthusiasm as another might display in describing an ascent of Mt. Everest. As he spoke, he strutted back and forth, eyeing the shelter. There were two of us in each side of it already, a full house. Neither pair wished to be crowded in together with this pompous fool. The moving van men wisely ignored him. I, foolish and softhearted, relented and invited him to join us.

Rain began in the night. It continued the next morning, but the boy and the movers set off early anyway. I tried waiting it out, which left me alone with the older hiker. We carried on an inane conversation for an hour, the sort of silly babble appropriate only to the most superficial of social events. It shamed me to descend to such a level. Finally I could tolerate him no longer and set off in the rain. The encounter left a bad taste in my mouth which persisted all morning.

The rain continued. And continued. It rained every day that I was on the Long Trail, and I was almost constantly soaked. Sometimes the deluge eased long enough for my clothing to begin to dry out, when another shower would strike with vengeance. Although not cold, the air was cool. The wetness made me cold whenever I was not climbing vigorously. The shelters failed to extend out over the fireplaces, so that building a fire in camp was impractical, and my clothes remained wet at night. I had dry garments to wear inside the shelters, but they did nothing to ease the shock of pulling on cold, clammy shorts and shirt in the morning.

To add to my woes, there was a large number of late-season hikers on the trail. Apparently the Long Trail has become an "in" place to go backpacking. It seemed as if all the neophyte hikers from Chicago and New York City were hiking it the week I was there. The foul weather forced us together in the lean-tos and cabins at night, so that one always felt cramped and crowded. The pleasant lonesome nights of Connecticut and Massachusetts were a distant memory. It would not have been so bad if my companions had been seasoned hikers, but most of them were rude, ignorant, loud, and surly. When I camped with them, it felt as if I had been abruptly transported from the forests of Vermont into the middle of the noxious cities from which they came.

There didn't seem to be too many hikers out on the trail itself, which was some solace. The trail was an unending green tunnel cut through the forest. At low elevations there were birches, beeches, and maples. At higher elevations there were balsams, fog, and bog. In either setting one felt as if he was in a world apart, with the irritations and problems of the "civilized" world screened from his consciousness by the trees and their mantle of drizzle and mist. Now and then one came to an open summit or an exposed ledge and looked down into the valley where a few farms had been carved out of the dark forest. These settlements were unpretentious and serene, and did not intrude on the harmony and restful seclusion of the trail.

I came to a steep and muddy gravel bank, and carelessly descending it, slipped and tumbled head over heels to the bottom of the embankment. My elbows, forearms, legs, and thigh and hip were lacerated by the sharp pebbles in the mud, and blood oozed through the wet clay that covered me in a dozen places. It was difficult to decide which caused me more pain—the physical injuries or the insult to my ego attendant upon taking such an ignominious fall. After picking myself up I began jumping up and down on the road in a fit of anger, flailing at my legs with my fists, and screaming unprintable profanity. After venting my anger, a bath in a nearby brook removed the coating of brown mud and blood, revealing that there were no serious wounds.

One afternoon the rain stopped and the sun actually came out. I had stopped for lunch at Big Branch Shelter. Feeling a little sick, it was easy to rationalize stopping for the day at this pretty place. A roaring brook before the lean-to made pleasant background music as I cleaned up the litter, swept the shelter with a broom fashioned from twigs, and collected wood for a fire. A long afternoon of writing was interrupted toward evening by the arrival of a young couple. The girl was liberated—braless beneath her sweat-soaked T-shirt—but she was not well enough endowed to make the display interesting. In other respects, however, she was overabundantly endowed. Indeed, she was almost big and husky enough to play tackle for the Green Bay Packers. The name Moose Girl sprang unbidden to my mind. They were planning to walk the whole Long Trail and had been under way several days. It appeared that Moose Girl had not bathed during this time, because her body smell was well-nigh overpowering. She made no effort to bathe and did not even change her shirt. Fortunately for my olfactory sensibilities, the evening breeze put them to leeward. Both of them were stiff and unfriendly, angry because I was using a part of *their* shelter. They made curt responses to my attempts at conversation, so I soon gave up the effort and retired to my own thoughts. In the morning they ignored me completely. It felt good to take leave of their hostile company.

The Last 500 Miles

I was beginning to consider various alternative plans for the last month of the hike. Three-quarters of the distance was behind me now and I had been walking for three months. This left roughly 500 miles, and a month in which to walk them. I had been told that Mt. Katahdin was closed to climbing after October 15. I was not convinced that this was correct, but I had to consider the possibility. If I continued at precisely the same average pace the rest of the way, I would not reach Baxter Peak until October 17. It would be a sorry matter to arrive at the park a day or two after closing and be denied permission to walk the last five miles of the trail. I could probably go fast enough to finish before the deadline, but I did not want to do New Hampshire and Maine so rapidly. I anticipated that these two states would be the climax of the trip, and I wanted ample time to savor them. Another possibility was to eliminate planned visits to friends in Hanover and the White Mountains. This would save two or three days, but I had been looking forward for months to seeing them. I was anticipating with glee their reactions when I presented myself, looking like a wild man, and told them what I was doing. Surely I could not forego these pleasures! The last alternative was to go up to Mt. Katahdin after hiking through New Hampshire and traverse Maine from north to south, finishing at the New Hampshire border. I kept mulling over these possibilities as I finished the section on the Long Trail and turned east toward the Connecticut River.

People sometimes asked how I could stand going so long without a woman. The answer was that I seldom felt the loss. This surprised me at first, because in the outside world one of my most insistent needs is to have a woman around. However, sex and female companionship are not such basic needs as food and shelter. Most of my time and energy was expended hiking, planning, and performing necessary camp chores. The need to obtain adequate food and satisfactory shelter was a constant preoccupation, which left little time to dwell on sexual needs. The woods, the wild animals, the sky, and my fellow hikers usually furnished as much companionship as I needed. Whenever I saw a pretty girl on the trail or an attractive woman in town, desire immediately welled up within me, but an hour after the stimulation the desire would subside. Sometimes I met someone with whom a tête-à-tête was a possibility, but more time would have been needed to seduce her than I was willing to spare. In these situations I would exert self-control and march on.

The closest I came to succumbing was the day I left the Long Trail. The rain had stopped and the weather was clear and cold. After a 20-mile walk, during which I saw nary a soul on the trail, I approached the Gulf Lean-to anticipating a night alone. To my great surprise a pretty blonde girl and a great black dog were at the lean-to. She was so petite and attractive that I assumed she must be camped with her boy friend. She assured me that she was alone. Anne had hiked all the way from Baxter State Park alone, except for her dog. Looking more closely, I observed a worn pack and strong, tanned legs, confirming the veracity of her story. Her plan was to continue up the Long Trail to the Canadian border and then call it quits for the season. She unnerved me. After three months in the woods without an iota of feminine companionship, here I was alone for the night with a charming young woman. My defenses and offenses were down, and I became frightfully bashful and tongue-tied. She too was a bit flustered, but soon we loosened up and became friends. I gathered wood and she built the fire. We shared our food and sat close together before the blaze in the frosty evening, holding hands and talking. We went to bed, intimately curled up against one another, but chastely separated by the goose down in the sleeping bags. The poor dog, accustomed to sleeping beside his mistress but now relegated to the foot of the bunk, left the shelter and sulked alone in the forest all night.

The smell and feel of a warm, soft, female body curled up in my arms blew my mind. In the morning the last thing I wanted to do was to get up and leave her. How delightful it would have been to stay at the shelter alone with her, strolling around in the crisp bright woods and reveling in her company. However, my primary mission was to walk the trail, and if I stopped with her it seemed quite possible that I would say "to hell with the hike" and not finish it at all. It was important to me that I complete the trek, so we cooked our common meal and said a fond farewell. My head remained unglued for the next two days as I wandered along in an almost delirious trance. Then I came back to earth and was left with the memory of her clear smiling eyes as one of the finer recollections of the expedition.

The tenth package of supplies was waiting in Hanover, the home of Dartmouth College. Fall registration was in full progress. New students and veterans, long-hairs and short-hairs, professors and townies thronged the campus and the adjacent downtown area. Though I had never been in Hanover, I felt right at home. Since entering the North I had let my hair and beard grow. A bearded long-haired hiker seemed little out of the ordinary to these people. The worst I received from them was a glance of mild interest.

The last day of summer was my first day in New Hampshire. Appropriately enough, the weather turned cold, windy, and rainy on the first day of fall. The rain did not last long, but the cold persisted. There was not another warm day for the rest of the hike. Days were cool and nights cold. The weather was just right for tramping, but it was poor for camping and writing. My hands became so cold and stiff at night that they would hardly write, and my journals began to suffer. Complicating the problem was the rapidly decreasing length of the days. On the standard 20-mile day, I would arrive in camp with just enough daylight left to attend to basic camp chores. Writing had to be done either sometime during the day, which wreaked havoc with mileage, or by candlelight, which was often impractical due either to cold hands or breezes that made using a candle impossible. Up to this time my journal had always been current, but now it began to lag. Sometimes it fell two and even three days behind events, and I could bring it up to date only by stopping early in the afternoon, while there was still warming sunshine, and writing for the rest of the afternoon.

Smarts and Cube mountains were the first outposts of the White

Mountains. The day was cool and breezy. The sun shone from a deep blue sky; occasionally it was briefly obscured by a high flying patch of cumulus. The air was as clear as in the Uintah from the laundering of the previous night's storm, and the woods were damp and fresh. All the flowers and berries were gone now, and the birch leaves were fast turning golden. The steep eroded trail climbed 2,000 feet up Smarts Mountain to a little shelter which was held down by steel cables to prevent it from blowing away in storms. A Pittsburgh couple had spent the night there, terrified by the high wind, continuous lightning, and crashing thunder. Wind-whipped rain had poured into the shelter and soaked them. Now they stood outside in the morning sunshine, slowly warming themselves. The trail again descended steeply to Quinttown Valley, and then climbed steadily for another 2,000 feet to the top of Cube Mountain. I reveled in the moderate climbs and descents. There was physical exhilaration from the climb itself and mental elation upon reaching the peak. I sat down in a warm sheltered nook on the rocky summit of Cube Mountain and blew a kiss across the Connecticut River valley to Anne in the Green Mountains, clearly visible on the horizon. I took a last look at the farms and towns in the valleys below and then turned to welcome my old acquaintance, Moosilauke. Its upper reaches were enveloped by a dark and menacing cloud, and behind it the main body of the White Mountains stretched out to the northeast as far as I could see.

The climax of the trip was at hand. I could feel myself working into a remarkably free, almost transcendental state of mind. Each day as I traversed the White Mountains, my mental state became a little bit higher. I was in familiar territory. I had hiked virtually all of the Appalachian Trail between Moosilauke and the Mahoosucs in previous years. If pressed for time I could skip almost a hundred miles of trail that I had already walked, but I was not about to bypass the best part of the entire Appalachian Trail. Indeed, I had scheduled several extra days in the White Mountains so I could tramp through them slowly. Since I was on schedule, I felt no qualms about slowing down when I reached Mt. Moosilauke. The climb up this splendid mountain was long and steep, but the weather was ideal for hiking. I went from highway to summit without a rest stop, making only brief pauses to savor the woods or examine a view. Up from the cultivated valley I ascended, through deciduous forests golden with autumn leaves, through dark spruce woods, then out onto the open tundra of the summit ridge. I followed the old Carriage Road to the sheltered cabin beneath the summit, deposited my pack there, and scrambled to the top for lunch. From the ruins of the foundation of the old Summit

House I looked out to the east and north over a sweeping view of the White Mountains. One could delineate the course of the Appalachian Trail for the next 60 miles: first it descends from Moosilauke into Kinsman Notch, then up and over the Kinsmans, then down into Franconia Notch, then up again along the Liberty–Lincoln–Lafayette range, then across the Twins and Mt. Guyot, and finally along the magnificent ridge of the Presidential Range. To the south and east of this array of outstanding peaks lay a vast sea of forested mountains. As I studied the display, first one peak and then another struck a familiar chord. Soon I had picked out all the prominent summits and realized that I had climbed virtually every interesting peak within sight.

I had traveled 12 miles in the morning, a good distance for only half a day. There was not another human being on the mountain. It was too good an opportunity to pass by, so I decided to stay for the afternoon and sleep in the summit cabin rather than pressing on. Inside the cabin was a filthy mess, so I spent the first part of the afternoon cleaning it up, burning rubbish, boiling water for laundry, collecting firewood, and writing in my journal. Chores completed, I sat in the lee of the cabin, warmed by the late afternoon sun, meditating and looking out across the valleys and ranges. Birds twittered in the nearby dwarf trees, brown bunnies went thump-thump-thumping across the yellow-green lawn, and the wind made the cabin's guy wires hum. The sun set and it became too cold to remain outside. The wood-burning stove filled the cabin with warmth, and my candles filled it with light. After supper I once more climbed to the summit, this time by starlight. The stars have never seemed nearer and brighter. There were so many of them that the familiar constellations were almost obscured. The Milky Way was a broad, nebulous band running the length of the sky from north to south, and Orion was just beginning to climb up out of the East. Several times during the night I felt impelled to arise and go outside into the frigid air to gaze in wonder at the heavens. Long before sunrise I was awake, watching the changing colors of the sky and then, as the sun came up, seeing the golden light creeping down into the valleys. The valleys were filled with clouds and the higher peaks rose like islands above the fluffy white sea. On the mountaintop the air was perfectly clear, cold and sparkling.

I would like to have stayed up there alone for a week; it was with the greatest reluctance that I left the summit and began the descent to Kinsman Notch. Now the trail was familiar, an old friend. I remembered each pool, each cascade, the ladders and cables, and even individual rocks and trees on the route. A few lazy motorists passed by as I sprawled in the morning sunshine at the notch, and then I followed the well-remembered trail up and over Wolf Mountain, down to Eliza Brook, and then back up and over the two Kinsmans. The familiar white blazes disappeared at the notch, and it seemed strange, after following the blazes for 1,600 miles, to follow a trail devoid of them. Someone had left a woolen shirt at the Eliza Brook Shelter, and I scavenged it. My winter clothes were ahead at the Gorham Post Office, but meanwhile my light denim shirt was wholly inadequate protection on the exposed summits. The shirt was a godsend, and it served me well until I picked up my clothing in Gorham.

Even with the wool shirt the northwesterly gale chilled me as I crossed the open summits of the Kinsmans. It was good to descend back into the woods and down to the Kinsman Pond Shelter. The air was frigid there, but at least the trees took away the bite of the wind. In front of the dark shelter was a sea of mud. Some enterprising soul had built a flagstone pathway to the fireplace from the lean-to, and a large pile of rotten soggy, dead spruces stood next to the shelter. Within the dim recesses of the structure lay a long, dark bundle. I thought it must be a pile of abandoned supplies, and was startled when it moved and spoke, "Hello there. I'm George. Who are you? You know, it's been a day since anyone was here. I built a fire while I waited for you to come. It's right there. All you have to do is light it. People said there wasn't any good wood here, but I found lots of it. Just look at the pile I collected today. It's right outside. Go ahead— look at it. I'll bet you wonder what someone like me is doing here. Well, I'll tell you. I'm waiting for my baby to come out. I know I don't look pregnant, but I am. The reason you don't believe me is that the baby is gestating inside my mind. Naturally you can't see it growing there. I'm the only one who knows it's there, but when it's born, the world is going to be a different place. I don't know what it's going to be like, although I have some pretty good ideas. But I'm not telling anyone yet. It's going to be a big surprise, the biggest in all time. Then my name is going to be a household word. You don't realize it, but you will be famous too, just because you met me up here. Do you know, I like you? You're a good companion, I can see that already. You're an Aquarian, too, aren't you? I can tell. You can always pick out a dissimulating Aquarian. I'm one, too. I'm a catalyst. While my baby is growing and I'm just sitting and waiting for the day it pops out, I go around acting as a catalyst for people. They meet me one day and the next day their entire life changes. Everything that needed to come together comes together just because I catalyze them, and they are different people overnight. My baby has been growing for a year now. It's going to be born in a few months, no more than 90 days, that much I'm sure of."

George's peroration complete for the moment, I introduced myself, admitting that I was indeed an Aquarian. He immediately pointed out that "Aquarians are Leos inside, but they will never admit to it. That is why they always know the score with Leos and put them down. A Leo tries to get on an Aquarian whenever they meet, but he can't succeed because the Aquarian knows him already from the inside out." While I was considering this insight I set to work making camp in the rapidly ebbing light. The shelter floor was caked with dried mud, so I improvised a broom and swept it out before making up my bed. George's "fire" was a dense, airless heap of soggy paper, rotten spruce, and wet socks. I asked permission to take it apart and rebuild it in my own way, which he readily granted, and soon a blazing fire illuminated the interior of the shelter.

The prospect of a cup of tea and some warm stew lured George out of his bed. He was a good-looking man of 30, tall and broad-shouldered, his once fine musculature now turned to soft fat. He wore filthy jeans, a red wool plaid jacket, and a pair of black navy oxfords which were coming apart at the seams. He alternately sat by the fire and walked about to look at it from varying perspectives while I prepared our meal. All the while he continued his monologue. When I asked a question or interjected a comment, he initially responded appropriately, but soon he would go off on a thousand tangents. The central, obsessive theme in his disordered thought was his mental baby, which was soon to spring forth from his brow and revolutionize the course of human history. He was an intelligent, well-educated man, and like many another psychotic, he possessed some remarkable insights into people. In recent months he had wandered from one place to another while his baby gestated. He had used up his money, and progressively he had become more ragged and disheveled. But it didn't matter to him; he believed that in a few months his ordeal would be over. On a whim, he had walked up to Kinsman Pond 10 days earlier. He had stayed there ever since, scrounging food from hikers who chanced upon him at the shelter.

He could not tell me the nature of his baby. "It's not been born yet. How can I say?" But he expounded his theories about Aquarians at length. It was unclear whether he spoke of himself, of me, or of Aquarians in general. I suspected that his discourse concerned itself with all three. Some of his remarks struck home so accurately that he might have been looking straight into my soul. His performance was an excellent example of that marvelously clear, yet perverse insight of the psychotic. One of his analyses was certainly directed toward me. He said, "Jim, I can see that you have great bear power within you. Aquarians who are fortunate enough to have a bear inside them are a breed apart. The bear gives them great healing power. Most of the famous healers of the past—the Catholic saints and all—they all had bear power. They weren't all Aquarians, but the best of them were both Aquarians and bears. You'll make a great doctor because of your bear nature. You probably already are."

The fire began to die down, and we went to bed. The clouds disappeared over the southern horizon, and the sky became clear and star-studded. The wind picked up, increasing from a brisk breeze to a gale. It continued blowing, an icy blast out of the Arctic, as the sun rose. Leaving George to his solitary gestation, I walked down to Franconia Notch and hitched a ride to North Woodstock for a hot meal. I was not anxious to brave the exposed ridge of Mt. Lincoln and Mt. Lafayette, so I unconsciously dawdled all morning in town. Returning to the trail early in the afternoon, I started up the trail to Mt. Liberty. Even with the exertion from the steep trail and the warmth of the sun I had to wear long pants and the woolen shirt I had found to maintain body warmth. Just before leaving the shelter of the last trees to begin the six-mile above-timberline ridge walk over Mt. Lincoln and Mt. Lafayette, I donned my down jacket and long raincoat, and wrapped kerchiefs around my forehead, ears, and neck. I had no gloves, so I plunged my hands deep into the coat pockets. The wind on the exposed rocky summits was fierce, but not as bad as I had anticipated. The temperature was below freezing, as witnessed by horizontal icicles on bushes and tree limbs, but the wind was the real problem. Sometimes I was able to travel on the lee side of the mountain and escape the wind's full force, but usually I was exposed to its uninterrupted blast. It was necessary to lean 20 degrees into the gale to maintain my balance. It was a precarious stance for anyone carrying a heavy pack, and the least change in wind velocity made me stumble and almost fall. Coming around the corners of large rocks was especially bad, because the sudden blast could easily knock me down if I was not prepared. I traveled just as rapidly as I could, running whenever the terrain and my balance would permit it. All the while I took fleeting glances at familiar views from this superb mountain. The descent from Lafayette was on its exposed northern slope. No mountain blocked the wind here, and its full force tore at me. It must have had a velocity of 50 or 60 knots. Throwing caution to the winds, I ran full-tilt down the trail until the sanctuary of timberline was reached. It had taken me only 90 minutes to travel the six miles above the trees, but the effort was equivalent to a day's normal hiking. I was completely exhausted, and the remaining three miles over Mt. Garfield to the shelter were almost more than I could manage.

The old Garfield Pond Shelter was situated well down in the woods, protected from the wind. It was rather shabby and dark, but quite tolerable. I remembered it well, because I had spent a night there in 1966 with the end-to-ender who sparked my interest in hiking the entire Appalachian Trail. In 1971 it was replaced by a plank structure high on the north slope of Mt. Garfield. A clearing was brutally hacked out of the spruce forest for a helipad, and the prefabricated parts were flown in. The shelter is in the new AMC style—long, dark, ugly, and located in the middle of a quagmire of mud. This one had the additional defect of having been placed where there was insignificant wind protection. This defect was discovered only after the shelter had been assembled. Canvas tarps were jury-rigged across most of its front opening, but they did not prevent the shelter from being drafty and cold. It was crowded that night, too. Six other hikers shared the place with me, and one of them stole some of my provisions and a flashlight that I had recently purchased for evening writing.

I was glad to hit the trail again in the morning. It descended and descended. The delightful travel on a smooth path in the early autumn forest of birch and maple lulled my suspicions. When I noticed that the trail was swinging around to the south and continuing its descent, I became quite concerned, but persisted on my course. I had passed no trail intersections, so I did not see how I could have gone astray. Finally there was no denying that I had made an error and was descending straight into the Pemigewasset Wilderness. Infuriated by the mistake, I turned about and started to climb back up the hill. Rage lent strength to my legs, and I rapidly ascended the two miles to the missed intersection. The ridge trail continued inconspicuously to the left, and the side trail which I had followed actually looked more like the continuation of the main trail. The signs were around the corner and out of sight, so my error was understandable. This did little to ameliorate my chagrin at the fact that the one time I became lost on the trip was in familiar territory.

The run over South Twin, Guyot, and Zealand mountains was pleasant, recalling old memories. I regretted that I had to pass up Guyot Shelter as a camping place. It has a spectacular view. However, I wanted to call my friends and ask them to meet me at Crawford Notch the next morning and I thought there might be a phone in the Zealand Falls Hut, a few miles south of the notch. When I met a middle-aged lady hiking southbound with a light day-pack, I inquired if there might be a phone there. She snapped, "Of course not! Look in your guidebook. Any fool should know that! Don't you believe in planning your trip ahead of time? You tenderfeet who come up into the mountains and don't know a damn thing and expect everyone to take care of you make me furious. Is this the first time you've gone hiking in your life?" I was initially taken aback by her outburst—and then amused. Keeping a straight face as best I could, I told her that it was my *second* time out and that I had hiked the entire distance from Franconia Notch all by myself. She didn't seem to suspect that she was being twitted, and after making a few condescending remarks about my footgear, she clumped off in her shiny new Limmer boots.

I had had my fill of Appies for one day and had no desire to encounter others, whether at the Zealand Falls Hut or the Ethan Pond Shelter, so I found an isolated campsite on a charming brook a few hundred yards away from the trail and had a cozy, solitary camp. I had planned to go as far as Pinkham Notch before contacting the Fosters, but the thief at Garfield Pond Shelter left me with only a day's rations so I dropped down into Crawford Notch the next morning and called them. They were delighted to receive my call, and Max drove up to the notch to meet me in his white Volkswagen.

The agenda called for a picnic that afternoon. In all, eight of us sat together in the woods, discussing the changing season while sipping our whiskey and tea and devouring sandwiches. After eating we took a hike on a trail that Max and a friend had cut years before. It was rather overgrown, and part of the reason for the picnic was to clear it a bit. Armed with clippers and a saw, I attacked the brush with vigor. In so doing, I wreaked a sort of surrogate vengeance against the branches that had slapped my face and torn my clothing for the past three months.

Max agreed to provide logistical support for an assault on the Presidential Range the next day. In preparation for an early start, we went to bed at nine. We were up again at five in the morning and motored up to Crawford Notch. It was six o'clock when we reached the trail head, and there was just enough light for me to feel my way along the trail. I climbed easily in the cool air, carrying only a five-pound knapsack containing lunch and a parka. In contrast to the preceding three days, the air was still, but it was not quite so clear when I greeted the sun from the top of Webster Cliffs. The valleys were hazy, and one could only barely make out Moosilauke on the western horizon. This was to be the longest distance—25 miles—and the greatest amount of ascent and descent in one day on my entire trip. There were only 13 hours of daylight so late in the season, which meant that if I wanted to finish before darkness fell, I would have to move steadily, with a minimum of stops for rest and sight-seeing. Climbing was effortless. Walking, unencumbered by a 40-pound pack, was so easy that I practically bounced with every step. Despite numerous brief stops along the Crawford Path to admire the scenery, I was at the summit of Mt. Washington by 11:00. Save for those staying at the Mizpah Spring Hut, I did not encounter a soul on the long ascent.

The summit itself depressed me. The observatory buildings and the hotel were encrusted with ice, and clouds threatened to close down on the peak at any moment. The buildings were gray and shabby; they were scattered around in a disorganized, sloppy sprawl. Worst of all was the band of pushy tourists who had ascended the mountain via the Cog Railway or private automobile. They seemed to stare with revulsion at the shabby soul who had hiked up the hill under his own power.

As soon as I left Mt. Washington my depression lifted, and I regained the exhilaration that I had experienced while climbing. I cheated a bit in the afternoon, detouring the official Appalachian Trail and hiking the summit loops over Mt. Jefferson and Mt. Adams. While skirting Mt. Clay, I met a tall, rangy Viking with long hair and glossy yellow beard. We communicated instantly. There was no need to speak; we simply clasped hands briefly and passed.

The afternoon was fast wearing on, and my strength was ebbing as I made the last ascent of the day over Mt. Madison. My elation rapidly drained away when I descended to the trees. The last two hours were a matter of drearily trudging along with as much speed as I could muster—down into the Great Gulf, across the Peabody River, and finally along the Old Jackson Road to Pinkham Notch. I knew from previous hikes that it was a beautiful walk, but I was too tired to notice; I wanted only to get it done with. I reached the new AMC buildings in the notch at 7:00 P.M. It was as dark as when I had started my traverse that morning.

My strength and spirits rapidly revived while waiting for Max to come for me. I sat in the lounge sipping tea and listening with amusement to hikers planning their assaults on Mt. Washington. Would they feel belittled if they knew that the thin, bearded man overhearing their conversation had just passed the 1,700-mile mark on his hike?

Dinner back at Dundee was a gala affair. The solitary joy that I had experienced along the ridge was recaptured by the ritual two cocktails. We all laughed and celebrated as if some signal achievement had been accomplished. Indeed, I had long dreamed of hiking the

Presidential Range in one day, and I was delighted to have done so at last.

I had planned a similar expedition for the next day, the object being to hike over Wildcat, Carter, and Moriah mountains, but I was mentally and physically exhausted. Max was worn out too, so we canceled the hike. Instead, I spent the morning getting my gear in order for the next leg of the trip—collecting the package of supplies from Gorham, buying groceries, doing laundry, eliminating nonessentials from the pack. Max loaned me a fine woolen pair of long johns, which the Fosters affectionately dubbed "The Golden Fleece" because they had cost so much. I also borrowed a lightweight down bag to slip inside my own for added warmth in the frosty nights to come. On the return from Gorham we stopped at the Pinkham Notch Camp to find out the date Mt. Katahdin closed. The official word from Baxter State Park was that one could climb after October 15 only if he observed their winter climbing rules. These require written approval four weeks beforehand, confirmed arrangements for search airplanes and a rescue team in the event of emergency, a minimum of four climbers, and satisfaction of an extensive equipment list, including high altitude winter boots, snowshoes, crampons, ice ax, ropes, and heavy sleeping bag. I could not possibly meet all of these requirements, so I would have to climb Mt. Katahdin before closing day.

I could reach the park at such an early date only by pushing all the way at my fastest rate. Even so I would need good luck—excellent mileage every day, no bad weather, no injuries, and no sickness. I was tired—the long haul over the Presidential Range was a sort of dying gasp. I knew that another such effort was out of the question at this stage of the trip. I doubted that I had the strength to push along at 20 miles a day for three weeks, and in any event, the last thing I wanted to do was make a grind out of the closing days of the hike. Max must have read my thoughts, for he suggested that we drive to Baxter State Park immediately; then I could walk back to New Hampshire at my own pace. I knew that was the best solution, but dignity demanded that I mull it over until after lunch before accepting the offer. The decision made, I spent the afternoon helping Max pry rocks from one of the pastures and piling them on top of the rock walls which have been building in this fashion for nearly 200 years.

Max and his son Pete drove me to Baxter State Park and deposited me in the Roaring Brook Campground by midafternoon. This final piece of assistance climaxed four days of kindness and generosity. When I reached Crawford Notch I was tired out physically and mentally. All of my food and money was gone. (There was more of both waiting at Gorham, but this was three trail days distant, which seemed impossibly far away.) The supply package contained some cold weather clothing, but not nearly enough for the frigid days and nights that lay ahead. Not only did the Fosters round out my clothing and bedding, they nourished my body with elegant cuisine, excellent Scotch, and fine wines. They provided me a comfortable bed with a down comforter on which to rest my weary bones. They gave me invaluable assistance in making the Presidential Range hike. More than anything, they nurtured my soul with their alert minds and sprightly conversation. In short, they came through at a time when I needed help, when I had hit rock bottom and could no longer handle the situation by myself.

I camped in one of the shelters along Roaring Brook, a stream whose name describes it perfectly. I felt terribly forlorn and depressed the moment my friends departed. It was the same sort of feeling of desolation and despair one has as a small child when his parents deposit him for the first time at a summer camp and drive away, severing his last contact with the world he knows. I fervently wished that the trip was over, and dreaded the prospect of the long hike back to New Hampshire. The comforts of civilization at Dundee had reminded me of the privations I had endured for the last 100 days. I had had my fill of this austere life and wanted only to be done with it. I wanted to be with people again—to work, to love, to read, to play music.

The first morning in Maine dawned clear, cold, and breezy. Once more I was in high spirits, ready to resume the journey. The ranger stationed at Chimney Pond informed me that the peak was closed to climbers because of high winds. He said conditions might improve later in the morning, so I decided to wait at his cabin in the hope that he would lift his ban. Another hiker waited along with me. He was a lean sinewy man of 40 who had taken a hike to the base of Mt. Everest the previous year. Shortly after returning to his home in Washington he quit his job to hitchhike across the country, stopping to climb the highest mountain in each state.

Finally the ranger relented and let us start up the trail. I stepped outside the cabin and almost ran into a bull moose. He paid not the slightest attention to me and continued his browsing. After a few minutes he plunged into the water, quickly and powerfully churning his way across to the far shore.

One of the virtues of hiking Maine from north to south was the opportunity it gave me to meet several of the through hikers who had been ahead of me all summer. Six of them were no more than 10 days ahead at Pinkham Notch—Sam and Cathy Johnson, Elmer Boyd and Gene Fiducia, Ed McInerney, and my erstwhile traveling companion Dave Odell. I had definite mental images of each of these hikers, based on their entries in the registers and on descriptions given by southbound hikers who had encountered them. It was intriguing to consider the prospect of matching imagination against reality. Dave had been ahead of me all the way from Connecticut, usually by a margin of two days. The gap had narrowed in Massachusetts, and at the Vermont line I was only half a dozen miles back, but then he accelerated and the gap widened again. Meeting him again for the last time was something to look forward to.

I encountered the first end-to-ender on the summit of Baxter Peak. At first glance I knew he must be one. The young man bearing the well-worn pack was thin and bedraggled. Tiredly leaning on his staff, he appeared to be done in. There was no exalted triumph here. All that Ned Smith seemed to want was a hot bath and a soft bed. It was very cold and windy on top of the mountain. Both of us were lightly clad and could not tolerate standing still for long, so we shook hands and went our separate ways—Ned to his hot bath and I to my final weeks on the trail.

The autumn color in Maine was superb. In the White Mountains it had not reached its climax, but in northern Maine it attained its peak during the first 10 days of my return trip. From the mountaintops one looked out over limitless expanses of green forest, splashed with giant smears of crimson, gold, and orange, and studded with large blue lakes beneath a sky that was as deep and pure a blue as that in the Uintah. Down in the forest itself, one walked alternately on soft, untrammeled humus in the spruce woods and brilliant carpets of fresh-fallen red and yellow leaves in the deciduous woods. Sometimes the carpet of leaves was so thick it obscured the trail, and I proceeded in large measure on the basis of the feel of the ground beneath my feet. Amid the spruces the trail was so little traveled that it was soft and springy underfoot; often it was difficult to distinguish trail from non-trail. Following it was easy, however, for when I stepped off it, the ground texture changed and my feet instantly told me I had made a mistake. Then I backed up a few steps and found the trail again.

The third morning in Maine I was walking along what had once been a well-kept woods road. An abandoned telephone line sometimes hung from insulators on the trees and sometimes lay on the ground, its rusty surface concealed in the deep carpet of leaves. Occasionally I tripped on it. Once I fell on my face, the heavy pack pushing me right down to the ground. My glasses shattered on a rock, and I cursed because the spares I had carried all the way from Georgia were back in Dundee. I had left them there, thinking they were so much excess baggage. There was no feasible way to get hold of them on short notice, so I would have to myopically stumble along the rest of the way. To my surprise I rapidly adjusted to the loss of my glasses, and after two days hardly noticed their absence. Indeed, I became so habituated to doing without them that I did not remember to don the extra pair until some six days after I had returned to Salt Lake City.

The numerous lakes in Maine were a novelty. In the West I had camped at a lake more often than not, but lakes are rare along the Appalachian Trail to the south of Maine. The few lakes that are close to the trail are usually crowded with people and thus make poor campsites. In Maine lakes are common and, at least late in the year, they are unpopulated. I picked lakeside shelters to stay at whenever it was feasible to do so. The day my glasses broke, I had planned to walk 20 miles to a woodland shelter, but after only 13 miles I came to a little log lean-to at the foot of Nahmakanta Lake. The area was a bit littered, and a cold 30-knot wind blew off the lake right into the camp, so at first I decided to press on. However, after reluctantly going about a hundred yards I did an about-face and strode rapidly back to the shelter; it was just too good an opportunity to pass up. The charming old CCC shelter nestles at the foot of a huge pine whose upper branches form a protective canopy far above its roof. Inside there is only enough space for two to be comfortable, so it is cozy even for one. In lieu of bunks there is a thick carpet of dry pine needles on the floor. They mold to one's contours, providing a firm yet comfortable mattress. A few moments sufficed to pick up the litter, and the wind didn't bother me when I sat on the floor within the shelter. The lake is three miles long and a mile wide, and the wind blew straight down its axis, stirring up two-foot waves which washed up in breakers on the white sand beach before the lean-to. As the afternoon passed, I kept going down to the water to watch the surf with almost the same degree of fascination I feel at the seashore. After a brief period at the shore I would become chilled and return to the fire and warm up. When the sun set, a full moon rose over the lake, the wind abated, and the night was still and peaceful.

The trail was virtually devoid of hikers. Aside from Ned Smith and a few day-hikers on Mt. Katahdin, I met only five people during the week it took to hike to Monson. Four of them were through hikers and the fifth was also a long-distance hiker. Sometimes I saw or heard signs of logging but had the good fortune never to encounter the loggers themselves. It was good for the soul to be so utterly alone. After contending with crowds all the way from Shenandoah National Park to New Hampshire, wilderness solitude was a welcome change. I felt an urgent desire to be by myself during the last few weeks, to meditate, review, and synthesize the experience I had undergone during the summer. During the difficult days in the middle states I had received a card from a friend which counseled me to "keep it going." I adopted the phrase as a sort of motto at that time. Now my motto became "put it all together."

There were so many beautiful places that it was difficult to make steady progress. Almost every lean-to and lake called out to me to stop and camp, but both time and food were limited so I confined myself to an hour of swimming at a beach here, an hour lunching at a shelter there, and an occasional hour deep in contemplation in the dark of the forest. All of the shelters I stayed at were outstanding. My favorites were the old CCC lean-tos. The things I liked about them were the same qualities that endeared their southern counterparts to me—rustic construction, harmony with their surroundings, and well-chosen locations. Whoever sited the old Maine lean-tos made a point of erecting each one at the base of an enormous old tree. The massive sentinels gave a feeling of security and timeless tranquility to the camps. At one shelter the ancient tree had fallen to the forest floor and lay there decomposing. I felt a sense of genuine loss, as if I had lost an old and trusted friend.

The Maine Forest Service lean-tos are newer and likewise of superior construction. They are made from native materials for the most part—logs felled in the surrounding forest, stripped of their bark, and notched and assembled in log-cabin style. They are of one standard design, large and capacious, high enough to permit standing erect inside, with sleeping platforms made of peeled spruce poles. The shelter at Cooper Brook Falls is a good example. It is placed 10 yards from a deep pool on Cooper Brook. A pretty cascade tumbles 50 yards down a pocket-sized gorge and empties into the far end of the pool. In the register there were numerous rave notices about the beauty of the place. Intellectually I had to agree with them, but emotionally I did not. For some reason it did not click with me, and I was depressed while I stayed there.

My depression was probably related to the sadness I was experiencing because of the impending end of the hike. It had become a way of life, and I was reluctant to exchange its ascetic simplicity for the complex, anxious clangor of the other world. Nevertheless, it was necessary to start making plans for my return to civilization. There was quite a bind in regards to time: there was not enough of it to both complete the hike and do everything else that I wanted to accomplish before school began.

By pressing vigorously the last 18 days I could finish in time, but I did not want to charge through Maine without taking time to savor it. The difference in time between traveling the remaining distance at a relaxed pace and hiking at full speed would be no more than two days, but two extra days were simply not available. A possible alternative was to reduce the distance by 20 or 30 miles in some manner, which would effectively save one or two days. Earlier I had hiked the Appalachian Trail between Gorham and Pinkham Notch, a distance of 20 miles. If I omitted this section, there would be ample time. By so doing I would complete the trail, but I would have hiked only 99 percent of it in one season. The idea of deleting the section over Moriah, Carter, and Wildcat did not seem quite cricket; just thinking about it caused guilt and anxiety. In any event, it was a decision that did not have to be made immediately. Travel was easy, and I was making good mileage each day, yet having adequate time to enjoy myself. I could delay making a decision until my progress slowed.

Here and there in Maine one encounters sections of devastated land reminiscent at first of the TV newsreels of South Vietnam. Tree trunks and uprooted brush lay in wild confusion on land that has been plowed and churned into a topsy-turvy chaos. These are the areas where loggers have been at work. I consider logging a reasonable and necessary industrial activity, but why must the lumber barons devastate the forest so near the Appalachian Trail? Couldn't they leave a quarter of a mile free zone on either side of the trail, so that hikers can enjoy wilderness rather than ruins? Compared to the vast areas of timber in the state, such a narrow strip would be an insignificant amount of acreage. It saddened and angered me to walk through such areas. Fortunately they were infrequent.

My calculations suggested that I should begin to meet the through hikers about the fifth day after ascending Katahdin. Sure enough, on the fifth morning as I rested beside the East Branch of the Pleasant River I saw a pair of hikers approaching—a short blond youth and a stocky girl, both bearing worn packs. They could only be Sam and Cathy Johnson, a brother-sister team from southern New Hampshire. We exchanged greetings, and it soon came out that they were end-to-enders. I pretended to be out only on a short journey. With complete truth, I told them that I was hiking from Baxter Peak to New Hampshire, never mentioning the initial leg of the trek. Caught up in my amusing little game, I asked all the silly questions that people are wont to ask. They were completely taken in by the act and answered my queries willingly. It was incomprehensible to me that they would continue to gain pleasure from reiterating their tale. Neither of them had ever hiked before this summer. They read about the trail and took it as a challenge to hike it from end to end. They were clearly tired, and anxious to get the trip over with as quickly as possible. I tendered them my congratulations and we parted.

I reached the White Brook Lean-to in the afternoon and was brewing tea when a slender young man with shoulder-length golden locks and a long yellow beard came in. This was Elmer Boyd, the last through hiker to leave Georgia ahead of Dave and me. Soon his dark-bearded companion Gene Fiducia arrived. My initial annoyance at having company was tempered by the consideration that this pair was a part of the mystical group of figures "ahead of us" on the trail. They proved to be gregarious souls and afforded good company for the evening. Again I assumed the role of the short-distance hiker. It was a difficult performance; frequently I had to restrain myself from bursting out with incriminating remarks. I presented myself as a lifelong resident of Dundee, which at least allowed me to speak authoritatively of the White Mountains.

The next day I crossed the Chairback–Barren Mountain range, and to my great surprise and pleasure, found the Cloud Pond Shelter deserted when I arrived. The lean-to stood close to the shore, and its view was limited to a small bay. However, by walking five yards one came to the east shore of the pond itself. Big granite boulders along the shoreline made good diving platforms and I was able to tolerate the cold water for five minutes at a time. Having arrived in midafternoon, there was ample time to make camp, catch up my journal, and meditate.

The first exhilarating week in Maine came to an end in the friendly little town of Monson. As always, my first thought was to head for a restaurant. A big breakfast of ham, eggs, blueberry muffins, cream, and innumerable cups of coffee filled the gastric pit long enough to allow me to complete my errands and hit the trail again.

I had anticipated that I would meet Dave Odell at some point well north of Monson. It worried me when I didn't meet him, because it meant that he would arrive at Baxter State Park perilously close to the deadline. To my relief, he came marching down a woods road toward me just a few miles south of Monson. He was accompanied by a tall handsome hiker of 25 or thereabouts. Ed McInerney had started his walk in Georgia long before Dave and me and had maintained a good pace, but he had recently suffered two serious bouts of illness. Both times he had to stop and recuperate, losing many days each time. Dave overtook him at the beginning of the Mahoosucs. They had traveled together ever since. Dave looked thin and tired, but very happy. He had weathered tremendous difficulties, and now he was about to enter the homestretch. He could almost smell the end of the trail, and his delight at being so close radiated from his face. For once it was impossible for me to play my little game of anonymity. It was a joy to let my hair down, so to speak, and have a good old family reunion with Dave and Ed. None of us could spare much time, however, and after an animated half-hour of conversation, we parted ways for the last time.

It depressed me momentarily to say good-bye to them. Now there were no more through hikers to meet, nor, in all probability, any other northbound hikers whatsoever. In just a few days, Dave and Ed would reach the summit of Katahdin; then I would be the only end-to-ender left on the trail, as far as I knew. While all the other hikers sat inside sipping their brandy and smoking their cigars before blazing fireplaces, I would still be out in the woods, solitarily plugging along.

I did not fret very long over the future, for the "here and now" of it was that it was another marvelous fall day—clear and cool, with the foliage still at its zenith of color. An afternoon of steady walking, a still frosty night at another wilderness lake, and then a cold day of gray skies and snow flurries brought me to the hamlet of Caratunk on the east bank of the Kennebec River. The postmaster-storekeeper arranged accommodations for me, and the game warden, dressed in a scarlet and blue uniform which made him resemble a palace guard, drove me to the lodgings. The Smiths are an elderly couple who live in a large old house that formerly was the town's only hotel. Some years ago they closed down the operation, and now confine themselves to renting rooms to occasional Appalachian Trail hikers. The building was erected early in the 1800s as one of a series of stagehouses on the old Kennebec Valley route. In addition to the posthouse franchise, Mrs. Smith's ancestors owned several hundred thousand acres of virgin timberlands. Parcel by parcel, the land was sold off to the lumber companies, until now only a hundred acres remain in family hands. The house is heated by a huge, wood-burning stove which also serves as the kitchen range. Each year Mr. Smith hauls in a great pile of wood, which he has felled from the woods behind the house. Cut in stove-size lengths, it is stacked and serves as their winter supply of fuel. The night I stayed with them the first heavy frost of the fall was

Photo by Ross R. Rowlands

Moose in beaver pond, Maine.

Photo by Elmer L. Onstot

Mt. Katahdin from Rainbow Lake, Maine.

expected, so Mrs. Smith had picked all the late tomatoes and cucumbers. As I cooked my supper on the enormous old stove, I munched on a heaping bowl of vegetables she gave me. The house cats were enamored of my woolen shirt for some reason, and they vied for the opportunity to curl up on it, whether I was wearing it or had dropped it on a chair. The purring cats on my lap made me homesick for my own.

Dave and Ed had informed me that early in the morning one can walk upstream from the trail crossing to some rapids and wade across the Kennebec in water that is no more than knee-deep. It was only later in the day that the water rises and the logs come down. Mr. Smith strongly advised against fording, but I decided to give it a try in the morning. I felt that to use a boat was a cop out. The six through hikers I had met had all managed to wade across without difficulty. Even petite Anne, the girl I had shared a shelter with back along the way, had successfully forded the river. Early in the morning, with frost still heavy on the grass, I hiked the mile up to the ford. The sky rapidly clouded over and a chill wind arose. At the marked crossing there were no rapids to be seen. The cold water flowed smoothly and swiftly by, no more than two feet below the high-water mark. Clearly this was not the ebb tide I had been told to expect. A fisherman told me that the water was no more than thigh-deep, so I suppressed my doubts, found a sturdy birch pole, and plunged into the icy water. At first the crossing went well. Planting the pole in the stream bed firmly before each step, I advanced on the slick cobblestoned stream bottom. The swift cold water rose only to my thighs at first, then deepened with each step. Soon I was chest-deep, and my teeth were chattering with cold. The current tugged at the bulky pack and pushed against my side, trying its hardest to upset me. My body's warmth was draining at a phenomenal rate, and my strength flowed away just as rapidly. I could barely maintain my footing as the stream tugged and pushed at me. I decided that if the water rose any higher I would have to retreat. Twice I slipped and almost went under before the bottom began to slope up toward the west bank. When the water had receded to my waist, I advanced at a reckless rate the rest of the way in my haste to escape the frigid water. When I emerged into the freezing wind I was so cold that my hands would hardly function to remove my wet clothing. I put on all the dry clothes I had, did calisthenics for 15 minutes, built a fire, drank a pot of scalding tea, and was still cold. Two hours of vigorous hiking passed before the last of the numbing chill departed from my body.

It rained almost continuously for two days. The temperature stayed in the forties and fifties during the day, and I was as cold and uncomfortable as I can remember being on the entire trip. The only way to maintain warmth was to hike rapidly. Rest stops became infrequent: it was preferable to be tired and relatively warm than to rest and become chilled. It was depressing to encounter such inclement weather. Wet brush slapped constantly at my body and legs, each branch showering me with chilly water. The trail degenerated to slimy, boggy mud, and the grades became slippery abominations. In my misery I would have welcomed company, but not another soul was to be seen on the trail. At least mileage did not suffer. When one is too miserable to do anything save plod along through the mud and rain, the miles go by almost as rapidly as when the weather is fine and spirits high.

The two days and nights of rain finally came to an end. Starting at the Bigelow Range, the relatively flat terrain of the first 10 days in Maine gave way to real mountains once more. The trail rose and fell over respectable peaks the remainder of its distance. When the rain stopped, I was just starting up Sugarloaf Mountain. The day became clear, but it was very windy and cold. Even down in the forest I had to bundle up. The exposed rocky summit of Sugarloaf was bitterly cold and windy. I hastened over it as rapidly as my legs would carry me. Down in the trees again, hiking was enjoyable as long as I did not stop and become chilled.

The night was frigid; light snow dusted the ground. I worried about the traverse of the exposed summits of Saddleback Mountain as I lay on my fragrant bed of balsam boughs. The morning dawned cloudy; an icy wind from the North knifed through the trees. Not too much of the first two summits on the ridge—Saddleback Junior and The Horn—was above timberline but even so, exposure to the full force of the gale and its burden of stinging snowflakes was chilling. The two miles above timberline along the summit of Saddleback itself was an extremely severe traverse. I leaned into the ferocious wind as a blizzard of wind-whipped snow slashed at my face. All of my clothing worn at once was insufficient to maintain body warmth. However, despite my discomfort, the crossing of the open ridge was intoxicating and my spirits soared. I was almost disappointed when I reentered the forest. The day continued cold, but a crisp breeze and the appearance of blue skies once more made travel pleasurable. I spent another frigid night warmly bundled up in the two sleeping bags; in the morning the ground was frozen hard.

This marked the end of the inclement weather. It became warmer and there was no more rain. The sky was full of scattered cumuli each day, and the sun frequently showed its face. I stopped writing my journal. It became a distraction that interfered with the single-minded focusing of my thoughts. The world shrunk to the bit of woods that was within range of my vision and hearing. For the moment I was oblivious to all cares and considerations of the outside world. The past and the future were forgotten; only the moment was real. I gave up virtually all consideration of time, distance, food, and shelter, walking whenever and at whatever pace my legs felt inclined to take. No others were on the trail to interrupt my thoughts, and the rare motorist seen at the infrequent road crossings scarcely impinged on my consciousness. He was a non-person, a ghost who flitted past with no more substance than a breath of air.

For two days I hiked 20 miles daily, up and down one mountain after another. Then I came to the Mahoosuc Range. It was 20 miles to Gorham and 40 miles to Pinkham Notch. An unconscious decision to limit the three remaining days to the Mahoosuc was made, but I did not become aware that it had been made for another 36 hours. Daily mileage plummeted to eleven, eight, and then five miles. The woods, streams, and mountains kept calling out, "Stop here awhile. Rest and meditate." I stopped whenever the urge came upon me, sitting by a babbling brook, perching on an open summit, or sprawling deep in fresh-fallen leaves beneath a tree. Scrambling under, over, and around the Mahoosuc Notch's boulders consumed an hour (for one mile). It was the roughest single mile on the trail and one of the most interesting. I camped at Full Goose Shelter and hardly noticed its ugliness.

Late the next morning I arrived at my final camp, the Gentian Pond Shelter. This snug little log shelter is one of the most prettily located of them all. It has a view straight down into the Androscoggin Valley, with the Moriah–Carter Range for a backdrop. The bluish-violet pond lies a few rods to the right of the shelter, surrounded by a forest of birch and spruce. It is drained by a gurgling, cascading little rill which tumbles through a jagged defile in the gray granite before the shelter. I had the camp to myself. In preparation for the morrow's return to civilization I swam in the pond's cold water, scrubbed my clothing, and trimmed my hair and beard. Then I sunbathed on the flat slabs of white rock along the pond until the sun went behind the trees. As the afternoon shadows lengthened, I sat before the shelter meditating. As dusk fell, a honking flight of geese winged its way through the gorge before me and alighted on the pond's surface for the night. The valley lights came on and then the stars. I sat on the soft spruce needle floor of the shelter until late at night, gazing into the flames of my last fire.

The morning dawned cold and clear. Well before the sun rose from the valley, the geese had resumed their flight to the South. There was hardly a bird's voice to be heard; most of them had departed for their winter quarters. I was loathe to leave the shelter, but at last I roused from my reverie, packed, and started down the trail.

The five-mile walk to the valley lasted until midafternoon. My downhill steps dragged, and at the slightest pretext I stopped to contemplate the surroundings. I was overcome by sadness that the journey's end was at hand. The day continued cold, the sky became obscured by clouds, and a chill north wind blew. All the leaves had fallen from the trees along the ridge. Winter was imminent. At last the trail leveled out in the valley. Children's voices greeted me from the houses near the highway. The hike was at its end. I bid the trail farewell and walked the last few yards to the road.

Postscript

All told, including the approaches to Springer and Katahdin plus a few side trips, I walked slightly more than 2,000 miles in four months, at a daily average of 16.3 miles. During the course of the hike, I took off 8 days entirely and 16 half-days. This was about the right pace for me. If I had traveled much slower, I would probably have become bored. If I had gone much faster, I would have been completely worn out. It would have been good to have another two weeks, so that I could have been a bit less compulsive about making good daily progress. Starting a month earlier would have helped me avoid the cold weather in Maine. On the other hand, by starting so late, I missed some of the crowds in New England.

The farthest I hiked in a single day was 25 miles. The roughest single day's walk was the 15 miles along Tinker Mountain in Virginia. The Mahoosucs were far and away the most rugged section, but it was so much fun being there that the difficulty of the trail did not bother me. Insects and snakes were not a problem any place. Rain was by far the worst environmental problem. There was rain on 57 days, with 30 days of rain in the first 49. There is little one can do about precipitation other than suffer through it. It is intolerably boring to wait in a shelter for the precipitation to end, and if one decides to hike during a downpour, he will eventually become soaked regardless of what raingear he may wear. In the long run, I think one may as well simply dispense with ponchos and accept the drenchings as a fact of life.

The system of receiving supplies and mail at spaced post offices worked well. Eleven of twelve packages were received intact, and it is not the fault of the postal service that the twelfth failed to reach me. It would certainly be preferable to have someone available to provide logistical support along the trail, but that is hardly practical unless one has willing friends near it.

The combination of food packages, grocery stores, restaurants, wild fruits, and handouts from short-distance hikers kept me adequately, but unexcitingly, nourished. Food generally tasted good, regardless of its culinary excellence or poorness, because my appetite was so enormous and insatiable. As with equipment, food is primarily a matter of personal taste. After a little experience, one learns what appeals to him and satisfies his needs. The only really important criterion that it should satisfy is adequate nutritional value. In general, simple and natural foodstuffs fulfill this requirement best. Along the Appalachian Trail it is frequently possible to go a step further and enjoy fresh foods, both for their flavor and their improved nutrition. They do weigh a bit more, but a few extra pounds are virtually unnoticeable once one rounds into condition.

On the whole, I was satisfied with the performance of my equipment. Most of it was not ideally suited for the job. Generally speaking, I used what was available from my closet rather than buying things specifically for the trip. The important factor is the hiker, not his equipment. The Appalachian Trail is not the place for sophisticated gear: there is little call for fancy alpine tents, Vibram sole mountaineering boots, ultralight down sleeping bags, or Kelty packs. Simple, inexpensive items will do quite nicely, and it is a shame to ruin expensive, delicate items in the mud and rain of the Appalachians. The prime consideration in selecting equipment should be durability and utility, not cost and elegance. A case in point is boots. I saw countless $50 pairs of boots reduced to disintegrating heaps of leather and rubber by the trail conditions. If I were to hike the trail again, I would go to the K-Mart and buy a $12 pair of crepe sole work boots, with the confident expectation that they would last the entire trip. Another example is packs. The Kelty performed superbly; despite the wear and tear it will still suffice for many a wilderness expedition. However, it was a shame to subject it to such abuse. I would certainly not buy a Kelty for another Appalachian Trail traverse; rather I would obtain a cheap, rugged pack from a surplus store. The only additional item I would carry on a second trip is a lightweight tent. The shelters were far too crowded for my taste.

When the hike was ended, my reaction, surprisingly, was one of total indifference. I had no feeling whatsoever one way or the other about its completion. I was neither depressed nor elated. In fact I had very little emotion of any kind. I was not especially tired, nor was I ambitious and looking forward to returning to Salt Lake City and school. For the first two weeks afterward I hardly thought about the hike. I answered the inevitable questions as briefly as possible, having no interest in recalling the trip.

Until the end of the year I hardly thought again about the trail. Of course I was working at the hospital seven days a week and was very much involved with medicine, so there was little time to think about anything else. When the new year began, occasional fleeting recollections of the journey flashed through my mind—images of camps, views, people, feelings. A few times I managed to sneak away from the medical center for climbing and skiing. Surrounded by the deep snow and wild jagged peaks of the Wasatch, it might momentarily occur to me what a fantastic experience the Appalachian Trail trip had been. But it took writing my story for this book to really focus my attention on the hike again, to relive its joys and sorrows, to experience again its difficulties, frustrations, and rewards, to evaluate its significance.

I am pleased that I took the hike. It fulfilled a desire of many years standing to do something adventurous and demanding. It was an opportunity to see a vast amount of interesting territory, meet many interesting people, and sample different cultures. It was a marvelous break from schooling. After many years of college, graduate school, and premed studies, the two years of basic science curriculum at the medical school came close to being the straw that broke the camel's back. If I had continued right into the clinical years, I probably would have become embittered and sick of the whole business. After the hike I returned to the wards with a fresh outlook. Lastly, the hike gave me untold hours alone to work through a variety of unresolved conflicts and to make some major decisions regarding my future.

Would I do it again? *Certainly not!* Once is quite enough. Would

I take another similarly long-distance hike? No! One such journey is enough for a lifetime. . . . Nevertheless, as I have been writing this story in spare moments over the last three months, I have been in occasional correspondence with Dave Odell. He and four others have been making excellent progress on their hike of the Pacific Crest Trail; they will surely complete the trip from Mexico to Canada this summer. Sometimes I have a pang of regret that I cannot be there with them high in the mountain wilderness.

Sometimes Easy, Sometimes Difficult, but Always Good

By James Rutter

Started at MT. KATAHDIN on June 6, 1971
Finished at SPRINGER MOUNTAIN on November 5, 1971

On my second day walking I met a couple in a dense thicket of tangled evergreens. The trail was barely wide enough to let me pass over the moss- and root-covered ground; my pack caught continually on branches. The thicket was dark and had a smell of its own, something like a Christmas tree. Clouds were gathering and thunder was rumbling. Occasionally the resident white-throated sparrow called, PEAbody, PEAbody. Every grove had one. Neither the little bird nor PEAbody could ever be found, but you always heard the call.

The couple was smiling in spite of the swarms of blackflies and mosquitoes. The insects had a hard time getting to the man through his full beard. The girl kept waving them away. They had been together for some time, and out in the Maine woods for several days, but now they were separating because nothing would suit the girl except living by the sea, and the man had the notion that nothing would suit him except living in the city. They were a good couple and I tried to keep them together by suggesting they go to Boston, or even Chicago, where Lake Michigan acted like an ocean sometimes. No, they said, there was no such thing as the true ocean and a city co-existing. Because of the city's selfishness, anything as fragile as an ocean became solely an extension of the city.

I mentioned that I was walking to Georgia alone. It was a strange thing to say on only the second day of my hike, and it must have sounded like a put-on. The girl asked me if I was an experienced hiker. I had not thought about my hike in that way, and all I could say was that I felt I knew what I was doing. As an afterthought I added that I was mature and ready to learn. Day trips in the White

1826

Mountains, a week of hiking in the Alps, and years of dreaming over equipment catalogs could hardly be called experience. When we parted company the last comment the girl made was that I would certainly be experienced by the end of my hike.

I walked on alone, more aware of the heavy stillness of the forest, feeling empty until I became accustomed to the solitude again. My mind was busy with what the girl had said. According to her reasoning, I would be an expert by trail's end—worthy of being heard, of writing in books, of giving advice. I tried to figure out what experience was. It seemed to me that it was rarely obtained in schools and books; life was where you got most of it. In life, experience keeps accumulating even when things are bad. I began to wonder at what point on the trip I would become experienced. Surely at the end, as the girl had said. Probably I would be experienced 50 miles from the end, also. Maybe 200 miles from the end as well. But 500 miles? It was important to me, as I walked along that afternoon to know exactly when I would be experienced.

That second night of the hike was spent in my little orange tent on top of Rainbow Ledges in a rainstorm. Thousands of blackflies spent the night with me, congregated under my tent's rain fly. What occurred in the morning will come to be known in the annals of the Appalachian Trail as the Massacre of Rainbow Ledges. It was fought as I packed my soaking tent and sleeping bag to move on. The breeze had left with the storm and there was nothing to keep the thousands of flies away. I applied insect repellent until it stung. I mixed three repellents, only to have the flies come and drink it from my hand like birds at a fountain. The blackflies were like a dark cloud over the ledges that morning, coming at me again and again, while I slapped and slapped. Someday I am going back there in midwinter, when there are no flies, and put up a plaque:

HERE

ON JUNE 7, 1971

THE BATTLE OF RAINBOW LEDGES

WAS FOUGHT AND

JIM RUTTER ESCAPED WITH HIS LIFE

I went on down to Rainbow Lake with another piece of the experience puzzle in place. This piece said that experience was a neck with bloody welts and a heel with raw blisters. "Enough of this intellectual business," I thought. "Let's keep moving." For the time being my definition of experience had to be that as long as nothing came up that I couldn't handle, I was experienced. There could be no marker along the trail to announce your experience, no card in your pocket to affirm it.

As the trip progressed through the weeks of flies, the weeks of rain, and the days of hot roads, it seemed that about all I learned was that I got up in the morning, ate some, walked some, talked some, and went to bed at night to sleep some. I did not *feel* experienced. The peculiar thing, however, was that people began to look at me as if I definitely *was* experienced. So experienced, in fact, that by the time I was in the Great Smokies I had 1,800 miles of walking as proof. Furthermore, people believed I could give a part of my experience to them. It became a game of tag where I was *it*, and I was figuratively herded into a corner and searched for my secrets. I felt bad because I had no secrets to give. I thought of making some up, but I was afraid they would look into my bag of tricks, in this case a Kelty, and find no magic at all—only oatmeal, peanut butter, dirty socks, and perhaps a filthy pot. I mean, they could have taken all of my peanut butter, if they had wanted it, but they wanted secrets and obviously peanut butter was not the secret of walking 2,000 miles. This is what leads people astray. People think that experience has an appearance or manner, which, when copied, will result in giving them the genuine thing. It doesn't work that way, though, because experience is something *behind* the appearances. It comes by doing; it cannot be transferred, and most of the words that try to tell about it are only so much more appearance. Only so much more peanut butter. People waste a lot of time in life matching appearances when they should be cultivating feeling. Read on if you will then, not to learn about hiking experience, but for the words themselves, in the hope that they may offer something interesting.

I wonder if the best sports are not running and swimming. In these sports nothing more than the body and terrain are involved. Nothing separates the runner or the swimmer from the experience, and ideally, when you have had enough you stop and go about other things. As we move from running and swimming to other activities requiring equipment, such as football with its suit of armor, and downhill skiing with its fiberglass skis and plastic boots, a whole way of life springs up around the sport. Time is spent in the ski lodge and the country club lounge; money is spent at the sports equipment shop; magazines and literature are published. Finally, there is no separating the sport from the life surrounding it, and the equipment takes on a life of its own. The sport becomes preoccupied with equipment.

A case in point is skiing with its ski shows, ski shops, advertising, promotions, fashion, and so on. This is carried to its ultimate irony when the equipment business becomes such a big part of the sport that a person who tells what equipment he uses is banned from skiing competition. All of which has nothing to do with the fact that it is fun to ski down a slope. That is why Jean-Claude Killy, in spite of his astonishing feat of sweeping the Grenoble Alpine events, is a false hero, and also partially explains why Abebe Bikila, the barefoot winner of the Rome Olympic marathon, never became a legend in his time. He couldn't even endorse a pair of shoes as being better than his bare feet! Hiking and backpacking are sports that have become preoccupied with equipment. This is where I split with the manner in which the sport is practiced today. There is nothing more basic than walking. It is true when we are walking for days at a time it is necessary to take some things along, but we should keep the role of equipment in perspective. For whatever reason we go to the woods, let us not go there for the sake of our equipment. Let us realize we are in the woods to live, and not solely to use a stove or a sleeping bag. I can never understand the endless discussions about such things as whether the Optimus stove or the Primus stove is better. I do not see enough difference in these stoves to warrant the discussion, and I would no more presume to list the items a hiker should carry than I would tell him what he should have in his house. Guided by the fact that he wants to be warm, not hungry, and free from pain, he should be able to fashion a life-style for himself. So, having said all that, here are some comments that might prove useful.

PACK. The contour packframe has become standard equipment, although I never hesitate to mention that the equivalent of a Charlie Atlas body-building course can be had with a rucksack. It puts a good strain on the muscles; body builders, take note. Quality is important. With so many joints and fittings, no other piece of equipment has the packframe's potential for breakdown. My packframe happened to be a Kelty. The quality was there, and I liked the degree to which the top of the frame was bent toward my shoulders. This helped in getting the load closer to my back and more directly over my center of gravity. In theory at least, this made the load easier to carry. The only breakdown I had was that the bottom backband frayed and began to rip. Someone told me I had not kept it tight enough to prevent excessive back-and-forth motion, but other distance hikers have had the same problem, usually somewhere between 1,000 and 1,500 miles of use. A hiker can have a shoemaker sew some light leather on the area that comes in contact with the frame. In any case, it is the kind of breakdown you can see coming; you need not be caught in the woods with it. As for the packbag, I finally settled on the Kelty D4 model with the bottom zipper compartment, I used the large expedition packbag for a while, but found it too large for what I was carrying. Except for the first days after a pickup of food, I could fit all of my belongings, including a sleeping bag, inside the D4 bag for a compact and high load. Rain protection for the pack was provided by my poncho. The only contingency not covered by this arrangement was when I was sleeping under the poncho on a rainy night and had to hoist the pack up a tree away from bears; in that case the pack was out in the rain. I do not believe in gadgetry, such as the Kelty rain cover.

Quite a few hikers fail to observe the basic principle of good packing, which is to put the heaviest items high and close to your back. Every morning I tried to engineer the best possible load, and was never afraid to mound the contents above the top of the bag. I knew the flap would cover it. I also found that if the upper backband was somewhat loose it made the frame lay closer to the hiker's back.

BOOTS.   How many pairs of boots and resolings are necessary for a complete hike of the Appalachian Trail? There is too much individual variation for an answer. In New England a pair of Vibram soles lasted me 500 miles. In the South a pair of Vibram soles showed little wear after 425 miles. For the middle 1,000 miles I used wedge crepe soles and got around 300 miles a pair. I think this is the most sensible sole to use despite the relatively poor durability. The superior traction and wear of the Vibram soles were never as important to me as the comfort of crepe soles. The ordinary six-inch moccasin-toe work shoe was the best all-around shoe for me. Incidentally, I found Pennsylvania to be a rocky, almost painful, state to walk through. The section north of the Susquehanna River was especially difficult as the trail consists largely of small sharp stones which gave the effect of walking barefoot on nails.

SOCKS.   I carried three pairs of heavy wool socks at a time, and they went 400 miles before they were shrunken and misshapen and began to slip down into my boots. I tried silk inner socks, but when they were wet they lasted only two days before turning into cheesecloth. Regular-weight white cotton inner socks were standard with me. Conditioning is the only answer for blisters, although I had fewer problems with blisters when wearing light boots than I did when wearing the mediumweight hiking boots. Incidentally, the shoe repairmen along the way were the most pleasant merchants I met. They seemed happy to be their own boss, away from the factory and the production line. They also seemed to take genuine pride in their work.

PONCHO.   I used a poncho when walking in the rain. Its size was 106 by 68 inches and was made of lightweight waterproof nylon. When I was caught away from a shelter on a rainy night, I draped the poncho over a cord between two trees and it provided sufficient protection. The edges were held down with rocks or logs. Occasionally the poncho was used as a windbreak on a breezy ridge or in a drafty shelter. A groundsheet was necessary because the poncho was neither rugged enough nor big enough to serve this second duty. I bought a tube tent and got a great deal of satisfaction out of cutting the horrible thing into two pieces and using one piece as a groundsheet.

TENT.   I started out carrying a tent. It was a Sierra Design Solo, a one-man tent that was very nice. However, it was used mainly as protection against mosquitoes inside the Maine shelters, and in the White Mountains I began to use the poncho arrangement. I was willing to put up with occasional overcrowding in the shelters for the sake of a light load.

SLEEPING BAG.   I think a sleeping bag that contains from 1 to 1½ pounds of down, does not have sewn-through seams, and comes to a total weight of 3 to 3½ pounds, is best for the usual hiking season on the Appalachian Trail. A bag of this kind will usually give enough warmth, even on a chilly night when the hiker is wet and exhausted. The Trailwise Slimline bag I used went the five months of the trip without laundering. It was certainly dirty and had less loft at the end of the trip, but it never smelled. I never did carry a sleeping pad. Even in Maine in June the ground was warm enough for sleeping.

STOVE.   For most of the trip I didn't carry a stove. I did very little cooking, and it was easy to pick up a few sticks of wood to boil a cup of water for my evening rice. However, when the days became rainy and chilly in the fall it was pleasant to have a hot drink during the rest periods so I started carrying a Bleuet S-200 without the windscreen and plastic base. Foil kept some of the wind off, and I thought it was stable enough without the base. The Bleuet was convenient to operate and the fuel cartridges could be mailed in my food boxes, thus eliminating a search for white gas. Cooking on the trail for me usually meant just boiling water, then mixing in instant rice, oatmeal, tea, coffee, and so on. In boiling about 1½ quarts of water a day I found that one cartridge would last at least five days, and up to seven days if I was careful. The one drawback to the Bleuet is that the cartridge idea threatens our resources just as much as the one-way bottles and the paper products of our throwaway world.

INSECT REPELLENT.   I am sorry to report that I found nothing new that could challenge the blackfly's ownership of the Maine woods in the spring. However, they can be lived with. Witness the thousands of Maine residents and their children who tolerate this problem—just as a New Yorker tolerates his air pollution. Some relief is afforded by Woodsman's Fly Dope. No one agrees with me, though, in liking the smell. I didn't find the Cutter product to be as effective for blackflies, although mosquitoes were repelled by it. Mosquitoes are a more easily controlled pest than blackflies except when their sheer numbers make all remedies ineffective—except flight. In most situations I found the repellent issued to soldiers in Vietnam to be excellent against mosquitoes. Repellent mixtures vary from bottle to bottle within the same brand but on the average the military repellent contained 75% of diethyl toluamides (25% inert ingredients) as compared to Cutter's 30% of diethyl toluamides (roughly 67% inert ingredients).

ALLERGENIC PLANTS.   It is impossible to hike the Appalachian Trail without brushing or wading through poison ivy. People have varying degrees of natural immunity to this poison, but the immunity is decreased by repeated contact with the plant's allergen. A case of poison ivy will increase your sensitivity to both poison oak and poison sumac, and vice versa. It is the same allergen in all cases. It is when the stem is broken that the allergen is spread—this explains why it is not always disastrous to walk through patches of poison ivy. The allergen remains potent even when away from the plant. A highly alkaline soap, like brown laundry soap, is best for washing off your pack, clothing, or skin when contaminated. Some of the new nonphosphate detergents are highly alkaline. A soap with an oil base will spread, not remove, the resinous allergen. It is said that a person has 10 minutes at most to wash the allergen off. After that the ensuing allergy must run its course. In severe cases a steroid-type drug such as cortisone is prescribed to lessen the severity of the symptoms. I had a severe case of what was diagnosed as poison sumac. It had been an oversight on my part not to take the series of four preventive shots against the allergenic plants; the shots are supposed to be effective. Some doctors say they must be taken during the winter; other doctors will give them at any time, provided the patient is not already suffering from the allergy.

SNAKES.   The only poisonous snakes I saw on the trip were three copperheads; two were mating and had no interest in me, and the third withdrew under a stump beside my foot. I had the Cutter snakebite kit and studied the instructions whenever I thought about it. Most hikers have a good snake story, but few are bitten. This does not mean there is no danger; it only means that a hiker should be reasonably careful and not worry too much about it.

An inventory of the contents of my pack would be something like this (*indicates items worn while walking): sleeping bag, plastic groundsheet, poncho, cup, pot (3-cup size), 2 one-quart plastic bottles, spoon, salt-and-pepper shaker, jackknife, 2 plastic containers (for peanut butter and margarine), plastic bag of Ivory Snow, light wool shirt, light wash and wear shirt, *net undershirt, *shorts, gym shorts, *pants, *3 pr. heavy wool socks and 3 pr. light cotton socks, (one pair of each worn at one time), *boots, *glasses, *handkerchief, bandanna, hat (felt crusher), guidebook, paperback (usually one of the USA trilogy).

In a plastic bag I carried stamped envelopes, postcards, toilet paper, book matches, odd pieces of correspondence, pen. For the cooler fall weather I added an extra pair of pants, sweat shirt, sweater, windbreaker parka, long-sleeved cotton jersey, pair of heavy wool socks, pair of light cotton socks, Bleuet stove, fuel cartridges, boot grease. In a little red bag I carried a Cutter snakebite kit, compass, 30 feet of cord, 2 oz. Woodsman's Dope, 2 oz. Cutter's repellent, 2 oz. military-type repellent (Maine only), notebook, pencil, match safe, driver's license, $20–$30. I never used the compass, snakebite kit, match safe, and knife, but convention dictates carrying them. In a little blue bag I had vitamin tablets, Halazone tablets, moleskin, scissors, small razor and blades, needle and thread, toothbrush and paste (no salt, say dentists), half bar of soap.

FOOD.   The facade of objectivity wears thin on the subject of diet. What we like overrules the dieticians' tables. Here are some points to consider: Protein, not necessarily meat, should be made a dietary goal. Meat is a good source of high-grade protein, but its expense and trouble make it difficult for a hiker to carry. Meat is kept in our packs largely because of our national fixation about meat. A good book to read on this subject is *Diet for a Small Planet* by Frances Moore Lappé. It is basically a book on protein and demonstrates how this need can be met without a reliance on meat. The needs of the backpacker are neglected to a certain degree in this book; some foods are not discussed because they contain too many calories for the protein they give, and a backpacker's calorie problem is different from that of most people. Nevertheless, the book is worth studying.

The second dietary goal is calories. When the required protein is combined with the required calories, a meal may then be called substantial. This does not mean exotic menus or quantity without substance. A substantial meal is not turkey tetrazzini and freeze-dried ice cream. The food companies should go beyond names and prices, and print honest nutritional analyses on their chicken pilafs and beef taco comidas. Then the hiker could judge for himself if all of that delicate flavor and bulk are worth carrying.

Fat is overlooked as a backpacker's staple for many reasons: in large quantities it is difficult to digest, it is thought to be a factor in heart disease, it is hard to keep from spoiling in some forms, and it is heavy. The weight factor appears to be the chief reason backpackers do not carry fat in some form. People who have no qualms about eating sour cream dips and cream cheese spreads in their normal lives usually consider margarine as too heavy a luxury to carry in the woods, yet this argument has no foundation. A cup of sugar (almost 100% carbohydrate) weighs 8 ounces, and a cup of margarine (81% fat) also weighs 8 ounces. The difference here is that the hiker receives 765 more calories from the fat than he does from the sugar, which is clearly an advantage to the person concerned with what he is getting from the weight he carries. When the foods that a hiker is likely to eat in quantity are considered, they appear to support the argument that fat is heavy. For instance, one cup of oatmeal weighs 2¾ ounces as compared to 8 ounces for a cup of fat. The oatmeal is certainly lighter, but the fat contains 1,365 more calories; that is, almost twice as many calories on a weight basis, and *almost 5½ times as many calories on a volume basis*. These are the kind of facts we should consider when we think of a lightweight concentrated diet, not a label on a package that says "when reconstituted this package provides 1¼ pounds of food." The water you add does not add any energy.

Today it is almost impossible for us to imagine the old Arctic explorers going for months on nothing but pemmican. Fat and protein, onward, onward, mush! A hiker on the Appalachian Trail is not faced with the critical survival problems of the Arctic explorer, but a hiker who is on the trail for months, and who gets up every morning and uses his legs for 15 or 20 miles, going up mountains and through cold rain, must deal with the problem of an adequate diet. An increase of fat in the diet should be considered with the assurance that the rigorous daily activity uses up the fat and diminishes risk to the heart. It is not suggested that fat be eaten to the exclusion of other sources of calories, but as the diet becomes more fatty, the pack becomes lighter and more compact for the same amount of food. According to his tolerance, each hiker will have to arrive at the proper level of fat in his own diet, and leave to history the stories of Arctic explorers spooning down lard.

To most hikers flavor is a more important dietary goal than variety. Flavors that come through under any conditions for most people are chocolate, cheese, peanut butter, onion, pepper, and coffee. In hiking the Appalachian Trail I progressed through various foods until this representative menu evolved: BREAKFAST: oatmeal, margarine, sugar, cheese. LUNCH: peanut butter, margarine (with or without bread), lemonade. SUPPER: instant rice, pemmican, lemonade, vitamins. With this basic menu I consumed one-half quart of milk (made from dry milk), coffee, tea, Kendall mint cake, Baby Ruth candy bars, milk chocolate, pea soup in colder weather, salt, pepper, and onion flakes.

The pemmican was homemade. Low-grade beef was bought wholesale and dried to make jerky. The jerky was ground in a meat grinder, mixed with melted Crisco (2 cups of ground jerky to 1 cup melted Crisco), cooled, divided into 4- or 5-ounce portions, and wrapped in foil. It was difficult to eat this pemmican cold; it was better heated; broken up and cooked with rice it was delicious. Oatmeal, instant rice, and sometimes bread were foods with which the concentrated fatty foods were eaten. In the future I would hope to eliminate pemmican and mint cake from my diet and find other items to take their place. A backpacker shouldn't be restricted to shopping in mountaineering stores, or picking up food packages at post offices.

My general menu consisted of the foods mentioned, but this was by no means all that I ate on my trip. There were apples from orchards, meals at restaurants, the wonderful picnickers who shared their celery stalks and egg salad sandwiches, and the food given to me by other hikers who were on their way out of the woods and had food to spare. At times I thought of turning down food and living solely from my pack and my calculations, but that would have meant turning my back on a lot of kindness just for the sake of an experiment. Instead,

I lived in terms of what each day offered (and perhaps still lost much in the name of Georgia-or-Bust.)

The Rain

The warm rain fell as you walked and at first it was fun as the rain dripped off your hat and ran down your poncho to the ground. You tied a bandanna around your neck to soak the drips that would otherwise leak in and run down your chest. Soon your boots could not shed any more water and they began to darken and become heavy. The thick wool socks became sodden and with each footfall excess water squeezed through the boot seams: *squish*. Puddles collected on the trail: *splash*. Walking in the rainy forest was a continuous *squish-squish-splash*. The pant legs below the poncho were wet, of course, and the water, carried by capillary action, rose to your upper thighs. Body moisture, increased by the mile-after-mile exertion, was trapped by the poncho and absorbed by your undershirt; your hair absorbed the moisture that could not escape from under your hat. This was how you became wet from head to foot. It did not matter at first because it was not a cold rain, and the activity of walking was warming. Not until the lunch stop did you feel cold. While your tin cup of tea was steaming on the little stove you took off the wet undershirt and put on a warm sweater. Then, when it was time to start, you had to take off the comfortable sweater and put on the cold wet undershirt again. The start was made quickly and sometimes you even ran to warm numbed feet. It was pleasant to stop on rainy days after only half a day of walking. It was cozy to be in a sleeping bag in a shelter for the afternoon and spend the time reading and sleeping. But when two weeks of rain had settled in, this stopping could not be afforded as a daily luxury. It did not matter that the rain sometimes ceased, for if the woods were wet *you* were wet. After a stormy night the woods were very wet indeed. A full day of bright sun was needed to dry the forest. If a storm broke in the early morning hours the only glimpse of the sun would be at sunrise. The rising sun's warmth drew the moisture from the fields and valleys, collecting it in large clouds that made the breaking day quite dismal. It took only half an hour of walking to be wet again from head to foot—from brushing against bushes and grass, from crawling through blowdowns, and from showers caused by bumping into saplings. By early afternoon, if it was truly a breaking day, the sun would come through the clouds, the forest would dry, and you yourself could start to dry. That evening in camp all was dry except your feet, and you celebrated with a rise in spirits. While supper was cooking you washed a pair of socks and hung the sleeping bag to dry. Supper could be eaten while watching a sunset for the first time in two weeks. There was time for reading in the afterglow. The test of rain was over now, you told yourself, and you had passed. In the evening you went to sleep listening to a whip-poorwill and the crickets instead of rain on the shelter roof.

So the various combinations of rain and no rain occurred daily and continued for weeks. Rain in the morning, no rain in the afternoon. Rain in the afternoon, no rain at night. Rain at night and in the morn-ing both, but just fog during the afternoon. Some rain in the morning, some rain in the afternoon, some rain at night. On and on it went. Translated into its effect on the true hiking force, the spirit, the rain and body wetness became a cycle—joy in spite of it all, unhappiness, expectation, dashed hopes, hope, no hope, hope. Probably no one has ever made a hike of the Appalachian Trail without going through at least one solid week of rain, and probably no one has gone through such rain without having serious thoughts of quitting the trail. How to get through it, that was the thing. There was no point in worrying about keeping dry. The body was going to be wet. The secret lay in somehow waterproofing the spirit—wrapping the spirit in a plastic bag like a pair of dry socks, or better yet, teaching it to breathe under-water and to become a fish.

It had been raining for two weeks and although the hiker was learn-ing to be a fish in spirit, he was unhappy. Scrambling up an embank-ment brought him to the highway. After having been in the woods, it made him dizzy to see the rush of traffic. Up the highway about a mile there was a general store. If he was to continue he would need food. The air was misty and there was a spray caused by the log trucks speeding down the grade. As he walked horns blared at him, people waved, and one boy flashed him the peace sign. The hiker waved back, but he did not smile.

The store was warm and dimly lit. The shelves were packed with wares; the counters were cluttered and dusty. The storekeeper was stacking cans in the rear of the store. "Morning," he said, "be with you in a minute."

"No hurry. Wouldn't have a package here for me, would you?" The hiker gave his name.

"Sure do. Letter, too." The storekeeper went to the caged-off area of the store. The box was on top of a cabinet. "Here you go. Where you walking to?"

"I'm trying to get to Georgia. Been walking in rain for weeks, though."

"Giving it up?"

"I've come this far from Maine. I think I'll stick it out a little longer."

The hiker bought a bottle of Coke and a pint of chocolate ice cream. There was a bench in front of one of the counters. He sat down and opened the letter. There wasn't any bad news in it. Few people entered the store; one old man bought beer, a boy came for mail. A lady entered the store carrying a little girl. She put the little girl down and said, "Go and say hello to grandpa, Cindy." The lady talked with the hiker. "I was reading the other day about people like you." She searched among some newspapers and came up with an old *Time* magazine. The article told about how students leave college because it doesn't interest them, and how they try to find other things to do. The hiker went on to read the other articles. A notice under MILE-STONES startled him: *Died. Louis Armstrong.* It was good that the storekeeper was stacking cans and that Cindy was after candy with her grandmother, for the hiker could not have said anything just then. He had seen enough news, far too much news.

He took his box outside and loaded his pack. He bought peanut butter, margarine, a can of pinto beans for supper, and some pipe tobacco, then wrote a note home saying he would be walking slower than he had planned. Being on the Blue Ridge, he explained, did not mean that it was all level walking. There was a lot of up-and-down walking as well. Because of this, and the fact that he was hungrier than planned, could they please send an extra $10 to the next post office? He mentioned the rain and closed his letter.

"You stop back and see us again," said the lady.

"Good luck," said the storekeeper.

The Appalachian Trail followed the highway for another mile before it found a bridge to cross the river. On the other side the trail began to climb up to the ridge crest. In five miles the trail gained over 2,000 feet in elevation. At 3,500 feet the trail entered the clouds. The shelter was at 4,000 feet and the hiker got there just before dark. After eating he put his sleeping bag behind a curtain made with his poncho, which he hoped would keep the billowing clouds of mist from totally soaking the sleeping bag. It had been a day fuller than most. People to talk with even. They had been so friendly that it made him acutely aware of being alone now. There must be better things to do than walking to Georgia in the rain, he thought.

The Theory

The theory explained why, as months of hiking passed, it became more difficult to get to sleep. Properly stated in strict form: sleep seemed to be needed in inverse ratio to the number of days you had been hiking. As you hiked your body became conditioned; no longer were you exhausted at the end of the day. You were in better condition mentally, too. Instead of going through strength-robbing anxiety about forest demons, or the sky falling as you slept under it, or the lightning striking you, you felt that it was all quite natural, just as Davey Crockett did. So in the later stages of the hike, instead of falling asleep halfway through supper as you used to do, you were now looking for a party to go to. But at the same time the body had become wise about what you were putting it through. After so many days of bone-jarring footfalls, branches slapping you in the face, stumbling on cliff edges—your body began to brace itself against the probability that what had happened before was going to happen again. Didn't the body know it was self-defeating to be so protective at night—when some sleep would be nice? No, it didn't, and you lay there like a 100-pound bow someone had forgotten to unstring. And if that wasn't enough, getting near the end of this crazy stunt was exciting. Exciting? Electrifying was the word, and who could blame the mind for acting like a child on Christmas Eve? The physically fit body, needing less rest, was afflicted with conditioned hyperactivity. That was the theory and if this was a no-holds-barred, one-million-sheep-count night, you would really get into it. The greatest theories of man would be unleashed on that child to try to get him to turn the switch off. Victor Frankel, front and center. Yes, yes, Logotherapy, Paradoxical Intention. Right. Dr. Frankel would say, "You must try and make yourself *more* wide awake, try harder and harder *not* to go to sleep, then you will pop right off to sleep." All right, thank you. Dr. Berne, what might Transactional Analysis add? I see, the parent-of-my-mind must spank that child-of-my-mind. . . . No? You say that would produce conflict. Sorry, I misunderstood. Instead, the adult-of-my-mind must ask the child-of-my-mind to please turn the switch off because it won't make either Santa Claus or Georgia come any sooner. Excellent, very sensible, Dr. Berne, and you say afterwards the hyperactivity will just go away in several hours; nicely planned and in time for breakfast. Dr. Freud, I must insist, joy was never repressed at Christmas at home, and I am not resisting; it is the truth. Say, Mr. M.D., how about a couple of those emerald-green pearls called Chloral Hydrate? And some of that muscle relaxer, Artane. . . . Thus the psychological hiker counted his sheep.

Credit for this theory goes to an extraordinary hiker named Bill. The hiker met Bill at a shelter in Vermont. Bill was on a 190-day

Georgia-to-Maine walk, one of the slower traverses of the Appalachian Trail. This didn't bother Bill. When he finished he would have walked closer to 2,500 miles than the usual 2,000 miles. Nothing was out of the way for Bill, and never, in the interest of making another mile, did he forego the pleasure of stopping to talk with another hiker. Maine was at the end of the trail and it wasn't going anywhere. Bill lived the fine philosophy that says the goal matters nothing alongside all that led up to it. When the hiker came into the clearing by the lake several people were sitting at the lean-to and Bill was stooped over a smoky fire frying what looked like a thick piece of plaster.

"Hi, man. Where you from?"

"Come from Maine. Going to Georgia."

"Great," said Bill. "I'm up from Georgia." Bill had settled down for the day after having walked only half a mile. The hiker had come 10 miles and planned to go 10 more that afternoon. A few campers came to sit by the two trail aces and hear of the battles with the Red Baron. It was something a hiker could very easily overlook when planning a hike of the Appalachian Trail, but in traveling from north to south you might meet 5 or 10 comrades, Maine-bound. Hikers traveling south to north would be lucky to see a single oddball walking the "wrong way" from Maine. A lot was missed in not meeting the other aces.

The hiker fired up his stove to heat soup. In a plastic bottle he mixed lemonade. In a plastic bag he washed a pair of socks and hung them to dry alongside his airing sleeping bag. Bill watched the activity without comment. The hiker asked Bill what he was cooking.

"Oh!" Bill leaped up and ran to the fire. With a stick he turned the piece of plaster over. It was now dark brown and looked like a board. "Almost burnt," he said, coming back. "Flour and water. Fry it and put peanut butter on it."

"What else do you eat?"

"I'll show you." He took a faded canvas pack down from a nail; it was an old-timer, a Duluth, complete with tumpline. He had a 10-pound sack of flour and a 5-pound pail of peanut butter. "I figure I eat for a quarter a day. Flour and peanut butter. Three thousand calories. Then, there's my sugar." He pulled out a 5-pound sack of sugar. "Only use it to sweeten the tea I make from sassafras roots and checkerberry leaves. Here's my tobacco." It was a pound can of Prince Albert. "That's about it except for the books." In the bottom of the pack were hardbound books—Dostoevsky, Nietzsche, Jung. The hiker picked out the only paperback; it was Hesse's *Magister Ludi*.

"You needn't read this, Bill. It's a put-on," the hiker said.

"So's everything else, man." That ended that. "Tell me, how's Maine?"

The hiker told how deep the woods were, and how clear the lakes seemed. Bill sat there, legs crossed, in jeans and an undershirt waiting for more. His long hair was kept under control by a blue bandanna around his forehead. The hiker went on about the moose, the deep moose dung on Mt. Bigelow, and the blackflies. He told about the 17 days of fair weather. Bill sat there as if in a trance, listening. He was one of those rare individuals who asked a question because he honestly wanted to hear what you had to say. The hiker was not used to someone paying him such close attention. He was uneasy and began to skip around, talking of the Kennebec River and the Mahoosucs. He wanted Bill to talk and asked, "Was Cheoah Bald a tough climb?"

"No. You just rest when you get tired. What about Katahdin Iron Works?" Bill was still in Maine.

"Didn't see it. It's a long way off the trail. I don't know how much of it is left to see."

"I want to go and take a look at it. I don't want to miss it."

The hiker shouldered his pack. "Well, what's next for you, Bill?"

"Got a friend with a boat. Going sailing. I like Saskatchewan, too. Indians are real people."

At the main trail they shook hands and parted. Although it was Bill's theory as to why a hiker couldn't get to sleep, the hiker hadn't heard it from Bill when they met in the Green Mountains. It was months later, in the Great Smokies, when two college students told him about it. The two had collected leaves along the Appalachian Trail in Maine, and then rode to the South to collect more leaves for a comparison. Upon seeing the hiker, they said Bill had told them to be on the lookout for him. It is a small world and these hikers are a large family.

A Cabin in Vermont

The trail was a dirt track over a grassy hill and led through fields and patches of trees. From the hilltop you could look in all directions at scattered farms among the surrounding low hills. Two backpackers approached the hiker. They could not stop to talk, they said, because they were in a race with a Boy Scout troop for the next shelter. A short time later the hiker passed the Boy Scout troop. The scouts formed a parade in their green uniforms covered with badges and red scarves held by gold clasps. Following the leader was the flag bearer with the troop flag: a brown grizzly bear on a white field. From the top of the

mast hung blue and yellow streamers. The only thing missing from
the parade was a drummer to mark cadence. As the hiker passed
someone cautioned him not to step on "the asthmatic runt" behind.
Soon the hiker came to a Scout who had collapsed on the trail. A
uniformed leader stood over him. As the hiker came near, the leader
yelled at the boy, "Get off the trail and let the man through," and
shoved the struggling boy off the trail with his foot. The hiker looked
coldly at the leader; there had been plenty of room to get by. They
needed the likes of him in the marines, the hiker thought, but he said
nothing. Any remark he made would only add to the leader's anger,
which probably would be taken out on the boy. The hiker stooped
down to speak to the boy. "How's it going?" The boy was pale and
gasping. "It's my asthma. I'm resting."

"Got your respirator?"

"I've used it."

"While you're resting, let's make your pack easier to carry." The
hiker took the loosely rolled sleeping bag that was hanging outside
the pack and rolled it tighter so it would fit inside.

"Thank you, sir," the boy said.

"I'm just a friend. Never call a friend 'sir,'" the hiker said. As he
walked off the leader was muttering something about baby-sitting.

Beside the cabin a clear brook flowed over gravel and stones. It was
one of the last good streams before they became murky and slow in
the urban states. He began to cook supper. Living outside was so
natural by this time that the hiker never went inside even when rain
was imminent. Three men and a woman arrived at the shelter. One of
the men had a red nylon pack with a violin case sticking out of the
top, wore a pot on his head Johnny Appleseed style, and had a thin
scraggly beard. The hiker had to smile at him.

"Where you people from?"

"We joined up in New York. Just traveling together. Been hitching
some. We're into music." He took a harmonica out of his pocket and
started to play. "Sort of going to Canada. Staying where we like it."
He played some more. "It's nice here. I think we like it here." He
began to sing, still with the pot on his head. Someone yelled from the
cabin door that they needed his pot for supper.

After the hiker finished supper he sat on the picnic bench drinking
tea. The antics of the balladeer and the large supper had not taken his
mind off the asthmatic runt being kicked along the trail. He wondered
about the bad feelings that filled such a man and drove him to kick
people. Finally he picked up his pack and walked to the cabin door.

The musicians were eating at the table between the two wide bunk beds. A candle was burning, and the stove crackled in the corner. The hiker took out his sleeping bag.

"Do you get up early?" One of the men at the table spoke.

"I'm quiet when I leave. You won't hear me."

"We're into music. We play music at night. I mean loud music. Hard to sleep."

"No problem with me," the hiker said. People always thought they would disturb your sleep when they made noise while you were in the sack. The truth was that it did not matter to the hiker in the least.

The overture began after supper. A mandolin, guitar, fiddle, harmonica, flute. They never knew when it began to rain that night. It was only much later, when the tempo slackened, that rain could be heard—not as rain, but more like applause. It was background music for the moments when only the flute played a few notes over and over. The musicians used the rain as another instrument. It kept the silence from being too loud.

The music played and played, louder and louder. When it filled the cabin the music had nowhere to go and began to be absorbed by the table, the bunks, the people. The hiker, once an outsider, was with them now as the music filled him, too. They all would have been killed as the rich music penetrated like radiation, if it had not been for the music leaking out through the cracks into the damp dark woods; to the bird on a limb, and to the fox huddled in a rotten stump.

The hiker awoke at five o'clock. Everyone was sleeping. On the table was the cabin register. He entered his name and put MAINE TO GEORGIA next to it, ate some cold oatmeal and started down the trail. He turned and looked at the sleeping cabin just before it went out of sight. This is the way it always is, he thought. Leaving people while they slept and never saying good-bye. Or thank you. He continued on to Georgia, never once thinking of the asthmatic runt.

A Walk in Search of the Horizon

By Bruce Balderston

Started at SPRINGER MOUNTAIN on April 2, 1972
Finished at MT. KATAHDIN on August 26, 1972

I had been camping for over 10 years before I made my Appalachian Trail hike. I was introduced to the wilderness on a two-week family camping trip in Virginia, and my interest was stimulated when I joined the Boy Scouts after my family moved to New York City. In the Scouts I went camping about once a month, and for several years spent two weeks each summer at a Boy Scout camp. I became an Eagle Scout two months after my fifteenth birthday and it was at about this time that I began to find group camping less enjoyable.

During the summer of 1968 my father, my younger brother, and I started to hike the Appalachian Trail from Kent, Connecticut, to the Hudson River. We had planned to take a week for this 50-mile hike, but after two days we realized that we were ill-equipped, not in proper shape physically, and not enjoying ourselves, so we abandoned the trip. In the spring of 1969, after more experience, my brother and I took a week's trip south of the Hudson River on the Appalachian Trail. We camped at a lake off the trail, after using a map and compass to locate it. The first day was beautiful, pleasant and clear. During the night, however, the temperature dropped and snow fell for 22 hours, leaving an accumulation of 12 to 14 inches. We were camped in a sheltered area in a good mountain tent, so we didn't experience any discomfort.

In the summer of 1970 my brother and I made a two-week trip on the Appalachian Trail in the White Mountains. These were the first mountains of any size we had ever seen, and we found them beautiful but very rough. The day we climbed Mt. Washington we were introduced to our first mountain storm. The weather was beautiful in the morning at the base of the mountain, but by the time we reached the summit the temperature had dropped into the mid-forties and the wind was gusting to 80 miles an hour, according to information from the weather observatory. It would have been foolhardy to continue our hike above timberline in such weather, so we traveled at a lower altitude for the remainder of the trip. The rugged mountain trails, the changing weather, and the feeling of freedom and peace made this a magnificent experience.

On a weekend camping trip in October of 1971 I found a card that had been tacked to a shelter wall by two hikers on their way from Springer Mountain to Mt. Katahdin. I spent most of the weekend thinking about what a magnificent hike that would be. There were many things to be considered for such a trip—food, clothing, maps, medicines, equipment. In my case the time element was an important consideration as I was in my senior year at high school. Even in the face of all of these problems, however, I decided that hiking the Appalachian Trail was something I wanted to do, and that I would perhaps never have as good an opportunity again.

I summoned up enough courage to mention the hike to my parents, explained my tentative plans for food and equipment, and told them I thought I had a good chance of graduating from school early. At first they greeted the idea with apprehension, but finally said I could attempt the trip if I found a competent hiker to go with me. I had envisioned being alone on the trail for 2,000 miles as part of the adventure, but agreed with my parents that the dangers in such a hike were increased if it was attempted alone.

I arranged to graduate from high school early, and wrote to many organizations trying to locate someone to hike the trail with me. All of my efforts were futile until the local newspaper wrote a story about my hike. Through this story I met Gary Wiesendanger, who was just a year older than I was, and who lived only a few miles from my home. After talking the matter over, we decided to attempt the trip together.

One of the primary factors in backpacking, especially on long-distance trips, is proper equipment and the ability to use it efficiently. I had recently purchased a Camp Trails Skyline packbag and decided to use it because it was durable, convenient, and had excellent size. When I was on the trail I discovered that the seams leaked, and the contents of the bag got wet in a moderate to heavy rain. My parents sent me a Kelty rain cover which kept the pack and its contents dry in any rain, without exception. I am convinced that the rain cover is the most practical solution to this problem. In combination with this packbag I used the Camp Trails Cruiser aluminum packframe.

In Virginia I discovered that the welds in the joints of the frame had developed hairline cracks, and the cracks quickly grew larger. Fortunately, I had planned to spend a day with friends in Roanoke, Virginia, and was able to have the joints welded while I was there. At almost any other point on the trail this fault could have caused a serious problem. I would now advise the use of a Kelty frame over almost any other brand. I used a Camp Trails waist belt and found it excellent; it puts most of the pack's weight on the hips and legs.

Several months prior to planning the hike I had purchased a Blacks Icelandic down sleeping bag. The bag was a semi-mummy type, tapered toward the feet to conserve heat and weight, but not as confining as a mummy bag. It was box baffled, contained 1.38 pounds of prime goose down, and was rated by Blacks as being comfortable to 15° F. I found that the Egyptian cotton shell warmed up quickly and did not hold odors as do many nylon bags. The cotton was strong and had excellent breathability, for which I was most thankful in warm weather. Only once did I find myself a bit cold. This was at 4,500 feet on Tray Mountain in Georgia, with snow and wind blowing over me all night long.

I carried a Gerry foam pad of the open cell type, sheathed in a waterproof nylon case, weighing 18 ounces. For shelter, after much consideration, I chose a tube tent. A tube tent is merely a plastic tube about 9½ feet long, open at both ends. It is held up by a cord strung through the tube and tied to two trees. I chose this shelter primarily because of its weight and cost. I had an expensive two-man mountain tent, but it weighed 3½ pounds with the poles and stakes. The tube tent weighed under 1½ pounds, was easily repaired with plastic tape, and cost less than $3. The tube tent was not too successful, however. There was entirely too much condensation, even with both ends open. During storms the rain poured in and collected in pools under our sleeping bags. In Virginia the tube tent was cut up the middle and from then on was used as a tarp. As a flat piece of plastic it could be pitched in a variety of ways, according to weather conditions. After this alteration I was never wet again while sleeping under the tarp in the rain. I am convinced that a tarp, in combination with a ground cloth, is the most efficient shelter for a hiker who wants to keep weight at a minimum and does not expect to encounter extreme weather conditions. A plastic tarp is less expensive than a nylon tarp but is perhaps a bit harder to handle. We carried an 8-ounce folding Swedish saw and a light aluminum grill. We used a Svea cook kit which included two pots, a frying pan, two plastic bowls, two sets of spoons and forks, and two plastic drinking cups. The kit was a bit too large for our needs but the weight was reasonable. The only fault we found with this set was that the pots and pan were soft and easily dented. I later used a cook kit consisting of an aluminum bowl with a handle which could be used as a bowl or a frying pan, spoon and fork, small pot with cover, plastic cup, and Sierra cup. After 1,200 miles on the trail I started using a Bleuet stove. It eliminated the problem of making a fire and cooking in the rain, and enabled me to start hiking earlier in the morning. It was easy to use and did not blacken pots as a fire or a gasoline stove does. I also liked the Bleuet because the butane canisters could be shipped to me. In fact, I found it perfect for all of my needs; with it I could even cook breakfast while remaining in my sleeping bag.

I began the trip with a wool sweater, down vest, set of net underwear, two pairs of long pants, one pair of short pants, heavy shirt, two light shirts, woolen mittens and hat, rain parka, rain pants, several pairs of underwear, and five pairs of woolen socks. I also carried a pair of moccasins for wearing after the day's hike. The worst problem I had, as far as clothing was concerned, was keeping warm during rest stops in cold weather. I solved this problem to some extent by wearing less clothing while hiking, and hiking at slower speeds for longer periods of time. By doing this I sweated less and a wind parka was sufficient to keep me warm during short rest stops. When the weather got warmer I sent home my mittens and hat, net underwear, and sweater. I also sent my down vest home during the summer months, but had it sent back to me when I reached Maine. By the time I reached Maryland my short pants were in tatters so I cut down a pair of long pants. I sent the other pair of long pants home, but had them mailed back to me in New Hampshire as I needed them on cool days in the mountains.

Rain created a major problem with regard to clothing. I used a rain parka and rain pants because I knew from experience that a poncho offered little protection for the legs and was a nuisance on steep trails, in rocky areas, and in areas of dense growth. I purchased the rain pants in a large size for maximum ventilation and freedom of action, and split them in the crotch to help with the problem of condensation. I used a liquid nylon sealer on the seams to make sure they would be waterproof. The rain pants worked well, but I had condensation problems when using the parka. This problem was partly solved by wearing only a light shirt under the parka.

Many hikers take great care in selecting their equipment but don't pay much attention to selecting boots. I have flat feet and not particularly strong ankles, so with these weaknesses in mind I looked for a pair of boots with thick soles and good ankle support. About 10 days before I was to begin the hike I bought a pair of Fabiano boots with Vibram Montagna soles. I replaced the nylon laces with cotton-nylon laces as I had experienced some problems with nylon laces coming untied. Throughout the hike I wore a pair of Norwegian Ragg wool socks over a pair of nylon-wool athletic socks. On rainy days, or on days when I hiked a considerable distance, I would wear two pairs of the athletic socks under the Ragg socks. I had a few blisters during the first part of the hike because I had not broken in my boots sufficiently. However, with proper care and much use of gauze pads, tape, and moleskin, they gave me no real problem and did not affect my hiking. I found the Fabiano boots to be excellent. They provided enough support so that I avoided sprained or bruised ankles—both fairly common injuries among hikers in rugged areas. After 1,300 miles the boot soles were still in excellent condition as far as wear was concerned, but they had begun to separate from the top of the boots. When I reached the Hudson River and went home for two days I had the boots resoled. For the remaining 700 miles I had a lot of trouble with the new soles coming loose. I was constantly gluing them with contact cement. In Monson I bought a quantity of wood screws and put 12 or 14 screws in the sole of each boot. The screws worked perfectly, and I had no further problems with the boots.

I took great care with my first-aid kit for I knew I would be hiking in areas where medical attention was hours away. Minor accidents could result in discomfort and a loss of hiking time. I had a fairly good knowledge of first aid, and my kit included everything which I thought might be needed for minor medical problems. I also considered size and weight when planning the kit. In a tough plastic container I put a razor blade, tweezers, gauze and gauze pads, adhesive tape, cotton, iodine, Bacitracin (an antibiotic cream), bandages, a Cutter's snakebite kit, burn cream, Lomotil pills for diarrhea, and an assortment of thread, wire, and needles. I included an emergency candle and waterproof matches, neither of which I ever needed. The entire kit weighed about 14 ounces. In a small nylon bag I carried Pak-it-Soap (a concentrated biodegradable liquid soap), hand towel, collapsible toothbrush, small tube of toothpaste, and comb. I didn't carry a razor, and found no reason for shaving during the trip. Items carried in the outside pockets of the pack included a pocketknife, a compass and metal match, a pen, and a notebook in which I kept a daily account of the trek. I began the trip with a camera but after I lost several rolls of color film in the mails I sent the camera home.

Unless a hiker has a very good camera and above-average photographic skills, he cannot do justice to what he sees on the Appalachian Trail.

I wrote to Mr. Bill White, president of Stow-A-Way Products Company, Inc., Cohasset, Massachusetts, and Mr. White said his company would give me a discount on a large order of food. I set to work on a menu for 2 people for 3 meals a day for 140 days, and planned 10 different breakfasts and dinners and 7 different lunches. I tried to keep each meal under 16 ounces for 2 people and contain at least 1,200 calories per person. With the discount the total cost was $460. Gary and I added $40 worth of food from supermarkets, including milk crackers, meat spread, and Lipton's instant Stroganoff dinners. I attempted to plan meals that were fairly well-balanced nutritionally, and varied enough so they wouldn't be too boring. Later, on the trail, we found that the major fault with the meals was that they were a bit too elaborate. Some breakfasts consisted of Swiss cereal, milk, juice, honey, and dried fruit; others were of freeze-dried eggs and ham. At first we cooked corn bread or biscuits for breakfast, but later we cooked food like this in the evening so we could start earlier in the morning. Lunches were kept simple, consisting primarily of freeze-dried or canned meat spreads, milk crackers, fruit juice, candy, and possibly a 4-ounce can of cake for the two of us. To make up for the lack of fat in our diet we consumed large quantities of peanut butter, purchased at stores along the way. During our first weeks on the trail we became hungry within two hours or so after eating breakfast, so we started buying peanuts, raisins, and chocolate, and eating more snacks between meals.

The time involved in preparing some of the morning meals gave us a late start on the trail. If we got up at 6:30 A.M. it would be 9:00 or 9:30 by the time we had built a fire, cooked, washed dishes, and packed. A late start would force us to hike until sunset to reach our destination for the day. Dinners usually consisted of a one-course meal which could be cooked in 20 or 30 minutes, crackers, fruit juice, and candy or cake. About once or twice a week we would bake gingerbread or brownies. Both were welcome changes in our diet, but took a lot of time to prepare. We decided that it had been a mistake to take so much food that had to be cooked, especially when we were depending on wood fires.

The food from Stow-A-Way arrived in 12 boxes weighing about 320 pounds. Gary and I spent hours organizing the food on shelves in my basement. Before the food arrived we had figured out our food pickup points. As we planned to average 14 miles a day, our first food pickup would be at Fontana Dam, North Carolina—a distance we figured to be about 140 miles from Springer Mountain, or 10 days of hiking. We underestimated the distance and ran into a bit of difficulty, which I will tell about later. To Fontana Dam we sent a package of food for nine days and planned to buy a day's food. We calculated this would enable us to reach Flag Pond, Tennessee, some 168 miles up the trail. The package sent to Flag Pond was to last us nine days and 130 miles to Damascus, Virginia, where we were to pick up an 11-day food supply to take us nearly 160 miles to Roanoke —and so on.

We made sure there were post offices in the towns we had selected by consulting the National ZIP Code Directory, which lists all post offices in the United States. We addressed the packages to ourselves in care of general delivery, and mailed the first two packages before we left home. Gary's parents were to mail the remaining packages on a prearranged schedule. Post office officials will hold a general delivery package for a month and we were told it would take no more than a week to 10 days for packages from home to reach our farthest pickup point. We wrapped all of the packages securely, indicated that we were hiking the Appalachian Trail, and included our return addresses. In addition to food we put soap, matches, maps, and guidebooks in the packages. In several boxes we included extra clothing.

On the morning of April 1, we traveled on a crowded commuter train from Scarsdale to New York City, then took a taxi to the airport. By two o'clock we were in Atlanta where we were greeted by beautiful 75-degree weather. We started to hitchhike and got several short rides, but at sunset we had traveled less than 30 miles from Atlanta. We thought of sleeping in the fields but barking dogs ended that idea. Eventually we came to a church and thought we could sleep under the overhang of the roof. However, we discovered that a side door was unlocked, so we slept on the floor in the hall and had a toilet and water fountain at our disposal. The next morning we awoke early, packed, wrote a "thank you" note to the pastor of the church, and left. We were lucky to have had such a good place to sleep for it had rained and turned cold during the night.

We got a ride with a minister on his way to work at a rehabilitation center for criminals. He was interested in our hike, and went out of his way to drive us to Amicalola Falls State Park. We stood in the cold mist looking at the 3,000- or 4,000-foot peaks that surrounded us and wondered if we could average 14 miles a day over such mountains in all kinds of weather. Following old jeep trails we climbed

Photo by Lowell Branham

Jim Rutter at Fontana Dam, North Carolina.

Photo by James R. Wolf

Slaughter and Blood mountains, as seen from Lake Winfield
Scott, Georgia.

steeply to the summit of Springer Mountain. The sky had cleared but the wind had risen and it was getting colder. We signed the trail register and had lunch while looking out over seemingly endless mountains shrouded in mist.

We arrived at the first trail shelter, where it was very cold and windy during the night. By morning the wind had died down and although it was cool, it was a beautiful clear and sunny day. We put in a full day on the Appalachian Trail and hiked an exhausting 14 miles. The following morning frost covered everything; the woods were as still as a winter landscape painting. When we stopped for lunch a family from the Midwest gave us fruit and cookies and wished us luck. With our spirits lifted by this friendliness we continued on, making camp on the summit of Blood Mountain, which at 4,500 feet was the highest mountain on the Appalachian Trail in Georgia. We had little trouble sleeping that night after having covered a rough 14.5 miles.

The next day we hiked less than 13 miles before the weather turned bad and we made camp. We awoke to the sound of heavy rain on the walls of our tube tent. With great difficulty we ate and packed inside the tent. We hiked all day through cold rain and sleet, stopping only to eat lunch. Visibility was poor and it began to snow as we climbed Tray Mountain. The climb was long, steep, and very cold as the wind and snow increased in intensity. It was almost dark when we arrived at a shelter on the far side of the mountain. Here we met Tom Paradise, a hiker who was also on his way to Mt. Katahdin. That night snow blew in on us and by morning three inches of snow had fallen, with drifts up to eight inches. We hiked 11 miles by lunchtime, then stopped to dry our sleeping bags and boots at Dicks Creek Gap. Here we met Leo, a 40-year-old janitor at Brown University, who was also attempting to hike the entire trail. By evening Gary and I had made 17 miles and were feeling more confident about our hiking.

The following day on Standing Indian we encountered snow a foot deep, but for the next few days we made long satisfying hikes and became increasingly confident about our ability to tackle mountains which at first had appeared almost impossible to climb. In the distance the Great Smoky Mountains were beautiful with their snow-capped peaks. We discovered that we had underestimated the distance from Springer Mountain to Fontana Dam by 20 miles. Leo, who had been hiking with us, slept late one day and urged us to go on without him. That same day Tom Paradise told us he was not enjoying the trail and planned to abandon his trek. He gave us his remaining food and boarded a bus in a small town near the trail.

We planned to attempt to hike some 20 miles to Fontana Dam the next day, although Tom had told us this was one of the most rugged sections on the entire trail. We got an early start, and with packs that were light because our food supply was low, we pushed on, going up and down the steepest mountains we had encountered so far. Some of the slopes were so steep we had to use small trees to pull ourselves up. We often found ourselves walking sideways because the trail was too steep for normal walking. We cursed ourselves up the slopes, took short rests on the summit, quickly hiked down to the next gap, and so on. It was sundown when we reached the highway to Fontana Village. A farmer who lived close to the trail took pity on us and drove us to the village.

We rented a cabin for the night and called our parents. The fact that everyone in the restaurant stared at us did not keep us from eating two five-course meals with two or three desserts. Back in our cabin we took long hot showers, made hot chocolate, and went to bed. In the morning we took more showers, had a big breakfast, and went to the laundromat. We picked up our box of food at the post office and purchased extra food and first-aid supplies. Because the box of food was so heavy and had come such a long way its contents were in fairly bad shape, so we spent much of the morning repackaging the food.

We needed a camping and fire permit for the Great Smoky Mountains National Park, but at the entrance to the park the ranger apologized, saying he had left his permits back at the ranger station. This made little difference for there was a forest fire and the ranger had orders not to allow anyone to travel in the direction we were going until the fire was under control. By the time everything was straightened out it was early evening and we decided to stay over until the following morning.

The next evening we found six people in the seven-man shelter. We decided that Gary was to have the unoccupied bunk, and I would share a bunk with a female hiker. I must admit that I was not cold that night, but I *was* a bit crowded and very uncomfortable. At Hot Springs, North Carolina, Gary telephoned Stow-A-Way and ordered a new pack. I called home to inquire about college acceptances or rejections, and it was decided that I would attend Dickinson College in Carlisle, Pennsylvania, in the fall. We hiked on over the mountains, stopping at fire towers to talk with the lookouts. These men knew every valley and every good spring for miles around. At Camp Creek

Bald Firetower the lookout showed us detailed maps of the trail and told us the names of the lookouts we would meet in the days ahead. He pointed out nests of hawks and areas of past fires, and told us about the condition of springs in the area.

The day we were to pick up food in Flag Pond, Tennessee, we ran into a rain and sleet storm. It was the first bad weather we had experienced in a long time. In the Smokies the weather had been beautiful. There hadn't even been any haze, and this was a most unusual condition for the Great Smoky Mountains. Gary and I had been hiking in cold rain, sleet, and lightning for hours when we arrived at a shelter just as Jim Wolf, a through hiker from Pittsburgh, was leaving. We talked with him for a while, then he went on and Gary and I took off our wet clothes, got into our sleeping bags, and fell asleep immediately. When we awoke it was just after noon and the rain had ended. We got back on the trail, hoping to reach Flag Pond by dark. I began to feel sick, and the trail seemed to grow steeper and muddier. By the time we reached the highway it was dark and cold. We stopped at a farmhouse to inquire about motels in Flag Pond and learned that Flag Pond was not really a town but merely a post office. The man was kind enough to drive us to Erwin, many miles past Flag Pond, and we got a motel room for the night. I was very sick all night long and in the morning I was barely able to get out of bed. Gary took a bus to Flag Pond to pick up our food while I stayed in the room. On the second morning I felt as if I could hike so we took a bus back to the trail. However, it was several days before I was able to hike well.

One evening we were forced by darkness to camp on top of Beauty Spot. Thunder sounded and lightning flashed and heavy rains fell all night, blowing in on us and soaking our sleeping bags. When we reached a shelter the next morning we decided to stop and dry our clothes and sleeping bags. The following day we struggled up Roan Mountain, one of the steepest climbs we had encountered. We were rewarded by spectacular views of Mt. Mitchell, the highest mountain in the eastern United States. We spent the night at a shelter just below Grassy Ridge. Gary hiked to the summit of the ridge but after the tough 17-mile day I could do little more than start the dinner fire. The following day we crossed the most beautiful of the grassy balds—Yellow Mountain and Hump Mountain. The balds, with few or no trees, afford unobstructed views of the surrounding mountains. We caught up with Jim Wolf at the White Rocks Mountain Firetower and hiked through Laurel Fork with him. Laurel Fork is a magnificent gorge with thundering cascades of clear water and sheer rock walls on each side. Gary and I climbed to a point high above the gorge to watch the unending cascades of white water.

For the next two days we hiked in the rain and averaged 15 miles a day. The weather cleared as we reached Damascus, a small place nestled among the Virginia mountains which had been described to us as the friendliest town on the trail. We stayed with a Mrs. Wright, who has rooms for Appalachian Trail hikers. We picked up our food and mail at the post office, washed our clothes, and cleaned our equipment and ourselves. Jim Wolf arrived during the evening. We got a late start the next day because I had to see a doctor about a stomach problem I was having. I waited two hours to see the doctor two minutes. He was unable to diagnose my stomach trouble; his only advice was that if the pains persisted I should see a doctor immediately. We left Damascus loaded with food for 11 days. We encountered heavy rains for the next few days and Gary became ill and my stomach was still not feeling good. We decided to spend two days at a shelter in the hope that we would recover and that the rain would stop.

At the Walker Mountain Firetower we watched the sun setting on the placid farming valley far below. It was moments like this that made the dull hours of hiking, the cold rains, and the long climbs worth the effort. For the next few days it rained. Gary began to feel sick again, so we hiked only six or eight miles a day, spending the nights at shelters so we could stay as dry as possible. In the small town of Crandon we purchased extra food and talked with the store owners about the through hikers who had stopped there over the years. They mentioned the Skinners, who had hiked the trail several years before us, and Art Smith, a college student who was several weeks ahead of us on his way to Mt. Katahdin. He had come into the store during a snowstorm, very cold and out of food.

Outside of Pearisburg the trail followed a dirt road and, according to our map, turned left toward a ridge. We saw no double blazes indicating a turn so we continued along the dirt road. Finally we inquired at a house and were told that the trail had been changed but that the old blazes had not yet been removed. The old trail was interesting but it did not get us back on the present trail for at least 20 miles. The following day we hiked 20 miles to Niday Shelter and then went to Catawba, a small town just off the trail, where we were picked up by my friends, the Adamses. We spent a day at the Adamses' home, washing clothes, making equipment repairs, and checking food and guidebooks and maps. I had my packframe welded. Gary's boots were worn out, but after shopping around he decided to have his brother mail him another pair of boots like the ones he was wearing.

We hiked on through the Blue Ridge Mountains in the George Washington National Forest. The forest was a bit more rugged than we had expected as the trail dipped into valleys and then climbed to the ridgetops. On Long Mountain, near Snowden, on a climb of over 2,000 feet from the James River, we encountered rain, fog, and high winds. The weather cleared the following day as we hiked up Priest Mountain and from its 4,000-foot summit descended to the Tye River, making the day's hike about 20 miles. On the day we were to go into Waynesboro, Virginia, we hiked hard through the constant rain, up and down steep muddy hills, trying to get to the post office before it closed. At a Holiday Inn we asked how far it was to Waynesboro, explaining that we had come from Georgia on the Appalachian Trail and were en route to Mt. Katahdin in Maine. We were tired, dirty, and wet after hiking for hours in the rain. The people were very kind and gave us a ride to Waynesboro. We reached the post office 20 minutes before closing time. We picked up our food, mail, and Gary's boots, rented an inexpensive room, took hot showers, and had a long night's sleep.

The next morning we awoke to the sound of rain. The rain came down so hard the streets of Waynesboro were flooded. We decided to take a bus back to the trail, but we missed the bus, so our prospects for getting back on the trail that day didn't look good. In the bus station we saw a notice to the effect that anyone needing help should call an organization known as FISH. Gary called, and in 15 minutes a man and his son drove up in a station wagon and took us back to the trail.

We hiked 10 miles in 3½ hours and arrived at the southernmost shelter in the Shenandoah National Park. It rained hard all night and the stream which flowed past the shelter had swelled to a torrent by morning. We hiked only 10 miles in fog and drizzle that day, and the next morning, after hiking about six miles, Gary asked what I thought about the possibility of our splitting up. Gary said he realized that at the rate we were hiking I wouldn't complete the trail before I was due at college. We finally decided that splitting up would be best for both of us. It was not that we were not getting along. On the contrary, we were getting along exceptionally well, but Gary felt that he would be rushing the hike if he tried to finish by the end of summer. He wanted to spend more time at the interesting points along the trail. We were, at this point, about 10 days behind schedule.

We made camp early that day and split up our equipment as best we could. Gary was to go home, divide the food we still had there, purchase some new equipment, and come back to the trail and hike at his own pace. We wished each other good luck as Gary headed for the highway and I continued on. I hiked 19 miles that day, making camp at South River Shelter. The following morning I called home. My mother told me Gary had arrived late the night before. Because I now had quite a bit of experience, my parents said I could continue the hike alone if I wanted to. I had already decided to continue, and promised my parents I would call them every time I picked up food.

For the next few days I hiked 20 miles a day and enjoyed the beauty of the Shenandoah National Park. I was warned by several hikers about a bear at Elk Wallow Shelter. When I arrived at the shelter I found notes from hikers who had had their food stolen, packs torn, and sleep disturbed by the bear. I strung my pack from the rafters and made my bed on the top bunk. There was a picnic table in the entrance to the shelter and I wedged sticks between the table and the shelter walls, hoping the bear would make enough noise to awaken me if he tried to enter the shelter. A doe stayed around that evening, coming within 20 feet of me as I ate dinner. At about 4:00 A.M. I was awakened by a sound. At first I thought it was the doe, then I saw a bear roaming around in front of the shelter, less than 40 feet from my bunk. After a time he moved off and I went back to sleep.

I hiked swiftly through the remainder of Virginia and into West Virginia, averaging 22 miles a day. I arrived at the Potomac River, spent the night at a youth hostel, and in the morning got a ride into Harpers Ferry, which was my next food stop. It was still early so I took a tour of the town before the tourists arrived. I hiked up to Jefferson Rock and had a beautiful view up and down the river. I picked up my food and mail, washed clothing, bought additional food, and was back on the trail by early afternoon. High on a ridge I was caught in a rainstorm accompanied by a great deal of lightning. I felt like I was going to be struck by lightning at any moment, but fortunately I was only soaked by the rain. I crossed into Pennsylvania, still averaging 22 miles a day and feeling very confident now that I had completed the southern half of the trail. I breezed through Caledonia State Park, and the day before I crossed the Cumberland Valley I put in a long 27-mile day. I found the Cumberland Valley very interesting, and spent some time watching the farmers at work in their fields. Several times during the day showers cooled off the roads, which the trail followed for a long distance across the valley.

Jim Ross, who was also hiking the trail from Georgia to Maine, came into the shelter where I was staying that night. He told me he had been seeing my name in the trail registers all the way from Georgia. Jim was a cross-country runner at Bates College in Maine, where he went to school, and he planned to hike the trail in 100 days. I learned later that he had accomplished this goal. We spent the remainder of the day talking about our trail experiences, and hiked into Duncannon together the following morning. After consuming large breakfasts we picked up our mail and I went to do my laundry and Jim went to find a motel. In the early afternoon I headed back for the trail and arrived at Clarks Creek Valley Shelter just as the rain began to fall heavily. To my dismay I discovered that the shelter had collapsed. Fortunately, the roof was resting on what remained of the walls and I managed to crawl under it and get out of the rain. Less than an hour later Jim joined me. When he read his mail back in Duncannon he had learned that his girl friend planned to meet him at Delaware Water Gap. In order to be there on time he would have to average 35 miles a day for the next four days.

It rained all night and was still raining in the morning when Jim left. It didn't look as if the rain was going to stop so I finally took off, too. I hiked all day with feet soaked and glasses fogged—going along country roads, up two 1,000-foot climbs, and along wet slippery rocky ridges. The wetter I got the more determined I was to get to the next shelter that evening. It was almost dark when I arrived, but I was glad I had kept going for I was cheered up immensely by the group of hikers who were already at the shelter.

The next day I hiked to Port Clinton, picked up extra food, and went on for 28 miles, trying to make up for lost time. In Delaware Water Gap I slept on a picnic table and had to fight off the largest swarm of mosquitoes I had ever encountered. I wanted to get to the Hudson River, 100 miles away, in 3½ to 4 days. I took just enough food for four days and left without even bothering to wash my clothes. I was headed up toward Sunfish Pond when I heard a rattling sound and glanced down to see a 3½-foot rattlesnake. It looked huge to me. I jumped back, but the snake appeared to be very sluggish so I cautiously approached and made sure that it was indeed a rattlesnake. The snake did not appear to want to move from its sunny position. I wanted to be on my way but was not willing to step off into the brush because I thought there might be other snakes about. I tossed small stones until the snake eventually slithered off into the brush.

I stayed at Stokes Lean-to that evening, having covered about 25 miles. The following morning I got an early start and hiked all day, stopping every hour for a short rest. It was late when I finally made camp in a field, had a cold meal, and quickly fell asleep. The next morning I got an early start, knowing that I had to do about 35 miles. It was hot and I carried as much as two quarts of water. I was drinking about a pint and a half every 45 minutes. I hiked by moonlight for a while and finally slept in the open by Lake Tiorati. In the morning an easy 4-hour, 12-mile hike brought me to the Hudson River. I had averaged 20 miles a day for about a month and was three days ahead of schedule.

I spent two days at home and bought several pieces of equipment, including a Bleuet stove and two plastic canteens. The canteen I had been using had developed a fungal growth which I was unable to eliminate. On the afternoon of the third day my mother, father, and I drove to Bear Mountain and had a picnic before I went back on the trail. I averaged about 17 miles a day through New York and Connecticut. I found this country rather bland but serene. I was warned by a group of Boy Scouts that there was no water at Chase Mountain Lean-to so I filled a plastic water bottle with four quarts of water. I also filled my canteen, and with all of this added weight I climbed to the lean-to. The next day I hiked 17 miles, passing through a pleasantly forested area and over several barren rocky areas. I camped about two miles beyond Cornwall Bridge, Connecticut, in an area with many waterfalls. Just as I finished dinner it began to rain. I took advantage of the situation and went out into the rain and took a bath.

For the next two days I hiked through a number of old pine and hemlock stands. I climbed Barrack Mountain, Lions Head, and Bear Mountain, the highest mountain in Connecticut, and that evening I camped in the beautiful Sages Ravine, which was timbered with hemlocks and fed by a clear rushing stream. In the morning I crossed into Massachusetts, hiking over rough terrain. A family invited me to have lunch with them as I passed their home, and I answered many questions about my trip. I arrived at the place where I had planned to stay, but couldn't find either a shelter or a water source. (Later I was told that the shelter had burned down.) I pushed on and arrived at Mt. Wilcox Lean-to after an exhausting 26 miles.

According to the guidebook the water at October Mountain Lean-to was not suitable for drinking. Hikers were advised to get water at the home of Mrs. Fred Hutchinson, about a mile up the road. Mrs. Hutchinson had me sign her register, and spoke of the many Appalachian Trail hikers she had met over the years. She had a scrapbook in which she kept letters and newspaper clippings from long-distance hikers who had stopped at her home. She invited me to camp in her backyard, and in the morning had breakfast waiting for me. I promised to write to her when I finished the trail, and we corresponded several times. Less than two miles from Mrs. Hutchinson's house my right foot began to hurt rather badly. When I took off my boot I found that the toenail on my big toe was digging into the flesh. I knew that if this condition persisted it might end my trip. I forced cotton between the toenail and the skin, coated the area with an antibiotic cream to prevent infection, and bandaged the toe so pressure from the boot wouldn't make the condition any worse.

Several miles from the summit of Mt. Greylock a savage thunderstorm came up. I made it to Kitchen Brook Lean-to, having hiked almost 23 miles. I reached the summit of Mt. Greylock, at 8:30 the next morning, spent some time enjoying the solitude and the magnificent views, then hiked down to the highway and got a ride to Williamstown, Massachusetts, my next food stop. I was back on the trail in a matter of hours, and spent the night at a beautiful shelter on Vermont's Long Trail, which coincides with the Appalachian Trail for some 90 miles.

One day I stopped for lunch at Willis Ross Lake, which was magnificent with its border of towering pines and dense stands of ancient hemlocks. The lake was a beautiful blue and contrasted spectacularly with the dark greens of the forest and the blues, greens, and grays of the surrounding mountains. Along here I met a hiker whose name I had been seeing in the registers all the way from Georgia. He and a friend had left Springer Mountain about three weeks before me and I had not expected to meet him. He told me that he and his friend had split up and that he was slowing down. We talked for a couple of hours, then I pushed on and camped at Mad Tom Shelter. Although I had hiked only 15 miles, I decided to stop at Stony Brook Lean-to the next day because the area was so beautiful. I hadn't been at the shelter long when a large group of noisy children and their adult leaders arrived. I decided I wouldn't enjoy the area with so much noise, so I hiked on. In another five miles I came to Greenwall Shelter, making the day's total some 20 miles.

Jim Rutter, who had started at Mt. Katahdin and was on his way to Springer Mountain, was at the shelter. We exchanged suggestions, warnings, and experiences. The next morning I hiked to a nearby town to pick up extra food. I stayed at Governor Clement Shelter that evening, having hiked only 14 miles. The following day, after going 7 miles, I came to Pico Camp, an enclosed cabin with magnificent views of several of Vermont's largest mountains from its windows. I decided it was worth losing some hiking time to enjoy the scenery here. Late in the afternoon it began to rain, and before dark, as the rain increased, a group from a camp came to the shelter. That night there were 21 people sleeping on the table, under the table, and on the floor.

I arrived in Hanover, New Hampshire, after hiking 16 miles in five hours. At the Dartmouth Outing Club I was invited to use the shower room and given maps showing trail relocations. Later in the day I met a hiker whose feet had been giving him trouble so he was stopping at a nearby Dartmouth cabin. It looked like rain so I decided to stop, too. The rain fell heavily as we got into our sleeping bags, and we were both glad to be in the cabin.

We hiked about 14 miles the following day. It was a long steep climb up Smarts Mountain but well worth it for the magnificent view. Sitting in front of the Smarts Mountain Lean-to we looked out at the sunset over miles and miles of bluish-green mountains. That evening Mike, the fire warden, invited us to his cabin and we sipped tea and talked by lantern light. The next morning we climbed the tower with Mike and he pointed out the surrounding mountains, which included Mt. Moosilauke and Mt. Washington. Just as we were about to leave Mike spotted a small fire. A crew was sent into the area and the fire, which was thought to have been started by lightning, was soon extinguished. We congratulated Mike on his work and went on our way.

On the summit of Mt. Cube a storm blew up, with gusting winds and sweeping rain, and we arrived at Armington Camp in miserable condition. The Dartmouth Outing Club trail crew was staying at the cabin while working on trails in the area. We dried out and enjoyed good food, a warm fire, and a comfortable sleep as the rain pounded down through the cold night. The next day we hiked 14 miles to Great Bear Cabin. The following morning I left early and headed for the summit of Moosilauke. Above timberline visibility was bad and it was cool and gusty. The trail down the mountain was flooded with water and very slippery. Some sections of the slope had wooden ladders and cables to help the hiker.

I knew I was in for some rough hiking once I got into the White Mountains. Mt. Wolf was very tough; the trail was steep, narrow, and rocky. South Kinsman Mountain was the steepest rockiest mountain I had ever seen. The six-foot ledges offered no footing at times and I had to detour around them through the thick growth at the side of the trail. I spent the night at Kinsman Pond Shelter, exhausted by the day's hike although it was only 11 miles.

The following morning I hiked down to Franconia Notch and

quickly ascended to Liberty Spring. I rested there, enjoying the cold refreshing spring water. I continued to climb to the summit of Little Haystack Mountain at 4,500 feet. From this point the trail crossed a rocky ridge and went up Mt. Lincoln. The view from the summit of Mt. Lincoln was disappointing because of the haze and low cloud cover. However, it did afford a splendid view of the mountains in front of and behind me along the ridge. I ate lunch on the summit of Mt. Lafayette, having hiked a bit over nine miles. After lunch the trail was much rougher than I had expected but I pushed on, climbing steeply up the rocky trail over Mt. Garfield. I was exhausted by the 15-mile hike, and felt like I had been climbing all day instead of hiking.

The next morning visibility was poor as I began a difficult climb up South Twin Mountain. I could see nothing except the trail in front of me. I crossed over Mt. Guyot and at the Zealand Falls Hut it started to rain. By nightfall, when I arrived at Ethan Pond Shelter, I was wet, hungry, and exhausted. I had a good hot dinner and a good night's rest, but in the morning I was still tired from the previous day's hike of over 25 miles. The climb up Webster Cliffs from Crawford Notch put the climb of South Twin Mountain to shame. I stopped at Mt. Jackson for a snack and a long rest. The hike to Mizpah Spring Hut was not bad so I decided to push on. The visibility was so poor I could see nothing as I went on over Mt. Franklin and Mt. Monroe to Lakes-of-the-Clouds Hut.

The next morning I was feeling sick and got a late start. The weather had turned bad, and I had high gusty winds and poor visibility as I ascended to the summit of Mt. Washington. On the summit, according to the weather observatory, the winds were gusting to 40 miles an hour and the temperature was about 45° F. I decided to make camp at the first likely location. I hiked past Mt. Clay and skirted the summit of Mt. Jefferson, and finally spent the night in the emergency shelter in Edmands Col. I was very sick all night and felt no better the following morning. Several people stopped at the shelter and offered their help, but I told them I thought I would feel better after more sleep. I slept most of the day, eating and drinking very little.

The following morning I was still too weak to hike. I sat out in the sun, writing in my diary and thinking about my hike. The next morning I felt good and was on the trail by 6:30 A.M., climbing over Mt. Adams and Mt. Madison and getting excellent views from both mountains. I thought I would feel weak but I didn't so I pushed on, arriving in Pinkham Notch for a late lunch. I climbed to the summit of

Wildcat Mountain after passing over a number of small peaks, the Wild Kittens. I camped in Carter Notch that night, and in the morning, starting in the cool of predawn, climbed steeply out of Carter Notch to the summit of Carter Dome. At Imp Shelter I rested. The Carter Range had taken more out of me than I realized.

By early afternoon, after hiking about 12.5 miles in 7.5 hours, I arrived at Rattle River Shelter. I went on out to the highway and got a ride to Gorham, New Hampshire, where I picked up my food, washed clothes, and mailed postcards and letters. I got back to the shelter, had an early dinner, and was asleep before sunset. I awoke before sunrise, ate a quick breakfast, and was on the trail before the sun rose. The sky became overcast as I stopped for lunch at Gentian Pond, and I climbed Mt. Success in heavy fog. I crossed into Maine, and went over Mt. Carlo and the East Peak of Mt. Goose Eye in fog so thick that I could see no more than 30 feet ahead. I fell several times on the ledges as I descended from Goose Eye, and had a difficult time staying on the trail up the North Peak of Goose Eye. At Full Goose Shelter I decided to push on and camp nearer to Mahoosuc Notch.

The next morning, still feeling tired from the strenuous 20-mile hike of the previous day, I started through Mahoosuc Notch. A light rain began to fall, and I had been told that this was the worst thing that could happen to a hiker going through the notch. Mahoosuc Notch was a most interesting area, being closed in by what appeared in the fog to be almost sheer rock walls. It was strewn with massive boulders, many of them 10 feet high and 10 to 20 feet in length. The trail went over, under, and around these boulders. Underneath the boulders there were ice caves, and water flowed around the ice. I clawed my way over these massive boulders and slipped up and down muddy little hills in the cold rain. Several times I was forced to remove my pack, slide through cracks between the boulders, and drag my pack after me. About halfway through the notch I slipped on a muddy section of trail and fell backwards, landing with my pack in a crevice. I managed to grab a small tree and pulled myself out of the mud, cursing the slippery trail and the continuing rain. I finally got through the notch, a distance of less than a mile, in about two hours. Slipping and falling, I climbed Mahoosuc Arm. When I reached Speck Pond Shelter I decided to stay, although I had hiked only 4.5 miles. The following morning the sun was shining and my spirits were much better. I climbed Old Speck and took a side trip to the summit to see the view from the fire tower before starting down. Old Speck is supposed to be the steepest mountain on the trail as it descends some

2,600 feet in just over a mile and a half. I fell several times on the descent, and lost the heel from one of my boots.

At Frye Brook Lean-to it rained all night and was still drizzling the next morning. It was not a difficult hike to Squirrel Rock Lean-to but much of the time the trail went through shoulder-high wet grass. During the late afternoon, while I was resting in the shelter, it began to rain heavily. The rain lasted for several hours. At dark the rain stopped, but as I was falling asleep it began to rain again. In the morning, with wet boots and socks, I pushed on. It drizzled all morning. I lost the trail and followed an old woods road for about half an hour. Discovering my mistake, I retraced my steps and got back on the trail. At Elephant Mountain Lean-to I was greeted by another heavy thunderstorm. Rain fell for the remainder of the day and well into the evening. I had not seen anyone for five days and I was beginning to believe that the rain would never stop.

The following day, August 4, was my nineteenth birthday. I ascended Bemis Mountain in the dim early morning light, trying not to hike too fast as the trail was very slippery. I did fall, however, and cut my hand—but it was not a serious cut. At Sabbath Day Pond Lean-to I met two boys a year younger than myself who were out for several days of fishing. They had a lot of food, and upon learning that it was my birthday they cooked steak and made a fresh salad for dinner. I contributed a gingerbread cake topped with chocolate I had been saving for my birthday celebration.

The next morning the sky was clear and my spirits were high as I hiked through relatively level country. At Piazza Rock Lean-to it rained all night and when I got on the trail at six o'clock the sky was overcast. On the long ascent of Saddleback Mountain the sky darkened, and as I came out on the open face of the mountain the wind was gusting with such force that it was difficult to walk. Descending from Saddleback I fell and broke the clevis pin that held one of the shoulder straps to my packframe. With numbed hands I managed to replace the pin with a spare I carried and continued on over The Horn and Saddleback Junior. Just before I descended from Saddleback Junior the clouds disappeared and I got a magnificent view of the surrounding mountains. I had a clear sky for a while, but before I reached Poplar Ridge Lean-to it began to rain again.

The sky was still dark in the morning as I moved on. Because of the rain, Orbeton Stream was more like a swollen river than a stream. The trail climbed steadily, with many of the blazes obliterated by recent logging operations. I spent the night at Spaulding Mountain Lean-to with a group of kids from a nearby summer camp and got an early start the next morning, spurred on by the clear sky and cool air. From Spaulding Mountain I had excellent views of the mountains I had climbed the past few days, and also of Mt. Sugarloaf, which rose straight in front of me, an almost perfect cone. The ascent of Sugarloaf was rather easy even though the trail was running with water. From the summit I could see the rugged and beautiful Bigelow Range ahead. At the highway I got a ride to Stratton, but as it was Sunday I had to get a room and wait until the following morning for the post office to open. I washed my clothes, took several showers, and rested.

The ascent to The Horns Pond was difficult under the weight of my new food supply. I pushed on, however, enjoying the good weather. The ascent and descent of Little Bigelow Mountain was very tiring. When I came to a dirt road early in the evening I took a long rest before going on to Jerome Brook Lean-to. It was nearly dark when I arrived at the lean-to and I spent very little time in eating and getting to sleep. The next morning I met a hiker who was hiking from Mt. Katahdin to Grafton Notch, and a bit later I passed a girl with a large German shepherd dog who was also hiking south. I pushed on toward the Kennebec River and at a new shelter four miles short of the river I met several hikers who had tried unsuccessfully to wade across the Kennebec River. Two girls, Helen and Patti, who had hiked from Stratton, had arranged for a boat to take them across the river the next afternoon. They were from Summit, New Jersey, and were on vacation before leaving for college in the fall.

In the morning I arose before dawn and said good-bye to Patti, who was the only person awake. I had heard that the Kennebec River could be waded if the hiker went several hundred yards upstream from where the trail reached the river. I had been warned that the current was strong and logs were floated down it after eight o'clock in the morning. When I got to the river it was not yet seven o'clock. I wasted no time in lashing two logs together, wrapping my pack in my tarp, and securing it to the logs. I planned to cross the river wearing only short pants and boots, so I took off my socks and shirt. I also cut a heavy pole, as I had been told that a pole was a necessity. I tied a line from the log raft to my waist. Without the weight of the pack I thought I could easily get back on my feet if I fell, and with the raft tied to me, I was sure to be with my pack, wherever it went.

I started across, fighting the swift current. At midpoint the water was still no higher than my waist, but the current became swifter. I found it difficult to plant the pole firmly on the slippery rock bottom of the river, and difficult to maintain my footing. At one point I slipped and went under, but managed to hold on to my pole. I finally got out of the main flow of the current and made my way to shore. The pack had gone under water several times and most of my equipment, including my sleeping bag, was wet. I had not eaten breakfast because I was afraid I might get cramps while crossing the river, so in Caratunk I bought doughnuts and fresh orange juice at the grocery store. Several people, seeing that I was a hiker and also soaking wet, remarked on how wet the river had been lately. It was a comment I did not find very funny at the time.

I arrived at Pleasant Pond Mountain Lean-to around lunchtime and decided to stay. It looked like rain and I wanted to dry my sleeping bag and clothes. Late in the afternoon it rained heavily. Helen and Patti arrived at the shelter looking very wet and very tired. They had been ferried across the river in the rain and had hiked from Caratunk in more rain. The three of us spent the next night at a lean-to with Ron, a hiker who was heading south. Patti had been having trouble with her feet so Ron and I performed minor surgery on her blisters. The next morning I hiked over Moxie Bald Mountain and on to Breakneck Ridge Lean-to. Patti and Helen arrived about an hour and a half later and we had dinner together. We had planned to go to sleep early but Patti and Helen had a habit of laughing for long periods of time, and acting afraid of every sound in the dark—most of this fear being much overdramatized.

The next morning at Monson I found several packages and letters waiting for me. My brother had sent me a beautiful spinning rod, reel, and accessories, and I had a letter from the Appalachian Trail Conference congratulating me for a nearly finished trip. Patti and Helen were waiting to be picked up by Helen's parents. I met a Canadian hiker, Ross Rolands, and we hiked together and camped at Long Pond Stream Lean-to. I caught two good-sized rainbow trout which we ate for dinner.

A few days later, less than 50 miles from Mt. Katahdin, I hiked out to Nahmakanta Lake Camps and tried to purchase food. The owner of the camps apologized, saying he was nearly out of supplies himself, but he did give me some small Maine potatoes which he had grown. He wouldn't accept any money so I thanked him and hiked on. At Rainbow Lake Lean-to I met a boy and girl who had more food than they needed and they insisted that I eat whatever I wished.

I got my first view of Mt. Katahdin from Rainbow Ledges, and at the Abol Bridge Campsite store I purchased food and feasted that evening in celebration of seeing the mountain I had traveled 2,000 miles to climb. The following day, hiking the 10 miles to Katahdin Stream Campground, I stopped several times to swim and sit in the sun. I arrived at the campground in late afternoon, and it rained during the night and the next morning. I had planned to climb Mt. Katahdin but the trails were closed because of the bad weather. My father and two sisters arrived and we spent the day fishing.

The following morning I began the ascent of Mt. Katahdin. Visibility was poor and it was rather cool. I stopped for a snack on The Tableland, and then continued on toward Baxter Peak, the end of the trail. When I saw the sign marking the summit, which I had seen in many pictures, I began to run toward it. At last, after 4½ months of hiking, I had finished the entire Appalachian Trail—some 2,000 miles through 14 states!

The Appalachian Trail is a tribute to all of the people who have worked to make it possible. For the most part I found the condition of the shelters and the trail very good. I only regret that there are some people who abuse the wilderness through carelessness, and others who would like to abuse it in the name of progress. The Appalachian Trail gave me a chance to learn more about myself and about others—some good things and some bad. The trail meant a great deal to me not merely because I hiked along it but because I was able to live it. Life on the trail is more natural than most people are able to experience in their ordinary existence. I lived through snow, sleet, and days of cold rain, but I lived free, the way I think people ought to live. I learned to be alone but not lonely. I learned what it meant to be on my own, and how good mountain spring water tasted, and how precious a deep breath of cool air can be when you have struggled to reach a mountain peak.

"There is beauty and one needs to find it.
There is also a silence of hearts and desire
    and if one can find that also, then that is enough.
And there are moments that begin and end but never cease
    and we will have them forever."

—Patricia Fairfield, Cloud Pond Lean-to
Appalachian Trail, August 27, 1970

Some Questions and Answers

Question: When did you start hiking?

BRUCE BALDERSTON: The longest hike I had undertaken prior to hiking the Appalachian Trail was a 100-mile hike through the White Mountains over a 12-day period during the summer of 1969. I had been hiking for about six years before hiking the Appalachian Trail, but rather short ventures only.

BRADLEY W. GREULING: I started to "long hike" when I was about 14, although the family went camping before that. I was about five or six when I first went day-hiking with my family. We camped and hiked all over the Presidential Range.

JEFFREY HANCOCK: I began hiking at the age of four or five when my parents took me with them on a walk through the foothills of Mt. Chocorua from Tamworth, New Hampshire.

RICHARD HUDSON: Since about age 9 or 10 I had gone on solo trips starting in Indiana state parks and then on vacations to the Great Smokies.

CHARLES KONOPA: Although I'd hiked before, my first serious hiking began when I started on the Appalachian Trail.

THOMAS MCKONE: I started hiking when I was in sixth grade—11 years ago—when a group of my friends and I started making day hikes in a nearby state park. Although we often got a ride one or both ways to the park, we sometimes hiked the eight miles to the park, spent the day hiking in the park, and then hiked the eight miles home. So you see I did my first 20-mile day long before I started the Appalachian Trail—and I did it in sneakers, no less.

MARGARET SMITH: We've been hiking our whole lives but a greater emphasis was placed on hiking about six years ago in preparation for our first attempt at hiking the Appalachian Trail. We started to hike the trail in 1968 but failed when I developed arthritis in my left knee

1867

after completing only 120 miles. From 1968 until 1970 we often hiked to keep in shape for we knew we would try again.

NED SMITH: I started hiking in 1970 as a part of ski club summer activities. We hiked almost all of the Appalachian Trail in Georgia that summer.

BRIAN WINCHESTER: My first hike was a two-day hike into the Everglades, primarily to try out equipment and break in my boots. This was about three weeks before beginning the Appalachian Trail, and was the only hiking I had ever done.

ROBERT WINSLOW: While riding high on top of my father's shoulders, I attained my first summit, Whiteface Mountain in the Adirondacks, at the ripe old age of 14 months. I guess I must have liked what I saw as I've been climbing ever since.

Question: When did you first hear of the Appalachian Trail?

WALTER BOARDMAN: In 1938, while walking the trails of Bear Mountain State Park, I noted a reference to the Appalachian Trail.

GENE FIDUCIA: The first time I was really aware of the Appalachian Trail was about a month before I started my hike.

RICHARD HUDSON: My first walk on the trail was at Bear Mountain, New York, with my mother. We wanted to go from the Bear Mountain Inn to the summit, but not knowing about the white blazes, we lost the trail and didn't make it to the top.

CHARLES KONOPA: From a casual reference in some outdoor magazine. I've never ceased to be surprised that so few people know about this splendid trail.

THOMAS MCKONE: I first heard of the Appalachian Trail only a few months before I started my hike. I was fascinated with the idea of a foot trail running 2,000 miles from Georgia to Maine and immediately decided I wanted to hike it. I wrote to the Appalachian Trail Conference for information, ignorantly inquiring if anyone had ever hiked the whole trail.

JAMES RUTTER: I first heard of the Appalachian Trail on one of our family's yearly vacations. We crossed the trail and my father mentioned that it went all the way to Georgia. The idea intrigued me.

BRIAN WINCHESTER: In the fall of 1971 I started to feel restless. Figuring that I might hitch to various national parks and hike about in them, I started to look into the idea. Leafing through a *National Geographic* I happened to come across a reference, only a few lines long, to the Appalachian Trail. Right then I knew that was it!

Question: How much hiking had you done before you decided to hike the entire trail?

BRUCE BALDERSTON: Prior to hiking the trail I had hiked with the Boy Scouts during the summers.

HOWARD E. BASSETT: According to my records, I had hiked a total of 1,605 miles before I started on the Appalachian Trail.

GENE FIDUCIA: I had no hiking experience before I decided to hike the entire trail.

JAMES FOX: Quite a bit. At the University of Maryland we went hiking, caving, or climbing every other weekend or so.

EDWARD GARVEY: I had hiked on the Appalachian Trail and connecting trails from 1952 until 1969. Had hiked 700–800 miles of the Appalachian Trail.

ANDREW GIGER: I had hiked the Muir Trail in California, and in the Grand Tetons, Yosemite National Park, and the Coast Range in California. I had also been on many weekend and day hikes, and had climbed several California peaks: Mt. Whitney, Mt. Olancha, Mt. San Gorgonio, Mt. Diablo, Mt. Lassen, and Mt. Owens.

BRADLEY W. GREULING: Before I hiked the entire trail, I had gone on only one two-week trip with my brother Bruce. Before that I had gone on a few overnight and many day trips.

RICHARD HUDSON: Frequent day trips but few overnight.

CHARLES KONOPA: I didn't decide to complete the trail until the spring of 1970, a half-dozen years after I first set foot on it. By then I'd hiked over 1,000 miles on the Appalachian Trail and several thousand miles on other trails.

GARNETT MARTIN: Since the 1920s I've been taking short hikes. As for backpacking, I made a three-day hike in the Rockies just west of Denver to test my equipment and food for the Appalachian Trail. I had never been on the Appalachian Trail or even seen it before I started my through hike.

THOMAS MCKONE: For 11 years I had been a year-round day hiker and, more recently, a snowshoer. I went backpacking only once before starting the Appalachian Trail: Bob Winslow and I went on a two-day backpacking trip to try out our equipment. The trip was a total disaster; we could not get the stove started, and we forgot to bring pads to put under our sleeping bags although there was snow on the ground. Our boots froze, and we made only half the distance we started out to make. In two days we covered only 10 miles and had to hitchhike home. We charged this off to inexperience and started on the Appalachian Trail anyway.

BILL O'BRIEN: I had been hiking for about 13 years. My longest previous trip was for one week.

BRANLEY OWEN: About 6,000 miles.

JAMES RUTTER: The only other hiking I'd done were day trips in the White Mountains.

JIM SHATTUCK: I had done virtually no hiking before I decided to hike the entire Appalachian Trail.

Question: Why did you hike the entire trail?

BRUCE BALDERSTON: I hiked the Appalachian Trail because I wanted to be out in the wilderness for an extended period of time, because I was bored with high school, and because the trail presented a challenge, both physically and mentally.

HOWARD E. BASSETT: Because (a) I had all the time in the world, (b) I wanted to photograph the beautiful scenery along it, (c) my first wife had passed away and I wanted to "get hold of myself" again. It was good therapy.

WALTER BOARDMAN: Because it was there. What was beyond the immediate view? I had no idea of hiking the entire trail until several hundred miles had been covered during vacation walks. There was the appeal of wild-land walking without the problem of trespass. The continuity of the footway also had appeal. It was only after covering over half the total distance that serious thought was given to completion of the 2,000 miles.

CHUCK EBERSOLE: The years seemed to build up a greater and greater desire to see the good earth and all the wondrous things she had to show. My stock answer as to why I hiked such a lengthy trail was that there were a lot of trees I hadn't seen yet. The true answer was that I wanted to see everything that nature had to offer to the sight of a man eager and hungry to know her real self. This included trees, rocks, soil, birds, bugs, insects, bushes, tiny plants, worms, flowers, bud forms, the sky, clouds, storms, rainbows, waterfalls, falling rain, snow, sunrises, sunsets, twigs, branches, leaves, the way a bird sings, the sound of the wind through the trees, the roar of a storm, the bolting flashes of lightning, the sound of thunder as the hills rolled the sound around, walking in the rain, frost crystals, sunshine, the shapes and configurations of all mountains and hills and tree limbs and anything else etched against the sky, the earthy smells of wet soil, boggy places, fresh mint teas and herbs, and the sounds of creepy things in the night as well as slithery snake sounds over dry leaves by day, a beaver gnawing on sticks, the cry of a loon across the mist of a lake, the drumming of a forest grouse in springtime courtship, the gobble of a wild turkey, the bleat of a deer, the sight of turtles and salamanders, and the face of America in every single thing I looked at. That's how the trail called me.

GENE FIDUCIA: I didn't know what I was getting into when I decided to hike the entire trail. I had no idea what it would be like, but I thought it might be a fine way to spend a few months. It would give me a chance to see America in a way that I might never have again, and see a part of it that few people have seen. I wanted to do something I had never done before, to accept a challenge. I guess I could sum it up by saying I wanted to live a dream, to be an explorer in an age when there is less and less wilderness to explore.

JAMES FOX: Mostly to do something big, do it well, and succeed. Probably also to prove to myself that I *could* do it.

BRADLEY W. GREULING: I hiked the entire trail because it was a challenge, and I had the time and money at the same time. Also, my family and friends had always talked of doing it "some day."

JEFFREY HANCOCK: Hiking had become my dominant interest. Walking the trail seemed like the perfect way to see as much of the country as possible and practice my hiking. From the start I planned to hike the whole trail.

CHARLES KONOPA: For the satisfaction of completing the world's longest continuous marked footpath.

DOROTHY LAKER: The trail became like an absorbing book that refused to be set aside and finished another day. Each state the trail crossed was like a chapter in that book, and although it was possible to tell, very early, what might be expected farther along the way, there was no way to know for sure. And the uncertainty was the lure leading the walker on to the final chapter to discover how everything actually turned out.

GARNETT MARTIN: Hiking the Appalachian Trail was one of the projects in my overall plan for seeing some of the horizons beyond.

THOMAS MCKONE: This is the hardest question to answer. Even now I do not know exactly why I wanted to hike the Appalachian Trail. I just wanted to hike it. Perhaps it was the adventure of jumping into something big that I knew nothing about. Part of it was being close to nature. Part of it was getting away from school for a while. A great part of it was being in the mountains for a long period of time. But the most precise answer to this question is that it is unanswerable; anyone who has to ask this question will not understand the answer, anyway.

BILL O'BRIEN: I had done parts of the Appalachian Trail before, and wanted to see the whole thing while it was still there and I was still here.

JAMES RUTTER: I hiked the trail to see the country, to meet people, to build endurance for other sports, and because hiking is a favorite sport of mine.

JIM SHATTUCK: The idea had intrigued me ever since I first heard of the Appalachian Trail. Also, in 1966 I was 51 years old and between jobs, and it looked like my last chance.

CLIFFORD AND MARGARET SMITH: One reason was to observe the wilderness and another was to prove that we were physically capable of completing such a hike. A third reason was to get away from monotony.

BRIAN WINCHESTER: There is no simple answer. In the planning stages it simply seemed the thing to do, and one cannot be sure how long the mountains will be left unspoiled. Looking deeper, I know that I was searching for the reason for *my* life. The simpler, down-to-earth lifestyle has enormous appeal to me, so I wanted to find out if that was *my* answer.

ROBERT WINSLOW: There were many reasons. There was the uniqueness, the opportunity to learn, to live simply, to confront the essentials of life, and to live close to nature where I function best. Most of all, I went for the simple joy of it.

JAMES WOLF: My reasons for hiking the entire Appalachian Trail were:

(a) the personal challenge of achieving a goal notwithstanding adversity, of testing my perseverance and self-reliance—an "ego trip," as a fellow hiker described it; (b) the feeling of freedom from customary obligations of work and city living, the relaxation of a real vacation; (c) deepening my awareness and appreciation of all forms of life—an educational as well as an aesthetic experience; (d) a conscious desire to improve my physical condition, particularly in view of a poor cardiac history in my family; (e) encountering the unexpected, finding novel and pleasurable experiences and meeting interesting and friendly people as one always does in travel; (f) having the incidental pleasures of planning and recollection that enrich the months preceding and the years following a venture of this type.

Question: What challenges did the trail represent to you?

RAYMOND BAKER: The challenge was entirely physical. I had no qualms as far as loneliness was concerned. I found I could live with myself and be very happy in the process. There was always something interesting taking place in nature. The trail goes on and on and time passes quickly.

BRUCE BALDERSTON: The trail presented the challenge of being in the wilderness for an extended period of time, of facing and hiking through various weather conditions, and of hiking the 2,000 miles. It also presented planning problems: food, clothing, medical supplies, and so on.

HOWARD E. BASSETT: There were plenty of challenges: the Yellow Creek Mountains, the Nantahalas, the Smokies, the Presidential Range in the White Mountains, Mahoosuc Notch, and last but not the least, Mt. Katahdin.

WALTER BOARDMAN: There was always the challenge of the elements, weather, footing, streams, and hills. It was an opportunity to be on one's own.

CHUCK EBERSOLE: It represented not only a personal endurance contest on various long stretches, but seemed to satisfy the need of being able to live outdoors for as much as 3½ weeks at a time with only what I could carry on my back. Most of these times were from 5 to 10 days with many 2-week periods and several 3- to 3½-week stretches. There is great satisfaction in such independence.

GENE FIDUCIA: In the beginning, before going on the trail, the major challenge was whether I wanted to give up my security—the security of always having food, shelter, and water. There was a challenge in leaving all the pleasures of a summer at the shore and going into the unknown—and at the time the trail was very unknown to me. After being on the trail, the challenge of survival was the primary one. Finding shelter and water, arranging for food drops, map reading, scheduling mileage, trying to predict the weather—all of these things were challenging to me.

JAMES FOX: The planning, and the day-after-day determination to overcome all challenges until our goal was reached. Also living successfully with another person for 24 hours a day under conditions of stress.

BRADLEY W. GREULING: The trail gave me a chance to live with myself, depend on myself, and to discover things about myself that I might otherwise have had little time to learn.

RICHARD HUDSON: Perhaps the challenge of the trail's length. Not so much the entire length, as I never set out to walk it all in one trip, but the challenge of completing each section, whether it was a one-day trip, or my longest trip of 319 miles in Virginia.

CHARLES KONOPA: I had been sick, and I hoped hiking would be the means of repairing my body. If it didn't—well, at least an attempt would have been made.

DOROTHY LAKER: Being a slow walker, it was a challenge to me just to cover enough territory to finish before the snow fell. Not being in any way muscular, but tending rather toward fat, it was a challenge to carry the food and gear I considered necessary. Being very much afraid of high places, it was a challenge to pass the many steep places along the trail. Being a city person, it was a challenge to get through the many open pastures and past the cattle that frequently obscured the trail by standing or lying on the rocks that marked the way. The cattle never seemed friendly, and I didn't understand them.

THOMAS MCKONE: The greatest challenge the Appalachian Trail represented to me was the unknown. I began the Appalachian Trail with no idea of what I was getting into, only knowing that it was something great.

BILL O'BRIEN: The long solitude, and the physical and mental discipline required.

JIM SHATTUCK: The trail presented many challenges—mainly physical. I found that my ability to go at a better pace improved with time. I traveled throughout the winter and had to learn how to use snowshoes, but never really got used to the cold weather. I could stand it, but never enjoyed it when the temperature dropped below zero.

CLIFFORD AND MARGARET SMITH: We found our physical endurance challenged by such things as rain, heat, cold, and insects. A great amount of mental endurance was also needed.

NED SMITH: The trail represented both a physical and a mental challenge to me. Mostly mental. After the first week I knew I could handle the physical strain if no accidents befell me. I often thought of quitting during the long rainy days in Virginia.

ROBERT WINSLOW: To me the Appalachian Trail represented no challenge greater than placing one foot in front of another. It's that simple, really.

JAMES WOLF: Challenges represented by the trail: (a) physical: was I strong enough to do it? (b) character: did I have the will and the fortitude? (c) logistical: could I plan competently and efficiently? (d) trail skills: could I make a camp in the woods? cooking? (e) nature study: could I learn as much as I hoped about the flora and fauna? How about edible plants and poisonous ones?

Question: How many years had you been hiking before you started the whole trail?

HOWARD E. BASSETT: Off and on for 47 years. My first hike was across 10 miles of sandy, rocky, lava-type desert in southwestern Arizona in 1921. By the time I reached Yuma I had worn out a brand-new pair of shoes. The hike, with another young fellow, started in Araby, Arizona.

WALTER BOARDMAN: About 40 years.

GENE FIDUCIA: I had never hiked before going on the Appalachian Trail.

BRADLEY W. GREULING: I had only been backpacking for four years, although I had gone camping, climbing, and day-hiking a lot before that.

JEFFREY HANCOCK: I had been hiking seriously for only one summer before I hiked the Appalachian Trail.

DOROTHY LAKER: I had not been hiking at all before I hiked the Appalachian Trail. I just felt that any person could hike the trail, given the desire to do so, if they walked all day and rested all night. By repeating this cycle long enough they would complete the trail. The catch was to have sufficient incentive to sustain the action.

JAMES RUTTER: I'd been hiking for about 11 years.

Question: Did walking the trail make any essential change in your life? Any change in your philosophy?

BRUCE BALDERSTON: Hiking the trail has increased my self-confidence and increased my appreciation of the wilderness. I loathe, even more than I did before my hike, the segments of civilization that are slowly but surely destroying the wilderness areas of the United States. I am now questioning whether or not I should strive merely to make money and fall into the forms of society, or whether I would be better suited to living in a fairly remote wilderness area.

HOWARD E. BASSETT: I proved to myself that I could take care of most situations that might turn up. It helped me make friends and get along better with people.

WALTER BOARDMAN: My best thinking has always been done when walking in solitude. A weekend alone on the trail has been an invaluable remedy for the tensions of life as a school administrator.

GENE ESPY: Hiking the trail has given me more confidence and a better understanding and appreciation of others. I enjoyed the hike and feel indebted to the good people who work on the trail, and to the landowners. The mountain people I met along the trail were kind, hospitable, and interesting. Many who took me in for the night were poor, but they willingly shared what they had. Some of them had never traveled more than a few miles from their birthplace. My faith in mankind was renewed. Reading the Bible, meditating, and enjoying God in nature made my hike an uplifting religious experience.

GENE FIDUCIA: I am more confident since I completed the trail. If I set out to do something now, I know I will do it. I do not fear the unknown anymore. Meeting people on the trail and helping and being helped by them has strengthened my belief that having a common need brings people together. Living life to the fullest and helping people seems to bring happiness.

JAMES FOX: Changes—yes, definitely. I can do what I intend to do now, but I don't ever have to do some stunt to prove it again. Hiking the Appalachian Trail gave me the confidence and the survival skills to get along almost anywhere, under almost any conditions.

BRADLEY W. GREULING: I proved to myself that I could complete a job larger than doing the dishes. I could depend on myself and survive. As for changing my philosophy: after you have walked 2,000 miles you have to admit that the world is not as small as everyone says it is getting.

JEFFREY HANCOCK: Walking the Appalachian Trail did change my way of life. Hiking became my prime interest, indeed nearly my only interest for a time. I have since fallen in love with winter climbing and am toying with rock-climbing. Whenever things seem bleak or frustrating, I turn to the mountains.

RICHARD HUDSON: Yes. As a youth I never was able to participate in athletic activities because of my health. As each section of the trail was completed it gave me a great deal of satisfaction. By the time the entire trail was completed I had a more positive outlook on life, both on and off the trail.

CHARLES KONOPA: As my body repaired in scrambling up and down the hills, I felt a gradual quickening of mind and spirit. I came to realize that I was involved in the ageless rhythm of Creation, that the roots of my life were very deep and that my home was at once here and everywhere. Life was fulfillment in itself, not a commodity to be bartered for a vague goal which would only heighten my self-esteem.

DOROTHY LAKER: It made me appreciate the remote and wild areas more, and made me more concerned to see them preserved for the enjoyment of others.

THOMAS MCKONE: Hiking the Appalachian Trail gave me more faith in people. Previously, I wavered between optimism and pessimism. Now that I have seen the full possibilities of humanity, I can be nothing but optimistic. Hiking the Appalachian Trail also cured me of excessive worry about a career and the future, a worry that our society, and particularly our educational institutions, has inflicted upon young minds.

BILL O'BRIEN: I'll never again (what, *never?*) let work interfere with living. I'm a more relaxed person, I think, and have a stronger sense of kinship with all living things than ever before. I've always enjoyed each day's weather for itself, but the enjoyment seems sharper now.

JAMES RUTTER: The main change that I've noticed is that I'm more settled, less easily disturbed.

ERIC RYBACK: I found new respect for God, for nature, and for myself. I found that I could do almost anything if I said "I will" instead of "I would like to" or "I may."

JIM SHATTUCK: Walking the trail gave me a greater appreciation of civilization, including the neon lights, bars, and motels. After four or five days and nights in the cold it really felt good to come to a settlement which featured these adjuncts to civilization. I also felt a tie to civilization in the clothes I wore, my sleeping bag, food, and boots; if it weren't for civilization and its products, I couldn't have enjoyed the wilderness.

CLIFFORD AND MARGARET SMITH: We found that spending our whole lives working and waiting for a two-week vacation isn't what it's cracked up to be.

NED SMITH: Friends say I am more even-tempered. I have a deeper feeling for the woods. I now *need* to go hiking as often as possible. I thank God more often for sunny days and cool breezes.

BRIAN WINCHESTER: On the trail my spirit became much calmer, more appreciative of all the things of life. I seriously thought about living my entire life in the same style. However, more profound changes were to come after I had finished my hike. Returning to the "civilized world" proved to be a completely unfulfilling way of life, more so than it had been before. I truly believe that all of this was just to lead me to the point of accepting Jesus Christ as my Lord on January 1, 1972. When I had done this, my life was changed more than in all the years preceding. It seems that I've finally found what I was looking for.

ROBERT WINSLOW: This is the most difficult question to answer. Yes, hiking the Appalachian Trail has influenced my outlook on life. I learned how simply and cheaply it is possible to live and be happy. The Appalachian Trail hike also influenced my fundamental beliefs. Ever since birth, I and just about everyone else in the world have been raised on a myth—the supposition that this world is imperfect, and that we must always strive toward higher, greater goals, toward some great and glorious heaven or nirvana that is beyond our poor powers of comprehension. Occasionally, while walking alone, I have been able to comprehend the real meaning of the word "timelessness," and with it has come the realization that we are not evolving along some long path to perfection, but that each moment is already perfect.

Question: Would you hike the entire trail again, given the opportunity?

BRUCE BALDERSTON: No. There are too many places along the trail that did not appeal to me to make another traverse of the entire trail worthwhile. I would consider hiking certain sections of the trail again—the Shenandoah, the Smokies, the White Mountains, and Maine. However, many of these places are rather crowded during most of the year.

HOWARD E. BASSETT: This is a tough question. I would have to take into account the fact that I am older, that there are many restrictions on trail use now (building wood fires, for instance) and the difficulty of getting a compatible partner for the trip.

WALTER BOARDMAN: I would rather explore another great trail, although I have walked certain sections of the Appalachian Trail several times.

CHUCK EBERSOLE: My answer is an unqualified YES—not only for the second time which I've already completed, but for a possible third time which I've been contemplating for several years.

GENE ESPY: I would enjoy hiking the Appalachian Trail again.

GENE FIDUCIA: I would like to take all of my friends with me on the trail, and let them see what I have seen.

JAMES FOX: No way. It's been done. There are other things to do and other places to go.

BRADLEY W. GREULING: Yes. As I have grown and changed, I feel that hiking the trail again would be a whole new experience.

JEFFREY HANCOCK: I would hike the entire Appalachian Trail again, given the opportunity. However, the Pacific Crest Trail is my present objective.

RICHARD HUDSON: Yes, I would like to walk it in one trip next time, from either end. If done by sections again, I would start at one end, and then begin each hike where the last one ended, rather than jump around from one area to another as I did before.

CHARLES KONOPA: The possibilities of the Appalachian Trail are virtually endless. It provides natural sights, smells, and sounds that are not to be duplicated anywhere except possibly in the deciduous hardwood forests of Asia, which are related to the woodlands of eastern

North America. There are sections of the trail totaling about 400 miles that I intend to walk again. They include a number of the bald mountains, which are a feature almost uniquely that of the southern Appalachians.

DOROTHY LAKER: Certainly, given the opportunity.

GARNETT MARTIN: I do not anticipate backtracking, but I would enjoy hiking the Appalachian Trail again.

THOMAS MCKONE: There is so much world to see and so many things to do that I probably will never hike the Appalachian Trail again, but if I could live forever I would.

BRANLEY OWEN: I never intend to hike the entire Appalachian Trail again. As far as I'm concerned, only about a third of the trail is worth hiking for the second time. I would like to hike Maine, New Hampshire, Vermont and some parts of Virginia, North Carolina, Tennessee, and Georgia again.

JAMES RUTTER: Certainly I'd hike it again.

JIM SHATTUCK: Yes, I would hike the entire trail again if given the opportunity.

NED SMITH: I'm not sure. I would like to do it again, but I would want my wife with me and I'm not sure she could handle a full summer of extended camping. She likes hot showers too much.

BRIAN WINCHESTER: Oh, yes!

ROBERT WINSLOW: I think not. There are too many other places I haven't seen yet.

Question: Do you still hike?

RAYMOND BAKER: Yes, I still take short hikes occasionally. I have hiked the Long Trail and the high peaks of the Adirondacks. I also did some hiking in Hawaii.

BRUCE BALDERSTON: I only hike occasionally, since demands at school are great and my time is limited. I do plan to do some hiking this summer, perhaps in the Catskills in New York, or on the roughest, most remote trails I can find in the White Mountains.

HOWARD E. BASSETT: You bet I do—both long and short hikes, mostly in Connecticut, sometimes in New York and Massachusetts, and mostly on a regular basis: Sundays, Wednesdays, and Saturdays.

WALTER BOARDMAN: Responsibilities to others and especially work to save the environment have made it difficult to find time for hiking. Right now, I am trying to clear more time for walks in the parks and forests of the Southwest.

CHUCK EBERSOLE: Yes, I still hike. Short half-day hikes twice a week in my job as interpretive naturalist each summer in Idaho, plus frequent two-day hikes on my days off to distant high-mountain lakes for solitude, fishing, and photography, plus 10- and 12-day, 50- to 75-mile hikes in Canyonlands National Park in Utah during spring quarter break each mid-March: these include isolated canyons, Indian ruins of the Ancient Ones (Anasazi), swimming in the Colorado and Green rivers, collecting artifacts and fossils, photography, and so on.

GENE ESPY: I enjoy day hikes occasionally. About once a year I take a day hike on the Appalachian Trail.

JAMES FOX: I'd like to, but rarely get away.

BRADLEY W. GREULING: I have plans to hike more, but at present the Coast Guard and marriage take most of my time.

JEFFREY HANCOCK: I still hike all the time! This past summer I climbed 34 of the Adirondack 4,000-footers in six weekends. This winter will make my fourth among the ranks of the winter climbers. This year I will complete the 63 New England 4,000-footers in winter as I have but 12 left. I hope to complete the remaining Adirondack 4,000-footers in summer. Since completing the Appalachian Trail I have hiked the remainder of the Long Trail in Vermont and have completed the New England 4,000-footers in summer.

RICHARD HUDSON: I hike once a week on a club trip or solo. In the Catskills usually, or in New Hampshire, Vermont, or the Adirondacks on long weekends. On the few weekends I spend at home I walk on trails in the surrounding woods.

GARNETT MARTIN: I still hike. The distances differ—in one area it may be only five miles, in another up to 15 miles. My hiking is on a regular basis, three to four times a week, with no pack.

JAMES RUTTER: Haven't had a chance to do any more hiking. I'm only interested in trips lasting a week or longer now.

ERIC RYBACK: It's still thrilling to me. I will always walk, but never alone again. My brother Tim joined me for a Continental Divide trip.

JIM SHATTUCK: I still hike, but confine it to two or three weeks on annual vacation. I take occasional weekend hikes of 15 to 20 miles. These expeditions are in the Green Mountains, Adirondacks, or Berkshires.

CLIFFORD AND MARGARET SMITH: We take short hikes throughout Maine during the summer to places that hold special interest for us, such as Katahdin.

NED SMITH: I still take weekend hikes of 15 or 16 miles every chance I get.

ROBERT WINSLOW: I still hike regularly in the hills around my house and in western Connecticut. When the opportunity arises I spend a few days in the White Mountains.

Question: What are some of the values you find in hiking?

OWEN ALLEN: The key thing for me is that it is a time apart, when I am independent of my normal routine, and in a new setting that brings a restoring and strengthening perspective to life. In biblical terms, it restores my soul, and it's fun.

RAYMOND BAKER: A chance to be alone with nature, a time to think clearly, a time to cleanse the body and mind of impurities.

BRUCE BALDERSTON: Hiking gives me an opportunity to find solitude and mental relaxation. It gives me the rare opportunity to transcend this mad plastic hell and seek a peace that is more healthy. Hiking has the potential of helping man transcend his anthropocentric view of nature and society.

WALTER BOARDMAN: A better sense of proportion comes as I walk. Irritations with mankind melt away and peace of mind is restored. (I began this day with a three-mile walk along the ocean beach as the sun came up.)

ALBERT FIELD: Separation from noise, litter, and superficial people. A chance to see wildlife. Exercise with a purpose.

BRADLEY W. GREULING: This is a hard question to answer. Self-confidence, understanding yourself and other people—the list could go on and on. The answer depends a lot on the maturity of the individual hiker.

JEFFREY HANCOCK: I find peace and quiet, fresh air, friendly and interesting people, and nature in its most pristine form in my hiking.

Photo by Ross R. Rowlands

Bruce Balderston.

Photo by Ross R. Rowlands

Bruce Balderston at Cloud Pond Lean-to.

RICHARD HUDSON: It gives the satisfaction of completing what you set out to do. When you are thinking about survival in the wilderness, problems concerning home or work disappear from your thoughts.

DOROTHY LAKER: I enjoy a greater sense of well-being. Hiking promotes relaxation and peace of mind. It gets me away from the trivialities of the workaday world. It sets up a storehouse of pleasant memories for the rocking-chair age of 80. It provides a time for thinking and dreaming. It makes me very rich in new possessions—the mountaintops I crossed become mine, as do the shelters I stay at, and even though I am an absentee landlord, they are all still in my domain. It keeps my weight down (for a little while). I talk with many fine people along the way.

GARNETT MARTIN: Hiking brings you close to nature. It is fine exercise, and gives you a chance to meet and talk with people and study an area.

THOMAS MCKONE: I find that the best time to think is when I am walking. Even a short walk is valuable; it awakens my senses and makes me more sensitive to people, to ideas, and to nature and the world around me. A long backpacking hike is a special experience in walking: it takes a few weeks for the body and the mind to condition themselves, then comes the apotheosis.

BILL O'BRIEN: The feeling of peace and contentment; the pleasure of seeing the living beauty; the sense of accomplishment when you reach the top of a mountain.

JAMES RUTTER: The greatest value I find in hiking is that it offers a simple, healthy life.

ERIC RYBACK: An awareness of living the days one at a time.

JIM SHATTUCK: I think hiking teaches patience. It gives peace of mind, and a sense of perspective on problems which would otherwise cause undue tensions.

CLIFFORD AND MARGARET SMITH: Clean air, clean smells, and freedom.

BRIAN WINCHESTER: Time to think, reflect, question. A long hike teaches a respect for common things like water, food, fire, and companionship. You cannot realize the true value of these things until you are forced to do without them.

ROBERT WINSLOW: Food, water, and shelter took on a value that I had never really appreciated before.

Question: Is there any other long trail you want to hike or plan to hike?

RAYMOND BAKER: I am interested in the Pacific Crest Trail.

BRUCE BALDERSTON: I would eventually like to hike the Bruce Trail and the Long Trail. I may take a leave of absence from school to hike the Pacific Crest Trail.

HOWARD E. BASSETT: I surely would love to, but circumstances prevent any long-distance hiking just now.

WALTER BOARDMAN: The Bruce Trail and the Roman Wall in England.

CHUCK EBERSOLE: To hike the Pacific Crest Trail from Mexico to Canada has long been a dream of mine. I'm also interested in hiking the Bruce Trail in Canada and the Fingerlakes Trail across New York.

GENE FIDUCIA: If I had the time and the money I would like to hike every trail in the world.

ALBERT FIELD: I'd like to do them all!

EDWARD GARVEY: I would like to hike the Long Trail and at least a part of the Pacific Crest Trail.

ANDREW GIGER: I have tentative plans to hike the Pacific Crest Trail if my job allows it, if my health stays good, if it's feasible financially, and if several other factors are suitable.

BRADLEY W. GREULING: I would like to hike all of the trails you mention (Pacific Crest, Bruce, Long Trail, Great Divide Trail in Canada, and so on) besides making a trail of my own. If I get stationed near one or more of these trails, I will probably hike it (or them). As I have only been married a year, it will probably be a couple of years before I can hike the Appalachian Trail again in the way I want to.

JEFFREY HANCOCK: I had originally planned to hike the Pacific Crest Trail in 1973 after having obtained permission from the college to graduate in seven semesters. This project has now been delayed for at least a year, but I will be hiking that trail. I have no plans beyond that, although Mexico's volcanoes, Alaska's high peaks, and the many European mountains do tempt me.

RICHARD HUDSON: Time will decide. Will go West only if someone joins me. Trails in the East and West are not alike. Walking the entire Appalachian Trail may make a person experienced in the Appalachians but not on western trails, and vice versa.

DOROTHY LAKER: I have hiked the Cascade Crest Trail across Washington, the Oregon Skyline Trail, the John Muir Trail, the High Sierra Trail. I would like to hike the Long Trail, but I have no definite plans made.

THOMAS MCKONE: I am beginning to make plans to hike half the Pacific Crest Trail one year and the other half the following year. I have already hiked several sections of the Long Trail, and may be hiking much of the Bruce Trail later.

BILL O'BRIEN: I want to finish the Long Trail, and I hope to hike the Pacific Crest Trail, taking six months or so to do half of it, and then completing it the next year. It all depends on my wife's feelings and my physical shape. Mentally, I want to hike that trail.

BRANLEY OWEN: I want to do the parts of the Pacific Crest Trail that I think I will really enjoy, in the states of Washington and Oregon and in parts of California. I don't have any ambition to hike the whole trail just for the sake of saying I did it all.

JIM SHATTUCK: I would like to hike from Lands End, England, to John o'Groat's, Scotland; also I would like to walk across Indiana, Illinois, and Iowa. This would be casual traveling afoot with no definite trail. I have hiked the Long Trail in Vermont and the Northville–Placid Trail in the Adirondacks. Sometime I would like to try part of the Pacific Crest Trail and test my theories of logistics.

CLIFFORD AND MARGARET SMITH: Pacific Crest Trail hopefully in a few years.

NED SMITH: No. No time or money. If I were wealthy, I would walk them all.

BRIAN WINCHESTER: I would like very much to take some more long hikes. I have all sorts of ideas.

ROBERT WINSLOW: Plans for a number of trips are in the kettle. Some are quite simple, others are extremely grand and complex.

Question: If you were to hike the Appalachian Trail again (or go on any other long hike) what would you do differently?

RAYMOND BAKER: I would try to keep the weight of my pack as close to 25 pounds as possible. I would carry freeze-dried food, and a hunting knife instead of an axe. I would take a tarp and a ground cloth.

BRUCE BALDERSTON: If I hiked another long trail I would take more care in planning simple meals, and also take time to get into the best possible physical condition. One of the important things I learned from hiking the trail was that I could live on less food than I had been eating.

HOWARD E. BASSETT: I would plan to have more food, either in caches or mailed to farms or post offices. I would have better raingear; most of the time my raingear consisted of a space blanket; 80 percent of the time the wind blew it over my head. As for physical conditioning, I doubt if I would have to do any. A mediumweight sleeping bag (1½–2 pounds of goose down) should suffice. One thing for sure, I would take slides instead of snapshots. Showing snapshots to a group is too time-consuming.

WALTER BOARDMAN: I would take more time to learn the geophysical and historical background of the area in which I plan to hike.

CHUCK EBERSOLE: My food would be better planned for nutrition and bulk. My sleeping equipment would be definitely warmer. I think raingear can be overdone and I found that a rain hat and poncho were adequate. I have had a never-ending debate with myself: was the wetness that came from wearing a poncho worse than the wetness that came from not wearing one? Perspiration under the poncho seemed to wet me and chill me just as much as walking in the rain did. I licked the problem one time by taking everything off except shoes and shorts. I placed my clothing in a plastic bag and carried it, and as long as I walked rapidly I was not cold. When the rain stopped after three hours and 9 or 10 miles I donned my dry clothing and continued on with no ill effects. This occurred near Damascus, Virginia, and it was a cold rain.

GENE FIDUCIA: If I were to take another long hike, I would make myself familiar with the trail by reading about it. One addition to my equipment would be a lightweight tent. Food would be freeze-dried and set out on the trail ahead of time, hopefully three days apart, so I could carry the minimum weight. As for conditioning, I would just plan to take it easy for the first two weeks on the trail. That is what we did on our hike and it worked out fine.

ALBERT FIELD: I doubt if I would make changes. Since I took 11 years to do the trail, I refined my plans and methods to what was best for me. I would advise any serious hiker to get in condition with long hikes before starting on the trail itself.

JAMES FOX: Were I to do the Appalachian Trail again I'd take 100 to 120 days minimum, as the time of 95 days is just a shade too fast to enjoy it. I'd try poison ivy desensitization. I'd get a pair of Peter Limmer's custom boots. I've had a pair for eight years now, and I wish I'd had them to hike the trail.

BRADLEY W. GREULING: If I were to go on a long hike again, I would *definitely* purchase my supplies as I went along for two reasons: (1) I think having your packages mailed to you means that you carry more weight and (2) when you shop you get a feeling for the locality and its people. Most stores sell items that are liked in that particular area so you can tell a lot about the local people from their stores. It also gives the hiker a chance to pick up the weather reports. If one of the locals says, "That was a mighty big washout they had on Frog Ridge yesterday," you have learned something about the condition of the section. Who would know better than the local grocer?

JEFFREY HANCOCK: On another long hike I would use a combination of post office food drops, cached (buried) supplies, grocery stores, and resupply by meeting friends. The grocery store would be used to the greatest extent possible, supplemented by food mailed to post offices. Where neither method is possible, meeting with friends and/or caches would be used. I would obtain the relevant maps and guidebooks and go over the route carefully. Many hikers will laugh at this, but I enjoy this type of extensive preparation. I would carry a lightweight tent. I would use several different weights of sleeping bags for the warmer and colder parts of the hike. The Eddie Bauer Mummy Inner Bag, with a total weight of 31 ounces, would be sufficient for much of the hike, but a 10-degree bag would be desirable for the colder stretches. A shorty foam pad is definitely worth carrying. I would carry a rain suit again, but would use chaps instead of full-length pants for more adequate cooling.

RICHARD HUDSON: I would prefer to buy all food along the way except for one-pot dinner meals from Stow-A-Way, which are hard to replace for ease in cooking and tastiness. Post offices are too frequent and too near the trail to make any other type of cache points necessary.

DOROTHY LAKER: I would start out as early as possible in the year so I would have time to stop for swimming, berry picking, picture taking, and talking to people out hiking or living along the trail. Many times the hiker is presented with the opportunity of enjoying local holidays or hospitality, and it is nice to be able to accept. I would also be able to follow the blue-blazed side trails to points of interest that I usually had to pass by. I would mail more food, especially powdered eggs. And I'd take only real fruit crystals, either lemon, lime, grapefruit, or orange, and not the fruit drinks which are predominantly chemicals. A poncho was never too satisfactory a rain shield for me. I found the condensation too uncomfortable. Plastic raincoats always split and so did my plastic rain suit, so I guess I'd take a more expensive rain suit next time. The sheet of plastic over my rucksack and pack was not too good because it required unwrapping each time access to the packs was necessary. A waterproof pack would be my choice.

GARNETT MARTIN: Should I hike the Appalachian Trail again the only change would be in my raingear. I would have it custom-made to my own specifications.

THOMAS MCKONE: Having hiked the Appalachian Trail in one long hike, I would suggest hiking it in two or three long hikes. The main disadvantage of hiking the whole trail at once is that there is never enough time to savor each section of the trail. Of course, there will never be enough time to hike the whole trail as leisurely as one might like, but hiking the whole trail at once is sometimes more like an athletic feat than a walk in the woods. I believe fully in taking long hikes, long in the sense of a long *time*, for it is not until you are on the trail for a few weeks that you can enjoy the greatest pleasures of walking and of the woods. The amount of distance covered is rather unimportant. I started planning my hike only three months before I was to leave. As a result, I could not get the exact equipment I wanted, and never did get a good pair of boots. It is not too early to begin buying equipment and making plans a year ahead of time. I did not figure out my diet very closely and lost more weight than I should have.

BILL O'BRIEN: I'd set a pace that allowed more time for just sitting and looking at what I came to see. That's why I plan to take 12 months to do the 2,400 miles of the Pacific Crest Trail.

ERIC RYBACK: Study your equipment as if your life depended upon it— for it may.

JIM SHATTUCK: If I were to hike the Appalachian Trail again I would certainly not start off with the load of 62 pounds I had on August 24,

1966. I would start with the load and clothing I finished with on May 23, 1967. This involved no change of clothing and a total pack weight of roughly 35 pounds. Food would be only what I could pick up at local grocery stores, not a lot of stuff that must be purchased from special suppliers. Dehydrated milk, cheese, raisins, apricots, liverwurst, dehydrated soups, freeze-dried mashed potatoes, peanut butter, and much else are readily portable and available. Shelter would consist of a one-man hiking tent with a sewed-in floor, a fly, and mosquito netting. A two-thirds-length ground pad (closed cell) and a 4½-pound Thomas Black and Sons sleeping bag would comprise the nocturnal equipment.

CLIFFORD AND MARGARET SMITH: We would hike the Appalachian Trail from south to north because the insects would be gone in the northern states and we wouldn't experience a water shortage as we did on our north-to-south hike. We would carry a double sleeping bag which would be lighter and warmer. We would carry guidebooks so we would know where to find stores. We would also carry rain covers for our packs to prevent water from getting in around the zippers.

NED SMITH: I would start a month earlier and go slower.

ROBERT WINSLOW: I'm in love with my Kelty BB5. My Bean boots slip on wet rocks as much as Vibram soles do. I no longer carry Tang; I eat violets and drink spruce tea and carry a few vitamin C tablets. I also add soybeans and sunflower seeds to my gorp. I now carry my camera in a shoulder harness. I no longer carry margarine for lunch, and eat peanut butter and honey sandwiches. For cold and damp weather I now carry a Volarafoam pad.

Question: In retrospect, what were the values you received from your Appalachian Trail hike?

RAYMOND BAKER: A much, much, wider vision as far as conservation is concerned. There is no better place to study erosion than in the mountains where the forces of wind, frost, and rain carry the soil downhill at a deplorable rate when man disturbs the vegetative cover. We all owe a debt to the many unselfish people who labor to keep the trail cleared and the shelters in shape.

BRUCE BALDERSTON: I gained a great deal of self-confidence from my hike. When I began the hike I didn't have a realistic conception of the extent of 2,000 miles. I had never realized how far, how fast, and with what a small amount of equipment one could travel, given some experience and a degree of physical fitness.

HOWARD E. BASSETT: The values I received from my Appalachian Trail hike were different from those I expected. I had thought that such a long strenuous walk would exhaust me and perhaps cause me to give up hiking for a time, but such was not the case.

WALTER BOARDMAN: For many years I firmly believed that a better world could be achieved through education. Now I see that unless we make drastic changes in our treatment of nature, man is destined for extinction.

CHUCK EBERSOLE: The values I received were even more richly satisfying than I had expected.

GENE FIDUCIA: Before hiking the trail I would talk about the need to maintain our forests, wildlife, and waters, but I was just talking. I had never really experienced the feel of living with these things. The trail gave me a chance to evaluate my thoughts, my convictions, and my values, and to know, firsthand, the value of living in harmony with nature.

JAMES FOX: Awareness of self and nature, self-confidence, survival skills.

BRADLEY W. GREULING: I wanted to be one of those who had done it alone. I matured in my own eyes, and also in the eyes of my family and friends. I gained self-confidence. My own family-influenced values were quite sound, I suppose, as I was successful in my venture.

JEFFREY HANCOCK: The trip left me instilled with a love for hiking which I believe to be permanent!

CHARLES KONOPA: I had hoped that the strenuous effort of hiking would benefit me physically, and it did. Health returned. I did not expect or hope for more, but there was another benefit: a measure of tranquility was added to my physical well-being.

DOROTHY LAKER: Even though I had always lived in a city, I suspected that the forests were my natural country. My hikes confirmed this feeling. I found education, inspiration, relaxation, and contentment.

THOMAS MCKONE: Two great experiences of hiking the trail which I had not anticipated were the fine people I met and the weather. As a city dweller I had pretty much taken the weather for granted; on the

Appalachian Trail I discovered the great beauty of the weather, even of a storm. I doubt if I have ever been as close to the destructive powers of nature as the night Bob Winslow and I spent in a remote lean-to high in Laurel Fork Gorge in the midst of an extremely violent thunderstorm. But there is just as much beauty in the silence of the forest, in a cool breeze on a still summer night, in a light afternoon shower, in the wind blowing through the cracks of a lean-to at night, in waking on a May morning to find that an inch of powdery snow had crept silently into the shelter during the night.

BILL O'BRIEN: I know myself better. I'm more at ease with the world in general, and less irritated by trivia.

JIM SHATTUCK: In retrospect I received many lasting memories of the United States of America and have since been very happy to remain here. Europe and other traditional travel targets outside the United States can't compete if there is the option of putting my house on my back and stamping around the wilderness regions here at home. Also, distances no longer awe me. If my car is confined to the garage I can walk—this includes the 20 miles between New Haven and Guilford; it's a bit of a project, but a very enjoyable one.

CLIFFORD AND MARGARET SMITH: It wasn't as easy as we thought it would be. Our romantic ideas were greatly changed by water shortages, insects, heat, and cold.

NED SMITH: I discovered a strange thing about the business world as a result of my trip. When I quit my job to make the hike I felt sure I would be able to get another job of equal caliber. I thought the trip would show an employer that I was able to think for myself, was resourceful, was self-confident. When I got back, even though my old boss gave me good references, I could not get a job. One man said I did not present the image of a hardworking employee. Another said I showed disloyalty to my old employer. It seems that it is all right to quit to go to another job, but not to take time for yourself.

BRIAN WINCHESTER: I grew closer to nature, just as I'd expected. What I didn't expect was the wealth of friendships I discovered.

ROBERT WINSLOW: If I may paraphrase Thoreau a bit here: Tom McKone and I found employment in watching the progress of the seasons. We were the self-appointed inspectors of wild flowers, birds, butterflies, mountain summits, snowstorms, and rainstorms, and we did our job faithfully. I did not start the trail with any preconceived thoughts about values. I knew it would be a learning experience, and I remained open and receptive to whatever I happened to come upon.

Question: If you walked the trail again, would you go alone or would you try to find a companion?

RAYMOND BAKER: I walked alone and loved it. I would walk alone again unless I found someone I knew would be compatible.

BRUCE BALDERSTON: I hiked the trail with a friend for 700 miles and finished the remaining 1,300 miles by myself. I don't think I could have hiked the entire trail if I had started alone. I do enjoy hiking alone, but it is very comforting to have someone to eat with and talk with at the end of a day.

HOWARD E. BASSETT: I walked the trail alone, but I would certainly attempt to have a companion on a second trip. The Appalachian Trail Conference understandably frowns on lone hikers.

WALTER BOARDMAN: I prefer hiking alone, but am now more concerned about the consequences of a mishap than once was the case. I agree with those who recommend that two or three of similar interests and ability join together.

CHUCK EBERSOLE: At this point, I'm not quite decided on aloneness or companionship. I have walked parts of many trails both ways. Each has its advantages and disadvantages. I find that there are times when I definitely want aloneness—I crave solitude for a while—nights, days, and even a week or more—and it is always a beautiful experience for me. At other times I seem to desire companionship around a cheery campfire at night. A companion must always be just that—really companionable and not just some person plodding along.

GENE FIDUCIA: I think it is great to hike alone, but there are times when a hiking companion is welcomed. If you can find someone who *lets you feel that you're alone when hiking*, it is great to have a companion when you camp. It is very hard to find the perfect companion. I was fortunate, as I had a great hiking partner.

ALBERT FIELD: I did 87 days alone and enjoyed them. I did 77 with people and enjoyed them, too. I would try to get company before setting out on any long expedition.

JAMES FOX: Two people have important logistical advantages. Also, two can have more fun and support each other in the morale department, but I wouldn't go with just anyone for a partner. It would have to be a friendship more basic than just getting together for the trip.

ANDREW GIGER: Companionship would have been nice, but another person could have been a handicap if he hadn't wanted to walk as slow or as fast as I did. Or maybe he would have snored.

BRADLEY W. GREULING: Yes, I think I would go alone as I have found it difficult to hike with others.

JEFFREY HANCOCK: If I walked the trail again I would like to go with a companion. There are many things that must be viewed with a companion to be fully enjoyed.

RICHARD HUDSON: I would go alone if necessary, but would prefer the company of someone I could communicate with.

CHARLES KONOPA: I enjoy hiking with a congenial companion, but I do not hike for the sake of conviviality. There is pleasure in solitude. Wildlife is normally shy and the solitary hiker will see much more of it than if he were walking in company. To hike alone, especially in unpeopled areas, is more adventuresome.

DOROTHY LAKER: I could go again, either alone or with companions. If I did not go alone I would want to go with someone closely matched to my walking speed and ability. A very fast person would soon become discouraged with my pace, and a too leisurely person would make me impatient. We would also have to have compatible views on nature and conservation. I would not want to have to try to make a convert as I hiked, and since I feel strongly on these subjects, that is what it would come to.

GARNETT MARTIN: I hiked alone, and if the hike should be repeated it probably would be a solo trip again.

THOMAS MCKONE: I hiked 1,600 miles of the Appalachian Trail with Bob Winslow and the last 400-plus miles alone. No offense to Bob, but I found hiking alone was preferable. Being with the same person constantly for months at a time is too much to expect of almost any friendship. Throughout the hiking season there are enough people on the trail so that a backpacker can find someone to hike with for a few days or longer if he wishes. He can have companionship when he wants to, and yet have the independence he needs to feel totally free from the pressures of society and civilization. For shorter hikes I would be happy to have the companionship of a good friend, but for anything over four to six weeks I would prefer to go alone.

BILL O'BRIEN: I'd positively still do long-distance hiking alone. Or any other hike where I had a choice, for that matter. The solitude is a plus.

JAMES RUTTER: I'd hike again either way. I'd like to do it again with a close friend.

JIM SHATTUCK: If I walked the trail again I would like to have one or all of my family with me. However, I would not want to try to persuade anyone to go. This means I would probably go alone again. This wouldn't deter me because I feel anyone who walks the trail should be an independent unit and go at his own pace.

MARGARET SMITH: I feel it isn't safe traveling the trail alone because of the possibility of breaking a bone or getting bitten by a snake.

NED SMITH: I walked alone except for one week when I walked with a group of boys from a YMCA camp. I prefer to walk alone, but it would be nice to have company in camp. If I did the trail again I would take my wife.

BRIAN WINCHESTER: Yes, I would still go it alone.

ROBERT WINSLOW: For a long hike, even into remote wilderness, I would prefer to go alone. Silence and solitude are not only good companions, but good teachers as well. If my companion and I were joyously in love, if we were tuned in to the same wavelength, if our eyes and ears were as one, I would of course enjoy hiking with this person much more than hiking alone. The only other exception would be on expeditions to high mountains where support teams are necessary.

JAMES WOLF: I'm convinced the only way to do it is alone. It is fine to meet someone on the trail and hike more or less at the same pace for days or weeks, but in that case each hiker is a completely free agent. To become tied down to marching to some other piper's tune from the outset is an appalling prospect.

Question: What do you feel would be the most important advice you could give to anyone who wanted to hike the entire trail?

OWEN ALLEN: If you have a desire to hike the Appalachian Trail, do it!

RAYMOND BAKER: Love the woods and trails, put your mind at ease, and enjoy yourself.

BRUCE BALDERSTON: The most important thing about hiking the trail is having the determination to finish it, and to enjoy the adventure.

HOWARD E. BASSETT: With so many factors to take into consideration, this is a tough question to answer. Maybe I would say: take your time, especially over rocky terrain, and enjoy every turn in the trail. Why hurry?

WALTER BOARDMAN: A hiker must be in good physical condition for extended hikes. This is not only a question of muscles, but of the feet. A strong man, with good shoes, can still get into serious trouble if the feet have not been toughened by day-long foot travel. No one should embark upon a 10-day hike until he has conditioned himself by a three-day hike over rough territory.

CHUCK EBERSOLE: I can't answer this question in so many words. There are so many things to think about—each a valid point for discussion. I would say that if you want to hike the Appalachian Trail, for goodness' sake, hurry, do it! Nature is there and waiting to share a wonderful and unique experience with you.

ALBERT FIELD: Don't let the trail dominate you. *Enjoy* the walk. If the trail begins to control you, then get off of it for a while. (I think doing it all in one season is silly, and probably undertaken in order to boast of it. It is the *doing* it that is worthwhile, not having done it!)

EDWARD GARVEY: Be sure to have proper conditioning and proper preparation. A good pair of shoes, well broken in, is a must. Shakedown hikes in which the hiker will experience stresses and strains similar to those on the Appalachian Trail are highly recommended. Any equipment the hiker has purchased for the hike (stoves, tents, tarps) should be thoroughly tested.

ANDREW GIGER: Don't do it!

BRADLEY W. GREULING: Make sure your legs and feet are conditioned and your general health is good. For a young person: call home often. Take along a book to read. I found Tolkein a good author to read while I was living through my own adventure.

JEFFREY HANCOCK: Take a good camera after learning how to use it. Take a notebook and pencil and diligently record your thoughts. The pleasure found in these photographs and notes later on cannot be overstated. When you hike the trail do not rush through it. Go at a slower, more reasonable pace than mine. Be prepared to trudge for days at a time through heavy rain and mud, to go for several days at a time without seeing another person, to walk through miles of stinging nettles and hordes of mosquitoes, to fight off packs of dogs, and to sweat innumerable gallons of perspiration. At the end you will realize that it has all been worth the struggle.

RICHARD HUDSON: Hike Vermont's Long Trail first. It is the Appalachian Trail in condensed form; both are very easy and very rough. If you can survive a three-week trip on the Long Trail you should have no problems on the Appalachian Trail.

CHARLES KONOPA: My only advice would be to pace one's self. There is a fair amount of corporal punishment involved in hiking, especially mountain hiking, and to push the body beyond its limits is unreasonable. Hiking should be more than a rugged physical experience.

DOROTHY LAKER: Take enough time to enjoy yourself. The chances are you won't be making a second trip, and what you miss the first time you'll miss forever.

GARNETT MARTIN: Be sure you are in good physical condition. Have maps and a compass, and know how to orient your map with the terrain and how to plot a course with your compass.

THOMAS MCKONE: Get good boots!

BRANLEY OWEN: Buy a good pair of hiking boots, a good packframe, and a good sleeping bag.

ERIC RYBACK: Hike one step at a time. Don't look from Mt. Katahdin and say, "Wow, it's a long way to Georgia!"

JIM SHATTUCK: My advice to anyone walking the entire trail would be to listen to advice but use only that which you find helpful. Don't be reluctant to experiment. Don't get discouraged; your stamina will improve with distance and the trail is very patient with the beginner.

CLIFFORD AND MARGARET SMITH: Plan on five months to complete the trail and above all, be in top physical shape.

NED SMITH: I would advise people to plan carefully, but I met some who did no planning and they seemed to be getting along all right.

BRIAN WINCHESTER: Realize that there will be bad times with the good. If you ever contemplate quitting, resolve not to quit until a week later. By then you probably won't feel like quitting anymore. Remember that after those first few hard weeks are behind you, your outlook will brighten considerably.

ROBERT WINSLOW: The trail and the mountains have much to teach. Do not attack them, flow with them. Keep your eyes open; be silent for a while; listen.

Question: Any other comments on the Appalachian Trail in general?

RAYMOND BAKER: Sheer pleasure, even if your feet hurt. Wonderful views from high in the mountains. Wildlife and flowers are everywhere.

BRUCE BALDERSTON: The time I spent on the Appalachian Trail is time that I would not trade for anything that I could possibly imagine.

HOWARD E. BASSETT: Keep pack weight down as much as possible, but still try to be comfortable. Take along a good camera. The possibilities for good pictures are endless. Slides are best, and less expensive. Keep forest rangers and friends posted on your whereabouts, especially around the Mt. Washington area in New Hampshire. Rescue operations run into real money, and the rescued foot the bill, as a rule.

WALTER BOARDMAN: The Appalachian Trail is not a stunt in heroics or of endurance. The 2,000 miles as distance should not be the objective. It is rather an opportunity for one to find himself as a creature in nature. It is a way of life and an experience in living. By reason of increased use and abuse, the trail is deteriorating. Wood fires at camps, refuse disposal, trail erosion, and more than all else, the invasion of motor vehicles, present threats that may destroy it entirely.

ALBERT FIELD: We should make strong efforts to bar the trail to anyone except genuine hikers—but don't ask me how to do it. If anyone uses a wheel on any of the trail portions, the vehicle should be confiscated, and the rider should be imprisoned for a few weeks for the first offense. I would include snowmobiles in this; they are even worse than motorcycles.

JAMES FOX: I wish I could help maintain it. It's important that the trail is there for everyone.

BRADLEY W. GREULING: There is nothing "in general" that can be said about the trail. Every part of it has a specific effect on the hiker.

GARNETT MARTIN: Maintain it in as primitive a condition as possible.

BILL O'BRIEN: When I look at a map of the Appalachian Trail it is often hard for me to believe that I have walked all of it.

ERIC RYBACK: It was a grand experience. I had never been away from home before except for the night I had my tonsils out, or when I went to a buddy's house once in a while.

JIM SHATTUCK: "An army moves on its stomach," the saying goes, and this applies to the hiker also. Don't miss a chance to get a good meal if the trail brings you within easy reach of a restaurant. A good meal can make a tired hiker positively jet-propelled. Regardless of whether you are a journalist, historian, or biologist, the trail has something for you personally. In fact, if these three walked the trail together their written accounts would vary greatly due to their respective interests and frames of reference.

NED SMITH: It's a wonderful experience that will deteriorate as more and more people take to the woods.

ROBERT WINSLOW: The trail crews and the officers of the Appalachian Trail Conference have done a tremendous job. I wish to express my gratitude to them for making such an experience possible. All the people that I met along the trail, in towns or on the trail itself, were friendly, helpful, and generous, and definitely played an important role in making the Appalachian Trail such an enjoyable experience for me.

JAMES WOLF: It's much tougher than you would expect until you try to hike it.

Question: Any other comments on your own hike?

RAYMOND BAKER: I wouldn't trade it for anything.

BRADLEY W. GREULING: I think of the trip often. When I'm out on my ship and see a sunrise, or in the morning when I hear the first birds calling, I can see the mountains again. I think of the people I met along the way—some wonderful and some not so great, but all crucial to the learning experience that the trail was for me.

JIM SHATTUCK: Regarding my own hike, the night of February 28, 1966, and the early morning of March 1, 1966, on Sinking Creek Mountain will live with me forever as the nearest I have come to death. With the temperature at 27 degrees below zero, I really suffered. Yet, I would not have missed that experience because I called on the Lord for help and I really felt his presence.

JAMES WOLF: I think I am particularly fortunate because the way I went about planning and carrying out my hike has left me with particularly rich memories. My advance reading and studying of the route gave me a good frame of reference for the experience itself. My bird-watching and nature study provided an additional dimension that embellished the adventure to something more than a lengthy walk in the woods. I have a diary that will help me recapture those happy days as long as I live. Along with the diary, I have some 600 photographs, and each brings back a precious moment. And I continue to correspond with friends from far and wide with whom I shared some part of the trail.

Question: All hikers, and especially through hikers, have been asked many times, "But aren't you afraid of ————?" Were you afraid? Of what?

OWEN ALLEN: I can recall some anxious moments over several things: the possibility of a bear coming into our shelter after food in the packs; a skunk that did come into a shelter in the Shenandoah just after we had gone to bed; the possibility of a fall that would prevent us from completing the trip; some desperate bushwhacking up the side of Kinsman Mountain trying to locate the trail; and some especially unfriendly dogs—these and similar fears come to mind easily. However, I would rate these fears as being relatively on the rational side. There were two occasions when I was gripped by powerful and irrational fear. One was when a thunderstorm came along while we were on the ridgeline of the Smokies. I prayed earnestly for deliverance, and it helped. The other time was on Killington Peak. I have had a latent fear of darkness ever since I can remember, and occasionally something triggers this fear. It was a very dark and windy night on Killington, after we had witnessed an especially beautiful sunset from the peak. During the night I went to look for the privy with the flashlight and was overcome with an irrational foreboding, a strange fear of something lurking in the darkness. The feeling did not leave me until I was back in the shelter. It was the only experience of its kind I had during the whole trip. We waited out another thunderstorm in the shelter on the rocky top of Mt. Cube and nearby lightning bolts scared me deeply.

RAYMOND BAKER: The only real fear I had was the thought of a rattler crawling into my sleeping bag. The chance of this happening was so remote, however, that I put it from my mind completely. A pack of cur dogs can give you a hard time when passing through a small town, especially early in the morning.

BRUCE BALDERSTON: At the beginning of my trip I was afraid that if the going got too rough I might think about quitting. This fear was soon driven from my mind as I moved on and gained experience. I never came close to quitting. In certain areas that were known for snakes I was at times afraid that I would be bitten.

HOWARD E. BASSETT: The only thing I was "afraid" of were the pesky dogs that tried to nip my heels as I went through small settlements. A long thin strong stick or switch solved the problem pretty well. The sight of the stick normally kept the mutts at bay. As for snakes, just keep one eye on the trail! Bears usually see or hear a man long before he appears on the scene and they usually make tracks away from the trail without delay. Moose? Keep away from them in mating season. Generally, a moose will make tracks, pronto. (Moose mate in September or October, which is the time many through hikers are on the trail in Maine.—ED.) I never did come upon rabid animals, as far as I know. Darkness itself is nothing to be afraid of. If you move around in the dark try to have a small flashlight handy. Injuries are best taken care of before they happen. Try to figure out every one of the 5,000,000 steps you have to take to complete the trail.

WALTER BOARDMAN: "Was I afraid?" Of wild animals, *no*. Of a *few* people, yes. I am always wary of any wild animal that permits me to come close to it. Here is the rabies danger, but I never have really had to face that problem. Dogs can be a nuisance. Snakes—one needs to be vigilant but not afraid. When I hiked the Appalachian Trail, one could pretty largely trust those whom one met. On revisiting remote sections of the trail in the past few years I have experienced some concern. Shelters within easy walking distance of a highway sometimes shelter "characters" quite different from the people for whom the shelters were intended. Even so, the Appalachian Trail is safer than a city street.

CHUCK EBERSOLE: I grew up in the country and had tremendous curiosity but seldom experienced fear. While living in the jungle on various Pacific islands during World War II my curiosity grew to even greater limits, but I did develop deep and terrifying fears of many man-made and man-associated things. To this day I have not been able to completely lose some of those fears. The only Appalachian Trail fears I had concerned people in certain particular circumstances. I won't go into detail here, but we did have a few scares. Dogs were a bother many times, but nothing to fear. I liked most of the people I met, with the hill people and the country folks my favorites.

GENE FIDUCIA: There is nothing to fear on the trail as long as you are reasonably well prepared. By that I mean that you should have some knowledge of the animals in the area in which you will be hiking. Most animals are frightened of humans and will not bother you unless they are disturbed while eating, or they or their babies are challenged. There is one place where the hiker should be careful, and that is in the Great Smoky Mountains National Park, where bears are accustomed to humans and seek food from them. As for snakes, just keep your eyes open and be familiar with the treatment for snakebite. Carry a road map and know the location of the nearest town or main road, so that in case of injury or sickness you can leave the trail and get to a doctor.

ALBERT FIELD: I've never been aware of anything to fear on the trail. The bears that I met were all well-mannered. Most moose were rather distant, and the one that allowed me to approach seemed quite gentle. Dogs are potentially dangerous when guarding their home turf, but I met no dogs on guard. It is true that rabid animals can be dangerous, and I would advise all hikers to be aware of the symptoms of rabies. Snakes are much overrated as dangers. I really can't imagine anyone other than a sick child being afraid of the dark. The night is full of interest and of beauty. It is peaceful and gentle, or if the weather is wild it is exciting—but it isn't fearsome, as far as I'm concerned. It's not that I cannot be afraid. I've been afraid of an amateur holdup artist with a gun; I've been afraid of dangerous spots on mountains. What of injuries and sickness? On the trail sickness probably would not become a threat so quickly as to become dangerous, but accidents are something else; I've sprained an ankle and might have been seriously incapacitated. Do I fear an accident? No. I'm aware of the possibility, and if I'm alone, a little more careful.

JAMES FOX: The most dangerous animal is the human one—the kind that tosses beer cans out of a car at you or heaves bottles at you when you are in your sleeping bag. And after our fight with a cow I was much more *respectful* of cows, to say nothing of bulls. As Paul Gerhard wrote later when he was on a mountain climb, "There was nothing that fear could solve. It was a luxury we could not afford."

EDWARD GARVEY: I had hiked the Appalachian Trail for so many years that it was like an old friend. I had no particular fear of any of the things I could encounter, figuring that they were no more than the ordinary risks that we encountered in everyday living. Even after my close call with a rattlesnake, I was not too concerned. After all, cars cause 60,000 deaths annually. Snakes cause only 15 deaths a year.

BRADLEY W. GREULING: Yes, I was afraid—not of anything or anyone else—but of myself and my possible incompetence. I thought perhaps I wouldn't be able to complete the hike because of a lack of something in *me*. These fears worked themselves out slowly and finally I could say, "Yes, I've done it!"

JEFFREY HANCOCK: Snakes were one of my big worries before I started the trail. However, I found that they were no particular problem. I think my greatest fear initially was that I would be too lonely to continue and would come back home after having spent so much of my parents' time and money preparing for the trip. I do think, though, that I was more afraid of disappointing myself than anyone else. Soon the problems I had with my feet made me forget my loneliness.

RICHARD HUDSON: I have been asked about snakes more than any other thing. I did not fear them, but I was shook-up one day in Tennessee when I almost stepped on a rattlesnake, then in a few feet came to some baby snakes. As for loneliness, I looked forward to finding a shelter empty when I reached it. As I took most of my trips out of season, I usually did have the shelters to myself. I always hoped others would show up for company in the evening, but if they didn't, I was happy to have the place to myself by the time I went to sleep.

CHARLES KONOPA: There have been moments of apprehension. Sometimes, when crawling up difficult ledges where hand and footholds were few, I have wished that I were elsewhere. Near Angels Rest in Virginia, as lightning snapped nearby and left the acrid smell of ozone, I dropped my pack with its metal frame and got down in the muck. Being caught in an open field by a strafing jet was the last time I had felt quite so helpless—or lain quite so flat. In the Georgia–North Carolina boundary area where there is much talk of bears, and where I met a number of them, I began to dream of bears. Sleeping on the ground one night in the Smokies I awoke suffocating, flat on my back. A bear was pressing its solid weight against my chest. A storm was gathering and a flicker of heat lightning revealed a dark form. I was desperately gathering my vital forces for a single elemental shout and a leap from my sleeping bag when another flicker revealed that my antagonist was the large stump of a chestnut tree killed by the blight! So much for fear, bear stories, and the power of imagination.

DOROTHY LAKER: Snakes? No problems except with rattlers, and then just with the first one. After that I was careful but not especially worried. Bears were not an active worry. At the time of confrontation, each incident was different. Some of the bears ran and some of them scared me. If I saw a moose across a lake or in a beaver pond, no problem. When they are coming down the trail toward you—oh, yes, they scare you. With regard to rabid animals: several times small animals came up to me in a too-tame fashion. I tried to leave their vicinity rapidly, but I never really considered rabies a problem. Several dog packs were encountered in the woods and were a cause of temporary apprehension, but nothing happened. Hunting dogs were found several times, but these usually were shy or friendly. Then, of course, I was bitten by a dog once. As for people: several times men followed me through the woods—yes, I was frightened on these occasions. The hikers I met were all fine folks. Afraid of the dark: no. Injuries and sickness: I never thought this could happen to me; it was always the other person I pictured with these problems.

GARNETT MARTIN: To be honest, my answer to this question is that I was not afraid. I was concerned, but not afraid, when camping near areas that were available to certain elements from large population centers. As a precaution I would move off the trail to pitch my tent, but not so far that my camp could not be seen in the daytime.

BILL O'BRIEN: I was only afraid that something would prevent me from finishing the trip. I had some uneasy times in thunderstorms but it was not real fear. I exercised normal caution about snakes. It was a time when I felt that I was being "taken care of," really. My encounter with a gang of wild youths at the William Brien Memorial Lean-to in New York was probably my most unpleasant moment on the trail. Again, the feeling was more of caution than of fear. When the bear cubs went up the trees in Maine I probably released some extra adrenalin, and after being bitten in Pennsylvania, I'm now more wary of little dogs that run up barking. I love the dark for the stars and the silhouettes, and the people I met were almost invariably a pleasure.

BRANLEY OWEN: I wasn't afraid, but I was annoyed by the porcupines in New England. They bothered me when I was trying to sleep.

ERIC RYBACK: Yes, I was afraid many times. I am still afraid even after hiking the Pacific Crest Trail. You must learn to trust in God and in yourself. If you can't, you should hike in groups. Everyone must find his own way.

JIM SHATTUCK: Regarding fear and nervousness: because this was my first hike everything was new. Just sleeping on the ground or in a lean-to took some getting used to. However, after the first hundred miles this was no problem. Unusual circumstances like meeting a bear face-to-face in the Maine woods or having a Smoky Mountains bobcat snuggle up to my tent on a rainy night gave me, and would still give me, quite a thrill. As a general observation, I found that really wild animals want no trouble with a hiker. If they can get away that's all they ask. It's the domestic dogs that really disturb the peace. They will growl, bark, yap, and charge. I found that by grabbing the bill of my cap and taking a quick step or two in their direction, the dogs' advances would turn to instant retreat. The noise would continue, but from a safe distance.

MARGARET SMITH: I was afraid of snakes but I found that my fear stemmed from ignorance, and as I became exposed to them I found they weren't so frightening. I was also afraid of thunderstorms but after being in a great many of them on the trail I learned to control my fears. My husband had learned to cope with nearly everything and if he had any fear he didn't show it.

NED SMITH: I was always being asked if I had seen any snakes. I only saw one, and I wasn't afraid of it. At first I was afraid of the noises in the night after I had gone to bed. I got over that after the first week. When I planned the trip I was afraid of the bad people who would try to rob me. I met only fine people on the trail, so that fear soon left me. Each time I fell, which was about once a day, I was afraid that I might really hurt myself, but that fear only bothered me right after I had fallen.

ROBERT WINSLOW: Fear results from a failure to see things as they really are. In addition to such questions as "What kind of a gun did you carry?" I was actually asked, on the summit of Mt. Moosilauke no less, if I wasn't afraid of trees falling on me. For me, going to the woods or going to the mountains is going home. I have no fears.

JAMES WOLF: Sure I was afraid, but only in the sense that I'm afraid of an automobile accident or being held up on the city streets; it isn't anything you allow yourself to worry about. There are risks on the Appalachian Trail, but I accepted them instead of worrying about them. One way to avoid fear and panic is to plan ahead and minimize the risks. For example, I was concerned that night might overtake me while I was without shelter if I continued on the trail near Blood Mountain in Georgia. I was in deep snow, and it would have been a bad situation, so I did the sensible thing and left the trail for the day.

The trail is crowded with people during the summer months; the likelihood of being stranded and unable to obtain assistance for any period of time is remote. A nagging concern, though not a fear, was the question of crossing the Kennebec River. It took me months of frustrating effort before I was finally able to arrange a canoe crossing. I think I was more concerned about wet clothing, bees, and poison ivy than most hikers. By carrying a number of changes of clothes, I could always continue to hike instead of having to lay over or wear wet things.

Birds along the Appalachian Trail

(An Annotated List of Observations from Georgia to Maine)

By James R. Wolf

Pause along the Appalachian Trail for a moment. Very likely the silence will be broken by a song, a chirp, a trill, or the chatter of a chickadee. From the tops of the trees to the forest floor your progress will be marked by countless birds, bold or shy, many more than you will see. By the time you have walked 2,000 miles, you will have learned much about them and just as much from them. For each kind has its own personality and habits, its own unique way of adapting to its environment.

No two travelers will have the same experience. Their observations will reflect differences in the season, the time they devote to looking and listening, their equipment (binoculars and field guides), and their prior familiarity with the birds that they might encounter. And luck, too.

I maintained a continuous record of the birds for my 171 days along the trail, from March 23 through September 10, 1971, except for a few days of bad weather. Though it isn't possible to concentrate every minute while hiking with a heavy pack, I tried not to miss too much.

It was very helpful to know the songs and calls of many of the species and to learn new ones along the way. Some of the birds that are easily identifiable by ear are the towhee, blue jay, cardinal, crow, ovenbird, whippoorwill, wood pewee, wood thrush, hermit thrush, white-throated sparrow, red-eyed vireo, white-breasted nuthatch, tufted titmouse, and the chickadees. Among others that can be learned with some study are the black-throated blue and black-throated green warblers, song and field sparrows, kingfisher, phoebe, brown thrasher, and great crested flycatcher. In compiling my daily lists I would include birds which I had heard and recognized as well as those that I had seen.

A field guide is helpful, but unfortunately too heavy to be carried conveniently on a long hike. For several portions of the trip I abandoned mine. There were occasions in New England when I was uncertain of an identification; in those cases I made field notes and tried to interpret them much later when I had reference books available.

Migration is an important factor. In summer, many species would be found farther south than I recorded them. On the other hand, some northern species that were common in Virginia in May might be relatively rare there at any other time.

The towhee was the commonest of the birds, even though it was absent at both the southern and northern ends of the trail. The blue jay was observed on more days than any other species, but never in great numbers at any one time. The observations of the dozen most common species may be summarized as follows:

Species	Individuals Counted	No. of Days Counted	No. of Days Species Was Most Common Bird
Towhee	1142	103	46
Grackle	569	52	14
Ovenbird	470	87	8
Junco	457	82	33
Robin	434	103	7
Blue jay	420	118	6
Wood thrush	365	91	0
Wood pewee	307	82	1
Red-eyed vireo	266	65	4
Black-capped chickadee	265	78	9
Crow	247	83	4
Cowbird	201	32	3

A total of 128 species, plus a few additional hypotheticals, are included in the bird list which I have prepared on the basis of my hike. In describing the frequency of observations, I have generally used four classifications:

Abundant: observed nearly every day, usually five or more per day.

Common: observed several times a week, usually less than five per day.

Fairly common: observed about two or three times a week.

Uncommon: observed about once per week or less.

In some cases, the classification applies only to a particular habitat (such as "rural sections" or "around human settlements") instead of the more characteristic forests. A single description, such as "fairly common" or "common," applied to a long stretch does not necessarily imply a completely uniform distribution over the entire distance; some averaging is resorted to for purposes of brevity.

References to "Tennessee" signify the short section between Elk Park and the Virginia boundary. "Western New England" includes Connecticut, Massachusetts, and Vermont. "Northern New England" refers to Vermont, New Hampshire, and Maine.

The absence from my list of such species as the Tennessee warbler and the least flycatcher may be misleading. These, and several others, are not really familiar to me and may have been overlooked.

A final word. Not so many years ago peregrine falcons nested in the Great Smokies near the Appalachian Trail. The trail will be more rewarding when—and if—they ever return. For this long path is not merely 2,000 miles of well-trodden turf. It is the stage for a symphony of nature. The peregrine falcon, and every other plant and animal as well, is vital to the harmony of the piece. Happy is the hiker who can play with the orchestra, keep in tune, and never miss a beat.

Loons—Order Gaviiformes
>   1. *Common loon.* Observed only in Maine, where it was found at Sabbath Day and Moxie ponds, and Lower Joe Mary and Nahmakanta lakes.

Waterfowl—Order Anseriformes
>   2. *Black duck.* Two ducks flushed from the Housatonic River at Kent, Connecticut. Another probable one at Wachipauka Pond, New Hampshire.
>   3. *American goldeneye.* Seen in Maine at East Carry Pond and Moxie Pond.

Vultures, Hawks, and Falcons—Order Falconiformes
>   4. *Turkey vulture.* Fairly common in Georgia and North Carolina south of the Great Smokies. Fairly common from Walker Mountain, Virginia, to the Hudson River. Farther north, just a single specimen at Mt. Everett, Massachusetts. Maximum count: 10, at Delaware Water Gap, Pennsylvania.
>   5. *Goshawk.* Single birds in densely forested areas on Middle Carter in the White Mountains and on Barren Mountain in the eastern section of Maine.
>   6. *Sharp-shinned hawk.* A single brief observation, on Apple

Orchard Mountain, Virginia. The characteristic notched tail of the bird was recorded at the time.

7. *Red-tailed hawk.* Uncommon. Listed at Blood Mountain, Georgia; near Lynchburg Reservoir, Virginia; near Linden, Virginia; and atop Wawayanda Mountain, New Jersey.

8. *Red-shouldered hawk.* A single specimen, along Craig Creek, Virginia. Though the bird was only seen while circling upward on a thermal, identification was reasonably certain.

9. *Broad-winged hawk.* Uncommon. Observed five times between Yellow Mountain on the Tennessee–North Carolina border and Harriman State Park, New York.

10. *Golden eagle.* April 8, from an outcrop on the summit of Cheoah Bald, North Carolina. Identification as a golden (instead of bald) eagle based upon pattern of white in the tail.

11. *Marsh hawk.* A single bird, evidently migrating, near the summit of Mt. Katahdin on September 10.

12. *Osprey.* Just one positive identification, at Wachipauka Pond, New Hampshire. (A second osprey, observed at a distance, was listed at The Pinnacle in Shenandoah National Park on June 7; its presence there at that time of year seems very improbable.)

13. *Pigeon hawk.* A steel blue hawk, recorded as a pigeon hawk, sped across the summit of Snowbird Mountain along the Tennessee–North Carolina border north of the Great Smokies on April 17. This observation is extremely exceptional and, in the absence of corroborating reports of similar sightings by others, might be regarded as hypothetical. However, if the bird was a falcon, as its style of flight—and its shape, as recalled—suggest, then it was definitely a pigeon hawk.

14. *Sparrow hawk.* One observed being mobbed by a kingbird near Churchtown in the Cumberland Valley, Pennsylvania. Also seen on Saddleback Mountain, Maine.

Gallinaceous Birds—Order Galliformes

15. *Turkey.* A single turkey in the Flattop Game Management Area north of Spivey Gap (U.S. 19W) near the Tennessee–North Carolina border. Another, a few hundred yards off the Appalachian Trail, near Pickles Branch south of Roanoke, Virginia.

16. *Spruce grouse.* Fairly common in the White Mountains and in spruce forests in Maine.

17. *Ruffed grouse.* Fairly common from Tray Mountain, Georgia, north through New York. Uncommon in New England. Often encountered with chicks, especially in June.

18. *Bobwhite.* Uncommon. Observed in rural country between Groseclose, Virginia, and the Susquehanna River on eight dates.

19. *Ring-necked pheasant.* Never seen. Identified by call in farmland in Cumberland Valley, Pennsylvania.

Herons—Order Ciconiiformes

20. *Great blue heron.* A single observation, at Stratton Brook Pond near Bigelow, Maine.

21. *Green heron.* In valleys near Elk Park, North Carolina, and Crandon and Webbs Mill, Virginia.

Cranes and Allies—Order Gruiformes

22. *American coot.* This marsh bird, in migration, was flushed from the ground in an oak forest on Levelland Mountain, Georgia, on March 29. It was only 20 feet away and field marks were clearly visible. A surprising observation.

Shorebirds and Gulls—Order Charadriiformes

23. *Killdeer.* Along roads in cleared lands near Groseclose, Virginia, and Unionville and Webatuck, New York.

24. *Spotted sandpiper.* Readily identified at water-edges near Elk Park, North Carolina; Craig Creek and Lynchburg Reservoir Dam, Virginia; and Pemadumcook Lake, Maine.

25. *Solitary sandpiper.* A single specimen, found with a spotted sandpiper, at a small farm pond near the Tennessee–North Carolina border north of Elk Park, North Carolina.

26. *Greater yellowlegs.* One bird, close to the Wallkill River near Unionville, New York. Listing as this species (instead of lesser yellowlegs) based on range description in J. Bull, *Birds of the New York Area.*

27. *Herring gull.* Gulls, identified as this species instead of ring-billed because of range data, were seen along the Hudson and Kennebec rivers, and at Pemadumcook and Nahmakanta lakes in Maine. (Thoreau had the same problem: his *Maine Woods* lists "Larus argentatus?")

Pigeons and Doves—Order Columbiformes

28. *Rock dove.* This species, the domestic pigeon, was fairly common in Pennsylvania. Elsewhere it was observed only a few times. Just one record, three birds in flight above Humpback Mountain, Virginia, was made in a wild setting away from human habitation.

29. *Mourning dove.* Fairly common from Shenandoah National Park through New York. Not found elsewhere.

Cuckoos—Order Cuculiformes

30. *Yellow-billed cuckoo.* One record, in the scrub along the dirt road through the game lands west of Port Clinton, Pennsylvania.

31. *Black-billed cuckoo.* Single birds observed near Three Springs Shelter in northern Virginia; in High Point State Park, New Jersey; and on West Mountain, New York.

Owls—Order Strigiformes

32. *Great horned owl.* One identified with fair certainty by size, flight, color, and habitat near Poor Mountain on the Blue Ridge in Georgia. Also listed in Pennsylvania and New Jersey by call.

Goatsuckers—Order Caprimulgiformes

33. *Whippoorwill.* Never seen. Heard at dawn and dusk fairly commonly between Nolichucky River (near Erwin, Tennessee) and Delaware River.

34. *Nighthawk.* A single specimen, in the center of Hanover, New Hampshire.

Swifts and Hummingbirds—Order Apodiformes

35. *Chimney swift.* Fairly common, probably as migrants, in southern Virginia. Uncommon thereafter to Hanover, New Hampshire, where the last observation (the largest one, with 14 birds counted) was made.

36. *Ruby-throated hummingbird.* At Three Springs Shelter, Virginia; also single observations in Massachusetts and Vermont; in Maine, at Squirrel Rock Shelter and Chairback Mountain Camps.

Kingfishers—Order Coraciiformes

37. *Belted kingfisher.* Along canal towpath in Maryland; Cono-

doguinet Creek, Pennsylvania; Wachipauka Pond, New
Hampshire. Fairly common in Maine.

Woodpeckers—Order Piciformes

38. *Flicker.* Absent in White Mountains. Otherwise fairly common in all sections north of the Great Smokies.

39. *Pileated woodpecker.* Fairly common south of the Great
Smokies and in the general vicinity of Damascus, Virginia.
Uncommon thereafter, with northernmost observation near
Port Clinton, Pennsylvania.

40. *Red-bellied woodpecker.* Near the ruins of the old Bagtown
Hotel in Maryland and at Toms Run Shelter in Pennsylvania.

41. *Redheaded woodpecker.* Just one, in a sycamore along
Black Creek, in the Vernon Valley of New Jersey.

42. *Yellow-bellied sapsucker.* Fairly common in Nantahala
Mountains, North Carolina; less common in Georgia and in
mountains north of the Great Smokies along the Tennessee–
North Carolina boundary. Uncommon in Massachusetts and
northern New England.

43. *Black-backed three-toed woodpecker.* One female, near the
Elephant Mountain Lean-to in Maine.

44. *Hairy woodpecker.* Fairly common in southern sections and
in New York and New England. Uncommon, Virginia
through New Jersey.

45. *Downy woodpecker.* Fairly common, especially in Pennsylvania; observed in all stretches except in Massachusetts,
Vermont, and New Hampshire, where it was unaccountably
scarce or absent.

Perching Birds—Order Passeriformes

Tyrant Flycatchers—Family Tyrannidae

46. *Eastern kingbird.* Fairly common, in suitable rural habitat,
from Tennessee through Vermont.

47. *Great crested flycatcher.* Common from Holston Mountain,
Tennessee, through southern Massachusetts.

48. *Eastern phoebe.* Common from Virginia to Connecticut
River, nearly always in immediate vicinity of trailside shelters. Thereafter only near Monson, Maine.

49. *Acadian flycatcher.* Surprisingly scarce. One was observed
in upland deciduous forest near Ashby Gap in northern
Virginia.

50. *Wood pewee.* Abundant from Virginia through New York. Common in Connecticut and Massachusetts. Fairly common in northern New England. Maximum count: 17, on June 14 in northern Maryland.

Swallows—Family Hirundinidae

51. *Tree swallow.* Observed in rural sections of Connecticut and Massachusetts, particularly in the Housatonic Valley.
52. *Bank swallow.* Recorded, but not carefully studied, along the Housatonic River near Cornwall Bridge, Connecticut.
53. *Rough-winged swallow.* Listed twice in Tennessee and once, below the Lynchburg Reservoir Dam, in Virginia.
54. *Barn swallow.* Common in rural lowland sections, and around water, from Fontana Dam, North Carolina, north to the Androscoggin River, New Hampshire. Maximum count: 26, on August 1, around Hanover, New Hampshire.
55. *Cliff swallow.* These were seen from the bridge crossing the Susquehanna River.
56. *Purple martin.* On the outskirts of Duncannon, Pennsylvania. Also, a few hundred feet from the Appalachian Trail near Hunters Run, Pennsylvania.

Jays and Crows—Family Corvidae

57. *Gray jay.* Seen only in Maine, where it was fairly common at shelters between Elephant Mountain and Mt. Katahdin.
58. *Blue jay.* Common in all sections; often abundant between Pennsylvania and Massachusetts. Maximum: 14, on July 18, in the central part of Massachusetts.
59. *Raven.* Fairly common along ridgetops between Great Smokies and Shenandoah National Parks, and in the White Mountains and Maine.
60. *Crow.* Common from Georgia through Massachusetts. Uncommon in northern New England.

Chickadees and Titmice—Family Paridae

61. *Black-capped chickadee.* Common in Great Smokies and Shenandoah National Parks, and from Pennsylvania through Maine. Maximum count: 12, on August 25, near Bigelow, Maine.
62. *Carolina chickadee.* Common from Georgia through Maryland.
63. *Brown-capped chickadee.* Common in the White Mountains

and Maine, often in same locations as black-capped.

64. *Tufted titmouse.* Common between Georgia and the Delaware River. Thereafter, a single observation (two birds) a few miles east of the Hudson River, at the limits of the species range.

Nuthatches—Family Sittidae

65. *White-breasted nuthatch.* Fairly common from Georgia to western New Hampshire. Uncommon in Maine.

66. *Red-breasted nuthatch.* Fairly common in the Great Smokies. Individuals at Roan Mountain on the Tennessee–North Carolina boundary and at Killington Peak, Vermont. Fairly common in Maine.

Creepers—Family Certhiidae

67. *Brown creeper.* Uncommon. Observed in the Great Smokies, near Plantain Pond in southern Massachusetts, and several times in Maine.

Wrens—Family Troglodytidae

68. *House wren.* Fairly common in farm country from eastern Pennsylvania through Connecticut. Also observed occasionally in Tennessee and southern Virginia.

69. *Winter wren.* Common in the Great Smokies. Fairly common in the White Mountains and western Maine. Also observed in Dean Ravine, Connecticut, and on three occasions in Vermont.

70. *Carolina wren.* Uncommon. Only a few observations, the northernmost in Virginia a few miles from the Potomac River.

Mockingbirds and Thrashers—Family Mimidae

71. *Mockingbird.* Fairly common in and near the Cumberland Valley, Pennsylvania, at the northern limits of its range. Occasionally seen in rural country in Virginia.

72. *Catbird.* First seen April 29 on Yellow Mountain on Tennessee–North Carolina boundary. Fairly common Virginia through Massachusetts, particularly around Shenandoah National Park. Also recorded near Smarts Mountain and at Gentian Pond, New Hampshire, and at Bodfish Farm, Maine.

73. *Brown thrasher.* Fairly common from Georgia through Connecticut.

Photo courtesy Gene G. Fiducia

Gene Fiducia.

Photo by James R. Wolf

Spring beauty in Bradley Gap, Tennessee—North Carolina border.

Thrushes and Bluebirds—Family Turdidae

74. *Robin.* Uncommon south of the Great Smokies. Thereafter common through Vermont (abundant from Potomac to Housatonic rivers). Fairly common in New Hampshire and Maine, especially approaching Mt. Katahdin. Maximum count: 20, on June 15, including golf course at Caledonia State Park, Pennsylvania.

75. *Wood thrush.* From Hot Springs, North Carolina, on April 20 to Sherburne Pass, Vermont, this thrush was always common, often abundant. It remained fairly common as far as Mt. Cube, New Hampshire; but thereafter it was recorded only once, near Little Wilson Stream, Maine. Maximum count: 12, on June 23, west of Port Clinton, Pennsylvania.

76. *Hermit thrush.* One observation during migration, on April 18, at Max Patch Mountain on the Tennessee–North Carolina border. Fairly common in northern New England, especially in the Green Mountains and approaching Mt. Katahdin.

77. *Olive-backed thrush.* One migrant seen on Floyd Mountain, Virginia, on May 23. Also observed near bottom of Peabody Brook Trail, New Hampshire.

78. *Veery.* Fairly common in Tennessee and southern Virginia during migration. Uncommon in New England.

79. *Eastern bluebird.* Fairly common through Virginia (including April migrants on the Blue Ridge and in the Great Smokies). Absent thereafter, except for a single record near Pawling, New York.

Gnatcatchers and Kinglets—Family Sylviidae

80. *Blue-gray gnatcatcher.* Recorded during migration season on April 22 at Big Butt on the Tennessee–North Carolina border. This is not a bird of the mountains and closer examination would have been desirable.

81. *Golden-crowned kinglet.* Fairly common in the Great Smokies, on Roan Mountain on the Tennessee–North Carolina border, and in the White Mountains and Maine.

82. *Ruby-crowned kinglet.* Carefully studied on Baldpate Mountain, Maine. Another probable record on Sugarloaf Mountain, Maine.

Pipits—Family Motacillidae

(*Water pipit.* Hypothetical. A single unsatisfactory observation, along a burned section of trail near Charlies Bunion in the Great Smokies, on April 14.)

Waxwings—Family Bombycillidae

83. *Cedar waxwing.* Fairly common in Maine. Only other observation near Cheshire, Massachusetts.

Starlings—Family Sturnidae

84. *Starling.* Common around human settlements from Hot Springs, North Carolina, to Pawling, New York.

Vireos—Family Vireonidae

85. *White-eyed vireo.* Seen only once, singing along Trout Creek near the Craig Creek Valley in Virginia.
86. *Yellow-throated vireo.* Only one observation, near Hortontown, New York.
87. *Blue-headed (solitary) vireo.* Common from Georgia to Roanoke, Virginia. Uncommon in northern Virginia and again in Maine. Absent Maryland through New Hampshire. (This may be incorrect; some may have been heard, but listed as red-eyed vireos by mistake.) Maximum count: 10, on April 22, near Big Butt on the Tennessee–North Carolina border.
88. *Red-eyed vireo.* Common north of Roanoke, Virginia, through western portions of New Hampshire; abundant in the Taconics and Green mountains. Uncommon in White Mountains and Maine. Maximum count: 16, on July 26, around Little Rock Pond, Vermont.
(*Warbling vireo.* Though possibly confused with red-eyed, listed several times in mid-May in general vicinity of Pearisburg, Virginia, and once in August at Stratton Brook Pond, Maine.)

Wood Warblers—Family Parulidae

89. *Black-and-white warbler.* The earliest warbler, in Georgia on April 1. Fairly common from Spivey Gap on the Tennessee–North Carolina border to Roanoke, Virginia. Uncommon farther north, except in Maine where it was again fairly common.
90. *Worm-eating warbler.* Seen only once, but well, on Feathercamp Ridge north of Damascus, Virginia.
91. *Nashville warbler.* Fairly common east of the Kennebec

River in Maine. (No bird guide was carried here, but identification based on field notes seems reliable.)

92. *Parula warbler.* One specimen, along Cooper Brook in Maine.

93. *Yellow warbler.* Surprisingly scarce. Only one observed clearly, in Sinking Creek Valley, Virginia.

94. *Black-throated blue warbler.* Common from Spivey Gap on the Tennessee–North Carolina border to Roanoke, Virginia, and in Massachusetts and Vermont. Fairly common in Maine. Also heard in Shenandoah National Park.

95. *Myrtle warbler.* Fairly common from Gorham, New Hampshire, to Mt. Katahdin. Also on Killington Peak, Vermont.

96. *Black-throated green warbler.* Fairly common from Davenport Gap north of the Great Smokies through central Virginia. Uncommon from there through New York. Common in western New England, especially in Green Mountains. Fairly common in New Hampshire and Maine.

97. *Blackburnian warbler.* Just one observation, in the Loft Mountain section of Shenandoah National Park.

98. *Chestnut-sided warbler.* Uncommon between Shady Valley, Tennessee, and Bennington, Vermont, except in Shenandoah National Park where it was fairly common.

99. *Blackpoll warbler.* This bird was identified at Peru Peak, Vermont, and at Carter Dome in the White Mountains on the basis of a series of notes with a crescendo-diminuendo effect. It was never positively identified by sight. (See next species.)

(*Pine warbler.* Hypothetical. Identification based upon field notes. Several observations between Sabbath Day Pond and the Kennebec River in Maine were listed as this species, but may have been blackpoll warbler in fall plumage.)

100. *Ovenbird.* First found on April 21 near Little Laurel Lean-to on Tennessee–North Carolina border. Abundant from there through New York. Common north as far as Bromley Mountain, Vermont. Fairly common north of Mt. Sugarloaf, Maine. Maximum count: 22, on June 21, in St. Anthonys Wilderness, Pennsylvania.

101. *Louisiana water thrush.* Observed near streams at Cove Creek Lean-to, Virginia, and Pine Grove Furnace, Pennsylvania, and along Dunnfield Creek, New Jersey.

102. *Yellowthroat.* Fairly common from southern Pennsylvania

through Green Mountains. Thereafter recorded positively only twice, near Norwich, Vermont, and Nahmakanta Lake, Maine.

103. *Yellow-breasted chat*. Observed on two successive days in northern Virginia, near Three Springs Shelter and on Loudoun Heights. Neither seen nor heard any other time.

104. *Canada warbler*. Noted during May migration north of Cherry Tree Lean-to, and on Pearis and Apple Orchard mountains, Virginia. Uncommon in New England.

105. *American redstart*. First seen near Crandon, Virginia. Fairly common from Three Ridges mountain, Virginia, to Potomac River, and in Vermont and Maine (but only one observation in New Hampshire, in the Carter Range).

Weaver Finches—Family Ploceidae

106. *House sparrow*. Common around human settlements from Hot Springs, North Carolina, north.

Blackbirds and Orioles—Family Icteridae

107. *Eastern meadowlark*. Fairly common around fields from Tennessee through New Jersey and especially in southern Virginia.

108. *Redwing*. Fairly common from Georgia to the Delaware River. Common to Hanover, New Hampshire; occasional sizable flocks, especially in Unionville, New York, area.

109. *Orchard oriole*. Male and female carefully studied north of Groseclose, Virginia. Also seen in Sinking Creek Valley, Virginia.

110. *Baltimore oriole*. Fairly common from near Groseclose, Virginia (May 9), through New York. Thereafter, one observation, near West Hartford, Vermont.

111. *Common grackle*. Numbers highly variable. First observed at Hot Springs, North Carolina. Common in Tennessee and Virginia. Abundant north of Shenandoah National Park through New York, with flocks often encountered in areas infested by gypsy moth caterpillars. Common to Hanover, New Hampshire. Uncommon thereafter except for a large flock near Pleasant Pond, Maine. Maximum count: 53 (at least), on June 20, east of the Susquehanna River.

112. *Cowbird*. Common from Tennessee through Massachusetts. Maximum count: 34, on July 9, near Pawling, New York.

Tanagers—Family Thraupidae

113. *Scarlet tanager.* Fairly common from Tennessee north through the Green Mountains.

Grosbeaks, Finches, and Sparrows—Family Fringillidae

114. *Cardinal.* Fairly common, except at high elevations, from the Nantahala River through Virginia. Common Maryland through New York. Uncommon in Connecticut and Massachusetts, including an observation on the outskirts of Blackinton, Massachusetts, at the edge of the species range.

115. *Rose-breasted grosbeak.* Fairly common (migrating?) in Virginia, commencing May 4. Uncommon from Hudson River to Monson, Maine.

116. *Indigo bunting.* Fairly common from Teas, Virginia, to Stokes State Forest, New Jersey. Observed thereafter only once, along Bolles Brook, near Bennington, Vermont.

117. *Evening grosbeak.* A flock of four, on August 20, feeding on cherries on the trail up Elephant Mountain, Maine.

118. *Purple finch.* A female observed in the Housatonic Valley, east of Jug End, Massachusetts, on July 16.

119. *Goldfinch.* Fairly common from Tennessee to Glencliff, New Hampshire. In Maine, recorded only once, along road south of Bodfish Farm.

120. *Towhee.* Common from Nantahala River through the Great Smokies. Abundant north to Massachusetts–Vermont border. Fairly common in Vermont, last seen on Smarts Mountain, New Hampshire. Maximum counts: 69, on June 23, in game lands west of Port Clinton, Pennsylvania; 45, on June 17, in vicinity of Pine Grove Furnace, Pennsylvania.

121. *Vesper sparrow.* Recorded at Bradley Gap, near Hump Mountain on the Tennessee–North Carolina boundary on April 29, and twice within the next few days in rural Tennessee.

122. *Slate-colored junco.* Common from Georgia to Damascus, Virginia (except abundant in the Great Smokies). Fairly common at higher elevations in Virginia. Absent between Skyland in Shenandoah National Park and Mt. Everett, Massachusetts. Common in Massachusetts and northern New England. Maximum count: 28, on April 15, in virgin forest north of False Gap in the Great Smokies.

123. *Chipping sparrow.* Fairly common in all sections north of the Great Smokies, except in New Hampshire where it was

seen only in the outskirts of Hanover. Maximum count: 8, on April 30 near Elk Park, North Carolina, and on July 2 near Unionville, New York.

124. *Field sparrow.* Fairly common in most sections from Georgia through New York (uncommon in Virginia north of Groseclose). Also observed near Cheshire, Massachusetts, and Bennington, Vermont.

125. *White-crowned sparrow.* One migrant seen at close range near Groseclose, Virginia, on May 10.

126. *White-throated sparrow.* Uncommon from the Nantahala River to Crandon, Virginia. Common from Tyringham, Massachusetts, to Mt. Katahdin. Maximum count: 10, on July 20, on Mt. Greylock, Massachusetts.

127. *Fox sparrow.* A single observation, extremely late in the year for this northbound migrant, near Chattahoochee Gap, Georgia, on March 30.

128. *Song sparrow.* Fairly common from Georgia to Roanoke, Virginia (except for the Great Smokies, where it was absent). Uncommon from Roanoke through Pennsylvania. Common from New Jersey to Hanover, New Hampshire. Maximum count: 8, on July 9, around Pawling, New York.

Mileage–Climb Data Summaries

By James R. Wolf

MILEAGE. Mileages are primarily derived from guidebooks. (When I hiked, the *Guide to the Appalachian Trail in Central and Southwestern Virginia* was out-of-print, however, and some estimates were necessary in this stretch.) In a few places, guidebook distances were modified to compensate for relocations or very occasional errors.

ELEVATIONS. Elevations (rounded to the nearest 50 feet) generally are taken from topographical maps. In some cases, particularly where the present route is not shown on the map, data are based upon pocket-altimeter readings.

CLIMB. The recorded values represent the gross feet climbed on a northbound hike. This is the sum of every rise (rounded to the nearest 50 feet) between the two indicated points, again using maps and hiking experience as the sources of the data. To calculate the climb between the same two points in a southbound direction, where A is the southern point and B is the northern point:
1. Subtract the elevation of B from the elevation of A (this will give a minus figure if B is higher than A).
2. Add the value from (1) to the Climb from Prior Point appearing opposite B.
3. The sum calculated in step (2) is the amount of climb involved southbound to go from B to A.

Where shelters are approximately 0.2 mile or more from the main trail, the side-trail distance is indicated. However, the elevation and the mileages from the terminals are recorded for the point at which the trail to the shelter intersects the Appalachian Trail.

All information pertains to the Appalachian Trail route in the spring and summer of 1971. Guidebooks and the *Appalachian Trailway News* may be consulted for subsequent relocations.

1921

THE APPALACHIAN TRAIL
Southern Division:
Springer Mountain, Georgia, to Rockfish Gap, Virginia

Miles from Springer Mountain	Mileage between Points	Location	Elevation	Climb from Prior Point	Miles from Rockfish Gap	Miles from Mt. Katahdin
		GEORGIA				
		Approach Trail				
6.9	0.0	Amicalola Falls	2,500	0	744.2	2,014.4
2.3	4.6	Nimblewill Gap	3,100	1,100	739.6	2,009.8
0.0	2.3	Springer Mountain	3,800	1,150	737.3	2,007.5
		Appalachian Trail				
0.0	0.0	Springer Mountain	3,800	0	737.3	2,007.5
1.6	1.6	Big Stamp Gap Lean-to	3,150	150	735.7	2,005.9
6.1	4.5	Three Forks	2,550	250	731.2	2,001.4
9.6	3.5	Hawk Mountain Lean-to	3,400	1,200	727.7	1,997.9
14.1	4.5	Cooper Gap	2,850	900	723.2	1,993.4
18.7	4.6	Gooch Gap Lean-to	2,850	1,450	718.6	1,988.8
22.4	3.7	Woody Gap (Georgia Highway 60)	3,150	750	714.9	1,985.1
27.4	5.0	Jarrard Gap	3,250	1,150	709.9	1,980.1
30.3	2.9	Blood Mountain Shelter	4,450	1,350	707.0	1,977.2
32.4	2.1	Neels Gap (U.S. Routes 19 and 129)	3,150	0	704.9	1,975.1
38.1	5.7	Tesnatee Gap Lean-to	3,150	1,600	699.2	1,969.4
43.4	5.3	Low Gap	3,050	1,450	693.9	1,964.1
50.1	6.7	Rocky Knob Lean-to	3,700	1,250	687.2	1,957.4
53.0	2.9	Unicoi Gap (Georgia Highway 75)	2,950	550	684.3	1,954.5
58.8	5.8	Tray Mountain Lean-to (0.3 mile off trail)	4,200	2,350	678.5	1,948.7
64.2	5.4	Addis Gap Lean-to (0.5 mile off trail)	3,300	1,100	673.1	1,943.3
69.6	5.4	Dicks Creek Gap (U.S. Route 76)	2,650	1,550	667.7	1,937.9
74.0	4.4	Plumorchard Gap Lean-to	3,100	1,600	663.3	1,933.5
78.3	4.3	Bly Gap	3,850	1,400	659.0	1,929.2
		NORTH CAROLINA				
83.8	5.5	Deep Gap	4,350	1,800	653.5	1,923.7
84.6	0.8	Standing Indian Lean-to	4,750	400	652.7	1,922.9
86.3	1.7	Standing Indian	5,450	700	651.0	1,921.2
92.3	6.0	Carter Gap Lean-to	4,550	550	645.0	1,915.2
98.3	6.0	Albert Mountain	5,250	1,650	639.0	1,909.2
98.8	0.5	Big Spring Gap Lean-to	4,950	50	638.5	1,908.7

THE APPALACHIAN TRAIL

Southern Division:
Springer Mountain, Georgia, to Rockfish Gap, Virginia

Miles from Springer Mountain	Mileage between Points	Location	Elevation	Climb from Prior Point	Miles from Rockfish Gap	Miles from Mt. Katahdin
103.9	5.1	Rock Gap Lean-to	3,750	400	633.4	1,903.6
104.6	0.7	Wallace Gap				
		(U.S. Route 64)	3,700	50	632.7	1,902.9
111.5	6.9	Siler Bald	4,750	1,800	625.8	1,896.0
112.7	1.2	Wayah Gap	4,150	50	624.6	1,894.8
116.4	3.7	Wayah Bald	5,350	1,200	620.9	1,891.1
121.9	5.5	Cold Springs Lean-to	4,950	1,100	615.4	1,885.6
125.5	3.6	Tellico Gap	3,850	450	611.8	1,882.0
126.3	0.8	Wesser Bald	4,650	800	611.0	1,881.2
129.7	3.4	Wesser Creek Lean-to	2,450	0	607.6	1,877.8
132.7	3.0	Wesser (U.S. Route 19)	1,700	0	604.6	1,874.8
138.6	5.9	Sassafras Gap Lean-to				
		(0.3 mile off trail)	4,400	3,100	598.7	1,868.9
141.6	3.0	Locust Cove Gap	3,650	800	595.7	1,865.9
144.0	2.4	Stekoah Gap	3,150	650	593.3	1,863.5
146.7	2.7	Brown Fork Gap	3,550	-1,500	590.6	1,860.8
151.7	5.0	Yellow Creek Gap	2,950	1,150	585.6	1,855.8
152.6	0.9	Cable Gap Lean-to	2,850	150	584.7	1,854.9
155.4	2.8	North Carolina				
		Highway 28	1,950	650	581.9	1,852.1
157.6	2.2	Fontana Dam	1,700	150	579.7	1,849.9
162.0	4.4	Shuckstack crest	3,900	2,300	575.3	1,845.5
163.3	1.3	Birch Spring Lean-to	3,750	400	574.0	1,844.2
165.3	2.0	Doe Knob	4,500	850	572.0	1,842.2

NORTH CAROLINA–TENNESSEE

Miles from Springer Mountain	Mileage between Points	Location	Elevation	Climb from Prior Point	Miles from Rockfish Gap	Miles from Mt. Katahdin
167.7	2.4	Mollies Ridge Lean-to	4,600	750	569.6	1,839.8
169.8	2.1	Spence Field Lean-tos	4,900	850	567.5	1,837.7
174.0	4.2	Thunderhead	5,500	800	563.3	1,833.5
178.2	4.2	Derrick Knob Lean-to	4,900	1,150	559.1	1,829.3
180.5	2.3	Cold Spring Knob	5,250	750	556.8	1,827.0
183.7	3.2	Silers Bald Lean-to	5,500	950	553.6	1,823.8
185.3	1.6	Double Springs				
		Gap Lean-to	5,500	500	552.0	1,822.2
188.1	2.8	Clingmans Dome	6,650	1,200	549.2	1,819.4
191.0	2.9	Mt. Collins	6,200	650	546.3	1,816.5
191.3	0.3	Mt. Collins Lean-to				
		(0.5 mile off trail)	6,000	0	546.0	1,816.2
193.9	2.6	Indian Gap	5,250	250	543.4	1,813.6
195.6	1.7	Newfound Gap				
		(U.S. Route 441)	5,050	350	541.7	1,811.9

THE APPALACHIAN TRAIL

Southern Division:
Springer Mountain, Georgia, to Rockfish Gap, Virginia

Miles from Springer Mountain	Mileage between Points	Location	Elevation	Climb from Prior Point	Miles from Rockfish Gap	Miles from Mt. Katahdin
198.5	2.9	Ice Water Spring Lean-tos	5,900	1,100	538.8	1,809.0
202.0	3.5	False Gap Lean-to	5,300	300	535.3	1,805.5
205.8	3.8	Pecks Corner Lean-to (0.4 mile off trail)	5,550	800	531.5	1,801.7
208.6	2.8	Mt. Sequoyah	6,000	800	528.7	1,798.9
210.8	2.2	Tri-Corner Knob Lean-to	5,900	450	526.5	1,796.7
212.8	2.0	Guyot Spring	6,250	450	524.5	1,794.7
218.5	5.7	Cosby Knob Lean-to	4,750	700	518.8	1,789.0
225.5	7.0	Davenport Gap Lean-to	2,550	900	511.8	1,782.0
226.4	0.9	Davenport Gap (Tennessee Highway 32 and North Carolina Highway 284)	2,000	0	510.9	1,781.1
228.0	1.6	Big Pigeon River (Interstate 40)	1,350	100	509.3	1,779.5
230.9	2.9	Painter Creek	2,750	1,450	506.4	1,776.6
233.4	2.5	Snowbird Mountain	4,250	1,500	503.9	1,774.1
235.9	2.5	Groundhog Creek Lean-to (0.2 mile off trail)	2,900	150	501.4	1,771.6
238.6	2.7	Brown Gap	3,500	1,000	498.7	1,768.9
241.3	2.7	Max Patch Road	4,300	1,050	496.0	1,766.2
246.3	5.0	Walnut Mountain Lean-to	4,250	800	491.0	1,761.2
248.8	2.5	Bluff Mountain	4,700	1,000	488.5	1,758.7
252.3	3.5	Garenflo Gap	2,500	50	485.0	1,755.2
255.7	3.4	Deer Park Mountain Lean-to	2,350	500	481.6	1,751.8
258.9	3.2	Hot Springs (U.S. Routes 25 and 70)	1,350	300	478.4	1,748.6
263.8	4.9	Rich Mountain	3,550	2,200	473.5	1,743.7
266.4	2.6	Spring Mountain Lean-to	3,550	750	470.9	1,741.1
270.0	3.6	Allen Gap (Tennessee Highway 70 and North Carolina Highway 208)	2,250	400	467.3	1,737.5
274.5	4.5	Little Laurel Lean-to	3,650	1,650	462.8	1,733.0
277.4	2.9	Bearwallow Gap	4,400	1,150	459.9	1,730.1
280.5	3.1	Jerry Cabin Lean-to	4,150	250	456.8	1,727.0
282.2	1.7	Big Butt	4,800	650	455.1	1,725.3
286.9	4.7	Locust Ridge Lean-to	3,350	250	450.4	1,720.6

THE APPALACHIAN TRAIL

Southern Division:
Springer Mountain, Georgia, to Rockfish Gap, Virginia

Miles from Springer Mountain	Mileage between Points	Location	Elevation	Climb from Prior Point	Miles from Rockfish Gap	Miles from Mt. Katahdin
288.4	1.5	Devil Fork Gap (North Carolina Highway 212)	3,100	200	448.9	1,719.1
291.5	3.1	Frozen Knob	4,600	2,000	445.8	1,716.0
296.2	4.7	Sams Gap (U.S. Route 23)	3,800	900	441.1	1,711.3
299.4	3.2	Low Gap	4,300	1,300	437.9	1,708.1
301.8	2.4	Big Bald	5,500	1,300	435.5	1,705.7
304.1	2.3	Little Bald	5,200	350	433.2	1,703.4
307.5	3.4	Spivey Gap (U.S. Route 19W)	3,200	550	429.8	1,700.0
312.0	4.5	No Business Lean-to	3,200	850	425.3	1,695.5
315.2	3.2	Temple Ridge	3,250	450	422.1	1,692.3
317.7	2.5	Nolichucky River	1,700	50	419.6	1,689.8
321.9	4.2	Curley Maple Gap Lean-to	3,050	1,400	415.4	1,685.6
325.3	3.4	Indian Grave Gap	3,350	1,000	412.0	1,682.2
327.7	2.4	Beauty Spot Gap	4,300	1,050	409.6	1,679.8
331.6	3.9	Picnic area	4,750	900	405.7	1,675.9
334.4	2.8	Cherry Gap Lean-to	3,950	400	402.9	1,673.1
337.2	2.8	Iron Mountain Gap (Tennessee Highway 107 and North Carolina Highway 26)	3,700	700	400.1	1,670.3
342.1	4.9	Homestead	4,200	1,400	395.2	1,665.4
345.3	3.2	Hughes Gap	4,050	1,200	392.0	1,662.2
347.9	2.6	Roan Mountain	6,150	2,300	389.4	1,659.6
349.9	2.0	Carvers Gap (Tennessee Highway 143 and North Carolina Highway 261)	5,500	100	387.4	1,657.6
351.6	1.7	Grassy Ridge Lean-to	5,850	650	385.7	1,655.9
355.8	4.2	Big Yellow Bald Mountain	5,450	1,100	381.5	1,651.7
357.5	1.7	Hump Mountain	5,550	650	379.8	1,650.0
360.5	3.0	U.S. Route 19E	3,100	0	376.8	1,647.0
		TENNESSEE				
365.0	4.5	Walnut Mountain Road	3,450	1,000	372.3	1,642.5
370.4	5.4	Moreland Gap Lean-to	3,800	1,050	366.9	1,637.1

THE APPALACHIAN TRAIL

Southern Division:
Springer Mountain, Georgia, to Rockfish Gap, Virginia

Miles from Springer Mountain	Mileage between Points	Location	Elevation	Climb from Prior Point	Miles from Rockfish Gap	Miles from Mt. Katahdin
373.1	2.7	White Rocks Mountain Fire Tower	4,100	950	364.2	1,634.4
377.1	4.0	Laurel Fork Lean-to	2,150	250	360.2	1,630.4
379.0	1.9	Tennessee Highway 67	1,850	100	358.3	1,628.5
382.0	3.0	South Pierce Lean-to	2,800	1,350	355.3	1,625.5
384.6	2.6	Wilbur Lake	1,650	450	352.7	1,622.9
386.2	1.6	Watauga Dam Road	2,250	850	351.1	1,621.3
390.6	4.4	Vanderventer Lean-to	3,450	1,650	346.7	1,616.9
395.8	5.2	Turkeypen Gap	3,950	1,050	341.5	1,611.7
397.5	1.7	Iron Mountain Lean-to	4,050	350	339.8	1,610.0
402.3	4.8	Tennessee Highway 91	3,500	600	335.0	1,605.2
405.2	2.9	Rich Knob Lean-to	4,050	550	332.1	1,602.3
408.6	3.4	Low Gap (U.S. Route 421)	3,400	400	328.7	1,598.9
411.9	3.3	McQueens Knob	3,900	800	325.4	1,595.6
413.3	1.4	Abingdon Gap Lean-to	3,800	250	324.0	1,594.2
419.6	6.3	Tennessee–Virginia line	3,200	650	317.7	1,587.9
		VIRGINIA				
423.8	4.2	Damascus	1,950	50	313.5	1,583.7
430.2	6.4	Sandy Flats Lean-to	3,350	1,850	307.1	1,577.3
435.5	5.3	Straight Branch Lean-to	3,700	1,050	301.8	1,572.0
440.7	5.2	Cherry Tree Lean-to	4,450	1,200	296.6	1,566.8
447.9	7.2	Virginia Highway 16	3,300	900	289.4	1,559.6
449.9	2.0	Raccoon Branch Lean-to (0.2 mile off trail)	3,750	650	287.4	1,557.6
452.9	3.0	Teas	2,500	200	284.4	1,554.6
456.6	3.7	Virginia Highway 16	3,250	1,000	280.7	1,550.9
460.6	4.0	Killinger Creek Lean-to	3,600	1,300	276.7	1,546.9
467.0	6.4	Interstate 81	2,400	500	270.3	1,540.5
471.3	4.3	Little Brushy Mountain	3,350	1,150	266.0	1,536.2
475.3	4.0	Walker Mountain Lean-to	3,950	1,450	262.0	1,532.2
482.5	7.2	Monster Rock Lean-to	3,750	650	254.8	1,525.0
483.5	1.0	Big Walker Lookout (U.S. Routes 21 and 52)	3,450	50	253.8	1,524.0
487.6	4.1	Big Bend	3,900	700	249.7	1,519.9
493.0	5.4	Turkey Gap Lean-to	3,700	450	244.3	1,514.5
500.2	7.2	High Rock Lean-to	3,750	950	237.1	1,507.3
503.7	3.5	Crandon (Virginia Highway 42)	2,250	200	233.6	1,503.8
507.3	3.6	Virginia Secondary Road 606	2,100	150	230.0	1,500.2

THE APPALACHIAN TRAIL

Southern Division:
Springer Mountain, Georgia, to Rockfish Gap, Virginia

Miles from Springer Mountain	Mileage between Points	Location	Elevation	Climb from Prior Point	Miles from Rockfish Gap	Miles from Mt. Katahdin
513.1	5.8	Wapiti Lean-to	2,450	550	224.2	1,494.4
515.4	2.3	Honey Spring				
		Patrol Cabin	3,750	1,300	221.9	1,492.1
519.7	4.3	Doc's Knob Lean-to	3,500	250	217.6	1,487.8
526.6	6.9	Angels Rest	3,550	950	210.7	1,480.9
528.5	1.9	Pearisburg				
		(U.S. Route 460)	1,800	0	208.8	1,479.0
529.9	1.4	New River	1,600	0	207.4	1,477.6
532.6	2.7	Clendennin Creek	2,100	900	204.7	1,474.9
534.8	2.2	Peters Mountain crest	3,400	1,300	202.5	1,472.7
538.3	3.5	Peters Mountain Bald	3,500	450	199.0	1,469.2
543.5	5.2	Pine Swamp Spring	3,800	1,150	193.8	1,464.0
545.5	2.0	Big Stony Creek				
		(Virginia Secondary				
		Highway 635)	2,350	0	191.8	1,462.0
548.8	3.3	Bailey Gap Lean-to	3,550	1,500	188.5	1,458.7
552.6	3.8	Stony Creek Fire Tower	4,150	800	184.7	1,454.9
556.1	3.5	War Branch Lean-to	2,350	200	181.2	1,451.4
561.2	5.1	Big Pond Lean-to	3,600	1,850	176.1	1,446.3
564.2	3.0	Virginia Highway 42	2,100	100	173.1	1,443.3
566.8	2.6	Sinking Creek				
		Mountain crest	3,150	1,100	170.5	1,440.7
569.9	3.1	Bruisers Knob	3,450	500	167.4	1,437.6
576.6	6.7	Sinking Creek Road	3,250	450	160.7	1,430.9
577.4	0.8	Niday Lean-to	2,900	0	159.9	1,430.1
580.6	3.2	Webbs Mill	1,450	0	156.7	1,426.9
583.3	2.7	Trout Creek Lean-to	1,700	250	154.0	1,424.2
586.0	2.7	Dragons Tooth	3,050	1,500	151.3	1,421.5
589.4	3.4	Catawba Creek	1,750	300	147.9	1,418.1
593.0	3.6	Virginia Highway 311	1,950	900	144.3	1,414.5
596.7	3.7	McAfee Knob	3,200	1,250	140.6	1,410.8
601.5	4.8	Tinker Mountain	3,000	1,000	135.8	1,406.0
603.2	1.7	Lamberts Meadow	2,000	0	134.1	1,404.3
606.9	3.7	Ruckers Knob	2,100	850	130.4	1,400.6
613.1	6.2	Interstate 81	1,200	650	124.2	1,394.4
617.4	4.3	Fullhardt Knob Lean-to	2,650	1,500	119.9	1,390.1
621.3	3.9	Curry Creek	1,600	350	116.0	1,386.2
623.4	2.1	Wilson Creek Lean-to	1,450	450	113.9	1,384.1
626.1	2.7	Black Horse Gap	2,400	1,000	111.2	1,381.4
631.2	5.1	Bobbletts Gap Lean-to				
		(0.2 mile off trail)	2,100	650	106.1	1,376.3
633.9	2.7	Bearwallow Gap	2,250	400	103.4	1,373.6

THE APPALACHIAN TRAIL
Southern Division:
Springer Mountain, Georgia, to Rockfish Gap, Virginia

Miles from Springer Mountain	Mileage between Points	Location	Elevation	Climb from Prior Point	Miles from Rockfish Gap	Miles from Mt. Katahdin
640.1	6.2	Cove Creek Lean-to	1,000	750	97.2	1,367.4
643.3	3.2	Virginia Secondary				
		Highway 714	1,500	1,300	94.0	1,364.2
648.8	5.5	Cornelius Creek Lean-to	3,100	2,350	88.5	1,358.7
652.3	3.5	Apple Orchard Mountain	4,150	1,600	85.0	1,355.2
654.4	2.1	Thunder Hill Lean-to	4,000	200	82.9	1,353.1
658.0	3.6	Petites Gap	2,350	450	79.3	1,349.5
660.3	2.3	Marble Spring Lean-to	2,350	800	77.0	1,347.2
661.7	1.4	Hickory Stand Mountain	2,400	150	75.6	1,345.8
666.0	4.3	Matts Creek Lean-to	800	300	71.3	1,341.5
668.5	2.5	James River				
		(U.S. Route 501)	650	500	68.8	1,339.0
671.0	2.5	Johns Hollow Lean-to	1,000	350	66.3	1,336.5
673.1	2.1	Little Rocky Row	2,450	1,450	64.2	1,334.4
676.7	3.6	Saltlog Gap	2,650	750	60.6	1,330.8
679.3	2.6	Punchbowl Spring Lean-to				
		(0.2 mile off trail)	2,550	800	58.0	1,328.2
681.9	2.6	Rice Mountain	2,200	650	55.4	1,325.6
684.0	2.1	Lynchburg Reservoir				
		Dam	1,000	0	53.3	1,323.5
687.8	3.8	Brown Mountain				
		Creek Lean-to	1,350	650	49.5	1,319.7
689.6	1.8	U.S. Route 60	2,050	700	47.7	1,317.9
692.9	3.3	Bald Knob	4,050	2,000	44.4	1,314.6
695.9	3.0	Wiggins Spring Lean-to				
		(0.5 mile off trail)	3,500	500	41.4	1,311.6
697.7	1.8	Salt Log Gap	3,250	350	39.6	1,309.8
699.9	2.2	Lovingston Spring	3,700	700	37.4	1,307.6
703.1	3.2	Fish Hatchery Road	3,450	450	34.2	1,304.4
707.6	4.5	The Priest Lean-to	3,900	1,750	29.7	1,299.9
712.5	4.9	Tye River	900	150	24.8	1,295.0
714.5	2.0	Harpers Creek Lean-to	1,900	1,000	22.8	1,293.0
717.3	2.8	Three Ridges	3,900	2,000	20.0	1,290.2
720.5	3.2	Maupin Field Lean-to	2,750	100	16.8	1,287.0
721.8	1.3	Reeds Gap	2,600	350	15.5	1,285.7
726.1	4.3	Laurel Springs Gap	2,850	1,050	11.2	1,281.4
728.7	2.6	Humpback Mountain	3,650	950	8.6	1,278.8
730.6	1.9	Humpback Gap				
		Parking Area	2,350	50	6.7	1,276.9
734.8	4.2	Blue Ridge Parkway	2,250	1,150	2.5	1,272.7
737.3	2.5	Rockfish Gap				
		(U.S. Route 250)	1,900	100	0.0	1,270.2

THE APPALACHIAN TRAIL

Central Division:
Rockfish Gap, Virginia, to Massachusetts–Vermont Line

Miles from Springer Mountain	Miles from Rockfish Gap	Mileage between Points	Location	Elevation	Climb from Prior Point	Miles from Vermont Line	Miles from Mt. Katahdin
737.3	0.0	0.0	Rockfish Gap	1,900	0	707.7	1,270.2
740.6	3.3	3.3	McCormick Gap	2,450	850	704.4	1,266.9
742.4	5.1	1.8	Beagles Gap	2,550	450	702.6	1,265.1
744.9	7.6	2.5	Jarmans Gap	2,200	450	700.1	1,262.6
			SHENANDOAH NATIONAL PARK				
747.0	9.7	2.1	Sawmill Run Shelter				
			(0.3 mile off trail)	2,300	400	698.0	1,260.5
748.5	11.2	1.5	Turks Gap	2,600	400	696.5	1,259.0
750.5	13.2	2.0	Wildcat Ridge Parking Area	3,000	550	694.5	1,257.0
754.5	17.2	4.0	Skyline Drive	2,650	600	690.5	1,253.0
756.3	19.0	1.8	Blackrock Gap	2,350	250	688.7	1,251.2
757.0	19.7	0.7	Blackrock Gap Shelter				
			(0.2 mile off trail)	2,750	400	688.0	1,250.5
759.3	22.0	2.3	Dundo Picnic Grounds	2,800	350	685.7	1,248.2
764.2	26.9	4.9	Loft Mountain Development	3,200	650	680.8	1,243.3
766.3	29.0	2.1	Ivy Creek Shelter	2,900	250	678.7	1,241.2
770.1	32.8	3.8	Pinefield Shelter	2,450	700	674.9	1,237.4
772.2	34.9	2.1	Simmons Gap	2,250	400	672.8	1,235.3
775.4	38.1	3.2	Powells Gap	2,300	750	669.6	1,232.1
778.3	41.0	2.9	High Top Shelter	3,150	900	666.7	1,229.2
781.4	44.1	3.1	Swift Run Gap				
			(U.S. Route 33)	2,350	450	663.6	1,226.1
784.0	46.7	2.6	South River Shelter				
			(0.3 mile off trail)	2,900	850	661.0	1,223.5
787.7	50.4	3.7	PATC Pocosin Cabin	3,200	800	657.3	1,219.8
789.7	52.4	2.0	Lewis Mountain				
			Campground and Lodge	3,450	350	655.3	1,217.8
790.5	53.2	0.8	Bear Fence Mountain Shelter				
			(0.2 mile off trail)	3,150	0	654.5	1,217.0
793.8	56.5	3.3	Hazel Top Mountain	3,800	1,000	651.2	1,213.7
797.5	60.2	3.7	Lewis Spring Shelter	3,350	150	647.5	1,210.0
798.0	60.7	0.5	Big Meadows Lodge				
			(0.3 mile off trail)	3,600	250	647.0	1,209.5
800.1	62.8	2.1	Fishers Gap	3,100	0	644.9	1,207.4
803.3	66.0	3.2	Hawksbill Gap Shelter				
			(0.3 mile off trail)	3,650	700	641.7	1,204.2
806.4	69.1	3.1	Skyland Lodge	3,650	500	638.6	1,201.1
809.6	72.3	3.2	Shavers Hollow Shelter				
			(0.3 mile off trail)	3,000	550	635.4	1,197.9
812.8	75.5	3.2	Byrd Shelter No. 3	3,250	750	632.2	1,194.7

THE APPALACHIAN TRAIL
Central Division:
Rockfish Gap, Virginia, to Massachusetts–Vermont Line

Miles from Springer Mountain	Miles from Rockfish Gap	Mileage between Points	Location	Elevation	Climb from Prior Point	Miles from Vermont Line	Miles from Mt. Katahdin
815.8	78.5	3.0	Thornton Gap (U.S. Route 211)	2,300	250	629.2	1,191.7
817.0	79.7	1.2	Pass Mountain Shelter (0.2 mile off trail)	2,800	500	628.0	1,190.5
818.9	81.6	1.9	Beahms Gap	2,500	250	626.1	1,188.6
819.8	82.5	0.9	Byrd Shelter No. 4	2,800	400	625.2	1,187.7
824.0	86.7	4.2	Elk Wallow Shelter	2,300	550	621.0	1,183.5
825.2	87.9	1.2	PATC Range View Cabin	2,950	650	619.8	1,182.3
828.5	91.2	3.3	Little Hogback Parking Overlook	3,000	650	616.5	1,179.0
830.2	92.9	1.7	Gravelly Springs Shelter (0.2 mile off trail)	2,650	150	614.8	1,177.3
832.6	95.3	2.4	North Marshall Mountain	3,350	800	612.4	1,174.9
835.7	98.4	3.1	Jenkins Gap	2,350	150	609.3	1,171.8
838.0	100.7	2.3	Indian Run Shelter (0.5 mile off trail)	2,500	650	607.0	1,169.5
840.0	102.7	2.0	Shenandoah National Park Boundary	2,050	0	605.0	1,167.5

NORTHERN VIRGINIA

Miles from Springer Mountain	Miles from Rockfish Gap	Mileage between Points	Location	Elevation	Climb from Prior Point	Miles from Vermont Line	Miles from Mt. Katahdin
841.7	104.4	1.7	Chester Gap (U.S. Route 522)	1,300	0	603.3	1,165.8
844.2	106.9	2.5	Mosby Shelter	1,800	750	600.8	1,163.3
847.2	109.9	3.0	Linden (Virginia Highway 55)	900	50	597.8	1,160.3
852.6	115.3	5.4	Trico Fire Tower	2,200	1,350	592.4	1,154.9
859.2	121.9	6.6	Ashby Gap (U.S. Route 50)	1,000	200	585.8	1,148.3
866.7	129.4	7.5	Three Springs Shelter	1,500	1,300	578.3	1,140.8
870.3	133.0	3.6	Snickers Gap (Virginia Highway 7)	1,050	200	574.7	1,137.2

VIRGINIA–WEST VIRGINIA

Miles from Springer Mountain	Miles from Rockfish Gap	Mileage between Points	Location	Elevation	Climb from Prior Point	Miles from Vermont Line	Miles from Mt. Katahdin
872.9	135.6	2.6	Sand Spring	1,050	450	572.1	1,134.6
875.8	138.5	2.9	Wilson Gap Shelter	1,350	750	569.2	1,131.7
878.2	140.9	2.4	Laurel Spring	1,350	350	566.8	1,129.3
883.2	145.9	5.0	Keys Gap Shelter	900	350	561.8	1,124.3
889.4	152.1	6.2	Potomac River	350	550	555.6	1,118.1

MARYLAND

Miles from Springer Mountain	Miles from Rockfish Gap	Mileage between Points	Location	Elevation	Climb from Prior Point	Miles from Vermont Line	Miles from Mt. Katahdin
891.3	154.0	1.9	Weverton Shelter	250	0	553.7	1,116.2

THE APPALACHIAN TRAIL

Central Division:
Rockfish Gap, Virginia, to Massachusetts–Vermont Line

Miles from Springer Mountain	Miles from Rockfish Gap	Mileage between Points	Location	Elevation	Climb from Prior Point	Miles from Vermont Line	Miles from Mt. Katahdin
892.1	154.8	0.8	Weverton Cliffs	850	600	552.9	1,115.4
897.8	160.5	5.7	Crampton Gap	900	900	547.2	1,109.7
898.4	161.1	0.6	Crampton Gap Shelter				
			(0.3 mile off trail)	1,150	250	546.6	1,109.1
902.6	165.3	4.2	Rocky Run Shelter				
			(0.2 mile off trail)	1,100	700	542.4	1,104.9
904.5	167.2	1.9	Turners Gap (U.S.				
			Alternate Route 40)	1,050	200	540.5	1,103.0
906.4	169.1	1.9	Monument Knob	1,500	650	538.6	1,101.1
909.6	172.3	3.2	Interstate 70				
			and U.S. Route 40	1,250	350	535.4	1,097.9
910.0	172.7	0.4	Pine Knob Shelter	1,400	150	535.0	1,097.5
913.4	176.1	3.4	Black Rock Springs	1,500	500	531.6	1,094.1
917.8	180.5	4.4	Smithsburg–Wolfsville Road				
			(Maryland Highway 17)	1,400	400	527.2	1,089.7
919.0	181.7	1.2	Maryland Highway 77	1,400	200	526.0	1,088.5
922.3	185.0	3.3	Devils Racecourse Shelter				
			(0.5 mile off trail)	1,700	900	522.7	1,085.2
926.7	189.4	4.4	Pen Mar	1,200	300	518.3	1,080.8

PENNSYLVANIA

928.6	191.3	1.9	Mackie Run Shelter	1,200	450	516.4	1,078.9
932.7	195.4	4.1	Antietam Shelter	900	350	512.3	1,074.8
933.8	196.5	1.1	Tumbling Run Shelter	1,050	150	511.2	1,073.7
936.8	199.5	3.0	Snowy Mountain				
			Fire Tower	2,100	1,250	508.2	1,070.7
941.0	203.7	4.2	Raccoon Run Shelters	1,100	0	504.0	1,066.5
942.9	205.6	1.9	U.S. Route 30	950	50	502.1	1,064.6
945.2	207.9	2.3	Quarry Gap Shelters	1,450	600	499.8	1,062.3
950.0	212.7	4.8	PATC Milesburn Cabin	1,700	850	495.0	1,057.5
952.4	215.1	2.4	Birch Run Shelters	1,750	200	492.6	1,055.1
953.6	216.3	1.2	Arendtsville–Shippensburg				
			Road	2,000	250	491.4	1,053.9
956.1	218.8	2.5	Tumbling Run	1,600	100	488.9	1,051.4
958.4	221.1	2.3	Toms Run Shelters	1,300	250	486.6	1,049.1
961.8	224.5	3.4	Pine Grove Furnace	900	100	483.2	1,045.7
965.8	228.5	4.0	Piney Mountain	1,450	650	479.2	1,041.7
969.0	231.7	3.2	Tagg Run Shelters	700	200	476.0	1,038.5
972.2	234.9	3.2	Pennsylvania Highway 94	850	400	472.8	1,035.3
975.1	237.8	2.9	Whiskey Spring	750	450	469.9	1,032.4
978.1	240.8	3.0	Dark Hollow Shelter				
			(0.3 mile off trail)	650	350	466.9	1,029.4

THE APPALACHIAN TRAIL

Central Division:
Rockfish Gap, Virginia, to Massachusetts–Vermont Line

Miles from Springer Mountain	Miles from Rockfish Gap	Mileage between Points	Location	Elevation	Climb from Prior Point	Miles from Vermont Line	Miles from Mt. Katahdin
982.0	244.7	3.9	Yellow Breeches Creek	500	500	463.0	1,025.5
983.7	246.4	1.7	Allen (Churchtown)	500	50	461.3	1,023.8
988.5	251.2	4.8	Pennsylvania Turnpike	450	50	456.5	1,019.0
989.4	252.1	0.9	U.S. Route 11	450	0	455.6	1,018.1
992.5	255.2	3.1	Conodoguinet Creek	350	0	452.5	1,015.0
994.8	257.5	2.3	Pennsylvania Highway 944	550	250	450.2	1,012.7
996.5	259.2	1.7	Darlington Shelter	1,150	600	448.5	1,011.0
998.9	261.6	2.4	Pennsylvania Highway 850	500	50	446.1	1,008.6
1,003.3	266.0	4.4	Thelma Marks Memorial Shelter	1,300	850	441.7	1,004.2
1,006.6	269.3	3.3	Duncannon	350	0	438.4	1,000.9
1,008.3	271.0	1.7	Susquehanna River	350	0	436.7	999.2
1,009.1	271.8	0.8	Susquehanna Shelter	700	350	435.9	998.4
1,013.3	276.0	4.2	Pennsylvania Highway 225	1,250	750	431.7	994.2
1,015.9	278.6	2.6	Shaffer Shelter	1,200	100	429.1	991.6
1,019.7	282.4	3.8	Shikellimy Rocks	1,300	300	425.3	987.8
1,022.6	285.3	2.9	Pennsylvania Highway 325	600	200	422.4	984.9
1,026.7	289.4	4.1	Horseshoe Trail Junction	1,500	1,050	418.3	980.8
1,029.1	291.8	2.4	Yellow Springs	1,350	100	415.9	978.4
1,033.7	296.4	4.6	Rausch Gap	1,000	100	411.3	973.8
1,035.1	297.8	1.4	Second Mountain	1,200	400	409.9	972.4
1,039.4	302.1	4.3	Swatara Gap	450	0	405.6	968.1
1,048.2	310.9	8.8	Pennsylvania Highway 645	1,200	1,300	396.8	959.3
1,050.1	312.8	1.9	Applebee Shelter	1,400	350	394.9	957.4
1,053.3	316.0	3.2	Shuberts Gap	1,200	350	391.7	954.2
1,056.9	319.6	3.6	Pennsylvania Highway 183	1,450	500	388.1	950.6
1,059.7	322.4	2.8	Pine Spring	1,550	200	385.3	947.8
1,063.3	326.0	3.6	Neys Shelter	1,350	50	381.7	944.2
1,067.4	330.1	4.1	Auburn Lookout	1,400	400	377.6	940.1
1,070.5	333.2	3.1	Port Clinton	400	50	374.5	937.0
1,072.7	335.4	2.2	Pocahontas Spring	1,250	1,000	372.3	934.8
1,075.6	338.3	2.9	Windsor Furnace	900	250	369.4	931.9
1,078.9	341.6	3.3	The Pinnacle	1,600	800	366.1	928.6
1,084.2	346.9	5.3	Eckville	500	100	360.8	923.3
1,086.2	348.9	2.0	Dans Pulpit	1,650	1,150	358.8	921.3
1,090.5	353.2	4.3	Allentown Hiking Club Shelter	1,550	150	354.5	917.0
1,094.8	357.5	4.3	U.S. Route 309	1,350	200	350.2	912.7
1,096.9	359.6	2.1	New Tripoli Shelter (0.2 mile off trail)	1,400	150	348.1	910.6
1,098.7	361.4	1.8	Baer Rocks	1,600	250	346.3	908.8

THE APPALACHIAN TRAIL
Central Division:
Rockfish Gap, Virginia, to Massachusetts–Vermont Line

Miles from Springer Mountain	Miles from Rockfish Gap	Mileage between Points	Location	Elevation	Climb from Prior Point	Miles from Vermont Line	Miles from Mt. Katahdin
1,101.3	364.0	2.6	Bake Oven Knob Shelter	1,400	150	343.7	906.2
1,104.8	367.5	3.5	Lehigh Furnace Gap	1,350	100	340.2	902.7
1,109.4	372.1	4.6	George W. Outerbridge Shelter	1,000	250	335.6	898.1
1,110.1	372.8	0.7	Lehigh River (Pennsylvania Highway 873)	400	0	334.9	897.4
1,115.4	378.1	5.3	Little Gap	1,100	1,100	329.6	892.1
1,117.7	380.4	2.3	Campsite (no water)	1,600	550	327.3	889.8
1,122.9	385.6	5.2	Smith Gap	1,600	200	322.1	884.6
1,130.2	392.9	7.3	Hahns Lookout	1,300	300	314.8	877.3
1,131.3	394.0	1.1	Wind Gap	1,000	0	313.7	876.2
1,138.0	400.7	6.7	Wolf Rocks	1,600	750	307.0	869.5
1,140.5	403.2	2.5	Kirkridge Shelter	1,500	200	304.5	867.0
1,144.4	407.1	3.9	Mt. Minsi Fire Tower	1,500	250	300.6	863.1
1,147.1	409.8	2.7	Delaware Water Gap (Interstate 80)	400	50	297.9	860.4

NEW JERSEY

Miles from Springer Mountain	Miles from Rockfish Gap	Mileage between Points	Location	Elevation	Climb from Prior Point	Miles from Vermont Line	Miles from Mt. Katahdin
1,151.8	414.5	4.7	Sunfish Pond	1,400	1,050	293.2	855.7
1,153.9	416.6	2.1	Mt. Mohican	1,550	200	291.1	853.6
1,156.9	419.6	3.0	Camp Mohican Road	1,100	100	288.1	850.6
1,160.2	422.9	3.3	Blairstown Road	1,250	550	284.8	847.3
1,164.4	427.1	4.2	Flatbrookville Road	1,350	350	280.6	843.1
1,169.1	431.8	4.7	Rattlesnake Mountain	1,500	450	275.9	838.4
1,171.4	434.1	2.3	Stokes Lean-to (0.2 mile off trail)	1,150	250	273.6	836.1
1,175.1	437.8	3.7	Culvers Gap (U.S. Route 206)	900	450	269.9	832.4
1,179.0	441.7	3.9	Gren Anderson Lean-to (0.2 mile off trail)	1,300	600	266.0	828.5
1,180.5	443.2	1.5	Sunrise Mountain	1,650	550	264.5	827.0
1,183.7	446.4	3.2	High Point No. 3 Lean-to	1,450	300	261.3	823.8
1,185.9	448.6	2.2	High Point No. 2 Lean-to (0.3 mile off trail)	1,450	250	259.1	821.6
1,188.5	451.2	2.6	New Jersey Route 23	1,500	300	256.5	819.0
1,189.9	452.6	1.4	High Point No. 1 Lean-to	1,200	200	255.1	817.6
1,192.7	455.4	2.8	Mt. Salem	800	50	252.3	814.8

NEW JERSEY–NEW YORK

Miles from Springer Mountain	Miles from Rockfish Gap	Mileage between Points	Location	Elevation	Climb from Prior Point	Miles from Vermont Line	Miles from Mt. Katahdin
1,195.8	458.5	3.1	Unionville (New York Route 284)	500	100	249.2	811.7

THE APPALACHIAN TRAIL
Central Division:
Rockfish Gap, Virginia, to Massachusetts–Vermont Line

Miles from Springer Mountain	Miles from Rockfish Gap	Mileage between Points	Location	Elevation	Climb from Prior Point	Miles from Vermont Line	Miles from Mt. Katahdin
1,197.7	460.4	1.9	Wallkill River	400	100	247.3	809.8
1,199.8	462.5	2.1	Pochuck Mountain	1,150	750	245.2	807.7
1,203.9	466.6	4.1	Black Creek	400	300	241.1	803.6
1,205.1	467.8	1.2	New Jersey Route 94	450	100	239.9	802.4
1,207.1	469.8	2.0	Wawayanda Mountain	1,350	900	237.9	800.4
1,212.0	474.7	4.9	Warwick Turnpike	1,150	650	233.0	795.5
			NEW YORK				
1,213.7	476.4	1.7	Bowen Road	1,000	100	231.3	793.8
1,215.7	478.4	2.0	Cascade Lake	1,100	450	229.3	791.8
1,218.1	480.8	2.4	Overlook Point	1,300	550	226.9	789.4
1,222.3	485.0	4.2	Mt. Peter				
			(New York Route 17A)	1,150	350	222.7	785.2
1,225.4	488.1	3.1	Dutch Hollow Road	700	450	219.6	782.1
1,228.4	491.1	3.0	Bramertown Road	900	700	216.6	779.1
1,231.6	494.3	3.2	Old Orange Turnpike	800	750	213.4	775.9
1,233.4	496.1	1.8	New York Route 17	550	600	211.6	774.1
1,235.2	497.9	1.8	William Brien				
			Memorial Lean-to	1,000	650	209.8	772.3
1,237.9	500.6	2.7	Fingerboard Lean-to	1,350	700	207.1	769.6
1,239.4	502.1	1.5	Lake Tiorati Circle	1,050	100	205.6	768.1
1,241.6	504.3	2.2	Letterrock Lean-to	1,100	350	203.4	765.9
1,243.7	506.4	2.1	Palisades Interstate Parkway	700	400	201.3	763.8
1,246.6	509.3	2.9	Seven Lakes Parkway	600	700	198.4	760.9
1,249.5	512.2	2.9	Hudson River	200	800	195.5	758.0
1,251.5	514.2	2.0	Hemlock Spring	550	700	193.5	756.0
1,254.1	516.8	2.6	U.S. Route 9	400	50	190.9	753.4
1,256.2	518.9	2.1	Old Albany Post Road	600	450	188.8	751.3
1,258.4	521.1	2.2	Indian Lake Lean-to	650	200	186.6	749.1
1,263.1	525.8	4.7	Candlewood Hill	950	850	181.9	744.4
1,267.7	530.4	4.6	Canopus Lake				
			(New York Route 301)	900	550	177.3	739.8
1,270.2	532.9	2.5	Raymond Torrey Memorial				
			Lean-to	950	300	174.8	737.3
1,272.2	534.9	2.0	Shenandoah Mountain	1,300	450	172.8	735.3
1,273.7	536.4	1.5	Taconic State Parkway	600	50	171.3	733.8
1,277.1	539.8	3.4	Farmers Mills Lean-to	700	500	167.9	730.4
1,280.1	542.8	3.0	New York Route 52	800	150	164.9	727.4
1,281.6	544.3	1.5	Interstate 84	950	300	163.4	725.9
1,286.2	548.9	4.6	Holmes				
			(New York Route 216)	750	400	158.8	721.3

THE APPALACHIAN TRAIL

Central Division:
Rockfish Gap, Virginia, to Massachusetts–Vermont Line

Miles from Springer Mountain	Miles from Rockfish Gap	Mileage between Points	Location	Elevation	Climb from Prior Point	Miles from Vermont Line	Miles from Mt. Katahdin
1,290.0	552.7	3.8	New York Route 55A	500	600	155.0	717.5
1,291.6	554.3	1.6	New York Route 22	500	50	153.4	715.9
1,296.1	558.8	4.5	Pawling Nature Preserve	800	600	148.9	711.4
1,299.5	562.2	3.4	Webatuck Lean-to (0.2 mile off trail)	650	450	145.5	708.0
1,301.1	563.8	1.6	Webatuck	350	0	143.9	706.4
1,305.6	568.3	4.5	New York–Connecticut line	1,250	1,000	139.4	701.9
			CONNECTICUT				
1,307.5	570.2	1.9	Thayer Brook	450	200	137.5	700.0
1,309.1	571.8	1.6	Connecticut Highway 341	400	700	135.9	698.4
1,311.2	573.9	2.1	Macedonia Brook Road	450	450	133.8	696.3
1,312.8	575.5	1.6	Chase Mountain Lean-to	950	700	132.2	694.7
1,315.0	577.7	2.2	Macedonia Lean-to	950	800	130.0	692.5
1,318.9	581.6	3.9	St. Johns Ledges	1,000	600	126.1	688.6
1,320.0	582.7	1.1	Mountain Brook Lean-to	450	50	125.0	687.5
1,326.3	589.0	6.3	Cornwall Bridge	450	400	118.7	681.2
1,331.4	594.1	5.1	Cathedral Pines Road	750	800	113.6	676.1
1,333.3	596.0	1.9	Mohawk No. 1 Lean-to	1,450	800	111.7	674.2
1,334.5	597.2	1.2	Bunker Hill Lean-to	1,400	150	110.5	673.0
1,334.8	597.5	0.3	Red Mountain Lean-to	1,450	100	110.2	672.7
1,336.7	599.4	1.9	Connecticut Highway 43	1,000	200	108.3	670.8
1,340.4	603.1	3.7	Yelping Hill Road	1,200	800	104.6	667.1
1,343.8	606.5	3.4	Pine Knoll Lean-to	1,150	400	101.2	663.7
1,345.3	608.0	1.5	Dean Ravine Lean-to	850	50	99.7	662.2
1,349.2	611.9	3.9	Falls Village	600	900	95.8	658.3
1,351.4	614.1	2.2	Limestone Spring Lean-to	1,000	450	93.6	656.1
1,353.7	616.4	2.3	U.S. Route 44	750	500	91.3	653.8
1,356.6	619.3	2.9	Lions Head	1,750	1,100	88.4	650.9
1,359.9	622.6	3.3	Bear Mountain	2,300	850	85.1	647.6
1,361.3	624.0	1.4	Sages Ravine	1,500	0	83.7	646.2
			MASSACHUSETTS				
1,364.3	627.0	3.0	Race Mountain	2,350	900	80.7	643.2
1,366.4	629.1	2.1	Mt. Everett	2,600	650	78.6	641.1
1,368.8	631.5	2.4	Mt. Bushnell	1,900	300	76.2	638.7
1,371.5	634.2	2.7	Jug End Road	850	100	73.5	636.0
1,376.2	638.9	4.7	U.S. Route 7	650	50	68.8	631.3
1,378.3	641.0	2.1	Homes Road	1,100	500	66.7	629.2
1,383.2	645.9	4.9	Massachusetts Highway 23	1,000	900	61.8	624.3
1,387.8	650.5	4.6	Mt. Wilcox Lean-to	1,600	1,000	57.2	619.7

THE APPALACHIAN TRAIL
Central Division:
Rockfish Gap, Virginia, to Massachusetts–Vermont Line

Miles from Springer Mountain	Miles from Rockfish Gap	Mileage between Points	Location	Elevation	Climb from Prior Point	Miles from Vermont Line	Miles from Mt. Katahdin
1,391.1	653.8	3.3	Beartown Mountain Road	1,800	650	53.9	616.4
1,394.5	657.2	3.4	Tyringham	900	0	50.5	613.0
1,397.0	659.7	2.5	Goose Pond	1,550	700	48.0	610.5
1,400.5	663.2	3.5	Massachusetts Thruway	1,400	600	44.5	607.0
1,403.5	666.2	3.0	Finerty Pond	1,900	950	41.5	604.0
1,407.5	670.2	4.0	October Mountain Lean-to	1,950	600	37.5	600.0
1,413.1	675.8	5.6	Warner Hill	2,050	700	31.9	594.4
1,418.2	680.9	5.1	Dalton	1,050	250	26.8	589.3
1,423.1	685.8	4.9	Gore Pond	2,000	1,250	21.9	584.4
1,427.1	689.8	4.0	Cheshire	950	0	17.9	580.4
1,430.8	693.5	3.7	Kitchen Brook Lean-to	2,100	1,200	14.2	576.7
1,434.8	697.5	4.0	Mt. Greylock	3,500	1,750	10.2	572.7
1,438.1	700.8	3.3	Wilbur Clearing Lean-to (0.2 mile off trail)	2,300	250	6.9	569.4
1,441.1	703.8	3.0	Massachusetts Highway 2	650	200	3.9	566.4
1,445.0	707.7	3.9	Massachusetts–Vermont line	2,350	1,750	0.0	562.5

THE APPALACHIAN TRAIL
Northern Division:
Massachusetts–Vermont Line to Mt. Katahdin, Maine

Miles from Springer Mountain	Miles from Massachusetts	Mileage between Points	Location	Elevation	Climb from Prior Point	Miles from Mt. Katahdin
			VERMONT			
1,445.0	0.0	0.0	Massachusetts–Vermont line	2,350	0	562.5
1,447.8	2.8	2.8	Seth Warner Shelter	2,200	450	559.7
1,449.9	4.9	2.1	Power line	2,900	850	557.6
1,455.0	10.0	5.1	Congdon Camp	2,200	700	552.5
1,457.5	12.5	2.5	Harmon Hill	2,350	500	550.0
1,459.9	14.9	2.4	Vermont Highway 9	1,200	50	547.6
1,461.5	16.5	1.6	Fay Fuller Camp	1,400	200	546.0
1,466.9	21.9	5.4	Glastenbury Mountain Shelter	3,600	2,200	540.6
1,471.2	26.2	4.3	Caughnawaga Shelter	2,750	550	536.3
1,474.6	29.6	3.4	Story Spring Shelter	2,800	1,100	532.9
1,476.3	31.3	1.7	Stratton Road	2,200	200	531.2
1,480.8	35.8	4.5	Willis Ross Camp	2,550	500	526.7
1,480.9	35.9	0.1	Bigelow Shelter	2,550	0	526.6
1,481.0	36.0	0.1	Vondell Shelter	2,550	0	526.5
1,481.4	36.4	0.4	Stratton View Shelter	2,550	0	526.1
1,483.3	38.3	1.9	South Bourn Pond Shelter	2,600	250	524.2
1,483.7	38.7	0.4	North Bourn Pond Shelter	2,600	0	523.8
1,486.8	41.8	3.1	Swezey Shelter	2,250	50	520.7
1,487.3	42.3	0.5	Old Swezey Camp	2,300	50	520.2
1,488.3	43.3	1.0	Prospect Rock	2,150	50	519.2
1,493.5	48.5	5.2	Vermont Highway 11	1,850	700	514.0
1,494.2	49.2	0.7	Bromley Camp	2,100	250	513.3
1,498.6	53.6	4.4	Mad Tom Shelter	2,450	1,200	508.9
1,502.9	57.9	4.3	Peru Peak Shelter	2,600	1,300	504.6
1,503.5	58.5	0.6	Griffith Lake Shelter	2,600	50	504.0
1,507.6	62.6	4.1	Lost Pond Shelter	1,900	400	499.9
1,509.3	64.3	1.7	Big Branch Shelter	1,450	0	498.2
1,512.5	67.5	3.2	Lula Tye Shelter	1,850	550	495.0
1,512.9	67.9	0.4	Little Rock Pond Shelter	1,850	0	494.6
1,517.8	72.8	4.9	Greenwall Shelter	2,000	950	489.7
1,519.7	74.7	1.9	Vermont Highway 140	1,250	0	487.8
1,522.2	77.2	2.5	Sunnyside Camp	1,500	750	485.3
1,525.0	80.0	2.8	Vermont Highway 103	800	400	482.5
1,525.8	80.8	0.8	Clarendon Shelter	1,200	400	481.7
1,528.6	83.6	2.8	North Shrewsbury Road	1,400	750	478.9
1,531.5	86.5	2.9	Governor Clement Shelter	1,900	500	476.0
1,534.4	89.4	2.9	Tamarack Shelter	3,700	1,850	473.1
1,535.5	90.5	1.1	Cooper Lodge	3,900	300	472.0
1,538.4	93.4	2.9	Pico Camp	3,450	150	469.1
1,541.1	96.1	2.7	Sherburne Pass (U.S. Route 4)	2,150	150	466.4

THE APPALACHIAN TRAIL
Northern Division:
Massachusetts–Vermont Line to Mt. Katahdin, Maine

Miles from Springer Mountain	Miles from Massachusetts	Mileage between Points	Location	Elevation	Climb from Prior Point	Miles from Mt. Katahdin
1,543.0	98.0	1.9	Vermont Highway 100	1,600	350	464.5
1,545.1	100.1	2.1	Ottauquechee River	1,200	50	462.4
1,549.2	104.2	4.1	Stony Brook Lean-to	1,400	1,250	458.3
1,550.9	105.9	1.7	Old Chatauguay Road	1,650	750	456.6
1,554.9	109.9	4.0	The Lookout	2,400	1,300	452.6
1,557.6	112.6	2.7	Gulf Lean-to	1,550	200	449.9
1,559.6	114.6	2.0	Vermont Highway 12	900	0	447.9
1,561.3	116.3	1.7	Barnard Brook Road	800	500	446.2
1,563.9	118.9	2.6	South Pomfret Road	950	950	443.6
1,568.9	123.9	5.0	Bunker Hill	1,500	1,300	438.6
1,571.3	126.3	2.4	West Hartford			
			(Vermont Highway 14)	400	0	436.2
1,575.3	130.3	4.0	Happy Hill Cabin	1,450	1,150	432.2
1,577.7	132.7	2.4	Old Newton Cabin site	1,150	200	429.8
1,580.2	135.2	2.5	Connecticut River	400	150	427.3

NEW HAMPSHIRE

Miles from Springer Mountain	Miles from Massachusetts	Mileage between Points	Location	Elevation	Climb from Prior Point	Miles from Mt. Katahdin
1,580.9	135.9	0.7	Hanover	500	100	426.6
1,582.3	137.3	1.4	Velvet Rocks Lean-to	900	450	425.2
1,586.4	141.4	4.1	Etna–Hanover Center Road	950	600	421.1
1,588.9	143.9	2.5	Harris Cabin	1,450	600	418.6
1,592.6	147.6	3.7	Moose Mountain Road	900	400	414.9
1,595.4	150.4	2.8	Holts Ledge Cabin	1,350	1,050	412.1
1,596.7	151.7	1.3	Lyme–Dorchester Road	850	0	410.8
1,602.4	157.4	5.7	Smarts Mountain Lean-to	3,200	2,400	405.1
1,606.1	161.1	3.7	Quinttown	1,150	50	401.4
1,607.8	162.8	1.7	Mt. Cube Lean-to	1,550	500	399.7
1,609.4	164.4	1.6	North Peak of Mt. Cube	2,900	1,400	398.1
1,610.9	165.9	1.5	New Hampshire Highway 25A	1,250	0	396.6
1,612.7	167.7	1.8	Upper Baker Pond	900	50	394.8
1,616.8	171.8	4.1	Lake Armington Cabin	1,400	550	390.7
1,620.4	175.4	3.6	Wachipauka Lean-to			
			(0.6 mile off trail)	1,700	400	387.1
1,623.4	178.4	3.0	Glencliff	1,100	150	384.1
1,625.0	180.0	1.6	Great Bear Cabin	1,750	650	382.5
1,628.6	183.6	3.6	Moosilauke Winter Cabin	4,800	3,050	378.9
1,631.7	186.7	3.1	Beaver Brook Shelter	1,900	0	375.8
1,631.9	186.9	0.2	Kinsman Notch (New			
			Hampshire Highway 112)	1,850	0	375.6
1,636.5	191.5	4.6	South Peak of Mt. Wolf	3,500	2,450	371.0
1,638.8	193.8	2.3	Eliza Brook Shelter	3,400	150	368.7

THE APPALACHIAN TRAIL

Northern Division:
Massachusetts–Vermont Line to Mt. Katahdin, Maine

Miles from Springer Mountain	Miles from Massachusetts	Mileage between Points	Location	Elevation	Climb from Prior Point	Miles from Mt. Katahdin
1,641.2	196.2	2.4	South Kinsman Mountain	4,350	1,950	366.3
1,642.7	197.7	1.5	Kinsman Pond Shelter	3,800	350	364.8
1,644.6	199.6	1.9	Lonesome Lake Hut	2,750	200	362.9
1,647.4	202.4	2.8	Franconia Notch			
			(U.S. Route 3)	1,400	0	360.1
1,649.8	204.8	2.4	Liberty Spring Campsite	3,850	2,500	357.7
1,653.7	208.7	3.9	Mt. Lafayette	5,250	1,850	353.8
1,657.7	212.7	4.0	Garfield Campsite	3,900	450	349.8
1,660.2	215.2	2.5	Galehead Hut	3,800	1,450	347.3
1,663.0	218.0	2.8	Guyot Shelter			
			(0.5 mile off trail)	4,550	1,300	344.5
1,667.1	222.1	4.1	Zealand Falls Hut	2,600	400	340.4
1,671.7	226.7	4.6	Ethan Pond Shelter	2,750	350	335.8
1,674.7	229.7	3.0	Crawford Notch			
			(U.S. Route 302)	1,300	150	332.8
1,679.1	234.1	4.4	Nauman Shelters			
			(0.2 mile off trail)	3,850	2,950	328.4
1,680.4	235.4	1.3	Mizpah Spring Hut	3,800	200	327.1
1,685.1	240.1	4.7	Lakes-of-the-Clouds Hut	5,000	1,750	322.4
1,686.6	241.6	1.5	Mt. Washington	6,300	1,300	320.9
1,690.2	245.2	3.6	Edmands Col	4,950	450	317.3
1,692.4	247.4	2.2	Madison Hut	4,800	650	315.1
1,695.8	250.8	3.4	West Branch of Peabody River	2,250	550	311.7
1,699.6	254.6	3.8	Pinkham Notch Camp	2,050	600	307.9
1,703.1	258.1	3.5	Wildcat Col	3,750	2,200	304.4
1,705.1	260.1	2.0	Carter Notch Hut	3,300	800	302.4
1,707.6	262.6	2.5	Zeta Pass	3,900	1,700	299.9
1,712.1	267.1	4.5	Imp Shelter	3,300	1,000	295.4
1,717.8	272.8	5.7	Rattle River Shelter	1,100	1,100	289.7
1,719.3	274.3	1.5	U.S. Route 2	800	0	288.2
1,721.1	276.1	1.8	Peabody Brook	800	150	286.4
1,726.1	281.1	5.0	Gentian Pond Shelter	2,150	1,950	281.4
1,730.7	285.7	4.6	New Hampshire–Maine line	2,950	2,200	276.8

MAINE

1,731.2	286.2	0.5	Carlo Col Shelter			
			(0.3 mile off trail)	3,200	300	276.3
1,735.5	290.5	4.3	Full Goose Shelter	3,050	1,650	272.0
1,740.4	295.4	4.9	Speck Pond Shelter	3,450	2,000	267.1
1,744.0	299.0	3.6	Grafton Notch Lean-to	1,600	900	263.5
1,747.3	302.3	3.3	East Peak of Baldpate	3,800	2,750	260.2

THE APPALACHIAN TRAIL
Northern Division:
Massachusetts–Vermont Line to Mt. Katahdin, Maine

Miles from Springer Mountain	Miles from Massachusetts	Mileage between Points	Location	Elevation	Climb from Prior Point	Miles from Mt. Katahdin
1,750.7	305.7	3.4	Frye Brook Lean-to	1,100	0	256.8
1,754.1	309.1	3.4	Surplus Pond	2,050	1,050	253.4
1,758.2	313.2	4.1	C Pond	1,300	50	249.3
1,761.0	316.0	2.8	Squirrel Rock Lean-to	1,200	250	246.5
1,764.0	319.0	3.0	Maine Highway 5	1,450	550	243.5
1,768.6	323.6	4.6	Elephant Mountain Lean-to	2,900	1,650	238.9
1,775.9	330.9	7.3	Bemis Stream	1,500	1,200	231.6
1,777.1	332.1	1.2	Maine Highway 17	2,000	500	230.4
1,779.6	334.6	2.5	Sabbath Day Pond Lean-to	2,400	400	227.9
1,785.8	340.8	6.2	Maine Highway 4	1,800	200	221.7
1,791.1	346.1	5.3	Piazza Rock Lean-to	2,050	900	216.4
1,794.8	349.8	3.7	Saddleback Mountain	4,100	2,050	212.7
1,796.4	351.4	1.6	The Horn	4,000	600	211.1
1,799.7	354.7	3.3	Poplar Ridge Lean-to	3,000	900	207.8
1,802.0	357.0	2.3	Orbeton Stream	1,600	150	205.5
1,806.8	361.8	4.8	Spaulding Mountain Lean-to	3,100	1,500	200.7
1,810.3	365.3	3.5	Mt. Sugarloaf	4,250	1,800	197.2
1,812.9	367.9	2.6	Mt. Sugarloaf Lean-to	1,900	50	194.6
1,814.8	369.8	1.9	Maine Highway 27	1,300	0	192.7
1,818.1	373.1	3.3	Stratton Brook Pond	1,250	200	189.4
1,821.8	376.8	3.7	Horns Pond Lean-tos	3,100	1,850	185.7
1,824.8	379.8	3.0	Myron H. Avery Memorial Lean-to	3,800	1,600	182.7
1,828.7	383.7	3.9	Little Bigelow Mountain	3,000	1,500	178.8
1,833.5	388.5	4.8	Flagstaff Lake	1,150	50	174.0
1,835.4	390.4	1.9	Jerome Brook Lean-to	1,200	500	172.1
1,838.2	393.2	2.8	West Carry Pond	1,300	400	169.3
1,844.5	399.5	6.3	East Carry Pond Camps	1,250	300	163.0
1,845.5	400.5	1.0	East Carry Pond Lean-to	1,250	0	162.0
1,851.8	406.8	6.3	Pierce Pond Lean-to	1,150	450	155.7
1,855.2	410.2	3.4	Kennebec River	500	0	152.3
1,855.9	410.9	0.7	Caratunk	550	50	151.6
1,860.8	415.8	4.9	Pleasant Pond Mountain Lean-to	1,350	900	146.7
1,865.6	420.6	4.8	Moxie Pond	950	1,050	141.9
1,868.8	423.8	3.2	Joes Hole Brook Lean-to	1,150	250	138.7
1,873.8	428.8	5.0	Moxie Bald Lean-to	1,200	1,300	133.7
1,879.3	434.3	5.5	Marble Brook	1,000	100	128.2
1,880.8	435.8	1.5	Breakneck Ridge Lean-to	1,350	350	126.7
1,884.3	439.3	3.5	Blanchard	600	100	123.2
1,889.8	444.8	5.5	Monson	850	450	117.7

THE APPALACHIAN TRAIL

Northern Division:

Massachusetts–Vermont Line to Mt. Katahdin, Maine

Miles from Springer Mountain	Miles from Massachusetts	Mileage between Points	Location	Elevation	Climb from Prior Point	Miles from Mt. Katahdin
1,894.9	449.9	5.1	Old Stage Road Lean-to	1,350	850	112.6
1,897.4	452.4	2.5	Stanchfield Cabin	1,000	100	110.1
1,901.0	456.0	3.6	Little Wilson Campsite	550	150	106.5
1,904.6	459.6	3.6	Bodfish Farm	600	500	102.9
1,907.5	462.5	2.9	Long Pond Stream Lean-to	1,000	450	100.0
1,911.5	466.5	4.0	Cloud Pond Lean-to (0.2 mile off trail)	2,500	1,800	96.0
1,913.8	468.8	2.3	Fourth Mountain	2,400	500	93.7
1,918.2	473.2	4.4	Chairback Gap Lean-to	1,950	1,050	89.3
1,921.6	476.6	3.4	Chairback Mountain Camps	1,100	50	85.9
1,924.1	479.1	2.5	The Hermitage	700	50	83.4
1,928.7	483.7	4.6	White Brook Lean-to	1,300	750	78.8
1,934.9	489.9	6.2	White Cap Mountain Lean-to	1,700	2,200	72.6
1,936.7	491.7	1.8	West Branch Ponds Road	1,550	50	70.8
1,943.2	498.2	6.5	East Branch Tote-road Lean-to	1,100	100	64.3
1,946.6	501.6	3.4	Yoke Pond side road	1,300	300	60.9
1,949.9	504.9	3.3	Cooper Brook Falls Lean-to	950	0	57.6
1,957.7	512.7	7.8	Antlers Camps	500	0	49.8
1,961.0	516.0	3.3	Potaywadjo Spring Lean-to	600	400	46.5
1,963.6	518.6	2.6	Mahar Campground	500	0	43.9
1,968.2	523.2	4.6	Nahmakanta Lake Lean-to	650	300	39.3
1,972.7	527.7	4.5	Wadleigh Pond Lean-to	950	700	34.8
1,975.5	530.5	2.8	Nahmakanta Lake Camps	650	200	32.0
1,980.1	535.1	4.6	Rainbow Lake Dam	1,050	650	27.4
1,981.9	536.9	1.8	Rainbow Lake Lean-to	1,050	50	25.6
1,983.5	538.5	1.6	Rainbow Lake Camp	1,050	150	24.0
1,986.9	541.9	3.4	Rainbow Ledges	1,500	600	20.6
1,989.5	544.5	2.6	Hurd Brook Lean-to	700	100	18.0
1,992.9	547.9	3.4	Penobscot West Branch	600	200	14.6
1,997.0	552.0	4.1	Nesowadnehunk Stream	600	0	10.5
2,000.3	555.3	3.3	Daicey Pond	1,100	500	7.2
2,002.3	557.3	2.0	Katahdin Stream Campground	1,100	50	5.2
2,005.9	560.9	3.6	The Gateway	4,500	3,400	1.6
2,007.5	562.5	1.6	Baxter Peak, Mt. Katahdin	5,250	750	0.0

RECAPITULATION OF MILEAGE-CLIMB DATA

BY SECTION

Miles from Springer Mountain (At Starting Point)	Miles from Springer Mountain (At Ending Point)	Section or Division	Starting Point	Ending Point	Miles	Total Climb (Northbound)	Average Climb per Mile (Northbound)	Total Climb (Southbound)	Average Climb per Mile (Southbound)	Average Climb per Mile (Northbound + Southbound)
0.0	78.3	Georgia	Springer Mountain	Bly Gap	78.3	20,050	256	20,000	255	256
78.3	165.3	North Carolina	Bly Gap	Doe Knob	87.0	22,700	261	22,050	253	257
165.3	360.5	North Carolina–Tennessee	Doe Knob	U.S. Route 19E	195.2	49,700	255	51,100	262	258
360.5	419.6	Tennessee	U.S. Route 19E	Tennessee–Virginia Line	59.1	12,300	208	12,200	206	207
419.6	737.3	Southern Virginia	Tennessee–Virginia Line	Rockfish Gap	317.7	65,250	205	66,550	209	207
737.3	744.9	Rockfish Gap	Rockfish Gap	Jarmans Gap	7.6	1,750	230	1,450	191	211
744.9	840.0	Shenandoah National Park	Jarmans Gap	Shenandoah National Park Boundary	95.1	17,950	189	18,100	190	190
840.0	870.3	Northern Virginia	Shenandoah National Park Boundary	Snickers Gap	30.3	3,850	127	4,850	160	144
870.3	889.4	Virginia–West Virginia	Snickers Gap	Potomac River	19.1	2,450	128	3,150	165	147
889.4	926.7	Maryland	Potomac River	Pen Mar	37.3	6,100	164	5,250	141	152
926.7	1,147.1	Pennsylvania	Pen Mar	Delaware Water Gap	220.4	23,500	107	24,300	110	108
1,147.1	1,192.7	New Jersey	Delaware Water Gap	Mt. Salem	45.6	5,650	124	5,250	115	120
1,192.7	1,212.0	New Jersey–New York	Mt. Salem	Warwick Turnpike	19.3	2,900	150	2,550	132	141

RECAPITULATION OF MILEAGE-CLIMB DATA (Continued)

Miles from Springer Mountain (At Starting Point)	Miles from Springer Mountain (At Ending Point)	Section or Division	Starting Point	Ending Point	Miles	Total Climb (Northbound)	Average Climb per Mile (Northbound)	Total Climb (Southbound)	Average Climb per Mile (Southbound)	Average Climb per Mile (Northbound + Southbound)
		BY SECTION								
1,212.0	1,305.6	New York	Warwick Turnpike	New York–Connecticut Line	93.6	15,300	163	15,200	162	163
1,305.6	1,361.3	Connecticut	New York–Connecticut Line	Sages Ravine	55.7	11,000	197	10,750	193	195
1,361.3	1,445.0	Massachusetts	Sages Ravine	Massachusetts–Vermont Line	83.7	15,250	182	14,400	172	177
1,445.0	1,580.2	Vermont	Massachusetts–Vermont Line	Connecticut River	135.2	26,500	196	28,450	210	203
1,580.2	1,730.7	New Hampshire	Connecticut River	New Hampshire–Maine Line	150.5	45,500	302	42,950	285	294
1,730.7	2,007.5	Maine	New Hampshire–Maine Line	Mt. Katahdin	276.8	49,750	180	47,450	171	176
		BY DIVISION								
0.0	737.3	Southern Division	Springer Mountain	Rockfish Gap	737.3	170,000	231	171,900	233	232
737.3	1,445.0	Central Division	Rockfish Gap	Massachusetts–Vermont Line	707.7	105,700	149	105,250	149	149
1,445.0	2,007.5	Northern Division	Massachusetts–Vermont Line	Mt. Katahdin	562.5	121,750	216	118,850	211	214
		BY ENTIRE TRAIL								
0.0	2,007.5	Appalachian Trail	Springer Mountain	Mt. Katahdin	2,007.5	397,450	198	396,000	197	198

Appalachian Trail Graphs

By James R. Wolf

The graphs are based upon my Georgia-to-Maine hike extending from March 23, 1971, to September 10, 1971. They are intended to provide a basis for the comparison of different sections of the trail in terms of three criteria: the amount of climbing involved, hiking speed, and the condition of the footpath. The variables employed—in order of decreasing reliability—are distances, elevation changes, and point-to-point hiking times. Temperature data are supplied as an additional item of general interest.

CLIMB. Topographical maps were used as the original source of elevation data. Every rise was recorded to the nearest 50 feet. Data were subsequently corrected by on-the-trail experience. Mileages were primarily derived from guidebooks. The charted values represent the gross feet climbed over a five-day period (including the two days preceding and the two days following the indicated date) divided by the mileage hiked in the same period.

PACE. The duration of each day's hike was recorded to the nearest quarter-hour. This time was increased or decreased to compensate for special conditions, such as the omission of rest stops because of rain or the addition of extra stops for resupply or sight-seeing. The adjusted time is thus based on a typical pace, which would include a one-hour lunch break and, additionally, a 15-minute rest after each hour or so of uninterrupted hiking. The charted values represent the total adjusted time hiked over a five-day period divided by the mileage hiked in the same period.

FOOTPATH ROUGHNESS. Examination of the trip log disclosed that, on the average, the adjusted time required for a given day's hike would be one hour for each 2.3 miles plus an additional hour for each 700 feet of rise. Thus for each day a par or nominal time could be calculated for the distance actually covered. A comparison of the actual adjusted time hiked with this nominal time reflects factors, other than elevation changes, that affect hiking progress. Rockiness or deadfalls, for example, increase the actual time required; road walking, on the other hand, will reduce this time. The charted values, identified as an index of footpath roughness, represent the ratio of the actual adjusted time for a five-day period to the nominal time calculated according to the above formula for the same period.

TEMPERATURE. Thermometer readings were taken each morning and evening and once or twice during the day. A daily 24-hour mean temperature was estimated using these readings as a guide. The charted values represent the average of this daily mean temperature with those of the two preceding and two subsequent days.

THE APPALACHIAN TRAIL

Southern Division: Springer Mountain, Georgia
to Rockfish Gap, Virginia

5-Day Moving Averages of Selected Data

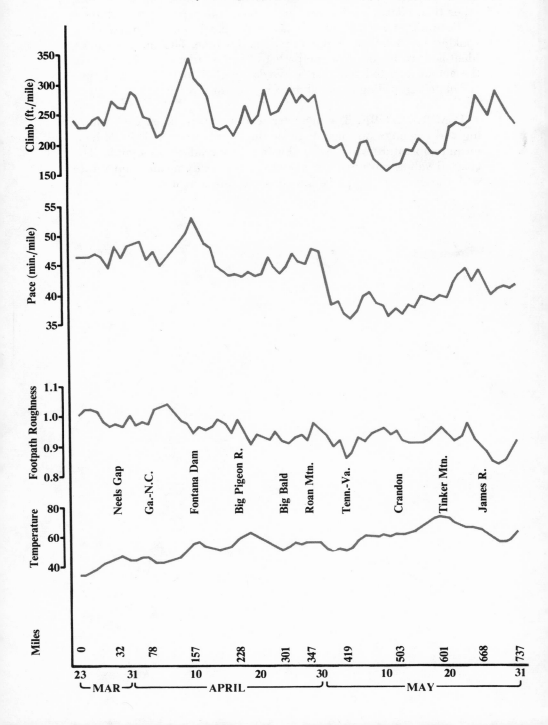

Photo by Garnett W. Martin

Wild turkey chicks on Big Tinker Mountain, near Roanoke, Virginia.

Photo by Elmer L. Onstott

Mt. Katahdin from a point on Nesowadnehunk Road about fourteen miles from the foot of the mountain.

THE APPALACHIAN TRAIL

*Central Division: Rockfish Gap, Virginia
to Massachusetts - Vermont Boundary*

5-Day Moving Averages of Selected Data

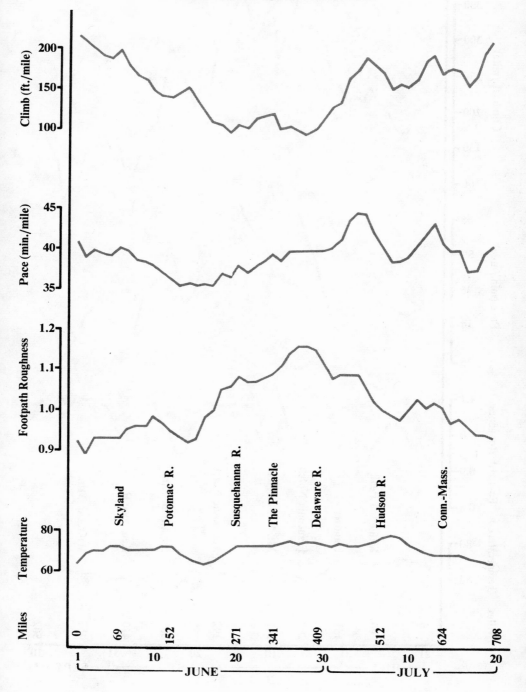

THE APPALACHIAN TRAIL

Northern Division: Massachusetts-Vermont Boundary to Mt. Katahdin, Maine

5-Day Moving Averages of Selected Data

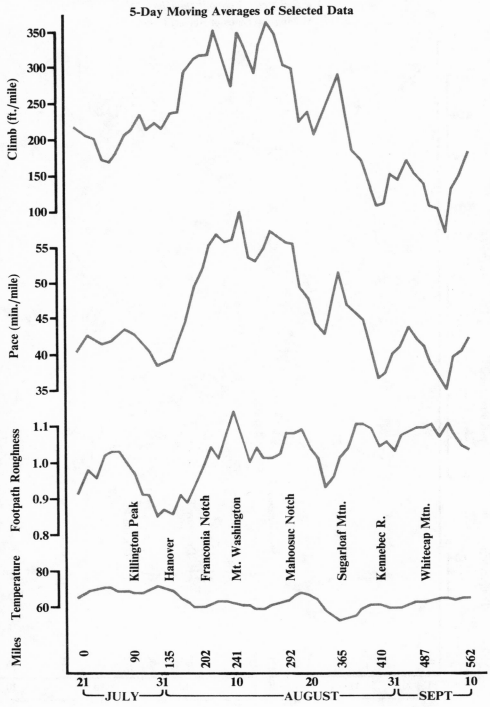

Picture Taking
on a Through Hike

By Garnett W. Martin

When you're deciding to take a camera along on your through hike of the Appalachian Trail, ask yourself these questions: will I want color or black-and-white pictures? Extreme close-ups of flowers? Shots of wild game? Birds? Just average subjects?

Various accessories will be needed to successfully handle these different pictures. The weight factor, and space available, may limit the number of accessories as well as the type of camera. Plan your picture taking just as you have planned the through hike; check and recheck every item for possible elimination.

A picture is worth more than pages of notes or written text. Do not forget to take pictures of the old chimneys, old houses, groups of shade trees, old wells, rock fences, old rock foundations, and cemeteries along the trail. Without words these subjects say "people lived here, worked here, died here; this was their community."

Make your pictures the story of the trail as it appeared to you as you hiked it. Make them say: "This is the Appalachian Trail."

The camera I decided to take on my through hike was a Kodak 35, with range finder, f/3.5 lens, exposure time 1/200 of a second. I had used it for years and knew the functional gadgets and its capabilities as a typist knows her keyboard. I sent it in to the Eastman Kodak Company for all needed repairs and cleaning (complete overhaul) well in advance of my starting date for the through hike. (Later, just before leaving on a two-year tour, I purchased a new Retina IV and accessories. I lost many pictures because I had not learned the use of all of its gadgets, or the camera's capabilities.)

My accessories for the Appalachian Trail hike were: (1) Kodak filter, skylight number 1A, series 6, used to reduce the blue haze and give warmth to the picture—I kept this filter on all the time as it protected the lens; (2) polarizing screen, Tiffen series 6, used for more color saturation, and it renders a more favorable sky; (3) Kodak Parta lens, 2+, 13¾-inch distance with camera set at four feet; (4) Kodak lens cleaning paper—a must.

Know your camera and equipment. Know the settings and controls on your camera by touch; know the hyperfocal settings for the various depths of field and what the different lens will do in a given situation. Leave the shutter in cocked position as little as possible. I leave the advancing of the film until I am ready for the next picture. This keeps less tension on the mechanism.

The meter is an important accessory. I used Weston, Master IV, Model 745. Know your exposure meter as you do your camera. At times you should choose between exposure readings from reflected light and incident light, especially on close-ups. When there is considerable contrast in the subject, average the readings when you have no other means of controlling the situation, unless you wish to favor one or the other of the readings.

Select the type and speed film, either color or black-and-white, that is best suited for your project. I used Kodachrome II, daylight type, K-135, ASA 25.

Here are some hints on picture taking that I've developed or borrowed over the years: learn to see beauty, form, lines, and color. This will help to improve the composition of your picture.

Normally one is standing, kneeling, or sitting when taking a picture, but do not hesitate to go flat on your belly, hang on a limb, or maybe stand on your head. However, I never used the "stand-on-your-head" position along the trail. If your desire is compelling, you will get the picture.

If you think you have an important shot, do not wait for a more favorable moment—shoot at once. Then follow up with more exposures as the situation changes. If you wait, you may lose the picture.

The parallax error is a problem with some cameras in shooting close-ups, especially at less than two feet. One way to overcome this, and not have a pack of gadgets along, is to experiment with a number of exposures and learn just where the lower edge of the subject should be in the picture frame.

Make a habit of keeping your settings for a normal exposure; thus you are ready for most pictures. It is easier to move to a desired setting from a known position. When you move from forest (dark area) to open area (lighter) your normal setting will need to be adjusted for the existing light conditions.

Try and have a "main subject" in the picture, a center of interest.

This will give your picture the appearance of being selective, and create interest.

When your center of interest is recognized as a moving object, such as a horse and carriage or truck-trailer, and you want it to appear to be moving, keep the subject in the half (or nearly so) of the frame from which the entry is being made.

Where you have a point of interest which may be used to lead the viewer into your picture, place it in the lower left of the frame.

The grey sky and/or unwanted foreground should be eliminated from your picture, or be effectively reduced.

In taking shots of distant subjects, frame your picture to a favorable degree, thus giving depth to the picture. Normally you will not take a reading of the light values of the frame.

Backlighting can be used to create some outstanding pictures, especially of the fall colors. Take into consideration all light values that will appear in your picture.

Study your subject for the best approach, from several angles, and make an overall shot. Then, move in for a close-up of the point of interest. These two shots will in most instances create considerable interest and comment from your viewers.

There were some interesting experiences in a few of my pictures. I was on the trail in the Jefferson National Forest east of Damascus, Virginia, when I stopped dead in my tracks—then put my camera in position with slow, even movements. The ruffed grouse just four feet in front of me flew down the trail, pretending to have a broken wing as she flapped along, leaving her covey of chicks. I was fast enough to cover the chicks with my cap before they scattered. How was I to get them from under my cap and take their picture? I took my handkerchief and worked it under the cap and chicks, and turned them over. I set my camera and waited a few minutes for the chicks to become quiet, then eased off the handkerchief. I made four exposures, then let them go free.

On the slope of Tinker Mountain, just west of Roanoke, Virginia, I flushed a wild turkey hen with her chicks. Two of the young turkeys made the mistake of running down the trail—I outran them and captured the two. What could I do with a wild turkey chick in each hand? A possible solution flashed quickly through my mind. I put one in each of my pant pockets, removed my pack, and found some twine, I then tied the chicks' feet, placed them on the leaves, and proceeded with my picture taking. Several times I had to give some attention to the old turkey hen as she moved in for a fight; once I thought I would need to protect myself.

In a rocky wooded area northeast of Roanoke, Virginia, I came upon four young men hunting rattlesnakes. I asked if I might take their picture. "Sure," was their reply. After I took some pictures we talked about "catching rattlesnakes." One of the men asked about the trail I had passed over.

"About a hundred yards back there are no more rocks, and it's fairly open area and level," I said. They decided to work the remaining hundred yards of rocky area.

"If you would like to take a picture of a rattlesnake, wait at the old gravel road. We'll be back in a few minutes," one of the men said.

They returned and a large rattlesnake (it had fourteen rattles and a button) was poured from the sack onto the gravel road. I made a number of exposures of the snake in different positions. While in a semicoiled position one of the men put a green leaf under its tail so the rattles would show up well in the picture (the gravel base and the snake were about the same color).

We were working at a distance of about four feet from the snake. When it was time for the creature to go back into the sack, the man with the gloves, boots, and forked stick picked the snake up and held it waist-high and close in. His shirt was open and his bare body was part of the background. At two feet I got an excellent picture; it even showed the snake's fangs.

East of Duncannon, Pennsylvania, the trail went through grass about knee-high. With my walking stick I gently touched what I thought might be a dead snake lying across the trail. It winced. On closer examination I recognized it as a harmless blacksnake five feet in length. I eased my walking stick under it, picked it up, and moved it to an open area for a picture. When I put it down it took a semicoiled, open position with its head and a couple of feet of its body five or six inches above the ground—in an open striking position. I made several exposures and then continued my hike, leaving behind a peaceful and very cooperative snake.

Photography along the Appalachian Trail

By Elmer L. Onstott

Had it not been for my interest in photography, it is doubtful if I would have hiked the Appalachian Trail even though I had other good reasons for doing so. In my case, travel and pictures are two interests which go together. I want more than a fading memory of the interesting places and things that I see when traveling. A diary is useful as far as it goes, but for a record I prefer pictures.

My interest in photography dates back to the end of World War I. In February, 1919, while still a soldier in the U.S. Army, I bought my first camera. Since then I have owned a camera continuously. Some of my most treasured mementos are pictures made more than 50 years ago.

Photography can record, in minute detail, just what we see. But more than that, it can be a medium through which the photographer can express ideas about people, places, and events. The traveler who looks diligently for picture possibilities will actually *see* more than he would see otherwise. Pictures can be shared with others.

Most amateurs, when looking at a striking photograph, want to know what camera was used. They feel that if they only had a similar camera they, too, could produce a masterpiece.

There are thousands of amateur photographers walking about with some of the world's finest camera equipment hanging around their necks, yet when it comes to pictures they have little or nothing to show. In fact, back in the thirties when the 35-mm camera was becoming popular, there was a type of photographer who had no prints to show at all. What he had to show was a roll of developed negatives. These negatives were his pride and joy. He would proudly unroll the film for your inspection with the remark, "Aren't they sharp and crisp?"

The camera I used on my hike over the Appalachian Trail was durable, time-tested, and dependable. The Model G Leica which I purchased in 1938 was a veteran of 30 years' use without an overhaul. It

1953

was equipped with a 50-mm f/3.5 Nikor lens, a 35-mm f/3.5 Leitz Elmar lens, and a 90-mm f/4 Leitz Elmar telephoto lens. All the lenses have good resolution, but the 35-mm f/3.5 wide-angle Leitz Elmar lens is the sharpest. My experience in testing several lenses for resolution seems to indicate that 28-mm and 35-mm lenses have a higher resolution than lenses of longer focal length.

Additional equipment included a tripod, gadget bag, exposure meter, and self-timer. My photographic equipment weighed eight pounds. I am probably the first person to carry a tripod from Georgia to Maine on foot, and I believe it is quite possible that I may be the last. I suffered a lot to get the tripod and gadget bag over the trail. The tripod was attached to the bottom of the large gadget bag, making a combination that was awkward to carry. Moreover, the tripod and gadget bag made it difficult for me to regain my balance if I started to fall, and made me take many hard falls.

To prevent the tripod and bag from swinging, and to relieve the weight on my right shoulder, I held the tripod with my left hand. Even with this method, I suffered sharp pains in my right shoulder for the first 700 miles of my journey. As a result of holding the tripod, my left hand was swollen during the hours of hiking for the more than six months that I lived on the trail. I had become resigned to the prospect of enduring the pain in my shoulder all the way to Maine when, to my great surprise and relief, the pains vanished as I entered Shenandoah National Park. Carrying a tripod from Georgia to Maine with or without pain is a great inconvenience, to say the least. However, the reward was many pictures that otherwise I would not have had. I really should have found a place on the packframe for the tripod, while the gadget bag should have been left at home.

Camera equipment, like all gear and the hiker himself, is subjected to the rigors, abuse, and accidents that occur on the trail.

A few miles from Mt. Katahdin, while crossing Hurd Brook, I slipped on wet moss and fell. Almost before I knew it I was wedged tightly between two boulders and was partly in the brook. It must have taken me ten minutes to free myself. Most of the contents of my gadget bag, including the Leitz wide-angle lens, fell into a foot of water. I was so certain the lens was flooded that I made no special effort to recover it. It must have been under water for at least 15 minutes. You can imagine my surprise when I opened the leather case and found only two or three drops of water on the lens cap! The air trapped in the lens case no doubt prevented the water from flowing into the case, which in any event must have had watertight seams. I gathered up my wet gear and carried it to the Hurd Brook Lean-to, where I spent the remainder of the afternoon and a good part of the night drying it by the campfire.

For persons whose interest in photography is limited to "aiming and shooting," the Konica Auto-S2 or the Olympus 35 should be of interest. Those who are interested in the more sophisticated type of photographic equipment will find there is a wide field to choose from. Unfortunately, the automatic and the semi-automatic features of all cameras are delicate and extremely sensitive to shock. They must be handled with great care.

We may buy the most expensive camera equipment, but as someone has said, "The picture-taking possibilities of a box camera have not been exhausted yet." I believe that is true; I know it is true in my case.

The selection of interesting subject matter and good composition are important factors in making pictures that excel. Those who are interested in composition may do well to study *Better Pictures through Good Composition* by Ray E. Koken. This good little book is available for $1.00 from Ray E. Koken, 261 Melbourne Ave., Youngstown, Ohio 44512.

Another important tool, and perhaps the most important of all, is LIGHT. Light in its many variations from sunrise to sunset offers unlimited picture possibilities. The angle at which light falls on the subject may make the difference between a picture that is interesting and one that is not interesting. There is need for knowledge and experience here.

One of the easiest things to do on the Appalachian Trail (as well as elsewhere) is to pass by picture opportunities without seeing them. The ability to SEE or THINK in terms of making pictures is something that each individual will have to develop in his own way. Most certainly it is not, like a piece of gear, an item that can be bought; it is a part of YOU.

However, after living on the Appalachian Trail for more than six months, I can offer a few suggestions as to what to look for in picture possibilities. First of all, what is the Appalachian Trail? Where does it begin—and end? And what is it like? Try to answer the questions with your camera, by showing the beginning and the end of the trail and how the footway passes over crests of mountains, crosses valleys, roads, and highways, passes through wilderness. How does the trail cross streams? Show the bridges and footlogs, beaver dam walkways and stepping stones. Where and how is the trail marked? Show paint blazes and the metal Appalachian Trail signs, signboards, cairns, and posts. Where do you get water? Show springs, brooks, ponds, and the hand pump in a mountain farmer's yard. There will be many opportunities to make pictures of landscapes. To give scenic scale and to sharpen interest, have a well-placed human figure in the picture area. Don't overlook the few towns the trail passes through.

Wild flowers, trees, and animals are fair game with the camera, too. And how about the weather? Everybody talks about the weather! Why not do something about it with your camera? Weather in its various moods will give atmosphere to many of your pictures along the way.

There are a number of good color films available to the photographer. I prefer Kodachrome II.

It is up to the photographer to select, from a world of confusion, the scenes, places, and things that tell the story of the Appalachian Trail. The tools he will use are his mind and his eyes, light and composition, and his camera. The picture possibilities are unlimited—or should I say—limited only by the skill, effort, and imagination of the photographer?

The Appalachian Trail Conference

The Appalachian Trail Conference is the private nationwide organization that represents citizens' interests in the Appalachian Trail. It is comprised of trail-maintaining and trail-supporting organizations and individual members. Dues of individual members (other than ex officio members) are $7 a year. Members receive the *Appalachian Trailway News* and certain other publications, but not the guidebooks, as a part of their membership. Persons desiring to become life members may do so for a membership fee of $200.

The conference is incorporated in the District of Columbia as a nonprofit organization. It is not endowed or government supported. Funds are derived from contributions by the organizations belonging to the conference, the dues of individual members, and gifts from those interested in the objectives of the conference. Contributions to it are deductible on income tax returns. (See Commissioner of Internal Revenue letter IT:P:ER/CSG, August 4, 1950.)

The conference is largely a volunteer amateur recreational group. Many of the services needed to keep up conference activities and to maintain the trail are contributed by those interested in the project. Meetings of the conference are held every two years. Control of the affairs of the conference is vested in the board of managers, which is elected by the membership. The conference's chief executive officer serves as chairman. Administration functions are conducted by an executive director.

The conference coordinates the efforts of the trail-maintaining clubs, which under the National Trails System Act still do a major share of the clearing and marking of the trail. The personal stewardship exercised over trail sections by club members and other individuals has had a strong influence on the nature of the trail, and this influence continues. The conference strives to keep a close liaison with all the governmental agencies, federal and state, that are involved in the trail program. The conference is represented on the Appalachian National Trail Advisory Council, which was established to advise the Secretary of the Interior on the selection of the rights-of-way, the marking, and the administration of the trail. By virtue of a National Park Service—Appalachian Trail Conference agreement, the conference has a voice in setting the guidelines, standards, and regulations that help determine the character and use of the trail.

Conference activities include publishing booklets and leaflets on

1957

construction and maintenance of trails, guidebooks for the various sections of the trail, and general information on trail use. Headquarters of the Appalachian Trail Conference are in Harpers Ferry, West Virginia 25425. The post office address is Box 236. Here inquiries are answered, services are provided for members and others, publications are prepared and sold, reports on trail conditions are passed to maintaining groups, and the activities of officers, trail workers, and government officials are coordinated.

Route of the Appalachian Trail
(Adapted from the Federal Register)

Maine

From the summit cairn on Baxter Peak atop Mt. Katahdin in Baxter State Park, the Appalachian Trail leads west across The Tableland, descends the Hunt Spur, crosses Katahdin Stream, passes Daicey Pond, and descends to the Penobscot West Branch, leaving Baxter State Park at 9.65 miles from the start. It then proceeds east a short distance, crosses Abol Bridge, and continues west and southwest across Hurd Brook and over Rainbow Ledges, and proceeds past Rainbow, Nahmakanta, and Lower Joe Mary lakes. The trail then follows Cooper Brook to Crawford Pond, turns south to the East Branch of Pleasant River, follows the river west about four miles, then crosses and continues southwest. Before reaching Third West Branch Pond it turns south, traverses White Cap Mountain, turns west, crosses the West Branch of Pleasant River, and continues south. After skirting the east end of Long Pond it ascends the Barren–Chairback Range.

The trail then follows Bodfish Valley south, crosses Little Wilson Stream, turns west, crosses the stream again, then goes south to Monson (post office and grocery). Here it turns west, passing through Blanchard (no post office or grocery), over Breakneck Ridge, by Bald Mountain Pond, and over Moxie Bald, then skirts Moxie Pond via Joes Hole, continues west over Pleasant Pond Mountain, and reaches the Kennebec River at Caratunk (post office and grocery).

Across the Kennebec, the trail continues west to Pierce Pond, then south around East Carry Pond and leads west, skirting West Carry Pond and the south end of Flagstaff Lake. Ascending Little Bigelow Mountain, it continues across the crest and over Myron H. Avery Peak, West Peak, and South Horn, then drops to Maine Highway 27 at Bigelow Village (no post office or grocery). It climbs Mt. Sugarloaf, crosses Orbeton Stream, ascends Saddleback Junior, passes Piazza Rock, and crosses Maine Highway 4 about five miles south of Rangeley (post office and grocery). Both of the Long Ponds and Sabbath Day Pond are passed, then the four summits of Bemis Mountain are crossed. After passing along the lower slope of Elephant Mountain the trail follows the East Branch of Black Brook, goes through

Sawyer Notch, passes C Pond, follows Mountain Brook by Surplus Pond, crosses the West Branch of Ellis River, and continues to Frye Brook.

The trail then ascends over Little Baldpate Mountain, continues over the East and West Peaks of Baldpate, enters Grafton Notch State Park, and descends into Grafton Notch. The trail follows the highway south for 0.5 mile, where it again turns west and steeply ascends Old Speck Mountain.

From the summit of Old Speck there is a steep descent to Speck Pond. The trail then continues southwesterly through Mahoosuc Notch and along the Mahoosuc Range over Fulling Mill and Goose Eye mountains to Carlo Col at the Maine–New Hampshire line.

New Hampshire

From the Maine–New Hampshire border in the Mahoosuc Mountain Range west of Carlo Col the Appalachian Trail continues southwesterly over the twin summits of Mt. Success, passes Gentian Pond and Moss Pond, and at Dream Lake leaves the ridge. The trail then descends southerly along Peabody Brook to the Androscoggin Valley, crossing the Androscoggin River on a highway bridge and then immediately crossing the Canadian National Railroad and U.S. Route 2. West on the highway it is 3.6 miles to Gorham (post office and grocery).

From the crossing of Route 2 the trail climbs southerly out of the valley along Rattle River, enters the White Mountain National Forest, and reaches the ridge of the Carter–Moriah Mountain Range. It follows southwesterly over the summits of Mt. Moriah, North Carter Mountain, Mt. Lethe, and Middle and South Carter mountains to Zeta Pass. It then ascends and crosses Mt. Hight and Carter Dome, drops to Carter Notch, and ascends steeply to Wildcat Mountain, crosses its several summits and descends westerly to the Pinkham Notch Scenic Area, crossing New Hampshire Highway 16 in Pinkham Notch. The trail then goes northerly, crossing the Mt. Washington Carriage Road, and traverses through and then along the perimeter of the Great Gulf Wilderness Area to the summit of Mt. Madison in the Presidential Range. Turning south, and continuing generally along the west boundary of the wilderness area, the trail descends to Madison Hut, ascends and crosses the western flank of Mt. Adams, descends to Edmands Col, ascends and crosses the eastern flank of Mt. Jefferson and the western flank of Mt. Clay, and leaves the wilderness' southern boundary at the edge of the Great Gulf.

The trail continues south, crosses the Cog Railway, ascends the cone near the summit of Mt. Washington, and descends southerly to the Lakes of the Clouds. Continuing generally along the ridge of the Presidential Range the trail goes southerly, passing close to or over the summits of Mt. Monroe, Mt. Franklin, Mt. Eisenhower, Mt. Pierce, Mt. Jackson, and Mt. Webster to the eastern edge of Crawford Notch, and leaves the White Mountain National Forest to enter Crawford Notch State Park. It follows and then descends from the Webster Cliffs, crosses the Saco River on a footbridge, crosses U.S. Route 302, and ascends to Willey House Station. It crosses the Maine Central Railroad and then, going northwesterly, ascends the western face of the notch, leaves the state park, and reenters the national forest as it passes south of Mt. Willey to Ethan Pond.

It then continues in a generally westerly direction, through Zealand Notch, over Zealand Mountain, along Zealand Ridge, over Mt. Guyot, along the ridge to South Twin Mountain, down to Galehead, along the ridge to Mt. Garfield, down to Garfield Pond, and along the ridge up to the North Peak, and then southerly to Mt. Lafayette. The trail continues south along the Franconia Ridge over Mt. Lincoln and Little Haystack Mountain, and just north of Mt. Liberty turns west and descends past Liberty Spring, enters Franconia Notch State Park, and descends to and crosses U.S. Route 3. North Woodstock (post office and grocery) is six miles south on the highway.

From the crossing of Route 3 the trail bears northwesterly and follows Cascade Brook up to Lonesome Lake where it bears west, reenters the White Mountain National Forest, and ascends to North Kinsman Mountain. Here the trail turns south, descends to a power line and passes Mt. Wolf, then descends steeply to Kinsman Notch, where it passes through the Society for the Protection of New Hampshire Forests' Lost River Reservation and crosses New Hampshire Highway 112. Steeply ascending southwesterly along Beaver Brook, the trail enters the national forest, passes near the summits of Mt. Blue and Mt. Moosilauke, and then descends the southwest side of Moosilauke, leaves the national forest, descends a paved road, and reaches New Hampshire Highway 25 in the village of Glencliff (post office but no grocery).

Turning northwesterly the trail follows the abandoned Boston and Maine Railroad, reenters the national forest, passes Wachipauka Pond, leaves the national forest (last time) at its western boundary, and crosses New Hampshire Highway 25C. Continuing southwesterly, the trail passes Lake Armington and Upper Baker Pond, crosses New Hampshire Highway 25A, ascends to the summit of Mt. Cube, passes abandoned Quinttown, ascends along Mousley Brook to the summit of

Smarts Mountain, and descends to and crosses the Lyme–Dorchester Road. It ascends Holts Ledge, continuing southwesterly in a valley between Bear Hill and Holts Ledge to the crossing of Hewes Brook Road. It continues up the north face of Moose Mountain and drops along the west side of Moose Mountain ridge, then westerly crosses farm country and dirt roads, surmounts a ridge, and then follows hard-surfaced Wheelock Street through Hanover (post office and grocery).

Vermont

The trail crosses the Connecticut River on New Hampshire Highway 120, entering Vermont, where a hard-surfaced road is followed westerly until the trail reenters the woods. The trail then crosses a ridge, drops to Dothan Brook, ascends to Griggs Mountain, descends to and follows down along Podunk Brook to Vermont Highway 14 to West Hartford (post office and grocery). The trail goes westerly over Bunker Hill, then through the woods to Thistle Hill, descends to cross a ravine, ascends again passing through field and forest to cross the Pomfret–South Pomfret Road, passes the southern flank of Topman Hill, descends to cross Barnard Brook, ascends and crosses the ridge of Frazier Hill and descends to Vermont Highway 12.

Continuing westerly, the trail leaves the rolling Connecticut Valley farmland to enter dense mature forest, ascends woods roads around Cobb Hill, passes near The Lookout, traverses several ridges, and descends to the old Chatauguay Road, which it follows down to cross the North Branch of the Ottauquechee River. Then it ascends to the crest of a ridge and descends through the drainage basin of Stony Brook, crosses another ridge and descends to River Road. Killington Post Office and the village of Sherburne Center are approximately 1.5 miles south on River Road. Continuing westerly, the trail crosses the Ottauquechee River on a bridge and ascends over a ridge to Kent Pond and Vermont Highway 100. Crossing the highway, the trail passes through the Gifford Woods State Park camping area, enters the Green Mountain National Forest, ascends westerly to the east flank of Deer Leap Mountain, turns south, descends and leaves the national forest, and crosses U.S. Route 4 at Sherburne Pass.

The trail then begins its southerly route, following the contours of the ridges of the Green Mountains. Ascending the north flank of Pico Peak, it follows the ridge, traverses the west flank of Killington Peak and the east flank of Little Killington Peak, and descends to cross and follow Cold River to the North Clarendon–North Shrewsbury Road. It crosses over a ridge to Beacon Hill and descends to and crosses

Vermont Highway 103. North Clarendon (post office and grocery) is two miles north on the highway.

After crossing the highway the trail goes over the Clarendon Gorge of the Mill River on a footbridge and follows a ridge, passes between Bear Mountain and Button Hill, and descends to and crosses Vermont Route 140, where the trail reenters the national forest. Continuing south, the trail crosses two dirt roads, ascends to White Rocks Mountain, descends and crosses Homer Stone Brook, ascends to Little Rock Pond, and descends to and crosses Forest Service Road No. 10. Continuing southerly, the trail descends to and crosses Big Branch on a footbridge, ascends to Baker Peak, descends to Griffith Lake, ascends to and follows the ridge over Peru Peak and Styles Peak, drops to Mad Tom Notch, ascends to Bromley Mountain, and descends to and crosses Vermont Highway 11/30. Manchester Center (post office and grocery) is about six miles west on the highway. It continues south along the ridge east of Spruce Peak to Prospect Rock, thence along a plateau area past Bourn Pond and Stratton Pond to descend gradually to the Arlington–West Wardsboro Road. Crossing the road, it proceeds southerly along the ridge, passes Story Spring and South Alder Brook, passes over the summit of Glastenbury Mountain, and descends along the ridge west of Bolles Brook to the crossing of Vermont Highway 9. Bennington (post office and grocery) is four miles west on the highway.

After crossing the highway the trail ascends over Harmon Hill, descends to Stamford Stream, ascends along the stream passing east of Sucker Pond, traverses the ridge, crosses County Road and, continuing on the flat ridge to the Vermont–Massachusetts border, leaves the Green Mountain National Forest.

Massachusetts

The trail enters the Clarksburg State Forest, continues south along the ridge of East Mountain, then descends into the Hoosic Valley, leaving the state forest and entering Blackinton (grocery but no post office). The trail crosses the Boston and Maine Railroad and Hoosic River on a footbridge, crosses Massachusetts Highway 2, ascends from the valley to the Mt. Williams Reservoir, which it skirts to the west, then enters the Mt. Greylock State Reservation and ascends southerly to the north flank of Prospect Mountain, where it turns east to descend and cross Notch Road, and ascends to the summit of Mt. Williams. The trail then goes southerly along the ridge, passing over

Mt. Fitch, Mt. Greylock, Saddle Ball Mountain, and Jones Nose, where it descends to and follows along Kitchen Brook, leaves the reservation by woods road, and turns easterly to cross Massachusetts Highway 8 at Cheshire (post office and grocery).

Continuing easterly on town roads the trail crosses the Penn Central Railroad and then heads southerly, skirts west of the Cobbles, passes Gore and Anthony ponds on North Mountain, and descends into Dalton (post office and grocery). The trail continues through Dalton, crossing Massachusetts Highway 8, passing under the Penn Central Railroad, ascending Grange Hall Road to turn southerly, and then ascending onto a plateau. It passes over Tully Mountain and Warner Hill, enters the Pittsfield Watershed Area, crosses Blotz Road, traverses upland country, leaves the watershed area, and then turns west on Beach Road, south on Pittsfield Road to Washington Town Hall (no post office or grocery), and west on Branch Road into the October Mountain State Forest. The trail continues southerly through the forest going over Bald Top, crosses County Road, skirts Finerty Pond, ascends to a ridge and passes over Walling and Becket mountains, and then descends to and crosses U.S. Route 20, Greenwater Brook, and the Massachusetts Turnpike Toll Road.

The trail then bears southwesterly, crosses a ridge, passes around the east end of Upper Goose Pond, ascends to, follows, and descends from a ridge to the south end of Goose Pond. Thence following old dirt roads, it traverses over another ridge, descends to the Tyringham Valley, follows paved roads through Tyringham (grocery but no post office), crosses the valley to its west side, follows an old dirt road over another ridge, enters Beartown State Forest, and crosses Beartown Mountain Road. Going westerly the trail crosses East Brook, traverses a ridge, crosses Mt. Wilcox Road, and ascends to Mt. Wilcox. It then turns south, recrosses Mt. Wilcox Road, passes around the east end of Benedict Pond, leaves the state forest, crosses Blue Hill Road, and descends to and follows Massachusetts Highway 23 to the west to Monument Valley Road. The trail then begins the ascent of East Mountain, enters East Mountain State Forest, traverses upland, leaves the forest, descends to and crosses Homes Road, ascends and crosses a ridge south of June Mountain, and descends into the Housatonic Valley.

A series of roads are followed across the valley as the trail goes westerly following Boardman Street, Kellogg Road (cross Housatonic River), U.S. Route 7 (post offices and grocery stores are in Great Barrington, three miles to the north, and Sheffield, three miles to the south, on Route 7), and Lime Kiln Road (cross Penn Central Railroad), crosses Massachusetts Highway 41, and follows Jug End Road. The trail ascends Jug End and gains and follows a ridge south over Mt. Bushnell entering Mt. Everett Reservation. It skirts to the east of Mt. Undine and Guilder Pond, passes over Mt. Everett, leaves the reservation, goes over Mt. Race, and then descends to Plantain Pond.

The trail descends south past Bear Rock Falls, turns west to Sages Ravine Brook, then turns south to begin the ascent of Bear Mountain, crosses the Massachusetts–Connecticut line, and ascends to the summit of Bear Mountain.

Connecticut

From the summit of Bear Mountain, the trail descends south along the ridge, ascends Lion Head, and crosses a pasture to Cobble Road. The trail follows Cobble Road and U.S. Route 44 east, enters Salisbury Town Forest, and continues east, crossing an abandoned pasture to a wooded col on the slope of Prospect Mountain. The trail now descends southeast through Amesville (no post office or grocery) and crosses the Housatonic River on the "Iron Bridge" at the outskirts of Falls Village (post office but no grocery). A hard-surfaced road is taken south for 1.5 miles and then railroad tracks and U.S. Route 7 are crossed.

The trail ascends over Barrack Mountain to Music Mountain Road, jogs east along the road, then ascends through Dean Ravine. The trail recrosses Music Mountain Road, enters the Housatonic State Forest, crosses West Yelping Hill Road, continues southeast through the forest, crosses Yelping Hill Road, reaches Connecticut Highway 4, and crosses a ridge to the ski area in the Mohawk State Forest. The trail descends through the primeval area of Cathedral Pines, ascends a slope of Coltsfoot Mountain, traverses Dark Entry Ravine, and follows U.S. Route 7 through Cornwall Bridge (post office and grocery). Leaving Cornwall Bridge, the trail goes over the Housatonic River, crosses and recrosses Connecticut Highway 4, and proceeds south along old roads near the Housatonic River.

Turning west over St. Johns Ledges and Calebs Peak, the trail enters Macedonia Brook State Park and crosses Fuller Mountain Road, continues west and southwest, then ascends Cobble Mountain, turns south traversing hills of the state park, and leaving the park descends to Macedonia Brook Road. Then the trail jogs right along the road, turns left, crosses a ridge, and descends to Connecticut Highway 341. A half mile east on the highway is Kent (post office and grocery). The trail follows the highway west for a short distance, turns left on a local improved road, then right, traversing Mt. Algo. The trail crosses Thayer Ravine Brook and ascends Schaghticoke Mountain. On the westerly slope of the mountain, the trail crosses the Connecticut–New York line.

New York

The trail enters New York on Schaghticoke Mountain, descends to Dog Tail Corners, continues south-southwest over an outlet from Ellis Pond, and crosses Ten Mile River and New York Highway 55 at Webatuck (no post office or grocery), and proceeds in a southwesterly direction just to the west of a marsh on the west shoulder of Leather Hill. The trail then passes through the Pawling Nature Preserve, proceeds along the top of Hammersly Ridge just west of Quaker Lake, turns sharply west-northwest, and comes to New York Route 22. One mile to the south is Pawling (post office and grocery). The trail crosses Route 22 and later New York Route 55A, climbs Mt. Tom, and descends to New York Route 216 at Holmes (post office and grocery). From this point the trail goes generally west to New York Route 52.

Turning southwest it proceeds just west of the height of land of the Hosner Mountains, crosses the Taconic State Parkway at the junction with Miller Hill Road, and goes south on Shenandoah Mountain. The trail enters Clarence Fahnestock State Park from the north, 0.3 mile from the Taconic Parkway, continues west of Canopus Lake, then goes south along Canopus Creek to a point south of Sunken Mine Pond, where it turns southwest and proceeds to Moneyhole Mountain.

The trail crosses Moneyhole Mountain, leaves the park, and descends to Nelsons Corners. It then proceeds southwesterly to the Catskill Aqueduct, follows this south to Phillips Brook Road, goes west on this for about 0.6 mile, then goes south over Fort Hill. The trail picks up a secondary road to Cat Rock Road, follows Cat Rock Road for about 0.4 mile, turns sharply west, then continues southwesterly over Canada Hill north of Anthonys Nose, and crosses the Hudson River on Bear Mountain Bridge.

The trail enters the Bear Mountain–Harriman State Parks' section of Palisades Interstate Park right after it crosses the Hudson. It passes the Bear Mountain Inn, goes over Bear Mountain and West Mountain crossing Palisades Parkway, and continues to Seven Lakes Drive at the north end of Lake Tiorati. It then goes southwest along Fingerboard Mountain, then west over Surebridge Mountain, and passes north of Island Pond. It then goes over Green Pond Mountain, descends, and crosses over the New York State Thruway at Arden (post office but no grocery) and climbs Arden Mountain, where it leaves Bear Mountain–Harriman State Parks.

The trail then continues westerly, crosses Orange Turnpike, goes north of Little Dam Pond, goes over Buchanan Mountain, and climbs Mombasha High Point. It then crosses New York Highway 17A, slabs the east side of Bellvale Mountain, with Greenwood Lake to the east, and then continues southwest, entering New Jersey on Bearfort Mountain.

New Jersey

The trail enters New Jersey in the Abram S. Hewitt State Forest and passes above Upper Greenwood Lake. Proceeding westerly, the trail crosses the Warwick Turnpike north of Parker Lake and enters Wawayanda State Park. It slabs the east side of Wawayanda Mountain, descending westerly to Vernon Valley, and continues west on Maple Grange Road. It then goes northwesterly over Pochuck Mountain, descends and enters New York State at Liberty Corners, and continues northwesterly on the road to Unionville (post office and grocery). It continues west on roads, reenters New Jersey near Rockport, continues through Mt. Salem, and crosses New Jersey Highway 519 where it climbs to top of the Kittatinny Ridge at High Point Memorial State Park.

The trail stays on the highest part of the ridge and crosses New Jersey Highway 23, passes Lake Rutherford, enters Stokes State Forest, passes the pavilion atop Sunrise Mountain, and crosses U.S. Route 206 in Culvers Gap (a mile east on the highway is the community of Culvers Lake—grocery but no post office). Lake Kittatinny is passed and the trail enters the Delaware Water Gap National Recreation Area, ascends Rattlesnake Mountain (now called Paradise Hill) and Mt. Mohican, skirts Sunfish Pond, and descends to the Delaware River in Delaware Water Gap.

Pennsylvania

The Appalachian Trail crosses the river on the Interstate 80 bridge and enters Pennsylvania in the village of Delaware Water Gap (post office and grocery). It ascends past Lake Lenape and reaches the crest of the Blue Mountain on Mount Minsi. The trail follows the crest of the ridge traveling west, crosses Totts Gap, and leaves the Delaware Water Gap National Recreation Area. It traverses Fox and Wind gaps, passes through Pennsylvania State Game Lands across Smith and Little gaps, leaves the game lands, dips down into Lehigh Gap, and crosses the Lehigh River on the Pennsylvania Highway 873 bridge.

At the west end of the bridge the trail ascends Blue Mountain (crossing Lehigh Furnace Gap, Bake Oven Knob, and Pennsylvania Highway 309) and follows the crest for nine miles, when the trail turns sharp left (south), descending just east of Hawk Mountain Sanctuary, and goes through the village of Eckville (no post office or grocery), and ascends Blue Mountain. At the top of the mountain it turns east, crossing the Pinnacle Rocks, then turns south around the valley rim, descends into a hollow, passes the Hamburg Reservoir, again ascends Blue Mountain, crosses over to the north side, and descends to Schuylkill Gap in the village of Port Clinton (post office and grocery).

After passing through the village and crossing the Schuylkill River, it turns left and ascends very steeply to the crest of Blue Mountain, where it reenters Pennsylvania State Game Lands, follows the trail and game feeding roads to Pennsylvania Highway 183, which is followed for 0.5 mile, and dips into Schubert Gap. Two miles later, going around the Kessel it reaches Pennsylvania Highway 501. It follows the ridge, crossing Pennsylvania Highway 645, continues on the ridge crest, and descends into Swatara Gap, leaving the game lands at the bottom of the mountain. Crossing Swatara Creek on an iron bridge, it then passes under Interstate 81 while following Pennsylvania Highway 72, and turns left, following secondary roads across the valley to Ditzler's Farm.

It enters the woods of the Pennsylvania State Game Lands from Rausch Gap, then continues northwest through St. Anthonys Wilderness, reaches the crest of Stony Mountain, descends to Clarks Valley, and crosses Pennsylvania Highway 325 at end of the game lands. After ascending Peters Mountain, the trail turns left (west) following the ridge crest, crosses Pennsylvania Highway 225, then follows the ridge to its end and descends to the Susquehanna River at Clarks Ferry. The trail crosses the river on the bridge carrying U.S. Routes 22 and 322 and on the west bank follows High Street through the village of Duncannon (post office and grocery), crosses Sherman Creek, and ascends Cove Mountain passing Hawk Rock.

It then follows the crest of Cove Mountain to Grier Point, there crossing Pennsylvania Highway 850. Then it ascends the north side of Blue Mountain to Deans Gap. After descending the south side of Blue Mountain it crosses Pennsylvania Highway 994 just east of Donnellytown, and crosses Conodoguinet Creek and the Cumberland Valley using secondary roads and trails. It crosses under Interstate 81 and then U.S. Route 11 west of New Kingstown and goes over the Pennsylvania Turnpike. Following Old Stone House Road, it passes through Churchtown (Allen Post Office and grocery), then crosses the Reading Railroad tracks and Yellow Breeches Creek. From here it follows the first ridge of South Mountain and goes around the boundary of the York YMCA Camp. It crosses Whiskey Spring Road, Rocky Ridge, and Old Town Road before descending the ridge to cross Pennsylvania Highway 94 and enter Michaux State Forest. The trail crosses Trents Hill, Pennsylvania Highway 34, the Reading Railroad, and Hunters Run Road. It ascends to the ridge of Piney Mountain, passing the Tagg Run Shelters, then follows the ridge southwest and passes Pole Steeple Trail, descends to Fuller Lake, and reaches Pennsylvania Highway 233 in Pine Grove Furnace State Park. The trail leaves the state park on crossing Pennsylvania Highway 233 and reenters Michaux State Forest. It crosses Camp Michaux on the abandoned Old Shippensburg Road.

The trail then ascends to the ridge of South Mountain, passes through the Tumbling Run Game Preserve and Caledonia State Park, and crosses U.S. Route 30 in this park. It skirts Old Forge State Picnic Grounds to the south and leaves Michaux State Forest at the crossing of Pennsylvania Highway 16 northeast of Pen Mar (no post office or grocery).

Maryland

In Maryland the trail skirts the edge of Pen Mar through the Western Maryland Railway's abandoned park and traverses the Fort Ritchie military installation on the road to High Rock. It follows the ridge of South Mountain, continuously passing through Greenbrier State Park (at U.S. Route 40 and Interstate 70), Washington Monument State Park, Turners Gap at U.S. Route 40A, and Gathland State Park. At Weverton Bluff the trail bears west along the towpath of the Chesapeake and Ohio Canal National Monument and crosses the Potomac River over the Sandy Hook Bridge on U.S. Route 340. The village of Harpers Ferry (post office and grocery) is 1.3 miles further to the west along the C & O towpath and via the plank walkway on the first railroad bridge beyond the confluence of the Potomac and Shenandoah rivers.

West Virginia

In West Virginia the trail touches the perimeter of Harpers Ferry National Historical Park on Loudoun Heights above U.S. Route 340 and for about 16 miles follows the ridge generally along the West Virginia–Virginia line to a point 2 miles north of Snickers Gap. (Again on the crest of Peters Mountain north of Pearisburg, Virginia, the trail follows along the West Virginia–Virginia line for over 8 miles.)

Virginia

The trail crosses Virginia Highway 7 at Snickers Gap just west of Bluemont (post office). The trail parallels the highway in a westerly direction for a short distance, then continues south along the west slope of the Blue Ridge Mountains. South of U.S. Route 50 at Ashby Gap the trail is generally just west of the Fauquier County line. It crosses Virginia Highway 55 in Linden (post office and grocery) and U.S. Route 522 at Chester Gap.

From Chester Gap the trail goes southwest to enter Shenandoah National Park and ascends to the ridge, crossing the Skyline Drive at Compton Gap. For 96 miles the trail follows the ridge in the park, crossing U.S. Route 211 and Virginia Highway 33 at their intersections with Skyline Drive and making occasional additional crossings of the Skyline Drive. The trail remains on the ridge leaving the park and then descends to the Blue Ridge Parkway, crossing Interstate 64 and U.S. Route 250 at Rockfish Gap. Waynesboro (post office and grocery) is three miles west on the highway.

From Rockfish Gap, the trail follows Virginia Highway 610 until crossing the Blue Ridge Parkway and entering George Washington National Forest. The trail ascends Elk Mountain, descends into Mill Creek, ascends Dobie Mountain, follows a ridge crest through Humpback Gap, crosses The Rocks and Humpback Mountain, and descends to Laurel Springs Gap. After passing to the west of Devils Knob, the trail descends to Reeds Gap, crosses Bee Mountain, ascends to and follows Three Ridges, passes by Chimney Rock, descends to Harpers Creek, crosses the Tye River via a bridge, and follows Virginia Highway 56 to the northwest for 0.5 mile.

The trail leaves the highway, follows Cripple Creek, ascends the north slope of The Priest, follows the ridge crest, crosses Maintop Mountain, Porters Ridge, and Elk Pond Mountain, and passes to the east of Rocky Mountain. It descends to Salt Log Gap, crosses Tar Jacket Ridge, descends to Hog Camp Gap, crosses Cole Mountain, descends to Cow Camp Gap, crosses Bald Knob, and descends to U.S. Route 60. It follows Brown Mountain Creek and Swapping Camp Creek to the Lynchburg Reservoir, passes to the south of the reservoir, follows Little Irish Creek, ascends Rice Mountain, follows the ridge crest, crosses the Blue Ridge Parkway, ascends to Punchbowl Mountain, follows the ridge across Bluff Mountain, descends, passes to the west of Silas Knob, and follows the ridge crest across Saddle Gap. It then crosses Big Rocky Row and Little Rocky Row, descends John Hollow to the confluence of Cashaw Creek and the James River, and crosses the James River on U.S. Route 501 at Snowden (post office and grocery).

The trail turns right ascending the slope on the west side of the James River, where it enters the Glenwood Ranger District of the Jefferson National Forest, and gradually curves south to Marble Springs on the ascent to High Cock Knob. In a short distance the trail descends into Petites Gap, then crosses and recrosses the Blue Ridge Parkway, after which it circles the peak of Apple Orchard Mountain, the highest peak in the area. It next circles the headwaters of Cornelius Creek, leads across Floyd Mountain, and follows the crest of Bryant Ridge until it drops off into Jennings Creek, then ascends to the crest of Cove Mountain.

A steady ascent around the headwaters of Bearwallow Creek brings the trail across the Blue Ridge Parkway, where the trail and the parkway run parallel for a few miles due to the extremely narrow ridge. The trail then passes in the vicinity of Fullhardt Knob, after which it leaves the Jefferson National Forest and descends to U.S. Route 11. Cloverdale (post office and grocery) is a mile south on roads.

The trail follows Route 11 and then U.S. Route 220 for short distances, underpasses Interstate 81, and climbs to Tinker Ridge, which is followed around Carvins Cove Lake. It traverses the Big Tinker Cliffs, goes over McAfee Knob, and drops to Virginia Highway 311 on Catawba Mountain. Catawba (post office and grocery) is a mile west on the highway.

Highway 311 is crossed and the trail passes along the mountain, fords Catawba Creek and ascends Cove Mountain to the northwest, where it enters the New Castle Ranger District of the Jefferson National Forest, then descends northwest along Trout Creek in the Broad Run Wildlife Research Area and crosses Craig Creek at Webbs

Mills. Next it ascends along Turnpike Creek to the crest of Sinking Creek Mountain, at which point it leaves the New Castle Ranger District and enters the Blacksburg Ranger District of the Jefferson National Forest. Sinking Creek Mountain is followed for about 10 miles.

After crossing Virginia Highway 42, the trail ascends Johns Creek Mountain at Kelly Knob and follows the ridge crest north to Rocky Gap, descending and crossing Johns Creek. Then it ascends to Lone Pine Peak, turns west, passes Mountain Lake Scenic Area, and follows the crest of Potts Mountain and Big Mountain. At Bailey Gap it descends to Interior (no post office or grocery). After crossing White Rock Mountain the trail descends into the Stony Creek valley before ascending Peters Mountain. The trail then follows along the Virginia–West Virginia border for 8.6 miles. Before reaching the New River it turns south and follows Hemlock Ridge to the U.S. Route 460 bridge over the New River. The highway is followed for 1.3 miles before the trail turns right into a street at the edge of Pearisburg (post office and grocery). A half mile later the trail enters woods and climbs steeply up Pearis Mountain.

From Angels Rest, following southwest along the crest of Pearis Mountain, the trail crosses Sugar Run Gap and Sugar Run Mountain before descending into Dismal Creek valley and Kimberling Creek valley. It crosses through Lick Skillet Gap to Virginia Highway 42 and the village of Crandon (grocery but no post office).

The trail crosses the highway and Walker Creek valley, then ascends steeply to the crest of Walker Mountain, where it enters the Wythe Ranger District of the Jefferson National Forest. Walker Mountain is followed southwest for about 30 miles.

At Redding Gap beyond Big Walker Fire Tower the trail turns left and descends steeply to Reed Creek. Then it ascends and follows Gullion Mountain (Brushy Mountain) and descends Davis Hollow to Interstate 81 and then U.S. Route 11. The trail, after crossing the valley of the Holston River, then climbs Glade Mountain and crosses Locust Mountain to Brushy Mountain, which is followed southwest descending to Rye Valley, where it enters Mt. Rogers National Recreation Area and leaves the Wythe Ranger District. After crossing Rye Valley, the trail circles the summit of High Point and descends to Virginia Highway 16. Then it traverses the north slope of Hurricane Mountain. Shortly after reaching the crest of Hurricane Mountain the trail descends to the southeast and crosses Virginia Secondary Road 603. It then ascends the north slope of Pine Mountain to Wilburn Ridge and continues to the summit of Mt. Rogers, the highest peak in Virginia, and follows Elk Garden Ridge.

From Elk Garden Gap it ascends over Whitetop Mountain, passes

Buzzard Rock, skirts Beech Mountain, then follows Lost Mountain and descends to Creek Junction, passing by Taylor Valley. After crossing U.S. Route 58 it ascends Feathercamp Ridge and drops into the town of Damascus (post office and grocery). From the intersection of U.S. Route 58 and Virginia Highway 91, the trail follows the streets through Damascus and ascends the northeast end of Holston Mountain. About 2.5 miles from the junction of U.S. Route 58 and Virginia Highway 91 the trail enters the Purchase Area of the Jefferson National Forest.

After another 1.6 miles the trail leaves Virginia and the Jefferson National Forest. It then enters the state of Tennessee and the Cherokee National Forest.

Tennessee

Continuing into Tennessee, the trail enters the Kettlefoot Wildlife Management Area and follows the crest of Holston Mountain, sometimes crossing to one side or another of the crests and summits. About eight miles from the Virginia–Tennessee line the trail passes through McQueens Gap. Continuing along the crest of Holston Mountain, it passes by McQueens Knob Fire Tower, through Double Springs Gap, over Locust Pole Knob, and gradually descends to Low Gap, where U.S. Route 421 crosses Holston Mountain.

The trail continues southwest, generally along the crest of Holston Mountain, for another three miles, crossing Locust Knob and circling north and east of Rich Knob. In the gap northwest of Rich Knob, the trail leaves the crest of Holston Mountain and proceeds in a southeasterly direction on national forest land along Cross Mountain. At the lowest point on Cross Mountain, the trail crosses Tennessee Highway 91. It continues southeasterly for a mile, then turns abruptly southwest and follows the crest of Iron Mountain for about 15 miles. It then descends along the southwest end of Iron Mountain. One mile farther it reaches a paved access road, which leads to the Watauga Dam Visitors Center.

Beyond the road, the trail ascends southwesterly to a summit, then descends steeply in a northwesterly direction to Wilbur Lake. Immediately beyond Wilbur Lake the trail turns left and ascends steeply for about two miles to the summit of Iron Mountain. It continues southwesterly along the crest of Iron Mountain for another 2.3 miles and descends its south slope to Tennessee Highway 67. Hampton (post office and grocery) is 1.2 miles west on the highway.

The trail crosses the highway and follows Laurel Fork upstream.

For the next 2.5 miles the trail follows close by the stream bed, passing by the so-called "Buckled Rock." On reaching Laurel Falls it climbs away from the stream until coming to what was formerly a logging railroad bed. Following the railroad bed it enters Dennis Cove and ascends southwesterly along Coon Den Branch to the crest of the northwest spur of White Rocks Mountain, which is followed to White Rocks Mountain Fire Tower. Beyond the fire tower the trail continues southeast, then gradually more easterly along the crest of White Rocks Mountain on the edge of the Laurel Fork Wildlife Management Area.

Passing through Moreland Gap it enters Walnut Mountain Road and continues southeasterly, still following the crest of White Rocks Mountain. After two miles the trail turns sharp right from the Walnut Mountain Road and follows lesser roads and trails in a south to southeasterly direction to U.S. Route 19E inside the North Carolina line. Elk Park, North Carolina (post office and grocery), is 1.6 miles to the east on the highway.

Tennessee–North Carolina

The Tennessee–North Carolina line is followed in general all the way to Doe Knob in the Great Smokies. The trail ascends the northern spur of Hump Mountain and then descends southwesterly to Bradley Gap. Beyond Bradley Gap it ascends along the east slope of Little Hump Mountain and climbs to the summit of Yellow Mountain (shown on some maps as Little Hump Mountain). The trail continues southwest to the junction of Big Yellow Mountain (sometimes locally known as Big Yellow Bald).

Here the trail turns northwest and follows along the crest and along the Tennessee–North Carolina line to Yellow Mountain Gap. From Yellow Mountain Gap the trail ascends westerly, then descends in a south to southwesterly direction. After passing through Buckeye Gap, it ascends to the summit of Elk Hollow Ridge and continues westerly along the main ridge crest, still following the Tennessee–North Carolina line. After ascending about one mile it goes around the northern slope of Grassy Ridge Bald, passes over Jane Bald, through Engine Gap, over Round Bald, and descends to Carvers Gap, through which passes Tennessee Highway 143 and North Carolina Highway 261.

From Carvers Gap the trail zigzags up the slope of Roan High Knob, passing to the north of the summit. Beyond Coltens Cliff, the trail leaves the summit of Roan Mountain and descends along the state line, passing through Ash Gap and over Beartown Mountain and through Hughes Gap. From Hughes Gap the trail ascends to the north to the summit of Little Rock Knob, where it turns westward and generally descends following the ridge crest and the state line.

Seven miles from Hughes Gap the trail swings southwesterly and descends to Iron Mountain Gap, through which Tennessee Highway 107 and North Carolina Highway 26 pass. From Iron Mountain Gap the trail ascends to the southwest along the state-line ridge crest, passing over the summit of Little Bald Knob. It then descends to the northwest, passing south of Piney Ball, and descends to Cherry Gap. From Cherry Gap the trail follows the main state-line ridge crest southwesterly and then goes west to Low Gap. Beyond Low Gap the trail ascends on the north slope of Unaka Mountain until it reaches and follows Unaka Mountain Road. At Pleasant Garden it begins a descent to the southwest to Deep Gap (shown as Beauty Spot Gap on U.S. Geodetic Survey maps). It passes over Beauty Spot, descends to the north side of Indian Grave Gap, and continues to the Nolichucky River via Curley Maple Gap and Jones Branch.

The Nolichucky River is crossed on an old concrete highway bridge. Erwin, Tennessee (post office and grocery), is 3.7 miles to the northeast by road. From the west side of the bridge the trail ascends to the west and then south along Cliff Ridge. Cliff Ridge merges with Temple Ridge, which is followed to the southwest to a point a short distance below Temple Hill Fire Tower. From this point the trail descends southeasterly to Temple Hill Gap. Beyond it proceeds to the east and southeast, maintaining a nearly constant elevation around the north and east side of No Business Knob. At Devils Creek Gap the trail crosses the state line from Tennessee into North Carolina and ascends to the east and then descends to the south to reach U.S. Route 19W east of Spivey Gap. At Spivey Gap it crosses U.S. Route 19W. Climbing Little Bald Mountain the trail passes through a treeless sag known as Big Stamp. Beyond the summit of Big Bald it descends westward to Low Gap, Street Gap, and Sams Gap, where U.S. Route 23 is crossed.

After crossing Route 23 the trail ascends High Rock Knob and continues to Rice Creek Gap. Four miles beyond, the trail turns right and the ridge crest is followed to Sugarloaf Gap, where the trail descends to Boone Cove Gap and Devil Fork Gap. From Devil Fork Gap the trail skirts the left side of Flint Mountain, crosses the ridge-line into Tennessee, and reenters North Carolina at Flint Gap.

Ascending northward, the trail crosses briefly again into Tennessee as it skirts right of the summit of Green Ridge Knob and then stays in North Carolina close to the crest, passing left of Gravel Knob and over Big Butt. Here the trail turns southwestward along the Tennessee side to Chestnut Log Gap, follows closely the state-line crest over Bald Mountain to the Phillips Hollow Trail and goes along the Tennessee side into Bearwallow Gap. From the gap the trail skirts the North Carolina slope below the state-line crest at Jones Meadow, circles the south side of the summit of Camp Creek Bald, and rejoins the state line just beyond on Seng Ridge.

The trail descends close to the state line and crosses Allen Gap at the junction of North Carolina Highway 208–Tennessee Highway 70. Continuing along the state line between the Andrew Johnson and the Rich Laurel Wildlife Management Areas, the trail ascends to Buzzard Roost Ridge and passes through Deep Gap and over Spring Mountain and into Hurricane Gap, where forest service roads from both states join. Proceeding to Rich Mountain the trail leaves the state line for 16 miles, descending Roundtop Ridge to the French Broad River and Hot Springs, North Carolina (post office and grocery).

The trail follows U.S. Routes 70 and 25 through Hot Springs and then ascends the west bank of North Carolina Highway 209 to the French Broad Ranger Headquarters of the National Forests in North Carolina. The trail ascends Deer Park Mountain and passes through Taylor Hollow Gap and into Garenflo Gap. Ascending from Garenflo Gap, it passes over Bluff Mountain and around the south slope of Tennessee Bluff, rejoins the state line, and crosses briefly into Cocke County, Tennessee, just before coming into Kale Gap and crossing back to North Carolina. A half mile further on, the trail loops into Tennessee over the summit of Walnut Mountain and returns to the state line at Lemon Gap. Here the trail follows Rich Mountain, then Max Patch Mountain.

Generally following the state-line crest, the trail passes through Brown Gap, ascends Harmon Den Mountain, drops into Deep (Ground Hog Creek) Gap, and crosses Wildcat Top and the West Peak of Snowbird Mountain. At Spanish Oak Gap the trail turns sharp left from the state line, descends by a wide loop near the head of Painter Creek in North Carolina, then swings westward to cross into Tennessee and descends to pass under Interstate 40 and then over the Big Pigeon River on the road bridge one mile downstream from the North Carolina state line at Waterville. From the south end of Browns Bridge across the Big Pigeon River, one mile west of the Tennessee–North Carolina line, the trail traverses privately owned land for 1.5 miles, going south along the right (east) bank of Tobes Creek.

Crossing State Line Branch, the trail turns east along the stream for 0.5 mile and goes north to the ridge crest, which it follows east and then south to Davenport Gap. After crossing North Carolina Highway 284 in Davenport Gap, the trail traverses Great Smoky Mountains National Park for 68.36 miles.

For the first 64 miles it closely follows the crest of the Great Smoky Mountains (which is the state line between Tennessee and North Carolina), sometimes in one state and sometimes in the other, and often directly on the state line. From Davenport Gap the trail reaches the crest at a point 0.5 mile west of Mt. Cammerer, then crosses a spur on the Tennessee side of Sunup Knob, crosses the crest of Rocky Face Mountain, and traverses Low Gap. From Low Gap it traverses the North Carolina slope of Cosby Knob and the Tennessee side of Ross Knob, goes through Camel Gap and around the Tennessee side of Camel Hump Knob, traverses the North Carolina side of Inadu Knob, goes through Yellow Creek Gap and Deer Creek Gap, crosses Pinnacle Lead (a spur off Old Black), traverses the Tennessee slope of Mt. Guyot, and crosses Guyot Spur, entering on the Tennessee side of the Research Reservation.

The trail continues around the Tennessee side of Tri-Corner Knob (North Carolina side of the Research Reservation begins here), goes through Big Cove Gap, traverses the North Carolina slope of Mt. Chapman, goes through Chapman Gap, crosses the summit of Mt. Sequoyah, goes through Copper Gap, crosses Eagle Rocks, goes around the North Carolina side of Pecks Corner (intersection of Hughes Ridge and the state line; the North Carolina side of the Research Reservation ends here), crosses Woolly Tops Lead (the Tennessee side of the Research Reservation ends here), passes around the Tennessee side of Laurel Top, and goes through False Gap.

The trail then crosses the crest of Porters Mountain on the Tennessee side, passes through Porters Gap, continues along the Sawteeth, goes around the Tennessee end of Richland Mountain, goes through Dry Sluice Gap, goes around the Tennessee side of Charlies Bunion, traverses the North Carolina slope of Mt. Kephart, then continues to Newfound Gap, where U.S. Route 441 is crossed. From Newfound Gap the trail crosses Mt. Mingus Ridge, passes through Indian Gap and Little Indian Gap, crosses the summit of Mt. Collins, passes through Collins Gap, and crosses the summits of Mt. Love and Clingmans Dome. From Clingmans Dome it crosses Mt. Buckley, passes through Double Springs Gap, crosses Jenkins Knob, continues along "The Narrows," and reaches the summit of Silers Bald. From Silers Bald the trail passes through Buckeye Gap, crosses the North Carolina side of Cold Spring Knob, crosses Hemlock Knob, traverses a slope of Mt. Davis, passes through Sams Gap, crosses Derrick Knob and Chestnut Bald, goes through Sugar Tree Gap and Starkey Gap, traverses the North Carolina slope of Brier Knob near the summit, passes through Mineral Gap and Beechnut Gap, and crosses the summit of Thunderhead.

From Thunderhead the trail crosses Rocky Top, Spence Field, and Mt. Squires, passes through Maple Sugar Gap and McCampbell Gap, traverses the North Carolina side of McCampbell Knob and Russell Field, and passes through Little Abrams Gap and Big Abrams Gap. After reaching the crest of Locust Knob it crosses Devils Tater Patch, passes through Ekaneetlee Gap, goes around the North Carolina side of Powell Knob, passes through Mud Gap, and reaches the summit of Doe Knob.

North Carolina

At Doe Knob the trail leaves the crest of the Great Smokies and turns south into North Carolina. It traverses the west slope of Greer Knob and passes through Birch Spring Gap, Red Ridge Gap, and Sassafras Gap. From Sassafras Gap it follows a jeep road south for about 0.3 mile to a point 0.1 mile southwest of Shuckstack, where it leaves the road and continues south down the ridge. It then turns east and passes through a gap between Shuckstack and Little Shuckstack, goes around the west side of Little Shuckstack, and descends to a hard-surfaced road.

The road is followed for 0.6 mile to Fontana Dam on the Little Tennessee River, where the trail exits from Great Smoky Mountains National Park. The trail crosses the Little Tennessee River on the walkway along the top of Fontana Dam and enters the Nantahala National Forest. After following a curving ridge crest for about a mile, the trail exits from national forest land, passes by the east side of a swimming pool, and immediately crosses a hard-surfaced road. The village of Fontana Dam (post office and grocery) is two miles to the southwest. The trail crosses North Carolina Highway 28, and reenters the Nantahala National Forest.

From Highway 28 the trail leads south to Walker Gap and then to Black Gum Gap. It continues east along the ridge crest, traverses the south slope of High Top, passes through Cable Gap, traverses the south slope of Tommy Knob, and continues to Yellow Creek Gap. From Yellow Creek Gap it goes south to Cody Branch and continues

Photo by Owen F. Allen

Lochlen Gregory on the Knife Edge, Mt. Katahdin, Maine.

Photo by Robert Winslow

Tom McKone on trail in North Carolina.

southeast to Cody Gap. There the trail turns south, reaches the crest of Cheoah Mountain, continues along the ridge crest in an east-south-east direction, and passes through Brown Fork Gap, Sweetwater Gap, and Stekoah Gap. From Stekoah Gap the trail continues southeast through Simp Gap and Locust Cove Gap and crosses the summit of Cheoah Bald.

From Cheoah Bald the trail continues northeast through Sassafras Gap, crosses the summit of Swim Bald, traverses "The Jump-Up," passes through Grassy Gap, traverses the south slope of Tyre Top, follows the crest of the ridge running south of Tyre Top for about a mile, then leaves a crest and goes east to a dirt road in the gap in Flint Ridge. The trail now descends the southwest slope of Flint Ridge to the Nantahala River, crosses the river on an iron bridge, and reaches U.S. Route 19 in Wesser (grocery but no post office).

Leaving the highway, the trail reenters the Nantahala National Forest and continues to the summit of Wesser Bald. From Wesser Bald it follows the crest of the Nantahala Mountains southward, passing through Tellico Gap and traversing the western spurs of Rocky Bald, Black Bald, Tellico Bald, and Copper Bald. From Copper Bald the trail traverses Burningtown Gap and Licklog Gap, enters the Wayah Wildlife Management Area, and surmounts Wayah Bald. It follows the west slope around Wine Spring Bald, then switches back to the east slope of the ridge leading southward along the east slope of Siler Bald, and continues southeast, traversing the west slope of Sheep Knob before turning south to Panther Gap. Continuing, the trail traverses the east slope of Panther Knob, continues south to Swinging Lick Gap, turns east to Winding Stair Gap, traverses the west slope of Rocky Cove Knob and the west shoulder of Buck Knob, and crosses U.S. Route 64 in Wallace Gap. The town of Franklin (post office and grocery) is 15 miles to the east on the highway. From Wallace Gap the trail enters the Standing Indian Wildlife Management Area, follows White Oak Bottoms Road south to Rock Gap, traverses the west slope of Little Bald Mountain, goes through Glassmine Gap, and regains the main ridge crest on the north side of Big Pinnacle.

The trail continues south through Big Spring Gap, crosses the summit of Albert Mountain, descends to Bear Pen Gap, traverses the east side of Big Butt, drops to Mooney Gap and Bettys Creek Gap, and continues along the crest of Little Ridgepole Mountain to Ridgepole Mountain, where the Nantahala Mountains end. From Ridgepole Mountain the trail continues along the Blue Ridge and traverses Carter Gap, turns west to Coleman Gap, traverses the north slope of

Little Bald Mountain, goes through Beech Gap, turns north to the crest of Standing Indian, and traverses Deep Gap. From Deep Gap the trail goes west along the south end of Yellow Mountain to Wateroak Gap, turns southwest, crosses Chunky Gal Mountain, passes through Whiteoak Stamp, traverses the west side of Big Kitchens Knob, crosses Little Mountain, and traverses Sassafras Gap.

It then goes around the shoulder near the top of Court House Bald and through Court House Bald Gap, traverses the west side of Sharp Top, and continues to Bly Gap on the North Carolina–Georgia line, where the trail exits from the Nantahala National Forest.

Georgia

The trail enters Georgia and the Chattahoochee National Forest at Bly Gap and runs generally south, passing to the east of Rich Knob and going over Rocky Knob and Wheeler Knob and through Blue Ridge, Plumorchard, and Cowart gaps. It crosses U.S. Route 76 and Dicks Creek east of Dicks Creek Gap, passes between the Swallow Creek Wildlife Management Area and the Lake Burton Game Management Area, continues through Parks Gap and crosses York Ridge at Muley Mountain. It crosses Moccasin Creek and climbs Bramlet Ridge at Hellhole Mountain, then runs west along the crest of Bramlet Ridge to Dismal Mountain.

From Dismal Mountain the trail swings in a southwesterly arc, traversing the Swag of the Blue Ridge, Steeltrap and Wolfpen gaps, and the top of Tray Mountain. It continues through Tray Gap, where the trail crosses Forest Service Road 79, and proceeds to Indian Grave Gap, crosses Forest Service Road 283, ascends Rocky Mountain, where it runs along the crest of the ridge, and then drops down to Unicoi Gap and Georgia Highway 75.

Ascending Blue Mountain through the Chattahoochee Wildlife Management Area, the trail continues through Henson Gap to Red Clay Gap, where it again changes to a southerly course, then crosses the headwaters of the Chattahoochee River and follows generally the course of the river to Low Gap Creek, where it leaves the river and ascends to the summit of Poe Knob and there changes to a southwesterly course.

It passes through Cool Springs Gap, crosses Richard B. Russell Scenic Highway (Georgia Highway 348) near Piney Mountain, passes the Raven Cliffs Scenic Area, and enters the Chestatee Wildlife Management Area. To the south of Wildcat Mountain it descends into the deep gorge of Town Creek, ascends and crosses Big Ridge at the south end of Cowrock Mountain, goes over Turkey Pen Mountain and Levelland Mountain, and crosses U.S. Route 19/129 in Neels Gap. Leaving the gap, the trail enters the Blood Mountain Archaeological Area and climbs to the top of Blood Mountain, highest elevation on the Georgia section of the trail.

From Blood Mountain the trail assumes a northwesterly direction to follow Duncan Ridge, crossing Slaughter Mountain and passing through Wolfpen Gap, where it crosses Georgia Highway 180 and goes over Wildcat Knob and Coosa Bald. Then in a westerly direction it goes over Buckeye Knob and on to Mulky Gap, where it crosses Forest Service Road 4 and continues west, crossing Akin Mountain, Fish Knob, Gregory Knob, and Rhodes Mountain.

At this point the trail again assumes a southerly course, passes over Licklog Mountain and Wallalah Mountain, and crosses Georgia Highway 60 at Little Skeenah Creek. Following the crest of Toonowee Mountain into the Blue Ridge Wildlife Management Area it crosses the Toccoa River and passes through Sapling Gap, goes over John Dick Mountain, and on to Three Forks and Forest Service Road 58, where three streams join to form Noontootla Creek. Here the trail crosses the stream and Forest Service Road 58, then ascends Rich Mountain and follows the length of the ridge, drops down to cross Forest Service Road 42, and ascends to the summit of Springer Mountain, southern terminus of the Appalachian Trail.

NOTE: *The official route of the Appalachian Trail as published in the* Federal Register *for October 9, 1971, differs from the present route insofar as it describes the footway as it will be when several approved relocations are made. The principal relocations will be in northern Virginia, where several private landowners have objected to the trail crossing their property and it has had to take to hard-surfaced roads, and in Georgia between Blood Mountain and Springer Mountain where the present route lies in the path of the proposed extension to the Blue Ridge Parkway. The guidebooks available from the Appalachian Trail Conference in 1973, as listed in the bibliography, describe the present route.—*ED.

Trail Maintaining Organizations

Section of Trail	Name of Organization or Individual	Mileage

Mt. Katahdin to park boundary **10.15**
Baxter State Park

Park boundary to Penobscot West Branch **4.40**
Boy Scout Troop, Springfield, Maine

Penobscot West Branch to Rainbow Lake Camps **9.43**
Richard Carleton

Rainbow Lake Camps to Pollywog Stream **8.00**
Gary Herrick AND *Percy Turner*

Pollywog Stream to Nahmakanta Lake Lean-to **7.30**
John W. Clarke

Nahmakanta Lake Lean-to to Mahar Campground **4.55**
Boy Scout Troop, Fort Kent, Maine

Mahar Campground to Lower Joe Mary Lake **5.90**
Andre de Saint-Rat

Lower Joe Mary Lake to Kokadjo-B Pond Road **11.10**
Wilson J. Acord

Kokadjo-B Pond Road to West Branch Ponds Road **10.00**
Lendall Parsons

West Branch Ponds Road to White Cap Mountain **3.85**
Mr. AND *Mrs. Damon J. Justin*

White Cap Mountain to Long Pond **11.11**
Sierra Club group

Long Pond to Bodfish Farm **16.96**
Colby College Woodsmen's Club

Bodfish Farm to Monson **14.80**
Husson College Outing Club

Monson to Blanchard **5.52**
Future Farmers of America, Foxcroft Academy

1982

TRAIL MAINTAINING ORGANIZATIONS 1983

Section of Trail	*Name of Organization or Individual*	*Mileage*
Blanchard to Moxie Pond		16.55
	University of Maine Outing Club	
Moxie Pond to Kennebec River		12.42
	Lukin Barette AND *Antoine Brousseau*	
Kennebec River to Pierce Pond		3.41
	Pine Island Camp	
Pierce Pond to East Carry Pond Camps		7.32
	Melvin McCorrison	
East Carry Pond Camps to Long Falls Dam Road		9.16
	Boy Scout Troop No. 470, Fairfield, Maine	
Long Falls Dam Road to former Maine Highway 16		2.17
Little Bigelow Mountain to Myron H. Avery Peak		2.73
	Maine Trail Trotters	
Former Maine Highway 16 to Little Bigelow Mountain		5.17
	Robert E. Libby	
Myron H. Avery Peak to The Horns Pond		3.41
	Bowdoin Outing Club	
The Horns Pond to Bigelow Village		7.08
	Maine Chapter, Appalachian Mountain Club	
Bigelow Village to Mt. Sugarloaf		4.78
	Farmington State College Outing Club	
Mt. Sugarloaf to Orbeton Stream		8.34
	James Robjent	
Orbeton Stream to Saddleback Mountain		7.20
	David AND *Mike Field*	
Saddleback Mountain to Maine Highway 5		30.70
	Bates College Outing Club	
Maine Highway 5 to Andover-B Hill Road		13.03
	Gould Academy Outing Club	
Andover-B Hill Road to Grafton Notch		7.20
Old Speck summit to Kinsman Notch		110.15
	Appalachian Mountain Club	
Grafton Notch to Old Speck summit		1.65
	Mrs. J. L. Faulkner	

1984 TRAIL MAINTAINING ORGANIZATIONS

Section of Trail Name of Organization or Individual	Mileage

Kinsman Notch to Vermont Highway 12 .... 75.32
Dartmouth Outing Club

Vermont Highway 12 to Vermont–Massachusetts line 112.93
Green Mountain Club

Vermont–Massachusetts line to Washington Town Hall 37.19
Mt. Greylock Ski Club

Washington Town Hall to Tyringham 13.63
Metawampe Club

Tyringham to Massachusetts–Connecticut line 32.98
Berkshire Chapter, Appalachian Mountain Club

Massachusetts–Connecticut line to Connecticut–New York
line 56.05
Connecticut Chapter, Appalachian Mountain Club,
AND *Seymour R. Smith*

Connecticut–New York line to New Jersey–Pennsylvania line 158.79
New York–New Jersey Trail Conference

New Jersey–Pennsylvania line to Fox Gap 7.20
Springfield Trail Club

Fox Gap to Wind Gap 8.60
Back to Nature Hiking Club of Philadelphia (Batona)

Wind Gap to Little Gap 15.90
Delaware Valley Chapter, Appalachian Mountain Club

Little Gap to Lehigh Furnace Gap 10.40
Philadelphia Trail Club

Lehigh Furnace Gap to Bake Oven Knob Road 4.40
Tri-County Corner to Swatara Gap 52.30
Blue Mountain Eagle Climbing Club

Bake Oven Knob Road to Tri-County Corner 11.30
Allentown Hiking Club

Swatara Gap to Rausch Creek 5.60
William Etchberger (for the BMECC)

Rausch Creek to Pennsylvania Highway 325 .... 11.10
Brandywine Valley Outing Club

Pennsylvania Highway 325 to Pennsylvania Highway 225 ... 9.30
Susquehanna Appalachian Trail Club

Section of Trail   *Name of Organization or Individual*   *Mileage*

Pennsylvania Highway 225 to Susquehanna River 5.00
York Hiking Club

Susquehanna River to Pine Grove Furnace 46.27
Mountain Club of Maryland

Pine Grove Furnace to Shenandoah National Park 123.60
Potomac Appalachian Trail Club

Shenandoah National Park (1.77 miles south of Chester Gap
to Jarmans Gap) 95.08
Potomac Appalachian Trail Club AND *National Park Service*

Jarmans Gap to Rockfish Gap 7.70
Potomac Appalachian Trail Club WITH *Old
Dominion Appalachian Trail Club*

Rockfish Gap to Laurel Springs 11.11
Shenandoah–Rockfish Appalachian Trail Club

Laurel Springs to Reeds Gap 4.56
Old Dominion Appalachian Trail Club

Reeds Gap to James River 54.17
*Natural Bridge Appalachian Trail Club
AND George Washington National Forest*

James River to Bearwallow Gap 34.52
*Natural Bridge Appalachian Trail Club
AND Jefferson National Forest*

Bearwallow Gap to Black Horse Gap 7.45
*Natural Bridge Appalachian Trail Club
AND Blue Ridge Parkway*

Black Horse Gap to Interstate 81 . . . .   12.43
Catawba Mountain (Virginia Highway 311) to Crandon
(Virginia Highway 42) 92.42
Roanoke Appalachian Trail Club AND
Jefferson National Forest

Interstate 81 to Catawba Mountain 19.93
Crandon to Big Walker Lookout (U.S. Routes 21/52) 21.17
Virginia Tech Outing Club

Big Walker Lookout to Virginia Highway 16 on Brushy
Mountain 25.26
Piedmont Appalachian Trail Hikers AND
Jefferson National Forest

Section of Trail	*Name of Organization or Individual*	*Mileage*

Virginia Highway 16 on Brushy Mountain to Teas 3.65
Mt. Rogers Appalachian Trail Club AND
Jefferson National Forest

Teas to Virginia–Tennessee line 49.50
Mt. Rogers Appalachian Trail Club AND
Mt. Rogers National Recreation Area

Virginia–Tennessee line to Watauga Dam Road 37.76
Wilbur Lake to Spivey Gap 77.01
Tennessee Eastman Hiking Club AND
Cherokee National Forest

Watauga Dam Road to Wilbur Lake 1.58
Tennessee Eastman Hiking Club

Spivey Gap to Sams Gap 11.30
Carolina Mountain Club AND *Cherokee National Forest*

Sams Gap to Big Pigeon River 68.33
Carolina Mountain Club AND *National
Forests in North Carolina*

Big Pigeon River to Davenport Gap 1.60
Smoky Mountains Hiking Club

Great Smoky Mountains National Park (Davenport Gap to
Fontana Dam) 68.36
Smoky Mountains Hiking Club AND
National Park Service

Fontana Dam to Nantahala River 26.83
Smoky Mountains Hiking Club AND
National Forests in North Carolina

Nantahala River to North Carolina–Georgia line 54.44
Nantahala Hiking Club AND *National
Forests in North Carolina*

North Carolina–Georgia line to Springer Mountain 79.04
Amicalola Falls Approach Trail (6.9 miles to Springer Mountain)
Georgia Appalachian Trail Club AND
Chattahoochee National Forest

Bibliography

HOW TO FIND THESE BOOKS: Try your library first. If they have the books you are interested in, you can inspect or read them before buying. The average bookstore will have only a few of these books in stock. However, most bookstores will have copies of BOOKS IN PRINT and PAPERBACK BOOKS IN PRINT, both published by the R. R. Bowker Co. If the books you want are listed, the bookstore can order them for you. If they are not listed in either of these reference works, the books are probably out of print, although some publishers' books are not listed in these references. In cases where the book or booklet is seldom available in retail stores, the address of the publisher or distributor is given.

If the books can't be located by the above methods, the next places to try are antiquarian (used) bookstores. If they don't have copies of the out-of-print books you want, they can advertise for them in *Antiquarian Bookman*. With the aid of a good librarian, good booksellers in the new and antiquarian fields, and a little letter writing, you should be able to find any book that interests you. A lot of trouble, perhaps, but then knowledge never did come easy. Use the author's full name and the exact title of the book when inquiring.

Birds

Cruikshank, Allan D. and Helen G. *1001 Questions Answered about Birds*. New York: Dodd, Mead & Co., 1958.
Answered, among others, are specific questions about bird habitats, behavior, bird song, senses, and special physical characteristics.

Long, William J. *Wings of the Forest*. Garden City, N.Y.: Doubleday & Co., 1957.
Captivating sketches of forest birds by the well-known New England naturalist.

Peterson, Roger Tory. *Field Guide to the Birds*. Boston: Houghton Mifflin Co., 1968. Hardcover and paperback.
The birds of eastern North America are identified by the "Peterson System" of patternistic drawings. Also given are each species' range, habitat, food, and voice.

Pettingill, Olin Sewall, Jr., ed. *Enjoying Maine Birds: An Aid to Finding, Studying, and Attracting Birds in Maine*. 1960. 85 pp., 6 by 9 in., 6 oz., Maine Audubon Society, 57 Baxter Boulevard, Portland, Maine 04111.

Familiar Maine birds are described in line drawings and text. A checklist and calendar graph are included, along with short articles on bird conservation in Maine, banding, migration, photography, and various subjects of ornithological interest.

Reed, Chester A. *Bird Guide—Land Birds East of the Rockies*. Garden City, N.Y.: Doubleday & Co., 1951.
Over 300 color photographs of 222 species. The guide will fit a shirt pocket.

Stupka, Arthur. *Notes on the Birds of Great Smoky Mountains National Park*. Knoxville: University of Tennessee Press, 1963.
A compilation of data on birds observed in the park. Given are altitudinal range, frequency of sighting in the case of seldom-seen species, dates of arrival and departure for most migrants, nesting information, and mortality counts along park roads and in the vicinity of ceilometer beacons at the Knoxville airport. Since the reader of this book is likely to be a bird-watcher in possession of an illustrated bird guide, no description of the species is furnished.

The Blue Ridge Parkway

Jolley, Harley E. *The Blue Ridge Parkway*. Knoxville: University of Tennessee Press, 1969.
A history of the Blue Ridge Parkway, the 469-mile noncommercial top-of-the-mountains strip of asphalt linking the Shenandoah and Great Smoky Mountains National Parks. Originally begun as a make-work project in the depth of the depression in the 1930s, the parkway is today one of the most scenic highways for its length within the borders of the United States. The changes it has made in the economy of the hill people and the controversy and political infighting that accompanied its construction are described. Included are many photographs and a detailed log of the route.

Cooking

Bunnelle, Hasse, with Shirley Sarvis. *Cooking for Camp and Trail*. San Francisco: Sierra Club, 1972.
Notes on individual and group food planning for a hike (or other outing), kinds of foods and beverages, methods of camp cooking, and recipes ranging from the fairly Spartan to the exotic.

Griffin, Thomas H. *Backpack Trail Cooking*. Ramona, Calif.: Sentinel Publications, 1970. 52 pp.
Thomas H. Griffin has been backpacking since 1935, and the information in this booklet is designed to get the noncooking beginner past that first important meal on the trail. The recipes are easy, often combining dehydrated foods with canned foods to make one-pot meals.

Mendenhall, Ruth Dyer. *Backpack Cookery*. 1966. 36 pp. Glendale, Calif.: La Siesta Press.
Recipes and hints for meal making on the trail.

Early History

Blacker, Irwin R., and Harry M. Rosen. *The Golden Conquistadores.* Indianapolis: Bobbs-Merrill Co., 1960.

A short chronicle of the luckless Hernando De Soto expedition, May 1539–September 1543, is related in Chapter 7, "De Soto Tries to Establish a Colony and Opens a Continent." The conquistadores were the first Europeans—and Africans—to set foot in the southern Appalachians. The Appalachian Trail crosses their ghostly track at Wallace Gap near Franklin, North Carolina.

Eifert, Virginia S. *Tall Trees and Far Horizons: Adventures and Discoveries of Early Botanists in America.* New York: Dodd, Mead & Co., 1965.

Sketches of the Bartrams, Peter Kalm, Michaux, Nuttall, and others who probed the Appalachian region for botanical treasure.

Wright, Louis B. *The American Heritage History of the Thirteen Colonies.* New York: American Heritage Publishing Co., 1967.

Of the 14 states through which the Appalachian Trail passes, 10 were among the British political units called the Thirteen Colonies when they banded together to seek independence. This well-illustrated book deals with the reactions of transplanted Europeans to the strange, sometimes frightening, environment of a new continent.

Ecology

Farb, Peter, and the *Life* editors. *Ecology.* New York: Time Inc., 1963.

An introduction to the relationship between organisms and their environment. Many illustrations.

Leopold, Aldo. *A Sand County Almanac.* New York: Oxford University Press, 1949. Hardcover and paperback.

In Part III, in his essays "Conservation Esthetic," "Wilderness," "Wildlife in American Culture," and "The Land Ethic," the noted naturalist looks at the science of land health.

MacKaye, Benton. *From Geography to Geotechnics.* Edited by Paul T. Bryant. Urbana: University of Illinois Press, 1968.

———. *The New Exploration: A philosophy of regional planning.* 1928. Paperback reprint. Urbana: University of Illinois Press, 1970. Introduction by Lewis Mumford.

Both of these books consist of selections from the essays of the man who inspired the Appalachian Trail. MacKaye believes, as passionately as did another man from Massachusetts, Thoreau, that wilderness is a basic need. The theme of his writings is how to use our resources without poisoning the environment and thus in the end making impossible the unalienable American right of "pursuit of Happiness." MacKaye was 95 on March 6, 1974.

Ferns

Durand, Herbert. *Field Book of Common Ferns.* Rev. ed. New York: G. P. Putnam's Sons, 1949.
Describes in lively text 50 ferns, including those principal species that have made of Vermont and Maine our national fernery.

Parsons, Frances T. *How to Know the Ferns.* 2d ed. Paperback. New York: Dover Publications, 1961.
This classic first appeared in 1899.

Forest

Farb, Peter, and the *Life* editors. *The Forest.* New York: Time Inc., 1961.
An examination of the forest and its importance to man. Emphasis is on the North American forests.

Frome, Michael. *Whose Woods These Are: The Story of the National Forests.* Garden City, N.Y.: Doubleday & Co., 1962.
An account of the public forests—history, timber and mineral politics, anecdotes.

Platt, Rutherford. *The Great American Forest.* Englewood Cliffs, N.J.: Prentice-Hall, 1965.
Includes authoritative information on the eastern hardwood forest and the North Woods, both of which are the milieu of the Appalachian Trail.

Thoreau, Henry David. *The Maine Woods.* Arranged with notes by Dudley C. Lunt. New Haven, Conn.: College & University Press, 1950.
The Maine Woods combines Thoreau's accounts of the three trips that he made into the Mt. Katahdin and northern Maine area during the middle of the last century. Because of the sparseness of population there is a certain thin background of unchangeability about the region. The reader who walks on the Appalachian Trail will find what has changed and what has not changed in the Maine woods. There is an appendix made up of excerpts— a list of birds sighted, flowers and shrubs recognized, items of clothing and gear for an "excursion."

General

The American Guide Series, also known as the "WPA Guides to the States," was compiled during the Great Depression by writers who kept body and typewriter together laboring on this project for the federal government's Works Progress Administration. The guides were cited as the first nationwide portrait of the American people and have been used as reference works ever since. They are mines, sometimes deep, sometimes shallow, of documented information on history, folkways, religion, geology, racial elements, the arts, economy, plant and animal life, communities, and place names. For the states traversed by the Appalachian Trail there are:

Connecticut, A Guide to Its Roads, Lore, and People. Boston: Houghton Mifflin Co., 1938.

Georgia, A Guide to Its Towns and Countryside. Reprint. Atlanta: Tupper & Love, 1954.

Maine, A Guide 'Down East.' 2d ed. Rockland, Me.: The Courier-Gazette, 1970. Also *Maine, A Guide to the Vacation State.* 2d ed. Boston: Houghton Mifflin Co., 1969.

Maryland, A Guide to the Old Line State. New York: Oxford University Press, 1940.

Massachusetts, A Guide to Its Places and People. Boston: Houghton Mifflin Co., 1937.

New Hampshire, A Guide to the Granite State. Boston: Houghton Mifflin Co., 1938.

New Jersey, A Guide to Its Present and Past. New York: Hastings House, 1939.

New York, A Guide to the Empire State. New York: Oxford University Press, 1940.

The North Carolina Guide. Chapel Hill: University of North Carolina Press, 1955. Its predecessor was *North Carolina, A Guide to the Old North State.* 1939.

Pennsylvania, A Guide to the Keystone State. New York: Oxford University Press, 1940.

Tennessee, A Guide to the State. New York: Hastings House, 1939.

Vermont, A Guide to the Green Mountain State. 3d ed. rev. Boston: Houghton Mifflin Co., 1968.

Virginia, A Guide to the Old Dominion. 1940. Reprint. New York: Oxford University Press, 1948.

West Virginia, A Guide to the Mountain State. New York: Oxford University Press, 1941.

In the Regions of America Series, published by Harper & Row, New York, four volumes deal with states through which the Appalachian Trail passes:

Fishwick, Marshall. *Virginia: A New Look at the Old Dominion.* 1959.

Hill, Ralph Nading. *Yankee Kingdom: Vermont and New Hampshire.* 1960.

Rich, Louise Dickinson. *State O' Maine.* 1964.

Wallace, Paul. *Pennsylvania: Seed of a Nation.* 1962.

The Rivers of America Series, published by Rinehart & Co., unless another publisher is listed, portrays famous rivers and their people, geographical regions, and history. The following volumes deal in part with segments of the Appalachian Trail:

Carmer, Carl. *The Hudson.* 1939. The Appalachian Trail crosses the Hudson River in New York on Bear Mountain Bridge, 40 miles upstream from the center of New York City.

———. *The Susquehanna.* New York: David McKay, 1967. The Appalachian Trail crosses the Susquehanna River on Clarks Ferry Bridge at Duncannon, Pennsylvania.

Coffin, Robert P. Tristram. *Kennebec, Cradle of Americans*. 1937. The Appalachian Trail fords the Kennebec River at Caratunk, Maine.

Davis, Julia. *Valley and a Song: The Story of the Shenandoah River*. 1963. The Appalachian Trail follows the rim of the Blue Ridge overlooking the Shenandoah River as it runs through northern Virginia and across the northeastern tip of West Virginia to join the Potomac River at Harpers Ferry, West Virginia.

Dykeman, Wilma. *The French Broad*. 5th ed. Knoxville: University of Tennessee Press, 1966. The Appalachian Trail crosses the French Broad River at Hot Springs, North Carolina.

Gutheim, Frederick. *The Potomac*. 1949. The Appalachian Trail crosses the Potomac River on the Sandy Hook Bridge a mile east of Harpers Ferry, West Virginia.

Hard, Walter. *The Connecticut*. 1947. The Appalachian Trail crosses the Connecticut River at Hanover, New Hampshire.

Niles, Blair. *The James*. 1939. The Appalachian Trail crosses the James River at Snowden, Virginia.

Smith, Chard Powers. *The Housatonic: Puritan River*. 1946. The Appalachian Trail crosses the Housatonic River on highway bridges at Cornwall Bridge and Falls Village, Connecticut; at a point three miles south of Great Barrington, Massachusetts; and at Dalton, Massachusetts.

Brooks, Maurice G. *The Appalachians*. Boston: Houghton Mifflin Co., 1965.
Knowledgeable essays on the mountains and its citizens, winged and legged and green-leafed. A discussion of the Canadian Appalachians is included.

Connelly, Thomas L. *Discovering the Appalachians: What to Look for from the Past and in the Present along America's Eastern Frontier*. Harrisburg, Pa.: Stackpole Books, 1968.
Information on the region encompassed by the Appalachian Mountains.

Baker, Raymond. *Campfires along the Appalachian Trail*. New York: Carlton Press, 1971. 120 pp. An adaptation of Raymond Baker's book appears in Volume I of *Hiking the Appalachian Trail*.

Garvey, Edward B. *Appalachian Hiker: Adventure of a Lifetime*. Oakton, Va.: Appalachian Books, 1971. 397 pp. An adaptation of Edward B. Garvey's book appears in Volume II of *Hiking the Appalachian Trail*.

Geology

Lane, Ferdinand C. *The Story of Mountains*. Garden City, N.Y.: Doubleday & Co., 1951.
Describes the principal mountain systems of the world. A brief account of the beginnings of the Appalachians is included in Chapter XVII.

Ogburn, Charlton, Jr. *The Forging of Our Continent*. New York: American Heritage Publishing Co. in association with the Smithsonian Institution, 1968.

The chapters "The Appalachians: I" and "The Appalachians: II" contain facts and conjecture on the origins of the Appalachian Mountains.

The Great Smokies

Bowman, Elizabeth Skaggs. *Land of High Horizons.* 4th ed. 1944. Kingsport, Tenn.: Southern Publishers, 1938.
An account of the white and red mountain people of the Smokies and of the beginnings of the national park. Included is the tragic story of the "Trail of Tears," when all of the Cherokees (our first southern mountaineers) who could be rounded up were driven from the Appalachians and forced into exile in order that white men could take over their country.

Campbell, Carlos C. *Birth of a National Park in the Great Smoky Mountains.* Knoxville: University of Tennessee Press, 1960.
The story of the formation of Great Smoky Mountains National Park and of the people who fought for it and the people who fought against it. After a series of touch-and-go incidents, the park was established in 1934. It quickly became America's most visited national park.

Frome, Michael. *Strangers in High Places: The Story of the Great Smoky Mountains.* Garden City, N.Y.: Doubleday & Co., 1966.
Almost 400 pages of information—sometimes humorous, often sad, occasionally glorious—about the Smokies and their colorful denizens: Cherokees, naturalists, explorers, loggers, park superintendents, politicians, moonshiners and revenuers, bears and boars. Includes an intriguing description of Horace Kephart.

Hutchins, Ross E. *Hidden Valley of the Smokies: With a Naturalist in the Great Smoky Mountains.* New York: Dodd, Mead & Co., 1971.
The writer, an entomologist who grew up in a mile-high valley of the Montana Rockies with surrounding peaks soaring to two miles, opens his book with the observation that in Hidden Valley, "near the crest of the Great Smoky Mountains, at less than 5,000 feet, I look down across a jumbled mass of mountains that is almost frightening in its immensity." This is a highly readable report on the geology and many of the insects, plants (useful and deadly), and animals of this fastness, whose worn-down mountains rank among the world's oldest, and whose variety of wildlife and lushness of vegetation verges on the tropical.

Peattie, Roderick, ed. *The Great Smokies and the Blue Ridge: The Story of the Southern Appalachians.* New York: Vanguard Press, 1943.
Among the subjects explored by the contributors to this book are mountain men and women, the southern hardwood forest, wild flowers of the Blue Ridge, and a section entitled "Through the Year in the Great Smoky Mountains National Park, Month by Month" by Arthur Stupka.

Great Smoky Mountains National Park

Stupka, Arthur. *Great Smoky Mountains National Park.* Washington, D.C.: Government Printing Office, 1960.

Can be obtained from Superintendent of Documents, Washington, D.C. 20402. A useful guide to the natural wonders of the Great Smoky Mountains. One chapter treats of the ubiquitous black bear. A generalized map of the park is included.

Guidebooks

The following 10 guidebooks, which between them cover the length of the Appalachian Trail, are obtainable from the Appalachian Trail Conference, P.O. Box 236, Harpers Ferry, West Virginia 25425. Each guide measures about 5 by 7 by 1 inch, weighs approximately half a pound, and has plastic covers. Trail data are prepared in both directions, that is, south to north and north to south, so that the description may be read in the direction of travel. The guides, listed consecutively from Maine to Georgia, are:

Guide to the Appalachian Trail in Maine. 7th ed. 1969. Looseleaf, 346 pp., 9 maps.
Trail data between Mt. Katahdin in north central Maine and the Maine–New Hampshire line on a ridge of Carlo Col, about 8 air miles east of Berlin, New Hampshire (277 trail miles).

Guide to the Appalachian Trail in New Hampshire and Vermont. 2d ed. 1968. Looseleaf, 274 pp., 6 maps.
Trail data between the Maine–New Hampshire line and the Vermont–Massachusetts line at the southern end of the Green Mountains 3.2 trail miles from Blackinton, Massachusetts (287 trail miles).

Guide to the Appalachian Trail in Massachusetts and Connecticut. 2d ed. 1968. Looseleaf, 210 pp., 4 maps.
Trail data between the Vermont–Massachusetts line and the Connecticut–New York line on Schaghticoke Mountain 4.3 trail and highway miles from Kent, Connecticut (139 trail miles).

Guide to the Appalachian Trail in New York and New Jersey. 7th ed. 1972. Not looseleaf, 231 pp., 1 page of maps.
Trail data between Kent, Connecticut, and the Connecticut–New York line (4.3 trail and highway miles), and between the Connecticut–New York line and the crossing of the Delaware River on the New Jersey–Pennsylvania line at the village of Delaware Water Gap, Pennsylvania (158 trail miles).

Guide to the Appalachian Trail in Pennsylvania. 2d ed. 1970. Looseleaf, 130 pp., maps.
Trail data between the New Jersey–Pennsylvania line and the Susquehanna River at Duncannon, Pennsylvania (140 trail miles), and between the Susquehanna River and the village of Pen Mar on the Pennsylvania–Maryland line (81 trail miles).

Guide to the Appalachian Trail from the Susquehanna River to the

Shenandoah National Park. 7th ed. 1970. Looseleaf, 186 pp., no maps. (For maps of the route *see* Maps, Appalachian Trail Conference.)

Trail data through southern Pennsylvania between the Susquehanna River and the village of Pen Mar on the Pennsylvania–Maryland line (81 trail miles), and through Maryland, West Virginia, and Virginia between the Pennsylvania–Maryland line and U.S. Route 522 at Chester Gap, which is 1.77 trail miles short of the northern boundary of Shenandoah National Park and 6 highway miles east of Front Royal, Virginia (86 trail miles).

Guide to the Appalachian Trail and Side Trails in the Shenandoah National Park. 7th ed. 1970. Looseleaf, 258 pp., no maps. (For maps of the park *see* Maps, Appalachian Trail Conference.)

Includes Appalachian Trail data from U.S. Route 522 through Shenandoah National Park to U.S. Route 250 at Rockfish Gap, which is 7.6 trail miles beyond the southern boundary of the park and 5 highway miles east of Waynesboro, Virginia (105 trail miles).

Guide to the Appalachian Trail in Central and Southwestern Virginia. 5th ed. 1972. Looseleaf, 294 pp., 3 maps.

Trail data between U.S. Route 250 and the Virginia–Tennessee line on Holston Mountain 3.4 trail miles beyond Damascus, Virginia (336 trail miles).

Guide to the Appalachian Trail in Tennessee and North Carolina: Cherokee, Pisgah, and Great Smokies. 3d ed. 1971. Looseleaf, 353 pp., 3 maps.

Trail data between Damascus, Virginia, and the Virginia–Tennessee line (3.4 trail miles); between the Virginia–Tennessee line and the Big Pigeon River, which is 1.5 miles from the northeastern boundary of Great Smoky Mountains National Park (196 trail miles); and from the Big Pigeon River through Great Smoky Mountains National Park to its southwestern boundary at Fontana Dam, North Carolina (70 trail miles). A number of side trails in the Great Smokies are also included.

Guide to the Appalachian Trail in the Great Smokies, the Nantahalas, and Georgia. 3d ed. 1971. Looseleaf, 325 pp., 3 maps.

Trail data from the Pig Pigeon River through the Great Smoky Mountains National Park to Fontana Dam, North Carolina (70 trail miles), and between Fontana Dam and Springer Mountain in northern Georgia (159 trail miles). Also included are the 6.9-mile approach trail from Amicalola Falls State Park to Springer Mountain and a number of side trails in the Great Smokies and Joyce Kilmer Memorial Forest.

Also available from the Appalachian Trail Conference is the *Katahdin Section of Guide to the Appalachian Trail in Maine.* 7th ed. 1969. Looseleaf, 194 pp. This is a guide to the trails of the Mt. Katahdin area. One of its two maps, "The Katahdin Region," may be purchased separately. This map embraces the Mt. Katahdin trail system and the region between the East and West branches of the Penobscot River.

A useful compendium of trail data known as the *Mileage Fact Sheet* is sold by the conference. It gives the locations of shelters, water holes, grocery stores, post offices, lodgings, and restaurants along the Appalachian Trail. Its purpose is to assist the long-distance hiker in planning his stops to rest, relieve thirst, buy food, make phone calls, and receive and send mail—it is of no value in trail finding.

Hiking Equipment and Preparation

Brower, David R., and others. *Going Light—With Backpack or Burro*. San Francisco: Sierra Club, 1951.
Of particular interest are the chapters "Women" (their special problems) and "Especially for Men" (also about women).

Fletcher, Colin. *The Complete Walker*. New York: Alfred A. Knopf, 1968.
Excellent discussion of modern backpacking ideas and gear. This book probably has influenced more contemporary backpackers than all other books put together. Some of Fletcher's ideas are more applicable to the drier West Coast than to the eastern part of the United States, but *The Complete Walker* is a gold mine for any hiker anywhere, and highly entertaining, to boot.

Lightweight Equipment for Hiking, Camping, and Mountaineering. 13th ed. 1972. 78 pp. Potomac Appalachian Trail Club, 1718 N Street, N.W., Washington, D.C. 20036. Also available from the Appalachian Trail Conference, P.O. Box 236, Harpers Ferry, West Virginia 25425.
Suppliers, prices, weights, and other information are given concerning hundreds of items of clothing and gear useful to the hiker, camper, and climber. Indispensable for the beginner.

Manning, Harvey. *Backpacking: One Step at a Time*. Seattle: The REI Press, 1972.
Harvey Manning puts his 30 years of outdoor recreational experience to work at describing suitable gear for the backpacker and dispensing sound advice on such subjects as "How to Walk," "Suffer the Little Children" (taking the younger members of the family on the trail). "When the Way Grows Rough," and "The New Ethic" that follows the old New England adage of "Eat it up, wear it out, make it do, do without." A chapter on boots is outstanding.

Rethmel, R. C. *Backpacking*. Minneapolis: Burgess Publishing Co., 1970.
A sensible short guide.

Rutstrum, Calvin. *Paradise below Zero*. New York: Macmillan Co., 1968.
Probably the best handbook for cold weather camping. Proper clothing and sleeping bags are described, as are the psychological and physical adjustments necessary for long journeys when the sun lies low on the horizon and the temperature slides below the freezing mark.

———. *The Wilderness Route Finder*. New York: Macmillan Co., 1967.
How to use a map and compass; why we get lost and how to prevent it;

how to find one's way in unfamiliar territory. The author lays to rest such cherished notions as that moss always grows heaviest on the north side of a tree.

Suggestions for Appalachian Trail Users. 7th ed. 1970. 36 pp. The Appalachian Trail Conference, P.O. Box 236, Harpers Ferry, West Virginia 25425.
Includes comments on trail etiquette, men's and women's apparel, and other matters of importance to the Appalachian Trail traveler.

Wood, Robert S. *Pleasure Packing—How to Backpack in Comfort.* San Francisco: Condor Books, 1972.
Thoughtful discussion of footwear, sleeping bags, and other backpacking equipment. Other sections deal with first aid and survival, camping, family trips, and trout fishing. This is one of the three best books available on present-day backpacking; all three give proper emphasis to lightweight equipment and to the ecological and aesthetic problems of camping and hiking. The other two "best books" are Colin Fletcher's *The Complete Walker* and Harvey Manning's *Backpacking: One Step at a Time,* both listed elsewhere in this bibliography.

Hobbies

Hillcourt, William. *The New Field Book of Nature Activities and Hobbies.* Rev. ed. New York: G. P. Putnam's Sons, 1970.
Hundreds of outdoor projects, encompassing close to 1,000 suggestions for nature activities and hobbies, are described. Among the suggestions are "Start a life list of all the trees you see," "Visit the location of the more important minerals of your state," "Learn to attract birds by 'squeaking,'" "Write a short article describing an experience in nature," "Make a collection of mosses," "Put up a salt lick and list animals attracted to it." The book includes a project index that is useful in pinpointing specific activities.

Indians

Brandon, William. *The American Heritage Book of Indians.* New York: American Heritage Publishing Co., 1961.
The chapters "War in the Forest," "The Anvil of America," and "The Dispossessed" treat of the Indians of the Appalachian region.

Underwood, Thomas Bryan, and Moselle Stack Sandlin, eds. *Cherokee Legends and the Trail of Tears.* Knoxville: S. B. Newman Printing Co., 1956. Obtainable from The Museum of the Cherokee Indian, Cherokee, North Carolina 28719.
This booklet contains a number of Cherokee legends adapted from the Nineteenth Annual Report of the Bureau of American Ethnology, and an account by John G. Burnett of the expatriation, officially called the "Removal," of the Cherokees from their homeland in the southern Appalachians

in 1838/39. Private Burnett, a soldier of the federal escort, wrote of this "Trail of Tears" in the form of a birthday letter to his children and grandchildren when he was an old man. A sketch map shows the route taken on the forced march to Indian Territory in Oklahoma. About 4,000 Cherokees died of disease and hardship on the way.

Information Folders

The Appalachian Trail winds through two national parks and two national recreation areas, and for over a hundred miles in Virginia it roughly parallels and frequently crosses the Blue Ridge Parkway, and for a mile and a half in Maryland, between Sandy Hook Bridge at the crossing of the Potomac River and Weverton Shelter, it follows the towpath of the disused Chesapeake and Ohio Barge Canal. Information folders on these preserves (all but one of which are administered by the National Park Service) are obtainable from:

Blue Ridge Parkway, P.O. Box 1710, Roanoke, Virginia 24008.

C & O Canal National Historical Park, P.O. Box 859, 120 North Potomac Street, Hagerstown, Maryland 21740.

Delaware Water Gap National Recreation Area, Highway I-80 Office, Columbia, New Jersey 07832.

Great Smoky Mountains National Park, Gatlinburg, Tennessee 37738.

Mount Rogers National Recreation Area, U.S. Forest Service, Marion, Virginia 24354.

Shenandoah National Park, Luray, Virginia 22835.

A folder on Harpers Ferry, which adjoins the Appalachian Trail at the Potomac River, may be procured from Harpers Ferry National Historical Park, P.O. Box 117, Harpers Ferry, West Virginia 25425.

Information Packet

The Appalachian Trail Conference, P.O. Box 236, Harpers Ferry, West Virginia 25425, will send to interested persons an information packet describing the Appalachian Trail and its route. Included is a price list of guidebooks and other publications concerning the trail. The conference requests 25 cents to cover postage and stationery costs.

Insects

Borror, Donald J., and Richard E. White. *A Field Guide to the Insects of America North of Mexico.* Boston: Houghton Mifflin Co., 1970.

Covers nearly 600 families of insects and presents 1,300 drawings, of which 142 are in color. Emphasis is on identification.

Lutz, Frank E. *Field Book of Insects of the United States and Canada, Aiming to Answer Common Questions.* Rev. ed. New York: G. P. Putnam's Sons, 1948.

The somewhat baroque title of this work, which first appeared in 1918, explains its intent. Most of the species mentioned inhabit the northeastern United States. Nearly 600 insects are illustrated. Collecting, preserving, and mounting are discussed.

Zim, Herbert S., and Clarence Cottam. *Insects: A Guide to Familiar American Insects.* 160 pp., 4 by 6 in., 4 oz. A Golden Nature Guide. New York: Golden Press, 1951.
A beginner's manual to 225 common insect species occurring within the United States and southern Canada. Illustrated in color by James Gordon Irving.

Maps

A few maps that do not appear in the guidebooks are sold separately by the Appalachian Trail Conference, P.O. Box 236, Harpers Ferry, West Virginia 25425. They include:

PENNSYLVANIA: three maps showing the Appalachian Trail from the Susquehanna River at Duncannon, Pennsylvania, to Whiskey Spring Road to U.S. Route 30 to the Pennsylvania–Maryland line at the village of Pen Mar (81 miles).

MARYLAND: one sheet of two maps showing the Appalachian Trail from the Pennsylvania–Maryland line to the Maryland–Virginia line at the Potomac River just east of Harpers Ferry, West Virginia (37 miles).

NORTHERN VIRGINIA: two maps (northern and southern sections) showing the Appalachian Trail from the Potomac River to Virginia Highway 7 to U.S. Route 522 at Chester Gap (49 miles).

SHENANDOAH NATIONAL PARK, VIRGINIA: three maps (northern, central, and southern sections) showing the Appalachian Trail from U.S. Route 522 to U.S. Route 211 to U.S. Route 33 to U.S. Route 250 in Rockfish Gap (105 miles).

The Appalachian Trail appears on many oil company and public road maps. These maps, however, are usually in such minute scale as to be of limited help to the hiker other than in locating the trail and the more prominent access points. More useful are the maps of several states whose small area or uncluttered countryside permit the route to stand out rather more boldly when printed on single large sheets. Free official road maps of these states may be acquired by writing to:

Maine State Highway Commission, Augusta, Maine 04330.

Maryland Department of Economic Development, State Office Building, Annapolis, Maryland 21401.

Massachusetts Department of Public Works, 100 Nashua Street, Boston, Massachusetts 02114.

New Hampshire Division of Economic Development, Concord, New Hampshire 03301.

Vermont Development Department, Info/Travel Division, Montpelier, Vermont 05602.

The supervisors of the eight national forests on the path of the Appalachian Trail will send on request a recreational map showing their forest, its developed campgrounds, and the trail. In addition, three of the forests print special, larger scale maps of the Appalachian Trail. These special maps are issued by the George Washington National Forest (through the Pedlar Ranger District from U.S. Route 250 in Rockfish Gap east of Waynesboro, Virginia, to the James River at Snowden, Virginia, 70 trail miles), the Jefferson National Forest (from the James River to the Virginia–Tennessee line near Damascus, Virginia, 267 trail miles), and the Chattahoochee National Forest (from Bly Gap on the North Carolina–Georgia line to Springer Mountain, 78 trail miles, and the 6.9-mile approach trail from Amicalola Falls State Park to Springer Mountain). Addresses of the forests, which are listed here in geographic order from Maine to Georgia, are:

White Mountain National Forest, Laconia, New Hampshire 03246.

Green Mountain National Forest, Rutland, Vermont 05701.

George Washington National Forest, Federal Building, Harrisonburg, Virginia 22801.

Jefferson National Forest, P.O. Box 2847, 920 Jefferson Street, Roanoke, Virginia 24016.

Cherokee National Forest, P.O. Box 400, Cleveland, Tennessee 37311.

Nantahala National Forest and Pisgah National Forest, P.O. Box 2750, Asheville, North Carolina 28802.

Chattahoochee National Forest, P.O. Box 1437, Gainesville, Georgia 30501.

Palisades Interstate Park, which is on the palisades of the Hudson River, is a chain of 13 parks in New York and New Jersey. The Appalachian Trail traverses only the Harriman and Bear Mountain sections, both of them New York state parks. The route totals about 16 miles. A map that shows the footpaths and shelters may be obtained from the Palisades Interstate Park Commission, Administration Building, Bear Mountain, New York 10911. A small charge is made.

Also obtainable by the hiker are topographic maps of the U.S. Geological Survey. They are printed in several scales and offer a wealth of detail. On the smaller scale maps, however, it may be necessary to employ a magnifying glass to pick out the trails. Each Appalachian Trail guidebook, previously noted, names the USGS topographic maps appropriate to its particular area. Maps may be purchased from various sources, but are almost always available from the Distribution Section, U.S. Geological Survey, 1200 South Eads Street, Arlington, Virginia 22202. The same source will send free on request indexes of maps available for each state.

Similar to the U.S. Geological Survey maps, but printed in raised relief on semiflexible plastic, are the topographic maps sold by Hubbard Press, P.O. Box 442, Northbrook, Illinois 60062. These, too, are printed in several colors (woodland shown in green tint and watercourses in blue, for example). Approximate average size of the maps is 22 by 33 inches. They were made by the federal government and formerly were available only from the U.S. Army Topographic Command. The region traversed by the Appalachian Trail is covered by 19 maps in all. Following are the names of the individual maps together with the latitude and longitude encompassed and the stretch of Appalachian Trail in each. (Refer to an atlas to locate the specific areas covered.) The maps and the checkpoints are listed in order as the trail runs from north to south. Mileages given are trail mileages and are approximate.

"Millinocket": lat. 46°–45° N, long. 68°–70° W. Trail from Mt. Katahdin, Maine, to the west side of the Kennebec River, 0.8 mile south of Caratunk, Maine.

"Sherbrooke": lat. 46°–45° N, long. 70°–72° W. Trail from the west side of the Kennebec River, 0.8 mile south of Caratunk, Maine, to the top of Spaulding Mountain, 7 miles south of Bigelow Village, Maine.

"Lewiston": lat. 45°–44° N, long. 70°–72° W. Trail from the top of Spaulding Mountain, 7 miles south of Bigelow Village, Maine, to the south slope of Mt. Moosilauke 2 miles north of Glencliff, New Hampshire.

"Portland": lat. 44°–43° N, long. 70°–72° W. Trail from the south slope of Mt. Moosilauke 2 miles north of Glencliff, New Hampshire, to Upper Baker Pond, 10.5 miles south of Glencliff.

"Glens Falls": lat. 44°–43° N, long. 72°–74° W. Trail from Upper Baker Pond, 10.5 miles south of Glencliff, New Hampshire, to an unnamed summit (elevation 3,450 feet) on Glastenbury Mountain 9.5 miles north of Vermont Highway 9.

"Albany": lat. 43°–42° N, long. 72°–74° W. Trail from an unnamed summit (elevation 3,450 feet) on Glastenbury Mountain 9.5 miles north of Vermont Highway 9 to a point 1 mile south of the Lions Head and 1.5 miles north of Salisbury, Connecticut.

"Hartford": lat. 42°–41° N, long. 72°–74° W. Trail from a point 1 mile south of the Lions Head and 1.5 miles north of Salisbury, Connecticut, to Bear Mountain at the crossing of the Hudson River in New York.

"Scranton": lat. 42°–41° N, long. 74°–76° W. Trail from Bear Mountain at the crossing of the Hudson River in New York to Sunfish Pond in New Jersey 4.5 miles north of Delaware Water Gap, Pennsylvania.

"Newark": lat. 41°–40° N, long. 74°–76° W. Trail from Sunfish Pond in New Jersey 4.5 miles north of Delaware Water Gap, Pennsylvania, to the crest of Blue Mountain 2 miles north of Port Clinton, Pennsylvania.

"Harrisburg": lat. 41°–40° N, long. 76°–78° W. Trail from the crest of Blue Mountain 2 miles north of Port Clinton, Pennsylvania, to a point on South Mountain 0.5 mile north of the Arendtsville–Shippensburg Road in Pennsylvania.

"Baltimore": lat. 40°–39° N, long. 76°–78° W. Trail from a point on South Mountain 0.5 mile north of the Arendtsville–Shippensburg Road in Pennsylvania to 2 miles south of Ashby Gap on U.S. Route 50 near Paris, Virginia.

"Charlottesville": lat. 39°–38° N, long. 78°–80° W. Trail from 2 miles south of Ashby Gap on U.S. Route 50 near Paris, Virginia, to the summit of Elk Mountain 3 miles south of Rockfish Gap on U.S. Route 250 in Virginia.

"Roanoke": lat. 38°–37° N, long. 78°–80° W. Trail from the summit of Elk Mountain 3 miles south of Rockfish Gap on U.S. Route 250 in Virginia to Ruckers Knob on Tinker Ridge 15 miles north of Catawba, Virginia.

"Bluefield": lat. 38°–37° N, long. 80°–82° W. Trail from Ruckers Knob on Tinker Ridge 15 miles north of Catawba, Virginia, to a point on Big Walker Mountain 3.5 miles north of U.S. Routes 21/52 in Virginia.

"Winston-Salem": lat. 37°–36° N, long. 80°–82° W. Trail from a point on Big Walker Mountain 3.5 miles north of U.S. Routes 21/52 in Virginia to the crest of Iron Mountain opposite Doeville, Tennessee.

"Johnson City": lat. 37°–36° N, long. 82°–84° W. Trail from the crest of Iron Mountain opposite Doeville, Tennessee, to the summit of Little Bald on the Tennessee–North Carolina line 3.5 miles south of Spivey Gap, North Carolina, on U.S. Route 19W.

"Knoxville": lat. 36°–35° N, long. 82°–84° W. Trail from the summit of Little Bald on the Tennessee–North Carolina line 3.5 miles south of Spivey Gap, North Carolina, to the shoulder of Court House Bald 6.5 miles south of Standing Indian and 1.5 miles north of Bly Gap on the North Carolina–Georgia line.

"Greenville": lat. 35°–34° N, long. 82°–84° W. Trail from the shoulder of Court House Bald 6.5 miles south of Standing Indian and 1.5 miles north of Bly Gap on the North Carolina–Georgia line to Woody Gap on Georgia Highway 60.

"Rome": lat. 35°–34° N, long. 84°–86° W. Trail from Woody Gap on Georgia Highway 60 to Springer Mountain and Amicalola Falls State Park in Georgia.

Note: After the trail is relocated to avoid the extension of the Blue Ridge Parkway into Georgia, the checkpoint on the "Greenville" and the "Rome" maps of Woody Gap on Georgia Highway 60 will be replaced by Chestnut Mountain 10 miles northwest of, but south on the trail from, Blood Mountain.

Medicine and Survival

Bleything, Dennis. *Primitive Medical Aid in the Wilderness.* 1971. 64 pp., 3½ by 4½ in., 1 oz. Life Support Technology, Inc., 4320 S.W. Lloyd Avenue, Beaverton, Oregon 97005.
Discusses problems of first aid when professional assistance is far away.

Burt, Calvin P., with Ronald L. Dawson and Frank G. Heyl. *Survival in the Wilderness.* 1969. 61 pp., 3½ by 4½ in., 1 oz. Life Support Technology, Inc., 4320 S.W. Lloyd Avenue, Beaverton, Oregon 97005.
Advice on coping with emergency situations in the backcountry.

Darvill, Fred T., Jr., M.D. *Mountaineering Medicine (A Wilderness Medical Guide).* 42 pp., 4 by 7 in., 1½ oz. Skagit Mountain Rescue Unit, P.O. Box 2, Mount Vernon, Washington 98273.
Manual of simple medical treatments.

First Aid Manual. 1971. 47 pp., 4 by 6 in., 1 oz. American Medical Association, 535 North Dearborn Street, Chicago, Illinois 60610.
A list of do's and don'ts.

Lathrop, Theodore G., M.D. *Hypothermia: Killer of the Unprepared.* Rev. ed. 1970. 23 pp. The Mazamas, 909 N.W. Nineteenth Avenue, Portland, Oregon 97029.

Causes, avoidance, and treatment of overexposure, with case histories and wind-chill chart.

Moonshiners

Carr, Jess. *The Second Oldest Profession: An Informal History of Moonshining in America.* Englewood Cliffs, N.J.: Prentice-Hall, 1972.

The locale of this book is the southern highlands, an area even today generously dotted with tubs of fermenting mash presided over by secretive men who on the whole are "rather solemn, businesslike, and frequently downright mean." The author, himself a mountain man, takes the reader through a history of distilling strong liquors and on a tour to an illicit still in operation. On its 750-mile run from the mountains of Georgia to the Shenandoah, the Appalachian Trail passes through the heart of moonshine country.

New England

Thomson, Betty Flanders. *The Changing Face of New England.* New York: Macmillan Co., 1958.

An introduction to the distinctive New England landscape—the Taconics, Berkshires, Green and White mountains, geology, glaciation, monadnocks, woods, and flowers—and weather.

The Northern Appalachians

Bliss, L. C. *Alpine Zone of the Presidential Range.* 1963. 67 pp., 6 by 9 in., 3½ oz. Appalachian Mountain Club, 5 Joy Street, Boston, Massachusetts 02108.

Interesting compilation of facts about the geologic formations, climate and microclimate (in this case the climate at ground level), and flora of the timberline region of the Presidentials. Over 40 of the more common alpine plants are described.

Burt, Allen F. *The Story of Mount Washington.* Hanover, N.H.: Dartmouth Publications, 1960.

The interesting history of the Mount Washington region.

Egan, Joseph B. *Donn Fendler, Lost on a Mountain in Maine.* Welles Publishing Co., 1939.

The story of a 12-year-old boy who, after ascending on the Appalachian Trail from Katahdin Stream Campground to Baxter Peak, became lost in fog on the summit of Mount Katahdin. Although search began in the very hour of his disappearance, and it was a search in which four to five hundred people were to join, nine days passed before Donn Fendler was seen again. Vividly described is the feeling of being lost, an overwhelming sensation that can be so terrifying that it provokes the lost person to cast off his clothing and run blindly until overcome by exhaustion or accident.

A fascinating narrative in itself, this story may also help hikers remember to keep their survival kit with them at all times in wilderness areas.

Mount Washington. 1962. 16 pp. Mount Washington Observatory News Bulletin, 87 Canal Street, Salem, Massachusetts 01970.
A quick look at summit history, buildings, weather, Cog Railway, and Carriage Road.

Peattie, Roderick, ed. *The Berkshires: The Purple Hills.* New York: Vanguard Press, 1948.
Birds, flora (some edible), history, and folkways of the Berkshire Hills of Massachusetts.

Poole, Ernest. *The Great White Hills of New Hampshire.* Garden City, N.Y.: Doubleday & Co., 1946.
The author wrote this engrossing collection of White Mountain history, anecdotes, and personal experiences in his stone house facing the Franconia Range. Included are chapters on the mountain farmers ("these are deep people"), on wildlife, and on climbing (Thoreau sprained an ankle on one of his two ascents of Mt. Washington).

Sherrard, Elizabeth M., ed. *A Brief Guide to the Natural History of the White Mountains.* 44 pp., 6 by 9 in., 3 oz. Audubon Society of New Hampshire, 63 North Main Street, Concord, New Hampshire 03301.
Consists of articles by authorities in the fields of history (geologic and human), animal life (insects, birds, mammals, fishes, reptiles, amphibians), trees, and wild flowers.

Photography

Baufle, Jean-Marie, and Jean-Philippe Varin. *Photographing Wildlife.* Translated from the French by Carel v. Amerogen. New York: Oxford University Press, 1972.
Combines practical how-to-do-it with awareness of other values. The animals are given their due and so is the wildlife photographer, hopefully defined as a "naturalist in spirit . . . filled with respect for life that does not belong to him, a man who wants to share his emotions and his enthusiasm with others." Technical equipment, the authors say, should not be regarded as "all-important"; the cameraman also needs perseverance, willingness to expend physical effort (walking with a load of gear is emphasized), stamina, and resourcefulness plus "confidence in [his] good luck." There are discussions on clothing for the field, stalking, and "the hide" (hiding places and blinds). Many illustrations, diagrams, and tables.

Kinne, Russ. *The Complete Book of Nature Photography.* New York: American Photographic Book Publishing Co., 1971.
Advice on the study of nature with the camera. Also investigated are cameras, lenses, film, and specialized equipment. There are chapters on photographing rocks, gems, and minerals, plants and flowers, birds, insects,

mammals (including nocturnal species), underwater and marine subjects, and reptiles and amphibians. Suggestions are detailed, e.g., "a medium-telephoto lens is the only safe way to get quality close-ups of poisonous snakes." Numerous illustrations. This book seems to be nearer and dearer to the hearts of young photographers than any other. If you have a youngster who is interested in nature photography, this book would be an ideal gift, but it is by no means written on a juvenile level.

Koken, Ray E. *Better Pictures through Good Composition.* 40 pp., 5 by 6 in., 2 oz. Ray E. Koken, 261 Melbourne Avenue, Youngstown, Ohio 44512.
Lists 12 basic rules of good composition, which is the pleasing arrangement of objects, mass, lines, and contrasts or colors to form a harmonious whole. Each rule is simply explained and graphically illustrated.

Poisonous Plants

Bleything, Dennis. *Poisonous Plants in the Wilderness.* 1971. 64 pp., 3½ by 4½ in., 1 oz. Life Support Technology, Inc., 4320 S.W. Lloyd Avenue, Beaverton, Oregon 97005.
Describes over 30 species of common plants that are toxic to humans. Although the prudent hiker is unlikely to sample such horrors as the fly amanita (the mushroom's typical aspect of a warty scurf on a bright red camp is discouragement enough), the curious may find the booklet's information to be its own reward.

Reptiles

Conant, Roger. *A Field Guide to Reptiles and Amphibians of the United States and Canada East of the 100th Meridian.* Boston: Houghton Mifflin Co., 1958.
Snakes, frogs, turtles, and other crawlers and low hoppers are identified and their modus operandi reported. Described also are the northern copperhead and the timber rattlesnake, both pit vipers, the only poisonous snakes found on the Appalachian Trail.

Dobie, J. Frank. *Rattlesnakes.* Boston: Little, Brown & Co., 1965.
Legends, yarns, and considerable gossip about rattlers.

Klauber, Laurence M. *Rattlesnakes: Their Habits, Life Histories, and Influence on Mankind.* 2 vols. Berkeley: University of California Press, 1956.
The definitive work on rattlesnakes.

Rocks and Minerals

Pough, Frederick H. *A Field Guide to Rocks and Minerals.* Boston: Houghton Mifflin Co., 1953.
A practical and useful book. Illustrated.

Zim, Herbert S., and Paul R. Shaffer. *A Guide to Familiar Minerals, Gems, Ores and Rocks.* A Golden Nature Guide. New York: Golden Press, 1957.
Beginner's guide to the basic stuff of which the earth is made.

Shenandoah National Park

Pollock, George Freeman. *Skyland—The Heart of the Shenandoah National Park.* Berryville, Pa.: Chesapeake Book Co., 1960.
The prehistory of the park and one of the best accounts ever written about the people of the Shenandoah highland.

The Sky

Menzel, Donald H. *A Field Guide to the Stars and Planets, Including the Moon, Satellites, Comets, and Other Features of the Universe.* Illustrations furnished by Ching Sung Yu. Boston: Houghton Mifflin Co., 1964.
A practical and simplified guide to what the author calls the "free show put on by the heavens."

Southern Mountain People

Hannum, Alberta Pierson. *Look Back with Love: A Recollection of the Blue Ridge.* New York: Vanguard Press, 1969.
Glimpses of a "separate" people, the Scotch (mostly) and German inhabitants of "Shakespeare's America." Stories of the past and the present.

Kephart, Horace. *Our Southern Highlanders: A Narrative of Adventure in the Southern Appalachians and a Study of Life among the Mountaineers.* Rev. ed. New York: Macmillan Co., 1913.
This is the classic work on Appalachia. It has been in print for 60 years and is still regularly quoted. The independence of mind of the mountain people is stressed. Two among other not-too-well-known instances are cited: they were the first Americans to establish a republic—in 1772 in the Watauga region of Tennessee, which is traversed by the Appalachian Trail; during the Civil War 180,000 riflemen, from Alabama to Virginia, served the Union—far more than joined the Confederate ranks. Every hiker in the southern highlands will appreciate the mountaineers' comment on the incline of their hills: "Goin' up, you can might' nigh stand up straight and bite the ground; goin' down, a man wants hobnails in the seat of his pants." Not too exaggerated at that, for 85 percent of the land of Appalachia has a "steeper slope than one foot in five."

Parris, John. *Roaming the Mountains.* Asheville, N.C.: Citizen-Times Publishing Co., 1955.
A newspaperman meets the individualistic people of the hills.

Raine, James Watt. *The Land of Saddlebags: A Study of the Mountain People of Appalachia.* Published jointly by the Council of Women for

Home Missions and the Missionary Education Movement, New York, 1924.
Examines the nature of the southern mountaineer, with his Elizabethan speech, lack of class consciousness, and love of liberty.

Trees

Li Hui-lin. *Trees of Pennsylvania, the Atlantic States, and the Lake States.* Philadelphia: University of Pennsylvania Press, 1972.
Pennsylvania, with its meaning of "Penn's Woods," lives up to its name in variety: the geographic ranges of many trees overlap in the state and most of the species of temperate eastern North America grow within its borders. This book describes 118 species, including all that are native to Pennsylvania plus a few introduced species that have become "extremely naturalized." The black-and-white photographs are good and the line drawings are first-rate.

Peattie, Donald Culross. *A Natural History of Trees of Eastern and Central North America.* Boston: Houghton Mifflin Co., 1950.
The sober title does scant justice to the contents of this book, verdant from the researches and deft pen of the late naturalist. Here are histories of many of the trees of the forests threaded by the Appalachian Trail, trees that helped shape Indian culture and the European-type civilization that followed.

Platt, Rutherford. *1,001 Questions Answered about Trees.* New York: Grosset & Dunlap, 1959.
A short course in arboreal knowledge, informative as a forest ranger guiding a nature walk.

———. *A Pocket Guide to Trees.* (Original title was *American Trees, A Book of Discovery*, 1952.) New York: Pocket Books.
A guide to many of America's distinctive tree species with descriptions that sometimes burst into lyric prose. "Hemlock," for instance, "is music in the form of a tree. It is a tall, graceful spiral like a Christmas card evergreen, but with sweeping, curved lines, instead of the stiff staccato of spruce."

Stupka, Arthur. *Trees, Shrubs, and Woody Vines of Great Smoky Mountains National Park.* Knoxville: University of Tennessee Press, 1964.
This is a tree watcher's manual of frequency of the species (whether common or rare), their localities, including habitat and altitudinal range within the park, flowering times, measurements of a number of the more impressive specimens, and similar arboreal matters.

The following small but useful tree identification guides are published by Nature Study Guild, P.O. Box 972, Berkeley, California 94701:

Watts, May Theilgaard. *Master Tree Finder.* 1963. 58 pp., 4 by 6 in., 2 oz.
An excellent pocket guide that identifies by their leaves more than 300 native and introduced species growing east of the Rocky Mountains.

————. *Tree Finder.* 1963. 38 pp., 3 by 5 in., ¾ oz.

Identifies over 100 of the more common eastern and midwestern species by their leaves. The small number of identifications somewhat limits this manual's utility.

Watts, May Theilgaard, and Tom Watts. *Winter Tree Finder.* 1963. 58 pp., 4 by 6 in., 2 oz.

Twigs, bark, nuts, and other features are used to identify nearly 250 deciduous (leaf-dropping) trees that grow east of the Rockies.

Weather

Watts, Alan. *Instant Weather Forecasting.* London: Adlard Coles Ltd., 1968. Distributed in the United States by Dodd, Mead & Co., New York.

How to predict weather from the appearance of the sky. There are 24 cloud-sky color photographs with explanations. The facts necessary for forecasting (with a hoped-for accuracy rate of 75 percent) are presented in a logical form that reduces the mystery of what is a most complex subject. This small book was written about weather as experienced in the British Isles, and the wind scale on the reproduced Beaufort chart does not exceed 55 miles an hour, a velocity which the author says is "seldom experienced inland." The high Appalachians of northern New England, just to name one area, very frequently experience winds of much greater velocity. Nonetheless, this book will serve quite well over much of the United States and Canada, particularly the eastern seaboard as far south as Georgia.

Wild Flowers

Mountain Flowers of New England. 1964. Appalachian Mountain Club, 5 Joy Street, Boston, Massachusetts 02108.

Describes over 200 flowering alpine plants of New England, New York, and Quebec. Illustrated in color.

Stupka, Arthur. *Wildflowers in Color.* New York: Harper & Row, 1965.

A field guide to the conspicuous flowers and fruits of more than 250 plants that flourish in the southern Appalachian Mountains. Colored photographs.

Watts, May Theilgaard. *Flower Finder.* 1955. 60 pp., 4 by 6 in., 1½ oz. Nature Study Guild, P.O. Box 972, Berkeley, California 94701.

Identified are over 240 spring wild flowers and flower families growing east of the Rocky Mountains and north of the Great Smoky Mountains.

Wild Foods

These two books depict edible wild flowers and tell how to cook them or use for beverages.

Angier, Bradford. *Free for the Eating.* Harrisburg, Pa.: Stackpole Books, 1966.

————. *More Free-for-the-Eating Wild Foods.* Harrisburg, Pa.: Stackpole Books, 1969.

Bleything, Dennis. 1972. *Edible Plants in the Wilderness*. 2 vols., each 64 pp., 3½ by 4½ in., 1 oz. Life Support Technology, Inc., 4320 S.W. Lloyd Avenue, Beaverton, Oregon 97005.
Both volumes include instructions for preparing common American wild plants as food.

Gibbons, Euell. *Stalking the Wild Asparagus*. New York: David McKay, 1970.
How to recognize, gather, and prepare many nutritious plants that grow wild in woods, fields, and streams.

Hesler, L. R. *Mushrooms of the Great Smokies*. Knoxville: University of Tennessee Press, 1960.
The Great Smoky Mountains constitute an amazing mushroom garden. Over 900 kinds of mushrooms are on the list of fungi discovered there and mycologists believe the total might eventually reach 1,500. This field guide describes in text and photographs 48 edible and poisonous common mushrooms and mushroom relatives. The luminous, hallucinogenic, and auto-digestive properties of certain fungi are briefly noted.

Wildlife

Long, William J. *The Spirit of the Wild*. Garden City, N.Y.: Doubleday & Co., 1956.
————. *Ways of Wood Folk*. Boston: Ginn & Co., 1899.
Fascinating personal observations of the ways of moose, bears, foxes, beaver, and other creatures in the woods of New England and New Brunswick.

North, Sterling. *Raccoons are the Brightest People*. New York: E. P. Dutton & Co., 1966.
Anecdotes about a feral animal that is learning to cope with our civilization.

Rue, Leonard Lee, III. *The World of the White-tailed Deer*. Philadelphia: J. B. Lippincott Co., 1962.
A close look at North America's most populous large wild animal and the one that the trail traveler most frequently sees.

Terres, John K. *From Laurel Hill to Siler's Bog—The Walking Adventures of a Naturalist*. New York: Alfred A. Knopf, 1969.
Firsthand glimpses of the gray fox, flying squirrel, wild turkey, cottontail, golden mouse, turkey vulture, and other wildlings of the North Carolina countryside.

Van Wormer, Joe. *The World of the Black Bear*. Philadelphia: J. B. Lippincott Co., 1966.
The virtues—and shortcomings—of *Ursus americanus* receive understanding treatment.